Hilgard's Introduction to
PSYCHOLOGY

Hilgard's Introduction to
PSYCHOLOGY

TWELFTH EDITION

RITA L. ATKINSON
University of California, San Diego

RICHARD C. ATKINSON
University of California, San Diego

EDWARD E. SMITH
University of Michigan

DARYL J. BEM
Cornell University

SUSAN NOLEN-HOEKSEMA
University of Michigan

HARCOURT BRACE COLLEGE PUBLISHERS

Fort Worth   Philadelphia   San Diego   New York   Orlando   Austin   San Antonio
Toronto   Montreal   London   Sydney   Tokyo

PUBLISHER	*Ted Buchholz*
EDITOR IN CHIEF	*Christopher P. Klein*
DEVELOPMENTAL EDITOR	*Karee Galloway/Amy Hester*
SENIOR PROJECT EDITOR	*Steve Welch*
PRODUCTION MANAGER	*Debra A. Jenkin*
ART DIRECTOR	*Jim Dodson/Melinda Welch*
PICTURE EDITOR	*Lili Weiner*
PERMISSIONS EDITOR	*Sheila Shutter*
COMPOSITOR	*Monotype Composition Company, Inc.*

Cover Photo © Y. Kawasaki/Photonica
Cover Design by Melinda Welch

ISBN: 0-15-501554-0
Library of Congress Catalog Card Number: 94-73797
Copyright © 1996, 1993, 1990, 1987, 1983, 1979, 1975, 1971, 1967, 1962, 1957
BY HARCOURT BRACE & COMPANY
COPYRIGHT 1953 BY HARCOURT BRACE & COMPANY
COPYRIGHT RENEWED 1990, 1985, 1981 BY ERNEST R. HILGARD

REQUESTS FOR PERMISSION TO MAKE COPIES OF ANY PART OF THE WORK SHOULD BE MAILED TO: PERMISSIONS DEPARTMENT, HARCOURT BRACE & COMPANY, 6277 SEA HARBOR DRIVE, ORLANDO, FLORIDA 32887-6777.

ADDRESS FOR EDITORIAL CORRESPONDENCE: HARCOURT BRACE COLLEGE PUBLISHERS, 301 COMMERCE STREET, SUITE 3700, FORT WORTH, TX 76102.

ADDRESS FOR ORDERS: HARCOURT BRACE & COMPANY, 6277 SEA HARBOR DRIVE, ORLANDO, FL 32887-6777. 1-800-782-4479, OR 1-800-433-0001 (IN FLORIDA).

COPYRIGHT ACKNOWLEDGMENTS BEGIN ON P.746, WHICH CONSTITUTES A CONTINUATION OF THIS COPYRIGHT PAGE.

PRINTED IN THE UNITED STATES OF AMERICA

5 6 7 8 9 0 1 2 3 4   069   9 8 7 6 5 4 3 2 1

PREFACE

As many readers know, Ernest (Jack) Hilgard was the sole author of the first edition of this book, which was published in 1953. Professor Hilgard had been teaching very popular courses in introductory psychology at Yale and Stanford since 1928 and had been courted by publishers to write his own textbook for decades. He simply did not feel he had time to write his own textbook until he gave up the chairmanship of the Stanford Psychology Department in 1951 to become Dean of the Graduate Division at Stanford (in 1951 it was less time-consuming to be Dean than Chair of a Department). In addition, he felt that the field was ready for a new introductory textbook, in part at least because the final edition of Robert Woodworth's book, which had dominated the field, had been published in 1947.

In writing *Introduction to Psychology,* Professor Hilgard sought to engage students in raising important psychological questions and in learning how to answer these questions. He states, "In planning my own book, I resolved to have the student very much in mind, just as I had done in my lecturing. I never approved fully of frontal lecturing that talked *at* the students instead of engaging them in seeking their own answers to some of the questions that were raised, or encouraging them to interrupt with questions when my expository remarks were unclear. In the outlining of the book and in its writing, I tried to remain faithful in this commitment to involve the student's participating interest."

One way that Professor Hilgard piqued the intrinsic interest of students was to focus the first chapter of the book on developmental psychology, including development during the years that most students were living. He also devoted more space than did other textbooks to the application of psychology to personal and social problems. He knew that students were interested in the problems faced by clinical and counseling psychologists and by vocational and industrial psychologists, and he felt that students would be more motivated to learn fundamental concepts in psychology if they understood how these concepts could be used to overcome important problems. Finally, he introduced "critical discussion" sections that addressed controversial issues in detail, a feature that was brand new to psychology textbooks.

In addition to appealing to students' interests, Hilgard sought to provide a comprehensive and rigorous review of current theory and research in psychology. He accomplished this goal, covering more scholarly material than any previous introductory text had attempted to cover, while presenting research in language that students could grasp.

The first edition of *Introduction to Psychology* was received enthusiastically, and sold 145,000 copies. In subsequent editions, Hilgard added chapters on biology, sensation and perception, statistics, and psychological measurement. His revisions were lauded, and the third edition of the book sold 415,000 copies. Eventually, the book was translated into French, German, Hebrew, Italian, Portuguese, Spanish, and Chinese. The textbook remains one of the best-selling introductory psychology textbooks in the world.

Hilgard retired to Emeritus Professor status at Stanford in 1969, but continued to revise the textbook for 18 years. In 1967, he began taking on coauthors to ensure that the rapidly expanding subfields of psychology were covered by experts in these subfields. Richard Atkinson became a coauthor in 1967, bringing his expertise in cognitive and biological psychology. In 1971, Rita Atkinson, a clinical psychologist, joined the team, revising the chapters in her area and coordinating the efforts of the authors. Daryl Bem joined the team in 1975, and eventually took responsibility for the material on development, personality, and social psychology. In 1979, Edward Smith began contributing his expertise in cognitive psychology. Finally, in 1992, Susan Nolen-Hoeksema joined the team to revise the material on health and clinical psychology.

Over the 43 years from the first to the twelfth edition, *Introduction to Psychology* has continued to enjoy a reputation for "scholarly sophistication," "extensive coverage," and "plain language" (Pfeiffer, 1980, p. 119). Instructors have come to know that they can rely on this textbook to provide a critical analysis of the major issues in historical and contemporary psychology in a manner that students find engaging and comprehensible.

THE TWELFTH EDITION

Our decision to change the title of the twelfth edition to *Hilgard's Introduction to Psychology* was made to honor the contributions of Ernest Hilgard to this book and to the teaching of introductory psychology. We remain committed to Hilgard's goals of presenting a comprehensive and scholarly overview of psychology in an engaging manner. As active researchers in psychology, we also bring to this twelfth edition developments at the cutting edge of modern psychology. Thus, we believe this edition of the book conveys the best of the old and the new.

Throughout the history of psychology, one of the questions most frequently asked by students has to do with "the nature–nurture issue." Whether the specific topic is social development, personality, or intelligence, students want to know whether the main determinants of a phenomenon are biological or due to learning. The answer to this question is typically "both," and a major task of teachers of psychology is to help students understand the complex interplay of nature and nurture in producing most psychological phenomena. In this twelfth edition, we have revised every chapter with the goal of helping students understand the dynamic between nature and nurture in psychology. We also have added a section at the end of every chapter, titled "Biological–Psychological Perspectives," in which we summarize and integrate the contributions of biological and nonbiological approaches to the phenomena of interest in that chapter.

Some highlights of the other significant changes in this twelfth edition are as follows:

- We have expanded discussions of the impact of culture and gender on psychological phenomena in many chapters. This is in response to the growing interest in culture and gender among students and to the increasing body of research on these topics. For example, Chapter 3, "Psychological Development," includes a comparative discussion of theories of sex typing, and Chapter 16, "Abnormal Psychology," has a new section on the effects of culture and gender on psychotherapy. Also, Appendix I, "A Brief History of Psychology," has been updated to reflect the important contributions that women have made in psychology.
- In the past few years, major advances have been made in the use of PET, MRI, and CAT technologies to study neurological processes in learning, memory, sensation and perception, as well as in psychopathology. We have expanded discussions of the use of these technologies in psychological research, and of ground-breaking findings from this research, throughout this twelfth edition. For example, Chapter 5, "Perception," includes a new discussion of recent scanning techniques that have documented the existence of separate object and location systems in the human brain; Chapter 8, "Memory," includes a new discussion of the biological basis of memory, as well as a discussion of how implicit and explicit memory are implemented in the brain; and Chapter 9, "Thought and Language," includes new sections on the neural basis of concept acquisition and the neural basis of imagery.
- Chapter 10, "Basic Motives," has been rewritten and now opens with a new section on reward and incentive motivation, which is appropriately followed by a new discussion of drug addiction and reward systems in the brain. In addition, the coverage of sexuality and sexual orientation has been rewritten, and the chapter includes a revised presentation of homeostasis and drives, obesity, and dieting and set points.
- We have extended the discussion of the heritability of abilities and personality traits in Chapter 12, "Individual Differences," in an attempt to clarify the common misconceptions students have about the heritability of individual differences. This chapter includes coverage of the assessment of individual differences, the interaction between nature and nurture, and the continuity of personality across the life course.
- In Chapter 14, "Stress, Health, and Coping," we have added an introduction to the field of health psychology and greatly expanded the coverage of new developments in health psychology, one of the fastest growing areas of psychology.

- The biological models and treatments for psychological disorders are discussed in greater detail in Chapters 15, "Abnormal Pschology," and 16 "Methods of Therapy," reflecting the rapid advancements in this field.
- In Chapter 17, "Social Beliefs and Attitudes," we have tackled a controversial area increasingly discussed in the mass media, the sociobiological approaches to sex differences in mating strategies.

We are proud of the heritage of this book and think it is fitting that this heritage is acknowledged with Ernest Hilgard's name on the cover of the book. With this and future editions we intend to continue this tradition, producing a book that is scholarly, state-of-the-art, and well written. We want students to gain a solid background in psychology and to be inspired to know more about psychology.

We extend our sincere appreciation to the following introductory psychology instructors, who contributed to this revision through insightful manuscript reviews and stimulating telephone discussions.

James Ackil, *Western Illinois University*

Cynthia Allen, *Westchester Community College*

Eileen Astor-Stetson, *Bloomsburg University*

Gordon D. Atlas, *Alfred University*

Raymond R. Baird, *University of Texas, San Antonio*

N. Jay Bean, *Vassar College*

John B. Best, *Eastern Illinois University*

Randolph Blake, *Vanderbilt University*

Terry Blumenthal, *Wake Forest University*

Richard W. Bowen, *Loyola University*

Thomas Brothen, *University of Minnesota*

James P. Buchanan, *University of Scranton*

James F. Calhoun, *University of Georgia*

Charles S. Carver, *University of Miami*

Avshalom Caspi, *University of Wisconsin*

Paul Chara, *Loras College*

Stephen Clark, *Vassar College*

Richard Eglfaer, *Sam Houston State University*

Gilles Einstein, *Furman University*

Judith Erickson, *University of Minnesota*

G. William Farthing, *University of Maine*

Mary Ann Fischer, *Indiana University Northwest*

Barbara L. Fredrickson, *Duke University*

William Rick Fry, *Youngstown State University*

Richard Gist, *Johnson County Community College*

W. B. Perry Goodwin, *Santa Clara University*

Paul Greene, *Iona College*

Elizabeth Hillstrom, *Wheaton College*

David Holmes, *University of Kansas*

William L. Hoover, *Suffolk County Community College*

Ralph Hupka, *California State University*

Fred A. Johnson, *University of the District of Columbia*

Wesley P. Jordan, *St. Mary's College of Maryland*

Grace Kannady, *Kansas City Kansas Community College*

Charles Ksir, *University of Wyoming*

Joan Lauer, *Indiana University/Purdue University*

Elissa M. Lewis, *Southwest Missouri State University*

Marc A. Lindberg, *Marshall University*

Richard Lippa, *California State University, Fullerton*

Joseph Lowman, *University of North Carolina*

James V. Lupo, *Creighton University*

Michael Martin, *University of Kansas*

Fred Maxwell, *Southwest Missouri State University*

Mary Benson McMullen, *Indiana University*

Steven E. Meier, *University of Idaho*

Sheryll Mennicke, *University of Minnesota*

Thomas Miller, *University of Minnesota*

Thomas Miller, *University of Oklahoma*

Jannay Morrow, *Vassar College*

Dean Murakami, *American River College*

Gregory L. Murphy, *University of Illinois at Urbana-Champaign*

David Neufeldt, *Hutchinson Community College*

Michael O'Hara, *University of Iowa*

Paul V. Olczak, *SUNY, Geneseo*

Carrol Perrino, *Morgan State University*

Jacqueline B. Persons, *Oakland, California*

Steve Platt, *Northern Michigan University*

Tom Posey, *Murray State University*

Janet Proctor, *Purdue University*

David Raskin, *University of Utah*

Cheryl A. Rickabaugh, *University of Redlands*

Steven Robbins, *Haverford College*

Tim Robinson, *Gustavus Adolphus*

Irvin Rock, *University of California, Berkeley*

Brian H. Ross, *University of Illinois at Urbana-Champaign*

Gene Sackett, *University of Washington*

D. Kim Sawrey, *University of North Carolina, Wilmington*

Robert Smith, *George Mason University*

Steven Smith, *Texas A&M University*

Joan Stanton, *Wheaton College*

Tim Strauman, *University of Wisconsin, Madison*

Francine Tougas, *University of Ottawa*

Stuart Valins, *SUNY, Stonybrook*

Frank Vattano, *Colorado State University*

Paul J. Wellman, *Texas A&M University*

Carsh Wilturner, *Green River College*

We are additionally grateful to Chandra Mehrotra, *College of Saint Scholastica;* Bill Graziano, *Texas A&M University;* Richard A. Kasschau, *University of Houston;* Jack Rossman, *Macalister College;* and David Pitlenger, *Marietta College,* for their participation in a prerevision focus group discussion.

CONTENTS IN BRIEF

CONTENTS

PART 3   **CONSCIOUSNESS AND PERCEPTION**

PART 4 **LEARNING, REMEMBERING, AND THINKING**

PART 5 MOTIVATION AND EMOTION

PART 8   **SOCIAL BEHAVIOR**

A WORD TO THE STUDENT

HOW TO READ A TEXTBOOK: THE PQRST METHOD

central topic in psychology is the analysis of learning and memory. Almost every chapter of this book refers to these phenomena; Chapter 7 ("Learning and Conditioning") and Chapter 8 ("Memory") are devoted exclusively to learning and memory. In this section we review a method for reading and studying information presented in textbook form. The theoretical ideas underlying this method are discussed in Chapter 8; the method is described here in greater detail for readers who wish to apply it in studying this textbook.

This approach for reading textbook chapters, called the PQRST method, has been shown to be very effective in improving a reader's understanding of and memory for key ideas and information. The method takes its name from the first letter of the five steps one follows in reading a chapter—*Preview*, *Question*, *Read*, *Self-recitation*, *Test*. The steps or stages are diagramed in the figure. The first and last stages (Preview and Test) apply to the chapter as a whole; the middle three stages (Question, Read, Self-recitation) apply to each major section of the chapter as it is encountered.[*]

STAGE P (PREVIEW) In the first step, you preview the entire chapter by skimming through it to get an idea of major topics. This is done by reading the chapter outline and then skimming the chapter, paying special attention to the headings of main sections and subsections and glancing at pictures and illustrations. The most important aspect of the preview stage is to read carefully the summary at the end of the chapter once you have skimmed through the chapter. Take time to

consider each point in the summary; questions will come to mind that should be answered later as you read the full text. The preview stage will give you an overview of the topics covered in the chapter and how they are organized.

STAGE Q (QUESTION) As noted earlier, you should apply Stages Q, R, and S to each major section of the chapter as it is encountered. The typical chapter in this textbook has five to eight major sections, each section beginning with a heading set in large letters. Work through the chapter one section at a time, applying Stages Q, R, and S to each section before going on to the next section. Before reading a section, read the heading of the section and the headings of the subsections. Then turn the topic headings into one or more questions that you should expect to answer while reading the section. Ask yourself: "What are the main ideas the author is trying to convey in this section?" This is the Question Stage.

STAGE R (READ) Next, read the section carefully for meaning. As you read, try to answer the questions you asked in Stage Q. Reflect on

---

[*] The PQRST method as described here is based on the work of Thomas and H. A. Robinson (1982) and Spache and Berg (1978); their work, in turn, is based on the earlier contributions of R. P. Robinson (1970). In some sources, the name SQ3R is used instead of PQRST. The S, the Q, and the three Rs stand for the same five steps, but are relabeled as Survey, Question, Read, Recite, and Review. We find PQRST to be easier to remember than SQ3R.

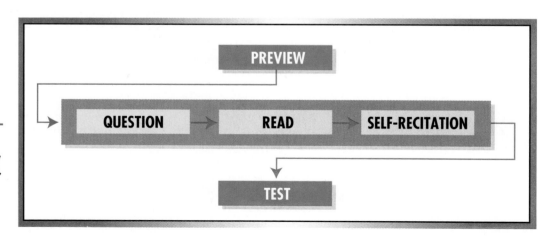

FIGURE 0-7

PQRST Method *The first and last stages apply to the chapter as a whole, and the middle three stages apply to each section of the chapter as it is encountered.*

what you are reading, and try to make connections to other things you know. You may choose to mark or underline key words or phrases in the text. Try, however, not to mark more than 10 to 15 percent of the text. Too much underlining defeats the intended purpose, which is to make key words and ideas stand out for later review. It is probably best to delay taking notes until you have read the entire section and encountered all the key ideas, so you can judge their relative importance.

STAGE S (SELF-RECITATION) After you have finished reading the section, try to recall the main ideas and recite the information. Self-recitation is a powerful means of fixing the material in your memory. Put the ideas into your own words and recite the information (preferably aloud or, if you are not alone, to yourself). Check against the text to be sure that you have recited the material correctly and completely. Self-recitation will reveal blanks in your knowledge and help you organize the information in your mind. After you have completed one section of the chapter in this way, turn to the next section and again apply Stages Q, R, and S. Continue in this manner until you have finished all sections of the chapter.

STAGE T (TEST) When you have finished reading the chapter, you should test and review all of the material. Look over your notes and test your recall for the main ideas. Try to understand how the various facts relate to one another and how they were organized in the chapter. The test stage may require that you thumb back through the chapter to check key facts and ideas. You should also reread the chapter summary at this time; as you are doing so, you should be able to add details to each entry in the summary. Don't put off the test stage until the night before an examination. The best time for a first review of the chapter is immediately after you have read it.

Research indicates that the PQRST method is very helpful and definitely preferable to simply reading straight through a chapter (Thomas & Robinson, 1982). Self-recitation is particularly important; it is better to spend a significant percentage of study time in an active attempt to recite than it is to devote the entire time to reading and rereading the material (Gates, 1917). Studies also show that a careful reading of the summary of the chapter before reading the chapter itself is especially productive (Reder & Anderson, 1980). Reading the summary first provides an overview of the chapter that helps organize the material as you read through the chapter. Even if you choose not to follow every step of the PQRST method, special attention should be directed to the value of self-recitation and reading the chapter summary as an introduction to the material.

The PQRST method and various other study skills, including taking lecture notes and preparing for and taking examinations, are discussed in an excellent book entitled *Building Better Study Skills: Practical Methods for Succeeding in College,* published by the American College Testing Program, Iowa City, Iowa. As its subtitle indicates, this book focuses on practical methods for achieving personal and academic success in college.

PSYCHOLOGY AS A SCIENTIFIC AND HUMAN ENDEAVOR

A NOTE TO THE STUDENT
A method for effectively reading a textbook is described in the section immediately before this chapter; you may wish to read this section before starting this chapter.

Today, you cannot afford *not* to know about psychology. It touches virtually every aspect of your life. It asks questions like: How does the way your parents raised you affect the way you raise your own children? What is the best way to break a drug dependency? Can a man care for an infant as ably as a woman? Can you recover a traumatic childhood experiences in more detail under hypnosis? How should instruments in a nuclear power plant be designed to minimize human error? What effect does prolonged stress have on your immune system? Is psychotherapy more effective than drugs in treating depression? Can learning be improved by the use of drugs that facilitate neural transmission? Psychologists are working on these and many other questions.

Psychology also affects our life through its influence on laws and public policy. Psychological theories and research have influenced laws concerning discrimination, capital punishment, pornography, sexual behavior, and personal responsibility for actions. For example, laws pertaining to sexual deviancy have changed markedly in the past 45 years as research has shown that many sexual acts previously classed as perversions are "normal" in the sense that most people engage in them. Consider also the effect of television violence on children. Only since psychological studies provided evidence of the harmful effects of such programs have people begun to argue that television programming must be modified so as to lessen the amount of violence during prime time.

Because psychology affects so many aspects of our life, it is essential that even those who do not intend to specialize in the field know something about its basic facts and research methods. An introductory course in psychology should give you a better understanding of why people think and act as they do, and provide insights into your own attitudes and reactions. It should also help you evaluate the many claims made in the name of psychology. Everyone has seen newspaper headlines like these:

- New form of psychotherapy facilitates recovery of repressed memories
- Anxiety controlled by self-regulation of brain waves
- Proof of mental telepathy found
- Hypnosis effective in the control of pain
- Emotional stability closely related to family size
- Homosexuality linked to parental attitudes
- Transcendental meditation facilitates problem solving
- Multiple personality linked to childhood abuse

There are two things you need to know to judge the likely truth of such claims. First, you need to know what psychological facts are already firmly established, so that you will know whether the new claim is compatible with these established facts; if it is not, there is reason to be cautious. Second, you need to know the kind of evidence necessary to give credence to a new claim or discovery, so that you can determine whether the arguments in support of the new claim meet the usual standards of scientific evidence; if they do not, again there is reason for skepticism. This book tries to supply both kinds of knowledge. First, it reviews the current state of knowledge in psychology—that is, it tries to present the most important findings in the field so that you know the established facts. Second, it examines the nature of research—that is, how a psychologist designs a research program that is capable of providing strong evidence for or against a hypothesis, so that you know the kind of evidence needed to back up a new claim.

In this chapter, we first consider the kinds of *topics* that are studied in psychology. Next

Psychological studies provide evidence that violent television programming may have harmful effects on young viewers.

we discuss the *perspectives* that psychologists adopt in investigating these topics. Then we describe the *research methods* used in psychological investigations, and after that discussion, we turn to various interdisciplinary approaches that involve psychology. Finally, we briefly describe the contents of the rest of the book.

SCOPE OF PSYCHOLOGY

Psychology can be defined as the *scientific study of behavior and mental processes.* An astonishing variety of topics fits this definition. To give you some grasp on this variety, we briefly describe five representative problems psychologists examine. (All of these problems will be discussed in more detail at various points in the text.)

BRAIN DAMAGE AND FACE RECOGNITION It is no surprise that when people suffer brain damage, they typically show impairment in their behavior. What is surprising is that sometimes when the damage is in a restricted region of the brain, the person may lose one specific capacity, but otherwise appear normal. A striking example of this occurs with people who are unable to recognize familiar faces as a result of damage to a particular region on the right side of their brain, yet can do just about everything else normally. This loss in face-recognition ability is referred to as "prosopagnosia," and sometimes it is astounding. Consider the famous case reported by the neurologist Oliver Sacks of a patient who actually mistook his wife for a hat (Sacks, 1985)! In another case, a person with prosopagnosia complained to a restaurant waiter that someone kept staring at him, only to be informed that he was looking in a mirror: He had been unable to recognize his own face!

Such cases tell us a lot about the way the normal brain works. They indicate that some psychological functions—like face recognition—are *localized* in a particular part of the brain. It is as if we have a special-purpose mechanism in our brain that does primarily one thing, as if the brain, or mind, were in part composed of a network of specialists, each doing its "own thing." (See Chapter 5 for further discussion.)

ATTRIBUTING TRAITS TO PEOPLE Suppose you witness the following scene at a crowded department store. Someone soliciting for a charity approaches a customer and, in front of numerous people, implores her to make a contribution; the woman proceeds to write a $50 check to the charity. Would you think the woman generous? Alternatively, would you think that the woman was pushed into making the donation? Logically, there is no reason to favor one explanation over the other. Countless experiments designed to study hypothetical situations like this one indicate that you would tend to see the woman as generous. Thus, when we have to decide whether someone's behavior (for example, donating the $50) reflects something unique about that *person,* or something about the *situation* in which the person is in, we tend to attribute the behavior (unconsciously) to the person (see Figure 1-1).

We are biased to see other people's actions as caused by their internal traits, not by the situations in which they find themselves. This bias often leads us into error. Some situational pressures can be so great that they cause just about everybody to act the same way, yet we persist in interpreting the act as an expression of an individual's personality. Errors caused by this bias are so pervasive that psychologists refer to the bias as the **fundamental attribution error** (see discussion in Chapter 18).

FIGURE 1-1

Trait Attribution *In deciding whether a substantial donation to charity is caused by the giver's traits or by the situation, we are biased toward believing that a trait was the critical factor.*

CHILDHOOD AMNESIA Most adults, even elderly ones, can recall events from their early years. But only up to a certain point. Virtually no one can accurately recall many events from the first 3 years of life. Consider a significant event like the birth of a sibling. If the birth occurred after you were 3 years old you may have some memory of it, the amount you recall being greater the older you were at the time of the birth. But if the birth occurred before age 3, most people have trouble correctly recalling a single incident about the event (see Figure 1-2).

This phenomenon, discovered by Sigmund Freud, is called **childhood amnesia**. It is particularly striking because our first three years are so rich in experience. So much is new in a way that it never will be again; we develop from helpless newborns to crawling, babbling infants to walking, talking children. But these remarkable transitions leave little trace on our memory, as we will see in Chapter 8.

WEIGHT CONTROL Roughly 35 million Americans are obese, which technically means they are 30 percent or more above the appropriate weight for their body structure and height. Unfortunately, obesity can be a stigma in our society. Obesity is also dangerous—it contributes to a higher incidence of diabetes, high blood pressure, and heart disease. At the other end of the spectrum, some people (especially young women) suffer from **anorexia nervosa,** a disorder in which people severely restrict their eating, sometimes to the point of self-imposed starvation. Anorexia can even result in death. The American pop singer Karen Carpenter died of anorexia in 1983.

Psychologists are interested in what factors lead people to eat too much or too little. One factor seems to be a history of deprivation. If rats are first deprived of food, then allowed to feed back to normal weights, and finally allowed to eat as much as they want, they eat more than other rats that have no history of deprivation. In this instance prior deprivation leads to subsequent overeating. This may explain why many cases of anorexia paradoxically record binge eating as well: The deprivation required to stay thin eventually leads to overeating.

EXPRESSION OF AGGRESSION Many people believe that they can lessen their aggressive feelings by expressing them either directly or vicariously. Psychological research indicates the

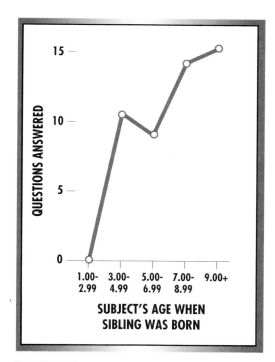

FIGURE 1-2

Recall of an Early Memory *In an experiment on childhood amnesia, college-age subjects were asked 20 questions about the events surrounding the birth of a younger sibling. The average number of questions answered is plotted as a function of the subject's age when the sibling was born. If the birth occurred before the subject's fourth year of life, no subject could recall a thing about it; if the birth occurred after that, recall increased with age at the time of the event. (After Sheingold & Tenney, 1982)*

opposite is more often the case. To study vicarious expression of aggression, researchers have looked at children's viewing of television. In one experiment, one group of children watched violent cartoons, while another group watched nonviolent cartoons for the same amount of time. The children who watched violent cartoons became more aggressive in their interactions with peers, whereas the children who viewed nonviolent cartoons showed no change in aggression. Moreover, these effects of television violence can be lasting: the more violent programs a boy watches at age 9, the more aggressive he is likely to be at age 19 (see Figure 1-3).

These five problems—face recognition, trait attribution, childhood amnesia, weight control, and expression of aggression—will surface again in our discussion of perspectives in psychology.

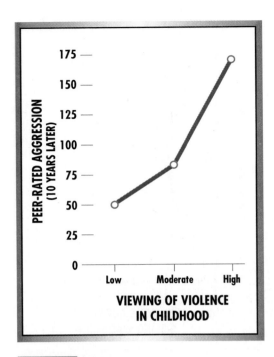

FIGURE 1-3

Relationship between Childhood Viewing of Violent Television and Adult Aggression   *A classic study shows that preference for viewing violent TV programs by boys at age 9 is related to aggressive behavior as rated by peers at age 19. (After Eron, Huesmann, Lefkowitz, & Walder, 1972)*

PERSPECTIVES IN PSYCHOLOGY

Any topic in psychology can be approached from a variety of perspectives. Indeed, this is true of any action a person takes. Suppose you walk across the street. From a **biological perspective**, this act can be described as involving the firing of the nerves that activate the muscles that move your legs. From a **behavioral perspective**, the act can be described without reference to anything within your body; rather, the green light is interpreted as a stimulus to which you respond by crossing the street. One may also take a **cognitive perspective** of crossing the street, focusing on the *mental processes* involved in producing the behavior. From a cognitive perspective, your action might be explained in terms of your goals and plans: your goal is to visit a friend, and crossing the street is part of your plan for achieving that goal.

While there are many possible ways to describe any psychological act, the following five perspectives represent the major approaches to the modern study of psychology. These five include the three mentioned above—biological, behavioral, and cognitive—plus two others: **psychoanalytic** and **phenomenological** (see Figure 1-4). Because some of these perspectives arose in reaction to other views, we first briefly consider the origin of psychological perspectives, and then describe the five contemporary perspectives.

ORIGINS OF PSYCHOLOGICAL PERSPECTIVES[*]

The roots of modern psychology can be traced to philosophy in the fourth and fifth centuries B.C. The great Greek philosophers Socrates, Plato, and Aristotle posed fundamental questions about mental life. For example: Do people perceive reality correctly? What is consciousness? Are people inherently rational or irrational? Are people capable of free choice? These questions, as important now as they were two thousand years ago, deal with the nature of *mind* and mental processes, rather than with the nature of *body* or *behavior,* and are precursors to a cognitive perspective.

The biological perspective has an equally long history. Hippocrates, usually credited as the "father of medicine," lived at roughly the same time as Socrates, and was much interested in *physiology* (the branch of biology that studies the normal functions of the living organism and its parts). He made many important observations about how the brain controls various organs of the body, which set the stage for the modern approach to physiology and the biological perspective in psychology.

Two millennia later, in the latter part of the nineteenth century, scientific psychology was born. The fundamental idea behind its inception was that mind and behavior—like planets or chemicals or human organs—could be the subject of scientific analysis. That is, by systematically varying the situations presented to people, their minds and behaviors could be analyzed into more basic components. The beginning of psychology involved some mixing of the questions of philosophy and the methods of physiology, but these two approaches were distinct enough to

---

[*] A more detailed history of psychology is presented in Appendix I.

emerge as the cognitive and biological perspectives to psychology.

The nineteenth-century version of the biological perspective differed markedly from the current version because relatively little was then known about the nervous system. Still, the development of this perspective has been more continuous than that of the cognitive perspective. The nineteenth-century cognitive perspective focused mainly on mental experiences, and its data were largely self-observations in the form of introspections. Introspection refers to an individual's observation and recording of the nature of his or her own perceptions, thoughts, and feelings; for example, self-reflections on one's immediate sensory impressions of a stimulus, such as the flash of a colored light. This extreme reliance on introspection, particularly for very rapid mental events, proved unworkable. Even after receiving extensive training in introspecting, different people produced very different introspections about simple sensory experiences, and little could be made of these differences. Introspectionism is not a critical part of the current cognitive perspective. As we will see, reactions by some psychologists to introspection played a role in the development of other modern perspectives.

MODERN PERSPECTIVES

Because the five perspectives of interest are discussed throughout the book, we provide here only a brief description of some main points. Also keep in mind that these approaches need not be mutually exclusive; rather, they may focus on different aspects of the same complex phenomenon.

BIOLOGICAL PERSPECTIVE The human brain contains well over 10 billion nerve cells and an almost infinite number of interconnections between these cells. It may well be the most complex structure in the universe. In principle, all psychological events correspond in some manner to the activity of the brain and nervous system. The biological approach to the study of human beings and other species attempts to relate overt behavior to electrical and chemical events taking place inside the body, particularly within the brain and nervous system. This approach seeks to specify the *neurobiological* processes that underlie

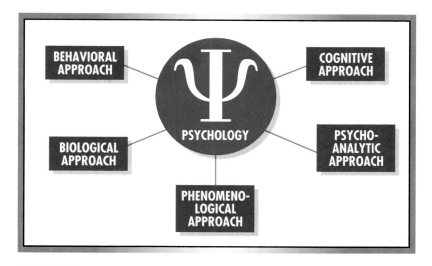

FIGURE 1-4

Perspectives in Psychology *The analysis of psychological phenomena can be approached from several perspectives. Each offers a somewhat different account of why individuals act as they do, and each can make a contribution to our conception of the total person. The Greek letter psi, ψ, is sometimes used as an abbreviation for psychology.*

behavior and mental processes. The biological approach to depression, for example, seeks to understand this disorder in terms of abnormal changes in the levels of **neurotransmitters**, which are chemicals produced in the brain that make possible the communication between **neurons**, or nerve cells.

We can use the problems described earlier to further illustrate the biological perspective. The study of face recognition in patients with brain damage indicates that particular regions of the brain are specialized for face recognition. The human brain is divided into right and left hemispheres, and the regions devoted to face recognition seem to be mainly in the right hemisphere. It turns out that there is substantial hemispheric specialization in humans; for example, in most right-handed people the left hemisphere is specialized for understanding language, and the right hemisphere is specialized for interpreting spatial relations.

The biological perspective has also made progress in the study of memory. The approach has emphasized the importance of certain brain structures, including the **hippocampus**, which is involved in consolidating memories. Childhood amnesia may be partly due to an immature hippocampus, since this brain structure is not fully developed until a year or two after birth.

The biological perspective has had similar successes in the study of motivation and emotion, particularly with other species. We know from work with rats, cats, and monkeys that there are certain regions in the brain that when electrically stimulated produce excessive overeating and obesity, and other nearby regions that when stimulated produce aggressive behavior. While human obesity and aggression involve far more than stimulation of these particular regions, these studies with animals provide some idea of the contribution that inborn biological mechanisms make to human motives and human emotions.

BEHAVIORAL PERSPECTIVE   A person eats breakfast, rides a bike, walks, talks, runs, blushes, laughs, and cries. These are forms of behavior—the activities of an organism that can be observed. With the behavioral approach, a psychologist studies individuals by looking at their behaviors rather than at their brains and nervous systems.

The view that behavior should be the sole subject matter of psychology was first advanced by the American psychologist John B.

By studying the brain activity of animals, researchers gain insight into the human brain. In this single-cell recording experiment, a microelectrode, which monitors the electrical activity of a single neuron, is implanted in the visual system of a monkey.

Watson in the early 1900s. Before that, the dominant nonbiological approach was the nineteenth-century cognitive perspective, with its emphasis on introspection. Watson noted that introspections have a private quality that distinguishes them from observations in other fields of science. Any qualified scientist can replicate an observation in the natural sciences, but the introspective observation can be reported by only one observer—the person engaging in the introspection. In contrast, other people *can* observe your behavior, including verbal behavior about your perceptions and feelings. Watson maintained that only by studying what people do—their behavior—is an objective science of psychology possible.

Watson's position came to be called **behaviorism**, and it helped shape the course of psychology during the first half of the twentieth century. One offshoot of behaviorism, **stimulus-response psychology**, is still influential. Stimulus-response psychology (S-R psychology) studies the relevant stimuli in the environment, the responses that are elicited by these stimuli, and the rewards or punishments that follow these responses. For example, an S-R analysis of your social life might focus on: which people you interact with (these would be the **social stimuli**), the kinds of responses you make to them (reinforcing, punishing, or neutral), the kinds of responses they in turn make to you (reinforcing, punishing, or neutral), and how the reinforcements sustain or disrupt the interaction.

Again we can use our sample problems to further illustrate the approach. With regard to obesity, some people may overeat (a specific response) only in the presence of specific stimuli, and learning to avoid these stimuli is part of many weight-control programs. With regard to aggression, children are more likely to express aggressive responses, such as hitting another child, when such responses are rewarded—the other child withdraws—than when their responses are punished—the other child counterattacks.

A strict behavioral approach does not consider the individual's mental processes. Psychologists other than behaviorists will often record what a person says about his or her conscious experiences (a verbal report), and from this objective data draw inferences about the person's mental activity. But, by and large, behavioral psychologists have chosen not to conjecture about the mental processes that intervene between the stimulus and the response (Skinner, 1981).* Today, few psychologists would regard themselves as strict behaviorists. Nevertheless, many modern developments in psychology have evolved from the work of behaviorists.

COGNITIVE PERSPECTIVE The modern cognitive perspective is in part a return to the cognitive roots of psychology, and in part a reaction to the narrowness of behaviorism and the S-R view (both of which tend to neglect complex human activities like reasoning, planning, decision making, and communication). Like the nineteenth-century version, the modern study of cognition is concerned with mental processes, such as perceiving, remembering, reasoning, deciding, and problem solving. Unlike the nineteenth-century version, however, modern cognitivism is not based on introspection. Thus, the modern study of cognition is premised on the assumptions that: (a) Only by studying mental processes can we fully understand what organisms do; and (b) we can study mental processes in an objective fashion by focusing on specific behaviors (just as the behaviorists do), but interpreting them in terms of underlying mental processes. In making these interpretations, cognitive psychologists often rely on an analogy between the mind and a computer. Incoming information is processed in various ways: It is selected, compared and combined with other information already in memory, transformed, rearranged, and so on. For example, the simple act of recognizing who it is when a friend phones and says "Hello" requires you (unconsciously) to compare her voice to samples of other peoples' voices that you have stored in your long-term memory.

We can use our sample problems to illustrate the cognitive perspective (which from here on refers to the modern version). Consider first the fundamental attribution error. When we interpret someone's behavior, essentially we are engaging in a form of *reasoning* (for example, given this behavior, what is its most likely cause), just as we may reason

about why a mechanical device functions the way it does. And it appears that our reasoning is biased in the sense that we favor traits (such as generosity) over situational pressures as causes.

The phenomenon of childhood amnesia also lends itself to a cognitive analysis. Perhaps we cannot remember events from the first few years of life because of a major developmental change in the way we organize our experience in memory. Such changes may be particularly pronounced around age 3 because at that point there is a great increase in our language abilities, and language offers us a new way of organizing our memories. A cognitive analysis can also be used in the study of aggression. If someone insults you, you are far less likely to return the verbal aggression if the person is a mental patient you do not know rather than an acquaintance. In both cases, mental patient and acquaintance, the stimulus situation is roughly the same; what differs is what you know about the other person, and it is this *knowledge* that controls your behavior.

PSYCHOANALYTIC PERSPECTIVE The psychoanalytic conception of human behavior was developed by Sigmund Freud in Europe about the same time behaviorism was evolving in the United States. Freud was a physician by training who was also interested in the cognitive developments then going on in Europe. In some respects his psychoanalysis was a blend of nineteenth-century versions of cognition and physiology. In particular, Freud combined then-current cognitive notions of consciousness, perception, and memory with ideas about biologically based instincts to forge a bold new theory of human behavior.

The basic assumption of Freud's theory is that much of our behavior stems from unconscious processes. By **unconscious process** Freud meant beliefs, fears, and desires a person is unaware of but that nevertheless influence behavior. He believed that many of the impulses that are forbidden or punished by parents and society during childhood are derived from innate instincts. Because each of us is born with these impulses, they exert a pervasive influence that must be dealt with in some manner. Forbidding them merely forces them out of awareness into the unconscious, where they remain to affect dreams, slips of speech, or mannerisms, and to

---

* Throughout this book you will find references, cited by author and date, that document or expand the statements made here. Detailed publishing information on these studies appears in the reference list at the end of the book.

manifest themselves as emotional problems, symptoms of mental illness, or, on the other hand, socially approved behavior such as artistic and literary activity. For example, if you feel a lot of anger toward a person whom you cannot afford to alienate, your anger may become unconscious, perhaps reflected indirectly in a dream about that person.

Freud believed that all of our actions have a cause but that the cause is often some unconscious motive rather than the rational reason we may give. Freud believed, in part, that we are driven by the same basic instincts as animals (primarily sex and aggression) and that we are continually struggling against a society that stresses the control of these impulses. While most psychologists do not completely accept Freud's view of the unconscious, they would probably agree that individuals are not fully aware of some important aspects of their personalities, and that these aspects may develop out of interactions with family during early childhood.

The psychoanalytic perspective suggests new ways of looking at some of our sample problems. According to Freud (1905), childhood amnesia arises because some emotional experiences in the first few years of life are so traumatic that allowing them to enter consciousness years later (that is, remembering

Sigmund Freud

them) would cause the individual to be overwhelmed by anxiety. With regard to obesity, it is known that some people overeat when anxious. The psychoanalytic perspective suggests that these people may be responding to an anxiety-producing situation by doing the one thing that has brought them comfort all their lives—namely, eating. And, of course, psychoanalysis has much to say about the expression of aggression. Freud claimed that aggression is an instinct, which means that people aggress to express an inborn need. While this proposal is not widely accepted in human psychology, it is in agreement with the views of some biologists and psychologists who study aggression in animals.

The number of psychologists who regard themselves as strict Freudians is on the decline, but many of the concepts in psychoanalytic theory remain influential.

PHENOMENOLOGICAL PERSPECTIVE   Unlike the other approaches we have considered, the phenomenological perspective focuses almost entirely on *subjective experience*. It is concerned with the individual's personal experience of events—the individual's **phenomenology**. This approach developed partly as a reaction to what phenomenologists perceived as the overly mechanistic quality of the other perspectives to psychology. Thus, phenomenological psychologists tend to reject the notion that behavior is controlled by external stimuli (behaviorism), or by the straightforward processing of information in perception and memory (cognitive psychology), or by unconscious impulses (psychoanalytic theories). Also, phenomenological psychologists have different goals than psychologists operating from the other perspectives: they are concerned more with describing the inner life and experiences of individuals than with developing theories or predicting behavior.

Some phenomenological theories are called *humanistic* because they emphasize those qualities that distinguish people from animals. For example, according to humanistic theories, an individual's principal motivational force is a tendency toward growth and self-actualization. All of us have a basic need to develop our potential to the fullest, to progress beyond where we are now. Although we may be blocked by environmental and social obstacles, our natural tendency is toward actualizing our potential. For example, a woman in a traditional marriage who had been raising her children for ten years may come to feel a strong desire to pursue an outside career, perhaps to develop a long-dormant interest in science that she feels the need to actualize.

Phenomenological or humanistic psychology has been more aligned with literature and the humanities than with science. For this reason, it is difficult to give detailed descriptions of what the phenomenological perspective would say about our sample problems, such as face recognition and childhood amnesia, because these are not the kinds of problems that phenomenologists study. In fact, some humanists reject scientific psychology altogether, claiming that its methods can contribute nothing to an understanding of human nature. This position, which is incompatible with our definition of psychology, seems far too extreme. The humanistic view makes a valuable point as a warning that psychology needs to focus its attention on solving problems relevant to human welfare rather than studying isolated bits of behavior that happen to lend themselves to an easy scientific analysis. But to assume that problems of mind and behavior can be solved by discarding all that we have learned from scientific methods of investigation seems wrong, and untenable.

RELATIONS BETWEEN PSYCHOLOGICAL AND BIOLOGICAL PERSPECTIVES

The behavioristic, cognitive, psychoanalytic, and phenomenological perspectives are all at the same level—they all rely on concepts and principles that are purely psychological (concepts such as reinforcement, perception, the unconscious, and self-actualization). Although these perspectives sometimes compete, as when they offer different explanations for the same phenomenon, they also agree that the explanations should be at the psychological level. This state of affairs contrasts with the biological perspective. The biological perspective is partly at a different level. In addition to using psychological concepts and principles, it also employs concepts and principles that are drawn from physiol-

ogy and other branches of biology (concepts such as neurons, neutrotransmitters, and hormones).

REDUCTIONISM There is a way, though, in which the biological perspective makes direct contact with the psychological perspectives. Biologically oriented researchers attempt to explain psychological concepts and principles in terms of their biological counterparts. For example, researchers might attempt to explain the normal ability to recognize faces *solely* in terms of neurons and their interconnections in a certain region of the brain. Because this attempt involves reducing psychological notions to biological ones, this kind of explanation is called **reductionism**. Throughout this book we will present examples in which reductionism has been successful; that is, situations in which what was once understood at only the psychological level is now understood at least in part at the biological level.

If reductionism can be successful, why bother with psychological explanations at all? To put it another way, is psychology just something to do until the biologists figure everything out? The answer is a resounding *No*. First and foremost, there seem to be many principles that can be stated *only* at the psychological level.

To illustrate, consider a principle about human memory, namely, that memory preserves the meaning of a message and not the actual symbols used to communicate the meaning. So, two minutes after reading these lines of text you will have no memory for the exact words used, although you will easily remember the meaning of the text. This principle seems to hold regardless of whether the message is read or heard. But some of the biological (brain) processes involved are different for reading and listening. The initial stages of reading involve the part of the brain that deals with vision, and the initial stages of listening involve the auditory part of the brain; consequently, any attempt to reduce our psychological principle to the biological level would end up with two separate subprinciples—one for reading and one for listening. The single overarching principle would therefore be lost. There are many examples of this sort, and they justify the need for a psychological level of explanation that is distinct from the biological level (Fodor, 1981).

A second reason for having a psychological level of explanation is that psychological concepts and principles can be used to direct biological researchers in their work. Given that the brain contains billions of brain cells and countless interconnections between these cells, biological researchers cannot hope to find something of interest by arbitrarily selecting some brain cells to study. Rather, they must have a way of directing their search to relevant groups of brain cells. Psychological findings can supply this direction. For example, if psychological research indicates that our ability to *discriminate* among spoken words (that is, to tell when they differ) obeys different principles than our ability to discriminate among different spatial positions, then biological psychologists might look in different regions of the brain for the neural basis of these two kinds of discrimination capacities (the left hemisphere for word discrimination, and the right for spatial-position discrimination). As another example, if psychological research indicates that learning a motor skill is a slow process that is hard to undo, then biological psychologists can direct their attention to brain processes that are relatively slow but that permanently alter connections between neurons (Churchland & Sejnowski, 1989).

Even given the above considerations, the push for reductionism, for recoding psychological accounts into biological ones, goes on at an ever-increasing rate. As a result, for many topics in psychology, we not only have psychological explanations of the phenomena of interest, but we also know something about how the relevant psychological concepts are implemented or executed in the brain (for example, what particular parts of the brain are involved and how they are interconnected). This kind of biological knowledge will typically fall short of total reductionism, but it is still terribly important. Memory researchers have long distinguished between short-term memory and long-term memory (which are psychological notions), but now they also know something about how these two kinds of memory are actually coded differently in the brain. Hence, for many of the topics that we cover in this book, we will review what is known at the biological level as well as at the psychological level. Indeed, if there is a grand theme to this book, and to current-day psychology in general, it

is that psychological phenomena can be understood at both the psychological and biological levels, where the biological analysis shows us how the psychological notions can be implemented in the brain. Both levels of analysis are clearly needed (though for some topics, including many dealing with social interactions, only psychological analyses have much to say).

The interplay between psychological and biological explanations is sometimes connected to the issue of whether certain behaviors of a person are caused by their genes or their learning. For example, is overeating among some obese people caused more by a genetic predisposition to gain weight, or to the learning of bad eating habits? Genes are, of course, part of biology, while learning is considered part of psychology. Consequently the issue is often cast as "biology versus psychology." But note that biological psychologists are trying to determine the brain basis of learning; to the extent they are successful, genes versus learning is *not* a question of biology versus psychology, but rather of two kinds of brain events, those reflecting the influence of genes and those reflecting the operations of experience.

METHODS OF PSYCHOLOGY

Now that we have some idea of the topics in psychology and the perspectives adopted in studying them, we can consider the research strategies that psychologists use to investigate them. In general, doing research involves two steps: (1) generating a scientific hypothesis and (2) testing that hypothesis. There is relatively little to say about the first step, but a great deal to say about the second one.

GENERATING HYPOTHESES

The first step in any research project is to generate a hypothesis about the topic of interest. If our concern is childhood amnesia, for example, we might generate the hypothesis that people can retrieve more memories of early family life if they are back in the exact place—say, their family home—where the incidents originally occurred. How does a researcher get such a hypothesis? There is no simple prescription for this, though fertile hypotheses are often derived from: (a) being an astute observer of naturally occurring situations—in which case you might have noticed that you can remember more about, say, high-school years when you are back home, and (b) being a scholar of the relevant scientific literature—in which case you might have read experiments about what kinds of cues aid in recovering old memories. How one puts together this background knowledge into a novel hypothesis is not well understood; it is a creative act, and psychology is only beginning to make progress in the study of creative, scientific thinking (Simon, 1989).

Note that a scientific hypothesis goes beyond common-sense observation. Common sense might lead one to say that, "Memory for earlier events gets better with the right cues." But without a definition of what "right" means, this claim cannot be tested scientifically. There is no way to know in advance which cues should lead to the hypothesized memory improvement.

Although not much may be known about how to think of a novel hypothesis, a good deal can be said about the methods needed to test it scientifically. The term "scientific" means that the research methods used to collect the data are (a) *unbiased*, in that they do not favor one hypothesis over another; and (b) *reliable*, in that they allow other qualified people to repeat the observations and obtain the same results. The various methods to be considered next have these two characteristics. Although some of the methods are used more by certain perspectives than others, each method can be used with each perspective. The major exception is that some phenomenological psychologists reject scientific methods entirely.

EXPERIMENTAL METHOD

CONTROL OF VARIABLES The typical scientific method is the experimental method. The investigator carefully controls conditions—often in a laboratory—and takes measurements in order to discover *relations among variables* (a variable is something that can occur with different values). For example, an experiment might seek to discover the relation between the variables of memory and sleep (e.g., whether one's ability to recover memories from childhood decreases with lack of sleep). To the extent that memory changes systematically with sleep, an orderly relation between these two variables has been found.

The ability to exercise precise control over variables distinguishes the experimental method from other methods of scientific observation. If the experimenter seeks to discover whether memory ability depends on the amount of sleep a person has had, the amount of sleep can be controlled by

A researcher in a sleep laboratory monitors the brain activity of a sleeping woman.

arranging to have several groups of subjects spend the night in the laboratory. Two groups might be allowed to go to sleep at 11:00 P.M. and 1:00 A.M., respectively, and a third group might be kept awake until 4:00 A.M. By waking all the subjects at the same time, for example, 7:00 A.M., and giving each the same memory task, the experimenter can determine whether the subjects with more sleep remember more than those with less sleep.

In this study, the amount of sleep is called the **independent variable** because it is independent of what the subject does (the subject does not determine how much sleep he or she gets; the experimenter does). The amount remembered is called the **dependent variable** because its values ultimately depend on the values of the independent variable. The independent variable is the variable that the experimenter manipulates, and the dependent variable is the variable the experimenter observes. The dependent variable is almost inevitably some measure of the subject's behavior. The phrase "is a function of" is used to express the dependency of one variable on another. Thus, for this experiment we could say that the subjects' ability to remember *is a function of* the amount of sleep they had.

To make this distinction between independent and dependent variables clearer, let's consider a new topic, the effect of marijuana on memory. In one typical experiment, when subjects arrived at the laboratory, they were given a dose of marijuana in a cookie. All subjects were given the same type of cookie and the same instructions. But the dosage level of the marijuana was different: one group of subjects received 5 milligrams of THC, the active ingredient in marijuana, a second group received 10 milligrams of THC, a third group got 15 milligrams, and a fourth group 20 milligrams.

After consuming the marijuana, the subjects were required to memorize several lists of unrelated words. One week later, the subjects were brought back to the laboratory and asked to recall as many words as possible. Figure 1-5 shows the percentage of words recalled for each of the four groups. Note that recall decreased as a function of the amount of marijuana taken at the time the subject studied the lists.

The experimenters had worked out a careful plan before bringing the subjects to the laboratory. Except for the dosage of mari-

juana, they held all conditions constant: the general setting for the experiment, the instructions to the subjects, the material to be memorized, the time allowed for memorization, and the conditions under which recall was tested. The only factor permitted to vary across the four groups was the dosage of marijuana—the independent variable. The dependent variable was the number of words recalled one week later. The marijuana dosage was measured in milligrams of THC; memory was measured by the percentage of words recalled. The experimenters could plot the relation between the independent and dependent variables as shown in Figure 1-5. Finally, the experimenters used sufficiently many subjects (a sample of 20 per group) to justify expecting similar results if the experiment were repeated with a different sample of subjects. The letter n is generally used to denote the number of subjects in each group; in this study, $n = 20$.

FIGURE 1-5

Marijuana and Memory *Subjects memorized word lists after taking varying dosages of THC (the active ingredient in marijuana). Recall tests administered a week later measured how much of the memorized material was retained. The figure shows the relationship between dosage level (independent variable) and recall score (dependent variable). (After Darley et al., 1973a)*

The experimental method can be used outside the laboratory as well as inside. For example, in research on obesity, it is possible to investigate the effects of different methods of weight control by trying these methods on separate but similar groups of obese individuals. The experimental method is a matter of logic, not of location. Still, most experiments take place in special laboratories, chiefly because precision instruments are usually necessary to control the presentation of stimuli and to obtain exact measures of behavior.

EXPERIMENTAL DESIGN The expression experimental design refers to the procedure used in collecting data. The simplest experimental designs are those in which the investigator manipulates one independent variable and studies its effect on one dependent variable (as was the case in the above marijuana study). Because everything is held constant except the independent variable, at the end of the experiment a statement like this can be made: "With everything else constant, when X is increased, Y also increases." Or, in other cases: "When X is increased, Y decreases." Almost any content can fit into this kind of statement, as is indicated by the following examples: (a) "When the dosage of THC is increased, the recall of memorized material decreases"; (b) "The more televised aggression children are exposed to, the more aggressively they will act with other children"; (c) "The more damage a patient has suffered in certain brain regions, the greater the impairment in the recognition of faces"; and (d) "The more prolonged stress one is under, the greater the likelihood of ulcers."

Sometimes an experiment focuses only on the influence of a single condition, which can be either present or absent (an independent variable with two values, presence and absence). The experimental design calls for an **experimental group** with the condition present and a **control group** with the condition absent. To illustrate, consider an experiment on how well college students can remember incidents that occurred during the third grade. The experimental group would be shown a picture of their third-grade classroom before trying to recall incidents, but the control group would not. If the experimental group recalled more incidents than the control group, the improvement could be attributed to the visual prompt.

Limiting an investigation to only one independent variable is too restrictive for some problems. It may be necessary to study how several independent variables interact to produce an effect on one or even several dependent variables. Studies involving the simultaneous manipulation of several variables are called **multivariate experiments** and are frequently used in psychological research. Thus, in the preceding study of the recall of third-grade events, in addition to varying whether or not a picture of the classroom is presented, the experimenter might also vary whether or not subjects are cued with the name of their third-grade teacher. Now there would be four groups of subjects: (1) pictures plus name, (2) picture but no name, (3) name but no picture, and (4) neither picture nor name. One might expect improvements in memory due to both the picture and the teacher's name: groups (2) and (3) would both do better than group (4), and group (1) would do best of all.

MEASUREMENT Psychologists using the experimental method often find it necessary to make statements about amounts or quantities. Sometimes the variables can be measured by physical means—for example, hours of sleep deprivation or dosage level of a drug. Other times variables have to be scaled in a manner that places them in some sort of order; in rating a patient's feelings of aggression, a psychotherapist might use a five-point scale ranging from "never" through "rarely," "sometimes," "often," and "always." Thus, for purposes of precise communication, numbers are assigned to variables; this process is referred to as **measurement**.

Experiments usually involve making measurements on not just one subject, but on a sample of many subjects. The outcome of the research is therefore data in the form of a set of numbers that must be summarized and interpreted. To accomplish this task, one needs to use **statistics**, the discipline that deals with sampling data from a population of individuals and then drawing inferences about the population from that sample. Statistics plays an important role not only in experimental research, but in other methods as well.* The most common statistic is the **mean**, which is

---
* This discussion is designed to introduce the problems of measurement and statistics. A more thorough discussion is provided in Appendix II.

simply the technical term for an arithmetic average. It is the sum of a set of scores divided by the number of scores. In studies involving an experimental and control group, there are two means to be compared: a mean for the scores of the subjects in the experimental group, and a mean for the scores of the subjects in the control group. The difference between these two means is, of course, what interests us.

If the difference between the means is large, we may accept it at face value. But what if the difference is small? What if our measures are subject to error? What if a few extreme cases are producing the difference? Statisticians have solved these problems by developing tests of the *significance of a difference*. A psychologist who says that the difference between the experimental group and the control group is "statistically significant" means that a statistical test has been applied to the data and that the observed difference is trustworthy or credible. In other words, the statistical test indicates that the difference observed is, in fact, due to the effect of the independent variable rather than an unlucky accident of chance factors or a few extreme cases.

CORRELATIONAL METHOD

NATURALLY OCCURRING DIFFERENCES   Not all problems are susceptible to the experimental method. There are many situations in which the investigator has no control over which subjects go in which conditions. For example, if we want to test the hypothesis that anorexic people are more sensitive to changes in taste than normal-weight people, we cannot select a group of normal-weight subjects and require half of them to become anorexic! Rather, we select people who are already anorexic or already of normal weight and see if they also differ in taste sensitivity. More generally, we can make use of the **correlational method** to determine whether some variable that is not under our control is associated, or *correlated*, with another variable of interest.

COEFFICIENT OF CORRELATION   In the above example, there were only two values of the weight variable—anorexic and normal. It is more common to have many values of each variable, and to determine the degree to which values on one variable are correlated with values on

another. This determination is made by using a statistic called the **coefficient of correlation**, symbolized by the lowercase letter *r*. The correlation coefficient is an estimate of the degree to which two variables are related and is expressed as a number between −1 and 1. No relation is indicated by 0; a perfect relation is indicated by 1 (+1 if the relation is positive and −1 if the relation is negative). As *r* goes from 0 to 1, the strength of the relation increases.

The nature of a correlation coefficient can be made clearer by examining a graphic presentation of data from a hypothetical study. As presented in Figure 1-6a, the study involves patients who are known in advance to have brain damage leading to at least some problems in face recognition (prosopagnosia). What is of interest is whether the degree of deficit, or error, in face recognition increases with the percentage of the relevant brain tissue that is damaged. Each point on the graph in Figure 1-6a represents the results for a single patient on a test of face recognition. For example, a patient who had only 10% brain damage made 15% errors on the face-recognition test, but a patient who had 55% brain damage made 95% errors. If errors in face recognition always increased with the percentage of brain damage, the points in the graph would consistently increase in moving from left to right; had they fallen on the diagonal line in the figure, the correlation would have been *r* = 1.0. A couple of points fall to either side of the line, though, so the correlation is about .90. A correlation of .90 indicates that there is a very strong relation between amount of the brain damage and errors in face recognition. In Figure 1-6a, the correlation is positive because *more errors* go with *more brain damage*. If instead of focusing on errors, we plot the percentage of *correct* responses on the face recognition test, we end up with the diagram in Figure 1-6b. Now the correlation is negative, roughly −.90, because *fewer correct responses* go with *more brain damage*. The diagonal line in Figure 1-6b is simply the inverse of the one in the previous figure. Finally, consider the diagram in Figure 1-6c. Here we have graphed the patients' percentage of errors on the face recognition test as a function of their height. Of course, there is no reason to expect a relation between height and face recognition performance, and the graph shows none. The points neither consistently increase nor consistently decrease in moving from left to right, but rather bounce around a horizontal line. The correlation is 0.

The numerical method for calculating a correlation coefficient is described in Appendix II. At this point, however, we will set forth some rules of thumb that will help you interpret correlation coefficients when you encounter them in later chapters.

A correlation can be either + or −. The sign of the correlation indicates whether the two variables are positively correlated (the values of the two variables either increase together or decrease together) or negatively correlated (as the value of one variable increases, the value of the other variable decreases). For example, suppose the number of times a student is absent from class correlates −.40 with the final course grade (the more absences, the lower the grade). On the other hand, the correlation between the number of classes *attended* and the course grade would be +.40. The strength of the relation is the same, but the sign indicates whether we are looking at classes missed or classes attended.

As the strength of the relation between two variables increases, *r* goes from 0 to 1. To appreciate this, consider a few known positive correlation coefficients:

- A correlation coefficient of about .75 between grades received in the first year of college and grades received in the second year.
- A correlation of about .70 between scores on an intelligence test given at age 7 and a retest of intelligence at age 18.
- A correlation of about .50 between the height of a parent and the adult height of the child.
- A correlation of about .40 between scores on scholastic aptitude tests given in high school and grades in college.
- A correlation of about .25 between scores on paper-and-pencil personality inventories and judgments of these individuals' personalities by psychological experts.

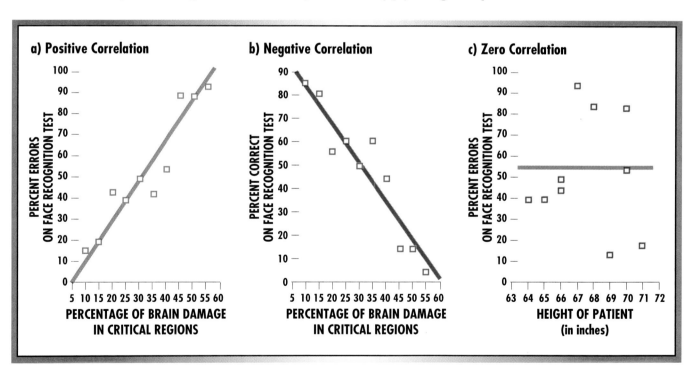

FIGURE 1-6

Scatter Diagrams Illustrating Correlations *These hypothesized data are based on ten patients, all of whom have some damage in those regions of the brain known to be involved in face recognition. In Figure 1-6a, the patients are ordered along the horizontal axis with respect to the amount of brain damage, with the patient represented by the leftmost point having the least brain damage (10%) and patient represented by the rightmost point having the most brain damage (55%). Each point on the graph represents a single patient's score on a test of face recognition. The correlation is a positive .90. In Figure 1-6b, the same data are depicted, but we now focus on the percentage of correct responses (rather than errors). Now the correlation is a negative .90. In Figure 1-6c, the patients' performance on the face recognition test is graphed as a function of their height. Now the correlation is 0.*

In psychological research, a correlation coefficient of .60 or more is judged to be quite high. Correlations in the range from .20 to .60 are of practical and theoretical value and useful in making predictions. Correlations between 0 and .20 must be judged with caution and are only minimally useful in making predictions.

TESTS   One familiar use of the correlation method involves tests that measure some aptitude, achievement, or other psychological trait. The test presents a uniform situation to a group of people who vary in some trait (such as mathematical ability, manual dexterity, or aggression). The variation in scores on the test can then be correlated with variations on another variable. For example, people's scores on a mathematical ability test can be correlated with their subsequent grades in a college math course; if the correlation is high, then the test score may be used to determine which of a new group of students should be placed in advanced sections.

The test is an important research instrument in psychology. It enables the psychologist to obtain large quantities of data from people with minimal disturbance of their daily routines and without elaborate laboratory equipment. The construction of tests requires many steps, which will be explored in detail in later chapters.

CAUSE-AND-EFFECT RELATIONS   There is an important distinction between experimental and correlational studies. In a typical experimental study, one variable (the independent variable) is systematically manipulated to determine its causal effect on some other variable (the dependent variable). Such cause-and-effect relations cannot be inferred from correlational studies. The fallacy of interpreting correlations as implying cause and effect can be illustrated with a couple of examples. The softness of the asphalt in the streets of a city may correlate with the number of sunstroke cases reported that day, but this does not mean that soft asphalt gives off some kind of poison that sends people to hospitals. Rather, variations in the two variables—softness of asphalt and number of sunstroke cases—are both being caused by a third factor—the heat of the sun. Another common example is the high positive correlation obtained for the number of storks seen nesting in French villages and the number of childbirths recorded in the same villages. We shall leave it to the reader's ingenuity to figure out possible reasons for such a correlation without postulating a cause-and-effect relation between storks and babies. These examples provide sufficient warning against giving a cause-and-effect interpretation to a correlation. When two variables are correlated, variation in one may *possibly* be the cause of variation in the other, but without further experiments, no such conclusion is justified.

FIGURE 1-7

Baboons Observed in Their Natural Habitat
Field studies can often tell us more about social behavior than experimental studies. Professor Shirley Strum has observed the same troop of baboons in Kenya for more than 20 years, identifying individual animals and making daily recordings of their behaviors and social interactions. Her data have provided remarkable information about the mental abilities of baboons and the role of friendships in their social system.

OBSERVATIONAL METHOD

DIRECT OBSERVATION   In the early stages of research, laboratory experiments and correlational studies may be premature and progress can best be made by observing the phenomenon of interest as it occurs naturally. Careful observation of animal and human behavior is the starting point for a great deal of research in psychology. For example, observation of primates in their native environment may tell us things about their social organization that will help in later laboratory investigations (see Figure 1-7). Motion pictures of newborn babies reveal the details of movement patterns shortly after birth and the types of stimuli to which babies are responsive. In making observations of naturally occurring behavior, investigators must be trained to observe and record accurately to avoid projecting their own biases into what they report.

Observational methods can require the use of a laboratory if the problem being studied is partly a biological one. For example, in their classic study of the physiological aspects of human sexuality, Masters and Johnson (1966) developed techniques that permitted direct observation of sexual responses in the laboratory. The data included (a) observations of behavior, (b) recordings of physiological changes, and (c) responses to questions asked about the subject's sensations before, during, and after sexual stimulation.

While Masters and Johnson of course agreed that human sexuality has many dimensions in addition to the biological one, their observations about the anatomical and physiological aspects of sexual response have been very helpful in understanding the nature of human sexuality, as well as in solving sexual problems.

SURVEY METHOD Some problems that are difficult to study by direct observation may be studied by indirect observation through the use of questionnaires or interviews. That is, rather than observe if people engage in a particular behavior, like exercising regularly, researchers simply ask them if they do. Since people may be trying to present themselves in a favorable light, this method is more open to bias than direct observation. Still, the **survey method** has produced many important results. For example, prior to the Masters and Johnson research on sexual response, most of the information on how people behave sexually (as opposed to how laws, religion, or society said they should behave) came from extensive surveys conducted by Alfred Kinsey and his associates 20 years earlier. Information from thousands of individual interviews was analyzed to form the basis of *Sexual Behavior in the Human Male* (Kinsey, Pomeroy, & Martin, 1948) and *Sexual Behavior in the Human Female* (Kinsey, Pomeroy, Martin, & Gebhard, 1953).

Surveys have also been used to observe people's political opinions, product preferences, health care needs, and so on. The Gallup poll and the U.S. census are probably the most familiar surveys. An adequate survey requires that a carefully pretested questionnaire be presented to a sample of people selected to ensure that they are representative of the population being studied.

CASE HISTORIES Still another means of indirectly observing someone is to obtain a biography of him or her. Now the researcher is asking people about what they have done in the past, rather than observing the behaviors of interest. For example, if the research is concerned with the effectiveness of a new kind of psychotherapy, the researcher might begin by obtaining from each client a biography. Biographies for scientific use are known as **case histories**, and are important sources of data for psychologists studying individuals.

Most case histories are prepared by *reconstructing the biography* of a person on the basis of remembered events and records. Reconstruction is necessary because the individual's history often does not become a matter of interest until that person develops some sort of problem; at such a time, knowledge of the past is important in understanding present behavior. The retrospective method may result in distortions of events or in oversights, compared to what direct observation would have uncovered, but it is often the only approach available.

INTERDISCIPLINARY APPROACHES

There are disciplines other than psychology that are interested in mind and behavior— biology, linguistics, and philosophy, to name just a few. Increasingly, researchers from these other disciplines are combining with psychologists to forge new, interdisciplinary approaches to the study of psychological phenomena.

These approaches promise to be of great importance in the next few decades. Of particular interest to us are two interdisciplinary approaches that favor a biological perspective, called cognitive neuroscience and evolutionary psychology, and two interdisciplinary

"How would you like me to answer that question? As a member of my ethnic group, income group, or religious category?"
Drawing by D. Fradon, ©1969
The New Yorker Magazine, Inc.

Because psychologists employ live subjects in their studies, they need to be sensitive to ethical issues that can arise in the conduct of research. Accordingly, the American Psychological Association (APA) and its counterparts in Canada and Great Britain have established guidelines for the care and treatment of both human and animal subjects (American Psychological Association, 1990). In the United States, federal regulations require any institution that conducts federally funded research to establish an internal review board, which reviews proposed studies to ensure that all subjects will be treated properly.

The first principle governing the ethical treatment of human subjects is *minimal risk*. The federal guideline specifies that, in most cases, the risks anticipated in the research should be no greater than those ordinarily encountered in daily life. Obviously a person should not be exposed to physical harm or injury, but deciding how much psychological stress is ethically justified in a research project is not always so clear-cut. In everyday life, of course, people are often impolite, they lie, and they make others anxious. When is it ethically justifiable for a researcher to do these same things to a subject in order to satisfy the goals of a research project? These are precisely the kinds of questions that the review boards consider on a case-by-case basis.

The second principle governing the ethical treatment of human subjects is *informed consent*. Subjects must enter a study voluntarily and be permitted to withdraw from it at any time without penalty if they so desire. They must also be told ahead of time about any aspects of the study that could be expected to influence their willingness to cooperate.

Like the principle of minimal risk, the requirement of informed consent is not always easy to implement. In particular, informed consent is sometimes at odds with another common requirement of research: that subjects be unaware of the hypotheses being tested in a study. If a researcher plans to compare subjects who learn lists of familiar words with subjects who learn lists of unfamiliar words, no ethical problem arises by simply telling subjects ahead of time that they will be learning lists of words: they do not need to know how the words vary from one subject to another. Nor are any serious ethical issues raised even if subjects are given a "surprise quiz" on words they didn't expect to be tested on. But what if the researcher seeks to compare subjects who learn words while in a neutral mood with subjects who learn words while they are angry or embarrassed? Clearly the research would not yield valid conclusions if subjects had to be

---

approaches that are more compatible with psychological perspectives, called cognitive science and cultural psychology. We briefly consider each of these approaches, starting with the biological ones.

COGNITIVE NEUROSCIENCE

Biological psychology is inherently interdisciplinary, since it seeks to establish relationships between psychological processes and biological ones. Until recently, most of this work used animal subjects and emphasized noncognitive processes. But there is a new movement afoot, called **cognitive neuroscience**, which uses human subjects, focuses on cognitive processes, and relies heavily on the methods and findings of **neuroscience** (that branch of biology dealing with the brain and central nervous system). In essence, cognitive neuroscience is an attempt by cognitive psychologists and neuroscientists to discover how mental activities are executed in the brain. The key idea is that cognitive psychology provides hypotheses about specific cognitive capacities—such as recognizing faces, or perceiving the distance of an object—and neuroscience supplies proposals about how these specific functions might be implemented or executed in the brain. This is a form of reductionism. In order for the approach to work, it seems that the cognitive capacities studied must be quite specific—for example, the recognition of human faces, rather than recognition in general (Kosslyn & Koenig, 1992). Our sample problem of face recognition deficits, or prosopagnosia, provides one example of cognitive neuroscience in action.

What is particularly distinctive about cognitive neuroscience is its reliance on new techniques for studying the brains of normal subjects (as opposed to brain-damaged ones) told ahead of time that they would be intentionally angered (by being treated rudely) or intentionally embarrassed (by being led to believe that they had accidentally broken a piece of equipment).

Accordingly, the guidelines specify that if such a study is permitted to proceed at all, subjects must be debriefed about it as soon as possible following their participation. The reasons for keeping them in ignorance—or deceiving them—about the procedures must be explained, and any residual anger or embarrassment must be dealt with so the subjects leave with their dignity intact and their appreciation for the research enhanced. The review board must be convinced that the debriefing procedures are adequate to this task.

A third principle of ethical research is the subjects' *right to privacy*. Information about a person that might be acquired during a study must be treated as confidential and not made available to others without his or her consent. One common practice is to separate the names or other identifying information about the subjects from the data once they have been collected. The data are then identified only by code or case numbers. In that way, nobody other than the experimenter has access to how any given subject responded.

About 7 to 8 percent of all psychological studies involve animals (mostly rodents and birds), and very few of these subject animals to painful or harmful procedures. Nevertheless, concern and controversy over the use, care, and treatment of animal subjects in research has increased in recent years, and both federal and APA guidelines require that any painful or harmful procedures imposed upon animals must be thoroughly justified in terms of the knowledge to be gained from the study. Specific rules also govern the living conditions and maintenance procedures that laboratory animals are entitled to.

Aside from the specific guidelines, the governing ethical principle should be that those who participate in psychology studies should be considered as full partners in the research enterprise. Some of the research discussed in this text was conducted before the ethical guidelines were formulated and would not be permitted by most review boards today. We will see a particularly notable example in Chapter 18 when we discuss the controversial studies of obedience by Stanley Milgram (1963, 1974).

while the subjects are performing some cognitive task. These **neuroimaging** or **brain scanning** techniques create visual images of a brain in action (a CAT scan creates an image of a brain, but does not show its activity), with an indication of which regions of the brain show the most neural activity during a particular task (see discussion in Chapter 2). We can illustrate this brand of cognitive neuroscience by studies of how people remember information for either brief or long periods. When subjects are required to remember information for a few seconds, neuroimaging results show increases in neural activity in regions in the front of the brain; when subjects have to remember information for a long period, there is an increase in activity in an entirely different region, one localized more in the middle of the brain. Thus, different mechanisms seem to be used for the short-term and long-term storage of information (Smith & Jonides, 1994; Squire et al., 1993).

Cognitive neuroscience relies on new techniques. Scientists can view a computer screen showing a PET scan to examine an individual's brain in action.

CRITICAL DISCUSSION SPECIALIZATIONS IN PSYCHOLOGY

We have tried to gain some understanding of the nature of psychology by looking at its topics, perspectives, and methods. We can further our understanding of what psychology is by looking at what different kinds of psychologists do, that is, at different specializations within psychology. About half the people who have advanced degrees in psychology work in colleges and universities. In addition to teaching, they may devote much of their time to research or counseling. Other psychologists work in the public schools, in hospitals or clinics, in research institutes, in government agencies, or in business and industry. Still others are in private practice and offer their services to the public for a fee. The first table gives the number and proportion of psychologists engaged in different specialized fields over a decade. The second table shows the dramatic increase in the number of women in psychology that occurred during a 15-year period.

We now turn to a brief description of some of these specializations.

BIOLOGICAL PSYCHOLOGY This is the specialization of those who adopt a biological perspective. Biological psychologists (also referred to as *physiological psychologists*) seek to discover the relationship between biological processes and behavior.

EXPERIMENTAL PSYCHOLOGY Experimental psychologists are usually behaviorist and cognitive psychologists who use experimental methods to study how people (and other animals) react to sensory stimuli, perceive the world, learn and remember, reason, and respond emotionally.

DEVELOPMENTAL, SOCIAL, AND PERSONALITY PSYCHOLOGY The categories of developmental, social, and personality psychology overlap. **Developmental psychologists** are concerned with human development and the factors that shape behavior from birth to old age. They might study a specific ability, such as how language develops in the growing child, or a particular period of life, such as infancy.

A large part of development is social. **Social psychologists** are interested in the ways interactions with other people influence attitudes and behavior. They are concerned also with the behavior of groups.

To the extent that personality is a product of developmental and social factors, the province of personality psychology overlaps both of these cat-

FIELD	1977		1987		
	No.	**%**	**No.**	**%**	**CHANGE**
Clinical	13,378	39.8%	28,147	49.9%	+10.1%
Counseling	2,712	8.1%	2,735	4.9%	−3.2%
School	1,084	3.2%	2,001	3.5%	+0.3%
Developmental	1,728	5.1%	2,903	5.1%	0
Educational	1,622	4.8%	1,438	2.6%	−2.2%
Social and Personality	2,450	7.3%	3,066	5.4%	−1.9%
Industrial/Organizational	1,974	5.9%	2,714	4.8%	−1.1%
Experimental, Comparative, & Physiological	4,598	13.7%	4.959	8.8%	−4.9%
Other	4,106	12.2%	8,415	14.9%	+2.7%
Total	33,652		56,378		

Fields of Specialization   *The number and percentage of all psychologists in the United States with doctoral-level degrees, in 1977, and again a decade later in 1987. Also shown are percent changes over the decade.* (After Pion, 1991)

EVOLUTIONARY PSYCHOLOGY

Evolutionary psychology is concerned with the biological *origins* of cognitive and other psychological mechanisms. In addition to psychology and biology, some of the major disciplines involved are branches of anthropology and psychiatry. The key idea behind evolutionary psychology, is that, just like biological mechanisms, psychological mechanisms must have evolved over millions of years by a process of natural selection. To say that a psychological mechanism has evolved by natural selection is to say that it has a genetic basis, and that it has proved useful in the past in solving some problems of survival egories. **Personality psychologists** focus on differences between individuals. They are interested in ways of classifying people for practical purposes, as well as in studying each individual's unique qualities.

CLINICAL AND COUNSELING PSYCHOLOGY The greatest number of psychologists are **clinical psychologists**, which means

they are engaged in the application of psychological principles to the diagnosis and treatment of emotional and behavioral problems—including mental illness, drug addiction, and marital and family conflict. Many clinical psychologists have a psychoanalytic perspective, though the behavioral, cognitive, and phenomenological perspectives are also well

represented. **Counseling psychologists** serve many of the same functions as clinical psychologists, although they often deal with less serious problems. They often work with high school or university students.

SCHOOL AND EDUCATIONAL PSYCHOLOGY Because the beginnings of serious emotional problems often appear in the early grades, many elementary schools employ psychologists whose training combines courses in child development, education, and clinical psychology. These **school psychologists** work with individual children to evaluate learning and emotional problems. In contrast, **educational psychologists** are specialists in learning and teaching. They may work in the schools, but more often they are employed by a university's school of education, where they do research on teaching methods and help train teachers.

INDUSTRIAL AND ENGINEERING PSYCHOLOGY **Industrial psychologists** (sometimes called **organizational psychologists**) typically work for a particular company. They are concerned with such problems as selecting people most suitable for particular jobs or developing job training programs. **Engineering psychologists** (sometimes called *human factors engineers*) seek to improve the relationship between people and machines; they help design machines to minimize the number of human errors.

| FIELD | 1975 | | | | 1993 | | | |
| | WOMEN | | MEN | | WOMEN | | MEN | |
	No.	(%)	No.	(%)	No.	(%)	No.	(%)
Clinical, Counseling, & School	371	(32.4)	773	(67.6)	1,222	(62.5)	732	(37.5)
Developmental	99	(54.7)	82	(45.3)	155	(76.7)	47	(23.2)
Educational	44	(32.8)	90	(67.2)	67	(73.6)	24	(26.4)
Experimental, Comparative, & Physiological	126	(25.3)	371	(74.7)	121	(51.9)	112	(48.1)
Industrial/ Organizational	10	(15.9)	53	(84)	73	(46.2)	85	(53.8)
Personality/ Social	81	(27.5)	214	(72.5)	79	(53.7)	68	(46.3)
Other	142	(32.5)	295	(67.5)	372	(58.6)	262	(46.3)
Subtotal	873	(31.5)	1,878	(68.5)	2,089	(61.1)	1,330	(38.9)

Recipients of Doctoral Degrees   *The number of individuals in the United States earning doctoral degrees in psychology in 1975 and fifteen years later in 1990, categorized by field of specialization. The percentages indicate the proportion of women and men receiving doctoral degrees.* (Based on data from The National Science Foundation (1988) and The National Research Council (1994).)

or in increasing the chances of reproducing. To illustrate, consider a liking for sweets. Such a preference can be thought of as a psychological mechanism, and it has a genetic basis. Moreover, we have this preference because in our evolutionary past it succeeded in increasing our ancestors' chances of survival (the fruit that tasted the sweetest had the

highest nutritional value), which increased the chances of the continued survival of the relevant genes (Symons, 1991).

There are a couple of ways in which adopting an evolutionary perspective can affect the study of psychological issues. For one thing, from an evolutionary perspective certain topics are of particular importance because of

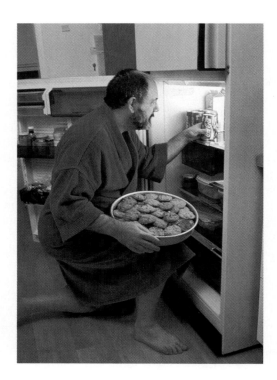

Could a liking for sweets save the human species? In our evolutionary past, a liking for sweets produced a preference for the most nutritional fruits.

lem solving; and (b) overlap with other disciplines interested in these processes, such as philosophy and computer science. The field's major objectives are to discover how information is represented in the mind (**mental representations**) and what types of computations can be carried out on these representations to bring about perceiving, remembering, reasoning, and so on. In addition to psychology, the disciplines involved are anthropology, linguistics, philosophy, aspects of neuroscience, and artificial intelligence. (The latter is a branch of computer science concerned with developing computers that act intelligently and computer programs that can simulate human thought processes.) The diagram in Figure 1-8 lists the contributing disciplines.

A central idea behind **cognitive science** is that the human cognitive system can be understood as though it were a giant computer engaged in a complex calculation. Just as a computer's complex calculation can be broken down into a set of simpler computations, such as storing, retrieving, and comparing symbols or representations, so a person's action can be decomposed into elementary mental components. Moreover, the elementary mental components may also involve storing, retrieving, and comparing symbols. There is a further parallel between a computer's calculations and mental computations. A computer's activity may be analyzed at different levels—including the level of hardware with its emphasis on chips, and the level of representation-and-algorithm with its emphasis on data structures and processes; similarly, human cognitive activity may also be analyzed at the level of "hardware" or neurons, and the level of mental representations and processes. The ideas of *mental computation* and *levels of analysis,* then, are among the cornerstones of cognitive science (Osherson, 1990).

One development within cognitive science that deserves special mention is **connectionism**. The hallmark of this approach is that mental representations and processes are described in terms that are similar to neurons and their interconnections. Thus, instead of talking about the storage, retrieval, and comparison of symbols, connectionist researchers talk about the activation of a unit and the spread of its activation to other units it is connected to. While the units and connec-

their link to survival or successful reproduction. Such topics include how we select our heterosexual mates, how we deal with those who have dominance over us, and how we handle our own aggressive feelings, and these topics are among the most investigated by evolutionary psychologists (Buss, 1991). An evolutionary perspective can also provide some new insights about familiar topics. We can illustrate this point by reconsidering one of our sample problems. Recall that in our description of obesity, we noted that a history of deprivation can lead to overeating in the future. Evolution theory provides an interpretation of this puzzling phenomenon. Until very recently in evolutionary history, people experienced deprivation *only* when food was scarce. An adaptive psychological mechanism for dealing with scarcity is a propensity to overeat when food *is* available. Hence evolution may have selected for the tendency to overeat following deprivation.

COGNITIVE SCIENCE

Cognitive science describes those areas of psychological research that (a) are concerned with cognitive processes like perceiving, remembering, reasoning, deciding, and problem-

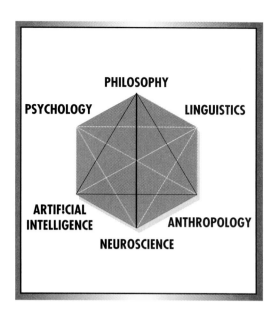

FIGURE 1-8

Cognitive Science   *The figure shows the fields involved in cognitive science and their interrelationships. Artificial intelligence refers to a branch of computer science concerned with (a) using computers to simulate human thought processes; and (b) devising computer programs that act "intelligently" and can adapt to changing circumstances. This figure was included in an unpublished report commissioned by the Sloan Foundation (New York City) in 1978; the report was prepared by leading researchers in cognitive science.*

tions involved have some properties of real neurons (for example, they are subject to activation and inhibition), they do not have all the properties of neurons. The units in a connectionist network are to be thought of at a more abstract level than real neurons; consequently, there are at least two levels of analysis in connectionism (Churchland, 1990).

Cultural Psychology

Scientific psychology in the West has often assumed that people in all cultures have exactly the same psychological processes. Increasingly, this assumption is being challenged by proponents of **cultural psychology,** an interdisciplinary movement involving psychologists, anthropologists, sociologists, and other social scientists. Cultural psychology is concerned with how the culture in which an

individual lives—its traditions, language, and worldview—influences the mental representation and psychological processes of that individual.

We can illustrate the cultural approach by a couple of examples that involve contrasts between Western and Eastern cultures. In the West—North America and much of Western and Northern Europe—we think of ourselves as separate and autonomous agents, with our individuality being made up of our specific abilities and traits. In contrast, many cultures in the East—including those of India, China, and Japan—emphasize the interrelations of people to one another, rather than their individuality. Furthermore, Easterners tend to pay more attention than do Westerners to social situations. These differences lead Easterners to explain the behavior of another person differently than do Westerners. Rather than explaining a piece of behavior solely in terms of a person's traits, Easterners appeal to the social situation in which the behavior occurred. This has profound implications for one of our sample problems, trait attribution. Because they rely less on trait attributions, Indian subjects, for example, are *less* likely than American subjects to commit the fundamental attribution error (Miller, 1984).

These differences between East and West in explaining behavior can also have educational implications. Because of their emphasis on collectivism rather than individualism, Asian students tend to study together more than American students. Such group study may be a useful technique, and it may be part of the reason why Asian students outperform their American counterparts in mathematics and some other subjects. In addition, when an American student is having difficulty in mathematics, both the student and teacher tend to attribute the difficulty to the individual abilities of the student; when a comparable case arises in a Japanese school, student and teacher are more likely to look to the situation—the student-teacher interaction in the instructional context—for an explanation of the poor performance (Stevenson, Lee & Graham, 1993).

Throughout this book, we will see illustrations of the four interdisciplinary approaches that we have just summarized. These cases will be sufficiently common that we will not bother to flag them as "interdisciplinary."

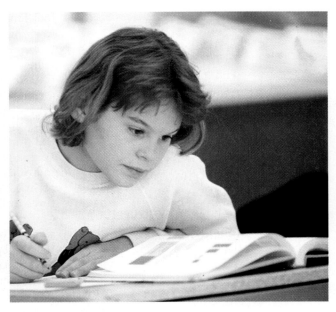

An emphasis on collectivism may be a reason why Asian students outperform American students, whose culture emphasizes individualism.

OVERVIEW OF THE BOOK

Psychologists today are in the process of investigating thousands of different phenomena. They range from microelectrode studies of how individual brain cells change during learning to studies of the effects of population density and overcrowding on social behavior. We have tried to arrange the topics in this book so that the understanding of the issues in each chapter will provide a background for the study of problems in the next.

To understand how people interact with their environment, we need to know something about their biological equipment. We also need to provide some background about biology so that you can better appreciate research done in the biological perspective. In Part 2 ("Biological and Developmental Processes"), the first chapter describes how the nervous and endocrine systems function to integrate and control behavior. Because behavior also depends on the interaction between inherited characteristics and environmental conditions, this chapter includes a discussion of genetic influences on behavior. The second chapter in Part 2 provides an overview of the individual's psychological development from infancy through adolescence and adulthood. By noting how cognitive abilities, attitudes, and personality develop, and the problems that must be faced at different stages of life, we can appreciate more fully

the kinds of questions to which psychology seeks answers.

With this as background, we move on to Part 3 ("Perception and Consciousness"), where we will survey how humans and other species acquire information about the external world. Such information must first be registered by the sense organs, which mediate the sensations of light, sound, touch, smell, and taste. We first discuss the nature of sensory information, and then consider how such information is organized into meaningful patterns and recognized as instances of familiar objects or events. For example, this is where face recognition will be discussed. Organization and recognition are parts of the *process* of perception. The *products* of perception often emerge in consciousness, and we will examine the characteristics of human consciousness under both normal and altered states.

In Part 4 ("Learning, Remembering, and Thinking"), we will first consider how organisms learn about their environment, ranging from the learning of simple relations like red light follows yellow light to the complex knowledge taught in college courses. We will also consider how such information is remembered both in short-term and long-term memory. For example, this is where childhood amnesia will be discussed. We will also discuss how remembered information is used for purposes of reasoning and problem solving. In addition, we take up the critical problem of language—how we communicate what we know.

Part 5 ("Motivation and Emotion") deals with the forces that energize and direct behavior. Such forces include basic motives such as hunger and sex, as well as emotions such as joy, fear, and anger. Both obesity and aggression will be discussed in Part 5.

The ways in which individuals differ from one another is the substance of Part 6 ("Personality and Individuality"). We will consider differences in both mental abilities and personality, paying close attention to how these differences are measured.

Dealing with stress and emotional problems are the major topics in Part 7 ("Stress,

Psychopathology, and Therapy"). We will consider the ways that stressful events can affect both emotional and physical health. In addition, we will discuss the biological and psychological causes of severe mental disorders and the various therapies that have been developed to deal with such problems and disorders.

Part 8 ("Social Behavior") is concerned with social interactions. We will discuss how we think, feel, and act in social situations, and how social situations in turn influence our thoughts, feelings, and actions. We will discuss how we perceive and interpret the behaviors of other people (as in trait attribution); how beliefs and attitudes are shaped; and how groups influence their members and vice versa.

BIOLOGICAL-PSYCHOLOGICAL PERSPECTIVES

Beginning with Chapter 3, each chapter typically contains research done from more than one perspective. For example, our treatment of consciousness (Chapter 6) reflects both the biological and cognitive perspectives, and our treatment of personality (Chapter 14) includes behavioristic and psychoanalytic perspectives as well. Of particular interest will be how the biologically based work connects to research done from psychological perspectives. Often, we will see that researchers first propose a concept or distinction at the psychological level, and that subsequently other researchers find out how that concept or distinction is implemented in the brain. We saw an example of this when we noted that there has long been a psychological distinction between short-term and long-term memory, but only recently are investigators finding the brain basis of this distinction. Sometimes, however, findings initially obtained in biologically oriented research have led other investigators to explore the phenomenon at the psychological level. For example, consider again the finding that damage to the brain in a particular region can lead to the loss of a specific function like face recognition. This phenomenon has led psychological researchers to explore the idea that, rather than having a general capacity to recognize objects, people have a number of specific recognition capacities that are used with different kinds of objects. These patterns of interplay between biological and psychological research will recur in most of the following chapters.

📖 CHAPTER SUMMARY

1. *Psychology* may be defined as the *scientific study of behavior and mental processes.* The variety of topics covered by this definition is illustrated by considering five specific problems: (a) *brain damage and face recognition,* in which people with damage to certain parts of their brain lose the ability to recognize familiar faces; (b) *attributing traits to*

people, wherein we interpret another person's behavior in terms of some underlying trait; (c) *childhood amnesia,* the inability to remember events from the first few years of life; (d) *causes of obesity,* including psychological and biological factors; and (e) the *expression of aggression,* and whether such expression leads to more or less aggression.

2. The *roots of psychology* can be traced to the fourth and fifth centuries B.C. The Greek philosophers Socrates, Plato, and Aristotle posed fundamental questions about the mind, while Hippocrates, the "father of medicine," made many important observations about how the brain controlled other organs. *Scientific psychology* was born in the latter part of the nineteenth century, when the idea took hold that mind and behavior could be the subject of scientific analysis.

3. The study of psychology can be approached from several viewpoints. The *biological perspective* relates our actions to events taking place inside the body, particularly the brain and nervous system. The *behavioral* perspective considers only those external activities of the organism that can be observed and measured. The *cognitive* perspective is concerned with mental processes such as perceiving, remembering, reasoning, deciding, and problem solving, and with relating these processes to behavior. The *psychoanalytic* perspective emphasizes unconscious motives stemming from sexual and aggressive impulses. The *phenomenological* perspective focuses on the person's subjective experiences and motivation toward self-actualization. A particular area of psychological investigation often can be analyzed from a number of these viewpoints.

4. The *biological* perspective differs from the other viewpoints in that its principles are partly drawn from biology. Often biological researchers attempt to explain psychological principles in terms of biological ones (*reductionism*). While there are some principles that can be stated only at psychological levels, increasingly, behavioral phenomena are being understood at both the biological and psychological levels.

5. Doing psychological research involves generating a hypothesis, and then testing it with a scientific method. When applicable, the *experimental method* is preferred for studying problems because it seeks to control all variables except the ones being studied. The *independent variable* is the one manipulated by the experimenter; the *dependent variable* (usually some measure of the subject's behavior) is the one being studied to determine if it is affected by changes in the independent variable. In a simple *experimental design,* the experimenter manipulates one independent variable and observes its effect on one dependent variable.

6. In many experiments, the independent variable is something that is either present or absent. The simplest experimental design includes an *experimental group* (with the condition present for one group of subjects) and a *control group* (with the condition absent for another group of subjects). If the difference in *means* between the experimental and control groups is *statistically significant,* we know that the experimental condition had a reliable effect; that is, the difference is due to the independent variable, not to chance factors or a few extreme cases.

7. If an investigator has no control over which subjects go in which conditions, a *correlational method* may be used. This method determines whether a naturally occurring difference is associated with another difference of interest. The degree of correlation between two variables is measured by the *correlation coefficient, r.* It is a number between -1 and 1. No relationship is indicated by 0; a perfect relationship is indicated by 1. As r goes from 0 to 1, the strength of the relationship increases. The correlation coefficient can be positive or negative, depending on whether one variable increases with another $(+)$ or one variable decreases as the other increases $(-)$.

8. Another approach to research is the *observational* method, in which one observes the phenomenon of interest. Researchers must be trained to observe and record accurately to avoid projecting their own biases into what they report. Phenomena that are difficult to observe directly may be observed indirectly by *surveys* (questionnaires and interviews) or by *reconstructing a case history.*

9. Two interdisciplinary approaches that psychology is involved in take a biological perspective, *cognitive neuroscience* and *evolutionary psychology.* Cognitive neuroscience is an effort by cognitive psychologists and *neuroscientists* (biologists who specialize in the brain and nervous system) to discover how mental activities are executed in the brain. The key idea is to integrate information from cognitive psychology about specific psychological functions with information from neuroscience about how these functions might be implemented in the brain. Evolutionary psychology is concerned with the evolutionary origin of cognitive and other psychological mechanisms. Its key idea is that such mechanisms have evolved over millions of years by a process of *natural selec-*

tion. This approach has led psychologists to look at topics of particular evolutionary significance, such as the choosing of a mate.

10. There are also two interdisciplinary approaches that take a more psychological perspective, *cognitive science* and *cultural psychology.* Cognitive science deals with the nature of intelligent processes, and in addition to psychology involves disciplines like artificial intelligence, linguistics, and philosophy. Its key ideas are that mental processes may be understood as *computations* and that mental activity may be analyzed at various levels. Cultural psychology is a joint venture of psychologists, anthropologists, and other social scientists. It deals with how the culture that an individual lives in influences that person's mental representations and processes.

FURTHER READING

The topical interests and theories of any contemporary science can often be understood best according to its history. Several useful books are Hilgard, *Psychology in America: A Historical Survey* (1987); Wertheimer, *A Brief History of Psychology* (3rd ed., 1987); and Schultz, *A History of Modern Psychology* (4th ed., 1987). Also of interest is Kimble, Wertheimer, and White's *Portraits of Pioneers in Psychology* (1991). A brief history of psychology is presented in Appendix II.

The various conceptual approaches to psychology are discussed in Medcof and Roth (eds.), *Approaches to Psychology* (1988); Anderson, *Cognitive Psychology and Its Implications* (3rd ed., 1990); Peterson, *Personality* (1988); Royce and Mos (eds.), *Humanistic Psychology: Concepts and Criticism* (1981); and Lundin, *Theories and Systems of Psychology* (3rd ed., 1985).

The methods of psychological research are presented in Wood, *Fundamentals of Psychological Research* (3rd ed., 1986); Snodgrass, Levy-Berger, and Haydon, *Human Experimental Psychology* (1985); Ray and Ravizza, *Methods Toward a Science of Behavior and Experience* (3rd ed., 1988); and Elmes, Kantowitz, and Roediger, *Research Methods in Psychology* (3rd ed., 1989). For more of an emphasis on the thinking skills needed to do psychological research, see Stanovich's *Thinking Straight About Psychology* (1992).

A simple but elegant introduction to basic concepts in statistics is Phillips, *How to Think About Statistics* (revised ed., 1992). A good introduction to cognitive neuroscience is provided by Kosslyn and Koenig, *Wet Mind: The New Cognitive Neuroscience* (1992). For an introduction to evolutionary psychology, see Barkow, Cosmides, and Tooky, *The Adapted Mind* (1990).

A general introduction to cognitive science is given in Gardner, *The Mind's New Science: A History of the Cognitive Revolution* (1985) and in Osherson, *Invitation to Cognitive Science* (Vols. 1–3) (1990). For an introduction to cultural psychology see Shewder's *Cultural Psychology* (1990).

To find out more about career opportunities in psychology and the training required to become a psychologist, write to the American Psychological Association (1400 North Uhle Street, Arlington, Va., 22201) for a copy of the booklet, *A Career in Psychology.*

BIOLOGICAL AND DEVELOPMENTAL PROCESSES

PART 2

2
CHAPTER

NEUROBIOLOGICAL BASIS OF PSYCHOLOGY

Behavior, from blinking an eye to playing basketball to writing a computer program, depends on the integration of many different processes within the body. This integration is provided by the nervous system, with help from the endocrine system. Consider, for example, all the processes that must coordinate effectively for you to stop your car at a red light. First you must see the light; this means that the light must register on one set of your sense organs, your eyes. Neural impulses from your eyes are relayed to your brain, where the stimulus is analyzed and compared with information about past events stored in your memory: you recognize that a red light in this context means "stop." The process of moving your foot to the brake pedal and pressing it is initiated by the motor areas of the brain that control the muscles of your leg and foot. In order to send the proper signals to these muscles, the brain must know where your foot is as well as where you want it to go. The brain maintains a register of the position of body parts relative to one another, which it uses to plan directed movements. You do not stop the car with one sudden movement of your leg, however. A specialized part of your brain receives continuous feedback from leg and foot muscles so that you are aware of how much pressure is being exerted and can alter your movements accordingly. At the same time, your eyes and some of your other body senses tell you how quickly the car is stopping. If the light turned red as you were speeding toward the intersection, some of your endocrine glands would also be activated, leading to increased heart rate, more rapid respiration, and other metabolic changes associated with fear; these processes speed your reactions in an emergency. Your stopping at a red light happens quickly and seems automatic; yet it involves a variety of complex messages and adjustments. The information for these activities is transmitted by large networks of nerve cells.

Our nervous system, sense organs, muscles, and glands enable us to be aware of and to adjust to our environment. Our perception of events depends on how our sense organs detect stimuli and how our brain interprets information coming from the senses. Much of our behavior is motivated by such needs as hunger, thirst, and the avoidance of fatigue or pain. Our ability to use language, to think,

and to solve problems depends on a brain that is incredibly complex. Indeed, the specific patterns of electrical and chemical events in the brain are the very basis of our most intricate thought processes.

Virtually all aspects of behavior and mental functioning can be better understood with some knowledge of the underlying biological processes. Elsewhere in this book, as we encounter such topics as perception, motivation, and language, we will go into more detail on the specific neurobiological mechanisms involved. The purpose of this chapter is not to provide a comprehensive survey of the linkages between biology and psychology, but to serve as an introduction to some basic neurophysiological ideas that will be elaborated upon later as we discuss various psychological phenomena.

PROPERTIES OF NEURONS

The basic unit of the nervous system is a specialized cell called the **neuron**. It is important to understand neurons because they undoubtedly hold the secrets of how the brain works and, in turn, the nature of human consciousness. We know their role in the transmission of nerve impulses, and we know how some neural circuits work; but we are just beginning to unravel their more complex functioning in memory, emotion, and thought.

NEURONS AND NERVES

Although neurons differ markedly in size and appearance, they have certain common characteristics (see Figure 2-1). Projecting from the cell body are a number of short branches called **dendrites** (from the Greek word *dendron,* meaning "tree"). The dendrites and cell body receive neural impulses from adjacent neurons. These messages are transmitted to other neurons (or to muscles and glands) by a slender tubelike extension of the cell called an **axon**. At its end the axon branches into a number of fine collaterals that end in small swellings called **synaptic terminals**.

The synaptic terminal does not actually touch the neuron that it will stimulate. Rather, there is a slight gap between the

FIGURE 2-1

Schematic Diagram of a Neuron *Arrows indicate the direction of the nerve impulse. Some axons are branched; the branches are called collaterals. The axons of many neurons are covered with an insulating myelin sheath that helps to increase the speed of the nerve impulse.*

synaptic terminal and the cell body or dendrites of the receiving neuron. This junction is called a **synapse** and the gap itself is called the **synaptic gap**. When a neural impulse travels down the axon and arrives at the synaptic terminals, it triggers the secretion of a chemical called a **neurotransmitter**. The neurotransmitter diffuses across the synaptic gap and stimulates the next neuron, thereby carrying the impulse from one neuron to the next. The axons from a great many neurons synapse on the dendrites and cell body of a single neuron (see Figure 2-2).

Although all neurons have these general features, they vary greatly in size and shape (see Figure 2-3). A neuron in the spinal cord may have an axon three to four feet long, running from the end of the spine to the muscles of the big toe; a neuron in the brain may cover only a few thousandths of an inch.

Neurons are classified into three categories depending on their general function. **Sensory neurons** transmit impulses received by **receptors** to the central nervous system. The receptors are specialized cells in the sense organs, muscles, skin, and joints that detect physical or chemical changes and translate these events into impulses that

FIGURE 2-2

Synapses at the Cell Body of a Neuron *Many different axons, each of which branches repeatedly, synapse on the dendrites and cell body of a single neuron. Each branch of an axon ends in a swelling called a synaptic terminal, which contains chemicals that are released and transmit the nerve impulse across the synapse to the dendrites or cell body of the receiving cell.*

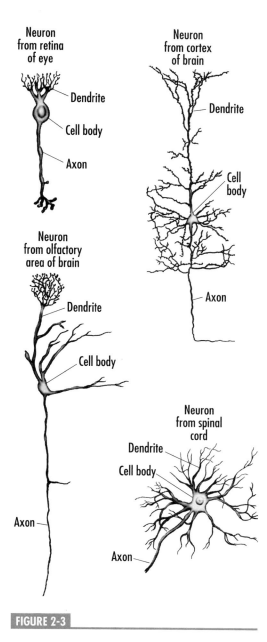

Neuron
from retina
of eye

Dendrite

Cell body

Axon

Neuron
from olfactory
area of brain

Dendrite

Cell body

Axon

Neuron
from cortex
of brain

Dendrite

Cell
body

Axon

Neuron
from spinal
cord

Dendrite

Cell body

Axon

FIGURE 2-3

Shapes and Relative Sizes of Neurons   *The axon of a spinal cord neuron (not shown in its entirety in the figure) may be several feet long.*

travel along the sensory neurons. **Motor neurons** carry outgoing signals from the brain or spinal cord to the effector organs, namely the muscles and glands. **Interneurons** receive the signals from the sensory neurons and send impulses to other interneurons or to motor neurons. Interneurons are found only in the brain, eyes, and spinal cord.

A **nerve** is a bundle of elongated axons belonging to hundreds or thousands of neurons. A single nerve may contain axons from both sensory and motor neurons.

In addition to neurons, the nervous system consists of a large number of nonneural cells, called **glial cells**, that are interspersed among—and often surround—neurons. Glial cells outnumber neurons 9 to 1 and take up more than half the volume of the brain. The name *glia,* derived from the Greek work for glue, suggests one of their functions, namely to provide structural support to hold neurons in place. In addition, they provide nutrients that are crucial to the neurons' health and appear to "keep house" in the brain by cleaning up the neuronal environment (particularly at synapses), thereby maintaining the signaling capacity of neurons. Uncontrolled proliferation of glial cells is the cause of almost all brain tumors.

Estimates of the number of neurons and glial cells in the human nervous system vary widely, depending on the method used to make the determination; as yet, there is no agreement among scientists on the best estimate. In the human brain alone, the estimates range from 10 billion to 1 trillion neurons; whatever the estimate for neurons, the number of glial cells is about 9 times that number (Groves & Rebec, 1992). These are astronomical figures, but this number of cells is undoubtedly necessary to support the complexities of human behavior.

ACTION POTENTIALS

Information moves along a neuron in the form of an electrochemical impulse that travels from the dendritic area down to the end of the axon. The ability to generate this traveling impulse, or **action potential**, is unique to neurons and is due to a multitude of **ion channels** and **ion pumps** that are embedded in the cell membrane. Ion channels are doughnut-shaped protein molecules that form pores across the cell membrane. These protein structures regulate the flow of electrically charged ions, such as sodium (Na^+), potassium (K^+), calcium (CA^{++}) or chloride (Cl^-), by opening and closing their pores. Each ion channel is selective, permitting (usually) only one type of ion to flow through it when open. Separate protein structures, called ion pumps, help to maintain an uneven distribution of the various ions across the cell

FIGURE 2-4

Action Potential   *(a) During an action potential, sodium gates in the neuron membrane open, and sodium ions enter the axon, bringing a positive charge with them. (b) After an action potential occurs at one point along the axon, the sodium gates close at that point and open at the next point along the axon. When the sodium gates close, potassium gates open, and potassium ions flow out of the axon, carrying a positive charge with them. (Modified from Starr and Taggart, 1989)*

membrane by pumping them into or out of the cell. In this way, the resting neuron maintains high concentrations of Na$^+$ outside the cell and low concentrations inside. The overall effect of these ion channels and pumps is to make the cell membrane polarized, with a positive charge on the outside and a negative charge on the inside.

When the resting neuron is stimulated, the voltage difference across the cell membrane is reduced. If the voltage drop is large enough, Na$^+$ channels open briefly at the point of stimulation and Na$^+$ ions flood into the cell. This process is called **depolarization;** now the inside of that area of the cell membrane becomes positive relative to the outside. Neighboring Na$^+$ channels sense the voltage drop and in turn open causing the adjacent area to depolarize. This self-propagating process of depolarization (repeating itself down the length of the cell body) is called the **neural impulse.** As the impulse travels down the neuron, the Na$^+$ channels close behind it

and the various ion pumps are activated to quickly restore the cell membrane to its resting state (see Figure 2-4).

The speed of the neural impulse as it travels down the axon can vary from about 2 to 200 miles per hour, depending on the diameter of the axon, with larger ones generally being faster. The speed can also be affected by whether or not the axon is covered with a **myelin sheath.** The sheath consists of specialized glial cells that wrap themselves around the axon, one after another, with small gaps between one and the next (refer back to Figure 2-1). The insulating function of the myelin sheath allows the nerve impulse to virtually jump from gap to gap, thus greatly increasing the speed of transmission. The myelin sheath is characteristic of higher animals, and is particularly prevalent in those areas of the nervous system where speed of transmission is critical. *Multiple sclerosis,* characterized by severe sensory and motor nerve dysfunction, is a disease in which the body destroys its own myelin.

SYNAPTIC TRANSMISSION

The synaptic junction between neurons is of tremendous importance because it is there that nerve cells transfer signals. A single neuron discharges, or fires, when the stimulation reaching it via multiple synapses exceeds a certain threshold. The neuron fires in a single, brief pulse and is then inactive for a few thousandths of a second. The strength of the neural impulse is constant and cannot be triggered by a stimulus unless it reaches threshold level; this is referred to as the **all-or-none principle** of action. The nerve impulse, once started, travels down the axon to its many axon terminals.

As we have said, neurons do not connect directly at a synapse; there is a slight gap across which the signal must be transmitted (see Figure 2-5). When a nerve impulse moves down the axon and arrives at a synaptic terminal, it stimulates **synaptic vesicles** in the terminal. These vesicles are small spherical structures that contain neurotransmitters; when stimulated they discharge the neurotransmitters. The neurotransmitter molecules diffuse across the synaptic gap and bind to **neuroreceptor molecules** in the cell membrane of the receiving neuron. The neurotransmitter molecule and the neuroreceptor molecule fit together in the same way that one piece of a jigsaw puzzle fits another, or the way a key fits a lock. This *lock-and-key action* of the two molecules causes a change in the permeability of the receiving neuron. When locked to their receptors some neurotransmitters have an excitatory effect and increase permeability in the direction of depolarization; others are inhibitory and decrease the permeability. Thus, the excitatory effect increases the likelihood that the neuron will fire, and the inhibitory effect decreases the likelihood.

A given neuron may receive many thousands of synapses from a network of other neurons. Some of these neurons release neurotransmitters that are *excitatory,* while others release neurotransmitters that are *inhibitory.* Depending on their pattern of firing, different axons will release their neurotransmitter substances at different times. If—at a particular moment and at a particular place on the cell membrane—the excitatory effects on the receiving neuron become large relative to the inhibitory effects, then depolarization occurs and the neuron fires an all-or-none impulse.

Once a neurotransmitter substance is released and diffuses across the synaptic gap, its action must be very brief. Otherwise, it will exert its effects for too long, and precise control will be lost. The brevity of the action is achieved in one of two ways. For some neurotransmitters, the synapse is almost immediately cleared of the chemical by **reuptake**, the process in which the neurotransmitter is reabsorbed by the synaptic terminals from which it was released. Reuptake cuts off the action of the neurotransmitter and spares the axon terminals from having to manufacture more of the substance. The effect of other neurotransmitters is terminated by **degradation**, the process in which enzymes in the membrane of the receiving neuron react with the neurotransmitter to break it up chemically and make it inactive.

NEUROTRANSMITTERS AND NEURORECEPTORS

More than 70 different neurotransmitters have been identified, and others surely will be discovered. Moreover, some neurotransmitters can bind to more than one type of

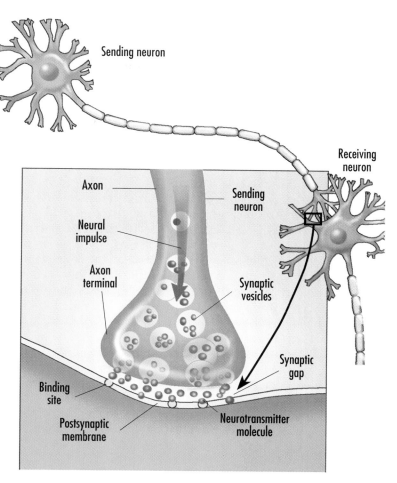

FIGURE 2-5

Release of Neurotransmitters into a Synaptic Gap *The neurotransmitter is carried to the presynaptic membrane in synaptic vesicles, which fuse with the membrane and release their contents into the synaptic gap. The neurotransmitters diffuse across the gap and combine with receptor molecules in the postsynaptic membrane.*

Electron micrograph of a neuron densely packed with synapses

MOLECULAR PSYCHOLOGY

When the neural impulse reaches the end of an axon, neurotransmitter molecules are released that cross the synaptic gap and combine with receptor molecules in the membrane of the receiving neuron. The lock-and-key action of the two molecules changes the electrical properties of the target cell, making firing either a bit more likely (excitation) or a bit less likely (inhibition).

To serve its function, every key requires a lock and every neurotransmitter requires a receptor. Many commonly used drugs interact with receptor molecules in very much the same way as neurotransmitters. Molecules of these drugs are shaped enough like those of the neurotransmitters to work as if they were keys to the lock of receptor molecules.

A good example of look-alike molecules are opiates, a class of drugs that includes heroin and morphine. In molecular shape, opiates resemble a group of neurotransmitters in the brain called endorphins, which have the effect of blocking pain. The discovery that opiates mimic naturally occurring substances in the brain has prompted considerable research on the chemical control system in the body that copes with stress and pain. Individuals who appear indifferent to pain may have an unusual ability to increase the production of these natural painkillers when they are needed. Research with one of the endorphins, called *enkephalin,* has helped explain why a painkiller like morphine can be addictive. Under normal conditions, enkephalin binds to a certain number of opiate receptors. Morphine relieves pain by binding to the receptors that are left unfilled. Too much morphine can cause a drop in enkephalin production, leaving opiate receptors unfilled. The body then requires more morphine to fill the unoccupied receptors and to reduce pain. When morphine is discontinued, the opiate receptors are left unfilled, causing painful withdrawal symptoms. The fact that the brain synthesizes substances that resemble opiates has been invoked to explain all sorts of effects. Joggers tout the theory that physical exertion increases enkephalin production to induce a "runner's high." Acupuncturists say their needles actuate enkephalins that act as natural anesthetics. There is, however, no definitive evidence to support these claims.

Drugs that influence mental functioning and mood, such as opiates, are called psychoactive drugs. By and large, they produce their effects by altering one of the various neurotransmitter-receptor systems. Different drugs can have different actions at

receptor molecule, causing different effects. For example, there are neurotransmitters that are excitatory at some sites in the nervous system and inhibitory at other sites because two different types of receptor molecules are involved.

Acetylcholine (ACh) is a neurotransmitter found at many synapses throughout the nervous system. In general, it is an excitatory transmitter, but it can be inhibitory depending on the type of receptor molecule in the membrane of the receiving neuron. ACh is particularly prevalent in an area of the forebrain called the hippocampus, which plays a key role in the formation of new memories (Squire, 1987).

Alzheimer's disease, a devastating disorder that affects many older people, involves impairment of memory and other cognitive functions. It has been demonstrated that neurons in the forebrain producing ACh tend to degenerate in Alzheimer patients, and consequently the brain's production of ACh is reduced; the less ACh the forebrain produces, the more serious the memory loss.

ACh is also released at every synapse at which a neuron terminates at a skeletal muscle fiber. The ACh is directed onto small structures called *end plates,* located on the muscle cells. The end plates are covered with receptor molecules that, when activated by ACh, trigger a molecular linkage inside the muscle cells that results in their contraction. Certain drugs that affect ACh can produce muscle paralysis. For example, botulinum toxin, which forms from bacteria in improperly canned foods, blocks the release of ACh at nerve-muscle synapses and can cause death when the muscles for breathing become paralyzed. Some nerve gases developed for warfare and many pesticides cause paralysis by destroying the enzyme that degrades ACh once the neuron has been fired; when the degradation process fails there is an uncontrolled buildup of ACh in the nervous system and normal synaptic transmission becomes impossible.

Norepinephrine (NE) is a neurotransmitter that is produced mainly by neurons in the brain stem. Two well-known drugs, cocaine and amphetamines, prolong the action of NE the same synapse. One drug might mimic the effect of a specific neurotransmitter, another might occupy the receptor site so that the normal neurotransmitter is blocked out, and still others might affect the reuptake or degradation processes. The drug action will either increase or decrease the effectiveness of synaptic transmission.

Two drugs, **chlorpromazine** and **reserpine,** have proved useful in treating schizophrenia (a mental illness to be discussed in Chapter 16). Both drugs act on norepinephrine and dopamine systems, but their antipsychotic action is primarily due to their effect on the neurotransmitter dopamine. It appears that chlorpromazine blocks dopamine receptors, and reserpine reduces dopamine levels by destroying storage vesicles in the synaptic terminals. The effectiveness of these drugs in treating schizo-

phrenia has led to the **dopamine hypothesis,** which postulates that schizophrenia is due to an excess of dopamine activity in critical cell groups within the brain. The key evidence for the hypothesis is that antipsychotic drugs seem to be clinically effective to the extent that they block the transmission of impulses by dopamine molecules.

Research on neurotransmitter-receptor systems has increased our understanding of how drugs work. In an earlier period, psychoactive drugs were discovered almost entirely by accident and their development took years of research. Now, as we gain more knowledge about neurotransmitters and receptors, new drugs can be designed and developed in a systematic way.

During the last 10 years, a great deal has been learned about the molecular basis of interneural communi-

cation. The emerging picture is that thousands of different types of molecules are involved—not just transmitter and receptor molecules but also the enzymes that manufacture and degrade them and various other molecules that modulate their action. Of course, each time a new molecule is identified, we have discovered the potential for at least two diseases or forms of mental illness; some people will surely have too much of that molecule and others too little. Research on these problems has proved so productive that the field has been given the name *molecular psychology* (Franklin, 1987). The basic idea behind this new discipline is that mental processes and their aberrations can be analyzed in terms of the molecular interplay that takes place between neurons.

by slowing down its reuptake process. Because of the delay in the reuptake, the receiving neurons are activated for a longer period of time, thus causing the stimulating psychological effects of these drugs. In contrast, **lithium** is a drug that speeds up the reuptake of NE, causing a person's mood level to be depressed. Any drug that causes NE to increase or decrease in the brain is correlated with an increase or decrease in the individual's mood level.

Another prominent neurotransmitter is **gamma-aminobutyric acid (GABA).** This substance is one of the major inhibitory transmitters in the nervous system. For example, the drug *picrotoxin* blocks GABA receptors and produces convulsions because (without GABA's inhibiting influence) there is a lack of control in muscle movement. The tranquilizing properties of certain drugs used to treat patients suffering from anxiety are related to a facilitation of GABA inhibitory activity.

Some mood-altering drugs, such as **chlorpromazine** and **LSD,** create their effects by causing an excess or deficiency of specific

neurotransmitters. Chlorpromazine, a drug used to treat schizophrenia, blocks the receptors for the neurotransmitter **dopamine** and allows fewer messages to get through. Too much dopamine at the synapse may cause schizophrenia; too little dopamine results in Parkinson's disease. LSD is similar in chemical structure to the neurotransmitter **serotonin,** which affects emotion. Evidence shows that LSD accumulates in certain brain cells, where it mimics the action of serotonin and overstimulates the cells.

The excitatory neurotransmitter **glutamate** is present in more neurons of the central nervous system than any other transmitter. There are at least three subtypes of glutamate receptors, and one in particular is believed to play a role in learning and memory. It is called the **NMDA receptor** after the chemical (N-methyl D-aspartate) that is used to detect it. Neurons in the hippocampus (an area near the center of the brain) are particularly rich in NMDA receptors, and several lines of evidence indicate that this area is critical in the formation of new memories.

FIGURE 2-6

NMDA Receptors and LTP   *The diagram illustrates a possible mechanism by which NMDA receptors could effect a long-term change in the strength of a synaptic connection (LTP). When neurotransmitters (blue triangles) are released from the first signaling neuron, they activate non-NMDA receptors in the receiving neuron (1) that partially depolarize the cell membrane (2). This partial depolarization sensitizes the NMDA receptors so that they can now be activated by glutamate transmitters (brown squares) coming from the second signaling neuron (3). Activating the NMDA receptors causes their associated calcium channels to open (4). As the calcium ions flow into the cell, they interact with various enzymes (5) presumably in ways that restructure the cell membrane (6). This restructuring makes the receiving neuron more sensitive to neurotransmitters from the first neuron, so that in time it can activate the receiving neuron on its own, thus inducing LTP.*

The NMDA receptor is not like other receptors in that successive signals from two different neurons are required in order to activate it. The signal coming from the first neuron sensitizes the cell membrane in which the NMDA receptor is embedded. Once sensitized, a second signal (glutamate transmitters coming from another neuron) will activate the receptor. When such converging signals occur, the NMDA receptor allows a very large number of calcium ions to flow

FIGURE 2-7

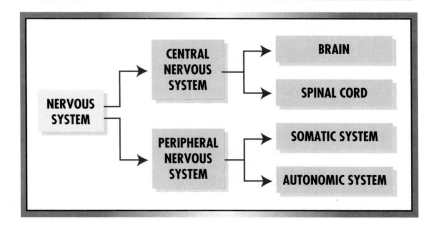

into the neuron. That influx of ions appears to cause a long-term change in the membrane of the neuron making it more responsive to the initial signal when it recurs at a later time—a phenomenon known as **long-term potentiation**, or LTP (see Figure 2-6).

Such a mechanism, in which two convergent signals strengthen a synapse, provides a possible explanation of how separate events become associated in memory. For example, in an associative learning experiment, the sound of a bell is immediately followed by the sight of food. When a dog sees the food, it salivates. But with repeated pairings of the bell and food, the dog learns to salivate to the sound of the bell alone—possibly indicating that the "bell" signal and the "food" signal have converged at the synapses causing salivation. With enough pairing of the bell and food, those synapses are strengthened by LTP so that eventually the bell alone will cause the dog to salivate. The NMDA mechanism offers an intriguing theory of how events are associated in memory—a theory that is being actively pursued (Malinow, 1994; Zalutsky & Nicoll, 1990).

DIVISIONS OF THE NERVOUS SYSTEM

All parts of the nervous system are interrelated. But for purposes of discussion, the nervous system can be separated into two major divisions, each having two subdivisions (see Figure 2-7).

The **central nervous system** includes all the neurons in the brain and spinal cord. The **peripheral nervous system** consists of the nerves connecting the brain and spinal cord to the other parts of the body. The peripheral nervous system is further divided into the *somatic system* and the *autonomic system*.

The sensory nerves of the **somatic system** transmit information about external stimulation from the skin, muscles, and joints to the central nervous system; they make us aware of pain, pressure, and temperature variations. The motor nerves of the somatic system carry impulses from the central nervous system to the muscles of the body, where they initiate action. All the muscles we use in making voluntary movements, as well as involuntary adjustments in posture and balance, are controlled by these nerves.

The nerves of the **autonomic system** run to and from the internal organs, regulating such processes as respiration, heart rate, and digestion. The autonomic system, which plays a major role in emotion, is discussed later in this chapter.

Most of the nerve fibers connecting various parts of the body to the brain are gathered together in the spinal cord, where they are protected by the bony spinal vertebrae. The spinal cord is remarkably compact— barely the diameter of your little finger. Some of the simplest stimulus-response reflexes are carried out at the level of the spinal cord. One example is the knee jerk, the extension of the leg in response to a tap on the tendon that runs in front of the kneecap. Frequently a doctor uses this test to determine the efficiency of the spinal reflexes. The natural function of this reflex is to ensure that the leg will extend when the knee is bent by the force of gravity, so the organism remains standing. When the knee tendon is tapped, the attached muscle stretches, and a signal from sensory cells embedded in the muscle is transmitted through sensory neurons to the spinal cord. There the sensory neurons synapse directly with motor neurons, which transmit impulses back to the same muscle, causing it to contract and the leg to extend. Although this response can occur solely in the spinal cord without any assistance from the brain, it can be modulated by messages from higher nervous centers. If you grip your hands just before the knee is tapped, the extension movement is exaggerated. Or if you consciously want to inhibit the reflex just before the doctor taps the tendon, you can do so. The basic mechanism is built into the spinal cord, but it can be modified by higher brain centers.

CENTRAL CORE AND LIMBIC SYSTEM

Some brain structures are clearly demarcated. Others gradually merge into each other; this leads to debate about their exact boundaries and the functions they control. For descriptive purposes, we can think of the human brain as composed of three concentric layers: (a) a *central core;* (b) the *limbic system;* and (c) the *cerebral hemispheres* (together known as the *cerebrum*). Figure 2-8 shows how these layers fit together; it can be

FIGURE 2-8

Three Concentric Layers of the Human Brain
The central core and the limbic system are shown in their entirety, but the left cerebral hemisphere has been removed. The cerebellum of the central core controls balance and muscular coordination; the thalamus serves as a switchboard for messages coming from the sense organs; the hypothalamus (not shown but located below the thalamus) regulates endocrine activity and such life-maintaining processes as metabolism and temperature control. The limbic system is concerned with actions that satisfy basic needs and with emotion. The cerebral cortex (an outer layer of cells covering the cerebrum) is the center of higher mental processes, where sensations are registered, voluntary actions initiated, decisions made, and plans formulated.

compared with the more detailed labeling of the cross section of the human brain in Figure 2-9.

CENTRAL CORE OF THE BRAIN

The **central core** includes most of the brain stem. The first slight enlargement of the spinal cord as it enters the skull is the **medulla,** a narrow structure that controls breathing and some reflexes that help the organism maintain an upright posture. Also, at

Cerebrum

Corpus callosum

Thalamus

Pineal gland

Hypothalamus

Cerebellum

Pituitary gland

Midbrain

Pons

Medulla

Spinal cord

FIGURE 2-9

Human Brain *This schematic drawing shows the main structures of the central nervous system. (Only the upper portion of the spinal cord is shown.)*

this point the major nerve tracts coming up from the spinal cord cross over so that the right side of the brain is connected to the left side of the body, and the left side of the brain to the right side of the body.

CEREBELLUM Attached to the rear of the brain stem, slightly above the medulla, is a convoluted structure, the cerebellum. The cerebellum is concerned primarily with the coordination of movement. Specific movements may be initiated at higher levels, but their smooth coordination depends on the cerebellum. Damage to the cerebellum results in jerky, uncoordinated movements.

Until recently, most scientists thought that the cerebellum was concerned almost exclusively with the fine control and coordination of body movements. However, some surprising new evidence has identified direct neural connections between the cerebellum and frontal parts of the brain involved in language, planning, and reasoning (Middleton & Strick, 1994). These connecting circuits are much larger in human beings than in mon-

keys and other animals. This, and other evidence, suggests that the cerebellum may play a role in the control and coordination of higher mental functions much as it does in ensuring the dexterity of body movements.

THALAMUS AND HYPOTHALAMUS Located just above the brain stem inside the cerebral hemispheres are two egg-shaped groups of nerve cell nuclei that make up the thalamus. One region of the thalamus acts as a relay station and directs incoming information to the cerebrum from the sense receptors for vision, hearing, touch, and taste. Another region of the thalamus plays an important role in the control of sleep and wakefulness.

The **hypothalamus** is a much smaller structure, located just below the thalamus. Centers in the hypothalamus mediate eating, drinking, and sexual behavior. The hypothalamus regulates endocrine activity and maintains **homeostasis**. Homeostasis refers to the normal level of functioning characteristic of the healthy organism, such as normal body temperature, heart rate, and blood pressure.

Under stress, homeostasis is disturbed and processes are set into motion to correct the disequilibrium. For example, if we are too warm, we perspire; and if we are too cool, we shiver. Both of these processes tend to restore normal temperature and are controlled by the hypothalamus.

The hypothalamus also plays an important role in emotion and in our response to stress-producing situations. Mild electrical stimulation of certain areas in the hypothalamus produces feelings of pleasure, stimulation of adjacent regions produces sensations that are unpleasant. By its influence on the pituitary gland, which lies just below it (see Figure 2-9), the hypothalamus controls the endocrine system and in turn the production of hormones. This control is particularly important when the body must mobilize a complex set of physiological processes (the "fight-or-flight" response) to deal with emergencies. The hypothalamus has been called the "stress center" in recognition of its special role in mobilizing the body for action.

RETICULAR FORMATION A network of neural circuits that extends from the lower brain stem up to the thalamus, traversing through some of the other central core structures, is the **reticular formation**. This network of neurons plays an important role in controlling our state of arousal. When an electric current of a certain voltage is sent through electrodes implanted in the reticular formation of a cat or dog, the animal goes to sleep; stimulation by a current with a more rapidly changing waveform awakens the sleeping animal.

The reticular formation also plays a role in our ability to focus attention on particular stimuli. All of the sense receptors have nerve fibers that feed into the reticular system. The system appears to act as a filter, allowing some of the sensory messages to pass to the cerebral cortex (to conscious awareness) while blocking others. Thus, our state of consciousness at any moment appears to be influenced by a filtering process in the reticular formation.

LIMBIC SYSTEM

Around the central core of the brain are a number of structures that together are called the **limbic system** (refer back to Figure 2-8).

This system is closely interconnected with the hypothalamus and appears to impose additional controls over some of the instinctive behaviors regulated by the hypothalamus and brain stem. Animals that have only rudimentary limbic systems (for example, fish and reptiles) carry out activities such as feeding, attacking, fleeing from danger, and mating by means of stereotyped behaviors. In mammals, the limbic system seems to inhibit some of the instinctive patterns, allowing the organism to be more flexible and adaptive to changes in the environment.

One part of the limbic system, the **hippocampus**, plays a special role in memory. Surgical removal of the hippocampus or accidental damage to the structure demonstrates that it is critical for the storage of new events as lasting memories, but it is not necessary for the retrieval of older memories. Upon recovery from such an operation, the patient will have no difficulty recognizing old friends or recalling earlier experiences; he will be able to read and perform skills learned earlier in life. However, he will have little, if any, recall of events that occurred in the year or so just prior to the operation. He will not remember events and people he meets after the operation at all. For example, the patient will fail to recognize a new person with whom he may have spent many hours earlier in the day. He will do the same jigsaw puzzle week after week, never remembering having done it before, and will read the same newspaper over and over without remembering the contents (Squire, 1992).

The limbic system is also involved in emotional behavior. Monkeys with lesions in some regions of the limbic system react with rage at the slightest provocation, suggesting that the destroyed area was exerting an inhibiting influence. Monkeys with lesions in other areas of the limbic system no longer express aggressive behavior and show no hostility, even when attacked. They simply ignore the attacker and act as if nothing had happened.

Describing the brain in terms of three concentric structures—the central core, the limbic system, and the cerebrum (to be discussed in the next section)—must not lead us to think of these structures as independent of one another. We might use the analogy of a network of interrelated computers. Each has specialized functions, but they must work

A number of techniques have been developed to obtain detailed pictures of the living human brain without causing the patient distress or damage. Before these techniques were perfected, the precise location and identification of most types of brain injury could be determined only by exploratory neurosurgery, by a complicated neurological diagnosis, or by autopsy after the patient's death. The new techniques depend on sophisticated computer methods that have become feasible only recently.

One such technique is **computerized axial tomography** (abbreviated CAT or simply CT). This procedure involves sending a narrow X-ray beam through the patient's head and measuring the amount of radiation that gets through. The revolutionary aspect of the technique is that measurements are made at hundreds of thousands of different orientations (or axes) through the head. These measurements are then fed into a computer and, by making appropriate calculations, a cross-sectional picture of the brain is reconstructed that can be photographed or displayed on a television monitor. The cross-sectional slice can be at any level and angle desired. The term "computerized axial tomography" refers to the critical role of the computer, the many axes at which measurements are made, and the resulting image that is a cross-sectional slice through the brain (*tomo* is from the Greek word meaning "slice" or "cut").

A newer and even more powerful technique involves **magnetic resonance imaging** (abbreviated MRI). Scanners of this sort use strong magnetic fields, radio-frequency pulses, and computers to compose the image. In this procedure the patient lies in a doughnut-shaped tunnel surrounded by a large magnet that generates a powerful magnetic field.

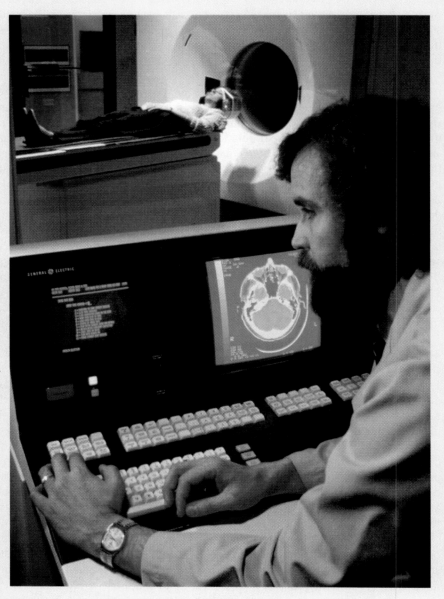

A technician administers an MRI, which generates a computerized cross section of the patient's brain.

When the anatomic part to be studied is placed in a strong magnetic field and explosed to a certain radio-frequency pulse, the tissues emit a signal that can be measured. As with the CT scanner, hundreds of thousands of such measurements are made and then manipulated by a computer into a two-dimensional image of the anatomic part. Among scientists, the technique is usually called *nuclear magnetic resonance* because what is being measured are variations in the energy level of hydrogen atom nuclei in the body caused by the radio frequency pulses. However, many physicians prefer to drop the term "nuclear" and simply call it magnetic resonance imaging, since they fear the public may confuse the reference to the nucleus of an atom with nuclear radiation.

MRI offers greater precision than the CT scanner in the diagnosis of diseases of the brain and spinal cord. For example, an MRI cross section of the brain shows features characteristic of multiple sclerosis that are not detected by a CT scanner; previously, diagnosis of this disease required hospitalization and a test in which dye is injected into the canal around the spinal cord. MRI is also useful in the detection of abnormalities in the spinal cord and at the base of the brain, such as herniated disks, tumors, and birth malformations.

While CT and MRI provide a picture of the anatomical detail of the brain, it is often desirable to assess the level of neural activity at different spots in the brain. A computer-based scanning procedure called **positron emission tomography** (abbreviated **PET**) provides this additional information. This technique depends on the fact that every cell in the body requires energy to conduct its various metabolic processes. In the brain, neurons use glucose (obtained from the bloodstream) as their principal source of energy. A small amount of a radioactive tracer compound can be mixed with glucose so that each molecule of glucose has a tiny speck of radioactivity (that is, a label) attached to it. If

Red areas indicate maximum brain activity; blue areas show minimum activity.

PET image shows three areas in the left brain active during a language task.

this harmless mixture is injected into the bloodstream, after a few minutes the brain cells begin to use the radio-labeled glucose in the same way they use regular glucose. The PET scan is essentially a highly sensitive detector of radioactivity (it is not like an X-ray machine, which *emits* X rays, but rather like a Geiger counter, which *measures* radioactivity). Neurons of the brain that are most active require the most glucose and, therefore, will be the most radioactive. The PET scan measures the amount of radioactivity and sends the information to a computer that draws a color cross-sectional picture of the brain, with different colors representing different levels of neural activity. The measurement of radioactivity is based on the emission of positively charged particles called *positrons*—hence the term "positron emission tomography."

Comparing PET scans of normal individuals with those of persons who have neurological disorders indicates that a variety of brain problems (epilepsy, blood clots, brain tumors, and so on) can be identified using this technique. For psychological research, the PET scan has been used to compare the brains of schizophrenics and has revealed differences in the metabolic levels of certain cortical areas (Andreasen, 1988). It has also been used to investigate the brain areas activated during such higher mental functions as listening to music, doing mathematics, or speaking, the goal being to identify the brain structures involved (Posner 1993).

The CT, MRI, and PET scanners are proving to be invaluable tools for studying the relationship between the brain and behavior. These instruments provide an example of how progress in one field of science forges ahead because of technical developments in another (Raichle, 1994; Pechura and Martin, 1991).

together to produce the most effective result. Similarly, the analysis of information coming from the senses requires one kind of computation and decision process (for which the cerebrum is well adapted), differing from that which controls a reflexive sequence of activities (the limbic system). The finer adjustments of the muscles (as in writing or playing a musical instrument) require another kind of control system, in this case mediated by the cerebellum. All these activities are organized into an integrated system that maintains the integrity of the organism.

THE CEREBRUM

The **cerebrum** is more highly developed in human beings than in any other organism. Its outer layer is called the **cerebral cortex;** in Latin, *cortex* means "bark." The cerebral cortex (often simply called the cortex) of a preserved brain appears gray because it consists largely of nerve cell bodies and unmyelinated fibers—hence the term "gray matter." The inside of the cerebrum, beneath the cortex, is composed mostly of myelinated axons and appears white.

STRUCTURE OF THE CEREBRUM

Each of the sensory systems (for example, vision, audition, and touch) project information to specific areas of the cortex. The movements of body parts (motor responses) are controlled by another area of the cortex. The rest of the cortex, which is neither sensory nor motor, consists of association areas. These areas are concerned with other aspects of behavior—memory, thought, and language—and occupy the largest area of the human cortex.

Before discussing some of these locations, we need to introduce a few landmarks in describing areas of the **cerebral hemispheres.** The two hemispheres are basically symmetrical, with a deep division between them running from front to rear. So, our first classification is the division into **right** and **left hemispheres.** Each hemisphere is divided into four *lobes:* the **frontal, parietal, occipital,** and **temporal.** The divisions between these

lobes are shown in Figure 2-10. The frontal lobe is separated from the parietal lobe by the **central fissure,** running from near the top of the head sideways to the ears. The division between the parietal lobe and the occipital lobe is less clear-cut; for our purpose, it suffices to say that the parietal lobe is at the top of the brain behind the central fissure and that the occipital lobe is at the rear of the brain. The temporal lobe is demarcated by a deep fissure at the side of the brain, the **lateral fissure.**

CORTICAL AREAS

PRIMARY MOTOR AREA   The primary motor area controls the voluntary movements of the body; it lies just in front of the central fissure (see Figure 2-11). Electrical stimulation at certain spots on the motor cortex produces movement of specific body parts; when these same spots on the motor cortex are injured, movement is impaired. The body is represented on the motor cortex in approximately upside-down form. For example, movements of the toes are mediated near the top of the head, tongue and mouth movements are mediated near the bottom of the motor area. Movements on the right side of the body are governed by the motor cortex of the left hemisphere; movements on the left side, by the right hemisphere.

PRIMARY SOMATOSENSORY AREA   In the parietal lobe, separated from the motor area by the central fissure, lies an area that if stimulated electrically produces a sensory experience somewhere on the opposite side of the body. It is as though a part of the body were being touched or moved. This is called the primary somatosensory area (body-sense area). Heat, cold, touch, pain, and the sense of body movement are all represented here.

Most of the nerve fibers in the pathways that radiate to and from the somatosensory and motor areas cross to the opposite side of the body. Thus, the sensory impulses from the right side of the body go to the left somatosensory cortex, and the muscles of the right foot and hand are controlled by the left motor cortex.

It seems to be a general rule that the amount of somatosensory or motor area associated with a particular part of the body is

FIGURE 2-10

Cerebral Hemispheres *Each hemisphere has several large lobes separated by fissures. In addition to these externally visible lobes, a large internal fold of cortex, called the insula, lies deep in the lateral fissure. (a) Lateral view. (b) Superior view. (c) Transverse section through cerebral cortex. Note the distinction between the more superficial gray matter (shown in dark pink) and the deeper white matter. (d) Photograph of human brain.*

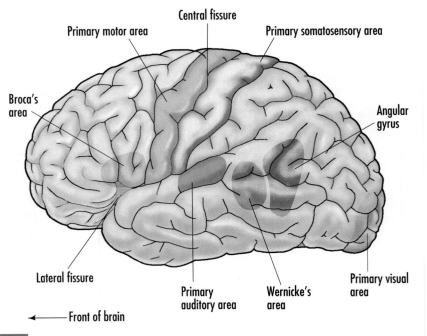

Central fissure
Primary motor area
Primary somatosensory area
Broca's area
Angular gyrus
Lateral fissure
Primary auditory area
Wernicke's area
Primary visual area

← Front of brain

FIGURE 2-11

Specialization of Function in the Left Cortex   *A major part of the cortex is involved in generating movements and in analyzing sensory inputs. These areas (which include motor, somatosensory, visual, auditory, and olfactory areas) are present on both sides of the brain. Other functions are found on only one side of the brain. For example, Broca's area and Wernicke's area are involved in the production and understanding of language, and the angular gyrus is involved in matching the visual form of a word with its auditory form; these functions exist only on the left side of the human brain.*

directly related to its sensitivity and use. For example, among four-footed mammals the dog has only a small amount of cortical tissue representing the forepaws, the raccoon—which makes extensive use of its forepaws in exploring and manipulating its environment—has a much larger representative cortical area, including regions for the separate fingers of the forepaw. The rat, which learns a great deal about its environment by means of its sensitive whiskers, has a separate cortical area for each whisker.

PRIMARY VISUAL AREA   At the back of each occipital lobe is an area of the cortex known as the primary visual area. Figure 2-12 shows the optic nerve fibers and neural pathways leading from each eye to the visual cortex. Notice that some of the optic fibers from the right eye go to the right cerebral hemisphere, whereas others cross over at a junction called the optic chiasma and go to the opposite hemisphere; the same arrangement holds true for the left eye. Fibers from the right sides of *both* eyes go to the right hemisphere

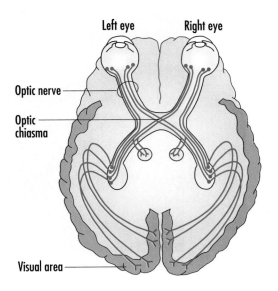

Left eye   Right eye

Optic nerve
Optic chiasma
Visual area

FIGURE 2-12

Visual Pathways   *Nerve fibers from the inner, or nasal, half of the retina cross over at the optic chiasma and go to opposite sides of the brain. Thus, stimuli falling on the right side of each retina are transmitted to the right hemisphere, and stimuli impinging on the left side of each retina are transmitted to the left hemisphere.*

of the brain, and fibers from the left sides of both eyes go to the left hemisphere. Consequently, damage to the visual area of one hemisphere (say, the left) will result in blind fields in the left sides of both eyes, causing a loss of vision to the right side of the environment. This fact is sometimes helpful in pinpointing the location of a brain tumor or other abnormalities.

PRIMARY AUDITORY AREA   The primary auditory area (found on the surface of the temporal lobe at the side of each hemisphere) is involved in the analysis of complex auditory signals. It is particularly concerned with the temporal patterning of sound, as in human speech. Both ears are represented in the auditory areas on both sides of the cortex; however, connections to the contralateral side are stronger.

ASSOCIATION AREAS   The many large areas of the cerebral cortex that are not directly concerned with sensory or motor processes are called association areas. The *frontal association areas* (the parts of the frontal lobes in front of the motor area) appear to play an important role in thought processes required for problem solving. In monkeys, for example, lesions in the frontal lobes destroy the ability to solve a delayed-response problem. In this kind of problem, food is placed in one of two cups while the monkey watches, and the cups are covered with identical objects. An opaque screen is then placed between the monkey and the cups; after a specified period of time the screen is removed, and the monkey is allowed to choose one of the cups. Normal monkeys can remember the correct cup after delays of several minutes, but monkeys with frontal lobe lesions cannot solve the problem if the delay is more than a few seconds (French & Harlow, 1962).

The *posterior association areas* are located near the various primary sensory areas and appear to consist of subareas, each serving a particular sense. For example, the lower portion of the temporal lobe is related to visual perception. Lesions in this area produce deficits in the ability to recognize and discriminate different forms. A lesion here does not cause loss of visual acuity, as would a lesion in the primary visual area of the occipital lobe; the individual "sees" the forms (and can trace the outline) but cannot identify the shape or distinguish it from a different form (Goodglass & Butters, 1988).

ASYMMETRIES IN THE BRAIN

On casual examination, the two halves of the human brain look like mirror images of each other. But closer examination reveals asymmetries. When brains are measured during autopsies, the left hemisphere is almost always larger than the right hemisphere. Also, the right hemisphere contains many long neural fibers that connect widely separate areas of the brain, whereas the left hemisphere contains many shorter fibers that provide rich interconnections within a limited area (Hillige, 1993).

As early as 1861, the French physician Paul Broca examined the brain of a patient who had suffered speech loss, and he found damage in an area of the left hemisphere just above the lateral fissure in the frontal lobe. This region, known as **Broca's area** and shown in Figure 2-11, is involved in the production of speech. Destruction of the equivalent region in the right hemisphere usually does not result in speech impairment. The areas involved in understanding speech and in the ability to write and understand written words are also usually located in the left hemisphere. Thus, a person who suffers a stroke that damages the left hemisphere is more likely to show language impairment than one whose damage is confined to the right hemisphere. A few left-handed people have speech centers located in the right hemisphere, but the great majority have language functions in the left hemisphere (the same as right-handed individuals).

Although the left hemisphere's role in language has been known for some time, only recently has it been possible to investigate what each hemisphere can do on its own. In the normal individual, the brain functions as an integrated whole; information in one hemisphere is immediately transferred to the other by way of a broad band of connecting nerve fibers called the **corpus callosum**. This connecting bridge can cause a problem in some forms of epilepsy, because a seizure starting in one hemisphere may cross over and trigger a massive discharge of neurons in the other. In an effort to prevent such generalized seizures in some severe epileptics, neurosurgeons have surgically severed the corpus callosum. The operation has proved successful for some individuals, resulting in a decrease in seizures. In addition, there appear to be no undesirable aftereffects; the patients seem to function in everyday life as well as individuals whose hemispheres are still connected. It took some very special tests to demonstrate how mental functions are affected by separating the two hemispheres. A little more background information is needed to understand the experiments we are about to describe.

We have seen that the motor nerves cross over as they leave the brain, so that the left cerebral hemisphere controls the right side

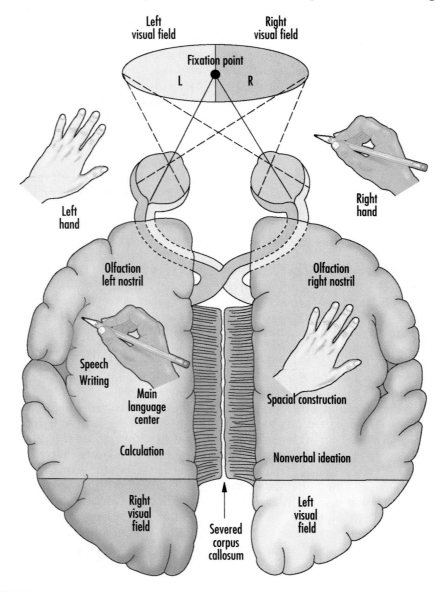

FIGURE 2-13

Sensory Inputs to the Two Hemispheres   *With the eyes fixated straight ahead, stimuli to the left of the fixation point go to the right cerebral hemisphere, and stimuli to the right go to the left hemisphere. The left hemisphere controls movements of the right hand, and the right hemisphere controls the left hand. Hearing is largely crossed in its input, but some sound representation goes to the hemisphere on the same side as the ear that registered it. The left hemisphere controls written and spoken language and mathematical calculations. The right hemisphere can understand only simple language; its main ability seems to involve spatial construction and pattern sense.*

of the body and the right hemisphere controls the left. We noted also that the area for the production of speech (Broca's area) is located in the left hemisphere. When the eyes are fixated directly ahead, images to the left of the fixation point go through both eyes to the right side of the brain and images to the right of the fixation point go to the left side of the brain (see Figure 2-13). Thus, each hemisphere has a view of that half of the visual field in which "its" hand normally functions; for example, the left hemisphere sees the right hand in the right visual field. In the normal brain, stimuli entering one hemisphere are rapidly communicated, by way of the corpus callosum, to the other, so that the brain functions as a unit. We will see what happens when the corpus callosum in an individual is severed—leaving a **split brain**—and the two hemispheres cannot communicate.

SPLIT-BRAIN SUBJECTS

Roger Sperry pioneered work in this field and was awarded the Nobel prize in 1981 for his research in neuroscience. In one of Sperry's test situations, a subject (who has undergone a split-brain operation) is seated in front of a

screen that hides his hands from view (see Figure 2-14a). His gaze is fixed at a spot on the center of the screen and the word "nut" is flashed very briefly (one-tenth of a second) on the left side of the screen. Remember that this visual signal goes to the right side of the brain, which controls the left side of the body. With his left hand, the subject can easily pick up the nut from a pile of objects hidden from view. But he cannot tell the experimenter what word flashed on the screen because speech is controlled by the left hemisphere and the visual image of "nut" was not transmitted to that hemisphere. When questioned, the split-brain subject seems unaware of what his left hand is doing. Since the sensory input from the left hand goes to the right hemisphere, the left hemisphere receives no information about what the left hand is feeling or doing. All information is fed back to the right hemisphere, which received the original visual input of the word "nut."

It is important that the word be flashed on the screen for no more than one-tenth of a second. If it remains longer, the subject's eyes move so that the word is also projected to the left hemisphere. If the split-brain subject can move his eyes freely, information goes to both cerebral hemispheres; this is one reason why the deficiencies caused by severing the

(a)   (b)   (c)

FIGURE 2-14

Testing the Abilities of the Two Hemispheres *(a) The split-brain subject correctly retrieves an object by touch with the left hand when its name is flashed to the right hemisphere, but he cannot name the object or describe what he has done.*
(b) The word "hatband" is flashed so that "hat" goes to the right cerebral hemisphere and "band" goes to the left hemisphere. The subject reports that he sees the word "band" but has no idea what kind of band. (c) A list of common objects (including "book" and "cup") is initially shown to both hemispheres. One word from the list ("book") is then projected to the right hemisphere. When given the command to do so, the left hand begins writing the word "book," but when questioned the subject does not know what his left hand has written and guesses "cup."

A great deal of our information about brain mechanisms for language comes from observations of patients suffering from brain damage. The damage may be due to tumors, penetrating head wounds, or the rupture of blood vessels. The term **aphasia** is used to describe language deficits caused by brain damage.

As already noted, Broca observed in the 1860s that damage to a specific area on the side of the left frontal lobe was linked to a speech disorder called *expressive aphasia*. Individuals with damage in Broca's area have difficulty enunciating words correctly and speak in a slow, labored way. Their speech often makes sense, but it includes only key words. Nouns are generally expressed in the singular, and adjectives, adverbs, articles, and conjunctions are likely to be omitted. However, these individuals have no difficulty understanding either spoken or written language.

In 1874, Carl Wernicke, a German investigator, reported that damage to another site in the cortex (also in the left hemisphere, but located in the temporal lobe) was linked to a language disorder called *receptive aphasia*. People with damage in this location, *Wernicke's area*, are not able to comprehend words; they can hear words, but they do not know their meaning. They can produce strings of words without difficulty and with proper articulation, but there are errors in word usage and their speech tends to be meaningless.

Based on an analysis of these defects, Wernicke developed a model for language production and understanding. Although the model is 100 years old, its general features still appear to be correct. Norman Geschwind has built on these ideas and developed the theory known as the *Wernicke-Geschwind model* (Geschwind, 1979). According to the model, Broca's area is assumed to store *articulatory codes* that specify the sequence of muscle actions required to pronounce a word. When these codes are transferred to the motor area, they activate the muscles of the lips, tongue, and larynx in the proper sequence and produce a spoken word (see figure).

Wernicke's area, on the other hand, is where auditory codes and the meanings of words are stored. If a word is to be spoken, its auditory code must be activated in Wernicke's area and transmitted by a bundle of nerves to Broca's area, where it activates the corresponding articulatory code. In turn, the articulatory code is transmitted to the motor area for the production of the spoken word.

If a word spoken by someone else is to be understood, it must be transmitted from the auditory area to Wernicke's area, where the spoken form of the word is matched to its auditory code, which in turn activates the word's meaning. When a written word is presented, it is first registered in the visual area and then relayed to the *angular gyrus,* which associates the visual form of the word with its auditory code in Wernicke's area; once the word's auditory code has been found, so has its meaning. Thus, the meanings of words are stored along with their acoustical codes in Wernicke's area. Broca's area stores articulatory codes, and the angular gyrus matches the written form of a word to its auditory code; neither of these two areas, however, stores information about word meaning. The meaning of a word is retrieved only when its acoustical code is activated in Wernicke's area.

The model explains many of the language deficits shown by aphasics. Damage restricted to Broca's area disrupts speech production but has less effect on the comprehension of spoken or written language. Damage to Wernicke's area disrupts all aspects of langauge comprehension, but the individual can still articulate words properly (since Broca's area is intact) even though the output is meaning-

corpus callosum are not readily apparent in a person's daily activities.

Further experiments demonstrate that the split-brain subject can communicate through speech only what is going on in the left hemisphere. Figure 2-14b shows another test situation. The word "hatband" is flashed on the screen so that "hat" goes to the right hemisphere and "band" to the left. When asked what word he saw, the subject replies, "band." When asked what kind of band, he makes all sorts of guesses—"rubber band," "rock band," "band of robbers," and so forth—and only hits on "hatband" by chance. Tests with

other word combinations (such as "keycase" and "suitcase") show similar results. What is perceived by the right hemisphere does not transfer to the conscious awareness of the left hemisphere. With the corpus callosum severed, each hemisphere seems oblivious to the experiences of the other.

If the split-brain subject is blindfolded and a familiar object (such as a comb, toothbrush, or keycase) is placed in his left hand, he appears to know what it is; for example, he can demonstrate its use by appropriate gestures. But he cannot express his knowledge in speech. If asked what is going on while he is less. The model also predicts that individuals with damage in the angular gyrus will not be able to read but will have no problem in comprehending speech or in speaking. Finally, if damage is restricted to the auditory area, a person will be able to read and to speak normally, but he or she will not be able to comprehend spoken speech.

There are some research findings that the Wernicke-Geschwind model does not adequately explain. For example, when the langauge areas of the brain are electrically stimulated in the course of a neurosurgical operation, both receptive and expressive functions may be disrupted at a single site. This suggests that some brain areas may share common mechanisms for producing and understanding speech. We are still a long way from a comprehensive model of language function, but there can be no doubt that some aspects of language function are highly localized in the brain (Hellige, 1994; Geschwind & Galaburda, 1987).

Wernicke-Geschwind Model *The left panel illustrates the sequence of events when a spoken word is presented and the individual repeats the word in spoken form. Neural impulses from the ear are sent to the primary auditory area, but the word cannot be understood until the signal is next transmitted to Wernicke's area. In Wernicke's area, the word's acoustical code is retrieved and transmitted via a bundle of nerve fibers to Broca's area. In Broca's area, an articulatory code for the word is activated, which in turn directs the motor area. The motor area drives the lips, tongue, and larynx to produce the spoken word. In the right panel, a written word is presented and the individual is to speak the word. The visual input to the eye is first transmitted to the primary visual cortex and then relayed to the angular gyrus. The angular gyrus associates the visual form of the word with the related acoustical code in Wernicke's area. Once the acoustical code is retrieved and the meaning of the word is established, speaking the word is accomplished through the same sequence of events as before.*

manipulating the object, he has no idea. This is true as long as any sensory input from the object to the left (talking) hemisphere is blocked. But if the subject's right hand inadvertently touches the object or if it makes a characteristic sound (like the jingling of a keycase), the speaking hemisphere immediately gives the correct answer.

Although the right hemisphere cannot speak, it does have some linguistic capabilities. It recognized the meaning of the word "nut," as we saw in our first example, and it can write a little. In the experiment illustrated in Figure 2-14c, a split-brain subject is

first shown a list of common objects such as cup, knife, book, and glass. This list is displayed long enough for the words to be projected to both hemispheres. Next, the list is removed, and one of the words (for example, "book") is flashed briefly on the left side of the screen so that it goes to the right hemisphere. If the subject is asked to write what he saw, his left hand will begin writing the word "book." If asked what his left hand has written, he has no idea and will guess at any of the words on the original list. The subject knows he has written something because he feels the writing movements through his body. But because there is no communication between the right hemisphere that saw and wrote the word and the left hemisphere that controls speech, the subject cannot tell you what he wrote (Nebes & Sperry, 1971; Sperry, 1970, 1968).

HEMISPHERIC SPECIALIZATION

Studies with split-brain subjects indicate that the two hemispheres function differently. The left hemisphere governs our ability to express ourselves in language. It can perform complicated logical activities and is skilled in mathematical computations. The right hemisphere can comprehend only very simple language. It can, for example, respond to simple nouns by selecting objects such as a nut or comb, but it cannot comprehend more abstract linguistic forms. If it is presented with such simple commands as "wink," "nod," "shake head," or "smile," it seldom responds.

The right hemisphere, however, has a highly developed spatial and pattern sense. It is superior to the left hemisphere in constructing geometric and perspective drawings. It can assemble colored blocks to match a complex design much more effectively than the left hemisphere. When split-brain subjects are asked to use their right hand to assemble the blocks according to a picture design, they make numerous mistakes. Sometimes they have trouble keeping their left hand from automatically correcting the mistakes being made by the right hand.

Studies with normal individuals tend to confirm the different specializations of the two hemispheres. For example, verbal information (such as words or nonsense syllables) can be identified faster and more accurately when flashed briefly to the left hemisphere (that is, in the right visual field) than to the right hemisphere. In contrast, the identification of faces, facial expressions of emotion, line slopes, or dot locations occurs more quickly when flashed to the right hemisphere (Hellige, 1994). And **electroencephalogram** (EEG) studies indicate that electrical activity from the left hemisphere increases during a verbal task, whereas during a spatial task, EEG activity increases in the right hemisphere (Springer & Deutsch, 1989; Kosslyn, 1988).

One should not infer from this discussion that the two hemispheres work independently of each other. Just the opposite is true. The hemispheres differ in their specializations, but they integrate their activities at all times. It is this interaction that gives rise to mental processes greater than and different from each hemisphere's special contribution. As noted by Levy,

These differences are seen in the contrasting contributions each hemisphere makes to all cognitive activities. When a person reads a story, the right hemisphere may play a special role in decoding visual information, maintaining an integrated story structure, appreciating humor and emotional content, deriving meaning from past associations and understanding metaphor. At the same time, the left hemisphere plays a special role in understanding syntax, translating written words into their phonetic representations and deriving meaning from complex relations among word concepts and syntax. But there is no activity in which only one hemisphere is involved or to which only one hemisphere makes a contribution. (1985, p. 44)

AUTONOMIC NERVOUS SYSTEM

We noted earlier that the peripheral nervous system consists of two divisions. The somatic system controls the skeletal muscles and receives information from the skin, muscles, and various sensory receptors. The autonomic system controls the glands and the smooth muscles, which include the heart, the blood vessels, and the lining of the stomach and intestines. These muscles are called "smooth" because that is how they look when examined under a microscope. (Skeletal muscles, in contrast, have a striped appearance.) The autonomic nervous system derives its name from the fact that many of the activities it controls are autonomous, or self-regulating—such as digestion and circulation—and continue even when a person is asleep or unconscious.

The **autonomic nervous system** has two divisions, the **sympathetic** and the **parasympathetic**, which are often antagonistic in their actions. Figure 2-15 shows the contrasting effects of the two systems on various organs. For example, the parasympathetic system constricts the pupil of the eye, stimulates the flow of saliva, and slows the heart rate; the

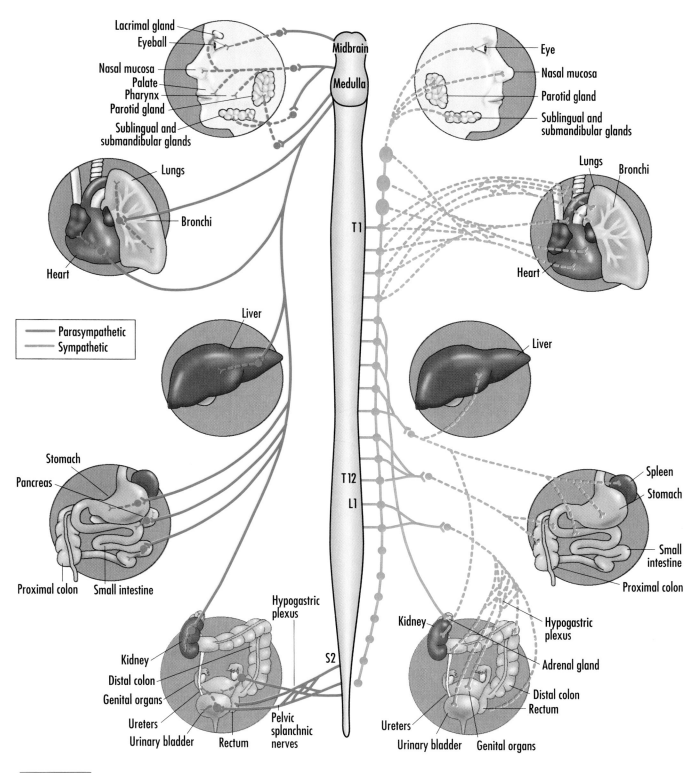

FIGURE 2-15

Motor Fibers of the Autonomic Nervous System *In this diagram the sympathetic division is indicated in blue and the parasympathetic is in red. Solid lines indicate preganglionic fibers and dashed lines indicate postganglionic fibers. Neurons of the sympathetic division originate in the thoracic and lumbar regions of the spinal cord; they form synaptic junctions with ganglia lying just outside the cord. Neurons of the parasympathetic division exit from the medulla region of the brain stem and from the lower (sacral) end of the spinal cord; they connect with ganglia near the organs stimulated. Most internal organs are innervated by both divisions, which function in opposition to each other.*

sympathetic system has the opposite effect in each case. The normal state of the body (somewhere between extreme excitement and vegetative placidity) is maintained by the balance between these two systems.

The sympathetic division tends to act as a unit. During emotional excitement, it simultaneously speeds up the heart, dilates the arteries of the skeletal muscles and heart, constricts the arteries of the skin and digestive organs, and causes perspiration. It also activates certain endocrine glands to secrete hormones that further increase arousal.

Unlike the sympathetic system, the parasympathetic division tends to affect one organ at a time. If the sympathetic system is thought of as dominant during violent and excited activity, the parasympathetic system may be thought of as dominant during quiescence. It participates in digestion and, in general, maintains the functions that conserve and protect bodily resources.

While the sympathetic and parasympathetic systems are usually antagonistic to one another, there are some exceptions to this principle. For example, the sympathetic system is dominant during fear and excitement; however, a not-uncommon parasympathetic symptom during extreme fear is the involuntary discharge of the bladder or bowels. Another example is the complete sex act in the male, which requires erection (parasympathetic) followed by ejaculation (sympathetic). Thus, although the two systems are often antagonistic, they interact in complex ways.

ENDOCRINE SYSTEM

We can think of the nervous system as controlling the fast-changing activities of the body by its ability to directly activate muscles and glands. The **endocrine system** is slower acting and indirectly affects the activities of cell groups throughout the body by means of chemicals called **hormones**. These hormones are secreted by the various endocrine glands into the bloodstream (see Figure 2-16). The hormones then travel through the body, acting in various ways on cells of different types. Each target cell is equipped with receptors that recognize only the hormone molecules meant to act on that cell; the receptors pull the appropriate hormone molecules out of the bloodstream and into the cell. Some endocrine glands are activated by the nervous system, while others are activated by changes in the internal chemical state of the body.

One of the major endocrine glands, the **pituitary**, is partly an outgrowth of the brain and lies just below the hypothalamus (refer back to Figure 2.9). The pituitary gland has been called the "master gland" because it produces the largest number of different hormones and controls the secretion of other endocrine glands. One of the pituitary hormones has the crucial job of controlling body growth. Too little of this hormone can create a dwarf, while oversecretion can produce a giant. Other hormones released by the pituitary trigger the action of other endocrine glands, such as the thyroid, the sex glands, and the outer layer of the adrenal gland. Courtship, mating, and reproductive behavior in many animals are based on a complex interaction between the activity of the nervous system and the influence of the pituitary on the sex glands.

The relationship between the pituitary gland and the hypothalamus illustrates the complex interactions that take place between the endocrine system and the nervous system. In response to stress (fear, anxiety, pain, emotional events, and so forth) certain neurons in the hypothalamus secrete a substance called **corticotropin-release factor** (CRF). The pituitary is just below the hypothalamus and CRF is carried to it through a channel-like structure. The CRF stimulates the pituitary to release **adrenocorticotrophic hormone** (ACTH), which is the body's major stress hormone. ACTH, in turn, is carried by the bloodstream to the adrenal glands and to various other organs of the body, causing the release of some 30 hormones, each of which plays a role in the body's adjustment to emergency situations. This sequence of events indicates that the endocrine system is influenced by the hypothalamus and thereby influenced by other brain centers via the hypothalamus.

The **adrenal glands** play an important role in determining an individual's mood, level of energy, and ability to cope with stress. The inner core of the adrenal gland secretes **epinephrine** and **norepinephrine** (also known as **adrenaline** and **noradrenaline**). Epinephrine acts in a number of ways to prepare the organism for an emergency, often in conjunction with the sympathetic division of the autonomic nervous system. Epinephrine, for example, affects the smooth muscles and the sweat glands in a way similar to that of the sympathetic system. It causes constriction of the blood vessels in the stomach and intestines and makes the heart beat faster (as anyone who has ever had a shot of adrenaline knows).

Norepinephrine also prepares the organism for emergency action. When it reaches the pituitary in its travels through the bloodstream, it stimulates the gland to release a hormone that acts on the outer layer of the adrenal glands; in turn, this second hormone stimulates the liver to increase the blood-sugar level so the body has energy for quick action.

The hormones of the endocrine system and the neurotransmitters of neurons have similar functions; they both carry *messages* between cells of the body. A neurotransmitter carries messages between adjacent neurons, and its effect is highly localized. In contrast, a hormone may travel a long distance through the body and act in various ways on many different types of cells. The basic similarity between these chemical messengers (despite their differences) is shown by the fact that some serve both functions. Epinephrine and norepinephrine, for example, act as neurotransmitters when released by neurons, and as hormones when released by the adrenal gland.

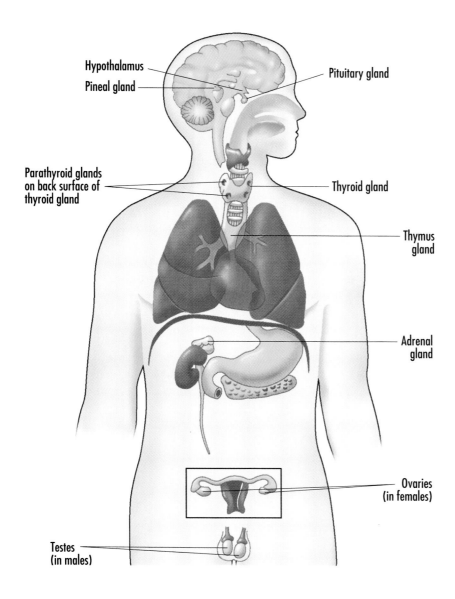

FIGURE 2-16

Some of the Endocrine Glands *Hormones secreted by the endocrine glands are as essential as the nervous system to the integration of the organism's activity. The endocrine system and the nervous system, however, differ in the speed with which they can act. A nerve impulse can travel through the organism in a few hundredths of a second. Seconds, or even minutes, may be required for an endocrine gland to produce an effect; the hormone, once released, must travel to its target site via the bloodstream—a much slower process.*

GENETIC INFLUENCES ON BEHAVIOR

To understand the biological foundations of psychology, we need to know something about hereditary influences. The field of **behavior genetics** combines the methods of genetics and psychology to study the inheritance of behavioral characteristics (Plomin, 1991). We know that many physical characteristics—height, bone structure, hair and eye color, and so on—are inherited. Behavioral geneticists are interested in the degree to which psychological characteristics—mental ability, temperament, emotional stability, and so on—are transmitted from parent to offspring (Bouchard, 1994).

CHROMOSOMES AND GENES

The hereditary units we receive from our parents and transmit to our offspring are carried by structures known as **chromosomes**, which are found in the nucleus of each cell in the body. Most body cells contain 46 chromosomes. At conception, the human being receives 23 chromosomes from the father's sperm and 23 chromosomes from the mother's ovum. These 46 chromosomes form 23 pairs, which are duplicated each time the cells divide (see Figure 2-17).

Each chromosome is composed of many individual hereditary units called **genes**. A gene is a segment of **deoxyribonucleic acid (DNA)**, which is the actual carrier of genetic information. The DNA molecule looks like a twisted ladder or a double-stranded helix (spiral), as shown in Figure 2-18. All DNA has the same chemical composition, consisting of a simple sugar (deoxyribose), phosphate, and four bases—adenine, guanine, thymine, and cytosine (A, G, T, C). The two strands of the DNA molecule are composed of phosphate and sugar, and the strands are held apart by pairs of bases. Due to the structural properties of these bases, A always pairs with T and G always pairs with C. The bases can occur in any sequence along a strand, and these sequences constitute the genetic code. The fact that many different arrangements of bases are possible is what gives DNA the ability to express many different genetic messages. The same four bases specify the characteristics of every living organism and, depending on their arrangement, determine whether a creature turns out to be a bird, a lion, a fish, or Michelangelo.

A segment of the DNA molecule, the gene, will give coded instructions to the cell, directing it to perform a specific function (usually to manufacture a particular protein). Although all cells in the body carry the same genes, the specialized nature of each cell is due to the fact that only 5 to 10 percent of the genes are active in any given cell. In the process of developing from a fertilized egg, each cell switches on some genes and switches off all others. When "nerve genes" are active, for example, a cell develops as a neuron because the genes are directing the cell to make the products that allow it to perform neural functions (which would not be possible if the genes irrelevant to a neuron, such as "muscle genes," were not switched off).

Genes, like chromosomes, exist in pairs. One gene of each pair comes from the sperm chromosomes and one gene comes from the ovum chromosomes. Thus, a child receives only half of each parent's total genes. The total number of genes in each human chromosome is around 1,000—perhaps higher. Because the number of genes is so high, it is extremely unlikely that two human beings would have the same heredity, even if they were siblings. The only exception is *identical twins,* who, because they developed from the same fertilized egg, have exactly the same genes.

FIGURE 2.17

Chromosomes *This photo (greatly enlarged) shows the 46 chromosomes of a normal human female. A human male would have the same pairs 1 through 22, but pair 23 would be XY rather than XX.*

DOMINANT AND RECESSIVE GENES Either gene of a gene pair can be a **dominant** gene or a **recessive** gene. When both members of a gene pair are dominant, the individual manifests the form of the trait specified by these dominant genes. When one gene is dominant and the other recessive, the dominant gene again determines the form of the trait. Only if the genes contributed by both parents are recessive is the recessive form of the trait expressed. The genes determining eye color, for example, act in a pattern of dominance and recessiveness; blue is recessive and brown is dominant. Thus, a blue-eyed child may have two blue-eyed parents, or one blue-eyed parent and one brown-eyed parent (who carries a recessive gene for blue eyes), or two brown-eyed parents (each of whom carries a recessive gene for blue eyes). A brown-eyed child, in contrast, never has two blue-eyed parents.

Some of the characteristics that are carried by recessive genes are baldness, albinism, hemophilia, and a susceptibility to poison ivy. Not all gene pairs follow the dominant-recessive pattern, and as we shall see, most human characteristics are determined by many genes acting together, rather than by a single gene pair.

Even though most human characteristics are not determined by the actions of a single gene pair, there are some striking exceptions. Of special interest from a psychological viewpoint are diseases like *phenylketonuria* (PKU) and *Huntington's disease* (HD), both of which involve deterioration of the nervous system and correlated behavioral and cognitive problems. Geneticists have identified the gene responsible for PKU and the gene responsible for HD.

PKU results from the action of a recessive gene that is inherited from each parent. The infant cannot digest an essential amino acid (phenylalanine), which then builds up in the body, poisoning the nervous system and causing irreversible brain damage. PKU children are severely retarded and usually die before the age of 30. If the PKU disorder is discovered at birth and the infants are placed on a diet that controls the level of phenylalanine, their chances of surviving with good health and intelligence are fairly high. Until the PKU gene was located, the disorder could not be diagnosed until an infant was at least 3 weeks old. Now it is possible to determine prenatally

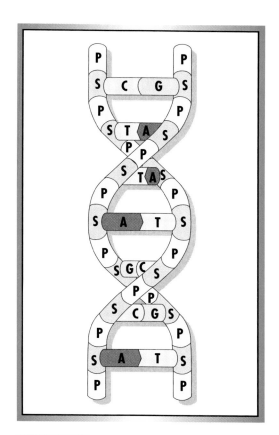

FIGURE 2-18

Structures of the DNA Molecule *Each strand of the molecule is made up of an alternating sequence of sugar (S) and phosphate (P); the rungs of the twisted ladder are made up of four bases (A, G, T, C). The double nature of the helix and the restriction on base pairings make possible the self-replication of DNA. In the process of cell division, the two strands of the DNA molecule come apart with the base pairs separating; one member of each base pair remains attached to each strand. Each strand then forms a new complementary strand using excess bases available in the cell; an A attached to a strand will attract a T, and so forth. By this process, two identical molecules of DNA come to exist where previously there was one.*

whether the fetus has the PKU gene so that the proper diet can begin at birth.

HD is caused by a single dominant gene. The long-term course of the disease involves a degeneration of certain areas in the brain and the ultimate outcome is death. Victims gradually lose their ability to talk and to control their movements, and they show a marked deterioration in memory and mental ability. The disease usually strikes when a person is 30 to 40 years of age. Before then there are no symptoms or other evidence of the disease. Once HD strikes, victims will typically live for 10 to 15 years with progressive deterioration and the agonizing experience of knowing what is happening to them.

Now that the Huntington gene has been isolated, geneticists can test individuals at risk and tell with virtual certainty whether or not they carry the gene. As yet, there is no cure for HD, but the protein produced by the gene has been determined. It is this protein that must in some way be responsible for HD and may provide a key for treating the disease.

SEX-LINKED GENES   Male and female chromosomes appear the same under a microscope, except for pair 23, which determines the sex of the individual and carries genes for certain traits that are sex-linked. A normal female has two similar-looking chromosomes in pair 23, called X chromosomes. A normal male has one X chromosome in pair 23 and one that looks slightly different, called a Y chromosome (refer back to Figure 2-17). Thus, the normal female chromosome pair 23 is represented by the symbol XX and the normal male pair by XY.

When most body cells reproduce, the resulting cells have the same number of chromosomes (46) as the parent cell. However, when sperm and egg cells reproduce, the

chromosome pairs separate, and half go to each new cell. Thus, egg and sperm cells have only 23 chromosomes. Each egg cell has an X chromosome, and each sperm cell has either an X or a Y chromosome. If an X-type sperm is the first to enter an egg cell, the fertilized ovum will have an XX chromosome pair and the child will be a female. If a Y-type sperm fertilizes the egg, the 23rd chromosome pair will be XY and the child will be a male. The female inherits one X chromosome from the mother and one from the father; the male inherits his X chromosome from the mother and his Y chromosome from the father. Thus, it is the father's chromosome contribution that determines a child's sex (see Figure 2-19).

The X chromosome may carry either dominant or recessive genes; the Y chromosome carries a few genes dominant for male sexual characteristics but otherwise seems to carry only recessive genes. Thus, most recessive characteristics carried by a man's X chromosome (received from his mother) are expressed since they are not blocked by dominant genes. For example, color blindness is a recessive sex-linked characteristic. A man will be color-blind if he inherits a color-blind gene on the X chromosome he receives from his mother. Females are less often color-blind, because a color-blind female has to have both a color-blind father and a mother who is either color-blind or who carries a recessive gene for color blindness. A number of genetically determined disorders are linked to the 23rd chromosome pair; these are called *sex-linked disorders*.

GENETIC STUDIES OF BEHAVIOR

Some traits are determined by single genes, but most human characteristics are determined by many genes: they are **polygenic**. Traits such as intelligence, height, and emotionality do not fall into distinct categories, but show continuous variation. Most people are neither dull nor bright; intelligence is distributed over a broad range, with most individuals located near the middle. Sometimes a specific genetic defect can result in mental retardation, but in most instances, a person's intellectual potential is determined by a large number of genes that influence the factors underlying different abilities. Of course, what

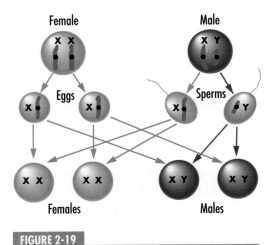

FIGURE 2-19

Sex of Offspring   *Females have XX cells and all of their eggs contain a single X chromosome. Males have XY cells; half of their sperm are X-bearing and half are Y-bearing. The sex of the offspring is determined by the sex chromosome contained in the sperm that fertilizes the egg.*

happens to this genetic potential depends on environmental conditions (Plomin, Owen & McGruffin, 1994).

SELECTIVE BREEDING One method of studying the heritability of traits in animals is by selective breeding. Animals that are high or low in a certain trait are mated with each other. For example, to study the inheritance of learning ability in rats, the females that do poorly in learning to run a maze are mated with males that do poorly; the females that do well are mated with the males that do well. The off-spring of these matings are tested on the same maze. On the basis of performance, the brightest are mated with the brightest and the dullest with the dullest. (To ensure that environmental conditions are kept constant, the offspring of "dull" mothers are some-times given to "bright" mothers to raise so that genetic endowment rather than ade-quacy of maternal care is being tested.) After a few rodent generations, a "bright" and a "dull" strain of rats can be produced (see Fig-ure 2-20).

Selective breeding has been used to show the inheritance of a number of behavioral characteristics. For example, dogs have been bred to be excitable or lethargic; chickens, to be aggressive and sexually active; fruit flies, to be more drawn or less drawn to light; and mice, to be more attracted or less attracted to alcohol. If a trait is influenced by heredity, it should be possible to change it by selective breeding. If selective breeding does not alter a trait, we assume that the trait is primarily dependent on environmental factors (Plomin, 1986).

TWIN STUDIES Since, ethically, breeding experi-ments cannot be carried out with human be-ings, we must look instead at similarities in behavior among individuals who are related. Certain traits often run in families. But fami-lies are not only linked genetically, they also share the same environment. If musical tal-ent runs in the family, we do not know whether inherited ability or parental empha-sis on music is more important to this devel-opment. Sons of alcoholic fathers are more likely than sons of nonalcoholic fathers to de-velop alcoholism. Do genetic tendencies or environmental conditions play the major role? In an effort to answer questions of this

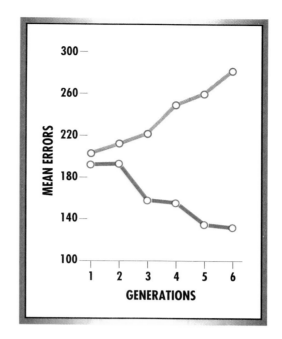

FIGURE 2-20

Inheritance of Maze Learning in Rats *Mean error scores of "bright" (green line) and "dull" (purple line) rats selectively bred for maze-running ability. (After Thompson, 1954)*

sort, psychologists have turned to studies on twins.

Identical twins develop from a single fer-tilized egg and thus share the same heredity; they are also called **monozygotic** since they come from a single zygote, or fertilized egg. Fraternal twins develop from different egg cells and are no more alike genetically than are ordinary siblings; they are also called **dizygotic**, or two-egged. Fraternal twins are about twice as common as identical twins. As Figure 2-21 indicates, there are other types of twins, but they are extremely rare.

Studies comparing identical and fraternal twins help to sort out the influence of envi-ronment and heredity. Identical twins are found to be more similar in intelligence than fraternal twins, even when they are separated at birth and reared in different homes (see Chapter 13). Identical twins are also more similar than fraternal twins in some person-ality characteristics and in susceptibility to the mental disorder of schizophrenia (see Chapter 15). Twin studies have proved to be a useful method of investigating genetic influ-ences on human behavior.

IDENTICAL TWINS

1. Accounting for about 1 in 250 births, identical twins are created when a single egg is fertilized by one sperm.

2. The egg splits into halves. Each develops into a fetus with the same genetic composition.

FRATERNAL TWINS

1. Twice as common as identicals, fraternals arise when two eggs are released at once.

2. If both are fertilized by separate sperm, two fetuses form. Genetically they are just ordinary siblings.

HALF-IDENTICAL TWINS

1. A rare type, half-identicals form when a precursor to an egg splits evenly and is fertilized by two sperm.

2. The fetuses have about half of their genes in common—those from the mother.

FIGURE 2-21

Types of Twins *Besides identical and fraternal twins, there may be "half-identical" twins. Half-identicals arise when a precursor to a true ovum divides into identical halves and is fertilized by two sperm. Thus they are more alike than fraternals, but less alike than identicals.*

Identical twins.

ENVIRONMENTAL INFLUENCES ON GENE ACTION The inherited potential with which an individual enters the world is very much influenced by the environment that he or she encounters. This interaction will be made clear in later chapters, but two examples will suffice to illustrate the point here. The tendency to develop diabetes is hereditary, although the exact method of transmission is unknown. Diabetes is a disease in which the pancreas does not produce enough insulin to burn carbohydrates as an energy source for the body. Scientists assume that genes determine the production of insulin. But people who carry the genetic potential for diabetes do not always develop the disease; for example, if one identical twin has diabetes, the other twin will develop the disorder in only about half the cases. Not all of the environmental factors that contribute to diabetes are known, but one variable that seems fairly certain is obesity. A fat person requires more insulin to metabolize carbohydrates than a thin person. Consequently, an individual who carries the genes for diabetes is more likely to develop the disorder if he or she is overweight.

A similar situation is found in the mental illness called **schizophrenia**. As we shall see in Chapter 15 substantial evidence indicates a hereditary component to the disorder. If one identical twin is schizophrenic, chances are high that the other twin will exhibit some signs of mental disturbance. But whether or not the other twin develops the full-blown disorder will depend on a number of environmental factors. The genes may predispose, but the environment shapes the outcome.

📖 CHAPTER SUMMARY

1. The basic unit of the nervous system is a specialized type of cell called a *neuron*. Projecting from the cell body of the neuron are a number of short branches called *dendrites* and a slender tubelike extension called the *axon*. Stimulation of the dendrites and cell body leads to a neural impulse that travels down the length of the axon. *Sensory neurons* transmit signals from sense organs to the brain and spinal cord; *motor neurons* transmit signals from the brain and spinal cord to muscles and glands. A *nerve* is a bundle of elongated axons belonging to hundreds or thousands of neurons.

2. A stimulus moves along a neuron as an electrochemical impulse that travels from the dendrites to the end of the axon. This traveling impulse, or *action potential,* is caused by a self-propagating mechanism called *depolarization* that changes the permeability of the cell membrane to different types of *ions* (electrically charged atoms and molecules) that float in and about the cell.

3. An action potential, once started, travels down the axon to many small swellings at the end of the axon called *synaptic terminals.* These terminals release chemical substances, called *neurotransmitters,* that are responsible for transferring the signal from one neuron to an adjacent one. The neurotransmitters diffuse across a small gap between the juncture of the two neurons (called the *synapse*) and bind to *neuroreceptors* in the cell membrane of the receiving neuron. Some neurotransmitter-receptor bindings cause the cell membrane to depolarize while others cause it to polarize. If depolarization reaches a threshold level, an action potential is fired down the length of the receiving neuron. The occurrence of the action potential is an all-or-none event. There are many different kinds of neurotransmitter-receptor interactions and they help explain a range of psychological phenomena.

4. The nervous system is divided into the *central nervous system* (the brain and spinal cord) and the *peripheral nervous system* (the nerves connecting the brain and spinal cord to other parts of the body). Subdivisions of the peripheral nervous system are the *somatic system* (which carries messages to and from the sense receptors, muscles, and the body surface) and the *autonomic system* (which connects with the internal organs and glands).

5. The human brain is composed of three concentric layers: a *central core,* the *limbic system,* and the *cerebrum.*

a. The central core includes the *medulla,* responsible for respiration and postural reflexes; the *cerebellum* is concerned with motor coordination; the *thalamus* is a relay station for incoming sensory information; and the *hypothalamus* is important in emotion and in maintaining homeostasis. The *reticular formation,* which crosses through several of the above structures, controls the organism's state of wakefulness and arousal.

b. The *limbic system* controls some of the instinctive activities (feeding, attacking, flee-

ing from danger, mating) regulated by the hypothalamus; it also plays an important role in emotion and memory.

c. The *cerebrum* is divided into two *cerebral hemispheres.* The convoluted surface of these hemispheres, the *cerebral cortex,* plays a critical role in discrimination, decision making, learning, and thinking—the higher mental processes. Certain areas of the cerebral cortex represent centers for specific sensory inputs or for control of specific movements. The remainder of the cerebral cortex consists of *association areas.*

6. When the *corpus callosum* (the band of nerve fibers connecting the two cerebral hemispheres) is severed, significant differences in the functioning of the two hemispheres can be observed. The left hemisphere is skilled in language and mathematical abilities. The right hemisphere can understand some language but cannot communicate through speech; it has a highly developed spatial and pattern sense.

7. The *autonomic nervous system* is made up of the *sympathetic* and the *parasympathetic* divisions. Because its fibers mediate the action of the smooth muscles and of the glands, the autonomic system is particularly important in emotional reactions. The sympathetic division is active during excitement and the parasympathetic during quiescence.

8. The *endocrine glands* secrete hormones into the bloodstream that are important for emotional and motivational behavior. They complement the nervous system in integrating behavior, and their action is closely tied to the activity of the hypothalamus and the autonomic nervous system.

9. An individual's hereditary potential, transmitted by the *chromosomes* and *genes,* influences psychological and physical characteristics. Genes are segments of *DNA* molecules, which store genetic information. Some genes are *dominant,* some *recessive,* and some *sex-linked.* Most human characteristics are *polygenic*—that is, determined by many genes acting together, rather than by a single gene pair.

10. *Selective breeding* (mating animals that are high or low in a certain trait) is one method of studying the influence of heredity. Another method for sorting out the effects of environment and heredity is *twin studies,* in which the characteristics of *identical twins* (who share the same heredity) are compared with those of *fraternal twins* (who are no

more alike genetically than ordinary siblings). Behavior depends on the *interaction* between heredity and environment; the genes set the limits of the individual's potential, but what happens to this potential depends on the environment.

FURTHER READING

Introductions to physiological psychology are Carlson, *Foundations of Physiological Psychology* (1988); Groves and Rebec, *Introduction to Biological Psychology* (4th ed., 1992); Kolb and Whishaw, *Fundamentals of Human Neuropsychology* (3rd ed., 1989); Schneider and Tarshis, *An Introduction to Physiological Psychology* (3rd ed., 1986); and Rosenzweig and Leiman, *Physiological Psychology* (2nd ed., 1989).

For a review of the molecular basis of neural processes, see Alberts et al. *Molecular Biology of the Cell* (2nd ed., 1989). Also see Squire, *Memory and Brain* (1987) for a discussion of the neural basis of memory and cognition; and Crick, *The Astonishing Hypothesis: The Scientific Search for the Soul (1994)* for a discussion of human consciousness in terms of neural mechanisms.

A survey of genetic influences on behavior is provided by Plomin, De Fries, and McClearn, *Behavioral Genetics: A Primer* (2nd ed., 1989). For a review of psychoactive drugs and their effects on the body, brain, and behavior, see Julien, *A Primer of Drug Action* (6th ed., 1992) and Julien, *Drugs and the Body* (1988).

For a survey of research on the function of the two cerebral hemispheres, see Springer and Deutsch, *Left Brain, Right Brain* (3rd ed., 1989) and Hellige, *Hemispheric Asymmetry: What's Right and What's Left* (1994).

PSYCHOLOGICAL DEVELOPMENT

O f all mammals, human beings require the longest period of maturation and learning before they are self-sufficient. In general, the more complex an organism's nervous system is, the longer the time required to reach maturity. A lemur (a primitive primate) can move about on its own shortly after birth and is soon able to fend for itself; an infant monkey is dependent on its mother for several months, a chimpanzee for several years. But even a chimpanzee—one of our closest relatives—will be a functioning adult member of its species long before a human of the same age.

Developmental psychologists are concerned with how and why different aspects of human functioning develop and change across the life span. These include *physical development,* such as changes in height and weight and the acquisition of motor skills; *cognitive development,* such as changes in thought processes, memory, and language abilities; and *personality and social development,* such as changes in self-concept, gender identity, and interpersonal relationships.

The development of particular psychological abilities and functions is treated in more detail in later chapters. For example, perceptual development is discussed in Chapter 5, concept acquisition and language development in Chapter 9, sexual development in Chapter 10, and personality development in Chapters 12 and 13. In this chapter, we provide a general overview of psychological development across the life span and consider two central questions: (a) How do biological factors interact with events in the child's environment to determine the course of development (often called the "nature-nurture" question)? and (b) Is development best understood as a gradual, continuous process of change or as a series of abrupt, qualitatively distinct stages?

INTERACTION BETWEEN NATURE AND NURTURE

The question of whether heredity ("nature") or environment ("nurture") is more important in determining the course of human development has been debated through the centuries. For example, the seventeenth-century British philosopher John Locke rejected the prevailing notion of his day that babies were miniature adults who arrived in the world fully equipped with abilities and knowledge and who simply had to grow in order for these inherited characteristics to appear. On the contrary, Locke believed that the mind of a newborn infant is a "blank slate" (**tabula rasa**). What gets written on this slate is what the baby experiences—what he or she sees, hears, tastes, smells, and feels. According to Locke, all knowledge comes to us through our senses. It is provided by experience; no knowledge or ideas are built in.

The advent of Charles Darwin's theory of evolution (1859), which emphasizes the biological basis of human development, led to a return of the hereditarian viewpoint. With the rise of behaviorism in the twentieth century, however, the environmentalist position once again gained dominance. Behaviorists such as John B. Watson and B. F. Skinner argued that human nature is completely malleable: Early training can turn a child into any kind of adult, regardless of his or her heredity. Watson stated the argument in its most extreme form: "Give me a dozen healthy infants, well-formed, and my own specified world to bring them up in, and I'll guarantee to take any one at random and train him to be any type of specialist I might select—doctor, lawyer, artist, merchant-chief, and, yes, even beggar-man and thief, regardless of his talents, penchants, tendencies, abilities, vocations, and race of his ancestors" (1930, p. 104).

Today most psychologists agree not only that both nature and nurture play important roles but that they interact continuously to guide development. For example, we shall see in Chapter 12 that the development of many personality traits, such as sociability and emotional stability, appear to be influenced about equally by heredity and environment; similarly, we shall see in Chapter 15 that psychiatric illnesses can have both genetic and environmental determinants.

Even development that seems most obviously to be determined by innate biological timetables can be affected by environmental events. At the moment of conception, a remarkable number of personal characteristics are already determined by the genetic structure of the fertilized ovum. Our genes program our growing cells so that we develop into a person rather than a fish or chimpanzee. They decide our sex, the color of our skin, eyes, and hair, and general body size, among other things. These genetic determinants are expressed in development through the process of **maturation**—innately determined sequences of growth and change that are relatively independent of environmental events.

For example, the human fetus develops within the mother's body according to a fairly fixed time schedule, and fetal behavior, such as turning and kicking, also follows an orderly sequence that depends on the stage of growth. However, if the uterine environment is seriously abnormal in some way, maturational processes can be disrupted. For example, if the mother contracts German measles during the first 3 months of pregnancy (when the fetus's basic organ systems are developing according to the genetically programmed schedule), the infant may be born deaf, blind, or brain-damaged, depending on which organ system was in a critical stage of development at the time of infection. Maternal malnutrition, smoking, and consumption of alcohol and drugs are among the other environmental factors that can affect the normal maturation of the fetus.

Motor development after birth also illustrates the interaction between genetically programmed maturation and environmental influence. Virtually all children go through the same sequence of motor behaviors in the same order: rolling over, sitting without support, standing while holding onto furniture, crawling, and then walking. But children go through the sequence at the different rates, and developmental psychologists began very early in the history of the discipline to ask whether learning and experience play an important role in such differences.

Although early studies suggested that the answer was no (McGraw, 1935/1975; Dennis & Dennis, 1940; Gesell & Thompson, 1929), more recent studies indicate that practice or extra stimulation can accelerate the appearance of motor behaviors to some extent. For example, newborn infants have a stepping reflex; if they are held in an upright position with their feet touching a solid surface, their legs will make stepping movements that are similar to walking. A group of infants who were given stepping practice for a few minutes several times a day during the first two months of life began walking five to seven weeks earlier than babies who had not had this practice (Zelazo, Zelazo, & Kolb, 1972).

The development of speech provides another example of the interaction between genetically determined characteristics and experience. In the course of normal development, all human infants learn to speak, but not until they have attained a certain level of neurological development; no infant less than a year old speaks in sentences. But children reared in an environment in which people talk to them and reward them for making speechlike sounds talk earlier than children who do not receive such attention. For example, children reared in middle-class American homes begin to speak at about 1 year of age. Children reared in San Marcos, a remote village in Guatemala, have little verbal interaction with adults and do not utter their first words until they are over 2 years old (Kagan, 1979).

Virtually all children go through the same sequence of motor behaviors in the same order.

STAGES OF DEVELOPMENT

In explaining the sequence of development, several psychologists have proposed that there are discrete, qualitatively distinct steps or **stages of development**. Many of us use this concept informally. We think of the life span as being divided into the stages of infancy, childhood, adolescence, and adulthood. Parents might say that their adolescent is going through a "rebellious stage." Developmental psychologists, however, have a more precise concept in mind: The concept of stages implies that (a) behaviors at a given stage are organized around a dominant theme or coherent set of characteristics; (b) behaviors at one stage are qualitatively different from behaviors that appear at earlier or later stages; and (c) all children go through the same stages in the same order. Environmental factors may speed up or slow down development, but the order of stages is invariant; a child cannot achieve a later stage without going through an earlier one first.

Not all psychologists agree that development proceeds according to an invariant sequence of qualitatively distinct stages. Some argue that many of the tasks designed to test stage theories actually require several underlying information-processing skills if the child is to succeed on them (for example, attention, memory, specific factual knowledge). Because these component skills develop at different rates, development on the overall tasks may appear to be discontinuous, but the underlying component skills themselves are developing in a smooth and continuous manner. A closely related argument is that the tasks used to assess the stages are not narrowly designed enough to test only the specific ability under examination. A child may actually possess the requisite ability but fail the task because he or she lacks one of the other abilities it requires. As a result, children's abilities have been frequently underestimated by the stage theorists. We will examine the evidence for and against the stage theories as we proceed.

Closely related to the concept of stages is the idea that there may be **critical periods** in human development—crucial time periods in a person's life during which specific events must occur for development to proceed normally. Critical periods have been firmly established for some aspects of the physical devel-opment of the human fetus. For example, the period 6 to 7 weeks after conception is critical for the normal development of the fetus's sex organs. Whether the primitive sex organ develops into a male or female sexual structure depends on the presence of male hormones, regardless of the XX or XY arrangement of chromosomes. The absence of male hormones means that female sexual organs will develop in either case. If male hormones are injected later in development, they cannot reverse the changes that have already taken place.

During postnatal development, there is a critical period for the development of vision. If children who are born with cataracts have them removed before the age of 7, their vision will develop fairly normally. But if a child goes through the first seven years without adequate vision, extensive permanent disability will result (Kuman, Fedrov, & Novikova, 1983).

The existence of critical periods in the psychological development of the child has not been established. It is probably more accurate to say that there are sensitive periods—periods that are optimal for a particular kind of development. If a certain behavior is not well established during this sensitive period, it may not develop to its full potential. For example, the first year of life may be sensitive for the formation of close interpersonal attachments. The preschool years may be especially significant for intellectual development and language acquisition. Children who have not had sufficient exposure to language prior to the age of 6 or 7 years may fail to acquire it altogether (Goldin-Meadow, 1982). The experiences of the child during such sensitive periods may shape his or her future course of development in a manner that will be difficult to change later.

CAPACITIES OF THE NEWBORN

At the end of the nineteenth century, psychologist William James suggested that the newborn child experiences the world as a "buzzing, blooming confusion," an idea that was still prevalent as late as the 1960s. We now know that newborn infants enter the world with all sensory systems functioning and are well prepared to learn about their new environment.

Because babies cannot explain what they are doing or tell us what they are thinking, developmental psychologists have had to design some very ingenious procedures to study the capacities of young infants. The basic method is to introduce some change in the baby's environment and observe his or her responses. For example, an investigator might present a tone or a flashing light and then see if there is a change in heart rate or if the baby turns its head or sucks more vigorously on a nipple. In some instances, the researcher will present two stimuli at the same time to determine if infants look longer at one than the other. If they do, it indicates that they can tell the stimuli apart and may indicate that they prefer one to the other.

VISION

Because the visual system is not well developed at birth, newborns have poor visual acuity, their ability to change focus is limited, and they are very nearsighted. An adult with normal vision is said to have 20/20 vision; a nearsighted adult with 20/30 vision is able to see at 20 feet what an adult with normal vision can see at 30 feet. Using this same index, a newborn has 20/660 vision. At 6 months this has improved to 20/100; and by 2 years, the child can see almost as well as an adult (Courage & Adams, 1990).

Despite their visual immaturity, newborns spend a lot of time actively looking about. They scan the world in an organized way and pause when their eyes encounter an object or some change in the visual field. They are particularly attracted to areas of high visual contrast, such as the edges of an object. Instead of scanning the entire object, as an adult would, they keep looking at areas that have the most edges. They also prefer complex patterns to plain ones, prefer patterns with curved lines to patterns with straight lines, and they are especially interested in faces (Fantz, 1961) (see Figure 3-1).

The possibility that there is an inborn, unlearned preference for faces initially aroused great interest, but later research showed that infants are not attracted to faces per se but to

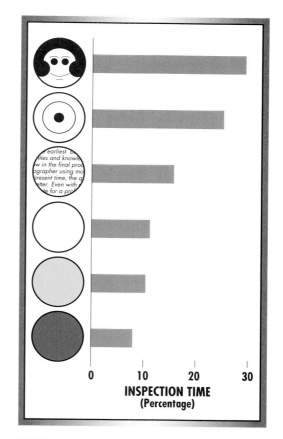

FIGURE 3-1

Visual Preferences *Newborns as young as 10 hours to 5 days old were shown disks that differed in particular ways—a facelike circle, a bull's-eye, an array of fine print, and disks colored white, yellow, or red. Infants could tell the difference between them and looked at different patterns different lengths of time.*

stimulus characteristics such as curved lines, high contrast, interesting edges, movement, and complexity—all of which faces possess (Banks & Salapatek, 1983; Aslin, 1987). Newborns look mostly at the outside contour of a face, but by 2 months they focus their attention on the inside of the face—the eyes, nose, and mouth (Haith, Bergman, & Moore, 1977). At this point parents may notice with delight that the baby has begun to make eye contact.

HEARING

Newborn infants will startle at the sound of a loud noise. They will also turn their heads toward the source of a sound. Interestingly, the head-turning response disappears at about 6 weeks and does not reemerge until 3 or 4 months of age, at which time the infants will also search with their eyes for the source of the sound. The temporary disappearance of the head-turning response probably represents a maturational transition from a reflexive response controlled by subcortical areas of the brain to a voluntary attempt to locate the sound source. By 4 months, they will reach in the correct direction toward the source of a sound in the dark; by 6 months they show a marked increase in their responsiveness to sounds that are accompanied by interesting sights and are able to pinpoint the location of sound more precisely, an ability that continues to improve into their second year (Hillier, Hewitt, & Morrongiello, 1992; Ashmead et al., 1991; Field, 1987).

Newborn infants can also detect the difference between very similar sounds, such as two tones that are only one note apart on the musical scale (Bridger, 1961), and they can distinguish sounds of the human voice from other kinds of sounds. We will see in Chapter 9 that they can also distinguish a number of critical characteristics of human speech. For example, 1-month-old infants can tell the difference between such similar sounds as "pa" and "ba." Interestingly, infants can distinguish between some speech sounds better than adults. These are sounds that adults "hear" as identical because they are not distinguished in their native language (Aslin, Pisoni, & Jusczyk, 1983). By 6 months of age, the child will have picked up enough information about the language that it will also have begun to "screen out" sounds it does not use (Kuhl et al., 1992). Thus, human infants appear to be born with perceptual mechanisms already tuned to the properties of human speech that will help them in their mastery of language (Eimas, 1975).

TASTE AND SMELL

Infants can discriminate differences in taste shortly after birth. They prefer sweet-tasting liquids to those that are salty, bitter, sour, or bland. The characteristic response of the newborn to a sweet liquid is a relaxed expression resembling a slight smile, sometimes accompanied by lip-licking. A sour solution produces pursed lips and a wrinkled nose. In response to a bitter solution, the baby will open its mouth with the corners turned down and stick out its tongue in what appears to be an expression of disgust.

Newborns can also discriminate among odors. They will turn their heads toward a sweet smell, and their heart rate and respiration will slow down, indicating attention. Noxious odors, such as ammonia or rotten eggs, cause them to turn their heads away; heart rate and respiration accelerate, indicating distress. Infants are even able to discriminate subtle differences in smells. After nursing for only a few days, an infant will consistently turn its head toward a pad saturated with its mother's milk in preference to one saturated with another mother's milk (Russell, 1976). Only breast-fed babies show this ability to recognize the mother's odor (Cernoch & Porter, 1985). When bottle-fed babies are given a choice between their familiar formula and the smell of a lactating breast, they will choose the latter (Porter et al., 1992). Thus, there seems to be an innate preference for the odor of breast milk. In general, the ability to distinguish among smells has a clear adaptive value: It helps infants avoid noxious substances, thereby increasing their likelihood of survival.

LEARNING AND MEMORY

It was once thought that infants could neither learn nor remember. This is not the case, and evidence for early learning and remembering comes from several studies. In one, infants only a few hours old learned to turn their heads right or left, depending on whether they heard a buzzer or a tone. In order to taste a sweet liquid, the baby had to turn to the right when a tone sounded and to turn to the left when a buzzer sounded. In only a few trials, the babies were performing without error—turning to the right when the tone sounded and to the left when the buzzer sounded. The experimenter then reversed the situation so that the infant had to turn the opposite way when either the buzzer or the tone sounded. The babies mastered this new task quickly (Siqueland & Lipsitt, 1966).

By the time they are 3 months old, infants have quite good memories. When a mobile over an infant's crib was attached by a ribbon to one of the baby's limbs, 3-month-old infants quickly discovered which arm or leg would

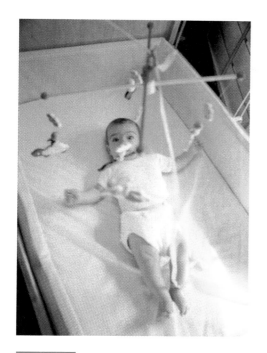

FIGURE 3-2

Early Learning *If a mobile is attached so the infant's movements activate the mobile, the infant soon discovers this relationship and seems to delight in activating the mobile with the appropriate kick. Two-month-old babies can learn to do this, but soon forget. Three-month-old babies can remember the correct action over several days.*

(DeCasper & Prescott, 1984; DeCasper & Fifer, 1980; Brazelton, 1978) (see Figure 3-3).

These several preferences appear to have their source in the infant's prenatal experience with sounds. Microphones placed near the fetus's head in the uterus reveal that the average sound level is quite high, about the level we experience when we are in a moving car (Birnholz & Benacerraf, 1983). One of the major sounds heard against the background noise is the mother's heartbeat, and the newborn's familiarity with this sound is apparently comforting. Groups of newborn infants were exposed to recordings of a human heart beating at different rates. One group heard the sound of a heart beating at the rate of 80 beats per minute, the normal rate they would have heard in the uterus; a second group heard a heart beating at 120 times per minute; the third group heard no special sounds. Newborns who heard the normal heartbeat gained more weight and cried less during the 4-day experiment than did newborns who heard no special sounds. Newborns exposed to the accelerated heartbeat became so upset that the investigator discontinued that part of the experiment (Salk, 1973). A study using a more elaborate

move the mobile. When the infants were placed in the same situation eight days later, they remembered which arm or leg to move (Hayne, Rovee-Collier, & Borza, 1991; Rovee-Collier & Hayne, 1987) (see Figure 3-2).

More startling is evidence that infants have already learned and remembered something from their prebirth experiences in the uterus. We noted earlier that newborn infants can distinguish the sound of the human voice from other sounds. They also prefer the human voice over other sounds. Infants tested within a few days of birth will learn to suck on an artificial nipple in order to turn on recorded speech or vocal music, but they will not suck as readily in order to hear nonspeech sounds or instrumental music (Butterfield & Siperstein, 1972). They also prefer heartbeat sounds and female voices to male voices, and they prefer their mothers' voices to those of other women. But they do not prefer their fathers' voices to those of other men

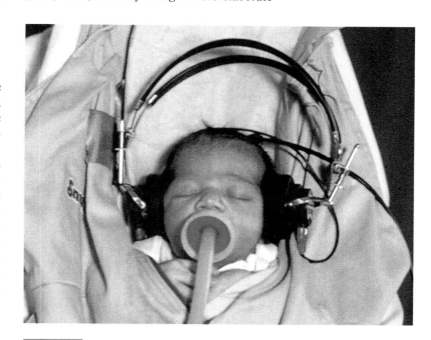

FIGURE 3-3

Preference for Sounds
A newborn can indicate a preference for certain sounds—like the mother's voice—by sucking more vigorously on a nipple when it causes the preferred sounds to be played through the earphones.

CRITICAL DISCUSSION

CAN NEWBORNS IMITATE?

For years, proud parents have claimed that their babies imitate their facial expressions—smiling, frowning, or sticking out the tongue in response to similar antics by the parents. It is beyond dispute that adults love to imitate babies, but the claim that young babies imitate adults encountered skepticism from developmental psychologists until recently.

Certainly the limited visual capacities and uncoordinated nature of a newborn infant would seem to rule out the possibility of very early imitation. Imitation would seem to require the infant to encode the visual image of the adult face into memory, translate this perception into corresponding motor commands, and then perform these commands. Moreover, because imitation requires individuals to reproduce a set of self-generated movements that they cannot themselves see or monitor visually, the famous Swiss psychologist, Jean Piaget, believed that imitation cannot develop until the child is able to form mental images—at about 18 months (Piaget, 1962).

Despite these apparent difficulties, many well-controlled observations suggest that parents may have been right all along. In one early study, researchers tested infants who were only 36 *hours* old! An adult "model" would hold the infant in her arms, do two knee bends, and click her tongue in order to get the infant's attention directed to her face. She would then hold her face in one of three facial expressions—happy, sad, or surprised—until the infant looked away. This was repeated with the same expression until the infant looked at the face for less than 2 seconds. The procedure was then repeated with the two other expressions.

This procedure showed, first, that the infants could, indeed, discriminate the three different facial expressions: They stopped paying attention to the repeated presentation of each expression but then began to pay close attention again when the adult switched to a different facial expression. More importantly, the babies appeared to imitate these new expressions (see the photographs below). An observer who could not see the model and who did not know what expressions were being presented to the infant was able to determine at greater than chance accuracy the facial expression of the model from the facial movements of the infants (Field, Woodson, Greenberg, & Cohen, 1982). Another early study found similar results (Meltzoff & Moore, 1983, 1977)

There have also been unsuccessful attempts to reproduce these results (Abravanel & Sigafoos, 1984; McKenzie & Over, 1983; Hayes & Watson, 1981; Jacobson, 1979). But in all of these, the newborns had been exposed to the drugs often used in labor and delivery and this may have impaired their abilities. When infants in

An observer who watched the facial expressions of 36-hour-old infants was able to guess with significant accuracy the facial expression being modeled by the adult.

procedure confirmed that the recorded sound of a heartbeat is rewarding to a newborn infant (DeCasper & Sigafoos, 1983).

The mother's voice can also be heard in the uterus, which would appear to explain why a newborn infant prefers her voice over others. And perhaps most startling of all is some evidence that the unborn infant may actually be learning in the uterus to discriminate some of the sound properties of individual words. In a quite extraordinary experiment, pregnant women recited speech passages from children's stories aloud each day during the last six weeks of pregnancy. For example, some women recited the first 28 paragraphs of the Dr. Seuss story *The Cat in the Hat*. Other pregnant women recited the last 28 paragraphs of the same story but with the main nouns changed so that it was now about "the dog in the fog" instead of the "cat in the hat." By the time the infants were born, they had heard one of the selected stories for a total of about $3\frac{1}{2}$ hours.

Two or three days after the infants were born, they were permitted to suck on a special pacifier wired to record sucking rates

Nepal were tested only minutes after a drug-free birth, they, too, showed clear imitation (Reissland, 1988). It also appears that newborns can imitate head movements and not just facial expressions (Meltzoff & Moore, 1989).

It is actually easier to evoke imitation in newborns than it is in babies who are 2 to 3 months old. It has been suggested that this early form of imitation may be a kind of reflex that disappears to be replaced later in life with a more cognitively or socially mature form of imitation. We noted in the text that newborn infants have a reflexive head-turning response to sounds that disappears at about 6 weeks and is replaced at 3 or 4 months of age by a more purposeful search with their eyes for the source of a sound. Imitation may follow this same pattern. On the other hand, newborns imitate a wide variety of facial expressions, and they do so even after the adult is no longer displaying the expression; this argues against the view that this ability to imitate is simply a reflex (Meltzoff, 1990). Moreover, 2- to 3-month-old babies are perfectly capable of imitating; the only reason they are slower to do so than newborns is that they attempt to play social games with any adult who makes interesting faces or gestures (Meltzoff & Moore, 1992).

There is an amusing anecdote about this controversy. One of Piaget's graduate students had been testing 7-week-old babies and was convinced that they were imitating her. She went to him with her discovery:

"Do you remember what I am doing?" she said. "I am sticking out my tongue at the babies, and do you know what they are doing?"

"You may tell me," Piaget murmured.

"They are sticking their tongues right back at me! What do you think of that?"

The venerable professor puffed on his pipe for a moment as he contemplated the challenge to his theory. "I think that is very rude," he said. (*Time*, 1983)

(like the apparatus shown in Figure 3-3). In this study, the pattern of sucking turned a tape recording of a story on or off. One sucking pattern turned on a recording of the story the infants had heard before birth; a contrasting pattern of sucking turned on a recording of one of the matched stories that the infant had not heard before. Some of the infants heard recordings of their own mother's voice; others heard recordings of an unfamiliar woman's voice. The results showed that the infants preferred the familiar story to the unfamiliar story—even when the two stories were read by an unfamiliar voice (DeCasper & Spence, 1986).

In sum, the research we have described in this section on the capacities of the infant challenges the view of the newborn as experiencing the world as "buzzing, blooming confusion" as well as the view that the child enters the world as a *tabula rasa* or blank slate. Clearly, the infant enters the world prepared to perceive and comprehend reality and to learn quickly the relations between events that are important for human development.

COGNITIVE DEVELOPMENT IN CHILDHOOD

PIAGET'S STAGE THEORY

Although most parents are aware of the intellectual changes that accompany their children's physical growth, they would have difficulty describing the nature of these changes. The ways in which contemporary psychologists describe these changes have been most profoundly influenced by the Swiss psychologist Jean Piaget (1896–1980), widely acknowledged to be one of the century's most influential thinkers.

Prior to Piaget, psychological thinking about children's cognitive development was dominated by the biological-maturation perspective, which gave almost exclusive weight to the "nature" component of development, and by the environmental-learning perspective, which gave almost exclusive weight to the "nurture" component. In contrast, Piaget focused on the interaction between the child's naturally maturing abilities and his or her interactions with the environment. Piaget saw the child as an active participant in this process rather than as a passive recipient of biological development or externally imposed stimuli. In particular, Piaget believed that the child should be viewed as an inquiring scientist who conducts experiments on the world to see what happens. ("What does it feel like to suck on the teddy-bear's ear?" "What happens if I push my dish off the edge of the table?")

The results of these miniature experiments lead the child to construct "theories"—Piaget called them *schemas* (or the singular, **schema**)—of how the physical and social worlds operate. Upon encountering a novel object or event, the child attempts to understand it in terms of a pre-existing schema. (Piaget called this the process of **assimilation**; the child attempts to *assimilate* the new event to the pre-existing schema.) If the old schema is not adequate to accommodate the new event, then the child—like a good scientist—modifies the schema and thereby extends his or her theory of the world. (Piaget called this process of revising the schema **accommodation.**) (Piaget & Inhelder, 1969).

Piaget also differed from other psychologists earlier in this century in his experimental methodology. Piaget's first job as a postgraduate student in psychology was as an intelligence tester for Alfred Binet, inventor of the IQ test (see Chapter 12). But Piaget found himself more interested in the children's *wrong* answers than in their intelligence test scores. Why did children make the errors they did? What distinguished their reasoning from that of adults? He began to observe his own three children closely as they played, frequently presenting them with simple scientific and moral problems and asking them to explain how they arrived at their answers. This informal clinical method of observing and interviewing a small number of children was quite alien to experimentally oriented American psychologists of the day. They criticized this approach as unscientific, and it was only slowly that they began to appreciate the importance of Piaget's work.

We emphasize these main features of Piaget's contribution here because even psychologists who now believe he was wrong about many features of cognitive development nevertheless accept his general portrait of the child as an active information-seeker and agree with his emphasis on the interaction between biological maturation and the environment. Moreover, many contemporary developmental psychologists use research methods that strongly reflect Piaget's influence. For clarity, we will first present Piaget's theory and his interpretations of the evidence, postponing our discussion of criticisms, and alternative interpretations to the subsequent section, "Evaluating Piaget."

On the basis of his observations, Piaget became convinced that children's abilities to think and to reason progress through a series of qualitatively distinct stages as they mature. He divided cognitive development into 4 major stages and a number of substages within each. The major stages and their prominent features are listed in Table 3-1.

SENSORIMOTOR STAGE Noting the close interplay between motor activity and perception in infants, Piaget designated the first two years of life as the **sensorimotor stage.** During this period, infants are busy discovering the relationships between their actions and the consequences of these actions. They discover, for example, how far they have to reach to grasp an object, what happens when they push their food dish over the edge of the table, and that their hand is part of their body and the

STAGE	CHARACTERIZATION
1. Sensorimotor (birth–2 years)	Differentiates self from objects
	Recognizes self as agent of action and begins to act intentionally; for example, pulls a string to set a mobile in motion or shakes a rattle to make a noise
	Achieves object permanence: realizes that things continue to exist even when no longer present to the senses
2. Preoperational (2–7 years)	Learns to use language and to represent objects by images and words
	Thinking is still egocentric: has difficulty taking the viewpoint of others
	Classifies objects by a single feature; for example, groups together all the red blocks regardless of shape or all the square blocks regardless of color
3. Concrete operational (7–11 years)	Can think logically about objects and events
	Achieves conservation of number (age 6), mass (age 7), and weight (age 9)
	Classifies objects according to several features and can order them in series along a single dimension, such as size
4. Formal operational (11 years and up)	Can think logically about abstract propositions and test hypotheses systematically
	Becomes concerned with the hypothetical, the future, and ideological problems

TABLE 3-1

Piaget's Stages of Cognitive Development   *The ages given are averages. They may vary considerably depending on intelligence, cultural background, and socioeconomic factors, but the order of progression is assumed to be the same for all children. Piaget has described more detailed phases within each stage; only a general characterization of each stage is given here.*

crib rail is not. Through countless "experiments," infants begin to develop a concept of themselves as separate from the external world.

An important discovery during this stage is the concept of **object permanence**, an awareness that an object continues to exist even when it is not present to the senses. If a cloth is placed over a toy that an 8-month-old is reaching for, the infant immediately stops and appears to lose interest. The baby seems neither surprised nor upset, makes no attempt to search for the toy, and acts as if the toy has ceased to exist (see Figure 3-4).

In contrast, a 10-month-old will actively search for an object that has been hidden under a cloth or behind a screen. The older baby seems to realize that the object exists even though it is out of sight and has thus attained the concept of object permanence. This implies that the baby possesses a *mental representation* of the missing object. But even at this age, search is limited. If the infant has had repeated success in retrieving a toy hidden in one place, he or she will continue to look for it in that spot even after watching an adult conceal it in a new location. The baby repeats the action that produced the toy earlier rather than looking for it where it was last seen. Not until about 1 year of age will a child consistently look for an object where it was last seen to disappear, regardless of what happened on previous trials.

PREOPERATIONAL STAGE   By about $1\frac{1}{2}$ to 2 years of age, children have begun to use language.

FIGURE 3-4

Object Permanence
When the toy is hidden by a screen, the infant acts as if the toy no longer exists. From this observation, Piaget concluded that the infant had not yet acquired the concept of object permanence.

FIGURE 3-5

Concept of Conservation
A 4-year-old acknowledges that the two balls of clay are the same size. But when one ball is rolled into a long thin shape, she says that it has more clay. Not until she is several years older will she state that the two different shapes contain the same amount of clay.

Words, as symbols, can represent things or groups of things, and one object can represent (symbolize) another. Thus, in play a 3-year-old may treat a stick as if it were a horse and ride it around the room; a block of wood can become a car; one doll can become a father and another, a baby.

Although 3- and 4-year-olds can think in symbolic terms, their words and images are not yet organized in a logical manner. Piaget calls the 2- to 7-years stage of cognitive development **preoperational**, because the child does not yet comprehend certain rules or *operations*. An operation is a mental routine for separating, combining, and otherwise transforming information mentally in a logical manner. For example, if water is poured from a tall narrow glass into a short wide one, adults know that the amount of water has not changed because they can reverse the transformation in their minds; they can imagine pouring the water from the short glass back into the tall glass, thereby arriving back at the original state. In the preoperational stage of cognitive development, a child's understanding of reversibility and other mental operations is absent or weak. As a result, according to Piaget, preoperational children have not yet attained **conservation**. They fail to understand that the amount of water is conserved when it is poured from the tall glass to the short one.

This lack of conservation is also illustrated by a procedure in which a child is given some clay to make into a ball that is equal to another ball of the same material. After doing this, the child declares them to be "the same." Then, leaving one ball for reference, the experimenter rolls the other into a long sausage shape while the child watches. The child can plainly see that no clay has been added or subtracted. In this situation, children about 4 years of age say that the two objects no longer contain the same amount of clay: "The longer one contains more," they say (see Figure 3-5). Not until the age of 7 do most children say the clay in the longer object is equal in amount to that in the reference ball.

Piaget believed that a key feature of the preoperational stage is that children are unable to center attention on more than one aspect of the situation at a time. Thus in the clay conservation task, the preoperational child cannot attend to both the length and the thickness of the clay ball simultaneously. Similarly, Piaget believed that preoperational thinking is dominated by visual impressions. A change in the visual appearance of the clay influences the preoperational child more than less obvious but more essential qualities, such as mass or weight.

The young child's reliance on visual impressions is made clear by an experiment on the conservation of number. If two rows of checkers are matched one for one against each other, young children will say, correctly, that the rows have the same number of checkers (see Figure 3-6). If the checkers in one row are brought closer together to form a cluster, 5-year-olds say there are now more checkers in the straight row—even though no checkers have been removed. The visual impression of a long row of checkers overrides the numerical equality that was obvious when the checkers appeared in matching rows. In contrast, 7-year-olds assume that if the number of objects was equal before, it must remain equal. At this age, numerical equality has become more significant than visual impression.

MORAL JUDGMENTS Cognitive development underlies not only the child's understanding of the physical world, but of the social world as well. Because understanding moral rules and social conventions is important in any society, Piaget was interested in how children come to understand such rules. He was skeptical that parental influence was as powerful in the development of this understanding as then-current theories claimed. Rather, he thought that children's understanding of moral rules and social conventions would have to match their overall level of cognitive development.

Interestingly, Piaget based his initial theorizing in this area on observations he made of children of different ages playing marbles, a popular game with most European children at the time. He asked these children questions about the origins, meaning, and importance of the game rules they were following. From their answers, he formulated four stages of children's developing understanding of rules. The first two stages fall within the preoperational period we are discussing in this section (Piaget, 1932/1965).

The first stage emerges at the beginning of the preoperational period when children begin to engage in symbolic play. Children at this stage will participate in a kind of "parallel play," playing amidst other children with shared objects but not in any socially organized way. Each child tends to follow a set of idiosyncratic rules, according to his or her own private wishes. For example, the child might sort the marbles of different colors into groups or roll the big ones across the room, followed by all the small ones. These "rules" give the child's play some regularity, but the child changes these rules frequently and arbitrarily, and they serve no collective purpose such as cooperation or competition.

The second stage puts an abrupt end to this easygoing view of rules. Beginning about age 5, the child develops a sense of obligation to follow rules, treating them as absolute moral imperatives handed down by some authority—possibly parents or God. Rules are permanent, sacred, and not subject to modification. Obeying them to the letter is more important than any human reason for changing them. For example, children at this stage reject the suggestion that the position of the starting line in the marble game might be changed to accommodate younger children who might want to play.

From this and other studies, Piaget came to the view that children at this stage subscribe to a **moral realism**, a confusion between moral and physical laws. Moral rules are predetermined and permanent aspects of the world—just like the law of gravity. When asked what would happen if they violated some moral rule (like lying or stealing), children at this stage often expressed the view that punishment would surely result—God would punish them or they would be hit by a car.

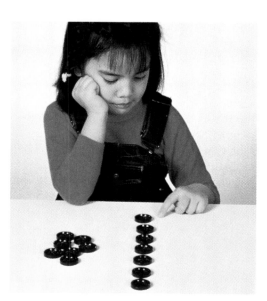

FIGURE 3-6

Conservation of Number
When the two rows of seven checkers are evenly spaced, most children report that they contain the same amount. When one row is then clustered into a smaller space, children under 6 or 7 will say the original row contains more.

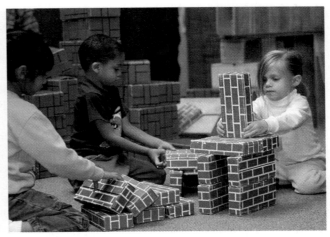

Although young children participate in parallel play with one another, it is only when they become older that they begin to understand the rules tht govern social interactions.

At this same stage, children judge an act more by its consequences than by the intentions behind it. For example, Piaget told children several pairs of stories. In one pair, a boy broke a teacup while trying to steal some jam when his mother was not home; another boy, who was doing nothing wrong, accidentally broke a whole trayful of teacups. "Which boy is naughtier?" Piaget asked. Preoperational children tended to judge as naughtier the person in the stories who did the most damage, regardless of the intentions or motivation behind the act. Similarly, a child who tells her mother that she saw a "dog as big as a cow" is judged to be naughtier than one who tells her mother that she received a good grade in school when she did not. Why? Because a dog could not be as big as a cow, and hence this is the bigger lie. Preoperational children do not differentiate between deliberate, opportunistic lies and harmless exaggerations or misstatements.

OPERATIONAL STAGES   Between the ages of 7 and 12, children master the various conservation concepts and begin to perform still other logical manipulations. They can order objects on the basis of a dimension, such as height or weight. They can also form a mental representation of a series of actions. Five-year-olds can find their way to a friend's house but cannot direct you there or trace the route with paper and pencil. They can find the way because they know they have to turn at certain places, but they have no overall picture of the route. In contrast, 8-year-olds can readily draw a map of the route. Piaget calls this period the **concrete operational stage:** Although children are using abstract terms, they are

doing so only in relation to concrete objects— that is, objects to which they have direct sensory access.

Piaget's third stage of moral understanding also begins about this time. The child begins to appreciate that some rules are social conventions—cooperative agreements that can be arbitrarily decided and changed if everyone agrees. Children's moral realism also declines: When making moral judgments, children now give weight to "subjective" considerations like a person's intentions, and they see punishment as a human choice, not an inevitable, divine retribution.

At about the age of 11 or 12, children arrive at adult modes of thinking, becoming able to reason in purely symbolic terms. Piaget called this the **formal operational stage.** In one test for formal operational thinking, the child tries to discover what determines the amount of time that a pendulum will swing back and forth (its period of oscillation). The child is presented with a length of string suspended from a hook and several weights that can be attached to the lower end. He or she can vary the length of the string, change the attached weight, and alter the height from which the bob is released.

In contrast to children still in the concrete operational stage—who will experiment by changing some of the variables, but not in a systematic way—adolescents of even average ability will set up a series of hypotheses and proceed to test them systematically. They reason that if a particular variable (weight) affects the period of oscillation, the effect will appear only if they change one variable and hold all others constant. If this variable seems to have no effect on the time of swing, they rule it out and try another. Considering all the possibilities—working out the consequences for each hypothesis and confirming or denying these consequences—is the essence of what Piaget called formal operational thought.

The beginning of the formal operational stage also coincides with the fourth and final stage in children's understanding of moral rules. Youngsters show an interest in generating rules to deal even with situations they have never encountered. This stage is marked by an ideological mode of moral reasoning, which addresses wider social issues rather than just personal and interpersonal situations.

The American psychologist Lawrence Kohlberg extended Piaget's work on moral reasoning to include adolescence and adulthood (Kohlberg, 1976, 1969). He sought to determine if there are universal stages in the development of moral judgments by presenting moral dilemmas in story form. For example, in one story a man whose dying wife needs a drug he cannot afford pleads with a druggist to let him buy the drug at a cheaper price. When the druggist refuses, the man decides to steal the drug. Subjects are asked to discuss the man's action.

By analyzing answers to several such dilemmas, Kohlberg arrived at six developmental stages of moral judgment grouped into three levels (see Table 3-2). The answers are scored on the basis of the reasons given for the decision, not on the basis of whether the action is judged right or wrong. For example, agreeing that the man should have stolen the drug because "If you let your wife die, you'll get in trouble" or disagreeing because "If you steal the drug, you'll be caught and sent to jail" are both scored at Stage 1. In both instances, the man's actions are evaluated as right or wrong on the basis of anticipated punishment.

Kohlberg believed that all children are at Level I until about age 10, when they begin to evaluate actions in terms of other people's opinions (Level II). Most youngsters reason at this level by age 13. Following Piaget, Kohlberg argues that only those who have achieved formal operational thought are capable of the kind of abstract thinking necessary for Level III, postconventional morality. The highest stage, Stage 6, requires formulating abstract ethical principles and upholding them to avoid self-condemnation.

Kohlberg reports that fewer than 10 percent of his adult subjects show the kind of "clear-principled" Stage-6 thinking exemplified by the following response of a 16-year-old to the man's dilemma: "By the law of society [the man] was wrong but by the law of nature or of God the druggist was wrong and the husband was justified. Human life is above financial gain. Regardless of who was dying, if it was a total stranger, man has a duty to save him from dying" (Kohlberg, 1969, p. 244).

Kohlberg has presented evidence for this sequence of stages in children from several cultures, including America, Mexico, Taiwan, and Turkey (Colby, Kohlberg, Gibbs, & Lieberman, 1983; Nisan & Kohlberg, 1982). On the other hand, there is evidence that people use different rules for different situations and

LEVEL I:	**PRECONVENTIONAL MORTALITY**
Stage 1	Punishment orientation (Obeys rules to avoid punishment)
Stage 2	Reward orientation (Conforms to obtain rewards, to have favors returned)
LEVEL II:	**CONVENTIONAL MORALITY**
Stage 3	Good-boy/good-girl orientation (Conforms to avoid disapproval of others)
Stage 4	Authority orientation (Upholds laws and social rules to avoid censure of authorities and feelings of guilt about not "doing one's duty")
LEVEL III:	**POSTCONVENTIONAL MORALITY**
Stage 5	Social-contract orientation (Actions guided by principles commonly agreed on as essential to the public welfare; principles upheld to retain respect of peers and, thus, self-respect)
Stage 6	Ethical principle orientation (Actions guided by self-chosen ethical principles, which usually value justice, dignity, and equality; principles upheld to avoid self-condemnation)

TABLE 3-2

Stages of Moral Reasoning *Kohlberg believed that moral judgment develops with age according to these stages.* (After Kohlberg, 1969)

that the stages are not sequential (Kurtines & Greif, 1974). The theory has also been criticized for being "male centered," because it places a "masculine" style of abstract reasoning based on justice and rights higher on the moral scale than a "feminine" style of reasoning based on a care and concern for others (Gilligan, 1982).

EVALUATION OF PIAGET

It should be clear from even this brief summary of Piaget's ideas that his theory is a major intellectual achievement; it has revolutionized the way we think about children's cognitive development and has inspired an enormous amount of research over the decades. Many studies support Piaget's observations about the sequences in cognitive development.

But newer and more sophisticated methods of testing the intellectual functioning of infants and preschool children reveal that Piaget underestimated their abilities. As we noted earlier, many of the tasks designed to test stage theories actually require several underlying information-processing skills if the child is to succeed at them, such as attention, memory, and specific factual knowledge. A child may actually possess the requisite ability under examination but fail the task because he or she lacks one of the other required but irrelevant skills.

OBJECT PERMANENCE. These points are sharply illustrated by studies of object permanence, the awareness that an object continues to exist even when it is not present to the senses. As we described earlier, when infants younger than 8 months are shown a toy that is then hidden or covered while they watch, they act as if it no longer exists; they do not attempt to search for it. Even after 8 months, a baby that has repeatedly succeeded in retrieving a toy hidden in one place will continue to look for it in that spot even after watching an adult conceal it in a new location.

Note, however, that successful performance on this test requires the child not only to understand that the object still exists—object permanence—but also to remember where the object was hidden and to display some physical action that indicates he or she is searching for it. Because Piaget believed

that early cognitive development depends on sensorimotor activities, he did not seriously entertain the possibility that the infant might know the object still exists but not be able to reveal this through searching behavior—that children's minds might be ahead of their motor abilities.

This possibility was tested in a set of studies that did not require the child to actively search for the hidden object. As shown in the top section of Figure 3-7, the apparatus consisted of a screen hinged at one edge to the top of a table. The screen began in a position lying flat on the table. As the infant watched, the screen was rotated slowly away from the infant like a drawbridge, through its upright position at 90 degrees, and then continued until it had rotated through a complete 180-degree arc and was again lying flat on the table. The screen was then rotated in the opposite direction, toward the infant.

When the infants were first shown the rotating screen, they looked at it for almost a full minute; but after repeated trials, they lost interest and turned their attention elsewhere. At that point, a brightly painted box appeared on the table beyond the hinge where it would be hidden as the screen moved into its upright position. (The infant was actually seeing a reflected image of a box, not the actual box.) As shown in Figure 3-7, the infants were then shown either a possible event or an impossible event. One group of infants saw the screen rotate from its starting position until it reached the point where it should bump against the box; at that point, the screen stopped and then moved back to its starting position. The other group saw the screen rotate to the upright position but then continue to rotate all the way to the other side of the 180-degree arc just as though there were no box in the way.

The investigators reasoned that if the infants thought the box still existed even when it was hidden by the screen, they would be surprised when it seemed to pass through the box—an impossible event—and, hence, look at the screen longer than they would when the screen seemed to bump into the box before returning to its starting point. This is exactly what happened. Even though the impossible event was perceptually identical to an event they had seen repeatedly and lost interest in, they found it more interesting than a physically possible event they had never seen before—the screen stopping halfway through the arc and then reversing direction (Baillargeon, Spelke, & Wasserman, 1985).

It should be noted that the infants in this experiment were only $4\frac{1}{2}$ months old; they thus displayed object permanence 4–5 months earlier than Piaget's theory predicts. A replication of this study found that some infants as young as $3\frac{1}{2}$ months also had object permanence (Baillargeon, 1987).

CONSERVATION Piaget's conservation tasks provide a second instance in which the careful analysis of the component skills required for successful task performance has uncovered earlier competence than his theory anticipates. For example, if test conditions are carefully arranged in conservation experiments so that the children's responses do not depend on their language ability (their understanding of what the experimenter means by "more" or "longer"), then even 3- and 4-year-olds can show that they possess number conservation; that is, they can distinguish between the essential feature, the number of items in a set, and the irrelevant feature, the way in which the items are arranged spatially (Gelman & Gallistel, 1978).

In one study of number conservation, two sets of toys were lined up in one-to-one correspondence (as in Figure 3–6 described earlier). The experimenter identified one row as the child's and one as her own and then asked the child for the initial judgment of equality. For example, "These are your soldiers and these are my soldiers. What's more, my soldiers, your soldiers or are they both the same?" After this initial judgment, the experimenter spread out one of the rows of toys and repeated the question.

As Piaget and others had previously reported, 5-year-old children failed to conserve, stating that the spread-out row was "more soldiers." But the investigator introduced a second set of conditions. Instead of describing the toys as individual soldiers, she said: "This is my army and this is your army. What's more, my army, your army or are they both the same?" With this simple change of wording, most of the children were able to conserve, judging the two "armies" to be the same size, even when one of them was spread out. By prompting the children to interpret the display as an aggregate or collection rather than as a set of individual items, their judgments of equality were less likely to be influenced by irrelevant perceptual transfor-

HABITUATION EVENT

TEST EVENTS

Possible event

Impossible event

FIGURE 3-7

Testing Object Permanence *Infants are shown a rotating screen until they no longer attend to it. A box is placed where it can be hidden by the screen and the infants then see either a possible event (the screen rotates until it would hit the box and then returns to its starting position) or an impossible event (the screen appears to pass right through the box). Infants attend more to the impossible event, indicating that they realize the hidden box still exists.* (Adapted from Baillargeon, 1987)

mations. Moreover, when asked to justify their equality judgments, most of the children in the "army" condition showed they understood the underlying principle. Many explicitly referred to numbers (for example, counting the soldiers to demonstrate equal numbers); others noted that nothing had been added or taken away; and still others referred explicitly to the irrelevance of the transformation (for example, "You just spread them"). The same results were found when the objects were "football players" versus a "football team," "animals" versus an "animal party," or "pigs" versus a "pig family" (Markman, 1979).

MORAL JUDGMENTS We saw earlier that preoperational children treat arbitrary rules of games and social conventions like divine moral prescriptions that cannot be changed by simple agreement among participants. More recent research suggests, however, that even preoperational children can and do make distinctions between social conventions and moral prescriptions.

In one study, for example, 7-year-old children were given a list of actions and asked to indicate which ones would be wrong even if there were no rules against them. There was widespread agreement among these children that lying, stealing, hitting, and selfishness would be wrong even if there were no rules against them. In contrast, they thought that there was nothing wrong with chewing gum in class, addressing a teacher by first name, boys entering the girls' bathroom, or eating lunch with the finger—as long as there were no rules against these acts. Moreover, they could make a further distinction between rules governing conduct that affects other people and rules governing conduct that affects only oneself. For example, they believed that it was *legitimate* for a school to have rules against chewing gum in class, addressing a teacher by first name, and so forth. But they felt that it should be "the person's own business" and hence that there should be no rules against watching television on a sunny day (when parents want children out playing), interacting with a forbidden friend, and boys wearing long hair (Nucci, 1981).

In a similar study, 7-year-old children were about evenly divided in deciding whether it would be okay for a boy to wear a dress to school even if "the principal decided that there is no rule in the school against it." But 82 percent of them thought it would be okay for a boy to do so "in a country that had no rule against it" (Turiel, 1983). We will discuss the violation of gender norms later in the chapter.

ALTERNATIVES TO PIAGET

There is general agreement among developmental psychologists that the kinds of findings we have reviewed here seriously challenge Piaget's theory and reveal that he underestimated children's abilities. But there is no consensus on which is the best alternative to pursue.

INFORMATION-PROCESSING APPROACHES We have already noted that many of the experiments challenging Piaget's views were inspired by investigators who view cognitive development as the acquisition of several separate information-processing skills. Accordingly, they believe that the standard Piagetian tasks

fail to separate these several skills from the critical skill that the task is allegedly designed to assess. But beyond that, information-processing theorists disagree among themselves about the challenge their views pose to Piaget.

For example, they disagree on the major question of whether development is best understood as a series of qualitatively distinct stages or as a continuous process of change. Some believe that the entire notion of stages should be abandoned (for example, Klahr, 1982). For them, the appearance of qualitative discontinuities in development is an illusion that arises from the careless mixing in the assessment tasks of information-processing skills at different stages of development; the separate skills develop smoothly and continuously.

But other information-processing theorists see themselves as modifying and extending the Piagetian stage model itself; they believe that gradual changes in information-processing skills do, in fact, lead to discontinuous, stagelike changes in children's thinking (for example, Case, 1985). These theorists are sometimes referred to as neo-Piagetians. Another group of neo-Piagetians agrees that there are genuine stages but that they occur only within more narrow domains of knowledge. For example, a child's language skills, mathematical understanding, social reasoning, and so forth may all develop in stagelike fashion, but each domain proceeds at its own pace, relatively independently of the others (for example, Mandler, 1983).

KNOWLEDGE ACQUISITION APPROACHES Some developmental psychologists who question the existence of qualitative stages of cognitive development believe that after infancy, children and adults have essentially the same cognitive processes and capacities and that the difference between them is primarily the adult's more extensive knowledge base. By knowledge, they do not just mean a larger collection of facts, but a deeper understanding of how facts in a particular domain are organized.

This distinction between facts and the organization of facts is nicely illustrated by a study that compared a group of 10-year-olds who were competing in a chess tournament with a group of college students who were chess amateurs. When asked to memorize and recall lists of random numbers, the college students easily outperformed the 10-year-olds. But when tested on their ability to recall actual game positions of the chess pieces on the board, the 10-year-old chess experts did better than the 18-year-old chess amateurs (Chi, 1978). Thus the relevant difference between the two groups is not different stages of cognitive development or different information-processing abilities (for example, memory capacity), but domain-specific knowledge. Because the 10-year-olds had a deeper grasp of the underlying structure of chess, they were able to organize and reconstruct the arrangements from memory by "chunking" the separate pieces of information into larger meaningful units (for example, a king-side attack by white) and by eliminating from consideration implausible placements of the pieces. An earlier study comparing adult chess masters with adult chess amateurs showed similar results (Chase & Simon, 1973). (We discuss experts versus amateur problem solvers in Chapter 9.)

Increasing knowledge of the world rather than a qualitative shift in cognitive development may also account for children's increasing ability to solve Piaget's conservation tasks as they get older. For example, the child who does not know that mass or number is the critical feature that defines what is meant by "more clay" or "more checkers" is likely to judge that the quantity has changed when only its visual appearance has changed. An older child may simply have learned the essential defining feature of "more." If this hypothesis is correct, then a child who fails to show conservation in one domain may show conservation in another, depending upon his or her understanding of the domain.

Evidence for this was obtained in a study in which kindergarten children were told about a series of "operations" that doctors or scientists had performed. Some operations altered an animal so that it looked like a different animal; other operations altered an animal so that it looked like a plant (see the stimulus photographs in Figure 3-8). For example, the child was told that

> the doctors took a horse [shows child picture of horse] and did an operation that put black and white stripes all over its body. They cut off its mane and braided its tail. They trained it to stop neighing like a horse, and they trained it to eat wild grass instead of oats and hay. They also trained it to live in the wilds in Africa instead of in a

> stable. When they were all done, the animal looked just like this [shows picture of zebra]. When they were finished, was this animal a horse or a zebra? (Keil, 1989, p. 307)

On operations that transformed one kind of animal to another, a majority of the children failed to conserve; about 65 percent agreed that the horse had been genuinely changed into a zebra. But when faced with the transformation of an animal to a plant, only about 25 percent agreed that the porcupine had been genuinely changed into a cactus (Keil, 1989). (Additional variations demonstrated that this could not be explained simply because the animals looked more like each other than plants and animals did.)

Studies like these demonstrate that in some domains, preoperational children can ignore dramatic changes in visual appearance and conserve because they have learned that an invisible but essential defining feature of the object has remained unchanged. We will see a similar experiment in the later section on gender identity and sex typing, where we examine whether preoperational children believe that girls can be changed into boys and vice versa.

SOCIOCULTURAL APPROACHES   Although Piaget emphasized the child's interaction with the environment, the environment he had in mind was the immediate physical environment. The child is seen as an inquiring physical scientist whose task it is to discover the true nature of the world and the universal rules of logical and scientific thought. The larger social and cultural context in which the child is embedded plays virtually no role in Piaget's theory. Even his discussion of social and moral rules implies that there is a universal, logical "right" way to think about such rules, which the child seeks to discover.

But not all knowledge is of this type. Much of what the developing child must learn is the particular and arbitrary ways in which his or her culture views reality, what roles different persons—and different sexes—are expected to play, and what rules and norms govern social relationships in his or her particular culture. In these areas, there are no universally valid facts or correct views of reality to be discovered. Thus for cultural anthropologists and other social scientists who take a sociocultural approach to development, the child

FIGURE 3-8

Testing Conservation
Children are told how doctors or scientists operated on an animal until it looked like a different animal (horse-to-zebra) or on an animal until it looked like a plant (porcupine-to-cactus). Children who say that the animal is "really" the new animal or plant are failing to show conservation; children who say that the animal is still "really" the original animals are showing conservation.

should be seen not as a physical scientist seeking "true" knowledge but as a newcomer to a culture who seeks to become a native by learning how to look at social reality through the lenses of that culture (Bem, 1993, 1987; Shweder, 1984). We will return to this theme in the section on gender identity and sex typing later in the chapter.

PERSONALITY AND SOCIAL DEVELOPMENT

TEMPERAMENT

First-time parents are often surprised that their newborn seems to possess a distinctive personality from the very beginning; when they have a second child, they are often sur-

prised at how different the second is from the first. These parental observations are correct. As early as the first weeks of life, infants show individual differences in activity level, responsiveness to change in their environment, and irritability. One infant cries a lot; another cries very little. One endures diapering or bathing without much fuss; another kicks and thrashes. One is responsive to every sound; another is oblivious to all but the loudest noises. Infants even differ in "cuddliness." Some seem to enjoy being cuddled and mold their bodies to the person holding them; others stiffen and squirm and do less body adjusting (Korner, 1973). Such mood-related personality characteristics are called **temperaments.**

The study of temperaments is now a very active research area, and there are disagreements on just how temperaments should be defined, identified, and measured. It is also not yet clear to what extent temperaments in early childhood constitute the building blocks for the individual's later personality (Kohnstamm, Bates, & Rothbart, 1989).

The observation that temperamental differences among children arise so early challenges the traditional view that all of an infant's behaviors are shaped by the early environment. Parents of a fussy baby, for example, tend to blame themselves for their infant's difficulties. But research with newborns makes it increasingly clear that many temperamental differences are inborn, and that the relationship between parent and infant is reciprocal—in other words, the infant's behavior also shapes the parent's response. An infant who is easily soothed, who snuggles and stops crying when picked up, increases the parent's feelings of competency and attachment. The infant who stiffens and continues to cry, despite efforts to comfort it, makes the parent feel inadequate and rejected. The more responsive a baby is to the stimulation provided by the parent (snuggling and quieting when held, attending alertly when talked to or played with), the easier it is for the parent and child to establish a loving bond.

One pioneering study of temperament that has followed the same children over time began in the 1950s with a group of 140 middle- and upper-class infants in the United States. The initial data were gathered through interviews with parents and were later supplemented by interviews with teachers and by tests given directly to the children. The infants were scored on nine traits, which were later combined to define three broad temperament types: Infants who were playful, regular in their sleeping and eating patterns, and adapted readily to new situations were classified as *easy* (about 40 percent of the sample); infants who were irritable, irregular in sleeping and eating patterns, and responded intensely and negatively to new situations were classified as *difficult* (about 10 percent of the sample); infants who were low in activity level, tended to withdraw from new situations in a mild way, and required more time than easy infants to adapt to new situations were classified as *slow to warm up* (about 15 percent of the sample). The remaining 35 percent of the infants were not rated high or low on any of the defining dimensions (Thomas et al., 1963). Of the original sample, 133 subjects have now been followed into adult life and have again been assessed on temperament and psychological adjustment.

The results provide mixed evidence for the continuity of temperament. On the one hand, temperament scores across the first five years of these children's lives were significantly correlated with one another; children with "difficult" temperaments were more likely than "easy" children to have school problems later on; and adult measures of both temperament and adjustment were significantly correlated with measures of childhood temperament obtained at ages 3, 4, and 5. On the other hand, all the correlations were low (about .3) and most of the nine traits considered separately showed little or no continuity across time (Thomas & Chess, 1986, 1977; Chess & Thomas, 1984).

The researchers emphasize that the continuity and discontinuity of temperament is a function of the interaction between the child's **genotype** (inherited characteristics) and the environment. In particular, they believe that the key to healthy development is a *goodness of fit* between the child's temperament and the home environment. When parents of a difficult child provide a happy, stable home life, the child's negative, difficult behaviors decline with age (Belsky, Fish, & Isabella, 1991). Thomas and Chess cite the case of Carl, a boy with one of the most difficult temperaments from the first few months of life through 5 years of age. Because Carl's father took delight in his son's "lusty" temperament and allowed for his initial negative reactions to new situations, Carl flourished and became increasingly "easy." At age 23, he was clearly classified into the "easy" temperament group. Nevertheless, Carl's original temperament often emerged briefly whenever life circumstances changed. For example, when he started piano lessons in late childhood, he again showed an intense negative response, followed by slow adaptability and eventual positive, zestful involvement. A similar pattern emerged when he entered college (Thomas & Chess, 1986).

EARLY SOCIAL BEHAVIOR

By 2 months of age, the average child will smile at the sight of its mother's or father's face. Delighted with this response, parents will go to great lengths to encourage repetition.

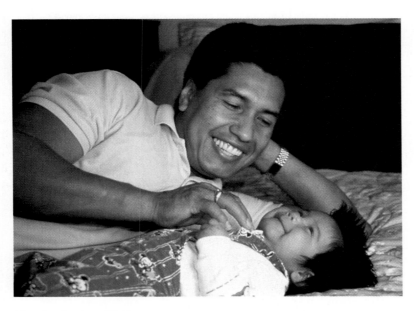

Infants throughout the world begin to smile at about the same age—as do blind children—implying that maturation is more important than conditions of rearing in determining the onset of smiling.

Indeed, the infant's ability to smile at such an early age may have evolved historically precisely because it strengthened the parent-child bond. Parents interpret these smiles to mean that the infant recognizes and loves them, encouraging them to be even more affectionate and stimulating in response. A mutually reinforcing system of social interaction is thus established and maintained.

Infants all over the world begin to smile at about the same age, whether raised in a remote African village or a middle-class American home. This suggests that maturation is more important in determining the onset of smiling than are the conditions of rearing. Blind babies also smile at about the same age as sighted infants (in response to their parents' voices or touch rather than faces), which indicates that smiling is an innate response (Eibl-Eibesfeldt, 1970).

By their third or fourth month, infants show that they recognize and prefer familiar members of the household—by smiling or cooing more when seeing these familiar faces or hearing their voices—but infants are still fairly receptive to strangers. At about 7 or 8 months, however, this indiscriminate acceptance changes. Many infants begin to show wariness or actual distress at the approach of a stranger (even while being held by a parent) and, at the same time, to protest strongly when left in an unfamiliar setting or with an unfamiliar person. Parents are often disconcerted to find that their formerly gregarious infant, who had always happily welcomed the

attentions of a baby sitter, now cries inconsolably when they prepare to leave—and continues to cry for some time after they have left.

Although not all infants show this "stranger anxiety"—it appears to be part of an infant's distinctive temperament—the number of infants who do show it increases dramatically from about 8 months of age until the end of the first year. Similarly, distress over separation from the parent—a distinct but related phenomenon also partially related to inborn temperament—reaches a peak between 14 to 18 months and then gradually declines. By the time they are 3 years old, most children are secure enough in their parents' absence to be able to interact comfortably with other children and adults.

The waxing and waning of these two fears appears to be only slightly influenced by conditions of child rearing. The same general pattern has been observed among American children reared entirely at home and among those attending a day-care center. Figure 3-9 shows that although the percentage of children who cry when their mothers leave the room varies across different cultures, the age-related pattern of onset and decline is very similar (Kagan, Kearsley, & Zelazo, 1978).

How do we explain the systematic timing of these fears among children who show them? Two factors seem to be important in both their onset and their decline. One is the growth of memory capacity. During the second half of the first year infants gain in their ability to remember past events and to compare past and present. This makes it possible for the baby to detect, and sometimes to fear, unusual or unpredictable events. The emergence of "stranger anxiety" coincides with the emergence of fears to a variety of stimuli that are unusual or unexpected; a weird-looking mask or a jack-in-the-box that brings smiles to a 4-month-old often causes an 8-month-old to look apprehensive and distressed. As children learn that strangers and unusual objects are not generally harmful, such fears gradually diminish.

It also seems reasonable to assume that memory development is involved in separation anxiety. The infant cannot "miss" the parent unless he or she can recall that parent's presence a minute earlier and compare this with the parent's absence now. When the parent leaves the room, the infant is aware that something is amiss—a kind of object permanence—which can lead to distress. As the child's memory improves for past instances of separation and return, the child becomes better able to anticipate the return of the absent parent, and anxiety declines.

The second factor is the growth of autonomy. One-year-olds are still highly dependent on care from adults, but children of 2 or 3 can head for the snack plate or toy shelf on their own. Also, they can use language to communicate their wants and feelings. Thus, dependency on caregivers in general and on familiar caregivers in particular decreases, and the issue of the parent's presence becomes less critical for the child.

ATTACHMENT

An infant's tendency to seek closeness to particular people and to feel more secure in their presence is called **attachment**. The young of other species show attachment to their mothers in different ways. An infant monkey clings to its mother's chest as she moves about; puppies climb over one another in their attempts to reach the warm belly of their mother; ducklings and baby chicks follow their mother about, making sounds to which she responds and going to her when they are frightened. These early responses to the mother have a clear adaptive value: They prevent the organism from wandering away from the source of care and getting lost.

Psychologists at first theorized that attachment to the mother developed because she was the source of food, one of the infant's most basic needs. But some facts did not fit. For example, ducklings and baby chicks feed themselves from birth, yet they still follow their mothers about and spend a great deal of time with them. The comfort they derive from the mother's presence cannot come from her role in feeding. A series of well-known experiments with monkeys showed that there is more to mother-infant attachment than nutritional needs (Harlow & Harlow, 1969).

Infant monkeys were separated from their mothers shortly after birth and placed with two artificial "mothers" constructed of wire mesh with wooden heads. The torso of one mother was bare wire; the other was covered with foam rubber and terry cloth, making it more cuddly and easy to cling to (see Figure 3-10). Either mother could be equipped to

FIGURE 3-9

Children's Stress at Mother's Departure *Even though the percentages of children who cry when their mothers leave the room varies from culture to culture, the age-related pattern of onset and decline of such distress is similar across cultures.* (From Kagan, Kearsley, & Zelazo, 1978)

provide milk by means of a bottle attached to its chest.

The experiment sought to determine whether the "mother" that was always the source of food would be the one to which the young monkey would cling. The results were clear-cut: No matter which mother provided food, the infant monkey spent its time clinging to the terry-cloth mother. This purely passive but soft-contact mother was a source of security. For example, the obvious fear of the infant monkey placed in a strange environment was allayed if the infant could make contact with the cloth mother. While holding on to the cloth mother with one hand or foot, the monkey was willing to explore objects that were otherwise too terrifying to approach.

Although contact with a cuddly, artificial mother provides an important aspect of

FIGURE 3-10

A Monkey's Response to an Artificial Mother
Although fed via a wire mother, the infant spends more time with the terry-cloth mother. The terry-cloth mother provides a safe base from which to explore strange objects.

"mothering," it is not enough for satisfactory development. Infant monkeys raised with artificial mothers and isolated from other monkeys during the first 6 months of life showed various types of bizarre behavior in adulthood. They rarely engaged in normal interaction with other monkeys later on (either cowering in fear or showing abnormally aggressive behavior), and their sexual responses were inappropriate. When female monkeys that had been deprived of early social contact were successfully mated (after considerable effort), they made poor mothers, tending to neglect or abuse their first-born infants—although they became better mothers with their later-born children. Note, however, that these monkeys were deprived of all social contact. Monkeys with artificial mothers do fine as adults if they are allowed to interact with their peers during the first 6 months.

Although we should be careful in generalizing from research on monkeys to human development, there is evidence that the human infant's attachment to the primary caregiver serves the same functions. Most of the work on attachment in human infants originated with the psychoanalyst John Bowlby in the 1950s and 1960s. His theory is an integration of concepts from psychoanalytic theory, ethology, and cognitive psychology. According to attachment theory, a child's failure to form a secure attachment to one or more persons in the early years is related to

an inability to develop close personal relationships in adulthood (Bowlby, 1973).

ASSESSING ATTACHMENT

Mary Ainsworth, one of Bowlby's associates, made extensive observations of children and their mothers in Uganda and the United States and then developed a laboratory procedure for assessing the security of a child's attachments from about 12–18 months of age (Ainsworth, Blehar, Waters, & Wall, 1978). The procedure is called the *Strange Situation* and comprises the following sequence of episodes:

1. The mother and the child enter the experimental room. The mother places the baby on the floor surrounded by toys and then goes to sit at the opposite end of the room.

2. A female stranger enters the room, sits quietly for one minute, converses with the mother for a minute, and then attempts to engage the baby in play with a toy.

3. The mother leaves the room unobtrusively. If the baby is not upset, the stranger returns to sitting quietly. If the baby is upset, the stranger tries to soothe him or her.

4. The mother returns and engages the baby in play while the stranger slips out.

5. The mother leaves again, this time leaving the baby alone in the room.

6. The stranger returns. If the baby is upset, the stranger tries to comfort him or her.

7. The mother returns and the stranger slips out.

Each episode is designed to last three minutes but can be shortened if the baby becomes too upset or lengthened if the baby needs additional time to get involved in play. The baby is observed through a one-way mirror during the entire sequence, and several observations are recorded: baby's activity level and play involvement, crying and other distress signs, proximity to and attempts to gain attention of the mother, proximity to and willingness to interact with the stranger, and so on. On the basis of their behaviors, babies are categorized into three main groups. Note that the groups differ from one another primarily in terms of the children's behaviors during the reunion episodes (episodes 4 and 7).

Securely Attached Whether or not they are upset at the mother's departures (episodes 3 and 5), babies who are classified as securely attached seek to interact with her when she returns. Some are content simply to acknowledge her return from a distance, while continuing to play with the toys. Others seek physical contact with her. Still others are completely preoccupied with the mother throughout the entire session, showing intense distress when she leaves. In all, 60–65 percent of American babies are classified into this category.

Insecurely Attached: Avoidant These babies show conspicuous avoidance of interaction with the mother in the reunion episodes. Some ignore the mother almost entirely; some display mixed attempts to interact and to avoid interacting. Avoidant babies may pay little attention to the mother when she is in the room and often do not seem distressed when she leaves. If distressed, they are as easily comforted by the stranger as by the mother. About 20 percent of American babies are classified into this category.

Insecurely Attached: Ambivalent Babies are classified as ambivalent if they show resistance to the mother during the reunion episodes. They simultaneously seek and resist physical contact. For example, they may cry to be picked up and then squirm angrily to get down. Some act very passive, crying for the mother when she returns but not crawling toward her and then showing resistance when she approaches. About 10 percent of American babies are classified into this category.

Because some babies did not seem to fit any of these categories, more recent studies have included a fourth category, called *disorganized* (Main & Solomon, 1986). Babies in this category often show contradictory behaviors. For example, they may approach the mother while taking care not to look at her, approach her and then show dazed avoidance, or suddenly cry out after having first settled down. Some seem disoriented, appear emotionless, or look depressed. About 10–15 percent of American babies are now placed into this category, with the percentages being much higher among babies who are maltreated or who come from homes with parents who are in psychiatric treatment.

SENSITIVE RESPONSIVENESS In attempting to account for differences in attachment among babies, researchers have directed most of their attention to the behavior of the primary caregiver, usually the mother. The main finding has been that it is a caregiver's "sensitive responsiveness" to the baby's needs that produces secure attachment. This is evident as early as the baby's first three months of life. For example, mothers of securely attached babies usually respond promptly when the baby cries and behave affectionately when they pick him or her up. They also tailor their responses closely to the baby's needs (Clarke-Stewart, 1973). In feeding, for example, they use an infant's signals to determine when to begin and end feeding, they attend to the baby's food preferences, and they pace their feeding to the baby's speed of eating.

In contrast, mothers of babies who show either type of insecure attachment respond more on the basis of their own wishes or moods than to signals from the baby. For example, they will respond to the baby's cries for attention when they feel like cuddling the baby but will ignore such cries at other times (Stayton, 1973).

Mothers of insecurely attached babies who show the avoidant pattern in the Strange Situation appear to hold their babies as much as mothers of securely attached babies, but they do not seem to enjoy the close bodily contact as much and sometimes act in a rejecting manner. They are especially likely to refuse contact when the baby is distressed and most needs comforting. They also tend to be rigid and compulsive, often giving care "according to the book" rather than responsively to the infant. Researchers propose that the result for the baby is a conflict between approaching and avoiding contact with the mother (Lyons-Ruth, Cornnell, Zoll, & Stahl, 1987; Belsky, Rovine, & Taylor, 1984; Ainsworth, Blehar, Waters, & Wall, 1978).

Mothers of insecurely attached babies who show the ambivalent pattern in the Strange Situation are inconsistent in their care. Sometimes they respond sensitively to their infants; sometimes they are inaccessible; at yet other times, they are intrusive, interfering with the baby's activity. Like the mothers of avoidant infants, the problem is not that they interact too little or too much, but that the nature and timing of their interaction does not consistently match the infant's needs. The result is that such babies are often frustrated in their attempts to seek contact. This generates the mixture of contact seeking and anger observed in the Strange Situation. Such babies also become much more distressed at little everyday separations than securely attached babies do (Ainsworth, 1989).

INFANT TEMPERAMENT   Not all developmental psychologists agree that the caregiver's responsiveness is the major cause of an infant's attachment behaviors. They call attention to the baby's own inborn temperament (Kagan, 1984; Campos et al., 1983). For example, perhaps the temperaments that make some babies "easy" also make them more securely attached than do the temperaments of "difficult" babies. And, as we noted earlier, a parent's response to a child is often itself a function of the child's own behavior. For example, mothers of difficult babies tend to spend less time playing with them (Green, Fox, & Lewis, 1983). Attachment patterns may reflect this interaction between a baby's temperament and the parents' responsiveness.

In reply, attachment theorists point to data that favor the caregiver responsiveness hypothesis. For example, it has been found that an infant's crying changes over the first year much more than the mother's responsiveness to the crying does. Moreover, the mother's responsiveness over a 3-month period predicts the infant's crying over the next three months significantly better than the infant's crying predicts the mother's subsequent responsiveness to crying. In short, the mother appears to influence the infant's crying more than the infant influences the mother's responsiveness to crying (Bell & Ainsworth, 1972). In general, the mother's behavior appears to be the most important factor in establishing a secure or insecure attachment (Isabella & Belsky, 1991).

More recent research may provide a resolution to this debate. Recall that the attachment classification in the Strange Situation is not based primarily on the baby's distress when the mother leaves but on how the baby reacts when she returns. It now appears that an infant's temperament predicts the former but not the latter (Vaughn, Lefever, Seifer, & Barglow, 1989; Frodi & Thompson, 1985). For example, babies with "easy" temperaments are not typically distressed when the mother leaves. When she returns, they either tend to greet her happily—thus showing one of the securely attached patterns—or they show the avoidant pattern of insecure attachment. Babies with "difficult" temperaments are typically distressed when the mother leaves. When she returns, they either tend to seek her out and cling to her—thus showing one of the securely attached patterns—or they show the ambivalent pattern of insecure attachment (Belsky & Rovine, 1987). Thus the overall reaction of a child to the departure and return of his or her primary caregivers is a function of both their responsiveness to the child and his or her own temperament.

ATTACHMENT AND LATER DEVELOPMENT   A baby's attachment classification has been found to remain quite stable when retested in the Strange Situation several years later—unless the family experiences major changes in life circumstances (Main & Cassidy, 1988; Thompson, Lamb, & Estes, 1982). Stressful life changes are likely to affect parental responsiveness to the baby that, in turn, affects the baby's feelings of security.

The patterns of early attachment also appear to be related to how children cope with new experiences during the next few years. For example, in one study, 2-year-olds were given a series of problems requiring the use of tools. Some of the problems were within the child's capacity; others were quite difficult. The toddlers, who had been rated as securely attached when they were 12 months of age, approached the problems with enthusiasm and persistence. When they encountered difficulties, they seldom cried or became angry; rather, they sought help from the adults who were present. Those who had been rated earlier as insecurely attached behaved quite differently. They became easily frustrated and angry, seldom asked for help, tended to ignore or reject directions from the adults, and quickly gave up trying to solve the problems (Matas, Arend, & Sroufe, 1978).

Another study looked at the social behavior of nursery school children (age 3½ years) whose attachment relationships had been assessed at 15 months of age. The children rated as securely attached earlier tended to be the social leaders: They were active in initiating and participating in activities and were sought out by the other children. Their teachers rated them as self-directed and eager to learn. The insecurely attached children tended to be socially withdrawn and hesitant about participating in activities. Their teachers rated them as less curious about new things and less forceful in pursuing their goals. These differences were not related to intelligence (Waters, Wippman, & Sroufe, 1979).

These studies suggest that children who are securely attached by the time they enter their second year of life are better equipped to cope with new experiences and relationships. However, we cannot be certain that the quality of children's early attachments is directly responsible for their later competence in problem-solving and social skills. Parents who are responsive to their children's needs in infancy probably continue to provide effective parenting during early childhood—encouraging autonomy and efforts to cope with new experiences, yet ready with help when needed. Thus, the child's competency and social skills at age 3½ may reflect the current state of the parent-child relationship rather than the relationship that existed two years earlier. Moreover, children's temperaments—which, as we saw earlier, affects their behavior in the Strange Situation—might also be influencing their later competency as preschoolers.

GENDER IDENTITY AND SEX TYPING

With rare exceptions, the human species comes in two sexes, and most children acquire a firm sense of themselves as either male or female. They acquire what developmental psychologists call a **gender identity**. But most cultures elaborate the biological distinction between male and female into a sprawling network of beliefs and practices

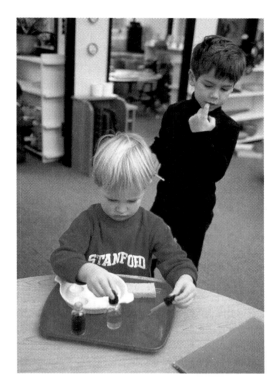

Children who were rated as insecure in their attachment relationships at 15 months of age tended to be socially withdrawn and hesitant about participating in activities in later years when they were in nursery school.

that permeate virtually every domain of human activity. Societies have both formal rules and informal norms that specify how men and women should behave; which roles they must, or are permitted to, fill; and even which personality characteristics they may "appropriately" possess. Different cultures may define the socially correct behaviors, roles, and personality characteristics differently from one another, and these may change over time within a culture—as they have in America over the past 25 years. But whatever its current definition, each culture still strives to transform male and female infants into masculine and feminine adults.

The acquisition of behaviors and characteristics that a culture considers sex-appropriate is called **sex typing**. Note that gender identity and sex typing are not the same thing. A girl may have a firm acceptance of herself as female and still not adopt all of the behaviors that her culture considers feminine or avoid all behavior labeled masculine.

But are gender identity and sex typing simply the product of cultural prescriptions and expectations or are they, in part, a product of "natural" development? Theories disagree on this point. We will examine four of them here.

PSYCHOANALYTIC THEORY The first psychologist to attempt a comprehensive account of gender identity and sex typing was Sigmund Freud, whose psychoanalytic theory contains a stage theory of **psychosexual development** within it (Freud, 1933/1964). Psychoanalytic theory and its limitations are discussed in more detail in Chapter 13; here we will give only a sketch of the concepts relevant to Freud's theory of gender identity and sex typing.

According to Freud, children begin to focus on the genitals at about age 3; he called this the beginning of the **phallic stage** of psychosexual development. Specifically, both sexes become aware that boys have a penis and that girls do not. During this same stage, they also begin to have sexual feelings toward their opposite-sex parent and feel jealous and resentful of their same-sex parent; Freud called this the **Oedipal conflict.** As they mature further, both sexes eventually resolve this conflict through **identification** with their same-sex parents, modeling their behaviors, attitudes, and personality attributes on those parents in an attempt to be like them. Thus, the process of forming a gender identity and becoming sex typed begins with the child's discovery of the genital differences between the sexes and ends with the child's identification with the same sex parent (Freud, 1925/1961).

Psychoanalytic theory has always been controversial, and many object to its explicit assumption that "anatomy is destiny." The theory implies that rigid sex typing—even stereotyping—is universally inevitable and unmodifiable. More important, however, the empirical evidence does not support the conclusion that a child's discovery of genital sex differences or identification with the same-sex parent is an influential determinant of sex typing (McConaghy, 1979; Maccoby & Jacklin, 1974; Kohlberg, 1966).

SOCIAL-LEARNING THEORY In contrast to psychoanalytic theory, social-learning theory has a much more straightforward account of sex typing. It emphasizes both the rewards and punishments that children receive for sex-appropriate and sex-inappropriate behaviors, respectively, and the ways in which children learn sex-typed behavior through their observation of adults (Bandura, 1986; Mischel, 1966). For example, children observe that

adult male and female behaviors differ and develop hypotheses about what is appropriate for themselves (Perry & Bussey, 1984). Observational learning also enables children to imitate and thus to acquire sex-typed behaviors by modeling the significant same-sex adults they admire. Thus, like psychoanalytic theory, social-learning theory has its own concept of modeling and identification, but it is based on observational learning rather than on inner conflict resolution. (Learning theory in general is discussed further in Chapter 7; social-learning theory, in particular, is discussed further in Chapter 13.)

Two broader points are worth emphasizing about social-learning theory. Unlike psychoanalytic theory, social-learning theory treats sex-typed behaviors like any other learned behaviors; no special psychological principles or processes must be postulated to explain how children become sex typed. Second, if there is nothing special about sex-typed behaviors, then sex typing itself is neither inevitable nor unmodifiable. Children become sex typed because sex happens to be the basis on which their culture chooses to base reward and punishment. If a culture becomes less sex typed in its ideology, children will become less sex typed in their behavior.

Many lines of evidence support the general social-learning account of sex typing. Parents do differentially reward and punish sex-appropriate and sex-inappropriate behaviors as well as serve as the child's first models of masculine and feminine behavior. From infancy on, most parents dress boys and girls differently and provide them with different toys (Rheingold & Cook, 1975). Observations made in the homes of preschool children have found that parents reward their daughters for dressing up, dancing, playing with dolls, and simply following them around but criticize them for manipulating objects, running, jumping, and climbing. In contrast, parents reward their sons for playing with blocks but criticize them for playing with dolls, asking for help, or even volunteering to be helpful (Fagot, 1978). Parents tend to demand more independence of boys and to have higher expectations of them; they also respond less quickly to boys' requests for help and focus less on the interpersonal aspects of a task. And finally, parents punish boys both verbally and physically more often than girls (Maccoby & Jacklin, 1974).

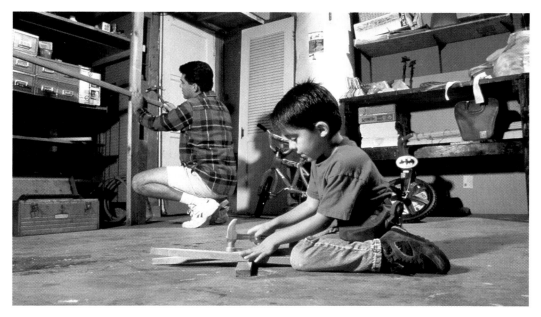

Both psychoanalytic theory and social learning theory propose that children become sex-typed by modeling the behavior of the parent or another adult of the same sex. The theories differ markedly in what motivates this modeling, however.

Some have suggested that in reacting differently to boys and girls, parents may not be imposing their own stereotypes on them but simply reacting to real innate differences between the behaviors of the two sexes (Maccoby, 1980). For example, even as infants, boys demand more attention than girls do, and research suggests that human males are innately more physically aggressive than human females (Maccoby & Jacklin, 1974). This could be why parents punish boys more often than girls.

There may be some truth to this, but it is also clear that adults approach children with stereotyped expectations that lead them to treat boys and girls differently. For example, adults viewing newborn infants through the window of a hospital nursery believe they can detect sex differences. Infants thought to be boys are described as robust, strong, and large-featured; identical-looking infants thought to be girls are described as delicate, fine-featured, and "soft" (Luria & Rubin, 1974). In one study, college students viewed a videotape of a 9-month-old infant showing a strong but ambiguous emotional reaction to a jack-in-the-box. The reaction was more often labeled "anger" when the child was thought to be a boy and "fear" when the same infant was thought to be a girl (Condry & Condry, 1976). When an infant was called "David" in another study, "he" was actually treated more roughly by subjects than when the same infant was called "Lisa" (Bem, Martyna, & Watson, 1976).

Fathers appear to be more concerned with sex-typed behavior than mothers, particularly with their sons. They tend to react more negatively than mothers (interfering with the child's play or expressing disapproval) when their sons play with "feminine" toys. Fathers are less concerned when their daughters engage in "masculine" play, but they still show more disapproval than mothers do (Langlois & Downs, 1980).

But if parents and other adults treat children in sex-stereotyped ways, children themselves are the real "sexists." Peers enforce sex-stereotyping much more severely than parents. Indeed, parents who consciously seek to raise their children without the traditional sex-role stereotypes—by encouraging the child to engage in a wide range of activities without labeling any activity as masculine or feminine or by playing nontraditional roles within the home—are often dismayed to find their efforts undermined by peer pressure. Boys, in particular, criticize other boys when they see them engaged in "girls'" activities. They are quick to call another boy a sissy if he plays with dolls, cries when he is hurt, or shows tender concern toward another child in distress. In contrast, girls seem not to object to other girls playing with "boys'" toys or engaging in masculine activities. (Langlois & Downs, 1980).

This points up a general phenomenon: The taboos in our culture against feminine behavior for boys are stronger than those against masculine behavior for girls. Being a male "sissy" is far less acceptable than being a female "tomboy." Four- and 5-year-old boys are more likely to experiment with feminine toys and activities (such as dolls, a lipstick and mirror, hair ribbons) when no one is watching than when an adult or another boy is present. For girls, the presence of an observer makes little difference in their choice of play activities (Kobasigawa, Arakaki, & Awiguni, 1966; Hartup & Moore, 1963).

In addition to parental and peer influences, children's books and television programs play an important part in promoting sex-role stereotypes. Until recently, most children's books portrayed boys in active, problem-solving roles. They were the characters who displayed courage and heroism, persevered in the face of difficulty, constructed things, and achieved goals. Girls were usually much more passive. Female storybook characters were likely to display fear and avoidance of dangerous situations; they would give up easily, ask for help, and watch while someone else achieved a goal. Similar differences have been noted in the sex roles portrayed in children's television programs (Sternglanz & Serbin, 1974).

Attempts to modify children's sex-role stereotypes by exposing them to television programs in which the stereotypes are reversed (for example, the girls win in athletic events or a girl is elected president) have shown some success (Davidson, Yasuna, & Tower, 1979). But exposure to television cannot counteract real-life experiences.

This was apparent when 5- and 6-year-olds were shown films in which the usual sex-typed occupations were reversed: The doctors were women and the nurses were men. When questioned about the films afterward and shown pictures of the actors, the children tended to relabel the occupations of the characters, to identify the female actor as the nurse and the male actor as the doctor. On the other hand, having a mother who worked outside the home or being exposed to female physicians and male nurses in real life increased the likelihood that the child would accept the less conventional roles (Cordua, McGraw, & Drabman, 1979).

These several phenomena of sex typing are fairly well explained by social-learning theory. On the other hand, there are some observations that social-learning theory cannot easily explain. First, it treats the child as the passive recipient of environmental forces: Society, parents, peers, and the media all "do it" to the child. This view of the child is inconsistent with the observation, implied above, that children themselves construct and enforce their own exaggerated version of society's gender rules on themselves and their peers more insistently than do most of the adults in their world. Second, there is an interesting developmental pattern to the child's view of gender rules. For example, a majority of 4-year-olds and a majority of 9-year-olds believe that there should be no sex-based restrictions on one's choice of occupation: Let women be doctors and men be nurses if they wish. Between these ages, however, children hold more rigid opinions. Thus about 90 percent of 6- and 7-year-olds believe that there *should* be sex-based restrictions on occupations (Damon, 1977).

Do these observations sound familiar? If you think these children sound like Piaget's preoperational moral realists, you are right. Which is why psychologist Lawrence Kohlberg (1966) developed a cognitive-developmental theory of sex typing based directly on Piaget's theory of cognitive development.

COGNITIVE-DEVELOPMENTAL THEORY   In accounting for gender identity and sex typing, social-learning theory puts its emphasis on the latter, describing how children acquire and come to prefer sex-typed behaviors because they are rewarded for them. This process begins long before gender identity emerges. Thus children begin to show preferences for same-sex peers and sex-typed play activities when they are as young as 2 years old, well before they develop any conceptual awareness that these actions are correlated with sex (Jacklin & Maccoby, 1978). Although 2-year-olds can identify their own sex in a photograph of themselves and are usually able to identify the sex of a stereotypically dressed man or woman in a photograph, they cannot accurately sort photographs into "boys" and "girls" or predict another child's toy preferences on the basis of sex (Thompson, 1975).

At about $2\frac{1}{2}$ years, however, a more conceptual awareness of sex and gender begins to emerge, and it is at this point that cognitive-developmental theory becomes relevant for explaining what happens next. In particular, the theory proposes that gender identity plays a critical role in sex typing. The sequence is: "I am a girl [boy]; therefore I want to do girl [boy] things" (Kohlberg, 1966). In other words, it is the motive to behave consistently with one's gender identity—not to obtain external rewards—that prompts children to behave in sex-appropriate ways. As a result they willingly take on the task of sex typing themselves—and their peers.

Gender identity itself develops slowly over the years from 2 to 7, in accord with the principles of the preoperational stage of cognitive development. In particular, preoperational children's overreliance on visual impressions and their consequent inability to conserve an object's identity when its appearance changes becomes relevant to their concept of sex. Thus 3-year-olds can separate pictures of boys and girls, but many of them cannot say whether they themselves will be a mommy or a daddy when they grow up (Thompson, 1975). The understanding that a person's sex remains the same despite changes in age and appearance is called **gender constancy**, a direct analog of conservation with water, clay, and checkers.

For example, Kohlberg asked children if a doll's sex could be changed if they wanted it to. Most 4-year-olds said that it could be, but most 6-year-olds said it could not be. The children who showed gender constancy—who said the doll's sex could *not* be changed—also conserved on the clay conservation task described earlier in this chapter.

The preoperational child's moral realism is also pertinent here:

> The physical constancies underlying . . . gender . . . tend to be identified with divine or moral law, and the need to adapt to the physical realities of one's identity is viewed as a moral obligation. . . . [Children] view same-sex behavior as morally required, and . . . express punitive sentiments to children who deviate from sex-typed behavior. (Kohlberg, 1966, p. 122)

This, then, is why preoperational children seem to be even more sexist and less tolerant of gender nonconformity in themselves and others than are adults. This is why bewildered feminist parents of preoperational children find that their careful nonsexist childrearing practices do not seem to "take" despite their best efforts (but see the Critical Discussion, "Can Sex Education Prevent Childhood Sexism?").

The cognitive-developmental theory of gender identity and sex typing is currently the most influential account of gender development within the field. But the shortcomings of Piaget's theory also apply to Kohlberg's special case of Piaget's theory. Thus, just as Piaget's more standard conservation tasks have been criticized, so too have the gender constancy tasks (Bem, 1989). For example, children who claim that a doll's sex can be changed at will may not understand that the experimenter wants them to pretend that the doll is a stand-in for a real person. Literally speaking, these children are right and the experimenter is wrong!

And just as developmental psychologists have shown that children can conserve at much younger ages than Piaget thought if the tasks are better designed, so too it seemed to some researchers that children would display gender constancy long before 6 or 7 years of age if ambiguities, such as the one just cited, are removed. For example, in one study of gender constancy in the self, the investigators asked "If you wore [opposite-sex] clothes, what would you *really* be, a boy or a girl?" Over 90 percent of 4-, 5-, and 6-year-olds responded correctly (Martin & Halverson, 1983). Another study took photographs of some of the subject's classmates dressed up in opposite-sex clothes and then asked whether the child in each photograph was a boy or a girl. Virtually all 3-, 4-, and 5-year-olds responded correctly (Miller, 1984).

Earlier we saw that psychologists who adopt a knowledge acquisition approach to cognitive development believe that children often fail conservation tasks because they simply do not possess sufficient knowledge of the relevant domain. We saw, for example, children who conserved on animal-to-plant transformations but failed to conserve on animal-to-animal transformations. Children will ignore dramatic changes in visual appearance—and hence conserve—only when they understand that some essential defining feature of an object has not changed.

This suggests that a child's gender constancy might also depend on his or her understanding of maleness and femaleness. But what do we adults know about sex that children do not? One answer is genitalia. For all practical purposes, genitalia constitute the essential defining feature of maleness and femaleness. Can young children who understand this conserve on a realistic gender constancy task?

In a study designed to test this possibility, three full-length, color photographs of toddlers between the ages of 1 and 2 were used as stimuli (Bem, 1989). As shown in Figure 3-11, the first photograph showed the toddler completely nude with the genitalia fully visible. The second photograph showed the same toddler dressed (and the boy bewigged) like a child of the opposite sex; the third photograph showed the toddler dressed normally—like a child of his or her own sex.

(Because of the sensitive nature of child nudity in our culture, each photograph was taken in the toddler's own home with at least one parent present. Parents provided written consent to use the photographs in the research, and parents of the two children who appear in Figure 3-11 also gave written consent to have these photographs published. Finally, parents of the children who served as subjects in the study gave written permission for their children to participate in a study in which they would be asked questions about pictures of nude toddlers.)

Using these 6 photographs, children between 3 years and $5\frac{1}{2}$ years of age were tested for gender constancy. First the experimenter showed the child the photograph of the nude toddler, who was given a sex-ambiguous name (for example, "Gaw"), and asked the child to identify the toddler's sex: "Is Gaw a boy or a girl?" Next the experimenter showed the child the sex-inconsistent photograph, making sure the child realized that this was the same toddler as in the nude photograph. The experimenter explained that the picture was taken one day when the toddler was playing dress-up and had put on opposite-sex clothes (and, in the case of the boy, put on a girl's wig). The nude photograph was removed and the child was asked to identify the sex of the toddler while looking only at the

FIGURE 3-11

Testing Gender Constancy   *After seeing the photograph of a nude toddler, children are asked to identify the sex of that same toddler from pictures in which the toddler is dressed in sex-inconsistent clothing and sex-consistent clothing. Children who can correctly identify the toddler's sex across all the pictures have attained gender constancy. (From Bem, 1989, pp. 653–654)*

sex-inconsistent picture: "What is Gaw really—a boy or a girl?" Finally, the child was asked to identify the sex of the same toddler from the sex-consistent picture. This procedure was then repeated with the other set of three photographs. The children were also asked to explain their answers. A child was considered to have attained gender constancy only if he or she correctly identified the sex of the toddler all six times.

A set of photographs of different toddlers was used to assess whether the children knew that genitalia constitute the defining feature of sex. Again, children were asked to identify the sex of the pictured toddlers and to explain their answers. The easiest part of the test required the child to point out which of two nude toddlers was a boy and which a girl. The most difficult part of the test showed photographs of toddlers who were nude from the waist down but dressed in sex-inconsistent clothes from the waist up. In order to cor-

rectly identify the toddler's sex in these photographs, a child would have to know not only that genitalia indicate sex, but that when the genital indicators are in conflict with culturally defined indicators of sex (such as clothing, hairstyles, and toys), the genital indicators have priority. Note that the constancy task itself is even harder because children had to give priority to the genital indicators even when those indicators were no longer visible in the photograph (as in the second photograph of each set in Figure 3-11).

The results showed that 40 percent of the 3-, 4-, and early 5-year-old children displayed gender constancy. This is much earlier than predicted by the cognitive developmental theory of Piaget and Kohlberg. More importantly, a full 74 percent of those who passed the genital knowledge test displayed gender constancy, compared with only 11 percent (three children) of those who failed the gender knowledge test. Children who passed the gender knowledge test were also more likely to show personal gender constancy: They correctly answered the question "If, like Gaw, you were playing dress-up games one day and you put on a girl's [boy's] wig . . . and girls' [boys'] clothes, what would you really be, a boy or a girl?

These results on gender constancy reveal that, like Piaget's general theory, Kohlberg's special theory about gender identity and sex typing underestimates the preoperational child's potential level of understanding. But there is a more important shortcoming of the theory: It fails to address why children should organize their self-concepts around their maleness or femaleness in the first place. Why should sex have priority over other potential categories of self-definition? It was this question that the next theory, gender schema theory, was designed to answer (Bem, 1985).

GENDER SCHEMA THEORY We noted earlier that the sociocultural approach to psychological development views the developing child not as a physical scientist seeking universally true knowledge but as a newcomer to a culture who seeks to become a native by learning how to look at reality through the lenses of that culture.

We also noted that most cultures elaborate the biological distinction between male and female into a network of beliefs and practices that permeate virtually every domain of human activity. Accordingly, the child needs to learn many specific details of this network: What are the culture's rules and norms about sex-appropriate behaviors, roles, and personality characteristics? As we have seen, both social-learning theory and cognitive-developmental theory provide reasonable explanations for how the developing child might acquire this information.

But the culture is also teaching the child a much deeper lesson, namely that the distinction between male and female is so important that it should become a set of lenses for looking at everything. Consider, for example, the child who first enters a day-care center offering a variety of new toys and activities. There are many potential criteria the child could use for deciding which toys and activities to try. Should she consider indoor or outdoor activities? Does he prefer a toy that involves artistic production or one that requires mechanical manipulation? How about an activity that one can do with other children? Or one that can be done in solitude? But of all the potential criteria, the culture emphasizes one above all others: "Be sure to consider first and foremost whether the toy or activity is appropriate for your sex." At every turn, the child is encouraged to look at the world through the lenses of gender, and it is these lenses that Bem calls the **gender schema** (Bem, 1993, 1985, 1981). And it is because children learn to evaluate their behavioral alternatives through these lenses that gender schema theory is a theory of sex typing.

As anthropologists have pointed out, the natives of a culture are typically not aware of the lenses they wear. Lenses are transparent to the wearer—who looks *through* the lenses of the culture, not *at* them. For this same reason, parents and teachers do not teach children about the gender schema directly. Instead, the lesson is silently embedded in the daily practices of the culture.

Consider, for example, a teacher who wishes to treat children of both sexes equally. Accordingly, she lines them up at the drinking fountain by alternating boys and girls. If a boy is selected to be hall monitor on Monday, then a girl will be hall monitor on Tuesday. Equal numbers of boys and girls must be selected for the class play. This teacher believes she is teaching her students the importance of sex equality. She is right, but she is also unwittingly teaching them the importance of sex. The students learn that no matter how

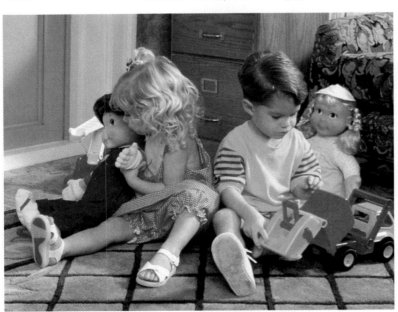

Several theories attempt to account for the development of sex typing in children.

CRITICAL DISCUSSION | *CAN SEX EDUCATION PREVENT CHILDHOOD SEXISM?*

The experiment on gender constancy described in the text shows that children as young as 3 years old are able to understand that one's maleness and femaleness is a permanent biological fact; it does not change just because one dresses like the opposite sex.

Sandra Bem, the researcher who conducted the study, and Daryl Bem (one of the authors of this text) believe that children who have a biologically grounded definition of sex may also have firmer gender identities—a more secure sense of themselves as male or female—because they do not have to fear that they will "lose" their maleness or femaleness if they engage in gender nonconforming behavior. Such children might thus be less sex-stereotyped in their own attitudes and behaviors, more able to resist social pressure to conform to society's gender rules, and more tolerant of others who do not conform.

In contrast, children who equate a person's sex with cultural indicators like clothing and hairstyle may be more sex-stereotyped as a result. Some support for this possibility comes from a study of 27-month-old children who were asked to identify the sex of conventionally clothed children in photographs taken from mail-order shopping catalogues. Children who could do this correctly—about half the children—were designated "early labelers."

Observations of these children revealed that, compared with the other children, early labelers spent twice as much of their time in sex-typed toy play. Moreover, their fathers were more likely than other fathers to believe that boys and girls should have different kinds of toys, that children of different sexes should not see each other naked, and that children should not be given sexual information. They were also more likely to dread answering their children's questions about sex and to hold more traditional views about women. No such differences were observed among the mothers (Fagot & Leinbach, 1989). These findings are consistent with our earlier observation that fathers are more concerned with sex-typed behaviors than mothers.

The Bems thus believe that teaching children as early as possible that the genitalia are the essential defining feature of maleness and femaleness might immunize them against an unquestioning acceptance of the culture's gender rules. The preoperational child's "moral realism" might actually prompt these gender-liberated future citizens to be even more adamant and radical than their feminist parents in opposing sexism and sex stereotyping.

The difference between children with and without a genitally grounded gender constancy is amusingly illustrated by the Bems' own son, Jeremy, who naively decided to wear barrettes to nursery school one day. Several times another little boy insisted that Jeremy must be a girl because "only girls wear barrettes." After repeatedly asserting that "wearing barrettes doesn't matter; being a boy means having a penis and testicles," Jeremy finally pulled down his pants in order to make his point more graphically. The other boy was not impressed. He simply said, "Everybody has a penis; only girls wear barrettes!"

Freud believed that a child's early discovery of the genital differences between the sexes led inexorably to conventional sex typing. There is a certain delicious irony in the possibility that a child's early discovery of the genital differences between the sexes should become a feminist weapon against conventional sex typing.

unrelated to sex an activity might seem, one cannot engage in it without attending to the male-female distinction. Even learning the pronouns of our language—he, she, him, her—requires wearing the lenses of gender.

Children also learn to apply the lenses of gender to themselves, to organize their self-concepts around their maleness or femaleness, and to judge their self-worth in terms of their answer to the question: Am I masculine or feminine enough? It is in this way that gender schema theory is a theory of gender identity as well as a theory of sex typing.

Gender schema theory, then, is the answer to the question that Bem believes Kohlberg's cognitive-developmental theory of gender identity and sex typing fails to address: Why should children organize their self-concepts around their maleness or femaleness in the first place? Like cognitive-developmental theory, gender schema theory views the developing child as an active agent in his or her own socialization. But like social-learning theory, gender schema theory implies that sex typing is neither inevitable nor unmodifiable. Children become sex typed because sex happens to be a major focus around which their culture chooses to organize its view of reality. If the culture becomes less sex typed in its ideology, children will become less sex typed in their behaviors and self-concepts.

DEVELOPMENT AFTER CHILDHOOD

Development does not end with childhood. It is a continuous process extending from birth through adolescence and adulthood to old age. Bodily changes occur throughout life, affecting the individual's attitudes, cognitive processes, and behavior. The kinds of problems people must cope with change throughout the life span, too.

The psychoanalyst Erik Erikson proposed a series of eight stages to characterize development throughout life. He called them **psychosocial stages** because he believed that the psychological development of individuals depends on the social relations established at various points in life. At each stage, there are special problems or crises to be confronted. These hypothesized stages are shown in Table 3-3.

Erikson believed that a person—child or adult—must successfully negotiate each crisis in order to be prepared for the psychosocial tasks that follow. Thus, infants must learn during the first year of life that their parents or caregivers can be trusted to provide food, comfort, and unconditional love. If and when such trust develops, then the child feels safe in trying out more autonomy in the second year. Parents who get exasperated when their toddler acts stubborn and defiant in the second year of life should congratulate themselves because their child trusts them enough to know that they will not withdraw their love when he or she is naughty. And, to the extent that parents encourage a sense of autonomy during the second year, their children learn to control their impulses and to feel pride in their accomplishments. Overprotection—restricting what the child is permitted to do—or ridiculing unsuccessful attempts may cause the child to doubt his or her abilities.

During the preschool years (ages 3 through 5), children progress from simple self-control to an ability to initiate activities and carry them out. Again, parental attitudes—encouraging or discouraging—can make children feel inadequate (or guilty, if the child initiates an activity that the adult views as shameful).

During the elementary-school years, children learn the skills valued by society. These include not only reading, writing, and physical skills, but also the ability to share responsibility and to get along with other people. To the extent that efforts in these areas are successful, children develop feelings of competence; unsuccessful efforts result in feelings of inferiority.

ADOLESCENCE

Adolescence refers to the period of transition from childhood to adulthood. Its age limits are not clearly specified, but it extends roughly from age 12 to the late teens, when physical growth is nearly complete. During this period, the young person develops to sexual maturity and establishes an identity as an individual apart from the family.

TABLE 3-3

Stages of Psychosocial Development *Erikson defines eight major life stages in terms of the psychosocial problems, or crises, that must be resolved.* (After Erikson, 1963)

STAGES	PSYCHOSOCIAL CRISES	FAVORABLE OUTCOME
1. First year of life	Trust versus mistrust	Trust and optimism
2. Second year	Autonomy versus doubt	Sense of self-control and adequacy
3. Third through fifth years	Initiative versus guilt	Purpose and direction; ability to initiate one's own activities
4. Sixth year to puberty	Industry versus inferiority	Competence in intellectual, social, and physical skills
5. Adolescence	Identity versus confusion	An integrated image of oneself as a unique person
6. Early adulthood	Intimacy versus isolation	Ability to form close and lasting relationships; to make career commitments
7. Middle adulthood	Generativity versus self-absorption	Concern for family, society, and future generations
8. The aging years	Integrity versus despair	A sense of fulfillment and satisfaction with one's life; willingness to face death

SEXUAL DEVELOPMENT Puberty, the period of sexual maturation that transforms a child into a biologically mature adult capable of sexual reproduction, takes place over a period of 3 or 4 years. It starts with a period of very rapid physical growth (the **adolescent growth spurt**) accompanied by the gradual development of the reproductive organs and **secondary sex characteristics** (breast development in girls, beard growth in boys, and the appearance of pubic hair in both sexes).

Menarche, the first menstrual period, occurs relatively late in puberty—about 18 months after a girl's growth spurt has reached its peak velocity. The first menstrual periods tend to be irregular, and ovulation (the release of a mature egg) does not usually begin until a year or so after menarche. A boy's first ejaculation typically occurs about 2 years after the growth spurt begins. The first seminal fluid does not contain sperm; the number of sperm and their fertility gradually increase.

There is wide variation in the age at which puberty begins and the rate at which it progresses. Some girls attain menarche as early as 11, others as late as 17; the average age is 12 years, 9 months. Boys, on the average, experience their growth spurt and mature 2 years later than girls. They begin to ejaculate semen with live sperm sometime between age 12 and 16; the average age is $14\frac{1}{2}$ years. The wide variation in the timing of puberty is strikingly apparent in seventh- and eighth-grade classrooms. Some of the girls may look like mature women with fully developed breasts and rounded hips, while others may still have the size and shape of little girls. Some of the boys may look like gangly adolescents, while others may look much as they did at the age of 9 or 10. (See the discussion of hormonal changes at puberty in Chapter 10.)

PSYCHOLOGICAL EFFECTS OF PUBERTY Conventional wisdom holds that adolescence is a period of "storm and stress" characterized by moodiness, inner turmoil, and rebellion. But research does not support this pessimistic view. One study followed more than 300 adolescents as they progressed from the sixth through the eighth grades, assessing them and their parents twice a year through interviews and psychological tests. They were assessed again during their last year of high school (Petersen, 1989). Most of the adolescents made it through this period without major turmoil. The data do indicate, however, that puberty does have significant effects on body image, self-esteem, moods, and relationships with parents and members of the opposite sex.

Some of these effects may be linked directly to the hormonal changes of puberty (reviewed in detail by Buchanan, Eccles, & Becker, 1992), but most are related to the personal and social effects of the body's physical changes and, most importantly, the timing of those changes. Being an early or late maturer (one year earlier or later than average) affects adolescents' satisfaction with their appearance and their body image. In general seventh- and eighth-grade boys who have reached puberty reported positive moods more often than their prepubertal male classmates. and they tend to be more satisfied with their weight and their overall appearance than later maturing boys—a reflection of the importance of strength and physical prowess for males in our society. But early maturing boys also tend to have less self-control and emotional stability than later-maturing boys; they are more likely to smoke, drink, use drugs, and be in trouble with the law (Duncan et al., 1985). In contrast, late-maturing boys feel the worst about themselves in seventh grade, but typically end up as the healthiest group by their senior year in high school (Petersen, 1989).

Early maturation has the opposite effect on the self-esteem of girls. Compared with later maturers, earlier maturers experience more depression and anxiety (Brooks-Gunn & Ruble, 1983), have lower self-esteem (Simmons & Blyth, 1988), and are generally less satisfied with their weight and appearance. They tend to be embarrassed by the fact that their bodies are more womanly in shape than those of their female classmates—particularly since the current standards for female attractiveness as promoted by the media emphasize the lean look. Although early maturers also achieve early popularity, this is partly because they are seen as sexually precocious. They are also more likely to have conflict with their parents, to drop out of school, and to have both emotional and behavioral problems (Caspi & Moffitt, 1991; Stattin & Magnusson, 1990).

Again, however, it is important to emphasize that for both sexes in the large-scale longitudinal study early adolescence was relatively trouble-free for more than half of those studied. About 30 percent of the group had only intermittent problems. Only 15 percent were caught in a "downward spiral of trouble and turmoil"; emotional and academic problems that were evident in the eighth grade continued or worsened into twelfth grade (Petersen, 1989).

IDENTITY DEVELOPMENT As shown in Table 3-3, Erikson believed that the major task confronting the adolescent is to develop a sense of identity, to find answers to the questions "Who am I?" and "Where am I going?" Although Erikson coined the term **identity crisis** to refer to this active process of self-definition, he believed that it is an integral part of healthy psychosocial development. Similarly, most developmental psychologists believe that adolescence should be a period of "role experimentation" in which young persons can explore alternative behaviors, interests, and ideologies. Many beliefs, roles, and ways of behaving may be "tried on," modified, or discarded in an attempt to shape an integrated concept of the self.

Developing a personal identity—answering the questions "Who am I?" and "Where am I going?"—is a major task of adolescence.

Adolescents try to synthesize these values and appraisals into a consistent picture. If parents, teachers, and peers project consistent values, the search for identity is easier. In a simple society in which identification models are few and social roles are limited, the task of forming an identity is relatively easy. In a society as complex as ours, it is a difficult task for many adolescents. They are faced with an almost infinite array of possibilities of how to behave and what to do in life. As a result, there are large differences among adolescents in how the development of their identity proceeds. Moreover, any particular adolescent's identity may be at different stages of development in different areas of life (for example, sexual, occupational, ideological).

Ideally the identity crisis should be resolved by the early or mid-twenties so that the individual can move on to other life tasks. When the process is successful, the individual is said to have achieved an identity; this usually means having arrived at a coherent sense of one's sexual identity, vocational direction, and ideological worldview—even though these can and should remain open to change during subsequent development. Until the identity crisis is resolved, the individual has no consistent sense of self or set of internal standards for evaluating his or her self-worth in the major areas of life. As shown in Table 3-3, Erikson called this unsuccessful outcome *identity confusion.*

Erikson's theory about adolescent identity development has been tested and extended by James Marcia (1980, 1966). On the basis of semistructured, open-ended interviews, Marcia concluded that there are four **identity statuses** or positions on Erikson's identity-formation continuum, which are distinguished on the basis of whether the person perceives an identity issue and whether a resolution has been reached:

- *Identity Achievement* Those in this status have passed through an identity crisis, a period of active questioning and self-definition. They have committed to ideological positions they have worked out for themselves and decided on an occupation. They have begun to think of themselves as a future doctor, not just a pre-med chemistry major. They have re-examined their family's religious and political beliefs and discarded those that don't seem to fit their identity.

- *Foreclosure* Those in this status are also committed to occupational and ideological positions, but they show no signs of ever having gone through an identity crisis. They have accepted the religion of their families without question. When asked about political positions, they often say they have never really given it much thought. Some of them seem committed and cooperative; others simply seem rigid, dogmatic, and conforming. They give the impression that they would be lost if some major event occurred to challenge their unexamined rules and values.

- *Moratorium* These are the young people currently in the midst of an identity crisis. They are actively seeking answers but are still finding the conflicts between their parents' plans for them and their own interests unresolved. They may express a set of political or religious beliefs with great intensity for a while only to abandon them after a period of reconsideration. At best, they seem sensitive, ethical, and open-minded; at worst, they appear anxiety-ridden, self-righteous, and vacillating (Scarr, Weinberg, & Levine, 1986).

- *Identity Diffusion* This is Marcia's term for Erikson's identity confusion category. Some of those in this category may have had an identity crisis in the past; some have not. But in either case, they still have no integrated sense of themselves. They say it might be "interesting" to go to law school or start a business, but they are not taking steps to move in either direction. They say they are not interested in religion or politics. Some seem cynical ("Politics is all just crap"); others just seem shallow and confused. Some, of course, are still too young to have reached the identity development of adolescence.

As expected, the percentage of adolescents who have attained identity achievement steadily increases from pre-high school years to college upperclass years, while the percentage of those remaining in identity diffusion steadily decreases. The state of identity crisis—moratorium—peaks during the first two years of college. In general, studies show that the level of identity achievement is considerably higher for vocational choice than for political ideology (Waterman, 1985).

EARLY ADULTHOOD

During the early adult years, people commit themselves to an occupation, and many marry or form other types of intimate relationships. As Table 3-3 indicates, Erikson saw identity as a precursor to intimacy. He believed that adolescents who have not yet formed a satisfactory identity would find it difficult to become involved in an intimate, mutually satisfying relationship because their preoccupation with themselves would make it difficult to attend to the other person's needs. There is another point of view, however, that argues that adolescence begins not with a search for identity but with a need for intimacy and that the construction of self-identity is made possible by participating in intimate interpersonal relations (Sullivan, 1953). There is not enough research to decide between these two points of view; most likely, intimacy and identity interact throughout the periods of adolescence and early adulthood.

MIDDLE ADULTHOOD

For many people, the middle years of adulthood (roughly ages 40 to 65) are the most productive period. People in their forties are usually at the peak of their careers. Women who have devoted earlier years primarily to home responsibilities often turn to career or other activities as their children pass through and beyond adolescence.

Erikson uses the term *generativity* to refer to a concern with guiding and providing for the next generation. Feelings of satisfaction in middle adulthood come from helping teenage children become adults, providing for others who need help, and seeing one's contributions to society as valuable.

There is also a widespread view that this is the time of the "midlife crisis"—a time when individuals begin to realize that they have not achieved the goals they set for themselves as young adults or that they are not doing anything of much importance. Several longitudinal studies have reported that men in their

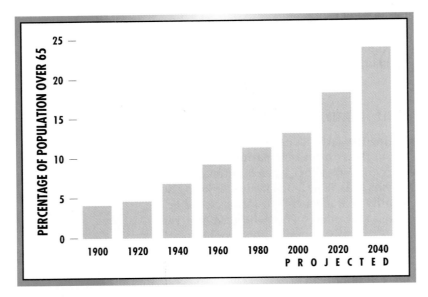

FIGURE 3-12

Aging America   *The percentage of the population in the United States over age 65 is increasing at a steady rate and is projected to continue to increase. For babies born in the United States today, life expectancy is an unprecedented 72.7 years for a boy and 79.6 years for a girl. For those who survive through middle age, the expected length of life is dramatically longer. A man who reaches 65 today can expect to live until 79.5 and a woman, to 83.7.* (U.S. Bureau of the Census, 1991)

early forties experience a period of emotional turmoil centered on conflicts about sexual relationships, family roles, and work values (Levinson, Darrow, Klein, Levinson, & McKee, 1978; Vaillant, 1977). And a similar

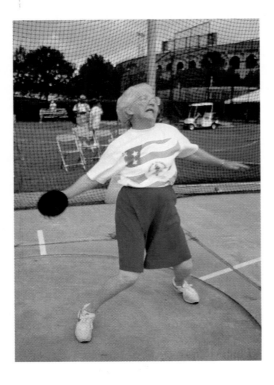

Because of better medical care, improved diet, and increasing interest in physical fitness, more people are reaching older age in excellent health.

midlife crisis has been proposed for women (Sheehy, 1976). The transition to middle adulthood, according to this view, is a time of upheaval not unlike a second adolescence, during which life goals are reevaluated and questions such as "Who am I?" and "Where am I going?" become important again.

But many researchers question the concept of midlife crisis as a developmental stage that most people experience. They find little evidence that people in their forties report more symptoms of emotional distress than younger or older people (Schaie & Willis, 1991; Costa & McCrae, 1980). And studies of how middle-aged women react to events such as menopause and children leaving home report that few perceive these changes as traumatic (Neugarten, 1968).

It is true that middle age is often a time of transition. As people approach the midpoint in life, their view of the life span tends to change. Instead of looking at life in terms of time since birth, as younger people do, they begin to think in terms of years left to live. Having faced the aging or death of their parents, they begin to realize the inevitability of their own death. At this point, many people restructure their lives in terms of priorities, deciding what is important to do in the years remaining. A man who has spent his years building a successful business may leave it to return to school. A woman who has raised her family may develop a new career or become active in politics. A couple may leave their jobs in the city to purchase a small farm. Although some people find this kind of reevaluation and change stressful enough to constitute a midlife crisis, most perceive it as a challenge rather than a threat.

THE AGING YEARS

People older than 65 now compose approximately 12 percent of the population, a percentage that is expected to approach 20 percent by the year 2020 (see Figure 3–12). Because of better medical care, improved diet, and increasing interest in physical fitness, more people are reaching the ages of 65, 75, and older in excellent health.

Normal aging is a gradual process that brings some changes: slower reflexes, dimmer eyesight and hearing, decreased stamina. But the more extreme debilities that we associate with old age are the result of disease, such as Alzheimer's, which destroys mental and physical functioning; abuse of the body by improper diet or use of alcohol and cigarettes; and failure to keep physically and mentally active. The number of individuals in ther 60s and 70s who work under demanding schedules and make important decisions (such as judges, corporate heads, and political leaders) attests to the fact that cognitive abilities need not diminish with age. Research on successful aging is now an active area of research in developmental psychology (Baltes & Baltes, 1990).

Erikson's last psychosocial crisis—integrity versus despair—is concerned with the way a person faces the end of life. Old age is a time of reflection, of looking back on the events of a lifetime. To the extent that an individual has successfully coped with the problems posed at each of the earlier stages of life, he or she has a sense of wholeness and integrity, of a life well-lived. If the elderly person looks back on life with regret, seeing it as a series of missed opportunities and failures, the final years will be ones of despair.

BIOLOGICAL-PSYCHOLOGICAL PERSPECTIVES

We noted in Chapter 1 that a full understanding of human behavior requires that we adopt both biological and psychological perspectives. In this chapter, this requirement is exemplified by the joint contributions of both "nature" and "nurture" to an individual's development throughout the life span.

For example, we have seen how children's maturing cognitive abilities influence not only how they conceive of the physical world but their moral and social worlds as well. We have noted that the age at which social and emotional behaviors such as smiling or displaying distress at the departure of the primary caregiver appear tends to be the same across diverse cultures, thereby implicating biological maturation. But we have also seen that the percentage of children who show distress at a caregiver's departure varies across cultures, showing the influence of the environment. Similarly, a child's reactions to the departure and reappearance of the primary caregiver turn out to be a function of both his or her inborn temperament and the caregiver's responsive sensitivity earlier in the child's development.

 CHAPTER SUMMARY

1. Two central questions in developmental psychology are: a) How do biological factors ("nature") interact with environmental experiences ("nurture") to determine the course of development? and b) Is development best understood as a *continuous process* of change or as a series of qualitatively distinct *stages?* A related questions is: Are there *critical* or *sensitive periods* during which specific experiences must occur for psychological development to proceed normally?

2. Genetic determinants express themselves through the process of *maturation:* innately determined sequences of growth or bodily changes that are relatively independent of the environment. Motor development, for example, is largely a maturational process because all children master skills such as crawling, standing, and walking in the same sequence

and at roughly the same age. But even these can be modified by an atypical or inadequate environment.

3. Infants are born with all sensory systems functioning and well prepared to learn about the environment. There is even some evidence that newborns respond differentially to sounds they heard while still in the uterus.

4. Piaget's theory describes stages in *cognitive development;* proceeding from the *sensorimotor stage* (in which an important discovery is *object permanence*), through the *preoperational stage* (symbols begin to be used), and the *concrete operational* stage (*conservation* concepts develop), to the *formal operational* stage (hypotheses are tested systematically in problem solving). The character of a child's *moral judgments* also corresponds to this sequence of stages.

5. New methods of testing reveal that Piaget's theory underestimates children's abilities, and alternative approaches have emerged. *Information-processing* approaches view cognitive development as reflecting the gradual development of processes such as attention and memory. Other theorists emphasize the child's increase in *domain-specific knowledge*. Still others focus on the influence of the *social and cultural context*.

6. As early as the first weeks of life, infants show individual differences in activity level, responsiveness to change in their environment, and irritability. Such mood-related personality characteristics are called *temperaments* and appear to be inborn. It is not yet clear to what extent they constitute the building blocks for the individual's later personality. Continuity of temperament across the life span is a function of the interaction between the child's inherited characteristics and the environment.

7. Some early social behaviors, such as smiling, reflect innate responses that appear at about the same time in all infants, including blind infants. The emergence of many later social behaviors—including wariness of strangers and distress over separation from primary caregivers—appears to depend on the child's developing cognitive skills.

8. An infant's tendency to seek closeness to particular people and to feel more secure in their presence is called *attachment*. Attachment can be assessed in a procedure called the *Strange Situation,* a series of episodes in which a child is observed as the primary caregiver leaves and returns to the room. On the basis of the child's reactions, he or she is classified as (a) *Securely Attached;* (b) *Insecurely Attached: Avoidant;* or (c) *Insecurely Attached: Ambivalent.* Securely attached infants tend to have primary caregivers who respond sensitively to their needs. A child's temperament also influences his or her behavior in the Strange Situation. Securely attached children tend to cope with new experiences better than insecurely attached children later in childhood.

9. *Gender identity* is the degree to which one regards oneself as male or female. It is distinct from *sex typing,* the acquisition of those characteristics and behaviors society considers appropriate for one's sex. Freud's *psychoanalytic theory* holds that gender identity and sex typing develop from the children's early discovery of the genital differences between the sexes and children's eventual *identification* with the same-sex parent. *Social-learning theory* emphasizes a) the *rewards and punishments* that children receive for sex-appropriate and sex-inappropriate behaviors and b) a process of *identification* with same-sex adults that is based on *observational learning*.

10. A *cognitive-developmental theory* of gender identity and sex typing developed by Kohlberg is based on Piaget's theory of cognitive development. Once children can identify themselves as male or female, they are motivated to acquire sex-typed behaviors. Their understanding of sex and gender corresponds to Piaget's stages of cognitive development, especially their understanding of *gender constancy,* the realization that a person's sex remains constant despite changes of age and appearance. Like its parent theory, cognitive-developmental theory underestimates children's degree of understanding.

11. *Gender schema theory,* developed by Sandra Bem, seeks to explain why children base their self-concept on the male-female distinction in the first place. It emphasizes the culture's role in teaching children to view the world through a set of *gender lenses*. Like cognitive-developmental theory, gender schema theory sees children as active agents in promoting their own sex typing; like social-learning theory, it rejects the conclusion that traditional sex typing is inevitable and unmodifiable.

12. Development is a lifelong process: Individuals change both physically and psychologically, and they encounter new adjustment problems throughout life. Erikson's *psychosocial stages* describe problems, or crises, in social relations that must be confronted at various points in life. These range from "trust versus mistrust" during the first year of life, through "intimacy versus isolation" in early adulthood, to "integrity versus despair" as individuals face death.

13. Puberty has significant effects on an adolescent's body image, self-esteem, moods, and relationships; but most adolescents make it through this period without major turmoil. Compared with their prepubertal classmates, early maturing boys report greater satisfaction with their appearance and more frequent positive moods; in contrast, early maturing girls report more depression, anxiety, family

conflict, and dissatisfaction with their appearance than do their prepubertal classmates. According to Erikson's theory, forming a personal sense of identity is the major task of the adolescent period.

FURTHER READING

Comprehensive textbooks on development include Cole and Cole, *The Development of Children* (2nd ed., 1993); and Mussen, Conger, Kagan, and Huston, *Child Development and Personality* (7th ed., 1989). A general text on development through the life course is Goldhaber, *Life-Span Human Development* (1986). For a discussion of the major approaches to the study of development, see Miller, *Theories of Developmental Psychology* (2nd ed., 1989).

Books focusing on infancy include Osofsky (ed.), *Handbook of Infant Development* (2nd ed., 1987); Lamb and Bornstein, *Development in Infancy: An Introduction* (2nd ed., 1987); and Rosenblith, *In the Beginning: Development from Conception to Age Two Years* (2nd ed., 1992). A four-volume overview of the major theories and research in child development may be found in Mussen (ed.), *Handbook of Child Psychology* (4th ed., 1983).

Cognitive Development (3rd ed., 1992) by Flavell presents a thorough introduction to this topic. *The Development of Memory in Children* (3rd ed., 1989) by Kail provides a readable summary of research on children's memory. *Children's Thinking* (1986) by Siegler is written from the perspective of information-processing theories. For a brief introduction to Piaget, see Phillips, *Piaget's Theory: A Primer* (1981).

Two books on children's moral and social reasoning are Damon, *Social and Personality Development: From Infancy Through Adolescence* (1983), and Turiel, *The Development of Social Knowledge: Morality and Convention* (1983). Kohnstamm, Bates, and Rothbart (eds.), *Temperament in Childhood* provides a good summary of research in this active area; and Bem, *The Lenses of Gender* (1993) provides a sociocultural approach to issues of sex and gender.

Adolescent development is dealt with in Steinberg *Adolescence* (2nd ed., 1989); and Kimmel and Wiener, *Adolescence: A Developmental Transition* (1985).

For the later years, see Woodruff and Birren, *Aging: Scientific Perspectives and Social Issues* (2nd ed., 1983); Perlmutter and Hall, *Adult Development and Aging* (2nd ed., 1992); and Baltes and Baltes (eds), *Successful Aging* (1990).

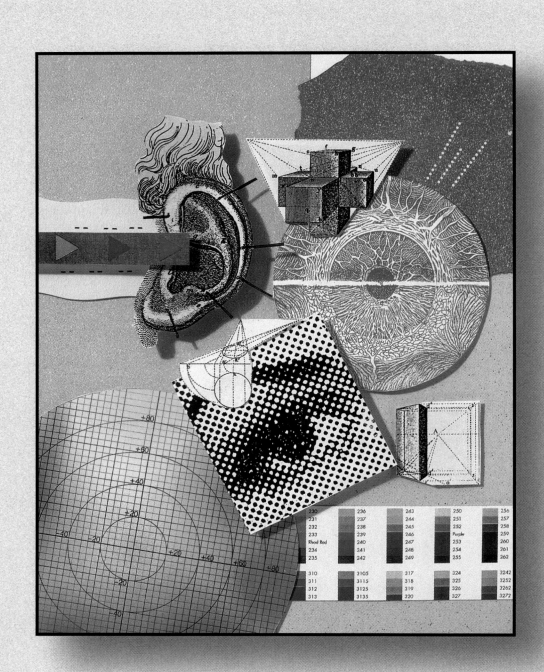

CONSCIOUSNESS AND PERCEPTION

Your face is your most distinctive part. The shape and size of your eyes, ears, nose, and mouth are what make you look so different from others. But the primary purpose of your facial features is not to make you recognizable; it is to enable you to sense the world. Our eyes see it, our ears hear it, our noses smell it, our mouths taste it, and these along with a few other senses provide us with most of the knowledge that we have about the world. The next time you look at your face in a mirror, think of it as an elaborate sensing system, mounted on the platform you call your body, that allows you to explore the outside world.

It is a remarkable fact that the world we know through our senses is not the same as the world that other species know through their senses. Each of our sense organs is tuned to receive a particular range of stimuli that is relevant to our survival, and is insensitive to stimuli outside this range. Different species have different ranges of sensitivity because they have different survival needs. Dogs, for example, are far more sensitive to smells than we are because they rely heavily on odors for activities critical to survival, like locating food, marking trails, and identifying kin.

In this chapter, we discuss some of the major properties of the senses, with an emphasis on human senses. Some of the research we review deals with psychological phenomena while other work deals with the biological bases of these phenomena. In virtually no other area of psychology have the biological and psychological approaches worked together so fruitfully. At both levels of analysis, a distinction is often made between *sensation* and *perception*. At the psychological level, sensations are experiences associated with simple stimuli (a flashing red light, for example), and perception involves the subsequent integration and meaningful interpretation of these sensations ("it's a fire engine"). At the biological level, sensory processes involve the sense organs and the neural pathways that emanate from them, which are concerned with the initial stages of acquiring stimulus information; perceptual processes involve higher levels of the cortex, which are known to be more related to meaning. This distinction is useful for organizing chapters, but it is somewhat arbitrary. Psy-

chological and biological events that occur early in the processing of a stimulus can sometimes affect its eventual meaningful interpretation; furthermore, from the perspective of the nervous system, there is no sharp break between the initial uptake of stimulus information by the sense organs and the brain's subsequent use of that information. Still, we employ the sensation-perception distinction in what follows, with this chapter treating sensory processes, and Chapter 5 perceptual processes.

The bulk of the present chapter is organized around the different senses: vision, hearing, smell, taste, and touch; the latter includes pressure, temperature, and pain. In everyday life, a number of senses are often involved in any act—we see a peach, feel its texture, taste and smell it as we bite into it, and hear the sounds of our chewing. For purposes of analysis, however, we consider the senses one at a time. Before beginning our analysis of individual senses, or **sensory modalities**, we will discuss some properties that are common to all senses.

COMMON PROPERTIES OF SENSORY MODALITIES

In this section we consider two properties common to all sensory modalities. The first one describes sensory modalities at a psychological level, while the second focuses on the biological level. (The Critical Discussion on decision processes in detection describes a third common property.)

SENSITIVITY

One of the most striking aspects about our sensory modalities is that they are extremely sensitive at detecting the presence of an object or event, or a change in an object or event. Some indication of this sensitivity is given in Table 4-1. For five of the senses, we have provided an estimate of the minimal stimulus that they can detect. What is most noticeable about these minimums is how low they are—that is, how sensitive the corresponding sensory modality is. This is particu-

SENSE	MINIMUM STIMULUS
Vision	A candle flame seen at 30 miles on a dark, clear night
Hearing	The tick of a clock at 20 feet under quiet conditions
Taste	One teaspoon of sugar in 2 gallons of water
Smell	One drop of perfume diffused into the entire volume of six rooms
Touch	The wing of a fly falling on your cheek from a distance of 1 centimeter

TABLE 4-1

Minimum Stimuli   *Approximate minimum stimuli for various senses.* (After Galanter, 1962)

larly true for vision. A classic experiment by Hecht, Shlaer, and Pirenne (1942) demonstrated that human vision is virtually as sensitive as is physically possible. The smallest unit of light energy is a quantum. Hecht and his colleagues showed that a person can detect a flash of light that contains only 100 quanta. Furthermore, they showed that only 7 of these 100 quanta actually contact the critical molecules in the eye that are responsible for translating light into vision, and that each of these 7 quanta affects a different molecule. The critical receptive unit of the eye (a molecule) is therefore sensitive to the minimal possible unit of light energy.

ABSOLUTE THRESHOLDS   Suppose you came across an alien creature, and you wanted to determine how sensitive it is to light. What would you do? Perhaps the most straightforward action would be to determine the minimum amount of light the creature could detect. This is the key idea behind measuring sensitivity. That is, the most common way to assess the sensitivity of a sensory modality is to determine the minimum magnitude of a stimulus that can be reliably discriminated from no stimulus at all—for example, the weakest light that can be reliably discriminated from darkness. This minimum magnitude is referred to as the **absolute threshold**.

The procedures used to determine such thresholds are called **psychophysical methods**. In one commonly used method, the experimenter first selects a set of stimuli with magnitudes varying around the threshold

(for example, a set of dim lights varying in intensity). The stimuli are presented to a subject one at a time in random order, and the subject is instructed to say "yes" if the stimulus is detected and "no" if it is not. Each stimulus is presented many times, and the percentage of "yes" responses is determined for each stimulus magnitude.

Figure 4-1 is a graph of the percentage of "yes" responses as a function of stimulus magnitude (light intensity, for example). The data are typical of those obtained in this kind of experiment; the percentage of "yes" responses rises gradually as intensity is increased. The subject detects some stimuli with intensities as low as three units, yet occasionally fails to detect some with intensities of eight units. When performance is characterized by such a graph, psychologists have agreed to define the absolute threshold as the value of the stimulus at which it is detected 50 percent of the time. Thus, for the data displayed in Figure 4-1, the absolute threshold is six units. (The absolute threshold may vary considerably from one individual to the next, and vary within an individual

FIGURE 4-1

Psychometric Function   *Plotted on the vertical axis is the percentage of times the subject responds, "Yes, I detect the stimulus"; on the horizontal axis is the measure of the magnitude of the physical stimulus. Such graphs are called* psychometric functions, *and they may be obtained for any stimulus dimension.*

from time to time, depending on the person's physical and motivational state.)

DETECTING CHANGES IN INTENSITY   The world is constantly changing, and it is of obvious survival value to us to be able to spot these changes. Not surprisingly, psychologists have devoted a good deal of effort to studying our ability to detect changes in intensity.

Just as there must be a certain minimum stimulus before we can perceive anything, so there must be a certain difference between two stimulus magnitudes before we can reliably distinguish one from the other. For instance, two tones must differ in intensity by a certain amount before one is heard as louder than the other; they must also differ in frequency by a certain amount before one is heard as different in pitch from the other. The minimum difference in stimulus magnitude or stimulus quality necessary to tell two stimuli apart is called the **difference threshold,** or the **just noticeable difference.** Like the absolute threshold, the just noticeable difference is defined statistically. Using an experimental method like the one we described earlier, the just noticeable difference is the amount of change necessary for a subject to detect a difference between two stimuli on 50 percent of the trials.

An experiment to determine a just noticeable difference, or **jnd** for short, might proceed as follows. A spot of light (standard) is flashed, and above it another spot of light (increment) is flashed for a shorter duration. The standard spot is the same on every trial but the increment spot varies in intensity from trial to trial. The subject responds "yes" or "no" to indicate whether or not the increment seems more intense than the standard. If the subject can discriminate an intensity of 51 watts in the increment from a standard of 50 watts on half the trials, then the jnd is 1 watt under these conditions.

Experiments like this have a long history. In 1834 Ernst Weber, a German physiologist, performed such a study and discovered one of the most robust findings in all of psychology. He found that the more intense the stimulus is to begin with, the larger the change must be for the subject to notice it. He measured jnds for intensity for several senses, including vision and hearing. He noted that a jnd increased with the intensity of the standard, and proposed that the jnd is a constant fraction of stimulus intensity (**Weber's law**). For

example, if a jnd is 1 at an intensity of 50, it will be 2 at 100, 4 at 200, and so forth (the jnd always being 0.02 of the intensity of the standard in this example). This relation between the intensity of a standard and a jnd may be written as

$$\frac{\Delta I}{I} = k$$

where I is the intensity of the standard, ΔI is the increase in the intensity for a jnd, and k is a constant proportion, called **Weber's constant** (0.02 in our example).

Since Weber's pioneering study, many similar experiments have been performed. The results from one involving light intensities are presented in Figure 4-2. The data are

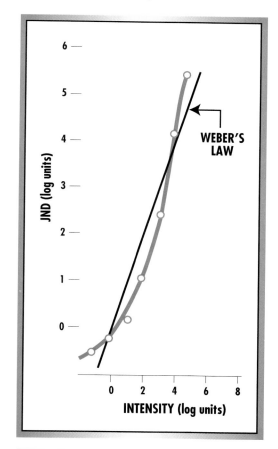

FIGURE 4-2

Jnd for Light   *Here the subject's task was to detect the difference between a flash of light at some intensity I and this same flash plus intensity ΔI. The jnd (measured in logarithmic units) was determined at several different intensities (also measured in logarithmic units). The graph shows that the size of the jnd increases with intensity in a way that corresponds only roughly to Weber's law. In other cases, Weber's law holds more accurately.*(After Geisler, 1978)

STIMULUS DIMENSION	WEBER'S CONSTANT
Sound frequency	.003
Sound intensity	.15
Light intensity	.01
Odor concentration	.07
Taste concentration	.20
Pressure intensity	.14

TABLE 4-2

Weber's Constant *Approximate values of Weber's constant for various stimulus dimensions.*

given by the curved line, and the predictions from Weber's law are depicted by the straight line. While Weber's law does not match the data in detail, it does provide a very good approximation. This is true in general. Weber's law is useful in other ways as well. Thus, the values of Weber's constants can be used to contrast the sensitivity of different sensory modalities. The smaller the constant, the more sensitive we are to a change in intensity in that modality. Table 4-2 provides Weber's constants for different modalities, and makes it clear, for example, that we are more sensitive to smell than taste. This means that as you add more spice to a dish you are cooking, you will be able to smell the difference before you can taste it.

Soon after Weber proposed his law, it was generalized by Gustav Fechner (1860), a German physicist. Fechner assumed not only that a jnd is a constant fraction of stimulus intensity, but also that one jnd is perceptually equal to any other jnd. (The perceived magnitude of a stimulus is therefore simply the number of jnds it is above the absolute threshold.) From these two assumptions, Fechner derived the relation that the perceived magnitude of a stimulus, P, is proportional to the logarithm of its physical intensity, I; that is,

$$P = c \log I.$$

This relation is known as **Fechner's law.** To see what it tells us, suppose $c = 1$. Then,

doubling I, say from 10 to 20 units, increases P only from 1 to approximately 1.3 units. Hence, doubling a light's intensity does not double its perceived brightness (a 100-watt bulb does not look twice as bright as a 50-watt bulb), doubling a sound's intensity does not double its perceived loudness, and so on for smell, taste, touch, and the other senses. More generally, as the physical intensity of a stimulus increases, its perceived magnitude increases rapidly at first, and then more and more slowly (see Figure 4-3). Like Weber's law, Fechner's law is only an approximation; modern researchers have proposed many variations on it to fit a wide variety of experimental results (Stevens, 1957). Nevertheless, the logarithmic relation has been useful in many practical applications of sensory psychology.

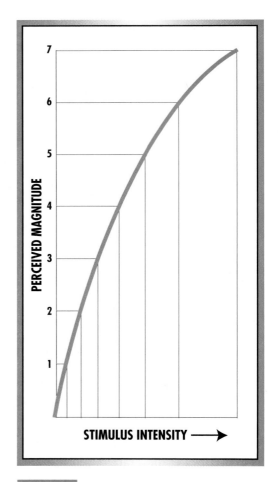

FIGURE 4-3

Fechner's Law *As the physical intensity of a stimulus increases, our perception of it increases rapidly at first, and then more slowly.*

SENSORY CODING

Now that we know something about the sensitivity of the different senses, we can inquire into the biological bases of sensation.

FROM RECEPTORS TO THE BRAIN The brain has a formidable problem in sensing the world. Each sense responds to a certain kind of stimulus—light energy for vision, mechanical energy for audition and touch, chemical energy for smell and taste. But the brain understands none of this. It speaks only the language of electrical signals associated with neural discharges. Somehow, each sensory modality must first translate its physical energy into electrical signals, so that these signals can eventually make their way to the brain. This translation process is called **transduction**. It is accomplished by specialized cells in the sense organs, called **receptors**. The receptors for vision, for instance, are located in a thin layer on the inside of the eye; each visual receptor contains a chemical that reacts to light, and this reaction triggers a series of steps that results in a neural impulse. The receptors for audition are fine hair cells located deep in the ear; the vibrations in the air that are the stimulus for sound succeed in bending these hair cells, which results in a neural impulse. Similar descriptions apply to the other sensory modalities.

A receptor is a specialized kind of nerve cell or **neuron** (see Chapter 2), and once activated, it passes its electrical signal to connecting neurons. The signal travels until it reaches its receiving area in the cortex, with different receiving areas for different sensory modalities. Somewhere in the brain—perhaps in the cortical receiving area, perhaps elsewhere in the cortex—the electrical signal results in conscious sensory experience. Thus, when we experience a touch, the experience is "occurring" in our brain, not in our skin. However, the electrical impulses in our brain that directly mediate the experience of touch are themselves caused by electrical impulses in touch receptors that are located in the skin. Similarly, our experience of a bitter taste occurs in our brain, not in our tongue; but the brain impulses that mediate the taste experience are themselves caused by electrical impulses in taste receptors on the tongue. In this way our receptors play a major role in relating external events to conscious experience. Numerous aspects of our conscious perceptions are caused by specific neural events that occurred in the receptors. For these reasons, we emphasize receptor events in our treatment of sensation.

CODING INTENSITY AND QUALITY Our sensory systems evolved to pick up information about objects and events in the world. What kind of information do we need to know about an event, say, the brief flash of a bright red light? Clearly it would be useful to know its intensity (bright), quality (red), duration (brief), location, and onset. Each of our sensory systems provides some information about these various attributes, though most research had focused on the attributes of *intensity* and *quality* (or nature), and these will be our main concerns in this chapter. To illustrate these two attributes of sensory experience, when we see a bright red color patch, we experience the quality of redness at an intense level; when we hear a faint, high-pitched tone, we experience the quality of the pitch at a nonintense level.

The receptors and their neural pathways to the brain must therefore code both intensity and quality. The question of interest is, how do they do this? Researchers who study these coding processes need a way of determining which specific neurons are activated by which specific stimuli. The usual means is to record from single cells in the receptors and neural pathways to the brain while the subject is presented various inputs or stimuli. By such means, one can determine exactly which attributes of a stimulus a particular neuron is responsive to.

A typical single-cell recording experiment is illustrated in Figure 4-4. This is a vision experiment, but the procedure is similar for studying other senses. Prior to the experiment, the animal (in this case a monkey) has undergone a surgical procedure in which thin wires are inserted into selected areas of its visual cortex. The surgery, of course, is done under sterile conditions and by surgeons using appropriate anesthesia. The thin wires are *microelectrodes,* insulated except at their tips, that can be used to record electrical activity of the neurons they are in contact with. Once implanted, these microelectrodes cause no pain, and the monkey moves around and lives quite normally. During the experiment proper, the monkey is placed in a

Oscilloscope

Amplifier

Microelectrode

Screen

Receptive field

Light

FIGURE 4-4

Single Cell Recording   *An anesthetized monkey is placed in a device that holds its head in a fixed position. A stimulus, often a flashing or moving bar of light, is projected onto the screen. A microelectrode implanted in the visual system of the monkey monitors activity from a single neuron, and this activity is amplified and displayed on an oscilloscope.*

testing apparatus, and the microelectrodes are connected to recording and amplifying devices. The monkey is then exposed to various visual stimuli. For each stimulus, one can determine which neurons respond to it

by seeing which microelectrodes produce sustained signals. Because the electrical signals are tiny, they must be amplified and displayed on an oscilloscope, which converts the electrical signals into a graph of the changing electrical voltage. Most neurons emit a series of nerve impulses that appear on the oscilloscope as vertical spikes. Even in the absence of a stimulus, many cells will respond at a slow rate *(spontaneous activity)*. If a stimulus is presented to which the neuron is sensitive, a fast train of spikes will be seen.

With the aid of single-cell recordings, researchers have learned a good deal about how sensory systems code intensity and quality. The primary means for coding the intensity of a stimulus is in terms of the number of neural impulses in each unit of time, that is, the rate of neural impulses. We can illustrate with touch. If someone lightly touches your arm, a series of electrical impulses will be generated in a nerve fiber. If the pressure is increased, the impulses stay the same in size but increase in number per unit time (see Figure 4-5). The same story holds for other modalities. In general, the greater the intensity of the stimulus, the higher the rate of neural firing and the greater the perceived magnitude of the stimulus.

The intensity of a stimulus can also be coded by alternative means. One alternative is that intensity is coded by the *temporal pattern* of the electrical impulses. At low intensities, nerve impulses are relatively spaced in time and the exact time between successive impulses is variable. At high intensities, though, the time between impulses may be quite constant (see Figure 4-5). Another alternative is that intensity is coded by the sheer number of neurons activated; the more intense the stimulus, the more neurons recruited.

Coding the quality of a stimulus is a more complex matter, and one that will continually crop up in our discussion. The key idea behind coding quality is due to Johannes Müller, who in 1825 proposed that the brain can distinguish information from different sensory modalities—like lights and sounds—because they involve different sensory nerves (some nerves lead to visual experiences, others to auditory experiences, and so on). Müller's idea of **specific nerve energies** received support from subsequent research demonstrating that neural pathways originating in different receptors terminate in different areas of the cortex. There is now a good deal of consensus that the brain codes the qualitative differences between sensory modalities by the specific neural pathways involved.

But what about the distinguishing qualities *within* a sense? How do we tell red from green, or sweet from sour? It is likely that again the coding is based on the specific neurons involved. To illustrate, there is evidence that we distinguish sweet from sour tastes by virtue of the fact that each kind of taste has its own nerve fibers. Thus, *sweet fibers* respond primarily to sweet tastes, *sour fibers* primarily to sour tastes, and ditto for *salty fibers* and *bitter fibers*.

But *specificity* is not the only plausible coding principle. A sensory system may also use the pattern of neural firing to code the quality of a sensation. While a particular nerve fiber may respond maximally to a sweet taste, it may respond to other tastes as well, but to varying degrees. One fiber may respond best to sweet tastes, less to bitter tastes, and even less to salty tastes; a sweet-tasting stimulus would thus lead to activity in a large number of fibers, with some firing more than others, and this particular pattern of neural activity would be the system's code for sweet. A different pattern across neural fibers would be the code for bitter. As we will see when we discuss the senses in detail, both specificity and patterning are used in coding quality.

FIGURE 4-5

Coding Intensity   *Response of a nerve fiber from the skin to (a) soft, (b) medium, and (c) strong pressure applied to the fiber's receptor. Increasing the stimulus strength increases both the rate and regularity of nerve firing in this fiber. (After Goldstein, 1989)*

sion, first we consider the nature of the stimulus energy to which vision is sensitive; next we describe the visual system with particular emphasis on how its receptors carry out the transduction process; and then we consider how the visual modality processes information about intensity and quality.

VISUAL SENSE

Humans are generally credited with the following senses: (a) vision; (b) audition; (c) smell; (d) taste; (e) touch (or the *skin senses*); and (f) the *body senses* (which are responsible for sensing the position of the head relative to the trunk, for example). Since the body senses do not always give rise to conscious sensations of intensity and quality, we will not consider them further in this chapter.

Only vision, audition, and smell are capable of obtaining information that is at a distance from us (often vital to our survival), and of this group vision is the most finely tuned in the human species. In discussing vi-

LIGHT AND VISION

Each sense responds to a particular form of physical energy, and for vision the physical stimulus is light. Light is *electromagnetic radiation*, a kind of energy that emanates from the sun and the rest of the universe, and that constantly bathes our planet. Electromagnetic energy includes not only light but also cosmic rays, X rays, ultraviolet and infrared rays, and radio and television waves. Think of electromagnetic energy as traveling in waves, with wavelengths (the distance from one crest of a wave to the next) varying tremendously from the shortest cosmic rays (4 trillionths of a centimeter) to the longest radio

The notion of an absolute threshold dates back to the early 1800s. The key idea is that an absolute threshold is a fixed, sensory barrier; above the threshold people can detect a stimulus; below it they cannot. (This seemingly all-or-none property suggests that a threshold *should* be defined as the value of the stimulus that can be detected 100 percent of the time. The reason the threshold is *in fact* defined by 50 percent detection is that on any trial of an experiment, many factors can go wrong: The sense organ may not function perfectly, the subject's attention may wander, etc.) The idea of a threshold as a fixed barrier implies that what subjects do in experiments is report whether or not the stimulus passed the threshold. Detailed research on this issue, however, indicates that rather than observers simply reporting whether a stimulus crossed a fixed barrier, they are instead making a relatively complex decision about whether their sensory experience is due to a stimulus or to random activity in their sensory system.

PROBLEMS WITH THRESHOLDS

Researchers have long been aware of certain difficulties in establishing thresholds. To illustrate the problems, suppose we want to determine the likelihood that a subject will detect a weak auditory signal—a faint tone, briefly presented. On each trial of an experiment, the auditory signal is presented and the subject indicates whether or not she heard it. Suppose that on 100 such trials the subject reported hearing the signal 89 times. How should this result be interpreted? Because the subject knows that the same signal will be presented on each trial, and because she will often be uncertain whether to respond "yes" or "no" on a given trial, she may unconsciously tend toward "yes" answers to impress the experimenter with her ability. To deal with this problem, experimenters introduce *catch trials*—

FIGURE 1

trials with no signals—to see how the subject responds.

The results shown in Figure 1 are typical of a subject's performance in an experiment involving several hundred trials, 10 percent of which were catch trials. These results represent the proportion of times the subjects answered "yes" or "no" when the signal was or was not presented. For example, on 89 percent of the trials on which a signal was presented, the subject said "yes." We refer to this as the probability of a *hit*. The probability of a hit is a kind of measure of an absolute threshold: If it is around .5 (50 percent), the stimulus is at threshold, whereas if the probability is greater than .5 the stimulus is above threshold. If a subject says "yes" on a trial in which no signal was presented, the response is called a *false alarm*. In the example, the probability of a false alarm is .52. This result suggests that even a zero stimulus can cross the threshold, which seems at odds with the idea of an absolute threshold.

The notion of a threshold runs into more problems when we do an experiment that varies the percentage of catch trials. Suppose that the subject is tested for several days with the same auditory signal but with the percentage of catch trials varied from day to day. Results of an experiment in which the percentage of catch trials ranged from 10 to 90 percent are given in the table to the right. These

data show that hits and false alarms both decrease as the proportion of catch trials increases. Presumably, with more catch trials, subjects come to *expect* trials with no signals, and accordingly are biased to say "no." Given that expectancy affected the probability of a hit, it follows that expectancy can affect the absolute threshold. But again, this is at odds with the idea that a threshold is fixed and with the idea that it is a purely *sensory* barrier. Results like these have led to an alternative theory of how people detect sensory stimuli.

THEORY OF SIGNAL DETECTION

The alternative theory is referred to as the **theory of signal detection**. It assumes that there is always some random activity or *noise* in sensory systems; hence, *there is no such thing as a zero stimulus*. A person in a detection task is always in the position of deciding whether the sensory activity experienced is more likely to be caused by a presented signal than by random noise in his or her sensory system. Thus, the task of detecting weak stimuli requires a decision process, rather than simply reporting whether a sensory barrier has been passed.

Two factors affect the decision that must be made. One factor is the subject's *sensitivity* to the stimulus—how well he can hear a faint tone or see a dim light. The other factor is the subject's *criterion*—how willing he is to say "yes." The subject's sensitivity is assumed to be influenced by the intensity of the stimulus; his criterion is influenced by expectancies and motives. A subject's criterion will be lower when a stimulus is expected than when it is not (Green & Swets, 1966).

According to the theory of signal detection, one can get separate measures of a subject's sensitivity and criterion by plotting on the same graph the hit and false-alarm probabilities obtained in an experiment. We have plotted the probability of hits and false alarms from the table in the upper graph of Figure 2. Note, for example, that the point on the graph farthest to the right is for data obtained when 10 percent of the trials were catch trials; referring to the table, we see the hit probability plotted on the vertical axis is .89 and the false-alarm probability on the horizontal axis is .52. When all five points are plotted, an orderly picture emerges. The points fall on a symmetric, bow-shaped curve. The fact that these points fall on the same curve implies that they all reflect the same sensitivity. That is, while every point on this curve reflects a different performance (different hit and false-alarm probabilities), these differences reflect only the criterion and not the subject's sensitivity. Thus, if we performed other experiments with the same signal but different percentages of catch trials, the hit and false-alarm probabilities would differ from those in the table but would fall somewhere on this curve. This curve is called the **receiver-operating-characteristic curve** (ROC) because it measures the operating characteristics of a person receiving signals.

While points along the same ROC curve indicate changes in criteria, different ROC curves indicate changes in sensitivity. The points that are plotted in the upper graph in Figure 2 are for a particular signal intensity.

When the signal is more intense, sensitivity is greater and the ROC curve arches higher; when the signal is weaker, sensitivity is less and the ROC curve is closer to the diagonal line. The curvature of the ROC curve is therefore determined by the subject's sensitivity, and the measure used for the curvature is called d'. The lower graph in the figure gives ROC curves for values of d' ranging from 0 to 2. Thus, hit and false-alarm probabilities can be converted into a d' value measuring the subject's sensitivity to a signal. Manipulating the percentage of catch trials may affect hits and false alarms for a fixed signal, but the various probabilities will fall on an ROC curve corresponding to a particular d' value (Egan, 1975).

Given this view of detecting signals, we need to reinterpret the threshold measurements obtained in other experiments. From the perspective of the theory of signal detection, a threshold is defined as the stimulus intensity at which d' has a particular value, such as 1. Still, the older methods for determining thresholds remain convenient indicators of sensitivity.

The theory of signal detection is used for more than explaining the results of laboratory experiments. It has proven very valuable in understanding real-life tasks. Consider the job of a radiologist who has to inspect X ray images for signs of lung cancer. Like the subjects in the experiments described above, the radiologist has to distinguish weak signals (true signs of lung cancer) from background noise (other anomalies in the X ray). Analogous to the subjects' performance in the above experiments, the radiologist will be more likely to say "yes" ("it looks cancerous") the more she expects a true signal, that is, the more she expects the patient to have cancer (based on other tests); and our radiologist will be less likely to say "yes" the higher the cost of a false alarm, that is, the more the patient will be severely disturbed by hearing a tentative cancer diagnosis.

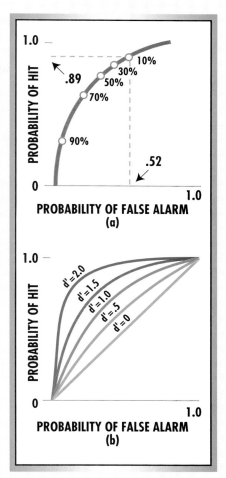

FIGURE 2

Plotting ROC Curves from Data *(a) A plot of the same data from the table in the form of an ROC curve. The percentages on this curve indicate the percentages of catch trials. (b) ROC curves for several different values of d'. The more intense the signal, the higher the value of d'; the d' value for the data in the table is 1.18.*

Hence, when these expectancy and motivational factors are varied, radiologists' frequency of reporting cancerous X rays will change in the expected directions—for example, where cancer is already expected, the radiologist will be more likely to interpret an ambiguous aspect of the X ray as a sign of cancer. Being aware of these influences is very important for medicine.

PERCENT CATCH TRIALS	HITS	FALSE ALARMS
10	.89	.52
30	.83	.41
50	.76	.32
70	.62	.19
90	.28	.04

Hits and False Alarms *The table presents data on the relationship between hits and false alarms as the percentage of catch trials is increased.*

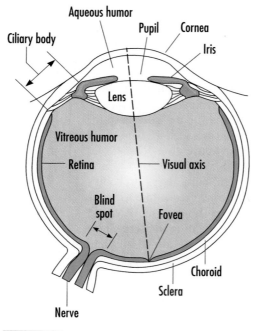

FIGURE 4-6

Top View of Right Eye *Light entering the eye on its way to the retina passes through the following:* cornea; aqueous humor; lens; *and* vitreous humor. *The amount of light entering the eye is regulated by the size of the* pupil, *a small hole toward the front of the eye formed by the* iris. *The iris consists of a ring of muscles that can contract or relax, thereby controlling pupil size. The iris gives the eyes their characteristic color (blue, brown, and so forth).*

waves (several miles). Our eyes are sensitive to only a tiny bit of this continuum—wavelengths of approximately 400 to 700 nanometers. Since a nanometer is one-billionth of a meter, visible energy makes up only a *very* small part of electromagnetic energy. Radiation within the visible range is called *light;* we are blind to all other wavelengths.

VISUAL SYSTEM

The human visual system consists of the eyes, several parts of the brain, and the pathways connecting them. (Go back to Figure 2-10 for a simplified illustration of the visual system.) Our primary concern will be with the inner workings of the eyes. The eye contains two systems, one for forming the image and the other for transducing the image into electrical impulses. The critical parts of these systems are illustrated in Figure 4-6.

The image-forming system works like a camera. Its function is to focus light reflected from objects, so as to form an image of the object on the *retina,* a thin layer at the back of the eyeball (see Figure 4-7). The image-forming system itself consists of the cornea, the pupil, and the lens. Without them, we could see light but not pattern. The **cornea** is the transparent front surface of the eye: light enters here, and rays are bent inward by it to begin image formation. The **lens** completes the process of focusing the light on the **retina** (see Figure 4-7). To focus objects at different distances, the lens changes shape. It becomes more spherical for near objects and flatter for far ones. In some eyes, the lens does not become flat enough to bring far objects in focus, although it focuses near objects well; people with such eyes are said to be *myopic* (nearsighted). In other eyes, the lens does not become spherical enough to focus on near objects, although it focuses well on far objects; people with such eyes are said to be *hyperopic* (farsighted). Such optical defects are common and can easily be corrected with eyeglasses or contact lenses. The **pupil**, the third component of the image-forming system, is a circular opening that varies in diameter in response to the light level. It is largest

FIGURE 4-7

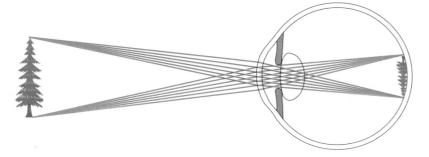

Image Formation in the Eye *Each point on an object sends out light rays in* all *directions, but only some of these rays actually enter the eye. Light rays from the same point on an object pass through different places on the lens. If a sharp image is to be formed, these different rays have to be brought back together (converge) at a single point on the retina. For each point on the object, there will be a matching point in the retinal image. Note that the retinal image is inverted and is generally much smaller than the actual object. Note also that most of the bending of light rays is at the cornea.*

in dim light and smallest in bright light, thereby ensuring enough light to maintain image quality at different light levels.

All of the preceding serves to focus the image on the back of the eyeball, to the retina. There the transduction system takes over. The heart of the system is the receptors. There are two types of receptor cells, **rods** and **cones,** so called because of their distinctive shapes (see Figure 4-8). The two kinds of receptors are specialized for different purposes. Rods are designed for seeing at night; they operate at low intensities and lead to colorless sensations. Cones are best for seeing during the day; they respond to high intensities and result in sensations of color. Curiously, the rods and cones are located in the layer of the retina farthest from the cornea (note the direction-of-light arrow in Figure 4-8). The retina also contains a network of neurons, plus support cells and blood vessels.

When we want to see the details of an object, we routinely move our eyes so that the object projects onto the center of our retina, onto a region called the **fovea.** The reason we do this has to do with the distribution of receptors across the retina. In the fovea, the receptors are plentiful and closely packed; outside of the fovea, in the *periphery,* there are fewer receptors. Not surprisingly, the fovea is the region of the eye that is best at seeing details (try reading this book while looking off the side of the page).

Given that light reflected from an object has made contact with a receptor cell, how exactly does the receptor transduce the light into electrical impulses? The rods and cones contain chemicals, called **photopigments** that absorb light. The absorption of light by the photopigments starts a process that results in a neural impulse. Once this transduction step is completed, the electrical impulses must make their way to the brain via connecting neurons. The responses of the rods and cones are first transmitted to **bipolar cells,** and from bipolar cells to other neurons called **ganglion cells** (refer to Figure 4-8). The long axons of the ganglion cells extend out of the eye to form the **optic nerve** to the brain. At the place where the optic nerve leaves the eye, there are no receptors; we are blind to a stimulus in this region (see Figure 4-9). We do not notice this partial blindness—this hole in our visual field—because the brain automatically fills it in (Ramachandran & Gregory, 1991).

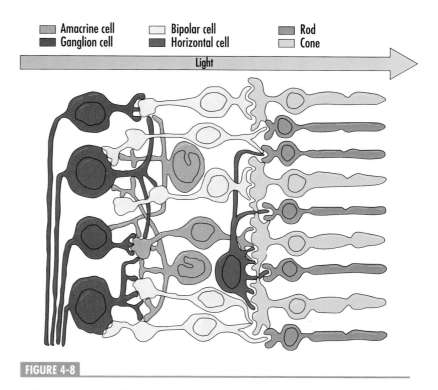

FIGURE 4-8

Schematic Picture of the Retina *This is a schematic drawing of the retina based on an examination with an electron microscope. The bipolar cells receive signals from one or more receptors and transmit those signals to the ganglion cells, whose axons form the optic nerve. Note that there are several types of bipolar and ganglion cells. There are also sideways or lateral connections in the retina. Neurons called horizontal cells make lateral connections at a level near the receptors; neurons called amacrine cells make lateral connections at a level near the ganglion cells.* (After Dowling & Boycott, 1966)

SEEING LIGHT

SENSITIVITY AND ACUITY   Our sensitivity to a light's intensity is determined by the rods and cones. There are two critical differences between rods and cones that explain a number of phenomena involving perceived intensity, or *brightness*. One difference is that, on the average, more rods connect to a single ganglion cell than do cones; rod-based ganglion cells therefore get more inputs than cone-based ones. Secondly, rods and cones differ in where they are located. The fovea of the retina contains many cones but no rods, but the periphery (the rest of the retina) is rich in rods and relatively sparse in cones. The fact that more rods connect to a ganglion cell than do cones leads to the consequence that vision is more sensitive when based on rods than on cones. Exactly how this comes about it illustrated in Figure 4-10. The left side of the figure shows three adjacent cones, *each*

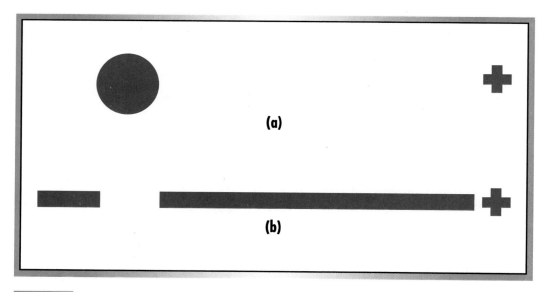

FIGURE 4-9

Locating Your Blind Spot *(a) With your right eye closed, stare at the cross in the upper right-hand corner. Put the book about a foot from your eye and move it forward and back. When the blue circle on the left disappears, it is projected onto the blind spot. (b) Without moving the book and with your right eye still closed, stare at the cross in the lower right-hand corner. When the white space falls in the blind spot, the blue line appears to be continuous. This phenomenon helps us to understand why we are not ordinarily aware of the blind spot. In effect, the visual system fills in the parts of the visual field that we are not sensitive to; thus, they appear like the surrounding field.*

of which is connected (indirectly) to a single ganglion cell; the right side contains three adjacent rods, *all* of which are connected (indirectly) to the same ganglion cell. To see the implication of these differences in the "wiring" of cones and rods, suppose that three very dim adjacent spots of light are presented to either the rods or cones. When presented to the cones, each spot of light may be too weak to lead to a neural impulse in its associated receptor, and consequently no neural response will occur in the ganglion cell. But when these same dim spots are presented to the rods, the activation from the

three receptors can combine, and the sum may be sufficient to lead to a neural response in the ganglion cell. Thus, connecting multiple rods to a single ganglion cell allows for a convergence of neural activation, and this convergence is why rod-based vision is more sensitive than cone-based vision.

But this advantage in sensitivity comes at a price, namely, that rod-based vision is less acute than cone-based vision (*acuity* is our ability to see details). Look again at the two diagrams in Figure 4-10, but now suppose that the three adjacent spots of light are relatively bright. When presented to the cones,

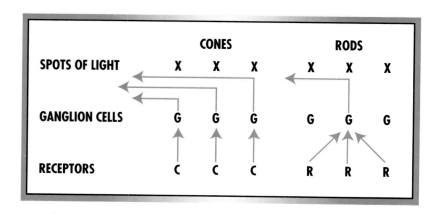

FIGURE 4-10

How Cones and Rods Connect to Ganglion Cells *A schematic diagram shows the difference between how cones and rods connect to ganglion cells. The Xs represent spots of light, the Gs ganglion cells, the Cs cones and the Rs rods. To simplify matters, we have omitted bipolar cells, which are between receptors and ganglion cells. The lines emanating from the ganglion cells are axons that will become part of the optic nerve.*

each spot of a light may lead to a neural response in its associated receptor, which in turn will lead to neural impulses in three different ganglion cells; these three different messages will be sent to the brain, and the system will therefore have a way of knowing that there are three different things out there. In contrast, when the three adjacent bright spots of light are presented to the rods, the neural activation in each receptor again converges with that in the others, leading to the activation of a single ganglion cell; hence only one message is sent to the brain, and the system has no way of knowing that there is more than one thing out there. In short, the way that receptors connect to ganglion cells explains the differences between rods and cones in sensitivity and acuity.

Another consequence of these differences is that we are better able to detect a dim light in the rod-rich periphery than in the fovea. So while acuity is greater in the fovea than in the periphery, sensitivity is greater in the periphery. Greater sensitivity in the periphery may be established by measuring a subject's absolute threshold for light flashes presented in a dark room. The threshold is lower (which means sensitivity is greater) when the subject looks off to the side so that the light falls on the periphery, than when the subject looks directly at the flash so that the light falls on the fovea.

LIGHT ADAPTATION   Thus far we have emphasized that we are sensitive to change. The other half of the coin is that, if a stimulus does not change, we adapt to it. A good example of **light adaptation** occurs when you enter a dark movie theater from a bright street. At first you can see hardly anything in the dim light reflected from the screen. However, in a few minutes you are able to see well enough to find a seat. Eventually you are able to recognize faces in the dim light. When you re-enter the bright street, almost everything will seem painfully bright at first and it will be impossible to discriminate among these bright lights. Everything will look normal in less than a minute, though, because adaptation to this higher light level is rapid. Figure 4-11 shows how the absolute threshold decreases with time in the dark. The curve has two limbs. The upper limb is due to the cones and the lower limb to the rods. The rod system takes much longer to adapt, but it is sensitive to much dimmer lights.

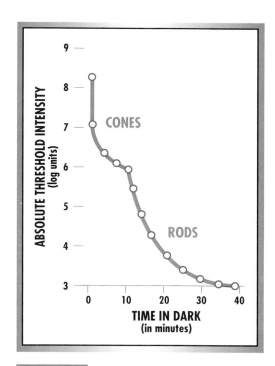

FIGURE 4-11

The Course of Light Adaptation   *Subjects look at a bright light until the retina has become light adapted. When the subjects are then placed in darkness, they become increasingly sensitive to light, and their absolute thresholds decrease. This is called light adaptation. The graph shows the threshold at different times after the adapting light has been turned off. The purple data points correspond to threshold flashes whose color could be seen; the orange data points correspond to flashes that appeared white regardless of their wavelength. Note the sharp break in the curve at about 10 minutes; this is called the rod-cone break. A variety of tests show that the first part of the curve is due to cone vision and the second part to rod vision. (Data are approximate, from various determinations.)*

SEEING COLOR

All light is alike except for wavelength. Our visual system does something wonderful with wavelength—it turns it into color, with different wavelengths resulting in different colors. For example, *short-wavelength* lights, those 450–500 nanometers, appear blue; *medium-wavelength* lights, those roughly 500–570 nanometers, appear green; and *long-wavelength* lights, those about 620–700 nanometers, appear red (see Figure 4-12). In what follows, our discussion of color perception considers only wavelength. This is perfectly adequate for cases in which the origin of a color sensation is an object that emits

FIGURE 4-12

Solar Spectrum   *The numbers given are the wavelengths of the various colors in nanometers (nm).*

light, such as the sun or a light bulb. Usually, however, the origin of a color sensation is an object that reflects light when a light source illuminates it. In these cases, our perception of the object's color is partly determined by the wavelengths the object reflects and partly by other factors. One such factor is the characteristic color of the object. Thus, we tend to see a rose as red even when it is illuminated by yellow-green light, yet if an unfamiliar object were illuminated by this light we would see it as yellow-green. This effect of characteristic color is why our favorite blue jacket always looks navy blue to us, regardless of the changes in light.

Color Appearance   Seeing color is in some ways a subjective experience. But to study color scientifically we have to use a common vocabulary to describe it. Consider a spot of light seen against a dark background. Phenomenologically it can be described by three dimensions: lightness, hue, and saturation. *Lightness* refers to how white a light appears (it is different from brightness, in that a dimly lit object may still appear white). The other two dimensions say something about the color itself. *Hue* refers to the quality described by the color name, such as red or greenish-yellow. *Saturation* means the colorfulness or purity of the light: Unsaturated colors appear pale (for example, pink); saturated colors appear to contain no white. Albert Munsell, an artist, proposed a scheme for specifying colored surfaces by assigning them one of ten hue names and two numbers, one indicating saturation and the other brightness. The colors in the Munsell system are represented by the *color solid* (see Figure 4-13).

FIGURE 4-13

Color Solid   *The three dimensions of color can be represented on a double cone. Hue is represented by points around the circumference, saturation by points along the radius, and lightness by points on the vertical axis. A vertical slice taken from the color solid will show differences in saturation and lightness of a single hue.*

FIGURE 4-14

Wavelength Discrimination   *This graph shows the difference threshold for wavelength at various wavelengths. In this experiment, lights of the two wavelengths were presented side by side, and the subjects had to judge whether they were the same or different. Over most of the range we can discriminate a change of 1 to 3 nanometers.* (After Wright, 1946)

Given a means for describing colors, we can ask how many colors we are capable of seeing. Within the 400–700 nanometer range to which we are sensitive, we can discriminate 150 hues, suggesting we can distinguish about 150 wavelengths. This means that, on the average, we can discriminate two wavelengths that are only 2 nanometers apart; that is, the jnd for wavelengths is 2 nanometers (see Figure 4-14). Given that each of the 150 discriminable colors can have many different values of lightness and many different values of saturation, the estimated number of colors that we can discriminate is over seven million! Furthermore, according to estimates of the National Bureau of Standards, we have names for about 7,500 of these colors (Judd & Kelly, 1965); it is hard to think of any other domain of experience that is so extensively coded in our language. These numbers give some indication of the importance of color to our lives (Goldstein, 1989).

COLOR MIXTURE   Remarkably, all the hues that we can discriminate can be generated by mixing together just a few basic colors. Suppose that we project different colored lights to the same region of the retina. The result of this light mixture will be a new color. For example, a mixture of 650-nanometer light (red) and 500-nanometer light (green) in the proper proportion will look yellow; in appearance the mixture will perfectly match a yellow light of 580 nanometers. Mixtures of

lights other than this particular one can also result in a light that perfectly matches a yellow light of 580 nanometers. Thus, light mixtures whose physical components are grossly different can appear to be identical.

A cautionary note is in order. Here and throughout this section we are referring to mixing lights, called an **additive mixture**; we are *not* referring to mixing paints or pigments, a **subtractive mixture** (see Figure 4-15). The rules of color mixture are different for mixing colors (paints) and mixing lights. This is to be expected. In mixing paints, the physical stimulus is itself altered (the mixture takes place outside the eye) and hence is a topic of study for physics. In contrast, in mixing lights, the mixture occurs in the eye itself, and thus is a topic for psychology.

With regard to mixing lights, in general, *three wavelengths of light can be combined to match almost any color of light* as long as one light is drawn from the long-wave end of the spectrum (red), another light is drawn from the middle (green or green-yellow), and the third light is from the short end (blue or violet). This finding is sometimes referred to as the *three primaries* law. To illustrate the law, a subject in an experiment on color matching might be asked to match the color of a test light by mixing together three other colored lights. As long as the three mixture lights are drawn from the three parts of the spectrum—for example, 450 (blue), 560 (green), and 640 nanometers (red)—the

FIGURE 4-15

Additive and Subtractive Color Mixtures   *Additive color mixture (illustrated by the figure at the left) combines lights. Red and green lights are mixed to appear yellow; green and purple appear blue; and so on. In the center where the three colors overlap, the mixture appears white.*

Subtractive color mixture (illustrated in the figure at the right) takes place when pigments are mixed or when light is transmitted through colored filters placed one over another. Usually blue-green and yellow will mix to give green, and complimentary colors like blue and yellow will combine to appear black.

subject will always be able to match the test light. The subject will not, however, be able to match any test light if he or she is provided only two mixture lights—for example, the 450- and 640-nanometer lights. The number three, therefore, is significant.

Because some lights that are grossly different physically look identical to humans, we have to conclude that we are blind to the differences. Without this blindness, color reproduction would be impossible. Realistic color reproduction in television or photography relies on the fact that a wide range of colors can be produced by mixing just a few colors. For example, if you examine your television screen with a magnifying glass you will find that it is composed of tiny dots of only three colors (blue, green, and red). Additive color mixture occurs because the dots are so close together that their images on your retina overlap. (See Figure 4-16 for a way of representing color mixtures.)

COLOR DEFICIENCY   While most people match a wide range of colors with a mixture of three primaries, other people can match a wide range of colors by using mixtures of only two primaries. Such people, referred to as *dichromats,* have deficient color vision, as they

confuse some colors that people with normal vision (*trichromats*) can distinguish. But dichromats can still see color. Not so for *monochromats,* who are unable to discriminate wavelength at all. Monochromats are truly *color-blind.* (Screening for color blindness is done with tests like that shown in Figure 4-17, a simpler procedure than conducting color mixture experiments.) Most color deficiencies are genetic in origin. Color blindness occurs much more frequently in males (2%) than in females (.03%), because the critical genes are recessive genes on the X chromosome (Nathans, Thomas, & Hogness, 1986).

THEORIES OF COLOR VISION   Over the years, two major theories of color vision have arisen. The first of these was initially proposed by Thomas Young in 1807. Fifty years later, Hermann von Helmholtz further developed Young's theory.

According to the **Young-Helmholtz** or **trichromatic theory,** even though there are many different colors that we can discriminate, there are only three types of receptors (cones) for color. Each receptor is sensitive to a wide range of wavelengths, but is most responsive in a narrow region. As shown in Fig-

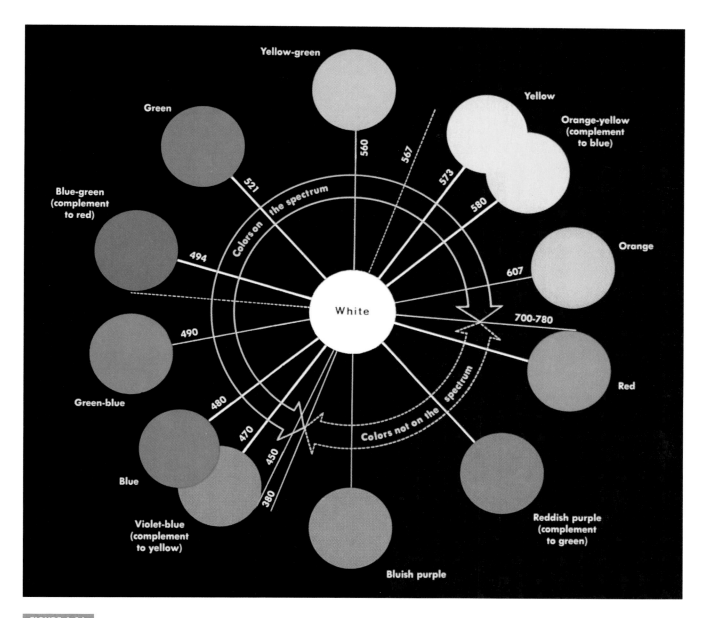

FIGURE 4-16

Color Circle   *A simple way to represent color mixture is by means of the color circle. The* spectral colors *(colors corresponding to wavelengths in our region of sensitivity) are represented by points around the circumference of the circle. The two ends of the spectrum do not meet; the space between them corresponds to the nonspectral reds and purples, which can be produced by mixtures of long and short wavelengths. The inside of the circle represents mixtures of lights. Lights toward the center of the circle are less saturated (or whiter); white is at the very center. Mixtures of any two lights lie along the straight line joining the two points. When this line goes through the center of the circle, the lights, when mixed in proper proportions, will look white; such pairs of colors are called complementary colors.*

ure 4-18, the *short wavelength receptor* is maximally sensitive to short wavelengths (blues), the *medium wavelength receptor* is most sensitive to medium wavelengths (greens and yellows), and the *long wavelength receptor* is maximally sensitive to long wavelengths (reds). The joint action of these three

receptors determines the sensation of color. That is, a light of a particular wavelength stimulates the three receptors to different degrees, and the specific ratios of activity in the three receptors leads to the sensation of a specific color. Hence, with regard to our earlier discussion of coding quality, the trichromatic

FIGURE 4-17

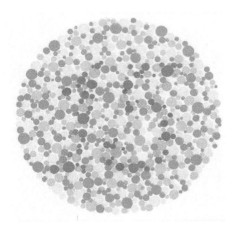

Color Blindness   *Two plates used in color blindness tests. In the left plate, individuals with certain kinds of red-green blindness will see only the number 5; others see only the 7; still others, no number at all. Similarly, in the right plate, people with normal vision see the number 15, whereas those with red-green blindness see no number at all.*

theory holds that the *quality* of color is coded by the *pattern* of activity of three receptors rather than by specific receptors for each color.

The trichromatic theory explains the facts about color vision that we mentioned previously. First, we can discriminate different wavelengths because they lead to different responses in the three receptors. Second, the law of three primaries follows directly from trichromatic theory. We can match a mixture of three widely spaced wavelengths to any color, because the three widely spaced wavelengths will activate the three different recep-

FIGURE 4-18

Trichromatic Theory   *Response curves for the short-, medium-, and long-wave receptors proposed by trichromatic theory. These curves enable us to determine the relative response of each receptor to light of any wavelength. In the example shown here, the response of each receptor to a 500-nanometer light is determined by drawing a line up from 500 nanometers and noting where this line intersects each curve. (After Wald & Brown, 1965)*

tors, and activity in these receptors is what lies behind perception of the test color. (Now we see the significance of the number three.) Third, this trichromatic theory explains the various kinds of color deficiencies by positing that one or more of the three types of receptors is missing: dichromats are born missing one type of receptor, whereas monochromats are born missing two of the three types of receptors. In addition to accounting for these long-known facts, trichromatic theory led biological researchers to a successful search for three kinds of receptors. We now know that three kinds of cones exist in the human retina.

Despite its successes, the trichromatic theory cannot explain some well-established findings about the phenomenology of color. In 1878 Ewald Hering observed that all colors may be described phenomenologically as consisting of one or two of the following sensations: red, green, yellow, and blue. Hering also noted that nothing is perceived to be reddish-green or yellowish-blue; rather, a mixture of red and green may look yellow, and a mixture of yellow and blue may look white. These observations suggested that red and green form an *opponent pair,* as do yellow and blue, and that the colors in an opponent pair cannot be perceived simultaneously. Further support for the notion of opponent pairs comes from studies in which a subject first stares at a colored light and then looks at a neutral surface. The subject reports seeing a color on the neutral surface that is the complement of the original one (see Figure 4-19).

These phenomenological observations led Hering to propose an alternative theory of color vision called **opponent-color theory.** Hering believed that the visual system contains two types of color-sensitive units. One type of unit responds to red or green, the

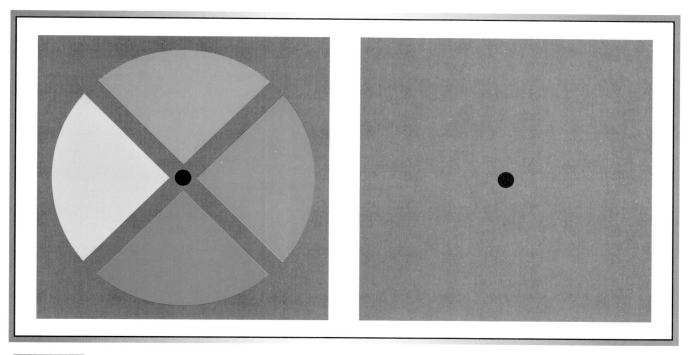

Complementary Afterimages   *Look steadily for about a minute at the dot in the center of the colors, then transfer your gaze to the dot in the gray field at the right. You should see a blurry image with colors that are complementary to the original: The blue, red, green, and yellow are replaced by yellow, green, red, and blue.*

other to blue or yellow. Each unit responds in opposite ways to its two opponent colors: the red-green unit, for example, increases its response rate when a red is presented and decreases it when a green is presented. Because a unit cannot respond in two ways at once, if two opponent colors are presented white is perceived (see Figure 4-20). Opponent-color theory is able to explain Hering's observations about color, and other facts as well. The theory accounts for why we see the hues that we do. We perceive a single hue—red or green or yellow or blue—whenever only one type of opponent unit is out of balance, and we perceive combinations of hues when both types of units are out of balance. Nothing is perceived as red-green, or as yellow-blue, because a unit cannot respond in two ways at once. Furthermore, the theory explains why subjects who first view a colored light and then stare at a neutral surface reported seeing the complementary color; if the subject first stares at red, for example, the red component of the unit will become fatigued, and consequently the green component will come into play.

We therefore have two theories of color vision—trichromatic and opponent-color—in which each theory can explain some facts but not others. The two theories were treated as competitors for decades, until researchers proposed that the theories be reconciled into a two-stage theory in which the three types of receptors in trichromatic theory feed into the color-opponent units at a *higher level* in the visual system (Hurvich & Jameson, 1957).

LIGHT OF 450 NM

HUE: BLUE + RED = VIOLET

Opponent-Process Theory *The diagram shows how an opponent process responds to light of a particular wavelength. The light is in the short-wave region of the visible spectrum, 450 nanometers. This will affect both the blue-yellow and the red-green systems. It will tip the blue-yellow balance toward blue, and the red-green balance toward red. The resulting hue will be a mixture of red and blue (that is, violet).* (After Hurvich & Jameson, 1957)

This resolution suggests that there should be neurons in the visual system that function as color-opponent units *and* that are at a higher level than the retina (which contains the three kinds of receptors of trichromatic theory). Such *color-opponent* neurons were discovered in the thalamus, a neural way-station between the retina and the visual cortex. (De-Valois & Jacobs, 1984). These cells are spontaneously active, increasing their activity rate in response to one range of wavelengths and decreasing it in response to another. Thus, some cells at a higher level in the visual system fire more rapidly if the retina is stimulated by a blue light, and less rapidly when the retina is exposed to a yellow light; such cells seem to be the biological basis of the blue-yellow opponent pair.

This research on color vision is a striking example of the successful interaction between psychological and biological approaches to a problem. Trichromatic theory suggested there must be three kinds of color receptors, and subsequent biological research established that there were three kinds of cones in the retina. Opponent-color theory said that there must be other kinds of units in the visual system, and biological researchers subsequently found opponent-color cells in the thalamus. Furthermore, a successful integration of the two theories required that the trichromatic cells feed into the opponent-color ones, and this too was confirmed by subsequent biological research. On numerous occasions, then, outstanding work at the psychological level pointed the way for biological discoveries. It is no wonder that many scientists have taken the analysis of color vision as a prototype for the analysis of other sensory systems.

AUDITORY SENSE

Along with vision, audition is our major means of obtaining information about the environment. For most of us, it is the major channel of communication and the vehicle for music. As we will see, it all comes about because small changes in sound pressure can move a membrane in our inner ear back and forth.

Our discussion of audition will follow the same plan as our discussion of vision. We will first consider the nature of the physical stimulus that audition is sensitive to, then describe the auditory system with particular emphasis on how the receptors execute the transduction process, and finally consider how the auditory system codes the intensity of sound and its quality.

SOUND WAVES

Sound originates from the motion or vibration of an object, as when the wind rushes through the branches of a tree. When something moves, the molecules of air in front of it are pushed together. These molecules push other molecules and then return to their original position. In this way, a wave of pressure changes (a *sound wave*) is transmitted through the air, even though the individual air molecules do not travel far. This wave is analogous to the ripples set up by throwing a stone into a pond.

A sound wave may be described by a graph of air pressure as a function of time. A pressure-versus-time graph of one type of sound is shown in Figure 4-21. The graph depicts a **sine wave** (so called, because it corresponds to a sine-wave function in mathematics). Sounds that correspond to sine waves are called *pure tones.* They are important in the analysis of audition because more complex sounds can be analyzed into pure tones, that is, decomposed into a number of different sine waves. Pure tones vary with respect to a couple of aspects that determine how we experience the tone. One aspect is the tone's frequency. The frequency of a tone is the number of cycles per second (called *hertz*), which reflects the rate at which the molecules move back and forth (see Figure 4-21). Frequency is the basis of our perception of pitch, which is one of the most noticeable qualities of a sound.

Another aspect of a pure tone is its *intensity,* the pressure difference between the peak and trough in a pressure-versus-time graph (see Figure 4-21). Intensity underlies our sensation of loudness. Sound intensity is usually specified in **decibels**; an increase of 10 decibels corresponds to a change in sound power of 10 times; 20 decibels, a change of 100 times; 30 decibels, a change of 1,000 times; and so forth. Table 4-3 shows the intensities of some familiar sounds, and indicates that some of them are so intense as to endanger our

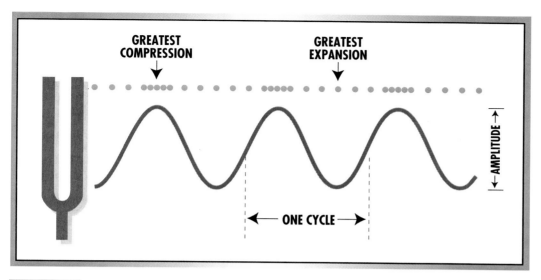

FIGURE 4-21

Pure Tone *As the tuning fork vibrates, it produces successive waves of compression and expansion of the air, which correspond to a sine wave. Such a sound is called a pure tone. It can be described by giving its frequency and intensity. If the tuning fork makes 100 vibrations per second, it produces a sound wave with 100 compressions per second and a frequency of 100 hertz. The intensity (or amplitude) of a pure tone is the pressure difference between the peaks and the troughs. The waveform of any sound can be decomposed into a series of sine waves of different frequencies with various amplitudes and phases. When these sine waves are added together, the result is the original waveform.*

hearing. Note in particular that the sound level at a rock concert is 10,000 times the level necessary to produce deafness, given enough time. (The difference between 80 db and 120 db is 4 log steps, or 10,000 times.)

AUDITORY SYSTEM

The auditory system consists of the ears, parts of the brain, and the various connecting neural pathways. Our primary concern will

DECIBEL LEVEL	EXAMPLE	DANGEROUS TIME EXPOSURE
0	Lowest sound audible to human ear	
30	Quiet library, soft whisper	
40	Quiet office, living room, bedroom away from traffic	
50	Light traffic at a distance, refrigerator, gentle breeze	
60	Air conditioner at 20 feet, conversation, sewing machine	
70	Busy traffic, office tabulator, noisy restaurant (constant exposure)	Critical level begins
80	Subway, heavy city traffic, alarm clock at 2 feet, factory noise	More than 8 hours
90	Truck traffic, noisy home appliances, shop tools, lawn mower	Less than 8 hours
100	Chain saw, boiler shop, pneumatic drill	2 hours
120	Rock concert in front of speakers, sandblasting, thunderclap	Immediate danger
140	Gunshot blast, jet plane	Any exposure is dangerous
180	Rocket launching pad	Hearing loss inevitable

TABLE 4-3

Decibel Ratings and Hazardous Time Exposures of Common Sounds *This table gives the intensities of common sounds in decibels. An increase of 3 decibels corresponds to a doubling of sound power. The sound levels given correspond approximately to the intensities that occur at typical working distances. The right-hand column gives the exposure times at which one risks permanent hearing loss.*

A Cross-Section of the Ear   *This drawing shows the overall structure of the ear. The inner ear includes the cochlea, which contains the auditory receptors, and the vestibular apparatus (semicircular canals and vestibular sacs), which is the sense organ for our sense of balance and body motion.*

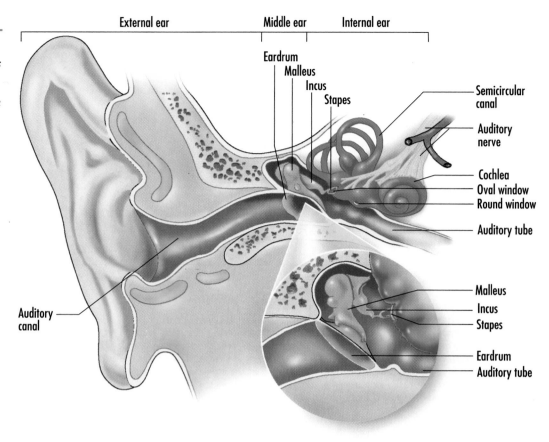

be with the ears; this includes not just the appendages on the sides of the head, but the entire hearing organ, most of which lies within the skull (see Figure 4-22).

As with the eye, the ear contains two systems. One system amplifies and transmits the sound to the receptors, whereupon the other system takes over and transduces sound into neural impulses. The *transmission system* involves the **outer ear,** which consists of the external ear (or *pinna*) along with the *auditory canal,* and the **middle ear,** which consists of the **eardrum** and a chain of three bones, called the *malleus, incus,* and *stapes.* The transduction system is housed in a part of the **inner ear** called the **cochlea,** which contains the receptors for sound.

Let us take a more detailed look at the transmission system (see Figure 4-23). The outer ear aids in the collection of sound, and funnels it through the auditory canal to a taut membrane called the *eardrum.* The eardrum is the outermost part of the middle ear. It is set into vibration by sound waves funneled to it through the auditory canal. The middle ear's job is to transmit these vi-

brations of the eardrum across an air-filled cavity to another membrane, the *oval window,* which is the gateway to the inner ear and the receptors. The middle ear accomplishes this transmission by means of a mechanical bridge built of the malleus, incus, and stapes. The vibrations of the eardrum move the first bone, which then moves the second, which in turn moves the third, which results in vibrations of the oval window. This mechanical arrangement not only transmits the sound wave, but greatly amplifies it as well.

Now consider the transduction system. The cochlea is a coiled tube of bone. It is divided into sections of fluid by membranes, one of which, the **basilar membrane,** supports the auditory receptors (Figure 4-23). The receptors are called **hair cells** because they have hairlike structures that extend into the fluid. Pressure at the oval window (which connects the middle and inner ear) leads to pressure changes in the cochlear fluid, which in turn causes the basilar membrane to vibrate, resulting in a bending of the hair cells and an electrical impulse. By this complex

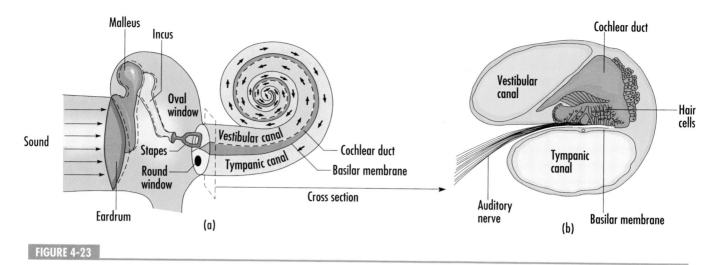

FIGURE 4-23

Schematic Diagram of the Middle and Inner Ear   *(a) Movement of the fluid within the cochlea deforms the basilar membrane and stimulates the hair cells that serve as the auditory receptors. (b) Cross section of the cochlea showing the basilar membrane and the hair cell receptors.*

process, a sound wave is transduced into an electrical impulse. The neurons that synapse with the hair cells have long axons that form part of the auditory nerve. Most of these auditory neurons connect to single hair cells. There are about 31,000 auditory neurons in the auditory nerve, many fewer than the one million neurons in the optic nerve (Yost & Nielson, 1985). The auditory pathway from each ear goes to both sides of the brain and has synapses in several nuclei before reaching the auditory cortex.

HEARING SOUND INTENSITY

Recall that in vision we are more sensitive to some wavelengths than others. There is a comparable phenomenon in audition. We are more sensitive to sounds of intermediate frequency than we are to sounds near either end of our frequency range. This is illustrated in Figure 4-24, which shows the absolute threshold for sound intensity as a function of frequency. Many people have some deficit in hearing and consequently have a threshold higher than those shown in Figure 4-24. There are two basic kinds of hearing deficits. In one, thresholds are elevated roughly equally at all frequencies as the result of poor conduction in the middle ear (**conduction loss**). In the other kind of hearing loss, the threshold elevation is unequal, with large elevations occurring at higher frequencies. This

pattern is usually a consequence of inner-ear damage, often involving some destruction of the hair cells (**sensory-neural loss**). Hair cells,

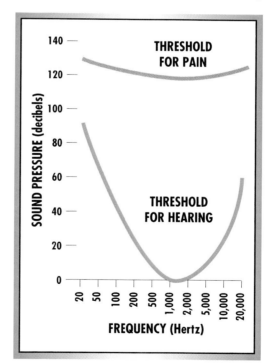

FIGURE 4-24

Absolute Threshold for Hearing   *The lower curve shows the absolute intensity threshold at different frequencies. Sensitivity is greatest in the vicinity of 1,000 hertz. The upper curve describes the threshold for pain. (Data are approximate, from various determinations.)*

Sitting or standing in front of the speakers at a rock concert can cause permanent hearing loss.

once destroyed, do not regenerate. Sensory-neural loss occurs in many older people. That is why the elderly often have trouble hearing high-pitched sounds. Sensory neural loss is not reserved for the elderly, though. It occurs in young people who are exposed to excessively loud sound. Rock musicians, airport-runway crews, and pneumatic drill operators commonly suffer major, permanent hearing loss. For example, Pete Townsend, the well-known guitarist of the rock group The Who, suffered severe sensory neural loss because of his continuous exposure to loud rock music; he has since alerted many young people to this danger.

It is natural to assume that the perceived intensity of a sound is the same at both ears, but in fact there are subtle differences. A sound originating on our right side, for example, will be heard as more intense by our right than our left ear; this is because our head causes a "sound shadow," which decreases the intensity of the sound reaching the far ear. Rather than this being a limitation on our hearing, we take advantage of this **interaural intensity** difference by using it to localize where the sound is coming from (as if we were reasoning "if the sound is more intense at my right than my left ear, it must be coming from my right side"). Likewise, a sound originating on our right side will arrive at the right ear a split-second before it reaches the left ear (and vice versa for a sound originating on the left). We also take

advantage of this *interaural time* difference to localize the sound ("if the sound arrived at my right ear first, it must be coming from the right").

HEARING PITCH

PITCH AND FREQUENCY   When hearing a pure tone, we experience not only its loudness but also its pitch. Just as color is the prime quality of light, so pitch is the prime quality of sound, ordered on a scale from low to high. And just as color is determined by the frequency of light, pitch is determined by the frequency of sound. As frequency increases, pitch increases. As with the wavelength of light, we are very good at discriminating the frequency of a sound. Young adults can hear frequencies between 20 and 20,000 hertz (cycles per second), with the jnd being less than 1 hertz at 100 hertz and increasing to 100 hertz at 10,000 hertz.

However, there is nothing analogous to color mixture in audition. When two or more frequencies are sounded simultaneously, we can hear the pitch associated with each frequency, provided that they are sufficiently separated. When the frequencies are close together, the sensation is more complex but still does not sound like a single, pure tone. In color vision, the fact that a mixture of three lights results in the sensation of a single color led to the idea of three types of receptors. The absence of a comparable phenomenon in audition suggests that, if there are receptors specialized for different frequencies, then there must be many different types of such receptors.

THEORIES OF PITCH PERCEPTION   As was the case with color vision, two kinds of theories have been proposed to account for how the ear codes frequency into pitch.

The first kind of theory originated with Lord Rutherford, a British physicist, in 1886. He proposed that a) a sound wave causes the entire basilar membrane to vibrate, and the rate of vibration matches the frequency of the sound; and b) the rate at which the membrane vibrates determines the rate of impulses of nerve fibers in the auditory nerve. Thus, a 1,000-hertz tone causes the basilar membrane to vibrate 1,000 times per second, which causes nerve fibers in the auditory nerve to fire at 1,000 impulses per second, and the brain interprets this as a particular pitch. Because this theory proposes that pitch depends on how the sound varies with time, it is called a **temporal theory** (it is also called a **frequency theory**).

Rutherford's hypothesis soon ran into a major problem. Nerve fibers were shown to have a maximum firing rate of about 1,000 impulses per second, so how do we perceive the pitch of tones whose frequency exceeds 1,000 hertz? Weaver (1949) proposed a way to salvage temporal theories. He argued that frequencies over 1,000 hertz could be coded by different groups of nerve fibers, each group firing at a slightly different pace. If one group of neurons is firing at 1,000 impulses per second, for example, and then 1 millisecond later a second group of neurons begins firing at 1,000 impulses per second, the combined rate of impulses per second for the two groups will be 2,000 impulses per second. This version of temporal theory received support from the discovery that the pattern of nerve impulses in the auditory nerve follows the waveform of the stimulus tone even though individual cells do not respond on every cycle of the wave (Rose, Brugge, Anderson, & Hind, 1967).

However, the ability of nerve fibers to follow the waveform breaks down at about 4,000 hertz; nevertheless, we can hear pitch at much higher frequencies. This suggests that there must be another means of coding the quality of pitch, at least for high frequencies.

The second kind of theory of pitch perception dates back to 1683 when Joseph Guichard Duverney, a French anatomist, proposed that frequency was coded into pitch mechanically by *resonance* (Green & Wier, 1984). To appreciate this proposal, it is helpful to first consider an example of resonance. When a tuning fork is struck near a piano, the piano string that is tuned to the frequency of the fork will begin to vibrate. To say that the ear works the same way is to say that the ear contains a structure like a stringed instrument, with different parts of this structure being tuned to different frequencies, so that when a frequency is presented to the ear the corresponding part of the structure vibrates. This idea proved to be roughly correct; the structure turned out to be the basilar membrane.

In the 1800s, Hermann von Helmholtz developed the resonance hypothesis into the **place theory** of pitch perception. It holds that each specific place along the basilar membrane will, when it responds, lead to a particular pitch sensation. The fact that there are many places on the membrane is compatible with there being many different receptors for pitch. Note that place theory does not imply that we hear with our basilar membrane; rather, the places on the membrane that vibrate most determine what neural fibers are activated, and that determines the pitch that we hear. This is an example of a sensory modality coding quality by the specific nerves involved.

How the basilar membrane actually moves was not established until the 1940s when Georg von Békésy measured its movement through small holes drilled in the cochleas of guinea pigs and human cadavers. Von Békésy's findings required a modification of place theory; rather than behaving like a piano with separate strings, the basilar membrane behaved more like a bed sheet when someone shakes it at one end. Specifically, von Békésy showed that the whole membrane moves for most frequencies, but the place of maximum movement depends on the specific frequency sounded. High frequencies cause vibration at the near end of the basilar membrane; as frequency increases, the vibration pattern moves toward the oval window (Békésy, 1960). For this and other research on audition, von Békésy received a Nobel prize in 1961.

CRITICAL DISCUSSION   *ARTIFICIAL EARS AND EYES*

The science fiction fantasy of replacing defective sense organs with artificial, functioning ones is becoming a reality. Researchers have been working for several years on artificial replacements (called *prostheses*) for damaged eyes and ears, some of which have been approved by the United States Food and Drug Administration. This work has important implications for both the reduction of sensory handicaps and for our understanding of sensory processes.

Research on auditory prostheses has concentrated on devices that apply electrical stimulation to the auditory nerve. They are designed to aid people whose hair cells (the receptors) have been destroyed, and consequently suffer a total sensory-neural hearing loss, but whose auditory nerve is intact and functional. Most of these devices use an electrode, which is inserted through the round window into the cochlea, to stimulate the neurons along the basilar membrane (a *cochlea implant*). Because the electrode goes directly into the cochlea, the functional part of the ear is bypassed (including the receptors); the cochlea is simply a convenient place to stimulate auditory neurons where they are accessible and laid out in an orderly array.

In addition to the stimulating electrode, a cochlea implant has three other components that operate in sequence: (a) a microphone located near the external ear that picks up sound; (b) a small battery-operated electronic processor (worn on the outside of the body) that converts the sound into electrical signals; and (c) a transmission system that transmits the electrical signal through the skull and to the electrode implanted in the cochlea. The last step in this process is accomplished by radio transmission to avoid running a wire through the skull.

A relatively simple device of this kind was developed in the early 1970s by William House (see the figure). The House implant extends only 6 millimeters into the cochlea and has only one electrode. The signal applied to this electrode is an electrical wave having essentially the same form as the sound wave. When sound is presented to a deaf patient using this device, he or she hears a complex noise that varies in loudness. These devices have been implanted in hundreds of profoundly deaf people. Most of the recipients believe that the device provides a marked improvement over their previously deaf state. With it, they at least hear sounds and have some ability to discriminate intensity.

More recent developments include devices with multiple electrodes. One of the most sophisticated of these, the Nucleus 22 Channel Cochlear Implant, has 22 electrodes. These extend further into the cochlea and are designed to independently stimulate several sets of neurons along the basilar membrane. Because the cochlea is only the size of a pea, with a solid bony shell and very delicate interior structures, there are difficult technical problems involved in designing and implanting the electrodes. Accompanying most of these multichannel implants is a more elaborate electronic processor that filters the sound into separate frequencies, one for each electrode. The sound wave in each frequency band is converted into an electrical signal and applied to one of the electrodes. Although results vary greatly, some patients show good performance, including word recognition scores of more than 70 percent (Loeb, 1985). Some cochlear implants have been performed with children, and again some of the results are encouraging (Staller, 1991).

The multiple-electrode devices are based on the place theory of pitch perception. In the normal ear, mechanical means are used to get different frequencies to vibrate specific parts of the basilar membrane, which lead to the activation of specific nerve fibers. In the multiple-electrode device, electronic filtering is used to accomplish this same task. The electronically filtered signal is sent to the identical place that it would be applied in the normal ear. To some extent the success of the device supports the theory.

However, use of the multiple-electrode devices has turned up some findings that don't fit well with place theory. According to the latter, when electrical stimulation is applied to a single small region on the basilar membrane, a sound with a particular pitch should be heard and this pitch varies with place. However, the sound that is heard with a multiple-electrode device is not at all like a pure tone; it is more like the "quacking of

Like temporal theories, place theories explain many phenomena of pitch perception, but not all. A major difficulty for place theory arises with low-frequency tones. With frequencies below 50 hertz, all parts of the basilar membrane vibrate roughly the same amount. This means that all receptors are equally activated, which implies that we have no way of discriminating between frequencies below 50 hertz. In fact, though, we can discriminate frequencies as low as 20 hertz.

Hence, place theories have problems explaining our perception of low-frequency tones, while temporal theories have problems ducks" or the "banging of garbage cans," even though it does have a crude pitch. Nor do results with multiple-electrode devices provide much support for temporal theories of pitch. Temporal theorists might expect that the sensation would change when the frequency of electrical stimulation changes. In fact, this produces only slight changes. The results suggest that another factor, apart from place alone or temporal pattern alone, is involved in pitch perception. This may be a complex spatiotemporal pattern of stimulation along the basilar membrane that cannot be mimicked by a few electrodes (Loeb, 1985).

The development of artificial eyes for the blind has not progressed as far as the development of artificial ears. The problem is not one of picking up the optical image; a video camera can do this well. Rather, the problem is putting the image's information into the visual system in a form that the brain can use. Research has focused on the direct electrical stimulation of the visual cortex in volunteer subjects who are either blind or undergoing brain surgery. If we know what a person sees when different places in the cortex are electrically stimulated, then by controlling the electrical stimulation it should be possible to evoke different experiences. The next step would be to use a video camera to form an image of the scene in front of a blind person and then evoke an experience of that scene.

Results obtained thus far suggest we are a long way from developing an artificial eye. When a small region of the visual cortex is stimulated with a weak electrical signal, the person experiences rudimentary, visual sensations. These sensations have been described as small spots of light that are seen in front of the person in different directions. They range in size from that of a "grain of rice" to a "coin." Most are white, but some are colored. If several places in the visual cortex are stimulated simultaneously, the corresponding spots will usually be experienced together. Although multiple stimulation of the visual cortex provides the basis for a crude pattern vision (Dobelle, Meadejovsky, & Girvin, 1974), it is questionable whether this approach will lead to a successful prosthesis for damaged eyes. The neural input to the visual cortex is so complicated that it is unlikely to be adequately duplicated by artificial means.

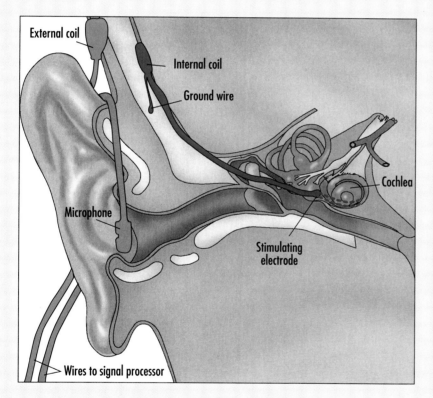

Labels: External coil, Internal coil, Ground wire, Cochlea, Microphone, Stimulating electrode, Wires to signal processor

Cochlear Implant   *This diagram illustrates the auditory prosthesis developed by William House and his associates. Sound is picked up by a microphone and filtered by a signal processor (not shown) worn outside the body. The electrical waveform produced by the processor is then transmitted by radio waves through the skull to the electrode inside the cochlea.*

dealing with high-frequency tones. This led to the idea that pitch depends on both place and temporal pattern, with temporal theory explaining our perception of low frequencies and place theory explaining our perception of high frequencies. It is not clear, however, where one mechanism leaves off and the other takes over. Indeed, it is possible that frequencies between 1000 and 5000 hertz are handled by both mechanisms (Goldstein, 1989).

OTHER SENSES

Senses other than vision and audition lack the richness of patterning and organization that have led sight and hearing to be called the "higher senses." Still these other senses are vitally important. In discussing each of these other senses, as with vision and audition we will consider the nature of the stimulus energy to which the sensory modality is sensitive, how the receptors carry out the transduction process, and how the sensory modality codes intensity and quality.

SMELL

EVOLUTIONARY SIGNIFICANCE   Before turning to our usual considerations about a sensory modality, it is useful to view the sense of smell from an evolutionary perspective and consider its development in other species.

Smell is one of the most primitive and most important of the senses. The sense organ for smell has a position of prominence

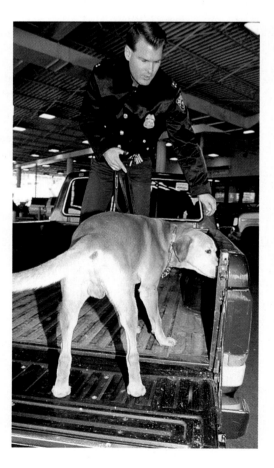

A dog's acute sense of smell is helpful in law enforcement, as this drug-sniffing canine demonstrates.

in the head appropriate to a sense intended to guide the organism. Smell has a more direct route to the brain than any other sense: the receptors, which are in the nasal cavity, are connected without synapse to the brain. Moreover, unlike the receptors for vision and audition, the receptors for smell are exposed directly to the environment—they are right there in the nasal cavity with no protective shield in front of them. (In contrast, the receptors for vision are behind the cornea, and those for audition are protected by the outer and middle ears.)

Smell (or **olfaction**) aids in the survival of our species; smell is needed for the detection of spoiled food or escaping gas, and a loss of smell can lead to a dulled appetite. Still, smell is even more essential for the survival of many other animals. Not surprisingly, then, a larger area of the cortex is devoted to smell in other species than in our own. In fish, the olfactory cortex makes up almost all of the cerebral hemispheres; in dogs, about one-third; in humans, only about one-twentieth. These differences are related to differences in sensitivity among the species. Taking advantage of the superior smell capability of dogs, both the United States Postal Service and the Bureau of Customs have trained them to check unopened packages for heroin. And specially trained police dogs can sniff out hidden explosives.

Because smell is so well developed in other species, it is often used as a major means of communication. Insects and some higher animals secrete chemicals, known as **pheromones**, that float through the air to be sniffed by other members of the species. For example, a female moth can release a pheromone so powerful that males are drawn to her from a distance of several miles. It is clear that the male moth responds only to the pheromone and not to the sight of the female; the male will be attracted to a female in a wire container even though she is blocked from view, but not to a female that is clearly visible in a glass container from which the scent cannot escape.

Insects use smell to communicate death as well as "love." After an ant dies, the chemicals formed from its decomposing body stimulate other ants to carry the corpse to a refuse heap outside the nest. If a living ant is experimentally doused with the decomposition chemicals, it is carried off by other ants to the

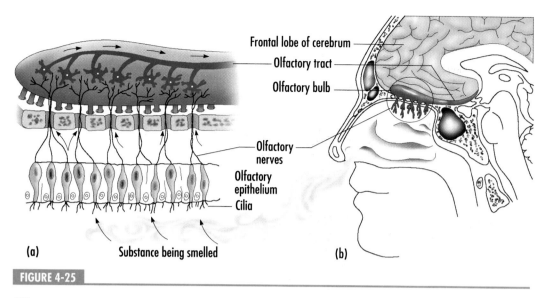

Frontal lobe of cerebrum
Olfactory tract
Olfactory bulb

Olfactory nerves
Olfactory epithelium
Cilia

(a)   Substance being smelled   (b)

Olfactory Receptors *(a) Detail of a receptor interspersed among numerous supporting cells. (b) The placement of the olfactory receptors in the nasal cavity.*

refuse heap. When it returns to the nest, it is carried out again. Such premature attempts at burial continue until the "smell of death" has worn off (Wilson, 1963).

Do we humans have a remnant of this primitive communication system? Experiments indicate that we can use smell at least to tell ourselves from others, and males from females. In one study, subjects wore undershirts for 24 hours without showering or using deodorant. The undershirts were collected by the experimenter. He then presented each subject with three shirts to smell: one was the subject's own shirt, another was a male's, and the third was a female's. Based only on odor, most subjects could usually identify their own shirt and tell which of the other shirts was worn by males or females (Russell, 1976). Other studies suggest that we may communicate subtler matters by odor. Women who live or work together seem to communicate where they are in their menstrual cycle by means of smell, and over time this results in a tendency for their menstrual cycles to synchronize and begin at the same time (Russell, Switz, & Thompson, 1980; McClintock, 1971).

OLFACTORY SYSTEM The volatile molecules given off by a substance are the stimulus for smell. The molecules leave the substance, travel through the air, and enter the nasal passage (see Figure 4-25). The molecules must also be soluble in fat, because the receptors for smell are covered with a fatlike substance.

The olfactory system consists of the receptors in the nasal passage, regions of the brain, and interconnecting neural pathways. The receptors for smell are located high in the nasal cavity. When the cilia (hairlike structures) of these receptors are contacted by molecules of odorant, an electrical impulse results; this is the transduction process. This impulse travels along nerve fibers to the **olfactory bulb**, a region of the brain that lies just below the frontal lobes. The olfactory bulb in turn is connected to the olfactory cortex on the inside of the temporal lobes. (Interestingly, there is a direct connection between the olfactory bulb and the part of the cortex known to be involved in the formation of long-term memories; perhaps this is related to the idea that a distinctive smell can be a powerful aid in retrieving an old memory.)

SENSING INTENSITY AND QUALITY Human sensitivity to the intensity of a smell depends dramatically on the substance involved. Absolute thresholds can be as low as 1 part per 50 billion parts of air. Still, as noted earlier, we are far less sensitive to smell than other species. Dogs, for example, can detect substances in concentrations 100 times lower than concentrations humans can detect (Moulton, 1977). Our relative lack of sensitivity is not due to our having less sensitive olfactory receptors.

Rather, we just have fewer of them: roughly 10 million receptors for people versus 1 billion for dogs.

Though we rely less on smell than other species, we are capable of sensing many different qualities of odor. Estimates vary, but a healthy person appears to be able to distinguish between 10,000 and 40,000 different odors, with women generally doing better than men (Cain, 1988). Professional perfumers and whiskey blenders can probably do even better—perhaps discriminating 100,000 odors (Dobb, 1991). Furthermore, we know something about how the olfactory system codes the quality of odors at the biological level. The situation is most unlike the coding of color in vision where three kinds of receptors suffice. In olfaction, many kinds of receptors seem to be involved; an estimate of 1,000 kinds of olfactory receptors is not unreasonable in light of recent work (Buck & Axel, 1991). Rather than coding a specific odor, each kind of receptor may respond to many different odors (Matthews, 1972). So quality may be partly coded by the pattern of neural activity even in this receptor-rich sensory modality.

TASTE

Taste gets credit for a lot of experiences that it does not provide. We say that a meal "tastes" good; but when smell is eliminated by a bad cold our dinner becomes an impoverished experience, and we may have trouble telling red wine from vinegar. Still, taste (or **gustation**) is a sense in its own right. Even with a bad cold, we can tell salted from unsalted food.

In what follows, we will talk about the taste of particular substances, but note that the substance being tasted is not the only factor that determines its taste. Our genetic makeup and experience also affect taste. For example, people vary in their sensitivity to the bitter taste in caffeine and saccharin, and this difference among people appears to be genetically determined (Bartoshuk, 1979). As another case in point, Indians living in the Karnataka province of India eat many sour foods, and experience citric acid and quinine as pleasant tasting; most of us experience the opposite. This particular difference between people seems to be a matter of experience, for Indians who have been raised in a western country find citric acid and quinine unpleasant (Moskowitz et al., 1975).

GUSTATORY SYSTEM The stimulus for taste is a substance that is soluble in saliva, which is a fluid much like salt water. The gustatory system includes receptors that are located on the tongue, as well as on the throat and roof of the mouth; the system also includes parts of the brain and interconnecting neural pathways. In what follows, we focus on the receptors on the tongue. These taste receptors occur in clusters, called *taste buds,* on the bumps of the tongue and around the mouth. At the ends of the taste buds are short, hairlike structures that extend out and make contact with the solutions in the mouth. This contact results in an electrical impulse; this is the transduction process. The electrical impulse then travels to the brain.

SENSING INTENSITY AND QUALITY Sensivity to different taste stimuli varies from place to place on the tongue. While any substance can be detected at almost any place on the tongue (except the center), different tastes are best detected in different regions. Sensitivity to salty and sweet substances is best near the front of the tongue; sour is best along the sides; and bitter is best on the soft palate (see Figure 4-26). In the center of the tongue is a region insensitive to taste (the place to put an unpleasant pill). While absolute thresholds for taste are generally very low, jnds for intensity are

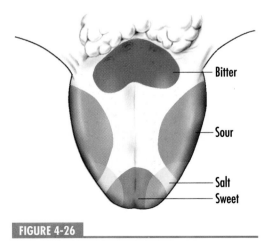

FIGURE 4-26

Taste Areas *Although any substance can be detected anywhere on the tongue—except in the center—different areas are maximally sensitive to different tastes. Thus the area labeled "sweet" is most sensitive to sweet tastes.*

relatively high (Weber's constant is often about 0.2). This means that if you are increasing the amount of spice in a dish usually you must add more than 20 percent or you will not taste the difference.

There is an agreed-upon vocabulary for describing tastes. Any taste can be described as one or a combination of the four basic taste qualities: sweet, sour, salty, and bitter (McBurney, 1978). These four tastes are best revealed in sucrose (sweet), hydrochloric acid (sour), sodium chloride (salty), and quinine (bitter). When subjects are asked to describe the tastes of various substances in terms of just the four basic tastes, they have no trouble doing this; even if given the option of using additional qualities of their own choice, they tend to stay with the four basic tastes (Goldstein, 1989).

The gustatory system codes taste in terms of both the specific nerve fibers activated and the pattern of activation across nerve fibers. There appear to be four types of nerve fibers, corresponding to the four basic tastes. While each fiber responds somewhat to all four basic tastes, it responds best to just one of them. Hence, it makes sense to talk of "salty fibers," whose activity signals saltiness to the brain. Thus, there is a remarkable correspondence between our subjective experience of taste and its neural coding.

PRESSURE AND TEMPERATURE

Traditionally, touch was thought to be a single sense. Today, it is considered to include three distinct skin senses, one responding to pressure, another to temperature, and the third to pain. This section briefly considers pressure and temperature, and the next discusses pain.

PRESSURE　The stimulus for sensed pressure is physical pressure on the skin. Although we are not aware of steady pressure on the entire body (such as air pressure), we can discriminate variations in pressure over the body surface. Some parts of the body are more effective than others at sensing the intensity of pressure; the lips, nose, and cheek are the most sensitive to pressure, while the big toe is least sensitive. These differences are closely related to the number of receptors that respond to the stimulus at each of these body

loci. In sensitive regions, we can detect a force as small as 5 milligrams applied to a small area. However, like other sensory systems, the pressure system shows profound adaptation effects. If you hold your friend's hand for several minutes without moving, you will become insensitive to it and cease to feel the hand.

The preceding focused on what happens when we experience pressure in a passive way, that is, when we are being touched. But what about when we are actively exploring the environment, that is, when we are doing the touching? Such *active touching* results in a different experience from its passive counterpart, and involves the activity of the motor senses, as well as the pressure sense. By active touch alone, we can readily identify familiar objects (Klatzky, Lederman, & Metzger, 1985). Though we rarely use active touch to identify many objects, we do use it often for recognizing coins, keys, and other small objects that we keep in our pockets and purses.

TEMPERATURE　The stimulus for temperature is the temperature of our skin. The receptors are neurons with free nerve endings just under the skin. In the transduction stage, *cold receptors* generate a neural impulse when there is a decrease in skin temperature, while *warm receptors* generate an impulse when there is an increase in skin temperature (Duclauz & Kenshalo, 1980; Hensel, 1973).

Food manufacturers employ tasters, who have highly discriminating senses of taste. Here, a taste expert samples varying blends of coffee.

After being in a swimming pool for a while, our temperature sense adapts to the change in temperature. However, when first dangling a foot into the water, we can detect the cooler temperature.

Hence, different qualities of temperature can be coded primarily by the specific receptors activated (as pitch is coded in audition). However, this specificity of neural reaction has its limits. Cold receptors respond not only to low temperatures but also to very high temperatures (above 45 degrees centigrade). Consequently a very hot stimulus will activate both warm and cold receptors, which in turn evoke a hot sensation.

Because maintaining body temperature is crucial to our survival, it is important that we can sense small changes in our skin temperature. When the skin is at its normal temperature, we can detect a warming of only 0.4 degrees centigrade and a cooling of just 0.15 degrees centigrade (Kenshalo, Nafe, & Brooks, 1961). Our temperature sense adapts completely to moderate changes in temperatures, so that after a few minutes the stimulus feels neither cool nor warm. This adaptation explains the strong differences of opinion about the temperature of a swimming pool between those who have been in it for a while and those first dangling a foot in it.

PAIN

Of all our senses, none captures our attention like pain. We may sometimes be blasé about the experiences of the other senses, but it is hard to ignore the experience of pain. Yet for all the discomfort it causes, we would be at risk if we had no sense of pain. It would be difficult for children to learn *not* to touch a hot stove, or to stop chewing their tongues. In fact, there are people born with a rare genetic disorder that makes them insensitive to pain, and they typically die young, from tissue deterioration resulting from wounds that could have been avoided with a sense of pain.

PAIN SYSTEM   Any stimulus that is intense enough to cause tissue damage is a stimulus for pain. It may be pressure, temperature, electric shock, or irritant chemicals. The effect of such a stimulus is to cause the release of chemical substances in the skin, which in turn stimulate distinct high-threshold receptors (the transduction stage). These receptors are neurons with specialized free nerve endings, and researchers have distinguished several types (Brown & Deffenbacher, 1979).

With regard to variations in the quality of pain, perhaps the most important distinction is between the kind of pain we feel immediately upon suffering an injury, called **phasic** pain, and the kind we experience after the injury has occurred, called **tonic** pain. Phasic pain is typically a sharp immediate pain that is brief in duration (rapidly rises and falls in intensity), and tonic pain is typically dull and long lasting.

To illustrate, if you sprain your ankle, immediately you feel a sharp undulating pain (phasic pain), but a short while after you start to feel the steady pain caused by the swelling (tonic pain). The two kinds of pain are mediated by two distinct neural pathways, and these pathways eventually reach different parts of the cortex. (Melzak, 1990).

NONSTIMULUS DETERMINANTS OF PAIN   More than any other sensation, the intensity and quality of pain is influenced by factors other than the immediate stimulus. These factors include the person's culture, expectations, and previous experience. The striking influence of culture is illustrated by the fact that some non-Western societies engage in rituals that at first blush seem unbearably painful to Westerners. A case in point is the hook-swinging ceremony practiced in some parts of India:

The ceremony derives from an ancient practice in which a member of a social group is chosen to represent the power of the gods. The role of the chosen man (or "celebrant") is to bless the children and crops in a series of neighboring villages during a particular period of the year. What is remarkable about the ritual is that steel hooks, which are attached by strong ropes to the top of a special cart, are shoved under his skin and muscles on both sides of his back [see Figure 4-27]. The cart is then moved from village to village. Usually the man hangs on to the ropes as the cart is moved about. But at the climax of the ceremony in each village, he swings free, hanging only from the hooks embedded in his back, to bless the children and crops. Astonishingly, there is no evidence that the man is in pain during the ritual; rather, he appears to be in a "state of exaltation." When the hooks are later removed, wounds heal rapidly without any medical treatment other than the application of wood ash. Two weeks later the marks on his back are scarcely visible (Melzak, 1973).

Clearly, pain is as much a matter of mind as of sensory receptors.

Phenomena like the above have led to the **gate control theory** of pain (Melzak & Wall, 1982; 1965). According to the theory, the sensation of pain requires not only that pain receptors on the skin be active, but also that a "neural gate" in the spinal cord be open and allow the signals from the pain receptors to pass to the brain (the gate closes when critical fibers in the spinal cord are activated). Because the neural gate can be closed by signals sent down from the cortex, the perceived intensity of pain can be reduced by mental state, as in the hook-swinging ceremony. What exactly is the "neural gate"? It appears to involve a region of the midbrain called the periaqueductal gray, or PAG for short; neurons in PAG are connected to other neurons that inhibit cells which would normally carry the pain signals arising in the pain receptors (Jesell & Kelly, 1991). So when the PAG neurons are active, the gate is closed; when the PAG neurons are not active, the gate is open.

Interestingly, the PAG appears to be the main place where strong pain killers like morphine affect neural processing. Morphine is known to increase neural activity in the PAG, which as we have just seen should result in a closing of the neural gate. Hence, the well-known analgesic effects of morphine fit with the gate control theory. Furthermore, our body produces certain chemicals, called *endorphins*, that act like morphine to reduce

FIGURE 4-27

Culture and Pain *Right: two steel hooks in the back of the "celebrant" in the Indian hook-swinging ceremony. Left: the celebrant hangs onto the ropes as a cart takes him from village to village. As he blesses the village children and crops, he swings freely suspended by the hooks in his back.* (After Kosambi, 1967)

pain, and these chemicals too are believed to have their effect by acting on the PAG in such a way as to close the neural gate.

There are other striking phenomena that fit with gate control theory. One is called *stimulation-produced analgesia,* in which stimulation of the PAG acts like an anesthetic. One can perform abdominal surgery on a rat using only PAG stimulation as the anesthetic, with the rat showing no sign of experiencing pain (Reynolds, 1969). A milder version of this phenomenon is familiar to all of us: Rubbing a hurt area relieves pain, presumably because pressure stimulation is closing the neural gate. A phenomenon related to stimulation-produced analgesia is the reduction in pain resulting from *acupuncture.* Acupuncture is a healing procedure developed in China in which needles are inserted into the skin at critical points; twirling these needles has been reported to eliminate pain entirely, making it possible to perform major surgery on a conscious patient

Acupuncture, a technique related to stimulation-produced analgesia, is often used to reduce pain.

(see Figure 4-28). Presumably, the needles stimulate nerve fibers that lead to a closing of the pain gate.

At the psychological level then, we have evidence that drugs, cultural beliefs, and various nonstandard medicinal practices can dramatically reduce pain. All of these factors, though, may have a common locus at the biological level. Here, then, is a case in which research at the biological level may actually unify findings at the psychological level.

FIGURE 4-28

Typical Acupuncture Chart   *The numbers indicate sites at which needles can be inserted, and then either twisted, electrified, or heated. An impressive analgesia results in many cases.*

BIOLOGICAL-PSYCHOLOGICAL PERSPECTIVES

The interplay between the psychological and biological research on pain is typical of the successful interaction between these two approaches to sensation. As we commented at the outset of this chapter, in perhaps no other area of psychology have the biological and psychological approaches worked so well together. Again and again, we have seen that neural events occurring in receptors can explain phenomena at the psychological level. Thus, in discussing vision, we showed how variations in sensitivity and acuity—which are psychological phenomena—can be understood as the direct consequence of how different kinds of receptors (rods versus cones) connect to ganglion cells. Also, with regard to vision, we pointed out how psychological theories of color vision led to breakthrough discoveries at the biological level (for example, the discovery of three kinds of cone receptors). The same story can be told for audition. The place theory of frequency perception was initially a psychological theory, and it led to Nobel prize–winning research in the physiology of the basilar membrane. If ever anyone needed justification for intertwining psychological and biological research, the study of sensation provides it.

📖 CHAPTER SUMMARY

1. At the psychological level, sensations are experiences associated with simple stimuli; at the biological level, sensory processes involve the sense organs and connecting neural pathways, and are concerned with the initial stages of acquiring stimulus information. The senses include vision; hearing (*audition*); smell (*olfaction*); taste (*gustation*); the *skin senses*, which include pressure, temperature, and pain; and the *body senses*.

2. One property common to all senses is a sensitivity for detecting change. Sensitivity to intensity is measured by the *absolute threshold*, the minimum amount of stimulus energy that can be reliably detected. Sensitivity to a change in intensity is measured by the *difference threshold* or *jnd*, the minimum difference between two stimuli that can be reliably detected. The amount of change needed for detection to occur increases with the initial intensity of the stimulus, and is approximately proportional to it (*Weber's law*).

3. Every sense modality must recode its physical energy into neural impulses. This *transduction* process is accomplished by the *receptors*. The receptors and connecting neural pathways code the *intensity* of a stimulus primarily by the rate of neural impulses and their patterns; they code the *quality* of a stimulus by the specific nerve fibers involved and their pattern of activity.

4. The stimulus for vision is electromagnetic radiation from 400 to 700 nanometers, and the sense organs are the eyes. Each eye contains a system for forming the image (including the *cornea, pupil,* and *lens*), and a system for transducing the image into electrical impulses. The transduction system is in the *retina,* which contains the visual receptors, the *rods* and *cones.*

5. Cones operate at high intensities, lead to sensations of color, and are found only in the center (or *fovea*) of the retina; rods operate at low intensities, lead to colorless sensations, and predominate in the *periphery* of the retina. Our sensitivity to a light's intensity is mediated by properties of the rods and cones. Of particular importance is the fact that more rods connect to a ganglion cell than do cones; because of this difference in connectivity, visual *sensitivity* is greater when based on rods than cones, but visual *acuity* is greater when based on cones than rods.

6. Different wavelengths of light lead to sensations of different colors. A mixture of three lights widely separated in wavelength can be made to match almost any color of light. This fact and others led to the development of *trichromatic* theory, which holds that the perception of color is based on the activity of three types of receptors (cones), each of which is maximally sensitive to wavelengths in a different region of the spectrum. There are four *basic color sensations:* red, yellow, green, and blue. Mixtures of these make up our experiences of color, except that we do not see reddish-greens and yellowish-blues. The latter facts can be explained by an *opponent-color theory.* It postulates red-green and yellow-blue *opponent processes* (each of which responds in opposite ways to its two opponent colors). Trichromatic and opponent-color theories have been successfully combined.

7. The stimulus for audition is a wave of pressure changes (a *sound wave*), and the sense organs are the ears. The ear includes: the *outer ear* (the external ear and the *auditory canal*); the *middle ear* (the *eardrum* and a chain of bones); and the *inner ear.* The inner ear includes the *cochlea,* which is a coiled tube that contains the *basilar membrane,* which supports the *hair cells* that serve as the receptors for sound. Sound waves transmitted by the outer and middle ear cause the basilar membrane to vibrate, which results in a bending of the hair cells, and eventuates in a neural impulse.

8. *Pitch,* the most striking quality of sound, increases with the frequency of the sound wave. The fact that we can hear the pitches of two different tones sounded simultaneously suggests there may be many receptors, which respond to different frequencies. *Temporal theories* of pitch perception postulate that the pitch heard depends on the temporal pattern of neural responses in the auditory system, which itself is determined by the temporal pattern of the sound wave. *Place theories* postulate that each frequency maximally stimulates one place along the basilar membrane, and the place of maximum movement determines which pitch is heard. There is room for both theories, as temporal theory explains our perception of low frequencies, and place theory accounts for our perceptions of high frequencies.

9. Smell is even more important to nonhuman species than to humans. Many species use specialized odors (*pheromones*) for communication, and humans seem to have a remnant of this system. The stimuli for smell are the molecules given off by a substance. The molecules travel by air and activate the olfactory receptors located high in the *nasal cavity*. There are many kinds of receptors (on the order of 1,000). A normal person can discriminate 10,000 to 40,000 different odors, with women generally doing better than men.

10. Taste is affected not only by the substance being tasted, but also by genetic makeup and experience. The stimulus for taste is a substance that is soluble in saliva; many of the receptors occur in clusters on the tongue (*taste buds*). Sensitivity varies from place to place on the tongue. Any taste can be described as one or a combination of the four basic taste qualities: *sweet, sour, salty,* and *bitter*. Different qualities of taste are coded partly in terms of the specific nerve fibers activated—different fibers respond best to one of the four taste sensations—and partly in terms of the pattern of fibers activated.

11. Two of the *skin senses* are *pressure* and *temperature*. Our sensitivity to pressure is greatest at the lips, nose, and cheeks, and least at the big toe. We are very sensitive to temperature, being able to detect a change of less than one degree centigrade. We code different kinds of temperatures primarily by whether *hot* or *cold receptors* are activated.

12. Any stimulus intense enough to cause tissue damage is a stimulus for pain. There are two distinct kinds of pain, mediated by different neural pathways: *phasic* pain, which is typically brief and rapidly rising and falling in intensity, and *tonic* pain, which is typically long lasting and steady. Sensitivity to pain is greatly influenced by factors other than the noxious stimulus, including expectations and cultural beliefs. These factors seem to have their influence by opening or closing a *neural gate* in the spinal cord and midbrain; pain is felt only when pain receptors are activated and the gate is open.

FURTHER READING

There are several good general texts on sensory processes and perception. A particularly clear one is Goldstein, *Sensation and Perception* (3rd ed., 1989). Other useful texts include: Barlow and Mollon, *The Senses* (1982); Coren and Ward, *Sensation and Perception* (3rd ed., 1989); Schiffman, *Sensation and Perception* (3rd ed., 1990); and Sekuler and Blake, *Perception* (1985).

For treatments of color vision, see Boynton, *Human Color Vision* (1979); and Hurvich, *Color Vision* (1981). Introductory books on audition include Moore, *An Introduction to the Psychology of Hearing* (2nd ed., 1982); and Yost and Nielson, *Fundamentals of Hearing* (2nd ed., 1985). For smell, see Engen, *The Perception of Odors* (1982); for touch,

Tactual Perception, edited by Schiff and Foulke (1982); and for pain, *The Psychology of Pain,* edited by Sternbach (2nd ed., 1986).

For reference, there are four multivolume handbooks, each of which has several chapters on sensory systems. They are the *Handbook of Perception* (1974–1978), edited by Carterette and Friedman; the *Handbook of Physiology: The Nervous System:* Section 1, Volume 3, *Sensory Processes* (1984), edited by Darian-Smith; the *Handbook of Perception and Human Performance:* Volume 1, *Sensory Processes and Perception* (1986), edited by Boff, Kaufman, and Thomas; and *Stevens' Handbook of Experimental Psychology: Volume 1* (1988), edited by Atkinson, Herrnstein, Lindzey, and Luce.

5
CHAPTER

PERCEPTION

Information may enter our senses in bits and pieces, but that is not how we *perceive* the world. We perceive a world of objects and people, a world that bombards us with integrated wholes, not piecemeal sensations. Only under unusual circumstances, or when we are drawing or painting, do we notice the individual features and parts of stimuli; most of the time we see three-dimensional objects and hear words and music.

Perception is the study of how we integrate sensory information into percepts of objects, and how we then use these percepts to get around in the world (a **percept** is a product of a perceptual process). Researchers are increasingly approaching the study of perception by asking what problems the perceptual system is designed to solve. Two general problems are repeatedly mentioned. The perceptual system must determine (a) *what* objects are out there (apples, tables, cats, and so on), and (b) *where* these objects are (arm's length on my left, hundreds of yards straight ahead, and so on). The same two problems are involved in auditory perception (*What* was that sound, a phone or a siren? *Where* was it coming from, the front or the back?), and in other sensory modalities as well.

In vision, determining what the objects are is referred to as the process of **pattern recognition**, or *recognition* for short. It is crucial for survival because often we have to know what an object is before we can infer some of its critical properties. So, once we know an object is an apple, we know it is edible; once we know an object is a wolf, we know not to disturb it. Determining where visual objects are is referred to as **spatial localization**, or *localization*. It is also necessary for survival. Localization is the means we use to navigate through our environment. Without such an ability, we would constantly be bumping into objects, failing to grasp things we are reaching for, and moving into the path of dangerous objects and predators.

In addition to localizing and recognizing objects, another goal of our perceptual system is to keep the appearance of objects constant, even though their impressions on our retinas are continually changing. Such **perceptual constancy** will be another concern to us.

In what follows, we first set the stage for our discussion by considering how the brain divides its perceptual tasks. Then we turn to what is known about the major goals of perception: localization, recognition, and perceptual constancy. Along the way, we will also discuss the role of attention. Finally, we consider the development of perception. Throughout the chapter, we will focus primarily on visual perception, because this is the area that has been most investigated. Keep in mind, though, that the goals of localization, recognition, and constancy seem to apply to all sensory modalities. With regard to recognition, for example, we can use our hearing to recognize a Mozart sonata, our smell to recognize McDonald's fries, our touch to recognize the quarter in our pants pocket, and our body senses to recognize that we are dancing a polka.

DIVISION OF LABOR IN THE BRAIN

In the past decade, a great deal has been learned about the neural processes that underlie perception. At a general level, that part of the brain concerned with vision—the *visual cortex*—operates according to a *division of labor* principle. Rather than all of the visual cortex participating in all or most aspects of perception, different regions of the visual cortex are specialized to carry out different perceptual functions (Kosslyn & Koenig, 1992).

RECOGNITION VERSUS LOCALIZATION SYSTEMS

The idea that localization and recognition are qualitatively different tasks is supported by findings that they are carried out by different regions of the visual cortex. Recognition of objects depends on a branch of the visual system that includes the cortical receiving area for vision (the first area in the cortex to receive visual information) and a region near the bottom of the cerebral cortex. In contrast, localization of objects depends on a branch of the visual system that includes the cortical receiving area for vision and a region of the cortex near the top of the brain (see Figure 5-1). Studies with nonhuman primates show that if the recognition branch of an animal's visual system is impaired, the animal can still perform tasks that require it to perceive spatial relations between objects (one in front of the other, for example), but it cannot perform tasks that require discriminating the actual objects—for example, tasks that require discriminating a cube from a cylinder; if the location branch is impaired, the animal can perform tasks that require it to distinguish a cube from a cylinder, but it cannot perform tasks that require it to know where the objects are in relation to one another (Mishkin & Appenzeller, 1987).

More recent research has used brain scanning techniques to document the existence of separate object and location systems in the *human* brain. The most widely used technique is PET (discussed in Chapter 2). Recall its basic logic. A subject first has a radioactive tracer injected into her bloodstream, and then is placed in a PET scanner while she performs various tasks. The PET scanner measures increases in radioactivity in various brain regions, which indicate increases in blood flow to those regions. Those regions that show the most increase in blood flow presumably are the ones that mediate performance in the task.

In one PET study, subjects performed two tasks, one a test of face recognition, which presumably taps object recognition, and the other a test of mental rotation, which presumably reflects localization. In the face-recognition task, on each trial subjects saw a *target* picture, and beneath it two *test* faces. One test face was the same person as that depicted by the target, except for changes in orientation and lighting; the other test face was of a different person. The subject's task was to decide which test face was the same as the target (see Figure 5.2a). While engaging in this task, there was an increase in blood flow in the recognition branch of the cortex (the branch terminating near the bottom of the cortex), but not in the localization branch (the branch terminating near the top of the cortex). Very different results were obtained with the mental rotation task. In this task, on each trial subjects saw a target display of a dot at some distance from a double line, and beneath that two test displays. One test display was the same as the target, except that it had been rotated, and the other test display contained a different configuration of the dot

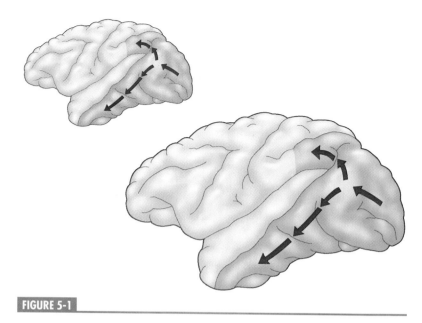

FIGURE 5-1

Two Cortical Visual Systems *The arrows going from the back of the brain toward the top depict the localization system; the arrows going from the back toward the bottom of the brain depict the recognition system.* (After Mishkin, Ungerleider, & Macko, 1983)

and lines (see Figure 5-2b). While engaging in this task, subjects showed an increase in blood flow in the localization branch of the cortex but not in the recognition branch. Localization and recognition are therefore carried out in entirely different regions of the visual cortex (Grady et al., 1992; Haxby et al., 1990).

COMPONENTS OF RECOGNITION

The division of labor in the visual cortex does not end with the split between localization and recognition. Rather, the different kinds of information that are used in recognition—color, shape, and texture, for example—appear to be processed by different subregions or cells of the recognition branch of the cortex.

The best evidence for the preceding claim comes from studies with nonhuman primates. These studies record electrical activity from single cells while the animal is exposed to various stimuli (see Figure 4-4 for a refresher on single-cell recordings). Such studies indicate that different attributes of an object are processed by different regions of the brain, or by different cells within a region. Thus, within the primary receiving area of the visual cortex, some cells respond only to

FIGURE 5-2

Recognition and Localization Tasks *Sample items from the face matching (a) and dot-location (b) matching tasks.* (From Grady et al, 1992)

simple shapes like lines and edges, and other cells respond only to colors, and still others respond only to movement. (Though we treat movement mainly as a component of localization—see below—it does play some role in recognition.) As information moves from the primary receiving area to other areas of the visual cortex, specialization becomes even more striking, as now one entire region will be devoted only to form, another only to color, and another only to motion (Keki, 1992).

The upshot is that the visual cortex consists of numerous "processing modules," each one specialized for a particular task. The more we learn about the neural basis of other sensory modalities, and other psychological functions as well, the more this modular, or division-of-labor, approach seems to hold.

LOCALIZATION

To know where the objects in our environment are, the very first thing that we have to do is *segregate* the objects from one another and from the background. Then the perceptual system can determine the position of the objects in a three-dimensional world, including their *distance* from us and their *movement* patterns. The idea that these three perceptual abilities—segregation, determining distance, and determining movement—be-

long together is supported by physiological findings indicating that all three abilities are mostly mediated by the same branch of the visual system (Livingstone & Hubel, 1988). We will discuss each of these perceptual abilities in turn.

SEGREGATION OF OBJECTS

The image projected on our retina is a mosaic of varying brightnesses and colors. Somehow our perceptual system organizes the mosaic into a set of discrete objects projected against a background. This kind of organization was of great concern to **Gestalt psychology,** an approach to psychology that began in Germany early in the twentieth century. The Gestalt psychologists emphasized the importance of perceiving whole objects or forms, and proposed a number of principles of how we organize objects.

FIGURE AND GROUND   In a stimulus that contains two or more distinct regions, we usually see part of it as a *figure* and the rest as *ground.* The regions seen as a figure contain the objects of interest—they appear more solid than the ground and appear in front of the ground. This is the most elementary form of perceptual organization. Figure 5-3 illustrates that **figure-ground organization** can be reversible. If you look at this picture for a few seconds, you will note that you can see as the figure either a vase *or* two profiles. Thus, you can see the same contour as part of one object or another. The fact that you can do this indicates that figure-ground organization is not part of the physical stimulus, but rather is an accomplishment of our perceptual system. Figure 5-4 illustrates a more complex reversible figure-ground effect. (Note that we can perceive figure-ground relations in senses other than vision. For example, we may hear the song of a bird against a background of outdoor noises, or the melody played by the violin against the harmonies of the rest of the orchestra.)

GROUPING OF OBJECTS   We see not only objects against a ground, but a particular grouping of the objects as well. Even simple patterns of lines or dots fall into groups when we look at them. In the top part of Figure 5-5, we tend to see three pairs of lines, with an extra line at the right. But notice that the stimulus can be described equally well as three pairs beginning at the right with an extra line at the left. The slight modification of the lines shown in the lower part of the figure causes us to perceive the second grouping.

The Gestalt psychologists proposed a number of determinants of grouping. One is *proximity:* elements that are near to one another will tend to be grouped together. This principle explains the preferred grouping of the lines in the top part of Figure 5-5. *Closure,* or our tendency to group elements to complete figures with gaps, explains the grouping preferred in the bottom part of the figure. In the bottom part of the figure, closure is a stronger factor than proximity.

Many determinants of grouping were first noted by Max Wertheimer (1912), the founder of Gestalt psychology. In modern times, researchers have shown that different ways of grouping objects have marked effects on perceptual performance. In one set of experiments, on each of the trials subjects were presented with a display (see Figure 5-6). The subject's task was to decide as quickly as possible whether or not the display contained a target letter, either a T or an F. On those trials in which the display contained a target, subjects responded faster when the target was relatively far from the nontargets, as in the display on the top, than when the target was relatively close to the nontargets, as in the display on the bottom. When the target was close to the nontargets, the principle of prox-

Reversible Figure and Ground   *The reversible goblet illustrates figure-ground reversal. Note that you can perceive either the light portion (the vase) or the dark portion (two profiles) as a figure against a background, but only one at a time. This vase was a gift to Queen Elizabeth II on her silver jubilee and shows her profile and that of Prince Philip* (from Rock, 1984).

The Slave Market with Disappearing Bust of Voltaire   *A reversible figure is in the center of this painting by Salvador Dali (1940). Two nuns standing in an archway reverse to form a bust of Voltaire.*

FIGURE 5-5

Perceptual Grouping

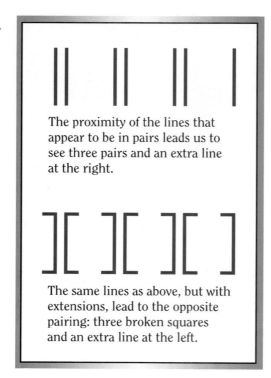

The proximity of the lines that appear to be in pairs leads us to see three pairs and an extra line at the right.

The same lines as above, but with extensions, lead to the opposite pairing: three broken squares and an extra line at the left.

FIGURE 5-6

Grouping by Proximity
Subjects found the target T faster when it was relatively far from the nontargets (a) than when it was relatively close to the nontargets (b). (After Banks & Prinzmetal, 1976)

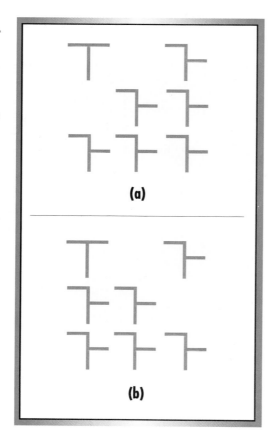

(a)

(b)

imity led the target and nontargets to be grouped together, which resulted in extra time being needed to extract the target.

Another determinant of grouping that deserves mention is *similarity,* our tendency to group together similar objects. If we replaced the T in the bottom display of Figure 5-6 with an O, subjects would be less likely to group it with the nontargets because an O is very dissimilar to the nontargets.

Although perceptual grouping has been studied mainly in visual perception, the same determinants of grouping appear in audition. Proximity clearly operates in audition (though it is proximity in time rather than in space): four drumbeats with a pause between the second and third will be heard as two pairs. Similarity and closure are also known to play important roles in hearing tones and more complex stimuli (Bregman & Reidnicky, 1975).

The research on perceptual grouping only scratches the surface of the Gestalt psychologists' contributions to our current understanding of perception. Other Gestalt insights will be noted throughout the chapter.

PERCEIVING DISTANCE

To know where an object is, we must know its distance or *depth.* Although perceiving an object's depth seems effortless, it is a remarkable achievement given the physical structure of our eyes.

DEPTH CUES   The retina, the starting point of vision, is a two-dimensional surface. This means the retinal image is flat and has no depth at all. This fact has led many students of perception (artists as well as scientists) to the idea of distance cues, two-dimensional aspects that a perceiver uses to infer distance in a three-dimensional world. There are a number of distance cues that combine to determine perceived distance. The cues can be classified as *monocular* or *binocular,* depending on whether they involve one or both eyes.

People using only one eye can perceive depth remarkably well by picking up monocular depth cues. Figure 5-7 illustrates four of these cues. The first is **relative size.** If an image contains an array of similar objects that differ in size, people interpret the smaller objects as being farther away (see Figure 5-7a). A second monocular cue is **superposition.** If one object is positioned so that it obstructs the view of the other, people perceive the overlapping object as being nearer (see Figure 5-7b).

A third cue is **relative height**. Among similar objects, those that appear higher are perceived as being farther away (see Figure 5-7c). A fourth cue is called **linear perspective**. When parallel lines appear to converge, they are perceived as vanishing in the distance (see Figure 5-7d). These four cues have been known to artists for centuries—they are called *pictorial cues* for this reason—and a single painting will often use more than one of the cues.

Another important monocular cue involves the use of motion. Have you ever noticed that if you are moving quickly—perhaps, on a fast-moving train—nearby objects seem to move quickly in the opposite direction while more distant objects move more slowly (though still in the opposite direction). The difference in speed with which these objects appear to move thus provides a cue as to their respective depths (this cue is referred to as **motion parallax**).

Seeing with both eyes rather than one has advantages for **depth perception**. Because the eyes are separated in the head, each eye perceives a three-dimensional object from a slightly different angle. Consequently each eye has a slightly different view of the object. Fusing these different views gives rise to an impression of depth. This can be demonstrated by a device called a *stereoscope*. The stereoscope displays a different photograph or drawing to each eye. If the two pictures are taken from slightly separated camera positions or drawn from slightly different perspectives, the viewer will experience vivid depth.

Binocular parallax is one cue that is responsible for this perception of depth. It hinges on the fact that any visible point will differ slightly in its direction to the two eyes. A related cue is **binocular disparity**; it is based on the difference between the retinal images on the two eyes when we look at an object from a distance. You can easily demonstrate these cues to yourself. Hold a pencil about a foot in front of you and, with only one eye open, line it up with a vertical edge of the wall opposite you. Then close that eye and open the other. The pencil will now appear in a different direction; the difference between these directions is binocular parallax. Also, the two edges that were lined up in the first eye will appear separated when you open the second eye, and indeed the images in the second eye are separated; the difference between the

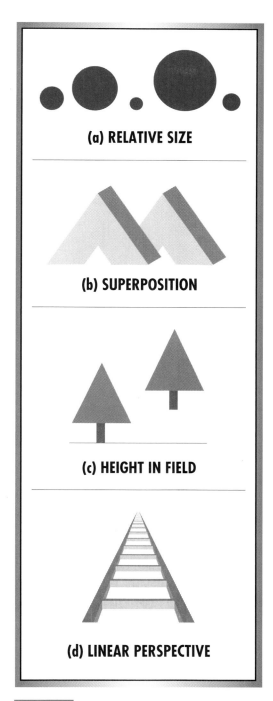

(a) RELATIVE SIZE

(b) SUPERPOSITION

(c) HEIGHT IN FIELD

(d) LINEAR PERSPECTIVE

FIGURE 5-7

Monocular Distance Cues   *The figure illustrates four monocular distance cues. These are used by artists to portray depth on a two-dimensional surface and are also present in photographs.*

retinal images in the two eyes is binocular disparity.

DIRECT PERCEPTION   The idea behind distance cues is that the observer notes a critical cue—

The Holmes–Bates stereoscope, invented by Oliver Wendell Holmes in 1861 and manufactured by Joseph Bates, creates a vivid perception of depth.

for instance, that one object appears larger than another—and then unconsciously infers distance information from the cue. This notion of **unconscious inference** was introduced by Helmholtz in 1909. While it continues to be a key idea in the study of perception (Rock, 1983), some psychologists have argued for another approach to depth perception.

Gibson (1979; 1966; 1950) claims that we do not infer depth, but rather perceive it directly. To appreciate Gibson's ideas, it is useful to consider *where* people routinely look for information about depth. Gibson argues that instead of looking for cues that characterize objects protruding in the air—such as relative size, superposition, and relative height—people look at information on the ground itself. The best example of such information is a **texture gradient** (see Figure 5-8). A texture gradient arises when we view a surface in perspective. The elements that make up the textured surface appear to be packed closer and closer together as the surface recedes. This gradient gives rise to a powerful impression of depth.

Unlike the standard distance cues, the gradient extends over a large visual area, and were you to move forward you could still determine your distance to any other point on the gradient. The gradient information on the retina, therefore, remains constant or, to use Gibson's term, *invariant*. Depth percep-

tion, according to Gibson, is a matter of directly perceiving such invariants. Thus, when we perceive depth in a scene, we need not process the information provided by scattered depth cues, but instead we can directly perceive the depth information provided by the texture gradient (Goldstein, 1989).

PERCEIVING MOTION

If we are to move around our environment effectively, we need to know not only the locations of static objects, but also the trajectories of moving ones. We need to know, for example, not only that the object located a few feet in front of us is a softball, but also that it is coming at us at a fast clip. This brings us to the issue of how we perceive motion.

STROBOSCOPIC MOTION   What causes us to perceive motion? The simplest idea is that we perceive an object is in motion whenever its image moves across our retina. This answer turns out to be too simple, though, for we can see motion even when *nothing* moves on our retina. This phenomenon was demonstrated in 1912 by Wertheimer in his studies of **stroboscopic motion** (see Figure 5-9). Stroboscopic motion is produced most simply by flashing a light in darkness and then, a few milliseconds later, flashing another light near the location of the first light. The light will seem to move from one place to the other in a way that is indistinguishable from real motion.

The motion that we see in movies is stroboscopic. The film is simply a series of still photographs (frames), each slightly different from the preceding. The frames are projected on the screen in rapid sequence, with dark intervals in between. The rate at which the frames are presented is critical. In the early days of motion pictures, the frame rate was 16 per second. This was too slow, and as a consequence movement in these early films appears too rapid, as well as jerky and disjointed. Today, the rate is usually 24 frames per second (with each frame typically shown a few times in succession to further reduce jumpiness).

INDUCED MOTION   Another case in which we perceive motion in the absence of movement

FIGURE 5-8

Examples of Texture Gradients   *The elements that make up the textured surface (rocks on left, people on right) appear to be packed closer and closer together as the surface recedes.*

across our retina is the phenomenon of in-duced motion. When a large object surrounding a smaller one moves, the smaller object may appear to be the one that is moving even if it is static. This phenomenon was first studied by the Gestalt psychologist, Duncker, in 1929. Duncker had subjects sit in a darkened room and observe a small luminous circle inside a larger luminous rectangular frame.

When the rectangle was moved to the right, subjects reported that the circle appeared to move to the left. This phenomenon may be at play on a windy night when the moon seems to be racing through the clouds.

REAL MOTION   Of course, our visual system is also sensitive to *real motion*—that is, motion induced by movement across the retina.

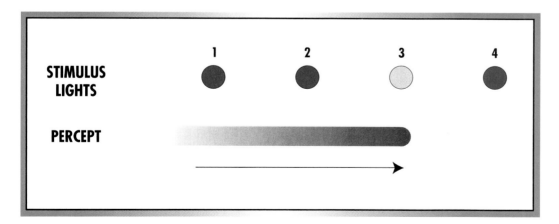

FIGURE 5-9

Stroboscopic Motion   *The four circles in the top row correspond to four lights. If these are flashed one after the other with a short dark interval in between, they will appear to be a single light in continuous motion, such as that suggested in the second row. This is stroboscopic motion; motion in movies and on television is of this kind.*

We are much better at detecting motion when we can see an object against a structured background *(relative motion)* than when the background is dark or neutral and only the moving object can be seen *(absolute motion)*. According to Gibson (1979; 1966), there is a distinctive pattern of information produced in relative motion. Specifically, as the object moves, it covers and uncovers parts of the background. Gibson argues that we can use this pattern to directly perceive motion, just as we can directly perceive depth.

Another important phenomenon in the study of real motion is called **selective adaptation**. Selective adaptation is a loss in sensitivity to motion that occurs when we view motion; the adaptation is selective in that we lose sensitivity to the motion viewed and to similar motions, but not to motion that differs significantly in direction or speed. If we look at upward-moving stripes, for example, we lose sensitivity to upward motion but our ability to see downward motion is not affected (Sekuler & Ganz, 1963). As with other types of adaptation, we do not usually notice the sensitivity loss but we do notice the aftereffect produced by adaptation. If we view a waterfall for a few minutes and then look at the cliff beside it, the cliff will appear to move upward. Most motions will produce such a **motion aftereffect** in the opposite direction.

With regard to how the brain implements the perception of real motion, some aspects of real motion are coded by specific cells in the visual cortex. These cells respond to some motions and not to others, and each cell responds best to one direction and speed of motion. The best evidence for the existence of such cells comes from studies with animals, in which the experimenter records from single cells in the visual cortex while the animal is presented stimuli with different patterns of motion (refer to Figure 4-4 again). Such single-cell recording studies have found cortical cells tuned to particular directions of movement. There are even cells specifically tuned to detect an object moving toward the head, clearly useful for survival (Regan, Beverly, & Cynader, 1979). Again, it is striking how the visual cortex distributes its various jobs over different areas and cells.

These specialized motion cells provide a possible explanation of selective adaptation and the motion aftereffect. Presumably, selective adaptation to an upward motion, for example, occurs because the cortical cells specialized for upward motion have become fatigued; because the cells specialized for downward motion are functioning as usual, they will dominate the processing and result in the aftereffect of downward motion.

However, there is more to the neural basis of real motion than the activation of specific cells. We can see motion when we track a luminous object moving in darkness (such as an airplane at night). Because our eyes follow the object, the image makes only a small, irregular motion on the retina (due to imperfect tracking), yet we perceive a smooth, continuous motion. Why? The answer seems to be that information about how our eyes are moving is sent from motor regions in the front of the brain to our visual cortex and influences the motion that we see. In essence, the visual system is being informed by the motor system that the latter is responsible for the lack of regular motion on the retina, and the visual system then corrects for this lack. In more normal viewing situations, there are both eye movements and large retinal-image movements. The visual system must combine these two sources of information to determine the perceived motion.

MOTION AND EVENT PERCEPTION Sometimes the motion of objects tells us not only about where the objects are, but also about what they are doing. Thus, our perception of motion is directly tied to our perception of events. A barking dog racing toward an intruder is perceived not just as a "moving dog" but as the event, "a dog is attacking."

Motion is particularly important in our perception of simple causal events. When two objects are in motion, we may perceive one as having *caused* the motion of the other. In a demonstration of this, Michotte (1963) used squares like those in Figure 5-10 as stimuli. When square A moves to square B, and then B immediately begins to move in the direction A was moving, subjects report that A caused B's movement; more specifically, A seems to launch B. (This perception of causality, however, obtains only when the interval between when A reaches B and when B starts to move is very brief, roughly, less than one-fifth of a second.) Furthermore, the perception of causality is not mediated by conscious inferences. The subject does not explicitly reason to herself that "A hit B and B moved, so A must have caused B to move." Rather, causality appears to be perceived without any intervening reasoning (Goldstein, 1989).

This remarkable ability to directly perceive physical causality is present in very young children (Leslie, 1987) and is as pronounced in members of Eastern cultures as it is in members of Western cultures (Morris, 1995).

RECOGNITION

We turn now to the second major function of perception: recognizing what an object is. Recognizing an object amounts to assigning it to a category—that's a shirt, that's a cat, that's a daisy, and so on. Of course, we can also recognize people, which amounts to assigning the visual input to a particular individual—that's Ben Murphy, or this is Irene Paull. In either case, objects or people, recognition allows us to infer many hidden properties of the object—if it's a shirt then it's made of cloth and I can wear it; if it's a cat then it may scratch me if I pull its tail; if it's Ben Murphy he'll want to tell me about his baseball exploits, and so on. Recognition is what allows us to go beyond the information given.

What attributes of an object do we use to recognize it? Shape, size, color, texture, orientation, and so on? While all of these attributes may make some contribution, shape appears to play the critical role. We can recognize a cup, for example, regardless of whether it is large or small (a variation in size), or brown or white (a variation in color), or smooth or bumpy (a texture variation), or presented upright or tilted slightly (an orientation variation). In contrast, our ability to recognize a cup is strikingly affected by variations in shape; if part of the cup's shape is occluded, we may not recognize it at all. One piece of evidence for the importance of shape to recognition is that we can recognize many objects about as well from simple line drawings, which preserve only the shapes of the objects, as from detailed color photographs, which preserve many attributes of the objects (Biederman & Ju, 1988).

The critical question then becomes: How do we use the shape of an object to assign it to its appropriate category? In dealing with

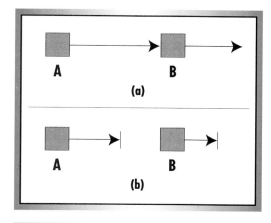

FIGURE 5-10

Motion and the Perception of Causality *When square A moves to square B, and B then immediately begins to move, subjects report that A "launches" B (a). The perception of causality is somewhat different when A stops before it reaches B (b).*

this question, first we focus on simple objects like letters of the alphabet, and later consider natural objects like animals and furniture.

EARLY STAGES OF RECOGNITION

Following Marr (1982), we may distinguish between *early* and *late* stages in recognizing an object. We will characterize these stages by what they accomplish. In early stages, the perceptual system uses information on the retina, particularly variations in intensity, to describe the object in terms of primitive components like lines, edges, and angles. The system uses these primitive components to construct a description of the object itself. In later stages, the system compares the object's description to shape descriptions of various categories of objects stored in visual memory and selects the best match. To recognize a particular object as the letter B, for example, is to say that the object's shape matches that of B's better than it matches that of other letters. Most of the processing in both the early and late stages of recognition are not available to consciousness. For now, our concern is with the early stages, which construct the shape description of the object.

FEATURE DETECTORS IN THE CORTEX Much of what is known about the primitive features of object perception comes from biological studies of other species (cats, monkeys) that use single-cell recordings in the visual cortex (refer back to Figure 4-4). These studies examine the sensitivity of specific cortical neurons when different stimuli are presented to the regions of the retina associated with these neurons; such a retinal region is called a **receptive field** of a cortical neuron. These single-cell studies were pioneered by Hubel and Wiesel (1968), who shared a Nobel prize in 1981 for their research.

Hubel and Wiesel identified three types of cells in the visual cortex that can be distinguished by the features to which they respond. **Simple cells** respond when the eye is exposed to a line stimulus (such as a thin bar or straight edge between a dark and a light region) at a particular orientation and position within their receptive field. Figure 5-11 illustrates how a simple cell will respond to a vertical bar and to bars tilted away from the vertical. The response decreases as the orientation varies from the optimal one. Other simple cells are tuned to other orientations and positions. A **complex cell** also responds to a bar or edge in a particular orientation, but it does not require that the stimulus be at a particular place within its receptive field. A complex cell responds to the stimulus anywhere within

its receptive field, and it responds continuously as the stimulus is moved across its receptive field. **Hypercomplex cells** require not only that the stimulus be in a particular orientation, but also that it be of a particular length. If a stimulus is extended beyond the optimal length, the response will decrease and may cease entirely. Since Hubel and Wiesel's initial reports, investigators have found cells that respond to shape features other than single bars and edges; for example, hypercomplex cells that respond to corners or angles of a specific length (Shapley & Lennie, 1985; De-Valois & DeValois, 1980).

All of the cells described above are referred to as **feature detectors**. Because the edges, bars, corners, and angles to which these detectors respond can be used to approximate many shapes, the feature detectors might be thought of as the building blocks of shape perception. As we will see later, though, this proposal seems more true of simple shapes like letters than of complex shapes like those of tables and tigers.

BEHAVIORAL INDICATORS OF FEATURES Cognitive researchers have developed behavioral tests of primitive features of objects that can be used with humans. One of the best-known tech-

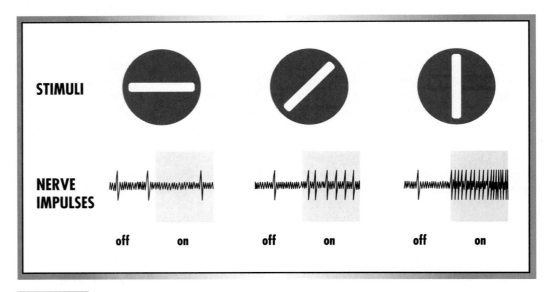

FIGURE 5-11

Response of a Simple Cell *This figure illustrates the response of a simple cortical cell to a bar of light. The stimulus is on the top, the response on the bottom; each vertical spike on the bottom corresponds to one nerve impulse. When there is no stimulus, only an occasional impulse is recorded. When the stimulus is turned on, the cell may or may not respond, depending on the position and orientation of the light bar. For this cell a horizontal bar produces no change in response, a bar at 45 degrees produces a small change, and a vertical bar produces a very large change.*

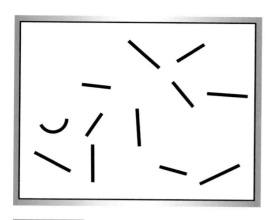

FIGURE 5-12

Searching for a Curve *The time it takes to find the curve does not depend on the number of straight lines surrounding it.* (After Treisman & Gormican, 1988)

niques was devised by Treisman (for example, Treisman & Gormican, 1988). On each trial of the task, subjects are presented an array of items and have to decide as quickly as possible whether the array contains a target. For example, the target might be a curve and the nontargets straight lines, as illustrated in Figure 5-12. What varies from trial to trial is the number of nontargets—which can be between 3 and 30—and the question of interest is how this number affects the time to detect the target. If the target is defined by a primitive feature, a viewer might be able to search an array for it in parallel, rather than examine each nontarget in series. Consequently, the number of nontargets should have no effect on the time to detect a primitive feature. This is exactly what happens with arrays like that in Figure 5-12, which suggests that curvature is a primitive feature of objects. Phenomenologically, the curve seems to "pop out" of the array; for this reason, a demonstration of parallel search in this task is referred to as the **pop-out effect**.

Treisman has found pop-out effects for a number of other features. Two such features are the length of a line (a long line pops out from an array of short ones) and the amount of brightness contrast between neighboring dots (a high-contrast pair pops out). These two features, like curvature, could well play a role in determining shape. However, other features that pass the pop-out test, such as color, have nothing to do with shape. These results indicate that the primitive features of objects are simple properties that characterize points and lines, with some but not all of these properties being related to shape.

RELATIONS BETWEEN FEATURES There is more to a description of a shape than just its features: Relations between features must also be specified. The importance of such relations is illustrated in Figure 5-13. The features of a printed T include a vertical line and a horizontal line, but unless these lines are combined in the right way, the resulting pattern is not a T. The description of a T must include the fact that the horizontal line is attached to the top of the vertical line at its center. It is this kind of relation between features that the Gestalt psychologists had in mind when they cautioned psychologists years ago that "the whole is different from the sum of its parts."

THE MATCHING STAGE AND CONNECTIONIST MODELS

Now that we have some idea of how an object's shape is described, we can consider how that description is matched to shape descriptions stored in memory to find the best match.

SIMPLE NETWORKS Much of the research on the matching stage has used simple patterns, specifically handwritten or printed letters or words. Figure 5-14 illustrates a proposal about how we store shape descriptions of letters. The basic idea is that letters are described in terms of certain features, and that knowledge about what features go with what letter is contained in a network of connections (hence the term, **connectionist models**). What is appealing about connectionist

FIGURE 5-13

Relations between Features *All forms include the features of a vertical line and a horizontal line, but only the rightmost form has the relation between features characteristic of the letter T.*

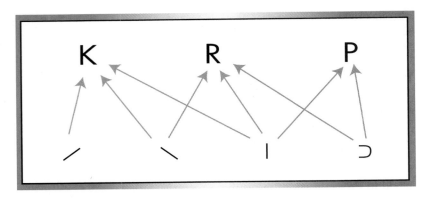

FIGURE 5-14

A Simple Network   *The bottom level of the network contains the features (ascending diagonal, descending diagonal, vertical line, and right-facing curve), the top level contains the letters, and a connection between a feature and a letter means the feature is part of the letter. Because the connections are excitatory, when a feature is activated the activation spreads to the letter.*

The network in Figure 5-14 tells us that Ks are described by an ascending diagonal, a descending diagonal, and a vertical line; Rs are described by a descending diagonal, a vertical line, and a right-facing curve, and Ps are described by a vertical line and a right-facing curve. (To keep the discussion simple, we will ignore relations between features.) To see how this network can be used to recognize (or match) a letter, consider what happens when the letter K is presented. It will activate the features of ascending diagonal, descending diagonal, and vertical line. All three of these features will activate the node for K; two of them—the descending diagonal and vertical line—will activate the node for R; and one of them—the vertical line—will activate the node for P. Only the K node has all of its features activated, and consequently it will be selected as the best match.

The above model is too simple to account for many aspects of recognition. To see what the model lacks, consider what happens when the letter R is presented (see Figure 5-14). It activates the features of descending diagonal, vertical line, and right-facing curve. Now both the nodes for R and P will have all their features activated, and the model has no way of deciding which of the two categories provides a better match. What the model needs to know to choose between these categories is that the presence of a descending diagonal means the input *cannot* be a P. This kind of negative knowledge is included in the augmented network in Figure 5-15. This network has everything the preceding one had, plus *inhibitory* connections (symbolized by solid circles at their ends) between features and letters that do not contain these features. When a feature is connected to a letter by an inhibitory connection, activating the feature *decreases* activation of the letter. When R is presented to the network in Figure 5-15, the descending diagonal sends inhibition to the P node thereby decreasing its overall level of activation; now the R node will receive the most activation and consequently will be selected as the best match.

models is that it is easy to conceive how these networks could be realized in the brain with its array of interconnected neurons. Thus, *connectionism* offers a bridge between psychological and biological models.

The bottom level of the network in Figure 5-14 contains the features—ascending diagonal, descending diagonal, vertical line, and right-facing curve, for example. The top level contains the letters themselves. We will refer to each of these features and letters as a *node* in the network. A connection between a feature and a letter node means that the feature is part of the letter. The fact that the connections have arrowheads at their ends means they are *excitatory* connections; if the feature is activated, the activation spreads to the letter (in a manner analogous to how electrical impulses spread in a network of neurons).

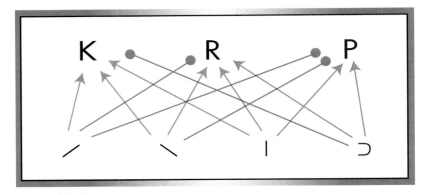

FIGURE 5-15

An Augmented Network   *The network contains inhibitory connections between features and letters that do not contain these features, as well as excitatory connections.*

The preceding discussion illustrates some critical properties of connectionist networks (Rumelhart & McClelland, 1986; McClelland & Rumelhart, 1986). The networks in Figures 5-14 and 5-15 are composed of only two kinds of entities: a) nodes designing features or patterns (such as the node for an upright line, or that at for the letter R); and b) connections between nodes that are either excitatory or inhibitory. All connectionist networks are restricted to just nodes and connections.* Furthermore, the networks in Figures 5-14 and 5-15 allow an object to be compared to all stored shape descriptions *simultaneously* (the feature information is passed to all letter nodes at once); this is in contrast to comparing the object to the stored shape descriptions one at a time or *sequentially*. Simultaneous processing (also called **parallel processing**) is characteristic of connectionist models.

NETWORKS WITH FEEDBACK The basic idea behind the model we just considered—that a letter must be described by the features it lacks as well as the features it contains—was originally proposed by researchers in artificial intelligence who were trying to write computer programs to simulate human letter perception (Selfridge & Neisser, 1960). Although the ideas were relatively successful for a time, ultimately they proved inadequate to explain findings about how context affects our ability to perceive letters. In particular, they could not explain why a letter is easier to perceive when presented as part of a word than when presented alone. Thus, if subjects are briefly presented a display containing either the single letter K or the word WORK, and are then asked whether the last letter was a K or a D, they are more accurate when the display contained a word than when it contained only a letter (see Figure 5-16).

To account for this result, our network of feature-letter connections has to be altered in a few ways. First, we have to add a level of words to our network, and along with it excitatory and inhibitory connections that go from letters to words (see Figure 5-17). In addition, we also have to add excitatory connections that go from words down to letters; these *top-down feedback* connections explain why a letter is more perceptible when presented briefly in a word than when presented briefly alone. When R is presented alone, for example, the features of vertical line, descending diagonal, and right-facing curve are activated, and this activation spreads to the node for R. Because the letter was presented very briefly, not all the features may have

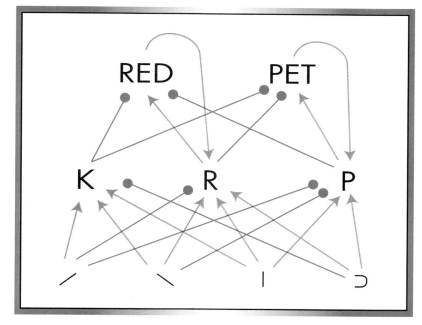

FIGURE 5-16

Perception of Letters and Words *This figure illustrates the sequence of events in an experiment that compares the perceptibility of a letter presented alone or in the context of a word. First, subjects saw a fixation point, followed by a word or a single letter, which was present for only a few milliseconds. Then the experimenter presented a stimulus that contained a visual mask in the positions where the letters had been, plus two response alternatives. The subjects' task was to decide which of the two alternatives occurred in the word or letter presented earlier.* (After Reicher, 1969)

FIGURE 5-17

---

* Each connection is usually accompanied by a number, or *weight*, indicating the strength of the connection.

Network with Top-Down Activation *The network contains excitatory and inhibitory connections between letters and words (as well as between features and letters), and some of the excitatory connections go from words to letters.*

been fully activated, and the activation culminating at the R node may not be sufficient for recognition to occur. In contrast, when R is presented in RED, there is activation not only from the features of R to the R node, but also from the features of E and D to their nodes; all of these partially activated letters then partially activate the RED node, which in turn feeds back activation to its letters via its top-down connections.

The upshot is that there is an additional source of activation for R when it is presented in a word—namely, that coming down from the word—and this is why it is easier to recognize a letter in a word than when it is presented alone. Many other findings about letter and word patterns have been shown to be consistent with this connectionist model (McClelland & Rumelhart, 1981).

RECOGNIZING NATURAL OBJECTS AND TOP-DOWN PROCESSING

We know quite a bit about the recognition of letters and words, but what about more natural objects—animals, plants, people, furniture, and clothing?

FEATURES OF NATURAL OBJECTS   The shape features of natural objects are more complex than lines and curves, and more like simple geometric forms. The features must be such that they can combine to form the shape of any recognizable object (just as lines and curves can combine to form any letter). The features of objects must also be such that they can be determined or constructed from more primitive features, such as lines and curves, because primitive features are the only information the system initially has available. These criteria have guided the search for a possible set of object features.

One proposal is that the features of objects include a number of geometric forms, such as cylinders, cones, blocks, and wedges, as illustrated in Figure 5-18a. These features are referred to as *geons* (a neologism of *geometric ions*), and they were developed by Biederman (1987). Biederman argues that a set of 36 geons like those in Figure 5-18a, combined according to a small set of spatial relations, is sufficient to describe the shapes of all objects that people can possibly recognize. To appreciate this point, note that the number of possible objects composed of just two geons is 36 × 36 (you can form a possible object by combining any two geons—see Figure 5-18b) while the number of possible three-geon objects is 36 × 36 × 36. The sum of these two numbers is already on the order of 30,000, and we have yet to consider objects made up of 4 or more geons. Furthermore, geons like those in Figure 5-18a can be distinguished solely in terms of primitive features. For example, geon 2 in Figure 5-18a, the cube, differs from geon 3, the cylinder, in that the cube has straight edges but the cylinder has curved edges; straight and curved edges are primitive features.

Evidence that geons are features comes from experiments in which subjects try to recognize pictured objects that are presented briefly. The general finding is that recognition of an object is good to the extent the geons of the object are perceptible. In one study, part of the shape of an object was deleted where this deletion either interfered with recovering the geons (see the right column of Figure 5-19) or not (middle column of Figure 5-19). Recognition of the objects was much better when there was no interference with the geons.

As usual, the description of an object includes not just its features but also the rela-

FIGURE 5-18

A Possible Set of Features (Geons) for Natural Objects   *(a) Wedges, cubes, cylinders, and cones may be features of complex objects. (b) When the features (geons) are combined, they form natural objects. Note that when the arc (geon 5) is connected to the side of the cylinder (geon 3), it forms a cup; when connected to the top of the cylinder, it forms a pail. (After Biederman, 1990)* tions between them. This is evident in Figure 5-18b. When the arc is connected to the side of the cylinder, it forms a cup; when connected to the top of the cylinder, it forms a pail. Once the description of an object's shape is constructed, it is compared to an array of geon descriptions stored in memory to find the best match. This matching process between the description of an object's shape and the descriptions stored in memory resembles the process described earlier for letters and words (Hummel & Biederman, 1992).

TOP-DOWN PROCESSES AND CONTEXT   A key distinction in perception is that between bottom-up and top-down processes. **Bottom-up processes** are driven solely by the input, whereas **top-down processes** are driven by a person's knowledge and expectations. To illustrate, recognizing that an object is a lamp on the basis of solely its geon description involves only bottom-up processes; one starts with primitive features of the input, determines the geon configuration of the input, and then compares this input description to stored shape descriptions. In contrast, recognizing that the object is a lamp partly on the basis of its being on a night table next to a bed involves some top-down processes; one brings to bear information other than that in the input. While most of the processes considered thus far in this chapter are bottom-up ones, top-down processes also play a major role in object perception.

Top-down processes are what lie behind the powerful effects that context has on our perception of objects and people. You expect to see your chemistry lab partner Sarah at the lab every Tuesday at 3 P.M., and when she enters the lab at that moment you hardly need to look to tell that it's she. Your prior knowledge has led to a powerful expectation, and little input is needed for recognition. But should Sarah suddenly appear in your home town during Christmas vacation, you may have substantial trouble recognizing her. She is *out of context*—your expectations have been violated, and you must resort to extensive bottom-up processing to tell that it is in fact she (we experience this as "doing a double take"). As this example makes clear, when the context is appropriate (that is, it predicts the input object), it facilitates perception; when inappropriate, the context impairs perception.

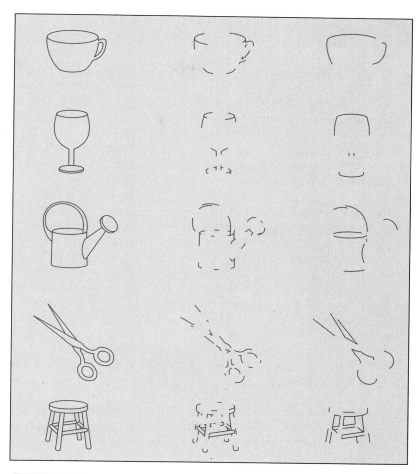

FIGURE 5-19

Object Recognition and Geon Recovery   *Items used in experiments on object recognition. The left column shows the original intact versions of the objects. The middle column shows versions of the objects where regions have been deleted, but the geons are still recoverable. The right column shows versions of the objects where regions have been deleted, and the geons are not recoverable. Recognition is better for the middle versions than for the rightmost versions.* (After Biederman, 1987)

The effects of context are particularly striking when the stimulus object is *ambiguous,* that is, can be perceived in more than one way. An ambiguous figure is presented in Figure 5-20; it can be perceived either as an old woman or as a young woman (though the old woman is more likely to be seen initially). If you have been looking at unambiguous pictures that resemble the young woman in Figure 5-20 (that is, if young women are the context), you will tend to see the young woman first in the ambiguous picture. This effect of *temporal context* is illustrated with another set of pictures in Figure 5-21. Look at the pictures as you would look at a comic strip, from left to right and top to bottom. The pictures in the middle of the series are

CRITICAL DISCUSSION

BREAKDOWN OF RECOGNITION

Recognizing an object is usually so automatic and effortless a process that we take it for granted. But the process can break down if people suffer brain damage (due to accidents or diseases like strokes). The general term for disorders in recognition is *agnosia*.

ASSOCIATIVE AGNOSIA   Of particular interest is a type of agnosia called **associative agnosia**. This is a syndrome in which patients with damage to particular regions of the cortex have difficulty recognizing objects only when they are presented visually. For example, the patient may be unable to name a comb when presented a picture of it, but can name it when allowed to touch it. The deficit is exemplified by the following case:

> For the first three weeks in the hospital the patient could not identify common objects presented visually and did not know what was on his plate until he tasted it. He identified objects immediately on touching them [but] when shown a stethoscope, he described it as "a long cord with a round thing at the end," and asked if it could be a watch. He identified a can opener as "could be a key." Asked to name a

cigarette lighter, he said, "I don't know." He said he was "not sure" when shown a toothbrush. Asked to identify a comb, he said, "I don't know." For a pipe, he said, "some type of utensil, I'm not sure." Shown a key, he said, "I don't know what that is; perhaps a file or a tool of some sort." (Reubens & Benson, 1971)

What aspects of object recognition have broken down in associative agnosia? Since these patients often do well on visual tasks other than recognition—such as drawing objects or determining whether two pictured objects match—the breakdown is likely to be in the later stages of recognition, where the input object is matched to stored object descriptions. One possibility is that the stored object descriptions have been lost or obscured (Damasio, 1985).

CATEGORY SPECIFIC DEFICITS   Some patients with associative agnosia have problems recognizing certain categories but not others. These category-specific deficits are of considerable interest because they may tell us something new about how normal recognition works.

The most frequent category-specific deficit is a loss just of the ability to

recognize faces, called **prosopagnosia**. When this deficit arises, there is always brain damage in the right hemisphere and often some lesser degree of damage in homologous regions of the left hemisphere. The deficit is illustrated by the following case:

> He could not identify his medical attendants. "You must be a doctor because of your white coat, but I don't know which one you are. I'll know if you speak." He failed to identify his wife during visiting hours. . . . He failed to identify pictures of Churchill, Hitler, and Marilyn Monroe. When confronted with such portraits he would proceed deductively, searching for the `critical' detail which would yield the answer. (Pallis, 1955)

A second kind of category deficit is a loss just of the ability to recognize words, called *pure alexia* (typically accompanied by damage in the left occipital lobe). Patients with this deficit are typically unimpaired in recognizing natural objects or faces. They can even identify individual letters. What they cannot do is recognize visually presented words. When presented a word, they will attempt to read it letter by letter. Because they

---

FIGURE 5-20

Ambiguous Stimulus
An ambiguous drawing that can be seen either as a young woman or as an old woman. Most people see the old woman first. The young woman is turning away, and we see the left side of her face. Her chin is the old woman's nose, and her necklace is the old woman's mouth. (After Boring, 1930)

ambiguous. If you view the figures in the sequence just suggested, you will tend to see these ambiguous pictures as a man's face. If you view the figures in the opposite order,

you will tend to see the ambiguous pictures as a young woman.

The stimulus object need not be ambiguous in order to demonstrate the effect of context. Suppose a person is first shown a picture of a scene, and is then briefly presented a picture of an unambiguous object to identify; identification will be more accurate if the object is appropriate to the scene. For example, after looking at a kitchen scene, a subject will correctly identify a briefly presented loaf of bread more often than he or she will a briefly presented mailbox (Palmer, 1975).

Because of top-down processing, our motives and desires can potentially affect our perceptions. If we are very hungry, a quick glance at a red ball on our kitchen table may register a tomato. Our desire for food has led us to think about food, and these expectations have combined with the input (a red, round take this approach, people with pure alexia can require as much as ten seconds to recognize a common word, with the amount of time needed substantially increasing with the number of letters in the word (Bub, Blacks, & Howell 1989).

Still another kind of category-specific deficit involves an impairment in the ability to recognize most living things, while recognition of nonliving things is relatively intact. (Occasionally, one finds a patient with the opposite problem—impaired on nonliving things, intact on living things—but this seems to be rare.)

In these cases, "living things" include animals, plants, and foods, whereas "nonliving things" typically include human-made objects or artifacts, particularly manipulable ones like tools. Thus, a patient with this kind of category-specific disorder might be unable to name pictures of familiar barnyard animals, but have no problem with household tools. (Warrington & Shallice, 1984).

Some of the suggested explanations of category-specific deficits have implications for normal recognition. One hypothesis is that the normal

recognition system is organized around different classes of objects— one subsystem for faces, another for words a third for animals, and so on—and these subsystems are localized in different regions of the brain. If a patient suffers only restricted brain damage, he or she may show a loss of one subsystem, but not others. Brain damage in a specific part of the right hemisphere, for example, might disrupt the face-recognition subsystem, but leave the other subsystems intact.

This kind of explanation, which again emphasizes the division-of-labor principle of the visual system, seems promising in explaining prosopagnosia and pure alexia, because the materials involved are so different and because often the deficit is so pure (Farah, 1990).

But researchers have been more reluctant to accept the idea that we have one mechanism for recognizing animals and another for recognizing artifacts. To account for a deficit with animals and other living things, two other hypotheses have gained favor. One is that living things, particularly animals, differ from artifacts in that

members of the same category are often similar in overall shape (think of various birds, or butterflies, or fish). As a consequence, one cannot recognize some animals based solely on their overall shape and instead must rely on other distinguishing criteria. If this extra processing is what is disrupted by brain damage, then it follows that brain damage will have more deleterious effects on the recognition of living things than the recognition of artifacts (Damasio, 1990). The second hypothesis of interest starts from the observation that perceptual information is more important than functional information in characterizing living things, but the two kinds of information are of about equal importance for artifacts. If brain damage is more likely to affect perceptual than functional information, it follows that the recognition of living things will be more impaired than the recognition of artifacts (Farah & McClelland, 1991). At this point, there is evidence for both hypotheses.

FIGURE 5-21

Effect of Temporal Context   *What you see here depends on the order in which you look at the pictures. The pictures in the middle of the series are ambiguous. If you have been looking at pictures of a man's face, they will appear to be distorted faces. If you have been looking at pictures of a woman, they will look like a woman.* (After Fisher, 1967) object) to yield the percept of a tomato. Our motives can also have a pernicious effect on perception. If we believe a man to be a child molester, for example, we are more likely to misperceive his innocent touching of a child as sexual.

Context effects and top-down processing also occur with letters and words, and play a major role in reading. When we read, we do not scan a line of text in a smooth continuous motion. Rather, our eyes are still for a brief period, then jump to another position on the line, are still for another brief period, then jump again (perhaps to a different line), and so on. The periods during which the eyes are still, called *fixations,* are when our visual system extracts information. Both the number of fixations we make, and the durations of these fixations, are greatly influenced by how much we know about the text, and hence by the amount of top-down processing we can invoke. When the material is unfamiliar—say, unfamiliar scientific material—there is little top-down processing. In such cases, we tend to fixate every word, except for certain function words like "a," "of," "the," and so on. As the material becomes more familiar, we can bring to bear our prior knowledge in top-down processes, and our fixations become wider spaced and shorter (Just & Carpenter, 1980; Rayner, 1978).

Top-Down Processes and Degraded Input   Top-down processing occurs even in the absence of context, if the input is sufficiently sparse or degraded. Suppose that at a friend's apartment you enter her dark kitchen and see a smallish black object in the corner. You think the object could be your friend's cat, but the perceptual input is too degraded to convince you of this, so you think of a particular feature of the cat, say, its tail, and then selectively attend to the region of the object likely to contain that feature if it is indeed a cat (Kosslyn & Koenig, 1992). This processing is top-down, as you have used some specific knowledge—that cats have tails—to generate an expectation, which then is combined with the visual input. Situations like this one are common in everyday life. Sometimes, if the input is very degraded, the expectations that we form may be way off the mark, as when we finally realize that our would-be cat in the kitchen is really our friend's purse.

ATTENTION

Our discussions of localization and recognition have often presupposed the notion of attention. To determine the motion of a plane, one must attend to its path; to recognize a particular object, one must first attend to it; and to determine if that black thing in your friend's kitchen has a tail, one must attend to the appropriate location of the object.

Attention involves selectivity. Most of the time we are bombarded with so many stimuli that we are unable to recognize all of them. As you sit reading, stop for a moment, close your eyes, and attend to the various stimuli that are reaching you. Notice, for example, the tightness of your left shoe. What sounds do you hear? Is there an odor in the air? You probably were not aware of these inputs before, because you had not selected them for recognition. The process by which we select is called **selective attention.**

In what follows, first we discuss the means by which we accomplish selectivity, next take up the question of when selectivity occurs relative to other processes, and then consider what is known about the neural basis of attention.

SELECTIVE LOOKING AND LISTENING

SELECTIVE LOOKING   How exactly do we direct our attention to objects of interest? The simplest means is by physically reorienting our sensory receptors so as to favor those objects. For vision, this means moving our eyes until the object of interest falls on the most sensitive region of the retina.

Studies of visual attention often involve observing a subject looking at a picture or scene. If we watch the subject's eyes it is evident that they are not stationary; rather, they are scanning. As was the case in reading, scanning is not a smooth continuous motion, but, rather, it involves successive fixations. There are a number of techniques for recording these eye movements. The simplest method is to monitor the eyes with a television camera in such a way that what the eye is gazing at is reflected on the cornea of the eye so it appears on television superimposed on the image of the eye. From this superimposed image, the experimenter can determine the point in the scene where the eye is fixated.

The eye movements used in scanning a picture ensure that different parts of the picture will fall on the fovea so that all of its details can be seen. (As noted in the previous chapter, the fovea has the best resolution.) The points on which the eyes fixate are not random. They tend to be places that are most informative about the picture, places where important features are located. For example, in scanning a photograph of a face, many fixations are in the regions corresponding to the eyes, nose, and mouth) (see Figure 5-22).

We can also selectively attend to something without moving our eyes. In experiments that demonstrate this, subjects have to detect when an object occurs. On each trial, the subject stares at a blank field, then sees a cue presented briefly, and then an object. The interval between the cue and object is too brief for the subject to move his eyes, but yet he can detect the object faster when it occurs in the cued location than elsewhere. Presumably, the subject is attending to the cued location even though he cannot move his eyes there (Posner, 1980).

SELECTIVE LISTENING   In audition, the closest thing to eye movements is moving our head so that our ears are directed at the source of interest. This mechanism of attention is of limited use in many situations, though. Consider, for example, a crowded party. The sounds of many voices bombard our ears, and their sources are not far enough apart that reorienting our ears would allow us to selectively follow one conversation. We are able, however, to use purely mental means to selectively attend to the desired message. Some of the cues that we use to do this are the direction of the sound, the lip movements of the speaker, and the particular voice characteristics of the speaker (pitch, speed, and intonation). Even in the absence of any of these cues, we can, with difficulty, select one of two messages to follow on the basis of its meaning.

Research on what is called the *cocktail party phenomenon* indicates that we remember very little of auditory messages that we do not attend to. A common procedure in this research is to put earphones on a subject and play one message through one ear and another message through the other ear. The

FIGURE 5-22

Eye Movements in Viewing a Picture   *Next to the picture of the young girl is a record of the eye movements made by a subject inspecting the picture.* (After Yarbus, 1967)

subject is asked to repeat (or *shadow*) one of the messages as it is heard. After proceeding in this way for a few minutes, the messages are turned off and the listener is asked about the unshadowed message. The person can report very little about it. The listener's remarks are usually limited to the physical characteristics of the sound in the unshadowed ear—whether the voice was high or low, male or female, and so forth; he or she can say almost nothing about the content of the message (Moray, 1969).

The fact that we can report so little about unattended auditory messages initially led researchers to the idea that nonattended stimuli are filtered out completely (Broadbent, 1958). However, there is now considerable evidence that our perceptual system processes nonattended stimuli to some extent (in vision as well as audition), even though they rarely reach consciousness. One piece of evidence for partial processing of nonattended stimuli is that we are very likely to hear the sound of our own name even when spoken softly in a nonattended conversation. This could not happen if the entire nonattended message were lost at lower levels of the perceptual

Although we may hear a number of conversations around us, as at a cocktail party, we remember very little of what we do not attend to.

system. Hence, a lack of attention does not block messages entirely, but rather *attenuates* them, much like a volume control that is turned down but not off (Treisman, 1969).

Early versus Late Selection

When does selectivity occur? Does it happen in the early stages of recognition—when constructing a description of the input—or only during the later stages—when comparing the input's descriptions to those of stored objects? The issue is important because it concerns whether we can selectively ignore something before we know what it means—**early selection**—or only after we know its meaning—**late selection.**

There is now evidence for both early and late selection. Some evidence for early selection comes from studies that record electrical activity in the auditory cortex (that part of the cortex that processes auditory information). These studies take as their starting point the findings that any auditory stimulus will trigger a sequence of brain waves, some of which occur early and are known to reflect processes prior to the determination of a stimulus' meaning. Thus, roughly 100 milliseconds after the onset of stimulus, there is a brain wave that is known to be insensitive to variations in meaning (hardly surprising given how early the wave occurs). This wave

has been measured when human subjects are performing attentional tasks. Consider an experiment in which in one condition subjects monitored one ear for targets, whereas in another condition they monitored both ears for targets. In the latter condition, subjects had to divide their attention, that is, divide their selectivity. If selectivity occurs early, the difference between conditions should have been reflected in the early brain wave described above. In fact, the amplitude of this wave was less when a target occurred in the divided attention condition than when it occurred in the other condition (Hillyard, 1985).

Evidence for late selection comes from experiments that use strictly behavioral techniques, and that try to show that the meaning of nonattended stimuli gets through. In one experiment, subjects wearing earphones listened to sentences spoken to one ear and ignored everything said in the other ear. The subjects were further required to paraphrase the sentence heard on the attended ear. Some of these sentences contained an ambiguous word, as in "The man walked by the bank," where "bank" could mean either a financial institution or a place by a river. How subjects paraphrased the sentence indicates how they interpreted the ambiguous word. At the same time the attended ear was hearing the ambiguous word, the unattended ear was exposed to a word related to one of its two meanings, say, "river." Subjects' paraphrases of the attended sentence was biased by what was presented at the unattended ear: For example, with "river" on the unattended ear, a likely paraphrase might be "The man strolled by the water." This effect could arise only if subjects were determining the meaning of unattended words. Hence, selection in this task was accomplished late (Lackner & Garrett, 1973).

THE NEURAL BASIS OF ATTENTION

In the past few years, there have been breakthroughs in our understanding of the neural basis of attention, particularly for visual attention. The research of interest has concerned two major questions: (1) What brain structures mediate the psychological act of selecting an object to attend to?, and (2) How does the subsequent neural processing differ for attended and non-attended stimuli? Let's consider these questions in turn.

It appears that the brain contains two separate systems that mediate the selection of inputs. One system is geared to *locations;* it is responsible for selecting one location among many, and for shifting from one location to the next. It is referred to as the *posterior system,* because the brain structures involved—part of the parietal cortex and some subcortical structures—are in the back of the brain (*posterior* means back). The other attentional system is geared to attributes of an object other than its location, for example, its shape or color. It is referred to as the *anterior system,* because the structures involved—the anterior cingulate and a subcortical structure—are in the front of the brain (*anterior* means front). In short, we can select an object for attention either by focusing on its location or on some other attribute, and two entirely different regions of the brain are used to implement these two kinds of selectivity.

To get some feel for the kind of evidence that is used to support the above claims, consider the case for the existence of the posterior system. Some critical findings come from PET scans of humans while they are engaged in selective-attention tasks. If a subject is instructed to shift his attention from one location to another, the cortical areas that show the greatest increase in blood flow—and hence neural activity—are the parietal

lobes of both hemispheres (Corbetta, Miezin, Shulman, & Petersen, 1993). Furthermore, when people who are known to have brain damage in these regions are tested in attentional tasks, they have great difficulty in shifting attention from one location to another (Posner, 1988). Hence, the same regions that are active when a normal brain accomplishes the task turn out to be the exact areas that are damaged when a patient cannot do the task. Moreover, when single-cell recording studies are done with nonhuman primates, cells in the very same brain regions are found to be active when attention must be switched from one location to the next (Moran & Desimone, 1985). Taken together, these findings converge on the idea that activity in parietal regions of the brain mediates attending to locations. There is comparable evidence for the involvement of frontal regions (the anterior system) in attending to nonlocational aspects of objects.

Consider now the second question. Once an object has been selected for attention, what changes occur in its neural processing? To make things concrete, consider an experiment in which a set of colored, geometric objects is presented, and the subject is instructed to attend only to the red ones and to indicate when a triangle is presented. The anterior system will shift attention to color, but what else changes in the neural processing of each stimulus? The answer is that those regions of the visual cortex that process color become more active than they would be if the subject were not selectively attending to color. More generally, those brain regions relevant to the attribute being attended to (be it color, shape, texture, motion, and so forth) will be amplified in activity (Posner & Dehaene, 1994). (There is also some suggestive evidence that brain regions relevant to unattended attributes will be inhibited.)

Some of the best evidence for this amplification of attended attributes again comes from PET studies. In one experiment (Corbetta et al., 1993), while having their brains scanned, subjects viewed moving objects of varying color and form. In one condition, subjects were instructed to detect changes among the objects in motion, and in another condition they were instructed to detect changes among the objects in color; hence, motion is the attended attribute in the first condition, color in the second condition.

FIGURE 5-23

PET Images Reveal
Differences in Cortical
Activity *In the first
condition, the subject
attends to an object's
motion. In the second
condition, the subject
attends to an object's
color.*

Even though the physical stimuli were identical in the two conditions, cortical areas
known to be involved in the processing of
motion were found to be more active in the
first condition, and areas involved in color
processing were more active in the second
condition (see Figure 5-23). Attention, then,
amplifies what is relevant, not only psychologically but biologically as well.

PERCEPTUAL CONSTANCIES

In addition to localization and recognition,
there seems to be another goal of our perceptual system—to keep the appearance of objects constant even though their impressions
on our retinas are changing. We have evolved
so that in general we represent—and experience—objects as they really are in the world
(real objects are constant in shape, size, color,
and brightness), not as they happen to impinge on our eyeball.

By and large, we perceive an object as remaining relatively constant regardless of
changes in lighting, the position from which
we view it, or its distance from us. Your car
does not appear to grow larger as you walk toward it, distort in shape as you walk around
it, or change in color when you view it in ar-

tificial light, even though the image on your
retina does undergo these changes. This
tendency toward constancy is referred to as
perceptual constancy. Although constancy is
not perfect, it is a salient aspect of visual
experience.

LIGHTNESS AND COLOR CONSTANCY

When an object is illuminated it reflects a
certain amount of the light. The amount reflected is related to the apparent *lightness* of
the object. The phenomenon of **lightness
constancy** refers to the fact that the perceived
lightness of a particular object may barely
change even when the amount of reflected
light changes dramatically. Thus, a black velvet shirt can look just as black in sunlight as
in shadow, even though it reflects thousands
of times more light when it is directly illuminated by the sun.

Although the above effect holds under
normal circumstances, a change in the surroundings can destroy it. Suppose that the
black shirt is put behind an opaque black
screen, and you view the shirt through a
peephole in the screen. This screen reduces
what you see through the opening to just the
actual light reflected from the shirt, independent of its surroundings. Now, when illuminated, the shirt looks white because the light
that reaches your eye through the hole is
more intense than that from the screen itself.
This demonstration provides a clue as to why
the lightness of an object usually remains
constant. When we perceive objects in natural settings, several other objects are usually
visible. Lightness constancy depends on the
relations among the intensities of light reflected from the different objects. Thus, normally we continue to see black velvet as black
even in sunlight because the velvet continues
to reflect a lesser percentage of its light than
does its surroundings. It is the relative percentage of light reflected that determines its
brightness (Gilchrist, 1978).

Similar principles apply to color. The tendency for an object to remain roughly the
same color with different light sources is
called **color constancy.** As was the case with
lightness constancy, color constancy can be
eliminated by removing the object from its
background. For example, if you look at a ripe
tomato through a tube that obscures the sur-

roundings and the nature of the object, the tomato may appear any color—blue, green, or pink—depending on the wavelengths reflecting from it. Hence color constancy, like lightness constancy, depends on a heterogeneous background (Maloney & Wandell, 1986; Land, 1977).

SHAPE AND LOCATION CONSTANCY

When a door swings toward us, the shape of its retinal image goes through a series of changes (see Figure 5-24). The door's rectangular shape produces a trapezoidal image, with the edge toward us wider than the hinged edge; then the trapezoid grows thinner, until finally all that is projected on the retina is a vertical bar the thickness of the door. Nevertheless, we perceive an unchanging door swinging open. The fact that the perceived shape is constant while the retinal image changes is an example of **shape constancy.**

Still another constancy involves the locations of objects. Despite the fact that a series of changing images strike the retina as we move, the positions of fixed objects appear to remain constant. We tend to take this **location constancy** for granted, but it requires that the visual system take account of both our movements and the changing retinal images. We discussed this kind of "accounting" earlier when we talked about the perception of motion. Essentially, the visual system must receive information from the motor system that the eyes are moving, and then take this information into account in interpreting image motion. If your visual system is informed that your eyes just moved 5 degrees to the left, it subtracts this out from the visual signal.

Shape constancy and location constancy also have implications for our earlier discussion of the goals of localization and recognition. In general, the constancies make the tasks of localization and recognition easier. If an object appeared to change its location every time we moved our eyes, determining its depth (an important part of localization) might be exceedingly difficult. If the shape of an object changed every time it or we moved, then the description of the object that we construct in the early stages of recognition would also change, and recognition might be an impossible task.

FIGURE 5-24

Shape Constancy *The various retinal images produced by an opening door are quite different, and yet we perceive a door of constant rectangular shape.*

SIZE CONSTANCY

The most studied of all the constancies is **size constancy,** the fact that an object's perceived size remains relatively constant no matter what its distance. As an object moves farther away from us, we generally do not see it as decreasing in size. Hold a quarter a foot in front of you and then move it out to arm's length. Does it appear to get smaller? Not noticeably so. Yet the retinal image of the quarter when it is 24 inches away is half the size of the

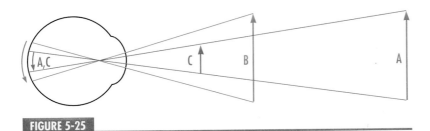

FIGURE 5-25

Retinal Image Size   *This figure illustrates the geometric relationship between the physical size of an object and the size of its image on the retina. Arrows A and B represent objects of the same size, but one is twice as far from the eye as the other. As a result, the retinal image of A is about half the size of the retinal image of B. The object represented by arrow C is smaller than that of A, but its location closer to the eye causes it to produce a retinal image of the same size as A.*

retinal image of the quarter when it is 12 inches away (see Figure 5-25).

DEPENDENCE ON DEPTH CUES   The moving quarter example indicates that when we perceive the size of an object, we consider something in addition to the size of the retinal image. That additional something is the *perceived distance* of the object. As long ago as 1881, Emmert was able to show that size judgments depend on distance. Emmert used an inge-

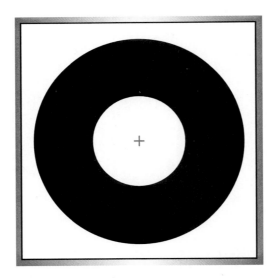

FIGURE 5-26

Emmert's Experiment   *Hold the book at normal reading distance under good light. Fixate on the cross in the center of the figure for about a minute, then look at a distant wall. You will see an afterimage of the two circles that appears larger than the stimulus. Then look at a piece of paper held close to your eyes; the afterimage will appear smaller than the stimulus. If the afterimage fades, blinking can sometimes restore it.*

nious method that involved judging the size of afterimages.

Emmert first had subjects fixate on the center of an image for about a minute (see Figure 5-26 for an example of such an image). Then subjects looked at a white screen and saw an afterimage. Their task was to judge the size of the afterimage; the independent variable was how far away the screen was. Because the retinal size of the afterimage was the same regardless of the distance of the screen, any variations in the judged size of the afterimage had to be due to its perceived distance. When the screen was far away, the afterimage looked large; when the screen was near, the afterimage looked small. Emmert's experiment is so easy to do that you can perform it on yourself.

Based on such experiments, Emmert proposed that the perceived size of an object increases with both: (a) the retinal size of the object; and (b) the perceived distance of the object. More specifically, perceived size is equal to the product of retinal size multiplied by perceived distance. This is known as the **size-distance invariance principle**. The principle explains size constancy in the following way. When the distance to an object increases, the object's retinal size decreases; but if distance cues are present, perceived distance will increase. Hence, the product of retinal size and perceived distance will remain approximately constant, which means that perceived size will remain approximately constant. To illustrate: When a person walks away from you, the size of her image on your retina gets smaller, but her perceived distance gets larger; these two changes cancel each other out, and your perception of the person's size remains relatively constant.

ILLUSIONS   The size-distance principle seems to be fundamental to understanding a number of size illusions. (An illusion is a percept that is false or distorted). A good example of a size illusion is the *moon illusion*. When the moon is near the horizon, it looks as much as 50 percent larger than when it is at its zenith, even though in both locations the moon produces the same size retinal image. One explanation of this illusion is that the perceived distance to the horizon is judged to be greater than that to the zenith; hence, it is the greater perceived distance that leads to the greater perceived size (Rock & Kaufman, 1962).

Another size illusion is the **Ames room** (named after its inventor, Adelbert Ames). Figure 5-27 shows a view of how the Ames room looks to an observer seeing it through a peephole. When the boy is in the left-hand corner of the room (photograph on the left) he appears much smaller than when he is in the right-hand corner (photograph on the right). Yet it is the same boy in both pictures! Here we have a case in which size constancy has broken down. Why? The reason lies in the construction of the room. Although the room looks like a normal rectangular room to an observer seeing it through the peephole, it is in fact shaped so that its left corner is almost twice as far from us as its right corner (see the diagram in Figure 5-28). Hence, the boy on the left is in fact much farther away than the one on the right, and consequently projects a smaller retinal image. We do not correct for this difference in distance, though, because we have been led to believe that we are looking at a normal room and thus assume that both boys are at the same distance from us. In essence, our assumption that the room is normal blocks our usual application of the size-distance invariance principle, and consequently size constancy breaks down.

Although all of the examples of constancy we have described are visual, constancies occur in the other senses as well. For example, a person will hear the same tune if the frequencies of all its notes double. Whatever the sensory modality, constancies depend on relations between features of the stimulus— between retinal size and distance in the case of size constancy, between the intensity of two adjacent regions in the case of lightness constancy, and so forth.

Why does the moon appear larger when it is on the horizon? Perceived distance is the key. When the distance is perceived as being greater, the size is also perceived to be greater.

FIGURE 5-27

The Ames Room *A view of how the Ames room looks to an observer viewing it through the peephole. The size of the boy and the dog depends on which one is in the left-hand corner of the room and which one is in the right-hand corner. The room is designed to wreak havoc with our perceptions. Because of the perceived shape of the room, the relative sizes of the boy and the dog seem impossibly different. Yet it is the same boy and dog in both photographs.*

FIGURE 5-28

True Shape of the Ames Room   *This figure shows the true shape of the Ames room. The boy on the left is actually almost twice as far away as the boy on the right; however, this difference in distance is not detected when the room is viewed through the peephole.* (After Goldstein, 1984)

PERCEPTUAL DEVELOPMENT

An age-old question about perception is whether our abilities to perceive are learned or innate—the familiar nature versus nurture problem. Contemporary psychologists no longer believe that this is an "either-or" question. No one today doubts that both genetics and learning influence perception; rather, the goal is to pinpoint the contribution of each, and to spell out their interaction. For the modern researcher, the question "Must we learn to perceive?" has given way to more specific questions: (a) What discriminatory capacity do infants have (which tells us something about inborn capacities), and how does this capacity change with age under normal rearing conditions? (b) If animals are reared under conditions that restrict what they can learn (referred to as **controlled stimulation**), what effects does this have on their later discriminatory capacity? (c) What effects does rearing under controlled conditions have on perceptual-motor coordination?

DISCRIMINATION BY INFANTS

Perhaps the most direct way to find out what human perceptual capacities are inborn is to see what capacities an infant has. At first, you might think that the research should con-

sider only newborns, because if a capacity is inborn it should be present from the first day of life. This idea turns out to be too simple, though. Some inborn capacities, such as form perception, can appear only after other more basic capacities, such as seeing details, have developed. Other inborn capacities may require that there be some kind of environmental input for an appreciable time in order for the capacity to mature. Thus the study of inborn capacities traces perceptual development from the first minute of life through the early years of childhood.

METHODS OF STUDYING INFANTS   It is hard for us to know what an infant perceives because it cannot talk or follow instructions, and has a fairly limited set of behaviors. To study infant perception, a researcher needs to find a form of behavior through which an infant indicates what it can discriminate. One behavior often used for this purpose is an infant's tendency to look at some objects more than others, and psychologists make use of this behavior in the **preferential looking method**.

This method is illustrated in Figure 5-29. Two stimuli are presented to the infant side by side. The experimenter, who is hidden from the infant's view, looks through a partition behind the stimuli and, by watching the infant's eyes, measures the amount of time that the infant looks at each stimulus. (Usually the experimenter will use a television camera to record the infant's viewing pattern to ensure accuracy.) From time to time, the stimulus positions are switched randomly. If an infant consistently looks at one stimulus more than the other, the experimenter concludes that the infant can tell them apart (discriminate between them).

A related technique is called the *habituation method* (Horowitz, 1974; Frantz, 1966). It takes advantage of the fact that, although infants look directly at novel objects, they soon tire of doing so (they habituate). Suppose that a novel object is presented for a while and then replaced by another object. To the extent the second object is perceived as identical or highly similar to the first one, the infant should spend little time looking at it; conversely, to the extent the second object is perceived as substantially different from the first one, the infant should spend a lot of time staring at it. By these means, an experimenter can determine whether two physical displays look the same to an infant, which is critical for studying the various perceptual constancies.

Using these techniques, psychologists have studied a variety of perceptual capacities in infants. Some of these capacities are needed to perceive forms, and hence are used in the task of recognition; other capacities studied in infants, particularly depth perception, are involved in the task of localization; and still other capacities are involved in the task of keeping the appearance of perceived objects constant.

PERCEIVING FORMS To be able to perceive an object, first one must be able to discriminate one part of it from another, an ability referred to as *visual acuity*. Related to acuity is *contrast sensitivity,* roughly the ability to discriminate between dark and light stripes under various conditions. (The dark and light stripes can correspond to different parts of a pattern, hence the relation between contrast sensitivity and acuity.)

The method typically used in studying acuity is preferential looking, with a pattern of stripes as one stimulus and a uniform gray field as the other stimulus. Initially, the stripes are relatively wide, and the infant prefers to look at the pattern rather than the uniform field. Then the researcher decreases stripe width until the infant no longer shows a preference. Presumably at this point the infant can no longer discriminate a stripe from its surrounding so that the pattern of stripes no longer has perceptible parts and looks like a uniform field. When first studied at about 1 month of age, infants can see some patterns, but their acuity is very low. Acuity increases rapidly over the first 6 months of life; then it increases more slowly, reaching adult levels between 1 and 5 years of age (Pirchio, Spinelli, Fiorentini, & Maffei, 1978; Teller, Morse, Borton, & Regal, 1974).

What do studies like this tell us about the infant's perceptual world? At 1 month, infants can distinguish no fine details; their vision can discriminate only relatively large objects. Such vision is sufficient, though, to perceive some gross characteristics of an object, including some of the features of a face (which create something like a pattern of dark and light stripes). Figure 5-30 uses the results of acuity and contrast-sensitivity experiments to simulate what a 1-, 2-, and 3-

FIGURE 5-29

Testing the Visual Preferences of an Infant

month-old infant sees when viewing a woman's face from a distance of 6 inches. At 1 month, acuity is so poor that it is difficult to perceive facial expressions (and indeed newborns look mostly at the outside contours of a face). By 3 months, acuity has improved to

FIGURE 5-30

Visual Acuity and Contrast Sensitivity *Simulations of what 1-, 2-, and 3-month-old infants see when they look at a woman's face from a distance of about six inches; the bottom right photograph is what an adult sees. The simulations of infant perception were obtained by first determining an infant's contrast sensitivity, and then applying this contrast-sensitivity function to the photograph on the bottom right.* (After Ginsburg, 1983) the point where an infant can decipher facial expressions (Goldstein, 1989). No wonder that infants seem so much more socially responsive at 3 months than 1 month.

Being able to discriminate dark from light edges is critical for seeing forms, but what about other aspects of object recognition? Our sensitivity to some of the shape features of objects is manifested early. When presented with a triangle, even a 3-day-old infant will direct its eye movements toward the edges and vertices, rather than look randomly over the form (Salapatek, 1975). Also, infants find some shapes more interesting than others. Infants tend to look more at forms that resemble human faces, which appears to be based on a preference for some of the features that comprise a face, like a preference for curved rather than straight contours (Fantz, 1970; 1961). By age 3 months, an infant can recognize something about the mother's face, even in a photograph, as revealed by an infant's preference to look at a photograph of the mother rather than one of an unfamiliar woman (Barrera & Maurer, 1981).

PERCEIVING DEPTH   Depth perception begins to appear at about 3 months of age but is not fully established until about 6 months. Thus, at 5½ months, but not before, infants will reach for the nearer of two objects, where nearness is signaled by the monocular cue of relative size. Further evidence about the development of monocular depth perception comes from studies of the **visual cliff**. The visual cliff (illustrated in Figure 5-31) consists of a center board placed across a sheet of glass, with a surface of patterned material located directly under the glass on the *shallow side,* and at a distance of a few feet below the glass on the *deep side.* (The appearance of depth in Figure 5-31—the cliff—is created by an abrupt change in the texture gradient.) An infant old enough to crawl (6–7 months) is placed on the center board; one of her eyes is patched to eliminate binocular depth cues. When the mother calls or beckons from the shallow side, the infant will consistently crawl toward her mother; but when the mother beckons from the deep side, the infant will not cross the "cliff." Thus when old enough to crawl, an infant's depth perception is relatively well developed.

PERCEIVING CONSTANCIES   Like the perception of form and depth, the perceptual constancies start to develop in the first few months of life. This is particularly true for shape and size constancy (for example, Kellman, 1984). We can illustrate the evidence for these claims by considering an experiment on size constancy that used the habituation method (infants habituate to looking at the same stimulus). Four-month-old infants were first presented one teddy bear for a while, and then shown a

FIGURE 5-31

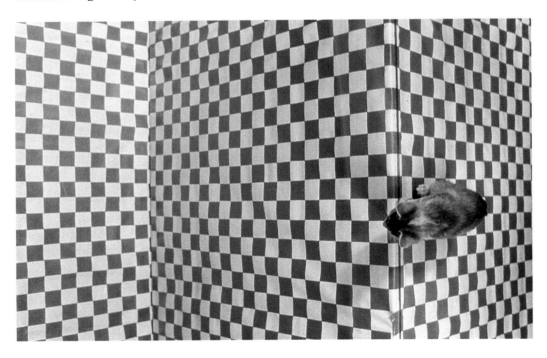

Visual Cliff   *The "visual cliff" is an apparatus used to show that infants and young animals are able to see depth by the time they are able to move about. The visual cliff consists of two surfaces, both displaying the same checkerboard pattern and covered by a sheet of thick glass. One surface is directly under the glass; the other is several feet below it. When placed on the center board between the deep and the shallow sides, the kitten refuses to cross to the deep side but will readily move off the board onto the shallow side.* (After Gibson & Walk, 1960)

second one. The second teddy bear was of two types: (1) identical in physical size to the original teddy, but presented at a different distance so that it produced a different-sized retinal image; and (2) different in physical size from the original teddy. If these infants had size constancy, they should perceive teddy (1) (same physical size) as identical to what they saw originally, and hence spend little time looking at it, compared to how much time they spend looking at teddy (2) (which is truly different from the original). This is exactly what happened (Granrud, 1986).

REARING WITH CONTROLLED STIMULATION

We turn now to the question of how specific experiences affect perceptual capacities. To answer this question, researchers have systematically varied the kind of perceptual experiences a young organism has, and then looked at the effects of this experience on subsequent perceptual performance. While the intent of these studies has usually been to study learning, the variations in experiences has sometimes affected innate processes.

ABSENCE OF STIMULATION The earliest experiments on controlled stimulation sought to determine the effects of rearing an animal in the total absence of visual stimulation. The experimenters kept animals in the dark for several months after birth until they were mature enough for visual testing. The idea behind these experiments was that if animals have to *learn* to perceive, they would be unable to perceive when first exposed to the light. The results turned out as expected: Chimpanzees reared in darkness for their first 16 months could detect light but could not discriminate patterns (Riesen, 1947). However, subsequent studies showed that prolonged rearing in the dark does more than prevent learning; it causes deterioration of neurons in various parts of the visual system. It turns out that a certain amount of light stimulation is necessary to maintain the visual system. Without any light stimulation, nerve cells in the retina and visual cortex begin to atrophy.

Though the above findings do not tell us much about the role of learning in perceptual development, they are important in themselves. In general, when an animal is deprived

of visual stimulation from birth, the longer the time of deprivation, the greater the deficit. Adult cats, on the other hand, can have one eye patched for a long period without losing vision in that eye. These observations led to the idea that a **critical period** exists for the development of inborn visual capacities, where a critical period is a stage in development during which the organism is optimally ready to acquire certain abilities. Lack of stimulation during a critical period for vision can permanently impair the visual system.

LIMITED STIMULATION Researchers no longer deprive animals of stimulation for a long period of time; instead they study the effects of rearing animals with stimulation in both eyes, but only of a certain kind. Researchers have raised kittens in an environment in which they see only vertical stripes, or only horizontal stripes. The kittens become blind to stripes in the orientation—horizontal or vertical—that they do not experience. And single-cell recording studies show that many cells in the visual cortex of a "horizontally reared" cat respond to horizontal stimuli and none responds to vertical stimuli, whereas the opposite pattern of results obtains for a "vertically reared" cat (Blakemore & Cooper, 1970; Hirsch & Spinelli, 1970). This blindness seems to be caused by the degeneration of cells in the visual cortex.

Of course researchers do not deprive humans of normal visual stimulation, but sometimes this happens naturally or as a consequence of medical treatment. For example, after eye surgery the operated eye is usually patched. If this happens to a child in the first year of life, the acuity of the patched eye is reduced (Awaya et al., 1973). This suggests that there is a critical period early in the development of the human visual system similar to that in animals; if stimulation is restricted during this period, the system will not develop normally. The critical period is much longer in humans than in animals. It may last as long as eight years, but the greatest vulnerability occurs during the first two years of life (Aslin & Banks, 1978).

None of these facts indicates that we have to learn to perceive. Rather, the facts show that certain kinds of stimulation are essential for the *maintenance and development* of perceptual capacities that are present at birth. But this does not mean that learning has no

FIGURE 5-32

Importance of Self-Produced Movements *Both kittens received roughly the same visual stimulation, but only the active kitten had this stimulation produced by its own movement.* (After Held & Hein, 1963)

effect on perception. For evidence of such effects, we need only consider our ability to recognize common objects. The fact that we can more readily recognize a familiar object than an unfamiliar one—a dog versus an aardvark, for example—must certainly be due to learning (because had we been reared in an environment rich in aardvarks and sparse in dogs, we could have recognized the aardvark more readily than the dog).

PERCEPTUAL-MOTOR COORDINATION   When it comes to coordinating perceptions with motor responses, learning plays a major role. The evidence for this comes from studies in which subjects receive normal stimulation but are prevented from making normal responses to that stimulation. Under such conditions, perceptual-motor coordination does not develop.

For example, in one classic study, two dark-reared kittens had their first visual experience in the "kitten carousel" illustrated in Figure 5-32. As the active kitten walked, it moved the passive kitten riding in the carousel. Although both kittens received roughly the same visual stimulation, only the active kitten had this stimulation produced by its movement. And only the active kitten successfully learned sensory-motor coordination; for example, when picked up and moved to-

ward an object, only the active kitten learned to put out its paws to ward off a collision.

Similar results have been obtained with humans. In some experiments people have worn prism goggles that distort the directions of objects. Immediately after putting on these goggles, a person temporarily has trouble reaching for objects and often bumps into things. If a person moves about and attempts to perform motor tasks while wearing the goggles, he or she learns to behave adaptively. The person is learning to coordinate his or her movements with the actual location of objects rather than with their apparent locations. On the other hand, if the person is pushed in a wheelchair, he or she does not adapt to the goggles. Apparently, self-produced movement is essential to prism adaption (Held, 1965).

In summary, the evidence indicates that we are born with considerable perceptual capacity. The natural development of some of these capacities may require years of normal input from the environment; hence, environmental effects early in development are often more indicative of innate than learned processes. But there clearly are learning effects on perception as well, which are particularly striking when perception must be coordinated with motor behavior.

BIOLOGICAL-PSYCHOLOGICAL PERSPECTIVES

This chapter, like the preceding one, has produced many examples of the interplay between psychological and biological approaches. To start things off, we introduced the critical biological findings that separate parts of the brain mediate localization and recognition, and that different brain regions or cells process different attributes of an object. These distinctions have proved as useful at the psychological level as at the biological level. Furthermore, throughout the chapter, we encountered cases in which specific psychological functions were implemented in the brain by specific cells or brain regions, including the functions of perceiving real motion, perceiving primitive features, and attending to locations. These cases are good examples of reductionism at work.

In the last section of the chapter, we saw another kind of interplay between biology and psychology, namely a concern with the relative contributions of genetics and learning in the development of perceptual abilities. (As noted in Chapter 1, thinking of learning as "psychological" makes sense to the extent that most of what we know about learning is at the psychological rather than biological level.) Here, what was most striking was the large role that inborn capacities played in perceptual development. We will be returning to this inborn versus learned contrast many times in the rest of this book.

CHAPTER SUMMARY

1. The study of perception deals with two major functions of the perceptual system: *localization*, or determining where objects are, and *recognition*, or determining what objects are. The study of perception also deals with how the perceptual system keeps the appearance of objects constant, even though their retinal images are changing. Another concern is with how our perceptual capacities develop.

2. The visual cortex operates according to a *division of labor* principle. Localization and recognition are carried out by different brain regions, with localization being mediated by a region near the top of the cortex and recognition by a region near the bottom of the cortex. Recognition processes are further subdivided into separate modules: for example, color, shape, and texture.

3. To localize objects, first we have to *segregate* objects from one another and then *organize* them into groups. These processes were first studied by *Gestalt* psychologists, who proposed principles of organization. One such principle is that we organize a stimulus into regions corresponding to *figure* and *ground*. Other principles concern the bases that we use to group objects together, including: *proximity, closure,* and *similarity*.

4. Localizing an object requires that we know its depth. *Depth perception* is usually thought to be based on *depth cues*. Monocular depth cues include *relative size, superposition, relative height, linear perspective,* and *motion parallax*. Binocular depth cues include *parallax* and *disparity*, with disparity due to the fact that any object provides slightly different images to the two eyes. An alternative to inferring distance on the basis of depth cues is Gibson's notion of *direct perception*, wherein a source of information like a *texture gradient* provides direct information about the depth of an object.

5. Localizing an object sometimes requires knowing the motion of moving objects. *Motion perception* can be produced in the absence of an object moving across our retina; one case of this is *stroboscopic motion* in which a series of rapid, still images induces apparent movement; another case of motion perception without a moving object is *induced motion* in which movement of a large object induces apparent movement of a smaller stationary object. *Real motion* (induced by an object moving across the retina) is implemented in the brain by specific cells in the visual system, as indicated by single-cell recordings and by experiments on *selective adaptation*.

6. Recognizing an object amounts to assigning it to a category and is based mainly on the shape of the object. In *early stages* of recognition, the visual system uses retinal information to describe the object in terms of *features* like lines and angles; neurons that detect such features (*feature detectors*) have been found in the visual cortex. In the *later stages* of recognition, the system matches the description of the object to shape descriptions stored in memory to find the best match.

7. Much of the research on the *matching stage* of recognition has used letter patterns. Matching can be explained by a *connectionist model* or network. The bottom level of the network contains features and the next level contains letters; an *ecitatory connection* between a feature and a letter means that the feature is part of a letter, while an *inhibitory connection* means the feature is not part of the letter. When a letter is presented, it activates some features in the network, which pass their activation or inhibition up to letters; the letter that receives the most activation is the best match to the input. The network can be expanded to include a level of words and to explain why a letter is easier to recognize when presented in a word than when presented alone.

8. The shape features of natural objects are more complex than lines, being more like simple geometric forms such as cylinders, cones, blocks, and wedges. A limited set of such forms may be sufficient in combination to describe the shapes of all objects that people can recognize.

9. *Bottom-up* recognition processes are driven solely by the input, and *top-down* recognition processes are driven by a person's knowledge and expectations. Top-down processes lie behind *context* effects in perception, because the context sets up a perceptual expectation, and when this expectation is satisfied less input information than usual is needed for recognition.

10. *Selective attention* is the process by which we select some stimuli for further processing while ignoring others. In vision, the primary means for directing our attention are *eye movements*. Most eye fixations are on the more informative parts of a scene. Selective attention also occurs in audition. Usually, we are able to *selectively listen* by using cues like the direction of the sound and the voice characteristics of the speaker. Our ability to selectively attend is mediated by processes that occur in the early stages of recognition, as well as by processes that occur only after the message's meaning has been determined.

11. Two separate brain systems seem to mediate the psychological act of selecting an object to attend to. The *posterior system* (back of the brain) is responsible for selecting on the basis of localization, and the *anterior system* (front of the brain) mediates selection on the basis of other attributes, such as shape and color. PET studies further show that once an object has been selected, those brain regions relevant to the attribute being attended to are amplified in activity.

12. Another major function of the perceptual system is to keep the appearance of objects the same in spite of large changes in the stimuli received by our sense organs. *Lightness constancy* refers to the fact that an object appears equally light regardless of how much light it reflects, and *color constancy,* means an object looks roughly the same color regardless of the light source illuminating it. In both cases, constancy depends on relations between object and background elements. Two other well-known constancies are *shape* and *location constancy.*

13. The most studied of all constancies is *size constancy,* the fact that any object's size remains relatively constant no matter what its distance from us. The perceived size of an object increases with both the *retinal size* of the object and the *perceived distance* of the object, in accordance with the *size-distance invariance principle.* Thus, as an object moves away from the perceiver, the retinal size decreases but the perceived distance increases, and the two changes cancel each other out, resulting in constancy. This principle can explain certain *illusions.*

14. Research on *perceptual development* is concerned with the extent to which perceptual capacity is inborn and the extent to which it is learned by experience. To determine inborn capacities, researchers study the discrimination capacities of infants using methods like *preferential looking* and *habituation. Acuity,* which is critical to recognition, increases rapidly over the first 6 months of life, then increases more slowly. *Depth perception* begins to appear at about 3 months of age, but is not fully established until about 6 months. The constancies begin to develop as early as 6 months.

15. Animals raised in darkness suffer permanent visual impairment, and animals raised with a patch over one eye become blind in that eye. Adult animals do not lose vision even when deprived of stimulation for long periods. These results suggest a *critical period* early in life, during which lack of normal stimulation produces an aberration in an innate perceptual capacity. If stimulation is controlled early in life, so that certain kinds of stimuli are absent, both animals and people become insensitive to the stimuli of which they have been deprived; again, this effect does not have much to do with learning. *Perceptual-motor* coordination must be learned, however. Both animals and people require *self-produced movement* to develop normal coordination.

FURTHER READING

Many of the textbooks listed under Further Reading in Chapter 4 also pertain to the topics considered in this chapter. Several additional sources are appropriate as well.

General treatments of perception are available in Kosslyn, *Invitation to Cognitive Science (Vol. 2): Visual Cognition,* (2nd ed., 1995); Coren and Ward, *Sensation and Perception* (3rd ed., 1989); and Rock, *The Logic of Perception* (1983). Gibson's distinctive approach to issues like depth and motion perception in particular, and to perception in general, is presented in *The Ecological Approach to Visual Perception* (1986). Marr's equally distinctive, cognitive-science approach to perception is given in his book *Vision* (1982). A more elementary introduction to some of Marr's work is presented in the early chapters of Johnson-Laird, *The Computer and the Mind* (1988).

Problems of recognition and attention are discussed in Spoehr and Lehmkuhle; *Visual Information Processing* (1982). Studies of brain mechanisms involved in recognition are discussed in Farah, *Visual Agnosia: Disorders of Object Recognition and What They Tell Us About Normal Vision* (1990); and Posner and Marin, (eds.), *Mechanisms of Attention* (1985). Recent advances in brain scanning are described in Posner and Raichle's, *Images of Mind* (1994). The connectionist approach to problems of recognition and localization are contained in an advanced, two-volume set by Rumelhart and McClelland, *Parallel Distributed Processing* (1986).

6 CHAPTER

CONSCIOUSNESS AND ITS ALTERED STATES

As you read these words, are you awake or dreaming? Hardly anyone is confused by this question. We all know the difference between an ordinary state of wakefulness and the experience of dreaming. We also recognize other *states of consciousness,* including those induced by drugs such as alcohol and marijuana.

A person's conscious awareness is readily subject to change. At this moment, your attention may be focused on this book; in a few minutes, you may be deep in reverie. To most psychologists, an *altered state of consciousness* exists whenever there is a change from an ordinary pattern of mental functioning to a state that *seems* different to the person experiencing the change. Although this is not a very precise definition, it reflects the fact that states of consciousness are personal and therefore subjective. Altered states of consciousness can vary from the distraction of a vivid daydream to the confusion and perceptual distortion of drug intoxication. In this chapter we will look at some altered states of consciousness that are experienced by everyone (sleep and dreams, for instance), as well as some that result from special circumstances (meditation, hypnosis, and the use of drugs).

ASPECTS OF CONSCIOUSNESS

Discussions about the nature of conscious experience and the functions of consciousness will occur throughout this book as we consider perception, memory, language, problem solving, and other topics. At this point, it would be helpful to present a general theory of consciousness that would provide a framework for considering these various topics as they are introduced later. Such an approach, however, is not feasible because there is no generally agreed-upon theory. Rather, there are almost as many theories of consciousness as there are individuals who have theorized about the topic. This state of affairs may be discouraging for some readers, particularly those whose prior exposure to science has been in areas where the facts are crystal clear and the theories are well established. Yet what can be more exciting or more challeng-

ing than venturing into territory that is still uncharted? As important discoveries are being made—in neurophysiology, evolutionary biology, genetics, and various fields of psychology—many observers believe that an explanation of consciousness is tantalizingly close (Crick, 1994). In the absence of a general theory, our discussion of consciousness can do little more than introduce some terms and concepts that will provide a perspective on the topic as it surfaces in later chapters.

What is consciousness? The early psychologists equated "consciousness" with "mind." They defined psychology as "the study of mind and consciousness" and used the **introspective method** to study consciousness. As noted in Chapter 1, both introspection as a method for investigation and consciousness as a topic for investigation fell from favor with the rise of **behaviorism** in the early 1900s. John Watson, the founder of behaviorism, and his followers believed that if psychology were to become a science, its data must be objective and measurable. Behavior could be publicly observed and various responses could be objectively measured. In contrast, an individual's private experiences revealed through introspection could not be observed by others or objectively measured. If psychology dealt with overt behavior, it would be dealing with *public events,* instead of *private events,* which are observable only to the experiencing person.

Behaviorism did not require as radical a change as its pronouncements seemed to imply. The behaviorists themselves dealt with private events when their research required them to do so. They accepted *verbal responses* as a substitute for introspection when the subject's own experiences were studied. What subjects said was objective, regardless of the uncertainties about the underlying subjective condition. Still, many psychologists continued to believe, regardless of the tenets of behaviorism, that when people said they experienced a series of colored afterimages after staring at a bright light, they probably did see colors in succession. That is, their words were not the whole story: The words referred to something of additional psychological interest. While behaviorists could deal with many phenomena in terms of verbal responses, their preoccupation with observable behavior caused them to neglect interesting psychological problems (such as dreaming, meditation, and hypnosis) because the subjective aspects made the topics irrelevant to them (Ericsson & Simon, 1993).

By the 1960s, psychologists began to recognize that the facts of consciousness are too pervasive and important to be neglected. This does not mean that psychology must again be defined exclusively as the study of consciousness; it means only that a complete psychology cannot afford to neglect consciousness. A strict behaviorist's insistence on confining psychology to the study of observable behavior is too limiting. If one can theorize about the nature of consciousness, and that theory leads to testable predictions about behavior, then such theorizing is a valuable contribution to understanding how the mind works.

CONSCIOUSNESS

Despite the re-emergence of the study of consciousness in psychology, there is still no common agreement on a definition of the term. Many textbooks simply define consciousness as the individual's current awareness of external and internal stimuli—that is, of events in the environment and of body sensations, memories, and thoughts. This definition identifies only one aspect of consciousness and ignores the fact that we are conscious also when we try to solve a problem or deliberately select one course of action over others in response to environmental circumstances and personal goals. Thus we are conscious when we monitor the environment (internal and external), but also when we seek to control ourselves and our environment. In short, consciousness involves a) *monitoring* ourselves and our environment so that percepts, memories, and thoughts are represented in awareness; and b) *controlling* ourselves and our environment so that we are able to initiate and terminate behavioral and cognitive activities (Kihlstrom, 1984).

MONITORING   Processing information from the environment is the main function of the body's sensory systems, leading to awareness of what is going on in our surroundings as well as within our own bodies. However, we could not possibly attend to all of the stimuli that impinge on our senses; there would be an information overload. Our consciousness focuses on some stimuli and ignores others. Often the information selected has to do with changes in our external or internal

worlds. While concentrating on this paragraph, you are probably unaware of numerous background stimuli. But should there be a change—the lights dim, the air begins to smell smoky, or the noise of the air conditioning system ceases—you would suddenly be aware of such stimuli.

Our attention is selective; some events take precedence over others in gaining access to consciousness and in initiating action. Events that are important to survival usually have top priority. If we are hungry, it is difficult for us to concentrate on studying; if we experience a sudden pain, we push all other thoughts out of consciousness until we do something to make it go away.

CONTROLLING   Another function of consciousness is to plan, initiate, and guide our actions. Whether the plan is simple and readily completed (such as meeting a friend for lunch) or complex and long-range (such as preparing for a lifetime career), our actions must be guided and arranged to coordinate with events around us. In planning, events that have not yet occurred can be represented in consciousness as future possibilities; we may envision alternative "scenarios," make choices, and initiate appropriate activities (Johnson-Laird, 1988).

Not all actions are guided by conscious decisions nor are the solutions to all problems carried out at a conscious level. One of the tenets of modern psychology is that mental events involve both conscious and nonconscious processes and that many decisions and actions are conducted entirely outside of the range of consciousness. The solution to a problem may occur "out of the blue" without our being aware that we have been thinking about it. And once we have the solution, we may be unable to offer an introspective account of how the solution was obtained. One can cite many examples of decision making and problem solving that occur at a nonconscious level, but this does not mean that *all* such behaviors occur without conscious reflection. Consciousness is not only a monitor of ongoing behavior, but plays a role in directing and controlling that behavior as well.

PRECONSCIOUS MEMORIES

From all that is going on around us now and from our store of knowledge and memories of past events, we can focus attention on only a few stimuli at a given moment. We ignore, se-lect, and reject all the time, so that the contents of consciousness are continually changing. Nonetheless, objects or events that are not the focus of attention can still have some influence on consciousness. For example, you may not be aware of hearing a clock strike the hour. After a few strokes, you become alert; then you can go back and count the strokes that you did not know you heard. Another example of peripheral attention (or nonconscious monitoring) is the **lunch-line effect** (Farthing, 1992). You are talking with a friend in a cafeteria line, ignoring other voices and general noise, when the sound of your own name in another conversation catches your attention. Clearly, you would not have detected your name in the other conversation if you had not, in some sense, been monitoring that conversation; you were not consciously aware of the other conversation until a special signal drew your attention to it. A considerable body of research indicates that we register and evaluate stimuli that we do not consciously perceive (Greenwald, 1992; Kihlstrom, 1987). These stimuli are said to influence us *subconsciously,* or to operate at a nonconscious level of awareness.

Many memories and thoughts that are not part of your consciousness at this moment can be brought to consciousness when needed. At this moment you may not be conscious of your vacation last summer, but the memories are accessible if you wish to retrieve them; then they become a part of your consciousness. Memories that are accessible to consciousness are called **preconscious memories.** They include specific memories of personal events, as well as the information accumulated over a lifetime, such as one's knowledge of the meaning of words, the layout of the streets of a city, or the location of a particular country. They also include knowledge about learned skills like the procedures involved in driving a car or the sequence of steps in tying one's shoe lace. These procedures, once mastered, generally operate outside conscious awareness, but when our attention is called to them we are capable of describing the steps involved.

The Unconscious

According to the psychoanalytic theories of Sigmund Freud and his followers, some memories, impulses, and desires are not ac-

"Good morning, beheaded—uhm I mean beloved"

Drawing by Dana Fradon; ©1979 The New York Magazine, Inc.

cessible to consciousness. Psychoanalytic theory assigns these to the **unconscious.** Freud believed that some emotionally painful memories and wishes are *repressed*—that is, diverted to the unconscious, where they may continue to influence our actions even though we are not aware of them. Thoughts and impulses repressed to the unconscious cannot enter our consciousness, but they can affect us in indirect or disguised ways—through dreams, irrational behaviors, mannerisms, and slips of the tongue. The term **"Freudian slip"** is commonly used to refer to unintentional remarks that are assumed to reveal hidden impulses. Saying "I'm sad you're better," when intending to say "I'm glad you're better," would be an example.

Freud believed that unconscious desires and impulses are the cause of most mental illnesses. He developed the method of psychoanalysis, the goal of which is to draw the repressed material to consciousness and, in so doing, cure the individual (see Chapter 16).

Most psychologists accept the idea that there are memories and mental processes that are inaccessible to introspection and accordingly may be described as unconscious. However, many would argue that Freud placed undue emphasis on the emotionally laden aspects of the unconscious and not enough on other aspects. They would include in the unconscious a large array of mental processes that we depend on constantly in our everyday lives but to which we have no conscious access (Kihlstrom, 1987). For example, during perception, the viewer may be aware of two objects in the environment but have no awareness of the mental calculations she performed almost instantaneously to determine that one is closer or larger than the other (see Chapter 5). Although we have conscious access to the outcome of these mental processes—in that we are aware of the size and distance of the object—we have no conscious access to their operations (Velmans, 1991).

In this section we have discussed four concepts—consciousness, nonconscious processes, preconscious memories, and the unconscious—and have tended to treat them as distinct categories. In actuality, however, not all processes and stored memories are so easily categorized. For this reason, some psychologists prefer not to make these types of distinctions, and instead talk about a *nonconscious-conscious continuum* that runs from one extreme of totally unconscious processes (through various gradations) to the other extreme of the most reflective form of consciousness (Farthing, 1992). Nevertheless, versions of these concepts are so pervasive that you need to be familiar with them, even though different psychologists talk about them somewhat differently.

DISSOCIATION

An important function of consciousness is the control of our actions. However, some activities are practiced so often that they become habitual, or automatic. Learning to drive a car requires intense concentration at first. We have to concentrate on coordinating the different actions (shifting gears, releasing the clutch, accelerating, steering, and so forth) and can scarcely think about anything else. However, once the movements become automatic, we can carry on a conversa-

Familiarity with a skill makes actions automatic, so that we can perform two tasks simultaneously.

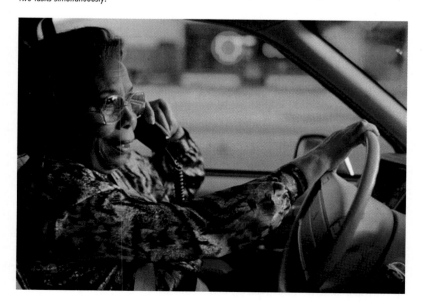

tion or admire the scenery without being conscious of driving—unless a potential danger appears that quickly draws our attention to the operation of the car.

AUTOMATIC PROCESSES

Skills, like driving a car or riding a bike, once well learned no longer require our attention. They become automatic, thereby permitting a relatively uncluttered consciousness to focus on other matters. Such *automatic processes* may have negative consequences on occasion, for example, when a driver cannot remember landmarks passed along the way.

The more automatic an action becomes, the less it requires conscious control. Another example is the skilled pianist who carries on a conversation with a bystander while performing a familiar piece. The pianist is exercising control over two activities—playing and talking—but does not think about the music unless a wrong key is hit, alerting her attention to it and temporarily disrupting the conversation. You can undoubtedly think of other examples of well-learned, automatic activities that require little conscious control. One way of interpreting this is to say that the control is still there (we can focus on automatic processes if we want to), but it has been *dissociated* from consciousness. (To "dissociate" means to sever the association of one thing from another.)

The French psychiatrist Pierre Janet (1889) originated the concept of **dissociation**. He proposed that under certain conditions some thoughts and actions become split off, or dissociated, from the rest of consciousness and function outside of awareness. Dissociation differs from Freud's concept of repression because the dissociated memories and thoughts are accessible to consciousness. Repressed memories, in contrast, cannot be brought to consciousness; they have to be inferred from signs or symptoms (such as slips of the tongue).

When faced with a stressful situation, we may temporarily put it out of our minds in order to be able to function effectively; when bored, we may lapse into reverie or daydreams. These are mild examples of dissociation; they involve dissociating one part of consciousness from another. More extreme examples of dissociation are demonstrated by cases of **dissociative identity disorder**.

DISSOCIATIVE IDENTITY DISORDER

Dissociative identity disorder, also called *multiple personality disorder,* is the existence in an individual of two or more distinct identities or personalities that alternate in controlling behavior. Usually, each personality has its own name and age and a specific set of memories and characteristic behaviors. In most cases there is a primary identity that carries the individual's given name and is passive, dependent, and depressed. The alternate identities typically have characteristics that contrast with the primary identity (for example, hostile, controlling and self-destructive (American Psychiatric Association, 1994). In some cases the personalities may even differ in such characteristics as handwriting, artistic or athletic abilities, and knowledge of a foreign language. The primary identity usually has no awareness of the experiences of the other identities. Periods of unexplained amnesia—the loss of memory for hours or days each week—can be a clue to the presence of dissociative identity disorder.

One of the most famous cases of multiple personality is that of Chris Sizemore, whose alternative personalities—Eve White, Eve Black, and Jane—were portrayed in the movie *The Three Faces of Eve* (Thigpen & Cleckley, 1957) and later elaborated more extensively in her autobiography *I'm Eve* (Sizemore & Pittillo, 1977). Another well-studied case is that of Jonah, a 17-year-old man who was admitted to a hospital complaining of severe headaches that were often followed by memory loss. Hospital attendants noticed striking changes in his personality on different days and the psychiatrist in charge detected three distinct secondary identities. The relatively stable personality structures that emerged are diagrammed in Figure 6-1 and can be characterized as follows:

* *Jonah.* The primary personality. Shy, retiring, polite, and highly conventional, he is designated "the square." Sometimes frightened and confused during interviews, Jonah is unaware of the other personalities.
* *Sammy.* He has the most intact memories. Sammy can coexist with Jonah or set Jonah aside and take over. He claims to be ready when Jonah needs legal advice or is in trouble; he is designated "the mediator." Sammy remembers emerging

at age 6, when Jonah's mother stabbed his stepfather and Sammy persuaded the parents never to fight again in front of the children.
* *King Young.* He emerged when Jonah was 6 or 7 years old to straighten out Jonah's sexual identity after his mother occasionally dressed him in girls' clothing at home and Jonah became confused about boys' and girls' names at school. King Young has looked after Jonah's sexual interests ever since; hence he is designated "the lover." He is only dimly aware of the other personalities.
* *Usoffa Abdulla.* A cold, belligerent, and angry person. Usoffa is capable of ignoring pain. It is his sworn duty to watch over and protect Jonah; thus he is designated "the warrior." He emerged at age 9 or 10, when a gang of boys beat up Jonah without provocation. Jonah was helpless, but Usoffa emerged and fought viciously against the attackers. He too is only dimly aware of the other personalities.

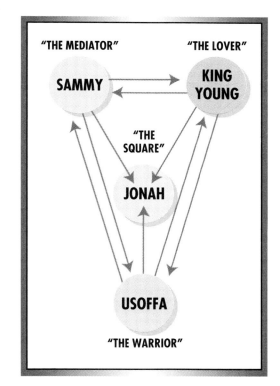

FIGURE 6-1

Jonah's Four Component Identities *The three personalities on the periphery have superficial knowledge of each other but are intimately familiar with Jonah, who in turn is totally unaware of them. (After Ludwig et al., 1972)*

The four personalities tested very differently on all measures having to do with emotionally laden topics but scored essentially alike on tests relatively free of emotion or personal conflict, such as intelligence or vocabulary tests.

Dissociative identity disorder reflects a failure to integrate various aspects of identity, memory, and consciousness. The dissociation is so complete that several different personalities seem to be living in the same body. Observers note that the switch from one personality to another is often accompanied by subtle changes in body posture and tone of voice. The new personality talks, walks, and gestures differently. There may even be changes in such physiological processes as blood pressure and brain activity (Putnam, 1989).

Individuals with dissociative identity disorders frequently report having experienced physical and sexual abuse during childhood. The accuracy of such reports is controversial, because childhood memories may be subject to distortion and because individuals with this disorder tend to be very vulnerable to suggestion. Nevertheless, defense against traumatic childhood experiences forms the basis of a hypothesis about how such disorders develop. The initial dissociation is assumed to occur in response to a traumatic event in childhood (usually between ages 4 and 6). The child copes with a painful problem by creating another personality to bear the brunt of the difficulty (Frischholz, 1985). In Jonah's case, Sammy (the mediator) emerged when Jonah had to deal with his mother's attack on his stepfather.

The child presumably learns to defend himself from the pain of abuse by dissociating the memory from consciousness. If the child is severely and repeatedly abused, this method of defense over time leads to dissociative identities in which only one or two subpersonalities are conscious of the abuse, while the others have no memory of the pain. It is adaptive for the child to keep the personalities separate, so that he can keep awareness of the abuse from his other selves. That way the feeling and memories of abuse do not continually flood the child's consciousness when he cannot handle it, for instance while at school or playing with friends (Braun, 1986). A large majority of individuals with multiple personalities are female, probably because they are more likely to be subjected to sexual abuse as children (Boon & Draijer, 1993).

Another factor in the development of dissociative identity disorder appears to be an enhanced susceptibility to self-hypnosis, a process by which one is able to put oneself at will into the kind of trance state characteristic of hypnosis (discussed later in this chapter). Dissociative identity patients often make excellent hypnotic subjects, and they report that the trance experience is identical to experiences they have had dating back to their childhood. One of the personalities of a patient said, "She creates personalities by blocking everything from her head, mentally relaxes, concentrates very hard, and wishes" (Bliss, 1980, p. 1392).

Once individuals discover that creating another identity relieves them of emotional pain, they are likely to create other personalities in the future when confronted by emotional problems. Thus, when Jonah was beaten by a gang of boys at age 10, he created another personality, Usoffa Abdulla, to handle the problem. Some dissociative identity patients become so accustomed to defending against problems by means of alternate personalities that they continue the process throughout adulthood, creating new personalities in response to new problems; thus they may end up with a dozen or more different personalities (Putnam, 1989).

Cases of dissociative identity disorder have always been fascinating but rare. However, recent years have seen a sharp rise in the number of cases reported in the United States. Some believe this increase reflects an increased awareness of the disorder among mental health professionals and, hence, identification of cases previously undiagnosed. Others believe that the disorder has been overdiagnosed in individuals who are highly suggestible (American Psychiatric Association, 1994).

SLEEP AND DREAMS

Sleep seems the opposite of wakefulness, yet the two states have much in common. We think when we sleep, as dreams show, although the type of thinking in dreams departs in various ways from the type we do while awake. We form memories while sleeping, as we know from the fact that we remember dreams. Sleep is not entirely quiescent: Some people walk in their sleep. People who are asleep are not entirely insensitive to the environment: Parents are awakened by their baby's cry. Nor is sleep entirely planless: Some people can decide to wake at a given time and do so.

STAGES OF SLEEP

Some people are readily aroused from sleep; others are hard to awaken. Research begun in the 1930s (Loomis, Harvey, & Hobart, 1937) has produced sensitive techniques for measuring the depth of sleep, as well as for determining when dreams are occurring (Dement & Kleitman, 1957). This research uses devices that measure electrical changes on the scalp associated with spontaneous brain activity during sleep, as well as eye movements that occur during dreaming. The graphic recording of the electrical changes, or brain waves, is called an **electroencephalogram,** or EEG (see Figures 6-2 and 6-3). The EEG measures the rapidly fluctuating average electrical potential of thousands of neurons that lie on the surface of the cortex under the electrode; it is a rather crude measure of cortical activity, but it has proved very useful in sleep research.

Analysis of the patterns of brain waves suggests that sleep involves five stages: four depths of sleep and a fifth stage, known as **rapid eye movement** (or REM) sleep. When a person closes her eyes and relaxes, the brain waves characteristically show a regular pattern of 8 to 12 hertz (cycles per second); these are known as **alpha waves.** As the individual drifts into *Stage 1* sleep, the brain waves become less regular and are reduced in amplitude. *Stage 2* is characterized by the appearance of **spindles**—short runs of rhythmical responses of 12 to 16 hertz—and an occasional sharp rise and fall in the amplitude of the whole EEG. The still deeper *Stages 3* and *4* are characterized by slow waves (1 to 2 hertz), which are known as **delta waves.** Generally the sleeper is hard to awaken during Stages 3 and 4, although she can be aroused by something personal, such as a familiar name or a child crying. A more impersonal

FIGURE 6-2

Arrangement of Electrodes for Recording the Electrophysiology of Sleep   *The diagram shows the way in which electrodes are attached to the subject's head and face in a typical sleep experiment. Electrodes on the scalp (1) record the patterns of brain waves. Electrodes near the subject's eyes (2) record eye movements. Electrodes on the chin (3) record tension and electrical activity in the muscles. A neutral electrode on the ear (4) completes the circuit through amplifiers (5) that produce graphical records of the various patterns.*

disturbance, such as a loud sound, may be ignored.

SUCCESSION OF SLEEP STAGES   After an adult has been asleep for an hour or so, another change occurs. The EEG becomes very active (even more so than when the subject is awake), but the subject does not wake. The electrodes placed near the subject's eyes detect rapid eye

FIGURE 6-3

Electrophysiological Activity During Sleep The figure presents EEG recordings during wakefulness and during the various stages of sleep. The Awake Stage (relaxed with eyes closed) is characterized by alpha waves (8–12 hertz). Stage 1 is basically a transition from wakefulness to the deeper stages of sleep. Stage 2 is defined by the presence of sleep spindles (brief bursts of 12–16 hertz waves) and K-complexes (a sharp rise and fall in the brain-wave pattern). Stages 3 and 4 are marked by the presence of delta waves (1–2 hertz), and the only difference between these two stages is the amount of delta wave found. Stage 3 is scored when 20 to 50 percent of the record contains delta waves, and Stage 4 for 50 percent or more.

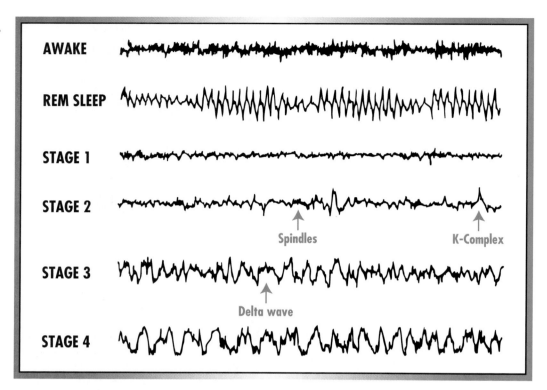

movements; these eye movements are so pronounced that one can even watch the sleeper's eyes move around beneath the closed eyelids. This stage is known as REM sleep; the other four stages are known as non-REM sleep (or NREM).

These various stages of sleep alternate throughout the night. Sleep begins with the NREM stages and consists of several sleep cycles, each containing some REM and some NREM sleep. Figure 6-4 illustrates a typical night's sleep for a young adult. As you can see, the person goes from wakefulness into a deep sleep (Stage 4) very rapidly. After about

70 minutes, Stage 3 recurs briefly, immediately followed by the first REM period of the night. Notice that the deeper stages (3 and 4) occurred during the first part of the night, whereas most REM sleep occurred in the last part. This is the typical pattern: the deeper stages tend to disappear in the second half of the night as REM becomes more prominent. There are usually four or five distinct REM periods over the course of an 8-hour night, with an occasional brief awakening as morning arrives.

The pattern of the sleep cycles varies with age. Newborn infants, for instance, spend

FIGURE 6-4

Succession of Sleep Stages *The graph provides an example of the sequence and duration of sleep stages during a typical night. The subject went successively through Stages 1 to 4 during the first hour of sleep. He then moved back through Stage 3 to REM sleep. Thereafter the subject cycled between NREM and REM periods with two brief awakenings at about 3½ and 6 hours of sleep.*

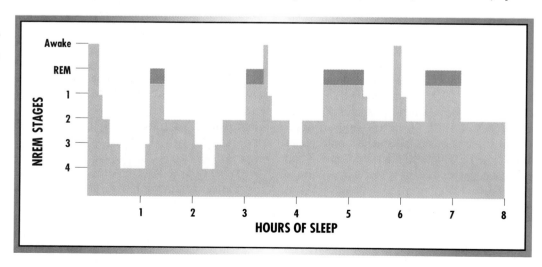

about half their sleeping time in REM sleep. This proportion drops to 20 to 25 percent of total sleep time by the age of 5 and remains fairly constant until old age, when it drops to 18 percent or less. Older people tend to experience less Stage 3 and 4 sleep (sometimes these stages disappear) and more frequent and longer nighttime awakenings. A natural kind of insomnia seems to set in as people grow older (Gillin, 1985).

REM AND NREM COMPARED The two types of sleep, REM and NREM, are as different from each other as each is from wakefulness. Indeed, some investigators consider REM not to be sleep at all, but rather a third state of existence in addition to wakefulness and NREM sleep.

During NREM sleep, eye movements are virtually absent, heart and breathing rates decrease markedly, there is increased muscle relaxation, and the metabolic rate of the brain decreases 25 to 30 percent compared to wakefulness. In contrast, during REM sleep very rapid eye movements occur in bursts lasting 10 to 20 seconds, heart rate increases, and the brain's metabolic rate increases somewhat compared to wakefulness. Further, during REM sleep we are almost completely paralyzed—only the heart, diaphragm, eye muscles, and smooth muscles (such as the muscles of the intestines and blood vessels) are spared. To summarize, NREM sleep is characterized by an idle brain in a very relaxed body, and REM sleep is characterized by a brain that appears to be wide awake in a virtually paralyzed body.

Physiological evidence indicates that in REM sleep the brain is isolated to a large extent from its sensory and motor channels; stimuli from other parts of the body are blocked from entering the brain, and there are no motor outputs. Nevertheless, the brain is still very active in REM sleep, being spontaneously driven by the discharge of giant neurons that originate in the brain stem. These neurons extend into parts of the brain that control eye movements and motor activities. Thus, during REM sleep the brain registers the fact that the neurons normally involved in walking and seeing are activated, even though the body itself is doing neither of these activities (Hobson, 1994).

Sleepers awakened during REM sleep almost always report having a dream, but when awakened during NREM sleep they will report a dream only about 25 percent of the time. The dreams reported when aroused from REM sleep tend to be visually vivid and have emotional and illogical features—they represent the type of experience we typically associate with the word "dream." The longer the period of REM sleep before being aroused, the longer and more elaborate is the reported dream. In contrast, NREM dreams are more like normal thinking, neither as visual nor as emotionally charged as REM dreams, and more related to what is happening in waking life. Thus, mental activity is different in REM and NREM periods, as indicated by the type of dream we report (bizarre and illogical versus thoughtlike) and the frequency of reporting a dream (almost always versus occasionally).

It is important to realize that we become conscious of a dream only if we awaken while dreaming. If we then pay attention and make an effort to remember the dream, some of it will be recalled at a later time. Otherwise, our dream is transient and fades quickly; we may know that we have had a dream but will be unable to remember its contents.

If you are interested in remembering your dreams, keep a notebook and pencil beside your bed. Tell yourself you want to wake up when you have a dream. When you do, immediately try to recall the details and then write them down. As your dream recall improves, look for patterns. Underline anything that strikes you as odd and tell yourself that the next time something similar happens, you are going to recognize it as a sign you are dreaming. The problem, of course, is that you will lose some sleep if you follow this regimen.

SLEEP DISORDERS

About 90 percent of adults sleep 6 to 9 hours per night, with the largest number sleeping 7½ to 8 hours. While some people sleep only 6 to 7 hours, most of these people have measurable signs of sleepiness during the daytime, even if they do not realize it. It appears that most adults require 8 to 9 hours of sleep to be free from daytime sleepiness (Kripke & Gillin, 1985). A *sleep disorder* exists whenever the inability to sleep well produces impaired daytime functioning or excessive sleepiness.

INSOMNIA The term **insomnia** is used in reference to complaints about a symptom, namely, dissatisfaction with the amount or quality of one's sleep. Whether or not a person has insomnia is almost always a subjective decision. Many people who complain of insomnia are found to have perfectly normal sleep when studied in a sleep laboratory, whereas others who do not complain of insomnia have detectable sleep disturbances (Trinder, 1988).

A perplexing feature of insomnia is that people seem to overestimate their sleep loss. One study that monitored the sleep of people who identified themselves as insomniacs found that only about half of them were actually awake as much as 30 minutes during the night (Carskadon, Mitler, & Dement, 1974). The problem may be that some people remember only time spent awake and think they have not slept because they have no memory of doing so. Table 6-1 provides some information on how to ensure that you have a restful sleep.

NARCOLEPSY AND APNEA Two relatively rare but severe sleep disorders are narcolepsy and apnea. A person with **narcolepsy** may fall asleep anytime, for example while writing a letter, driving a car, or carrying on a conversation. If a student falls asleep while a professor is lecturing, that may be perfectly normal;

but if a professor falls asleep while lecturing, that indicates narcolepsy. Individuals with this dysfunction have recurring, irresistible attacks of drowsiness, and simply fall asleep at inappropriate times. These episodes can occur several times a day in severe cases, and last from a few seconds to 15–30 minutes. Narcoleptics have difficulty keeping jobs because of their daytime sleepiness and are potentially dangerous if they are driving a car or operating machinery when an attack occurs. Approximately one in a thousand individuals suffers from debilitating narcolepsy, and the incidents of milder, unrecognized cases may be much higher.

Essentially, narcolepsy is the intrusion of REM episodes into daytime hours. During attacks victims go quickly into a REM state, so rapidly in fact that they may lose muscle control and collapse before they can lie down. Moreover, many will report experiencing hallucinations during an attack as reality is replaced by vivid REM dreams. Narcolepsy runs in families, and there is evidence that a specific gene or combination of genes confers susceptibility to the disorder (Hobson, 1988).

In **apnea**, the individual stops breathing while asleep. There are two reasons for apnea attacks. One reason is that the brain fails to send a "breathe" signal to the diaphragm and other breathing muscles, thus causing

---

TABLE 6-1

Advice for a Good Night's Sleep   *There is considerable agreement among researchers and clinicians on how to avoid sleep problems. These recommendations are summarized in the table; some are based on actual research, and others are simply the best judgments of experts in the field. (After Pion, 1991)*

REGULAR SLEEP SCHEDULE Establish a regular schedule of going to bed and getting up. Set your alarm for a specific time every morning and get up at that time no matter how little you may have slept. Be consistent about naps. Take a nap every afternoon or not at all; when you take a nap only occasionally, you probably will not sleep well that night. Waking up late on weekends can also disrupt your sleep cycle.

ALCOHOL AND CAFFEINE Having a stiff drink of alcohol before going to bed may help put you to sleep, but it disturbs the sleep cycle and can cause you to wake up early the next day. In addition, stay away from caffeinated drinks like coffee or cola for several hours before bedtime. Caffeine works as a stimulant even on those people who claim they are not affected by it, and the body needs 4 to 5 hours to halve the amount of caffeine in the bloodstream at any one time. If you must drink something before bedtime, try milk; there is evidence to support the folklore that a glass of warm milk at bedtime induces sleep.

EATING BEFORE BEDTIME Don't eat heavily before going to bed, since your digestive system will have to do several hours of work. If you must eat something before bedtime, have a light snack.

EXERCISE Regular exercise will help you sleep better, but don't engage in a strenuous workout just before going to bed.

SLEEPING PILLS Be careful about using sleeping pills. All of the various kinds tend to disrupt the sleep cycle, and long-term use inevitably leads to insomnia. Even on nights before exams, avoid using a sleeping pill. One bad night of sleep tends not to affect performance the next day, but hangover from a sleeping pill may.

RELAX Avoid stressful thoughts before bedtime and engage in soothing activities that help you relax. Try to follow the same routine every night before going to bed; it might involve taking a warm bath or listening to soft music for a few minutes. Find a room temperature at which you are comfortable and maintain it throughout the night.

WHEN ALL FAILS If you are in bed and have trouble falling asleep, don't get up. Stay in bed and try to relax. But if that fails and you become tense, then get up for a brief time and do something restful that reduces anxiety. Doing push-ups or some other form of exercise to wear yourself out is not a good idea.

breathing to stop. The other reason is that muscles at the top of the throat become too relaxed, allowing the windpipe to partially close, thereby forcing the breathing muscles to pull harder on incoming air, which causes the airway to completely collapse. During an apnea episode, the oxygen level of the blood drops dramatically, leading to the secretion of emergency hormones. This reaction causes the sleeper to awaken in order to begin breathing again.

Most people have a few apnea episodes a night, but people with severe sleep problems may have several hundred apneas per night. With each one, they wake up in order to resume breathing, but these arousals are so brief they are generally unaware of doing so. The result is that those who suffer from apnea can spend 12 or more hours in bed each night and still be so sleepy the next day that they cannot function and will fall asleep even in the middle of a conversation (Ancoli-Israel, Kripke, & Mason, 1987).

Sleep apnea is common among older men. Sleeping pills, which make arousal more difficult, lengthen periods of apnea (during which the brain is deprived of oxygen) and may prove fatal. Failure to awaken, and thereby terminate a period of apnea, is probably one of the main reasons people die in their sleep.

DREAMS

Dreaming is an altered state of consciousness in which remembered images and fantasies are temporarily confused with external reality. Investigators do not yet understand why people dream at all, much less why they dream what they do. However, modern methods of study have answered a great many questions about dreaming.

DOES EVERYONE DREAM? Although many people do not recall their dreams in the morning, REM-sleep evidence suggests that nonrecallers do as much dreaming as recallers. If you take people who have sworn that they never dreamed in their life, put them in a dream research laboratory and wake them from REM sleep, you will get dream recall at rates comparable to other people. If someone says "I never dream," what they mean is "I can't recall my dreams."

Researchers have proposed several hypotheses to account for differences in dream recall. One possibility is that nonrecallers simply have more difficulty than recallers in remembering their dreams. Another hypothesis suggests that some people awaken relatively easily in the midst of REM sleep and thus recall more dreams than those who sleep more soundly. The most generally accepted model for dream recall supports the idea that what happens on awakening is the crucial factor. According to this hypothesis, unless a distraction-free waking period occurs shortly after dreaming, the memory of the dream is not consolidated (Hobson, 1988; Koulack & Goodenough, 1976).

HOW LONG DO DREAMS LAST? Some dreams seem almost instantaneous. The alarm clock rings and we awaken to complex memories of a fire breaking out and fire engines arriving with their sirens blasting. Because the alarm is still ringing, we assume that the sound must have produced the dream. Research suggests, however, that a ringing alarm clock or other sound merely reinstates a complete scene from earlier memories or dreams. This experience has its parallel during wakefulness when a single cue may tap a rich memory that takes some time to tell. The length of a typical dream can be inferred from a REM study in which subjects were awakened and asked to act out what they had been dreaming (Dement & Wolpert, 1958). The time it took them to pantomime the dream was almost the same as the length of the REM sleep period, suggesting that the incidents in dreams commonly last about as long as they would in real life.

DO PEOPLE KNOW WHEN THEY ARE DREAMING? The answer to this question is "sometimes yes." People can be taught to recognize that they are dreaming, and their awareness does not interfere with the dream's spontaneous flow. For example, subjects have been trained to press a switch when they notice that they are dreaming (Salamy, 1970).

Some people have **lucid dreams** in which events seem so normal (lacking the bizarre and illogical character of most dreams) that the dreamers feel they are awake and conscious. Lucid dreamers report doing various "experiments" within their dreams to determine whether they are, in fact, awake or dreaming. A Dutch physician, van Eeden (1913), was one of the first to give an accurate account of initiating actions within a lucid dream to prove that events were not occurring normally. In a later report, Brown (1936) described a standard experiment in which he jumped and suspended himself in the air. If he did this successfully, he knew he was dreaming. Both Brown and van Eeden report an occasional "false awakening" within a dream. For example, in one of Brown's dreams, he discovered that he was dreaming and decided to call a taxicab as an indication of his control over events. When he reached into his pocket to see if he had some change to pay the driver, he thought that he woke up. He then found the coins scattered about the bed. At this point, he really awoke and found himself lying in a different position and, of course, without any coins.

CAN PEOPLE CONTROL THE CONTENT OF THEIR DREAMS?

Psychologists have demonstrated that some control of dream content is possible by making suggestions to subjects in the presleep period and then analyzing the content of the dreams that followed. In a carefully designed study of an *implicit predream suggestion*, researchers tested the effect of wearing red goggles for several hours prior to sleep. Although the researchers made no actual suggestion, and the subjects did not understand the purpose of the experiment, many subjects reported that their visual dream worlds were tinted red (Roffwarg, Herman, Bowe-Anders, & Tauber, 1978). In a study of the effect of an *overt predream suggestion*, subjects were asked to try to dream about a personality characteristic that they wished they had. Most of the subjects had at least one dream in which the intended trait could be recognized (Cartwright, 1974).

Another way of influencing dream content is through **posthypnotic suggestion.** In one extensive study using this method, detailed dream narratives were suggested to highly responsive hypnotic subjects. After the suggestion, the subject slept until roused from REM sleep. Some of the resulting dreams reflected the thematic aspects of the suggestion without including many of the specific elements, whereas other dreams reflected specific elements of the suggestion (Tart & Dick, 1970).

DREAM CONTENT Freud's theory that dreams are mental products that can be understood and interpreted was one of the earliest and most comprehensive attempts to explain the content of dreams without reference to the supernatural. In his book, *Interpretation of Dreams* (1900), Freud proposed that dreams provide the "royal road to a knowledge of the unconscious activities of the mind." He believed that dreams are a disguised attempt at *wish fulfillment.* By this he meant that the dream touches on wishes, needs, or ideas that the individual finds unacceptable and have been repressed to the unconscious (for example, Oedipal longings for the parent of the opposite sex). These wishes and ideas are the **latent content** of the dream. Freud used the metaphor of a censor to explain the conversion of latent content to **manifest content** (the characters and events that make up the actual narrative of the dream). In effect, Freud said, the censor protects the sleeper, enabling him to express repressed impulses symbolically while avoiding the guilt or anxiety that would occur if they were to appear consciously in undisguised form.

The transformation of latent content into manifest content is done by the "dream work," as Freud called it, the function of which is to code and disguise material in the unconscious in such a way that it can reach consciousness. However, sometimes the dream work fails, and anxiety awakens the dreamer. The dream essentially expresses the fulfillment of wishes or needs that are too painful or guilt-inducing to acknowledge consciously (Freud, 1933).

THEORIES OF DREAM SLEEP

A variety of theories have been advanced to explain the role of sleep and dreams. For our purposes it will be useful to summarize two theories, one proposed by Evans (1984) that takes a cognitive approach and the other by Crick and Mitchison (1986; 1983) that takes a neurobiological approach.

Evans's theory views sleep, particularly REM sleep, as a period when the brain disengages from the external world and uses this "off-line" time to sift through the information that was input during the day and to incorporate it into its existing memory. We are not consciously aware of the processing that occurs during REM sleep. During dreaming, however, the brain comes back on-line for a brief time and the conscious mind observes a small sample of the modification and reorganization of information taking place. The brain attempts to interpret this information the same way it would interpret stimuli coming from the outside world, giving rise to the kind of pseudo-event that characterizes dreams. Thus, according to Evans, dreams are nothing more than a small subset of the vast amount of information that is being scanned and sorted during REM sleep, a momentary glimpse by the conscious mind that we remember if we awaken. Evans believes that dreams can be useful in making inferences about the processing that occurs during REM sleep, but dreams represent an extremely small sample on which to base such inferences.

Crick and Mitchison base their theory on the fact that the cortex is made up of richly interconnected *neural networks* in which each neuron has the capacity to excite its neighbors. They believe that memories are encoded in these networks. The networks are like spiderwebs, and when one point in the web is excited, perhaps by hearing a few notes of a song, a pulse travels throughout the network, prompting recall of the rest of the song. The problem with such networks—whether electronic and made by human beings or neural and the product of evolution—is that they malfunction when overloaded with too much incoming information. An overloaded network "freezes up" and becomes dysfunctional. To deal with information overload, a mechanism is needed to debug and tune the network. With electronic networks, debugging mechanisms work best when the network is temporarily isolated from additional inputs; randomly activating the isolated network unfreezes it and makes it functional. By analogy, Crick and Mitchison argue that a debugging mechanism for neural networks is REM sleep: The hallucinatory quality of dreams is nothing more than the neural firing needed for the daily cleanup of the network.

As noted earlier, the brain is very active during REM sleep, barraged with neural signals traveling from the brain stem to the cortex. According to the theory, these signals erase the spurious memory associations formed during the previous day; we awaken with the network cleaned up and the brain

ready for new inputs. Crick and Mitchison suggest that trying to remember one's dreams—a key aspect of psychoanalysis—may not be a good idea. They believe that such remembering could help to retain patterns of thought that are better forgotten, the very patterns the system is attempting to tune out.

The two theories have some common features, but there are differences. Evans views REM sleep as a time when the brain modifies and reorganizes the vast array of information input during the day; Crick and Mitchison see REM sleep as a time when spurious or useless information is purged from memory. Evans regards conscious dreams as a surface indicator of the rich reorganizational process taking place during REM sleep; Crick and Mitchison suggest that dreams are little more than random noise with no real content. Both theories, however, assume that REM sleep plays a role in the storage of memories and in preparing the brain from one day to the next to deal with new information inputs. Neither theory assigns to dreams the rich symbolism and concealed meaning that typifies Freud's psychoanalytic approach to dream content.

PSYCHOACTIVE DRUGS

Since ancient times, people have used drugs to alter their state of consciousness—to stimulate or relax, to bring on sleep or prevent it, to enhance ordinary perceptions, or to produce hallucinations. Drugs that affect behavior, consciousness, and/or mood are called **psychoactive**. They include not only street drugs such as heroin and marijuana but also tranquilizers, stimulants, and such familiar drugs as alcohol, nicotine, and caffeine.

Table 6-2 lists and classifies the psychoactive drugs that are commonly used and abused. Drugs that are used to treat mental disorders (see Chapter 16) also affect mood and behavior and, thus, might be considered psychoactive. They are not included here, however, because they are seldom abused. By and large, their effects are not immediate (for example, most of the drugs used to treat depression take days or weeks before they begin to lift the individual's mood), and usually are not experienced as particularly pleasant. An

Our ability to store incoming information in memory for retrieval at later times is called *memory consolidation*. Researchers have long hypothesized that REM sleep facilitates the consolidation of long-term memories. Several studies with rats have demonstrated that being deprived of REM sleep interferes with the animal's performance on a task that was learned the previous day. And when rats are given intensive training on a difficult maze-learning task, the amount of time spent in REM sleep increases signifi-

cantly. However, until recently, studies designed to test for similar effects in humans either failed to do so or were at best equivocal (Dujardin, Guerrien, & Leconte, 1990; Horne & McGrath, 1984). The breakthrough with human subjects was achieved by Karni et al. (1994) using a unique type of learning task. On each trial a line segment is briefly flashed in the subject's peripheral field of vision; the subject's task is to correctly identify the orientation (angle) of the line. It is a very difficult task because the flash is extremely brief, but with daily

practice sessions—involving many trials—subjects eventually become quite proficient. However, the course of learning is atypical: Subjects show little improvement during a practice session, but when they return the next day, they are clearly better than they were at the end of the preceding session. Thus, while performance steadily improves over the course of several days, the improvement is not evident within a practice session but only from one day's session to the next. This is an ideal task to determine whether memory consolidation

---

exception would be the minor tranquilizers that may be prescribed for the treatment of anxiety disorders and are sometimes abused.

It may be difficult for students today to appreciate the major changes in patterns of drug-taking behavior that have occurred in the United States over the past 40 years. In the 1950s, very few Americans used drugs (other than nicotine and alcohol). Since the 1950s, we have moved from a relatively drug-free society to a drug-using society. Drug use, particularly among young people, increased steadily through the 1960s and 1970s. In the 1980s, however, drug use gradually declined, a trend that continued until 1992 (see Figure

6-5). The education of young people about the hazards of using drugs contributed to this decline. The turnaround that occurred in 1992 is a cause for concern because students' attitudes about the dangers of drug use appear to be softening (Johnston, O'Malley, & Bachman, 1995).

The drugs listed in Table 6-2 are assumed to affect behavior and consciousness because they act in specific biochemical ways on the brain. With repeated use, an individual can become dependent on any of them. *Drug dependence,* also called addiction, is characterized by (1) *tolerance*—with continued use, the individual must take more and more of

---

TABLE 6-2

PSYCHOACTIVE DRUGS THAT ARE COMMONLY USED AND ABUSED
Only a few examples of each class of drug are given. The generic name (for example, psilocybin) or the brand name (Xanax for alprazolam; Seconal for secobarbital) is used, depending on which is more familiar.

DEPRESSANTS (SEDATIVES)

Alcohol (ethanol)
Barbiturates
   Nembutal
   Seconal
Minor tranquilizers
   Miltown
   Xanax
   Valium
Inhalants
   Paint thinner
   Glue

OPIATES (NARCOTICS)

Opium and its derivatives
   Codeine
   Heroin
   Morphine
Methadone

STIMULANTS

Amphetamines
   Benzedrine
   Dexedrine
   Methedrine
Cocaine
Nicotine
Caffeine

HALLUCINOGENS

LSD
Mescaline
Psilocybin
PCP (Phencyclidine)

CANNABIS

Marijuana
Hashish

occurs during a specific stage of sleep.

Subjects were trained on the task in the evening before going to sleep in the laboratory. Some subjects were awakened by an electric bell every time the EEG showed that they were entering REM sleep. Other subjects had their sleep interrupted the same number of times, but during NREM sleep stages 3 and 4 (what is called slow-wave sleep). The following day all subjects were tested. Those with REM deprivation showed no improvement at all; their performance was the same as the night before. On the other hand, subjects who were awakened during slow-wave sleep improved significantly over the night.

This work, taken together with earlier research, tends to support the idea that REM sleep plays a role in the consolidation of memory. However, we still have a great deal to learn about the specific mechanisms involved and whether REM sleep by itself, or REM sleep in conjunction with other sleep stages, is the critical factor (Wilson & McNaughton, 1994; Winson, 1990). REM sleep is probably not a necessary condition for memory consolidation, but it may greatly facilitate the process. And it may be more important for the consolidation of complex skills and memories than it is for simple learning tasks. The consolidation of memory undoubtedly requires the meshing of new information with old memories, a process that could explain why dreams often involve a mix of life's current difficulties and past experiences (Ramachandran, 1995).

the drug to achieve the same effect; (2) *withdrawal*—if use is discontinued, the person experiences unpleasant physical and psychological reactions; (3) *compulsive use*—the individual takes more of the drug than intended, tries to control use but can't, and spends a great deal of time trying to obtain the drug.

The degree to which tolerance develops and the severity of withdrawal symptoms varies across drugs. Tolerance for opiates, for example, develops fairly quickly, and heavy users can tolerate a dosage that would be lethal to a nonuser; in contrast, marijuana smokers seldom build up much tolerance. Withdrawal symptoms are common and easily observed following heavy and sustained use of alcohol, opiates, and sedatives. They are common, but less apparent, for stimulants, and nonexistent after repeated use of hallucinogens. (American Psychiatric Association, 1994).

Although tolerance and withdrawal are the primary characteristics of drug dependence, they are not necessary for a diagnosis. A person who shows a pattern of compulsive use without any signs of tolerance or withdrawal, as some marijuana users do, would still be considered drug dependent.

Drug dependence is usually distinguished from *drug abuse*. A person who is not dependent on a drug (that is, shows no symptoms of tolerance, withdrawal, or compulsive craving) but who continues to use the drug despite serious consequences is said to abuse the drug.

For example, an individual whose overindulgence in alcohol results in repeated accidents, work absenteeism, or marital problems (without signs of dependency) would be said to abuse alcohol.

DEPRESSANTS

Drugs that depress the central nervous system include tranquilizers, barbiturates (sleeping pills), inhalants (volatile solvents and aerosols), and ethyl alcohol. Of these, the one

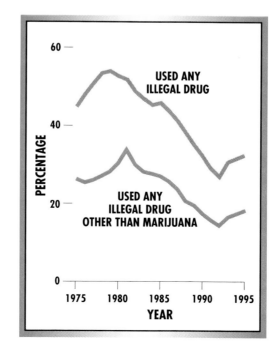

FIGURE 6-5

Illegal Drug Use *The percentage of American high school seniors who reported using an illegal drug in the 12-month period prior to graduation. Drugs included in the upper curve are marijuana, hallucinogens, cocaine, heroin, and any nonprescribed use of opiates, stimulants, sedatives, and tranquilizers. The lower curve excludes marijuana. (After Johnston, O'Malley, & Bachman, 1995)* most used and abused is alcohol; consequently, that is the drug on which our discussion of depressants will focus. Before proceeding, however, a word about inhalants is appropriate. Solvents and aerosols are cheap and easily obtained legally. Volatile solvents include gasoline, paint thinner, cleaning solutions, and glue; the psychoactive chemicals are various hydrocarbons. Aerosols, such as spray paint, contain toxic forms of alcohol. Users typically warm the substance and inhale the vapors through the mouth (huffing) or nose (sniffing).

Inhalant abuse does not affect many people, but it is a source of concern because (1) the abusers are very young (boys as young as 7 have been found sniffing glue or gasoline); (2) some of these solvents can produce permanent brain damage; and (3) abuse in the elementary and secondary schools is on the increase (Johnston, O'Malley, & Bachman, 1995)

ALCOHOL AND ITS EFFECTS   Most societies, primitive or industrialized, consume alcohol. It can be produced by fermenting a wide variety of materials: grains, such as rye, wheat, and corn; fruits, such as grapes, apples, and plums; and vegetables, such as potatoes. Through the process of distillation, the alcoholic content of a fermented beverage can be increased to obtain "hard liquors" such as whiskey or rum.

Measuring the amount of alcohol in the air we exhale (as in a breath analyzer) gives a reliable index of alcohol in the blood. Consequently, it is easy to determine the relationship between **blood alcohol concentration** (BAC) and behavior. At concentrations of .03 to .05 percent in the blood (30 to 50 milligrams of alcohol per 100 milliliters of blood), alcohol produces lightheadedness, relaxation, and release of inhibitions. People say things they might not ordinarily say; they tend to become more sociable and expansive. Self-confidence may increase, but motor reactions will begin to slow (a pair of effects that makes it dangerous to drive after drinking).

At a BAC of .10 percent, sensory and motor functions become noticeably impaired. Speech becomes slurred, and people have difficulty coordinating their movements. Some people tend to become angry and aggressive; others grow silent and morose. The drinker is seriously incapacitated at a level of .20 percent,

and a level above .40 percent may cause death. The legal definition of intoxication in most states is a BAC of .10 percent (one-tenth of 1 percent).

How much can a person drink without becoming legally intoxicated? The relationship between BAC and alcohol intake is not simple. It depends on a person's sex, body weight, and speed of consumption. Age, individual metabolism, and experience with drinking are also factors. Although the effects of alcohol intake on BAC vary a great deal, the average effects are shown in Figure 6-6. Moreover, it is not true that beer or wine is less likely to make someone drunk than so-called hard drinks. A 4-ounce glass of wine, a 12-ounce can of beer, and 1.2 ounces of 80-proof whiskey have about the same Alcohol content and will have about the same effect.

ALCOHOL USAGE   Drinking is viewed as an integral part of social life for many college students. It promotes conviviality, eases tensions, releases inhibitions, and generally adds to the fun. Nevertheless, social drinking can create problems in terms of lost study time, poor performance on an exam because of feeling hung over, and arguments or accidents while intoxicated. Clearly the most serious problem is accidents: Alcohol-related automobile accidents are the leading cause of death among 15- to 24-year-olds. When the legal drinking age was lowered from 21 to 18 years of age in a number of states, traffic fatalities of 18- and 19-year-olds increased 20 to 50 percent. All states have since raised their minimum drinking age, and a significant decrease in traffic accidents has followed.

About two-thirds of American adults report that they drink alcohol. At least 10 percent of them have social, psychological, or medical problems resulting from alcohol use. Probably half of that 10 percent are dependent on alcohol. Heavy or prolonged drinking can lead to serious health problems. High blood pressure, stroke, ulcers, cancers of the mouth, throat, and stomach, cirrhosis of the liver, and depression are some of the conditions associated with the regular use of substantial amounts of alcohol.

Despite the fact that it is illegal for anyone under the age of 21 to purchase alcoholic beverages, experience with alcohol is almost universal among young people (67% of eighth-graders have tried it, 81% of high

FIGURE 6-6

DRINKS IN A TWO-HOUR PERIOD
(1.2 ozs. 80-proof liquor or 12 ozs. beer)

WEIGHT												
100	1	2	3	4	5	6	7	8	9	10	11	12
120	1	2	3	4	5	6	7	8	9	10	11	12
140	1	2	3	4	5	6	7	8	9	10	11	12
160	1	2	3	4	5	6	7	8	9	10	11	12
180	1	2	3	4	5	6	7	8	9	10	11	12
200	1	2	3	4	5	6	7	8	9	10	11	12
220	1	2	3	4	5	6	7	8	9	10	11	12
240	1	2	3	4	5	6	7	8	9	10	11	12

BE CAREFUL DRIVING
BAC TO .05%

DRIVING IMPAIRED
.05%–.09%

DO NOT DRIVE
.10% & UP

BAC and Alcohol Intake
Approximate values of blood-alcohol concentration as a function of alcohol consumption in a 2-hour period. For example, if you weigh 180 pounds and had four beers in two hours, your BAC would be between .05 and .09 percent and your driving ability would be seriously impaired. Six beers in the same 2-hour period would give you a BAC of over .10 percent—the level accepted as proof of intoxication. (After National Highway Traffic Safety Administration)

school seniors, and 91% of college students). More disturbing is the widespread occurrence of "binge drinking" (defined for research purposes as having five or more drinks in a row). In national surveys, 28% of high school seniors and 44% of college students report binge drinking (Johnston, O'Malley, & Bachman, 1994; Wechsler et al., 1994). Since college-bound seniors in high school are *less* likely to engage in heavy drinking than students who are not college bound, the college crowd clearly caught up with and surpassed their peers after high school. Lost study time, missed classes, injuries, engaging in unprotected sex, and trouble with police are some of the problems reported by binge-drinking college students. Because of these problems, an increasing number of universities no longer permit alcohol on campus. The Drug Free School and Campuses Act passed by Congress in 1989 requires institutions to make alcohol education programs and counseling services available to students and employees.

Alcohol can also produce risks for a developing fetus. Mothers who drink heavily are twice as likely to suffer repeated miscarriages and to produce low birth-weight babies. A condition called fetal alcohol syndrome, characterized by mental retardation and multiple deformities of the face and mouth, is caused by drinking during pregnancy. The amount of alcohol needed to produce this syndrome is unclear, but it is thought that as little as a few ounces of alcohol a week can be

detrimental (Streissguth, Clarren, & Jones, 1985).

OPIATES

Opium and its derivatives, collectively known as **opiates,** are drugs that diminish physical sensation and the capacity to respond to stimuli by depressing the central nervous system. (These drugs are commonly called "narcotics," but opiates is the more accurate term; the term "narcotics" is not well defined and covers a variety of illegal drugs.) Opiates are medically useful for their painkilling properties, but their ability to alter mood and

Ages 16 through 25 are peak drinking years for most people.

reduce anxiety has led to widespread illegal consumption. Opium, which is the air-dried juice of the opium poppy, contains a number of chemical substances, including morphine and codeine. Codeine, a common ingredient in prescription painkillers and cough suppressants, is relatively mild in its effects (at least at low doses). Morphine and its derivative, heroin, are much more potent. Most illegal opiate use involves heroin because, being more concentrated, it can be concealed and smuggled more easily than morphine.

HEROIN USAGE   Heroin can be injected, smoked, or inhaled. At first, the drug produces a sense of well-being. Experienced users report a special thrill, or rush, within a minute or two after an intravenous injection. Some describe this sensation as intensely pleasurable, similar to an orgasm. Young people who sniff heroin report that they forget everything that troubles them. Following this, the user feels fixed, or gratified, with no awareness of hunger, pain, or sexual urges. The person may "go on the nod," alternately waking and drowsing while comfortably watching television or reading a book. Unlike a person intoxicated by alcohol, the heroin user can readily produce skilled responses to agility and intellectual tests and seldom becomes aggressive or assaultive.

The changes in consciousness produced by heroin are not very striking; there are no exciting visual experiences or feelings of being transported elsewhere. It is the change in

mood—the feeling of euphoria and reduced anxiety—that prompts people to *start* using this drug. However, heroin is very addictive; even a brief period of usage can create physical dependency. After a person has been smoking or "sniffing" (inhaling) heroin for a while, tolerance builds up, and this method no longer produces the desired effect. In an attempt to recreate the original high, the individual may progress to "skin popping" (injecting under the skin) and then to "mainlining" (injecting into a vein). Once the user starts mainlining, stronger and stronger doses are required to produce the high, and the physical discomforts of withdrawal from the drug become intense (chills, sweating, stomach cramps, vomiting, headaches). Thus, additional motivation to continue using the drug stems from the need to avoid physical pain and discomfort.

The hazards of heroin use are many; the average age at death for frequent users is 40 (Hser, Anglin & Powers, 1993). Death from an overdose is always a possibility because the concentration of street heroin fluctuates widely. Thus, the user can never be sure of the potency of the powder in a newly purchased supply. Death is caused by suffocation resulting from depression of the brain's respiratory center. Heroin use is generally associated with a serious deterioration of personal and social life. Because maintaining the habit is costly, the user often becomes involved in illegal activities to acquire funding.

Additional dangers of heroin use include AIDS (acquired immune deficiency syndrome), hepatitis, and other infections associated with unsterile injections. Sharing drug needles is an extremely easy way to be infected with the AIDS virus; blood from an infected person can be trapped in the needle or syringe, and then injected directly into the bloodstream of the next person who uses the needle. The sharing of needles and syringes by those who inject drugs is the most rapidly increasing way that the AIDS virus is being spread.

OPIOID RECEPTORS   In the 1970s, researchers made a major breakthrough in understanding opiate addiction with the discovery that opiates act on very specific neuroreceptor sites in the brain. Neurotransmitters travel across the synaptic junction between two neurons and bind to neuroreceptors, trig-

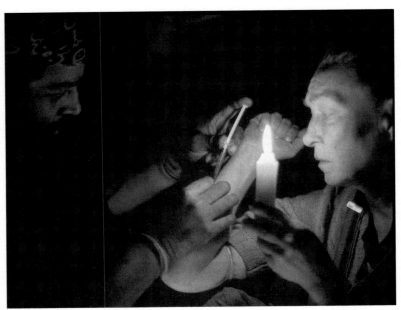

Drug users who share needles increase their risk of contracting AIDS.

gering activity in the receiving neuron (see Chapter 2). In molecular shape, the opiates resemble a group of neurotransmitters called **endorphins**. These endorphins bind to **opioid receptors**, producing sensations of pleasure as well as reducing discomfort (Julien, 1992). Heroin and morphine relieve pain by binding to opioid receptors that are unfilled (see Figure 6-7). Repeated heroin use causes a drop in endorphin production; the body then needs more heroin to fill the unoccupied opioid receptors in order to reduce pain. The person experiences painful withdrawal symptoms when heroin is discontinued because many opioid receptors are left unfilled (since the normal endorphin production has decreased). In essence, the heroin has replaced the body's own natural opiates (Koob and Bloom, 1988).

These research findings have led to the development of new drugs that operate by modulating the opioid receptors. The drug-abuse medications, generally, fall into two classes: *agonists* and *antagonists*. Agonists bind to the opioid receptors to produce a feeling of pleasure, thereby reducing the craving for opiates; but they cause less psychological and physiological impairment than the opiates. Antagonists also lock onto the opioid receptors, but in a way that does not activate them; the drug serves to "block" the receptors so that the opiates cannot gain access to them. Thus there is no feeling of pleasure and the craving is not satisfied (see Figure 6-7).

Methadone is the best-known agonist drug for treating heroin-dependent individuals. It is addictive in its own right, but it produces less psychological impairment than heroin and has few disruptive physical effects. When taken orally in low doses, it suppresses the craving for heroin and prevents withdrawal symptoms.

Naltrexone, an antagonist drug, blocks the action of heroin because it has a greater affinity for the opioid receptors than does heroin itself. Naltrexone is often used in hospital emergency rooms to reverse the effects of a heroin overdose. But as a treatment for heroin addiction, it has not proved generally effective. Interestingly, naltrexone does reduce the craving for alcohol. Alcohol causes the release of endorphins, and naltrexone, by blocking opioid receptors, reduces the pleasurable effects of alcohol and consequently the desire for it (Winger, Hoffman, & Woods, 1992).

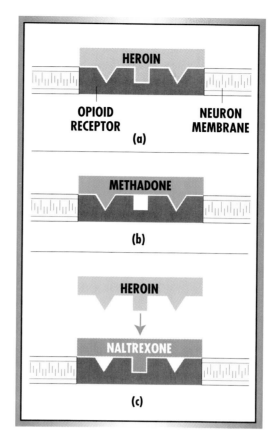

FIGURE 6-7

Drug-Abuse Medications *(a) Heroin binds to opioid receptors and produces a feeling of pleasure—mimicking the body's naturally occurring endorphins. (b) Methadone, an agonist drug, will also bind to opioid receptors and produce a pleasant sensation. The drug reduces both the craving for heroin and the associated withdrawal symptoms. (c) Naltrexone, an antagonist drug, acts to block the opioid receptors so that heroin cannot gain access to them. The craving for heroin is not satisfied and the drug has not proved generally effective as a treatment method.*

STIMULANTS

AMPHETAMINES   In contrast to depressants and opiates, stimulants are drugs that increase alertness and general arousal. **Amphetamines** are powerful stimulants, sold under such trade names as Methedrine, Dexedrine, and Benzedrine and known colloquially as "speed," "uppers," and "bennies." The immediate effects of consuming such drugs are an increase in alertness and a decrease in feelings

PET scans show the effects of opiates on the neural activity of different brain areas.

of fatigue and boredom. Strenuous activities that require endurance seem easier when amphetamines are taken. As with other drugs, the ability of amphetamines to alter mood and increase self-confidence is the principal reason for their use. People also use them to stay awake.

Low doses that are taken for limited periods to overcome fatigue (as during nighttime driving) seem to be relatively safe. However, as the stimulating effects of amphetamines wear off, there is a period of compensatory let-down during which the user feels depressed, irritable, and fatigued. He or she may be tempted to take more of the drug. Tolerance develops quickly, and the user needs increasingly larger doses to produce the desired effect. Since high doses can have dangerous side effects—agitation, confusion, heart palpitations, and elevated blood pressure—medications containing amphetamines should be used with caution.

When tolerance develops to the point at which oral doses are no longer effective, many users inject amphetamines into a vein. Large intravenous doses produce an immediate pleasant experience (a flash or rush); this sensation is followed by irritability and discomfort, which can be overcome only by an additional injection. If this sequence is repeated every few hours over a period of days, it will end in a "crash," a deep sleep followed by a period of lethargy and depression. The amphetamine abuser may seek relief from this discomfort by turning to alcohol or heroin.

Long-term amphetamine use is accompanied by drastic deterioration of physical and mental health. The user, or "speed freak," may develop symptoms that are indistinguishable from those of acute schizophrenia (see Chapter 16). These symptoms include persecutory delusions (the false belief that people are persecuting you or out to get you) and visual or auditory hallucinations. The delusions may lead to unprovoked violence. For example, in the midst of an amphetamine epidemic in Japan (during the early 1950s when amphetamines were sold without prescription and advertised for "elimination of drowsiness and repletion of the spirit"), 50 percent of the murder cases in a 2-month period were related to amphetamine abuse (Hemmi, 1969).

COCAINE   Like other stimulants, **cocaine,** or "coke," a substance obtained from the dried leaves of the coca plant, increases energy and self-confidence; it makes the user feel witty and hyperalert. In the early part of this century, cocaine was widely used and easy to obtain; in fact, it was an ingredient in the early recipe of Coca-Cola. Its use then declined, but recently its popularity has been increasing, even though it is now illegal.

Cocaine can be inhaled or it can be made into a solution and injected directly into a vein. It can also be converted into a flammable compound known as *crack* and smoked.

One of the earliest studies of the effects of cocaine is reported by Freud (1885). In an account of his own use of cocaine, he was at first highly favorable to the drug and encouraged its use. He noted

> ... the exhilaration and lasting euphoria, which in no way differs from the normal euphoria of the healthy person. ... You perceive an increase of self-control and possess more vitality and capacity for work. ... In other words, you are simply normal, and it is so hard to believe that you are under the influence of any drug. ... Long intensive mental or physical work is performed without any fatigue. ... This result is enjoyed without any of the unpleasant after-effects that follow exhilaration brought about by alcohol. (1885/1974, p. 9)

Freud soon withdrew this unreserved support, however, after he treated a friend with cocaine and the results were disastrous. The friend developed a severe addiction, demanded larger dosages of the drug, and was debilitated until his death.

Inhaling cocaine.

Despite earlier reports to the contrary, and as Freud soon discovered, cocaine is highly addictive. In fact, it has become more addictive and dangerous in recent years with the emergence of crack. Tolerance develops with repeated use, and withdrawal effects, while not as dramatic as with the opiates, do occur. The restless irritability that follows the euphoric high becomes, with repeated use, a feeling of depressed anguish. The down is as bad as the up was good and can be alleviated only by more cocaine (see Figure 6-8).

Heavy cocaine users can experience the same abnormal symptoms as high-level amphetamine users. A common visual hallucination is flashes of light ("snow lights") or moving lights. Less common but more disturbing is the feeling that bugs are crawling under the skin—"cocaine bugs." The hallucination may be so strong that the individual will use a knife to cut out the bugs. These experiences occur because cocaine is causing the sensory neurons to fire spontaneously (Weiss, Mirin, & Bartel, 1994).

Studies of babies exposed to cocaine before birth indicate that the drug is causing an epidemic of damaged infants, some of whom will be impaired for life because the mother used cocaine during pregnancy. The damaging effects include retarded growth in the womb, neurological abnormalities, malformed genital and urinary organs, and brain-damaging strokes. The research indicates that even a single exposure to cocaine during pregnancy can cause lasting damage. Cocaine readily crosses the placenta and the fetus converts a significant portion into norcocaine—an even more potent drug. Norcocaine does not leave the womb; the fetus excretes it into the amniotic fluid and then swallows it, re-exposing itself repeatedly to the drug. While a single dose of cocaine and its metabolites clear out of an adult body in about 2 days, a fetus is exposed for 5 or 6 days. As a consequence, almost no cocaine-exposed baby escapes its damaging effects (Julien, 1992).

Just as there is a heroin–AIDS connection, injecting cocaine can lead to AIDS and other diseases if drug needles are shared among several people. In some ways AIDS may be more of a problem for cocaine users than for heroin users. One reason is "binge use," with cocaine users sharing a needle for injection many times in a short period, unlike heroin addicts, who fall asleep after injection.

HALLUCINOGENS

Drugs whose main effect is to change perceptual experience are called **hallucinogens,** or *psychedelics.* Hallucinogens typically change the user's perception of both his or her internal and external worlds. Usual environmental stimuli are experienced as novel events—for example, sounds and colors seem dramatically different. Time perception is so altered that minutes may seem like hours. The user may experience auditory, visual, and tactile hallucinations and will have a decreased ability to differentiate between himself and his surroundings.

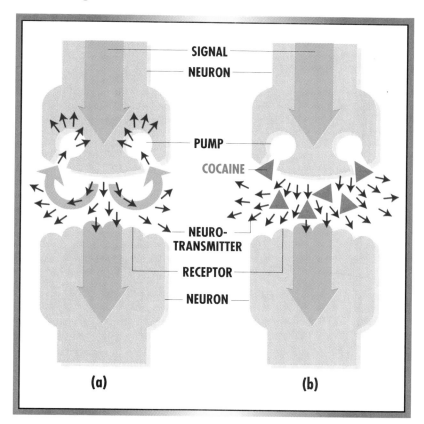

FIGURE 6-8

Molecular Effects of Cocaine *(a) A nerve impulse causes the release of neurotransmitters that carry the signal across the synapse to a receiving neuron. Some of the neurotransmitters are then reabsorbed into the originating neuron (reuptake process), while the rest are broken up chemically and made inactive (degradation process). These processes are discussed in Chapter 2. (b) Several lines of research indicate that cocaine blocks the reuptake process for three neurotransmitters (dopamine, serotonin, and norepinephrine) that are involved in the regulation of mood. With reuptake hampered by cocaine, the normal effects of these neurotransmitters are amplified; in particular, an excess of dopamine is associated with feelings of euphoria. However, prolonged cocaine use produces a shortage of these neurotransmitters, because their reuptake for later use is blocked; that is, the body degrades them at a faster rate than it can manufacture them. With the normal supply depleted by repeated cocaine use, eurphoria is replaced by anxiety and depression.*

Some hallucinogenic drugs are derived from plants—such as mescaline from cactus and psilocybin from mushrooms. Others are synthesized in the laboratory, such as LSD (lysergic acid diethylamide) and PCP (phencyclidine).

LSD   The drug LSD, or "acid," is a colorless, odorless, tasteless substance that is often sold dissolved on sugar cubes or pieces of paper. It is a potent drug that produces hallucinations at very low doses. Some users have vivid hallucinations of colors and sounds, and others have mystical or semireligious experiences. Anyone can have an unpleasant, frightening reaction (or "bad trip"), even those who have had many pleasant LSD experiences. Another adverse LSD reaction is the flashback, which may occur days, weeks, months, or even years after the last use of the drug. The individual experiences illusions or hallucinations similar to those experienced when using the drug. Since LSD is almost completely eliminated from the body within 24 hours after it is taken, the flashback is probably a restoration of memories of the prior experience.

More threatening to the LSD user is the loss of reality orientation that can occur with the drug. This alteration in consciousness can lead to an irrational and disoriented behavior and, occasionally, to a panic state in which the victim feels that he cannot control what he is doing or thinking. People have jumped from high places to their deaths when in this state. LSD was popular during the 1960s, but its use declined, probably due to widespread reports of severe drug reactions. There are some indications, however, of a renewed interest in LSD and other hallucinogens (Johnston, O'Malley, & Bachman, 1995).

PCP   Although it is sold as a hallucinogen (under such street names as "angel dust," "Shermans," and "superacid"), PCP is technically classified as a dissociative anesthetic. It may cause hallucinations, but it also makes the user feel dissociated or apart from the environment.

PCP was first synthesized in 1956 for use as a general anesthetic. It had the advantage of eliminating pain without producing a deep coma. However, its legal manufacture was discontinued when doctors found that the drug produced agitation, hallucinations, and a psychotic-like state resembling schizophrenia among many patients. Because the ingredients are cheap and the drug is relatively easy to manufacture in a kitchen laboratory, PCP is widely used as an adulterant of other, more expensive street drugs. Much of what is sold as THC (the active ingredient of marijuana) is really PCP.

PCP can be taken in liquid or pill form, but more often it is smoked or snorted. In low doses it produces an insensitivity to pain and an experience similar to a moderately drunken state—one of confusion, loss of inhibition, and poor psychomotor coordination. Higher doses produce a disoriented, co-malike condition. Unlike the person who experiences LSD, the PCP user is unable to observe his or her drug-induced state and frequently has no memory of it.

CANNABIS

The **cannabis** plant has been harvested since ancient times for its psychoactive effects. The dried leaves and flowers, or **marijuana**, is the form in which it is most often used in this country, while the solidified resin of the plant, called **hashish** ("hash"), is commonly used in the Middle East. Marijuana and hashish are usually smoked, but may be taken orally mixed with tea or food. The active ingredient in both substances is THC (tetrahydrocannabinol). Taken orally in small doses (5 to 10 milligrams), THC produces a mild high; larger doses (30 to 70 milligrams) produce severe and longer-lasting reactions that resemble those of hallucinogenic drugs. As with alcohol, the reaction often has two stages: a period of stimulation and euphoria followed by a period of tranquillity and sleep.

Regular users of marijuana report a number of sensory and perceptual changes: a general euphoria and sense of well-being, some distortions of space and time, and changes in social perception. Not all marijuana experiences are pleasant. Sixteen percent of regular users report anxiety, fearfulness, and confusion as a "usual occurrence," and about one-third report that they occasionally experience such symptoms as acute panic, hallucinations, and unpleasant distortions in body image (Negrete & Kwan, 1972; Halikas, Goodwin, & Guze, 1971;). Individuals who use marijuana regularly (daily or almost daily) often report both physical and mental lethargy; about a third show mild forms of depression, anxiety, or irritability (American Psychiatric Association, 1994). It should be noted that marijuana smoke contains even larger amounts of known carcinogens than tobacco.

Marijuana interferes with performance on complex tasks. Motor coordination is significantly impaired by low to moderate doses; and reaction time for automobile braking and the ability to negotiate a twisty road course are adversely affected (Institute of Medicine, 1982). These findings make it clear that driving while under the drug's influence is dangerous. The number of automobile accidents related to marijuana use is difficult to determine because, unlike alcohol, THC declines rapidly in the blood, quickly going to the fatty tissues and organs of the body. A blood analysis two hours after a heavy dose of marijuana may show no signs of THC, even though an observer would judge the person to be clearly impaired. It is estimated that one-fourth of all drivers involved in accidents are under the influence of marijuana alone or marijuana in combination with alcohol (Jones & Lovinger, 1985).

The effects of marijuana may persist long after the subjective feelings of euphoria or sleepiness have passed. A study of aircraft pilots using a simulated flight-landing task found that performance was significantly impaired as much as 24 hours after smoking one marijuana cigarette containing 19 milligrams of THC—despite the fact that the pilots reported no awareness of any aftereffects on their alertness or performance (Yesavage, Leier, Denari, & Hollister, 1985). These findings have led to concern about marijuana use by those whose jobs involve public safety.

It is a common subjective experience that marijuana disrupts memory functions, and this observation is well documented by research. Marijuana has two clear effects on memory. (1) It makes short-term memory more susceptible to interference. For example, people may lose the thread of a conversation, or forget what they are saying in the middle of a sentence, due to momentary distractions (Darley et al., 1973a). (2) Marijuana disrupts learning; that is, it interferes with the transfer of new information from short-term to long-term memory (Darley et al., 1977; Darley et al., 1973b). These findings

suggest that trying to study while under the influence of marijuana is not a good idea; recall of the material will be poor.

MEDITATION

In **meditation,** a person achieves an altered state of consciousness by performing certain rituals and exercises. These exercises include controlling and regulating breathing, sharply restricting one's field of attention, eliminating external stimuli, assuming yogic body positions, and forming mental images of an event or symbol. The result is a pleasant, mildly altered subjective state in which the individual feels mentally and physically relaxed. Some individuals, after extensive meditation practice, may have mystical experiences in which they lose self-awareness and gain a sense of being involved in a wider consciousness, however defined. That such meditative techniques may cause a change in consciousness goes back to ancient times and is represented in every major world religion. Buddhists, Hindus, Sufis, Jews, and Christians all have literature describing rituals that induce meditative states.

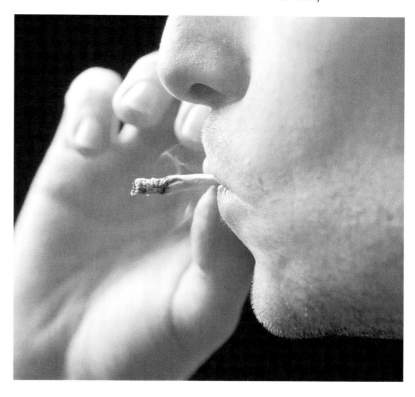

Marijuana impairs motor coordination and memory.

TRADITIONAL FORMS OF MEDITATION

Traditional forms of meditation follow the practices of *yoga,* a system of thought based on the Hindu religion, or *Zen,* which is derived from Chinese and Japanese Buddhism. Two common techniques of meditation are an *opening-up meditation,* in which the subject clears his or her mind for receiving new experiences, and a *concentrative meditation,* in which the benefits are obtained through actively attending to some object, word, or idea. The following is a representative statement of opening-up meditation:

> This approach begins with the resolve to do nothing, to think nothing, to make no effort of one's own, to relax completely and let go of one's mind and body . . . stepping out of the stream of ever-changing ideas and feelings which your mind is in, watch the onrush of the stream. Refuse to be submerged in the current. Changing the metaphor . . . watch your ideas, feelings, and wishes fly across the firmament like a flock of birds. Let them fly freely. Just keep a watch. Don't let the birds carry you off into the clouds. (Chauduri, 1965, pp. 30–31)

Here is a corresponding statement for concentrative meditation:

> The purpose of these sessions is to learn about concentration. Your aim is to concentrate on the blue vase. By concentration I do not mean analyzing the different parts of the vase, but rather, trying to see the vase as it exists in itself, without any connections to other things. Exclude all other thoughts or feelings or sounds or body sensations. (Deikman, 1963, p. 330)

After a few sessions of concentrative meditation, subjects typically report a number of effects: an altered, more intense perception of the vase; some time shortening, particularly in retrospect; conflicting perceptions, as if the vase fills the visual field and does not fill it; decreasing effectiveness of external stimuli (less distraction and eventually less conscious registration); and an impression of the meditative state as pleasant and rewarding.

Experimental studies of meditation provide only limited insight into the alterations of consciousness that a person can achieve when meditative practice and training extend over many years. In his study of the *Matra-mudra,* a centuries-old Tibetan Buddhist text, Brown (1977) has described the complex training required to master the technique. He has also shown that cognitive changes can be expected at different meditative levels. (In this type of meditation, people proceed through five levels until they reach a thoughtless, perceptionless, selfless state known as concentrative samadhi.)

MEDITATION FOR RELAXATION

A somewhat commercialized and secularized form of meditation has been widely promoted in the United States and elsewhere under the name of **transcendental meditation** or TM (Forem, 1973). The technique is easily learned from a qualified teacher who gives the novice meditator a **mantra** (a special sound) and instructions on how to repeat it over and over to produce the deep rest and awareness characteristic of TM.

A similar state of relaxation can be produced without the mystical associations of TM. Developed by Benson and his colleagues, the technique includes the following steps:

1. Sit quietly in a comfortable position and close your eyes.

2. Deeply relax all your muscles, beginning at your feet and progressing to your face. Keep them deeply relaxed.

3. Breathe through your nose. Become aware of your breathing. As you breathe out, say the word "one" silently to yourself. For example, breathe in . . . out, "one"; in . . . out, "one"; and so on. Continue for 20 minutes. You may open your eyes to check the time, but do not use an alarm. When you finish, sit quietly for several minutes at first with closed eyes and later with opened eyes.

4. Do not worry about whether you are successful in achieving a deep level of relaxation. Maintain a passive attitude and permit relaxation to occur at its own pace. Expect other thoughts. When these distracting thoughts occur, ignore them by thinking "oh well" and continue repeating "one." With practice, the response should come with little effort.

5. Practice the technique once or twice daily but not within two hours after a meal, since the digestive processes seem to interfere with the subjective changes. (Benson, Kotch, Crassweller, & Greenwood, 1977, p. 442)

During this kind of meditation, a person develops a reduced state of physiological arousal. Subjects report feelings quite similar to those generated by other meditative practices: peace of mind, a feeling of being at peace with the world, and a sense of well-being.

EFFECTS OF MEDITATION

Meditation is an effective technique for inducing relaxation and reducing physiological arousal. Almost all studies of the phenomenon report a significant lowering of the respiratory rate, a decrease in oxygen consumption, and less elimination of carbon dioxide. The heart rate is lowered, blood flow stabilizes, and the concentration of lactate in the blood is decreased (Dillbeck & Orme-Johnson, 1987). Also, there is a change in the EEG activity; these changes in brain waves suggest that cortical arousal is decreased during meditation, reflecting a reduced level of mental activity (Fenwick, 1987). Meditation has also proved effective in helping people with chronic feelings of anxiety (Eppley, Abrams & Shear, 1989) and in improving self-esteem (Alexander, Rainforth & Gelderloos, 1991).

A number of people involved in *sports psychology* believe that meditation can be useful in getting maximum performance from an athlete (Cox, Qiu, & Liu, 1993). Engaging in meditation helps reduce stress before an event, and with experience the athlete can learn to relax different muscle groups and appreciate subtle differences in muscle tension. The meditation may also involve forming mental images of the details of an upcoming event, such as a downhill ski race, until the athlete is in total synchrony with the flow of actions. The skier visualizes the release from the starting platform, speeding down the hill, and moving between the gates, and goes through every action in her mind. By creating visual sensations of a successful performance, the athlete is attempting to program the muscles and body for peak efficiency. Golfing great Jack Nicklaus developed this technique on his own years ago. In describing how he images his performance, Nicklaus wrote:

> I never hit a shot, even in practice, without having a sharp, in-focus picture of it in my head. It's like a color movie. First, I "see" the ball where I want it to finish, nice and white and sitting up high on the bright green grass.

Traditional forms of meditation have been practiced for hundreds of years as part of some Eastern religions.

> Then the scene quickly changes, and I "see" the ball going there: its path, trajectory, and shape, even its behavior on landing. Then there's a sort of fade-out, and the next scene shows me making the kind of swing that will turn the previous images into reality. Only at the end of this short, private, Hollywood spectacular do I select a club and step up to the ball. (1974, p. 79)

The research literature on meditation is of mixed quality, and some claims, particularly by those who have a commercial interest in the outcome, are suspect. Nevertheless, on balance, the evidence suggests that meditation may reduce arousal (especially in easily stressed individuals) and may be valuable for those suffering from anxiety and tension. To summarize, we quote from Harré and Lamb:

> The value of meditating for an individual depends on attitude and context. In the spiritual market place many contemporary cults of meditation, with their emphasis on gurus and membership of self-defining elitist institutions, may perhaps be seen as an expression of the disintegration of the family system in the modern West and attendant uncertainty regarding parental and sexual roles and mores. Young people, often desperate for guidance, find parental substitutes in strange places and are liable to become brainwashed practitioners of powerful psychosomatic exercises, access to which is made dependent on cult membership and financial contribution. Only where meditation is used as a means to personal development, insight and above all autonomy can its true potential be realized. (1983, p. 377)

Meditation can help an athlete relax and visualize the movements needed for a successful performance.

HYPNOSIS

Of all altered states of consciousness, none has raised more questions than **hypnosis**. Once associated with the occult, hypnosis has become the subject of rigorous scientific investigation. As in all fields of psychological investigation, uncertainties remain, but by now many facts have been established.

INDUCTION OF HYPNOSIS

In hypnosis, a willing and cooperative subject (the only kind that can be hypnotized under most circumstances) relinquishes some control over his behavior to the hypnotist and accepts some reality distortion. The hypnotist uses a variety of methods to induce this condition. For example, the subject may be asked to concentrate all thoughts on a small target (such as a thumbtack on the wall) while gradually becoming relaxed. A suggestion of sleepiness may be made because, like sleep, hypnosis is a relaxed state in which a person is out of touch with ordinary environmental demands. But sleep is only a metaphor. The subject is told that he will not really go to sleep but will continue to listen to the hypnotist.

The same state can be induced by methods other than relaxation. A hyperalert hypnotic trance is characterized by increased tension and alertness, and the trance-induction procedure is an active one. For example, in one study, subjects riding a stationary laboratory bicycle while receiving suggestions of strength and alertness were as responsive to hypnotic suggestions as were conventionally relaxed subjects (Banyai & Hilgard, 1976). This result denies the common equation of hypnosis with relaxation, but it is consistent with the trance-induction methods used by the whirling dervishes of some Muslim religious orders.

Modern hypnotists do not use authoritarian commands. Indeed, with a little training, subjects can hypnotize themselves (Ruch, 1975). The subject enters the hypnotic state when the conditions are right; the hypnotist merely helps set the conditions. The following changes are characteristic of the hypnotized state.

- *Planfulness ceases.* A deeply hypnotized subject does not like to initiate activity and would rather wait for the hypnotist to suggest something to do.
- *Attention becomes more selective than usual.* A subject who is told to listen only to the hypnotist's voice will ignore any other voices in the room.
- *Enriched fantasy is readily evoked.* A subject may find herself enjoying experiences at a place distant in time and space.
- *Reality testing is reduced and reality distortion is accepted.* A subject may uncritically accept hallucinated experiences (for example, conversing with an imagined person believed to be sitting in a nearby chair) and will not check to determine whether that person is real.
- *Suggestibility is increased.* A subject must accept suggestions in order to be hypnotized at all, but whether suggestibility is increased under hypnosis is a matter of some dispute. Careful studies have found some increase in suggestibility following hypnotic induction, although less than is commonly supposed (Ruch, Morgan, & Hilgard, 1973).
- *Posthypnotic amnesia is often present.* When instructed to do so, a highly responsive hypnotic subject will forget all or most of what transpired during the hypnotic session. When a prearranged release signal is given, the memories are restored.

Not all individuals are equally responsive to hypnosis, as Figure 6-9 indicates. Roughly

A therapist induces a hypnotic state.

5 to 10 percent of the population cannot be hypnotized even by a skilled hypnotist, and the remainder show varying degrees of susceptibility. However, if a person is hypnotized on one occasion, he probably will be equally susceptible on another (Piccione, Hilgard, & Zimbardo, 1989; Hilgard, 1961).

One might suspect that individuals who are highly responsive to hypnosis would also be highly suggestible or compliant in other social situations. However, research findings indicate that this is not true; personality tests designed to measure for compliance do not correlate significantly with hypnotic susceptibility. What does appear to be a good predictor of responsiveness to hypnosis is whether or not the individual has a rich imagination, enjoys daydreaming, and has the ability to generate vivid mental images (Crawford, 1989; Hilgard, 1979).

HYPNOTIC SUGGESTIONS

Suggestions given to a hypnotized subject can result in a variety of behaviors and experiences. The person's motor control may be affected, new memories may be lost or old ones reexperienced, and current perceptions may be radically altered.

CONTROL OF MOVEMENT Many hypnotic subjects respond to direct suggestion with involuntary movement. For example, if a person stands with arms outstretched and hands facing each other and the hypnotist suggests that the subject's hands are attracted to each other, the hands will soon begin to move together, and the subject will feel that they are propelled by some force that she is not generating. Direct suggestion can also inhibit movement. If a suggestible subject is told that an arm is stiff (like a bar of iron or an arm in a splint) and then is asked to bend the arm, it will not bend, or more effort than usual will be needed to make it bend. This response is less common than suggested movement.

Subjects who have been roused from hypnosis may respond with movement to a prearranged signal from the hypnotist. This is called a **posthypnotic response**. Even if the suggestion has been forgotten, subjects will feel a compulsion to carry out the behavior. They may try to justify such behavior as rational, even though the urge to perform it is

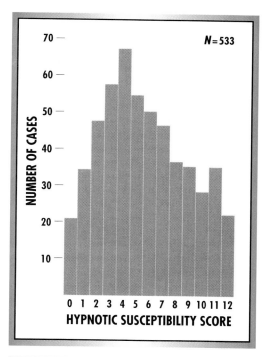

FIGURE 6-9

Individual Differences in Hypnotizability *After using a standard procedure designed to induce hypnosis, researchers administered 12 test suggestions from the Stanford Hypnotic Susceptibility Scale to 533 subjects. The object of the experiment was to test the appearance of hypnotic responses such as those described in the text (for example, being unable to bend one's arm or separate interlocked fingers when the hypnotist suggests these possibilities). The response was scored as present or absent, and the present responses were totaled for each subject to yield a score ranging from 0 (totally unresponsive) to 12 (most responsive). Most subjects fell in the middle ranges with a few very high and a few very low.* (After Hilgard, 1965)

impulsive. For example, a young man searching for a rational explanation of why he opened a window when the hypnotist took off her glasses (the prearranged signal) remarked that the room felt a little stuffy.

POSTHYPNOTIC AMNESIA At the suggestion of the hypnotist, events occurring during hypnosis may be "forgotten" until a signal from the hypnotist enables the subject to recall them. This is called **posthypnotic amnesia**. Subjects differ widely in their susceptibility to posthypnotic amnesia, as Figure 6-10 shows. The items to be recalled in this study were 10 actions the subjects performed while hypnotized. A few subjects forgot none or only one or two items; most subjects forgot four or five

THE HIDDEN OBSERVER

The concept of a **hidden observer** originated with Hilgard's (1986) observation that in many hypnotized subjects, a part of the mind that is not within awareness seems to be watching the subject's experience as a whole. His finding has been described as follows:

The circumstances of Hilgard's discovery of a doubled train of thought in hypnosis were suitably dramatic. He was giving a classroom demonstration of hypnosis using an experienced subject who, as it happened, was blind. Hilgard induced deafness, telling him that he would be able to hear when a hand was put on his shoulder. Cut off from what was going on around him, he became bored and began to think of other things. Hilgard showed the class how unresponsive he was to noise or speech, but then the question arose as to whether he was as unresponsive as he seemed. In a quiet voice, Hilgard asked the subject whether, though he was hypnotically deaf, there might be "some part of him" that could hear; if so, would he raise a forefinger? To the surprise of everyone—including the hypnotized subject—the finger rose.

At this, the subject wanted to know what was going on. Hilgard put a hand on his shoulder so he could hear, promised to explain later, but in the meantime asked the subject what he remembered. What he remembered was that everything had become still, that he was bored and had begun thinking about a problem in statistics. Then he felt his forefinger rise, and he wanted to know why.

Hilgard then asked for a report from "that part of you that listened to me before and made your finger rise," while instructing the hypnotized subject that he would not be able to hear what he himself said. It turned out that this second part of the subject's awareness had heard all that went on and was able to report it. Hilgard found a suitable metaphor to describe this detached witness—the *hidden observer* (Hebb, 1982, p. 53).

Thus, the hidden-observer metaphor refers to a mental structure that monitors everything that happens, including events that the hypnotized subject is not consciously aware of perceiving.

The presence of the hidden observer has been demonstrated in many experiments (Kihlstrom, 1985; Zamansky & Bartis, 1985). In studies on pain relief, subjects are able to describe how the pain feels, using automatic writing or speaking, at the same time that their conscious sys-

FIGURE 6-10

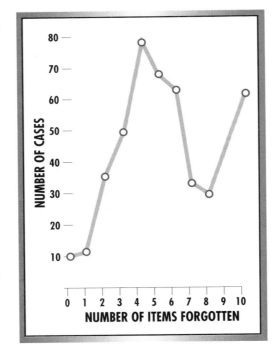

Distribution of Posthypnotic Amnesia *Subjects performed 10 actions while hypnotized and were then given posthypnotic amnesia instructions. When asked what occurred during hypnosis, subjects varied in the number of actions they failed to recall: The level of forgetting for a given subject ranged from 0 to 10 items. The experiment involved 491 subjects, and the graph plots the number of subjects at each level of forgetting. The plot shows a bimodal distribution for posthypnotic amnesia with peaks at 4 and 10 items forgotten.* (After Cooper, 1979)

items. However, a sizable number of subjects forgot all 10 items. This type of bimodal distribution, showing two distinct groups of subjects, has been found in many studies of posthypnotic amnesia. The group of subjects with the higher recall is larger and presumably represents the average hypnotic responders; the smaller group, the subjects who forgot all 10 items, has been described as hypnotic virtuosos. Differences in recall between the two groups following posthypnotic suggestion do not appear to be related to differences in memory capacity: Once the amnesia is canceled at a prearranged signal from the hypnotist, highly amnesic subjects remember as many items as those who are less amnesic. Some researchers have suggested that hypnosis temporarily interferes with the person's ability to retrieve a particular item from memory but does not affect actual memory storage (Kihlstrom, 1987).

AGE REGRESSION In response to hypnotic suggestion, some individuals are able to relive episodes from earlier periods of life, such as a birthday party at age 10. To some subjects, the episode seems to be pictured as if it were on a television screen; the subjects are conscious of being present and viewing the event but do not feel as if they are producing it. In another type of regression, subjects feel as if tem accepts and responds to the hypnotist's suggestion of pain relief. In other studies using automatic writing, hypnotized subjects have written messages of which they were unaware while their attention was directed to another task, such as reading aloud or naming the colors on a display chart (Knox, Crutchfield, & Hilgard, 1975). Hilgard and his colleagues have compared these phenomena to everyday experiences in which an individual divides attention between two tasks, such as driving a car and conversing at the same time or making a speech and simultaneously evaluating her performance as an orator.

Hidden-observer experiments, although replicated in many laboratories and clinics, have been criticized on methodological grounds. Skeptics argue that implied demands for compliance may have produced the results (see, for example, Spanos, 1986; Spanos & Hewitt, 1980). In an experiment designed to determine the role of compliance, researchers have shown that it is possible to distinguish the responses of the truly hypnotized from those of the merely compliant. They asked subjects of proven low hypnotizability to simulate hypnosis while highly responsive subjects behaved naturally. The experimenter did not know to which group each subject belonged. The simulators did conform to the implied demands in the way they were expected to, but their reports of the subjective experiences differed significantly from those individuals who were actually hypnotized (Zamansky & Bartis, 1985; Hilgard et al., 1978).

An unresolved problem is why some highly responsive hypnotized subjects do not have access to a hidden observer. One difference between the two groups has been reported. Subjects without a hidden observer are more "compliant" to suggestions of age regression—that is, they report feeling like children again—whereas those with a hidden observer invariably report a persistent duality of awareness. During age regression, they see themselves simultaneously as adult observers and as children. This division between an active participant and an observer is spontaneous and not suggested by the hypnotist (Laurence, 1980).

These are complex matters, not to be simply explained or lightly dismissed. They have implications not only for theories of hypnosis but for our view of consciousness in general. For a further discussion of this topic, see Hilgard (1986) and Farthing (1992).

they are reexperiencing the events. They may describe the clothing they are wearing, run a hand through their hair and describe its length, or recognize their elementary-school classmates. Occasionally, a childhood language, long forgotten, emerges during regression. For example, an American-born boy whose parents were Japanese and who had spoken Japanese at an early age but had forgotten it began speaking the language again while under hypnosis (Fromm, 1970).

POSITIVE AND NEGATIVE HALLUCINATIONS Some hypnotic experiences require a higher level of hypnotic talent than others. The vivid and convincing perceptual distortions of hallucinations, for instance, are relatively rare. Two types of suggested hallucinations have been documented: *positive hallucinations,* in which the subject sees an object or hears a voice that is not actually present; and *negative hallucinations,* in which the subject does not perceive something that normally would be perceived. Many hallucinations have both positive and negative components. In order not to see a person sitting in a chair (a negative hallucination), a subject must see the

Previously, when her hand was in the ice water, the subject felt no pain following suggestions of hypnotic anesthesia. By placing a hand on her shoulder, however, Dr. Hilgard can tap a "hidden observer" that reports the pain that the subject had felt at some level.

parts of the chair that would ordinarily be blocked from view (a positive hallucination).

Hallucinations can also occur as the result of posthypnotic suggestion. For example, subjects may be told that on arousal from the hypnotic state they will find themselves holding a rabbit that wants to be petted and that the rabbit will ask, "What time is it?" Seeing and petting the rabbit will seem natural to most of the subjects. But when they find themselves giving the correct time of day, they are surprised and try to provide an explanation for the behavior: "Did I hear someone ask the time? It's funny, it seemed to be the rabbit asking, but rabbits can't talk!" is a typical response.

Negative hallucinations can be used effectively to control pain. In many cases, hypnosis eliminates pain, even though the source of the pain—a severe burn or a bone fracture, for example—continues. The failure to perceive something (pain) that would normally be perceived qualifies this response as a negative hallucination. The pain reduction need not be complete in order for hypnosis to be useful in giving relief. Reducing pain by 20 percent can make the patient's life more tolerable. Experimental studies have shown that the amount of pain reduction is closely related to the degree of measured hypnotizability (Crasilneck & Hall, 1985; Hilgard & Hilgard, 1975).

PSI PHENOMENA

A discussion of consciousness would not be complete without considering some esoteric and mystical claims about the mind that have attracted widespread public attention. Of particular interest are questions about whether or not human beings (a) can acquire information in ways that do not involve stimulation of the known sense organs, or (b) can influence physical events by purely mental means. These questions are the source of controversy over the existence of **psi**, processes of information and/or energy exchange not currently explicable in terms of known science (in other words, known physical mechanisms). The phenomena of psi are the subject matter of **parapsychology** ("beside psychology") and include the following:

1. **Extrasensory perception (ESP)**. Response to external stimuli without any known sensory contact.
   a. **Telepathy**. Thought transference from one person to another without the mediation of any known channel of sensory communication (for example, identifying a playing card merely being thought of by another person).
   b. **Clairvoyance**. Perception of objects or events that do not provide a stimulus to the known senses (for example, identifying a concealed playing card whose identity is unknown to anyone).
   c. **Precognition**. Perception of a future event that could not be anticipated through any known inferential process (for example, predicting that a particular number will come up on the next throw of dice).

2. **Psychokinesis (PK)**. Mental influence over physical events without the intervention of any known physical force (for example, willing that a particular number will come up on the throw of dice).

EXPERIMENTAL EVIDENCE

Most parapsychologists consider themselves to be scientists applying the usual rules of scientific inquiry to admittedly unusual phenomena. Yet the claims for psi are so extraordinary and so similar to what are widely regarded as superstitions that some scientists declare psi to be an impossibility and reject the legitimacy of parapsychological inquiry. Such a priori judgments are out of place in science; the real question is whether the empirical evidence is acceptable by scientific standards. Many psychologists who are not yet convinced that psi has been demonstrated are nevertheless open to the possibility that new evidence might emerge that would be more compelling. For their part, many parapsychologists believe that several recent experimental procedures either provide that evidence already or hold the potential for doing so. We shall examine the most promising of these, the *ganzfeld procedure*.

The ganzfeld procedure tests for telepathic communication between a subject acting as the "receiver" and another subject who serves as the "sender." The receiver is sequestered in an acoustically isolated room and placed in a mild form of perceptual isolation: Translucent ping-pong ball halves are taped over the eyes and headphones are placed over the ears; diffuse red light illuminates the room, and white noise is played through the headphones. (White noise is a random mixture of sound frequencies similar to the hiss made by a radio tuned between stations.) This homogeneous visual and auditory environment is called the *ganzfeld,* a German word meaning "total field."

The sender sits in a separate acoustically isolated room, and a visual stimulus (picture, slide, or brief videotape sequence) is randomly selected from a large pool of similar stimuli to serve as the "target" for the session. While the sender concentrates on the target, the receiver attempts to describe it by providing a continuous verbal report of his or her ongoing imagery and free associations. Upon completion of the session, the receiver is presented with four stimuli—one of which is the target—and asked to rate the degree to which each matches the imagery and associations experienced during the ganzfeld session. A "direct hit" is scored if the receiver assigns the highest rating to the target stimulus.

More than 50 experiments have been conducted since the procedure was introduced in 1974; the typical experiment involves about 30 ganzfeld sessions in which a receiver attempts to identify the target transmitted by the sender. An overall analysis of 28 studies (comprising a total of 835 ganzfeld sessions conducted by investigators in 10 different laboratories) reveals that subjects were able to select the correct target stimulus 38 percent of the time. Because a subject must select the target from four alternatives, we would expect a success rate of 25 percent if only chance were operating. Statistically this result is highly significant; the probability that it could have arisen by chance is less than one in a billion (Bem & Honorton, 1994).

DEBATE OVER THE EVIDENCE

In 1985 and 1986, the *Journal of Parapsychology* published an extended examination of the ganzfeld studies, focusing on a debate between Ray Hyman, a cognitive psychologist and critic of parapsychology, and Charles Honorton, a parapsychologist and major contributor to the ganzfeld database. They agree on the basic quantitative results but disagree on points of interpretation (Hyman, 1994, 1985; Hyman & Honorton, 1986; Honorton, 1985). We shall use their debate as a vehicle for examining the issues involved in evaluating claims of psi.

The receiver (top photograph) and the sender (bottom photograph) in a ganzfeld experiment.

REPLICATION PROBLEM In science generally, a phenomenon is not considered established until it has been observed repeatedly by several researchers. Accordingly, the most serious criticism of parapsychology is that it has failed to produce a single reliable demonstration of psi that can be replicated by other investigators. Even the same investigator testing the same individuals over time may obtain statistically significant results on one occasion but not on another. The ganzfeld procedure is no exception; fewer than half (43 percent) of the 28 studies analyzed in the debate yielded statistically significant results.

The parapsychologists' most effective response to this criticism actually comes from within psychology itself. Many statisticians and psychologists are dissatisfied with psychology's focus on the **statistical significance level** as the sole measure of a study's success. As an alternative, they are increasingly adopting the technique of **meta-analysis**, a statistical technique that treats the accumulated studies of a particular phenomenon as a single grand experiment and each study as a single observation. Thus any study that obtains results in the positive direction—even though it may not be statistically significant itself—contributes to the overall strength and reliability of the phenomenon rather than simply being dismissed as a failure to replicate (Rosenthal, 1984; Glass, McGaw, & Smith, 1981).

From this perspective, the ganzfeld studies provide impressive replicability: 23 of the 28 studies obtain positive results, an outcome whose probability of occurring by chance is less than one in a thousand.

The power of a particular experiment to replicate an effect also depends on how strong the effect is and how many observations are made. If an effect is weak, an experiment with too few subjects or observations will fail to detect it at a statistically significant level—even though the effect actually exists. In the ganzfeld situation, if the effect actually exists and has a true direct-hit rate of 38 percent, then statistically we should expect studies with 30 ganzfeld sessions (the average for the 28 studies discussed above) to obtain a statistically significant psi effect only about one-third of the time (Utts, 1986).

In short, it is unrealistic to demand that any real effect be replicable at any time by any competent investigator. The replication issue is more complex than that, and meta-analysis is proving to be a valuable tool for dealing with some of those complexities.

INADEQUATE CONTROLS The second major criticism of parapsychology is that many, if not most, of the experiments have inadequate controls and safeguards. Flawed procedures that would permit a subject to obtain the communicated information in normal sensory fashion either inadvertently, or through deliberate cheating, are particularly fatal. This is called the problem of *sensory leakage*. Inadequate procedures for randomizing (randomly selecting) target stimuli are another common problem.

Methodological inadequacies plague all sciences, but the history of parapsychology is embarrassingly full of promising results that collapsed when the procedures were critically examined (Akers, 1984). One common charge against parapsychology is that preliminary, poorly controlled studies often obtain positive results but that as soon as better controls and safeguards are introduced, the results disappear.

Once a flaw is discovered in a completed experiment, there is no persuasive way of arguing that the flaw did not contribute to a positive outcome; the only remedy is to redo the experiment correctly. In a database of several studies, however, meta-analysis can evaluate the criticism empirically by checking to see if, in fact, the more poorly controlled studies obtained more positive results than did the better controlled studies. If there is a correlation between a procedural flaw and positive results across the studies, then there is a problem. In the case of the ganzfeld database, both critic Hyman and parapsychologist Honorton agree that flaws of inadequate security and possible sensory leakage do not correlate with positive results. Hyman claimed to find a correlation between flaws of randomization and positive results, but both Honorton's analysis and two additional analyses by nonparapsychologists dispute his conclusion (Harris & Rosenthal, 1988; Saunders, 1985). Moreover, a series of 11 new studies designed to control for flaws identified in the original database yielded results consistent with the original set of 28 studies (Bem & Honorton, 1994).

FILE-DRAWER PROBLEM Suppose that each of 20 investigators independently decides to conduct a ganzfeld study. Even if there were no genuine ganzfeld effect, there is a reasonable probability that at least one of these investigators would obtain a statistically significant result by pure chance. That lucky investigator would then publish a report of the experiment, but the other 19 investigators—all of whom obtained *null* results—are likely to become discouraged, put their data into a file drawer, and move on to something more promising. As a result, the scientific community would learn about the one successful study but have no knowledge of the 19 null studies buried away in the file drawers. The database of known studies would thus be seriously biased toward positive studies, and any meta-analysis of that database would arrive at similarly biased conclusions. This is called the **file-drawer problem.**

The problem is particularly tricky because it is impossible, by definition, to know how many unknown studies are languishing in file drawers somewhere. Nevertheless, parapsychologists offer two defenses against the charge that the file-drawer problem seriously compromises their database.

First, they point out that the *Journal of Parapsychology* actively solicits and publishes studies that report negative findings. Moreover, the community of parapsychologists is relatively small, and most investigators are cognizant of ongoing work in the various laboratories around the world. When conducting meta-analysis, parapsychologists actively attempt to scout out unpublished negative studies at conventions and through their personal networks.

But their major defense is statistical, and again meta-analysis provides an empirical approach to the problem. By knowing the overall statistical significance of the known database, it is possible to compute the number of studies with null results that would have to exist in file drawers to cancel out that significance. In the case of the ganzfeld database, there would have to be over 400 unreported studies with null results—the equivalent of 12,000 ganzfeld sessions—to cancel out the statistical significance of the 28 studies analyzed in the debate (Honorton, 1985). Not surprisingly, there is consensus that the overall significance of the ganzfeld studies cannot reasonably be explained by the file-drawer effect (Hyman & Honorton, 1986).

Rather than continue their debate, Hyman and Honorton issued a joint communiqué in which they set forth their areas of agreement and disagreement and made a series of suggestions for the conduct of future ganzfeld studies (Hyman & Honorton, 1986). Their debate and the subsequent discussion provide a valuable model for evaluating disputed domains of scientific inquiry.

Anecdotal Evidence

In the public's mind, the evidence for psi consists primarily of personal experiences and anecdotes. Such evidence is unpersuasive in science because it suffers fatally from the same problems that jeopardize the experimental evidence—nonreplicability, inadequate controls, and the file-drawer problem.

The replication problem is acute because most such evidence consists of one-time occurrences. A woman announces a premonition that she will win the lottery that day—and she does. You dream about an unlikely event that actually occurs a few days later. A "psychic" correctly predicts the assassination of a public figure. Such incidents may be subjectively compelling, but there is no way to evaluate them because they are not repeatable.

The problem of inadequate controls and safeguards is decisive because such incidents occur under unexpected and ambiguously specified conditions. There is thus no way of ruling out such alternative interpretations as coincidence (chance), faulty memories, and deliberate deception.

Finally, the file-drawer problem is also fatal. The lottery winner who announced ahead of time that she would win is prominently featured in the news. But the thousands of others with similar premonitions who did *not* win are never heard from; they remain in the file drawers. It is true that the probability of this woman's winning the lottery was very low. But the critical criterion in evaluating this case is not the probability that *she* would win but the probability that any *one* of the thousands who thought they would win would do so. That probability is much higher. Moreover, this woman has a personal file drawer that contains all those past instances in which she had similar premonitions and then lost.

The same reasoning applies to *precognitive dreams* (dreams that anticipate an unlikely event that then occurs a few days later). We tend to forget our dreams unless and until an event happens to remind us of them. We thus have no way of evaluating how often we might have dreamed of similar unlikely events that did *not* occur. We fill our database with positive instances and unknowingly exclude the negative instances.

Perhaps the fullest file drawers belong to the so-called psychics who make annual predictions in the tabloid newspapers. Nobody remembers the predictions that fail, but everybody remembers the occasional direct hits. In fact, these psychics are almost always wrong (Frazier, 1987; Tyler, 1977).

SKEPTICISM ABOUT PSI

If some of the experimental evidence for psi is as impressive as it seems, why hasn't it become part of established science? Why do we continue to be skeptical?

EXTRAORDINARY CLAIMS   Most scientists believe that extraordinary claims require extraordinary proof. A study reporting that students who study harder get higher grades will be believed even if the study was seriously flawed because the data accord well with our understanding of how the world works. But the claim that two people in a ganzfeld study communicate telepathically is more extraordinary; it violates most people's a priori beliefs about reality. We thus rightly demand a higher measure of proof from parapsychologists because their claims, if true, would require us to radically revise our model of the world—something we should not undertake lightly. In this way, science is justifiably conservative. Many open-minded nonparapsychologists are genuinely impressed by the ganzfeld studies, for example, but reasonably they can and do ask to see more evidence before committing themselves to the reality of psi.

Extraordinariness is a matter of degree. Telepathy seems less extraordinary to most of us than precognition because we are already familiar with the invisible transmission of information through space. We may not all understand how television pictures get to our living rooms, but we know that they do so. Why should telepathy seem that much more mysterious? Precognition, on the other hand, seems more extraordinary because we have no familiar phenomena in which information flows backward in time.

SKEPTICISM OF PSYCHOLOGISTS   Psychologists are a particularly skeptical group. A survey of over 1,000 college professors found that about 66 percent believe that ESP is either an established fact or a likely possibility. Moreover, these favorable views were expressed by a majority of professors in the natural sciences (55 percent), the social sciences excluding psychology (66 percent), and the arts, humanities, and education (77 percent). The comparable figure for psychologists was 34 percent (Wagner & Monnet, 1979).

Psychologists may be more skeptical than others for several reasons. First, they are the most familiar with past instances of extraordinary claims within psychology that turned out to be based on flawed experimental procedures, faulty inference, or even on fraud and deception. Over the history of research on parapsychology, there have been a disturbing number of cases where research claims have later proved to be based on fraudulent data. Those who follow developments in this field have so often encountered charlatans—some very clever—that they have good reason to be skeptical of new claims (Randi, 1982; Gardner, 1981).

Second, psychologists know that popular accounts of psychological findings are frequently exaggerated. For example, the genuinely remarkable findings from research on asymmetries in the human brain (see p. 00) have spawned a host of pop-psychology books and media reports containing unsubstantiated claims about left-brained and right-brained persons. Irresponsible reports about states of consciousness—including hypnosis and psi—appear daily in the media. It is thus pertinent to note that when the college professors in the survey cited above were asked to name the sources for their beliefs about ESP, they most frequently cited reports in newspapers and magazines.

Finally, research in cognitive and social psychology has sensitized psychologists to

A range of psychic offerings.

the biases and shortcomings in our abilities to draw valid inferences from our everyday experiences (see Chapter 18). This makes them particularly skeptical of anecdotal reports of psi where, as we saw above, our judgments are subject to many kinds of errors.

For these several reasons, then, much of the skepticism of psychologists toward psi is well founded, but some of it is not. The work using the ganzfeld procedure has withstood considerable scrutinizing and warrants consideration.

PSYCHOLOGICAL-BIOLOGICAL PERSPECTIVES

Advances in psychology often go hand in glove with a better understanding of the underlying neurobiological mechanisms. In this chapter, the discussions of sleep and psychoactive drugs were clearly advanced by a knowledge of related biological processes. In contrast, discussions of parapsychology, meditation, and hypnosis made virtually no reference to biological mechanisms, suggesting that our understanding of these phenomena is still at a very elementary stage.

This chapter's opening section on consciousness also made no reference to possible biological correlates. To be sure, consciousness is the most elusive of all psychological phenomena and there is little agreement on how to study the topic—let alone how to define it. Nevertheless, in recent years there has been a surge of speculation about consciousness, much of it at a neurophysiological level. The speculation, so far, has yielded little real progress in understanding consciousness, but some mention of the work is appropriate. We will briefly describe two developments that represent opposite extremes on a range of speculations about consciousness.

At one extreme are scientists who share an affinity with the philosophical concept of *materialism,* which holds that the brain and its billions of interacting neurons somehow give rise to conscious experience. A prominent advocate of this position is Francis Crick, one of this century's greatest scientists who shared a Nobel prize in 1962 for discovering the structure of DNA. In recent years his research has been in the areas of psychology and neuroscience; his avowed goal is to provide a scientific account of consciousness (Crick, 1994).

Crick believes that consciousness is synonymous with awareness, and that all forms of awareness—whether focused on objects in the external world or abstract mental images—involve the same underlying mechanism, one that combines attention and short-term memory (see Chapter 8). He makes specific proposals about the cortical areas involved in short-term memory and the way the brain's attentional processes focus on only a small portion of the information flooding into the sensory system. The sustained firing of neurons in these cortical areas is the basis of short-term memory, and it is this neural activity that represents consciousness awareness. Crick elaborates on these ideas in *The Astonishing Hypothesis,* a book published in 1994, and argues that as we expand our understanding of the neural mechanisms underlying short-term memory we will unravel the nature of human consciousness.

At the other extreme are those who reject the idea that consciousness can be explained in terms of a scientific theory—either neurobiological or psychological. This position is illustrated by Colin McGinn in his 1991 book, *The Problem of Consciousness.* He argues that the human brain is the product of evolution and accordingly has limitations on what it can perceive and understand. Just as a baboon or a chimpanzee cannot conceive of complex scientific ideas—such as that the earth goes around the sun and not vice versa—so human beings are prohibited from understanding how and why we have a subjective experience of the world. Consciousness, according to McGinn, will remain forever beyond human understanding.

The proposals of Crick and McGinn are but two examples of theories that have been advanced in recent years—not just by psychologists and neuroscientists but by physicists, computer scientists, philosophers, and mathematicians. These developments are so new that many introductory psychology textbooks make no reference to the work and in some of the textbooks the term "consciousness" is not even listed in the index. But the topic is central to psychology and should not be ignored.

📖 CHAPTER SUMMARY

1. A person's perceptions, thoughts, and feelings at any moment in time constitute that person's *consciousness*. An *altered state of consciousness* is said to exist when mental functioning seems changed or out of the ordinary to the person experiencing the state. Some altered states of consciousness, such as sleep and dreams, are experienced by everyone; others result from special circumstances, such as meditation, hypnosis, or the use of drugs.

2. The functions of consciousness are (a) *monitoring* ourselves and our environment so that we are aware of what is happening within our bodies and in our surroundings; and (b) *controlling* our actions so that they coordinate with events in the outside world. Not all events that influence consciousness are at the center of our awareness at a given moment. Memories of personal events and of the knowledge accumulated during a lifetime that are accessible but are not currently part of one's consciousness are called *preconscious memories*. Events that affect behavior even though we are not aware of perceiving them influence us *subconsciously*.

3. According to psychoanalytic theory, some emotionally painful memories and impulses are *not* available to consciousness because they have been repressed—that is, diverted to the *unconscious*. Unconscious thoughts and impulses influence our behavior even though they reach consciousness only in indirect ways through dreams, irrational behavior, and slips of the tongue.

4. The notion of a *dissociation* assumes that thoughts and memories may sometimes be *dissociated*, or split off, from consciousness, rather than repressed to the unconscious. Extreme examples are cases of *dissociative identity disorder*, in which two or more well-developed personalities alternate within the same individual.

5. *Sleep*, an altered state of consciousness, is of interest because of the rhythms evident in sleep schedules and in the depth of sleep. These rhythms are studied with the aid of the *electroencephalogram* (EEG). Patterns of brain waves show four stages (depths) of sleep, plus a fifth stage characterized by *rapid eye movements* (REMs). These stages alternate throughout the night. Dreams occur more often during REM sleep than during the other four stages (NREM sleep).

6. In 1900, Sigmund Freud proposed the most influential theory of dreams. It attributes psychological causes to dreams, distinguishing between the *manifest* and *latent content* of dreams and stating that dreams are wishes in disguise. Recent theories assume that REM sleep plays a role in the storage of memories and in preparing the brain from one day to the next to deal with new information inputs.

7. *Psychoactive drugs* have long been used to alter consciousness and mood. They include *depressants*, such as alcohol, tranquilizers and inhalants; *opiates*, such as heroin and morphine; *stimulants*, such as amphetamines and cocaine; *hallucinogens*, such as LSD and PCP; and *cannabis*, such as marijuana and hashish.

8. Repeated use of any of these drugs can result in *drug dependence*, which is characterized by *tolerance*, *withdrawal*, and *compulsive use*. *Drug abuse* refers to the continued use of a drug despite serious consequences by a person who has not reached the stage of dependence.

9. *Meditation* represents an effort to alter consciousness by following planned rituals or exercises such as those of yoga or Zen. The result is a somewhat mystical state in which the individual is extremely relaxed and feels divorced from the outside world. Simple exercises combining concentration and relaxation can help novices experience meditative states.

10. *Hypnosis* is a responsive state in which subjects focus their attention on the hypnotist and the hypnotist's suggestions. Some people are more readily hypnotized than others, though most people show some susceptibility. Characteristic hypnotic responses include enhanced or diminished *control over movements*, the distortion of memory through *posthypnotic amnesia*, *age regression*, and positive and negative *hallucinations*. The reduction of pain, as a variety of negative hallucination, is one of the beneficial uses of hypnosis.

11. There is considerable controversy over *psi*, the idea that human beings can acquire information about the world in ways that do not involve stimulation of known sense organs or can influence physical events by purely mental means. The phenomena of psi includes *extrasensory perception* (ESP) in its

various forms (telepathy, clairvoyance, precognition) and *psychokinesis,* movement of objects by the mind.

12. A number of carefully controlled studies (called *ganzfeld experiments*) have been conducted to evaluate ESP via telepathy. These experiments are subject to criticism (replicability, inadequate controls, file-drawer problems). However, a careful analysis of the results does not preclude the possibility of a real ESP effect. Nevertheless, most psychologists remain skeptical about ESP and psi in general, in part because so many past instances of extraordinary claims turned out to be based on flawed experimental procedures, faulty inferences, or even on fraud and deception.

FURTHER READING

Farthing, *The Psychology of Consciousness* (1992) provides a very readable overview of the problems of consciousness and its alterations. See, also, Hobson, *The Chemistry of Conscious States* (1994). For philosophical/psychological discussions of consciousness see Lycan, *Consciousness* (1987); Jackendoff, *Consciousness and the Computational Mind* (1990); and Churchland, *The Engine of Reason, the Seat of the Soul,* (1995).

Problems of dissociation are treated in Hilgard, *Divided Consciousness* (1986); Kluft (ed.), *Childhood Antecedents of Multiple Personality* (1985); and Putnam, *Diagnosis and Treatment of Multiple Personality Disorders* (1989).

Useful books on sleep and dreams include Hobson, *Sleep* (1989); Booztin, Kihlstrom, and Schacter (eds.), *Sleep and Cognition* (1990); Anch et al., *Sleep: A Scientific Perspective* (1988); and Hobson, *The Dreaming Brain* (1988).

General books on drugs include Julien, *A Primer of Drug Action* (6th ed., 1992); Goldstein, *Addiction: From Biology to Drug Policy* (1994); and Winger, Hofmann, and Woods, *A Handbook on Drug and Alcohol Abuse* (3rd ed., 1992). *Drug and Alcohol Abuse* (3rd ed., 1989) by Schuckit provides a guide to diagnosis and treatment. For a discussion of cocaine, see Weiss, Mirin, and Bartel, *Cocaine* (2nd. ed., 1994).

On meditative practices, see West (ed.), *The Psychology of Meditation* (1987); Goleman, *The Varieties of Meditative Experience* (1977); or Naranjo and Ornstein, *On the Psychology of Meditation* (1977). On meditation for relaxing, see Benson, *The Relaxation Response* (1976). For a discussion of relaxation and mental images in athletics, see Singer, Murphey and Tennant (eds.), *Handbook of Research on Sport Psychology* (1993); and Butt, *The Psychology of Sport* (2nd ed., 1988).

There are a number of books on hypnosis. Presentations that include methods, theories, and experimental results are Hilgard, *The Experience of Hypnosis* (1968); Fromm and Shor (eds.), *Hypnosis; Developments in Research and New Perspectives* (2nd ed., 1979); and Gheorghiu et al. (eds.), *Suggestion and Suggestibility: Theory and Research* (1989).

For a review of parapsychology, see Wolman, Dale, Schmeidler, and Ullman (eds.), *Handbook of Parapsychology* (1986); and Gardner, *Science: Good, Bad, and Bogus* (1981).

Learning,
Remembering,
and Thinking

LEARNING AND CONDITIONING

L earning pervades our lives. It is involved not only in mastering a new skill or academic subject but also in emotional development, social interaction, and even personality development. We learn what to fear, what to love, how to be polite, how to be intimate, and so on. Given the pervasiveness of learning in our lives, it is not surprising that we have already discussed many instances of it—how, for example, children learn to perceive the world around them, to identify with their own sex, and to control their behavior according to adult standards. Now, however, we turn to a more systematic analysis of learning.

Learning may be defined as a relatively *permanent* change in behavior that results from practice; behavior changes that are due to maturation (rather than practice), or to *temporary* conditions of the organism (such as fatigue or drug-induced states) are not included. All cases of learning are not the same, though. Four different kinds may be distinguished: (a) *habituation,* (b) *classical conditioning,* (c) *operant conditioning,* and (d) what we will call *complex learning.* **Habituation,** the simplest kind of learning, amounts to learning to ignore a stimulus that has become familiar and has no serious consequences—for example, learning to ignore the ticking of a new clock. Classical and operant conditioning both involve forming *associations*—that is, learning that certain events go together. In **classical conditioning,** an organism learns that one event follows another; for example, a baby learns that the sight of a breast will be followed by the taste of milk. In **operant conditioning,** an organism learns that a response it makes will be followed by a particular consequence; for example, a young child learns that striking a sibling will be followed by disapproval from his or her parents. **Complex learning** involves something in addition to forming associations; for example, applying a strategy when solving a problem, or constructing a mental map of one's environment. Our main focus will be on the last three kinds of learning. Before beginning our discussion of conditioning and learning, though, we need to consider how the various perspectives on psychology have been applied to the study of learning.

PERSPECTIVES ON LEARNING

Recall from Chapter 1 that three of the most important perspectives on psychology are the behavioristic, cognitive, and biological perspectives. As much as any area in psychology, the study of learning has involved all three of these perspectives.

Much of the early work on learning, particularly on conditioning, was done from a behavioristic perspective. Researchers studied how nonhuman organisms learn an association between stimuli or an association between a stimulus and a response. The focus was on external stimuli and responses, in keeping with the general behavioristic dictum that behavior is better understood in terms of external causes than mental ones. The behaviorist approach to learning made other key assumptions as well. One was that simple associations of the classical or operant kind are the building blocks of all learning. Thus something as complex as acquiring a language is presumably a matter of learning many associations (Staats, 1968). Another assumption was that the same basic laws of learning are in play regardless of what exactly is being learned or who exactly is doing the learning—be it a rat learning to run a maze or a child mastering long division (Skinner, 1971; 1938). These views lead behaviorists to focus on how the behaviors of nonhuman organisms, particularly rats and pigeons, are influenced by rewards and punishments in simple laboratory situations.

This work uncovered a wealth of findings and phenomena that continue to form the basis of much of what we know about associative learning. But, as we will see, the behaviorist assumptions have had to be modified in light of subsequent work. Understanding conditioning, not to mention complex learning, requires us to consider what the organism *knows,* about the relations between stimuli and response (even when the organism is a rat or a pigeon), thereby ushering in the cognitive perspective. Also, in cases of complex learning, strategies, rules, and the like must be considered in addition to associations, and again this requires us to adopt a cognitive approach. Furthermore, it now appears that there is *not* a single set of laws that underlies learning in all situations and for all organisms. In particular, different mechanisms of learning seem to be involved in different species, thereby ushering in the biological perspective.

The upshot is that the contemporary study of learning involves an integration of the three perspectives of interest. Accordingly, our treatment of both classical and operant conditioning will consider behaviorist, cognitive, and biological factors (our treatment of complex learning will concern mainly cognitive factors). We begin our discussion with behavioristic work, which introduces the essential phenomena.

CLASSICAL CONDITIONING

The study of **classical conditioning** began in the early years of the twentieth century when Ivan Pavlov, a Russian physiologist who had already won the Nobel prize for research on digestion, turned his attention to learning. While studying digestion, Pavlov noticed that a dog began to salivate at the mere sight of a food dish. While any dog will salivate when food is placed in its mouth, this dog had learned to associate the sight of the dish with the taste of food. Pavlov had happened upon a case of associative learning, and he decided to see whether a dog could be taught to associ-

ate food with other things, such as a light or a tone.

PAVLOV'S EXPERIMENTS

In Pavlov's basic experiment, a researcher first attaches a capsule to the dog's salivary gland to measure salivary flow. Then the dog is placed in front of a pan, in which meat powder can be delivered automatically. A researcher turns a light on in a window in front of the dog. After a few seconds, some meat powder is delivered to the pan, and the light is turned off. The dog is hungry, and the recording device registers copious salivation. This salivation is an **unconditioned response**, or UCR, for no learning is involved; by the same token, the meat powder is an **unconditioned stimulus**, or UCS. The procedure is repeated a number of times—light then food, light then food, and so on. Then, to test if the dog has learned to associate the light with food, the experimenter turns on the light but does not deliver any meat powder. If the dog salivates, it has learned the association. This salivation is a **conditioned response**, or CR, while the light is a **conditioned stimulus**, or CS. The dog has been taught, or conditioned, to associate the light with food and to respond to it by salivating. Pavlov's experiment is diagrammed in Figure 7-1.

EXPERIMENTAL VARIATIONS Psychologists over the years have devised many variations of Pavlov's experiments. To appreciate these variations, we need to note some critical aspects of the conditioning experiment. Each paired presentation of the conditioned stimulus (CS) and the unconditioned stimulus (UCS) is called a *trial*. The trials during which the subject is learning the association between the two stimuli is the **acquisition** stage of conditioning. During this stage, repeated pairings of the CS (light) and UCS (food) are said to strengthen, or **reinforce**, the association between the two, as illustrated in the left-hand curve of Figure 7-2. If the association is not reinforced (the UCS is omitted repeatedly), the response will gradually diminish; this is called **extinction** and is illustrated by the right-hand curve in Figure 7-2. Does extinction amount to unlearning the previously acquired association, or to learning to inhibit the CR when the CS is present? It can-

Ivan Pavlov with his assistants.

not involve true unlearning, because when an organism undergoes extinction and is then moved to a new context the conditioned response may reappear. This phenomenon, discovered by Pavlov, is referred to as *spontaneous recovery*. Modern researchers favor the idea that, as a result of extinction, the CS takes on an inhibitory signal as well as an excitatory one, but the inhibitory signal is tied to the context. If there is a change in the context, the inhibitory signal of the CS is lost, and the conditioned response can be recovered (Bouton, 1994).

Acquisition and extinction make intuitive sense if we view classical conditioning as learning to predict what will happen next. (This is the heart of the cognitive approach to conditioning that we will later consider.) When the prediction is successful (reinforced), the animal learns to keep making that prediction (acquisition); when things change in the world so that the prediction is outdated (not reinforced), the animal learns to inhibit that prediction (extinction).

CONDITIONING IN DIFFERENT SPECIES   Classical conditioning is pervasive in the animal kingdom and can occur with organisms as primitive as the flatworm. Flatworms contract their bod-

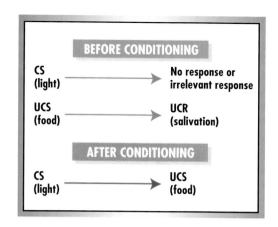

FIGURE 7-1

Diagram of Classical Conditioning   *The association between the unconditioned stimulus and the unconditioned response exists at the start of the experiment and does not have to be learned. The association between the conditioned stimulus and the unconditioned stimulus is learned. It arises through the pairing of the conditioned and unconditioned stimuli. (An association may also be learned between the conditioned stimulus and the conditioned response.)*

ies when subjected to mild electric shock, and if they experience sufficient pairings of shock (the UCS) and light (the CS), eventually they will contract to the light alone

FIGURE 7-2

Acquisition and Extinction of a Conditioned Response   *The curve in the panel on the left depicts the acquisition phase of an experiment. Drops of salivation in response to the conditioned stimulus (prior to the onset of the UCS) are plotted on the vertical axis; the number of trials, on the horizontal axis. After 16 acquisition trials, the experimenter switched to extinction; the results are presented in the panel at the right. (After Pavlov, 1927)*

(Jacobson, Fried, & Horowitz, 1967). Numerous human responses can also be classically conditioned. Many of these are involuntary responses. To illustrate, consider the plight of cancer patients who are undergoing chemotherapy treatments to stop the growth of their tumors. Chemotherapy involves injecting toxic substances into the patients, who as a result often become nauseated. After a number of chemotherapy sessions, patients sometimes become nauseated and sick upon entering the treatment room. The repeated pairing of the chemotherapy (the UCS) and the sight of the treatment room (the CS) has led the patients to associate the room with the chemotherapy, which results in the patients experiencing intestinal upset before their treatment even begins. A related phenomenon arises with young cancer patients who are given ice cream before the chemotherapy session. The ice cream may have been intended to lighten the child's distress about the impending treatment, but alas the ice cream becomes conditioned to the chemotherapy experience (now the ice cream is the CS and the chemotherapy the UCS). The upshot is that the children will be less likely to eat ice cream even outside the chemotherapy setting (Bernstein, 1978).

PHENOMENA AND APPLICATIONS

A number of phenomena greatly increase the generality of classical conditioning and make it an important kind of learning.

SECOND-ORDER CONDITIONING   Thus far in our discussion of conditioning, the UCS has always been biologically significant, such as food, cold, or shock. However, other stimuli can acquire the power of a UCS by being consistently paired with a biologically significant UCS. Recall the example of a dog exposed to a light (CS) followed by food (UCS), where the light comes to elicit a conditioned response. Once the dog is conditioned, the light acquires the power of a UCS. Thus, if the dog is now put in a situation in which it is exposed to a tone followed by the light (but no food) on each trial, the tone alone will eventually elicit a conditioned response even though it has never been paired with food. (There must also be other trials in which the light is again paired with food; otherwise, the originally

conditioned relation between light and food will extinguish.)

The existence of such *second-order* conditioning greatly increases the scope of classical conditioning, especially for humans for whom biologically significant UCSs occur relatively frequently. Now, all that is needed for conditioning to occur is the pairing of one stimulus with another, where the latter has previously been paired with a biologically significant event. Consider again our chemotherapy example. Suppose that for a particular patient the sight of the treatment room has become conditioned to the chemotherapy experience (a biologically significant event). If the patient is repeatedly presented a neutral stimulus, say a tone, followed by a picture of the treatment room, the patient may start to experience some unpleasant feeling to the tone alone.

GENERALIZATION AND DISCRIMINATION   When a conditioned response has been associated with a particular stimulus, other similar stimuli will evoke the same response. Suppose that a person is conditioned to have a mild emotional reaction to the sound of a tuning fork producing a tone of middle C. (The emotional reaction is measured by the **galvanic skin response**, or GSR, which is a change in the electrical activity of the skin that occurs during emotional stress.) The person will also show a GSR to higher or lower tones without further conditioning (see Figure 7-3). The more similar the new stimuli are to the original CS, the more likely they are to evoke the conditioned response. This principle, called **generalization**, accounts in part for an individual's ability to react to novel stimuli that are similar to familiar ones.

A process complementary to generalization is **discrimination**. Whereas generalization is a reaction to similarities, discrimination is a reaction to differences. Conditioned discrimination is brought about through selective reinforcement as shown in Figure 7-4. Instead of just one tone, for instance, now there are two. The low-pitched tone, CS_1, is always followed by a shock, and the high-pitched tone, CS_2, is not. Initially, subjects will show a GSR to both tones. During the course of conditioning, however, the amplitude of the conditioned response to CS_1 gradually increases while the amplitude of the response to CS_2 decreases. By this process of **differential reinforcement**, subjects are conditioned to discriminate between the two tones. The high-pitched tone, CS_2, has become a signal to inhibit the learned response.

Generalization and discrimination occur in everyday life. A young child who has learned to associate the sight of her pet dog with playfulness may initially approach all dogs. Eventually, through differential reinforcement, the child may expect playfulness only from dogs that look like hers. The sight of a threatening dog has come to inhibit the child's response of approaching dogs.

CONDITIONED FEAR   Classical conditioning plays a role in emotional reactions like fear. Suppose a rat is placed in an enclosed compartment in which it is periodically subjected to electric shock (by electrifying the floor). Just before the shock occurs a tone sounds. After repeated pairings of the tone (the CS) and the shock (the UCS), the tone alone will produce reactions in the rat that are indicators of fear, including stopping in its tracks and crouching; in addition, its blood pressure increases. The rat has been conditioned to be fearful when exposed to what was once a neutral stimulus.

It has been known since the seminal experiment of Watson and Rayner (1920) that humans too can be conditioned to be fearful. Many human fears may be acquired in this way, particularly in early childhood (Jacobs & Nadel, 1985). Perhaps the best evidence that they can be classically conditioned is that some of these fears, especially irrational ones, can be eliminated by therapeutic techniques based on classical-conditioning principles. A person with an intense fear of cats, for example, may overcome the fear by gradually and repeatedly being exposed to cats. Presumably, a cat was a CS for some noxious UCS a long time ago, and when the person now repeatedly experiences the CS without the UCS, the conditioned fear extinguishes. Note that if the person were not treated, he or she would simply avoid cats; consequently extinction would not occur, and the phobia would persist. (See Chapter 15 for a discussion of conditioning and phobias and Chapter 16 for conditioning therapies.)

CONDITIONING AND DRUG TOLERANCE   In most of our examples thus far the conditioned response resembles the unconditioned response. Pavlov's

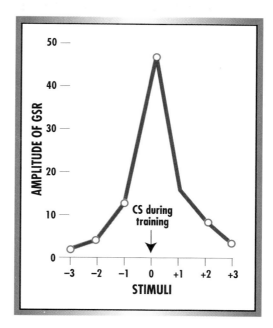

FIGURE 7-3

Gradient of Generalization   *Stimulus 0 denotes the tone to which the galvanic skin response (GSR) was originally conditioned. Stimuli +1, +2, and +3 represent test tones of increasingly higher pitch; stimuli −1, −2, and −3 represent tones of lower pitch. Note that the amount of generalization decreases as the difference between the test tone and the training tone increases.*

dogs salivate to the light (the CR) just as they do to the food (the UCR), cancer patients become nauseated at the sight of the treatment room (the CR) just as they do to the chemotherapy treatment (the UCR), and so on. But this is not always the case. There are situations in which the CR is the opposite of the UCR, and some of the most dramatic of these situations involve the use of drugs. Consider a case in which someone regularly takes injections of morphine. Since the sight of the injection is repeatedly followed by the

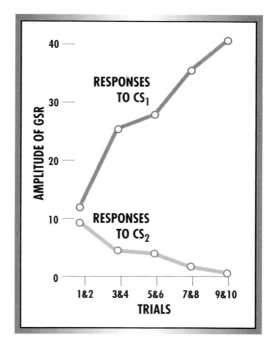

FIGURE 7-4

Conditioned Discrimination   *The discriminative stimuli were two tones of clearly different pitch (CS_1 = 700 hertz and CS_2 = 3,500 hertz). The unconditioned stimulus, an electric shock applied to the left forefinger, occurred only on trials when CS_1 was presented. The strength of the conditioned response, in this case the GSR, gradually increased following CS_1 and extinguished following CS_2. (After Baer & Fuhrer, 1968)* morphine, the injection functions as a CS, morphine as a UCS, and classical conditioning occurs. That is, the sight of the injection will be associated with the intake of morphine. However, while the response to morphine, the UR, is a reduced sensitivity to pain, the response to the sight of the injection, the CR, is an *increase* in sensitivity to pain. The CR is the opposite of the UR.

This phenomenon has implications for the development of *drug tolerance*. It is well known that as a person continues to use a drug like morphine, a given dose of the drug becomes progressively ineffective; the person must increase the dosage level to get the desired effect. While this development of drug tolerance is partly a matter of physiological adaptation, it appears also to be a matter of classical conditioning. With continued use of morphine, conditioning occurs that results in an increase in pain sensitivity, hence increasingly more morphine is needed to obtain the desired level of painkiller. It is not that the painkilling effect of morphine has decreased, but rather that the background level of pain sensitivity has increased. The same process is presumably operative in the use of heroin for nonmedical purposes. After repeated injections, the drug user's conditioned response to the injection is the opposite of the desired effect of a sense of well-being; consequently he must take a higher and higher dosage to produce the desired effect (Siegel, 1983, 1979).

PREDICTABILITY AND COGNITIVE FACTORS

Until now we have analyzed classical conditioning solely in terms of external or environmental events—one stimulus is consistently followed by another, and the organism comes to associate them. Although this behaviorist view was the dominant one for many years, there have long been researchers who argued that the critical factor behind conditioning is what the animal *knows* (Tolman, 1932). In this cognitive view, classical conditioning provides an organism with new knowledge about the relation between two stimuli; given the CS, it has learned to *expect* the UCS. In what follows, we consider the role played by cognitive factors in classical conditioning.

CONTIGUITY VERSUS PREDICTABILITY Since Pavlov, researchers have tried to determine the criti-

cal factor needed for classical conditioning to occur. Pavlov thought the critical factor was temporal contiguity of the CS and UCS—that is, the two stimuli must occur close together in time in order for an association to develop. There is, however, an alternative to temporal contiguity as the critical factor in classical conditioning, namely that the CS be a *reliable predictor* of the UCS. In other words, for conditioning to occur, there must be a higher probability that the UCS will occur when the CS has been presented than when it has not. This notion seems quite cognitive.

Rescorla (1967), in an important experiment, contrasted contiguity and predictability. On certain trials of the experiment, Rescorla exposed dogs to shock (the UCS), and on some of these trials he preceded the shock by a tone (the CS). The procedures for two of the groups from the experiment are illustrated in Figure 7-5. The number of temporally contiguous pairings of tone and shock was the same in both groups. The independent variable was that tones preceded all shocks in Group A, whereas in Group B shocks were as likely to be preceded by no tones as tones, so the tone had no real predictive power. The predictive power of the tone proved critical: Group A became rapidly conditioned, whereas Group B did not (as determined by whether or not the dog responded to the tone in such a way as to avoid the shock). In other groups in the experiment (not shown in Figure 7-5), the strength of the conditioning was directly related to the predictive value of the CS in signaling the occurrence of the UCS. Subsequent experiments support the conclusion that the predictive relation between the CS and UCS is more important than either temporal contiguity or the frequency with which the CS and UCS are paired (Rescorla, 1972).

What a dog is doing in the preceding experiment may be analogized to what a scientist usually does. Confronted with the possibility of an important negative occurrence like a thunderstorm, a scientist—a meteorologist—tries to find something that predicts the event. It cannot be something that merely occurs contiguously with thunderstorms, because many innocuous events will fit this bill (such as clouds and even the presence of trees). Rather, the meteorologist must search for events that are predictive of thunderstorms in that they tend to occur prior to thunderstorms but not at other times. Like-

FIGURE 7-5

Rescorla's Experiment   *The figure presents a schematic representation of two groups from Rescorla's study. For each group, the events for 16 trials are presented. Note that on some trials CS occurs and is followed by UCS (CS + UCS); on other trials CS or UCS occurs alone; and on still other trials, neither CS nor UCS occurs. The boxes to the far right give a count of these trial outcomes for the two groups. The number of CS + UCS trials is identical for both groups, as is the number of trials on which only the CS occurs. But the two groups differ in the number of trials on which UCS occurred alone (never in Group A and as frequently as any other type of trial in Group B). Thus, for Group A, the experimenter established a situation in which the tone was a useful (but not perfect) predictor that shock would follow shortly, whereas for Group B the tone was of no value in predicting subsequent shock. A conditioned response to CS developed readily for Group A but did not develop at all for Group B.*

wise, when a dog in the preceding experiment has to deal with the important, negative occurrence of shock, it too tries to find some event that can predict it. And like the meteorologist, the dog does not focus on events that merely co-occur with shock (such as the sight of the experimental apparatus, or the tone in Group B of the experiment); rather the dog looks for an event that tends to occur prior to any shock, but not at other times (the tone in Group A of the experiment), and hence is truly predictive of the shock.

The importance of predictability is also shown by the phenomenon of **blocking**, discovered by Kamin (1969). What Kamin showed is that if a CS is *redundant,* providing information that an organism already has, it will not be conditioned to the UCS. Kamin's experiment is outlined in Table 7-1. It involved three stages. In the first stage, an experimental group of animals was repeatedly

presented a light, the CS, followed by a shock, the UCS. The experimental animals easily learned the light-shock association. The control group of animals received no training in this first stage. In the second stage, both the experimental and control groups were repeatedly presented a light plus a tone, a compound CS, followed by a shock, the UCS. For the experimental animals, who had already learned to associate the light with shock, the tone was redundant. For the control animals that had no prior learning, the compound CS was informative. In the third and final stage of the experiment, the tone was presented alone to see whether it would produce a conditioned response. The control animals showed conditioned responses, but the experimental animals did not. For the experimental animals, the previously learned light-shock association *blocked* the learning of the new tone-shock association. Why? Presumably because the

	STAGE 1	**STAGE 2**	**STAGE 3**
Experimental Group	Light → Shock	Light + Tone → Shock	Tone → No Conditioned Response
Control Group		Light + Tone → Shock	Tone → Conditioned Response

TABLE 7-1

Experiment on Blocking   *The design of an experiment which shows that a previously learned association can block the learning of a new association.*(After Kamin, 1969)

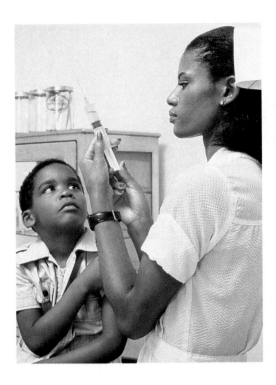

Knowing when to expect pain lessens anxiety.

earlier learning made the shock predictable, and once a UCS is predictable there is little possibility of further conditioning.

PREDICTABILITY AND EMOTION   Predictability is also important for emotional reactions. If a particular CS reliably predicts that pain is coming, then the absence of that CS predicts that pain is not coming and the organism can relax. The CS is therefore a "danger" signal, and its absence a "safety" signal. When such signals are erratic, the emotional toll on the organism can be devastating. When rats have a reliable predictor that shock is coming, they respond with fear only when the danger signal is present; if they have no reliable predictor, they appear to be continually anxious and may even develop ulcers (Seligman, 1975).

There are clear parallels to human emotionality. If a dentist gives a child a danger signal by telling her that a procedure will hurt, the child will be fearful until the procedure is over. In contrast, if the dentist always tells a child "it won't hurt" when in fact it sometimes does, the child has no danger or safety signals and may become terribly anxious whenever in the dentist's office. As adults, many of us have experienced the anxiety of being in a situation where something disagreeable is likely to happen but no warnings exist for us to predict it. Unpleasant

events are, by definition, unpleasant, but unpredictable unpleasant events are downright intolerable. (Further discussion of this point is included in Chapter 14.)

MODELS OF CLASSICAL CONDITIONING   The findings about predictability have led to a number of models of classical conditioning. The best known of these models was developed by Rescorla and Wagner (1972). Although it has less of a cognitive emphasis than the other models, like them it focuses on the notions of predictability and surprise. According to the **Rescorla-Wagner model**, the amount of conditioning on any trial depends on how *surprising* the UCS is, which in turn depends on how associated the UCS is with possible CSs. The more surprising the UCS, the greater the amount of conditioning on that trial. Early in learning the UCS is very surprising (no CSs yet predict it), and hence a good deal should be learned on each trial. Late in learning, there is at least one CS that predicts the UCS, hence the UCS is not very surprising and rather little is learned on each trial. This pattern—bigger learning gains early rather than later on—in fact characterizes the acquisition of a classically conditioned response (refer back to Figure 7-2).

Another assumption of the Rescorla-Wagner model is that the predictability of the UCS on any trial is determined by all the CSs present on that trial. For example, if there are two CSs present on a trial, say, a light and a tone, the amount of conditioning possible for one of the CSs, say, the tone, is less the more conditioning that has already occurred to the other CS, the light. This explains the blocking phenomenon described above. Essentially, CSs that occur together *compete* with one another for association strength, where the amount to be won in the competition is the amount of unpredictability left in the UCS.

Other models of classical conditioning give greater emphasis to cognitive factors. According to Wagner (1981), just as humans have a short-term memory in which they can rehearse information (see Chapter 8), so do other animals. And just as humans tend to rehearse in short-term memory primarily information that is unexpected, so lower animals do also. An animal's short-term memory plays a critical role in conditioning. Early in the course of conditioning, a UCS is novel and unpredictable. Consequently, the organism actively rehearses the CS–UCS connection in short-term memory; this rehearsal process is presumably what mediates the acquisition of a classically conditioned response. Once the UCS is no longer surprising, rehearsal decreases and no further learning occurs. This offers another explanation of the blocking phenomenon: once the UCS is completely predictable, there will be no rehearsal of any new association involving that UCS.

Another cognitive model views classical conditioning as the *generation* and *testing* of rules about what events are likely to follow other events (Holyoak, Koh, & Nisbett, 1989). According to this model, an animal is likely to generate a rule whenever two unexpected events occur in close proximity, or whenever an old rule fails. For a rat in a classical conditioning experiment, an unexpected light followed closely by an unexpected shock would lead to the generation of the rule, "If light, then shock." Once a rule is formed, it is strengthened every time it leads to a correct prediction and weakened every time it leads to an incorrect prediction. The "If light, then shock" rule, for example, would be strengthened whenever the light is in fact followed by the shock, and weakened whenever it is not. The rule model clearly predicts that predictability is necessary for conditioning to occur, because only correct predictions can strengthen a rule. The model also accounts for the blocking phenomenon: As long as a UCS is predicted by a known rule, no new rule involving that UCS will be generated.

BIOLOGICAL CONSTRAINTS

We mentioned earlier in the chapter that different species sometimes learn the same thing by different mechanisms. These phenomena were discovered by **ethologists**, biologists and psychologists who study animal behavior in the natural environment. The phenomena reveal that what an organism can learn by conditioning is constrained by its biology.

ETHOLOGICAL APPROACH   Ethologists, like behaviorists, are concerned with the behavior of animals, but ethologists place a greater emphasis on evolution and genetics than on learning. This emphasis has led ethologists to take a distinctive approach to learning,

namely to assume that it is rigidly constrained by an animal's genetic endowment and to show that different species will learn different things in different ways. (Early behaviorists, on the other hand, assumed that the laws of learning were the same for all species.) As ethologists put it, when an animal learns it must conform to a genetically determined "behavioral blueprint"; just as an architectural blueprint imposes constraints on the kinds of functions that a building may serve, so a behavioral blueprint imposes genetic constraints on the kinds of associations that an organism may learn. That is, animals are preprogrammed to learn particular things in particular ways.

CONSTRAINTS IN CLASSICAL CONDITIONING   Some of the best evidence for constraints in classical conditioning comes from studies of taste aversion. Consider first the basic phenomenon of taste aversion. In a typical study, a rat is permitted to drink a flavored solution, say, vanilla. After drinking it, the rat is mildly poisoned and made ill. When the rat recovers, it is again presented the vanilla solution. Now the rat scrupulously avoids the solution because it has learned to associate the vanilla taste with feeling ill. There is good evidence that such avoidance is an instance of classical conditioning: the initial taste of the solution is the CS, the feeling of being sick is the UCS, and after conditioning the taste signals that sickness is on its way.

According to early behaviorist ideas, a light or a sound might be expected to play the same signaling role as taste. That is, if a light is as effective a stimulus as taste, then an association between a light and feeling sick should be no more difficult to establish than one between a taste and feeling sick. But the facts turn out to be otherwise. This is shown by the experiment that is diagrammed in Table 7-2. In the first stage of the experiment, an experimental group of rats is allowed to lick at a tube that contains a flavored solution; each time the rat licks the tube, a click and a light are presented. Thus the rat experiences three stimuli simultaneously—the taste of the solution, as well as the light and the click. In the second stage of the experiment, rats in the experimental group are mildly poisoned. The question is: What stimuli—the taste or the light-plus-click—will become associated with feeling sick? To answer this, in the third and final stage of the study, rats in the experimental group are again presented the same tube; sometimes the solution in the tube has the same flavor as before but there is no light or click, while at other times the solution has no flavor but the light and click are presented. The animals avoid the solution when they experience the taste, but not when the light-plus-click is presented; hence, the rats have associated only taste with feeling sick. These results cannot be attributed to taste being a more potent CS than light-plus-click, as shown by the control condition of the experiment that is diagrammed in the bottom of Table 7-2. In the second stage, instead of being mildly poisoned, the rat is shocked. Now, in the final stage of the study, the animal avoids the solution only when the light-plus-click is presented, not when it experiences the taste alone (Garcia & Koelling, 1966).

Thus taste is a better signal for sickness than for shock, and light-plus-click is a better signal for shock than for sickness. Why does this selectivity of association exist? It does not fit with the early behaviorist idea that equally potent stimuli can substitute for one another; since taste and light-plus-click can both be effective CSs, and since being sick and being shocked are both effective UCSs, then either CS should have been associable with either UCS. In contrast, this selectivity of association fits perfectly with the ethological perspective and its emphasis on an animal's evolutionary adaptation to its environment. In their natural habitat, rats (like other mammals) rely on taste to select their food. Consequently, there may be a genetically determined, or "built-in," relation between taste and intestinal reactions, which fosters

an association between taste and sickness but not between light and sickness. Furthermore, in a rat's natural environment, pain resulting from external factors like cold or injury is invariably due to external stimuli. Consequently, there may be a built-in relation between external stimuli and "external pain," which fosters an association between light and shock but not one between taste and shock.

If rats learn to associate taste with sickness because it fits with their natural means of selecting food, then another species with a different means of selecting food might have trouble learning to associate taste with sickness. This is exactly what happens. Birds naturally select their food on the basis of looks rather than taste, and they readily learn to associate a light with sickness, but not a taste with sickness (Wilcoxin, Dragoin, & Kral, 1971). Here then is a perfect example of different species learning the same thing—what causes sickness—by different means. In short, if we want to know what may be conditioned to what, we cannot consider the CS and UCS in isolation; rather, we must focus on the two in combination and consider how well that combination reflects built-in relations. This conclusion differs considerably from the assumption that the laws of learning are the same for all species and situations.

In addition to what they tell us about the nature of conditioning, these findings have important practical applications as well. Coyotes, like rats, readily learn to associate taste with sickness. This fact gives ranchers in the western United States a means for stopping coyotes from killing sheep. The ranchers offer the coyotes sheep meat (mutton) that contains low levels of poisons (for example,

	STAGE 1	STAGE 2	STAGE 3
Experimental Group	Taste and Light + Click	Sickness	Taste → Avoid
			Light + Click → Don't Avoid
Control Group	Taste and Light + Click	Shock	Taste → Don't Avoid
			Light + Click → Avoid

TABLE 7-2

Experiment on Constraints and Taste Aversion *The design of an experiment which shows that taste is a better signal for sickness than shock, while light-plus-sound is a better signal for shock than sickness.* (After Garcia & Koelling, 1966).

lithium salts). The coyotes eat the mutton, become sick, and thereby learn to associate the taste of mutton with being sick. After that, the coyotes avoid sheep. The sheep have been saved without killing the coyotes, which themselves are threatened (Garcia, 1990).

NEURAL BASIS OF LEARNING

Our discussion of biological factors in learning thus far has focused on evolutionary theory. But the biology of neurons and their interconnections, which proved so important in our analysis of sensation and perception, is again relevant. There is a growing interest in the neural basis of classical conditioning and simple forms of learning like habituation. In what follows, we briefly discuss some of the key ideas behind this expanding research frontier.

STRUCTURAL CHANGES   It is useful to start by considering what kinds of approaches to the neural basis of learning will *not* work. One possibility is to look for a specific region in the cortex that is solely responsible for learning (much as there appear to be specific cortical regions that are responsible for processing color). Researchers today do not believe in such a "learning center." Rather, the evidence indicates that the products of long-term learning are distributed all over the cortex, perhaps with the visual aspects of what is learning being stored in mainly visual regions of the brain, the motor aspects of what is learning being stored in motor regions, and so on (Squire, 1982).

Another approach that will not work is to assume that whatever brain regions and neurons are involved in learning something remain active *thereafter*. While this idea seems to hold for short-term learning or memory (as discussed in the next chapter), researchers agree that it cannot apply to long-term learning (Carlson, 1986). If everything we learned led to a permanent increase in neural activation, our brains would become increasingly active each passing day; this is clearly not the case.

So what kind of neurological approach will work? Researchers believe that the neural basis of learning consists of structural changes in the nervous system, and increasingly they are looking for these changes at the level of neural connections.

To appreciate their ideas, you need to recall from Chapter 2 the basic structure of a neural connection and how it transmits an impulse. An impulse is transmitted from one neuron, to another by the axon of the sender. Because the axons are separated by the *synaptic gap,* the sender's axon secretes a *neurotransmitter,* which diffuses across the gap and stimulates the receiving neuron. More precisely, when the neural impulse travels down the sender's axon, it triggers terminals at the end of the axon to release the neurotransmitter, and this neurotransmitter is then picked up by receptors on the receiving neuron. This entire structure is called a *synapse.* The key ideas regarding learning are: (1) that some structural change in the synapse is *the* neural basis of learning, and (2) the effect of this structural change is to make the synapse more efficient.

What would constitute evidence for this proposal? One thing would be to demonstrate that, after a learning episode, a synapse becomes more efficient, that is, fires more readily when stimulated again. Presently, this is difficult to demonstrate with organisms of any complexity—if you recorded from some specific neurons, how could you find a learning task that affects exactly those neurons? Researchers have chosen the strategy of first electrically stimulating a particular set of neurons (presumably, this simulates learning), and then checking for an increase in the rate of activity of these neurons when subsequently stimulated. Such increases have been found in a number of regions of the rabbit brain, and the increases can last for several months. This phenomenon is referred to as *long-term potentiation,* and it provides indirect support for the structural-change view of learning (Berger, 1984; Bliss & Lomo, 1973).

LEARNING IN SIMPLE ORGANISMS   We have not been very specific about what kinds of structural changes increase synaptic efficiency. There are several possibilities. One is that learning results in an increase in the amount of neurotransmitter secreted by the sending neuron, perhaps because of an increase in the number of axon terminals that secrete the neurotransmitter. Alternatively, there may be no increase in the amount of neurotransmitter sent, but there may be an increase in the amount of neurotransmitter taken up by the receiving neuron, perhaps because of an increase in the number of receptors. Other possibilities are that the synapse could change in size, or that entirely new synapses could be established (Carlson, 1986). Several possibilities may be correct, with different kinds of structural changes underlying different kinds of learning.

To study learning processes at this level of neural detail, researchers have to work with elementary forms of learning and with organisms that have simple nervous systems. One kind of elementary learning that we mentioned at the beginning of the chapter is *habituation*. This is the process by which an organism learns to weaken its reaction to a weak stimulus that has no serious consequences, such as tuning out the sound of a loud clock. A related case of learning is *sensitization*, whereby an organism learns to strengthen its reaction to a weak stimulus if a threatening or painful stimulus follows. For instance, we learn to respond more intensely to the sound of a piece of equipment if it is frequently followed by a crash. Habituation and sensitization are found at virtually all levels of the animal kingdom, but our present concern is with the snail. Snails have a simple and accessible nervous system, which makes them well suited for studying structural changes in the synapse that accompany elementary learning.

When a snail is lightly touched repeatedly, initially it responds, but within about ten trials it habituates to the touch. Researchers have shown that this habituation learning is accompanied by a *decrease* in the amount of neurotransmitter secreted by a sending neuron. This snail also manifests sensitization. Now a light touch to the body is accompanied by a strong stimulus to the tail, and after a few trials of this procedure, the snail's response to the touch becomes more pronounced. Sensitization learning has been shown to be mediated by an *increase* in the amount of neurotransmitter secreted by the sending neuron (Kandel, Schwartz & Jessel, 1991). These findings provide relatively direct evidence that elementary learning is mediated by structural changes at the neuronal level. (The details of the synaptic processes are given in the Critical Discussion.)

What about associative learning? Do structural changes like the one described above

mediate classical conditioning? The fact that classical conditioning is similar to sensitization—both involve changing one's response to a weak stimulus on the basis of another stronger stimulus—suggests that the two kinds of learning might have a similar neural basis. Indeed, researchers have proposed a neural account of classical conditioning that is remarkably similar to that for sensitization (Hawkins & Kandel, 1984).

OPERANT CONDITIONING

In classical conditioning, the conditioned response often resembles the normal response to the unconditioned stimulus: Salivation, for example, is a dog's normal response to food. But when you want to teach an organism something novel—such as teaching a dog a new trick—you cannot use classical conditioning. What unconditioned stimulus would make a dog sit up or roll over? To train the dog, you must first persuade it to do the trick and *afterward* reward it with either approval or food. If you keep doing this, eventually the dog will learn the trick.

Much of real-life behavior is like this: Responses are learned because they *operate* on, or affect, the environment. Referred to as **operant conditioning**, this kind of learning occurs in our own species, as well as in other species. Alone in a crib, a baby may kick and twist and coo spontaneously. When left by itself in a room, a dog may pad back and forth; sniff; or perhaps pick up a ball, drop it, and play with it. Neither organism is responding to the onset or offset of a specific external stimulus. Rather, they are operating on their environment. Once the organism performs a certain behavior, however, the likelihood that the action will be repeated depends on its consequences. The baby will coo more often if each such occurrence is followed by parental attention, and the dog will pick up the ball more often if this action is followed by petting or a food reward. If we think of the baby as having a goal of parental attention, and the dog as having a goal of food, then operant conditioning amounts to learning that a particular behavior leads to attaining a particular goal (Rescorla, 1987).

LAW OF EFFECT

The study of operant conditioning began at the turn of the century with a series of experiments by E. L. Thorndike (1898). Thorndike, much influenced by Darwin's theory of evolution, was trying to show that learning in animals is continuous with learning in humans. A typical experiment proceeded as follows. A hungry cat is placed in a cage whose door is held fast by a simple latch, and a piece of fish is placed just outside the cage. Initially, the cat tries to reach the food by extending its paws through the bars. When this fails, the cat moves about the cage, engaging in a variety of different behaviors. At some point it inadvertently hits the latch, frees itself, and eats the fish. The researchers then place the cat back in its cage and put a new piece of fish outside. The cat goes through roughly the same set of behaviors until once more it happens to hit the latch. The procedure is repeated again and again. Over trials, the cat eliminates many of its irrelevant behaviors, eventually efficiently opening the latch and freeing itself as soon as it is placed in the cage. The cat has learned to open the latch in order to obtain food.

It may sound as if the cat is acting intelligently, but Thorndike argued that there is little "intelligence" operative here. There is no moment in time at which the cat seems to have an insight about the solution to its problem. Instead, the cat's performance improves gradually over trials. Rather than insight, the cat appears to be engaging in *trial-and-error* behavior, and when a reward immediately follows one of these behaviors, the learning of the action is strengthened. Thorndike referred to this strengthening as the **law of effect**. He argued that in operant learning, the law of effect selects from a set of random responses just those responses that are followed by positive consequences. The process is similar to evolution, in which the law of *survival of the fittest* selects from a set of random species variations just the changes that promote survival of the species. The law of effect, then, promotes the survival of the *fittest responses* (Schwartz, 1989).

SKINNER'S EXPERIMENTS

B. F. Skinner was responsible for a number of changes in how researchers conceptualize

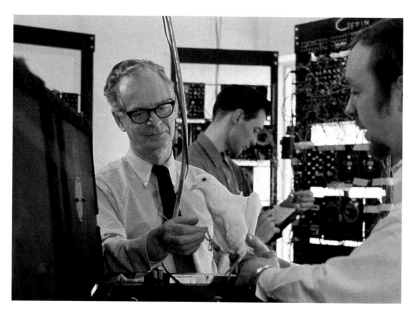

B.F. Skinner

and study operant conditioning. His method of studying operant conditioning is simpler than Thorndike's—there is only one response involved, for instance—and it has been widely accepted.

EXPERIMENTAL VARIATIONS In a Skinnerian experiment, a hungry animal—usually a rat or a pigeon—is placed in a box like the one shown in Figure 7-6, which is popularly called a "Skinner box." The inside of the box is bare except for a protruding bar with a food dish

FIGURE 7-6

Apparatus for Operant Conditioning *The photograph shows a Skinner box with a magazine for delivering food pellets. The computer is used to control the experiment and record the rat's responses.*

In the text, we presented some key information about the structural changes in synapses that underlie habituation and sensitization. That discussion, though, touched only the surface of this breakthrough research.

Consider then, in more detail, some of the research of Eric Kandel and his associates. They use snails in their work because the neurons of a snail are similar in structure and function to those of a human, yet its nervous system is simple enough to allow researchers to study individual neurons. Indeed, the total number of neurons in a snail is only in the thousands (compared to billions in a human). Also, some of the snail's neurons of interest are among the largest and most accessible in nature. Moreover, the neurons of a snail are collected into discrete groups (or **ganglia**) of 500 to 1,500 neurons, and a single ganglion can control an instance of habituation or sensitization. This makes it possible to give a "cell-by-cell" account of elementary learning.

The *Aplysia,* a large marine animal, is the snail of choice for researchers, and the behavior of particular inter-

est is a withdrawal response. As shown in Figure 1, the *Aplysia's* gill is housed in a cavity that is covered by a protective sheet called the *mantle shelf;* the sheet ends in a fleshy spout called a *siphon.* When the siphon is stimulated by touch, both the siphon and gill contract into the cavity. The withdrawal is controlled by a single ganglion and is subject to habituation and sensitization.

In studies of habituation, the researchers lightly touch the snail's siphon on each trial of the experiment. In the initial trials, the gill-withdrawal reflex is strong, but it gradually weakens after 10 or 15 trials. Essentially, the *Aplysia* has learned to recognize the stimulus as trivial. What cellular events mediate this habituation behavior? The stimulus to the siphon activates 24 sensory neurons, each of which activates the 6 motor neurons in the gill that innervate the contracting muscle. The structure of the system can be understood by looking at the neural connections for a single sensory neuron and a single motor neuron (see the top of Figure 2). The small triangles in the figure depict synaptic connections between neu-

FIGURE 1

Gill Withdrawal in the *Aplysia* *When the siphon is stimulated, the animal retracts its gill into the protective sheet of the mantle cavity; this sheet is called the mantle shelf.* (After Kandel, 1979)

beneath it. A small light above the bar can be turned on at the experimenter's discretion. Left alone in the box, the rat moves about, exploring. Occasionally it inspects the bar and presses it. The rate at which the rat first presses the bar is the *baseline* level. After establishing the baseline level, the experimenter activates a food magazine located outside the box. Now, every time the rat presses the bar, a small food pellet is released into the dish. The rat eats the food pellet and soon presses the bar again; the food *reinforces* bar pressing, and the rate of pressing increases dramatically. If the food magazine is disconnected so that pressing the bar no longer delivers food, the rate of bar pressing will diminish. Hence, an operantly conditioned response (or, simply, an *operant*) un-

dergoes *extinction* with nonreinforcement just as a classically conditioned response does. The experimenter can set up a *discrimination* test by presenting food only if the rat presses the bar while the light is on, hence conditioning the rat through selective reinforcement. In this example, the light serves as a **discriminative stimulus** that controls the response.

Thus, operant conditioning increases the likelihood of a response by following the behavior with a reinforcer (often something like food or water). Because the bar is always present in the Skinner box, the rat can respond to it as frequently or infrequently as it chooses. The organism's *rate of response* is therefore a useful measure of the operant's strength; the more frequently the response rons, where a synaptic gap must be bridged by a chemical neurotransmitter. In the *Aplysia,* a neurotransmitter released by the sensory neuron onto the motor neuron causes initial gill withdrawal, and a decrease in the amount of this neurotransmitter is what mediates the habituation of gill withdrawal. That is, after a sufficient number of trials, a touch of the siphon no longer results in the release of enough neurotransmitter to cause the gill motor neuron to fire. Thus, this form of elementary learning is due to chemically induced changes in synaptic connections between neurons (Kandel, 1979).

Sensitization functions in a similar, though more complex, manner. To sensitize gill withdrawal, again the researchers apply a weak tactile stimulus to the siphon, but this time they also apply simultaneously a strong stimulus to the tail. After a number of such trials, gill withdrawal becomes more pronounced. Some of the mediating neural connections are illustrated in the bottom half of Figure 2. Since there are now two stimuli that need to be connected—the siphon touch and the tail stimulus—a bridge must be formed between the two

neural pathways. The bridge consists of neural connections from the tail that are added to the circuit from the siphon. The new connections include a synapse between a tail sensory neuron and a *facilitator interneuron* (a neuron that connects other neurons) and a synapse that connects the facilitator interneuron with the circuit that supports gill withdrawal. In essence, the neural activity from the strong stimulus to the tail modifies the neural connection that underlies gill withdrawal. Once more, learning is mediated by changes in the neurotransmitter that bridges the synaptic gap between the siphon's sensory neuron and the gill's motor neuron. But in this case, the change consists of an increase in the amount of the neurotransmitter released by the sensory neuron (Bailey, Chen, Keller, & Kandel, 1992; Castelluci & Kandel, 1976).

These results indicate that, at least for simple organisms, the biological basis of learning can be localized to the activity of specific neurons. It remains to be determined whether the same kinds of structural changes will characterize more advanced forms of learning in more complex organisms.

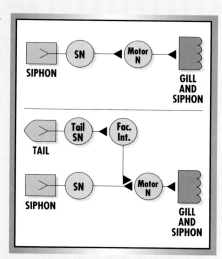

FIGURE 2

Neural Circuits for Habituation *The top panel illustrates the connection between a single sensory neuron (SN) and a single motor neuron (Motor N) for the gill-withdrawal reflex. Stimulation of the siphon excites the sensory neuron, which in turn excites the motor neuron to innervate the gill. Habituation of gill withdrawal is mediated by a change at the synaptic connection between the sensory and motor neurons. The bottom panel illustrates the connections involved in sensitization of gill withdrawal. Now, stimulation of the tail excites a facilitator interneuron (Fac. int.), which facilitates the impulse being sent from the siphon's sensory neuron.*

occurs during a given time interval, the greater its strength.

IMPLICATIONS FOR CHILD REARING Although rats and pigeons have been the favored experimental subjects, operant conditioning applies to many species, including our own. Indeed, operant conditioning has a good deal to tell us about child rearing. A particularly illuminating example of this is given by the following case. A young boy had temper tantrums if he did not get enough attention from his parents, especially at bedtime. Since the parents eventually responded, their attention probably reinforced the tantrums. To eliminate the tantrums, the parents were advised to go through the normal bedtime rituals and then to ignore the child's protests, painful though

that might be. By withholding the reinforcer (the attention), the tantrums should extinguish—which is just what happened. The time the child spent crying at bedtime decreased from 45 minutes to not at all over a period of only 7 days (Williams, 1959).

Another application of operant conditioning to child rearing focuses on the temporal relation between a response and its reinforcer. Laboratory experiments have shown that immediate reinforcement is more effective than delayed; the more time between an operant response and a reinforcer, the less the response strength. Many developmental psychologists have noted that the delay of reinforcement is an important factor in dealing with young children. If a child acts kindly to a pet, the act can best be strengthened by praising (rewarding) the child immediately, rather than waiting until later. Similarly, if a child hits someone without provocation, this aggressive behavior will more likely be eliminated if the child is punished immediately, rather than waiting until later.

SHAPING   Suppose you want to use operant conditioning to teach your dog a trick—for instance, to press a buzzer with its nose. You cannot wait until the dog does this naturally (and then reinforce it), because you may wait forever. When the desired behavior is truly novel, you have to condition it by taking advantage of natural variations in the animal's actions. To train a dog to press a buzzer with its nose, you can give the animal a food reinforcer each time it approaches the area of the buzzer, requiring it to move closer and closer to the desired spot for each reinforcer until finally the dog's nose is touching the buzzer. This technique of reinforcing only those variations in response that deviate in the direction desired by the experimenter is called **shaping** the animal's behavior.

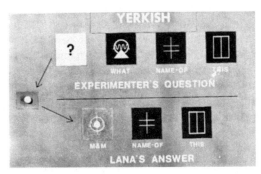

Animals have been taught very complex responses by means of shaping techniques. At the Yerkes Primate Research Center in Atlanta, a chimpanzee named Lana has learned to answer questions and to make requests by pressing symbols on a computer console. At bottom is an example of how the experiment works. A researcher outside the room asked Lana a question by pressing the symbols on the console for the words "What name of this" and also holding up candy. The chimpanzee answered by pressing the symbols for "M&M® name of this."

Animals can be taught elaborate tricks and routines by means of shaping. Two psychologists and their staff trained thousands of animals of many species for television shows, commercials, and county fairs (Breland & Breland, 1966). One popular show featured "Priscilla, the Fastidious Pig." Priscilla turned on the TV set, ate breakfast at a table, picked up dirty clothes and put them in a hamper, vacuumed the floor, picked out her favorite food (from among foods competing with that of her sponsor!), and took part in a quiz program, answering questions from the audience by flashing lights that indicated yes or no. She was not an unusually bright pig; in fact, because pigs grow so fast, a new "Priscilla" was trained every 3 to 5 months. The ingenuity was not the pig's but the experimenters', who used operant conditioning and shaped the behavior to produce the desired result. Pigeons have been trained by shaping of operant responses to locate persons lost at sea (see Figure 7-7), and porpoises have been trained to retrieve underwater equipment.

PHENOMENA AND APPLICATIONS

There are a number of phenomena that greatly increase the generality of operant conditioning, and that show its applications to human behavior.

CONDITIONED REINFORCERS   Most of the reinforcers we have discussed are called *primary* because, like food, they satisfy basic drives. If operant conditioning occurred only with primary reinforcers, it would not be that common in our lives because primary reinforcers are not that common. However, virtually any stimulus can become a *secondary* or **conditioned reinforcer** by being consistently paired with a primary reinforcer; conditioned reinforcers greatly increase the range of operant conditioning (just as second-order conditioning greatly increases the range of classical conditioning).

A minor variation in the typical operant-conditioning experiment illustrates how conditioned reinforcement works. When a rat in a Skinner box presses a lever, a tone sounds momentarily, followed shortly by a delivery of food (the food is a primary reinforcer; the tone will become a conditioned reinforcer). After the animal has been conditioned in this

Pigeon sitting   *Pigeon pecking key*   *Pigeon rewarded*

FIGURE 7-7

Search and Rescue by Pigeons *The Coast Guard has used pigeons to search for people lost at sea. The pigeons are trained, using shaping methods, to spot the color orange—the international color for life jackets. Three pigeons are strapped into a plexiglass chamber attached to the underside of a helicopter. The chamber is divided into thirds so that each bird faces a different direction. When a pigeon spots an orange object, or any other object, it pecks a key that buzzes the pilot. The pilot then heads in the direction indicated by the bird that responded. Pigeons are better suited than people for the task of spotting distant objects at sea. They can stare over the water for a long time without suffering eye fatigue, have excellent color vision, and can focus on a 60- to 80-degree area, whereas a person can only focus on a 2- to 3-degree area. (After Simmons, 1981)*

way, the experimenter begins extinction, so that when the rat presses the lever neither the tone nor the food occurs. In time, the animal ceases to press the lever. Then the tone is reconnected but not the food. When the animal discovers that pressing the lever turns on the tone, its rate of pressing markedly increases, overcoming the extinction even though no food follows. The tone has acquired a reinforcing quality of its own through classical conditioning; because the tone was reliably paired with food, it came to signal food.

Our lives abound with conditioned reinforcers. Two of the most prevalent are money and praise. Presumably, money is a powerful reinforcer because it has been paired so frequently with so many primary reinforcers—we can buy food, drink, and comfort, to mention just a few of the obvious things. And mere praise, without even the promise of a

primary reinforcer, can sustain many an activity.

GENERALIZATION AND DISCRIMINATION Again, what was true for classical conditioning holds for operant conditioning as well: Organisms generalize what they have learned, and generalization can be curbed by discrimination training. If a young child is reinforced by her parents for petting the family dog, she will soon generalize this petting response to other dogs. Since this can be dangerous (the neighbors might have a vicious watchdog), the child's parents may provide some discrimination training, so that she is reinforced when she pets the family dog but not the neighbor's.

Discrimination training will be effective to the extent there is a discriminative stimulus (or set of them) that clearly distinguishes cases where the response should be made from those where it should be suppressed. Our young child will have an easier time learning which dog to pet if her parents can point to an aspect of dogs that signals their friendliness (a wagging tail, for example). In general, a discriminative stimulus will be useful to the extent its presence predicts that a response will be followed by reinforcement while its absence predicts that the response will not be followed by reinforcement (or vice versa). Just as in classical conditioning, the predictive power of a stimulus seems critical for conditioning.

SCHEDULES OF REINFORCEMENT In real life, every instance of a behavior is rarely reinforced—sometimes hard work is followed by praise, but often it goes unacknowledged. If operant conditioning occurred only with continuous reinforcement, it might play a limited role in our lives. It turns out, however, that once a behavior is established, it can be maintained when it is reinforced only a fraction of the time. This phenomenon is known as **partial reinforcement**, and it can be illustrated in the laboratory by a pigeon that learns to peck at a key for food. Once this operant is established, the pigeon continues to peck at a high rate even if it receives only occasional reinforcement. In some cases, pigeons that were rewarded with food on the average of once every 5 minutes (12 times an hour) pecked at

the key as often as 6,000 times per hour! Furthermore, extinction following the maintenance of a response on partial reinforcement is much slower than extinction following the maintenance of a response on continuous reinforcement. This phenomenon is known as the *partial-reinforcement effect*. It makes intuitive sense because there is less difference between extinction and maintenance when reinforcement during maintenance is only partial.

When reinforcement occurs only some of the time, we need to know exactly how it is scheduled—after every third response? after every five seconds? It turns out that the **schedule of reinforcement** determines the pattern of responding. Some schedules are called **ratio schedules**, because with them reinforcement depends on the number of responses the organism makes. It's like being a factory worker who gets paid for piecework. The ratio can be either fixed or variable. On a *fixed ratio* schedule (called an FR schedule), the number of responses that has to be made is fixed at a particular value. If the number is 5 (FR 5), 5 responses are required for reinforcement, if 50 (FR 50), 50 responses are required, and so on. In general, the higher the ratio, the higher the rate at which the organism responds, particularly when the organism is initially trained on a relatively low ratio, say FR 5, and then is continuously shifted to progressively higher ratios, culminating say in FR 100. It is as if our factory worker initially got 5 dollars for every 5 hems sewn, but then times got tough and he needed to do 100 hems to get 5 dollars. But perhaps the most distinctive aspect about behavior under an FR schedule is that there is a pause in responding right after the reinforcement occurs (see the left side of Figure 7-8). It is hard for the factory worker to start on a new set of hems right after he just finished enough for a reward.

On a *variable ratio* schedule (a VR schedule), one still gets reinforced only after making a certain number of responses but that number varies unpredictably. Thus in a VR 5 schedule, the number of responses needed for reinforcement may sometimes be 1, other times 10, with an average of 5. Unlike the behavior with FR schedules, there are no pauses when the organism is operating under a VR schedule (see the left side of Figure 7-8), presumably because the organism has no way of

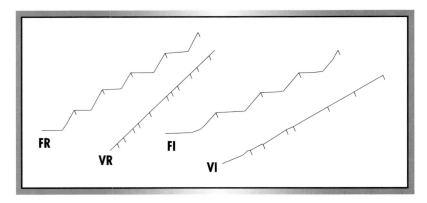

FIGURE 7-8

Typical Patterns of Responding on the Four Basic Schedules of Reinforcement
Each curve plots an animal's cumulative number of responses as a function of time; the slope of the curve thus indicates the animal's rate of responding. The curves on the left are for ratio schedules. In the curve for the FR schedule, note the horizontal segments—these correspond to pauses (they show no increase in the cumulative number of responses). The curves on the right are for interval schedules. In the curve for the FI schedule, again the horizontal segments correspond to pauses. (Adapted from Schwartz, 1989)

detecting that it is far from a reinforcement. A good example of VR schedule in everyday life is the operation of a slot machine. The number of responses (plays) needed for reinforcement (payoff) keeps varying, and the operator has no way of predicting when reinforcement will occur. VR schedules can generate very high rates of responding (as casino owners appear to have figured out).

Other schedules are called **interval schedules**, because with them reinforcement is available only after a certain time interval has elapsed. Again the schedule can be either fixed or variable. On a *fixed interval* (FI) schedule, the organism is reinforced for its first response after a certain amount of time has passed since its last reinforcement. On an FI 2 (minutes) schedule, for example, reinforcement is available only when 2 minutes have elapsed since the last reinforced response; responses made during that 2-minute interval have no consequence. One distinctive aspect of responding on an FI schedule is a pause that occurs immediately after reinforcement. (This post-reinforcement pause can be even longer than the one that occurs in FR schedules.) Another distinctive aspect of responding on an FI schedule is an increase in the rate of responding as the end of the interval approaches (see the right side of Figure 7-8). A good example of an FI schedule in everyday life is mail delivery, which comes just once a day (FI 24 hours), or in some places twice a day (FI 12 hours). Thus, right after your mail is delivered you would not check it again (this is your pause), but as the end of the mail-delivery interval approaches you will start checking again.

On a *variable interval* schedule (a VI schedule), reinforcement still depends on a certain interval having elapsed, but the interval's duration varies unpredictably. In a VI 10 (minute) schedule, for example, sometimes the critical interval may be 2 minutes, sometimes 20 minutes, and so on, with an average of 10 minutes. Unlike the variations in responding found under an FI schedule, organisms tend to respond at a uniform high rate when the schedule is a VI 1 (see the right side of Figure 7-8). For an example of a VI schedule in everyday life, consider redialing a busy number. In order to get reinforced (getting your call through), you have to wait some time interval after your last response (dialing), but the length of that interval is unpredictable.

AVERSIVE CONDITIONING

We have talked about reinforcement as if it were almost always positive (food, for example). But negative or aversive events, such as shock or a painful noise, are often used in conditioning. There are different kinds of **aversive conditioning**, depending on whether the aversive event is used to weaken an existent response or to learn a new response.

PUNISHMENT In punishment training, a response is followed by an aversive stimulus or event, which results in the response being weakened or suppressed on subsequent occasions. Suppose a young child who is learning to use crayons starts drawing on the wall (this is the undesirable response); if he is slapped on the hand when he does this (the punishment), he will learn not to do so. Similarly, if a rat learning to run a maze is shocked whenever it chooses a wrong path, it will soon learn to avoid past mistakes. In both cases, punishment is used to decrease the likelihood of an undesirable behavior.*

Although punishment can suppress an unwanted response, it has several disadvantages. First, its effects are not as predictable as the results of reward. Reward essentially says, "Repeat what you have done"; punishment says, "Stop it!" but fails to give an alternative. As a result, the organism may substitute an even less desirable response for the punished one. Second, the by-products of punishment may be unfortunate. Punishment often leads to dislike or fear of the punishing person (parent, teacher, or employer) and of the situation (home, school, or office) in which the punishment occurred. Finally, an extreme or painful punishment may elicit aggressive behavior that is more serious than the original undesirable behavior.

These cautions do not mean that punishment should never be employed. It can effectively eliminate an undesirable response if an

---

* It is worth noting the relation between the terms *reward* and *punisher* on the one hand, and *positive* and *negative reinforcers* on the other. *Reward* can be used synonymously with *positive reinforcer*—an event whose occurrence following a response increases the probability of that response. But a *punisher* is not the same as a *negative reinforcer*. Negative reinforcement means termination of an aversive event following a response; this increases the probability of that response. Punishment has the opposite effect: It decreases the probability of a response.

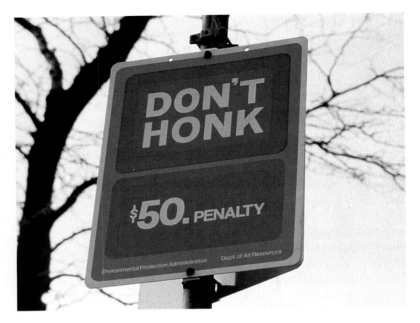

The threat of punishment is an effective motivator.

alternative response is rewarded. Rats that have learned to take the shorter of two paths in a maze to reach food will quickly switch to the longer one if they are shocked in the shorter path. The temporary suppression produced by punishment provides the opportunity for the rat to learn to take the longer path. In this case, punishment is an effective means of redirecting behavior because it is informative, and this seems to be the key to the humane and effective use of punishment. A child who gets a shock from an electrical appliance may learn which connections are safe and which are hazardous.

ESCAPE AND AVOIDANCE   Aversive events can also be used in the learning of new responses. Organisms can learn to make a response to terminate an ongoing aversive event, as when a child learns to turn off a faucet to stop hot water from flowing into his bath. This is called **escape learning**. Organisms can also learn to make a response to prevent an aversive event from even starting, as when we learn to stop at red lights to prevent accidents (and traffic tickets). This is called **avoidance learning**.

Often escape learning precedes avoidance learning. This is illustrated by the following experiment. A rat is placed in a box consisting of two compartments divided by a barrier. On each trial the animal is placed in one of the compartments. At some point, a warning tone is sounded, and five seconds later the floor of that compartment is electrified; to get away from the shock, the animal must jump the barrier into the other compartment. Initially, the animal jumps the barrier only when the shock starts—this is escape learning. But with practice, the animal learns to jump upon hearing the warning tone, thereby avoiding the shock entirely—this is avoidance learning.

Avoidance learning has generated a great deal of interest, in part because there is something very puzzling about it. What exactly is reinforcing the avoidance response? In the above study, what reinforces the animal for jumping the barrier? Intuitively, it seems to be the absence of shock, but this is a nonevent. How can a nonevent serve as a reinforcer? One solution to this puzzle holds that there are two stages to the learning. The first stage involves classical conditioning: Through repeated pairings of the warning (the CS) and the punishing event or shock (the UCS), the animal learns a fear response to the warning. The second stage involves operant conditioning: The animal learns that a particular response (jumping the barrier) removes an aversive event, namely fear. In short, what first appears to be a nonevent is actually fear, and we can think of avoidance as escape from fear (Rescorla & Solomon, 1967; Mowrer, 1947).

There is an alternative to this two-stage theory that emphasizes cognitive factors (Seligman & Johnston, 1973). According to this cognitive theory, avoidance training leads the animal to certain *expectancies,* namely: (a) If it responds (jumps the barrier, for example), no shock will occur, and (b) if it does not respond, shock will occur. These expectancies are strengthened whenever they are confirmed. The reason why the rat in the preceding study continues to jump the barrier upon hearing the warning tone is that the tone triggers its "respond—no shock" expectancy, and each jump strengthens this expectancy (there is in fact no shock). Moreover, this cognitive theory explains another important fact about avoidance responses—they are difficult to extinguish. Thus, if the shocker in the preceding study were disconnected, the rat would continue to jump the barrier. Why? Because turning off the shocker does nothing to alter the "respond—no shock" expectancy, and hence behavior continues to be controlled by that expectancy. Similarly, if we learned to avoid a once-dangerous situation (a faulty elevator, for example) we may continue to avoid the situation even after the danger is gone (the elevator has been fixed) because nothing has happened to refute our expectancy.

Control and Cognitive Factors

Our analysis of operant conditioning has tended to emphasize environmental factors— a response is consistently followed by a reinforcing event, and the organism learns to associate the response and the reinforcement. However, the cognitive theory of avoidance that we just discussed suggests that cognitive factors may play an important role in operant conditioning, just as they do in classical conditioning. As we will see, it is often useful to view the organism in an operant conditioning situation as acquiring new *knowledge* about response-reinforcer relations.

Contiguity Versus Control   As was the case in classical conditioning, we want to know what factor is critical for operant conditioning to occur. Again, one of the options is temporal contiguity: an operant is conditioned whenever reinforcement immediately follows the behavior (Skinner, 1948). A more cognitive option, closely related to predictability, is that of control: An operant is conditioned only when the organism interprets the reinforcement as being controlled by its response. Some important experiments by Maier and Seligman (1976) provide more support for the control view than for the temporal contiguity view. (See also the discussion of control and stress in Chapter 15.)

Their basic experiment includes two stages. In the first stage, some dogs learn that whether they receive a shock or not depends on (is controlled by) their behavior, while other dogs learn that they have no control over the shock. Think of the dogs as being tested in pairs. Both members of a pair are in a harness that restricts their movements, and occasionally they receive an electric shock. One member of the pair, the "control" dog, can turn off the shock by pushing a nearby panel with its nose; the other member of the pair, the "yoked" dog, cannot exercise any control over the shock. Whenever the control dog is shocked, so is the yoked dog; and whenever the control dog turns off the shock,

the yoked dog's shock is also terminated. The control and yoked dogs therefore receive the same number of shocks.

To find out what the dogs learned in the first stage, a second stage is needed. In this second stage, the experimenter places both dogs in a new apparatus—a box divided into two compartments by a barrier. This is the same avoidance-testing device that we considered a moment ago. As before, on each trial a tone is first sounded, indicating that the compartment that the animal currently occupies is about to be subject to electric shock; to avoid shock, the animal must learn to jump the barrier into the other compartment when it hears the warning tone. Control dogs learn this response rapidly. But the yoked dogs are another story. Initially the yoked dogs make no movement across the barrier, and as trials progress their behavior becomes increasingly passive, lapsing finally into utter helplessness. Why? Because during the first stage the yoked dogs learned that shocks were not under their control, and this belief in noncontrol made conditioning in the second stage impossible. If a belief in noncontrol makes operant conditioning impossible, then a belief in control may be what makes it possible. Many other experiments support the notion that operant conditioning occurs only when the organism perceives reinforcement as being under its control (Seligman, 1975). See Chapter 15 for a detailed discussion of learned helplessness.

Contingency Learning   We can also talk about the previous results in terms of *contingencies*. We can say that operant conditioning occurs only when the organism perceives a contingency between its responses and reinforcement. In the first stage of the preceding study, the relevant contingency is between pushing a panel and the shock ending; perceiving this contingency amounts to determining that the likelihood of shock ending is greater when the panel is pushed than when it is not. Dogs that do not perceive this contingency in the first stage of the study appear not to look for any contingency in the second stage. This contingency approach makes it clear that the results with operant conditioning fit with the findings about the importance of predictability in classical conditioning: Knowing that a CS predicts a UCS can be interpreted as showing that the organism has detected a contingency between the two stimuli. Thus, in both classical and operant conditioning, what the organism seems to learn is a contingency between two events.

Our ability to learn contingencies develops very early, as shown by the following study of 3-month-old infants. All infants in the experiment were lying in their cribs, with their heads on pillows. Beneath each pillow was a switch that closed whenever the infant turned its head. For subjects in the control group, whenever they turned their heads and closed the switch, a mobile on the opposite side of the crib was activated. For these infants, there was a contingency between head-turning and the mobile moving—the mobile being more likely to move with a head turn than without. These infants quickly learned to turn their heads, and they reacted to the moving mobile with signs of enjoyment (they smiled and cooed). The situation is quite different for subjects in the experimental group. For these infants, the mobile was made to move roughly as often as it did for the experimental subjects, but whether it moved or not was not under their control: There was no contingency between head-turning and the mobile moving. These infants did not learn to turn their heads more frequently. Moreover, after a while they showed no signs of enjoying the mobile moving. With no control over the mobile, it appears to have lost some of its reinforcing character.

Water squirting (a natural behavior for walruses) can be easily conditioned to occur on command.

BIOLOGICAL CONSTRAINTS

As was the case with classical conditioning, biology imposes constraints on what may be learned in operant conditioning. The constraints involve response-reinforcer relations. To illustrate, consider pigeons in two experimental situations; *reward learning,* where the animal acquires a response that is reinforced by food; and *escape learning,* where the animal acquires a response that is reinforced by the termination of shock. In the case of reward, pigeons learn much faster if the response is pecking a key rather than flapping their wings. In the case of escape, the opposite is true: Pigeons learn faster if the response is wing flapping rather than pecking (Bolles, 1970).

As was the case in classical conditioning, the results seem inconsistent with the assumption that the same laws of learning apply to all situations, but they make sense from an ethological perspective. The reward case with the pigeons involved eating, and pecking (but not wing flapping) is part of the bird's natural eating activities. Hence, a genetically determined connection between pecking and eating is reasonable. Similarly, the escape case involved a danger situation, and the pigeon's natural reactions to danger include flapping its wings (but not pecking). Birds are known to have a small repertoire of defensive reactions, and they will quickly learn to escape only if the relevant response is one of these natural defensive reactions. In sum, rather than being a means for learning arbitrary associations, operant conditioning also honors the behavioral blueprint.

COMPLEX LEARNING

According to the cognitive perspective, the crux of learning—and of intelligence in general—lies in an organism's ability to mentally represent aspects of the world, and then to *operate* on these **mental representations** rather than on the world itself. In many cases, what is mentally represented are associations between stimuli or events; these cases correspond to classical and operant conditioning. In other cases, what is represented seems more complex. It might be a map of one's environment or an abstract concept like *cause*. Also, there are cases where the operations performed on mental representations are more complex than associative processes. The operations may take the form of a mental trial and error, in which the organism tries out different possibilities in its mind. Or the operations may make up a multistep strategy, in which we take some mental steps only because they enable subsequent ones. The idea of a strategy in particular seems at odds with the assumption that complex learning is built out of simple associations. In what follow, we consider phenomena in learning that directly point to the need to consider non-associative representations and operations. Some of these phenomena involve animals, whereas others involve humans performing tasks that are similar to conditioning.

COGNITIVE MAPS AND ABSTRACT CONCEPTS

An early advocate of the cognitive approach to learning was Edward Tolman, whose research dealt with the problem of rats learning their way through complex mazes (Tolman, 1932). In his view, a rat running through a complex maze was not learning a sequence of right- and left-turning responses but rather was developing a **cognitive map**—a mental representation of the layout of the maze.

More recent research provides strong evidence for cognitive maps in rats. Consider the maze diagrammed in Figure 7-9. The maze consists of a center platform with eight identical arms radiating out. On each trial, the researcher places food at the end of each arm; the rat needs to learn to visit each arm (and obtain the food there) without returning to those it has already visited. Rats learn this remarkably well; after 20 trials, they will virtually never return to an arm they have already visited. (Rats will do this even when the maze has been doused with after-shave lotion to eliminate the odor cues about which arms still have food.) Most important, a rat rarely employs the strategy that would occur to humans—such as always going through the arms in an obvious order, say clockwise. Instead, the rat visits the arms randomly, indicating that it has not learned a rigid sequence of responses. What, then, has it learned? Probably, the rat has developed a maplike

FIGURE 7-9

Maze for Studying Cognitive Maps *With food placed at the end of every arm, the rat's problem is to find all the food without retracing its steps. The pattern shown here reflects perfect learning: This rat visited each arm of the maze only once, eating whatever it found there; it did not go back to an empty arm even one time.*

representation of the maze, which specifies the spatial relations between arms, and on each trial it makes a mental note of each arm that it has visited (Olton, 1979; 1978).

More recent studies, which involve primates rather than rats, provide even stronger evidence for complex mental representations. Particularly striking are studies showing that chimpanzees can acquire abstract concepts that were once believed to be the sole province of humans. In the typical study, chimpanzees learn to use plastic tokens of different shapes, sizes, and colors as words.

Using the technique developed by Premack, an experimenter tests a chimpanzee's ability to use language by manipulating plastic chips that represent specific words.

For example, they might learn that one token refers to "apples" and another to "paper," where there is no physical resemblance between the token and the object. The fact that chimpanzees can learn these references suggests they understand concrete concepts like "apple" and "paper." More impressively, they also have abstract concepts like "same," "different," and "cause." Thus, chimpanzees can learn to use their "same" token when presented either two "apple" tokens or two "orange" ones, and their "different" token when presented one "apple" and one "orange" token. Likewise, chimpanzees seem to understand causal relations. They will apply the token for "cause" when shown some cut paper and scissors, but not when shown some intact paper and scissors (Premack, 1985a; Premack & Premack. 1983).

INSIGHT LEARNING

While many early researchers tried to study complex learning with species far removed from humans (like rats and pigeons), other early researchers assumed that the best evidence for complex learning would come from other primate species. Among these researchers, Wolfgang Köhler's work with chimpanzees, carried out in the 1920s, re-

mains particularly important. The problems that Köhler set for his chimpanzees left some room for insight, because no parts of the problem were hidden from view (in contrast, the workings of a food dispenser in a Skinner box are hidden from the animal's view). Typically, Köhler placed a chimpanzee in an enclosed area with a desirable piece of fruit, often a banana, out of reach. To obtain the fruit, the animal had to use a nearby object as a tool. Usually the chimpanzee solved the problem, and did it in a way that suggested it had some insight. The following description from Köhler is typical:

> Sultan [Köhler's most intelligent chimpanzee] is squatting at the bars but cannot reach the fruit which lies outside by means of his only available short stick. A longer stick is deposited outside the bars, about two meters on one side of the object and parallel with the grating. It cannot be grasped with the hand, but it can be pulled within reach by means of the small stick. [See Figure 7-10 for an illustration of a similar multiple-stick problem.] Sultan tries to reach the fruit with the smaller of the two sticks. Not succeeding, he tears at a piece of wire that projects from the netting of his cage, but that too is in vain. Then he gazes about him (there are always in the course of these tests some long pauses, during which the animals scrutinize the whole visible area). He suddenly picks up the little stick once more, goes up to the bars directly opposite to the long stick, scratches it towards him with the "auxiliary," seizes it, and goes with it to the point opposite the objective (the fruit), which he secures. From the moment that his eyes fall upon the long stick, his procedure forms one consecutive whole, without hiatus, and although the angling of the bigger stick by means of the smaller is an action that could be complete and distinct in itself, yet observation shows that it follows, quite suddenly, on an interval of hesitation and doubt—staring about—which undoubtedly has a relation to the final objective, and is immediately merged in the final action of the attainment of the end goal. (Köhler, 1925, pp. 174–75)

Several aspects of the performance of these chimpanzees are unlike those of Thorndike's cats or Skinner's rats and pigeons. For one thing, the solution was sudden, rather than being the result of a gradual trial-and-error process. Another point is that once a chimpanzee solved a problem, thereafter it would solve the problem with few irrelevant moves. This is most unlike a rat in a Skinner box, which continues to make irrelevant responses for many trials. Also, Köhler's chimpanzees

FIGURE 7-10

Multiple Stick Problem   *Using the shorter sticks, the chimpanzee pulls in a stick long enough to reach the piece of fruit. It has learned to solve this problem by understanding the relationship between the sticks and the piece of fruit.*

could readily transfer what they had learned to a novel situation. For example, in one problem, Sultan was not encaged, but some bananas were placed too high for him to reach, as shown in Figure 7-11. To solve the problem, Sultan stacked some boxes strewn around him, climbed the "platform," and grabbed the bananas. In subsequent problems, if the fruit was again too high to reach, Sultan found other objects to construct a platform; in some cases, Sultan used a table and a small ladder, and in one case Sultan pulled Köhler himself over and used the experimenter as a platform.

There are, therefore, three critical aspects of the chimpanzee's solution: its suddenness, its availability once discovered, and its transferability. These aspects are at odds with the trial-and-error behaviors of the type observed by Thorndike, Skinner, and their students. Instead, the chimpanzee's solutions may reflect a *mental* trial and error. That is, the animal forms a mental representation of the problem, manipulates components of the representation until it hits on a solution, and then enacts the solution in the real world. The solution, therefore, appears sudden because the researchers do not have access to the chimpanzee's mental process. The solution is available thereafter because a mental representation persists over time. And the solution is transferable because the representation is either abstract enough to cover more than the original situation, or malleable enough to be extended to a novel situation.

Köhler's work suggests that complex learning often involves two phases. In the initial phase, problem solving is used to derive a solution; in the second phase, the solution is stored in memory and retrieved whenever a similar problem situation presents itself. Hence complex learning is intimately related to memory and thinking (the topics of the next two chapters). Moreover, this two-phase structure characterizes not just chimpanzee learning, but also many cases of complex learning in humans. Indeed, it has recently been incorporated into artificial intelligence programs that try to simulate human learning (Rosenbloom, Laird & Newell, 1991).

PRIOR BELIEFS

Research on animal learning has tended to emphasize the learning of *perfectly pre-*

FIGURE 7-11

Chimpanzee Constructing a Platform   *To reach the bananas hanging from the ceiling, the chimpanzee stacks boxes to form a platform.*

dictable relations. For example, in most studies of classical conditioning, the CS is followed by the UCS 100 percent of the time. But in real life, relations between stimuli or events are usually less than perfectly predictable. The study of associative learning with less than perfect relations has been conducted mainly with humans. Many of these studies have used tasks that are quite novel and that do not make much contact with the learner's *prior beliefs*. In such cases, subjects are very sensitive to the degree of the objective relation between the stimuli (Wasserman, 1990; Shanks, 1987). But our concern here is with studies that use tasks that do make contact with the learner's prior beliefs. These studies show that prior beliefs can determine what is learned, which indicates that learning involves processes in addition to those that form associations between inputs.

In the studies of interest, a different pair of stimuli is presented on each trial—say, a picture and a description of a person—and the subject's task is to learn the relation between the members of the pairs—say, that pictures of tall men tend to be associated with brief descriptions. Some striking evidence for the role of prior beliefs comes from cases in which, objectively, there is *no* relation between the stimuli, yet subjects "learn" such a relation. In one experiment, subjects were concerned with the possible relation between the drawings that mental patients made and the symptoms that the patients manifested. On each trial of the experiment, subjects were presented a patient's drawing of a person and one of six symptoms, including the symptoms "suspiciousness of other people" and "concerned with being taken care of." The subject's task was to determine whether any of the signs in the drawing—some aspect of the eyes or mouth, for instance—were associated with any of the symptoms. In fact, the six symptoms had been randomly paired with the drawings so that there was no association between sign (drawing) and symptom. Yet subjects consistently reported there were such relations, and the relations they reported were ones they probably believed *before* participating in the experiment: for example, that large eyes are associated with suspiciousness, or that a large mouth is associated with a desire to be taken care of by others. These nonexistent but plausible relations are referred to as **spurious associations** (Chapman & Chapman, 1967).

In the preceding study, prior beliefs about the stimuli determined what was "learned." Since prior beliefs are part of one's knowledge, these results attest to the cognitive nature of such learning. However, the preceding study does not say anything about how learning proceeds when there is in fact an objective association to be learned. This issue was analyzed in the following research.

On each of a set of trials, subjects were presented two measures of an individual's honesty taken from two completely different situations. For example, one measure might have been how often a young boy copied another student's homework in school, and the second measure might have been an indication of how often that same boy was dishonest at home. It is well known that most people believe (erroneously) that two measures of the same trait (like honesty) will always be highly correlated. This is the critical prior belief. In fact, the objective relation between the two honesty measures varied across conditions of the experiment, sometimes being quite low, and the subjects' task was to estimate the strength of this relation by choosing a number between 0 (which indicated no relation) and 100 (a perfect relation). The results showed that subjects consistently overestimated the strength of the relation. Their prior belief that an honest person is honest in all situations led them to see more than was there (Jennings, Amabile, & Ross, 1980).

In the preceding study, sometimes the learner's prior beliefs were not in agreement with the objective association to be learned. In these cases, the beliefs and data were in conflict. In such situations, typically people will go with their prior beliefs. If people believe that two different measures of an individual's honesty should be highly related, for example, they may "detect" such a relation even when there is no objective association. However, as the data (the objective association) is made increasingly salient, eventually our prior beliefs will capitulate, and we learn what is in fact there (Alloy & Tabachnik, 1984).

The results of the preceding studies are reminiscent of what we called *top-down processing* in perception (see Chapter 5). Recall that top-down processing refers to situations in which a perceiver combines her expectation of what she is likely to see with the actual input to yield a final percept. In *top-down processing in learning*, the learner combines her prior belief about an associative relation with the objective input about that relation to yield a final estimate of the strength of that relation.

The effects of prior beliefs on learning have important implications for education. In particular, when teaching someone about a topic, say, the biology of digestion, one cannot ignore his or her prior beliefs about the subject matter. The student will often try to assimilate the new information to the earlier beliefs. Educationally, it may be best to get these prior beliefs out in the open, so that they can be confronted by the instructor if they are in fact erroneous (Genter & Collins, 1983).

In sum, this line of research demonstrates the importance of prior beliefs in human learning, thereby strengthening the case for a cognitive approach to learning. In a way, however, the research also has a connection to the ethological approach to learning. Just as rats and pigeons may be constrained to learn only those associations that evolution has prepared them for, so we humans seem to be constrained to learn those associations that our prior beliefs have prepared us for. Without prior constraints of some sort, perhaps there would simply be too many potential associations to consider, and associative learning would be chaotic if not impossible.

BIOLOGICAL-PSYCHOLOGICAL PERSPECTIVES

Biological constraints are part of a biological approach to behavior. Hence the ethological research that we discussed in this chapter shows us a new way that biological and psychological approaches can interact. In particular, we saw how ethological concepts could make sense out of previous psychological findings (for example, pigeons learn faster in reward learning if the response is pecking, but faster in escape learning if the response is wing flapping). In addition to the contributions of ethology, again we noted how considerations of neural processing could also be successfully combined with psychological work. In particular, we discussed the neural bases of elementary learning processes, such as habituation and sensitization, pointing out possible neurochemical mediators of learning.

It is worth noting, though, that we had little to say about the biological bases of learning once we moved to complex learning. Here, virtually all of the work is at the psychological level, particularly the cognitive perspective. This state of affairs could soon change, though, because researchers increasingly are viewing complex learning as one of the next research frontiers.

CHAPTER SUMMARY

1. *Learning* may be defined as a relatively permanent change in behavior that results from practice. Four kinds of learning can be distinguished: (a) *habituation,* in which an organism learns to ignore a familiar and inconsequential stimulus; (b) *classical conditioning,* in which an organism learns that one stimulus follows another; (c) *operant conditioning,* in which an organism learns that a response leads to a particular consequence; and (d) *complex* learning, in which learning involves more than the formation of associations.

2. Early research on learning was done from a behavioristic perspective. It often assumed that: (a) behavior is better understood in terms of external causes than internal ones, (b) simple associations are the building blocks of all learning, and (c) the laws of learning are the same for different species and different situations. These assumptions have been modified in light of subsequent work. The contemporary analysis of learning includes cognitive factors and biological constraints as well as behavioristic principles.

3. In Pavlov's experiments, if a *conditioned stimulus* (CS) consistently precedes an *unconditioned stimulus* (UCS), the CS comes to serve as a signal for the UCS and will elicit a *conditioned response* (CR) that often resembles the *unconditioned response* (UCR). Stimuli that are similar to the CS also elicit the CR to some extent, though such *generalization* can be curbed by *discrimination training.* These phenomena occur in organisms as diverse as flatworms and humans. There are a number of important human applications of classical conditioning, including *conditioned fear* and *conditioned drug tolerance.* In the latter case, the conditioned response to a stimulus associated with drug use is the opposite of the effect caused by the drug.

4. Cognitive factors also play a role in conditioning. For classical conditioning to occur, the CS must be a reliable predictor of the UCS; that is, there must be a higher probability that the UCS will occur when the CS has been presented than when it has not. The importance of *predictability* is also evident in the phenomenon of *blocking:* If one CS reliably predicts a UCS, and another CS is added, the relation between the added CS and the UCS will not be learned. Models of classical conditioning center on the notions of predictability and surprise.

5. Findings of ethologists challenge the assumption that the laws of learning are the same for all species or for all situations that a given species encounters. According to ethologists, what an animal learns is constrained by its genetically determined "behavioral blueprint." Evidence for such constraints on classical conditioning comes from studies of *taste aversion.* While rats readily learn to associate the feeling of being sick with the taste of a solution, they cannot learn to associate sickness with a light. Conversely, birds can learn to associate light and sickness, but not taste and sickness. These differences are the result of innate differences between rats and birds in their food-gathering activities.

6. Operant conditioning deals with situations in which the response operates on the environment rather than being elicited by an unconditioned stimulus. The earliest systematic studies were performed by Thorndike, who showed that animals engage in *trial-and-error* behavior, and that any behavior followed by reinforcement is strengthened (the *law of effect*).

7. In Skinner's experiments, typically a rat or pigeon learns to make a simple response, such as pressing a lever, to obtain reinforcement. The rate of response is a useful measure of *response strength. Shaping* is a training procedure used when the desired response is novel; it involves reinforcing only those variations in response that deviate in the direction desired by the experimenter.

8. There are a number of phenomena that increase the generality of operant conditioning. One is *conditioned reinforcement,* wherein a stimulus associated with a reinforcer acquires its own reinforcing properties. Other relevant phenomena are *generalization* and *discrimination;* organisms generalize responses to similar situations, though this

generalization can be brought under the control of a *discriminative* stimulus. Finally, there are *schedules of reinforcement.* Once a behavior is established, it can be maintained when reinforced only part of the time. Exactly when the reinforcement comes is determined by its schedule; either a *fixed ratio,* a *variable ratio,* a *fixed interval,* or a *variable interval* schedule.

9. The reinforcement in operant conditioning can be an aversive event like shock. There are three different kinds of *aversive conditioning.* In *punishment,* a response is followed by an aversive event, which results in the response being suppressed. In *escape,* an organism learns to make a response to terminate an ongoing aversive event. In *avoidance,* an organism learns to make a response to prevent the aversive event from even starting.

10. Cognitive factors are operative in operant conditioning. For operant conditioning to occur, the organism must believe that reinforcement is at least partly under its *control;* that is, the organism must perceive a *contingency* between its responses and reinforcement. Biological constraints also play a role in operant conditioning. There are constraints on what reinforcers can be associated with what responses. With pigeons, when the reinforcement is food, learning is faster if the response is pecking a key rather than flapping their wings; but when the reinforcement is termination of shock, learning is faster when the response is wing flapping rather than pecking a key.

11. According to the cognitive perspective, the crux of learning is an organism's ability to represent aspects of the world mentally and then to operate on these *mental representations* rather than on the world itself. In complex learning, the mental representations depict more than associations, and the mental operations may constitute a *strategy.* Studies of complex learning in animals indicate that rats can develop a *cognitive map* of their environments, as well as acquire abstract concepts like *cause.* Other studies demonstrate that chimpanzees can solve problems by insight, and then generalize these solutions to similar problems.

12. When learning relations between stimuli that are not perfectly predictive, people often invoke prior beliefs about the relations. This can lead to people detecting relations that are not objectively present (*spurious associa-*

tions). When the relation is objectively present, having a prior belief about it can lead to overestimating the relation's predictive strength; when an objective relation conflicts with a prior belief, the learner may favor the prior belief. These effects demonstrate *top-down processing* in learning.

FURTHER READING

Pavlov's *Conditioned Reflexes* (1927) is the definitive work on classical conditioning. Skinner's *The Behavior of Organisms* (1938) is the corresponding statement on operant conditioning. The major points of view about conditioning and learning, presented in their historical settings, are summarized in Bower and Hilgard, *Theories of Learning* (5th ed., 1981).

For a general introduction to learning, a number of textbooks are recommended. Schwartz's *Psychology of Learning and Behavior* (3rd ed., 1989) is a particularly well-balanced review of conditioning, including discussion of ethology and cognition. Other useful textbooks include Gordon's *Learning and Memory* (1989), Schwartz and Reisberg's *Learning and Memory* (1991), and Domjan

and Burkhard's *The Principles of Learning and Behavior* (1985). At the advanced level, the six-volume Estes (ed.), *Handbook of Learning and Cognitive Processes* (1975–1978), covers most aspects of learning and conditioning; and Honig and Staddon (eds.), *Handbook of Operant Behavior* (1977), provides a comprehensive treatment of operant conditioning.

The early cognitive approach is well described in two classics: Tolman's *Purposive Behavior in Animals and Men* (1932; reprint ed. 1967) and Köhler's *The Mentality of Apes* (1925; reprint ed. 1976). For a more recent statement of the cognitive approach to animal learning, see Roitblat's *Introduction to Comparative Cognition* (1986).

MEMORY

It seems, then, that we owe to memory almost all that we either have or are; that our ideas and conceptions are its work, and that our everyday perception, thought, and movement is derived from this source. Memory collects the countless phenomena of our existence into a single whole; and, as our bodies would be scattered into the dust of their component atoms if they were not held together by the attraction of matter, so our consciousness would be broken up into as many fragments as we had lived seconds but for the binding and unifying force of memory. (Hering, 1920)

Hering's words, spoken in his lecture to the Vienna Academy of Sciences many years ago, attest to the importance of memory in mental life. As Hering's comments about consciousness suggest, it is memory that gives us the sense of continuity on which our very notion of a *self* depends. When we think of what it means to be human, we must acknowledge the centrality of memory.

To appreciate the scientific study of memory, first we need to understand how researchers divide the field into manageable units, such as *short-term memory* and *long-term memory*. After describing the key distinctions, we will review the major findings about short-term memory, long-term memory, and what is called *implicit memory* (the kind of memory involved in learning a skill). Then we will take up a question of universal interest: How can memory be improved? We will conclude with a discussion of situations in which our memories are partly constructed.

DISTINCTIONS ABOUT MEMORY AND THEIR BIOLOGICAL BASES

Psychologists today make three critical distinctions about memory. The first concerns the three stages of memory: *encoding, storage,* and *retrieval.* The second distinction deals with different memories for storing information for short and long periods. The third distinction is about different memories being used to store different kinds of information (for example, one system for facts and another for skills). For each of these distinctions, there is evidence that the entities

being distinguished—say, short-term versus long-term memory—are mediated, in part, by different structures in the brain.

THREE STAGES OF MEMORY

PSYCHOLOGICAL DISTINCTION   Suppose one morning you are introduced to a student and told her name is Barbara Cohn. That afternoon you see her again and say something like, "You're Barbara Cohn. We met this morning." Clearly, you have remembered her name. But how exactly did you remember it?

Your minor memory feat can be broken into three stages (see Figure 8-1). First, when you were introduced, you somehow entered Barbara Cohn's name into memory; this is the **encoding stage.** You transformed a physical input (sound waves) that corresponds to her spoken name into the kind of code or representation that memory accepts, and you "placed" that representation in memory. Second, you retained—or stored—the name during the time between the two meetings; this is the **storage stage.** And, third, you recovered the name from storage at the time of your second meeting; this is the **retrieval stage.**

Memory can fail at any of these three stages. Had you been unable to recall Barbara's name at the second meeting, this could have reflected a failure in encoding, storage, or retrieval. Much of current research on memory attempts to specify the mental operations that occur at each of the three stages of memory and to explain how these operations can go awry and result in memory failure.

BIOLOGICAL BASIS   A number of recent studies suggest that the different stages of memory recruit different structures in the brain. The most striking evidence comes from

Theories of memory attribute forgetting to a failure at one or more of three stages encoding, storage, retrieval.

ENCODING	STORAGE	RETRIEVAL
Put into memory	**Maintain in memory**	**Recover from memory**

FIGURE 8-1

Three Stages of Memory   *Theories of memory attribute forgetting to a failure at one or more of these stages.* (After Melton, 1963)

brain-scanning studies that look for neuroanatomical differences between encoding and retrieval stages. These experiments involve two parts. In part 1, which taps encoding, subjects study a set of verbal items, for example, pairs consisting of categories and uncommon instances (*furniture-sideboard*); in part 2, which taps retrieval, subjects have to recognize or recall the items when cued with the category name. In both parts, PET measures of brain activity are recorded while subjects are engaged in their task. The most striking finding is that during encoding most of the activated brain regions are in the left hemisphere, and during retrieval most of the activated brain areas are in the right hemisphere (Shallice et al., 1994; Tulving et al., 1994). Thus the distinction between encoding and retrieval has a clear-cut biological bias.

SHORT-TERM VERSUS LONG-TERM MEMORY

PSYCHOLOGICAL DISTINCTION   The three stages of memory do not operate the same way in all situations. Memory seems to differ between those situations that require us to store material for a matter of seconds and those that require us to store material for longer intervals—from minutes to years. The former situations are said to tap **short-term memory,** and the latter reflect **long-term memory.**

We can illustrate this distinction by amending our earlier story about meeting Barbara Cohn. Suppose that during the first meeting, as soon as you had heard her name, a friend came up and you said, "Have you met Barbara Cohn?" In this case, remembering Barbara's name would be an example of short-term memory: You retrieved the name after only a second or two. Remembering her name at the time of your second meeting would be an example of long-term memory, because then retrieval would take place hours after the name was encoded.

When we recall a name immediately after encountering it, retrieval seems effortless, as if the name were still active, still in our consciousness. But when we try to recall the same name hours later, retrieval is often difficult because the name is no longer in our consciousness and, in some sense, has to be brought back.

BIOLOGICAL DISTINCTION   It has been known for a while that short-term and long-term memory are implemented by somewhat different brain structures. In particular, the *hippocampus,* a brain structure beneath the cortex and near the middle of the brain, is critical for long-term memory but not for short-term memory.

Much of the relevant evidence comes from experiments with rats and other nonhuman species. In some experiments, one group of rats is first subjected to damage to the hippocampus and the surrounding cortex, and a second group is subjected to damage in a completely different region, the front of the cortex. Both groups of rats then have to perform a *delayed-response* task: On each trial, first one stimulus is presented (say, a square), then after a delay a second stimulus is presented (say, a triangle), and the animal has to respond only when the second stimulus *differs* from the first. How well the animal does on this task depends on the kind of brain damage it has suffered and the length of the delay between the two stimuli. When the delay is long (15 seconds or more), animals with damage to the hippocampus perform poorly, but those with damage in the front of the cortex perform relatively normally. Because a long delay between stimuli requires long-term memory for storage of the first stimulus, these results fit with the idea that the hippocampus is critical for long-term memory. When the delay between the two stimuli is short (just a few seconds), the results reverse: Now animals with damage in the front of the cortex perform poorly, and those with hippocampal damage perform relatively normally. Because a short delay between stimuli requires short-term memory for storage of the first stimulus, these results indicate that regions in the frontal cortex are involved in short-term memory. Hence different brain regions implement short-term and long-term memory (e.g., Goldman-Rakic, 1987; Zola-Morgan & Squire, 1985)

What about evidence for this distinction in humans? Patients who happen to have suffered damage in certain brain regions provide an "experiment of nature." Specifically, some patients have suffered damage to the hippocampus and surrounding cortex, and consequently show a severe memory loss; because the hippocampus is located in the middle of the temporal lobe, these patients are said to have *medial-temporal-lobe amnesia.* Such patients have profound difficulty remembering material for long intervals but rarely have any trouble remembering material for a few seconds. Thus, a patient with medial-temporal-lobe amnesia may be unable to recognize his doctor when she enters the room—even though the patient has seen this doctor every day for years—yet will have no trouble repeating back the physician's full name when she is reintroduced (Milner, Corkin, & Teuber, 1968). Such a patient has a severe impairment in long-term memory but a normal short-term memory.

Other patients, however, show the opposite problem. They cannot correctly repeat a string of even three words, yet they are relatively normal when tested on their long-term memory for words. Such patients have an impaired short-term memory but an intact long-term memory. And their brain damage is never in the medial temporal lobe (Shallice, 1988). Thus, for humans as well as for other mammals, short-term and long-term memory are mediated by different brain structures.

DIFFERENT MEMORIES FOR DIFFERENT KINDS OF INFORMATION

Until about a decade ago, psychologists generally assumed that the same memory system was used for all materials. For example, the same long-term memory was presumably used to store both one's recollection of a grandmother's funeral and the skill one needs to ride a bike. Recent evidence indicates that this assumption is wrong. In particular, we seem to use a different long-term memory for storing *facts* (such as who the current president is) than we do for retaining *skills* (such as how to ride a bicycle). The evidence for this difference, as usual, includes both psychological and biological findings, but we will defer consideration of these findings until later in the chapter when we discuss in detail the kind of memory that stores skills.

We have, then, three important distinctions. Given these differences, ideally we would like to proceed as follows: first specify the different memory systems corresponding to different contents, and then for each one describe the nature of encoding, storage, and retrieval stages in its short-term and long-term memory. This goal is too ambitious given present knowledge. Most of what we know concerns memory for facts, particularly personal ones about our experiences. The kind of memory situation that we understand

best is one in which a person consciously recollects an event in the past, where this recollection is experienced as occurring in a particular time and place. This kind of memory, which is called **explicit memory,** will be the focus of most sections of the chapter. The next two sections consider the nature of encoding, storage, and retrieval in short-term and long-term explicit memory. Then we will examine what is known about another kind of memory, which includes memory for skills, and is referred to as **implicit memory.**

SHORT-TERM MEMORY

Even in those situations in which we must remember information for only a few seconds, memory involves the three stages of encoding, storage, and retrieval.

ENCODING

To encode information into short-term memory, we must attend to it. Since we are selective about what we attend to (see Chapter 5), our short-term memory will contain only what has been selected. This means that much of what we are exposed to never even enters short-term memory and, of course, will not be available for later retrieval. Indeed, many difficulties labeled "memory problems" are really lapses in attention. For example, if

Psychological and biological findings indicate that we use a different long-term memory for storing facts than for retaining skills.

When you look up a telephone number, do you remember it visually, acoustically, or semantically?

you bought some groceries and someone later asked you for the color of the checkout clerk's eyes, you might well be unable to answer, not because of a failure in your memory, but because you had not paid attention to the clerk's eyes in the first place.

ACOUSTIC CODING   When information is encoded into memory, it is entered in a certain code or representation. For example, when you look up a phone number and retain it until you have dialed it, in what form do you represent the digits? Is the representation visual—a mental picture of the digits? Is it acoustic—the sounds of the names of the digits? Or is it semantic (based on meaning)—some meaningful association that the digits have? Research indicates that we can use any of these possibilities to encode information into short-term memory, although we favor an acoustic code when we are trying to keep the information active by *rehearsing* it—that is, by saying it over and over to ourselves. **Rehearsal** is a particularly popular strategy when the information consists of verbal items such as digits, letters, or words. So in trying to remember a phone number, we are most likely to encode the number as the sounds of the digit names and to rehearse these sounds to ourselves until we have dialed the number.

In a classic experiment that provided evidence for an acoustic code, researchers briefly showed subjects a list of six consonants (for example, RLBKSJ); when the letters were removed, the subject had to write all six letters

in order. Although the entire procedure took only a second or two, subjects occasionally made errors. When they did, the incorrect letter tended to be similar in sound to the correct one. For the list mentioned, a subject might have written RLTKSJ, replacing the B with the similar-sounding T (Conrad, 1964). This finding supports the hypothesis that the subjects encoded each letter acoustically (for example, "bee" for B), sometimes lost part of this code (only the "ee" part of the sound remained), and then responded with a letter ("tee") that was consistent with the remaining part of the code. This hypothesis also explains why it is more difficult to recall the items in order when they are acoustically similar (for example, TBCGVE) than when they are acoustically distinct (RLTKSJ).

VISUAL CODING   If need be, we can also maintain verbal items in a visual representation. However, experiments indicate that though we can use a visual code for verbal material, the code fades quickly. To illustrate, after looking at the address 7915 THIRD AVENUE, you may have a visual code of it for a second or two. This representation would preserve visual details, such as the fact that the address is written in all capital letters. But after a couple of seconds, all that would remain would be the sound of the address (the acoustic code), and this code would not preserve information about the form of the letters (Posner & Keele, 1967).

This dominance of the acoustic code may apply mainly to verbal materials. When a person must store nonverbal items (such as pictures that are difficult to describe and therefore difficult to rehearse acoustically), the visual code becomes more important. While most of us can maintain some kind of visual image in short-term memory, a few people are able to maintain images that are almost photographic in clarity. This ability occurs mainly in children. Such children can look briefly at a picture and, when it is removed, still experience the image before their eyes. They can maintain the image for as long as several minutes, and when questioned, provide a wealth of detail, such as the number of stripes on a cat's tail (see Figure 8-2). Such children seem to be reading the details directly from an **eidetic image** (Haber, 1969). Eidetic imagery is very rare, though. Some studies with children indicate that only about

5 percent report visual images that are long-lasting and possess sharp detail. Moreover, when the criteria for possessing true photographic imagery are made more stringent—for example, being able to read an imaged page of text as easily from the bottom up as from the top down—the frequency of eidetic imagery becomes minuscule, even among children (Haber, 1979). The visual code in short-term memory, then, is something short of a photograph.

TWO SHORT-TERM MEMORY SYSTEMS   The existence of both acoustic and visual codes had led researchers to argue that short-term memory consists of two distinct stores or *buffers*. One is an *acoustic buffer,* which briefly stores information in an acoustic code; the second store is a *visual-spatial buffer,* which briefly stores information in a visual or spatial code (Baddeley, 1986). Some recent brain-scanning studies indicated that the two buffers are mediated by different brain structures.

In one experiment, on every trial subjects saw a sequence of letters in which both the identity and the position of the letter varied from item to item (see Figure 8-3). On some trials, subjects had to attend only to the identity of the letters, and their task was to determine whether each letter presented was identical to the one presented three back in the sequence. On other trials, subjects had to attend only to the position of the letters, and their task was to determine whether each letter's position was identical to the position of the letter presented three back (see Figure 8-3). Thus, the actual stimuli were identical in all cases, but what varied was whether the subjects were storing verbal information (the identities of the letters), or spatial information (the positions of the letters). Presumably, the verbal information was being kept in the acoustic buffer and the spatial information in the visual-spatial buffer. On both identity and spatial trials, PET measures of brain activity were recorded. The results indicated that, roughly, the two buffers are in different hemispheres. On trials in which subjects had to store verbal information (acoustic buffer), most of the brain activity was in the left hemisphere; on trials in which subjects had to store spatial information (visual-spatial buffer), most of the brain activity was in the right hemisphere. The two buffers seem to be distinct systems (Smith, Jonides, & Koeppe, 1996).

STORAGE

LIMITED CAPACITY   Perhaps the most striking fact about short-term memory is that it has a very limited capacity. On the average, the limit is seven items, give or take two (7 ± 2). Some people store as few as five items; others can retain as many as nine. It may seem strange to give such an exact number to cover all people when it is clear that individuals differ greatly in their memory abilities. These differences, however, are primarily due to long-term memory. For short-term memory, most normal adults have a capacity of 7 ± 2. This constancy has been known since the earliest

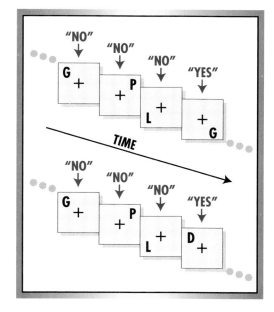

FIGURE 8-2

Testing for Eidetic Images   *This test picture was shown for 30 seconds to elementary school children. After removal of the picture, one boy saw in his eidetic image "about 14" stripes in the cat's tail. The painting, by Marjorie Torrey, appears in Lewis Carroll's* Alice in Wonderland, *abridged by Josette Frank.*

FIGURE 8-3

Experiment on Acoustic and Visual Buffers   *Subjects had to decide whether each item was identical to the one three back in the sequence. The top half of the figure shows a typical sequence of events in which subjects had to attend only to the identity of the letters, along with the responses required to each item. The bottom half of the figure shows the trial events when subjects had to attend only to the position of the letters, along with the responses required to each item.* (After Smith et al., 1995) days of experimental psychology. Hermann Ebbinghaus, who began the experimental study of memory in 1885, reported results showing that his own limit was seven items. Some 70 years later, George Miller (1956) was so struck by the constancy that he referred to it as the "magic number seven," and we now know that the limit holds in non-Western cultures as well as Western ones (Yu et al., 1985).

Psychologists determined this number by showing subjects various sequences of unrelated items (digits, letters, or words) and asking them to recall the items in order. The items are presented rapidly, and the subject does not have time to relate them to information stored in long-term memory; hence, the number of items recalled reflects only the storage capacity for short-term memory. On the initial trials, subjects have to recall just a few items, say, three or four digits, which they can easily do. Then the number of digits increases over trials until the experimenter determines the maximum number a subject can recall in perfect order. The maximum (almost always between five and nine) is the subject's **memory span**. This task is so simple that you can easily try it yourself. The next time you come across a list of names (a directory in a business or university building, for example), read through the list once and then look away and see how many names you can recall in order. It will probably be between five and nine.

CHUNKING   As we just noted, the memory-span procedure discourages subjects from connecting the to-be-remembered items to information in long-term memory. When such connections *are* possible, performance on the memory-span task can change substantially.

To illustrate this change, suppose you were presented the letter string SRUOYYLERECNIS. Because your memory span is 7 ± 2, you would probably be unable to repeat the entire letter sequence since it contains 14 letters. Should you notice, however, that these letters spell the phrase SINCERELY YOURS in reverse order, your task would become easier. By using this knowledge, you have decreased the number of items that must be held in short-term memory from 14 to 2 (the two words). But where did this spelling knowledge come from? From long-term memory, of course, where knowledge about words

is stored. Thus, you can use long-term memory to recode new material into larger meaningful units and then store those units in short-term memory. Such units are called **chunks,** and the capacity of short-term memory is best expressed as 7 ± 2 chunks (Miller, 1956). Chunking can occur with numbers as well. The string 149-2177-619-96 is beyond our capacity, but 1492-1776-1996 is well within it. The general principle is that we can boost our short-term memory by regrouping sequences of letters and digits into units that can be found in long-term memory (Bower & Springston, 1970).

FORGETTING   We may be able to hold on to seven items briefly, but in most cases they will soon be forgotten. Forgetting occurs either because the items *decay* with time, or because they are *displaced* by new items.

Information may simply decay in time. We may think of the representation of an item as a trace that fades within a matter of seconds. One of the best pieces of evidence for this hypothesis is that our short-term memory span holds fewer words when the words take longer to say; for example, the span is less for long words such as "harpoon" and "cyclone" than for shorter words such as "bishop" and "pewter" (try saying the words to yourself to see the difference in duration). Presumably this effect arises because as the words are presented we say them to ourselves, and the longer it takes to do this, the more likely it is that some of the words' traces will have faded before they can be recalled (Baddeley, Thompson, & Buchanan, 1975).

The other major cause of forgetting in short-term memory is the displacement of old items by new items. The notion of *displacement* fits with short-term memory having a fixed capacity. Being in short-term memory may correspond to being in a state of activation. The more items we try to keep active, the less activation there is for any one of them. Perhaps only about seven items can be simultaneously maintained at a level of activation that permits all of them to be recalled. Once seven items are active, the activation given to a new item will be usurped from items presented earlier; consequently these earlier items may fall below the critical level of activation needed for recall (Anderson, 1983).

It appears, then, that information at the forefront of our memory must soon give way.

RETRIEVAL

Let us continue to think of the contents of short-term memory as being active in consciousness. Intuition suggests that access to this information is immediate. You do not have to dig for it; it is right there. Retrieval, then, should not depend on the number of items in consciousness. But in this case intuition is wrong.

Evidence shows that the more items there are in short-term memory, the slower retrieval becomes. Most of the evidence for such a slowing comes from a type of experiment introduced by Sternberg (1966). On each trial of the experiment, a subject is shown a set of digits, called the *memory list,* that he or she must temporarily maintain in short-term memory. It is easy for the subject to maintain the information in short-term memory because each memory list contains between one and six digits. The memory list is then removed from view, and a probe digit is presented. The subject must decide whether the probe was on the memory list. For example, if the memory list is 3 6 1 and the probe is 6, the subject should respond "yes"; given the same memory list and a probe of 2, the subject should respond "no." Subjects rarely make an error on this task; what is of interest, however, is the *decision time,* which is the elapsed time between the onset of the probe and the subject's press of a "yes" or a "no" button. Figure 8-4 presents data from such an experiment, indicating that decision time increases directly with the length of the memory list. What is remarkable about these decision times is that they fall along a straight line. This means that each additional item in short-term memory adds a fixed amount of time to the retrieval process—approximately 40 milliseconds, which is ⅟₂₅th of a second. The same results are found when the items are letters, words, auditory tones, or pictures of people's faces (Sternberg, 1975). Psychologists have obtained similar results with groups as varied as schizophrenic patients, college students under the influence of marijuana, and people from preliterate societies.

These results have led some researchers to hypothesize that retrieval requires a search of short-term memory in which the items are examined one at a time. This **serial search** of short-term memory presumably operates at a rate of 40 milliseconds per item, which is too fast for people to be aware of it (Sternberg, 1966). However, thinking of short-term memory as a state of activation leads to a different interpretation of the results. Retrieval of an item in short-term memory may depend on the activation of that item reaching a critical level. That is, one decides a probe is in short-term memory if its representation is above a critical level of activation, and the more items in short-term memory the less activation for any one of them (Monsell, 1979). Such **activation models** have been shown to accurately predict many aspects of retrieval from short-term memory (McElree & Doesher, 1989).

SHORT-TERM MEMORY AS WORKING MEMORY

Short-term memory plays an important role in thought. When consciously trying to solve a problem, we often use short-term memory as a mental work space: we use it to store parts of the problem as well as information accessed from long-term memory that is relevant to the problem. To illustrate, consider what it takes to multiply 35 by 8 in your head. You need short-term memory to store the

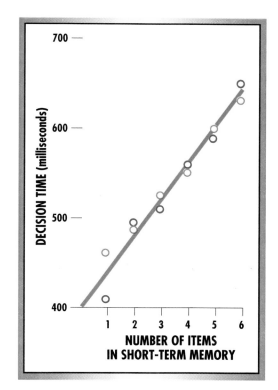

FIGURE 8-4

Retrieval as a Search Process *Decision times increase in direct proportion to the number of items in short-term memory. Blue circles represent "yes" responses; red circles, "no" responses. The times for both types of decision fall along a straight line. Because the decision times are so fast, they must be measured with equipment that permits accuracy in milliseconds (thousandths of a second). (After Sternberg, 1966)* given numbers (35 and 8), the nature of the operation required (multiplication), and arithmetic facts such as $8 \times 5 = 40$ and $8 \times 3 = 24$. Not surprisingly, performance on mental arithmetic declines substantially if you have to remember simultaneously some words or digits; try doing the above mental multiplication while remembering the phone number 745–1739 (Baddeley & Hitch, 1974). Because of its role in mental computations, researchers increasingly refer to short-term memory as "working memory," and conceptualize it as a kind of blackboard in which the mind performs its computations and posts the partial results for later use (Baddeley, 1986).

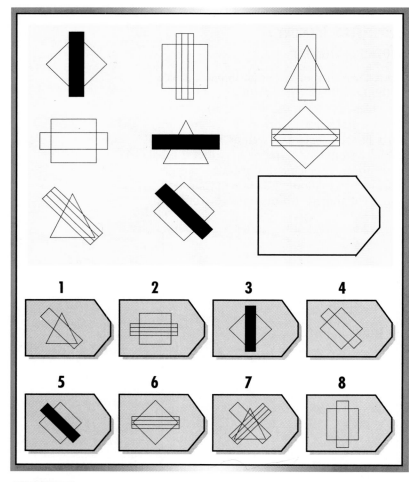

FIGURE 8-5

Illustration of a Geometric Analogy *The task is to inspect the forms in the 3 × 3 matrix, in which the bottom right entry is missing, and to determine which of the eight alternatives given below is the missing entry. To do this, you have to look across each row and determine the rules that specify how the forms vary, and to do the same thing for each column.* (After Carpenter, Just, & Shell, 1990)

Other research shows that short-term memory is used not only in doing numerical problems but also in solving a whole gamut of complex problems. One such class of problems are geometric analogies, which are sometimes used in tests of intelligence (e.g., Ravens, 1955). An illustrative geometric analogy is presented in Figure 8-5. Try to solve it, so that you can get an intuitive idea of the role of working memory in problem solving. You may note that you need working memory to store (1) the similarities and differences that you observe among the forms in a row, and (2) the rules that you come up with to account for these similarities and differences and that you then use to select the correct answer. It turns out that the larger one's working memory, the better one does on problems like these (even though there is relatively little variation among people in the capacity of working memory). Furthermore, when computers are programmed to simulate people solving problems like that in Figure 8-5, one of the most important determinants of how well the program does is the size of its working memory created by the programmer. There seems to be little doubt that part of the difficulty in many complex problems is the load they place on working memory (Carpenter, Just, & Shell, 1990).

The role that short-term or working memory plays in understanding language is more complicated. The short-term memory system we have described appears not to be involved in understanding relatively simple sentences. The best evidence for this comes from studies of brain-damaged patients with memory disorders. When presented with a list of unrelated words, some patients can correctly repeat only a single word (their memory span is 1), yet when presented with a whole sentence they can repeat the entire thing. In contrast, other brain-damaged patients have a normal memory span, yet are unable to repeat a simple sentence. These findings suggest that we have a special memory system for processing language. A patient who has a defective memory span but normal language understanding has an impaired short-term memory but an intact language memory. On the other hand, a patient who has a normal memory span but defective language understanding has the opposite memory problem. The special memory for language seems limited to relatively simple sentences, though. Once sentences become complex—for example, "The salesman that the doctor met departed"—short-term memory is brought in for help. Hence short-term memory serves as a backup in sentence understanding (McCarthy & Warrington, 1987a, b).

When it comes to higher-level language processes like following a conversation or reading a text, short-term memory appears to play a crucial role. When reading for understanding, often we must consciously relate new sentences to some prior material in the text. This relating of new to old seems to occur in short-term memory because people who have more short-term capacity score higher than others on reading comprehension tests (Just & Carpenter, 1992; Daneman & Carpenter, 1980).

TRANSFER FROM SHORT-TERM TO LONG-TERM MEMORY

From what we have seen so far, short-term memory serves two important functions: It stores material that is needed for short time periods, and it serves as a work space for mental computations. Another possible function is that short-term memory may be a way-station to long-term memory. That is, information may reside in short-term memory while it is being encoded or transferred into long-term memory (Raaijmakers, 1992; Atkinson & Shiffrin, 1971). While there are a number of different ways to implement the transfer, one of the most commonly investigated is rehearsal. Rehearsing an item not only maintains it in short-term memory but also causes it to be transferred to long-term memory.

Some of the best support for these ideas comes from experiments on free recall. In a **free-recall experiment**, subjects first see a list of, for example, 40 unrelated words that are presented one at a time. After all the words have been presented, subjects must immediately recall them in any order (hence the designation "free"). The results from such an experiment are shown in Figure 8-6. The chance of correctly recalling a word is graphed as a function of the word's position in the list. The part of the curve to the left in the graph is for the first few words presented, and the part to the right is for the last few words presented.

"Can we hurry up and get to the test? My short term-memory is better than my long-term memory."
©1985, reprinted courtesy of Bill Hoest and *Parade Magazine*.

Presumably, at the time of recall the last few words presented are still likely to be in short-term memory, whereas the remaining words are in long-term memory. Hence, we would expect recall of the last few words to be high, because items in short-term memory can easily be retrieved. Figure 8-6 shows this is the case. But recall for the first words presented is also quite good. Why is this? This is where rehearsal enters the picture. When the first words were presented, they were entered into short-term memory and rehearsed. Since there was little else in short-term memory, they were rehearsed often and were therefore likely to be transferred to long-term memory.

FIGURE 8-6

Results from Free-Recall Experiment   *Probability of recall varies with an item's position in a list, with the probability being highest for the last five or so positions, next highest for the first few positions, and lowest for the intermediate positions. Recall of the last few items is based on short-term memory, whereas recall of the remaining items is based on long-term memory.*
(After Glanzer, 1972; Murdock, 1962)

As more items were presented, short-term memory quickly filled up, and the opportunity to rehearse and transfer any given item to long-term memory decreased to a low level. So, only the first few items presented enjoyed the extra opportunity of transfer, which is why they were later recalled so well from long-term memory.

We do not want to place too much emphasis on rehearsal as a means of transfer, though. People have other, more effective ways of encoding information in long-term memory, as we are about to see.

LONG-TERM MEMORY

Long-term memory is involved when information has to be retained for intervals as brief as a few minutes (such as a point made earlier in a conversation) or as long as a lifetime (such as an adult's childhood memories). In experiments on long-term memory, psychologists generally have studied forgetting over intervals of minutes, hours, or weeks, but a few studies have involved years or even decades. Experiments that use intervals of years often involve the recall of personal experience (what is called *autobiographical memory*) rather than the recall of laboratory materials. In what follows, studies using both kinds of material are intermixed because they seem to reflect many of the same principles.

Our discussion of long-term memory will again distinguish between the three stages of memory—encoding, storage, and retrieval—but this time there are two complications. First, unlike the situation in short-term memory, important interactions between encoding and retrieval occur in long-term memory. In view of these interactions, we will consider some aspects of retrieval in our discussion of encoding, and will present a separate discussion of encoding-retrieval interactions. The other complication is that it is often difficult to know whether forgetting from long-term memory is due to a loss from storage or a failure in retrieval. To deal with this problem, we will delay our discussion of storage until after we have considered retrieval, so that we will have a clearer idea of what constitutes good evidence for a storage loss.

ENCODING

ENCODING MEANING For verbal materials, the dominant long-term memory representation is neither acoustic nor visual; instead, it is based on the meanings of the items. Encoding items according to their meanings occurs even when the items are isolated words, but it is more striking when the items are sentences. Several minutes after hearing a sentence, most of what you can recall or recognize is the sentence's meaning. Suppose you heard the sentence, "The author sent the committee a long letter." The evidence indicates that two minutes later you would do no better than chance in telling whether you had heard that sentence or one that has the same meaning: "A long letter was sent to the committee by the author" (Sachs, 1967).

Encoding meaning is pervasive in everyday memory situations. When people report on complex social or political situations, they may misremember many of the specifics (who said what to whom, when something was said, who else was there) yet can accurately describe the basic situation that took place. Thus, in the Watergate scandal of the early 1970s, the chief government witness (John Dean) was subsequently shown to have made many mistakes about what was said in particular situations, yet his overall testimony is generally thought to accurately describe the events that had taken place (Neisser, 1981).

Although meaning may be the dominant way of representing verbal material in long-term memory, we sometimes code other aspects as well. We can, for example, memorize poems and recite them word for word. In such cases, we have coded not only the meaning of the poem but the exact words themselves. We can also use an acoustic code in long-term memory. When you get a phone call and the other party says "hello," often you recognize the voice. In a case like this, you must have coded the sound of that person's voice in long-term memory. Visual impressions, tastes, and smells are also coded in long-term memory. Thus, long-term memory has a preferred code for verbal material (namely, meaning), but other codes can be used as well.

ADDING MEANINGFUL CONNECTIONS Often the items we have to remember are meaningful but the connections between them are not. In such cases, memory can be improved by creating real or artificial links between the items. For example, people learning to read music must remember that the five lines in printed music are referred to as EGBDF; although the symbols themselves are meaningful (they refer to notes on a keyboard), their order seems arbitrary. What many learners do is convert the symbols into the sentence "Every Good Boy Does Fine"; the first letter of each word names each symbol, and the relations between the words in the sentence supply meaningful connections between the symbols. These connections aid memory because they provide retrieval paths between the words: once the word "Good" has been retrieved, for example, there is a path or connection to "Boy," the next word that has to be recalled.

One of the best ways to add connections is to elaborate on the meaning of the material while encoding it. The more deeply or elaborately one encodes the meaning, the better memory will be (Craik & Tulving, 1975). If you have to remember a point made in a textbook, you will recall it better if you concentrate on its meaning rather than on the exact words. And the more deeply and thoroughly you expand on its meaning, the better you will recall it.

An experiment by Bradshaw and Anderson (1982) illustrates some of these points. Subjects read facts about famous people that they would later have to recall, such as "At a critical point in his life, Mozart made a journey from Munich to Paris." Some facts were elaborated by either their causes or consequences, as in "Mozart wanted to leave Munich to avoid a romantic entanglement." Other facts were presented alone. Later subjects were tested for memory of just the facts (not the elaborations). Subjects recalled more facts that were given elaborations than those presented alone. Presumably, in adding the cause (or consequence) to their memory representation, subjects set up a retrieval path from the cause to the target fact in the following manner:

Mozart journeyed from Munich to Paris

Mozart wanted to avoid a romantic entanglement in Munich

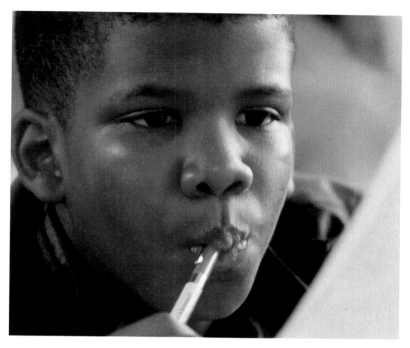

Over time, we tend to remember the meaning of a sentence rather than the exact words.

At the time of recall, subjects could retrieve the target fact directly, or indirectly by following the path from its cause. Even if they forgot the target fact entirely, they could infer it if they retrieved the cause.

Results like the above establish an intimate connection between understanding and memory. The better we understand some material, the more connections we see between its parts. Because these connections can serve as retrieval links, the better we understand, the more we remember.

RETRIEVAL

Many cases of forgetting from long-term memory result from a loss of *access* to the information rather than from a loss of the information itself. That is, poor memory often reflects a retrieval failure rather than a storage failure. (Note that this is unlike short-term memory, where forgetting is a result of decay or displacement, and retrieval is thought to be relatively error-free.) Trying to retrieve an item from long-term memory is like trying to find a book in a large library. Failure to find the book does not necessarily mean it is not there; you may be looking in the wrong place, or it may simply be misfiled.

EVIDENCE FOR RETRIEVAL FAILURES Common experience provides considerable evidence for retrieval failures. Everyone at some point has been unable to recall a fact or an experience, only to have it come to mind later. How many times have you taken an exam and not been able to recall a specific name, only to remember it after the exam? Another example is the "tip-of-the-tongue" experience in which a particular word or name lies tantalizingly outside our ability to recall it (Brown & McNeill, 1966). We may feel quite tormented until a search of memory (dredging up and then discarding words that are close but not quite right) finally retrieves the correct word.

A more striking example of retrieval failure is the occasional recovery by a person in psychotherapy of a memory that had previously been forgotten. Although we lack firm evidence for these observations, they at least suggest that some seemingly forgotten memories are not lost. They are just difficult to get at and require the right kind of **retrieval cue**, which is anything that can help us retrieve a memory.

For stronger evidence that retrieval failures can cause forgetting, consider the following experiment. Subjects were asked to memorize a long list of words. Some of the words were names of animals, such as dog, cat, horse; some names of fruits, such as apple, orange, pear; some names of furniture, and so on (see Table 8-1). At the time of recall, the subjects were divided into two groups. One group was supplied with retrieval cues such as "animal," "fruit," and so on; the other group, the control group, was not. The group given the retrieval cues recalled more words than the control group. In a subsequent test, when both groups were given the retrieval cues, they recalled the same number of words. Hence, the initial difference in recall between the two groups must have been due to retrieval failures.

Thus, the better the retrieval cues, the better our memory. This principle explains why we usually do better on a recognition test of memory than on a recall test. In a recognition test, we are asked if we have seen a particular item before (for example, "Was Bessie Smith one of the people you met at the wedding?"). The test item itself is an excellent retrieval cue for our memory of that item. In contrast, in a recall test we have to produce the memorized items with minimal retrieval cues (for example, "Recall the name of the woman you met at the party"). Since the retrieval cues in a recognition test are generally more useful than those in a recall test, recognition tests usually show better memory performance than recall tests (Tulving, 1974).

INTERFERENCE Among the factors that can impair retrieval, the most important is interference. If we associate different items with the same cue, when we try to use that cue to retrieve one of the items (the target item), the other items may become active and interfere

LIST TO BE MEMORIZED

dog	cotton	oil
cat	wool	gas
horse	silk	coal
cow	rayon	wood
apple	blue	doctor
orange	red	laywer
pear	green	teacher
banana	yellow	dentist
chair	knife	football
table	spoon	baseball
bed	fork	basketball
sofa	pan	tennis
knife	hammer	shirt
gun	saw	socks
rifle	nails	pants
bomb	screwdriver	shoes

RETRIEVAL CUES

animals	cloth	fuels
fruit	color	professions
furniture	utensils	sports
weapons	tools	clothing

TABLE 8-1

Examples From a Study of Retrieval Failures
Subjects not given the retrieval cues recalled fewer words from the memorized list than other subjects who did have the cues. This finding shows that problems at the retrieval stage of long-term memory are responsible for some memory failures. (After Tulving & Pearlstone, 1966)

with our recovery of the target. For example, if your friend, Dan, moves and you finally learn his new phone number, you will find it difficult to retrieve the old number. Why? You are using the cue "Dan's phone number" to retrieve the old number, but instead this cue activates the new number, which interferes with recovery of the old one. Or suppose that your reserved space in a parking garage, which you have used for a year, is changed. You may initially find it difficult to retrieve from memory your new parking location. Why? You are trying to learn to associate your new location with the cue "my parking place," but this cue retrieves the old location, which interferes with the learning of the new one. In both examples, the power of retrieval cues ("Dan's phone number" or "my parking place") to activate particular target items decreases with the number of other items associated with those cues. The more items associated with a cue, the more overloaded it becomes and the less effectively it can retrieve.

Interference can operate at various levels, including that of whole facts. In one experiment, subjects first learned to associate various facts with the names of professions. For example, they learned that:

The banker:

(1) was asked to address the crowd,

(2) broke the bottle, and

(3) did not delay the trip.

The lawyer:

(1) realized the seam was split, and

(2) painted an old barn.

The occupational names "banker" and "lawyer" were the retrieval cues here. Since "banker" was associated with three facts, and "lawyer" was associated with just two, "banker" should have been less useful in retrieving any of its associated facts than "lawyer" was in retrieving any of its associated facts ("banker" was the more overloaded cue). When subjects were later given a recognition test they did take longer to recognize any one of the facts learned about the banker than any one of those learned about the lawyer. In this study, then, interference slowed the speed of retrieval. Many other experiments show that in-

terference can lead to a complete retrieval failure if the target items are weak or the interference is strong (Anderson, 1983). Indeed, it has long been thought that interference is a major reason why forgetting from long-term memory increases with time; roughly, the relevant retrieval cues become more and more overloaded with time (see Figure 8-7).

RETRIEVAL MODELS   In attempting to explain interference effects, researchers have developed a variety of models of retrieval. As was the case when considering retrieval from short-term memory, some models of long-term-memory retrieval are based on a search process whereas others are based on an activation process.

The interference effects in the banker-lawyer experiment fit nicely with the idea that retrieval from long-term memory may be

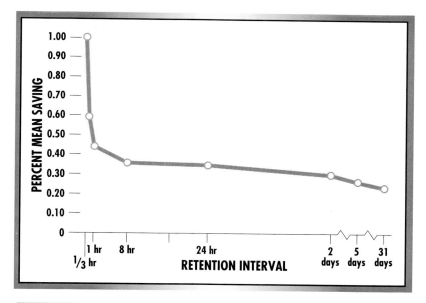

FIGURE 8-7

Forgetting as a Function of Time   *A forgetting curve graphs the decline in recall as a function of time. This forgetting curve, the first ever reported, comes from the work of Ebbinghaus (1885). He studied lists of 13 syllables that he repeated until he was able to recall the list without error on two successive trials. Then, after intervals ranging from 20 minutes to 31 days, he tested himself by determining how long it took him to relearn the list to the original level; the less the forgetting, the fewer trials should be needed to relearn the list. The figure plots a measure of ease of relearning (called savings) as a function of time; it suggests that one forgets a lot about an event within the first few hours, but after that the rate of forgetting slows down. While this curve is representative of memory for unrelated verbal materials, different kinds of curves are found with different kinds of material (for example, Bahrick and Phelphs, 1987). In all cases, interference is thought to play some role in the changes in forgetting with time.*

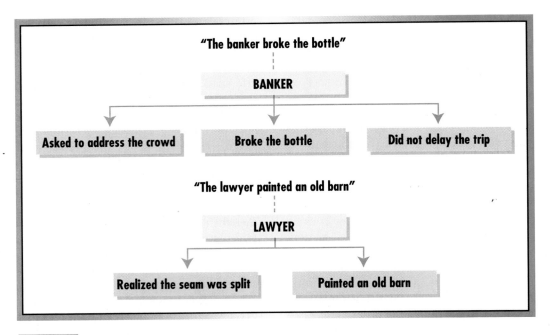

FIGURE 8-8

Retrieval as a Search Process Versus an Activation Process   *When presented the sentence, "The banker broke the bottle," the term "banker" accesses the banker representation in long-term memory; once at this representation, there are three paths to be searched. When presented "The lawyer painted an old barn," "lawyer" accesses the lawyer representation, from which there are two paths to be searched. Alternatively, the term "banker" may activate the banker representation, where this activation then spreads simultaneously along the three paths (and similarly for the "lawyer" example).*

thought of as a search process (e.g., Raaijmakers & Shiffrin, 1981). To illustrate, consider how a sentence from the preceding study, "The banker broke the bottle," might be recognized (see Figure 8-8). The term "banker" accesses its representation in memory, which localizes the search to the relevant part of long-term memory. Once there, three paths need to be searched to verify that "broke the bottle" was one of the facts learned about the banker. In contrast, if the test sentence was "The lawyer painted an old barn," there are only two paths to be searched. Since the duration of a search increases with the number of paths to be considered, retrieval will be slower for the "banker" sentence than the "lawyer" one. Retrieval generally is more difficult when more facts are associated with a retrieval cue, because each fact adds a path to be searched.

An alternative way to think about the retrieval process is in terms of activation. When trying to recognize "The banker broke the bottle," for example, the subject activates the representation for "banker," and the activation then spreads simultaneously along the three paths emanating from "banker" (see Figure 8-8). When sufficient activation reaches "broke the bottle," the sentence can

be recognized. Interference arises because the activation from the banker representation must be subdivided among the paths emanating from it. Hence, the more facts associated with "banker," the thinner the activation on each path, and the longer it will take for sufficient activation to reach any particular fact. So, thinking of retrieval in terms of spreading activation can also account for why interference slows retrieval (Anderson, 1983).

STORAGE

Retrieval failures are unlikely to be the only cause of forgetting. The fact that *some* forgetting is due to retrieval failures does not imply that *all* forgetting is. It seems most unlikely that everything we ever learned is still there in memory waiting for the right retrieval cue. Some information is almost certainly lost from storage (Loftus & Loftus, 1980).

Some evidence of storage loss comes from people who receive **electroconvulsive therapy** to alleviate severe depression (a mild electric current applied to the brain produces a brief epilepticlike seizure and momentary unconsciousness; see Chapter 16). In such cases, the patient loses some memory for events that occurred in the months just prior to the shock, but not for earlier events (Squire & Fox, 1980). These memory losses are unlikely to be due to retrieval failures, because if the shock disrupted retrieval then all memories should be affected, not just the recent ones. More likely, the shock disrupts storage processes that *consolidate* new memories over a period of months or longer, and information that is not consolidated is lost from storage.

Most research on storage in long-term memory is done at the biological level. Researchers have made substantial progress in determining the neuroanatomical bases of consolidation. The critical brain structures involved seem to be the hippocampus (which we discussed at the beginning of the chapter) and the cortex surrounding the hippocampus (which includes the *enthorhinal, perirhinal,* and *parahippocampal* cortices; they are involved in the exchange of information between the hippocampus and much of the cerebral cortex). The hippocampus' role in consolidation seems to be that of a cross-referencing system, linking together aspects of a particular memory that are stored in separate parts of the brain (Squire, 1992). While a global memory loss in humans usually occurs only when the surrounding cortex as well as the hippocampus is impaired, damage to the hippocampus alone can result in severe memory disturbance. This fact was demonstrated by a study that started with an analysis of a particular patient's memory problems (due to complications from coronary bypass surgery) and ended with a detailed autopsy of his brain following the patient's death; the hippocampus was the only brain structure damaged (Zola-Morgan, Squire, & Amaral, 1989).

A study with monkeys provides the best evidence we have that the function of the hippocampus is to consolidate relatively new memories. In the study, a group of experimental monkeys learned to discriminate between 100 pairs of objects. For each pair, there was food under one object, which the monkey got only if it picked that object. Since all the objects differed, the monkeys essentially learned 100 different problems. Twenty of these problems were learned 16 weeks before the researchers removed the monkeys' hippocampus; additional sets of 20 problems were learned either 12, 8, 4, or 2 weeks before the hippocampal surgery. Two

weeks after surgery, the researchers tested the monkeys' memory with a single trial of each of the 100 pairs. The critical finding was that the experimental monkeys remembered discriminations learned 8, 12, or 16 weeks before surgery as well as normal control monkeys, but remembered the discriminations learned 2 or 4 weeks before surgery less well than the control monkeys. Furthermore, the experimental monkeys actually remembered less about the discriminations learned 2 to 4 weeks before surgery than about the discriminations learned earlier. These results suggest that memories need processing by the hippocampus for a period of a few weeks, for it is only during this period that memory is impaired by removal of the hippocampus. Permanent long-term memory storage is almost certainly localized in the cortex, particularly those regions in which sensory information is interpreted (Squire, 1992; Zola-Morgan & Squire, 1990).

ENCODING-RETRIEVAL INTERACTIONS

In describing the encoding stage, we noted that operations carried out during encoding (for instance, elaboration) later make retrieval easier. Two other encoding factors also increase the chances of successful retrieval: a) organizing the information at the time of encoding, and b) ensuring that the context in which information is encoded is similar to that in which it will be retrieved.

ORGANIZATION The more we organize the material we encode, the easier it is to retrieve. Suppose you were at a conference at which you met various professionals—doctors, lawyers, and journalists. When later you try to recall their names, you will do better if initially you organize the information by profession. Then you can ask yourself, Who were the doctors I met? Who were the lawyers? And so forth. A list of names or words is far easier to recall when we encode the information into categories and then retrieve it on a category-by-category basis (e.g., Bower, Clark, Winzenz, & Lesgold, 1969).

CONTEXT It is easier to retrieve a particular fact or episode if you are in the same context in which you encoded it (Estes, 1972). For example, it is a good bet that your ability to retrieve the names of your classmates in

CONNECTIONIST MODELS OF MEMORY

As noted in Chapter 5, a new way to describe many psychological processes is in terms of connectionist models. In such models, knowledge is represented in a network of interconnected units that resemble neurons, and the knowledge is processed by activation and inhibition spreading among the units. One topic that has been a focus of connectionist modelling is long-term memory, and in what follows we illustrate some basic aspects of such memory models.

For ease of exposition, let us consider a simple memory task. On each trial of an experiment, a subject is visually presented a different triple of letters, such as RDK, and her task is to learn to verbally recall all three letters when cued with two of them (for example, when cued with RD, the subject should say "RDK"). Figure 1a shows a connectionist network that depicts the subject's memory at the outset of the task. The bottom, or *input,* level of the network contains units that represent the possible stimuli or input—these units represent the visual appearances of individual letters. The top, or *output,* level of the network contains units that represent possible responses or output—these units represent the pronunciations of individual letters. Encoding amounts to forming connections between certain input units and certain output units.

The basic principle assumed to guide encoding is this: When a triple

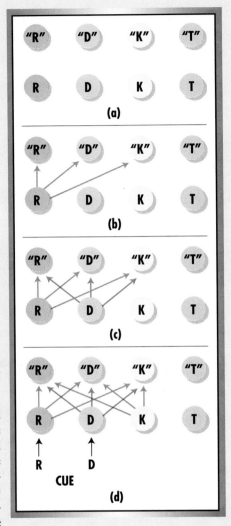

FIGURE 1

A Simple Network for Cued Recall *This network involves only excitatory connections between units. (a) The bottom level of the network contains input units, which represent the visual appearance of R, D, K, and T, while the top level contains output units that represent the pronunciations of the four letters. Presentation of RDK leads to the formation of: (b) excitatory connections between the input unit for R and the output units for "R," "D," and "K"; (c) excitatory connections between the input unit for D and the output units for "R," "D," and "K"; and (d) excitatory connections between the input unit for K and the output units for "R," "D," and "K." When RD is presented as a cue, the output units for "R," "D," and "K" all become active.*

of letters is presented, for each one the subject forms an excitatory connection between its input unit and the output units of all active letters. To illustrate, if RDK is presented, the subject would form excitatory connections between: (*i*) the input unit for R and the output units for "R," "D," and "K" (see Figure 1b); (*ii*) the input unit for D and the output units for "R," "D," and "K" (see Figure 1c); and (*iii*) the input unit for K and the output units for "R," "D," and "K" (see Figure 1d). (All connections would be formed at the same time.) The fact that these connections are excitatory (as indicated by the arrowheads at their ends) means that if the input units are activated, the excitation will spread to the corresponding output units in a manner analogous to how electrical impulses spread in a network of neurons. If a critical amount of activation reaches an output unit, that unit itself becomes active. This is how retrieval

is implemented in a connectionist network. Figure 1d, then, represents the resulting network. It explains how a subject can retrieve the names of all three letters in a triple when cued

the first and second grades would improve were you to walk through the corridors of your elementary school. Similarly, your ability to retrieve an emotional moment with a close friend—say, an argument with her in a restaurant—would be greater if you were back in the place where the incident occurred. This may explain why we are sometimes overcome with a torrent of memories about our earlier life when we visit a place we

once lived. The context in which an event was encoded is itself one of the most powerful retrieval cues possible, and a mass of experimental evidence supports this (see Figure 8-9 for a representative study).

Context is not always external to the memorizer—that is, not always a matter of environment. What is happening inside of us when we encode information—our internal state—is also part of context. For example, if with two of them. Suppose RD is presented as a cue. The cue will activate the input units for R and D, and this activation will spread to the output units for "R," "D," and "K." Assuming that two units of activation is sufficient to make a response unit available, all three letters will be verbally recalled, as the task requires.

The preceding analysis illustrates an important aspect of connectionist models: given part of a memorized pattern, the model will fill in the rest. Such *pattern completion* seems to be a fundamental aspect of human memory. Indeed, our general ability to retrieve full memories given just partial retrieval cues may be viewed as an instance of the pattern-completion nature of memory.

To illustrate a further point about connectionist models of memory, let us change one aspect of our memory task. Instead of the subject having to verbally recall all three letters in the cued-for triple, now she has to respond with just the letter that is not in the cue. For example, cued with RD, she should say "K." How can we alter the network in Figure 1d so that it will accomplish this new task? Since the subject must essentially *inhibit* saying the names of the input letters, let us add inhibitory connections (symbolized by solid circles at their ends) between the input and output unit for each letter (see Figure 2a—it differs from Figure 1d only in the addition of inhibitory connections). Now when RD is presented as

a cue, activation will again spread to the output units for "R," "D," and "K"; but inhibition will also be sent to the output units for "R" and "D," which will reduce the activation of these units. As a result, only the output unit for "K" will have the critical amount of activation needed to become active, and it will be given as a response, as the task requires. Thus, by the subtle interaction of excitatory and inhibitory connections, connectionist models can account for performance in a variety of tasks (Willshaw; 1981).

Such models can also explain interference effects. Suppose that in the preceding task, after memorizing RDK, our subject learns the triple RDT. Now, among other things, excitatory connections will be formed between the inputs unit for R and D and the output unit for "T" (see Figure 2b). These new connections will lead to interference when the subject is cued with RD. Such a cue will activate the output unit for "T" as well as that for "K" (see Figure 2b), and the two output units will compete with one another, resulting in poorer recall.

Connectionist models of interference have been intensively explored (Sloman & Rumelhart, 1991; McCloskey & Cohen, 1989). In some of these models, rather than units representing entire items (such as letters), each unit represents only a feature of an item. That is, the representation of each item is *distributed* over a set of

units. Connectionist models with such distributed representations are more powerful than the sort we have illustrated here.

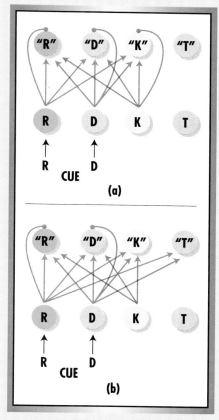

FIGURE 2

A Modified Network   *These networks contain inhibitory as well as excitatory connections. (a) The network after encoding inhibitory connections between each letter and its pronunciation; (b) the network after encoding excitatory connections between the input units for R and D and the output unit for "T."*

we experience an event while under the influence of a particular drug (for instance, alcohol or marijuana), perhaps we can best retrieve it when we are again in that drug-induced state. In such cases, memory would be partly dependent on the internal state during learning; this is called **state-dependent learning**. While the evidence on state-dependent learning is controversial, it suggests that memory does indeed improve when our in-

ternal state during retrieval matches that during encoding (Eich, 1980).

EMOTIONAL FACTORS IN FORGETTING

So far, we have treated memory as if it were divorced from emotion. But don't we sometimes remember material because of its emotional content? Or forget material because of

FIGURE 8-9

Effects of Environmental Context On Retrieval *In an experiment to demonstrate how context affects retrieval, one group of deep-sea divers learned a list of words while they were on the beach (panel a), whereas another group of divers learned the list while they were beneath 15 feet of water (panel c). Later, each group was divided in half and tried to recall the words in either the same environment they learned in (panels a' and c'), or in a different environment (panels b and d). There was no overall effect of whether the divers originally learned the words on land or under water. But divers who were tested in an environment different from the one they learned in recalled 40% less than divers who learned and recalled in the same environment.* (Godden & Baddeley, 1975).

its emotional content? There has been a great deal of research on these questions. The results suggest that emotion can influence long-term memory in at least five distinct ways.

The simplest idea is that we tend to think about emotionally charged situations, negative as well as positive, more than we think about neutral ones. We rehearse and organize exciting memories more than blander ones. For example, you may forget where you saw this or that movie; but if a fire breaks out while you are in a theater, that incident will dominate your thoughts for a while, and you will describe the setting over and over to friends, as well as think about the setting over and over to yourself, thereby rehearsing and organizing it. Since we know that re-

hearsal and organization can improve retrieval from long-term memory, it is not surprising that many researchers have found better memory for emotional than for unemotional situations (Neisser, 1982; Rapaport, 1942).

The second way that emotion can affect memory is via **flashbulb memories**. A flashbulb memory is a vivid and relatively permanent record of the circumstances in which you learned of an emotionally charged, significant event. An example would be the explosion of the space shuttle *Challenger* in 1986, which was witnessed by millions of people on television. Many people in their 20s remember exactly where they were when they learned of the *Challenger* disaster and exactly who told them about it, even though these are the kinds of details that we usually forget quickly. Americans 30 years of age or older may have flashbulb memories of the assassination attempt on Ronald Reagan in 1981, while those 40 or older may have such memories of the assassinations of John F. Kennedy and Martin Luther King, Jr., in the 1960s. Remarkably, there is even a published report indicating that Americans a century ago had flashbulb memories of the assassination of Abraham Lincoln. When Colegrove (1899) interviewed 179 people, 127 of them were able to give full particulars as to where they were and what they were doing when they heard of Lincoln's assassination.

What is responsible for such memories? According to Brown and Kulik (1977), extraordinarily important events trigger a *special memory mechanism,* one that makes a permanent record of everything the person is experiencing at the moment. It is as if we took a picture of the moment, which is why the recollection is dubbed a "flashbulb memory."

The idea of a special mechanism for emotional memories has proven controversial. Researchers who dispute the idea of a special memory mechanism point out that flashbulb memories become less retrievable with time, as do normal long-term memories. In one study, a few days after the *Challenger* explosion, people were asked where they were and what they were doing when they heard of the disaster; nine months later, the same people were asked the same questions. Although the people had unusually detailed memories of the event 9 months after it occurred, there was some forgetting during the interval (McCloskey, Wible, & Cohen, 1988). Results like these suggest that memory for national tragedies could be an instance of normal memory. The reason we remember the events so vividly is that we keep on hearing and talking about them, the way we do other emotionally charged situations.

Researchers who support the idea of a special mechanism for emotional memories also can cite evidence in their favor. Perhaps the most striking evidence comes from a recent study that focuses on the biological bases of memory. The key idea is that the storage of emotional memories involves the hormones adrenaline and noradrenaline, whereas the storage of normal memories does not. Consequently, if the biochemical effects of these two hormones are blocked, people should have trouble remembering emotional mater-

ial, but no problems remembering nonemotional material. These ideas were tested by the following experiment. Subjects watched a slide presentation accompanied by either an emotional narration (about a boy being taken to a hospital for emergency surgery), or a neutral narration (about a boy going to a hospital to visit his father, who works there). Before hearing the stories, half the subjects were administered a drug (propranolol) known to block the effects of adrenaline and noradrenaline, and the other half of the subjects were administered a placebo. One week later all subjects were given a memory test for the stories. The subjects administered the hormone-blocking drug recalled less information about the emotional story than did the subjects administered the placebo, but the two groups of subjects showed no difference on recall of the neutral story. These results imply that emotional material is indeed stored by a mechanism different from that used with neutral memories (Cahill, Prins, Weber, & McGaugh, 1994).

There are also cases in which negative emotions *hinder* retrieval, which brings us to the third way that emotion can affect memory. An experience that many students have at one time or another illustrates this:

You are taking an exam about which you are not very confident. You can barely understand the initial question, let alone answer it. Signs of panic appear. Although the second question really isn't hard, the anxiety triggered by the previous question spreads to this one. By the time you look at the third question, it wouldn't matter if it just asked for your phone number. There's no way you can answer it. You're in a complete panic.

For many people, the explosion of the space shuttle Challenger *is a flashbulb memory.*

What is happening to memory here? Failure to deal with the first question produced anxiety. Anxiety is often accompanied by extraneous thoughts, such as "I'm going to flunk out" or "Everybody will think I am stupid." These thoughts fill our consciousness and interfere with any attempt to retrieve the information relevant to the question; this may be why memory fails. According to this view, anxiety does not directly cause memory failure; rather, it causes, or is associated with, extraneous thoughts, and these thoughts cause memory failure by interfering with retrieval (Holmes, 1974).

Emotion may also affect memory by a kind of *context effect*. As we have noted, memory is best when the context at retrieval matches that at encoding. Since our emotional state during learning is part of the context, if the material we are learning makes us feel sad, then perhaps we can best retrieve that material when we feel sad again. Experimenters have demonstrated such an emotional-context effect in the laboratory. Subjects agreed to keep diaries for a week, recording daily every emotional incident that occurred and noting whether it was pleasant or unpleasant. One week after they handed in their diaries, the subjects returned to the laboratory and were hypnotized (they had been preselected to be highly hypnotizable). Half the subjects were put in a pleasant mood, and the other half were put in an unpleasant mood. All were asked to recall the incidents recorded in their diaries. For subjects in a pleasant mood, most of the incidents they recalled had been rated as pleasant when experienced; for subjects in an unpleasant mood at retrieval, most of the incidents recalled had been rated as unpleas-

ant when experienced. As expected, recall was best when the dominant emotion during retrieval matched that during encoding (Bower, 1981).

Thus far all of the means by which emotions can influence memory rely on principles already discussed—namely, rehearsal, interference, and context effects. The fifth view of emotion and memory, Freud's theory of the unconscious, brings up new principles. Freud proposed that some emotional experiences in childhood are so traumatic that allowing them to enter consciousness many years later would cause the individual to be totally overwhelmed by anxiety. (This is different from the example of the exam, where the anxiety was tolerable to consciousness.) Such traumatic experiences are said to be stored in the unconscious, or *repressed;* and they can be retrieved only when some of the emotion associated with them is defused. Repression, therefore, represents the ultimate retrieval failure: access to the target memories is *actively* blocked. This notion of active blocking makes the **repression hypothesis** qualitatively different from the ideas about forgetting we considered earlier. (For a discussion of Freud's theory, see Chapter 13.)

Repression is such a striking phenomenon that we would of course like to study it in the laboratory, but this has proved difficult to do. To induce true repression in the laboratory, the experimenter must have the subject experience something extremely traumatic; ethical considerations prohibit this. The studies that have been done have exposed subjects to only mildly upsetting experiences. The evidence from these studies lends mixed support to the repression hypothesis (Baddeley, 1990; Erdelyi, 1985).

"And then I say to myself, 'If I really wanted to talk to her, why do I keep forgetting to dial 1 first?'"
Drawing by Modell; ©1981 *The New Yorker Magazine,* Inc.

IMPLICIT MEMORY

Thus far we have been mainly concerned with situations in which people remember personal facts. In such cases, memory is a matter of consciously recollecting the past, and is said to be expressed *explicitly*. But there seems to be another kind of memory, the kind that is often manifested in skills and that shows up as an improvement on some perceptual, motor, or cognitive task without conscious recollection of the experiences that led to the improvement. For example, with practice we can steadily improve our ability to recognize words in a foreign language, but at the moment we are recognizing a word, and thereby demonstrating our skill, we need not have any conscious recollections of the lessons that led to our improvement. Here, memory is expressed *implicitly* (Schacter, 1989).

MEMORY IN AMNESIA

AMNESIA   Much of what we know about implicit memory we have learned from people who suffer **amnesia**. Amnesia refers to a partial loss of memory. It may result from very different causes, including accidental injuries to the brain, strokes, encephalitis, alcoholism, electroconvulsive shock, and surgical procedures (for example, removal of the hippocampus to reduce epilepsy). Whatever its cause, the primary symptom of amnesia is a profound inability to remember day-to-day events, and hence to acquire new factual information; this is referred to as **anterograde amnesia,** and it can be extensive. There is an intensively studied patient, identified as NA, who is unable to participate in a normal conversation because he loses his train of thought with the least distraction. Another patient identified as HM—the most intensively studied of all amnesiacs—reads the same magazines over and over and continually needs to be reintroduced to doctors who have been treating him for decades.

A secondary symptom of amnesia is an inability to remember events that occurred *prior* to the injury or disease. The extent of such **retrograde amnesia** varies from patient to patient. Aside from retrograde and anterograde memory losses, the typical amnesiac appears relatively normal: he or she has a normal vocabulary, the usual knowledge about the world (at least prior to the onset of the amnesia), and in general shows no loss of intelligence.

SKILLS AND PRIMING   A striking aspect of amnesia is that not all kinds of memory are disrupted. Thus, while amnesiacs are generally unable to either remember old facts about their lives or learn new ones, they have no difficulty remembering and learning perceptual and motor skills. This suggests that there is a dif-

ferent memory for facts than for skills. More generally, it suggests that explicit and implicit memory (which encode facts and skills, respectively) are different systems.

The skills preserved in amnesia include *motor skills,* such as tying one's shoelaces or riding a bike, and *perceptual skills,* such as normal reading or reading words that are projected into a mirror (and hence reversed). Consider the ability of reading mirror-reversed words. To do this well takes a bit of practice (try holding this book in front of a mirror and reading it). Amnesiacs improve with practice at the very same rate as normal subjects, though they may have no memory of having participated in prior practice sessions (Cohen & Squire, 1980). They show normal memory for the skill but virtually no memory for the learning episodes that developed it (the latter being *facts*).

A similar pattern emerges in situations where prior exposure to a stimulus facilitates or *primes* later processing of that stimulus. This pattern is nicely illustrated in the experiment outlined in Table 8-2. In stage 1 of the experiment, amnesiac and normal subjects were presented a list of words to study. In stage 2, stems of words on the list and stems of words not on the list were presented, and subjects tried to complete them (see Table 8-2). The normal subjects performed as expected, completing more stems when they were drawn from words on the list than when they were drawn from words not on the list.

STAGE 1	EXAMPLE
Present list of words for study	MOTEL
STAGE 2	
Present stems of list words and nonlist words for completion. Number of list words completed minus number of nonlist words completed = Priming	MOT BLA
STAGE 3	
Present original list of words plus new words for recognition	MOTEL STAND

TABLE 8-2

Procedure of an Experiment to Study Implicit Memory in Amnesia   (After Warrington & Weiskrantz, 1978)

  CHILDHOOD AMNESIA

One of the most striking aspects of human memory is that everyone suffers from a particular kind of amnesia: virtually no person can recall events from the first years of life, though this is the time when experience is at its richest. This curious phenomenon was first discussed by Freud (1905), who called it **childhood amnesia**.

Freud discovered the phenomenon by observing that his patients were generally unable to recall events from their first 3 to 5 years of life. At first you might think there is nothing unusual about this, because memory for events declines with time, and for adults there has been a lot of intervening time since early childhood. But childhood amnesia cannot be reduced to a case of normal forgetting. Most 30-year-olds can recall a good deal about their high school years, but it is a rare 18-year-old that can tell you anything about his or her third year of life; yet the time interval is roughly the same in the two cases (about 15 years).

In some studies, people have been asked to recall and date their childhood memories. For most subjects, their first memories are of something that occurred when they were age 3 or older; a few subjects, however, will report memories prior to the age of 1.

This little girl probably will not remember the events surrounding the birth of her baby brother.

A problem with these reports, however, is that we can never be sure that the "remembered" event actually occurred (the person may have reconstructed what he or she thought happened). This problem was overcome in an experiment in which subjects were asked a total of 20 questions about a childhood event that was known to have occurred—the birth of a younger sibling—the details of which could be verified by another person. The questions asked of each subject dealt with events that transpired during the mother's leaving for the hospital (for example, "What time of day did she leave?"), when the mother was in the hospital ("Did you visit her?"), and when the mother and infant returned home ("What time of

This difference is referred to as **priming**, because the words presented in stage 1 facilitated or primed performance on the stem completion problems of stage 2. Importantly, amnesiacs also completed more stems in stage 2 when they were drawn from words on the list than when they were drawn from words not on the list. In fact, the degree of priming for amnesiacs was exactly the same as that for normals! This finding indicates that when memory is manifested implicitly, as in priming, amnesiacs perform normally. Lastly, in stage 3 of the experiment, the original words were presented again along with some novel words, and subjects had to recognize which words had appeared on the list. Now amnesiacs remembered far fewer words than normals. Thus, when memory is tested explicitly, as in recognition, amnesiacs perform far below normals.

There is an interesting variation of the preceding study that further strengthens its conclusion. Suppose that in stage 2 subjects are instructed that it will help them in the stem completion task to try to think of the words presented earlier. This instruction makes stem completion into an explicit memory task (because conscious recollection is being emday did they come home?"). The subjects were college students, and their ages at the birth of their siblings varied from 1 to 17 years. The results are shown in the figure. The number of questions answered is plotted as a function of the subject's age when the sibling was born. If the sibling was born before the subject was 3 years old, the person could not recall a thing about it. If the birth occurred after that, recall increased with age at the time of the event. These results suggest an almost total amnesia for the first 3 years of life. More recent research, however, suggests that such recall may be improved if more cues are given and the cues are more specific (Fivush & Hamond, 1991). Still, the bulk of the evidence indicates that we should be skeptical about reports of memory from the first few years of life.

What causes childhood amnesia? Freud (1905) thought that it was due to the repression of sexual and aggressive feelings that a young child experiences toward his parents. But this account predicts amnesia only for events related to sexual and aggressive thoughts, when in fact childhood amnesia extends to all events. A more accepted explanation is that childhood amnesia is due to a massive difference between how young children encode

experience and how adults organize their memories. Adults structure their memories in terms of categories and schemata ("She's that kind of person," "It's that kind of situation"), while young children encode their experiences without embellishing them or connecting them to related events. Once a child begins to form associations between events and to categorize those events, early experiences become lost (Schachtel, 1982).

What causes the shift from early childhood to adult forms of memory? One factor is biological development. The hippocampus, a brain structure involved in consolidating memories, is not mature until roughly a year or two after birth. Therefore, events that take place in the first 2 years of life cannot be sufficiently consolidated and consequently cannot be recalled later. Other causes of the shift to adult memory are better understood at the psychological level. These include cognitive factors, particularly the development of language and the beginning of schooling. Both language and the kind of thinking emphasized in school provide new ways of organizing experiences, ways that may be incompatible with how the young child encodes experiences. Interestingly, language development reaches an early peak at age 3, while

schooling often begins at age 5; and the age span from 3 to 5 is when childhood amnesia seems to end.

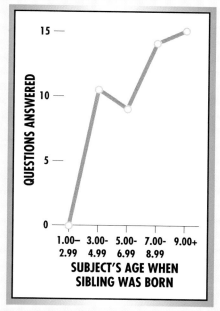

FIGURE 1

Recall of an Early Memory
In an experiment on childhood amnesia, college-age subjects were asked 20 questions about the events surrounding the birth of a younger sibling. The average number of questions answered is plotted as a function of the subject's age when the sibling was born. If the birth occurred before the fourth year of life, no subject could recall a thing about it; if the birth occurred after that, recall increased with age at the time of the event. (After Sheingold & Tenney, 1982)

phasized). Now amnesiacs show substantially less priming than normal subjects (Graf & Mandler, 1984).

A VARIETY OF MEMORY STORES

On the basis of work with various brain-damaged patients, researchers have proposed that both explicit and implicit memory come in various forms. One such proposal is presented in Figure 8-10. The basic distinction is between explicit and implicit memory. With

regard to implicit memory, a further distinction is made between perceptual-motor skills, such as reading mirror-reversed words, and priming, as occurs in word-stem completions. The reason for assuming that skills and priming may involve different memory stores is that there are patients with brain damage (those in the early stages of Alzheimer's disease) who are normal at learning motor skills but show less priming than normal. In contrast, there are other brain-damaged patients (those with Huntington's disease) who show normal priming but are impaired in learning new motor skills (Schacter, 1989).

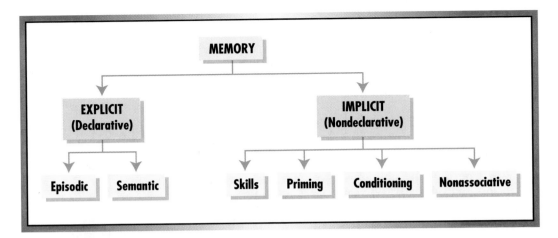

FIGURE 8-10

A Proposed Classification of Different Memory Stores *Squire et al. (1990) propose several different memory systems. The basic distinction is between explicit and implicit memory (which they refer to as* declarative *and* nondeclarative, *respectively). There are at least four known kinds of implicit memory, corresponding to the memory involved in skills, priming, conditioning, and certain nonassociative phenomenon (such as habituating to a repeated stimulus). There are two kinds of explicit memory, corresponding to semantic and episodic memory.*

The theory in Figure 8-10 also posits two kinds of explicit memory, which are referred to as *episodic* and *semantic*. Episodic facts refer to personal episodes, and semantic facts refer to general truths. To illustrate, your memory of your high-school graduation is an episodic fact, and so is your memory for what you had for dinner last night. In each of these cases, the episode is encoded with respect to you the individual (*your* graduation, *your* dinner, and so on), and often the episode is coded with respect to a specific time and place as well. All of this is in contrast to semantic facts, examples of which include your memory, or knowledge, that the word "bachelor" means an unmarried man, and that September has 30 days. In these cases, the knowledge is encoded in relation to other knowledge rather than in relation to yourself, and there is no coding of time and place. For example, you probably cannot remember much about the context in which you learned that February has 29 days every fourth year (Tulving, 1985).

Are episodic and semantic facts stored in different memories? The very existence of amnesia suggests that they might be. Aside from their severe memory loss, most amnesiacs seem to have normal intelligence. This implies they have a normal vocabulary and normal knowledge about the world, which in turn implies they are relatively normal

with respect to semantic knowledge. In most forms of amnesia, then, memory for semantic knowledge is spared but memory for personal episodes is disrupted, suggesting that the two types of facts are indeed stored in different memories.

The idea of different memories for different kinds of materials is not without its critics. Roediger (1990), for example, points out that studies with brain-damaged patients have already been used to distinguish 20–25 memory systems. This proliferation of memory systems seems implausible, and Roediger believes that much of the evidence used to argue for different kinds of memories can in fact be interpreted as indicating different retrieval processes operating on a common memory store. The general idea is that an item—for example, the word MOTEL—is represented in memory in terms of both its perceptual appearance and its meaning; implicit-memory situations require retrieval of perceptual information, and explicit-memory situations emphasize the retrieval of meaning. Still, the evidence favors the hypothesis that implicit and explicit tasks are accomplished by two different memory stores, particularly when the implicit task involves a perceptual-motor skill and the explicit task involves recall of a fact. Skill knowledge is "knowing how"; fact knowledge is "knowing that" (Ryle, 1949), and often the twain never meet. We know how to ride a bike, for example, but it is nearly impossible to describe it as a set of facts. The knowledge in a skill seems to be represented by the procedures needed to perform the skill, and such knowledge can be retrieved only by executing the procedures (Anderson, 1987).

IMPLICIT MEMORY IN NORMAL SUBJECTS

Studies that involve only normal subjects also suggest that there are separate systems for explicit and implicit memories. A number of these studies use stem completion as an implicit memory test, and recall or recognition as an explicit memory test. In one study, normal subjects went through the same three stages that were used in the preceding experiments—(1) original presentation of a list of words, (2) stem completion of list words and nonlist words, and (3) recognition of original words. The critical finding was that there was *no* correlation between the amount of priming a word showed in stage 2, which indicates how implicitly memorable it is, and how easy it was to recognize in stage 3, which indicates how explicitly memorable it is. That is, when the experimenter divided the words into those that were recognized and those that were not, the recognized words showed no more priming than the nonrecognized words. Performance on stem completion seems to be based on a completely different system than that involved in recognition (Tulving, Schacter, & Stark, 1982).

Other studies support the idea of two memory systems by showing that an independent variable that affects explicit memory has no effect on implicit memory, or vice versa. One such variable is whether or not people elaborate an item's meaning. Whereas elaborating a word's meaning boosts its subsequent recall, elaboration has no influence on whether a fragment drawn from that word will be completed (Graff & Mandler, 1984). An independent variable that works the opposite way is whether or not words are presented in the same modality during learning and a subsequent memory test. Subjects who were first presented a list of words auditorally, and subsequently had to recognize them when presented visually, do as well as subjects who were presented the words auditorally during

both learning and recognition. So a change in the modality of presentation has little effect on explicit memory. Such a change, however, significantly lowers performance on a test of implicit memory (Jacoby & Dallas, 1981).

Along with the psychological differences between implicit and explicit memory, there seem to be fundamental differences in how these two kinds of memories are implemented in the brain. The critical evidence comes from brain-scanning experiments (PET). In one experiment (Squire et al., 1992), subjects first studied a list of 15 words and then were exposed to three different conditions. The *implicit-memory* condition was the stem-completion task. Half the stems were drawn from the 15 words originally studied, and the other half were new; subjects were instructed to complete the stems with the first words that came to mind. The second condition of interest involved *explicit memory*. Again word stems were presented, but now subjects were instructed to use them to recall words from the initial list of 15. The third condition was a *control*. Word stems were presented, and subjects were instructed to complete them with the first words that came to mind, but now none of the stems were drawn from the words initially studied. The control condition, then, requires no memory. Subjects performed all three of these conditions while their brains were being scanned.

Consider first what the brain is doing during the explicit-memory task. From the material presented in the first section of this chapter, we might expect that: (1) the hippocampus is involved (remember, this structure is critical in forming long-term memories); and (2) most of the brain activity will be in the right hemisphere (because the task emphasized retrieval, and long-term retrieval involves mainly right-hemisphere processes). This is exactly what was found. More specifically, when the brain activity in the explicit-memory condition was compared to that in the control condition, there was increased activation in right-hemisphere hippocampal and frontal regions. Now consider the implicit-memory condition compared to the control condition; it showed *decreases* in activation rather than increases. That is, priming is reflected in less-than-usual neural activity, as if there has been a "greasing of the neural wheels." Implicit memory, then, has the opposite neural consequences of explicit memory, which demonstrates a deep biological difference between the two kinds of memory. (This is the biological evidence for the explicit-implicit distinction that we alluded to in the first section of this chapter.)

IMPROVING MEMORY

Having considered the basics of short-term and long-term memory, we are ready to tackle the question of improving memory. We will consider here mainly explicit memory (in part, because we are not sure of what other than sheer practice can improve implicit memory). First, we will consider how to increase the short-term memory span. Then we will turn to a variety of methods for improving long-term memory; these methods work by increasing the efficiency of encoding and retrieval.

CHUNKING AND MEMORY SPAN

For most of us, the capacity of short-term memory cannot be increased beyond 7 ± 2 chunks. However, we can enlarge the size of a chunk and thereby increase the number of items in our memory span. We demonstrated this point earlier: given the string 149-2177-619-96, we can recall all 12 digits if we recode the string into 1492-1776-1996 and then store just these three chunks in short-term memory. Although recoding digits into familiar dates works nicely in this example, it will not work with most digit strings because we have not memorized enough significant dates. But if a recoding system could be developed that worked with virtually *any* string, then short-term memory span for numbers could be dramatically improved.

There is a study of a particular subject who discovered such a general-purpose recoding system and used it to increase his memory span from 7 to almost 80 random digits (see Figure 8-11). The subject, referred to as SF, had average memory abilities and average intelligence for a college student. For a year and a half, he engaged in a memory-span task for about 3 to 5 hours per week. During this extensive practice, SF, a good long-distance runner, devised the strategy of recoding sets of four digits into running times. For example, SF would recode 3492 as "3:49.2—world class time for the mile," which for him was a single chunk. Since SF was familiar with many running times (that is, had them stored in long-term memory), he could readily chunk most sets of four digits. In those cases in which he could not (1771 cannot be a running time because the third digit is too large), SF tried to recode the four digits into either a familiar date or the age of some person or object.

Use of the above recoding systems enabled SF to increase his memory span from seven to 28 digits (because each of SF's seven chunks contains four digits). SF then built to nearly 80 digits by hierarchically organizing the running times. Thus, one chunk in SF's short-term memory might have pointed to three running times; at the time of recall, SF would go from this chunk to the first running time and produce its four digits, then move to the second running time in the chunk and produce its digits, and so on. One chunk was therefore worth 12 digits. In this way SF achieved his remarkable span of nearly 80 digits. It was due to increasing the *size* of a chunk (by relating the items to information in long-term memory), not to increasing the *number* of chunks that short-term memory can hold.

FIGURE 8-11

Number of Digits Recalled by SF   *This subject greatly increased his memory span for digits by devising a recoding system using chunking and hierarchical organization. Total practice time was about 215 hours.* (After Ericsson, Chase, & Faloon, 1980)

For when SF switched from digits to letters, his memory span went back to seven—that is, seven letters (Ericsson, Chase, & Faloon, 1980).

Since the report on SF, researchers have used the same procedure—constant practice on a memory-span task—to produce other short-term memory whizzes. One subject, referred to as DD, also a runner, used a similar method of recoding to running times, and was able to increase his memory span to 106 digits (Waldrop, 1987).

This research reflects a modern interest in improving short-term memory. In contrast, there has long been interest in how to improve long-term memory, which is the focus of the rest of this section. We will look first at how material can be encoded to make it easier to retrieve and then consider how the act of retrieval itself can be improved.

IMAGERY AND ENCODING

We mentioned earlier that we can improve the recall of unrelated items by adding meaningful connections between them at the time of encoding, for these connections will later facilitate retrieval. Mental images turn out to be particularly useful for connecting pairs of unrelated items, and for this reason imagery is the major ingredient in many **mnemonic** (memory-*aiding*) systems.

One famous mnemonic system is called the **method of loci** (*loci* is Latin for "places"). The method works especially well with an ordered sequence of arbitrary items, like unrelated words. The first step is to commit to memory an ordered sequence of places, say, the locations you would come upon in a slow walk through your house. You enter through the front door into a hallway, move next to the bookcase in the living room, then to the television in the living room, then to the curtains at the window, and so on. Once you can easily take this mental walk, you are ready to memorize as many unrelated words as there are locations on your walk. You form an image that relates the first word to the first location, another image that relates the second word to the second location, and so on. If the words are items on a shopping list—for example, "bread," "eggs," "beer," "milk," and "bacon"—you might imagine a slice of bread nailed to your front door, an egg hanging

from the light cord in the hallway, a can of beer in the bookcase, a milk commercial playing on your television, and curtains made from giant strips of bacon (see Figure 8-12). Once you have memorized the items this way, you can easily recall them in order by simply taking your mental walk again. Each location will retrieve an image, and each image will retrieve a word. The method clearly works and is a favorite among those who perform memory feats professionally.

FIGURE 8-12

A Mnemonic System
The method of loci aids memory by associating items (here, entries on a shopping list) with an ordered sequence of places.

TABLE 8-3

Key-word Method *Examples of key words used to link Spanish words to their English translations. For example, when the Spanish word muleta is pronounced, part of it sounds like the English word "mule." Thus, "mule" could be used as the key word and linked to the English translation by forming an image of a mule standing erect on a crutch.*

SPANISH	KEY WORD	ENGLISH
caballo	(eye)	horse
charco	(charcoal)	puddle
muleta	(mule)	crutch
clavo	(claw)	nail
lagartija	(log)	lizard
payaso	(pie)	clown
hiio	(eel)	thread
tenaza	(tennis)	pliers
jabon	(bone)	soap
carpa	(carp)	tent
pato	(pot)	duck

Imagery is also used in the **key-word method** of learning a foreign vocabulary. (See Table 8-3.) Suppose you had to learn that the Spanish word *caballo* means "horse." The key-word method has two steps. The first is to find a part of the foreign word that sounds like an English word. Since *caballo* is pronounced, roughly, "cob-eye-yo," "eye" could serve as the key word. The next step is to form an image that connects the key word and the English equivalent—for example, a giant eye being kicked by a horse (see Figure 8-13).

FIGURE 8-13

Foreign Language Learning *Mental images can be used to associate spoken Spanish words with corresponding English words. Here, possible images for learning the Spanish words for "horse" and "duck" are illustrated.*

Caballo → eye → Horse

Pato → pot → Duck

This should establish a meaningful connection between the Spanish and English words. To recall the meaning of *caballo,* you would first retrieve the key word "eye" and then the stored image that links it to "horse." The key-word method may sound complicated, but studies have shown that it greatly facilitates learning the vocabulary of a foreign language (Atkinson, 1975; Pressley, Levin, & Delaney, 1982).

ELABORATION AND ENCODING

We have seen that the more we elaborate items, the more we can subsequently recall or recognize them. This phenomenon arises because the more connections we establish between items, the larger the number of retrieval possibilities. The practical implications of these findings are straightforward: If you want to remember some fact, expand on its meaning. To illustrate, suppose you read a newspaper article about an epidemic in Brooklyn that health officials are trying to contain. To expand on this, you could ask yourself questions about the causes and consequences of the epidemic: Was the disease carried by a person or an animal? Was the disease transmitted through the water supply? To contain the epidemic, will officials go so far as to stop outsiders from visiting Brooklyn? How long is the epidemic likely to last? Questions about the causes and consequences of an event are particularly effective elaborations because each question sets up a meaningful connection, or retrieval path, to the event.

CONTEXT AND RETRIEVAL

Since context is a powerful retrieval cue, we can improve our memory by restoring the context in which the learning took place. If your psychology lecture always meets in one room, your recall of the lecture material may be better when you are in that room than in a different building entirely, because the context of the room is a retrieval cue for the lecture material. Most often, though, when we have to remember something, we cannot physically return to the context in which we learned it. If you are having difficulty remembering the name of a particular high-school classmate, you are not about to go back to your high school just to recall it. In these situations, however, you can try to recreate the context mentally. To retrieve the long forgotten name, you might think of different classes, clubs, and other activities that you were in during high school to see if any of these bring to mind the name you are seeking. When subjects used these techniques in an actual experiment, they were often able to recall the names of high-school classmates that they were sure they had forgotten (Williams & Hollan, 1981).

ORGANIZATION

We know that organization during encoding improves subsequent retrieval. This principle can be put to great practical use: we are capable of storing and retrieving a massive amount of information if only we organize it.

Some experiments have investigated organizational devices that can be used to learn many unrelated items. In one study, subjects memorized lists of unrelated words by organizing the words in each list into a story, as illustrated in Figure 8-14. Later, when tested for 12 such lists (a total of 120 words), subjects recalled more than 90 percent of the words. Control subjects, who did not use an organizational strategy, recalled little more than 10% of the words! The performance of the experimental subjects appears to be a remarkable memory feat, but anyone armed with an organizational strategy can do it.

At this point, you might concede that psychologists have devised some ingenious techniques for organizing lists of unrelated items. But, you argue, what you have to remember are not lists of unrelated items but stories you were told, lectures you have heard, and readings like the present chapter. Isn't this kind of material already organized, and doesn't this mean that the previously mentioned techniques are of limited value? Yes and no. Yes, this chapter is more than a list of unrelated sentences, but—and this is the critical point—there is always a problem of organization with any lengthy material, including this chapter. Later you may be able to recall that elaborating meaning aids learning, but this may not bring to mind anything about, say, acoustic coding in short-term memory. The two topics do not seem to be in-

A LUMBERJACK DARTed out of a forest, SKATEd around a HEDGE past a COLONY of DUCKs. He tripped on some FURNITURE, tearing his STOCKING while hastening toward the PILLOW where his MISTRESS lay.

A VEGETABLE can be a useful INSTRUMENT for a COLLEGE student. A carrot can be a NAIL for your FENCE or BASIN. But a MERCHANT of the QUEEN would SCALE that fence and feed the carrot to a GOAT.

One night at DINNER I had the NERVE to bring my TEACHER. There had been a FLOOD that day, and the rain BARREL was sure to RATTLE. There was, however, a VESSEL in the HARBOR carrying this ARTIST to my CASTLE.

FIGURE 8-14

Organizing Words into a Story *Three examples of turning a list of 10 unrelated words into a story. The capitalized items are the words on the list.* (After Bower & Clark, 1969)

timately related, but there is a relation between them: Both deal with encoding phenomena. The best way to see that relationship is to note the headings and subheadings in the chapter, because these show how the material in the chapter is organized. A most effective way to study is to keep this organization in mind. You might, for example, try to capture part of this chapter's organization by sketching a hierarchical tree like the one shown in Figure 8-15. Then you can use such a hierarchy to guide your memory search whenever you have to retrieve information about this chapter. It may be even more helpful, though, to make your own hierarchical outline of the chapter. Memory seems to benefit most when the organization is done by the rememberers themselves.

PRACTICING RETRIEVAL

Another way to improve retrieval is to practice it—that is, to ask yourself questions about what you are trying to learn. Suppose you have 2 hours in which to study an assignment that can be read in approximately 30 minutes. Reading and rereading the assignment four times is generally less effective than reading it once and asking yourself questions about it. You can then reread selected parts to clear up points that were difficult to retrieve the first time around, perhaps

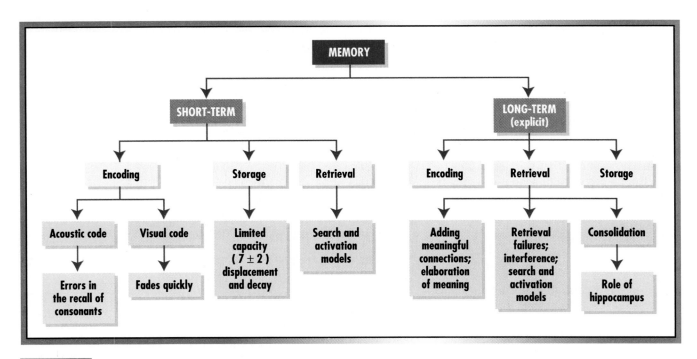

FIGURE 8-15

A Hierarchical Tree   *Creating hierarchical trees of chapters in textbooks can help students retrieve information about those chapters. This tree represents the organization of part of this chapter.*

elaborating these points so they become particularly well connected to each other and to the rest of the assignment. Attempting re-

FIGURE 8-16

Practicing Retrieval   *Recall can be improved by spending a large proportion of study time attempting retrieval rather than silently studying. Results are shown for tests given immediately and 4 hours after completing study. (After Gates, 1917)*

trieval is an efficient use of study time. This was demonstrated long ago by experiments using material like that actually learned in courses (see Figure 8-16).

A procedure akin to practicing retrieval may be useful in implicit memory situations. The procedure is referred to as **mental practice**, and it involves the imagined rehearsal of perceptual-motor skill in the absence of any gross body movements. For example, you might imagine yourself swinging at a tennis ball, making mental corrections when the imagined swing seems faulty, without even really moving your arm. Such mental practice can improve performance of the skill, particularly if the mental practice is interspersed with actual physical practice (Swets & Bjork, 1990).

PQRST METHOD

Thus far in this section we have considered particular principles of memory (for example, the principle that elaboration aids subsequent retrieval) and then shown their implications for improving memory. In establishing the practical application of memory principles, we can also go in the opposite direction. We can start with a well-known technique for improving memory and show how it is based on principles of memory.

One of the best-known techniques for improving memory is called the **PQRST method.** It is intended to improve a student's ability to study and remember material presented in a textbook (Thomas & Robinson, 1982). The method takes its name from the first letters of its five stages: *Preview, Question, Read, Self-Recitation,* and *Test.* We can illustrate the method by showing how it would apply to studying a chapter in this textbook. In the first stage, students preview the material in a chapter to get an idea of its major topics and sections. Previewing involves reading the chapter outline at the beginning of the chapter, skimming the chapter while paying special attention to the headings of main sections and subsections, and carefully reading the summary at the end of the chapter. This kind of preview induces students to organize the chapter, perhaps even leading to the rudiments of a hierarchical organization like that shown above. As we have repeatedly noted, organizing material aids one's ability to retrieve it.

The second, third, and fourth stages (Question, Read, and Self-Recitation) apply to each major section of the chapter as it is encountered. In this book, for example, a chapter typically has five to eight major sections, and students would apply the Question, Read, and Self-Recitation stages to each section before going on to the next one. In the Question stage, students carefully read the section headings and subsection headings and turn these into questions. In the Read stage, students read the section with an eye toward answering these questions. And in the Self-Recitation stage, the reader tries to recall the main ideas in the section and recites the information (either sub-vocally or, preferably, aloud). For example, if you were applying these stages to the present section of this chapter, you might look at the headings and make up such questions as "How much can the short-term memory span be increased?" or "What exactly is the PQRST method?" Next you would read this section and try to determine answers to your questions (for example, "One person was able to increase his short-term memory span to nearly 80 digits"). Then you would try to recall the main ideas (for example, "You can increase the size of a chunk but not the number of chunks"). The Question and Read stages almost certainly induce

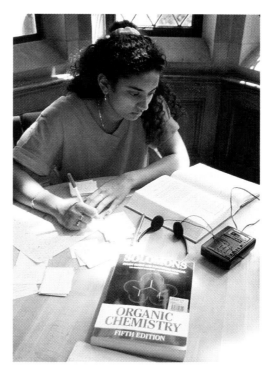

The PQRST method increases understanding and retention.

students to elaborate the material while encoding it; the Self-Recitation stage induces the student to practice retrieval.

The fifth, or Test, stage occurs after finishing an entire chapter. Students try to recall the main facts from what they have read and to understand how the various facts relate to one another. This stage prompts elaboration and offers further practice at retrieval. In summary, the PQRST method relies on three basic principles for improving memory: organizing the material, elaborating the material, and practicing retrieval. (For a more in-depth description of the method, see "A Word to the Student" preceding Chapter 1.)

CONSTRUCTIVE MEMORY

In previous chapters, we distinguished between bottom-up and top-down processes; **bottom-up processes** are driven by the input, whereas **top-down processes** are driven by the person's prior knowledge and expectancies. In Chapter 5 we noted that the perception of an object is based partly on the physical characteristics of the input object (bottom-up processes) and partly on the observer's expectations (top-down processes); in Chapter 7, we pointed out that learning is based partly on the contingencies in the input (bottom-up processes) and partly on the learner's prior beliefs (top-down processes).

The distinction can be applied to memory as well. Bottom-up processes work only on the input information, the actual items that have to be remembered, while top-down processes bring other knowledge to bear on the task. Most of the material we have covered thus far in the chapter deals with bottom-up processes. In this final section, we consider top-down processes, which add information to the input and result in what is called **constructive memory**.

When we hear a sentence or story, we often take it as an incomplete description of a real event, and we use our general knowledge about how the world works to construct a more detailed description of the event. How do we do this? By adding to the input sentences statements that are likely to follow from them. For example, on hearing "Mike broke the bottle in a barroom brawl," we are likely to infer that it was a beer or whiskey bottle, not a milk or soda bottle. We add this inference to our memory of the sentence itself. Our total memory therefore goes beyond the original information given. We fill in the original information by using our general knowledge about what goes with what (for example, that beer bottles go with bars). We do this because we are trying to explain to ourselves the events we are hearing about. Constructive memory, then, is a by-product of our need to understand the world. Many, if not most, real-life memory situations are constructive ones.

SIMPLE INFERENCES

Often when we read a sentence we draw inferences from it and store the inferences along with the sentence. This tendency is particularly strong when reading real text because inferences are often needed to connect different lines. To illustrate, consider the following story, which was presented to subjects in an experiment.

1. Provo is a picturesque kingdom in France.

2. Corman was heir to the throne of Provo.

3. He was so tired of waiting.

4. He thought arsenic would work well.

When reading this story, subjects draw inferences at certain points. At line 3, they infer that Corman wanted to be king, which permits them to connect line 3 to the preceding line. But this is not a necessary inference (Corman could have been waiting for the king to receive him). At line 4, subjects infer that Corman had decided to poison the king, so they can connect this line to what preceded it. Again, the inference is not a necessary one (there are people other than the king to poison, and there are other uses of arsenic). When subjects' memories were later tested for exactly which lines had been presented, they had trouble distinguishing the story lines from the inferences we just described. It is hard to keep separate what was actually presented from what we added to it (Seifert, Robertson, & Black, 1985).

Inferences can also affect memory for visual scenes. This point is strikingly illustrated in the following study. Subjects were shown a film of a traffic accident and then were asked questions about their memory of the accident. One question about the speed of the vehicles was asked in two different ways. Some subjects were asked, "How fast were the cars going when they smashed into each other?" whereas others were asked, "How fast were the cars going when they hit each other?" Subjects asked the "smashed" question might infer that the accident was a very destructive one, perhaps more destructive than they had actually remembered. These subjects were likely to use this inference to alter their memory of the accident to make it more destructive (see Figure 8-17). Subjects asked the "hit" question, however, should be less likely to do this, since "hit" implies a less severe accident than does "smashed."

This line of reasoning was supported by the results of a memory test given a week later. In this test, subjects were asked, "Did you see any broken glass?" There was no broken glass in the film of the accident, but subjects who had been asked the "smashed" question were more likely to say mistakenly that there had been glass than were subjects who had been asked the "hit" question. The "smashed" question may have led to reconstruction of the memory for the accident, and the reconstructed memory contained details, such as broken glass, that were never actually part of the accident (Loftus, Schooler, & Wagenaar, 1985).

The above results have important implications for eyewitness identification: A question phrased in a particular way ("smashed" rather than "hit") can alter the witness's memory structures that an attorney is trying to probe. The results also have implications for the controversy about whether some traumatic memories "recovered" from our past are true memories or instead are reconstructions (see the Critical Discussion, Recovered Memories or Reconstructed Memories?).

STEREOTYPES

Another means by which we fill in, or construct, memories is through the use of social **stereotypes**. A stereotype is a set of inferences about the personality traits or physical attributes of a whole class of people. We may, for example, have a stereotype of the typical German (intelligent, meticulous, serious) or of the typical Italian (artistic, carefree, fun loving). These descriptions rarely apply to many people in the class and can often be misleading guides for social interaction. Our concern here, however, is not with the effects of stereotypes on social interaction (see Chapter 18 for a discussion of this) but with the effects of stereotypes on memory.

When presented with information about a person, we sometimes stereotype that person (for example, "He's your typical Italian") and then combine the information presented with that in our stereotype. Our memory of the person is thus partly constructed from the stereotype. To the extent that our stereotype does not fit the person, our recall can be seriously distorted. Hunter, a British psychologist, provides a firsthand account of such a distortion:

> In the week beginning 23 October, I encountered in the university, a male student of very conspicuously Scandinavian appearance. I recall being very forcibly impressed by the man's nordic, Viking-like appearance—his fair hair, his blue eyes, and long bones. On several occasions, I recalled his appearance in connection with a Scandinavian correspondence I was then conducting and thought of him as the "perfect Viking," visualizing him at the helm of a longship crossing the North Sea in quest of adventure. When I again saw the man on 23 November, I did not recognize him, and he had to introduce himself. It was not that I had forgotten what he looked like but that his appearance, as I recalled it, had become grossly distorted. He was very different from my recollection of

FIGURE 8-17

Reconstructing a Memory of an Accident   *The picture at the top represents the subject's original memory of the accident. Then comes the "smashed" question, which leads the subject to draw inferences about the destructiveness of the accident. These inferences may be used to reconstruct the original memory so that it looks more like the picture on the bottom.* (After Loftus & Loftus, 1975)

> him. His hair was darker, his eyes less blue, his build less muscular, and he was wearing spectacles (as he always does). (Hunter, 1974, pp. 265–66)

Hunter's stereotype of Scandinavians seems to have so overwhelmed any information he actually encoded about the student's appearance that the result was a highly constructed memory. It bore so little resemblance to the student that it could not even serve as a basis for recognition.

SCHEMAS

Psychologists use the term **schema** (*schemas* for plural) to refer to a mental representation of a class of people, objects, events, or situations. Stereotypes are thus a kind of schema because they represent classes of people (for example, Italians, women, athletes). Schemas can also be used to describe our knowledge about how to act in certain situations. For example, most adults have a schema for how to

The findings about reconstructive memory, particularly studies like the "hit" versus "smashed" one, have important implications for a controversy involving reports of sexual abuse. Specifically, the last decade has witnessed a substantial number of cases in which someone, typically an adult, claims to have recovered a previously forgotten memory of sexual abuse during childhood, the recovery often occurring in the context of therapy or a therapy-like situation. In some of these cases, the person who has supposedly recovered the memory takes legal action against the alleged perpetrators (often their parents). These emotionally charged cases have attracted intense media coverage. The controversy arises because some professionals are convinced that the memories are authentic—that the incidents reported were originally repressed—whereas other experts are convinced that the memories are false—that the incidents reported never even occurred.

To make the controversy concrete, consider a variant of an actual case (described in Loftus, 1993). A woman in her late 20s began having recollec-

tions of being sexually abused by her father when she was between the ages of 5 and 8. She claimed that because of the trauma of that experience, her memories had been repressed for 20 years and were brought out only by counseling and therapy. She then sued her father for damages. Since the father vehemently denied the allegations, and since there were no witnesses to the abuse and no physical evidence of it, everything hinged on whether or not a jury would believe that the woman's memory was authentic.

Experts, as well as jurors, might have difficulty in determining whether the woman's memory was authentic. There are several reasons for taking her charges very seriously. For one thing, there is independent evidence that sexual abuse of children, regrettably, is relatively common in our society (Daro, 1988). In addition, there are many clinical reports of the repression of traumatic events (e.g., Mack, 1980). Furthermore, the woman may have symptoms like those frequently found in the victims of childhood abuse (though these tend to be common to many kinds of emo-

tional problems). But these considerations would not be decisive if the woman did not appear totally sincere in her allegations, totally convincing that she has suffered mental anguish.

Subjective impressions about a witness's honesty are critical, because for many people, including professionals, if someone is not reporting a true memory then they are lying. But this is where the research on constructive memory comes in. This work shows us there is an alternative to reporting a true memory and intentionally lying, namely that the person may be reporting a reconstructed memory. In the text we described an experiment in which subjects were led to believe that an accident they had witnessed was more serious than it initially appeared, and as a result, the subjects apparently embellished their memories of the accident to include some broken glass that was never there. When these subjects later recalled the presence of broken glass, they were not reporting something that happened, nor were they lying; they were reporting from a memory representation that was reconstructed rather

We often have mental representations of a class of people based upon their appearance, interests, race, social status, etc.

eat in a restaurant (enter the restaurant, find a table, get a menu from the waiter, order food, and so on). Perceiving and thinking in terms of schemas permits us to process large amounts of information swiftly and economically. Instead of having to perceive and remember all the details of each new person, object, or event we encounter, we can simply note that it is like a schema already in memory and encode and remember only its most distinctive features. The price we pay for such "cognitive economy," however, is that an object or event can be distorted if the schema used to encode it does not fit well.

Bartlett (1932) was perhaps the first psychologist to study systematically the effect of schemas on memory. He suggested that than being an accurate record of the events. In the same way, the woman in our story may be sincerely and truthfully reporting the contents of her memory representations, but these representations may be based on a reconstruction of the past, one that is *not* faithful to the events that actually occurred.

What kinds of external influences would lead someone to reconstruct memories of childhood so as to include abuse? A major possibility stems from the fact that many of the cases involve people in therapy: Some therapists may unwittingly implant suggestions that the client has been abused, and then suggest techniques that would lead the client to elaborate this reconstructed abuse (Loftus, 1993; Ganaway, 1989). Thus, one therapist concerned with repressed memories recommends in print, "When the client does not remember what happened to her, the therapist's encouragement to 'guess' or 'tell a story' will help the survivor regain access to the lost material" (Olio, 1989, p. 6). And a well-known self-help book tells its readers: "To say 'I was abused,' you do not need the kind of

recall that would stand up in a court of law. Often the knowledge that you were abused starts with a tiny feeling, an intuition. Assume your feelings are valid" (Bass & Davis, 1988, p. 22). These kinds of suggestions, though well intentioned, may be the stuff that reconstructed memories are made of. Furthermore, some therapists and other professionals investigating charges of abuse may encourage the person supposedly abused to try to visualize the details of the episode. Even if we have not been abused, we may be able to visualize and feel what it would be like to be so. Subsequently, we may find it difficult to distinguish between what we imagined and what actually occurred, as has repeatedly been shown in experimental studies (e.g., Johnson, 1990).

It is quite a stretch, though, from the laboratory studies of memories about relatively mundane events, like broken glass in an accident, to the kinds of traumatic memories that are at stake in allegations of sexual abuse. What we need are convincing studies that reconstruction goes on even when the events involved are significant. Such experiments are begin-

ning to appear. In one study, a teenager is convinced by trusted family members that he had been lost in a shopping mall when he was 5, an event that in fact had never happened. Days after this brainwashing, the teenager starts recounting facts and feelings about the episode that were not even mentioned in the indoctrination! He is embellishing a suggestion, resulting in a vivid memory of an event that never occurred (Loftus & Coan, 1994). Other studies suggest that younger children are particularly susceptible to this wholesale implantation of false memories (Ceci et al., 1981).

The upshot, then, is that "recovered" memories of traumatic events may sometimes be reconstructions, induced in part by others' suggestions and embellished by one's own top-down processes. Other times, however, the recovered memories may be authentic, and the crime they depict may actually have occurred. It is a matter of considerable difficulty to determine which situation we are dealing with when confronted with a particular case.

memory distortions, much like those that occur when we fit people into stereotypes, can occur when we attempt to fit stories into schemata. Research has confirmed Bartlett's suggestion. For example, after reading a brief story about a character going to a restaurant, subjects are likely to recall statements about the character eating and paying for a meal, even when those actions were never mentioned in the story (Bower, Black, & Turner, 1979).

Schemas seem to affect both the encoding and retrieval stages of long-term memory. If a particular schema is active when we read a story, we tend to encode mainly the facts that are related to the schema. We can illustrate with the following simple story:

1. Steven and Edgar went to a movie.

2. Steven and Edgar talked about business while waiting in line.

3. Steven liked the film, but Edgar thought it was too sentimental.

Assuming that Sentence No. 1 activates our movie schema, we are more likely to encode Sentence No. 3 than No. 2 because Sentence No. 3 is more related to the schema. In later recalling this story, if we could remember that it had to do with going to a movie, we could use our movie schema to search our memory: For example, was there anything in the story about a reaction to the film?

Thus, schemata can affect retrieval by guiding search processes (Brewer & Nakamura, 1984).

Situations in which memory is schema-driven and heavily constructive seem a far cry from the simpler situations we covered earlier. Consider, for example, memory for a list of unrelated words: Here, memory processes appear more bottom-up; that is, their function is more to *preserve* the input than to *construct* something new. However, there is a constructive aspect even to this simple situation, for techniques such as using imagery add meaning to the input. Similarly, when we read a paragraph about a schema-based activity we must still preserve some of its specifics if we are to recall it correctly in detail. Thus, the two aspects of memory—to preserve and to construct—may always be present, although their relative emphasis may depend on the exact situation.

BIOLOGICAL-PSYCHOLOGICAL PERSPECTIVES

We note, in closing, that progress in the study of memory has been made possible by dividing the field into manageable units—such as encoding in short-term memory or retrieval from explicit long-term memory—where these divisions rest on the interplay of psychological and biological approaches. We have used three basic distinctions to structure this chapter—three stages of memory, short-term versus long-term memory, and explicit versus implicit memory—and in each case we have supplied biological as well as psychological (cognitive) evidence. Interestingly, in all three cases, the psychological evidence was obtained first and then used to direct the subsequent biological work. Thus the cognitive distinction between short-term and long-term memory was made clearly in papers published about a century ago, yet it is only relatively recently that biologically oriented researchers have been able to demonstrate some of the neural bases for this key distinction.

Showing us how to divide up the field of memory is by no means the only contribution of biological work. Increasingly, researchers are determining the neural basis of components of the various kinds of memories. As examples, we now know something about the biological basis of storage in explicit, long-term memory (specifically, the role of the hippocampal system) and about storage in visual and verbal buffers of short-term memory. Such knowledge is not only useful in its own right, but may also prove helpful in combating the ravages of memory brought about by diseases of aging, such as stroke, senility, and Alzheimer's.

CHAPTER SUMMARY

1. There are three stages of memory: *encoding, storage,* and *retrieval*. Encoding refers to the transformation of information into the kind of code or representation that memory can accept; storage is the retention of the encoded information; and retrieval refers to the process by which information is recovered from memory. The three stages may operate differently in situations that require us to store material for a matter of seconds *(short-term memory)* and in situations that require us to store material for longer intervals *(long-term memory)*. Furthermore, different long-term memory systems seem to be involved in storing facts, which are part of *explicit memory,* and skills, which are part of *implicit memory.*

2. There is now some biological evidence for the above-mentioned distinctions. Recent brain-scanning studies of long-term memory indicate that most of the brain regions activated during encoding are in the left hemisphere, and that most of the regions activated during retrieval are in the right hemisphere. Evidence from both animal studies and studies of humans with brain damage indicates that different brain regions may mediate short-term and long-term memory. In particular, in both humans and other mammals, damage to the *hippocampal system* impairs performance on long-term memory tasks, but not short-term memory tasks.

3. Information in short-term memory tends to be encoded *acoustically,* although we can

also use a *visual code*. The most striking fact about short-term memory is that its storage capacity is limited to 7 ± 2 items, or *chunks*. While we are limited in the number of chunks, we can increase the size of a chunk by using information in long-term memory to *recode* incoming material into larger meaningful units. Information can be lost or forgotten from short-term memory. One cause of forgetting is that information *decays* with time; another is that new items *displace* old ones.

4. Retrieval slows down as the number of items in short-term memory increases. Some have taken this result to indicate that retrieval involves a *search process,* whereas others have interpreted the result in terms of an *activation process.*

5. Short-term memory seems to serve as a mental "work space" in solving various kinds of problems, such as mental arithmetic, geometric analogies, and answering questions about text. However, short-term memory does not seem to be involved in the understanding of relatively simple sentences. Short-term memory may also serve the function of being a way station to permanent memory, in that information may reside in short-term memory while it is being encoded into long-term memory.

6. Information in long-term memory is usually encoded according to its *meaning*. If the items to be remembered are meaningful but the connections between them are not, memory can be improved by adding meaningful connections that provide retrieval paths. The more one *elaborates* the meaning, the better memory will be.

7. Many cases of forgetting in long-term memory are due to *retrieval failures* (the information is there but cannot be found). Retrieval failures are more likely to occur when there is *interference* from items associated with the same retrieval cue. Such interference effects suggest that retrieval from long-term memory may be accomplished by a *sequential search* process or a *spreading activation* process.

8. Some forgetting from long-term memory is due to a loss from storage, particularly when there is a disruption of the processes that *consolidate* new memories. The biological locus of consolidation includes the *hippocampus,* a brain structure located below the cerebral cortex, and surrounding cortex. Recent work suggests that consolidation takes a matter of a few weeks.

9. Retrieval failures in long-term memory are less likely to happen when the items are *organized* during encoding and when the *context* at retrieval is similar to that at encoding. Retrieval processes can also be disrupted by *emotional factors*. In some cases, anxious thoughts interfere with retrieval of the target memory; in others, the target memory may be actively blocked *(repression hypothesis)*. In still other cases, emotion can enhance memory, as in *flashbulb memories*.

10. *Explicit memory* refers to the kind of memory manifested in recall or recognition, where we consciously recollect the past. *Implicit memory* refers to the kind of memory that manifests itself as an improvement on some perceptual, motor, or cognitive task with no conscious recollection of the experiences that led to the improvement. While explicit memory—particularly recall and recognition of facts—breaks down in *amnesia,* implicit memory is usually spared. This suggests that there may be separate storage systems for explicit and implicit memory.

11. Research with normal subjects also suggests that there may be separate systems for explicit and implicit memory. Much of this research has relied on a measure of implicit memory called *priming* (for example, the extent to which prior exposure to a list of words later facilitates completing stems of these words). Some studies reveal that an independent variable that affects explicit memory (amount of elaboration during encoding) has no effect on priming, while other studies show that a variable that affects implicit memory has no effect on explicit memory. Brain-scanning studies with normal subjects show that explicit memory is accompanied by increased neural activity in certain regions, but implicit memory is accompanied by a *decrease* in neural activity in critical regions.

12. Although we cannot increase the capacity of short-term memory, we can use *recoding* schemes to enlarge the size of a chunk and thereby increase the memory span. Long-term memory for facts can be improved at the encoding and retrieval stages. One way to improve encoding and retrieval is to use imagery, which is the basic principle underlying mnemonic systems such as the *method of loci* and the *key-word method*.

13. Other ways to improve encoding (and subsequent retrieval) are to elaborate the meaning of the items and to organize the material during encoding (hierarchical organization

seems preferable). The best ways to improve retrieval are to attempt to restore the encoding context at the time of retrieval and to practice retrieving information while learning it. Most of these principles for improving encoding and retrieval are incorporated into the *PQRST method* of studying a textbook, whose five stages are *Preview, Question, Read, Self-Recitation,* and *Test.*

14. Memory for complex materials, such as stories, is often *constructive.* We tend to use our general knowledge of the world to construct a more elaborate memory of a story or an event. Construction can involve adding simple *inferences* to the material presented; it can also involve fitting the material into *stereotypes* and other kinds of *schemata* (mental representations of classes of people, objects, events, or situations).

FURTHER READING

There are several recent introductory books on memory and cognition that are readable and up-to-date: Baddeley, *Human Memory* (1990); Anderson, *Cognitive Psychology and Its Implications* (3rd ed., 1990), Barsalou, *Cognitive Psychology for Cognitive Scientists* (1992); Medin and Ross, *Cognitive Psychology* (1992); Haberlandt, *Cognitive Psychology* (1993); and Best, *Cognitive Psychology* (1992). In addition to these textbooks, Neisser (ed.), *Memory Observed* (1982), provides a survey of remembering in natural contexts.

For an advanced treatment of theoretical issues in memory, see Anderson, *The Architecture of Cognition* (1983); Tulving, *Elements of Episodic Memory* (1983); the second volume of Atkinson, Herrnstein, Lindzey, and Luce (eds.), *Stevens' Handbook of Experimental Psychology* (2nd ed., 1988); and Baddeley, *Working Memory* (1986).

For a review of research on the biological bases of memory and learning, see Squire and Butters (eds.), *The Neuropsychology of Memory* (1984); and Squire, *Memory and Brain* (1987).

9
CHAPTER

THOUGHT AND LANGUAGE

The greatest accomplishments of our species stem from our ability to entertain complex thoughts, to communicate them, and to act on them. Thinking includes a wide range of mental activities. We think when we try to solve a problem that has been presented to us in class; we think when we daydream while waiting for that class to begin. We think when we decide what groceries to buy, plan a vacation, write a letter, or worry about a troubled relationship.

In all cases, thought can be conceived of as a "language of the mind." Introspection suggests that there is more than one language. One *mode of thought* corresponds to the stream of sentences that we seem to "hear in our mind"; this is referred to as *propositional thought* (because it expresses a proposition or claim). Another mode corresponds to images, particularly visual ones, that we can "see" in our mind; this is *imaginal thought*. Finally, there may be a third mode, *motoric thought,* which corresponds to sequences of "mental movements" (Bruner, Olver, Greenfield et al., 1966). While studies of cognitive development have paid some attention to motoric thought in children, research on thinking in adults has emphasized the other two modes, particularly the propositional one; this emphasis is reflected in the current chapter.

The first four sections of this chapter discuss major topics in propositional thinking. In the first section, we focus on concepts, which are the building blocks of thought, and discuss their use in classifying objects; this is the study of *concepts and categorization.* Then we consider how thoughts are organized in the service of drawing some conclu-sion; this is the study of *reasoning.* Next, we deal with how thoughts are communicated, which is the study of *language,* and then we consider the development of such communication, or the study of *language acquisition.* In the fifth section of the chapter, we turn to the imaginal mode of thought. In the final section, we will discuss thought in action—the study of *problem solving*—and consider the uses of both propositional and imaginal thought.

CONCEPTS AND CATEGORIZATION

We can think of a proposition as a statement that expresses a factual claim. "Mothers are hard workers" is one proposition, and "Cats are animals" is another. It is easy to see that such a thought consists of concepts—such as "mothers" and "hard workers" or "cat" and "animal"—combined in a particular way. To understand propositional thought, first we need to understand the concepts that compose it.

FUNCTIONS OF CONCEPTS

A **concept** represents an entire class—it is the set of properties that we associate with the class. Our concept of "cat" for example, includes, among other things, the properties of having four legs and whiskers. Concepts serve some major functions in mental life. One is that concepts foster *cognitive econ-*

Does flying and chirping make a bird? Your prototype for "bird" probably includes these features; however, they do not apply to certain kinds of birds, such as penguins and ostriches.

omy by dividing the world into manageable units. The world is full of so many different objects that if we treated each one as distinct, we would soon be overwhelmed. For example, if we had to refer to every single object we encountered by a different name, our vocabulary would have to be gigantic—so immense that communication might be impossible. (Think of what it would be like if we had a separate name for each of the seven million colors we can discriminate!) Fortunately, we do not treat each object as unique; rather, we see it as an instance of a concept. Thus, many different objects are seen as instances of the concept "cat," many others as instances of the concept "chair," and so on. By treating different objects as members of the same concept, we reduce the complexity of the world that we have to represent mentally.

Assigning an object to a concept is referred to as **categorization**. When we categorize an object, we treat it as if it has many of the properties associated with the concept, including properties that we have not directly perceived. Hence a second major function of concepts is that they allow us to *predict information* that is not readily perceived. For example, our concept of "apple" is associated with such hard-to-perceive properties as having seeds and being edible, as well as with readily visible properties like being round, having a distinctive color, and being found on trees. We may use the visible properties to categorize some object as an "apple" (the object is red, round, and hangs from a tree), and then infer that the object has the less visible properties as well (it has seeds and is edible). Concepts, then, enable us to go beyond the information given (Bruner, 1957)

We also have concepts of activities, such as "eating"; of states, such as "being old"; and of abstractions, such as "truth," "justice," or even the number "two." In each case we know something about the properties common to members of the concept. Widely used concepts like these generally are associated with a one-word name. This allows us to communicate quickly about experiences that occur frequently. We can also make up concepts on the spot, to serve some specific goal. For example, if you are planning an outing, you might generate the concept "things to take on a camping trip." These kinds of *goal-driven concepts* serve the function of facilitating planning. While such concepts are used relatively infrequently, and accordingly have relatively long names, they still provide us with some cognitive economy and predictive power (Barsalou, 1985).

PROTOTYPES

The properties associated with a concept seem to fall into two sets. One set of properties makes up the **prototype** of the concept, that is, those properties that describe the best examples of the concept. In the concept "bachelor," for example, your prototype might include such properties as a man who is in his 30s, lives alone, and has an active social life. The prototype is what usually comes to mind when we think of the concept. But while the prototype properties may be true of the typical examples of a bachelor, they are clearly not true of all instances (think of an uncle in his 60s who boards with his sister and rarely goes out). This means that a concept must contain something in addition to a prototype; this additional something is a **core** that comprises the properties that are most important for being a member of the concept. Your core of the concept "bachelor" would probably include the properties of being adult, male, and unmarried; these properties are essential for being a member of the concept (Armstrong, Gleitman, & Gleitman, 1983).

As another example, consider the concept "bird." Your prototype likely includes the properties of flying and chirping—which works for the best examples of "bird," such as robins and blue jays, but not for other examples, such as ostriches and penguins. Your core would likely specify something about the biological basis of birdhood—the fact that it involves having certain genes or, at least having parents that are birds.

Note that in both our examples—"bachelor" and "bird"—the prototype properties are salient but not perfect indicators of concept membership, whereas the core properties are more diagnostic of concept membership. However, there is an important difference between a concept like "bachelor" and a concept like "bird." The core of "bachelor" is a definition, and it can be easily applied. Thus, anyone who is adult, male, and unmarried must be a "bachelor," and it is relatively easy to determine whether someone has these defining properties. Concepts like this are said to be *well defined.* Categorizing a person or object into a well-defined category involves determining whether it has the core or defining properties. In contrast, the core of "bird" is hardly a definition—we may know only that genes are somehow involved, for example—and the core properties are hidden from view. Thus, if we happen upon a small animal, we can hardly inspect its genes or inquire about its parentage. All we can do is check whether it does certain things such as fly and chirp, and use this information to decide whether it is a bird. Concepts like "bird" are called **fuzzy**. Deciding whether an object is an instance of a fuzzy concept often involves determining its similarity to the concept's prototype (Smith, 1989). Importantly, most natural concepts seem to be fuzzy—they lack true definitions, and categorization relies heavily on prototypes.

Some instances of fuzzy concepts will have more prototype properties than other instances. Among birds, for example, a robin will have the property of flying, whereas an ostrich will not. The more prototype properties an instance has, the more typical people will consider that instance to be of the concept. Thus, of "bird," most people rate a robin as more typical than an ostrich; of "apple," they rate red apples as more typical than green ones (since red seems to be a property of the concept "apple"); and so on. The *typicality* of an instance has a major effect on its categorization. When people are asked whether or not a pictured animal is a "bird," a robin produces an immediate "yes," whereas a chicken requires a longer decision time. When young children are asked the same question, a robin will almost inevitably be correctly classified, whereas often a chicken will be declared a nonbird. Typicality also determines what we think of when we encounter the name of the concept. Hearing the sentence, "There is a bird outside your window," we are far more likely to think of a robin than a vulture, and what comes to mind will obviously influence what we make of the sentence (Rosch, 1978).

HIERARCHIES OF CONCEPTS

In addition to knowing the properties of concepts, we also know how concepts relate to one another. For example, "apples" are members (or a subset) of a larger concept, "fruit"; "robins" are a subset of "birds," which in turn are a subset of "animals." These two types of knowledge (properties of a concept and relationships between concepts) are represented in Figure 9-1 as a hierarchy. Such a hierarchy allows us to infer that a concept has a particular property even when it is not associated directly with that concept. Suppose you do not have the property of being sweet associated directly with "Golden Delicious apple." If you were asked, "Is a Golden Delicious apple sweet?" presumably you would enter your mental hierarchy at "Golden Delicious apple" (see Figure 9-1), trace a path from "Golden Delicious apple" to "fruit," find the property of being sweet stored at "fruit," and respond "yes." This idea implies that the time needed to establish a relation between a concept and a property should increase with the distance between them in the hierarchy. This prediction has been confirmed in experiments in which subjects were asked questions such as, "Is an apple sweet?" and "Is a Golden Delicious apple sweet?" Subjects took longer to answer the Golden Delicious apple question than the apple question, because the distance in the hierarchy between "Golden Delicious apple" and "sweet" is greater than that between "apple" and "sweet" (Collins & Loftus, 1975).

As the hierarchy in Figure 9-1 makes clear, an object can be identified at different levels. The same object is at once a "Golden Delicious apple," an "apple," and a "fruit." However, in any hierarchy, one level is the "basic" or preferred one for classification; this is the level at which we first categorize an object. For the hierarchy in Figure 9-1, the level that contains "apple" and "pear" would be the basic one. Evidence for this claim comes from studies in which people are asked to name pictured objects with the first names that come to mind. People are more likely to call a pictured Golden Delicious apple an "apple" than either a "Golden Delicious apple" or a "fruit." It seems then that we first divide the world into basic-level concepts (Mervis & Rosch, 1981). What determines which level is basic? The answer appears to be that the basic level is the one that has the most *distinctive properties*. In Figure 9-1, "apple" has several properties that are distinctive—they are not shared by other kinds of fruit (for example, red and round are not

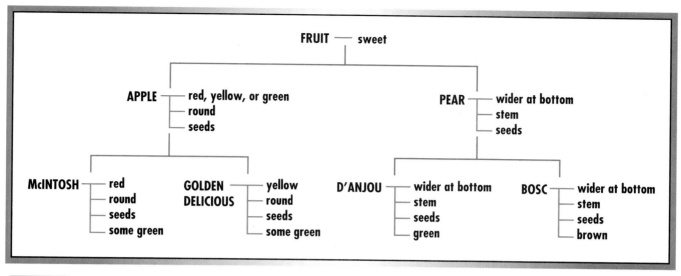

Hierarchy of Concepts   *Words in capital letters represent concepts; lowercase words depict properties of these concepts. The blue lines show relationships between concepts, and the red lines connect properties and concepts.*

properties of "pear"). In contrast, "Golden Delicious apple" has few distinct properties; most of its properties are shared by "MacIntosh apple," for example (see Figure 9-1). And "fruit," which is at the highest level of Figure 9-1, has few properties of any kind. Thus, we categorize the world first at what turns out to be the most informative level (Murphy & Brownell, 1985).

ACQUIRING CONCEPTS

How do we acquire the multitude of concepts that we have? Some concepts may be inborn, such as the concepts of "time" and "space." Other concepts have to be learned.

LEARNING PROTOTYPES AND CORES   We can learn about a concept in different ways: Either we are explicitly taught something about the concept, or we learn it through experience. Which way we learn depends on *what* we are learning. Explicit teaching is likely to be the means by which we learn cores of concepts, while experience seems to be the standard means by which we acquire prototypes. Thus, someone explicitly tells a child a "robber" is someone who takes another person's possessions with no intention of returning them (the core), while the child's experiences may lead him or her to expect robbers to be shiftless, disheveled, and dangerous (the prototype).

Children must also learn that the core is a better indicator of concept membership than the prototype is, but it takes a while for them to learn this. In one study, children aged 5 to 10 were presented with descriptions of items and had to decide whether or not they belonged to particular well-defined concepts. We can illustrate the study with the concept of "robber." One description given for "robber" depicted a person who matched its prototype but not its core:

> A smelly, mean old man with a gun in his pocket who came to your house and takes your TV set because your parents didn't want it anymore and told him he could have it.

Another description used for "robber" was of a person who matched its core but not its prototype:

> A very friendly and cheerful woman who gave you a hug, but then disconnected your toilet bowl and took it away without permission and no intention to return it.

The younger children often thought the prototypical description was more likely than the core description to be an instance of the concept. Not until age 10 did children show a clear shift from the prototype to the core as the final arbitrator of concept decisions (Keil & Batterman, 1984).

LEARNING THROUGH EXPERIENCE   There are at least three different ways in which one can learn a concept through experience with its instances. The simplest way is called the **exemplar strategy**, and we can illustrate it with a child learning the concept of "furniture." When the child encounters a known instance or exemplar—say, a table—she stores a representation of it. Later, when the child has to decide whether or not a new item—say, a desk—is an instance of "furniture," she determines the new object's similarity to stored exemplars of "furniture," including table. This strategy seems to be widely used by children, and it works better with typical instances than atypical ones. Because the first exemplars a child learns tend to be typical ones, new instances are more likely to be correctly classified to the extent they are similar to typical instances. Thus, if a young child's concept of "furniture" consisted of just the most typical instances (say, table and chair), she could correctly classify other instances that looked similar to the learned exemplars, such as desk and sofa, but not instances that looked different from the learned exemplars, such as lamp and bookshelf (Mervis & Pani, 1981). The exemplar strategy remains part of our repertory for acquiring concepts, as there is substantial evidence that adults often use it in acquiring novel concepts (for example, Estes, 1994).

But as we grow older we start to use another strategy as well, **hypothesis testing**. We inspect known instances of a concept, searching for properties that are relatively common to them (for example, many pieces of "furniture" are found in living spaces), and we hypothesize that these common properties are what characterize the concept. We then analyze novel objects for these critical properties, maintaining our hypothesis if it leads to a correct categorization about the novel object and revamping it if it leads us astray. The strategy thus focuses on abstractions—properties that characterize sets of instances rather than just single instances—and is tuned to finding core properties, since they are the ones common to most instances (Bruner, Goodenow & Austin, 1956).

Both the exemplar and hypothesis-testing strategies are driven solely by the input, the known instances, and give little weight to the learner's prior knowledge. In the preceding chapters, we have referred to such strategies as *bottom-up,* and contrasted them with *top-down* strategies, in which people make extensive use of their prior knowledge. In a top-down strategy of concept learning, people use their prior knowledge along with the known instances to determine the critical properties of a concept. An example is provided by the following study.

Two groups of adult subjects were presented the children's drawings shown in Figure 9-2. Their task was to describe the properties that characterized each category. One group of subjects was told that category 1 drawings were done by creative children, while category 2 drawings were done by noncreative children; the other group of subjects was told that category 1 drawings were done by city children, while category 2 drawings were done by farm children. The two groups of subjects therefore differed in the kind of prior knowledge they would bring to bear, either knowledge about creativity or knowledge about city versus farm living. This difference showed its effect in the descriptions of the categories that the two groups of subjects generated. The creative-noncreative group produced more descriptions of the two categories that emphasized the amount of detail in the drawing; for example,

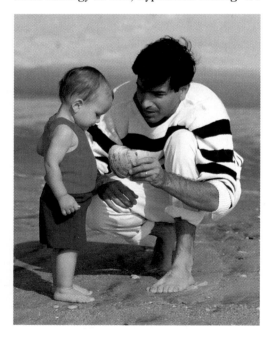

Parents can teach children to name and classify objects. Later, when the child sees another object, she may determine if it is of the same classification as the stored exemplar.

Creative kids will draw more detail—like eyelashes, teeth, curly hair, shading and coloring. Noncreative kids draw more stick-figurish people.

In contrast, the farm-city group generated more descriptions of the two categories that emphasized the clothing in the drawings; for example,

Farm kids will draw people with overalls, straw or farm hats. City kids will draw people with ties, suits.

Thus learners with different prior knowledge focused on different properties of the instances. Moreover, in some cases, differences in prior knowledge seem to have determined how the learners interpreted the properties in the first place. To illustrate, consider the pointed-to object in the fourth figure of category 1 (see Figure 9-2). Some subjects in the creative-noncreative group interpreted this object as a pocket, and mentioned it as evidence of greater detail. Some subjects in the farm-city group interpreted this same object as a purse, and mentioned it as evidence of an urban background. Prior knowledge therefore may affect every aspect of concept attainment (Wisniewski & Medin, 1991).

Neural Bases of Concept Acquisition

Our two bottom-up strategies of concept acquisition, exemplars and hypothesis testing, seem to be implemented by different regions of the brain. The best evidence for this claim comes from studies of adult patients with different kinds of brain damage trying to learn different kinds of concepts.

Use of the exemplar strategy hinges on the concept learner being able to retrieve known instances of the concept; for example, in deciding whether a novel object is an instance of "furniture," one might retrieve instances of desks or chairs. Clearly this involves retrieval from long-term memory, and as we saw in Chapter 8 such retrieval depends on brain structures in the medial temporal lobe, particularly the hippocampus. It follows, then, that someone with damage in these particular brain regions will have difficulty acquiring concepts that require use of the exemplar strategy. This is exactly what has been found. One study tested patients with medial-temporal-lobe damage as well as normal subjects on two different tasks. One task required subjects to learn to sort dot patterns into one

Category 1

Category 2

FIGURE 9-2

Top-Down Concept Learning *In an experiment on concept learning, one group of subjects was told that category 1 drawings were done by creative children and category 2 drawings by noncreative children, while another group of subjects was told that category 1 drawings were done by city children and category 2 drawings by farm children. The two groups of subjects offered different kinds of descriptions of the categories. Furthermore, the same feature (for example, the pointed-to-object in the fourth figure of category 1) was sometimes interpreted differently by the two groups. (After Wisniewski & Medin, 1991)*

of two categories, and the other task required subjects to learn to sort paintings into two categories that corresponded to two different artists. Independent evidence indicated that only the paintings task relied extensively on retrieving exemplars. The patients learned the dot pattern concepts as easily as the normal subjects, but performed far worse than the normals in acquiring the painting concepts. When concept learning depends on the exemplar strategy, damage to the brain structures that mediate long-term memory leads to an impairment in learning (Kolodny, 1994).

In contrast, the hypothesis-testing strategy seems to be mediated by structures in the front of the brain. The evidence for this claim comes from studies in which normal subjects and patients with frontal brain damage are compared in a concept-attainment

LINGUISTIC RELATIVITY HYPOTHESIS

In our discussion of concepts, we assume that words reflect existing concepts. We assume that language is designed to express propositional thought and, therefore, that the structure of language reflects the structure of thought. However, some have suggested that the relationship between language and thought is the other way around. Rather than thought determining language, it may be that language determines thought. This is the **linguistic relativity hypothesis** proposed by Benjamin Whorf (1956). Whorf argued that the kinds of concepts and perceptions we can have are affected by the particular language we speak. Therefore, people who speak different languages perceive the world in different ways. This provocative idea has caused considerable debate over the years.

Much of the evidence cited in favor of the hypothesis is based on vocabulary differences. For example, English has only one word for snow, whereas Eskimo has four. Consequently, speakers of Eskimo may perceive differences in snow that speakers of English do not. Do such observations constitute strong evidence for the linguistic relativity hypothesis? Critics of the hypothesis argue that they do not (for example, Brown, 1986; Slobin, 1979). According to the critics, language may embody distinctions that are important to a culture, but it does not create those distinctions, nor are its speakers the only ones who can perceive them. English

speakers may have the same capacity for perceiving variations in snow as Eskimo speakers, but since such variations are more important in Eskimo cultures than in Anglo cultures Eskimos assign different words to the variations whereas English speakers do not. The best evidence for this view is the development of jargons. For example, American skiers talk of "powder" and "corn," not just "snow." This growth in vocabulary may be accompanied by changes in perception: Eskimos and skiers are more likely to notice variations in snow than are Hawaiians. But the critical point is that such changes do not depend on the language spoken. If anything, the language seems to depend on changes in perception.

The linguistic relativity hypothesis has fared no better when it comes to explaining cultural variations in terms describing colors. At one time, many linguists believed that languages differed widely in how they divided the color spectrum and that this led to differences in the perception of colors. Subsequent research showed just the opposite. Berlin and Kay (1969), two anthropologists, studied the *basic color terms* of many languages. Basic color terms are simple, nonmetaphoric words that are used to describe the colors of many different objects. Berlin and Kay found striking commonalities in such terms across languages. For instance, every language takes its basic color terms from a restricted set of 11 names. In Eng-

lish these are "black," "white," "red," "yellow," "green," "blue," "brown," "purple," "pink," "gray," and "orange." No matter what color terms a particular language has, they inevitably correspond to some subset of the colors listed here. In addition, if a language uses fewer than 11 terms, the basic terms chosen are not arbitrary. If a language has only two terms (none has fewer), they correspond to "black" and "white"; if it has three, they correspond to "black," "white," and "red"; if it has six, they correspond to these three plus "yellow," "green," and "blue." Thus, the ordering of basic color terms seems to be universal, rather than varying from language to language as the linguistic relativity hypothesis might suggest.

In addition, people whose languages use corresponding basic color terms agree on what particular color is most typical of a color term. Suppose two different languages have terms corresponding to "red." When speakers of these languages are asked to pick the best example of red from an array of hues, they make the same choice. Even though the range of hues for what they would call red may differ, their idea of a typical red is the same. Further work by Rosch (1974) suggests that the Dani (a New Guinea people), whose language has only two basic color terms, perceive color variations in exactly the same way as people whose language has all 11. Dani subjects were given a set of red color patches to remember, and the patches

task that is known to invoke hypothesis testing. On each trial of the task, a card is presented that contains between one and three colored, geometric forms (for example, two red squares). From card to card, there is a variation in the number of forms on a card (1, 2, or 3), the type of forms (circles, squares, or triangles), and the color of the forms (red, green, or blue). The subject's task is to determine which one of these three attributes—number, form, or color—is relevant to the

concept, and then to sort the cards into three piles on the basis of that attribute. In addition, after the subject sorts a certain number of cards correctly, the experimenter switches the relevant attribute, and subjects have to discover the new critical attribute. For example, after learning that the concept is "color," and correctly sorting the cards into piles corresponding to red, green, and blue, the critical attribute might be switched to shape, and now the subject would have to sort the cards varied in how typical they were of "red." Later the subjects were presented a set of color patches and had to decide which ones they had seen before. Even though they had no word for "red," Dani subjects recognized more typical red colors better than the less typical ones. This is exactly what American subjects do in the comparable task. So the perception and memory of color give little support to the linguistic relativity hypothesis.

More recent experiments suggest that concepts of animals may also be universal. The experiments compare U.S. students and Maya Itza, a culture in the Guatemala rain forest that is relatively insulated from Western influences. The U.S. subjects were from southeastern Michigan, which happens to have a number of mammalian species that are comparable to those found in the Guatemala rain forest. Both groups of subjects were presented the names of these comparable species, asked first to group them into sets that go together, then to group these sets into higher-order groups that were related, and so on until all the species were in one group (corresponding to "mammals"). In this way, each subject creates a tree, with their initial groupings at the bottom and "mammal" at the top; this tree reflects their taxonomy of mammals. The trees or taxonomies created by the Maya Itza were quite similar to those created by the U.S. students. The correlation be-

tween the average Itza and average U.S. trees in fact was about .6. Moreover, both the Itza and U.S. taxonomies were highly correlated with the true scientific taxonomy. Apparently, all people base their concepts of animals on properties that they can easily observe (overall shape, or distinctive features like a bushy tail, movement pattern, or coloring), and these same properties are indicators of the evolutionary history of the species, which is what the scientific taxonomy is based on (Lopez et al., 1995).

We should not dismiss the linguistic relativity hypothesis too quickly, however. Few language domains have been investigated in the same detail as color and animal terms, and per-

haps support for the hypothesis will be found in other domains (for example in the grammar of a language, as suggested by Hunt & Agnoli, 1991). Also, the linguistic relativity hypothesis calls attention to an important point. In learning to make fine discriminations in a particular field, it is helpful to have a vocabulary that expresses these discriminations. As we gain expertise in a field (whether skiing, psychology, or something else), we enlarge our vocabulary for distinctions in that field. Jargons help us to think about and communicate these distinctions. Although a distinction must exist in someone's mind before a term can be created to embody it, the importance of that embodiment should not be underestimated.

Eskimos may perceive differences in snow that we do not.

into piles corresponding to circles, squares, and triangles. Patients with damage in the frontal cortex are markedly impaired on this task compared to normal subjects. The patients may learn the initially relevant attribute (color in the preceding example) as easily as normals, but they have severe problems in shifting to a new attribute when the experimenter switches the relevant attribute. Although the experimenter may repeatedly tell the subjects their sortings are incorrect,

the patients persist in sorting on the basis of the outmoded attribute. It is as if they cannot change their hypotheses on the basis of feedback (for example, Milner, 1964).

REASONING

When we think propositionally our sequence of thoughts is organized. Sometimes our thoughts are organized by the structure of long-term memory. A thought about calling your father, for example, leads to a memory of a recent conversation you had with him in your house, which in turn leads to a thought about fixing the house's attic. But memory associations are not the only means we have of organizing thought. The kind of organization of interest to us here manifests itself when we try to *reason.* In such cases, our sequence of thoughts often takes the form of an argument, in which one proposition corresponds to a claim, or *conclusion,* that we are trying to draw. The remaining propositions are reasons for the claim, or *premises* for the conclusion.

DEDUCTIVE REASONING

LOGICAL RULES   According to logicians, the strongest arguments are *deductively valid,* which means that it is impossible for the conclusion of the argument to be false if its premises are true (Skyrms, 1986). An example of such an argument is the following.

1. a. If it's raining, I'll take an umbrella.

   b. It's raining.

   c. Therefore, I'll take an umbrella.

How does the reasoning of ordinary people line up with that of the logician? When asked to decide whether or not an argument is deductively valid, people are quite accurate in their assessments of simple arguments. How do we make such judgments? Some theories of **deductive reasoning** assume that we operate like intuitive logicians and use logical rules in trying to prove that the conclusion of an argument follows from the premises. To illustrate, consider the following rule:

> If you have a proposition of the form *If p then q,* and another proposition *p,* then you can infer the proposition *q.*

Presumably, adults know this rule (perhaps unconsciously) and use it to decide that the previous argument is valid. Specifically, they identify the first premise ("If it's raining, I'll take an umbrella") with the *If p then q* part of the rule. They identify the second premise ("It's raining") with the *p* part of the rule, and

then they infer the *q* part ("I'll take an umbrella").

Rule-following becomes more conscious if we complicate the argument. Presumably, we apply our sample rule twice when evaluating the following argument:

2. a. If it's raining, I'll take an umbrella.

   b. If I take an umbrella, I'll lose it.

   c. It's raining.

   d. Therefore, I'll lose my umbrella.

Applying our rule to Propositions a and c allows us to infer "I'll take an umbrella"; and applying our rule again to Proposition b and the inferred proposition allows us to infer "I'll lose my umbrella," which is the conclusion. One of the best pieces of evidence that people are using rules like this is that the number of rules an argument requires is a good predictor of the argument's difficulty. The more rules that are needed, the more likely it is that people will make an error, and the longer it will take them when they do make a correct decision (Rips, 1983, 1994).

EFFECTS OF CONTENT   Logical rules do not capture all aspects of deductive reasoning. Such rules are triggered only by the logical *form* of propositions, yet our ability to evaluate a deductive argument often depends on the *content* of the propositions as well. We can illustrate this point by the following experimental problems. Subjects are presented four cards. In one version of the problem, each card has a letter on one side and a digit on the other (see the top half of Figure 9-3). The subject must decide which cards to turn over to determine whether the following claim is correct: "If a card has a vowel on one side, then it has an even number on the other side." While most subjects correctly choose the "E" card, fewer than 10 percent of them also choose the "7" card, which is the other correct choice. (To see that the "7" card is critical, note that if it has a vowel on its other side, the claim is disconfirmed.)

Performance improves drastically, however, in another version of the above problem (see the bottom half of Figure 9-3). Now the claim that subjects must evaluate is "If a person is drinking beer, he or she must be over 19." Each card has a person's age on one side, and what he or she is drinking on the other.

This version of the problem is logically equivalent to the preceding version (in particular, "Beer" corresponds to "E," and "16" corresponds to "7"); but now most subjects make the correct choices (they turn over the "Beer" and "16" cards). Thus, the content of the propositions affects our reasoning.

Results such as the above imply that we do not always use logical rules when faced with deduction problems. Rather, sometimes we use rules that are less abstract and more relevant to everyday problems, what are called **pragmatic rules**. An example is the *permission rule*, which states that "If a particular action is to be taken, often a precondition must be satisfied." Most people know this rule, and activate it when presented the drinking problem in the bottom half of Figure 9-3; that is, they would think about the problem in terms of permission. Once activated, the rule would lead people to look for failures to meet the relevant precondition (being under 19), which in turn would lead them to choose the "16" card. In contrast, the permission rule would not be triggered by the letter-number problem in the top half of Figure 9-3, so there is no reason for people to choose the "7" card. Thus, the content of a problem affects whether or not a pragmatic rule is activated, which in turn affects the correctness of reasoning (Cheng, Holyoak, Nisbett, & Oliver, 1986).

In addition to rules, subjects may sometimes solve the drinking problem by setting up a concrete representation of the situation, what is called a **mental model**. They may, for example, imagine two people, each with a number on his back and a drink in his hand. They may then inspect this mental model and see what happens, for example, if the drinker with "16" on his back has a beer in his hand. According to this idea, we reason in terms of mental models that are suggested by the content of the problem (Johnson-Laird, 1989).

The two procedures just described—applying pragmatic rules and constructing mental models—have one thing in common. They are determined by the content of the problem. This is in contrast to the application of logical rules, which should not be affected by problem content. Hence, our sensitivity to content often prevents us from operating as intuitive logicians.

INDUCTIVE REASONING

LOGICAL RULES Logicians have noted that an argument can be good even if it is not deductively valid. Such arguments are *inductively strong,* which means that it is *improbable* that the conclusion is false if the premises are true (Skyrms, 1986). An example of an inductively strong argument is as follows:

3. a. Mitch majored in accounting in college.

   b. Mitch now works for an accounting firm.

   c. Therefore, Mitch is an accountant.

This argument is not deductively valid (Mitch may have tired of accounting courses and taken a night-watchman's job in the only place he had contacts). Inductive strength, then, is a matter of probabilities, not certainties; and (according to logicians) inductive logic should be based on the theory of probability.

We make and evaluate inductive arguments all the time. In doing this, do we rely on the rules of probability theory as a logician or mathematician would? One probability

FIGURE 9-3

Content Effects in Deductive Reasoning   *The top row illustrates a version of the problem in which subjects had to decide which two cards should be turned over to test the hypothesis, "If a card has a vowel on one side, it has an even number on the other side." The bottom row illustrates a version of the problem where subjects had to decide which cards to turn over to test the hypothesis, "If a person is drinking beer, he or she must be over 19." (After Griggs & Cox, 1982; Wason & Johnson-Laird, 1972)* rule that is relevant is the **base-rate rule**, which states that the probability of something being a member of a class (such as Mitch being a member of the class of accountants) is greater the more class members there are (that is, the higher the base rate of the class). Thus, our sample argument about Mitch being an accountant can be strengthened by adding the premise that Mitch joined a club in which 90 percent of the members are accountants. Another relevant probability rule is the **conjunction rule**: the probability of a proposition cannot be less than the probability of that proposition combined with another proposition. For example, the probability that "Mitch is an accountant" cannot be less than the probability that "Mitch is an accountant and makes more than $40,000 a year." The base-rate and conjunction rules are rational guides to inductive reasoning—they are endorsed by logic—and most people will defer to them when the rules are made explicit. However, in the rough-and-tumble of everyday reasoning, people frequently violate these rules, as we are about to see.

HEURISTICS   In a series of ingenious experiments, Tversky and Kahneman (1983; 1973) have shown that people violate some basic rules of probability theory when making inductive judgments. Violations of the base-rate rule are particularly common. In one experiment, one group of subjects was told that a panel of psychologists had interviewed 100 people—30 engineers and 70 lawyers—and had written personality descriptions of them. These subjects were then given a few descriptions and for each one were asked to indicate the probability that the person described was an engineer. Some descriptions were prototypical of an engineer (for example, "Jack shows no interest in political issues and spends his free time on home carpentry"); other descriptions were neutral (for example, "Dick is a man of high ability and promises to be quite successful"). Not surprisingly, these subjects rated the prototypical description as more likely to be an engineer than the neutral description. Another group of subjects was given the identical instructions and descriptions, except they were told that the 100 people were 70 engineers and 30 lawyers (the reverse of the first group). The base rate of engineers therefore differed greatly between the two groups. This

difference had virtually no effect: Subjects in the second group gave essentially the same ratings as those in the first group. For example, subjects in both groups rated the neutral description as having a 50–50 chance of being an engineer (whereas the rational move would have been to rate the neutral description as more likely to be in the profession with the higher base rate). Subjects completely ignored the information about base rates (Tversky & Kahneman, 1973).

People pay no more heed to the conjunction rule. In one study, subjects were presented the following description:

> Linda is 31 years old, single, outspoken, and very bright. In college, she majored in philosophy . . . and was deeply concerned with issues of discrimination.

Subjects then estimated the probabilities of the following two statements:

4. Linda is a bank teller.

5. Linda is a bank teller and is active in the feminist movement.

Statement No. 5 is the conjunction of Statement No. 4 and the proposition "Linda is active in the feminist movement." In flagrant violation of the conjunction rule, most subjects rated No. 5 more probable than No. 4. Note that this is a fallacy because every feminist bank teller is a bank teller, but some female bank tellers are not feminists, and Linda could be one of them (Tversky & Kahneman, 1983).

Subjects in this study based their judgments on the fact that Linda seems more similar to a feminist bank teller than to a bank teller. Though they were asked to estimate *probability*, subjects instead estimated the *similarity* of Linda to the prototype of the concepts "bank teller" and "feminist bank teller." Thus, estimating similarity is used as a *heuristic* for estimating probability, where a heuristic is a short-cut procedure that is relatively easy to apply and can often yield the correct answer, but not inevitably so. That is, people use the *similarity heuristic* because similarity often relates to probability yet is easier to calculate. Use of the similarity heuristic also explains why people ignore base rates. In the engineer-lawyer study described earlier, subjects may have considered only the similarity of the description to their prototypes of "engineer" and "lawyer." Hence, given a description that matched the prototypes of "engineer" and "lawyer" equally well, subjects judged that engineer and lawyer were equally probable. Reliance on the similarity heuristic can lead to errors even by experts.

Reasoning by similarity shows up in another common reasoning situation, that in which we know some members of a category have a particular property and have to decide whether other category members have the property as well. In one study, subjects had to judge which of the following two arguments seemed stronger

6. a. All robins have sesamoid bones.

   b. Therefore all sparrows have sesamoid bones.

   versus

7. a. All robins have sesamoid bones.

   b. Therefore all ostriches have sesamoid bones.

Not surprisingly, subjects judged the first argument stronger, presumably because robins are more similar to sparrows than they are to ostriches. This use of similarity appears rational, inasmuch as it fits with the idea that things that have many known properties in common are likely to have unknown properties in common as well. But the veneer of rationality fades when we consider subjects' judgments on another pair of arguments:

7. a. All robins have sesamoid bones.

   b. Therefore all ostriches have sesamoid bones (same as the preceding argument).

   versus

8. a. All robins have sesamoid bones.

   b. Therefore all birds have sesamoid bones.

Subjects judged the second argument stronger, presumably because robins are more similar to the prototype of birds than they are to ostriches. But this judgment is a fallacy: Based on the same evidence (that robins have sesamoid bones), it cannot be more likely that *all* birds have some property than that all ostriches do, because ostriches

are in fact birds. Again, our similarity-based intuitions can sometimes lead us astray (Osherson, et al., 1990).

Similarity is not our only strong heuristic; another is the *causality heuristic*. People estimate the probability of a situation by the strength of the causal connections between the events in the situation. For example, people judge Statement No. 10 to be more probable than Statement No. 9:

9. Sometime during the year 2000, there will be a massive flood in California, in which more than 1,000 people will drown.

10. Sometime during the year 2000, there will be an earthquake in California, causing a massive flood, in which more than 1,000 people will drown.

Judging No. 10 to be more probable than No. 9 is another violation of the conjunction rule (and hence another fallacy). This time, the violation arises because in Statement No. 10 the flood has a strong causal connection to another event, the earthquake; whereas in Statement No. 9, the flood alone is mentioned and hence has no causal connections.

So our reliance on heuristics often leads us to ignore some basic rational rules, including the base-rate and conjunction rules. But we should not be too pessimistic about our level of rationality. For one thing, the similarity and causality heuristics probably lead to correct decisions in most cases. Another point is that under the right circumstances, we can appreciate the relevance of certain logical rules to particular problems and use them appropriately (Nisbett et al., 1983). Thus, in reading and thinking about this discussion, you were probably able to see the relevance of the base-rate and conjunction rules to the problems at hand.

LANGUAGE AND COMMUNICATION

Language is our primary means for communicating thought. Moreover, it is a universal means: Every human society has a language, and every human being of normal intelligence acquires his or her native language and uses it effortlessly. The naturalness of language sometimes lulls us into thinking that language use requires no special explanation. Nothing could be further from the truth. Some people can read, and others cannot; some can do arithmetic, and others cannot; some can play chess, and others cannot. But virtually everyone can master and use an enormously complex linguistic system. Why this should be so is among the fundamental puzzles of human psychology.

LEVELS OF LANGUAGE

Language use has two aspects: *production* and *comprehension*. In producing language, we start with a propositional thought, somehow translate it into a sentence, and end up with sounds that express the sentence. In comprehending language, we start by hearing sounds, attach meanings to the sounds in the form of words, combine the words to create a sentence, and then somehow extract a proposition from it. Thus, language use seems to involve moving through various levels, and Figure 9-4 makes these levels explicit. At the highest level are sentence units, including sentences and phrases. The next level is that of words and parts of words that carry meaning (the prefix "non" or the suffix "er," for example). The lowest level contains speech sounds. The adjacent levels are closely related to one another: The phrases of a sentence are built from words and prefixes and suffixes, which in turn are constructed from speech sounds. Language is therefore a multilevel system for relating thoughts to speech by means of word and sentence units (Chomsky, 1965).

There are striking differences in the number of units at each level. All languages have only a limited number of speech sounds; English has about 40 of them. But rules for com-

bining these speech sounds make it possible to produce and understand thousands of words (a vocabulary of 40,000 words is not unusual for an adult). Similarly, rules for combining words make it possible to produce and understand millions of sentences (if not an infinite number of them). Thus, two of the basic properties of language are that it is *structured* at multiple levels and that it is *productive*: Rules allow us to combine units at one level into a vastly greater number of units at the next level. Every human language has these two properties.

LANGUAGE UNITS AND PROCESSES

With the above as background, let us now consider the units and processes involved at each level of language. In surveying the relevant material, we usually take the perspective of a person comprehending language, a listener, though occasionally we switch to the perspective of a language producer, or speaker.

SPEECH SOUNDS If you could attend to just the sounds someone makes when talking to you, what would you hear? You would not perceive it as a continuous stream of sound, but rather as a sequence of discrete speech categories, called *phonemes*. A phoneme is a category in the sense that sounds that differ physically can be perceived as the same phoneme. For example, the sound corresponding to the first letter in "boy" is an instance of a phoneme symbolized as /b/. (Note that while phonemes may correspond to letters, they are speech sounds not letters.) In English, we divide all speech sounds into about 40 phonemes.

We are good at discriminating different sounds that correspond to different phonemes in our language, but poor at discriminating different sounds that correspond to the same phoneme. Consider, for example, the sound of the first letter in "pin" and the sound of the second letter in "spin" (Liberman, Cooper, Shankweiler, & Studdert-Kennedy, 1967); they are the same phoneme, /p/, and they sound the same to us even though they have different physical characteristics. The /p/ in "pin" is accompanied by a small puff of air, but the /p/ in "spin" is not (try holding your hand a short distance from your mouth as you say the two words). Thus,

Levels of Language *At the highest level are sentence units, including phrases and sentences. The next level is that of words and parts of words that carry meaning. The lowest level contains speech sounds.*

SENTENCE UNITS

WORDS, PREFIXES, AND SUFFIXES

SPEECH SOUNDS

our phonemic categories act as filters, in that they convert a continuous stream of speech into a sequence of familiar phonemes.

Every language has a different set of phonemes, which is one reason why we often have difficulty learning to pronounce foreign words. Another language may use phonemes that never appear in ours. It may take us a while even to hear the new phonemes, let alone produce them. For example, in the Hindi language, the two different /p/ sounds illustrated above correspond to two different phonemes. Or another language may not make a distinction between two sounds that our language treats as two phonemes. For example, in Japanese the English sounds corresponding to "r" and "l" (/r/ and /l/) are perceived as the same phoneme.

When phonemes are combined in the right way, we perceive them as words. Each language has its own rules about which phonemes can follow others. In English, for example, /b/ cannot follow /p/ at the beginning of a word (try pronouncing "pbet"). Such rules show their influence when we listen. We are more accurate in perceiving a string of phonemes whose order conforms to the rules of our language than a string whose order violates these rules. The influence of these rules is even more striking when we take the perspective of a speaker. For example, we have no difficulty pronouncing the plurals of nonsense words we have never heard before. Consider "zuk" and "zug." In accordance with a simple rule, the plural of "zuk" is formed by adding the phoneme /s/, as in "hiss." In English, however, /s/ cannot follow "g" at the end of a word, so to form the plural of "zug" we must use another rule—one that adds the phoneme /z/, as in "fuzz." We may not be aware of these differences in forming plurals, but we have no difficulty producing them. It is as if we "know" the rules for combining phonemes even though we are not consciously aware of the rules: We conform to rules we cannot verbalize.

WORD UNITS What we typically perceive when listening to speech are not phonemes but words. Unlike phonemes, words carry meaning. However, they are not the only smallish linguistic units that convey meaning. Suffixes such as "ly," or prefixes such as "un," also carry meaning; they can be added on to words to form more complex ones with different meanings, as when "un" and "ly" are added on to "time" to form "untimely." Any small linguistic unit that carries meaning is called a *"morpheme."*

Most morphemes are themselves words. Most words denote some specific content, such as "house" or "run." A few words, however, primarily serve to make sentences grammatical; such grammatical words, or *grammatical morphemes,* include what are commonly labeled articles and prepositions, such as "a," "the," "in," "of," "on," and "at." Some prefixes and suffixes also play primarily a grammatical role. These grammatical morphemes include the suffixes "ing" and "ed." Grammatical morphemes may be processed in a qualitatively different manner than content words. One piece of evidence for this is that there are forms of brain damage in which the use of grammatical morphemes is impaired more than the use of content words (Zurif, 1990). Also, as we shall see later, grammatical morphemes are acquired in a different manner than are content words.

The most important aspect of a word is, of course, its meaning. A word can be viewed as the name of a concept; hence, its meaning is the concept it names. Some words are *ambiguous* because they name more than one concept. "Club," for example, names both a social organization and an object used for striking. Sometimes we may be aware of a word's ambiguity, as when hearing the sentence "He was interested in the club." In most cases, however, the sentence context makes the meaning of the word sufficiently clear so we do not consciously experience any ambiguity—for example, "He wanted to join the club." Even in the latter cases, though, there is evidence that we *unconsciously* consider both meanings of the ambiguous word for a brief moment. In one experiment, a subject was presented a sentence like "He wanted to join the club," followed immediately by a test word that the subject had to read aloud as quickly as possible. Subjects read the test word faster if it was related to either meaning of "club" (for example, "group" or "struck") than if it was unrelated to either meaning (for example, "apple"). This suggests that both meanings of "club" were activated during comprehension of the sentence, and that either meaning could prime related words (Tanenhaus, Leiman, & Seidenberg, 1979; Swinney, 1979).

SENTENCE UNITS As listeners, usually we effortlessly combine words into sentence units, which include sentences as well as phrases. An important property of these units is that they can correspond to parts of a proposition. Such correspondences allow a listener to "extract" propositions (or thoughts) from sentences.

To understand these correspondences, first you have to appreciate that any proposition can be divided into a *subject* and a *predicate* (a description). In the proposition "Audrey has curly hair," "Audrey" is the subject and "has curly hair" is the predicate. In the proposition "The tailor is asleep," "the tailor" is the subject and "is asleep" is the predicate. And in "Teachers work too hard," "teachers" is the subject and "work too hard" is the predicate. It turns out that any sentence can be broken into phrases in such a way that each phrase corresponds either to the subject or the predicate of a proposition or to an entire proposition. For example, intuitively we can divide the simple sentence "Irene sells insurance" into two phrases, "Irene" and "sells insurance." The first phrase, which is called a *noun phrase* because it centers on a noun, specifies the subject of an underlying proposition. The second phrase, a *verb phrase,* gives the predicate of the proposition. For a more complex example, consider the sentence "Serious scholars read books." This sentence divides into two phrases, the noun phrase "serious scholars" and the verb phrase "read books." The noun phrase expresses an entire proposition, "scholars are serious"; the verb phrase expresses part (the predicate) of another proposition, "scholars read books" (see Figure 9-5). Again, sentence units correspond closely to proposition units, which provides a link between language and thought.

Thus, when listening to a sentence, people seem to first divide it into noun phrases, verb phrases, and the like, and then extract propositions from these phrases. There is a good deal of evidence for our dividing sentences into phrases and treating the phrases as units, with some of the evidence coming from memory experiments. In one study, subjects listened to sentences such as "The poor girl stole a warm coat." Immediately after each sentence was presented, subjects were given a probe word from the sentence and asked to say the word that came after it. People responded faster when the probe and the response words came from the same phrase ("poor" and "girl") than when they came from different phrases ("girl" and "stole"). Thus, each phrase acts as a unit in memory. When the probe and response are from the same phrase, only one unit needs to be retrieved (Wilkes & Kennedy, 1969).

Analyzing an incoming sentence into noun and verb phrases, and then dividing these phrases into smaller units like nouns, adjectives, and verbs, is called a **syntactic analysis** (*syntax* deals with the relations between words in phrases and sentences). Usually, in the course of understanding a sentence we perform such an analysis effortlessly and unconsciously. Sometimes, however, our syntactic analysis goes awry and we become

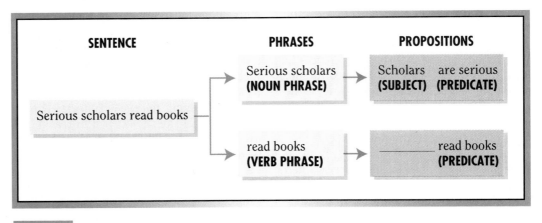

SENTENCE	PHRASES	PROPOSITIONS
Serious scholars read books	Serious scholars **(NOUN PHRASE)**	Scholars **(SUBJECT)** are serious **(PREDICATE)**
	read books **(VERB PHRASE)**	_____ read books **(PREDICATE)**

FIGURE 9-5

Phrases and Propositions *The first step in extracting the propositions from a complex sentence is to decompose the sentence into phrases. This decomposition is based on rules like "Any sentence can be divided into a noun phrase and a verb phrase."*

aware of the process. Consider the sentence, "The horse raced past the barn fell." Many people experience difficulty understanding this sentence. Why? Because on first reading, we assume that "The horse" is the noun phrase and "raced past the barn" the verb phrase, which leaves us with no place for the word "fell." To correctly understand the sentence, we have to repartition it so that the entire phrase "The horse raced past the barn" is the noun phrase, and "fell" is the verb phrase (that is, the sentence is just a shortened version of "The horse who was raced past the barn fell") (Garrett, 1990).

EFFECTS OF CONTEXT ON COMPREHENSION AND PRODUCTION

By way of summary, Figure 9-6 presents an amended version of our levels description of language. The figure suggests that producing a sentence is the inverse of understanding a sentence.

To understand a sentence, we hear phonemes, use them to construct the morphemes and phrases of a sentence, and finally extract the proposition from the sentence unit. We work from the bottom level up. To produce a sentence, we move in the opposite direction. We start with a propositional thought, translate it into the phrases and morphemes of a sentence, and finally translate these morphemes into phonemes.

Although this analysis describes some of what occurs in sentence understanding and production, it is oversimplified because it does not consider the *context* in which language processing occurs. Often the context makes what is about to be said predictable. After comprehending just a few words, we jump to conclusions about what we think the entire sentence means (the propositions behind it), and then use our guess about the propositions to help understand the rest of the sentence. In such cases, understanding proceeds from the highest level down as well as from the lowest level up (Adams & Collins, 1979).

Indeed, there are cases where language understanding is nearly impossible without some context. To illustrate, try reading the following paragraph:

The procedure is actually quite simple. First you arrange things into different groups. Of course, one pile may be

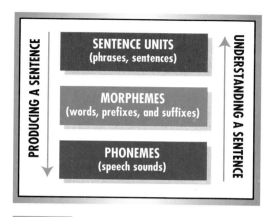

FIGURE 9-6

Levels of Understanding and Producing Sentences *In producing a sentence, we translate a propositional thought into the phrases and morphemes of a sentence and translate these morphemes into phonemes. In understanding a sentence, we go in the opposite direction—we use phonemes to construct the morphemes and phrases of a sentence and from these units extract the underlying propositions.*

sufficient, depending on how much there is to do. If you have to go somewhere else due to lack of facilities, that is the next step; otherwise you are pretty well set. It is important not to overdo things. That is, it is better to do too few things at once than too many. In the short run this may not seem important but complications can easily arise. A mistake can be expensive as well. At first the whole procedure will seem complicated. Soon, however, it will become just another facet of life. (After Bransford & Johnson, 1973)

In reading the paragraph, you no doubt had difficulty in trying to understand exactly what it was about. But given the context of "washing clothes," you can now use your knowledge about washing clothes to interpret all the cryptic parts of the passage. The "procedure" referred to in the first sentence is that of "washing clothes," the "things" referred to in the first sentence are "clothes," the "different groups" are "groups of clothing of different colors," and so on. Your understanding of the paragraph, if you reread it, should now be excellent.

Perhaps the most salient part of the context, though, is the other person (or persons) we are communicating with. In understanding a sentence, it is not enough to understand its phonemes, morphemes, and phrases; we must also understand the *speaker's intention* in uttering that particular sentence. For example, when someone at dinner asks you, "Can you pass the potatoes," usually you assume that their intention was not to find out if you are physically capable of lifting the potatoes, but rather to induce you to actually pass the potatoes. However, had your arm been in a sling, then given the identical question you might assume that the speaker's intention *was* to determine your physical capability. In both cases, the sentence (and proposition) is the same; what changes is the speaker's goal for uttering that sentence (Grice, 1975). There is abundant evidence that people extract the speaker's intention as part of the process of comprehension (Clark, 1984).

There are similar effects in the production of language. If someone asks you, "Where is the Empire State Building?" you will say different things depending on the physical context and the assumptions that you make about the questioner. If the question is asked of you in Detroit, for example, you might answer "In New York"; if the question is asked in Brooklyn you might say "Near Midtown Manhattan"; and if the question is asked in Manhattan, you might say "On 34th Street." In speaking, as in understanding, one must determine how the utterance fits the context.

DEVELOPMENT OF LANGUAGE

Our discussion of language should indicate the enormity of the task confronting children. They must master all levels of language—not only the proper speech sounds but also how these sounds are combined into thousands of words and how these words can be combined into sentences to express thoughts. It is a wonder that virtually all children in all cultures accomplish so much of this in a mere 4 to 5 years. We will first discuss what is acquired at each level of language and then consider how it is acquired—specifically what roles learning and innate factors play.

WHAT IS ACQUIRED?

Development occurs at all three levels of language. It starts at the level of phonemes, proceeds to the level of words and other morphemes, and then moves on to the level of sentence units, or syntax. In what follows, we adopt a chronological perspective, tracing the child's development in both understanding and producing language.

PHONEMES AND THEIR COMBINATION   Recall that adult listeners are good at discriminating different sounds that correspond to different phonemes in their language, but poor at discriminating different sounds that correspond to the same phoneme in their language. Remarkably, children come into the world able to discriminate different sounds that correspond to different phonemes in *any* language. What changes over the first year of life is that infants learn which phonemes are relevant to their language, and *lose* their ability to discriminate between sounds that correspond to the same phoneme in their language. (In essence, they lose the ability to make distinctions that will be of no use to them in understanding and producing their language.) These remarkable facts were determined by experiments in which infants were presented pairs of sounds in succession while they were sucking on pacifiers. Since infants suck more to a novel stimulus than to a familiar one, their rate of sucking can be used to tell whether they perceive two successive sounds as the same or different. Six-month-old infants increase their rate of sucking when the successive sounds correspond to different phonemes in *any* language, whereas 1-year-olds increase their rate of sucking only when the successive sounds correspond to different phonemes in their own language. Thus, a 6-month-old Japanese

Infant vocalization is an initial stage of language acquisition.

child can distinguish /l/ from /r/ but loses this ability by the end of the first year of life (Eimas, 1985).

While children learn which phonemes are relevant in their first year of life, it takes several years for them to learn how phonemes can be combined to form words. When children first begin to talk, they occasionally produce "impossible" words, like "dlumber" for "lumber." They do not yet know that in English /l/ cannot follow /d/ at the beginning of a word. By age 4, children have learned most of what they need to know about phoneme combinations.

WORDS AND CONCEPTS At about 1 year of age, children begin to speak. One-year-olds already have concepts for many things (including family members, household pets, food, toys, and body parts), and when they begin to speak, they are mapping these concepts onto words that adults use. The beginning vocabulary is roughly the same for all children. Children 1 to 2 years old talk mainly about people ("Dada," "Mama," "baby"), animals ("dog," "cat," "duck"), vehicles ("car," "truck," "boat"), toys ("ball," "block," "book"), food ("juice," "milk," "cookie"), body parts ("eye," "nose," "mouth"), and household implements ("hat," "sock," "spoon"). While these words name some of the young child's concepts, by no means do they name them all. Consequently, young children often have a gap between the concepts they want to communicate and the words they have at their disposal. To bridge this gap, children aged 1 to 2½ years old *overextend* their words to neighboring concepts. For example, a 2-year-old child might use the word "doggie" for cats and cows, as well as dogs (the child is not unsure of the word's meaning—if presented pictures of various animals and asked to pick the "doggie," the child makes the correct choice). At about the age of 2½ years, overextensions begin to disappear, presumably because the child's vocabulary begins to increase markedly, thereby eliminating many of the gaps (Clark, 1983; Rescorla, 1980).

Thereafter, vocabulary development virtually explodes. At 1½ years, a child might have a vocabulary of 25 words; at 6 years, the child's vocabulary is around 15,000 words. To achieve this incredible growth, children have to learn new words at the rate of almost 10 per day (Miller & Gildea, 1987; Templin, 1957). Children seem to be tuned to learning

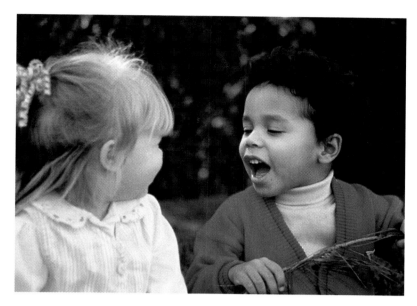

Children between 18 and 30 months of age learn to combine words in phrases and sentences.

new words. When they hear a word they do not know, they may assume it maps onto one of their concepts that is as yet unlabeled, and they use the context in which the word was spoken to find that concept (Markman, 1987; Clark, 1983).

FROM PRIMITIVE TO COMPLEX SENTENCES At 1½ to 2½ years, the acquisition of phrase and sentence units, or syntax, begins. Children start to combine single words into two-word utterances, such as "There cow" (where the underlying proposition is "There's the cow"), "Jimmy bike" (the proposition is "That's Jimmy's bike"), or "Towel bed" (the proposition is "The towel's on the bed"). There is a **telegraphic** quality about two-word speech. The child leaves out the grammatical words (such as "a," "an," "the," and "is"), as well as other grammatical morphemes (such as the suffixes "ing," "ed," and "s") and puts in only the words that carry the most important content. Despite their brevity, these utterances express most of the basic intentions of speakers, such as locating objects and describing events and actions.

Children progress rapidly from two-word utterances to more complex sentences that express propositions more precisely. Thus, "Daddy hat" may become "Daddy wear hat" and finally "Daddy is wearing a hat." Such expansions of the verb phrase appear to be the first complex constructions that occur in children's speech. The next step is the use of conjunctions like "and" and "so" to form compound sentences ("You play with the doll *and* I play with the blocks") and the use of grammatical morphemes like the past tense "ed." The sequence of language development is remarkably similar for all children.

LEARNING PROCESSES

Now that we have an idea about what children acquire in the language process, we can ask how they acquire it. Learning must play a role; that is why children who are brought up in an English-speaking household learn English and why children raised in a French-speaking household learn French. Innate factors must also play a role; that is why all children in a household learn language but none of the pets do (Gleitman, 1986). We discuss learning in this section and consider innate factors in the next section. In both discussions, we emphasize sentence units and syntax, for it is at this level of language that the important issues about language acquisition are most clearly illustrated.

IMITATION AND CONDITIONING   One possibility is that children learn language by *imitating* adults. While **imitation** plays some role in learning words (a parent points to a telephone, says "phone," and the child tries to repeat it), it cannot be the principal means by which children learn to produce and understand sentences. Young children constantly utter sentences they have never heard an adult say, such as "All gone milk." Even when children at the two-word stage try to imitate longer adult sentences (for example, "Mr. Miller will try"), they produce their usual telegraphic utterances ("Miller try"). In addition, the mistakes children make (for instance, "Daddy taked me") suggest that they are trying to apply rules, not simply trying to copy what they have heard adults say (Ervin-Tripp, 1964).

A second possibility is that children acquire language through **conditioning**. Adults may reward children when they produce a grammatical sentence and reprimand them when they make mistakes. For this to work, parents would have to respond to every detail in a child's speech. However, Brown, Cazden, and Bellugi (1969) found that parents do not pay attention to how the child says something as long as the statement is comprehensible. Also, attempts to correct a child (and hence to apply conditioning) are often futile.

CHILD:	Nobody don't like me.
MOTHER:	No, say, "nobody likes me."
CHILD:	Nobody don't like me.
MOTHER:	No, now listen carefully; say "nobody likes me."
CHILD:	Oh! Nobody don't LIKES me.

(McNeill, 1966, p. 49)

HYPOTHESIS TESTING   The problem with imitation and conditioning is that they focus on specific utterances (one can imitate or reinforce only something specific). However, children often learn something general, such as a rule; they seem to form a hypothesis about a rule of language, test it, and retain it if it works.

Consider the morpheme "ed." As a general rule in English, "ed" is added to the present tense of verbs to form the past tense (as in "cook–cooked"). Many common verbs, however, are irregular and do not follow this rule (like "go–went" and "break–broke"). Many of these irregular verbs express concepts that children use from the beginning. So at an early point, children use the past tense of some irregular verbs correctly (presumably because they learned them by imitation). Then they learn the past tense for some regular verbs and discover the hypothesis "add 'ed' to the present tense to form the past tense." This hypothesis leads them to add the "ed" ending to many verbs, including irregular ones. They say things such as "Annie goed home" and "Jackie breaked the cup," which they have never heard before. Eventually, they learn that some verbs are irregular and stop overgeneralizing their use of "ed."

How do children generate these hypotheses? There are a few *operating principles* that all children use as a guide to forming hypotheses. One is to pay attention to the ends of words. Another is to look for prefixes and suffixes that indicate a change in meaning. A child armed with these two principles is likely to hit the hypothesis that "ed" at the end of verbs signals the past tense, since "ed" is a word ending associated with a change in meaning. A third operating principle is to avoid exceptions, which explains why children initially generalize their "ed"-equals-past-tense hypothesis to irregular verbs. Some of these principles appear in Table 9-1 and they seem to hold for the 40 languages studied by Slobin (1985; 1971).

In recent years, there has been a challenge to the idea that learning a language involves learning rules. Some researchers have argued that what looks like an instance of learning a single rule may in fact be a case of learning numerous associations or *connections* (like those in the connectionist models we considered in Chapters 5 and 8). Consider again a child learning the past tense of verbs in English. Instead of learning a rule about adding "ed" to the present tense of a verb, perhaps children are learning associations between the past tense ending "ed" and various *phonetic properties* of verbs that can go with "ed." The phonetic properties of a verb include properties of the sounds that make up the verb, such as whether it contains an "alk" sound at the end. Thus, a child may learn (unconsciously) that verbs containing an "alk" sound at the end—such as "talk," "walk," and "stalk"—are likely to take "ed" as a past tense ending. This proposal has in fact been shown to account for some aspects of learning verb endings, including the finding that at some point in development children add the "ed" ending even to irregular verbs (Rumelhart & McClelland, 1987). However, other aspects of learning verb endings cannot be explained in terms of associations between sounds. For example, the word "break" and the word "brake" (meaning to a stop a car) are identical in sound, but the past tense of the former is "broke" whereas that of the latter is "braked." So a child must learn something in addition to sound connections. This additional knowledge seems best cast in terms of rules (for example, "If a verb is derived from a noun—as in the case of 'brake'—*always* add 'ed' to form the past tense"). Language learning thus seems to involve rules as well as associations (Pinker, 1991; Pinker & Prince, 1988).

INNATE FACTORS

As noted earlier, some of our knowledge about language is inborn, or innate. There are, however, controversial questions about the extent and nature of this innate knowledge. One question concerns its *richness*. If our innate knowledge is very rich, or detailed, then the process of language acquisition should be similar for different languages, even if the opportunities for learning differ among cultures. A second question about innate factors involves *critical periods*. As

---

1. Look for systematic changes in the form of words.

2. Look for grammatical markers that clearly indicate changes in meaning.

3. Avoid exceptions.

4. Pay attention to the ends of words.

5. Pay attention to the order of words, prefixes, and suffixes.

6. Avoid interruption or rearrangement of constituents (that is, sentence units).

TABLE 9-1

Operating Principles Used by Young Children
Children from many countries seem to follow these principles in learning to talk and to understand speech. (After Slobin, 1971)

---

noted in Chapter 5, a common feature of innate behavior is that it will be acquired more readily if the organism is exposed to the right cues during a critical time period. Are there such critical periods in language acquisition? A third question about the innate contribution to language concerns its possible *uniqueness:* Is the ability to learn a language system unique to the human species? We will consider these three questions in turn.

RICHNESS OF INNATE KNOWLEDGE All children, regardless of their culture and language, seem to go through the same sequence of language development. At age 1, the child speaks a few isolated words; at about age 2, the child speaks two- and three-word sentences; at age 3, sentences become more grammatical; and at age 4, the child sounds much like an adult. Because cultures differ markedly in the opportunities they provide for children to learn from an adult, the fact that this sequence is so consistent across cultures indicates that our innate knowledge about language is very rich.

Indeed, our innate knowledge of language seems to be so rich that children can go through the normal course of language acquisition even when there are no language users around them to serve as models or teachers. A group of researchers studied six deaf children of parents who could hear and who had decided not to have their children learn sign language. Before the children received any instruction in lip reading and vocalization, they began to use a system of gestures called **home sign.** Initially, their home sign was a kind of simple pantomime, but eventually it took on the properties of a language. For example, it was organized at both morphemic and syntactic levels, including individual signs and combinations of signs. In addition, these deaf children (who essentially created their own language) went through the same stages of development as normal hearing children. Thus, the deaf children initially gestured one sign at a time, then later put their pantomimes together into two- and three-concept "sentences." These striking results attest to the richness and detail of our innate knowledge (Feldman, Goldin-Meadow, & Gleitman, 1978).

CRITICAL PERIODS   Like other innate behaviors, language learning has some critical periods. This is particularly evident when it comes to acquiring the sound system of a new language—that is, learning new phonemes and their rules of combination. We have already noted that infants less than 1 year old can discriminate phonemes of any language, but lose this ability by the end of their first year. Hence, the first months of life are a critical period for honing in on the phonemes of one's native language. There also seems to be a critical period in acquiring the sound system of a second language. After a few years of learning a second language, young children are more likely than adults to speak it with-

out an accent, and better able to understand the language when it is spoken in noisy conditions (Snow, 1987; Lenneberg, 1967).

More recent work indicates there is also a critical period in learning syntax. The evidence comes from studies of deaf people who know American Sign Language (abbreviated ASL), which is a full-blown language and not a pantomime system. The studies of interest involved adults who had been using ASL for 30 years or more, but who varied in the age at which they learned the language. Though all subjects were born to hearing parents, some were native signers who were exposed to ASL from birth, others first learned ASL between ages 4 and 6 when they enrolled in a school for the deaf, and still others did not encounter ASL until after they were 12 (their hearing parents had been reluctant to let them learn a sign language rather than a spoken one). If there is a critical period for learning syntax, then the early learners should have shown a greater mastery of some aspects of syntax than the later learners, even 30 years after acquisition. This is exactly what the researchers found. Thus, with respect to understanding and producing words with multiple morphemes—like "untimely" which consists of the morphemes "un," "time," and "ly,"—native signers did better than those who learned ASL when entering school, who in turn did better than those who learned ASL after age 12. (Meier, 1991; Newport, 1990).

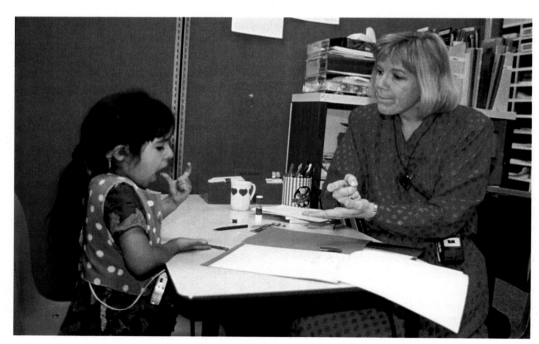

Research confirms a critical period in learning syntax. Deaf people who know American Sign Language prove to be better with the language if they learned it at an earlier age.

CAN ANOTHER SPECIES LEARN HUMAN LANGUAGE? Some experts believe that our innate capacity to learn language is unique to our species (Chomsky, 1972). They acknowledge that other species have communication systems but argue that these are qualitatively different from ours. Consider the communication system of the chimpanzee. This species' vocalizations and gestures are limited in number, and the *productivity* of its communication system is very low in comparison to human language, which permits the combination of a relatively small number of phonemes into thousands of words and the combination of these words into an unlimited number of sentences. Another difference is that human language is structured at several levels, whereas chimpanzee communications are not. In particular, in human language, a clear distinction exists between the level of words, or morphemes—at which the elements have meaning—and the level of sounds—at which the elements do not. There is no hint of such a *duality of structure* in chimpanzee communication, because every symbol carries meaning. Still another difference is that chimpanzees do not vary the *order* of their symbols to vary the meaning of their messages, while we do. For instance, for us, "Jonah ate the whale" means something quite different from "The whale ate Jonah"; there is no evidence for a comparable difference in chimpanzee communications.

The fact that chimpanzee communication is impoverished compared to our own does not *prove* that chimpanzees lack the capacity for a more productive system. Their system may be adequate for their needs. To determine if chimpanzees have the same innate capacity we do, we must see if they can learn our language.

In one of the best known studies of teaching our language to chimps, Gardner and Gardner (1972) taught a female chimpanzee named Washoe signs adapted from American Sign Language. Sign language was used because chimps lack the vocal equipment to pronounce human sounds. Training began when Washoe was about a year old and continued until she was 5. During this time, Washoe's caretakers communicated with her only by means of sign language. They first taught her signs by shaping procedures, waiting for her to make a gesture that resembled a sign, and then reinforcing her. Later Washoe learned signs simply by observing and imitating. By age 4, Washoe could produce 130 different signs and understand even more. She could also generalize a sign from one situation to another. For example, she first learned the sign for *more* in connection with *more tickling* and then generalized it to indicate *more milk*.

Other chimpanzees that were studied acquired comparable vocabularies. Some of these studies used methods of manual communication other than sign language. For example, Premack (1983; 1971) taught a chimpanzee named Sarah to use plastic symbols as words and to communicate by manipulating these symbols. In a series of similar studies, Patterson (1978) taught sign language to a gorilla named Koko, starting when Koko was 1 year old. By age 10, Koko had a vocabulary of more than 400 signs (Patterson & Linden, 1981).

Do these studies prove that apes can learn human language? There seems to be little doubt that the apes' signs are equivalent to our words and that the concepts behind some of these signs are equivalent to ours. But there are grave doubts about these studies showing that apes can learn to combine signs in the manner that humans combine words into a sentence. Thus, not only can people combine the words "snake," "Eve," "killed," and "the" into the sentence "The snake killed Eve," but we can also combine the same words in a different order to produce a sentence with a different meaning, "Eve killed the snake." Although the studies reviewed provide some evidence that apes can combine signs into a sequence resembling a sentence, little evidence exists to show that apes can alter the order of the signs to produce a different sentence (Brown, 1986; Slobin, 1979).

Even the evidence that apes can combine signs into a sentence has come under attack. In early work, researchers reported cases in which an ape produced what seemed to be a meaningful sequence of signs, such as "Gimme flower" and "Washoe sorry" (Gardner & Gardner, 1972). As data accumulated, it became apparent that, unlike human sentences, the utterances of an ape are often highly repetitive. Thus, "You me banana me banana you" is typical of the signing chimps but would be most odd for a human child. In the cases in which an ape utterance is more like a sentence, the ape may have simply been

BRAIN LOCALIZATION OF LANGUAGE

Given that innate factors play a large role in language acquisition, it is not surprising that regions of the human brain are specialized for language. In a Critical Discussion in Chapter 2 ("Language and the Brain"), we discussed how damage to certain regions of the left hemisphere results in *aphasia*, or language deficits. There we emphasized the relationship between the site of the brain damage and whether the resulting deficit was primarily one of production or comprehension. In the current discussion, we focus on the relation between the site of the damage and whether the deficit involves syntactic or conceptual knowledge.

Recall from Chapter 2 that there are two regions of the left hemisphere of the cortex that are critical for language: *Broca's area*, which lies in the frontal lobes, and *Wernicke's area*, which lies in the temporal region (see Figure 2-9). Damage to either of these areas leads to specific kinds of aphasia.

The disrupted language of a patient with *Broca's aphasia* is illustrated by the following interview in which "E" designates the interviewer and "P," the patient:

E: Were you in the Coast Guard?
P: No, er, yes, yes . . . ship . . . Massachu . . . chusetts . . . Coast Guard . . . years. [Raises hands twice with fingers indicating "19"]
E: Oh, you were in the Coast Guard for 19 years.

P: Oh . . . boy . . . right . . . right.
E: Why are you in the hospital?
P: [Points to paralyzed arm] Arm no good. [Points to mouth] Speech . . . can't say . . . talk, you see.
E: What happened to make you lose your speech?
P: Head, fall, Jesus Christ, me no good, str, str . . . oh Jesus . . . stroke.
E: Could you tell me what you've been doing in the hospital?
P: Yes sure. Me go, er, uh, P. T. nine o'cot, speech . . . two times . . . read . . . wr . . . ripe, er, rike, er, write . . . practice . . . get-ting better.

(Gardner, 1975, p. 61)

The speech is very disfluent. Even in simple sentences, pauses and hesitations are plentiful. This is in contrast to the fluent speech of a patient with *Wernicke's aphasia:*

Boy, I'm sweating, I'm awful nervous, you know, once in a while I get caught up. I can't mention the tarripoi, a month ago, quite a little, I've done a lot well, I impose a lot, while, on the other hand, you know what I mean, I have to run around, look it over, trebin and all that sort of stuff. (Gardner, 1975, p. 68)

In addition to fluency, there are other marked differences between Broca's and Wernicke's aphasias. The speech of a Broca's aphasic consists mainly of content words. It contains few grammatical morphemes and

complex sentences and, in general, has a telegraphic quality that is reminiscent of the two-word stage of language acquisition. In contrast, the language of a Wernicke's aphasic preserves syntax but is remarkably devoid of content. There are clear problems in finding the right noun, and occasionally words are invented for the occasion (as in the use of "tarripoi" and "trebin"). These observations suggest that Broca's aphasia involves a disruption at the syntactic stage, while Wernicke's aphasia involves a disruption at the level of words and concepts.

These characterizations of the two aphasias are supported by experiments. In a study that tested for a syntactic deficit, subjects had to listen to a sentence on each trial and show that they understood it by selecting a picture (from a set) that the sentence described. Some sentences could be understood without using much syntactic knowledge. For example, given "The bicycle the boy is holding is broken," one can figure out that it is the bicycle that is broken and not the boy, solely from one's knowledge of the concepts involved. Understanding other sentences requires extensive syntactic analysis. In "The lion that the tiger is chasing is fat," one must rely on syntax (word order) to determine that it is the lion who is fat and not the tiger. On those sentences that did not require much syntactic analysis, Broca's aphasics did almost as well as normals, scoring

---

imitating the sequence of signs made by its human teacher. Thus, some of Washoe's most sentencelike utterances occurred when she was answering a question; for example, the teacher signed "Washoe eat?" and then Washoe signed "Washoe eat time." Here, Washoe's combination of signs may have been a partial imitation of her teacher's combination, which is not how human children learn to combine words (Terrace et al., 1979).

The evidence considered thus far supports the conclusion that, although apes can develop a humanlike vocabulary, they cannot learn to combine their signs in the systematic way we do. However, a relatively recent study seems to challenge this conclusion (Greenfield & Savage-Rumbaugh, 1990). The researchers worked with a new kind of subject, a pygmy chimpanzee, whose behavior is thought to be more like that of humans than the behavior close to 90 percent correct. But with sentences that required extensive analysis, Broca's aphasics fell to the level of guessing (for example, given the sentence about the lion and tiger, they were as likely to select the picture with a fat tiger as the one with the fat lion). In contrast, the performance of Wernicke's aphasics did not depend on the syntactic demands of the sentence. Thus, Broca's aphasia, but not Wernicke's, seems to be partly a disruption of syntax (Caramazza & Zurif, 1976). The disruption is not total, though, in that Broca's aphasics are capable of handling certain kinds of syntactic analysis (Grodzinski, 1984).

Other experiments have tested for a conceptual deficit in Wernicke's aphasia. In one study, subjects were presented three words at a time and were asked to select the two that were most similar in meaning. The words included animal terms, such as "dog" and "crocodile," as well as human terms, such as "mother" and "knight." Normal subjects used the distinction between humans and animals as the major basis for their selections; given "dog," "crocodile," and "knight," for example, they selected the first two. Wernicke's patients, however, ignored this basic distinction. Although Broca's aphasics showed some differences from normals, their selections at least respected the human–animal distinction. A conceptual deficit is thus more pronounced in Wernicke's

aphasics than in Broca's aphasics (Zurif, Caramazza, Myerson, & Galvin, 1974).

Although Broca's and Wernicke's aphasias are the most studied, numerous other kinds of aphasias exist (Benson, Heilman, & Vallenstein, 1985). One of these is referred to as *conduction aphasia*. In this condition, the aphasic seems relatively normal in tests of both syntactic and conceptual abilities, but manifests a severe problem when asked to repeat a spoken sentence. A neurological explanation of this curious disorder is that while the brain structures mediating basic aspects of comprehension and production are intact, the neural connections between these structures are damaged. Hence, the patient can understand what is said because Wernicke's area is intact, and can produce fluent speech because Broca's area is intact, but cannot transmit what was understood to the speech center because the connecting links between the areas are damaged (Geschwind, 1972).

All of the above presupposes the idea that each kind of aphasia is caused by damage to a specific area of the brain. This idea may be too simple: The particular region mediating a particular linguistic function may vary from person to person. The best evidence for such individual differences comes from findings of neurosurgeons who are preparing to operate on patients with incurable

epilepsy. The neurosurgeon needs to remove some brain tissue but first has to be sure that this tissue is not mediating some critical function like language. Accordingly, prior to surgery and while the patient is awake, the neurosurgeon delivers small electric charges to the area in question and observes their effects on the patient's ability to name things. If electrical stimulation disrupts the patient's naming, the neurosurgeon knows to avoid this location in the operation. These locations are of great interest to students of language. Within a single patient, these language locations seem to be highly localized. A language location might be less than one centimeter in all directions from locations where electrical stimulations do not disrupt language. But, and this is the critical point, different brain locations have to be stimulated to disrupt naming in different patients. For example, one patient's naming may be disrupted by electrical stimulation to locations in the front of the brain but not by stimulation in the back of the brain, whereas another patient might show a different pattern (Ojemann et al., 1989). If different areas of the brain mediate language in different people, then presumably the areas associated with aphasias will also vary among people.

of the more widely studied common chimpanzee. The subject, a 7-year-old named Kanzi, communicated by manipulating symbols that stand for words. Unlike the case in previous studies, Kanzi learned to manipulate the symbols in a relatively natural way, for example, by listening to his caretakers as they uttered English words while pointing to the symbols. Most importantly, after a few years of language training, Kanzi demon-

strated some ability to vary word order to communicate changes in meaning. For example, if Kanzi were going to bite his half-sister Mulika he would signal "bite Mulika"; but if his sister bit him, he would sign "Mulika bite." Kanzi thus seems to have some syntactic knowledge, roughly that of a 2-year-old human.

These results are tantalizing, but they need to be interpreted with caution. For one

Panzee the chimp uses a communication keyboard. Chimpanzees may learn a kind of sign language, as this chimp makes the sign for toothbrush.

thing, so far Kanzi is among the few chimpanzees who have shown any syntactic ability; hence, there's a question of how general the results are. Another matter is that, although Kanzi may have the linguistic ability of a 2-year-old, it took him substantially longer to get to that point than it does a human; also, we do not yet know if Kanzi, or any other chimpanzee, can get much beyond that point. But perhaps the main reason to be skeptical about any ape developing comparable linguistic abilities to a human has been voiced by Chomsky (1991):

> If an animal had a capacity as biologically advantageous as language but somehow hadn't used it until now, it would be an evolutionary miracle, like finding an island of humans who could be taught to fly.

IMAGINAL THOUGHT

We mentioned at the beginning of the chapter that, in addition to propositional thought, we can also think in an imaginal mode, particularly in terms of visual images. Such visual thinking is the concern of the present section.

Many of us feel that we do some of our thinking visually. Often it seems that we retrieve past perceptions, or parts of them, and then operate on them in the way we would a real percept. To appreciate this point, try to answer the following three questions:

1. What shape are a German shepherd's ears?

2. What new letter is formed when an uppercase N is rotated 90 degrees?

3. How many windows are there in your parents' living room?

When answering the first question, most people report that they form a visual image of a German shepherd's head and "look" at the ears to determine their shape. When answering the second question, people report first forming an image of a capital *N,* then mentally "rotating" it 90 degrees and "looking" at it to determine its identity. And when answering the third question, people report imagining the room and then "scanning" the image while counting the windows (Kosslyn, 1983; Shepard & Cooper, 1982).

The above examples rest on subjective impressions, but they and other evidence suggest that imagery involves the same representations and processes that are used in perception (Finke, 1985). Our images of objects and places have visual detail: We see the German shepherd, the *N,* or our parents' living room in our "mind's eye." Moreover, the mental operations that we perform on these images seem to be analogous to the operations that we carry out on real visual objects: We scan the image of our parents' room in much the same way we would scan a real room, and we rotate our image of the *N* the way we would rotate the real object.

NEURAL BASIS OF IMAGERY

Perhaps the most persuasive evidence for imagery being like perception would be demonstrations that the two are mediated by the same brain structures. In recent years, a substantial amount of evidence of this sort has accumulated.

Some of the evidence comes from studies of brain-damaged patients, and shows that any problem the patient has in visual perception is typically accompanied by a parallel problem in visual imagery (for example, Farah et al., 1988). A particularly striking example of this arises with patients who have suffered damage in the parietal lobe of the right hemisphere, and as a result develop *visual neglect* of the left-side of the visual field. Although not blind, these patients ignore everything on the left side of their visual fields. A male patient, for example, may neglect to shave the left side of his face. This visual neglect extends to imagery, as established by the Italian neurologist Bisiach (for example, Bisiach & Luzzatti, 1978). Bisiach asked his patients with visual neglect to imagine a familiar square in their native Milan as it looks while standing in the square facing the church. The patients reported most objects on their right, but few on their left. When asked to imagine the scene from the opposite perspective, while standing in front of the church and looking out into the square, the patients neglected the objects they had previously reported (such objects were now on the left of the image). Thus, these patients manifested the same kind of neglect in imagery as they did in perception, which suggests that the damaged brain structures normally mediate imagery as well as perception.

Some recent studies use brain-scanning methods to demonstrate that, in normal subjects, the parts of the brain involved in perception are also involved in imagery. In one experiment, subjects performed both a mental arithmetic task ("Start at 50, and count down, subtracting by 3s") and a visual imagery task ("Visualize a walk through your neighborhood, making alternating right and left turns starting at your door"). While a subject was doing each task, the amount of blood flow in various areas of his or her cortex was measured. There was more blood flow in the visual cortex when subjects engaged in the imagery task than the mental arithmetic one. Moreover, the pattern of blood flow found during the imagery task was like that normally found in perceptual tasks (Roland & Friberg, 1985).

A recent PET experiment by Kosslyn et al. (1993) provides a striking comparison of the brain structures involved in perception and imagery. While having their brains scanned, subjects performed two different tasks, a *perception* task and an *imagery* task. In the *perception* task, first a block capital letter was presented on a background grid, and then an *X* was presented in one of the grid cells; the subject's task was to decide as quickly as possible whether or not the *X* fell on part of the block letter (see Figure 9-7). In the *imagery* task, the background grid was again presented, but without a block capital letter. Under the grid was a lowercase letter, and subjects had been previously instructed to generate an image of the capital version of the lowercase letter and to project it onto the grid. Then an *X* was presented in one of the grid cells, and subjects had to determine whether or not the *X* fell on part of the *imagined* block letter (see Figure 9-7). Unsurprisingly, the perception task resulted in heightened neural activity in parts of the visual cortex. But so did the imagery task. Indeed, the imagery task resulted in increased activity in those brain structures that are known to be among the first regions of the cortex to receive visual information. Thus imagery

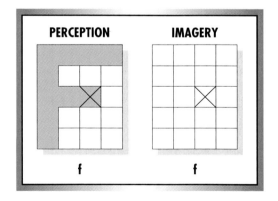

FIGURE 9-7

Imagery and Perception   *Tasks used to determine whether visual imagery involves the same brain structures as visual perception. In the* perception task, *subjects must decide whether or not the X fell on part of the block letter. In the* imagery task, *subjects generate an image of the block letter, and then decide whether or not the X fell on part of the (image of) the block letter. The subject knows which letter to image because the lowercase version of it is presented below the grid (the lowercase version is also presented in the perception task, just to keep things comparable).* (After Kosslyn et al. 1993)

FIGURE 9-8

Study of Mental Rotation
*Shown are examples of
the letters presented to
subjects in studies of
mental rotation. On each
presentation, subjects
had to decide whether
the letter was normal or
backward. Numbers indi-
cate deviation from the
vertical in degrees.* (After
Cooper & Shepard, 1973)

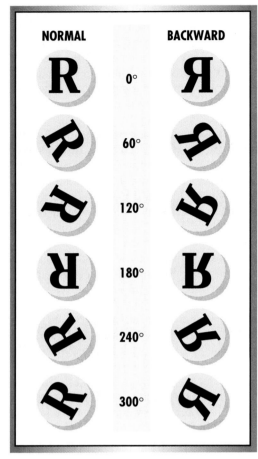

is like perception from the early stages of
cortical processing. Furthermore, when the
neural activations from the two tasks were directly compared, there was *more* activation

FIGURE 9-9

Decision Times in Mental
Rotation Study
*The time taken to decide
whether a letter had nor-
mal or reversed orienta-
tion was greatest when
the rotation was 180° so
that the letter was upside
down.* (After Cooper &
Shepard, 1973)

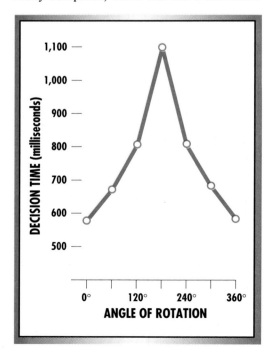

in the imagery than the perception task, presumably reflecting the fact that the imagery
task required more "perceptual work" than
the perception task. These results leave little
doubt that imagery and perception are mediated by the same neural mechanisms.

IMAGINAL OPERATIONS

We have noted that the mental operations
performed on images seem to be analogous to
those we carry out on real visual objects. Numerous experiments provide objective evidence for these subjective impressions.

One operation that has been studied intensively is mental rotation. In a classic experiment, subjects saw the capital letter R on
each trial. The letter was presented either
normally (R) or backward (Я) and in its usual
vertical orientation or rotated various degrees (see Figure 9-8). The subjects had to
decide if the letter was normal or backward.
The more the letter had been rotated from its
vertical orientation, the longer it took the
subjects to make the decision (see Figure
9-9). This finding suggests that subjects
made their decisions by mentally rotating the
image of the letter until it was vertical and
then checking whether it was normal or
backward.

Another operation that is similar in imagery and perception is that of scanning an
object or array. In an experiment on scanning
an image, subjects first studied the map of a
fictional island, which contained seven critical locations. The map was removed, and subjects were asked to form an image of it and
fixate on a particular location (for example,
the tree in the southern part of the island—
see Figure 9-10). Then the experimenter
named another location (for example, the
tree at the northern tip of the island). Starting at the fixated location, the subjects were
to scan their images until they found the
named location and were to push a button on
"arrival" there. The greater the distance between the fixated location and the named
one, the longer the subjects took to respond.
This suggests subjects were scanning their
images in much the same way they scan real
objects.

Another commonality between imaginal
and perceptual processing is that both are
limited by *grain size*. On a television screen,
for instance, the grain of the picture tube de-

termines how small the details of a picture can be and still remain perceptible. While there is no actual screen in the brain, we can think of our images as occurring in a *mental medium,* the grain of which limits the amount of detail we can detect in an image. If this grain size is fixed, then smaller images should be more difficult to inspect than larger ones. A good deal of evidence supports this claim. In one experiment, subjects first formed an image of a familiar animal— say, a cat. Then they were asked to decide whether or not the imaged object had a particular property. Subjects made decisions faster for larger properties, such as the head, than for smaller ones, such as the claws. In another study, subjects were asked to image an animal at different relative sizes—small, medium, or large. Subjects were then asked to decide whether their images had a particular property. Their decisions were faster for larger images than smaller ones. Thus, in imagery as in perception, the larger the image, the more readily we can see the details of an object (Kosslyn, 1980).

VISUAL CREATIVITY

There are innumerable stories about scientists and artists producing their most creative work through visual thinking (Shepard & Cooper, 1982). Although not solid evidence, these stories are among the best indicators that we have of the power of visual thinking. It is surprising that visual thinking appears to be quite effective in highly abstract areas like mathematics and physics. Albert Einstein, for example, said he rarely thought in words; rather, he worked out his ideas in terms of "more or less clear images which can be 'voluntarily' reproduced and combined." Thus Einstein claimed that he had his initial insight into the theory of relativity when he thought about what he "saw" when he imagined that he was chasing after and matching the speed of a beam of light. Perhaps the most celebrated example is in chemistry. Friedrich Kekule von Stradonitz was trying to determine the molecular structure of benzene (which turned out to have a ring structure). One night he dreamed that a writhing, snakelike figure suddenly twisted into a closed loop, biting its own tail. The structure of the snake proved to be the structure of benzene. A dream image had provided the solution to a

FIGURE 9-10

Scanning Mental Images *The subject scans the image of the island from south to north, looking for the named location. It appears as though the subject's mental image is like a real map and that it takes longer to scan across the mental image if the distance to be scanned is greater.* (After Kosslyn, Ball, & Reiser, 1978)

major scientific problem. Visual images can also be a creative force for writers. Samuel Coleridge's famous poem "Kubla Khan" supposedly came to him in its entirety as a prolonged visual image.

THOUGHT IN ACTION: PROBLEM SOLVING

For many people, solving a problem epitomizes thinking itself. In problem solving, we are striving for a goal but have no ready means of obtaining it. We must break the goal into subgoals and perhaps divide these subgoals further into smaller subgoals, until we reach a level that we have the means to obtain (Anderson, 1990).

We can illustrate these points with a simple problem. Suppose you need to figure out the combination of an unfamiliar lock. You know only that the combination has four numbers and that whenever you come across a correct number, you will hear a click. Your overall goal is to find the combination. Rather than trying four numbers at random, most people decompose the overall goal into four subgoals, each corresponding to finding one of the four numbers in the combination. Your first subgoal is to find the first number, and you have a procedure for accomplishing this—namely, turning the lock slowly while listening for a click. Your second subgoal is to find the second number, and you can use the same procedure, and so on for the remaining subgoals.

The strategies that people use to decompose goals into subgoals is a major issue in the study of problem solving. Another issue is how people mentally represent a problem, because this also affects how readily we can solve the problem. The following discussion considers both of these issues.

PROBLEM-SOLVING STRATEGIES

Much of what we know about strategies for decomposing goals derives from the research of Newell and Simon (see, for example, Newell & Simon, 1972). Typically, the researchers ask subjects to think aloud while trying to solve a difficult problem, and they analyze the subjects' verbal responses for clues to the underlying strategy. A number of general-purpose strategies have been identified.

One strategy is to reduce the difference between our *current state* in a problem situation and our *goal state,* wherein a solution is obtained. Consider again the combination lock problem. Initially, our current state includes no knowledge of any of the numbers, while our goal state includes knowledge of all four numbers. We therefore set up the subgoal of reducing the difference between these two states; determining the first number accomplishes this subgoal. Our current state now includes knowledge of the first number. There is still a difference between our current

state and our goal state, and we can reduce it by determining the second number, and so on. Thus, the critical idea behind **difference reduction** is that we set up subgoals that, when obtained, put us in a state that is closer to our goal.

A similiar but more sophisticated strategy is **means-ends analysis.** Here, we compare our current state to the goal state in order to find the most important difference between them; eliminating this difference becomes our main subgoal. We then search for a means or a procedure to achieve this subgoal. If we find such a procedure but discover that something in our current state prevents us from applying it, we introduce a new subgoal of eliminating this obstacle. Many common-sense problem-solving situations involve this strategy. Here is an example:

> I want to take my son to nursery school. What's the [most important] difference between what I have and what I want? One of distance. What [procedure] changes distance? My automobile. My automobile won't work. What is needed to make it work? A new battery. What has new batteries? An auto repair shop. (After Newell & Simon, 1972, as cited in Anderson, 1990, p. 232)

Means-ends analysis is more sophisticated than difference reduction because it allows us to take action even if it results in a temporary decrease in similarity between our current state and the goal state. In the above example, the auto repair shop may be in the opposite direction from the nursery school. Going to the shop thus temporarily increases the distance from the goal, yet this step is essential for solving the problem.

Another strategy is to work backward from the goal. This is particularly useful in solving mathematical problems, such as that illustrated in Figure 9-11. The problem is this: given that ABCD is a rectangle, prove that AD and BC are the same length. In **working backward,** one might proceed as follows:

> What could prove that AD and BC are the same length? I could prove this if I could prove that the triangles ACD and BDC are congruent. I can prove that ACD and BDC are congruent if I could prove that two sides and an included angle are equal. (After Anderson, 1990, p. 238)

We reason from the goal to a subgoal (proving the triangles congruent), from that subgoal to another subgoal (proving the sides and

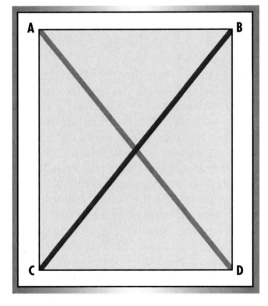

FIGURE 9-11

An Illustrative Geometry Problem   *Given that ABCD is a rectangle, prove that the line segments AD and BC are the same length.*

angle equal), and so on, until we reach a sub-goal that we have a ready means of obtaining.

The three strategies we have considered—difference reduction, means-ends analysis, and working backward—are extremely general, and can be applied to virtually any problem. These strategies, which are often referred to as **weak methods,** do not rest on any specific knowledge and may even be innate. People may especially rely on these weak methods when they are first learning about an area and are working on problems with unfamiliar content. We will soon see that when people gain expertise in an area they develop more powerful domain-specific procedures (and representations), which come to dominate the weak methods (Anderson, 1987).

REPRESENTING THE PROBLEM

Being able to solve a problem depends not only on our strategy for decomposing it but also on how we represent it. Sometimes a propositional representation works best; at other times, a visual representation or image is more effective. To illustrate, consider the following problem:

> One morning, exactly at sunrise, a monk began to climb a mountain. A narrow path, a foot or two wide, spiraled around the mountain to a temple at the summit. The monk ascended at varying rates, stopping many times along the way to rest. He reached the temple shortly before sunset. After several days at the temple, he began his journey back along the same path, starting at sunrise and again walking at variable speeds with many pauses along the way. His average speed descending was, of course, greater than his average climbing speed. Prove that there exists a particular spot along the path that the monk will occupy on both trips at precisely the same time of day. (Adams, 1974, p. 4)

In trying to solve this problem, many people start with a propositional representation. They may even try to write out a set of equations and soon confuse themselves. The problem is far easier to solve when it is represented visually. All you need do is visualize the upward journey of the monk superimposed on the downward journey. Imagine one monk starting at the bottom and the other at the top. No matter what their speed, at some time and at some point along the path the two monks will meet. Thus, there must be a spot along the path the monk occupied on both trips at precisely the same time of day. (Note that the problem did not ask you *where* the spot was.)

Some problems can be readily solved by manipulating either propositions or images. We can illustrate with the following simple problem: "Ed runs faster than David but slower than Dan; who's the slowest of the three men?" To solve this problem in terms of propositions, note that we can represent the first part of the problem as a proposition that has "David" as subject and "is slower than Ed" as predicate. We can represent the second part of the problem as a proposition with "Ed" as subject and "is slower than Dan" as predicate. We can then deduce that David is slower than Dan, which makes David the slowest. To solve the problem by imagery, we might, for example, imagine the three men's speeds as points on a line, like this:

Then we can simply "read" the answer to the question directly from the image. Apparently, some people prefer to represent such problems as propositions, while others tend to represent them visually (Johnson-Laird, 1985).

Learning aids help students visualize a math problem.

In addition to the issue of propositions versus images, there are questions about *what* gets represented. Often, we have difficulty with a problem because we fail to include something critical in our representation or because we include something in our representation that is *not* an important part of the problem. We can illustrate with an experiment. One group of subjects was posed the problem of supporting a candle on a door, given only the materials depicted in Figure 9-12. The solution was to tack the box to the door and use the box as a platform for the candle. Most subjects had difficulty with the problem, presumably because they represented the box as a container, not as a platform. Another group of subjects was given the identical problem, except that the contents of the box were removed. These subjects had more success in solving the problem, presumably because they were less likely to include the box's container property in their representation and more likely to include its supporter property. Studies like this and others covered in this section give some inkling of why many experts believe that getting a useful representation of a problem is half the battle in solving the problem.

EXPERTS VERSUS NOVICES

In a given content area (physics, geography, or chess, for instance), experts solve problems qualitatively differently than novices.

These differences are due to differences in the representations and strategies that experts and novices use. Experts have many more specific representations stored in memory that they can bring to bear on a problem. A master chess player, for example, can look for 5 seconds at a complex board configuration of over 20 pieces and reproduce it perfectly; a novice in this situation can reproduce only the usual 7 ± 2 items (see Chapter 8). Experts can accomplish this memory feat because, through years of practice, they have developed representations of many possible board configurations; these representations permit them to encode a complex configuration in just a few chunks. Further, these representations are presumably what underlies their superior chess game. A master may have stored as many as 50,000 configurations and has learned what to do when each one arises. Thus, master chess players can essentially "see" possible moves; they do not have to think them out the way novices do (Chase & Simon, 1973; Simon & Gilmartin, 1973).

Even when confronted with a novel problem, experts represent it differently than novices. This point is nicely illustrated in studies of problem solving in physics. An expert (say, a physics professor) represents a problem in terms of the physical principle that is needed for solution: For example, "this is one of those every-action-has-an-equal-and-opposite-reaction problems." In contrast, a novice (say, a student taking a first course in physics) tends to represent the same problem in terms of its surface features: For example, "this is one of those inclined-plane problems" (Chi, Glaser, & Rees, 1982).

Experts and novices also differ in the strategies they employ. In studies of physics problem solving, experts generally try to formulate a plan for attacking the problem before generating equations, whereas novices typically start writing equations with no general plan in mind (Larkin, McDermott, Simon, & Simon, 1980). Another difference is that experts tend to reason from the givens of a problem toward a solution, while novices tend to work in the reverse direction (the working-backward strategy). This difference in the direction of reasoning has also been obtained in studies of how physicians solve problems. More expert physicians tend to reason in a forward direction—from symptom to possible disease—while the less expert tend

FIGURE 9-12

Materials for Candle Problem   *Given the materials depicted, how can you support a candle on a door? The solution is shown on page 328.* (After Glucksberg & Weisberg, 1966)

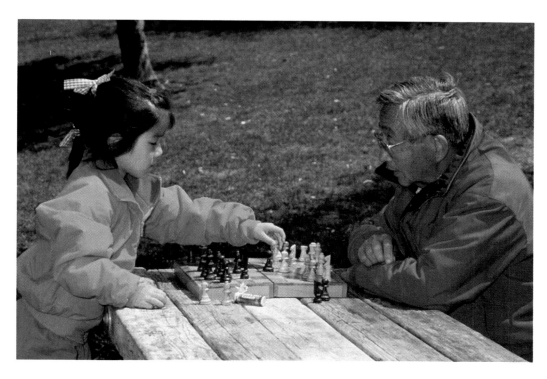

A novice player solves chess problems differently than an expert.

to reason in a backward direction—from possible disease to symptom (Patel & Groen, 1986).

The characteristics of expertise we have just discussed—a multitude of representations, representations based on principles, planning before acting, and working-forward—make up some of the domain-specific procedures that come to dominate the weak methods of problem solving discussed earlier.

COMPUTER SIMULATION

To study how people solve problems, researchers often use the method of **computer simulation**. After having people think aloud while solving a complex problem, researchers use their verbal reports as a guide in programming a computer to solve the problem. Then the output of the computer can be compared to aspects of people's performance on the problem—say, the sequence of moves—to see if they match. If they match, the computer program offers a theory of some aspects of problem solving. Computer simulation has played a major role in the development of the weak methods of problem solving as well as of expert procedures.

Why use computers in this way to learn about people? Perhaps the most interesting answer is Simon's claim: "The reason human beings can think is because they are able to carry out with neurons the simple kinds of processes that computers do with tubes or chips" (1985, p. 3). These simple processes include reading, outputting, storing, and comparing symbols; we do one thing if the symbols match and another if they differ. To the extent that we can closely simulate human problem solving on a computer, which uses just these simple processes, we have support for Simon's claim.

Consider what is involved in trying to write a computer program that simulates the way many of us solve simple algebraic equations. When confronted with the equation $3X + 4 = X + 10$, you might have learned to reason as follows:

The solution of the equation looks like an X followed by an = sign followed by a number—not any number, it has to be one that will fit the equation if I substitute it back in. If I start out with something that has a number on the left side where I don't want it, then I better get rid of it. So given $3X + 4 = X + 10$, I subtract the 4 (I know I have to subtract it from both sides). Then I have a new equation $3X = X + 6$. But I don't want an X on the right side of the equation. So I subtract it and now have $2X = 6$. Now I don't want a 2X, but instead just a plain X on the left side of the equation, so I divide by 2. Then I have $X = 3$. (After Simon, 1985, p. 6)

The solution to the candle problem.

3. If there is a number in front of the X on the left side of the equation, then divide both sides of the equation by it.

4. If you arrive at an equation that looks like "X = Number," quit and check your answer.

Although probably you do not articulate these rules, they may underlie your ability to solve algebraic equations. These rules can readily be translated into a computer program. A program is simply a detailed set of instructions (written in a language designed for a computer) that specifies every step the machine must take. Our rules can be treated as such instructions. Thus, simulation requires that we first be precise about the knowledge involved and then translate it into the language of a computer.

Some critics have challenged the basic analogy between computers and people: Computers, they say, can do only what they have been programmed to do. However, it is quite possible that humans can also do only what heredity and experience have "programmed" them to do. The analogy between computers and human minds remains appealing because these two kinds of entities are the most complex information-processing systems that we know of. Furthermore, as computer scientists continue to design computers to function more like people, the mind-computer analogy will grow even stronger.

The above reasoning can be captured by four rules:

1. If there is a number on the left side of the equation, then subtract it from both sides.

2. If there is an X or a multiple of X on the right side of the equation, then subtract it from both sides.

BIOLOGICAL-PSYCHOLOGICAL PERSPECTIVES

As usual, we close by noting the interplay between biological and psychological approaches to the topics of interest. Although most of the research on thought and language is at the psychological level (and adopts a cognitive perspective), we discussed a few cases in which the biological approach has made significant inroads. One case concerned concept learning. Two modes of concept learning that have been treated as different at the psychological level have now been shown to invoke different brain mechanisms. This case shows a pattern that we encountered numerous times in earlier chapters: A distinction first made at the psychological level is subsequently shown to hold at the biological level as well. Another instance of biological-psychological interplay concerned the neural basis of visual imagery. Unlike the usual situations in which we look to biological findings to document that two processes are different, in the case of imagery we used biological findings to argue that imagery and perception are partly the *same* process. In other respects, this research follows the usual pattern in that the claim of interest— that imagery and perception involve the same mechanisms—was first advanced at the psychological level. In this case, however, the recent biological findings are regarded as substantially more decisive than the earlier psychological ones (Kosslyn, 1994). Indeed, it is difficult to envision stronger evidence for imagery and perception being the same than the fact that they activate identical brain structures.

Still, there were fewer biological advances discussed in this chapter than in most previous ones. Perhaps this is due to thought processes being implemented by neural activity that is so widely dispersed throughout the brain that no meaningful localization is possible. Alternatively, the current lack of knowledge about the biological basis of thought may reflect that only recently have researchers found the tools and methods to attack this issue. The next two decades of research should tell us a great deal about whether the components of thought will admit of meaningful biological reduction.

CHAPTER SUMMARY

1. Thought occurs in different modes, including *propositional, imaginal,* and *motoric.* The basic component of a proposition is a *concept,* the set of properties that we associate with a class. Concepts provide us *cognitive economy,* by allowing us to code many different objects as instances of the same concept, and also permit us to *predict information* that is not readily perceptible.

2. A concept includes both a *prototype* (properties that describe the best examples) and a *core* (properties that are most essential for being a member of the concept). Core properties play a major role in *well-defined* concepts, such as "bachelor"; prototype properties dominate in *fuzzy* concepts such as "bird." Most natural concepts are *fuzzy.* Concepts are sometimes organized into hierarchies; in such cases, one level of the hierarchy is the *basic* or preferred level for categorization.

3. Children often learn the prototype of a concept by an *exemplar strategy.* With this technique, a novel item is classified as an instance of a concept if it is sufficiently similar to a known exemplar of the concept. As children grow older, they use *hypothesis testing* as another strategy for learning concepts. In addition to these bottom-up strategies, people use *top-down* strategies of concept learning in which they employ their prior knowledge along with the known instances to determine the properties of a concept. The two bottom-up strategies seem to be mediated by different structures in the brain, with structures in the *medial temporal lobe* being critical for the exemplar strategy, and structures in the *frontal lobes* being involved in hypothesis testing.

4. In reasoning, we organize our propositions into an argument. Some arguments are *deductively valid:* it is impossible that the conclusion of the argument is false if its premises are true. When evaluating a deductive argument, we sometimes try to prove that the conclusion follows from the premises by using logical rules. Other times, however, we use *heuristics*—rules of thumb—that operate on the content of propositions rather than on their logical form.

5. Some arguments are *inductively strong:* It is improbable that the conclusion is false if the premises are true. In generating and evaluating such arguments, we often ignore some of the principles of probability theory and rely instead on heuristics that focus on similarity or causality. For example, we may estimate the probability that a person belongs to a category by determining the person's similarity to the category's prototype. Or we may estimate the probability that some member of a category has a particular property by determining the similarity of that member to members known to have the property.

6. Language, our primary means for communicating thoughts, is structured at three levels. At the highest level are *sentence units,* including phrases that can be related to units of propositions. The next level is that of *words* and *parts of words* that carry meaning. The lowest level contains *speech sounds.* The phrases of a sentence are built from words (and other parts of words), whereas the words themselves are constructed from speech sounds.

7. A *phoneme* is a category of speech sounds. Every language has its own set of phonemes and rules for combining them into words. A

morpheme is the smallest unit that carries meaning. Most morphemes are words: Others are prefixes and suffixes that are added onto words. A language also has *syntactic* rules for combining words into phrases and phrases into sentences. Understanding a sentence requires not only analyzing phonemes, morphemes, and phrases, but also using context and understanding the *speaker's intention.*

8. Language development occurs at three different levels. Infants come into the world preset to learn phonemes, but they need several years to learn the rules for combining them. When children begin to speak, they learn words that name familiar concepts. In learning to produce sentences, children begin with one-word utterances, progress to two-word telegraphic speech, and then elaborate their noun and verb phrases.

9. Children learn language at least partly by testing hypotheses. Children's hypotheses appear to be guided by a small set of *operating principles,* which call the children's attention to critical characteristics of utterances, such as word endings. Innate factors also play a role in language acquisition. Our innate knowledge of language seems to be very rich and detailed, as suggested by the fact that all children seem to go through the same stages in acquiring a language. Like other innate behaviors, some language abilities are learned only during a *critical period.* It is a matter of controversy whether or not our innate capacity to learn language is unique to our species. Many studies suggest that chimpanzees and gorillas can learn signs that are equivalent to our words, but they have difficulty learning to combine these signs in the systematic manner that humans beings combine words.

10. Not all thoughts are expressed in propositions; some are manifested as *visual images.* Such images contain the kind of visual detail found in perceptions. Imagery seems to be like perception because it is mediated by the same parts of the brain. Thus, brain damage that results in certain perceptual problems, *visual neglect,* also results in comparable problems in imagery. Also, experiments using brain scanning techniques indicate that the specific brain regions involved in an imagery task are the same as those involved in a perceptual task. In addition, the mental operations performed on images (such as scanning and rotation) are like the operations carried out on perceptions.

11. Problem solving requires decomposing a goal into subgoals that are easier to obtain. Strategies for such decomposition include *reducing differences* between the *current state* and the *goal state; means-ends analysis* (eliminating the most important differences between the current and goal states); and *working backward.* Some problems are easier to solve by using a propositional representation; for other problems, a visual representation works best.

12. Expert problem solvers differ from novices in four basic ways: they have more representations to bring to bear on the problem; they represent novel problems in terms of solution principles rather than surface features; they form a plan before acting; and they tend to reason forward rather than working backward. A useful method for studying problem solving is *computer simulation,* in which one tries to write a computer program that solves problems the same way people do. This method requires that we be precise about the knowledge involved in solving the problem.

FURTHER READING

Two relatively recent introductions to the psychology of thinking are Osherson and Smith, *Invitation to Cognitive Science (Vol. 3): Thinking* (1990) and Garnham and Oakhill, *Thinking and Reasoning* (1994). The study of concepts is reviewed in Smith and Medin, *Categories and Concepts* (1981). Research on reasoning is reviewed by Kahneman, Slovic, and Tversky, *Judgment Under Uncertainty: Heuristics and Biases* (1982);

for more advanced treatments of reasoning, see Holland, Holyoak, Nisbett, and Thagard, *Induction: Processes of Inference, Learning, and Discovery* (1986), Johnson-Laird and Byrne, *Deduction* (1991), and Rips, *The Psychology of Proof* (1994). For an introduction to the study of imagery, see Kosslyn, *Ghosts in the Mind's Machine* (1983). For more advanced treatments of imagery, see Kosslyn, *Image and Mind* (1980), Shepard and Cooper,

Mental Images and Their Transformations (1982), and Kosslyn, *The Resolution of the Imagery Debate* (1994). For an introduction to problem solving, see Anderson, *Cognitive Psychology and Its Implications,* 3rd ed. (1990), Hayes, *The Complete Problem Solver,* 2nd ed. (1989), Mayer, *Thinking, Problem Solving, and Cognition* (1983); for an advanced treatment, see the classic by Newell and Simon, *Human Problem Solving* (1972).

Numerous books deal with the psychology of language. Standard introductions include Clark and Clark, *Psychology and Language: An Introduction to Psycholinguistics* (1977); and Foss and Hakes, *Psycholinguistics: An Introduction to the Psychology of Language* (1978). For more recent surveys, see Osherson and Lasnik, *Invitation to Cognitive Science* (Vol. 1): *Language* (1990); Tartter, *Language Processes* (1986); and Carroll, *Psychology of Language* (1985). For a more advanced treatment, particularly of issues related to Chomsky's theory of language and thought, see Chomsky, *Rules and Representations* (1980); and Fodor, Bever, and Garrett, *The Psychology of Language* (1974). For an introduction to early language development (and other aspects of language), see Pinker, *The Language Gene* (1994). For more advanced treatments, consult Brown, *A First Language: The Early Stages* (1973); and Pinker, *Language Learnability and Language Development* (1984).

PERSONALITY AND INDIVIDUALITY

BASIC MOTIVES

I f you could have whatever you desired, what would you choose? Try to imagine it vividly. Now that you have imagined what you most want, can you imagine living without it? Of course you can. But can you imagine not wanting it? Could you honestly not care about it? Now try the reverse exercise. Can you think of something that you now dislike, and by an act of will make yourself honestly want it?

Motivational processes determine the direction and intensity of goal-directed behavior. They are experienced by us subjectively as conscious desires. Most of us can choose whether or not to act on our desires. We can force ourselves to forgo what we desire, and we can make ourselves do what we would rather not. Perhaps we can even deliberately choose not to think about the desires that we refuse to act on. But it is considerably more difficult—perhaps impossible—to control our motivations directly. They seem to exist apart from our volition. When we are hungry, it is hard not to want food. When we are hot and thirsty, we cannot help wanting a cool breeze or cold drink. Conscious choice appears to be more the consequence, rather than the cause, of our motivational states. What does control our motivation, if not our own rational choice?

This question defines the psychology of **motivation.** The causes of motivation range from physiological events within our brain and body, at the most microscopic level, to our culture and social interactions with other individuals who surround us, at the most macroscopic level. This chapter will discuss the control of basic motivations, such as thirst, hunger, and sex. These motivations arise in large part out of our biological heritage and reveal general principles, shared by humans and animals, about how motivation and reward work to give direction to behavior. Social aspirations and cultural influences on motivation will be discussed later (Chapters 14–19).

For basic motivations like hunger, thirst, and sex, psychologists have traditionally made a distinction between two types of theories of motivation. The difference concerns where the motivation comes from, what causes it, and how the motivation controls behavior. On the one hand are **drive** theories, which stress the role of *internal factors* in motivation. Some internal drives, such as those related to hunger or thirst, have been said to reflect basic physiological needs. For motivations like sex or aggression, drive factors seem less tied to absolute physiological needs. After all, does one ever need to aggressively attack another in the same way that one needs to eat or drink? Still, aggression and sex have been said to have drive aspects both in the sense that internal factors like hormonal state often appear important and

Water is a necessity for human life, but the motivation to succeed is not. What lies at the heart of our motivation?

in the sense that they may have evolved originally to fulfill basic ancestral needs.

On the other hand are **incentive** theories of motivation, which stress the motivational role of *external events or objects* of desire. Food, drink, sexual partners, targets of attack, relationships with others, esteem, money and the rewards of success: All of these are incentives. Incentives are the objects of our motivation. After all, our motivations don't operate in a vacuum—when we want, we seem always to want *something*. The nature of this something pulls us in one or another particular direction. And so we seek out and work for that particular incentive. The goal might be tasty food, water to drink, a partner for interaction, the expulsion of an intruder, or the possession of a disputed resource. Many incentives share the common property of reward. They can produce pleasure and reinforce behavior that leads to them. Some incentives are *primary reinforcers,* able to act as rewards independent of prior learning. For example, a sweet taste or a sexual sensation may be pleasant the first time they are experienced. Other incentives are *secondary reinforcers,* which have gained their status at least partly through *learning* about their relation to other events. For example, money or a good grade can be effective incentives, based on our cultural experience with them and with what they represent. For animals, a conditioned stimulus that has been paired with food can serve as an effective reward. In every case, learning is crucial to the formation of secondary reinforcers. Although less important, learning may even play a part in modulating the effectiveness of some primary reinforcers. For example, you may have been hungry when you were born—but you weren't born with any idea of the foods that are now your favorites. Incentive theories of motivation focus especially on the relation of learning and experience to the control of motivation.

Incentive theory and drive theory provide different perspectives on the control of motivation. But the difference between the theoretical perspectives is primarily in their points of view rather than in substance. There is actually no conflict between the two. It is widely acknowledged that both types of process exist for almost every kind of motivation (Toates, 1986). It is simply easier for the purpose of study to focus on one type of control, so as to thoroughly understand it, before switching to another. For this reason, we will consider first incentive processes and then drive processes. Both incentive and drive factors operate together in real-life motivation, and they often interact (Figure 10-1). For example, drive factors can enhance the motivational effect of incentives. The taste of food, for instance, becomes more pleasant to most people when they are hungry (Cabanac, 1979). Have you ever skipped lunch so that you would better enjoy an evening feast? Or been scolded for snacking because it would "ruin your dinner"? Conversely, incentive factors can awaken drive states. Have you ever walked by the delicious aroma from a bakery or restaurant and suddenly realized that you were hungry?

FIGURE 10-1

A Model of Basic Motives *An external stimulus, such as the sight of food, is compared to the memory of its past reward value. At the same time, physiological signals of hunger and satiety modulate the potential value at the moment. These two types of information are integrated to produce the final incentive motivation for the external stimulus, which is manifested in behavior and conscious experience.* (Adapted from Toates, 1986)

REWARD AND INCENTIVE MOTIVATION

Motivation typically directs behavior towards a particular incentive that produces pleasure or alleviates an unpleasant state: food, drink, sex, and so forth. In other words, incentive motivation is characterized by **affect**, the production of pleasure or displeasure. Early psychologists argued that almost every sensation we have contains some degree of reward or displeasure, in addition to its other sensory quality and intensity (Wundt, 1904). According to this view, every experience falls somewhere along a "hedonic continuum." The continuum stretches from pleasant through neutral to unpleasant, and each experience falls along it as a point.

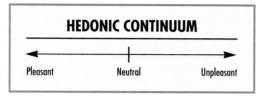

HEDONIC CONTINUUM

Pleasant   Neutral   Unpleasant

Regardless of whether this is true for all sensations, it is certainly so for our experience of incentives. Why should pleasure and displeasure be so pervasive? One possible answer stems from evolution and from the function of conscious pleasure. The ubiquity of affect in our experience of life has led some to suggest that pleasure has evolved to serve a basic psychological role (Cabanac, 1992). That role is to shape behavior by serving as a psychological "common currency" that reflects the value of each action we perform. Pleasure tends to be associated with stimuli

that enhance our biological good, namely, consequences that increase our survivability or that of our offspring. These include tasty food, refreshing drink, and sexual reproduction. Painful or frustrating consequences are associated with events that threaten our survival: physical damage, illness, or loss of resources. The rewarding consequences of an action, in other words, generally reflect whether the action is worth repeating. Pleasure may have evolved as a way for brains to keep track of the beneficial or deleterious consequences of past action, in order to better guide action in the future.

If pleasure is a kind of common currency for the value of diverse events, then it makes sense that the brain should have a way of translating different pleasures into their equivalent "dollar value" of common units. There is indeed evidence that the brain may have its own common neural currency for reward. It may even be the case that all incentives are rewarding precisely because they activate the same brain reward system. This neural currency appears to be related to the level of activity within the **mesolimbic dopamine system** (see Figure 10-2). The neurons

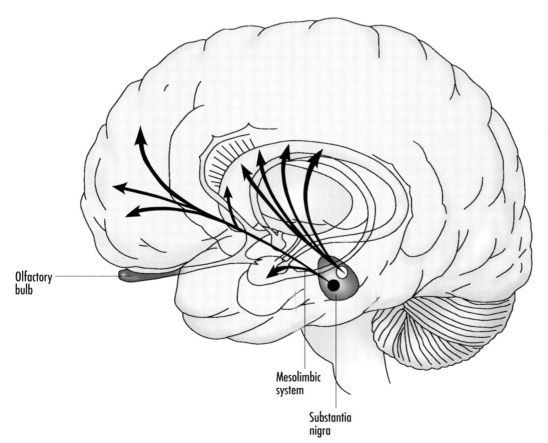

FIGURE 10-2

Two Major Dopamine Pathways *The mesolimbic system is apparently responsible for the symptoms of schizophrenia; the path to the basal ganglia is responsible for tardive dyskinesia, which sometimes results from use of neuroleptic drugs.* (Adapted from Valzelli, 1980)

Olfactory bulb

Mesolimbic system

Substantia nigra

Some motivations appear *instinctively* directed toward their incentive targets. The concept of **instinct**—which refers to an innate propensity to behave in a particular way—has had a long and controversial history in psychology. Psychologists of the nineteenth and early twentieth century invoked lists of instincts (18 according to one prominent theorist) to explain human behavior (McDougall, 1908). Beginning in the 1920s the concept fell into disrepute in American psychology, partly because the explanation was usually circular (for example, we might explain that birds build nests because they have an instinct to do so, but the only evidence we have of such an instinct is that birds do build nests); partly because every type of behavior seemed to qualify for its own instinct, which led to an ever-proliferating list (do you have an instinct to take psychology courses?); and partly because the emergence of behaviorism made psychologists look more to learning for explanations of behavior. The study of instinctive behavior, however, persisted among European zoologists known as ethologists (**ethology** is the branch of zoology that studies animal behavior),

Austrian ethologist Konrad Lorenz demonstrates how young ducklings follow him instead of their mother because he was the first moving object they saw after they were hatched.

and beginning in the 1950s, ethological concepts of instinct began to be incorporated into psychology. In the ethological sense, a pattern of behavior may be called instinctive if it is (a) *species-specific,* that is, it appears in all members of a species regardless of the environment in which they grew up and without being specifically learned; (b) a *fixed action pattern,* that is, it has a very stereotyped and predictable organization; and (c) *innately released,* that is, it can be triggered by some natural stimulus the first time the stimulus is encountered by an individual physically able to perform it. Crawling or walking for the first time by a young child, opening a nut for the first time by a young squirrel, or smiling or crying by a newborn human are all examples of instinctive behavior patterns. Even certain stereotyped patterns of learning may be instinctive in this sense.

of this system lie in the upper brain stem and send their axons up to the forebrain. As their name implies, these neurons use the neurotransmitter *dopamine* to convey their message.

The mesolimbic dopamine system is activated by natural rewards of many different kinds, such as tasty food or drink or a desired sexual partner. The same neurons are also activated by many drugs that humans and animals find rewarding: for example, cocaine, amphetamine, and heroin. The ability of virtually every reward, whether natural or artificial, to activate these neurons has led some

psychologists to conclude that activity in this neural system constitutes the brain's "common currency" for reward (Wise, 1982).

The function of the mesolimbic dopamine system seems to be especially important to the *motivational* property of rewards. Rather than creating a sensation of pleasure per se, its activity appears to dispose individuals to want to repeat the event that caused the increase, by seeking out and acquiring familiar incentives (Berridge & Valenstein, 1991). This may occur when a nibble of food whets your appetite for more. Even artificial activation of dopamine neurons can do the same

One of the most successful applications of the ethological approach has been the study of **imprinting**. As you may recall from Chapter 7, imprinting refers to the early rapid learning that allows a newborn or newly hatched animal to develop an attachment to its mother. Within the first hours of life, infants of many species are "programmed" to learn an emotional attachment to the closest social figure. Normally this would be their mother, but if a newly hatched duckling sees only a human being or even a moving inanimate object, such as a wooden hunting decoy, instead of its real mother, it will imprint on the person or object instead. Within the "critical period" during which imprinting can occur, exposure to an object for as little as 10 minutes is enough to establish an emotional attachment that will persist until the animal is grown. A duckling will follow the decoy if it is the first object it sees, will then attempt to remain close to the decoy even under adverse circumstances, and later will prefer to be near the decoy even if given a choice between it and a live duck (Hess, 1972).

Imprinting has several other consequences. The development of the bond between mother and offspring is called *maternal* imprinting. Another form is *sexual imprinting,* which is learned at the same time as maternal imprinting, but which isn't expressed in behavior until later life when the animal chooses a mate. In sexual imprinting, the infant learns from its parents the characteristics of what a "proper adult" should look like, and then as an adult chooses a mate of similar appearance. For example, a male duckling raised by its natural mother will later choose a mate that resembles her, but a male raised by a foster mother from a different duck species will choose a mate that resembles the foster mother rather than its biological mother. The greatest preference is for mates that *resemble but are not identical* to the sexual imprinting target. A mate that is just *slightly different* from the target is perceived as the most desirable (Bateson, 1978). Ethologists have interpreted this as due to a psychological mechanism that evolved to allow the chooser to pick a mate of the appropriate species while at the same time preventing inbreeding. A mate that looked identical to the imprinting target is likely to be a close relative; a mate just slightly different would be a better choice. Some psychologists have suggested that this mechanism may be related to why human romantic attachments so rarely develop between members of the same family.

Are humans capable of imprinting? Imprinting is strongest in species that are born and hatched already able to walk around and that mature quickly. Humans, by comparison, are born helpless and are slow to mature. Although traces of imprinting phenomena persist in humans, these are undoubtedly minor compared to the influence of culture.

When imprinting studies go awry

thing. For example, activation of the system by a stimulating electrode motivates animals to eat, drink, or engage in sex if the opportunity to do these things is available. Activation of the mesolimbic dopamine system by an electrode (or by a drug) is also rewarding by itself. Subjects will work to repeat the event that activates the system. In just the opposite way, if given different drugs that suppress the activity of the mesolimbic dopamine system, animals behave as if they do not want food, water, sex, or other natural incentives anymore. They also seem not to want artificial incentives, such as cocaine or rewarding electrical brain stimulation. Thus the mesolimbic dopamine system seems to be used by the brain to create wanting for a diverse array of natural and artificial incentives.

DRUG ADDICTION AND REWARD

Addiction is a powerful motivation for some people. The craving for certain drugs, such as opiates (for example, heroin or morphine), psychostimulants (amphetamine or cocaine) or synthetic "street versions" of these drugs, and certain other drugs (for example, alcohol), can become overwhelming. Addicts may crave their drugs so strongly that they will sacrifice job, family life and relationships, home and even freedom, to obtain it.

Taking a drug once, or even once in a while, does not constitute addiction. Many Americans have sampled at least one of these drugs without becoming addicted. Even regular use (for example, someone who often drinks wine with dinner) need not reflect addiction. Addiction occurs only when a pattern of *compulsive drug-taking* behavior has emerged and when a person *compulsively craves* the drug. What causes the transformation from "trying out" a drug, or from social or recreational use, into addiction?

Some drugs are especially powerful in their ability to produce addiction. Although people may sometimes be said to be "addicted" to food, sex, recreation, or their work, psychoactive drugs alone seem able to produce the kind of overwhelming addiction that ruins lives. Three major factors operate together to make drugs more addictive than other incentives. The first is the ability of most addictive drugs to overactivate brain systems of reward. Because drugs act directly on brain neurons, they can produce levels of activity in the mesolimbic dopamine system of reward that far surpass the levels produced by natural incentives. Drug euphoria can be a super-reward, because drugs can cause super-activation of brain reward systems. Euphoric drugs activate both pleasure (liking) and motivational (wanting) systems of brain reward, perhaps because they activate both opiate and dopamine neural systems of reward. Once experienced, the memory of such intense pleasure is a potent temptation to regain it again and again.

But the memory of pleasure by itself would not be sufficient to produce addiction, at least for many people, if it were not for additional factors. The second factor is the ability of addictive drugs, if taken repeatedly, to produce unpleasant withdrawal syndromes. As a drug is taken again and again, the brain systems of pleasure that it activates may become increasingly resistant to activation, in an effort to regain their normal balanced state. This is partly the cause of tolerance (the need for a greater amount of drug to achieve the same euphoria). In addition, after repeated exposure to the drug, the brain may activate processes that have consequences exactly *opposite* to those of the drug. These processes may help the brain remain in a balanced state when the drug is taken, but by themselves they are unpleasant. If the addict stops using the drug, the lack of activity in resistant pleasure systems, and the activation of unpleasant drug-opposite processes, can produce withdrawal. The aversive withdrawal state presents addicts with another motive to resume taking the drug, at least for as long as the withdrawal state lasts—typically several weeks.

Finally, addictive drugs may produce permanent changes in brain reward systems that cause craving even after withdrawal is over. The repeated use of drugs such as cocaine, heroin, or amphetamine, which activate the mesolimbic dopamine system, causes these neurons to become hyperactive or *sensitized*. Neural sensitization may be permanent, and it means that these neurons will be activated more highly by subsequent drugs and by drug-related stimuli. Since the mesolimbic dopamine brain system appears to mediate the motivational properties of reward (wanting) more than the pleasurable properties (liking), its hyperactivation in addicts may cause exaggerated craving for the drug (Robinson & Berridge, 1993). Neural sensitization lasts much longer than does withdrawal. This may be a reason why recovered addicts are in danger of relapse into drug use even after they have completed detoxification programs.

The combination of these factors sheds light on why drugs, more than other incentives, are able to produce addictions. Drugs directly activate brain mechanisms of pleasure to unmatched levels, produce withdrawal syndromes that drive a recovering addict back to the drug again, and perhaps permanently hyperactivate the brain systems that cause drug rewards to be wanted. This combination is hard to resist.

HOMEOSTASIS AND DRIVES

Our lives depend upon keeping certain things the same. If the temperature of your brain were to change by more than several degrees, you would quickly become unconscious. If the proportion of water within you were to rise or fall by more than a few percent, your brain and body could not function, and you would risk death. Humans and animals walk a tightrope of balance between physiological extremes. Like delicate and finely tuned machines, we cannot work unless our internal environment stays in balance. But unlike most machines, we've been designed to maintain this balance ourselves. Even when the outside world changes, our internal states remain relatively stable.

A great deal of basic motivation is directed towards helping to maintain our internal balance. In order to keep our internal world within the narrow limits of physiological survival, we have active control processes to maintain **homeostasis**. Homeostasis means to keep something the same ("homeo" means equal and "stasis" means to remain static or constant). A homeostatic control process is a system that actively works to maintain a constant state (that is, homeostasis).

Homeostatic control processes can be psychological, physiological, or mechanical. Perhaps the homeostatic control process with which you are most familiar is not psychological but rather a simple household device: the thermostat that runs your furnace or air conditioner. Thermostats are designed to maintain temperature homeostasis. When you set your thermostat to a particular temperature, that temperature is the *goal value* or **set point** that the homeostatic system tries to maintain. If the winter room temperature falls below the value you set, the thermostat is triggered: The discrepancy between its goal and the actual temperature causes it to activate the furnace. If the summer room temperature rises above the thermostat's set temperature for cooling, the thermostat activates the air conditioner. A thermostat coupled to both furnace and air conditioner can be used to keep your room at a stable temperature even as the seasons change. We have many physiological processes within us that work in homeostatic ways similar to the thermostat. These processes activate motivations that help to maintain homeostasis.

TEMPERATURE AND HOMEOSTASIS

If the temperature of your brain dropped by 10°C, you would lose consciousness. Even worse, if your brain temperature were to rise more than 10°C, above normal, you would

Symptoms of withdrawal can drive an addict to take drugs again.

die. Even though you may have been in very hot or cold weather, your brain remained largely protected within a narrow range of several degrees centigrade. Homeostatic control systems, both physiological and psychological, are the reason for this constancy.

Physiological responses such as sweating and shivering are part of the reason why your brain temperature remains so constant: These physiological responses provide cooling in the form of evaporation and heating in the form of muscle activity. Psychological reactions also come into play as you begin to feel uncomfortably hot. You may find yourself wanting to shed clothing, have a cool drink, or find shade. But what turns on these physiological and psychological responses in the first place?

When you are under a hot sun, your entire body begins to become hot. Conversely, if you remain too long unprotected in the cold, your entire body becomes hypothermic (too cold). But it is only within your brain that the change of temperature is actually detected. Neurons within several particular sites of the brain, especially within the *preoptic* (front) region of the *hypothalamus* at the base of the brain are essentially neural thermostats (Satinoff, 1983). They begin to operate differently as their own temperature changes. These neurons serve as both the thermometer and the homeostatic set point within you. When

Most of us have experienced a temporary change in set point. An illness can temporarily raise brain set points to several degrees above normal. Then the temperature they "seek" becomes higher, and a fever results. Physiological reactions that elevate body temperature are activated. You shiver, and your body temperature begins to rise above normal. But in spite of the rise in temperature, you may still feel cold—even in a warm room—until your hypothalamic neurons rise all the way to their elevated set point.

THIRST AS A HOMEOSTATIC PROCESS

If you go on a hunger fast, chances are that you could survive quite well (if uncomfortably) for up to several weeks as long as you drank plenty of fluids. But if you tried to go without water, you probably could not survive more than a week. And under a hot sun with nothing to drink, a person might not last beyond a single day. Water is crucial to human life. Thirst is our psychological manifestation of this need for water. What controls our thirst for water?

After going without water, or exercising under a hot sun, our body begins to deplete two kinds of fluid reservoirs as water gradually leaves through perspiration, respiration, or urination. Eating salty food also makes us thirsty because we deplete one of these reservoirs. The first type of reservoir is made up of water contained inside your body cells. This water is mixed with the protein, fat, and carbohydrate molecules, that form the structure and contents of the cell. The water inside your cells is your **intracellular reservoir**. The second type of reservoir is made up of the water that is outside any cell. This water is contained in blood and other types of body fluid. All of the water stored outside individual cells is called the **extracellular reservoir**. Losses from either one of these reservoirs can trigger thirst. We will first consider thirst caused by the extracellular reservoir.

We lose water from our body if we go without drinking or if we exercise in the heat. Water is extracted from our body by our kidneys in the form of urine, excreted by sweat glands in our skin, or breathed out of our lungs as vapor, and in each case it comes most directly from the blood supply: extracellular fluid. The loss reduces the volume of ex-

A breeze cools the skin by evaporation, pulling extra heat away from internal thermostats.

their temperatures diverge from their normal levels, their metabolism alters, which changes their activity or firing patterns. This triggers physiological reactions such as perspiration or shivering, which help to correct your temperature. In addition, this triggers the eventual generation of your conscious sensation of being too hot or too cold, which makes you want to seek shade or put on a coat, a behavioral solution to the same problem.

When you are too hot, a cool breeze can feel good. Likewise, when you are too cold, a hot bath feels pleasant. But as your own internal temperature changes, your perception of these outside events also changes. Although ordinarily your entire body changes temperature by a degree or two when you are in situations that make you feel very hot or cold, it is only the slight change in your brain temperature that causes the change in the way you feel. The brain can be "fooled" into feeling hot or cold by merely changing the temperature of a relatively few neurons in the hypothalamus. For example, cooling of the hypothalamus alone, by painlessly pumping cold liquid through a small loop of tubing that has been surgically implanted into the hypothalamus, motivates a rat to press a bar to turn on a heat lamp that warms its skin—even though its overall body temperature has not been lowered (Satinoff, 1964). The hypothalamic neurons have detected a change in their own temperature away from the normal set point.

tracellular fluid that remains. Just as the loss of air from a leaking tire leaves the tire shrunken and flabby, the loss of blood volume produces a reduction in blood pressure. You will not feel this slight change in blood pressure as a distinct sensation of pressure. Nonetheless, pressure receptors within your kidneys, heart, and major blood vessels detect the slight drop in blood pressure and send a signal to the brain that results in the experience of thirst.

The chain of events between pressure sensor and psychological thirst involves a complex series of signals that travel back and forth between the brain and body.

When pressure receptors detect a drop in blood pressure, they activate sensory neurons that relay a signal to the brain. Neurons in the hypothalamus next send an impulse to the pituitary gland, causing it to release **antidiuretic hormone** (*ADH*) into the bloodstream. ADH causes the kidneys to retain water from the blood as they filter it. Rather than send this water on to become urine, the kidneys instead deliver it back to the blood. This happens whenever you go without drinking for more than several hours. For example, you may have noticed that your urine appears more concentrated in color at such times (for instance, when you wake up after a night's sleep). In addition, the brain sends a neural signal to the kidneys that causes them to release a hormone of their own: *renin*. Renin interacts chemically with a substance that is in the blood to produce yet another hormone: **angiotensin**. This is the final and immediate cause that generates thirst in the brain. Angiotensin activates neurons deep within the brain, producing the desire to drink. You may recall that this entire chain of events is triggered by a drop in blood pressure caused by dehydration. Other events that cause dramatic loss of blood pressure can also produce thirst. For example, soldiers wounded on the battlefield, or injured people who have bled extensively may feel intense thirst. The cause of their craving is the activation of pressure receptors. Their activation triggers the same chain of renin and angiotensin production, which results in the experience of thirst (Fitzsimons, 1990).

A separate system for producing thirst usually operates in the brain in parallel with the extracellular thirst system that has just been described. This second system is con-

tained completely in the brain and does not rely on pressure detectors or hormonal signals from the body. The intracellular thirst system monitors the level of water inside neurons of the brain. Actually, most neurons are not monitored—only a relative few, located in the hypothalamus, are able to activate thirst in response to loss of intracellular water. But because changes in water availability affect all neurons nearly equally, these few neurons are able to monitor the general state of the entire brain. Intracellular thirst is caused by osmosis—the tendency of water to move from zones where it is plentiful to zones where it is relatively rare. It is primarily the concentration of "salt" ions of sodium, chloride, and potassium that determine whether water is plentiful or rare. As the body loses water, these concentrations begin to rise in the bloodstream. In essence, the blood becomes saltier. The higher concentrations within the blood cause water to migrate from the relatively dilute insides of body cells—including neurons—toward the blood. In a process something like sucking up a puddle of water with a paper towel, water is pulled out of the neurons and other cells. Neurons within the hypothalamus become activated when higher salt concentrations in the blood pulls water from them, thus causing them to become dehydrated. Their activation produces "osmotic" or intracellular thirst, leading again to a desire to drink. Drinking replaces water to the blood, reducing the concentration of salt, which in turn allows

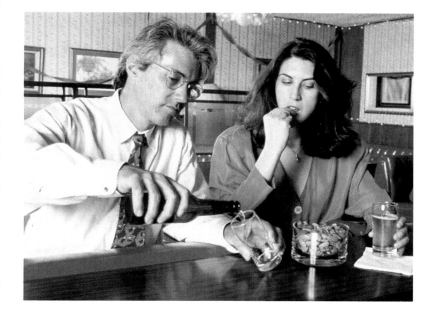

Most bar owners know that salty foods trigger hyperosmotic thirst and induce customers to drink more.

water to return to neurons and other cells. That is why people become thirsty after eating salty food—even though they might not have lost water. The salt in the food is absorbed into the blood, where the higher concentrations pull water out of neurons and other cells. When the hypothalamic neurons are forced to give up their water, thirst ensues. In fact, intracellular thirst can be triggered in animals by injections of tiny quantities of concentrated salty solutions directly onto the neurons of the hypothalamus (Epstein, 1982). These microinjections mimic the cause of normal intracellular thirst.

HUNGER

The control of hunger involves many of the same homeostatic concepts as thirst, but eating is much more complex than drinking. When we're thirsty, we generally need only water, and our thirst is directed to anything that will provide it. But there are lots of different things to eat. We need to eat a number of different kinds of things (proteins, carbohydrates, fats, minerals) in order to be healthy. We need to select the proper balance of foods that contain these things. Evolution has given our brains ways of helping us to select the foods we need (and to help avoid eating the things that might poison us). Some of these ways involve the basic taste preferences with which we were born. Others involve mechanisms for learning preferences for particular foods and aversions to others.

Flavor is the most important factor for food preferences. Flavor contains both taste and odor components, but taste has been the most important in human evolution. Humans are born "programmed" with elemental likes and dislikes for particular tastes. Even infants, for example, respond to sweet tastes with lip-smacking movements and facial expressions indicative of pleasure (Steiner, 1979). The same newborns respond to bitter tastes by turning away and pulling up their faces into expressions of disgust (apes, monkeys, and a number of other species of animals respond the same way). Modern food manufacturers have capitalized on our natural "sweet tooth" to devise sweet foods that spur many people to overconsume, which

contributes to the development of obesity. Why do we find sweet foods and drinks so attractive? Evolutionary psychologists have suggested that it is because sweetness is an excellent "label" that told our ancestors, foraging among unknown plants, that a particular food or berry was rich in sugar, a class of digestible carbohydrate. Eating sweet foods is an excellent way to gain calories—as any dieter knows—and calories were not in overabundance in our evolutionary past. A similar labeling explanation has been advanced for our dislike of bitterness. The naturally bitter compounds that occur in certain plants can make the plant toxic to humans. Bitter, in other words, is a label for a natural type of poison that occurs commonly. Ancestors who avoided bitter plants may have been more successful at avoiding such poisons (Rozin & Schulkin, 1990).

A second way of developing food preferences is through an array of individual learning and social learning mechanisms. One of these is preference based upon the postingestive consequences of a flavor. Experience with the nourishing consequences of a food leads to gradual liking for its taste through a process that is essentially a form of classical conditioning (Booth, 1991). Experience with other forms of taste-consequence pairings may also be the basis for developing preferences for other tastes that are initially not pleasant, such as alcohol or caffeine-containing coffee. Conversely, the same kind of process can work in the opposite direction to produce strong dislike or conditioned aversion for a particular food. If your first sample of a tasty food or drink is followed by symptoms of visceral illness (for example, strong nausea), you may find that the food seems not at all tasty the next time. The food hasn't changed, but you would have, because of your new associative memories, and the change would cause a food to subsequently be experienced as unpleasant. Conditioned aversions tend to be strong and permanent only if the food is new to the individuals at the time they become ill (because learned flavor preferences and aversions are a form of classical conditioning, and classical conditioning works best on stimuli that are previously unfamiliar). This is why someone who has become ill after drinking too much of a familiar alcoholic beverage may find the thought of that particular drink unpleasant for a few days, but then find it palatable afterward. The learned aversion is temporary, because the drink was familiar before illness was experienced.

HOMEOSTASIS AND INCENTIVE INTERACTION IN HUNGER

Whatever the particular foods one chooses, it is clear that we must eat in order to maintain energy homeostasis of our bodies. Body cells burn fuel in order to produce the energy required for the tasks they perform. Physical exercise, of course, causes muscle cells to burn extra fuel in order to meet the metabolic needs that energetic movement places on them. By burning more fuel, they draw upon stores of calories that have been deposited as body fat or as other forms of "stored energy." That's why weight-watchers exercise. As you read this, the neurons of your brain also burn fuel in order to meet the metabolic needs created as they fire electrical impulses and make and release neurotransmitters. The main fuel used by your brain neurons is *glucose,* a simple sugar. Without fuel, neurons cannot work. Unfortunately, your brain doesn't use more glucose when you "exercise it" by thinking hard. Those neurons are always active, and always consuming glucose, whether you are thinking hard or not. Concentrated thought or other psychological events may slightly alter the pattern of glucose use, but not the total amount. Thus you can't lose any weight by studying—regardless of how much you may "strengthen" your mind. Glucose is present in many fruits and other foods. It can also be manufactured easily by your liver out of other sugars or carbohydrates. Once you've eaten a meal, a great deal of glucose will be absorbed into your bloodstream by the process of digestion. Even more will be created by your liver as it converts other forms of nutrients. In this way, a meal replenishes the fuel needed by your brain neurons and your body's other cells.

Because our cells need fuel, we might expect hunger to be solely a homeostatic motivation: controlled entirely by the need to keep sufficient sources of energy available. Indeed, homeostasis is the dominant principal operating in the control of hunger.

Deficits in available fuels can trigger hunger and surpluses can inhibit it. But even though homeostasis is crucial to understanding the control of hunger, incentive factors are equally important. In fact, we can't understand hunger unless we look at the interaction between homeostasis and incentives.

The importance of interaction between homeostatic drive reduction and the taste and other incentive stimuli of food was made clear by a classic experiment by Miller and Kessen (1952). The general questions Miller and Kessen asked were whether hunger was essentially equivalent to homeostatic need for calories, and whether the motivation for food was merely the motivation to alleviate caloric deficits. They tackled this question by training rats to run down a short path for a milk reward. In one case, the rats received milk as a reward in the ordinary way: They drank it. In the other case, the rats received exactly the same amount of milk, but in a more direct way: The milk was gently pumped directly into their stomachs, through a tube passed into an artificial stomach opening or *fistula* that had been implanted weeks before. Both of these rewards provided exactly the same number of calories. Both reduced the rats' fuel deficit to the same degree. But the rats learned to run for the milk reward much better in the case when they were allowed to drink it. The milk was simply not a powerful motivator when it was given directly into the stomach, even though it reduced their hunger just as well as when it went into the mouth. They needed to both taste the reward and have it reduce hunger in order for it to become a powerful target for motivation.

Modern life presents an enticing array of food incentives.

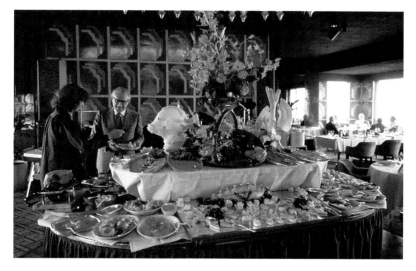

The importance of interaction between oral incentives and drive reduction to hunger has been demonstrated in many ways since that original experiment (Toates, 1986). Food that bypasses the normal route of voluntary tasting and swallowing is not strongly motivating for either animals or humans. For example, people who are fed entirely by intravenous or intragastric infusions of nutrients often also find these "meals" unsatisfying. They may feel an intense desire to have some food that they can put into their mouth—even if they are required to spit it out again after chewing it. The strong desire for oral stimulation—above and beyond the satisfaction of caloric needs—is also reflected in our widespread use of artificial sweeteners, which provide flavor without calories. Food incentives, in the form of the sensory experience involved in eating palatable foods and drinks, are both necessary and sufficient determinants of intake. They are as crucial to appetite as caloric drive reduction.

Learning processes are an important part of the interaction between physiological hunger signals and the incentive stimuli of eating that controls your feeling of appetite. This can be seen in the conditioned aspect of satiety. Dramatic demonstrations can be seen in animals in which the act of eating is "decoupled" from the ordinary caloric consequences by implantation of a stomach fistula, which allows food to leave the stomach as well as to be put in. If the fistula cap is removed, whatever is eaten will fall out through the fistula rather than be digested. This is called *sham feeding* because the meal is a sham in the sense that it provides no calories. Sham-fed animals eat normal amounts and then stop the first time they eat in this condition. Why do they stop rather than continue eating? The answer becomes clear if one observes food intake during subsequent meals: They gradually increase the amount eaten as they learn that the meal conveys fewer calories than it once did (Van Vort & Smith, 1987). If the fistula cap is replaced, so that everything is digested as it normally would be, the animals eat the "too large" amount for their next few meals. Gradually, their meal size declines to normal levels as they learn that the food is apparently calorie rich once again. These observations have led to the hypothesis of "conditioned satiety"—that the fullness we feel after a meal is at least in part a product of learning (Booth, 1987). Humans also are capable of conditioned satiety. In one experiment, people were asked to eat several meals of a distinctive food that was rich in calories and of another food that was low in calories. Later, when the subjects were given the two foods again, apparently the same as before but with the caloric content made equal, the subjects persisted in finding more satiating the food that had originally been higher in calories (Booth, 1990).

A final form of interaction between food incentives and homeostatic drive is the phenomenon called *alliesthesia* (Cabanac, 1979). This is the common experience that food (especially sweet food) tastes better when one is hungry. When people are asked to rate the palatability of sweet drinks, for example, either after a meal or after a period of several hours without food, they give higher palatability ratings to the same drink when they are hungry than when they have recently eaten. The physiological state of hunger/satiety, in other words, modulates the reward value of incentive tastes.

PHYSIOLOGICAL HUNGER CUES

You may have noticed that when you are hungry, your stomach sometimes "growls." At such moments, your stomach walls are engaged in muscular contractions, which sometimes creates the burbling movements of its contents that you hear. Stomach contractions are most frequent when you are hungry and likely to feel that your stomach is empty. The coincidence of these contractions with your feelings of hunger led early investigators to hypothesize that pressure sensors in the stomach detected emptiness and triggered both contractions and the psychological experience of hunger.

Later psychologists and physiologists found that this coincidence is really just that—a coincidence. Stomach sensations from contractions are not the real cause of hunger. In fact, people who have had their stomachs surgically removed for medical reasons, so that food passes directly to the intestines, still can have strong feelings of hunger even though they lack a stomach and its stretch receptors.

The stomach does have receptors that are important to changes in hunger, but these receptors are primarily chemical, not pressure. These chemical receptors have more to do with feelings of satiety—they are activated by sugars and other nutrients in stomach contents and send a neural signal to the brain—than with feelings of hunger.

The physiological signal for hunger is more directly related to the real source of calories for neurons and other cells: levels of glucose and other nutrients in the body. The brain itself is its own sensor for deficiencies in available calories. You may remember that brain neurons use glucose as their principal source of energy. Neurons in particular parts of the brain, especially in the brain stem and hypothalamus, are especially sensitive to levels of glucose. When the level falls too low, the activity of these neurons is disrupted. This signals the rest of the brain, producing hunger. Such hunger can be produced artificially in laboratory animals even if they have recently eaten. If chemicals that prevent neurons from burning glucose as a fuel are infused into an animal's brain, the animal will suddenly seek out food. Its brain has been fooled into sensing a lack of glucose, even though glucose was actually present, because the neurons have been disrupted in the same way as if glucose were low.

PERIPHERAL SIGNALS To some degree, hunger is what we feel when we have no feeling of satiety. As long as caloric food is in our stomach or intestine, or calorie stores are high within our body, we feel relatively sated. When these decline, hunger ensues. The control of hunger is therefore the reverse of the control of satiety. Many systems within us contribute to our feeling of satiety after a meal.

The first system is made up of the parts of our body that process food first: the stomach and intestine. Both the physical expansion of the stomach and the chemicals within the food activate receptors in the stomach's walls. These receptors relay their signal to the brain through the vagus nerve, which carries signals from many other body organs too. A second kind of satiety message comes from the duodenum, the part of the intestines that receives food directly from the stomach. This signal is sent to the brain as a chemical rather than through a nerve. When food reaches the duodenum, it causes this structure to release a hormone (*cholecystokinin,* or CCK) into the many blood vessels that run

through it. CCK helps promote physiological digestion, but it also has a psychological consequence. CCK travels through the blood until it reaches the brain, where it is detected by special receptors. This produces feelings of satiety. Hungry animals can be fooled into false satiety if microscopic amounts of CCK are infused into their brains shortly after they have begun a meal (Smith & Gibbs, 1994).

Perhaps surprisingly, the brain's most sensitive signal of nutrient availability comes from neuronal receptors that are separate from both the brain and from food: the liver (Friedman, 1990). Receptors in the liver are exquisitely sensitive to changes in blood nutrients after digestion. These signals are also sent to the brain through the vagus nerve. A hungry animal will stop eating almost immediately after a tiny infusion of nutrients into the blood supply that goes directly to the liver.

Why should the brain rely upon nutrient signals from the liver rather than upon its own detectors? The answer may be that the liver can more accurately measure the various types of nutrients used by the body. The brain detects chiefly glucose, but other forms of nutrients, such as complex carbohydrates, proteins, and fats, can be measured, stored, and sometimes converted into other nutrients by the liver. Its role as a general "currency exchange" for nutrients may allow the liver to make the best estimate of the total energy stores that are available to the body.

INTEGRATION OF HUNGER SIGNALS WITHIN THE BRAIN

Signals for hunger and satiety are processed by the brain in two stages to produce the motivation to eat. First, signals from hunger receptors in the brain itself and satiety signals relayed from the stomach and liver are added together in the brain stem to detect the overall level of need (Grill & Kaplan, 1990). This "integrated hunger assessment" is also connected in the brain stem to the sensory neural systems that process taste. Taste neurons in the brain stem may change their responsiveness during some forms of hunger and satiety (Scott & Mark, 1986). This may be partly the basis for why food tastes more palatable when we are hungry.

In order to become the conscious experience you know as hunger, and in order to

FIGURE 10-3

The Hypothalamus of the Brain

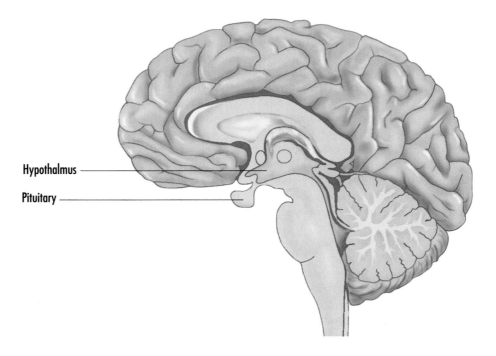

Hypothalmus ——————

Pituitary ——————

FIGURE 10-4

Damage to the ventromedial hypothalamus produces overeating and obesity.

stimulate the seeking of food, the hunger signal of the brain stem must be processed further in the forebrain. A chief site for hunger processing is the hypothalamus (see Figure 10-3). Hunger is affected in two dramatically different ways by manipulations of two parts of the hypothalamus: the lateral hypothalamus (the parts on each side) and the ventromedial hypothalamus (ventromedial means the lower ['ventral'] and middle [medial] portion). Destruction of the lateral hypothalamus produces an apparent total lack of hunger, at least until the rest of the brain recovers (Teitelbaum & Epstein, 1962). This phenomenon is called the *lateral hypothalamic syndrome*. Animals that have had small lesions made in their lateral hypothalamus may simply ignore food. They may even reject it as though it tasted bad (for example, they will grimace and vigorously spit it out). Unless they are fed artificially, they will voluntarily starve themselves to death. Nearly the exact opposite pattern of behavior is produced by a lesion of the ventromedial hypothalamus: the *ventromedial hypothalamic syndrome*. These animals eat voraciously. They consume large quantities of food, especially if it is palatable. Not surprisingly, these animals gain weight until they become quite obese, up to double their normal body weight (see Figure 10-4).

Other types of manipulation of these brain sites also appear to change hunger. For example, electrical stimulation of the lateral hypothalamus produces overeating: the exact opposite of a lesion of the lateral hypothalamus (and the same effect as a lesion of the ventromedial hypothalamus). An animal with a stimulating electrode in its lateral hypothalamus may begin to look for food and eat as soon as the stimulation begins and to stop eating once it ends. Stimulation of the ventromedial hypothalamus, conversely, will stop ordinary eating by a hungry animal.

Neurochemical stimulation of the hypothalamus works in similar ways. For example, certain compounds such as Neuropeptide Y, or opiate drugs such as morphine, can stimulate feeding when they are injected into the ventromedial hypothalamus. These drugs may temporarily stimulate hunger or make food taste better. Other drugs, such as amphetamines, can halt feeding when injected into parts of the lateral hypothalamus. Many prescription diet drugs are chemically similar to amphetamines. Such drugs might well help to inhibit a person's appetite by acting on neurons in the hypothalamus.

When the importance of the lateral hypothalamus and ventromedial hypothalamus to hunger were discovered around 1960, psychologists tended to view these sites simply as hunger or satiety centers. Since then, it has become clear that the concepts of "hunger center" or "satiety center" are too simplistic for a number of reasons. One is that these sites are not the sole centers for hunger or satiety in the brain. They interact with many other brain systems to produce their effects. In fact, some of the same effects can be produced by manipulating related brain systems instead of the hypothalamus. For example, many of the effects of manipulating the lateral hypothalamus itself can be duplicated by manipulating instead the mesolimbic dopamine system, which simply

passes through the hypothalamus. Lesions of only this dopamine-containing bundle of axons eliminate feeding, similar to lateral hypothalamic lesions. In fact, many early studies of lateral hypothalamic lesions actually destroyed both the mesolimbic dopamine system and neurons in the lateral hypothalamus itself. Conversely, the elicitation of feeding by electrical stimulation and by many drugs also depends partly on the activation of the mesolimbic system. Rather than just one or two centers, many neuroanatomical and neurotransmitter systems are involved in appetite and satiety.

One consequence of having many neural systems for appetite is that it is not possible to abolish eating by destroying just one site. Even for animals with lateral hypothalamic lesions, appetite will return eventually. If the rats are artificially fed for several weeks or months after their lesion, they will begin to eat again, but, they will eat only enough to maintain their lower body weight. They seem to have reached homeostasis at a lower set point. In fact, rats can be "protected" from the usual loss of eating that would follow a lateral hypothalamic lesion if they are put on a diet before the lesion that lowers their body weight (see Figure 10-5). This indicates that

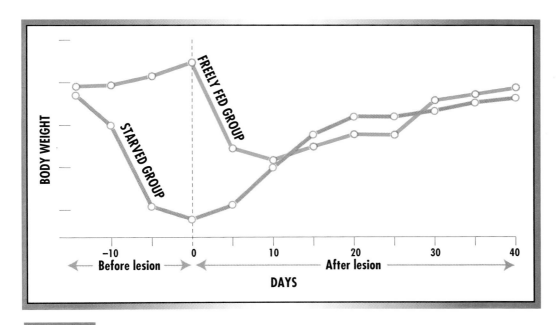

FIGURE 10-5

Body Weight and the Lateral Hypothalamus *Prior to lesioning the lateral hypothalamus, one group of rats was starved and another group was allowed to feed freely. Following surgery, the starved animals increased their food intake and gained weight and the freely fed group lost weight. Both groups stabilized at the same weight level.* (After Powley & Keesey, 1970)

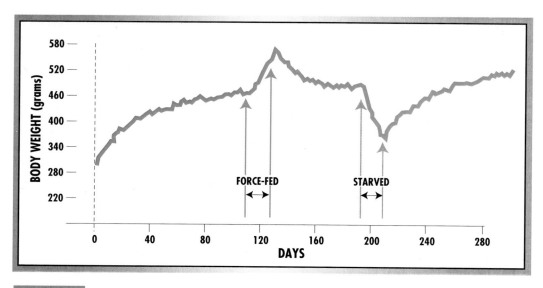

FIGURE 10-6

Effects of Forced Feeding and Starvation on Rats with VMH Lesions   *Following lesioning of the ventro-medial hypothalamus, the rat overeats and gains weight until it stabilizes at a new, obese level. Forced feeding or starvation alters the weight level only temporarily; the rat returns to its stabilized level.* (After Hoebel & Teitelbaum, 1966)

hypothalamic lesions don't actually destroy hunger. Instead, they may raise or lower the homeostatic set point for body weight that ordinarily controls hunger. Changing the set point is like resetting a thermostat: The system attempts to achieve the new body weight. The effect of ventromedial hypothalamic lesions also conform to this idea. Animals with those lesions do not gain weight infinitely. Eventually they stop at a new, obese body weight. At that point, they eat only enough to maintain the new set point. But if they are put on a diet and drop below that set point, they will resume overeating to regain that body weight when they are finally given the opportunity (see Figure 10-6). Once they regain that level of obesity, they will halt once again.

OBESITY AND ANOREXIA

We have emphasized homeostatic processes in hunger, but our eating behavior shows several departures from homeostasis. Some people's body weights are not as constant as the homeostatic viewpoint suggests. The most frequent deviation from homeostatic regulation of eating—at least for humans—is obe-

sity. It is common in our culture. Roughly 25 percent of Americans are obese, a condition often defined as being 30 percent or more in excess of one's appropriate body weight. The prevalence of obesity varies from group to group within society. Physical obesity occurs about equally in both sexes, but the psychological self-perception of being overweight is more common among women. More than 50% of American women, compared to more than 35% of men, consider themselves overweight (Brownell & Rodin, 1994; Horm & Anderson, 1993). In the United States, obesity is more prevalent in lower-class socioeconomic groups than higher-class ones; however, in developing countries, the reverse is true, as people are more likely to be obese the higher their socioeconomic status (Logue, 1991).

Obesity is a major health hazard. It contributes to a higher incidence of diabetes, high blood pressure, and heart disease. As if this were not bad enough, in our culture obesity can also be a social stigma, as obese people are often perceived as being indulgent and lacking in willpower. This allegation can be most unfair since, as we will see, in many cases a person's obesity is due to genetic factors rather than overeating. Given all of the problems associated with obesity, it is not surprising that each year millions of people spend billions of dollars on diets and drugs to lose weight.

Most researchers agree that obesity is a complex problem and can involve metabolic, nutritional, psychological, and sociological factors. Obesity probably is not a single disorder but a host of disorders that all have fatness as their major symptom (Rodin, 1981). The question of how one becomes obese is like that of how one gets to Pittsburgh—there are many ways to do it, and which one you "choose" depends on where you are coming from (Offir, 1982). In what follows, we will divide the factors that lead to weight gain into two broad classes: (a) genetics and (b) calorie intake (overeating). Roughly speaking, people may become obese because they are genetically predisposed to metabolize nutrients into fat even if they don't eat more than other people (metabolic reasons), or because they eat too much (for psychological or sociological reasons). Both factors may be involved in some cases of obesity, while in others just genetics or just overeating may be the culprit.

Genetic Factors in Obesity

It has long been known that obesity runs in families. In families in which neither parent is obese, only about 10% of the children will be obese; if one parent is obese, about 40 percent of the children will be too; and if both parents are obese, approximately 70 percent of the children will be too (Gurney, 1936). These statistics suggest a biological basis of obesity, but other interpretations are possible (perhaps the children are simply imitating their parents' eating habits). Recent findings, however, strongly support a genetic basis for obesity.

Twin Studies One way to get evidence about the role of genetics in obesity is to study identical twins. Since identical twins have the same genes, and since genes supposedly play a role in weight gain, identical twins should be alike in their patterns of weight gain.

In one experiment, 12 pairs of identical twins (all males) agreed to stay in a college dormitory for 100 days. The intent of the experiment was to get the twins to gain weight. Each man ate a diet that contained 1,000 extra calories per day. Also, the men's physi-

cal activity was restricted; they were not allowed to exercise, and instead spent much of their time reading, playing sedentary games, and watching television. By the end of the 100 days, all of the men had gained weight, but the amount gained varied considerably, from 9 to 30 pounds. However, and this is the critical point, there was hardly any variation in the amount gained within a pair of twins (the variation being between pairs of twins). Identical twins gained almost identical amounts. Moreover, identical twins tended to gain the weight in the same places. If one member of twins gained weight in his middle, so would the other member; if one member of another pair of twins gained the weight on his hips and thighs, so would the other member (Bouchard et al., 1990).

The above results make it clear that both calorie intake and genetics contribute to weight gain. The fact that all the men in the study gained weight shows that increased calories translates into increased weight (hardly surprising). The fact that how much weight the men gained varied from twins to twins but did not vary within a pair of twins shows that genetics determines how much we gain when we increase calorie intake. The above results also make it clear why we should not assume that obese people necessarily eat more than nonobese people. Despite eating roughly the same amount (1,000 extra calories), the weight gain of the twins varied. This difference between pairs of twins seems to arise from how their bodies metabolized the extra calories. The bodies tend to convert a larger proportion of calories into fat stores, and other bodies are likely to burn off

A genetic influence may be reflected in family patterns of body weight.

the same calories through different metabolic processes, regardless of how much is eaten (Ravussin, et al., 1988).

A critic might object to making too much of the preceding twins study. Identical twins not only have identical genes, but also very similar environments, and perhaps environmental factors were responsible for the identical twins being alike in weight gain. To eliminate this potential confounding, we need to study identical twins who have been reared apart and see how similar the members of a pair are in weight gain. Precisely this was done in a recent study conducted in Sweden. The researchers studied the weights of 93 pairs of identical twins reared apart, as well as that of 153 pairs of identical twins reared together. Members of a pair of twins reared apart were found to be remarkably similar in weight; indeed, they were as similar in weight as were pairs of twins reared together! Genes, then, are a major determinant of weight and weight gain.

FAT CELLS Given that genetics plays a role in weight gain, we now want to know some details of that role. In particular, what are the digestive and metabolic processes that are affected by genes and that mediate the weight gain? One answer involves fat cells, where all body fat is stored. There are 30 billion to 40 billion fat cells in the bodies of most normal adults, but the degree of excess weight carried by ordinary American adults varies by more than the 25% to 33% this figure would suggest. The additional variation comes from the size, rather than the mere number, of fat cells: the more calories one eats and fails to burn off, the larger the existing fat cells become. In one sample, obese subjects were found to have three times as many fat cells as normal subjects (Knittle & Hirsch, 1968). In other studies, researchers have shown that rats that have double the usual number of fat cells tend to be twice as fat as control rats. And when researchers cut some of the fat cells out of young rats, so that they had only half as many fat cells as their littermates, the operated-on rats grew up to be only half as fat as their littermates (Faust, 1984; Hirsch & Batchelor, 1976). Hence, there is a link between genes and the number of fat cells, and another link between the number of fat cells and obesity; by this chain, genes are connected to obesity.

DIETING AND SET POINTS When people take diet drugs, a variety of things can happen. The drug might suppress appetite directly: This would reduce the feeling of hunger. Another drug might suppress the set point at which body weight is regulated, rather than suppress appetite directly. For example, this has been suggested to be the consequence of diet drugs such as fenfluramine (Stunkard 1982). Such an effect would be equivalent to direct appetite suppression as long as body weight was higher than the lowered set point. Once body weight fell to the lower level, appetite would return to just the degree needed to stay at that weight. When a person stopped taking the drug, the set point would return to its higher level, and the person would regain the weight he or she had lost. Finally, some drugs, such as nicotine, may help people lose weight by elevating cells' metabolic rate, causing them to burn more calories than they would ordinarily even when the person is resting.

One reason why the set point hypothesis has become popular among psychologists is the strong tendency for obese adults, both humans and animals, to return to their original body weight after a particular diet has ended. In contrast to the young rats above, even surgical removal of fat deposits by liposuction appears less permanent a way to lose weight when it is performed on adult rats: The adults regain the fat elsewhere. This also appears to be true of liposuction performed on obese human adults (Vogt & Belluscio, 1987). Some investigators have suggested that once adult levels of fat tissue have been reached, they are kept at that level. The brain may detect changes in the level of body fat and influence hunger accordingly (Weigle, 1994). For example, an "obesity gene" recently discovered in mice has been suggested to code the ability of fat cells to produce a chemical "satiety signal" (Zhang et al., 1994). Mice that lack this gene become obese. Ordinarily, the more body fat one has, the more satiety signal is released into the blood. Whether human obesity involves a disruption in this satiety factor or gene is not yet known. But the possibility that the level of fat stores is kept constant may help explain why some obese people find it difficult not to regain weight that they lost through dieting.

In sum, there are various routes by which genes can be responsible for excessive weight gain, including having many and large fat cells, having a high set point, and having a low metabolic rate.

OVEREATING AND OBESITY

While physiological factors such as fat regulation and metabolic rate are important determinants of body weight, there is no question that overeating can also cause obesity. What are the psychological factors that characterize eating by people who are trying to lose weight?

BREAKDOWN OF CONSCIOUS RESTRAINTS   Some people stay obese by binge eating after they diet. An obese man may break his two-day diet and then overeat so much that he eventually consumes more calories than he would have had he not dieted at all. Since the diet was a conscious restraint, the breakdown of control is a factor in increased calorie intake.

To have a more detailed understanding of the role of conscious restraints, researchers have developed a questionnaire that asks about diet, weight history, and concern with eating (for example, How often do you diet? Do you eat sensibly in front of others, yet overeat when alone?). The results show that almost everyone—whether thin, average, or overweight—can be classified into one of two categories: people who consciously restrain their eating and people who do not. In addition, regardless of their actual weight, the eating behavior of restrained eaters is closer to that of obese individuals than to that of unrestrained eaters (Ruderman, 1986; Herman & Polivy, 1980). A laboratory study shows what happens when restraints are dropped. Restrained and unrestrained eaters (both of normal weight) were required to drink either two milk shakes, one milk shake, or none; they then sampled several flavors of ice cream and were encouraged to eat as much as they wanted. The more milk shakes the unrestrained eaters were required to drink, the less ice cream they consumed later. In contrast, the restrained eaters who had been preloaded with two milk shakes ate more ice cream than did those who drank one milk shake or none. Thus, individuals who are trying to restrain their eating, ignoring their ordinary impulse to eat more, may also come to

ignore the feelings of satiety that would ordinarily halt their desire to eat.

EMOTIONAL AROUSAL   Overweight individuals often report that they tend to eat more when they are tense or anxious, and experiments support this. Obese subjects eat more in a high-anxiety situation than they do in a low-anxiety situation, while normal-weight subjects eat more in situations of low anxiety (McKenna, 1972). Other research indicates that any kind of emotional arousal seems to increase food intake in some obese people. In one study, overweight and normal-weight subjects saw a different film in each of four sessions. Three of the films aroused various emotions: one was distressing; one, amusing; and one, sexually arousing. The fourth film was a boring travelogue. After viewing each of the films, the subjects were asked to taste and evaluate different kinds of crackers. The obese subjects ate significantly more crackers after viewing any of the arousing films than they did after seeing the travelogue. Normal-weight individuals ate the same amount of crackers regardless of which film they had seen (White, 1977).

The ability of emotional stress to elicit eating has been observed in other animals too. This may mean that stress can activate basic brain systems that, under some conditions, result in overeating (Rowland & Antelman, 1976).

RESPONSIVENESS TO EXTERNAL CUES   Compared to normal-weight people, obese individuals may be more sensitive to external hunger cues (the sight, aroma, and taste of food) and less sensitive to internal hunger cues (such as satiety signals from the intestines). One study examined the effects of taste on the eating behavior of underweight and overweight subjects. The subjects were allowed to eat as much vanilla ice cream as they wanted and then were asked to rate its quality. Some subjects were given a creamy, expensive brand; the others, a cheap brand with quinine added. Figure 10-7 plots the amount of ice cream subjects ate against their ratings of the ice cream. Overweight subjects ate much more ice cream when they rated it "excellent" than when they rated it "bad," while the ice-cream consumption by underweight subjects was less affected by taste. Other experiments indicate that while people do indeed differ

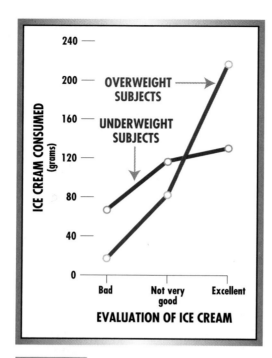

240 —

200 — **OVERWEIGHT SUBJECTS** →

160 —

UNDERWEIGHT SUBJECTS ↓

120 —

80 —

40 —

0 —

ICE CREAM CONSUMED (grams)

Bad   Not very   Excellent
                good

EVALUATION OF ICE CREAM

FIGURE 10-7

Taste and Obesity   *The effects of food quality on the amount eaten by overweight and underweight subjects. The subjects rated the quality of ice cream and could eat as much as they desired.* (After Nisbett, 1968)

in their *externality* (sensitivity to external cues), by no means are all obese people "externals," nor are all externals obese. Rather, there are externals and internals in every weight category, and only a moderate correlation exists between degree of externality and degree of obesity (Rodin, 1981).

DIETING AND WEIGHT CONTROL

Though genetic factors may limit the amount of weight we can comfortably lose, still, overweight people can generally lose weight by means of a weight control program. For a program to be successful, though, it must involve something other than just extreme dieting.

LIMITATIONS OF DIETING   Unfortunately, most dieters are not successful, and those who succeed in shedding pounds often regain them. This state of affairs seems to be partly due to two deep-seated human reactions to a temporary deprivation of food (which is what a diet is).

The first reaction is that deprivation per se can lead to subsequent overeating. In some experiments, rats were first deprived of food for four days, then allowed to feed back to their normal weights, and finally allowed to eat as much food as they wanted. These once-deprived rats ate more than did control rats that had no history of deprivation. Thus, prior deprivation leads to subsequent overeating, even after the weight lost from the deprivation has been regained (Coscina & Dixon, 1983).

The second reaction of interest is that deprivation decreases metabolic rate, and, as you may recall, the lower one's metabolic rate, the fewer calories expended and the greater one's weight. Consequently, the calorie reduction during dieting is partly offset by the lowered metabolic rate, making it difficult for dieters to meet their goal. The reduction in metabolic rate with dieting may also explain why many people find it harder and harder to lose weight with each successive diet: The body responds to each bout of dieting with a reduction in metabolic rate (Brownell, 1988).

Both reactions to dieting—binge eating and lowered metabolic rate—are understandable in terms of an evolutionary approach to psychology. Until very recently in historical time—and indeed, still in underdeveloped countries—whenever human beings experienced deprivation, it was because of scarcity of food in the environment. One adaptive response to such scarcity is to overeat and store in our bodies as much food as possible whenever it is available. Hence evolution may have selected for an ability to overeat following deprivation. This explains the overeating reaction. A second adaptive response to a scarcity of food in the environment is for organisms to decrease the rate at which they expend their limited amount of calories; hence, evolution may have selected for an ability to lower one's metabolic rate during deprivation. This explains the second reaction of interest. These two reactions have served our species well in times of famine, but once famine is not a concern, these reactions keep obese dieters overweight (Polivy & Herman, 1985).

WEIGHT CONTROL PROGRAMS   To lose weight and keep it off, it seems that overweight individuals need to establish a new set of permanent eating habits (as opposed to temporary dieting) and to engage in a program of exercise. Some support for this conclusion is given by the following study, which compared various methods for treating obesity.

For 6 months, obese individuals followed one of three treatment regimens: (a) behavior modification of eating and exercise habits, (b) drug therapy using an appetite suppressant (fenfluramine), and (c) a combination of behavior modification and drug therapy. Subjects in all three treatment groups were given information on exercise and extensive nutritional counseling, including a diet of no more than 1,200 calories per day. Subjects in the behavior modification groups were taught to become aware of situations that prompted them to overeat, to change the conditions associated with their overeating, to reward themselves for appropriate eating behavior, and to develop a suitable exercise regimen. In addition to the three treatment groups, there were two control groups: One consisted of subjects waiting to take part in the study, and the other comprised subjects who saw a physician for traditional office treatment of weight problems.

Table 10-1 presents the results of the study. The subjects in all three treatment groups lost more weight than the subjects in the two control groups, with the group combining behavior modification and drug therapy losing the most weight and the behavior-modification-only group losing the least. However, during the year after treatment, a striking reversal developed. The behavior-modification-only group regained far less weight than the two other treatment groups; these subjects maintained an average weight

Physical exercise lowers body weight by consuming energy stores in fat.

loss of 19.8 pounds by the end of the year, whereas the weight losses for the drug-therapy-only group and the combined-treatment group averaged only 13.8 and 10.1 pounds each.

What caused this reversal? An increased sense of self-efficacy may have been a factor. Subjects who received the behavior-modification-only treatment could attribute their weight loss to their own efforts, thereby strengthening their resolve to continue controlling their weight after the treatment ended. Subjects who received an appetite suppressant, on the other hand, probably attributed their weight loss to the medication and so did not develop a sense of self-control.

TABLE 10-1

Weight Loss Following Different Treatments
Weight loss in pounds at the end of 6 months of treatment and on a follow-up 1 year later. Subjects in the two control groups were not available for the 1-year follow-up. (After Craighead, Stunkard, & O'Brien, 1981)

	WEIGHT LOSS AFTER TREATMENT	WEIGHT LOSS ONE YEAR LATER
Treatment groups		
Behavior modification only	24.0	19.8
Drug therapy only	31.9	13.8
Combined treatment	33.7	10.1
Control groups		
Waiting list	2.9 (gain)	—
Physician office visits	13.2	—

Another possible factor stems from the fact that the medication had decreased the subjects' feelings of hunger, or temporarily lowered their set point, and consequently subjects in the drug-therapy-only group and the combined-treatment group may not have been sufficiently prepared to cope with the increase in hunger that they felt when the medication was stopped.

ANOREXIA

While obesity is our most frequent eating problem, the opposite problem has also surfaced in the form of **anorexia nervosa** and **bulimia**. Both of these disorders involve a pathological desire *not* to gain weight. This section treats anorexia, the next one bulimia.

CHARACTERISTICS Anorexia is distinguished by an extreme, self-imposed weight loss. Based on standards set by the American Psychiatric Association (1994), individuals should be diagnosed as being anorexic only if they weigh at least 15 percent less than their minimal normal weight. Some anorexics in fact weigh less than 50 percent of their normal weight. For females to be diagnosed as anorexic, in addition to the weight loss they must also

have stopped menstruating. The weight loss can lead to a number of dangerous side effects, including emaciation, susceptibility to infection, and other symptoms of undernourishment. In extreme cases, the side effects can lead to death. No wonder that one of the leading investigators of anorexia has described it as, "the relentless pursuit of thinness through self-starvation, even unto death" (Bruch, 1973).

Anorexia is relatively rare; its incidence in the United States is about 1 percent. However, this incidence represents more than a doubling since the 1960s, and the frequency may still be rising (McHugh, 1990). It is 20 times more likely to occur in women than men, particularly young women between their teens and their thirties. Moreover, most anorexics are white and upper-middle or upper class. Typically, anorexics are entirely focused on food, carefully calculating the amount of calories in anything they might consume. Sometimes this concern reaches the point of obsession, as when one anorexic commented to her therapist, "Of course I had breakfast; I ate my Cheerio"; or when another anorexic said, "I won't lick a postage stamp—one never knows about calories" (Bruch, 1973). The obsession with food and possible weight gains leads some anorexics to become

---

FIGURE 10-8

Distortions in Body Image *Anorexics and control subjects were allowed to adjust someone's photograph to between −20 percent and +20 percent of the photograph's actual width. An anorexic was more likely than a control subject to adjust a picture of herself so it was larger than actual size.* (After Garfinkel & Garner, 1982)

Actual size

Constricted image
(−20%)

Expanded image
(+20%)

compulsive exercisers, sometimes exercising vigorously several hours a day (Logue, 1991).

DISTORTIONS IN BODY IMAGE   It is a remarkable fact that despite the extreme loss of weight and the problems it leads to, the typical anorexic denies there is any problem and refuses to gain weight. In fact, anorexics frequently think that they look too fat. This suggests that anorexics have a distorted image of their own body, seeing themselves as heavier than they actually are. Indeed, there is experimental evidence for such a distortion. Anorexic and control subjects were given a device that allowed them to adjust someone's photograph to between −20 percent and +20 percent of the photograph's actual width (see Figure 10-8). An anorexic was more likely than a control subject to adjust a picture of herself so that it was larger than actual size; however, she showed no tendency to distort the sizes of other people (Garfinkel & Garner, 1982).

The preceding results suggest that anorexics' refusal to eat is mediated by their image of themselves as too fat. To some extent, this kind of distorted image may be held by many college-age women in our society, which could explain why this group of people is the most likely to become anorexic. Support for this idea is provided by the following experiment. Hundreds of male and female undergraduates were shown drawings of figures of their own sex. The figures of each sex were arranged on a scale running from very thin to very heavy, as shown in Figure 10-8. The subjects were asked to indicate: (a) the figure that looked most like their current shape; (b) the figure they most wanted to look like, that is, their *ideal;* and (c) the figure they felt would be most attractive to the opposite sex. The results, shown in Figure 10-9 are strikingly different for males and females. The men chose very similar figures for their current figure, their ideal figure, and the figure

FIGURE 10-9

Body Images of Male and Female Undergraduates
Male and female undergraduates were shown figures of their own sex and asked to indicate: (a) the figure that looked most like their current shape; (b) their ideal figure; and (c) the figure they felt would be most attractive to the opposite sex. Men selected very similar figures for all three choices, but women selected very different figures for their current figure and either their ideal figure or the figure they thought would be most attractive to the opposite sex. (Adapted from Fallon & Rozin, 1985)

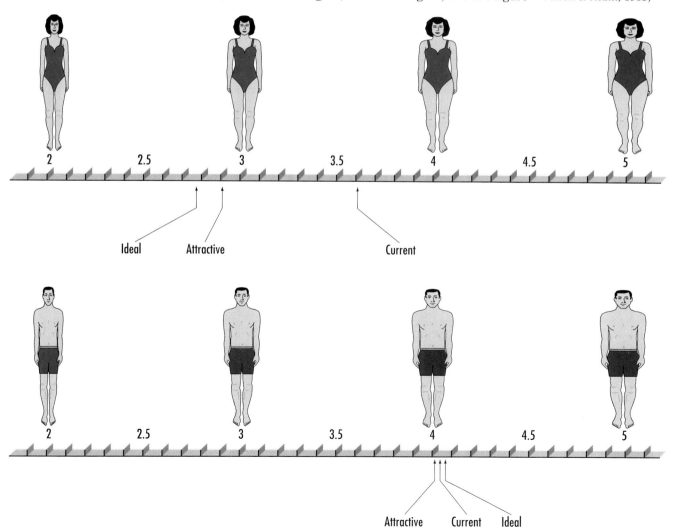

they thought most attractive to women; that is, men thought that their current weight was close to both their ideal and to what women would find attractive. The women, in contrast, chose very different figures for their current figure and either their ideal figure or the figure that they thought would be most attractive to the opposite sex (the latter two figures being relatively close). Clearly, the women were dissatisfied with their current weight, viewing themselves as too heavy to be attractive to men. But this turns out to be a distorted view. For when the male subjects were asked to choose the female figure to which they would be most attracted, their average choice was substantially heavier than the figures that women had chosen as either their ideal or as being most attractive to the opposite sex. Thus, college women mistakenly think that college men are attracted to very thin women. In short, college women, but not college men, were dissatisfied with their current weight in a way that could lead them to diet and perhaps become anorexic (Fallon & Rozin, 1985).

POSSIBLE CAUSES   A number of different kinds of causes of anorexia have been proposed, in-cluding personality factors, societal norms, and brain physiology. At this point in time, we lack firm evidence about any of the pro-posed causes.

That personality factors are involved is suggested by the fact that anorexics tend to be a certain kind of woman—young, white, and from an upwardly mobile family that stresses achievement. This kind of back-ground may lead to stressful family demands and expectations, and in this context a young woman's refusal to eat may seem (uncon-sciously) like a way of exerting control. An-other possibility that has been mentioned is that anorexia represents a denial of sexuality. In addition to not menstruating, girls who are severely underweight will lack other sex-ual characteristics, such as a truly feminine form (Bruch, 1973). A further indication that the cause may have something to do with fac-tors involving gender or sexual identity has come from the observation that, of the rel-atively few men who are anorexic, more are homosexual than would be expected by chance (Herzog, Norman, Gordon, & Pepose, 1984).

Many social scientists have suggested that social factors play a major role in anorexia,

FIGURE 10-10

Jayne Mansfield (left) represented a perfect fig-ure for the 1950s, while Julia Roberts (right) is considered the perfect figure for the 90s.

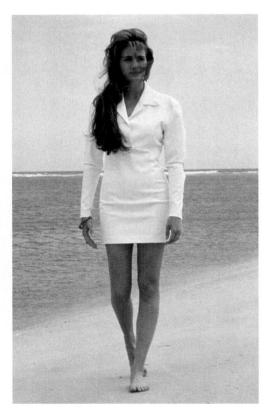

in particular our society's emphasis on thinness in women. This emphasis has increased markedly in the past 40 years, which fits with the claim that the incidence of anorexia has also increased during that period. An indication of this societal change is the change in what people regard as a "perfect" woman's figure. Figure 10-10 contains a photograph of Jayne Mansfield, who was popularly thought to have an ideal figure in the 1950s, next to a photograph of the actress Julia Roberts, one of today's ideals. Roberts is clearly much thinner than Mansfield. Presumably these "perfect" figures greatly influence women's own ideals, which results in women feeling their own figure is much heavier than their ideal (Logue, 1991).

Other researchers have focused on possible biological causes. One hypothesis is that anorexia is caused by malfunctions of the hypothalamus. The critical observation that led to this hypothesis is that sometimes the stop in menstruation in anorexics cannot be attributed to either weight loss or its side effects. Hence, there may be some common factor that is responsible for both irregularities in menstruation and anorexia. The most likely candidate is the hypothalamus, given that it is known to play a role in both eating and hormonal functions (Garfinkle & Garner, 1982).

BULIMIA

CHARACTERISTICS   Bulimia is characterized by recurrent episodes of *binge eating* (rapid consumption of a large amount of food in a discrete period of time), followed by attempts to purge the excess eating by means of vomiting and laxatives. The binges can be frequent and extreme. A survey of bulimic women found that most women binged at least once per day (usually in the evening), and that an average binge involved consuming some 4800 calories (often sweet or salty carbohydrate foods). However, because of the purges that follow the binges, a bulimic's weight may stay relatively normal; this allows bulimics to keep their eating disorder hidden. But there can be a large physiological cost for the bulimic's behavior; the vomiting and use of laxatives can disrupt the balance of the electrolyte potassium in the body, which can result in problems like dehydration, cardiac arrhythmias, and urinary infections.

Like anorexia, bulimia primarily afflicts young women. But bulimia is more frequent than anorexia, with an estimated 5 to 10 percent of American women affected to some degree. Rather than being restricted to just the upwardly mobile, bulimia is found in all racial, ethnic, and socioeconomic groups in our society.

POSSIBLE CAUSES   As was the case with anorexia, researchers have looked for explanations of bulimia in terms of personality, biological, and social factors.

With regard to personality factors, therapists who work with bulimic patients often see them as lacking a sense of identity and self-esteem. In line with this, depression seems to be relatively common in bulimics (Johnson & Larson, 1982). Such people may use food to fulfill their feelings of longing and emptiness. Researchers interested in biological factors in bulimia have also noted the link between bulimia and depression. It has been suggested that the same chemical disorder that underlies some cases of depression may also be the basis of some cases of bulimia; for example, a deficit of the neurotransmitter serotonin could be behind both depression and bulimia (Bruch, 1973). Bulimia may also be accompanied by changes in physiology related to hunger. For example, bulimics have been reported to have lower levels in their bloodstream of the hormone cholecystokinin (CCK), which helps produce ordinary feelings of satiety after a meal (Pirke et al., 1994).

As for social factors, again the culprit is often thought to be our society's recent overemphasis on thinner women. Indeed, some bulimic women are quite explicit that their disorder is a way of solving the problem of how to eat lots of high calorie food, yet stay as slim as current cultural norms prescribe. As one bulimic woman put it, "I thought I had the problem licked; I couldn't understand why everyone didn't eat and then vomit" (Garfinkel & Garner, 1982).

In closing our discussion of bulimia and anorexia, it is important to keep in mind three qualifications about the putative causes of these disorders. First and foremost, there is very little hard evidence for any of the possible causes that we have discussed. Most of what we know about anorexia and bulimia comes from clinical reports of patients with these disorders, and not from controlled experiments that can rigorously establish a causal link between some factor and self-starvation. Second, it seems highly unlikely that there is only one cause for anorexia and one for bulimia. As was the case with obesity, there may be many ways to get to anorexia or bulimia. Third, and finally, despite how little we know about the causes of these eating disorders, treatments for them have been developed. Typically, the treatments involve some form of therapy. Traditional psychotherapies can be useful in dealing with personality issues; behavior modification programs, like that described in our earlier discussion of weight control, seem quite useful in helping anorexics and bulimics bring their eating habits under control.

EARLY SEXUAL DEVELOPMENT

Just as are thirst and hunger, sexual desire is a powerful motivation. There are, however, important differences between sex and the motives of temperature, thirst, and hunger. Sex is a *social* motive—it typically involves another—whereas the survival motives concern only the biological self. In addition, motives such as hunger and thirst stem from tissue needs, while sex does not involve an internal deficit that needs to be regulated and remedied for the organism to survive. Consequently, social motives do not lend themselves to a homeostatic analysis.

With regard to sex, two critical distinctions should be kept in mind. The first stems from the fact that, although we begin to mature sexually at puberty, the basis for our sexual identity is established in the womb. We therefore distinguish between adult sexuality (that is, beginning with changes at puberty) and early sexual development. The second distinction is between the biological and environmental determinants of sexual behaviors and feelings. For many aspects of sexual development and adult sexuality, a fundamental question is the extent to which the behavior or feeling in question is a product of biology—particularly hormones—or environment and learning—early experiences and cultural norms—or of an interaction be-

tween the two. (This distinction between biology and environment is similar to one we drew earlier in our discussion of obesity. There we were concerned with genetic factors, which are of course biological, versus factors that tended to reflect learning and the environment.)

Most individuals, in order for social and sexual experiences to be gratifying in adult life, need to develop an appropriate **gender identity**—that is, males come to think of themselves as males, and females as females. This development is quite complex and begins in the womb.

PRENATAL HORMONES

For the first couple of months after conception, only the chromosomes of a human embryo indicate whether it will develop into a boy or girl. Up to this stage, both sexes are identical in appearance and have tissues that will eventually develop into testes or ovaries, as well as a genital tubercle that will become either a penis or a clitoris. But between 2 and 3 months, a primitive sex gland, or gonad, develops into testes if the embryo is genetically male (that is, has XY chromosomes—see Chapter 2) or into ovaries if the embryo is genetically female (XX chromosomes). Once testes or ovaries develop, they produce the sex hormones, which then control the development of the internal reproduction structures and the external genitals. The sex hormones are even more important for prenatal development than they will be later for expressions of adult sexuality.

The critical hormone in genital development is **androgen** (testosterone, which we have previously mentioned, is a kind of androgen). If the embryonic sex glands produce enough androgen, the newborn will have male genitals; if there is insufficient androgen, the newborn will have female genitals, *even* if it is genetically male (XY). Conversely, if androgens are added artificially, the newborn will have male genitals even if it is genetically female (XX). In other words, the presence or absence of a male (Y) chromosome normally influences sexual development simply by determining whether the embryo will secrete its own androgens. The anatomical development of the female embryo does not require female hormones, only the absence of male hormones. In short, nature will produce a female unless androgen intervenes.

The influence of androgen, called *androgenization,* extends far beyond anatomy. After it has molded the genitals, androgen begins to operate on the brain cells. Studies with rats provide direct evidence that prenatal androgen changes the volume and detailed structure of cells in the fetus' hypothalamus, an organ that regulates motivation in humans as well as rats (Money, 1988). These effects of androgen essentially masculinize the brain, and may be responsible for some masculine traits and behaviors that appear months or years later.

In a series of experiments, pregnant monkeys were injected with androgen (specifically, testosterone), and their female offspring were observed in detail. These female offspring showed some anatomical changes (penises instead of clitorises) and also acted differently than normal females. They were more aggressive in play, more masculine in sexual play, and less intimidated by approaching peers (Goy, 1968; Phoenix, Goy, & Resko, 1968). These findings indicate that some gender-typical behaviors (such as greater aggression for males) are partly hormonally determined in nonhuman animals.

Early hormonal abnormalities can also have the opposite consequence: to "feminize" the later sexual behavior of males. A striking example is that of "maternal stress": a change in the sexual behavior of male rats whose mothers experienced high emotional stress during their pregnancy (Ward, 1992). High levels of stress in a pregnant mother rat triggers hormonal events that result in a decrease in the amount of androgens produced by the male embryo's testes. That in turn results in a reduction of androgen that reaches the developing brain. The hypothalamus and other brain regions appear to develop differently in such embryos. When these male rats are adult, they show less male sexual behavior and may even show female patterns of copulation movements if they are mounted by another male. It is unknown whether similar effects on brain development or behavior occur in humans. Although some believe that these experiments may provide insights into the basis of human heterosexual versus homosexual orientation, there are differences between these animal models and human

Prenatal development: 4 months.

behavior. For example, male rats born to maternally stressed mothers tend to show less sexual behavior of any kind than ordinary male rats, but this is not true of gay men compared to heterosexual men. But these examples illustrate the importance of early hormonal environment for later sexual behavior of nonhuman animals, and they raise the possibility that prenatal hormones may be important for human sexual motivation too.

HORMONES VERSUS ENVIRONMENT IN HUMAN SEXUALITY

In humans, much of what is known about the effects of prenatal hormones and early environment has been uncovered by studies of humans who, for various reasons, were exposed to the prenatal hormones that would ordinarily be experienced by one sex, but then were raised in a social role that would ordinarily typify the opposite sex.

In most such cases, the assigned label and the sex role in which the individual is raised have a much greater influence on gender identity than do the individual's genes and hormones. For example, many thousands of women born during the 1950s and 1960s were exposed to an antimiscarriage drug, diethylstilbestrol, which had unexpected hormonelike effects on brain development. Ordinarily the testosterone secreted by a male embryo's testes is converted inside the embryo's brain to a substance similar to diethylstilbestrol. Pregnant women who took the drug thus unknowingly exposed their fetus to a chemical environment similar to that experienced by the developing brain of a normal male. For male fetuses, this would have little consequence: Their brains already were exposed to male patterns of chemical stimulation. But the female fetuses were exposed to an opposite-sex or malelike chemical stimulation for the length of time that their mothers took the drug. For the overwhelming majority of these daughters, the prenatal exposure had no detectable effect. Most women exposed prenatally to diethylstilbesterol went on to grow up similarly to other girls and to become indistinguishable from women with normal prenatal experience. Social environment, in other words, appears to be much more dominant in determining the sexual and gender development of these women than were prenatal hormones. On the other hand, this is not to say that prenatal chemical environment had absolutely no effect. Recent studies have detected several subtle differences that characterize at least some of the women exposed to diethylstilbestrol. For example, a slightly higher proportion of these women appear to be of homosexual/bisexual orientation than would be ordinarily expected. Sexual orientation is not identical to gender identity but in this case a slight effect of prenatal hormone on both may be reflected. Sexual orientation will be discussed in detail later. Similarly, these women appear to give slightly lower ratings on some measures of "maternal interest," such as finding infants attractive, even though they are not different from other women by most other measures of parental, sexual, or social behavior and attitudes (Ehrhardt, et al., 1989). Such studies suggest that although prenatal hormonal events may have some subtle consequences for later sexual and social development, their effect in humans is vastly reduced from the magnitude of their impact in nonhuman animals. For humans, social and cultural factors appear to be relatively dominant (Money, 1980).

But there are also studies that point to the opposite conclusion. The most famous occurred several years ago in remote villages of the Dominican Republic. It involved 18 genetic males, who, owing to a condition known as androgen insensitivity, were born with internal organs that were clearly male, but external genitals that were closer to females, including a clitorislike sex organ. In androgen insensitivity, the gonads develop as normal testes, and begin to secrete testosterone and other androgens. However, the receptor systems that would be activated by circulating androgens are missing in early life from at least some of the body tissues that would ordinarily be masculinized by the hormones. Even though androgens are secreted and present in the bloodstream of such a boy, they do not produce the male pattern of genital and physical development. All 18 were raised as girls, which was at odds with both their genes and their prenatal hormonal environment. When they reached puberty, the surge of male hormones produced the usual bodily changes and turned their clitorislike sex organs into penislike organs. The vast majority of these males-reared-as-females rapidly turned into males. They seemed to have little difficulty adjusting to a male gender identity; they went off to work as miners and woodsmen and some found female sexual partners. In this case, biology triumphed over environment (Imperato-McGinley, Peterson, Gautier, & Sturla, 1979). There is controversy, however, about these Dominican boys who appeared to be girls. They do not seem to have been raised as ordinary girls (not surprising, since they had ambiguous genitals). Rather, they seemed to have been treated as half-girl, half-boy, which could have made their subsequent transition to males easier (Money, 1987).

In other cases, the results of conflict between prenatal hormones and social rearing are less clear. In the most dramatic example, identical twin boys had a completely normal prenatal environment. But at the age of 7 months, in a tragic mistake, one of the boys had his penis completely severed in what was supposed to be a routine circumcision. Ten months later, the agonized parents authorized surgery to turn their child into a little girl—the testes were removed and a vagina was given preliminary shape. The child was then given female sex hormones and raised as a girl. Within a few years, the child seemed to have assumed a female gender identity: She preferred more feminine clothes, toys, and activities than her twin brother. The child appeared to be a normal girl in many ways, so most early investigators concluded this was a case in which social environment had won out. However, studies as the child reached puberty revealed that the outcome was more complex (Diamond, 1982). As a teenager, she was unhappy and appeared especially conflicted regarding her sexuality, even though, as far as is known, she had not been told about her original sexuality or sex-change operation. In interviews, she refused to draw a picture of a woman, and instead would draw only a man. Aspects of her "body language," such as walking gait and patterns of posture and movement, were masculine in appearance. Socially, she had considerably more than the usual degree of difficulty in forming relationships with her peers. In other words, it would seem rash to conclude that the attempt to control her gender identity through socialization, and to raise her as a "normal girl," had been completely successful. It is difficult to know the precise source of her difficulty in emotional and social adjustment, and there are several possibilities. But these include the possibility that her early brain development as a male placed constraints on her later ability to adapt to a female gender identity.

What can we conclude about gender identity? Clearly, prenatal hormones and environment are both major determinants of gender identity that typically work in harmony. When they clash, as they do in some individuals, most experts believe that environment will dominate. But this is a controversial area, and expert opinion may change as additional data are gathered.

ADULT SEXUALITY

Changes begin to occur in body hormone systems at puberty, which usually occurs between ages 11 and 14. These changes activate processes of psychological sexuality and trigger the development of physical sexual characteristics such as hair growth and breast development. Control of sexual hormone secretion in adults begins in the brain's hypothalamus (see Figure 10-11). The hypothalamus triggers a feedback loop of causes that affect first the pituitary gland, then the rest of the body, and then the brain itself once again. Thus reverberating signals related to sexual

function keep a loop operating between body and brain.

At puberty, the hypothalamus begins to secrete chemicals, called *gonadotropin releasing factors,* which stimulate the pituitary gland, which lies immediately below the hypothalamus. The function of the pituitary gland is to secrete hormones into the bloodstream. The pituitary gland's sexual hormones, called *gonadotropins,* circulate through the body to reach the **gonads**: ovaries in females and testes in males, which generate egg or sperm cells for sexual reproduction. Gonadotropin hormones activate the gonads, causing them to secrete sexual hormones of their own into the bloodstream.

In women, the hypothalamus releases its gonadotropin releasing factors on a monthly cycle, rising and falling approximately every 28 days. This stimulates the female pituitary to secrete two gonadotropin hormones: *follicle stimulating hormone* (FSH) and *luteinizing hormone* (LH), also on a monthly cycle. These hormones activate the ovaries. Follicle stimulating hormone stimulates the ovaries to generate *follicles,* clusters of cells in the

FIGURE 10-11

Hormonal System Involved in Sex *By way of hormones, the hypothalamus directs the pituitary, which in turn directs the gonads to secrete the sex hormones.*

ovaries that allow fertile eggs to develop. Once a follicle is generated, it begins to secrete the female hormone, **estrogen**. Estrogen is released into the bloodstream to affect the sexual development of the body and, in many species of animals, to activate sexual motivation in the brain. The second gonadotropin, luteinizing hormone, is released from the pituitary just slightly later than follicle stimulating hormone. Luteinizing hormone causes ovulation, the release of a mature fertile egg cell from the follicle. When the follicle releases its egg, it also secretes a second female hormone: **progesterone**, which prepares the uterus for implantation of a fertilized egg, and which, in some species of animals, also activates sexual motivation in the brain.

In men, the hypothalamus secretes gonadotropin releasing factor in a constant fashion rather than in a monthly cycle. This causes the male pituitary to constantly release its gonadotropin, called *interstitial cell stimulating hormone* (ICSH), into the bloodstream. ICSH causes male testes to produce mature sperm cells and to dramatically boost secretion of the male hormones called androgens—especially **testosterone**. Testosterone and other androgens stimulate the development of male physical characteristics and, in most species of animals, act on the brain to activate sexual desire (and in some species, to facilitate some forms of aggression).

EFFECTS OF HORMONES ON DESIRE AND AROUSAL

What role do these hormones play in adult sexual desire and arousal? In other species, sexual arousal is closely tied to variations in hormonal levels; in humans, however, hormones play less of a role. One way to assess the contribution of hormones to sexual arousal is to study the effects of removing the gonads: either the ovaries or the testes. This is called *gonadectomy*. (In males, removal of the testes is called *castration*.) In experiments with lower species (such as rats and guinea pigs), castration results in the rapid decline and eventual disappearance of sexual activity. For humans, of course, there are no controlled experiments; psychologists rely instead on observations of males with serious illnesses (for example, cancer of the testes)

who have undergone *chemical castration* (synthetic hormones administered to suppress or block the use of androgen). These studies typically show that some men lose their interest in sex, while others continue to lead a normal sex life (Walker, 1978; Money, Wiedeking, Walker, & Gain, 1976). Apparently, androgen contributes to sexual desire only in some cases.

Another way to measure the contribution of hormones to sexual desire and arousal in men is to look for a relation between hormonal fluctuation and sexual interest. For example, is a man more likely to feel aroused when his testosterone level is high? It turns out that testosterone level may have no effect on *copulatory function*—as indicated by the ability to have an erection—but does increase *desire*—as indicated by sexual fantasies (Davidson, 1988). [The major determinants of sexual desire in men, however, seem to be emotional factors; thus, for males (as well as females), the most common cause of low desire in couples seeking sex therapy is marital conflict (Goleman, 1988).]

Sexual desire is even less dependent on hormones in women. This contrasts with nonprimate species in which female sexual behavior is highly dependent on sexual hormones. In all other animals, removal of the ovaries results in cessation of sexual activity. The castrated female ceases to be receptive to the male and usually resists sexual advances. The major exception is the human female; following menopause (when the ovaries have ceased to function), sexual desire in most women does not diminish. In fact, some women show an increased interest in sex after menopause, possibly because they are no longer concerned about becoming pregnant. There is evidence to indicate that women's sexual desire is facilitated by trace amounts of sexual hormones in the bloodstream (Sherwin, 1988). However, the level required is so low that it may ordinarily be exceeded by most women and not play a significant role in changes in desire.

Studies looking at the relation between hormonal fluctuation and sexual arousal in premenopausal females lead to a similar conclusion: Normal changes in hormones have substantial control of arousal in other animals but not in humans. In female mammals, hormones fluctuate cyclically with accompanying changes in fertility. During the first part of the mammalian cycle (while the egg is being prepared for fertilization), the ovaries secrete estrogen, which prepares the uterus for implantation and also tends to arouse sexual interest. After ovulation occurs, both progesterone and estrogen are secreted. This *fertility* or **estrous cycle** is accompanied by a consequent variation in sexual motivation in most mammalian species. Most female animals are receptive to sexual advances by a male only during the period of ovulation, when the estrogen level is at its highest in the cycle (when they are "in heat"). Among primates, however, sexual activity is less influenced by the fertility cycle; monkey, ape, and chimpanzee females copulate during all phases of the cycle, although ovulation is still the period of most intense sexual activity. In the human female, sexual desire and arousal seems to be barely influenced by the fertility cycle, being affected much more by social and emotional factors.

In sum, the degree of hormonal control over adult sexual behavior decreases from the lower to the higher vertebrates. Still, even for humans there may be some hormonal control, as witnessed by the relation between testosterone and sexual desire in men.

NEURAL CONTROL

In one sense, the primary sex organ is the brain. The brain is where sexual desire originates and where sexual behavior is controlled. For humans, the sexual function of the brain extends to the control of sexual thoughts, images, and fantasies. Within the brain, sexual hormones can influence neural function in adult individuals. Sexual hormones also influence the actual physical growth and connection patterns of developing neurons in early life for all mammalian species, including humans (discussed below), and in adults for at least some species (Breedlove, 1994).

The nervous system is affected at many levels by sexual hormones. At the level of the spinal cord, neural circuits exist that control the movements of copulation. In males, these include erection of the penis, as well as pelvic movements and ejaculation. All of these actions can be elicited in a reflex fashion from men whose spinal cords were severed by injury and who have no conscious sensations

A young couple in love.

from their body. Similarly in females, clinical studies of women with spinal injury indicate that vaginal secretions in response to genital stimulation and pelvic movements may be controlled by neural reflex circuits within the spinal cord (Offir, 1982).

Higher levels of the brain, especially the hypothalamus, contain the neural systems that are important to more complex aspects of sexual behavior. For example, sexual pursuit and copulation can be elicited from both males and females of many animal species by electrical stimulation of hypothalamic regions. Even for humans, stimulation of brain regions near the hypothalamus has been reported to induce intense sexual feelings and desire (Heath, 1972). Conversely, lesions of the hypothalamus can eliminate sexual behavior for many species, including humans.

EARLY EXPERIENCES

The environment also has great influence on adult sexuality, one class of determinants being early experience. Experience is a major determinant of the sexual behavior of many mammals.

EXPERIMENTS WITH MONKEYS Experience can affect specific sexual responses. For instance, young monkeys exhibit in their play many of the postures required later for copulation. In wrestling with their peers, infant male monkeys display hindquarter grasping and

Sexual play among snow monkeys.

thrusting responses that are components of adult sexual behavior. Infant female monkeys retreat when threatened by an aggressive male infant and stand steadfastly in a posture similar to the stance required to support the weight of the male during copulation. These presexual responses appear as early as 60 days of age and become more frequent and refined as the monkey matures. Their early appearance suggests that they are innate responses to specific stimuli, and the modification and refinement of these responses through experience indicates that learning plays a role in the development of the adult sexual pattern.

Experience also affects the interpersonal aspect of sex. Monkeys raised in partial isolation (in separate wire cages, where they can see other monkeys but cannot have contact with them) are usually unable to copulate at maturity. The male monkeys are able to perform the mechanics of sex: They masturbate to ejaculation at about the same frequency as normal monkeys. But when confronted with a sexually receptive female, they do not seem to know how to assume the correct posture for copulation. They are aroused but aimlessly grope the female or their own bodies. Their problem is not just a deficiency of specific responses. These once-isolated monkeys have social or affectional problems: Even in nonsexual situations, they are unable to relate to other monkeys, exhibiting either fear and flight or extreme aggression. Apparently, normal heterosexual behavior in primates depends not only on hormones and the develop-

ment of specific sexual responses, but also on an affectional bond between two members of the opposite sex. This bond is an outgrowth of earlier interactions with the mother and peers, through which the young monkey learns to trust, to expose its delicate parts without fear of harm, to accept and enjoy physical contact with others, and to be motivated to seek the company of others (Harlow, 1971).

Although we must be cautious about generalizing these findings with monkeys to human sexual development, clinical observations of human infants suggest certain parallels. Human infants develop their first feelings of trust and affection through a warm and loving relationship with the mother or primary caretaker (see Chapter 3). This basic trust is a prerequisite for satisfactory interactions with peers. And affectionate relationships with other youngsters of both sexes lay the groundwork for the intimacy required for sexual relationships among adults.

CULTURAL INFLUENCES

Cultural influences constitute another class of environmental determinants that influence the expression of sexual desire. Unlike that of other primates, human sexual behavior is strongly determined by culture.

SEXUAL ACTIVITY IN DIFFERENT CULTURES   Every society places some restrictions on sexual behavior. Incest (sexual relations within the family), for example, is prohibited by almost all cultures. Other aspects of sexual behavior—sexual activity among children, homosexuality, masturbation, and premarital sex—are permitted in varying degrees by different societies. Among preliterate cultures studied by anthropologists, acceptable sexual activity varies widely. Some very permissive societies encourage autoerotic activities and sex play among children of both sexes and allow them to observe adult sexual activity. The Chewa of Africa, for example, believe that if children are not allowed to exercise themselves sexually, they will be unable to produce offspring later. The Sambia of New Guinea have institutionalized bisexuality: From prepuberty until marriage, a boy lives with other males and engages in homosexual practices (Herdt, 1984).

In contrast, very restrictive societies try to control preadolescent sexual behavior and to keep children from learning about sex. The Cuna of South America believe that children should be totally ignorant about sex until they are married; they do not even permit their children to watch animals give birth.

SEXUAL CHANGES WITHIN THE UNITED STATES   While the most obvious way to study cultural differences is to investigate practices in different countries, one can also look at culture changes that occur within a country. One such change occurred in the United States and other Western countries between the 1940s and the 1970s. In the 1940s and 1950s, the United States and most other Western countries would have been classified as sexually restrictive. Traditionally, the existence of prepubertal sexuality had been ignored or denied. Marital sex was considered the only legitimate sexual outlet, and other forms of sexual expression (homosexual activities, premarital and extramarital sex) were generally condemned and often prohibited by law. Of course, many members of these societies engaged in such activities, but often with feelings of shame.

Over the years, sexual activities became less restricted. Premarital intercourse, for example, became more acceptable and more frequent. Among American college-educated individuals interviewed in the 1940s, 27 percent of the women and 49 percent of the men had engaged in premarital sex by the age of 21 (Kinsey, Pomeroy, Martin & Gebhard, 1953; Kinsey, Pomeroy, & Martin, 1948). In contrast, several surveys of American college students in the 1970s reported percentages ranging from 40 to over 80 for both males and females (Tavris & Sadd, 1977; Hunt, 1974). There has been a gradual trend over the past several decades toward initiating sex at an earlier age. Roughly 50 percent of both men and women report having had sexual intercourse by age 16–17 (Laumann, Gagnon, Michael, & Michaels, 1994). Figure 10-12 gives the reported incidence of premarital intercourse in studies conducted over a 35-year span. Note that the change in sexual behavior was greater among women than men and that the biggest changes occurred in the late 1960s. These changes led many observers of the social scene in the 1970s to conclude that there had been a sexual revolution.

Today, it seems that the sexual revolution has been stymied by the fear of sexually transmitted diseases, particularly the acquired immunodeficiency syndrome, or AIDS. Furthermore, the revolution may always have pertained more to behavior than to feelings. In interviews conducted with American college-student couples in the 1970s, only 20 percent thought that sex between casual ac-

According to the theory described in the text, both heterosexual and homosexual attraction are based on the same principles.

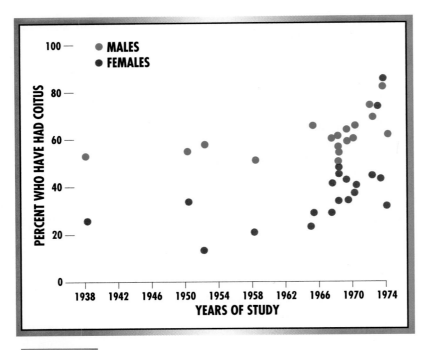

FIGURE 10-12

Reported Incidence of Premarital Coitus   *Each data point represents findings from a study of the incidence of premarital sex among college men and women. Note the marked upward trend starting in the 1960s.* (After Hopkins, 1977)

quaintances was completely acceptable (Peplau, Rubin, & Hill, 1977). In a similar vein, while women are becoming more like men with regard to sexual behavior, they continue to differ from men in certain critical attitudes toward sex before marriage. The majority of women who engage in premarital sex do so with only one or two partners with whom they are emotionally involved. Men, in contrast, are more likely to seek sex with multiple partners (Laumann et al., 1994). However, within a given 5-year period, the majority of both men and women are likely to have no more than one sexual partner (Laumann et al., 1994).

SEX DIFFERENCES

Studies of heterosexuals have shown that young men and women differ in their attitudes about sex; women are more likely than men to view sex as part of a loving relationship. Related to this, differences between women and men have been reported in the nature of the type of event that is most likely to elicit sexual jealousy: emotional infidelity or sexual infidelity. Whether measured by

self-report or by autonomic reactions such as heart rate, women react more strongly to the prospect of emotional infidelity (the prospect of their partner's forming a romantic relationship with someone else), regardless of whether their partner's infidelity involves an actual sexual act. By contrast, men react more strongly to the prospect of sexual infidelity, regardless of whether their partner's sexual liaison involves an emotional commitment (Buss, Larsen, Westen, & Semmelroth, 1992). Differences between the sexes apply to behavior as well as to attitudes. Women are likely to have fewer sexual partners than men if they engage in premarital sex. Differences between male and female patterns of sexual behavior persist regardless of sexual orientation. For example, lesbian couples are likely to have sex less frequently than heterosexual couples, and gay male couples have sex more often than heterosexual couples. Such differences can be viewed as reflecting a continuum of female-typical to male-typical characteristics (Buss, 1994).

SEXUAL ORIENTATION

An individual's **sexual orientation** is the degree to which he or she is sexually attracted to persons of the opposite sex and/or to persons of the same sex. Like Alfred Kinsey, the pioneering sex researcher of the 1940s, most behavioral scientists conceptualize sexual orientation as a continuum, ranging from exclusive heterosexuality to exclusive homosexuality. For example, on Kinsey's own 7-point scale, individuals who are attracted exclusively to persons of the opposite sex and who engage in sexual behavior only with such persons are at the heterosexual end of the scale (category 0); those who are attracted exclusively to persons of the same sex and who engage in sexual behavior only with such persons are at the homosexual end of the continuum (category 6). Individuals in categories 2–4 are usually defined as bisexual.

This oversimplifies the situation, however, because sexual orientation comprises several distinct components, including erotic attraction or sexual desire, sexual behavior, romantic attraction, and self-identification as a **heterosexual**, homosexual, or bisexual person. It is not uncommon for an individual to be at different points on the scale for different components. For example, many people who are sexually attracted to persons of the same sex have never participated in any homosexual behaviors; many who have had frequent homosexual encounters do not identify themselves as homosexual or bisexual persons. To further complicate matters, individuals may shift over time on one or more of the components.

FREQUENCY OF DIFFERENT SEXUAL ORIENTATIONS In a recent survey of sexuality in the United States, 10.1 percent of adult men and 8.6 percent of adult women in a national random sample reported at least one of the following: (a) they were currently attracted "mostly" or "only" to persons of their own sex; (b) they found having sex with someone of the same sex "somewhat" or "very" appealing; or (c) they had engaged in sexual behavior with a person of the same sex since age 18 (Laumann, Gagnon, Michael, & Michaels, 1994). These percentages are similar to the percent of people who report that they are left-handed (about 8 percent). In terms of self-identification, 2.8 percent of the men and 1.4 percent of the woman identified themselves as homosexual (or gay or lesbian) or bisexual—similar to the percent of people in the United States who identify themselves as Jewish (2–3 percent).

As the authors of the survey acknowledge, these percentages must be regarded as underestimates because many people are reluctant to report desires or behaviors that are still considered by some to be immoral or pathological. The problem was particularly acute in this survey because the interviews were conducted in the persons' own homes and were not always private; other family members—even children—were present in over 20 percent of the interviews.

LINKS TO CHILDHOOD The determinants of sexual orientation—specifically homosexuality—are currently the subject of debate in both the behavioral sciences and the mass media. At issue, once again, is the nature-nurture question, which we introduced in the chapter on development (Chapter 3) and discuss in detail in the chapter on individual differences (Chapter 12): Is an adult's sexual orientation primarily determined by earlier life experiences or by innate biological influences such as hormones or genes?

The best data on earlier life experiences comes from an intensive, large-scale interview study of approximately 1,000 homosexual and 500 heterosexual men and women living in the San Francisco Bay area (Bell, Weinberg, & Hammersmith, 1981a).*

The study uncovered one—and only one—major factor that predicted a homosexual orientation in adulthood for both men and women: childhood gender nonconformity. As shown in Table 10-2, when asked what play activities they had or had not enjoyed as children, homosexual men and women were much less likely than heterosexual men and women to report that they had enjoyed activities typical of their sex and much more likely to report that they had enjoyed activities typical of the other sex. Homosexual men and women were also less likely than their heterosexual counterparts to report that they had been masculine (for men) or feminine

---

* Footnote: When describing studies in which men and women with a homosexual orientation are explicitly compared with men and women with a heterosexual orientation, we will use the terms *homosexual men and women* in parallel with the terms *heterosexual men and women.* Otherwise we will adhere to the guidelines published by the American Psychological Association and refer to homosexual men and women as *gay men* and *lesbians,* respectively.

	HOMOSEXUAL MEN	HOMOSEXUAL WOMEN	HETEROSEXUAL MEN	HETEROSEXUAL WOMEN
Enjoyed Boys' Activities	37%	81%	90%	61%
Enjoyed Girls' Activities	48%	37%	11%	85%
Were Sex-Typed (Masculine for men; Feminine for women).	44%	20%	92%	76%
At least 1/2 of Childhood Friends were of the Opposite Sex	42%	60%	13%	40%

TABLE 10-2

Gender Nonconformity in Childhood *In a large-scale interview study, homosexual men and women were more likely than heterosexual men and women to report that were gender nonconforming during childhood* (After Bell, Weinberg, & Hammersmith, 1981b) (for women) as children. In addition to this gender nonconformity, homosexual men and women were more likely to have had more friends of the opposite sex.

Two features of the data in Table 10-2 are worth noting. First, the findings are quite strong and similar for men and women: Only about 37 percent of homosexual men and women enjoyed childhood activities typical of their sex compared with 85–90 percent of their heterosexual counterparts. In fact, homosexual men actually enjoyed typical boys' activities (such as football and baseball) less than did heterosexual women. Second, despite the strength of the findings, there are still many exceptions. For example, 44 percent of homosexual men reported that they were masculine as children (compared, however, with 92 percent of heterosexual men). The finding that childhood gender nonconformity predicts an adult homosexual outcome has now been confirmed in several other studies (Bailey & Zucker, 1995), including several that selected gender-nonconforming boys and followed them into adulthood (Zucker, 1990; Green, 1987).

In addition to the gender nonconformity finding, the San Francisco study also yielded many negative findings that were important because they disconfirmed common theories about the antecedents of a homosexual orientation. For example:

- A person's identification with the opposite-sex parent while growing up appears to have no significant effect on whether he or she turns out to be homosexual or heterosexual. This fails to confirm Freud's psychoanalytic theory (discussed in Chapter 13) as well as other theories based on the dynamics of the person's childhood family. And although gay men recalled somewhat poorer relationships with their fathers than did heterosexual men—which is consistent with psychoanalytic theory—this was also true for lesbians compared with heterosexual women. Moreover, the findings suggest that a poor father-child relationship is not a determinant of a homosexual outcome but a result of the father's disliking or rejecting his gender-nonconforming child, especially a feminine-acting son. As we noted in Chapter 3, fathers are much less tolerant of gender nonconformity than are mothers.

- Gay men and lesbians were no more likely than their heterosexual counterparts to report having their first sexual encounter with a person of the same sex. Moreover, they neither lacked heterosexual experiences during their childhood and adolescent years nor found such experiences unpleasant.

- A person's sexual orientation is usually determined by adolescence, even though he or she might not yet have become sexually active. Gay men and lesbians typically experienced same-sex attractions about 3 years before they had engaged in any "advanced" sexual activity with persons of the same sex.

These last two sets of findings indicate that, in general, homosexual feelings, not homosexual activities, are the crucial antecedents of an adult homosexual orientation. They thus disconfirm any simple behavioral learning theory of sexual orientation, including the popular, layperson's version which asserts that an individual can become gay by being "seduced" by a person of the same sex or by having an admired teacher, parent, or clergyperson who is openly gay. Cross-cultural data are also consistent with this conclusion. For example, in the Sambian culture of New Guinea, all boys engage in exclusively homosexual behaviors from prepuberty through late adolescence. At that point, virtually all of them get married and become exclusively heterosexual (Herdt, 1987, 1984).

Finally, it is clear from all the studies that one's sexual orientation is not simply a matter of choice. Gay men and lesbians do not choose to have erotic feelings toward persons of the same sex any more than heterosexual persons choose to have erotic feelings toward persons of the opposite sex. Behavioral scientists do disagree over the nature-nurture question—whether the major determinants of sexual orientation are rooted in biology or experience—but the public often misconstrues the question to be whether sexual orientation is determined by variables beyond the individual's control or is freely chosen. That is not the same question.

Because the results of the San Francisco study disconfirmed virtually all the major theories of homosexuality based on childhood or adolescent experiences, the investigators speculate that the origins of both childhood gender nonconformity and adult homosexual orientation may lie in the innate or prenatal biology of the individual, the topic to which we turn next.

HORMONES As we noted earlier in this chapter, sex hormones—especially the androgens—are involved in sexual motivation. This observation, which is especially marked in men, suggested to many early researchers the hypothesis that gay men might have lower androgen or testosterone levels than heterosexual men. But this hypothesis was not confirmed. Most studies showed no differences and those that did failed to control for other factors that are known to suppress androgen levels, such as stress or recreational drug use. Moreover, when gay men are given additional testosterone, their sexual motivation increases—as it does for men in general—but their sexual orientation does not change.

The role of hormones in prenatal development suggested a different hormonal hypothesis. Reasoning from research on rats in which prenatal testosterone "masculinizes" the brain and influences subsequent male-like mating responses, some researchers hypothesized that human males who get substantially lower than average amounts of testosterone as fetuses at a critical point in prenatal development will be predisposed toward a homosexual orientation in adult life. Similarly, female fetuses exposed to substantially higher than average amounts of testosterone may also be slightly predisposed toward a homosexual orientation in adult life (Ellis & Ames, 1987).

It is difficult to test hypotheses about prenatal hormones in humans, and most of the relevant studies have methodological flaws that prevent any firm conclusions (Adkins-Regan, 1988; Ehrhardt & Meyer-Bahlburg, 1981). For example, a well-known study followed girls who were exposed to extremely high levels of prenatal testosterone. These girls were born with ambiguous genitalia which were surgically corrected soon after birth. In interviews in middle childhood, these girls and their mothers reported that they were more likely to be "tomboys" than a group of control girls (Money & Ehrhardt, 1972). In early adulthood, they were more likely than control girls to have same-sex fantasies (Money, Schwartz, & Lewis, 1984). These results have often been interpreted as demonstrating that the testosterone had

"masculinized" the girls' brains during the prenatal period.

But other interpretations are possible. For example, these girls were also on cortisone medication, which could make them more physically active and, hence, more tomboy-like. This might influence their interactions with other girls, with boys, and with adults, and possibly change the way these individuals behave toward them. For this and other reasons, the study does not clearly demonstrate a direct link between prenatal hormones and adult sexual orientation.

Similar methodological problems make it difficult to interpret other findings relevant to the prenatal hormone hypothesis. For example, it has been reported that the hypothalamus of gay men differs in a small structural detail from those of heterosexual men (LeVay, 1993, 1991). As we noted earlier, the hypothalamus is a part of the brain intimately involved with sexual hormones and sexual behavior. But this finding is based on an examination of brains of men who had died, and the gay men had all died from complications of AIDS, but most of the control group of heterosexual men had not. We do not know whether the disease process itself might have affected the brain anatomy, although there is some evidence to suggest that AIDS is probably not the cause of the structural difference (LeVay, 1993).

GENES In contrast to the ambiguity of the hormonal evidence, the evidence for a link between genetic factors and an adult homosexual orientation now seems well established—even if its interpretation is not. The most compelling data come from studies of identical and fraternal twins. As we describe briefly in Chapter 2 and more at length in Chapter 12 (Individual Differences), identical twins share all their genes, whereas fraternal twins are like ordinary siblings in that they share only about half their genes. To the extent that identical twins are more alike on a trait than are fraternal twins, the trait has a genetic or heritable component (assuming that other factors, such as differential parental treatment of identical and fraternal twins can be ruled out).

In a study of gay men who had male twins, it was found that 52 percent of their identical twin brothers were also gay compared with only 22 percent of their fraternal twin brothers (Bailey & Pillard, 1991). In a comparable study of lesbians, 48 percent of their identical twin sisters were also lesbian, compared with only 16 percent of fraternal twin sisters. Moreover, only 6 percent of these women's adoptive sisters were lesbian, a further indication that a genetic link is involved (Bailey, Pillard, Neale, & Agyei, 1993). Finally, an analysis of 114 families of gay men, in conjunction with a chromosomal analysis of 40 families in which there were two gay brothers, showed some suggestive evidence for a genetic marker for homosexuality on the X chromosome, the chromosome that males receive from their mothers. Thus, gay men had more gay male relatives on the mother's side than on the father's side of the family (Hamer & Copeland, 1994; Hamer et al., 1993).

PUTTING IT ALL TOGETHER   Because most of the theories of homosexuality based on life experiences have failed to receive empirical support and the genetic evidence has become increasingly compelling, many researchers now appear to subscribe to a biological or "nature" explanation of sexual orientation—although they are careful to hedge this conclusion in their written work. Nevertheless, a recently proposed experience-based theory attempts to integrate the findings we have reviewed here. It is called the exotic-becomes-erotic theory of sexual orientation (D. Bem, 1995.)

The theory proposes, first, that genetic (and possibly other biological) factors do not influence adult sexual orientation per se but a child's temperament and personality traits. As we document in the chapter on individual differences (Chapter 12), about half of the variation among individuals in most personality traits can be attributed to genetic differences. In other words, there is solid evidence that most personality traits have a strong genetic or heritable component, including such childhood temperaments as emotionality, sociability, and activity level (Buss & Plomin, 1984, 1975).

Temperaments such as these predispose a child to enjoy some activities more than others: One child will enjoy rough-and-tumble play and competitive team sports; another will prefer to socialize quietly or play jacks or hopscotch. Some of these activities are more male-typical; others are more female-typical. Thus, depending on the sex of the child, he or she will be genetically predisposed to be gen-

der conforming or gender nonconforming. As shown in Table 10-2, children also tend to have friends who share their activity preferences; for example, the child—male or female—who shuns competitive team sports will avoid playing with boys and seek out girls as playmates. Accordingly, gender-conforming children will feel most similar to and most comfortable with children of their own sex; gender-nonconforming children will feel most similar to and most comfortable with children of the opposite sex.

The theory next proposes that dissimilarity and discomfort produce general (nonsexual) arousal. For the female-typical child, this arousal may be experienced as mild fear or apprehension in the presence of boys; for the male-typical child, it may be felt as antipathy or contempt in the presence of girls ("girls are yucky"). The clearest case is the "sissy" boy who is teased and tormented by other boys for his gender nonconformity and who is thereby likely to experience the strong arousal of fear and suppressed anger in their presence. The "tomboy" girl who is shunned by her female peers may experience similar emotionally toned arousal. The most common case, however, is probably the child who simply experiences the mild arousal produced by being in the presence of dissimilar peers.

Finally, the theory proposes that this general arousal is transformed in later years into erotic arousal or sexual attraction—after the original cause of the arousal may have diminished or disappeared. Evidence for this last step in the process comes, in part, from laboratory studies (described more amply in Chapter 17) in which male subjects were physiologically aroused in one of several nonsexual ways (for example, by running in place or by watching a videotape of a comedy routine or a grisly killing). When these men subsequently watched a videotape of an attractive woman, they found her more attractive and expressed more interest in dating and kissing her than did men who had not been physiologically aroused. Moreover, it did not matter what caused the initial arousal. This general finding has now been replicated in several studies (Allen, Kenrick, Linder, & McCall, 1989; White & Kight, 1984; Dutton & Aron, 1974; White, Fishbein, & Rutstein, 1981). In short, general physiological arousal can be subsequently experienced as, interpreted as, or actually transformed into sexual arousal.

Conversely, the theory implies that when children interact with peers with whom they are quite comfortable, no arousal (or, possibly, the extinction of arousal) occurs. Thus, gender-conforming children will come to have comfortable but nonerotic friendships with persons of the same sex and gender-nonconforming children will come to have comfortable but nonerotic friendships with persons of the opposite sex. Only the exotic becomes erotic. Indirect evidence for this comes from the observation that boys and girls raised collectively on communes (kibbutzim) in Israel rarely marry one another because they feel too much like brothers and sisters (Shepher, 1971).

This same process explains why virtually all Sambian men turn out to be predominantly heterosexual in adulthood despite having spent their entire adolescence engaging in homosexual activities. Although the majority of Sambian boys enjoy their homosexual activity, the context of close male bonding in which it occurs does not produce strongly charged homoerotic or romantic feelings; meanwhile, the boys are taught that women are both inferior and dangerous—which enhances the erotic appeal of women. More generally, the theory implies that across time and cultures, heterosexuality will be the predominant outcome because virtually all societies set up a sex-based division of labor that sets men and women apart and makes them dissimilar, exotic, and, hence, erotic to one another.

Other writers have also proposed that although similarity and familiarity may promote friendship and compatibility, it is dissimilarity, unfamiliarity, and a sense of the exotic that sparks sexual arousal and/or romantic feelings (for example, Bell, 1982; Tripp, 1987). Ethologists have even noted the effects of dissimilarity in the mating choices of nonhuman animals. As we discuss in the critical discussion (Imprinting—Interaction Between Learning and Instinct), some species prefer mates that resemble but are not identical to the sexual imprinting target they encountered prior to sexual maturity; a mate that is just slightly different from the target is perceived as the most desirable. Ethologists speculate that this preference prevents inbreeding because a mate that looks identical to the imprinting target is likely to be a close relative.

HETEROSEXUALITY As we have seen, Bem's theory of sexual orientation attempts to account symmetrically for the erotic attractions of both gay men and lesbians, thereby mirroring the symmetry of the data on gender nonconformity shown in Table 10-2. We have also seen that it attempts to account for heterosexual as well as homosexual attraction. In fact, the common question "what causes homosexuality?" is scientifically misconceived because it implicitly assumes either that heterosexuality needs no explanation or that its causes are self-evident. Those who have thought about it at all are likely to conclude that because only heterosexual behavior results in reproduction, it must be the "natural" outcome of evolution, and hence only deviations from heterosexuality (such as homosexuality) pose a scientific puzzle. Freud himself did not agree: "[heterosexuality] is also a problem that needs elucidation and is not a self-evident fact based upon an attraction that is ultimately of a chemical nature" (1905/1962, pp. 11–12). It is because we agree with Freud that we have called this section of the chapter "sexual orientation" and not "homosexuality."

The more general point here is that just because a behavior might be reproductively advantageous, it does not follow that evolution must necessarily "hardwire" it into the species. Consider again the ducks described in the critical discussion on instinct and imprinting. Clearly it would be reproductively advantageous for ducks to mate with other ducks. And yet, if they are raised by a foster mother of another species they will prefer a mate that resembles her to another duck; They will even prefer a human if he or she was the first moving object they saw after they were hatched. As long as the environment supports or promotes the reproductively successful behavior sufficiently often, it will not necessarily get programmed into the genes. And just as baby ducks will encounter mother ducks most of the time, so, too, human societies see to it that men and women will see each other as dissimilar sufficiently often to ensure that the species will not perish from the earth. It has even been proposed that by nurturing their nephews and nieces, lesbian aunts and gay uncles help the species along (Wilson, 1978).

BIOLOGICAL-PSYCHOLOGICAL PERSPECTIVES

Psychological and biological causes are so closely intertwined in the control of many human motivations as to virtually merge together into one stream of events. Causation works in both directions between biological and psychological events. First, we've seen that biological causes can control psychological motivations. For example, activation of a single brain system mediates the reward value of a diverse array of incentives. Many psychological states, such as feeling too hot or too cold, or being thirsty or hungry, are triggered directly by homeostatic signals. Sexual hormones (prenatal or later in life) may influence the intensity and direction of sexual desire. Even evolutionary aspects of biological causes, arising from the selection pressures that shaped our development, can be seen to have influenced motivation. For example, the tendency to prefer sweet foods above others, the automatic way in which we acquire certain learned food preferences and aversions, and the rigid rules of learning that operate during social imprinting all are motivational systems whose operation has been tuned by the need to cope with specific evolutionary pressures.

Second, psychological processes and experiences also control motivation and may feed back to control physiological responses. For example, repeated use of an addictive drug may permanently change particular brain systems. More commonly, the particular foods and drinks we desire are established as objects of choice largely by learning, and even the degree of satiety produced by a stomach full of food is influenced by previous experience. Our social attachments are determined largely by the consequences of earlier social interactions with particular individuals. When it comes to many motivational processes, biology and psychology are not separate domains, but rather two aspects of control that continually interact to direct motivational processes.

 CHAPTER SUMMARY

1. Motivational states direct and activate our behavior. We can consciously choose whether to act upon a motive, but the processes that directly control motivational states operate in advance of conscious choice. They arise from two sources: internal drive factors and external incentive factors.

2. Incentive factors are goals in the outside world, such as food, water, partners, and drugs. Incentives are the target of motivated behavior and are typically rewarding once acheived. Although some incentives—such as a sweet food when we are hungry—are by themselves powerful motivators, most incentives are established by learning.

3. Many different types of natural reward may activate the *mesolimbic dopamine system* of the brain. Activity in these neurons may constitute the neural basis for all rewards. Artificial activation of them, by rewarding drugs or electrical brain stimulation, causes increased motivation for both natural and artificial incentives. Changes in this system, produced by repeatedly taking drugs

that activate it, may partly cause the compulsive craving of *addiction*.

4. Drive factors tend to promote *homeostasis:* the preservation of a constant internal state. Homeostasis involves several components: a *goal value* or *set point* for the ideal internal state, a *sensory signal* that measures the actual internal state, a *comparison* between the goal value and the sensory signal, and finally, a *response* that brings the actual internal state closer to the goal value.

5. Our regulation of temperature is an example of homeostasis. The regulated variable is the temperature of the blood, and sensors for this are located in various regions of the body, including the *hypothalamus.* The ideal value and comparator are also located in the hypothalamus. Adjustments are either automatic physiological responses (for example, shivering) or voluntary behavioral ones (such as putting on a sweater).

6. Thirst is another homeostatic motive. There are two regulated variables, *intracellular fluid* and *extracellular fluid.* The loss of

intracellular fluid is detected by *osmotic sensors,* which are neurons in the hypothalamus that respond to dehydration. The loss of extracellular fluid is detected by *blood-pressure sensors,* which are neurons in major veins and body organs that respond to a drop in pressure. Intracellular and extracellular signals act in parallel to produce thirst.

7. Hunger has evolved to allow us to select an array of nutrients. Humans have innate taste *preferences,* as for sweetness, and innate *aversions,* as for bitterness, that guide our choice of foods. In addition, we may develop a wide variety of learned preferences and aversions. Homeostatic hunger signals, which arise when our bodies are low in calorie-containing fuels such as *glucose,* produce appetite in part by causing an individual to perceive food incentives as more attractive and pleasant.

8. Hunger is largely controlled by homeostatic *deficit* and *satiety* signals. Certain neurons in the brain, especially in the brain stem and hypothalamus, detect shortages in glucose availability and trigger hunger. Other nutrient detectors, especially in the liver, detect rising levels of energy stores and trigger satiety. A satiety signal, in the form of a hormone, *cholecystokinin,* is released from the intestines to help stop hunger and eating.

9. Two regions of the brain are critical for hunger: the *lateral hypothalamus* and the *ventromedial hypothalamus.* Destruction of the lateral hypothalamus leads to undereating; destruction of the ventromedial hypothalamus leads to overeating. Although these regions were originally thought to be centers for hunger and satiety, hunger is not destroyed by any lesion. Another interpretation of these effects is that the lateral and ventromedial regions of the hypothalamus exert reciprocal effects on the homeostatic set point for body weight. Damage to the lateral hypothalamus may lower the set point, and damage to the ventromedial hypothalamus may raise the set point. Diet drugs that alter appetite may work in part by affecting neurons in these regions of the hypothalamus.

10. People become obese primarily because: (a) they are genetically predisposed to be overweight or (b) they overeat (for psychological reasons). The influence of genes is mediated by their effect on *fat cells, metabolic rate,* and *set points.* As for overeating and obesity, obese people tend to overeat when they break a diet, eat more when emotionally aroused, and are more responsive than normal-weight individuals to external hunger cues. In treating obesity, extreme diets appear ineffective, because the deprivation leads to subsequent overeating and to a lowered metabolic rate. What seems to work best is to establish a new set of permanent eating habits and to engage in a program of exercise.

11. *Anorexia nervosa* is characterized by an extreme, self-imposed weight loss. Anorexia is 20 times more likely to occur in women than men. The weight loss may be mediated by a *distorted body image,* the anorexic erroneously thinking that she looks too fat. Possible causes of anorexia include personality factors (for example, a struggle for autonomy), society's overemphasis on thinness in women, and biological problems (for example, a dysfunctional hypothalamus). *Bulimia* is characterized by recurrent episodes of *binge-eating,* followed by attempts to purge the excess eating by means of vomiting and laxatives. Possible causes again include personality factors (for example, depression), society's emphasis on thinness, and biological factors (for example, a deficit in the neurotransmitter serotonin).

12. Prenatal hormones contribute to sexual development. If the embryonic sex glands produce enough androgen hormones, the embryo will have a male pattern of genital and brain development. If androgens are low or missing, the embryo will have a female pattern of genital and brain development. For nonhuman animals, prenatal hormones appear to be extremely powerful in determining later adult sexual behavior. For humans, prenatal hormones appear to be much less important, although they may still play a role in later sexual behavior. In cases in which the hormonal exposure of the embryo is typical of one sex but the social role and gender after birth is more typical of the opposite sex (due to hormone imbalance, prenatal drugs, or a postnatal accident), the development of the person seems to correspond most closely to the postnatal social gender.

13. The female hormones (*estrogen* and *progesterone*) and male hormones (*androgens*) are responsible for the body changes at puberty but play only a limited role in human sexual arousal. In contrast, there is substantial hormonal control over sex in lower species. Early social experiences with parents

and peers have a large influence on adult sexuality in primates and humans. Monkeys raised in isolation have sexual problems as adults. For humans, other environmental determinants of adult sexuality include cultural norms. Although western society has become increasingly flexible regarding female and male sex roles during the past 30 years, men and women may still differ in their attitudes toward sex and relationships.

14. Although it seems clear that for most people sexual orientation is caused, not freely chosen, the nature of the causes is obscure. Recent studies have bolstered the claim that biological, genetic, hormonal, or neural factors may partly determine whether an individual will be heterosexual or homosexual, but the evidence is not conclusive. It is also unknown whether biological factors may influence sexual orientation directly or whether they instead contribute to other traits, such as gender conformity, that indirectly influence the development of sexual orientation.

FURTHER READING

A general summary of incentive and drive theories of motivation, and their interaction with learning, is provided by Toates, *Motivational Systems* (1986). An overview of biological factors in motivation can be found in Kalat, *Biological Psychology* (4th ed., 1992); and in Carlson, *Physiology of Behavior* (5th ed., 1994). The neural substrates of reward are discussed in detail by Stellar and Stellar, *The Neurobiology of Motivation and Reward* (1985); and by Hoebel in *Stevens' Handbook of Experimental Psychology* (2nd edition, 1988). For analyses of factors controlling eating and drinking, see E. M. Stricker (ed.), *Neurobiology of Food and Fluid Intake, Handbook of Behavioral Neurobiology* 10 (1990); and Logue, *The Psychology of eating and Drinking* (1986). A discussion of diverse aspects of human sexuality can be found in McWhirter et al. (eds.), *Homosexuality/-Heterosexuality* (1990); and in LeVay, *The Sexual Brain* (1994).

EMOTIONS

The most basic feelings that we experience include not only motives such as hunger and sex but also emotions such as joy and anger. Emotions and motives are closely related. Emotions can activate and direct behavior in the same way that basic motives do. Emotions may also accompany motivated behavior: Sex, for example, is not only a powerful motive but a potential source of joy, as well.

Despite their similarities, motives and emotions need to be distinguished. One common distinction is that emotions are triggered from the outside, while motives are activated from within. That is, emotions are usually aroused by external events, and emotional reactions are directed toward these events; motives, in contrast, are often aroused by internal events (a homeostatic imbalance, for example) and are naturally directed toward particular objects in the environment (such as food, water, or a mate). Another distinction between motives and emotions is that a motive is usually elicited by a specific need, whereas an emotion can be elicited by a wide variety of stimuli (think of all the different things that can make you angry, for example). These distinctions are not absolute. An external source can sometimes trigger a motive, as when the sight of food triggers hunger. And the discomfort caused by a homeostatic imbalance—severe hunger, for example—can arouse emotions. Nevertheless, emotions and motives are sufficiently different in their sources of activation, subjective experience, and effects on behavior that they merit separate treatment.

COMPONENTS OF AN EMOTION

An intense emotion includes several general components (Lazarus, 1991; Frijda, Kuipers, & Schure, 1989). The component we most frequently recognize in an emotion is the subjective experience of the emotion—the affective state or feelings associated with the emotion. A second component is bodily reaction. When angered, for example, you may sometimes tremble or raise your voice, even though you don't want to. A third component

is the collection of thoughts and beliefs that accompany the emotion, and that seem to come to mind automatically. Experiencing joy, for example, often involves thinking about the reasons for the joy ("I did it—I'm accepted into college!"). A fourth component of an emotional experience is facial expression. When you experience disgust, for example, you probably frown, often with your mouth open wide and your eyelids partially closed. A fifth component concerns global reactions to the emotion; for example, a negative emotion may darken your outlook on the world. A sixth component is the action tendencies associated with the emotion—the set of behaviors that people tend to engage in when experiencing a certain emotion. Anger may lead you to aggression, for instance.

Thus, our list of the components of an emotion includes:

1. The subjective experience of the emotion

2. Internal bodily responses, particularly those involving the autonomic nervous system

3. Cognitions about the emotion and · associated situations

4. Facial expression

5. Reactions to the emotion

6. Action tendencies

None of these components, by itself, *is* an emotion. All these components come together to create a particular emotion. In addition, each of these components can influence the other components. For example, your cognitive appraisal of a situation can lead to a specific emotion: If you believe that a store clerk is trying to cheat you, you are likely to experience anger. But if you enter that situation already angry, you will be even more likely to appraise the clerk's behavior as dishonest. Emotion theorists are moving toward a *systems* perspective on emotion, in which the components of an emotion are seen as having reciprocal effects on each other (see Figure 11-1). The critical questions in modern emotions theories concern the detailed nature of each of these components and the specific mechanisms by which components influence each other. For example, one set of questions concerns how autonomic responses, beliefs and cognitions, and facial expressions contribute to the intensity of an experienced emotion. Do you feel angrier, for example, when you experience more autonomic arousal? Indeed, could you even feel angry if you had no autonomic arousal? Similarly, does the intensity of your anger depend on your having a certain kind of thought, or a certain kind of facial expression? In contrast to these questions about the intensity of an emotion, there are also questions about which components of an emotion are responsible for making the different emotions *feel* different. Which components *differentiate* the emotions? To appreciate the difference between questions about intensity and questions about differentiation, consider the possibility that autonomic arousal greatly increases the intensity of our emotions, but that the pattern of arousal is roughly the same for several emotions; if this were the case, autonomic arousal could not differentiate between emotions.

These questions will guide us as we consider in turn autonomic arousal, cognitive appraisal, and facial expression. We will then turn our attention to general reactions of an emotional experience. In the final part of the chapter, we will focus on an action tendency of an emotion, and consider in detail the topic of aggression. We will be concerned throughout primarily with the more intense affective states—like those involved in happiness, sadness, anger, fear, and disgust—although the ideas and principles that will emerge in our discussion are relevant to a variety of feelings.

AROUSAL AND EMOTION

PHYSIOLOGICAL BASIS

When we experience an intense emotion, such as fear or anger, we may be aware of a number of bodily changes—including rapid heartbeat and breathing, dryness of the throat and mouth, perspiration, trembling, and a sinking feeling in the stomach (see Table 11-1). Most of the physiological changes that take

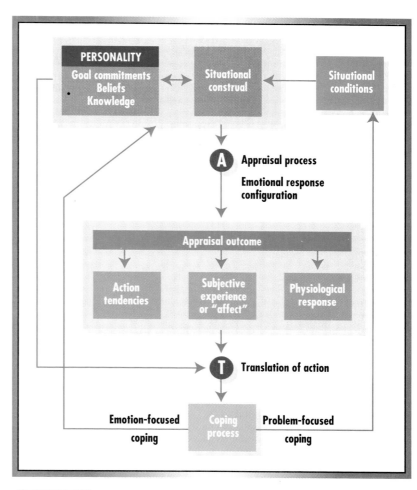

FIGURE 11-1

One Model of How the Components of Emotion Affect Each Other in a Dynamic System.   (After Lazarus, 1991)

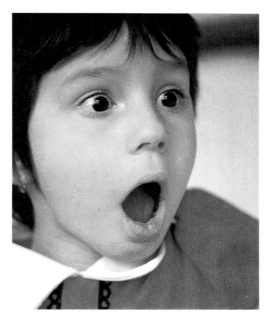

Facial expression is a component of emotion.

TABLE 11-1

Symptoms of Fear in Combat Flying *Based on reports of combat pilots during World War II. (After Shaffer, 1947)*

DURING COMBAT MISSIONS DID YOU FEEL . . . ?	SOMETIMES	OFTEN	TOTAL
A pounding heart and rapid pulse	56%	30%	86%
That your muscles were very tense	53	30	83
Easily irritated or angry	58	22	80
Dryness of the throat or mouth	50	30	80
Nervous perspiration or cold sweat	53	26	79
Butterflies in the stomach	53	23	76
A sense of unreality—that this could not be happening to you	49	20	69
A need to urinate very frequently	40	25	65
Trembling	53	11	64
Confused or rattled	50	3	53
Weak or faint	37	4	41
That right after a mission you were unable to remember the details of what had happened	34	5	39
Sick to the stomach	33	5	38
Unable to concentrate	32	3	35
That you had wet or soiled your pants	4	1	5

place during emotional arousal result from activation of the sympathetic division of the autonomic nervous system as it prepares the body for emergency action (see Chapter 2). The **sympathetic system** is responsible for the following changes (all of which need not occur at once):

1. Blood pressure and heart rate increase.

2. Respiration becomes more rapid.

3. The pupils dilate.

4. Perspiration increases while secretion of saliva and mucous decreases.

5. Blood-sugar level increases to provide more energy.

6. The blood clots more quickly in case of wounds.

7. Blood is diverted from the stomach and intestines to the brain and skeletal muscles.

8. The hairs on the skin become erect, causing goose pimples.

The sympathetic system gears the organism for energy output. As the emotion subsides, the **parasympathetic system**—the energy-conserving system—takes over and returns the organism to its normal state.

These activities of the autonomic nervous system are themselves triggered by activity in certain critical regions of the brain, including the **hypothalamus** (which, as we saw in the last chapter, plays a major role in many biological motives) and parts of the **limbic system**. Impulses from these areas are transmitted to nuclei in the brain stem that control the functioning of the autonomic nervous system. The autonomic nervous system then acts directly on the muscles and internal organs to initiate some of the bodily changes previously described, and acts indirectly by stimulating the adrenal hormones to produce other bodily changes.

Note that the kind of heightened physiological arousal we have described is characteristic of emotional states such as anger and fear, during which the organism must prepare for action—for example, to fight or flee. (The role of this fight-or-flight response in threatening or stressful situations is elaborated in Chapter 14.) Some of the same responses may also occur during joyful excitement or sexual arousal. During emotions such as sorrow or grief, however, some bodily processes may be depressed, or slowed down.

INTENSITY OF EMOTIONS

What is the relation between heightened physiological arousal and the subjective experience of an emotion? In particular, does our perception of our own arousal make up part of the experience of the emotion? To answer this question, researchers have studied the emotional life of individuals with spinal cord injuries. When the spinal cord is severed or lesioned, sensations below the point of injury cannot reach the brain. Since some of these sensations arise from the sympathetic nervous system, the injuries reduce the contributions of autonomic arousal to felt emotion. In one study, army veterans with spinal cord injuries were divided into five groups, according to the location on the spinal cord at which the lesion occurred. In one group, the lesions were near the neck (at the cervical level), with no innervation of the sympathetic system. In another group, the lesions were near the base of the spine (at the sacral level), with at least partial innervation of the sympathetic nerves. The other three groups fell between these two extremes. The five groups represented a continuum of bodily sensation: the higher the lesion on the spinal cord, the less the feedback of the autonomic nervous system to the brain.

The subjects were interviewed to determine their feelings in situations of fear, anger, grief, and sexual excitement. Each person was asked to recall an emotion-arousing incident prior to the injury and a comparable incident following the injury, and to compare the intensity of emotional experience in each case. The data for states of fear and anger are shown in Figure 11-2. The higher the person's lesion was on the spinal cord (that is, the less the feedback from the autonomic nervous system), the more his emotionality decreased following injury. The same relation was true for states of sexual excitement and grief. A reduction in autonomic arousal resulted in a reduction in the intensity of experienced emotion.

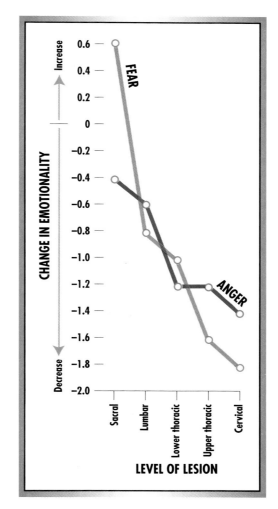

FIGURE 11-2

Relationship Between Spinal Cord Lesions and Emotionality *Subjects with spinal cord lesions compared the intensity of their emotional experiences before and after injury. Their reports were coded according to the degree of change: 0 indicates no change; a mild change ("I feel it less, I guess") is scored −1 for a decrease or +1 for an increase; and a strong change ("I feel it a helluva lot less") is scored −2 or +2. Note that the higher the lesion, the greater the decrease in emotionality following injury.* (After Schachter, 1971; Hohmann, 1962)

Comments by patients with the highest spinal cord lesions suggested that they could *react* emotionally to arousing situations, but that they did not really *feel* emotional. For example, "It's sort of a cold anger. Sometimes I act angry when I see some injustice. I yell and cuss and raise hell, because if you don't do it sometimes, I've learned people will take advantage of you; but it doesn't have the heat to it that it used to. It's a mental kind of anger." Or, "I say I am afraid, like when I'm going into a real stiff exam at school, but I don't really feel afraid, not all tense and shaky with the hollow feeling in my stomach, like I used to."

The preceding study is important, but it is not entirely objective—the emotional situations varied from person to person, and subjects rated their own experiences. A follow-up study provides a more objective situation: All subjects were exposed to the same situations, and their emotional experiences were rated by independent judges. Male subjects with spinal cord injuries were presented with pictures of clothed and nude females and were told to imagine that they were alone with each woman. Subjects reported their "thoughts and feelings," which then were rated by judges for expressed emotion. Patients who had higher lesions were rated as experiencing less sexual excitement than those whose lesions were lower on their spines (Jasmos & Hakmiller, 1975). Again, the less the feedback of the autonomic system to the brain, the less intense the emotion.

DIFFERENTIATION OF EMOTIONS

Clearly, autonomic arousal contributes to the intensity of emotional experience. But does it differentiate the emotions? Is there one pattern of physiological activity for joy, another for anger, still another for fear, and so on? This question dates back to a seminal paper that William James wrote over a century ago (James, 1884), in which he proposed that the perception of bodily changes *is* the subjective experience of an emotion: "We are afraid because we run"; "we are angry because we strike." The Danish physiologist Carl Lange arrived at a similar position at about the same time, but for him the bodily changes included autonomic arousal. Their combined position is referred to as the **James-Lange theory,** and it argues as follows: Because the perception of autonomic arousal (and perhaps of other bodily changes) constitutes the experience of an emotion, and because different emotions feel different, there must be a distinct pattern of autonomic activity for each emotion. The James-Lange theory therefore holds that autonomic arousal differentiates the emotions.

The theory came under severe attack in the 1920s (particularly that part of the theory dealing with autonomic arousal). The attack was led by the physiologist Walter Cannon (1927), who offered three major criticisms:

1. Since the internal organs are relatively insensitive structures and not well supplied with nerves, internal changes occur too slowly to be a source of emotional feeling.

2. Artificially inducing the bodily changes associated with an emotion—for example, injecting a drug such as epinephrine—does not produce the experience of a true emotion.

3. The pattern of autonomic arousal does not seem to differ much from one emotional state to another; for example, while anger makes our heart beat faster, so does the sight of a loved one.

The third argument, then, explicitly denies that autonomic arousal can differentiate the emotions.

Psychologists have tried to rebut Cannon's third point while developing increasingly more accurate measures of the subcomponents of autonomic arousal. Although a few experiments in the 1950s reported distinct physiological patterns for different emotions (Funkenstein, 1955; Ax, 1953), until the 1980s most studies on this topic had found little evidence for different patterns of arousal being associated with different emotions. A study by Levenson, Ekman, and Friesen (1990), however, provides strong evidence that there are autonomic patterns distinct to different emotions. Subjects produced emotional expressions for each of six emotions—surprise, disgust, sadness, anger, fear, and happiness—by following instructions about which particular facial muscles to contract. While they held an emotional expression for 10 seconds, the researchers measured their heart rate, skin temperature, and other indicators of autonomic arousal. A number of these measures revealed differences between the emotions (see Figure 11-3). Heart rate was faster for the negative emotions of anger, fear, and sadness than it was for happiness, surprise, and disgust; and the former three emotions themselves could be partially distinguished by the fact that skin temperature was higher in anger than in fear or sadness. Thus, even though both anger and the sight of a loved one make our heart beat faster, only anger makes it beat *much* faster; and though anger and fear have much in common, anger is hot and fear cold (no wonder people describe their anger as their "blood boiling," and their fear as "bone-chilling" or as "getting cold feet").

Recent work suggests that these distinctive arousal patterns may be universal. Levenson, Ekman and their colleagues studied members of the Minangkabau culture in Western Sumatra, a culture very different from ours. Again, subjects produced facial expressions for various emotions—this time, fear, anger, sadness, and disgust—while measures were taken of their heart rate, skin temperature, and other indicators of arousal. Although the magnitude of the physiological changes were less for the Sumatrans than those reported earlier for Americans, the patterns of arousal for the different emotions were the same; again, heart rate was faster for anger, fear, and sadness than for disgust, and skin temperature was highest in anger (Levenson, Ekman, Heider, & Friesen, 1992).

These results are important, but by no means do they provide unequivocal evidence for the James-Lange theory or the claim that autonomic arousal is the *only* component that differentiates the emotions. All the above studies demonstrated was that there are *some* physiological differences between emotions, not that these differences are perceived and experienced as *the* qualitative differences between the emotions. Even if autonomic arousal does help differentiate some emotions, it is unlikely that it differentiates *all* emotions; the difference between contentment and pride, for example, is unlikely to be found in visceral reactions. Also, the first two points that Cannon raised against the James-Lange theory still stand: Autonomic arousal is too slow to differentiate emotional experiences, and artificial induction of arousal does not yield a true emotion. For these reasons, many psychologists still believe that something other than autonomic arousal must be involved in differentiating the emotions. That something else (or part of it) is usually thought to be one's cognitive appraisal of the situation.

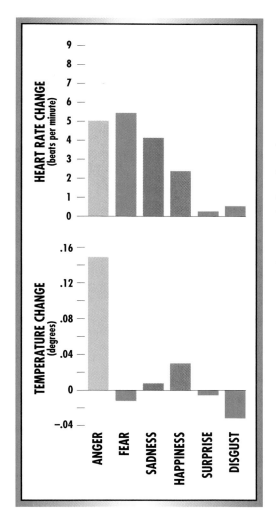

FIGURE 11-3

Arousal Differences for Different Emotions *Changes in heart rate (upper graph) and right finger temperature (lower graph). For heart rate, the changes associated with anger, fear, and sadness were all significantly greater than those for happiness, surprise, and disgust. For finger temperature, the change associated with anger was significantly different from that for all other emotions.* (After Ekman, Levenson, & Friesen, 1990)

COGNITION AND EMOTION

When we experience an event or action, we interpret the situation with respect to our personal goals and well-being ("I won the match and I feel happy" or "I failed the test and I feel depressed"). This interpretation is known as a **cognitive appraisal.**

INTENSITY AND DIFFERENTIATION OF EMOTIONS

Clearly, our appraisal of a situation can contribute to the intensity of our emotional experience. If we are in a car that starts to roll down a steep incline, we experience fear, if not terror; but if we know the car is part of a roller coaster, the fear is usually much less. If we are

USING AROUSAL TO DETECT LIES

If autonomic arousal is part of an emotion and if experiencing an emotion is a likely consequence of lying, then we can use the presence of autonomic arousal to infer that a person is lying. This is the theory behind the **lie-detector** test, in which a machine called a **polygraph** (meaning "many writings") simultaneously measures several physiological responses known to be part of autonomic arousal (see Figure 1). The measures most frequently recorded are changes in heart rate, blood pressure, respiration, and the galvanic skin response or **GSR** (a change in the electrical conductivity of the skin that occurs with emotional arousal).

In operating a polygraph, the standard procedure is to make the first recording while the subject is relaxed; this recording serves as a *baseline* for evaluating subsequent responses. The examiner then asks a series of carefully worded questions that the subject has been instructed to answer with a "yes" or "no" response. Some of the questions are "critical," which means that the guilty are likely to lie in response to them (for example, "Did you rob Bert's Cleaners on December 11?"). Other questions are "controls"; even innocent people are somewhat likely to lie in response to these questions (for example, "Have you ever taken something that didn't belong to you?"). Yet other questions are "neutral" (for example, "Do you live in San Diego?"). Critical questions are interspersed among control and neutral ones; sufficient time is allowed between questions for the polygraph measures to return to normal. Presumably, only the guilty should show greater physiological responses to the critical questions than to the others. Lie detection essentially rests on a "con game" of sorts, in which the examiner works hard to convince the subject that any attempt to deceive

In a polygraph, the arm cuff measures blood pressure and heart rate, the pneumograph around the rib cage measures rate of breathing, and the finger electrodes measure GSR. The recording on the right shows the physiological responses of a subject as he lies and as he simulates lying. The respiratory trace (top line) shows that he held his breath as he prepared for the first simulation. He was able to produce sizable changes in heart rate and GSR at the second simulation. (After Kubis, 1962)

the machine will be very obvious (Saxe, Dougherty & Cross, 1985). Instilling this belief in subjects may be more important than the pen tracings themselves.

However, the use of the polygraph in detecting lies is far from foolproof. A response to a question may show that a subject is aroused but not why he or she is aroused. An innocent subject may be very tense or may react emotionally to certain words in the questions and therefore appear to be lying when telling the truth. On the other hand, a practiced liar may show little arousal when lying. And a knowledgeable subject may be able to "beat" the machine by thinking about something exciting or by tensing muscles during neutral questions, thereby creating a baseline comparable to reactions to the critical questions. The recording in Figure 1 shows the responses to an actual lie and a simulated lie. In this experiment, the subject picked a number and then tried to conceal its identity from the examiner. The number was 27, and a marked change in heart rate and GSR can be seen when the subject denies number 27. The subject simulates

lying to number 22 by tensing his toes, producing noticeable reactions in heart rate and GSR.

Because of these and other problems, most state and federal courts will not admit polygraph tests; the courts that do generally require that both sides agree to its introduction. Such tests are frequently used, however, in preliminary criminal investigations and by employers interviewing prospective personnel for trusted positions.

Representatives of the American Polygraph Association have claimed an accuracy rate of 90 percent or better for polygraph tests conducted by a skilled operator. Critics, however, consider the accuracy rate to be much lower. For example, Lykken (1984) claims that in studies involving real-life situations, the lie-detector test is correct only about 65 percent of the time, and an innocent person has a 50-50 chance of failing the test. He argues that the polygraph detects not only the arousal that accompanies lying but also the stress that an honest person experiences when strapped to the equipment. Also, guilty people who are less so-

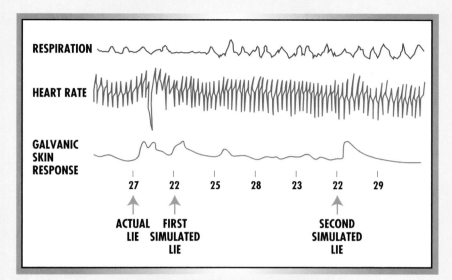

FIGURE 1

This recording shows the physiological responses of a subject as he lies and as he simulates lying. The respiratory trace (top line) shows that he held his breath as he prepared for the first simulation. He was able to produce sizable changes in heart rate and GSR at the second simulation. (After Kubis, 1962)

cialized may be less aroused while lying, and consequently harder to detect (Saxe, Dougherty, & Cross, 1985). Nevertheless, many businesses believe that the benefits of these tests outweigh the risks, and polygraph tests are often used in private industry. They are also widely used in law enforcement. The FBI, for example, administers several thousand polygraph tests per year, mostly to follow up leads and to verify specific facts—areas in which, experts agree, the polygraph is more useful. In criminal and private cases, anyone has the legal right to refuse a polygraph test. However, this is hardly a safeguard for someone whose refusal, for whatever reason, may endanger a career or job opportunity.

Another type of lie detector measures changes in a person's voice that are undetectable to the human ear. All muscles, including those controlling the vocal cords, vibrate slightly when in use. This tremor, which is transmitted to the vocal cords, is suppressed by activity of the autonomic nervous system when a speaker is under stress. When a tape recording of a person's voice is played through a device called a **voice-stress analyzer**, a visual representation of the voice can be produced on a strip of graph paper. The tremors of the vocal cords in the voice of a relaxed speaker resemble a series of waves (see the left-hand graph in Figure 2). When a speaker is under stress, the tremors are suppressed (see the right-hand graph in Figure 2).

The voice-stress analyzer is used in lie detection in essentially the same way as a polygraph; neutral questions are interspersed with critical questions, and recordings of the subject's responses to both are compared. If answers to the critical questions produce the relaxed wave form, the person is probably telling the truth (as far as we know, vocal cord tremors cannot be controlled voluntarily). A stressed wave form, on the other hand, indicates only that the individual is tense or anxious, not necessarily that he or she is lying.

There are, however, two serious problems with the use of the voice-stress analyzer in detecting lies. First, since the analyzer can work over the telephone, from radio or television messages, or from tape recordings, there is potential for the unethical use of this instrument. The second concern is the accuracy of the voice-stress analyzer. Some investigators claim that it is as accurate as the polygraph in distinguishing between the guilty and the innocent; others claim that it is no more accurate than chance. Much more research is required to determine the relationship between voice changes and other physiological measures of emotion (Lykken, 1980; Rice, 1978).

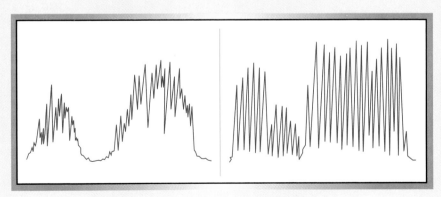

FIGURE 2

Effects of Stress on Voice Patterns   *A voice-stress analyzer produces graphic records of speech. The voice printout for a relaxed speaker resembles a series of waves, such as those shown on the left. The waves are produced by tiny tremors of the vocal cords. Under stress, the tremors are suppressed, producing a printout similar to that shown on the right. (After Holden, 1975)*

Two people can have different emotional reactions to an event because they interpret the event differently.

told by someone that he or she cannot stand the sight of us, we may feel very angry or hurt if that person is a friend, but feel barely perturbed if the person is a mental patient whom we have never met before. In these cases, and countless others, our cognitive appraisal of the situation determines the intensity of our emotional experience (Lazarus, 1991; Lazarus, Kanner, & Folkman, 1980).

Cognitive appraisal may also be heavily responsible for differentiating the emotions. Unlike autonomic arousal, appraisals are varied enough to distinguish among many different kinds of feelings, and the appraisal process itself may be fast enough to account for the speed with which some emotions arise. Also, we often emphasize cognitive appraisals when we describe the quality of an emotion. We say, "I felt angry because she was unfair" or "I felt frightened because I was abandoned"; unfairness and abandonment are clearly beliefs that result from a cognitive process.

These observations suggest that cognitive appraisals are often sufficient to determine the quality of emotional experience. This in turn suggests that if people could be induced to be in a neutral state of autonomic arousal, the quality of their emotion would be determined solely by their appraisal of the situation. Schachter and Singer (1962) first tested

this claim in an experiment that had a major impact on theories of emotion for the next two decades.

Subjects were given an injection of epinephrine, which typically causes autonomic arousal, such as an increase in heart and respiration rates, muscle tremors, and a jittery feeling. The experimenter then manipulated the information that the subjects were given regarding the effects of epinephrine. Some subjects were correctly informed about the arousal consequences of the drug (heart-rate acceleration, muscle tremors, and so on); other subjects were given no information about the physiological effects of the drug. The *informed* subjects had an explanation of their arousal; the *uninformed* subjects did not. Schachter and Singer predicted that how the uninformed subjects interpreted their symptoms would depend on the situation they were placed in. Subjects were left in a waiting room with another person, ostensibly another subject but actually a confederate of the experimenter; this confederate created either a happy situation (by making paper airplanes, playing basketball with wads of paper, and so on), or an angry situation (by complaining about the experiment, tearing up a questionnaire, and so on). The results of this study suggested that the uninformed subjects placed in the happy situation rated their feelings as more happy than the informed subjects in that situation did, and the uninformed subjects in the angry situation rated their feelings as more angry that the informed subjects in that situation did. In other words, subjects who had a physiological explanation for their arousal were less influenced in their subjective state by the situation than subjects who did not have the explanation.

The Schachter and Singer experiment was extremely influential, but that influence may not have been justified. The pattern of results in the study did not strongly support the experimenters' hypotheses, in that the differences between certain important groups did not reach statistical significance, and a placebo control group did not react to the experimental manipulations in a manner consistent with the hypotheses. In addition, the autonomic arousal may not have been the same in the happy and angry situations, and it certainly was not neutral.

Follow-up experiments to the Schachter and Singer study have found that subjects rate their experiences more negatively (less happy, or more angry) than the situation warrants, suggesting that the physiological arousal produced by epinephrine is experienced as somewhat unpleasant. Also, these follow-up experiments have sometimes had difficulty reproducing the Schachter and Singer results (Maslach, 1979; Marshall & Zimbardo, 1979). Hence, we need supporting evidence that completely neutral arousal may be misattributed.

A subsequent study supplied such evidence. Subjects first engaged in strenuous physical exercise and then participated in a task where they were provoked by a confederate of the experimenter. The exercise induced physiological arousal that was neutral and that persisted until the subject was provoked; this arousal should have combined with any that was elicited by the provocation, thereby resulting in a more intense experience of anger. In fact, subjects who exercised responded more aggressively to the provocation than subjects who did not (Zillman & Bryant, 1974).

The conclusions that emerge from this line of research are that an eliciting event typically results in both autonomic arousal and cognitive appraisal. The perceived arousal and cognitive appraisal are not experienced as inde-

pendent; rather, the arousal is *attributed* to the appraisal—"My heart is racing *because* I'm so angry about what Mary said." These studies indicate that both arousal and appraisal contribute to the intensity of experience—and that sometimes appraisal alone can determine the quality of experience. While research indicates that arousal may aid in differentiating emotions, it seems to play less of a role than does appraisal.

The top two sections of Figure 11-4 summarize how the components of an emotion interrelate for the two major theories we have discussed so far. Although each of these theories has been supported to some extent, they clearly oversimplify the emotion process. The components, autonomic arousal and cognitive appraisal, are themselves complex events that involve subcomponents, and these subcomponents do not all occur at the same time. For example, suppose an acquaintance says something insulting to you. You may first be aware of the unpleasantness of the remark, then feel a tinge of arousal, next appraise the remark more in detail while concurrently experiencing more arousal, and so on. Thus, autonomic arousal and cognitive appraisal are events stretched out in time, and the subcomponents that comprise these events can go on in parallel (Ellsworth, 1991).

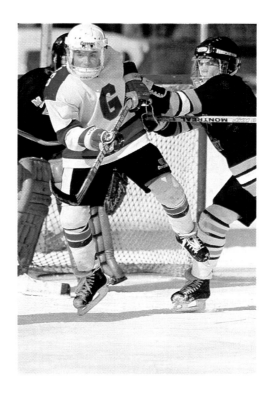

Physical arousal may intensify feelings of anger.

FIGURE 11-4

Major Theories of Emotion   *Different theories of emotion propose different relationships between the components of an emotion.*

DIMENSIONS OF APPRAISAL

In the third section of Figure 11-4 is a third major theory of emotion, which we have labeled *appraisal theory*. Actually, this is a group of theories that suggest it is people's appraisals of *situations* (not their appraisals of general physiological arousal) that lead to the subjective experience of emotion and the physiological arousal associated with the emotions. These appraisal theories can be divided into (a) theories that identify primary or fundamental emotions that everyone experi-

TABLE 11-2

Primary Emotions and Their Causes   *Eight primary emotions and their associated appraisals.* (After Plutchik, 1980)

EMOTION	APPRAISAL
Grief (Sorrow)	Loss of loved one
Fear	Threat
Anger	Obstacle
Joy	Potential mate
Trust	Group member
Disgust	Gruesome object
Anticipation	New territory
Surprise	Sudden novel object

ences and then specify the types of situations and appraisals that elicit those primary emotions, and (b) theories that identify the primary dimensions of appraisals and the specific emotions resulting from these appraisals.

According to the first group of appraisal theories, there is a relatively small set of "primary" emotions and each emotion is elicited by specific appraisals of an event. Table 11-2 lists several emotions (such as fear) and their respective triggering appraisals (threat). These primary emotions can be found in every human culture and throughout the animal kingdom. Some events may be appraised the same way by everyone. For example, large hissing snakes tend to be appraised as threats by most animals and humans. The types of threats that elicit the appraisals listed in Table 11-2 may differ across species and human cultures, however (Scherer, 1988). Among humans, for example, many Americans would be shocked to walk onto a beach to discover everyone is nude, but many Brazilians would be unmoved by such a scene, because nude sunbathing is more common in Brazil than in America.

The second group of appraisal theories is concerned with specifying primary dimensions of *appraisals* (rather than a primary set of emotions) and the emotional consequences of these dimensions. An example is given in Table 11-3. One dimension is the desirability of an anticipated event, and another is whether or not the event occurs. When we combine these two dimensions, we get four possible appraisals (the left-hand side of Table 11-3), each of which seems to produce a distinct emotion. (We are using only four emotions in our example just to keep things simple.) When a desired event occurs (such as falling in love), we experience *joy;* when a desired event does not occur (the person we are in love with does not love us), we experience *sorrow;* when an undesired event occurs (doing poorly on an exam), we experience *distress;* and when an undesired event does not occur (not doing poorly on an exam), we experience *relief.*

The preceding example invokes only two dimensions, but most theories of cognitive appraisal assume that multiple dimensions are involved. For example, Smith and Ellsworth (1987; 1985) found that at least six dimensions were needed to describe 15 different emotions (including, for example, anger, guilt, and sadness). These dimensions included: (a) the desirability of the situation (pleasant or unpleasant); (b) the effort that one anticipates spending on the situation; (c) the certainty of the situation; (d) the attention that one wants to devote to the situation; (e) the control that one feels over the situation; and (f) the control that one attributes to nonhuman forces in the situation. To illustrate how the last two dimensions operate, anger is associated with an unpleasant situation caused by another person, guilt is associated with an unpleasant situation brought about by one's self, and sadness is associated with an unpleasant situation controlled by circumstances. Thus, if you and your friend miss a concert that you had your heart set on hearing, you will feel anger if you missed it because your friend carelessly misplaced the tickets, guilt if you misplaced them, and sadness if the performance is cancelled due to a performer's illness. The virtue of this kind of approach is that it specifies the appraisal process in detail and accounts for a wide range of emotional experiences.

SOME CLINICAL IMPLICATIONS

The fact that cognitive appraisals can differentiate emotions helps make sense of a puzzling clinical observation. Clinicians report that sometimes a patient appears to be experiencing an emotion but is not conscious of it. That is, the patient has no subjective expe-

APPRAISAL DIMENSIONS	EMOTION
Desirable and occurs	Joy
Desirable and doesn't occur	Sorrow
Undesirable and occurs	Distress
Undesirable and doesn't occur	Relief

TABLE 11-3

Primary Appraisal Dimensions and Their Consequences *Combinations of two appraisal dimensions and their associated emotions.* (After Roseman, 1984; 1979)

rience of the emotion, yet reacts in a manner consistent with the emotion—for example, though the patient may not feel angry, he acts in a hostile manner. Also, at a later point he may experience the emotion and agree that in some sense he must have been having it earlier. Freud (1915/1976) thought that this phenomenon involved the repression of painful ideas, and modern work on appraisal and emotion is compatible with his hypothesis. Because the belief about a situation usually gives the emotion its quality, preventing that belief from entering consciousness (repression) prevents one from experiencing the quality of the emotion.

Another point of contact between clinical analysis and experimental research concerns emotional development. Clinical work suggests that a person's sensations of pleasure and distress change rather little as he or she develops from child to adult; what does develop, however, are the ideas associated with the sensations (Brenner, 1980). Thus, the

The sensation of joy may be the same whether we are 3 or 30 years of age.

sensation of joy may be the same when we are 3 or 30, but what makes us joyous is very different. This developmental pattern fits perfectly with the facts that we have reviewed about emotion. Sensations of pleasure and distress are probably due to feedback from autonomic arousal, and the nature of this arousal may not change much over the life span. In contrast, ideas associated with the sensations are simply emotional beliefs, and they should show the same kind of development as other aspects of cognition.

Finally, the work on appraisal fits with a phenomenon that is familiar not just to clinicians but to all of us: The extent to which a situation elicits an emotion depends on our experience. When confronted with an overly critical employer, some people will be merely annoyed while others will be enraged. Why the difference? Presumably because of differences in past experience: Perhaps those who are enraged suffered a hypercritical authority figure in the past, while those who are only annoyed had no such experience. A possible link between past experience and current emotion is the appraisal process; that is, our past experience affects our beliefs about the current situation, and these beliefs then influence the emotion we experience.

EMOTION WITHOUT COGNITION

Are there cases of emotion in which no cognitive appraisal seems to be involved? When a rat receives an electric shock for the first time, for example, presumably it has little to think about, and its emotional reaction is devoid of cognitive activity. Similarly, if you are suddenly punched in the face, you may experience an emotion before you interpret the event.

The preceding examples suggest there may be two kinds of emotional experiences: those that are based on cognitive appraisal and those that precede cognition (Zajonc, 1984; 1980). This dichotomy is supported by work on the physiology of emotion, which explores the brain structures involved in emotion. One such structure is the **amygdala**, a small, almond-shaped mass that is located in the lower brain and that is known to register emotional reactions. Until recently, it was thought that the amygdala receives all its inputs from the cortex; since the cortex is the

seat of cognition, the amygdala's inputs were thought to always involve cognitive appraisal. But newer research with rats has uncovered connections between sensory channels and the amygdala that do not go through the cortex; these direct connections may be the biological basis of **precognitive emotions** (emotions *not* based on appraisal). Thus, the amygdala is capable of responding to an alarming situation before the cortex does, which suggests that sometimes we can feel before we can think. To illustrate, if in the corner of your eye you see something that has the shape of a snake, your amygdala will send an alarm signal that makes you jump before your cortex can determine that the object in question is in fact a harmless piece of rope. Though this research is based on rats, there is reason to believe that the neural pathways involved exist in humans as well (Le Doux, 1989).

While we can have emotional experiences without conscious and deliberate cognitive appraisal, such experiences may be restricted to undifferentiated positive or negative feelings. If we define cognitive appraisal broadly to include primitive or automatic evaluations of situations that we have acquired through evolution, then we may be able to say that almost all emotions involve some type of appraisal (Lazarus, 1991).

EXPRESSION AND EMOTION

The facial expression that accompanies an emotion clearly serves to communicate that emotion. Since the publication of Charles Darwin's 1872 classic, *The Expression of Emotion in Man and Animals,* psychologists have regarded the communication of emotion as an important function, one with survival value for the species. Thus, looking frightened may warn others that danger is present, and perceiving that someone is angry tells us that he or she may be about to act aggressively. More recent work goes beyond the Darwinian tradition, suggesting that, in addition to their communicative function, emotional expressions contribute to the subjective experience of emotion, just as arousal and appraisal do. This is the emotion theory depicted in the panel of Figure 11-4.

Emotional expression in the mandrill monkey.

COMMUNICATION OF EMOTIONAL EXPRESSIONS

Certain facial expressions seem to have a universal meaning, regardless of the culture in which an individual is raised. The universal expression of anger, for example, involves a flushed face, brows lowered and drawn together, flared nostrils, a clenched jaw, and bared teeth. When people from five countries (the United States, Brazil, Chile, Argentina, and Japan) viewed photographs showing facial expressions of happiness, anger, sadness, disgust, fear, and surprise, they had little difficulty in identifying the emotion that each expression conveyed. Even members of remote groups that had had virtually no contact with Western cultures (the Fore and Dani peoples in New Guinea) were able to identify the facial expressions of people from Western cultures correctly. Likewise, American college students who viewed videotapes of emotions expressed by Fore natives identified the emotions accurately, although they sometimes confused fear and surprise (Ekman, 1982).

Facial expressions are universal in the emotions they convey. Photographs of people from New Guinea and from the United States demonstrate that emotions are conveyed by the same facial expressions. From left to right are happiness, sadness, and disgust.

The universality of certain emotional expressions supports Darwin's claim that they are innate responses with an evolutionary history. According to Darwin, many of the ways in which we express emotion are inherited patterns that originally had some survival value. For example, the expression of disgust or rejection is based on the organism's attempt to rid itself of something unpleasant that it has ingested. To quote Darwin (1872),

> The term "disgust," in its simplest sense, means something offensive to the taste. But as disgust also causes annoyance, it is generally accompanied by a frown, and often by gestures as if to push away or to guard oneself against the offensive object. Extreme disgust is expressed by movements around the mouth identical with those preparatory to the act of vomiting. The mouth is opened widely, with the upper lip strongly retracted. The partial closure of the eyelids, or the turning away of the eyes or of the whole body, are likewise highly expressive of disdain. These actions seem to declare that the despised person is not worth looking at, or is disagreeable to behold. Spitting seems an almost universal sign of contempt or disgust; and spitting obviously represents the rejection of anything offensive from the mouth.

While some facial expressions and gestures seem to be innately associated with particular emotions, others are learned from culture. One psychologist reviewed Chinese novels to determine how Chinese writers portray various human emotions. Many of the bodily changes in emotion (for example, flushing, trembling, goose pimples) represent the same symptoms of emotion in Chinese fiction as they do in Western writing. Other bodily expressions, however, convey very different emotions in Chinese fiction than they do in the West. The following quotations from Chinese novels would surely be misinterpreted by an American reader unfamiliar with the culture (Klineberg, 1938).

"They stretched out their tongues."
(They showed signs of surprise.)

"He clapped his hands."
(He was worried or disappointed.)

"He scratched his ears and cheeks."
(He was happy.)

"Her eyes grew round and opened wide."
(She became angry.)

Each culture has its own set of *display rules* for emotion. These rules specify the types of emotions people should experience in certain situations, and the behaviors appropriate for an emotion. As an example, in some cultures people who lose a loved one are expected to feel sad and to express the sadness by openly crying and wailing for the loved one to return. In other cultures, bereaved people are expected to sing, dance, and be merry. In Europe, two men greeting each other on the street may embrace and kiss, but in America these gestures of affection are taboo for men. Thus, superimposed on the basic expressions of emotion, which appear to be universal, are conventional forms of ex-

Cultures have different norms for expression of emotions such as affection.

pressions—a kind of language of emotion recognized by others within a culture, but often misunderstood by people from other cultures.

BRAIN LOCALIZATION

The emotional expressions that are universal (for example, those associated with joy, anger, and disgust) are also highly specific: Particular muscles are used to express particular emotions. This combination of universality and specificity suggests that a specialized neurological system may have evolved in humans to interpret the primitive emotional expressions. Recent evidence indicates that there is indeed such a system, and it is localized in the right cerebral hemisphere.

One source of evidence comes from studies in which pictures of emotional expressions are presented briefly to either the left side or the right side of the subject's visual field. Recall from Chapter 2 that a stimulus presented to the left visual field projects to the right hemisphere, and a stimulus presented to the right visual field projects to the left hemisphere. When subjects have to decide which of two emotions the picture manifests, they are faster and more accurate when the picture is projected to their right hemisphere. In addition, when the two halves of the face convey different emotions (one half may be smiling while the other half is frowning), the expression projected to the right hemisphere has the most impact on the subject's decision. Another source of evidence about the localization of emotional expressions comes from studies of patients who have suffered brain damage from strokes or accidents. Patients who have only right-hemisphere damage have more difficulty recognizing facial expressions of emotion than do patients who have only left-hemisphere damage (Etcoff, 1985).

Our system for recognizing emotional expressions seems to be highly specialized. In particular, it is distinct from our ability to recognize faces. Consider a **prosopagnosic**, a person who, because of damage to his cortex, has such extreme difficulty recognizing familiar faces that he sometimes fails to recognize his own face! He can, however, recognize emotional expressions: He can tell you that a particular person is happy even when he does not know that the person is his wife (Bruyer

et al., 1983). The abilities to recognize faces and to recognize emotions also are differentially affected by electrical stimulation of various regions of the right hemisphere: Face recognition is disrupted by stimulation in the region between the parietal and occipital lobes whereas emotion recognition is disrupted by stimulation of a particular region in the temporal lobe (Fried et al., 1982).

Emotions, in addition to being communicated by facial expressions, are also expressed by variations in voice patterns (particularly variations in pitch, timing, and stress). Some of these variations appear to be universal and specific: A sharp increase in pitch indicates fear, for example. The specialized neurological system for perceiving these emotional clues is again located in the right cerebral hemisphere, and the evidence for this is similar to that for facial expressions. Subjects are more accurate in identifying the emotional tone of a voice presented to the left ear (which projects information primarily to the right hemisphere) than one presented to the right ear (which projects primarily to the left hemisphere). And patients who have solely right-hemisphere damage have more trouble identifying emotions from voice clues than do patients who have solely left-hemisphere damage (Ley & Bryden, 1982).

INTENSITY AND DIFFERENTIATION OF EMOTIONS

FACIAL FEEDBACK HYPOTHESIS   The idea that facial expressions, in addition to their communicative function, also contribute to our experience of emotions is sometimes called the *facial feedback hypothesis* (Tomkins, 1962). According to the hypothesis, just as we receive feedback about (or perceive) our autonomic arousal, so we receive feedback about our facial expression, and this feedback combines with the other components of an emotion to produce a more intense experience. This implies that if you make yourself smile and hold the smile for several seconds, you will begin to feel happier; if you scowl, you will feel tense and angry. (Try it.)

In support of the facial feedback hypothesis, subjects who exaggerate their facial reactions to emotional stimuli report more emotional response than subjects who do not. In one study, subjects judged the pleasantness of various odors while posing either a smile or a frown. Posing a smile resulted in subjects perceiving the odors as more pleasant; posing a frown resulted in them perceiving the odors as less pleasant (Kraut, 1982). It is possible however, that subjects in this experiment "figured out" that when they posed a smile, for example, they were supposed to be happy, and this is why emotional expression affected the judgments. This possibility is ruled out by subsequent studies in which it is most unlikely that subjects noticed any connection between their facial expression and an emotion. In one experiment, subjects rated cartoons for funniness, while they held a pen either in their teeth or in their lips. Holding a pen in one's teeth forces your face into a smile, while holding it in one's lips forces your face into a frown (try it). As expected, the cartoons were rated as funnier when the pen was held in the teeth than when held in the lips (Strack, Martin, & Stepper, 1988). In addition to these studies which show a direct connection between expression and felt emotion, other experiments indicate that facial expressions may have an indirect effect on emotion by increasing autonomic arousal. Such an indirect influence was demonstrated in an experiment we discussed earlier, where producing particular emotional expressions led to changes in heartbeat and skin temperature. We therefore need to add emotional expression to our list of contributors to emotional experience.

Some researchers also believe that facial expressions can determine the *quality* of emotions. Since the expressions for the primary emotions are distinct and occur rapidly, they are at least plausible candidates for contributing to the differentiation of emotions. Tomkins (1980) has proposed that the feedback from a facial expression is inherently positive or negative, thereby suggesting a means by which facial expressions can distinguish the positive from the negative emotions. Should this suggestion prove true, we are back (in part) to the James-Lange theory mentioned earlier, which holds that emotion is the perception of certain bodily changes; facial expressions are bodily changes—we *are* happy *because* we smile.

BLOOD FLOW AND BRAIN TEMPERATURE   Exactly which aspects of a facial expression makes it inherently positive or negative? A possible answer may be found in the fact that the contraction of certain facial muscles can affect the blood flow in neighboring blood vessels. This, in turn, may affect cerebral blood flow, which can determine brain temperature, which in turn can facilitate and inhibit the release of various neurotransmitters—and the latter may well be part of the cortical activity that underlies emotion. For example, when smiling, the configuration of facial muscles may lead to a lowering of the temperature in a region of the brain in which the neurotransmitter serotonin is released; this temperature change may block the release of the neurotransmitter, resulting in a positive feeling. The critical path, then, moves from facial expression to blood flow to brain temperature to emotional experience (Zajonc, Murphy, & Inglehart, 1989).

This path from expression to emotion is supported by experiments. One study takes advantage of the fact that pronunciation of the German vowel "ü" (as in Für) requires extending a facial muscle that is contracted when smiling. This suggests that the facial expression associated with pronouncing ü can lead to a negative feeling. To test this hypothesis, German subjects read aloud stories that contained either many words with ü or no words with ü; the stories were equated for their content and emotional tone. When asked how much they liked the stories, subjects rated those with ü words as less favorable than those with no ü words. Also, while subjects read the stories, the temperature of their foreheads was measured to provide an estimate of brain temperature. Temperatures rose during stories with ü words but not during stories without such words. Thus, the facial expression needed to produce ü led to both increased brain temperature and negative feeling, which supports the proposed path from facial expression to brain temperature to emotional experience (Zajonc, Murphy, & Inglehart, 1989).

GENERAL REACTIONS TO BEING IN AN EMOTIONAL STATE

At the outset of this chapter we noted that one of the major components of an emotion involves the reactions to being in an emotional state. Although some reactions to being in an emotional state are specific to the emotion experienced—approaching someone when happy or withdrawing when frightened, for example—other reactions seem to apply to emotions in general. In particular, being in an emotional state: a) can energize or disrupt us; b) determine what we attend to and learn; and c) determine what kinds of judgments we make about the world.

ENERGY AND DISRUPTION

Being in an emotional state sometimes energizes people, but other times disrupts them—depending on the intensity of the experience, the individual who is experiencing it, and the duration of the experience. With regard to intensity, a mild level of emotional arousal tends to produce alertness and interest in the current situation. When emotions become intense, however, whether pleasant or unpleasant, they usually result in some disruption of thought or behavior. The curve in Figure 11-5 represents the relation between a person's level of emotional arousal and his or her effectiveness on a task. At very low levels of emotional arousal (for example, at the point of waking up), we may not attend well to sensory information, and our performance will be relatively poor. Performance is optimal at moderate levels of arousal. At high levels of emotional arousal, our performance begins to decline, probably because we cannot devote enough cognitive resources to the task. The optimum level of arousal and the shape of the curve differ for different tasks. A simple, well-learned routine would be much less susceptible to disruption by emotional arousal than a more complex activity that depends on the integration of several thought processes. During a moment of intense fear, you would probably still be able to spell your name but not be able to play chess well.

People vary at how emotionally aroused they become during crises, and thus at how much their behavior is disrupted. Studies of people faced with fires or sudden floods find that about 15 percent of people show organized, effective behavior, suggesting that their optimum level of emotional arousal has not been exceeded. The majority of people, about 70 percent, show various degrees of disorganization but are still able to function

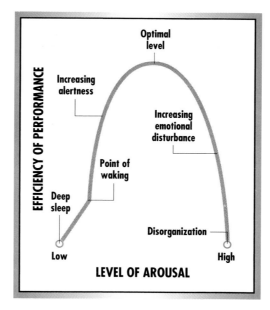

FIGURE 11-5

Emotional Arousal and Performance *The curve shows the hypothetical relationship between level of emotional arousal and efficiency of performance. The precise shape of the curve differs for various tasks.* (After Hebb, 1972)

with some effectiveness. The remaining 15 percent are so disorganized that they are unable to function at all; they may panic or exhibit aimless and completely inappropriate behavior, suggesting they are far above their optimal level of emotional arousal (Tyhurst, 1951).

Sometimes intense emotions are not quickly discharged but continue to remain unresolved. Perhaps the situation that makes a person angry (for example, prolonged conflict with a teacher or employer) or fearful (such as worry over the illness of a parent) continues for a long period. While the physiological changes that accompany anger and fear can have adaptive value (they mobilize us to fight or flee), when maintained too long they can exhaust our resources and even cause tissue damage. A chronic state of heightened arousal can thus take its toll on the individual's health. We will have more to say about the relationship between stress and the body's vulnerability to illness in Chapter 14.

ATTENTION AND LEARNING: MOOD CONGRUENCE

When experiencing an emotion, we tend to pay more attention to events that fit our mood than to events that do not. As a consequence, we learn more about the events that are congruent with our mood.

One experiment that demonstrates these phenomena involved three stages. In the first stage, subjects were hypnotized and induced to be in either a happy or sad mood (the subjects had been selected for being hypnotizable). In the second stage, the hypnotized subjects read a brief story about an encounter between two men—a happy character and a sad one. The story vividly described the events of the two men's lives and their emotional reactions. After reading the story, subjects were asked who they thought the central character was, and with whom they identified. Subjects who had been induced to be happy identified more with the happy character and thought the story contained more statements about him; subjects who had been induced to be sad identified more with the sad character and estimated that more story statements were about him. These results indicate that subjects paid more attention to the character and events that were congruent with their moods than to those that were not.

Evidence that subjects also *learned* more about mood-congruent events than mood-incongruent ones comes from the third part of the experiment. One day after reading the story, subjects, now in a neutral mood returned to the laboratory. They were asked to recall the story. Subjects recalled more about the character they had identified with: For the previously happy subjects, 55 percent of the facts they recalled were about the happy character; for the previously sad subjects, 80 percent of their recalled facts were about the sad character (Bower, 1981).

Exactly how does the congruence between one's mood and some new material affect the learning of that material? We know that we can learn new material better if we can relate it to information already in memory. One's mood during learning may increase the availability of memories that fit that mood, and such memories will be easier to relate to new material that also fits that mood. Suppose you hear a story about a student flunking out of school. If you are in a bad mood when hearing the story, some of your memories about failure experiences (particularly academic failures) may be easily accessible, and the similarity of these memories to the new fact of someone flunking out of school will make it easy to relate them. In contrast, if you are in a good mood when hearing the story, your most accessible memories may be too dissimilar to a school failure to foster a relation between the old memories and the new fact. So, our mood determines what memories are

more accessible, and those memories determine what is easy for us to learn at the moment (Isen, 1985; Bower, 1981).

EVALUATION AND ESTIMATION: MOOD EFFECTS

Our emotional mood can affect our evaluation of other people. Everyday experiences provide numerous examples of this. For example, when we are in a good mood, a friend's habit of constantly checking his appearance in a mirror may seem just an idiosyncrasy; when we are in a bad mood, we may dwell on how vain our friend is. Our mood affects our evaluation of inanimate objects as well. In one experiment, subjects were asked to evaluate their major possessions. Subjects who had just been put in a good mood by receiving a small gift rated their televisions and cars more positively than did control subjects who were in a neutral mood (Isen et al., 1978).

Our mood also affects our judgments about the frequency of various risks in the world. Bad moods lead us to see these risks as more likely; good moods lead us to see the risks as less likely. In an experiment dealing with estimating risks, subjects in the experimental group first read a newspaper story that recounted a tragic death, putting the subjects in a negative mood. Control subjects read a bland newspaper story, putting them in a neutral mood. Then all subjects were asked to estimate the frequencies of various fatalities, including diseases like leukemia and heart disease, and accidents like fires and floods. Subjects who were in a negative mood estimated the frequencies of these fatalities to be almost twice as great as did subjects in a neutral mood. Further, all that mattered for estimating frequencies was the subject's mood, not the content of the story that had put them in that mood. The tragic story that some experimental subjects read involved a case of leukemia, and the story that other experimental subjects read involved a death due to fire; both kinds of subjects overestimated the frequencies of leukemia and fire to the same degree. The similarity between the story and the risk had no effect on the estimate of frequency. It is as if the affect was separated from the content of the story, and only the affect guided subsequent estimates. Comparable results were obtained for the effects of being in a good mood. Reading a story about someone's good fortune led subjects to make relatively low estimates about the frequencies of various fatalities, and the extent to which subjects did this did not depend on the similarity between the story and the risk being evaluated (Johnson & Tversky, 1983).

Specific moods may have specific effects on our judgments of the world and of other people. In one study, subjects were put either into a sad mood or an angry mood by imagining themselves experiencing either a sad or angry event, then were asked to evaluate the possible causes of hypothetical events, such as missing an important flight or losing money. Subjects who were in an angry mood tended to attribute the hypothetical events to the mistakes of other people, but subjects in a sad mood tended to attribute the events to situations (for example, bad traffic was the reason for missing a flight). So the angry subjects were more ready to blame someone for negative events, and the sad subjects were more willing to acknowledge that an unlucky situation might have caused the events (Keltner, Ellsworth, & Edwards, 1993).

Being in a bad mood, then, makes the world seem a more dangerous place. Such a perception can reinforce the bad mood. Also, as noted earlier, being in a bad mood leads us to selectively attend and learn negative-toned facts; this too can reinforce a bad mood. A similar analysis applies to a good mood. It makes the world seem less risky, and leads us to attend and learn positively toned material. Thus, the general consequences of a mood serve to perpetuate that mood.

AGGRESSION AS AN EMOTIONAL REACTION

Emotions cause not only general reactions, but specific action tendencies as well. We may laugh when happy, withdraw when frightened, get aggressive when angry, and so forth. Among these typical action tendencies, psychologists have singled out one in particular for extensive study: aggression.

This special attention is partly due to the social significance of aggression. At the soci-

etal level, in an age when nuclear weapons are still widely available, a single aggressive act can spell disaster. At the individual level, many people experience aggressive thoughts and impulses frequently, and how they handle these thoughts will have major effects on their health and interpersonal relations. Another reason why psychologists have focused their research on aggression is because two major theories of social behavior make quite different assumptions about the nature of aggression. Freud's **psychoanalytic theory** views aggression as a drive, and **social-learning theory** views it as a learned response. Research on aggression helps us to evaluate these competing theories.

In the following discussion, we first describe these different views along with related research, and then consider how the views differ with respect to the effects of viewing aggression in the mass media. Keep in mind that what we mean by "aggression" is behavior that is *intended* to injure another person (physically or verbally) or to destroy property. The key concept in this definition is intent. If a person accidentally steps on your foot in a crowded elevator and immediately apologizes, you would not interpret the behavior as aggressive; but if someone walks up to you as you sit at your desk and steps on your foot, you would not hesitate to label the act as aggressive.

AGGRESSION AS A DRIVE

We will present only those aspects of psychoanalytic theory and social-learning theory

Is aggression a drive or a learned response?

that are relevant to aggression. Both theories will be presented in more detail in Chapter 13, where we focus on personality, and Chapters 15 and 16, where we discuss abnormal behavior and its treatment.

According to Freud's early psychoanalytic theory, many of our actions are determined by instincts, particularly the sexual instinct. When expression of these instincts is frustrated, an aggressive drive is induced. Later theorists in the psychoanalytic tradition broadened this **frustration-aggression hypothesis** to the following claim: Whenever a person's effort to reach *any* goal is blocked, an aggressive drive is induced that motivates behavior to injure the obstacle (person or object) causing the frustration (Dollard et al., 1939). There are two critical aspects of this proposal: One is that the usual cause of aggression is frustration; the other is that aggression has the properties of a basic drive—being a form of *energy* that *persists* until its goal is satisfied, as well as being an *inborn* reaction (hunger, sex, and other basic drives have these properties). As we will see, it is the drive aspect of the frustration-aggression hypothesis that has proved to be particularly controversial.

AGGRESSION IN OTHER SPECIES If aggression is really a basic drive like hunger, then we would expect other mammalian species to exhibit patterns of aggression that are similar to ours (just as they exhibit patterns of hunger that are similar to ours). The evidence on this issue has changed over the years. In the 1960s, early work in ethology suggested that there was a major difference between humans and other species—namely that animals have evolved mechanisms to control their aggressive instincts but humans have not (for example, Ardrey, 1966; Lorenz, 1966). Subsequent work in the 1970s and 1980s, however, suggested that animals may be no less aggressive than we are. The incidence of murder, rape, and infanticide among animals was shown to be much greater than was thought in the 1960s. One kind of murder involves border wars between chimpanzees (Goodall, 1978). In one well-documented case in the Gombe Stream National Park in Tanzania, a gang of five male chimpanzees defended their territory against any strange male that wandered into it. If the gang encountered a group of two or more strangers, their response would be raucous but not deadly; but if there was only one intruder, then one member of the gang might hold his arm, another a leg, while a third member pounded the intruder to death. Or a couple of members of the gang would drag the intruder over the rocks until he died. In another chimpanzee border war observed during the 1970s, a tribe of about 15 chimpanzees destroyed a smaller neighboring group by killing the members off one male at a time. Furthermore, at least for primates, females engage in as many aggressive acts as males, though their encounters are less deadly because their teeth are shorter and less sharp (Smuts, 1986).

While observations like these bring animal aggression more in line with human aggression, there still are many apparent differences. Only humans wage wide-scale wars, for example.

BIOLOGICAL BASIS OF AGGRESSION IN OTHER SPECIES Findings on the biological basis of aggression in animals provide evidence for an aggressive drive in at least some species. Some studies show that mild electrical stimulation of a specific region of the hypothalamus produces aggressive, even deadly, behavior in animals. When a cat's hypothalamus is stimulated via implanted electrodes, the animal hisses, its hair bristles, its pupils dilate, and it will strike at a rat or other objects placed in its cage. Stimulation of a different area of the hypothalamus produces quite different behavior: instead of exhibiting any of these rage responses, the cat coldly stalks and kills a rat.

Similar techniques have produced aggressive behavior in rats. A laboratory-bred rat that has never killed a mouse, nor seen a wild rat kill one, may live quite peacefully in the same cage with a mouse. But if the rat's hypothalamus is stimulated, the animal will pounce on its mouse cage mate and kill it with exactly the same response that is exhibited by a wild rat (a hard bite to the neck that severs the spinal cord). The stimulation seems to trigger an innate killing response that had previously been dormant. Conversely, if a neurochemical blocker is injected into the same brain site in rats that induces them to spontaneously kill mice on sight, the rats become temporarily peaceful (Smith, King, & Hoebel, 1970). In these cases, then, aggression has some properties of a drive, since it involves inborn reactions.

In higher mammals, such instinctive patterns of aggression are controlled by the cortex and therefore are influenced more by experience. Monkeys living in groups establish a dominance hierarchy: One or two males become leaders, and the others assume various levels of subordination. When the hypothalamus of a dominant monkey is electrically stimulated, the monkey attacks subordinate males but not females. When a low-ranking monkey is stimulated in the same way, it cowers and behaves submissively (see Figure 11-6). Thus, aggressive behavior in a monkey is not automatically elicited by stimulation of the hypothalamus; rather, the monkey's environment and past experiences also play a role. Humans are similar. Although we are equipped with neurological mechanisms that are tied to aggression, the activation of these mechanisms is usually under cortical control (except in some cases of brain damage). Indeed, in most individuals, the frequency with which aggressive behavior is expressed, the forms it takes, and the situations in which it is displayed are determined largely by experience and social influences.

BIOLOGICAL BASES OF AGGRESSION IN HUMANS   One biological factor that may be related to aggression in human males is testosterone level. As you may recall from Chapter 10, testosterone is a male sex hormone that is responsible for many male bodily characteristics and that has been linked to aggression in monkeys. Recent studies suggest that in humans as well, higher levels of testosterone are associated with higher levels of aggression. One large-scale study involved more than 4,400

male U.S. veterans. The men were given various psychological tests, some of which tapped aggressiveness; they also had blood samples taken from them so that their testosterone level could be determined. Men who had higher levels of testosterone were more likely to have a history of aggression. Since aggressive behavior in males can sometimes lead to antisocial behavior, we might expect that high testosterone would be an impediment to success in American life. Indeed, men with extremely high testosterone levels were more likely to have low-status than high-status positions (Dabbs & Morris, 1990).

These findings provide some evidence for a biological basis of aggression in humans, and hence for the view that aggression is like a drive. Still, in these studies the link between testosterone and aggression is often tenuous—large numbers of subjects are needed to find the effect—which suggests the need to look elsewhere for determinants of aggression.

AGGRESSION AS A LEARNED RESPONSE

Social-learning theory is concerned with human social interaction, but it has its origins in behavioristic studies of animal learning (such as those discussed in Chapter 7). It focuses on the behavior patterns that people develop in response to environmental contingencies. Some social behaviors may be rewarded while others may produce unfavorable results; through the process of differential reinforcement, people eventually select the more successful behavior patterns. Social-learning theory differs from strict be-

FIGURE 11-5

Brain Stimulation and Aggression *A mild electrical current is delivered to electrodes implanted in the monkey's hypothalamus via remote radio control. The animal's response (attack or flight) depends on its position in the dominance hierarchy of the colony.*

haviorism, however, in that it stresses the importance of cognitive processes. Because people can mentally represent situations, they are able to foresee the likely consequences of their actions and to alter their behavior accordingly.

Social-learning theory further differs from strict behaviorism in that it stresses the importance of **vicarious learning,** or learning by observation. Many behavior patterns are learned by watching the actions of others and observing what consequences they produce for them. A child who observes the pained expressions of an older sibling in the dentist's chair will probably be fearful when the time comes for his or her first dental appointment. Social-learning theory emphasizes the role of **models** in transmitting both specific behaviors and emotional responses. It focuses on such questions as what types of models are most effective and what factors determine whether the modeled behavior that is learned will actually be performed (Bandura, 1986; 1973).

With this emphasis on learning, it is no surprise that social-learning theory rejects the concept of aggression as a frustration-produced drive; the theory proposes instead that aggression is similar to any other learned response. Aggression can be learned through observation or imitation, and the more often it is reinforced, the more likely it is to occur. A person who is frustrated by a blocked goal or disturbed by some stressful event experiences an unpleasant emotion. The response that this emotion elicits will differ, depending on the kinds of responses the individual has learned to use in coping with stressful situations. The frustrated individual may seek help from others, aggress, withdraw, try even harder to surmount the obstacle, or anesthetize himself or herself with drugs or alcohol. The chosen response will be the one that has relieved frustration most successfully in the past. According to this view, frustration provokes aggression mainly in people who have learned to respond to adverse situations with aggressive behavior (Bandura, 1977).

Figure 11-7 shows how social-learning theory differs from psychoanalytic theory (the frustration-aggression hypothesis) in conceptualizing aggression. Social-learning theory assumes that (a) aggression is just one of several reactions to the aversive experience of frustration, and (b) aggression is a response with no drivelike properties, and consequently is influenced by anticipated consequences of behavior.

IMITATION OF AGGRESSION One source of evidence for social-learning theory is studies showing that aggression, like any other response, can be learned through imitation. Nursery-school children who observed an adult expressing various forms of aggression toward a large, inflated doll subsequently imitated many of the adult's actions, including unusual ones (see Figure 11-8). The experiment was expanded to include two filmed versions of aggressive modeling (one showing an adult behaving aggressively toward the doll, the other showing a cartoon character displaying the same aggressive behavior). The results were equally striking. Children who watched either of the two films behaved as aggressively toward the doll as children who had observed a live model displaying aggression. Figure 11-9 shows the measures of aggressive behavior for each of the groups and for two control groups who observed either no model or a nonaggressive model. The conclusion of such studies is that observation of either live or filmed models of aggression increases the

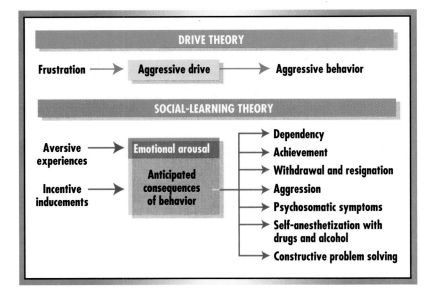

FIGURE 11-7

Two Views of Aggression *The diagram schematically represents the determinants of aggression according to psychoanalytic theory (the frustration-aggression hypothesis) and social-learning theory. From the viewpoint of social-learning theory, the emotional arousal caused by unpleasant experiences can lead to any number of different behaviors, depending on the behavior that has been reinforced in the past.*

FIGURE 11-8

Children's Imitation of Adult Aggression   *Nursery-school children observed an adult express various forms of aggressive behavior toward an inflated doll. After watching the adult, both boys and girls behaved aggressively toward the doll, performing many of the detailed acts of aggression the adult had displayed, including lifting and throwing the doll, striking it with a hammer, and kicking it.*

likelihood of aggression in the viewer. This may be part of the reason why children whose parents punish them severely are likely to be more aggressive than average; the parents provide the model (Eron, 1987).

REINFORCEMENT OF AGGRESSION   Another source of evidence for social-learning theory is that aggression is sensitive to reinforcement contingencies in the same manner that other learned responses are. A number of studies show that children are more likely to express the aggressive responses they learned by watching aggressive models when they are reinforced for such actions or when they observe aggressive models being reinforced. In one study, investigators observed children for

10 weeks, recording instances of interpersonal aggression and the events that immediately followed them, such as positive reinforcers of the aggression (victim winced or cried), punishment of the aggression (victim counterattacked), or neutral reactions (victim ignored the aggressor). For the children who showed the highest overall level of aggression, the most common reaction to their aggressive act was positive reinforcement. For the children who showed the least aggression, punishment was a common reaction. Children who were initially unaggressive, but occasionally succeeded in stopping attacks by counteraggression gradually began to initiate attacks of their own (their aggression was being positively reinforced). Clearly,

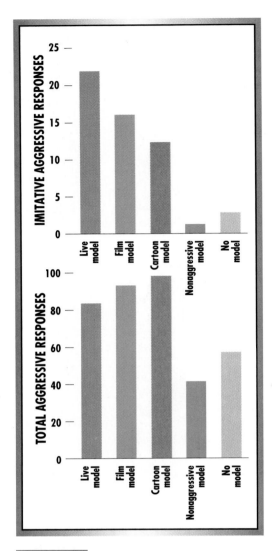

FIGURE 11-9

Imitation of Aggression *Observing aggressive models (either live or on film) greatly increases the amount of aggressive behavior that children display, compared to observing a nonaggressive model or no model at all. Note that observation of the live model results in the imitation of more specific aggressive acts, whereas observation of filmed (either real-life or cartoon) models instigates more aggressive responses of all kinds.* (After Bandura, 1973)

the consequences of aggression play an important role in shaping behavior (Patterson, Littman, & Bricker, 1967).

AGGRESSIVE EXPRESSION AND CATHARSIS

Studies that try to distinguish between aggression as a drive and aggression as a learned response often focus on **catharsis** (purging an emotion by experiencing it intensely). If aggression is a drive, then the expressions of aggression should be cathartic, resulting in a reduction in the intensity of aggressive feelings and actions (analogous to how eating leads to a reduction of hunger-based feelings and actions). On the other hand, if aggression is a learned response, the expression of aggression could result in an increase in such actions (if the aggression is reinforced). Currently, the evidence favors the learned-response view.

ACTING AGGRESSIVELY Psychologists have conducted numerous laboratory studies to determine whether or not aggression decreases once it has been partially expressed. Studies of children indicate that participation in aggressive activities either increases aggressive behavior or maintains it at the same level. Experiments with adults produce similar results. When given repeated opportunities to shock another person (who cannot retaliate), college students become more and more punitive. Subjects who are angry become even more punitive on successive attacks than subjects who are not angry. If aggression were cathartic, the angry subjects should reduce their aggressive drive by acting aggressively and become less punitive the more they aggress (Green & Quanty, 1977; Berkowitz, 1965).

Some evidence about catharsis is also taken from real-life situations. In one case, California aerospace workers who had been laid off were first interviewed about how they felt about their companies and supervisors, and subsequently were asked to describe their feelings in writing. If aggression were cathartic, men who expressed a lot of anger in the interviews should have expressed relatively little in the written reports. The results, however, showed otherwise: The men who let out anger in conversation expressed even more in their reports. Fuming in conversation may have kindled the aggression. Another study looked at the relation between the hostility of a country (vis-à-vis its neighboring countries) and the kinds of sports it plays. More belligerent cultures were found to play more combative games. Again, aggression seems to breed aggression rather than dissipate it (Ebbesen, Duncan, & Konečni, 1975).

These results argue against aggression being cathartic. However, there are circumstances in which the expression of aggression may decrease its incidence. For example, behaving aggressively may arouse feelings of anxiety in the aggressors that inhibit further aggression, particularly if they observe their actions have led to injuries. But in these instances, the effect on aggressive behavior can be explained without concluding that an aggressive drive is being reduced. Also, although expressing hostile feelings in action does not usually reduce the aggression, it may make the person feel better. But this may happen because the person feels more powerful and more in control, rather than because the person has reduced an aggressive drive.

VIEWING VIOLENCE Most of the studies we have discussed deal with the consequences of directly expressing aggression. What about the effects of indirectly or vicariously expressing aggression through watching violence on television or in the movies? Is viewing violence cathartic, providing fantasy outlets for an aggressive drive? Or does it elicit aggression by modeling violent behavior? We have already seen that children will imitate live or filmed aggressive behavior in an experimental setting, but how will they react in more natural settings? The amount of media violence to which we are exposed makes this an important question. This is particularly true for children, for whom the amount of violence in certain television programs contin-

ues to increase. For example, in 1980 there was an average of 18.6 violent acts per hour in Saturday morning cartoons; by 1990, this number had risen to 26.4 (*New York Times,* 1990).

Several experimental studies have controlled children's viewing of television: One group watched violent cartoons for a specified amount of time each day; another group watched nonviolent cartoons for the same amount of time. The amount of aggression the children showed in their daily activities was carefully recorded. The children who watched violent cartoons became more aggressive in their interactions with their peers, whereas the children who viewed nonviolent cartoons showed no change in interpersonal aggression (Steuer, Applefield, & Smith, 1971).

The above study involves an experimental group and a control group. However, most studies that deal with children's viewing habits are correlational; they determine the relation between the amount of exposure to televised violence and the degree to which children use aggressive behavior to solve interpersonal conflicts. This correlation is clearly positive (Singer & Singer, 1981), even for children in Finland, which has a limited number of violent programs (Lagerspetz, Viemero, & Akademi, 1986). Correlations, however, do not imply causal relationships. It may be that children who are aggressive prefer to watch violent television programs— that is, having an aggressive nature causes one to view violence, rather than vice versa.

Children often imitate what they see on television.

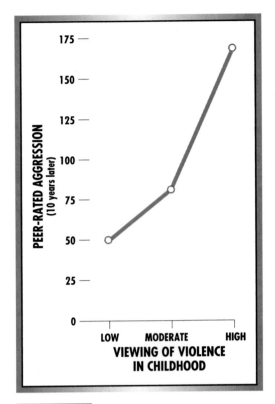

FIGURE 11-10

Relationship Between Childhood Viewing of Violent Television and Adult Aggression
Preference for viewing violent television programs by boys at age 9 is positively correlated with aggressive behavior at age 19. (After Eron, Huesmann, Lefkowitz, & Walder, 1972)

To evaluate this alternative hypothesis, a study traced television viewing habits over a 10-year period. More than 800 children between the ages of 8 and 9 years were studied. Investigators collected information about each child's viewing preferences and aggressiveness (as rated by schoolmates). Boys who preferred programs that contained a considerable amount of violence were found to be much more aggressive in their interpersonal relationships than boys who preferred programs that contained little violence. So far, the evidence is of the same nature as that in previous studies. But 10 years later, more than half of the original subjects were interviewed concerning their television preferences, given a test that measured delinquency tendencies, and rated by their peers for aggressiveness. Figure 11-10 shows that high exposure to violence on television at age

9 is positively related to aggressiveness in boys at age 19. Most important, the correlation remains significant even when statistical methods are used to control for the degree of childhood aggressiveness, thereby reducing the possibility that the initial level of aggression determines both childhood viewing preferences and adult aggressiveness.

It is interesting that the results showed no consistent relation between the television viewing habits of girls and their aggressive behavior at either age. This agrees with the results of other studies indicating that girls tend to imitate aggressive behavior much less than boys do unless specifically reinforced for doing so. In our society, girls are less likely to be reinforced for behaving aggressively. And since most of the aggressive roles on television are male, females are less likely to find aggressive models to imitate. For boys, however, the majority of studies point to the conclusion that viewing violence does increase interpersonal aggression, particularly in young children. Indeed, this conclusion is supported by a review of 28 studies on this issue (Wood, Wong, & Chachere, 1991). This argues against aggression catharsis and the view that aggression is a drive.

Our survey of aggression has by no means considered all of its possible causes. Common causes of anger and aggression include a loss of self-esteem or a perception that another person has acted unfairly (Averill, 1983); neither of these factors has figured centrally in our discussion of aggression as a drive versus aggression as a learned response. Also, many societal factors are involved in the instigation of aggression; conditions of poverty, overcrowding, the actions of authorities such as the police, and the values of one's cultural group are only a few. Some of these social influences will be considered in Chapter 18. In sum, aggression may often occur when a person is frustrated, but it does not always follow frustration; there are many social conditions and cues that either increase or decrease a person's tendency to act aggressively (Berkowitz, 1981).

The study of aggression makes it clear that an emotional reaction is a complex event. Similarly, each component of an emotion that we considered—autonomic arousal, cognitive appraisal, and emotional expression—is itself a complex event involving multiple factors.

BIOLOGICAL-PSYCHOLOGICAL PERSPECTIVES

Each of the theories of emotion described in this chapter has addressed how the biological components of emotion (such as physiological arousal and universal facial expressions) and the psychological components of emotion (such as cognitive appraisals) interact in the emotion process. These theories differ in which components of emotion are said to cause the other components. The James-Lange theory and the facial feedback hypothesis suggest that the biological components of emotion are most influential in producing the subjective experience of an emotion. The Schachter-Singer theory and appraisal theories place the psychological components of emotion central to the subjective experience of emotion. In addition, we saw that, although there may be common, perhaps biologically determined, ways of expressing some emotions across cultures, social situations, such as cultural display rules, can influence the ways people display emotions and perhaps even the emotions they feel in certain situations. Taken together, the research reviewed in this chapter suggests that in most cases, the biological and psychological components of emotion probably have reciprocal influences on each other in a dynamic process that evolves over time. A situation may initially elicit a mild emotion, but as a person evaluates the situation more deeply the emotion may intensify and his physiological arousal may increase. The effects of the emotion on his memory for similar events from the past and on his appraisals of this event may further intensify his subjective experience of emotion. Over time, then, feedback loops between the biological and psychological components of an emotion can influence the development of the emotion. We will return to discussions of the feedback between the biological and psychological components of emotion when we discuss stress in Chapter 14 and emotional disorders in Chapters 15 and 16.

CHAPTER SUMMARY

1. The components of an emotion include the *subjective experience of emotion, autonomic arousal cognitive appraisal, emotional expression, general reactions* to the emotion and action tendencies. One critical question is, What is the nature of these components? Other critical questions are, How do arousal, appraisal, and expression contribute to the intensity of an emotional experience? and Which components *differentiate* the emotions?

2. Intense emotions usually involve physiological arousal caused by activation of the *sympathetic division* of the *autonomic nervous system.* People who have spinal cord injuries, which limit feedback from the autonomic nervous system, report experiencing less intense emotions. Autonomic arousal may also help differentiate the emotions, since the pattern of arousal (for example, heartbeat, skin temperature) differs for different emotions.

3. A *cognitive appraisal* is an analysis of a situation that results in an emotion. Such appraisals affect both the intensity and quality of an emotion. When people are induced into a state of undifferentiated arousal, the quality of their emotional experience may be influenced by their appraisal of the situation. There are cases of emotion, however, in which no conscious or deliberate cognitive appraisal seems to be involved (for example, fear experiences that were acquired in childhood by classical conditioning). These *precognitive emotions* appear to be mediated by distinct neural pathways in the brain.

4. The facial expressions that accompany primary emotions have a universal meaning: People from different cultures agree on what emotion a person in a particular photograph is expressing. Cultures may differ in the factors that elicit certain emotions and in rules for the proper display of emotion. The ability to recognize emotional expression is localized

in the right cerebral hemisphere and is neurologically distinct from the ability to recognize faces. In addition to their communicative functions, emotional expressions may also contribute to the subjective experience of an emotion (the *facial feedback hypothesis*). In support of this hypothesis, people report more of an emotional experience when they exaggerate their facial reactions to emotional stimuli.

5. Being in an emotional state has some general consequences. One is that emotion can sometimes energize people, but at other times disrupt them. A mild emotion produces alertness, but an intense emotion can be disruptive. Another general reaction to being in an emotional state is that we tend to pay more attention to and learn more about events that fit our mood than to events that do not. Another consequence is that our emotional mood affects our evaluation of people and objects, as well as our estimation of what will happen in the future. When in a bad mood, we estimate various risks in life to be relatively frequent; when in a good mood, we estimate these risks to be relatively infrequent.

6. *Aggression* is a typical action tendency in response to anger (though it can occur for other reasons as well). According to early *psychoanalytic theory*, aggression is a *frustration-produced drive;* according to *social-learning theory*, aggression is a *learned response.*

7. The hypothesis that aggression is a basic drive (like hunger) receives some support from studies showing a biological basis of aggression. In lower animals, aggression is controlled by neurological mechanisms in the *hypothalamus.* Stimulation of the hypothalamus of a rat or cat can lead to a rage or killing response. In humans and other higher mammals, aggressive behavior is largely under cortical control, and hence more affected by past experiences and social influences. Even in humans, though, there may be some biological bases of aggression (like *testosterone level* in men).

8. In keeping with the social-learning theory of aggression, aggressive responses can be learned through *imitation* and increased in frequency when positively reinforced. Children are more likely to express aggressive responses when they are reinforced for such actions (for example, their victims wince or cry) than when they are punished for the actions (their victims counterattack).

9. Evidence indicates that aggression either increases subsequent aggressive behavior or maintains it at the same level. Thus, when given repeated opportunities to shock another person (who cannot retaliate), college students become more and more punitive. The indirect or vicarious expression of aggression has similar effects: There is a positive relation between the amount of exposure children have to television violence and the extent to which they act aggressively.

FURTHER READING

For an introduction to various views on emotion, some chapters in Mook, *Motivation* (1987) are very useful. For a more technical treatment of emotion, see Lazarus, *Emotion and Adaptation* (1991); Frijda, *The Emotions* (1986); Mandler, *Mind and Emotion* (1982); and Plutchik and Kellerman (eds.), *Emotion: Theory, Research, and Experience* (1980). The role of cognition in emotion is discussed in detail in Ortony, Clore, and Collins, *The Cognitive Structure of Emotions* (1988).

Interesting books on facial expressions and emotion include Ekman's *Emotion in the Human Face* (2nd ed., 1982) and his *Telling Lies: Clues to Deceit in the Marketplace, Politics and Marriage* (1985). For a review and critical analysis of lie detection procedures, see Lykken, *A Tremor in the Blood: Uses and Abuses of the Lie Detector* (1980).

The psychoanalytic theory of emotion is presented in two books by Freud: *Beyond the Pleasure Principle* (1920/1975) and *New*

Introductory Lectures on Psychoanalysis (1933/1965). For the social-learning approach, see Bandura, *Social Learning Theory* (1977).

Books on aggression include Bandura, *Aggression: A Social Learning Analysis* (1973); Tavris, *Anger: The Misunderstood Emotion* (1984); Hamburg and Trudeau (eds.), *Biobehavioral Aspects of Aggression* (1981); and Averill, *Anger and Aggression: An Essay on Emotion* (1982).

PERSONALITY AND INDIVIDUALITY

INDIVIDUAL DIFFERENCES

I n many ways, every person is like every other person. The biological and psychological processes discussed in this book—development, consciousness, perception, learning, remembering, thinking, motivation, and emotion—are basically the same for all of us. But in other ways, every person is different from every other person. Each of us has a distinctive pattern of abilities, beliefs, attitudes, motivations, emotions, and personality traits that makes us unique. It is this individuality that concerns us in this section of the book.

In this chapter we survey some of the methods for measuring intellectual abilities and personality, discuss the biological and environmental factors that produce individual differences, and consider the extent to which an individual's personality changes or remains the same across the course of life. In Chapter 13, we review formal theories of personality and discuss their underlying philosophies of human nature.

We also return to a major theme that we introduced in the earlier chapter on psychological development (Chapter 3): the interaction between nature and nurture. There we discussed how innate biological factors interact with events in an individual's environment to determine the course of development, focusing particularly on factors that make us all alike. We considered, for example, how innately determined sequences of maturation cause all children to go through the same stages of development in the same sequence, relatively independently of differences in their rearing environments. In this chapter we focus on those biological and environmental factors that individualize us and make us different from one another.

ASSESSMENT OF INDIVIDUAL DIFFERENCES

Many industrialized societies rely heavily on the objective assessment of individual differences, particularly differences in cognitive or intellectual abilities. Children in elementary school are often placed in instructional groups on the basis of their performances on such tests. Aptitude or ability tests are part of the admissions procedure in many colleges and most professional and graduate schools. In addition, many industries and government agencies select job applicants and place or promote employees on the basis of test scores.

Tests for assessing interests, attitudes, and personality traits are also familiar to most of us. In helping students to make career choices, counselors can offer better advice if they know something about the student beyond academic ability. In selecting individuals for high-level positions, employers often seek to assess a candidate's interactional styles, ability to handle stress, and so on. Decisions about the kind of treatment that will be most beneficial to an emotionally disturbed person or that will help to rehabilitate a felon require an objective assessment of similar individual differences.

Beyond these practical concerns, methods of assessment are essential to theory and research on individual differences. In fact, several personality theorists (discussed in Chapter 13) have developed assessment methods tailored to their particular approaches.

CHARACTERISTICS OF A GOOD TEST

Because tests and other assessment instruments play important practical and scientific roles, it is essential that they measure accurately what they are intended to measure. Specifically, they must have *reliability* and *validity*.

RELIABILITY   If a test or method of assessment is reliable, it will give reproducible and consistent results. If a test yielded different results when it was administered on different occasions or scored by different people, it would be unreliable. A simple analogy is a rubber yardstick. If we did not know how much it stretched each time we took a measurement, the results would be unreliable no matter how carefully we make each measurement.

Reliability is typically assessed by correlating two sets of scores. For example, the same test might be given to the same group of people on two occasions. If the test is reliable, then their scores on the first occasion should correlate highly with their scores on the second. If they do, then the test is said to have **test-retest reliability** or **temporal stability**.

In actual practice, of course, one would not usually want to give the same exact test to the same people twice. But there are many situations in which one would want to give equivalent forms of the same test—for example, when college-bound high school seniors want to take the Scholastic Assessment Test (SAT) more than once. To ensure that two forms of the same test yield equivalent scores, both forms are administered to the same population and the two forms correlated. If they correlate highly, then the test is said to have **alternate form reliability**. Some of the questions on the SAT do not actually count toward the student's score but are being statistically evaluated so they can be used on future, equivalent forms of the test.

Another common measure of reliability is **internal consistency**, the degree to which the separate questions or items on a test are all measuring the same thing. This can be assessed by correlating the scores obtained by a group of individuals on each item with their total scores. Any item that does not correlate with the total score is an unreliable item; it is failing to contribute to what the test is measuring. Discarding unreliable items "purifies" a test by increasing its internal consistency. As the number of reliable items on a test increases, the reliability of the test's total score also increases.

Most tests and assessment instruments are scored objectively, often by computer. But sometimes one must evaluate intellectual performance or social behavior subjectively. An essay examination is a familiar example. To assess the reliability of such subjective judgments, two or more sets of ratings made by independent judges are correlated. For example, two observers might independently rate a group of nursery school children for aggression or two or more judges might be asked to read past U.S. presidential inaugural addresses and to rate them for optimism or to count the number of negative references to Iraq. If the correlation between raters or judges is high, then the method is said to possess **interrater agreement** or **interjudge reliability**.

In general, a well-constructed, objectively scored test of ability should have a reliability of .90 or greater. For personality tests and subjective judgments, reliability coefficients of .70 can sometimes be satisfactory for research purposes, but inferences about partic-

ular individuals must be made with great caution. But as noted above, the reliability of a test's total score increases as the number of reliable items on the test increases. One can apply the same reasoning to subjective judgments and increase the reliability of the method by adding more judges, raters, or observers. For example, if ratings of two observers correlate only .50, the researcher can add a third, comparable observer and thereby raise the interjudge reliability of their summed ratings to .75; adding a fourth rater would raise the reliability to .80.

VALIDITY Reliability assesses the degree to which a test is measuring *something*, but high reliability does not guarantee that the test is measuring what it is intended to measure; it does not guarantee that the test has **validity**. For example, if the final examination in your psychology course contained especially difficult vocabulary words or trick questions, it might be a test of your verbal ability or test sophistication rather than of the material learned in the course. Such an examination might be *reliable*—students would achieve about the same scores on a retest and the separate items might all be measuring the same thing—but it would not be a *valid* test of achievement for the course. A test of sense of humor containing jokes that are hard to understand might well be reliable, but the test might be measuring intelligence, educational achievement, or social class rather than sense of humor.

In some instances the validity of a test can be assessed by correlating the test score with some external criterion. This correlation is called a validity coefficient. For example, the relatively strong positive correlation between scores on the SAT and freshman grades in college indicates that the test has reasonable validity. This kind of validity is called **criterion** or **empirical validity**. Because of sensitivity to race and sex discrimination, the courts are increasingly requiring companies or government agencies that use tests for personnel selection to provide evidence that those tests correlate with on-the-job performance—that they have criterion or empirical validity.

A special kind of validity, which applies especially to tests used in personality research, is called **construct validity**. If a researcher is designing a test to measure some concept or construct that is part of a theory, it is not always possible to compute a single coefficient that would indicate its criterion validity because it is not clear what the external criterion should be. How, for example, should a researcher assess the validity of a test for achievement motivation? One can think of a number of possibilities. The test could be given to business executives to see if the test correlates with their salaries. Perhaps the test will correlate with teachers' ratings of the ambitiousness of their students. The problem is that there is no single criterion the researcher is willing to accept as the ultimate "true" answer. It would be reassuring if the test correlated with executive salaries, but if it did not, the researcher would not be willing to judge the test to be invalid. This is known as the **criterion problem** in personality psychology: There is no measure of "truth" against which to validate the test. Accordingly, the researcher attempts instead to establish its construct validity.

This is done through the process of research itself. The researcher uses his or her theory both to construct the test and to generate predictions from the theory. Studies using the test are then conducted to test those predictions. To the extent that the results of several converging studies confirm the theory's predictions, both the theory and the test are validated simultaneously. Most often, mixed results suggest ways in which both the theory and the test need to be modified.

ASSESSMENT OF INTELLECTUAL ABILITIES

HISTORICAL BACKGROUND The first person to attempt to develop tests of intellectual ability was Sir Francis Galton a century ago. A naturalist and mathematician, Galton developed an interest in individual differences from the evolutionary theory of his cousin, Charles Darwin. Galton believed that certain families are biologically superior—stronger and smarter—than others. Intelligence, he reasoned, is a question of exceptional sensory and perceptual skills, which are passed from one generation to the next. Because all information is acquired through the senses, the more sensitive and accurate an individual's perceptual apparatus, the more intelligent the person. In 1884, Galton administered a battery of tests (measuring such variables as head size, reac-

tion time, visual acuity, auditory thresholds, and memory for visual forms) to more than 9,000 visitors at the London Exhibition. To his disappointment, he discovered that eminent British scientists could not be distinguished from ordinary citizens on the basis of their head size and that measurements such as speed of reaction were not particularly related to other measures of intelligence. Although his test did not prove very useful, Galton did invent the correlation coefficient, which—as we have already seen—plays an important role in psychology.

The first tests that approximated contemporary intelligence tests were devised by the French psychologist Alfred Binet. In 1881, the French government passed a law making school attendance compulsory for all children. Previously, slow learners had usually been kept at home; now teachers had to cope with a wide range of individual differences. The government asked Binet to create a test that would detect children who were too slow intellectually to benefit from a regular school curriculum.

Binet assumed that intelligence should be measured by tasks that required reasoning and problem-solving abilities rather than perceptual-motor skills. In collaboration with another French psychologist, Théophile Simon, Binet published a scale in 1905, which he revised in 1908 and again in 1911.

Binet reasoned that a slow or dull child was like a normal child retarded in mental growth. On tests, the slow child would perform like a normal child of younger age,

Alfred Binet with his daughters.

whereas the mental abilities of a bright child were characteristic of older children. Binet devised a scale of test items of increasing difficulty that measured the kinds of changes in intelligence ordinarily associated with growing older. The higher a child could go on the scale in correctly answering items, the higher his or her **mental age (MA)**. The concept of mental age was critical in Binet's method; using this method, one could compare the MA of a child with his or her **chronological age (CA)** as determined by date of birth.

STANFORD-BINET INTELLIGENCE SCALE   The test items originally developed by Binet were adapted for American schoolchildren by Lewis Terman at Stanford University. He standardized the administration of the test and developed age-level norms by giving the test to thousands of children. In 1916, he published the Stanford revision of the Binet tests, now referred to as the Stanford-Binet Intelligence Scale; it was revised in 1937, 1960, 1972, and, most recently, in 1986. Despite its age, the Stanford-Binet is still one of the most frequently used psychological tests.

Test materials from the 1986 Stanford-Binet Intelligence Scale.

Terman retained Binet's concept of mental age. Each test item was age-graded at the level at which a substantial majority of the children pass it. A child's mental age could be obtained by summing the number of items passed at each level. In addition, Terman adopted a convenient index of intelligence suggested by the German psychologist William Stern. This index is the **intelligence quotient**, commonly known as the IQ. It expresses intelligence as a ratio of mental age to chronological age:

$$IQ = \frac{MA}{CA} \times 100$$

The 100 is used as a multiplier so that the IQ will have a value of 100 when MA is equal to CA. If MA is lower than CA, then the IQ will be less that 100; if MA is higher than CA, then the IQ will be more than 100.

The most recent revision of the Stanford-Binet uses Standard Age Scores instead of IQ scores. These can be interpreted in terms of percentiles, which show the percentage of subjects in the standardization group falling above or below a given score (Thorndike, Hage, & Sattler, 1986). And although the concept of IQ is still used in intelligence testing, it is no longer actually calculated using this equation. Instead, tables are used to convert raw scores on the test to standard scores that are adjusted so the mean at each age equals 100.

In line with the current view of intelligence as a composite of different abilities, the 1986 revision groups its tests into four broad areas of intellectual abilities: *verbal reasoning, abstract/visual reasoning, quantitative reasoning,* and *short-term memory* (Sattler, 1988). A separate score is obtained for each area; Table 12-1 gives some examples of items, grouped by area.

WECHSLER INTELLIGENCE SCALES   In 1939, David Wechsler developed a new test because he thought the Stanford-Binet depended too heavily on language ability and was also not appropriate for adults. The Wechsler Adult Intelligence Scale, or WAIS (1939, 1955, 1981), is divided into two parts—a *verbal* scale and a *performance* scale—which yield separate scores as well as a full-scale IQ. The test items are described in Table 12-2. Later he developed a similar test for children, the Wechsler Intelligence Scale for Children (WISC) (1958, 1974, 1991).

TABLE 12-1

Stanford-Binet Items
Typical examples of items from the 1986 Stanford-Binet Intelligence Scale for a 6- to 8-year-old.

VERBAL REASONING

Vocabulary   Defines words, such as "dollar" and "envelope."

Comprehension   Answers questions, such as "Where do people buy food?" and "Why do people comb their hair?"

Absurdities   Identifies the "funny" aspect of a picture, such as a girl riding a bicycle on a lake or a bald man combing his head.

Verbal Relations   Tells how the first three items in a sequence are alike and how they differ from the fourth: scarf, tie, muffler, shirt.

QUANTITATIVE REASONING

Quantitative   Performs simple arithmetic tasks, such as selecting a die with six spots because the number of spots equals the combination of a two-spot die and a four-spot die.

Number Series   Gives the next two numbers in a series, such as

$$20 \quad 16 \quad 12 \quad 8 \quad \underline{\quad} \quad \underline{\quad}.$$

Equation Building   Builds an equation from the following array:

$2\ 3\ 5\ +\ \ =$. One correct response would be $2\ +\ 3\ =\ 5$.

ABSTRACT/VISUAL REASONING

Pattern Analysis   Copies a simple design with blocks.

Copying   Copies a geometrical drawing demonstrated by the examiner, such as a rectangle intersected by two diagonals.

SHORT-TERM MEMORY

Bead Memory   Shown a picture of different-shaped beads stacked on a stick. Reproduces the sequence from memory by placing real beads on a stick.

Memory for Sentences   Repeats after the examiner sentences such as "It is time to go to sleep" and "Ken painted a picture for his mother's birthday."

Memory for Digits   Repeats after examiner a series of digits, such as 5-7-8-3, forward and backward.

Memory for Objects   Shown pictures of individual objects, such as a clock and an elephant, one at a time. Identifies the objects in the correct order of their appearance in a picture that also includes extraneous objects; for example, a bus, a clown, an *elephant*, eggs, and a *clock*.

Items on the performance scale require the manipulation or arrangement of blocks, pictures, or other materials. The Wechsler scales also provide scores for each of the subtests, so the examiner has a clearer picture of the individual's intellectual strengths and weaknesses. For example, a discrepancy between verbal and performance scores prompts the examiner to look for specific learning problems such as reading disabilities or language handicaps.

Both the Stanford-Binet and the Wechsler scales show good reliability and validity. They have test-retest reliabilities of about .90, and both are fairly valid predictors of achievement in school, with validity coefficients of about .50 (Sattler, 1988).

GROUP ABILITY TESTS   The Stanford-Binet and the Wechsler scales are individual ability tests; that is, they are administered to a single individual by a specially trained tester. Group ability tests, in contrast, can be administered to a large number of people by a single examiner and are usually in pencil-and-paper form.

The Scholastic Assessment Test and the American College Test (ACT) are both examples of group-administered, general-ability tests likely to be familiar to most college students in the United States. Virtually all 4-year colleges require applicants to take one of these as a way of setting a common standard for students from high schools with different curricula and grading standards. The SAT underwent a major revision in 1994 and now involves a new essay section and open-ended (rather than multiple-choice) mathematics questions, among other changes. These changes, like some of those in recent revisions of the ACT, are in response to recent high school curriculum trends that place a

TABLE 12-2

Tests Composing the
Wechsler Adult
Intelligence Scale   *The
tests of the Wechsler
Intelligence Scale for
Children are similar with
some modifications.*

TEST	DESCRIPTION
VERBAL SCALE	
Information	Questions tap a general range of information; for example, "How many nickels make a dime?"
Comprehension	Tests practical information and ability to evaluate past experience; for example, "What is the advantage of keeping money in a bank?"
Arithmetic	Verbal problems testing arithmetic reasoning.
Similarities	Asks in what way certain objects or concepts (for example, *egg* and *seed*) are similar; measures abstract thinking.
Digit span	A series of digits presented auditorily (for example, 7-5-6-3-8) is repeated in a forward or backward direction; tests attention and rote memory.
Vocabulary	Tests word knowledge.
PERFORMANCE SCALE	
Digit symbol	A timed coding task in which numbers must be associated with marks of various shapes; tests speed of learning and writing.
Picture completion	The missing part of an incompletely drawn picture must be discovered and named; tests visual alertness and visual memory.
Block design	Pictured designs must be copied with blocks; tests ability to perceive and analyze patterns.
Picture arrangement	A series of comic-strip pictures must be arranged in the right sequence to tell a story; tests understanding of social situations.
Object assembly	Puzzle pieces must be assembled to form a complete object; tests ability to deal with part-whole relationships.

premium on more sophisticated reading, writing, and mathematics skills.

Correlations between SAT scores and freshman grade point averages vary across studies, with a median correlation of about .38 for the verbal section of the SAT and .34 for the mathematics section (Linn, 1982). When these correlations are corrected for the fact that many students with very low scores do not end up attending college (and hence cannot be included in the calculation of the validity correlation), the resulting correlations are about .50. This means that about 44 percent of students in the top fifth of the distribution of SAT scores will also be in the top fifth of the distribution of freshman grade point averages, compared with only 4 percent of students in the bottom fifth of the SAT score distribution. Thus, SAT scores improve prediction considerably, but it is also clear that the freshman grades of students with identical SAT scores will vary widely.

FACTORIAL APPROACH   Some psychologists view intelligence as a general capacity for comprehension and reasoning that manifests itself in

various ways. This was Binet's assumption. Although his test contained many kinds of items, Binet observed that a bright child tended to score higher than dull children on all of them. He assumed, therefore, that the different tasks sampled a basic underlying ability. Similarly, despite the diverse subscales that compose the WAIS, David Wechsler also believed that "intelligence is the aggregate or global capacity of the individual to act purposefully, to think rationally, and to deal effectively with his environment" (Wechsler, 1958).

Other psychologists, however, question whether there is such a thing as "general intelligence." They believe that intelligence tests sample a number of mental abilities that are relatively independent of one another. One method of obtaining more precise information about the kinds of abilities that determine performance on intelligence tests is **factor analysis**. This mathematical technique is used to determine the minimum number of *factors*, or abilities, that are required to explain the observed pattern of correlations for an array of different tests. The basic idea is

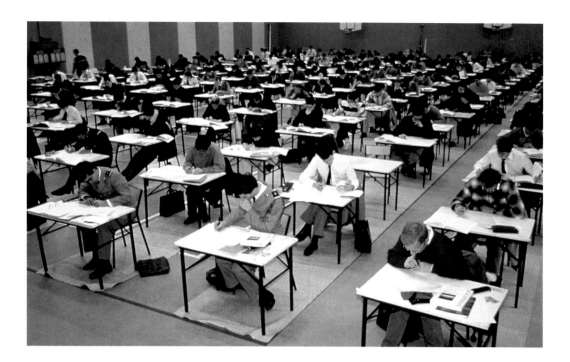

that two tests that correlate very highly with each other are probably measuring the same underlying ability. The factor analysis of data from an array of tests tells us how many distinguishable factors enter the set of correlations and the weight or influence of each factor. A more detailed explanation of factor analysis is given in Table 12-3.

It was actually the originator of factor analysis, Charles Spearman (1904), who first proposed that all individuals possess a general intelligence factor (called *g*) in varying amounts. A person could be described as generally bright or generally dull, depending on the amount of *g* he or she possessed. According to Spearman, the *g* factor is the major determinant of performance on intelligence test items. In addition, special factors, each called *s,* are specific to particular abilities or tests. For example, tests of arithmetic or spatial relationships would each tap a separate *s.* An individual's tested intelligence would reflect the amount of *g* plus the magnitude of the various *s* factors. Performance in mathematics would be a function of a person's general intelligence and mathematical aptitude.

A later investigator, Louis Thurstone (1938), objected to Spearman's emphasis on general intelligence, feeling that it could be broken down into a number of primary abilities using factor analysis. After many rounds of administering tests, factor analyzing the results, purifying the scales, and retesting, Thurstone identified seven factors which he used to construct his *Test of Primary Mental Abilities.*

Revised versions of this test are still widely used, but its predictive power is no greater than the predictability of general intelligence tests, such as the Wechsler scales. Thurstone's hope of discovering the basic elements of intelligence through factor analysis was not fully realized for several reasons. His primary abilities are not completely independent; indeed, the significant intercorrelations among them provide support for the concept of a general intelligence factor that underlies the specific abilities. In addition, the number of basic abilities identified by factor analysis depends on the nature of the test items. Other investigators, using different test items and alternative methods of factor analysis, have identified from 20 to 150 factors to represent the range of intellectual abilities (Guilford, 1982; Ekstrom, French, & Harman, 1979; Ekstrom, French, Harman, & Derman, 1976).

This lack of consistency in the number and kinds of factors raises doubts about the value of the factorial approach. Nevertheless, factor analysis continues to be a principal technique for studying intellectual performance (Comrey & Lee, 1992; Carrol, 1988), and we will meet it again when we discuss personality traits.

Factor Analysis   *An example of the data and major steps involved in factor analysis.*

What are the data that enter into factor analysis, and what are the major steps in the analysis? The data are simply scores on a variety of tests designed to measure various psychological contents or processes. Each of a large number of individuals obtains a score for each of a number of tests. All these scores can then be intercorrelated; that is, we know how the scores of many individuals on Test 1 relate to their scores on Test 2, and so on. These intercorrelations yield a table of correlations known as a *correlation matrix*. An example of such a correlation matrix, based on only nine tests, is given below.

TESTS	2	3	4	5	6	7	8	9
1	.38	.55	.06	−.04	.05	.07	.05	.09
2		.36	.40	.28	.40	.11	.15	.13
3			.10	.01	.18	.13	.12	.10
4				.32	.60	.04	.06	.13
5					.35	.08	.13	.11
6						.01	.06	.07
7							.45	.32
8								.32

The three gray boxes of correlations indicate that these are groups of tests with something in common not shared by other tests (that is, they show high correlations). The inadequacy of making such a judgment from a table of correlations of this kind is shown by noting the additional high correlations of Test 2 with Tests 4, 5, and 6, not included in the outlined clusters. We can use factor analysis to tell us more precisely what underlies these correlations. If the correlation matrix contains a number of statistically significant correlations and a number of near-zero correlations, it is apparent that some tests measure similar abilities of one kind and that others measure abilities of other kinds. The purpose of factor analysis is to be more precise about these underlying abilities.

INFORMATION-PROCESSING APPROACH   Until the 1960s, research on intelligence was dominated by the factorial approach. However, with the development of cognitive psychology and its emphasis on **information-processing models** (see Chapter 9), a new approach emerged. This approach is defined somewhat differently by different investigators, but the basic idea is to try to understand intelligence in terms of the cognitive processes that operate when we engage in intellectual activities (Hunt, 1990; Carpenter, Just, & Shell, 1990). The information-processing approach asks:

1. What mental processes are involved in the various tests of intelligence?

2. How rapidly and accurately are these processes carried out?

3. What types of mental representations of information do these processes act upon?

Rather than try to explain intelligence in terms of factors, this approach attempts to identify the mental processes that underlie intelligent behavior. The information-processing approach assumes that individual differences on a given task depend on the specific processes that different individuals bring into play and the speed and accuracy of these processes. The goal is to use an information-processing model of a particular task to identify appropriate measures of the component processes. These measures may be as simple as the response to a multiple-choice item, or they may include the subject's speed of re-

Factor analysis then uses mathematical methods to compute the correlation of each of the tests with each of several possible underlying factors. Such correlations between test scores and factors are known as *factor loadings;* if a test correlates .05 on factor I, .10 on factor II, and .70 on factor III, it is most heavily "loaded" on factor III. For example, the nine tests with the above correlation matrix yield the *factor matrix* below.

TESTS	FACTORS		
	I	II	III
1	.75	−.01	.08
2	.44	.48	.16
3	.72	.07	.15
4	.08	.76	.08
5	−.01	.49	−.01
6	.16	.73	.02
7	−.03	.04	.64
8	.02	.05	.66
9	−.01	.10	.47

The gray boxes in the factor matrix show which tests are most highly correlated with each of the underlying factors. The clusters are the same as the clusters in the correlation matrix but are now assigned greater precision. The problem of Test 2 remains because it is loaded almost equally on factor I and factor II; it is obviously not a "factor-pure" test. Having found the three factors that account for the intercorrelations of the nine tests, the factors can be interpreted by studying the content of the tests most highly weighted on each factor. The factor analysis itself is strictly a mathematical process, but the naming and interpretation of the factors depends on psychological considerations.

sponse or the eye movements and cortical-evoked potentials associated with the response. The idea is to use whatever information is needed to estimate the efficiency of each component process.

The information-processing approach can be illustrated by the work of Sternberg (1985) and his *componential model* of intelligence. He assumes that the test taker possesses a set of mental processes, which he calls *components,* that operate in an organized way to produce the responses observed on an intelligence test. There are many components that fall into the five classes given in Table 12-4. Sternberg selects a specific task from an intelligence test and uses it in a series of experiments to try to identify the components involved in the task.

For example, consider analogy problems of the following kind:

lawyer is to *client* as *doctor* is to _____

(a) *medicine*   (b) *patient*

A series of experiments with such problems led Sternberg to conclude that the critical components were the *encoding process* and the *comparison process.* The subject encodes each of the words in the analogy by forming a mental representation of the word—in this case, a list of attributes of the word that are retrieved from long-term memory. For example, a mental representation of the word "lawyer" might include the following attributes: college-educated, versed in legal procedures, represents clients in court, and so on.

COMPONENTS	PROCESSES
Metacomponents	Higher-order control processes used for executive planning and decision making in problem solving.
Performance components	Processes that execute the plans and implement the decisions selected by metacomponents.
Acquisition components	Processes involved in learning new information.
Retention components	Processes involved in retrieving information previously stored in memory.
Transfer components	Processes involved in carrying over retained information from one situation to another.

TABLE 12-4

Components of Intelligence *Sternberg's scheme for classifying the many component processes operative in solving problems.* (After Sternberg, 1985)

Once the subject has formed a mental representation for each word in the analogy, the comparison process scans the representations looking for matching attributes that solve the analogy.

Other processes are involved in analogy problems, but Sternberg has shown that individual differences on this task are principally determined by the efficiency of the encoding and comparison processes. The experimental evidence shows that individuals who score high on analogy problems (skilled performers) spend more time encoding and form more accurate mental representations than do individuals who score low on such problems (less-skilled performers). In contrast, during the comparison stage, the skilled performers are *faster* than the less-skilled performers in matching attributes, but both are *equally accurate*. Thus the better test scores for skilled performers are based on the increased accuracy of their encoding process, but the time they require to solve the problem is a complicated mix of slow encoding speeds and fast comparisons (Galotti, 1989; Pellegrino, 1985).

A factorial approach and an information-processing approach provide complementary interpretations of performance on intelligence tests. Factor-based tests are useful in identifying broad areas of strengths and weaknesses. They may indicate that a person is strong in word fluency and verbal comprehension but weak in reasoning. If additional testing is conducted, an information-processing analysis could provide a diagnostic profile of the processes responsible for the observed deficiency. A process analysis may indicate a deficiency at the level of metacomponents (such as the choice of strategies used to attach the problem), or retention components (such as slow or inaccurate recall of relevant information), or transfer components (such as poor ability to transfer what has been learned in one situation to another).

MULTIPLE INTELLIGENCES   In an attempt to generalize his componential approach, Sternberg argues that current tests tap primarily "academic intelligence" and ignore components of practical intelligence such as the ability to adapt to changing and uncertain circumstances or to motivate oneself to accomplish important tasks (Sternberg, 1985).

An even broader critique of current tests is offered by Howard Gardner (1983), who believes that there are at least six distinct kinds of intelligence that are independent of one another, each operating as a separate system (or module) in the brain according to its own rules. These are (a) linguistic; (b) logical-mathematical; (c) spatial; (d) musical; (e) bodily-kinesthetic; and (f) personal. The first three are familiar components of intelligence and are measured by standard intelligence tests. Gardner believes that the last three deserve comparable status and that Western society has emphasized the first three types of intelligence to the virtual exclusion of the others.

In particular, Gardner argues that musical intelligence—which includes the ability to perceive pitch and rhythm—has been more important than logical-mathematical intelligence throughout most of human history. Bodily-kinesthetic intelligence involves the control of one's own body and the ability to manipulate objects skillfully: Examples are dancers, gymnasts, artisans, and neurosurgeons. Personal intelligence has two components. *Intra*personal intelligence is the ability to monitor one's own feelings and emotions, discriminate among them and use the information to guide one's actions. *Inter*personal intelligence is the ability to notice and understand the needs and intentions of others and to monitor their moods as a way of predicting how they will behave.

Gardner analyzes each kind of intelligence from several viewpoints: the cognitive operations involved, the appearance of prodigies and other exceptional individuals, evidence from cases of brain damage, manifestations in different cultures, and the possible course of evolutionary development. For example, certain kinds of brain damage can impair one type of intelligence and have no effect on the others.

As we have noted, conventional IQ tests are good predictors of college grades, but they are less valid for predicting later job success or career advancement. Measures of other abilities, such as personal intelligence, may help explain why some people with brilliant college records fail miserably in later life, while lesser students become charismatic leaders (Kornhaber, Krechevsky, & Gardner, 1990). Even so, however, the accumulated evidence shows that intelligence, as measured by standard intelligence tests, is still the best single predictor of overall success in increasingly technological societies like ours (Herrnstein & Murray, 1994). For better or worse, the narrow focus of standard intelligence tests reflects the narrow range of

abilities that are most likely to be rewarded in the society at large.

ASSESSMENT OF PERSONALITY

Personality can be defined as the distinctive and characteristic patterns of thought, emotion, and behavior that define an individual's personal style of interacting with the physical and social environment. When we are asked in daily life to describe an individual's personality, we are likely to use personality trait terms—adjectives such as intelligent, extraverted, conscientious, and so forth. Personality psychologists have historically attempted to devise formal methods of describing and measuring personality by systematizing the ways in which we use personality trait terms in daily life. In particular, they attempt to go beyond our everyday trait conceptions of personality in three ways. First, they seek to reduce the potential set of trait terms to a manageably small set that will still encompass the diversity of human personality. Second, they attempt to ensure that their instruments for measuring personality traits are reliable and valid. Finally, they do empirical research to discover the relationships among traits and between traits and specific behaviors.

One way to begin the task of deriving a comprehensive but manageable number of traits is to consult a dictionary. The assumption is that through linguistic evolution, the language will encode most, if not all, of the important distinctions among individuals that make a difference in everyday life. The language embodies the accumulated experience of the culture, and the unabridged dictionary is the written record of that experience. In the 1930s, two personality psychologists actually undertook this task by going through the unabridged dictionary. They found approximately 18,000 words that refer to characteristics of behavior—nearly 5 percent of the English lexicon. Next, they reduced the list to about 4,500 terms by eliminating obscure words and synonyms. Finally, they organized the list into psychologically meaningful subsets (Allport & Odbert, 1936).

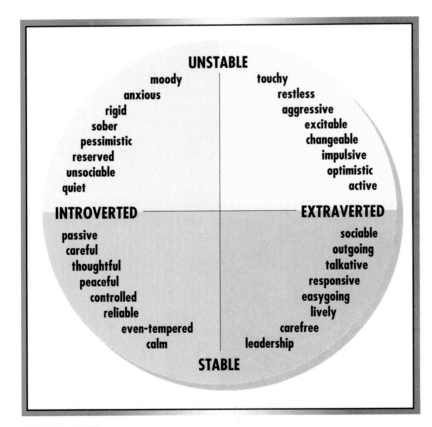

UNSTABLE

moody
anxious
rigid
sober
pessimistic
reserved
unsociable
quiet

touchy
restless
aggressive
excitable
changeable
impulsive
optimistic
active

INTROVERTED ——————— **EXTRAVERTED**

passive
careful
thoughtful
peaceful
controlled
reliable
even-tempered
calm

sociable
outgoing
talkative
responsive
easygoing
lively
carefree
leadership

STABLE

FIGURE 12-1

Eysenck's Personality Factors   *The figure shows the two major factors that emerge from factor-analytic studies of the intercorrelations between traits by Eysenck and others. The Stable-Unstable axis defines the neuroticism factor; the Introverted-Extraverted axis defines the extraversion factor. The other terms around the circle indicate where other traits are placed with respect to these two factors. (After Eysenck & Rachman, 1965)*

Subsequent researchers have used such trait terms to obtain personality ratings of an individual. Peers who know the individual well are asked to rate him or her on a scale of each trait. For example, a rater might be asked to rate the person on the trait of friendliness using a 7-point scale that ranges from "not at all friendly" to "very friendly." Often such scales are labeled at the two ends with opposite traits—for example, "domineering-submissive" or "conscientious-unreliable." Individuals can also be asked to rate themselves on the scales.

For example, Raymond Cattell (1966; 1957) first condensed the Allport-Odbert list to under 200 terms and then obtained both peer and self-ratings. He then used the method of factor analysis, which we described earlier, to determine how many underlying personality factors could account for the pattern of correlations among the trait ratings. His analysis yielded 16 factors.

A similar procedure was used by the British psychologist Hans Eysenck to arrive at two personality factors: introversion-extraversion—a dimension first identified by the psychoanalyst Carl Jung—and emotional instability-stability, which he calls **neuroticism** (Eysenck, 1953). (Eysenck has also proposed a third dimension, but it is not as well established or researched as the other two (Eysenck & Eysenck, 1976).)

Introversion-extraversion refers to the degree to which a person's basic orientation is turned inward toward the self or outward toward the external world. At the introversion end of the scale are individuals who are shy and prefer to work alone; they tend to withdraw into themselves, particularly in times of emotional stress or conflict. At the extraversion end are individuals who are sociable and prefer occupations that permit them to work directly with other people; in times of stress, they seek company. Neuroticism (instability-stability) is a dimension of emotionality, with moody, anxious, temperamental, and maladjusted individuals at the neurotic or unstable end, and calm, well-adjusted individuals at the other. Figure 12-1 shows how these two dimensions combine to organize a number of subtraits that are correlated with the factors.

How many basic personality factors are there? Even with a rigorous analytic procedure like factor analysis, there is no definitive answer. Thus Cattell arrived at 16 and

Eysenck arrived at 2 (or 3). Other investigators arrive at still different numbers. We encountered a similar situation earlier when we noted that the number of factors defining the concept of intelligence could be 1 (Spearman's general intelligence factor, g), 7 (Thurstone's primary mental abilities), or as many as 150 (Guilford, 1982).

Some of the discrepancy occurs because different traits are initially put into the analysis; some occurs because different types of data are being analyzed (for example, peer-ratings versus self-ratings); and some occurs because different factor analytic methods are employed. But much of the disagreement is a matter of taste. A researcher who prefers a more differentiated or fine-grained description of personality will set a lower criterion for a factor and thus accept more factors, arguing that important distinctions would be lost if the factors were further merged. Another researcher, like Eysenck, will prefer to merge several lower-level factors into more general ones, arguing that the resulting factors will be more stable (more likely to reemerge in other analyses). For example, when Cattell's 16 factors are themselves factor analyzed, Eysenck's 2 factors emerge as superfactors. One can thus think of a hierarchy of traits in which each broad general trait is composed of several subordinate, narrower traits.

Despite these disagreements, however, a consensus is emerging among many trait researchers that five trait dimensions may provide the best compromise (John, 1990). Although the five factors—now called the "Big Five"—were originally identified through a factor analysis of the Allport-Odbert trait list (Norman, 1963), the same five have now emerged from a wide variety of personality tests (McCrae & Costa, 1987; Digman & Inouye, 1986). There is still disagreement about how best to name and interpret the factors, but one reasonable way to summarize them is with the acronym OCEAN: Openness to experience, Conscientiousness, Extraversion, Agreeableness, and Neuroticism. Table 12-5 displays some representative examples of the trait scales that characterize each of the five factors. Many personality psychologists consider the discovery and validation of the Big Five to be one of the major breakthroughs of contemporary personality psychology.

TRAIT FACTOR	REPRESENTATIVE TRAIT SCALES
Openness	Conventional-Original Unadventurous-Daring Conservative-Liberal
Conscientiousness	Careless-Careful Undependable-Reliable Negligent-Conscientious
Extraversion	Retiring-Sociable Quiet-Talkative Inhibited-Spontaneous
Agreeableness	Irritable-Good-natured Ruthless-Soft-hearted Selfish-Selfless
Neuroticism	Calm-Worrying Hardy-Vulnerable Secure-Insecure

TABLE 12-5

Five Trait Factors *The table presents five trait factors that reliably emerge when a wide variety of assessment instruments are factor analyzed. The adjective pairs are examples of trait scales that characterize each of the factors.* (After McCrae & Costa, 1987)

PERSONALITY INVENTORIES Most personality tests do not actually ask individuals to directly rate themselves on personality trait dimensions. Instead, they are asked a set of questions about how they react in certain situations. For example, they might be asked to indicate how much they agree or disagree with the statement "I often try new and foreign foods" or "I really like most people I meet." Such questionnaires—called **personality inventories**—resemble structured interviews in that they ask the same questions of each person, and the answers are usually given in a form that can be easily scored, often by computer. Each item on a personality inventory is composed to exemplify a particular personality trait, and subsets of similar items are summed to give the individual a score on each trait scale. For example, the item "I often try new and foreign foods" is on the Openness to experience scale of one inventory designed to measure the Big Five; the item "I really like most people I meet" is on the Extraversion scale.

Items on most personality inventories are initially composed according to the developer's theory of each trait and then retained or discarded from the final inventory depending on whether they correlate or fail to correlate with other items on the same scale. Often a large number of trial items are placed on a preliminary form of the inventory that is administered to a large number of people. Their responses are then factor-analyzed to determine which subsets of items intercorrelate and whether these subsets actually belong to the trait scale for which they were originally devised.

A very different method of test construction, called the **criterion-keyed method**, was used to develop one of the most popular of all personality inventories, the Minnesota Multiphasic Personality Inventory (MMPI). The original MMPI was developed to provide a pencil-paper version of a psychiatric interview (Hathaway & McKinley, 1943). It consists of more than 550 statements concerning attitudes, emotional reactions, physical and psychological symptoms, and experiences. The subject responds to each statement by answering "true," "false," or "cannot say."

Here are four representative items:

- I have never done anything dangerous for the thrill of it.
- I daydream very little.
- My mother or father often made me obey, even when I thought it was unreasonable.
- At times my thoughts have raced ahead faster than I could speak them.

Instead of formulating items on the basis of a theory, designers of the MMPI gave hundreds of test items like these to groups of individuals. Each group was known to differ from the norm on a particular criterion. For example, to develop a scale of items that distinguish between paranoid and normal individuals, the same questions were given to two groups. The criterion group consisted of individuals who were hospitalized with the diagnosis of paranoid disorder; the control group comprised people who were similar to the criterion group in age, sex, socioeconomic status, and other important variables but who had never been diagnosed as having psychiatric problems. Only the questions that discriminated between the psychiatric group and the control group were retained on the inventory. Questions that at face value might seem to distinguish normal from paranoid

individuals (for instance, "I think that most people would lie to get ahead") may or may not do so when put to an empirical test. In fact, patients diagnosed as paranoid were significantly *less* likely to respond "true" to this statement than were normal individuals. On the final test, the responses to each item are scored according to their correspondence to answers given by the different criterion groups.

In addition to its content scales, the MMPI was the first major inventory to incorporate a number of validity scales within it. These are scales that attempt to determine whether the person has answered the test items carefully and honestly. If an individual's scores on any of these scales is too high, then his or her scores on the content scales must be interpreted with particular caution or disregarded altogether. These scales have been helpful but not completely successful at detecting invalid scores. Table 12-6 lists the 3 validity and 10 content scales usually scored on the MMPI.

Because the MMPI is derived from differences between criterion and control groups, it does not really matter whether what the person says is true. What is important is the fact that he or she says it. If schizophrenics answer "true" and control subjects answer "false" to the statement "My mother never loved me," their answers distinguish the two groups regardless of how their mothers actually behaved. This is an advantage of a test based on the criterion-keyed method over one based on a test constructor's assumption that certain answers indicate specific personality traits. The disadvantage is that one does not really have a theoretical understanding of the connection between the test responses and the personality characteristics they identify.

The MMPI, published in 1943, is based on research that began in 1939. There are now more than 8,000 published studies on the MMPI, and it has been translated into at least 15 languages. There are even several private companies that provide computer-based scoring and interpretation of the inventory.

Over the years, the MMPI has been criticized for the weak reliability and validity of some of its scales. It also became evident that the original inventory was getting out of date and should be revised. But the enormous amount of existing data on the original version discouraged most researchers from ever undertaking such a daunting task. Neverthe-

SCALE NAME	SCALE ABBREVIATION	INTERPRETATION OF HIGH SCORES
Lie	L	Denial of common frailties
Frequency	F	Invalidity of profile
Correction	K	Defensive, evasive
Hypochondriasis	Hs	Emphasis on physical complaints
Depression	D	Unhappy, depressed
Hysteria	Hy	Reacts to stress by denying problems
Psychopathic deviancy	Pd	Lack of social conformity; often in trouble with the law
Masculinity-femininity	Mf	Feminine orientation (males); masculine orientation (females)
Paranoia	Pa	Suspicious
Psychasthenia	Pt	Worried, anxious
Schizophrenia	Sc	Withdrawn, bizarre thinking
Hypomania	Ma	Impulsive, excitable
Social introversion-extraversion	Si	Introverted, shy

TABLE 12-6

MMPI Scales *The first three scales are "validity" scales, which help to determine whether the person has answered the test items carefully and honestly. For example, the F (Frequency) scale measures the degree to which infrequent or atypical answers are given. A high score on this scale usually indicates that the individual was careless or confused in responding. (However, high F scores often accompany high scores on the Schizophrenia scale, which measures bizarre thinking.) The remaining "clinical" scales were originally named for categories of psychiatric disorders, but interpretation now emphasizes personality attributes rather than diagnostic categories.*

less, it has now been done. The MMPI-2 was published in 1989 and incorporates a number of significant revisions while maintaining the basic features of the original, including most of the original items. The new standardization involves a much larger and a more diversified sampling that is more representative of the United States population (Graham, 1990). The difficult job of assessing the comparability of scores between the new and original versions is now underway.

Overall, the MMPI has been most valuable in distinguishing in a general way between abnormal and normal populations and can be used to evaluate the overall severity of a particular individual's disturbance (Meehl & Dahlstrom, 1960). It is less successful, however, in making finer distinctions among various forms of psychopathology (Kleinmuntz, 1982)

Although the MMPI was originally designed to identify people with serious personality disorders, it has been widely used to study normal populations. But because the MMPI does not adequately sample some of the traits useful in describing the normal personality, the California Psychological Inventory (CPI) was devised, using many of the same items. The CPI scales measure such traits as dominance, sociability, self-acceptance, responsibility, and socialization. The comparison groups for some of the scales were obtained by asking high-school and college students to designate the classmates they would rate high or low on the trait in question. Thus, for the dominance scale, the criterion group consisted of students who were described by their peers as high in dominance (aggressive, confident, self-reliant) and the control group consisted of students who were described by their peers as low in dominance (retiring, lacking in self-confidence, inhibited). Items that revealed a statistically significant difference between the criterion group and the control group formed the dominance scale. The CPI is still one of the most widely validated personality inventories available for use with normal populations (Megargee, 1972).

Q SORT One special method for measuring personality traits is called the **Q sort**. (The Q in Q sort was arbitrarily chosen and has no particular meaning.) In this method, a rater or sorter describes an individual's personality by sorting a set of approximately 100 cards into piles. Each card contains a personality statement (for example, "Has a wide range of interests" and "Is self-defeating"). The rater sorts the cards into 9 piles, placing those cards that are least descriptive of the individual in pile 1 on the left and those that are most descriptive in pile 9 on the right. The other cards are distributed in the intermediate piles, with those that seem neither characteristic nor uncharacteristic of the individual going into the middle pile (pile 5). Thus each Q item receives a score ranging from 1 to 9, with higher numbers indicating that the item is more characteristic of the person. (Some Q sorts use fewer or more than 9 piles, but the technique is the same.)

At first glance, this would seem no different from asking raters to rate the individual on a set of traits, using a 9-point rating scale. And, in fact, the item scores can be used in this way if the researcher wishes. But there is an important difference. When filling out rating scales, a rater is implicitly comparing the individual with other individuals (for example, a rating of "very friendly" implies that the individual is very friendly compared with other individuals). When performing a Q sort, however, a rater is explicitly comparing each trait with other traits *within* the same individual (for example, placing the item "friendly" in pile 9 implies that, compared with other traits, friendliness stands out as particularly descriptive of the individual).

Two Q sorts can be compared with each other quantitatively by computing a correlation between them, thereby assessing the degree to which two individuals are similar to one another in their overall personality configurations. If the two Q sorts are descriptions of the same individual at two different times then the correlation assesses the test-retest reliability of the Q sort or the continuity of the individual's overall personality

profile over time. If two Q sorts are descriptions of a single individual made by two raters, then the correlation assesses the interjudge reliability of the Q sort or the degree to which two persons perceive the same individual in the same way. (For example, in marital counseling, it could be helpful to assess the degree to which two spouses agree or disagree in their perceptions of each other.) Finally, if one of the Q sorts is a description of some hypothetical personality type, then the correlation between an individual's Q sort and the hypothetical sort assesses the degree to which the person is similar to that personality type. For example, one researcher had clinical psychologists construct Q sorts of the hypothetical "optimally adjusted personality." The correlation between a person's Q sort and this hypothetical sort can thus be directly interpreted as an adjustment score (Block 1961/1978, 1971).

PROJECTIVE TESTS The fixed structure of personality inventories—specific questions to which the individual must respond by selecting one of the answers presented—is not well-suited to assessing certain aspects of personality. For example, personality psychologists who follow in Freud's psychoanalytic tradition (discussed in Chapter 13) are particularly interested in assessing unconscious wishes, motivations, and conflicts. Accordingly, they prefer tests that resemble Freud's technique of free association, in which the individual is free to say whatever comes to mind. For this reason, they developed **projective tests**. A projective test presents an ambiguous stimulus to which the person may respond as he or she wishes. Because the stimulus is ambiguous and does not demand a specific response, it is assumed that the individual *projects* his or her personality onto the stimulus and thus reveals something about himself or herself. Projective tests have also been useful in areas of personality other than psychoanalytic theory. Two of the most widely used projective techniques are the Rorschach Test and the Thematic Apperception Test (TAT).

RORSCHACH TEST The Rorschach Test, developed by the Swiss psychiatrist Hermann Rorschach in the 1920s, consists of a series of 10 cards, each displaying a rather complex inkblot like the one shown in Figure 12-2. Some of the blots are in color; some are black and white. The subject is instructed to look at one card at a time and report everything the inkblot resembles. After the subject has finished the 10 cards, the examiner usually goes over each response, asking the subject to clarify some responses and to tell what features of the blot gave a particular impression.

The subject's responses may be scored in various ways. Three main categories are location (whether the response involves the entire inkblot or a part of it), determinants (whether the subject responds to the shape of the blot, its color, or differences in texture and shading), and content (what the response represents). Most testers also score responses according to frequency of occurrence; for example, a response is "popular" if many people assign it to the same inkblot.

Several elaborate scoring systems have been devised based on these categories. But most of these systems proved to have limited predictive value. Consequently, many psychologists base their interpretations on an impressionistic evaluation of the response record, as well as on the subject's general reaction to the test situation (for example, whether the individual is defensive, open, competitive, cooperative, and so on).

In 1974, a system was introduced that attempted to extract and combine the validated portions of all the scoring systems into one complete system. It has undergone extensive revision and is now supplemented by a computer scoring service and software for microcomputers (Exner, 1986). Although this system looks more promising than previous efforts, not enough studies have accumulated to evaluate its validity with any confidence.

THEMATIC APPERCEPTION TEST Another popular projective test, the Thematic Apperception Test (TAT), was developed at Harvard University by Henry Murray in the 1930s. The subject is shown as many as 20 ambiguous pictures of persons and scenes, similar to the one in Figure 12-3, and is asked to make up a story about each. The subject is encouraged to give free rein to his or her imagination and to tell whatever story comes to mind. The test is intended to reveal basic themes that recur in a person's imaginative productions. Apperception is a readiness to perceive in certain ways based on prior experiences. People interpret ambiguous pictures according to their apperceptions and elaborate stories in terms of pre-

FIGURE 12-2

Rorschach Inkblott
The subject is asked to tell what is seen in the blot; it may be viewed from any angle.

ferred plots or themes that reflect personal fantasies. If particular problems are bothering the subject, they may become evident in a number of the stories or in striking deviations from the usual theme in one or two stories. When shown a picture similar to the one in Figure 12-3, a 21-year-old male told the following story:

> She has prepared this room for someone's arrival and is opening the door for a last general look over the room. She is probably expecting her son home. She tries to place everything as it was when he left. She seems like a very tyrannical character. She led her son's life for him and is going to take over again as soon as he gets back. This is merely the beginning of her rule, and the son is definitely cowed by this overbearing attitude of hers and will slip back into her well-ordered way of life. He will go through life plodding down the tracks she has laid down for him. All this represents her complete domination of his life until she dies. (Arnold, 1949, p. 100)

Although the original picture shows only a woman standing in an open doorway looking into a room, the subject's readiness to talk about his relationship with his mother led to this story of a woman's domination of her son. Facts obtained later confirmed the clinician's interpretation that the story reflected the subject's own problems.

FIGURE 12-3

Thematic Apperception Test *This picture is similar to the pictures used on the Thematic Apperception Test. The pictures usually have elements of ambiguity so that the subject can "read into" them something from personal experience or fantasy.*

In analyzing responses to the TAT cards, the psychologist looks for recurrent themes that may reveal the individual's needs, motives, or characteristic way of handling interpersonal relationships.

PROBLEMS WITH PROJECTIVE TESTS Many other projective tests have been devised. Some ask the subject to draw pictures of people, houses, trees, and so on. Others involve completing sentences that start with "I often wish . . . ," "My mother . . . ," or "I feel like quitting when they. . . ." In fact, any stimulus to which a person can respond in an individualistic way could be considered the basis for a projective test. But most projective tests have not been subjected to enough research to establish their usefulness in assessing personality.

In contrast, the Rorschach Test and the TAT have been intensively researched. The results, however, have not always been encouraging. Reliability of the Rorschach Test has been generally poor because the interpretation of responses is too dependent on the clinician's judgment; the same test protocol may be evaluated quite differently by two trained examiners. And attempts to demonstrate the Rorschach's ability to predict behavior or discriminate between groups have met with limited success. The comprehensive system, mentioned above, may prove more successful.

The TAT has fared somewhat better. When specific scoring systems are used (for example, to measure achievement motives or aggressive themes), the interscorer reliability is fairly good. But the relationship of TAT scores to overt behavior is complex. Preoccupations are not necessarily acted on. A person who produces a number of stories with aggressive themes may not actually behave aggressively. In fact, the individual may be compensating for a need to inhibit aggressive tendencies by expressing such impulses in fantasy. When inhibitions about expressing aggression and strength of aggressive tendencies are estimated from the TAT stories, the relationship to behavior becomes more predictable. Among boys whose tests indicated that they were not very inhibited, the correlation between amount of aggression in the TAT stories and overt aggression was .55. Among boys showing a high degree of inhibition, the correlation between the number of aggressive themes and overt aggression was −.50 (Olweus, 1969).

Defenders of the Rorschach Test and the TAT point out that it is not fair to expect accurate predictions based on test responses alone; responses to inkblots and story themes are meaningful only when considered in light of additional information, such as the person's life history, other test data, and observations of behavior. The skilled clinician uses the results of projective tests to make tentative interpretations about the individual's personality and then verifies or discards them, depending on further information. The tests are helpful in suggesting possible areas of conflict to be explored.

We will see further examples of personality testing methods in Chapter 13, where we discuss theories of personality.

INTERACTION BETWEEN NATURE AND NURTURE

If you were asked why one person is taller than another, you would probably give a "nature" explanation: The taller person has inherited taller "height genes" from his or her parents than the shorter person. Even though health and nutrition can affect a person's growth, you would be correct in assuming that, in general, environmental factors play a very minor role in determining a person's height. If, however, you were asked why one person prefers classical music to jazz but another person has the reverse preference, you would be much more inclined to give a "nurture" (environmental) explanation. The possibility that there might be genes for musical preference seems unlikely.

But might there be genes for musical *talent?* Or intelligence, sociability, or sexual orientation? Here the answers are not obvious. Moreover, advocates of particular political positions and social policies frequently invoke one answer or another in support of their viewpoint (for example, Herrnstein & Murray, 1994; also see the discussion of sexual orientation in Chapter 10). Because these debates reveal widespread public misunderstanding about the empirical issues involved, we will describe in some detail the reasoning and methods behavioral scientists use to assess how genetic and environmental factors contribute to individual differences.

SOURCES OF VARIANCE

We begin with Figure 12-4, which displays the results of a hypothetical examination given to two classes of students. Within each class, each student's score is displayed as a point in a graph known as a frequency distribution. The horizontal axis lists the scores, divided into intervals; the vertical axis plots the number of scores falling within each interval. As explained in more detail in Appendix II, two main features of this distribution are of interest. The first is each class's mean (average) score, which is calculated by summing the scores and dividing by the number of scores. In this case, the mean score for both classes is 70.

The second important feature of the distribution—and the one that most concerns us here—is the degree to which the scores within each class differ from one another. We can see in the figure that the scores from Class A are much more variable, more spread out, more different from one another than are the scores from Class B. This feature of a distribution can be quantified by computing its *variance:* Each score is first subtracted from the mean score for the class; these differences are then squared (which gets rid of negative signs) and their mean is calculated (by summing them and dividing by the num-

The ways in which biological (nature) and environmental (nurture) factors interact to make us different from one another is a major topic in the study of individual differences.

ber of scores). When this is done for the data in Figure 12-4, the variance for Class A turns out to be 300; for Class B, it is 150, confirming quantitatively our visual impression that Class A is more variable than Class B.

Now consider the scores for Class A. Why are they different from one another? Why do some students do better than others? What accounts for the variance we observe? One obvious possibility is that some students studied for the exam longer than other students. To find out whether and to what extent this is true, we can conduct a hypothetical experiment in which we "control for" the variable of study time by requiring all students to study exactly 3 hours for the exam, no more and no less. If study time really does affect students' scores, then what can we expect to happen to the variance of the distribution?

First, some of the students who would have studied longer than 3 hours and done quite well will now do less well than they would have, thereby moving their scores down closer to the class average. For example one or more of the three students in Class A who obtained scores between 90 and 100 might not perform as well. Second, some of the students who would have studied less than 3 hours and not done very well will now do better, thereby moving their scores up closer to the class average; the student who obtained the score between 30 and 39 might now do better. In other words, the students' scores will bunch closer together: The variance of their scores will decrease. The distribution of their scores will now look more like Class B than Class A.

In fact, if the distribution for Class A represents the scores that students would have

FIGURE 12-4

Variance of Exam Scores in Two Classes
An inspection of these two frequency distributions shows that the scores for Class A are more variable, more spread out, more different from one another than are scores for Class B—even though the means of the two classes are identical (70). This difference in variability between the two distributions can be quantified by computing each of their variances. For Class A, the variance is 300; for Class B, the variance is 150, or 50 percent smaller.

Theoretically, we could test for any other potential sources of variance in the same way. If we think that having a good breakfast might affect students' scores, then we could feed all the students the same breakfast (or deny breakfast to all the students) and observe whether we reduce the variance as a result. In general, holding constant any variable that "makes a difference" will reduce the variance of the scores. In the extreme case, if we held all the relevant variables constant, the variance would diminish to zero: Every student would obtain the same score.

It is important to note, however, that we cannot say what will happen to the mean of the distribution when we hold a variable constant. For example, if the students would have studied for the exam an average of only 2 hours, then by requiring them all to study 3 hours, we will raise the class average. If, however, the students would have studied 4 hours on the average, then we will lower the class average by limiting everybody to only 3 hours of study time.

HERITABILITY

We are now prepared to ask the "nature" question: To what extent do some students do better than others on the exam because they are genetically more capable than others? Put more technically, what proportion of the variance in exam scores is accounted for by genetic differences among the students? Analogously, if we had measured each student's height, then we would ask what proportion of the variance in height was accounted for by their genetic differences. In general, the proportion of variance in any trait accounted for by genetic differences among the individuals in a population is called the trait's **heritability**, a number that ranges from 0 to 1. The more individual differences on a trait are due to genetic differences, the closer the heritability is to 1. For example, the heritability of height, which is heavily influenced by genetics, ranges from about .85 to .95 across different studies.

Now, however, we face a difficulty. We cannot experimentally determine how much of the variance in exam scores is accounted for by students' genetic differences the way we did for study time because that would require

obtained if we had not controlled for study time and the distribution for Class B represents the scores that they would obtain if study time were held constant, then, by controlling (holding constant) study time, we will have reduced the variance from 300 to 150, a reduction of ½ or 50 percent. Technically, we would say that study time accounts for 50 percent of the variance in these scores. In this hypothetical example, then, a major reason the exam scores differed from one another is that students differed in how much time they spent studying.

holding the genetic variable constant—making all the students into genetic clones. But we can take advantage of the fact that nature sometimes does produce genetic clones: They are called identical twins.

As we described briefly in Chapter 2, identical twins (who are called **monozygotic** twins because they come from a single zygote, or fertilized egg) share all their genes. Fraternal twins (called **dizygotic** twins because they develop from two separate eggs) are like ordinary siblings in that they share about half their genes. To the extent that identical twins are more alike on a trait than are fraternal twins, the trait has a genetic or heritable component (assuming that other factors, such as differential parental treatment of identical and fraternal twins can be ruled out).

For example, across many studies the mean correlation between IQ scores of 4,672 pairs of identical twins was .86; the comparable correlation for 5,533 sets of fraternal twins was .60. The difference in correlations implies that IQ has a genetic component. To calculate the heritability from these two correlations, one simply doubles the difference between them: $2 \times (.86 - .60) = .52$. In other words, about half of the variance in IQ scores is due to genetic differences (Bouchard & McGue, 1981).

Similar studies have examined the heritability of personality traits. One large Swedish study assessed the traits of extraversion (sociability) and emotional stability in a sample of more than 12,000 pairs of adult twins. On both traits, there were correlations of .5 between members of identical-twin pairs and .2 between members of fraternal-twin pairs, yielding a heritability estimate of $[2 \times (.5 - .2)]$ or .6 (Floderus-Myred, Petersen, & Rasmuson, 1980).

One difficulty in interpreting the results of twin studies, however, is that identical twin pairs may be treated more alike than fraternal twin pairs, which may account for their greater personality similarities. Ideally one should study sets of identical twins who had been separated at birth and raised in unrelated environments. Fortunately, an ongoing research project comes close to fulfilling these conditions: the Minnesota Study of Twins Reared Apart (Bouchard, 1984). As of 1990, more than 50 pairs of identical twins had been brought to the laboratory for study.

On average, these twin pairs had been separated at 10 weeks of age and had not seen each other again until 34 years later; some had not met until the study brought them together. The Minnesota researchers have now compared these twins with those in an earlier Minnesota study on twins reared together (Bouchard et al., 1990; Tellegen et al., 1988; Lykken, 1982).

Surprisingly, these studies reveal that twins reared apart are just as similar to one another as twins reared together across a wide range of personality characteristics. The median correlations were .49 for identical twins reared apart and .52 for identical twins reared together; the corresponding correlations for fraternal twins were .21 and .23. These results permit us to conclude with greater confidence that identical twins are more similar to each other on personality characteristics than are fraternal twins because they are more similar genetically.

If one has a set of identical twin pairs who were reared separately, one does not even need a comparison group of fraternal twins to estimate heritabilities. Any correlation between pairs of identical twins reared apart in unrelated environments must arise entirely from their genetic similarities. In other words, for such twins, the correlation is directly equal to the heritability. In the Minnesota study, for example, the correlation between IQ scores for identical twins reared apart—and, hence, the heritability of IQ—was .72. (This is much higher than the heritability estimate of .52 that we calculated by comparing the correlations from identical and fraternal twin pairs reared together. We will return to this discrepancy later.)

For the most part, the correlations found in the Minnesota studies are in accord with results from many other twin studies. In general, the highest heritabilities are found in measures of abilities and intelligence (.6–.7); the next highest heritabilities are typically found in measures of personality (about .5); and the smallest heritabilities are found for religious and political beliefs and vocational interests (.3–.4).

MISUNDERSTANDINGS ABOUT HERITABILITY   The recurring public debate over nature-nurture questions reveals widespread misunderstanding about the concept of heritability. Thus it is

The participants in the Minnesota Study of Twins Reared Apart were assessed on a number of ability and personality measures. In addition, they participated in lengthy interviews, during which they were asked questions about such topics as childhood experiences, fears, hobbies, musical tastes, social attitudes, and sexual interests. A number of startling similarities were found.

The twins with the most dramatically different backgrounds are Oskar Stohr and Jack Yufe. Born in Trinidad of a Jewish father and a German mother, they were separated shortly after birth. The mother took Oskar to Germany, where he was raised by his grandmother as a Catholic and a Nazi. Jack remained with his father, was raised as a Jew, and spent part of his youth on an Israeli kibbutz. The families never corresponded, and the two brothers now lead quite different lives. They were in their late forties when they participated in the study and had met only once before about 20 years earlier. Remarkable similarities were evident when the pair showed up for the study. Both men were wearing blue double-breasted epauletted shirts, mustaches, and wire-rimmed glasses. Their manner-

These twins, separated at birth, showed remarkable similarities in interests and habits when they first met at age 31.

isms and temperaments were similar, and they shared certain idiosyncrasies: Both liked spicy foods and sweet liqueurs, were absentminded, flushed the toilet before using it, liked to dip buttered toast in their coffee, and enjoyed surprising people by sneezing in elevators.

Another pair of twins with fairly different backgrounds are now British housewives who were separated during World War II and were raised by families of different socioeconomic statuses. Both twins, who had never met before, arrived for their inter-

views wearing seven rings on their fingers.

There are not, of course, toast-dipping or ring-loving genes; such similarities reflect similarities in the heritable components of more basic personality characteristics. But as we shall see, it is unlikely that genetics alone can account for the extraordinary similarities of twins reared apart. Morever, there are other puzzling findings that emerge from twin studies, which we will discuss later in this section.

important to be clear about the following points:

- Heritability is not an individual measure.

The heritability of a trait refers to differences *among* individuals within a population, not to proportions of a trait *within* an individual. To say that height has a heritability of .9 does not mean that 90% of your height came from your genes and 10% came from the environment.

- Heritability is not a fixed attribute of a trait.

Heritability refers to an attribute of a trait in a particular population at a particular point in time. If something happens to change the variability of a trait in a population, the heritability of the trait will also change. For example, if everyone in our society were suddenly to be given equal educational opportunities, the variance of intellectual performance in the society would decrease; everybody's scores on standardized measures of intellectual ability would be more similar. (This is what happened in our hypothetical experiment when we required everyone to study the same length of time for the exam.) And because heritability is the

Environmental factors can influence mean levels of intellectual ability and personality traits—even though those traits have high heritabilities.

proportion of variance due to inherited differences among individuals, the heritability would *increase* because the proportion of the variance due to an important environmental factor, education, would have decreased.

• Heritability does not tell us about the source of mean differences between groups.

One of the most contentious and recurring debates in American society is whether average differences in the scores of different ethnic groups on standardized ability and intelligence tests are due to genetic differences between the groups. In the early twentieth century, the debate concerned the relatively low IQ scores obtained by Hungarian, Italian, and Jewish immigrants when they were tested upon their arrival at Ellis Island in New York; the test scores of these groups implied that the majority of them were "feeble-minded" (Kamin, 1974). Today the debate concerns the lower scores obtained by black, Hispanic, and Native Americans compared with white Americans (Herrnstein & Murray, 1994).

The heritability of IQ is often invoked in these debates to support the genetic argument. But this is based on a logical fallacy, as illustrated by the following "thought experiment":

We fill a white sack and a black sack with a mixture of different genetic varieties of corn seed. We make certain that the proportions of each variety of seed are identical in each sack. We then plant the seed from the white sack in fertile Field A, while that from the black sack is planted in barren Field B. We will observe that within Field A, as within Field B, there is considerable variation in the height of individual corn plants. This variation will be due largely to genetic factors (seed differences). We will also observe, however, that the average height of plants in Field A is greater than that in Field B. That difference will be entirely due to environmental factors (the soil). The same is true of IQs: differences in the average IQ of various human populations could be entirely due to environmental differences, even if within each population all variation were due to genetic differences! (Eysenck & Kamin, 1981, p. 97).

• Heritability does not tell us about the effects of environmental changes on the mean level of a trait.

Another incorrect claim about heritability that is sometimes expressed in the public debates is that a trait with high heritability cannot be changed by a change in the environment. (For example, it is sometimes argued that it is futile to use preschool intervention programs to help disadvantaged children enhance their intellectual abilities because those abilities have high heritabilities.)

But between the years of 1946 and 1982, the height of young adult males in Japan increased by 3.3 inches, due mainly to improving nutrition of the Japanese during this period (Angoff, 1988). And yet height was then and is now one of the most heritable traits we know. Then as now, taller Japanese parents have taller children than do shorter Japanese parents. Similarly, a survey covering 14 countries has shown that the average IQ test score has significantly increased in recent years (Flynn, 1987). Heritability is about variances, not means.

PERSONALITY-ENVIRONMENT INTERACTIONS

GENOTYPE-ENVIRONMENT CORRELATION   In shaping an individual's personality, genetic and environmental influences are intertwined from the moment of birth. Parents give their biological offspring both their genes and a home environment, and both are functions of the parents' own genes. As a result, there is a built-in correlation between the child's inherited characteristics (genotype) and the environment in which he or she is raised. For example, because general intelligence is partially heritable, parents with high intelligence are likely to have children with high intelligence. But parents with high intelligence are also likely to provide an intellectually stimulating environment for their children—both through their own interactions with them and through the books, music lessons, trips to museums, and other intellectual experiences that are likely to be a part of their home. Because the child's genotype and environment are positively correlated in this way, he or she will get a double-dose of intellectual advantage. Similarly, children born to parents with low intelligence are likely to encounter a home environment that further exacerbates whatever intellectual disadvantage they may have inherited directly.

Some parents may deliberately construct an environment that is negatively correlated with the child's genotype. For example, introverted parents may encourage social activities in order to counteract the child's own likely introversion: "We make an effort to have people over because we don't want Chris to grow up to be as shy as we are." Parents of a very active child may try to provide more interesting quiet activities. But whether the correlation is positive or negative, the pertinent point is that the child's genotype and

environment are not simply independent sources of influence that add together to shape the child's personality.

In addition to being correlated with the environment, a child's genotype also shapes the environment itself (Bouchard, et al., 1990; Scarr, 1988; Scarr & McCartney, 1983; Plomin, DeFries, & Loehlin, 1977). In particular, the environment becomes a function of the child's personality through three forms of interaction: *reactive, evocative,* and *proactive.*

REACTIVE INTERACTION   Different individuals exposed to the same environment interpret it, experience it, and react to it differently. An anxious, sensitive child will experience and react to harsh parents differently than will a calm, resilient child; the sharp tone of voice that provokes the sensitive child to tears might pass unnoticed by his sister. An extraverted child will attend to people and events around her; her introverted brother will ignore them. A brighter child will get more out of being read to than a less bright child. In other words, each child's personality extracts a subjective psychological environment from the objective surroundings, and it is that subjective environment that shapes subsequent personality development. Even if parents provided exactly the same environment for all their children—which they usually do not—it will not be psychologically equivalent for all of them. **Reactive interaction** occurs throughout life. One person will interpret a hurtful act as the product of deliberate hostility and react to it quite differently from the person who interprets that same act as the product of unintended insensitivity.

EVOCATIVE INTERACTION   Every individual's personality evokes distinctive responses from others. An infant who squirms and fusses when picked up will evoke less nurturance from a parent than one who likes to be cuddled. Docile children will evoke a less controlling style of child-rearing from parents than will aggressive children. For this reason, we cannot simply assume that an observed correlation between the child-rearing practices of a child's parents and his or her personality reflects a simple cause-and-effect sequence. Instead, the child's personality can shape the parents' child-rearing style, which, in turn, further shapes his or her personality. **Evocative interaction** also occurs throughout life: Gracious people evoke gracious environments; hostile people evoke hostile environments.

Proactive Interaction As children get older, they can move beyond the environments imposed by their parents and begin to select and construct environments of their own. These environments, in turn, further shape their personalities. A sociable child will choose to go to the movies with friends rather than to stay home alone and watch television; her sociable personality prompts her to select an environment that further reinforces her sociability. And what she cannot select, she will construct: If nobody invites her to the movies, she will organize the event herself. As the term implies, **proactive interaction** is a process through which individuals become active agents in their own personality development.

The relative importance of these several kinds of personality-environment interaction shifts over the course of development (Scarr, 1988; Scarr & McCartney, 1983). The built-in correlation between a child's genotype and his or her environment is strongest when the child is young and confined almost exclusively to the home environment. As the child gets older and begins to select and construct his or her own environment, this initial correlation decreases and the influence of proactive interaction increases. As noted, reactive and evocative interactions remain important throughout life.

Some Unsolved Puzzles Studies of twins have produced a number of puzzling patterns that still are not completely understood. We noted earlier, for example, that the estimate of heritability for IQ is much higher when it is based on identical twin pairs reared apart than it is when based on a comparison of identical and fraternal twins pairs reared together. Moreover, the striking similarities of identical twins do not seem to diminish across time or separate rearing environments. In contrast, the similarities of fraternal twins (and non-twin siblings) diminish from childhood through adolescence even when they are reared together; the longer they live together in the same home, the less similar they become (Scarr, 1988; Scarr & McCartney, 1983).

Some of these patterns would emerge if the genes themselves interact with one another so that inheriting all one's genes in

A sociable child displaying proactive interaction will select and construct situations that further promote and sustain his or her sociable personality.

common (as identical twins do) is more than twice as effective as inheriting only half one's genes in common (as fraternal twins and non-twin siblings do). This could come about if a trait depends on a particular combination of genes.

Consider, for example, the trait of having blue eyes (which we will oversimplify a bit to make the point). Suppose that two parents each have a blue-eye gene and a brown-eye gene. For one of their children to get blue eyes, he or she must inherit a blue gene from the father *and* a blue gene from the mother; the three other combinations (brown-brown, brown-blue, blue-brown) will give the child brown eyes. In other words, any child of theirs has a 1-in-4 chance of getting blue eyes. But because identical twins inherit identical genes from their parents, they will also inherit the same combination of genes; if one gets blue eyes, so will the other. In contrast, if a fraternal twin inherits a blue gene from *both* parents, the chances that the other twin will also do so is still only 1 out of 4—not 1 out of 2. Thus, inheriting all one's genes in common is here more than twice as effective as inheriting only half one's genes in common. There is evidence for this kind of gene-gene interaction for some personality traits, especially extraversion (Lykken, McGue, Tellegen, & Bouchard, 1992; Pedersen, Plomin, McClearn, & Friberg, 1988). But personality-environment interactions could also be partially responsible for these patterns.

Consider identical twins. Because they have identical genotypes, they also react to

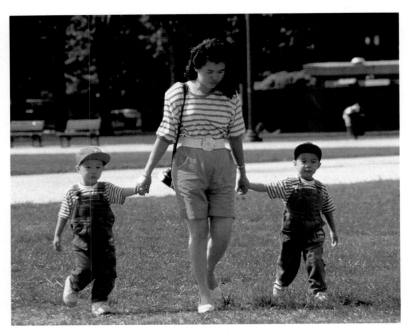

Because identical twins have identical genotypes, the processes of personality-environment interaction promote and sustain their similarity across time—even if they grow up in unrelated environments.

situations in similar ways (reactive interaction); they evoke similar responses from others (evocative interaction); and their similar, genetically guided talents, interests, and motivations lead them to seek out and construct similar environments (proactive interaction). The important point is that these processes all operate whether the twins are reared together or apart. For example, two identical twins separated at birth will still be treated in similar ways by other people because they each independently evoke similar responses from others.

Proactive interaction operates in the same way. Each twin's personality prompts him or her to select friends and environments that happen to be similar to the friends and environments chosen by the other twin. But friends and environments that are similar will treat each twin in similar ways. And so it goes. Because the twins begin with identical genotypic personalities, all the processes of personality-environment interaction act together to promote and sustain their similarity across time—even if they have never met after birth.

In contrast, the environments of fraternal twins and nontwin siblings increasingly diverge as they get older—even within the same home. They are most alike in early childhood when parents impose a common environment. (Although even here, siblings will react somewhat differently from each other and evoke different responses from the

parents.) But as soon as they begin to select and construct environments outside the home, their moderately different talents, interests, and motivations will take them down increasingly divergent paths, thereby producing increasingly divergent personalities.

Shared Versus Nonshared Environments Twin studies permit researchers to estimate not only how much of the variation among individuals is due to genetic variation, but also how much of the environmentally related variation is due to those aspects of the environment that family members share with one another (for example, the socioeconomic status of the family) as compared with aspects of the environment that family members do not share (for example, friends outside the family). Surprisingly, differences due to the shared aspects of the environment seem to account for almost none of the environmental variation: After their genetic similarities are subtracted out, two children from the same family seem to be no more alike than two children chosen randomly from the population (Plomin & Daniels, 1987). This implies that the kinds of variables that psychologists typically study (such as child-rearing practices, socioeconomic class of the family, parents' education) are contributing virtually nothing to individual differences in personality. How can this be so?

One possible explanation might be that the reactive, evocative, and proactive processes act to diminish the differences between environments as long as those environments permit some flexibility of response. A bright child from a neglecting or impoverished home is more likely than a less bright sibling to absorb more information from a television program (reactive interaction), to attract the attention of a sympathetic teacher (evocative interaction), and to go to the library on his or her own (proactive interaction). This child's genotype acts to counteract the potentially debilitating effects of the home environment, and therefore he or she develops differently from a less bright sibling. Only if the environment is severely restrictive will these personality-driven processes be thwarted (Scarr, 1988; Scarr & McCartney, 1983). This explanation is supported by the finding that the most dissimilar pairs of identical twins reared apart are those in which one was reared in a severely restricted environment.

Although this explanation seems plausible, there is no direct evidence that it is correct. In any case, it appears that research will have to shift from the usual comparisons of children from different families to comparisons of children within the same families—with particular attention paid to the personality-environment interactions within those families.

CONTINUITY OF PERSONALITY ACROSS THE LIFE COURSE

When you look back over your life, you can probably discern personal patterns and styles that have always seemed a part of your personality. Perhaps you have always been shy or had a problem with procrastination. At the same time, you can probably identify ways in which you have changed; perhaps you are less impulsive than you used to be or better able to relate to others. Sometimes you might be able to identify specific experiences that have changed you. Going to college often affects attitudes, values, and personality in far-reaching ways. Understanding the interplay of continuity and change in personality across the life course is a basic task for both personality and developmental psychology. (For example, we discussed the continuity of childhood temperaments in Chapter 3, the chapter on psychological development.)

EVIDENCE FOR CONTINUITY

The only effective way to investigate continuity and change in personality over the life course is to conduct longitudinal studies, studies that observe or assess the same persons over time. But because these are very difficult to conduct (see the Critical Discussion, Studying Personality the Long Way), there are only a handful of longitudinal studies that cover extensive time periods.

Two of the most ambitious longitudinal studies ever conducted are housed at the Institute of Human Development (IHD) at the University of California in Berkeley. Investi-

gators began the *Berkeley Guidance Study* in 1929 by contacting the parents of every third baby born in Berkeley over an 18-month period and asking them to enroll their newborns in the study; in all, 248 infants and their families were included. The *Oakland Growth Study* began in 1932 with 212 fifth-grade children in Oakland, California. The children from both samples were studied intensively through adolescence and were interviewed again when the Berkeley subjects were about 30, 40, and 50 and the Oakland subjects were about 37, 47, and 57. IHD has generously made its archive available to many investigators around the world.

As described in the Critical Discussion, independent clinical psychologists described the IHD subjects when they were in junior high school (age 13), senior high school (age 16), and as adults (age 30 or 37). The three personality profiles for each subject were correlated with one another to assess the continuity of the overall personality across these time intervals.

The results show that in general there was strong continuity of personality from early to later adolescence; the mean correlations were .77 and .75 for men and women, respectively. The correlations between senior high and adulthood were lower but still quite impressive: .56 for men and .54 for women.

The strongest continuities were related to intelligence and intellectual interests. For example, the continuities from adolescence to adulthood for the item "Appears to have a high degree of intellectual capacity" were .60 and .61 for men and women, respectively. The corresponding correlations for the item "Genuinely values intellectual and cognitive matters" were .59 and .51. Table 12-7 lists correlations for other personality characteristics that showed substantial continuities.

SOURCES OF CONTINUITY

Studies of individuals across the life course typically find that measures of intellectual performance show the strongest continuities; personality variables like extraversion, emotional stability, and impulse control are next; and political attitudes and measures of self-opinions (for example, self-esteem, life satisfaction) are last—showing correlations between .2 and .4 over 5–10-year intervals

TABLE 12-7

Continuity of Personality
The table lists some of the personality characteristics that showed the greatest continuity over the years from early adolescence to adulthood. (After Block, 1971)

Q ITEMS	CORRELATIONS FROM JUNIOR HIGH TO SENIOR HIGH SCHOOL	CORRELATIONS FROM SENIOR HIGH SCHOOL TO ADULTHOOD
MALES		
Is a genuinely dependable and responsible person	.58	.53
Tends toward undercontrol of needs and impulses; unable to delay gratification	.57	.59
Is self-defeating	.50	.42
Enjoys aesthetic impressions; is aesthetically reactive	.35	.58
FEMALES		
Basically submissive	.50	.46
Emphasizes being with others; gregarious	.39	.43
Tends to be rebellious and nonconforming	.48	.49
Is concerned with philosophical problems (for example, religion, values, meaning of life)	.45	.42

We display proactive interaction when we tend to select friends and spouses who share our interests and personalities, and who thereby promote and sustain the continuity of our own personalities.

(Conley, 1985; 1984). Note that these results tend to parallel those from heritability studies: Traits with higher heritabilities generally show stronger continuities, suggesting that the underlying genetic basis of many intellectual and personality characteristics may contribute to their temporal stability. In general, however, it is not the genotype itself that directly produces continuity, but the interaction of the genotype with the environment—acting through the same processes we

discussed earlier when we examined the initial shaping of personality in childhood. In particular, the processes of reactive, evocative, and proactive interaction all act to create environments for the individual that are themselves a function of his or her personality.

For example, in our earlier discussion of proactive interaction, we cited the sociable child who, in selectively choosing to enter and create social situations, creates environments for herself that further reinforce her sociability. We do the same thing when we choose friends and spouses. Because we are likely to choose companions who share our values and personality traits, they are likely, in turn, to reinforce those values and traits.

Evidence for this process was obtained in a classic study of women attending Bennington College in the 1930s. Most of them came from politically conservative homes, but they became increasingly liberal during their 4 years at the college. Follow-up studies of these women 25 and 50 years later showed that most of them had retained their liberal attitudes. Interviews revealed that they had remained liberal, in part, because they acquired politically liberal friends and married politically liberal husbands who reinforced their political attitudes (Alwin, Cohen, & Newcomb, 1991; Newcomb, Koenig, Flacks, & Warwick, 1967; Newcomb, 1943).

CRITICAL	
DISCUSSION	*STUDYING PERSONALITY THE LONG WAY*

Only investigators with a strong ability to delay gratification or an unselfish devotion to science undertake longitudinal studies. For studies designed to span many years, the original investigators may not even be around to reap the final rewards; their studies may outlive them. Other practical reasons also deter most would-be investigators. Longitudinal studies are expensive, and funding cannot usually be guaranteed over the required time interval. Second, subjects who start out in the study move away, die, decide to discontinue their participation, or cannot otherwise be located for follow-up. In general, the administrative tasks involved in conducting such a study take as much time and effort as collecting the data. For these reasons, many longitudinal studies are conducted under the auspices of research institutes rather than by independent investigators.

In addition to the practical problems, there is a more substantive problem that arises in many long-term longitudinal studies. As the interests of the field change over time,

the kinds of data collected in a longitudinal study also change. A study that begins with a focus on academic achievement may fail to gather personality information that later investigators wish to have. Sometimes assessment instruments used early in the study become obsolete and are discarded for better instruments as the study progresses. All of these factors make it difficult to compare later observations with earlier ones.

This was the major problem with the two studies discussed in the text that were conducted at the Institute of Human Development (IHD) in Berkeley. Not only were noncomparable measurements made at different times, but the two studies were themselves not comparable to each other in many ways. These problems were elegantly solved by Jack Block, who used the Q-sort method of personality description to standardize the data (Block, 1961/1978; Block, 1971).

As we noted in our earlier discussion of the Q-sort method, a rater (sorter) is given a set of cards, each containing a personality statement (for example, "Is cheerful"), and is

asked to describe an individual's personality by sorting the cards into piles. The rater places statements that are least descriptive of the individual in pile 1 on the left and those that are most descriptive in pile 9 on the right. The other statements are distributed in the intermediate piles, thereby assigning each Q item a score ranging from 1 to 9.

In the IHD studies, all the data on a single subject from the junior high years were placed into a single folder. Two to four clinical psychologists independently examined the folder and prepared Q-sort descriptions of the subject. A different set of sorters did the same thing for the data gathered during the senior high period. And finally, the interviewers and independent clinicians prepared Q-sort descriptions of the subjects when they were interviewed as adults in 1960, 1970, and 1980. This total procedure thus converted a bewildering variety of data to a set of independent but standardized personality descriptions on each subject at different ages that could be directly compared with one another.

There is also evidence for this process of proactive interaction in the domain of personality. When the subjects who participated in the Berkeley Guidance Study were interviewed in 1970 and 1980, so were their spouses, thereby providing Q sorts of subjects and spouses that could be directly correlated with each other. Two researchers examined those Q sorts to see whether spouses who were more alike in personality would produce greater personality continuity in each other. To do this, they compared the similarity of each couple's Q sorts from 1970 with the personality continuity of each spouse in the period from 1970 to 1980 (Caspi & Herbener, 1990).

When the researchers divided the couples into three groups of equal size on the basis of the similarity between the spouses' 1970 Q sorts, they found that the least similar

spouses showed individual continuities of .4 from 1970 to 1980; moderately similar spouses showed individual continuities of .5; and the most similar spouses showed continuities of .6. Further analyses demonstrated that these findings were not simply due to spouses' similarities in age, social class, or education.

The study also found that spouses who were more similar in personality were also more similar in their enjoyment of daily activities like visiting friends, going out for dinner, and participating in community activities and professional meetings. They also reported less marital conflict and greater closeness, friendliness, and marital satisfaction than less similar spouses. (This last finding exemplifies a well-known phenomenon. We discuss the similarity-produces-liking effect further in Chapter 17.)

CONTINUITY OF MALADAPTIVE PERSONALITY PATTERNS   It is easy to appreciate why we might be motivated to create environments for ourselves that sustain those aspects of our personalities that bring us happiness and personal satisfaction. But the same processes of reactive, evocative, and proactive interaction can also act in more coercive ways to sustain maladaptive personality patterns as well.

For example, consider an adolescent boy who has tantrums. His ill temper may provoke school authorities to expel him (evocative interaction) or cause him to experience school so negatively (reactive interaction) that he quits as soon as he is legally permitted to do so (proactive interaction). In either case, leaving school cuts short his education, which is likely to lead to lower occupational status. This low occupational status might then lead to an erratic worklife—frequent job changes, bouts of unemployment—which, in turn, might disrupt his marriage and lead to divorce. In this hypothetical scenario, these occupational and marital outcomes are *cumulative* consequences of his childhood personality. Once set in motion by childhood tantrums, the chain of events takes over and culminates in the adult outcomes—even if he is no longer ill tempered as an adult.

Now consider a different scenario that could produce the same outcome. The boy's tantrums might coerce his parents into giving in to his demands (evocative interaction), thereby reinforcing his behavior. This reinforcement not only short-circuits the learning of more controlled ways of behaving that might have greater adaptability in the long run, but it also increases the likelihood that

he will react in similar ways when similar situations arise in the future (reactive interaction). Thus, he will continue to be ill tempered as an adult, losing his temper when frustrations arise on the job or when conflicts arise in his marriage. This, in turn, can lead to an erratic worklife, low-level occupational status, and divorce. In this scenario, the same occupational and marital outcomes are *contemporary* consequences of his current personality rather than cumulative consequences of earlier events like quitting school.

Although these scenarios are hypothetical, they are based on actual research findings showing evidence for both cumulative and contemporary consequences of child ill-temperedness. Using the IHD archive from the Berkeley Guidance Study, the investigators first identified subjects in the archive who had had severe and frequent tantrums in late childhood (8–10 years old). The investigators traced the continuities and consequences of this ill-temperedness across the subsequent 30 years of the subjects' lives (Caspi, Bem, & Elder, 1989; Caspi, Elder, & Bem, 1987).

ILL-TEMPERED MEN   Beginning with male subjects, the investigators first asked the continuity question: Do ill-tempered boys become ill-tempered men? The answer was yes. Correlations between the tantrum scores in late childhood and the Q-sort ratings 20 years later reveal that ill-tempered boys were later described as significantly more undercontrolled, irritable, and moody than their peers.

The investigators then examined the subjects' work histories. The major finding was that ill-tempered boys who came from middle-class homes suffered a progressive deterioration of socioeconomic status as they moved through life. They were somewhat more likely than their peers to terminate their formal education earlier; the occupational status of their first jobs was significantly lower, and by midlife (age 40), their occupational status was indistinguishable from that of men born into the working class. A majority held jobs of lower occupational status than those held by their fathers at a comparable age. They also had more erratic worklives, changing jobs more frequently and being unemployed more often between ages 18 and 40.

Having established an overall correlation between childhood ill-temperedness and occupational outcomes, the investigators then

Do ill-tempered children become ill-tempered adults?

asked about the path between these two things. Did these subjects become occupationally disadvantaged because their earlier ill-temperedness started them down a particular path (cumulative consequences) or because their current ill-temperedness handicapped them in the world of work (contemporary consequences)? To answer this, the investigators used a correlational procedure called **path analysis,** which divides an overall correlation into separate components or paths. Figure 12-5 shows the results of this analysis; the arrows show the significant path correlations that were found.

As the figure shows, there is a significant path or correlation for males from childhood ill-temperedness to less education and a continuing significant path from less education to low occupational status. In other words, childhood ill-temperedness leads to less education (ill-tempered boys quit school sooner), which, in turn, leads to low occupational status. But at the same time, there is no *direct* path from ill-temperedness to low occupational status. Together, these results imply that low occupational status is a cumulative consequence of earlier childhood ill-temperedness, not a contemporary consequence of current adult ill-temperedness: The reason that ill-tempered males held low occupational status at age 40 is that they had quit school sooner.

The path from childhood ill-temperedness to an erratic worklife shows the opposite pattern. There is no significant path from less education to an erratic worklife, but there is a significant direct path from childhood ill-temperedness to an erratic worklife. This implies that an erratic worklife is a contemporary consequence of adult ill-temperedness, not a cumulative consequence of less education. Ill-tempered males appear to have a more erratic worklife at age 40, in part, because they are still ill-tempered—perhaps exploding on the job when frustrations arise.

Finally, there is a significant correlation between low occupational status and an erratic worklife, but we cannot determine the direction of causality because these two variables are present at the same time. Ill-tempered men may become frustrated with low-status jobs and thus become erratic by quitting or being fired. Alternatively, their erratic worklife may keep them out of better jobs, thus forcing them into lower-status jobs. Both sequences could be in effect.

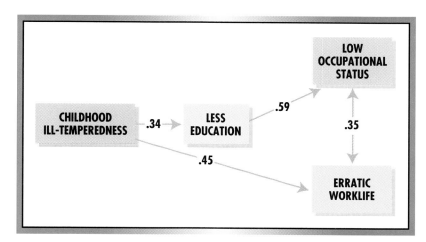

FIGURE 12-5

Path Analysis for Male Ill-Temperedness *The figure traces the separate paths from childhood ill-temperedness to low occupational status and an erratic worklife at age 40 for middle-class men. Childhood ill-temperedness leads to lower occupational status because ill-tempered children quit school sooner (cumulative consequences). Childhood ill-temperedness leads directly to an erratic worklife because the subjects remain ill-tempered as adults, and this handicaps them in the world of work (contemporary consequences). (After Caspi, Elder, & Bem, 1987)*

A history of childhood ill-temperedness also affects the domestic sphere. Almost half (46 percent) of men with histories of childhood ill-temperedness had divorced by age 40, compared with only 22 percent of other men.

ILL-TEMPERED WOMEN Like the men, women who had been ill-tempered as young girls also showed personality continuity. Compared with other women, these women were described by both their husbands and their children at the time of the 1970 interviews as less adequate, more ill-tempered mothers.

The Berkeley subjects became adults between 1945 and 1960, a time of quite traditional sex roles in America. As a result, few of the women had occupations outside the home, and the investigators were not able to analyze their occupational status as they had done for the men. But this was also a time when a woman's socioeconomic status was defined by her husband's occupation, and so the investigators looked at the occupational status of these women's husbands. They found that compared with other women, women with a history of childhood ill-temperedness married men who had lower occupational status both at the time of marriage and at midlife. By comparing the jobs held by their husbands at the time of marriage with those held by their fathers at a comparable age, the investigators found that 40 percent of the ill-tempered women moved down in socioeconomic status when they married compared with only 24 percent of other women.

Ill-temperedness in childhood not only consigned these women to marriages at a socioeconomic level lower than that of their childhood homes, but it also contributed to the deterioration of these relationships. Over a quarter (26 percent) of these women had divorced by age 40, compared with only 12 percent of other women. Husbands of those ill-tempered women who were married at the time of the 1970 interviews reported more marital conflict than husbands of other women.

SOURCES OF DISCONTINUITY

Despite the evidence for the continuity of ill-temperedness discussed above, the correlations themselves are still relatively low, leaving room for many exceptions: Ill-tempered children do not inevitably become ill-tempered adults. Often a person will encounter a transforming event or series of events—such as going to college or entering therapy—that starts him or her on a new path and thereby initiates personality change. Individuals whose personalities are at odds with their environments may be directly pressured to change by those who find their patterns of behavior unpleasant; and finally, many individuals make efforts at one time or another to change their own personality patterns in order to achieve greater happiness. These several sources of change can thus create discontinuities in personality across the life course.

One frequent source of pressure for change arises from society's sex-role norms. For example, one extensive longitudinal study found that boys but not girls showed continuity from childhood to early adulthood on tra-

Men who were dependent as children tend to have nurturant personalities.

ditionally male-appropriate personality traits like aggression, and that girls but not boys showed continuity on traditionally female-appropriate traits like dependency (Kagan & Moss, 1962). There was also some evidence that behavior inconsistent with sex-role expectations in childhood may not be entirely suppressed but may be expressed in adulthood in more socially acceptable ways.

This possibility was explored further by the same investigators who had conducted the study of ill-temperedness, again using the IHD archives from the Berkeley Guidance Study (Caspi, Elder, & Bem, 1989). For this study, they selected subjects who had been strongly dependent on adults in late childhood and then traced the continuity of this dependency across the subsequent 30 years of the subjects' lives. Because dependency is discouraged for boys and men in our society, the investigators were particularly interested in whether this trait would survive the sex-role pressures on the male subjects. Do dependent boys become dependent men?

The answer this time was both more complex and more interesting. Compared with other men, those who had histories of childhood dependency were characterized in adulthood as calm, warm, giving, sympathetic, insightful, undefensive, incisive, and socially poised. Although they sought reassurance from others—a possible echo of their earlier childhood dependency—others felt nurturant toward them and sought them out for advice. It appears that the negative childhood attribute of dependency had been transformed into a related but remarkably positive nurturant personality style in adulthood. We thus see both continuity and discontinuity.

Not unexpectedly, the warm, nurturant adult style of these men conferred its most obvious advantages in the domestic sphere. These men were significantly more likely to have an intact first marriage at midlife than other men (83 percent versus 62 percent); their wives expressed more satisfaction with their marriages than wives of other men; and, they and their wives agreed more with one another on such child-rearing practices as discipline, affection, and attention. Dependent adolescent boys who worry about being insufficiently assertive should take note—as should adolescent girls who will someday come to appreciate nurturant, lovable men and wonder where to find them.

BIOLOGICAL-PSYCHOLOGICAL PERSPECTIVES

We noted in Chapter 1 that a full understanding of human behavior requires that we adopt both biological and psychological perspectives. In this chapter, we have noted how the study of intellectual abilities is being increasingly nourished by discoveries in brain anatomy and function. We have also seen how findings in behavioral genetics contribute directly to our knowledge of the complex interactions between "nature" and and "nurture" in shaping and maintaining an individual's personality across the course of life. Psychologists who want to understand human abilities and personality must now be increasingly acquainted with the neighboring disciplines of neurobiology and behavioral genetics.

 # CHAPTER SUMMARY

1. Tests for assessing intelligence or personality must demonstrate that they yield reproducible and consistent results *(reliability)* and that they measure what they are intended to measure *(validity)*.

2. The first successful intelligence tests were developed by the French psychologist Alfred Binet, who proposed the concept of *mental age*. A bright child's mental age is above his or her chronological age; a slow child's mental age is below his or her chronological age. The concept of the *intelligence quotient* (IQ), the ratio of mental age to chronological age (multiplied by 100), was introduced into the revision of the Binet scales (the Stanford-Binet). Many intelligence test scores are still expressed as IQ scores, but they are no longer actually calculated according to this formula.

3. Both Binet and Wechsler, developer of the Wechsler Adult Intelligence Scale (WAIS), assumed that intelligence is a general capacity for reasoning. Similarly, Spearman proposed that a general factor *(g)* underlies performance on different kinds of test items. A method for determining the kinds of abilities that underlie performance on intelligence tests is *factor analysis.*

4. An alternative approach to intelligence is the *information-processing approach,* which seeks to understand intellectual behavior in terms of the underlying cognitive processes brought into play when an individual attempts to solve an intelligence test problem.

5. Some critics believe that there are multiple intelligences and that current tests tap primarily "academic intelligence," rather than practical intelligence or other aspects of intelligent behavior (for example, musical or interpersonal intelligence). Thus, conventional intelligence tests are better at predicting college grades than they are for predicting later job success or career advancement.

6. To arrive at a comprehensive but manageable number of personality traits on which individuals can be assessed, investigators first collected all the trait terms found in the unabridged dictionary (about 18,000); these were then reduced to a smaller number. Ratings of individuals on these terms were factor-analyzed to determine how many underlying dimensions were needed to account for the correlations among the scales. Although different investigators arrive at different numbers of factors, the recent consensus is that 5 factors provide the best compromise. These have been labeled the "Big Five" and form the acronym OCEAN: Openness to experience, Conscientiousness, Extraversion, Agreeableness, and Neuroticism.

7. *Personality inventories* are questionnaires on which individuals report their reactions or feelings in certain situations. Responses to subsets of items are summed to yield scores on separate scales or factors within the inventory. Although items on most inventories are composed or selected on the basis of a theory, they can also be selected on the basis of their correlation with an external criterion—the *criterion-keyed method* of test construction. The best known example is the Minnesota Multiphasic Personality Inventory (MMPI), which is designed to identify individuals with psychological disorders. For example, an item to which schizophrenics answer "true"

significantly more often than do nonschizophrenics would be selected as an item for a schizophrenia scale.

8. Psychologists who take the psychoanalytic approach prefer less structured assessment instruments called *projective* tests, such as the Rorschach Test and the Thematic Apperception Test (TAT). Because the test stimuli are ambiguous, it is assumed that the individual *projects* his or her personality onto the stimulus, thereby revealing unconscious wishes and motives.

9. A major task in psychology is to discover how genetic/biological factors ("nature") and environmental factors ("nurture") contribute to differences among individuals. Behavioral scientists typically quantify the extent to which a group of people differs from one another on some measure of a trait or ability by computing the *variance* of the scores obtained. The more the individuals in the group differ from one another, the higher the variance. Researchers can then seek to determine how much of that variance is due to different causes. The proportion of variance in a trait that is accounted for (caused by) genetic differences among the individuals is called the *heritability* of the trait. Because heritability is a proportion, it ranges from 0 to 1. For example, the heritability of height is approximately .90: Differences among people in their heights are due almost entirely to differences in their genetic makeup.

10. Heritabilities can be estimated by comparing correlations obtained on pairs of identical twins (who share all their genes) and correlations obtained on pairs of fraternal twins (who, on the average, share about half of their genes). If identical twin pairs are more alike on the trait than fraternal twin pairs, then the trait probably has a genetic component. Heritabilities can also be estimated from the correlation between identical twin pairs who have been raised apart from one another in different environments. Any correlation between such pairs must be due to their genetic similarities.

11. There are many misunderstandings about heritability: (a) It is about differences among individuals. It does not indicate how much of a trait in an individual is due to genetic factors; (b) It is not a fixed attribute of a trait. If something happens to change the variability of a trait in a group, the heritability will also change; (c) Heritability is about the *vari-*

ance within a group. It does not indicate the source of *mean* differences *between* groups; (d) Heritability does indicate how much possible environmental changes might change the mean level of a trait in a population.

12. In shaping personality, genetic and environmental influences do not act independently of one another but are intertwined from the moment of birth. Because a child's personality and his or her home environment are both a function of the parents' genes, there is a built-in correlation between the child's *genotype* (inherited personality characteristics) and that environment.

13. Three dynamic processes of personality-environment interaction are (a) *reactive interaction*—different individuals exposed to the same environment experience it, interpret it, and react to it differently; (b) *evocative interaction*—an individual's personality evokes distinctive responses from others; and (c) *proactive interaction*—individuals select or create environments of their own. As a child gets older, the influence of proactive interaction becomes increasingly important.

14. Studies of twins have produced a number of puzzling patterns: Heritabilities estimated from identical twins reared apart are much higher than estimates based on comparisons between identical and fraternal twins; identical twins reared apart are as similar to each other as identical twins reared together, but fraternal twins and nontwin siblings become less similar over time, even when they are reared together. These patterns are probably due, in part, to interactions among genes, so that having all one's genes in common is more than twice as effective as having only half of one's genes in common. Such patterns might also be due in part to the three processes of personality-environment interaction (reactive, evocative, and proactive).

15. After their genetic similarities are subtracted out, children from the same family seem to be no more alike than children chosen randomly from the population, a surprising finding. This implies that the kinds of variables that psychologists typically study (such as child-rearing practices and the family's socioeconomic status) contribute virtually nothing to individual differences in personality. Research will have to look more closely at differences between different children within the same family. This finding, too, might be partially accounted for by the

three processes of personality-environment interaction.

16. *Longitudinal studies* observe the same individuals over time and provide the only effective way to assess the continuity of personality through the life course. In general, measures of intellectual performance show the strongest continuities; personality variables like extraversion, emotional stability/instability, and impulse control are next; political attitudes and measures of self-opinions (for example, self-esteem, life satisfaction) are last.

17. The three processes of personality-environment interaction influence the continuity of personality. For example, continuity produced by proactive interaction occurs when we choose friends and spouses who are compatible with our personalities, and they, in turn, reinforce our personalities.

18. Maladaptive personality patterns can also be sustained over the life course through the processes of personality-environment interaction. These produce *cumulative consequences* when an individual's early personality selects or channels him or her into particular life paths. They produce *contemporary consequences* when the early personality is itself carried forward into adulthood, where it evokes distinctive responses from the environment.

FURTHER READING

For an introduction to individual differences and psychological testing, see Kaplan and Sacuzzo, *Psychological Testing* (3rd ed., 1993); Cronbach, *Essentials of Psychological Testing* (4th ed., 1984); Kail and Pellegrino, *Human Intelligence: Perspectives and Prospects* (1985); Murphy and Davidshofer, *Psychological Testing: Principles and Applications* (2nd ed., 1991); Sattler, *Assessment of Children* (1988); Sternberg (ed.), *Human Abilities: An Information-Processing Approach* (1984); and Anastasi, *Psychological Testing* (6th ed., 1989).

For a more general overview of intellectual abilities, see Sternberg, *Intelligence Applied: Understanding and Increasing Your Intellectual Skills* (1986); and Brody, *Intelligence* (2nd ed., 1992). A theory of multiple intelligences is presented in Gardner, *Frames of Mind: The Theory of Multiple Intelligence* (1983). For a historical perspective on intelligence tests and the controversies associated with them, see Fancher, *The Intelligence Men: Makers of the IQ Controversy* (1985). A recent and very controversial book on intelligence in American society is Herrnstein and Murray, *The Bell Curve* (1994). For personality assessment, see Aiken, *Assessment of Personality* (1989) or any of the personality textbooks listed at the end of Chapter 13.

Plomin, *Nature and Nurture* (1990) provides an accessible discussion of behavioral genetics, including the twin method of assessing heritability. For a complete discussion of the differences among children from the same family, see Dunn and Plomin, *Separate Lives: Why Siblings Are So Different* (1990). A more advanced treatment of the genetics of intelligence is Plomin, DeFries, and McClearn, *Behavioral Genetics: A Primer* (2nd ed., 1989). Plomin and McClearn (eds.), *Nature, Nurture & Psychology* (1993) provide a collection of essays on the nature-nurture problem in several areas.

Studies based on the longitudinal archives housed at the Institute of Human Development in Berkeley can be found in Eichorn et al. (eds.), *Present and Past in Middle Life* (1981); and Block, *Lives Through Time* (1971).

13 CHAPTER

PERSONALITY

ersonality was defined in Chapter 12 as the distinctive and characteristic patterns of thought, emotion, and behavior that define an individual's personal style of interacting with the physical and social environments. Accordingly, one of the first tasks of personality psychology is to describe individual differences—the diverse ways in which individuals differ from one another. The previous chapter (Individual Differences) described the most common approach to this task, the trait approach.

By itself, however, the trait approach is not a theory of personality but a general orientation and set of methods for assessing stable characteristics of persons. By themselves personality traits do not tell us anything about the dynamic processes of personality functioning, and trait psychologists who have sought complete theories of personality have had to look to other approaches to address the second major task of personality psychology: synthesizing the many processes that influence an individual's interactions with the physical and social environments—biology, development, learning, thinking, emotion, motivation, and social interaction—into an integrated account of the total person. This task requires going far beyond the general nature-nurture interactions discussed in Chapter 12 and makes the study of personality one of the most ambitious subfields of psychology.

In this chapter, we shall look at the three theoretical approaches to personality that have dominated the history of personality psychology in the twentieth century: the psychoanalytic approach, the behavioristic approach, and the phenomenological approach. In doing so, we shall also return to a theme touched on briefly in Chapter 1 by comparing the portraits of the human personality that emerge from their different philosophies of human nature: To what degree are our beliefs, emotions, and actions free and in what ways are they determined by causes beyond our control? Are we basically good, neutral, or evil? Fixed or modifiable? Active or passive in controlling our destinies? What constitutes psychological health or lack of health? These are not empirical questions, and theories of personality do not attempt to answer them explicitly. But each approach does have implicit answers—underlying presumptions

about human nature that give the approach a distinctive flavor. Historically, these more philosophical factors have been as important as the empirical data in provoking controversies and in winning converts for the competing accounts of personality.

Today, however, most personality psychologists would not identify themselves as "pure" adherents to any one of these three approaches, and the differences among the approaches are themselves no longer as sharp as they once were. This is because most contemporary personality theorists, whatever their historical allegiances, have joined the rest of psychology in becoming more "cognitive." As we proceed, we will point out how each approach has become more cognitive in recent years.

PSYCHOANALYTIC APPROACH

Sigmund Freud, the creator of psychoanalytic theory, is one of the towering intellectual figures of the twentieth century. Whatever its shortcomings as a scientific theory, the psychoanalytic account of personality remains the most comprehensive and influential theory of personality ever created. Its impact extends well beyond psychology, influencing the social sciences, the humanities, the arts, and society generally. Even though psychoanalytic theory plays a less central role in psychology today than it did 50 or 60 years ago, many of its ideas have been absorbed into the mainstream of psychological thinking. Even parents who have done nothing more than raise their children with the occasional guidance of psychiatrist Benjamin Spock's best-selling *Baby and Child Care* are more like Freudian psychologists than they realize.

Freud began his scientific career as a neurologist, treating patients suffering from various "nervous" disorders by using conventional medical procedures. Because these often failed, he used but then later abandoned the technique of hypnosis. Eventually, he discovered the method of **free association**, in which a patient is instructed to say everything that comes to mind, regardless of how trivial or embarrassing it may seem. By listening carefully to these verbal associations, Freud detected consistent themes that he believed were manifestations of unconscious wishes and fears. He found similar themes in the recall of dreams and early childhood memories.

Freud compared the human mind to an iceberg. The small part that shows above the surface of the water is the **conscious**—our current awareness—and the **preconscious**, all the information that is not currently "on our mind," but which we could bring into consciousness if called upon to do so (for example, the name of the president of the United States). The much larger mass of the iceberg below the water represents the **unconscious**, a storehouse of impulses, wishes, and inaccessible memories that affect our thoughts and behavior. This **topographic model** was Freud's earliest attempt to map out the nature of the human mind. He was not the first to discover unconscious mental influences—even Shakespeare includes them in his plays—but Freud gave them primary importance in the everyday functioning of the normal personality.

Closely allied with Freud's focus on unconscious processes was his belief in the determinism of human behavior. **Psychological determinism** is the doctrine that all thoughts, emotions, and actions have causes. Freud maintained not only that all psychological events are caused, but that most of them are caused by unsatisfied drives and unconscious wishes. In one of his earliest publications, *The Psychopathology of Everyday Life* (1901), Freud argued that dreams, humor, forgetting, and slips of the tongue ("Freudian slips") all serve to relieve psychological tension by gratifying forbidden impulses or unfulfilled wishes.

Freud's writings fill 24 volumes. His first major contribution, *The Interpretation of Dreams*, was published in 1900, and his final treatise, *An Outline of Psychoanalysis*, was published in 1940, a year after his death. We can present only the barest outline of Freud's theory of personality here.

PERSONALITY STRUCTURE

Freud discovered that his topographic model was too simple to describe the human personality, and so he went on to develop his structural model, which divided personality into three major systems that interact to govern human behavior: the *id,* the *ego,* and the *superego.*

THE ID   The id is the most primitive part of the personality, from which the ego and the superego later develop. It is present in the newborn infant and consists of the basic biological impulses (or drives): the need to eat, to drink, to eliminate wastes, to avoid pain, and to gain sexual (sensual) pleasure. Freud believed that aggression is also a basic biological drive (see Chapter 11). In fact, he believed that the sexual and aggressive drives were the most important instinctual determinants of personality throughout life. The id seeks immediate gratification of these impulses. Like a young child, the id operates on the **pleasure principle**: It endeavors to obtain pleasure and to avoid pain, regardless of the external circumstances.

THE EGO   Children soon learn that their impulses cannot always be gratified immediately. Hunger must wait until someone provides food. Relieving bladder or bowel pressure must be delayed until the bathroom is reached. Certain impulses—playing with one's genitals or hitting someone—may be punished by a parent. A new part of the personality, the **ego**, develops as the young child learns to consider the demands of reality. The

"Very well, I'll introduce you. Ego, meet Id. Now get back to work."

ego obeys the **reality principle**: The gratification of impulses must be delayed until the situation is appropriate. It is essentially the executive of the personality: It decides what actions are appropriate and which id impulses will be satisfied and in what manner. The ego mediates among the demands of the id, the realities of the world, and the demands of the superego.

THE SUPEREGO   The third part of the personality is the **superego**, which judges whether actions are right or wrong. More generally, the superego is the internalized representation of the values and morals of society and comprises the individual's conscience as well as his or her image of the morally ideal person (called the *ego ideal*). The superego develops in response to parental rewards and punishments.

Initially, parents control children's behavior directly by reward and punishment. Through the incorporation of parental standards into the superego, a child brings behavior under his or her own control. Children no longer need anyone to tell them it is wrong to steal; their superego tells them. Violating the superego's standards, or even the impulse to do so, produces anxiety—which was originally the anxiety over the loss of parental love. According to Freud, this anxiety is largely unconscious but may be experienced as guilt. If parental standards are overly rigid, the individual may be guilt ridden and inhibit all aggressive or sexual impulses. In contrast, an individual who fails to incorporate any standards for acceptable social behavior will have few behavioral constraints and may engage in excessively self-indulgent or criminal behavior. Such a person is said to have a weak superego.

The three components of personality are often in opposition: The ego postpones the gratification that the id wants immediately, and the superego battles with both the id and the ego because behavior often falls short of the moral code it represents. In the well-integrated personality, the ego remains in firm but flexible control; the reality principle governs. In terms of his earlier topographic model, Freud proposed that all of the id and most of the ego and superego are submerged in the unconscious; small parts of the ego and superego are in either the conscious or preconscious (See Figure 13-1).

PERSONALITY DYNAMICS

CONSERVATION OF ENERGY   The science of physics was remarkably successful in the nineteenth century, and Freud was greatly influenced by the German physicist Hermann von Helmholtz, who argued that physiological events could also be explained by the same principles that had been so successful in physics. Freud was particularly impressed by the principle of the conservation of energy—which states that energy may be changed into different forms but is neither created nor destroyed—and he postulated that humans are also closed energy systems. There is a constant amount of psychic energy for any given individual, which Freud called **libido** (Latin for lust), reflecting his view that the sexual drive was primary.

One corollary of the conservation of energy principle is that if a forbidden act or impulse is suppressed, its energy will seek an outlet somewhere else in the system, possibly appearing in disguised form. The desires of the id contain psychic energy that must be expressed in some way, and prohibiting their

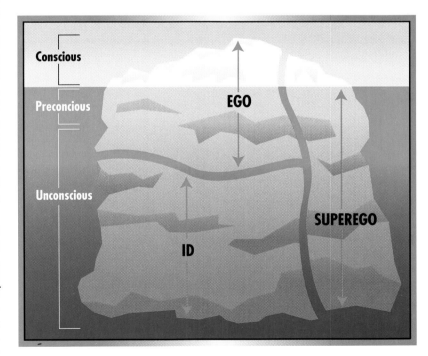

FIGURE 13-1

Freud's Structural Model of the Mind   *In Freud's "iceberg" model of the mind, all of the id and most of the ego and superego are submerged in the unconscious. Small parts of the ego and superego are either in the conscious or preconscious.*

expression does not abolish them. Aggressive impulses, for example, may be displaced to racing sports cars, playing chess, or to a sarcastic sense of humor. Dreams and neurotic symptoms are also manifestations of psychic energy that has been prevented from direct expression.

Anxiety and Defense   Individuals with an urge to do something forbidden experience anxiety. One way of reducing this anxiety is to express the impulse in a disguised form that will avoid punishment either by society or by its internal representative, the superego. Freud described several additional strategies the individual can use to prevent or reduce anxiety. These strategies are called the ego's **mechanisms of defense**. The most basic defense mechanism is **repression**, in which the ego pushes a threatening thought or forbidden impulse out of awareness into the unconscious; from the outside it appears that the individual has simply forgotten the thought or impulse. Individuals differ both in their thresholds for anxiety and in the defenses they use to deal with such anxiety. Anxiety and mechanisms of defense are central to Freud's theory of psychopathology and will be examined more at length in Chapter 14, the chapter on stress and coping.

Toilet training is one of a child's first experiences with imposed control.

Personality Development

Freud believed that during the first 5 years of life, the individual progresses through several developmental stages that affect personality. Applying a broad definition of sexuality, he called these periods **psychosexual stages**. During each stage, the pleasure-seeking impulses of the id focus on a particular area of the body and on activities connected with that area.

Freud called the first year of life the **oral stage** of psychosexual development. During this period, infants derive pleasure from nursing and sucking and begin to put anything they can reach into their mouths. Freud called the second year of life the beginning of the **anal stage** and believed that children find pleasure during this time both in withholding and in expelling feces. These pleasures come into conflict with parents who are attempting toilet training, the child's first experience with imposed control. In the **phallic stage**, from about age 3 to age 6, children begin to derive pleasure from fondling their genitals. They observe the differences between males and females and begin to direct their awakening sexual impulses toward the parent of the opposite sex

It is during the phallic stage that children must resolve the **Oedipal conflict**. Freud described this conflict most clearly in the case of a boy. Around the age of 5 or 6, the boy's sexual impulses are directed toward the mother. This leads him to perceive his father as a rival for his mother's affection. Freud called this situation the Oedipal conflict, after Sophocles' play in which Oedipus Rex unwittingly kills his father and marries his mother. According to Freud, the boy also fears that his father will retaliate against these sexual impulses by castrating him. Freud labeled this fear *castration anxiety* and considered it to be the prototype of all later anxieties provoked by forbidden internal desires. In a normal case of development, the boy simultaneously reduces this anxiety and settles for vicarious gratification of his feelings toward his mother by *identifying* with his father—internalizing an idealized perception of his father's attitudes and values. The same process in a girl—resulting in her identification with her mother—is analogous but more complicated, and even more controversial. (See the Critical Discussion, Controversial Tests of Freud's Oedipal Theory.)

Resolution of the Oedipal conflict terminates the phallic stage and is succeeded by the **latency period,** which lasts from about age 7 to age 12. During this sexually quiescent time, children become less concerned with their bodies and turn their attention to the skills needed for coping with the environment. Finally, adolescence and puberty usher in the **genital stage**, the mature phase of adult sexuality and functioning

Freud felt that special problems at any stage could arrest (or *fixate*) development and have a lasting effect on the individual's personality. Libido would remain attached to the activities appropriate for that stage. Thus, a person who was weaned very early and who did not have enough sucking pleasure might become fixated at the oral stage. As an adult, this person may be excessively dependent on others and overly fond of such oral pleasures as eating, drinking, and smoking. Such a person is called an *oral personality.* A person fixated at the anal stage of psychosexual development may be abnormally concerned with cleanliness, orderliness, and saving and may tend to resist external pressure—the *anal personality.* Inadequate resolution of the Oedipal conflict can lead to a weak sense of morality, difficulties with authority figures, and many other problems.

MODIFICATIONS OF FREUD'S THEORIES

Freud modified his theories throughout his life. Like a good scientist, he remained open to new data, revising earlier positions as new observations accumulated that could not be accommodated by the original theory. For example, he completely revised his theory of anxiety quite late in his career. Freud's theory has been further extended by his daughter Anna, who has played a particularly important role in clarifying the mechanisms of defense (1946/1967) and in applying psychoanalytic theory to the practice of child psychiatry (1958).

But if Freud was open to new data, he was emphatically not open to dissenting opinions. He was particularly adamant that his colleagues and followers not question the libido theory and the centrality of sexual motivation in the functioning of personality. This dogmatism forced a break between Freud and many of his most brilliant associates—some of whom went on to develop rival theories

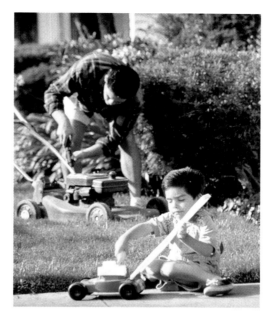

According to psychoanalytic theory, a child resolves the Oedipal conflict by identifying with the same-sex parent.

that placed more emphasis on motivational processes other than sexuality. These former associates included Carl Jung and Alfred Adler, as well as later theorists such as Karen Horney, Harry Stack Sullivan, and Erich Fromm.

These dissidents and other, more recent psychoanalytic theorists all place more stress on the role of the ego. They believe that the ego is present at birth, develops independently of the id, and performs functions other than finding realistic ways of satisfying id impulses. These ego functions are learning how to cope with the environment and making sense of experience. Ego satisfactions include exploration, manipulation, and competency in performance. This approach ties the concept of the ego more closely to cognitive processes.

One important part of this new direction is called **object relations theory,** which deals with a person's attachments and relationships to other people over the course of life. Object relations theorists have not rejected the concept of the id or the importance of biological drives in motivating behavior, but they have an equal interest in such questions as the degree of psychological separateness from parents, the degree of attachment to and involvement with other people versus self-preoccupation, and the strength of the individual's feelings of self-esteem and competency.

Although we did not identify it as such, Erik Erikson's stage theory of development—which we discussed in Chapter 3—is an example of a revised psychoanalytic theory.

CONTROVERSIAL TESTS OF FREUD'S OEDIPAL THEORY

Over the years, many personality psychologists have attempted to test portions of psychoanalytic theory, using a wide variety of experimental and observational techniques. One particularly intriguing set of experimental studies has attempted to test Freud's Oedipal theory using a procedure called *subliminal psychodynamic activation*. Subjects in these experiments look into a tachistoscope, a device that enables the experimenter to flash images on a screen for very short exposure times. When an image is exposed for only 4 thousandths of a second, subjects are unable to describe it, but the investigators hypothesize that the image has nevertheless registered in the unconscious. If this is true, then the technique enables investigators to present threatening materials directly to the unconscious and to see if it influences behavior as psychoanalytic theory predicts. There are now more than 100 studies using this technique (Weinberger & Silverman, 1987).

In a test of the Oedipal conflict, male subjects competed in a dart-throwing game for cash prizes both before and after seeing images in the tachistoscope. According to Freud, such competition should raise unresolved early Oedipal desires to symbolically defeat their fathers. One group of men saw the phrase "Beating Dad is Wrong," accompanied by a picture of two men looking unhappily at each other; a second group saw the phrase "Beating Dad is OK" with a picture of two smiling men; and a control group saw the phrase "People Are Walking" with a picture of people walking. As predicted, subjects who saw the phrase "Beating Dad is Wrong" obtained lower dart-throwing scores than they had before seeing

the phrase—presumably because the phrase heightened Oedipal feelings; subjects who saw the phrase "Beating Dad is OK" increased their scores; and, control subjects did not change (Silverman, Ross, Adler, & Lustig, 1978). In further tests, it was found that the phrase "Beating Mom is Wrong" had no effect on dart-throwing scores, but the phrase "Winning Mom is OK" increased them (Silverman & Fishel, 1981). These findings, too, are in accord with the Oedipal theory.

These striking findings have attracted a lot of attention and many skeptics find them hard to accept. There have been several articles critical of the methodology (for example, Balay & Shevrin, 1988; Allen & Condon, 1982) and attempts to replicate the experiments have sometimes failed (for example, Haspel & Harris, 1982; Heilbrun, 1980). Nevertheless, the subliminal psychodynamic activation procedure has been used successfully by other researchers (Geisler, 1986; Dauber, 1984; Frauman, Lynn, Hardaway, & Melteni, 1984). Although these successful studies did not specifically examine the Oedipal hypotheses, they do provide additional support for a critical element of psychoanalytic theory: the influence of unconsciously perceived information on behavior.

A very different kind of test of the Oedipal theory comes from anthropology. Psychoanalytic theorists often cite the cross-cultural taboo against incest as evidence for the universality of the Oedipal conflict; the taboo is seen as society's attempt to control Oedipal rivalry within the family. The anthropologist Bronislaw Malinowski (1927) had read Freud's account of how boys often reveal their Oedipal

hostility toward their fathers in dreams in which the father is maimed or killed. According to Freud, such dreams symbolically fulfill the boy's wish to get rid of the rival for his mother's affection. Malinowski collected dream reports from adolescent boys in the Trobriand Islands, where uncles rather than fathers are responsible for disciplining them. He found no instances of dreams in which fathers suffered but several in which uncles met with disaster, implying that it is the discipline, not Oedipal rivalry, that creates the hostility.

Because Freud's own observations were drawn from a culture in which the father was both the mother's lover and the son's disciplinarian, he had no way of determining which function created the son's hostility. The Trobriand Island culture provided Malinowski with a natural laboratory in which the two functions were separated. Psychoanalytic theorists, however, can counterargue that Malinowski's study is not a valid test because he interviewed adolescent boys, who would have resolved the Oedipal conflict many years earlier in their development. (Also see Spiro, 1982, for a refutation of Malinowski's conclusion.) However, there is other anthropological evidence that is also not supportive of psychoanalytic theory (Daly & Wilson, 1990).

As these examples make clear, testing psychoanalytic theory is challenging and exciting. Even though psychoanalytic theory plays a smaller role in psychology today than it did several years ago—or than it does today in some other disciplines such as literature—we have not yet seen the end of the story.

Erikson himself was trained as a psychoanalyst by Anna Freud, and he perceived his own views as expanding rather than altering Freudian theory. Instead of viewing develop-

mental stages in terms of their psychosexual functions, Erikson sees them as *psychosocial* stages involving primarily ego processes. For Erikson, the important feature of the first

Because psychoanalytic theory portrays humans as basically evil, Freud saw the events leading up to World War II as the natural consequence of the human aggressive drive when it is not held in check.

year of life is not that it focuses on oral gratification, but that the child is learning to trust (or mistrust) the environment as a satisfier of needs. The important feature of the second year of life is not that it focuses on anal concerns such as toilet training, but that the child is learning autonomy. Toilet training just happens to be a frequent arena of conflict in which the child's striving for autonomy clashes with new obedience demands by parents. Erikson's theory also adds more stages in order to encompass the entire life span.

PSYCHOANALYTIC PORTRAIT OF HUMAN NATURE

At the beginning of this chapter, we noted that each approach to personality carries with it an intrinsic philosophy of human nature. To what extent are we free or determined? Good, neutral, or evil? Fixed or modifiable? Active or passive? What constitutes psychological health?

Our description of Freud's theory has already hinted at many of his views on these matters. Freud is often compared with Copernicus and Darwin. Like these two other intellectual pioneers, Freud was accused of undermining the stature and dignity of humanity. The astronomer Copernicus demoted the earth from its position as center of the universe to one of several planets moving around a minor star; Darwin demoted the human

species to a descendant of apes. Freud took the next step by emphasizing that human behavior is determined by forces beyond our control, thereby depriving us of our free will and psychological freedom. By emphasizing the unconscious status of our motivations, he deprived us of our rationality; and, by stressing the sexual and aggressive nature of those motivations, he dealt the final blow to our dignity.

Psychoanalytic theory also draws a dark portrait of human nature as basically evil. Without the restraining forces of society and its internalized representative, the superego, humans would destroy themselves. Freud was a deeply pessimistic man. He was forced to flee from Vienna, when the Nazis invaded in 1938, and died in September 1939, the month World War II began. He saw these events as the natural consequence of the human aggressive drive when it is not held in check.

According to psychoanalytic theory, the human personality is also relatively fixed; our personalities are basically determined by inborn drives and by environmental events in the first five years of life. Only extensive psychoanalysis can undo some of the negative consequences of early experiences, and it can do so in only limited ways. We also emerge from psychoanalytic theory as relatively passive creatures. Although the ego is in an active struggle with the id and superego, we are relatively impotent, passive pawns of this drama being played out in our unconscious.

And finally, for Freud, psychological health consisted of firm but flexible ego control over the impulses of the id. As Freud noted, the goal of psychoanalysis was to ensure that "Where id is, there ego shall be" (1933).

EVALUATION OF PSYCHOANALYTIC APPROACH

Psychoanalytic theory is so broad in scope that it cannot simply be pronounced true or false. But whether it is correct or incorrect in its particulars is virtually irrelevant to its overall impact on our culture and to the value of some of its scientific contributions. For example, Freud's method of free association opened up an entirely new database of observations that had never before been explored systematically. Second, the recognition that our behavior often reflects a compromise between our wishes and our fears accounts for many of the apparent contradictions in human behavior better than any other theory of personality; as a theory of **ambivalence**, psychoanalytic theory has no peer. Third, Freud's recognition that unconscious processes play an important role in much of our behavior is almost universally accepted—although these processes are now often reinterpreted in learning-theory or information-processing terms.

Nevertheless, as a scientific theory, the psychoanalytic account has been persistently criticized for its inadequacy (for example, Grünbaum, 1984). One of the main criticisms is that many of its concepts are ambiguous and difficult to define or measure objectively. Also, psychoanalytic theory assumes that very different behaviors may reflect the same underlying motive. For example, a mother who resents her child may be abusive, or she may deny her hostile impulses by becoming overly concerned and protective toward the child— what Freud would call a **reaction formation** (see Chapter 14). When opposite behaviors are claimed to result from the same underlying motive, it is difficult to confirm the presence or absence of the motive or to make predictions that can be empirically verified.

A more serious criticism concerns the validity of the observations that Freud obtained through his psychoanalytic procedure. Critics have pointed out that it is often not clear what Freud's patients told him spontaneously about past events in their lives, what he may have planted in their minds, and what he simply inferred. For example, Freud reported that many of his patients recalled being seduced or sexually molested as children. At first he believed them, but then decided that these reports were not literally true, but reflected patients' own early sexual fantasies. He regarded this realization as one of his major theoretical insights. But one writer argued that Freud's original assumption about the reality of the seductions was probably more accurate, an argument that seems more reasonable in light of our increased awareness of child sexual abuse (Masson, 1984).

Other critics have gone further and suggested that Freud may have questioned his patients so persistently with leading questions and suggestions that they were led to reconstruct memories of seductions that never occurred—a hypothesis that Freud considered but rejected (Powell & Boer, 1994). (See the Critical Discussion of reconstructed memories in Chapter 8.) Others charge that in many cases, Freud simply inferred that seduction had occurred even though the patient never reported such an incident; he actually substituted his theoretical expectations for data (Esterson, 1993; Scharnberg, 1993).

When Freud's theories have actually been empirically tested, they have achieved a mixed record. (See the Critical Discussion, Controversial Tests of Freud's Oedipal Theory.) Efforts to link adult personality characteristics to psychosexually relevant events in childhood have generally met with negative outcomes (Sears, Maccoby, & Levin, 1957; Sewell & Mussen, 1952). When relevant character traits *are* identified, they appear to be related to similar character traits in the parents (Hetherington & Brackbill; 1963; Beloff, 1957). Thus, even if a relationship were to be found between toilet-training practices and adult personality traits, it could have arisen because both are linked with a parental emphasis on cleanliness and order. In such a case, a simple learning-theory explanation— parental reinforcement and the child's modeling of the parents—would be a more economical explanation of the adult traits than the psychoanalytic hypothesis.

This outcome should also remind us that Freud based his theory on observations of a very narrow range of people—primarily upper-middle-class men and women in Victorian Vienna who suffered from neurotic symptoms. In hindsight, many of Freud's cultural biases are now obvious, particularly in his theories about women. For example, his theory that female psychosexual development is shaped largely by "penis envy"—a girl's feelings of inadequacy because she doesn't have a penis—is almost universally rejected as reflecting the sex bias of Freud and the historical period in which he lived. A little girl's personality development during the Victorian era was surely shaped more decisively by her awareness that she lacked the greater independence, power, and social status of her brother than by her envy of his penis.

Despite these criticisms, however, the remarkable feature of Freud's theory is how well it did manage to transcend its narrow observational base. For example, many experimental studies of the defense mechanisms and reactions to conflict have supported the theory in contexts quite different from those in which Freud developed the theory (for example, Erdelyi, 1985; Holmes, 1974; Blum, 1953; Sears, 1944; 1943.)

In general, the structural theory (ego, id, and superego), the psychosexual theory, and the energy concept have not fared well over the years. Even some psychoanalytic writers are prepared to abandon or to modify them substantially (for example, Schafer, 1976; Kline, 1972;). On the other hand, Freud's dynamic theory—his theory of anxiety and the mechanisms of defense—has withstood the test of time, research, and observation. There is a continuing interest in reformulating psychoanalytic theory in more testable terms and subjecting it to further experimental evaluation.

BEHAVIORISTIC APPROACH

In contrast to the psychodynamic approach to personality, the behavioristic approach emphasizes the importance of *environmental,* or *situational,* determinants of behavior. Behavior is the result of a continuous interaction between personal and environmental variables. Environmental conditions shape behavior through learning; a person's behavior, in turn, shapes the environment. Persons and situations influence each other recipro-

cally. To predict behavior, we need to know how the characteristics of the individual interact with the characteristics of the situation (Bandura, 1986). In its contemporary formulation, the behavioristic approach is now called the social-learning approach or the social cognitive approach and is the descendant of behaviorism and its outgrowth, **stimulus-response psychology,** which were dominant in the first half of this century (see Chapter 1 and Appendix I).

SOCIAL LEARNING AND CONDITIONING

OPERANT CONDITIONING The effect of other people—the rewards and punishments they provide—is an important influence on an individual's behavior. Accordingly, one of the most basic principles of social-learning theory is **operant conditioning** and the processes related to it that we discussed in Chapter 7. The basic tenet of social-learning theory is that people behave in ways that are likely to produce reinforcement, and individual differences in behavior result primarily from differences in the kinds of learning experiences a person encounters in the course of growing up.

Although individuals learn many behavior patterns through direct experience, by being rewarded or punished for behaving in a certain manner, they also acquire many responses through observational learning. People can learn by observing the actions of others and by noting the consequences of those actions. It would be a slow and inefficient process indeed if all of our behavior had to be learned through the direct reinforcement of our responses. Similarly, the reinforcement that controls the expression of learned behaviors may be direct (tangible rewards, social approval or disapproval, or alleviation of aversive conditions), vicarious (observation of someone receiving reward or punishment for behavior similar to one's own), or self-administered (evaluation of one's own performance with self-praise or self-reproach).

Because most social behaviors are not uniformly rewarded in all settings, the individual learns to discriminate the contexts in which certain behavior is appropriate and those in which it is not. To the extent that a person is rewarded for the same response in many different situations, **generalization** takes place, ensuring that the same behavior will occur in a variety of settings. Thus, a boy who is reinforced for physical aggression at home, as well as at school and at play, is likely to develop a personality that is pervasively aggressive. More often, aggressive responses are differentially rewarded, and learned discriminations determine the situations in which the individual will display aggression (for example, aggression is acceptable on the football field but not in the classroom). For this reason, social-learning theorists challenge the usefulness of characterizing persons with trait terms like "aggressive," arguing that such terms obscure the cross-situational variability of behavior, a challenge to which we will return later.

CLASSICAL CONDITIONING   Operant conditioning and its related processes apply to **behavior,** the major focus of social-learning approaches. To account for **emotion** or *affect,* social-learning theorists add classical conditioning to their account of personality (see Chapter 7). For example, when a child is punished by a parent for engaging in some forbidden activity, the punishment elicits the physiological responses that we associate with guilt or anxiety. Subsequently, the child's behavior may itself elicit those same responses; he or she will feel guilty when engaging in the forbidden behavior. In the terminology of classical conditioning, we would say that the behavior becomes a **conditioned stimulus** by being paired with the **unconditioned stimulus** of punishment; the anxiety becomes the **conditioned response.** For the social-learning theorist, it is classical conditioning that produces the internalized source of anxiety that Freud labeled the superego. Like operant conditioning, classical conditioning can also operate vicariously and can generalize to stimuli that have not been directly conditioned.

COGNITIVE VARIABLES   Social-learning theory has come a long way from its roots in early radical behaviorism, which explicitly avoided any reference to internal cognitive processes. As early as 1954, Julian Rotter was introducing cognitive variables into the behavioristic approach (1954, 1982), and Albert Bandura, one of the leading contemporary theorists in this area, even calls his version of the approach

social *cognitive* theory. His theory emphasizes *reciprocal determinism,* in which external determinants of behavior (such as rewards and punishments) and internal determinants (such as beliefs, thoughts, and expectations) are part of a system of interacting influences that affect both behavior and other parts of the system (1986).

INDIVIDUAL DIFFERENCES   We noted earlier that personality psychology seeks to specify both the variables on which individuals differ from one another and the general processes of personality functioning. Trait approaches have focused on the first task, describing personality differences in detail while saying virtually nothing about the general dynamic processes of personality functioning. Psychoanalytic theory has attempted to do both. In contrast, the social-learning approach has focused primarily on process, with little attention devoted to describing individual differences. Because the approach sees every individual's personality as the unique product of an idiosyncratic reinforcement history and emphasizes the degree to which behavior varies across situations, it has not attempted to classify individuals into types or to rate them on traits. But social-learning theorist Walter Mischel has attempted to incorporate individual differences into social learning theory by introducing the following set of cognitive variables:

1. *Competencies: What can you do?* Competencies include intellectual abilities, social and physical skills, other special abilities.

2. *Encoding strategies: How do you see it?* People differ in the way they selectively attend to information, encode (represent) events, and group the information into meaningful categories. An event perceived by one person as threatening may be seen by another as challenging.

3. *Expectancies: What will happen?* Expectations about the consequences of different behaviors will guide the individual's choice of behavior. If you cheat on an examination and are caught, what do you expect the consequences to be? If you tell your friend what you really think of him or her, what will happen to

your relationship? Expectations about our own abilities will also influence behavior: We may anticipate the consequences of a certain behavior but fail to act because we are uncertain of our ability to execute the behavior.

4. *Subjective values: What is it worth?* Individuals who have similar expectancies may choose to behave differently because they assign different values to the outcomes. Two students may expect a certain behavior to please their professor; however, this outcome is important to one student but not to the other.

5. *Self-regulatory systems and plans:* How can you achieve it? People differ in the standards and rules they adopt for regulating their behavior (including self-imposed rewards for success or punishments for failure), as well as in their ability to make realistic plans for reaching a goal. (After Mischel, 1993, 1973)

All of these person variables (sometimes referred to as cognitive social-learning person variables) interact with the conditions of a particular situation to determine what an individual will do in that situation.

RESEARCH METHODS

Because of their primary focus on behavior and its situational determinants, psychologists who take a social-learning approach to personality have developed several methods for recording behavior in naturalistic settings. One group of researchers has constructed an elaborate electronic system for recording the behavior of children in free-play settings. By holding down buttons on a console, a single observer is able to record up to 12 categories of behavior simultaneously (for example, "talking," "sitting"). The continuous record of behavior is sufficiently precise to enable researchers to relate even small changes in a child's behavior to events and to other children's behavior in the situation (Lovaas, Freitag, Gold, & Kassorla, 1965). Another research program has developed ingenious methods for recording the detailed interactions between highly aggressive children and their family members in everyday settings like the dinner table (Patterson, 1976).

Many behavioral assessments are conducted in conjunction with therapeutic techniques based on social-learning principles (see Chapter 16). In one study of height phobia, fear of heights was assessed by measuring the distance that individuals would climb on a fire escape. After receiving therapy, they were assessed again by having them take an elevator to a roof garden and attempt to count passing cars below for 2 minutes (Lazarus, 1961).

Individuals are often assessed by training them to be self-observers. For example, individuals in behavioral therapy are often asked to keep daily diaries of their activities in order to help the therapist pinpoint sources of anxiety. One study of adolescents provided each subject with an electronic paging device. Whenever they were beeped by the experimenter during the day, they stopped whatever they were doing and filled out a form, recording their current activity and their current level of self-esteem (Savin-Williams & Jaquish, 1981).

As psychologists who take a social-learning approach have become more cognitive in recent years, they have also begun to measure cognitions relevant to behavior, such as expectancies. In one study, patients who had suffered heart attacks were given a list of daily situations that might cause emotional strain (such as complaining to an unsympathetic sales person about poor service) and were asked to indicate whether they thought they could manage the situation and, if so, to rate

"Leave us alone! I am a behavior therapist! I am helping my patient overcome a fear of heights!"

how confident they felt about doing so (Bandura et al., 1985). And finally, social-learning researchers have occasionally recorded physiological variables in order to assess ongoing emotional reactions to situations.

THE CONSISTENCY PARADOX

By emphasizing the situational influences on human behavior, the social-learning approach has persistently challenged the common assumption that persons display cross-situational consistencies in their behavior. This assumption is so embedded in our thinking that it is practically synonymous with our definition of personality and lies behind the notion that we all possess personality traits. Although the assumption is most explicit in trait theories of personality, it is also present in psychoanalytic theory. For example, even when overt behaviors appear inconsistent—as when a mother who resents her child shows hostility on one day and exaggerated love and concern the next—psychoanalytic theory assumes that a consistent unconscious motivation produces both behaviors.

But dissenting voices were heard as long ago as the sixteenth century, when the French essayist Michel de Montaigne wrote an essay titled "Of the Inconsistency of Our Actions." In it, he sounded very much like a contemporary behaviorist in his insistence that the situation ("neighboring circumstances") determines behavior:

> In view of the natural instability of our conduct, it has often seemed to me that even good authors are wrong to insist on weaving a consistent and solid fabric out of us. . . . He who would judge [us] in detail and distinctly, bit by bit would more often hit upon the truth. . . . The surest thing, in my opinion, would be to trace [our actions] to the neighboring circumstances without getting into any further research and without drawing from them any other conclusions. (1580/1943, pp. 118, 120)

The consistency issue was first addressed empirically 65 years ago, when a series of studies explicitly set out to assess consistency across situations. The best known of these studies was the classic investigation of character by Hartshorne and May in the late 1920s. They gave 11,000 elementary and high school students a large number of behavioral tests designed to measure the traits of altru-

ism, self-control, and honesty in a number of different situations—at home, in the classroom, during athletic competition, and in church. To test honesty, for instance, the children were placed in situations where they had a chance to be dishonest while believing they would not be detected—to keep some of the money they were given to play with, to cheat on a test, to report falsely about the number of push-ups they could do, or the amount of work done at home. The correlations among behaviors in the different situations turned out to be quite low. For example, the average correlation between any two tests used to measure honesty was only .23. These low correlations led Hartshorne and May to conclude that neither honesty nor dishonesty is a unified character trait; behavior is specific to the situation (Hartshorne & May, 1929).

The debate was reactivated some 40 years later by Walter Mischel (1968). After reviewing additional studies that had accumulated since the Hartshorne-May inquiry, Mischel also concluded that people are quite variable in their behavior across situations. He reported that correlations between measures of the same trait in two different situations were quite low in most studies—typically less than .30. Similarly, correlations between trait measures on personality tests and actual behavioral observations of the same traits in real situations were also low. (Mischel, 1968).

The paradox that sustains the debate and accounts for its historical durability is this: Our intuitions tell us that individuals are consistent; the research tells us that they are not. Intuitions or research? Which one is wrong?

Recent research in social psychology lends some support to those who believe that our intuitions about consistency might be wrong (see the Critical Discussion, Six Reasons Why Our Intuitions About Consistency Are Wrong). Nevertheless, personality psychologists have responded to this challenge in several ways, proposing alternative "solutions" to the consistency paradox. We shall look at three of them here.

AGGREGATION SOLUTION   The first solution to the consistency paradox is essentially a methodological argument against the studies that show low cross-situational correlations. In discussing test construction in Chapter 12,

Six Reasons Why Our Intuitions About Consistency Are Wrong

Research by social psychologists on the processes of social inference has revealed a number of biases and shortcomings in our abilities to draw valid judgments from the data of everyday experience. (We discuss some of these in Chapter 17.) This research suggests that there are a number of plausible reasons why our intuitions might be in error about consistency. Here are six:

1. Our preconceived notions of how people behave may lead us to generalize beyond our actual observations. We may fill in the missing data according to our implicit personality theories of which traits and behaviors go together. Moreover, research shows that when we expect two behaviors to be correlated, we tend to see them as correlated even when they are not. Stereotypes of how a gay person, a librarian, or an athlete behaves may cause us to attribute greater consistency to a person's actions than actual observations warrant.

2. Many features of an individual remain fairly constant—physical appearance, manner of speaking, expressive gestures, and so on. These constancies help to create an impression that the personality is consistent as well.

3. Our presence can cause people to behave in certain ways. Thus, our acquaintances may appear to behave consistently because we are present as a stimulus during every observation we make. They may behave quite differently when we are not there.

4. Because the actions of another person are such a salient feature of any scene, we tend to

Because we see Tom Brokaw so frequently, we mistakenly assume we know how he would behave in other situations.

overestimate the extent to which behavior is caused by personality characteristics and underestimate the importance of situational forces that may cause the person to act as he or she does. If we observe someone behaving aggressively, we assume that the person has an aggressive disposition and will behave similarly in other settings, even though the situational factors may be quite different. This tendency to underestimate situational influences on behavior has been called the **fundamental attribution error** (see Chapter 17).

5. The set of situations in which we observe most individuals is usually more limited than we realize. For example, we are so familiar with the warm, sincere personalities of the network news anchors on the national nightly newscasts that we would be shocked if we learned that one of them cheated on a spouse or kicked the family poodle. Because we see them so often, we mistakenly assume that we also see them in a variety of situations. As a result we feel we

know them well and readily generalize about their behavior, assuming a consistency that is unwarranted. This example is particularly telling, because the behavior of news anchors is so severely constrained and so situationally determined that it could not possibly convey very much about their personalities. If they deviated even slightly from their prescribed role—if they uttered an obscenity or stood up to stretch, for example—they would soon be off the air.

6. Our language entices us to think about human behavior in trait terms. As we noted in Chapter 12, there are about 18,000 trait terms in our language, nearly 5 percent of the entire lexicon. In contrast, we have an impoverished and awkward vocabulary for labeling situations. But language is not only a cause of how we think, it is also the result of how we think. The fact that our language is so unbalanced in this way probably indicates that we have always found it more important to classify persons rather than situations.

we noted that as the number of items on a test increases, the reliability of the entire test increases. For example, the correlation between any two items on the Wechsler Adult Intelligence Scale (WAIS) is only about .16. Clearly it would be absurd to expect an individual's answer to a single item to correlate with his or her intelligence in nontest situations; in other words, a one-item test would have virtually no validity. But because many such items are summed or aggregated on the WAIS, the reliability of the total test score is .96, and its validity—its correlation with many nontest behaviors—is quite impressive.

Now consider the studies that find little cross-situational consistency in behavior. Most are based on only one or two measures of behavior. For example, a typical study may try to relate helpfulness in one situation (giving money to charity) with helpfulness in another (coming to the aid of a person in distress). This is analogous to trying to correlate one item on the WAIS with one of the other items. Low correlations should be expected. Other studies may correlate an individual's score on a scale measuring aggression with an aggressive behavior in a laboratory experiment. Because the aggression scale is an aggregate of many items, it is probably reliable, but the likely unreliability of the single laboratory measure of aggression is rarely considered and almost never actually assessed.

In other words, a more accurate estimate of cross-situational consistency would be obtained if investigators combined several behavioral measures of the same trait to arrive at an **aggregated score**, just as they have always done with their tests. For example, much higher correlations are found in the Hartshorne and May study when aggregated scores are used. When the children's aggregated scores on half of the honesty tests are correlated with those on the other half of the tests, the correlation is .72. This is much higher than the average correlation of .23 between any two tests for honesty and indicates considerable consistency (Rushton, Jackson, & Paunonen, 1981).

The method of aggregation can also be used to demonstrate the stability of traits over time. In one study, observers followed people for 4 weeks and rated them on variables related to their sociability or their tendency to be impulsive. Although the correlations for any 2 days were quite low, the ratings averaged over the first 14 days correlated .81 with the ratings averaged over the second 14 days (Epstein, 1977). Thus, it appears that we can find considerable consistency in traits, given a large enough sample of behavior.

The aggregation solution also resolves another paradox. In Chapter 12, we reported impressive continuities between childhood personality characteristics (such as ill-temperedness and dependency) and adult outcomes 30 years later (such as occupational status and marital stability). But how can this be so if behaviors are not even consistent across situations measured within days of each other? The answer is that the childhood personality characteristics comprised aggregated observations over 3 years and the adult outcomes similarly reflected the consequences of many aggregated behaviors. We cannot predict whether a boy who has a tantrum one day when he is 10 will have a fight with his wife one day when he is 40. But we can predict from the sum of his tantrums over three years in late childhood to a divorce precipitated by several adult years of marital strife.

PERSON-CENTERED SOLUTION   The second proposed solution to the consistency paradox is a conceptual one that argues that our intuitions capture the reality of personality more faithfully than does the research (Bem, 1983; Bem & Allen, 1974). It is an extension of the personality psychology of Gordon Allport, an influential trait theorist who died in 1967. Allport argued that the usual trait approach in which individuals are compared with one another on a common set of traits failed to capture a person's individuality and that the focus should be instead on the unique patterning or configuration of traits within the individual. The important differences among individuals are not expressed in terms of where they stand on a common set of traits but in terms of *which* traits centrally organize their individual personalities.

We shall refer to the first strategy as the *trait-centered approach* and Allport's strategy as the *person-centered approach*. The important difference between the two approaches is illustrated by Allport's response to the findings of Hartshorne and May that the children they observed in their study were not consistently honest or dishonest across situations. He noted that the low correlations "prove only that children are not consistent *in the same way,* not that they are inconsistent with themselves" (1937, p. 250). What did he mean by this?

Consider the two behaviors of lying and stealing, which were relatively uncorrelated in the study. One child may lie in order to avoid hurting the feelings of the teacher, but another may steal pennies in order to buy social acceptance from his or her peers. The first child might be consistently empathic and sensitive across situations, the second child consistently insecure about acceptance across situations. But for neither of these two children do the behaviors of lying and stealing belong together in a common category representing an honesty-dishonesty dimension. Honesty and dishonesty are categories in the head of the investigator, not categories that capture the coherence of either of these children's behaviors. If Hartshorne and May had measured empathy and sensitivity across situations, the first child would have shown up as consistent; if they had measured insecurity across situations, the second child would have shown up as consistent. As Allport said, the children are not inconsistent with themselves; they are only inconsistent with the investigator's theory that lying and stealing represent "the same thing." This, according to Allport, is the fallacy of the trait-centered approach to personality.

In contrast, our intuitions appear to follow the person-centered strategy. Consider how we approach the task of describing a friend. We do not invoke a fixed set of trait terms that we apply to everyone. Instead, we first review our friend's behavior and then select a small set of traits that strike us as pertinent *precisely because* they seem to conform to the consistent patterns in our friend's behavior.

If Dick always does his schoolwork early, is meticulous about his personal appearance, and is always punctual, it may well occur to us to describe him as conscientious. In contrast, if Jane is always conscientious about her schoolwork but sloppy about her appearance and never punctual, we may well describe her as a workaholic who has time for little else. The important point is that we are not likely to characterize her as someone who is inconsistently conscientious. That is, we do not first impose a trait term—"conscientious"—on her and then judge her to be

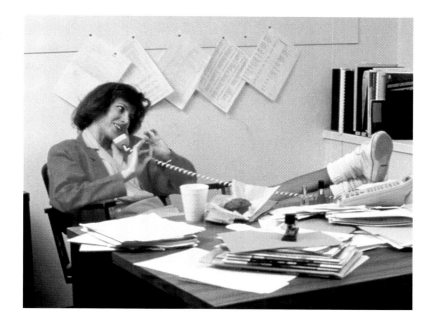

A person who is neat in one area, such as personal appearance, may not be neat in others. Nevertheless, our intuitions are not likely to see the person as inconsistent.

inconsistent. Instead, we first attempt to discern a recognizable consistent pattern to her behaviors and only then to put a label on that pattern.

This, then, is the essence of our intuitive approach to personality, and the person-centered approach argues that in terms of the underlying logic and fidelity to reality, our intuitions about consistency are right; the research, wrong (Bem 1983; Bem & Allen, 1974).

INTERACTIONAL SOLUTION   The interactional solution to the consistency paradox reflects the more general recognition by personality psychologists that behavior is a function of the interaction between the person and the situation. In Chapter 12, we described three forms of interaction through which situations become a function of the individual's personality. First, we do not react simply to the objective features of situations but to our subjective interpretations of them (*reactive interaction*). Second, our personalities evoke distinctive responses from others (*evocative interaction*).

The third process—the one that is most pertinent to the consistency paradox—is *proactive interaction:* Our personalities lead us to seek out some situations and to avoid others. A domineering person will seek out confrontations; a submissive person will avoid them. Moreover, once in a situation, we will seek to shape it to be compatible with our

An abrasive person will both provoke others to be abrasive in return (evocative interaction) and seek out (or create) abrasive confrontations (proactive interaction).

personality: The sociable student will suggest moving the seminar to the lawn or the local hangout. Proactive interaction produces cross-situational consistencies in behavior because we intentionally select and create situations in which we can behave in ways most comfortable for us and we selectively avoid situations in which we might behave differently—in ways that are inconsistent with our personalities.

This analysis has implications for the methods psychologists use to study personality. The hallmark of the experimental laboratory is the control of conditions: Subjects assigned to the same condition must interpret it in the same way if valid inferences are to be drawn. Moreover, subjects should be randomly assigned to conditions. But if individuals differ from one another primarily in their interpretations of situations, in the characteristic responses they evoke from others in situations, and in their proactive selection and shaping of situations, then psychologists who use only the laboratory to study personality will never see its major manifestations. Everyday life does not randomly assign us to conditions (Ross & Nisbett, 1991).

BEHAVIORISTIC PORTRAIT OF HUMAN NATURE

Like the psychoanalytic approach, the behavioristic approach to personality is very deterministic. In contrast to the psychoanalytic approach, however, it pays very little attention to biological determinants of behavior and focuses exclusively on environmental determinants. It has also been strongly influenced by the ideas of Darwin. Just as evolution works through natural selection to shape the species to be adaptive to its ecology, so the processes of learning—especially operant conditioning—shape the individual's behavioral repertoire to be adaptive to his or her environment. Inherently, we are neither good nor evil, but extraordinarily modifiable by environmental experiences in our personal histories and contemporary situational circumstances. As we noted in Chapter 3, John Watson, founder of the behaviorist movement in the United States, claimed that he could raise an infant to be anything, regardless of the infant's "talents, penchants, tendencies, abilities, vocations, and race of his [or her] ancestors."

Few social-learning theorists would take such an extreme view today. Nevertheless, social-learning theory shares with its behavioristic predecessors a strong optimism about our ability to change human behavior by changing the environment. Such a view is nicely congruent with American pragmatism and American ideology about equality, so it is not surprising that behaviorism was popular in the United States. Interestingly, the former Soviet Union—whose communist ideology also emphasized equality—has always shared America's view that human behavior is quite modifiable by the environment. Thus, it is not accidental that both these societies have embraced a conditioning-based view of human behavior (the Soviet Union was the birthplace of Pavlov and classical conditioning). In contrast, more traditional, class-based societies like England and Germany have produced Charles Darwin, ethologists and trait theorists—all of whom see human personality as more fixed by biology.

Even though the human personality that emerges from the social-learning approach is modifiable, it still has a passive quality to it. We still seem to be shaped primarily by forces beyond our control. This portrait is changing, however, as social-learning approaches increasingly emphasize the individual's active role in selecting and modifying the environment, thereby permitting the person to become a causal force in his or her own life. As we shall see, however, this is still not sufficiently active for the humanistic theorists. In particular, they do not believe that it is sufficient to define psychological health merely as optimal adaptation to the environment.

EVALUATION OF BEHAVIORISTIC APPROACH

Through its emphasis on specifying the environmental variables that evoke specific behaviors, social-learning theory has made a major contribution to both clinical psychology and personality theory. It has led us to see human actions as reactions to specific environments, and it has helped us to focus on the way in which environments control our behavior and how they can be changed to modify behavior. As we will see in Chapter 16, the systematic application of learning principles has proved successful in changing many maladaptive behaviors.

Social-learning theorists have been criticized for overemphasizing the importance of situational influences on behavior and thus losing the person in personality psychology (Carlson, 1971), and there is still some merit in this criticism despite the recent cognitive processes and variables that have been incorporated into the theories. But the debate initiated by the social-learning theorists over the cross-situational consistency of personality has forced other personality psychologists to reexamine their fundamental assumptions. As a result, personality psychologists have emerged with a clearer understanding of the interactions between persons and situations and an enhanced appreciation of each person's individuality.

PHENOMENOLOGICAL APPROACH

The phenomenological approach to the study of personality focuses on the individual's *subjective experience*—his or her personal view of the world. Phenomenological theories differ from the theories we have discussed so far in that they generally are not concerned with the person's motivational or reinforcement history or with predicting behavior. They focus instead on how the individual perceives and interprets events in his or her current environment; that is, the focus is on the individual's **phenomenology**. Among the subvarieties of the phenomenological approach, the most central is *humanistic psychology*.

HUMANISTIC PSYCHOLOGY

During the first half of this century, the psychoanalytic and behavioristic approaches were dominant in psychology. In 1962, a group of psychologists founded the Association of Humanistic Psychology. They offered **humanistic psychology** as a "third force," an explicit set of alternative assumptions and concerns to those that characterized the other two approaches. To define its mission, the association adopted a set of four principles:

1. *The experiencing person is of primary interest.* Humans are not simply objects of study. They must be described and understood in terms of their own subjective views of the world, their perceptions of self, and their feelings of self-worth. The central question each person must face is "Who am I?" In order to learn how the individual attempts to answer this question, the psychologist must become a partner with the individual in the quest for existential meaning.

2. *Human choice, creativity, and self-actualization are the preferred topics of investigation.* Humanistic psychologists reject the psychoanalytic approach, believing that a psychology based on crippled personalities could only produce a crippled psychology. They also reject behaviorism, a psychology devoid of consciousness derived primarily from the study of lower organisms. People are not simply motivated by basic drives like sex or aggression or physiological needs like hunger and thirst. They have a need to develop their potentials and capabilities. Growth and self-actualization should be the criteria of psychological health, not merely ego control or adjustment to the environment.

3. *Meaningfulness must precede objectivity in the selection of research problems.* The humanistic psychologists believe that too often psychological research is guided by the methods available rather

than by the importance of the problems to be investigated. They argue that we should study important human and social problems, even if that sometimes means adopting less rigorous methods. And while psychologists should strive to be objective in collecting and interpreting observations, their choice of research topics can and should be guided by values. In this sense, research is not value-free; values are not something psychologists should pretend not to have or feel they have to apologize for.

4. *Ultimate value is placed on the dignity of the person.* Persons are basically good. The objective of psychology is to understand, not to predict or control people. Even referring to them as "subjects" is considered by many humanistic psychologists to degrade their dignity as full partners in the quest for understanding human personality.

Psychologists who share the values of the association come from diverse theoretical backgrounds. For example, the trait theorist Gordon Allport was also a humanistic psychologist, and we have already pointed out that several psychoanalysts such as Carl Jung, Alfred Adler, and Erik Erikson held humanistic views of motivation that diverged

from Freud's views. But it is Carl Rogers and Abraham Maslow whose theoretical views lie at the center of the humanistic movement.

CARL ROGERS   Like Freud, Carl Rogers (1902–1987) developed his theory from his work with patients or clients in the clinic (Rogers, 1951, 1959, 1963, 1970). Rogers was impressed with what he saw as the individual's innate tendency to move in the direction of growth, maturity, and positive change. He came to believe that the basic force motivating the human organism is the actualizing tendency—a tendency toward fulfillment or actualization of all the capacities of the organism. A growing organism seeks to fulfill its potential within the limits of its heredity. A person may not always clearly perceive which actions lead to growth and which actions are regressive. But once the course is clear, the individual chooses to grow rather than to regress. Rogers did not deny that there are other needs, some of them biological, but he saw them as subservient to the organism's motivation to enhance itself.

Rogers' belief in the primacy of actualization forms the basis of his nondirective or **client-centered therapy.** This method of psychotherapy assumes that every individual has the motivation and ability to change and that the individual is the person best qualified to decide on the direction that such change should take. The therapist's role is to act as a sounding board while the individual explores and analyzes his or her problems. This approach differs from psychoanalytic therapy, during which the therapist analyzes the patient's history to determine the problem and devise a course of remedial action. (See Chapter 16 for a discussion of various approaches to psychotherapy.)

THE SELF   The central concept in Rogers' theory of personality is the *self.* The self, or **self-concept** (Rogers uses the terms interchangeably), became the cornerstone of his theory. The self consists of all the ideas, perceptions, and values that characterize "I" or "me"; it includes the awareness of "what I am" and "what I can do." This perceived self, in turn, influences both the person's perception of the world and his or her behavior. For example, a woman who perceives herself as strong and competent perceives and acts upon the world quite differently from a woman who considers

Carl Rogers Writing on the Phenomenological Approach
"The best vantage point for understanding behavior is from the internal frame of reference of the individual himself.
"The organism has one basic tendency and striving—to actualize, maintain, and enhance the experiencing organism.
"When the individual perceives and accepts into one consistent and integrated system all his sensory and visceral experiences, then he is necessarily more understanding of others and is more accepting of others as separate individuals."
(Rogers, 1951)

herself weak and ineffectual. The self-concept does not necessarily reflect reality: A person may be highly successful and respected but still view himself or herself as a failure.

According to Rogers, the individual evaluates every experience in relation to this self-concept. People want to behave in ways that are consistent with their self-image; experiences and feelings that are not consistent are threatening and may be denied admittance to consciousness. This is essentially Freud's concept of repression, although Rogers felt that such repression is neither necessary nor permanent. (Freud would say that repression is inevitable and that some aspects of the individual's experiences always remain unconscious.)

The more areas of experience that a person denies because they are inconsistent with his or her self-concept, the wider the gulf between the self and reality and the greater the potential for maladjustment. An individual whose self-concept is incongruent with personal feelings and experiences must defend himself or herself against the truth because the truth will result in anxiety. If the incongruence becomes too great, the defenses may break down, resulting in severe anxiety or other forms of emotional disturbance. The well-adjusted person, in contrast, has a self-concept that is consistent with thought, experience, and behavior; the self is not rigid, but flexible, and can change as it assimilates new experiences and ideas.

The other self in Rogers' theory is the *ideal* self. We all have a conception of the kind of person we would like to be. The closer the ideal self is to the real self, the more fulfilled and happy the individual becomes. A large discrepancy between the ideal self and the real self results in an unhappy, dissatisfied person.

Thus, two kinds of incongruence can develop: one, between the self and the experiences of reality; the other, between the self and the ideal self. Rogers had some hypotheses about how these incongruences may develop.

In particular, Rogers believed that people are likely to become more fully functioning if they are brought up with *unconditional positive regard*. This means that they feel themselves valued by parents and others even when their feelings, attitudes, and behaviors are less than ideal. If parents offer only condi-

tional positive regard—valuing the child only when he or she behaves, thinks, or feels correctly—the child is likely to distort his or her self-concept. For example, feelings of competition and hostility toward a younger sibling are natural, but parents disapprove of hitting a baby brother or sister and usually punish such actions. Children must somehow integrate this experience into their self-concept. They may decide that they are bad and so may feel ashamed. They may decide that their parents do not like them and so may feel rejected. Or they may deny their feelings and decide they do not want to hit the baby. Each of these attitudes contains a distortion of the truth. The third alternative is the easiest for children to accept, but in so doing, they deny their real feelings, which then become unconscious. The more people are forced to deny their own feelings and to accept the values of others, the more uncomfortable they will feel about themselves. Rogers suggested that the best approach is for the parents to recognize the child's feelings as valid while explaining the reasons why hitting is not acceptable.

MEASURING REAL-IDEAL SELF-CONGRUENCE   In Chapter 12, we described a method of assessment called the Q-sort technique, in which a rater or sorter is given a set of cards, each containing a personality statement (for example, "Is cheerful") and is asked to describe an individual's personality by sorting the cards into piles. The rater places statements that are least descriptive of the individual in a pile on the left and those that are most descriptive in a pile on the right. The other statements are distributed in the intermediate piles, thereby assigning each Q item a score corresponding to the pile in which it is placed. Two Q sorts can be compared with each other by computing a correlation between their item scores, thereby assessing the degree to which the two sorts are similar to one another.

Carl Rogers pioneered the use of the Q sort as an instrument for examining the self-concept. Rogers' Q set contains statements like "I am satisfied with myself"; "I have a warm emotional relationship with others"; and "I don't trust my emotions." In Rogers' procedure, individuals first sort themselves as they actually are—their *real self*—and then sort themselves as they would like to be—their *ideal self*. The correlation between the two sorts indexes the self-ideal discrepancy. A low or negative correlation corresponds to a large *self-ideal discrepancy,* implying feelings of low self-esteem and lack of personal worth.

By repeating this procedure several times during the course of therapy, Rogers could assess the effectiveness of therapy. In one study, correlations between self and ideal Q sorts of individuals seeking therapy averaged −.01 prior to therapy, but increased to +.34 following therapy. Correlations for a matched control group not receiving therapy did not change (Butler & Haigh, 1954). In other words, the therapy had significantly reduced these individuals' perception of the discrepancy between their real selves and their ideal selves. Note that this could occur in two ways: An individual could change his or her concept of the real self so that it is closer to the ideal self or change the concept of the ideal self so that it is more realistic. Therapy can produce changes of both kinds.

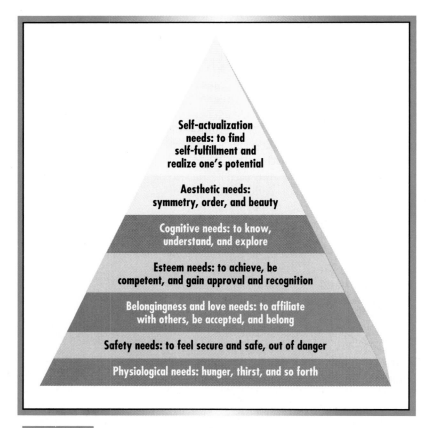

FIGURE 13-2

Maslow's Hierarchy of Needs   *Needs that are low in the hierarchy must be at least partially satisfied before needs that are higher in the hierarchy become important sources of motivation.* (After Maslow, 1970)

ABRAHAM MASLOW   The psychology of Abraham Maslow (1908–1970) overlaps with that of Carl Rogers in many ways. Maslow was first attracted to behaviorism and carried out studies in primate sexuality and dominance. He was already moving away from behaviorism when his first child was born, after which he remarked that anyone who observes a baby cannot be a behaviorist. He was influenced by psychoanalysis, but eventually became critical of its theory of motivation and developed his own. Specifically, he proposed that there is a **hierarchy of needs,** ascending from the basic biological needs to the more complex psychological motivations that become important only after the basic needs have been satisfied (see Figure 13-2). The needs at one level must be at least partially satisfied before those at the next level become important determiners of action. When food and safety are difficult to obtain, the satisfaction of those needs will dominate a person's actions and higher motives are of little significance. Only when basic needs can be satisfied easily will the individual have the time and energy to devote to aesthetic and intellectual interests. Artistic and scientific endeavors do not flourish in societies in which people must struggle for food, shelter, and safety. The highest motive—**self-actualization**—can be fulfilled only after all other needs are fulfilled.

Maslow decided to study *self-actualizers*—men and women who had made extraordinary use of their potential. He began by studying the lives of eminent historical figures such as Spinoza, Thomas Jefferson, Abraham Lincoln, Jane Addams, Albert Einstein, and Eleanor Roosevelt. In this way, he was able to create a composite picture of a self-actualizer. The distinguishing characteristics of such persons are listed in Table 13-1, along with some of the behaviors that Maslow believed could lead to self-actualization.

Maslow extended his study to a population of college students. Selecting students who fit his definition of self-actualizers, Maslow found this group to be in the healthiest 1 percent of the population; these students showed no signs of maladjustment and were making effective use of their talents and capabilities (Maslow, 1970).

Many people experience transient moments of self-actualization, which Maslow called *peak experiences*. A peak experience is an experience of being characterized by hap-

Martin Luther King fulfilled Maslow's criteria for a self-actualizer.

Eleanor Roosevelt was one of Maslow's examples of a self-actualizer.

piness and fulfillment—a temporary, non-striving, nonself-centered state of perfection and goal attainment. Peak experiences may occur in different intensities and in various contexts: creative activities, appreciation of nature, intimate relationships with others, parental experiences, aesthetic perceptions, or athletic participation. After asking a large number of college students to describe any experience that came close to being a peak experience, Maslow attempted to summarize their responses. They spoke of wholeness, perfection, aliveness, uniqueness, effort-lessness, self-sufficiency, and the values of beauty, goodness, and truth.

PERSONAL CONSTRUCT THEORY

George Kelly (1905–1966) was one of the first personality psychologists to give cognitive processes a central role in an individual's functioning. Whereas humanistic psychologists are concerned with how individuals feel about themselves and their personal worth, Kelly's **personal construct theory** takes a more cognitive approach to the individual's phenomenology. Kelly objected that personality psychologists typically characterized an individual on dimensions that they themselves had constructed; he believed that the goal should be to discover instead the dimensions that individuals themselves use to interpret or to *construe* themselves and their

social worlds. These dimensions are the individual's own **personal constructs**, and they constitute the basic units of analysis in Kelly's theory (1955).

CHARACTERISTICS OF SELF-ACTUALIZERS

Perceive reality efficiently and are able to tolerate uncertainty
Accept themselves and others for what they are
Spontaneous in thought and behavior
Problem-centered rather than self-centered
Have a good sense of humor
Highly creative
Resistant to enculturation, although not purposely unconventional
Concerned for the welfare of humanity
Capable of deep appreciation of the basic experiences of life
Establish deep, satisfying interpersonal relationships with a few, rather than many, people
Able to look at life from an objective viewpoint

BEHAVIORS LEADING TO SELF-ACTUALIZATION

Experience life as a child does, with full absorption and concentration
Try something new rather than sticking to secure and safe ways
Listen to your own feelings in evaluating experiences rather than to the voice of tradition or authority or the majority
Be honest; avoid pretenses or "game playing"
Be prepared to be unpopular if your views do not coincide with those of most people
Assume responsibility
Work hard at whatever you decide to do
Try to identify your defenses and have the courage to give them up

TABLE 13-1

Self-Actualization
Listed are the personal qualities that Maslow found to be characteristic of self-actualizers and the behaviors he considered important to the development of self-actualization. (After Maslow, 1967)

More generally, Kelly believed that individuals should be viewed as intuitive scientists. Like formal scientists, they observe the world, formulate and test hypotheses about it, and make up theories about it. Like the psychologists who study them, human subjects also construe or abstract behavior—categorizing, interpreting, labeling, and judging themselves and their world. And, like scientists, individuals can entertain invalid theories, beliefs that hinder them in daily life and lead them to bias their interpretations of events and persons, including themselves.

In Kelly's view, the purpose of therapy or counseling is to help the person construct more effective interpretations, construals, or theories of the world. If a client claims that he is unable to stand up to authority, the therapist's job is not to determine the truth or falsity of the assertion but to encourage the individual to explore what the implications of viewing himself that way are for his daily life and to consider alternative hypotheses about his behaviors. In order to get clients to construe themselves and their social worlds from different perspectives, Kelly used the technique of role playing. For example, the client who claimed he cannot stand up to authority might be asked to role-play his boss, construing the situation as he thinks his boss might. This often helped clients to interpret their own behaviors differently.

Because typical trait tests of personality do not meet Kelly's basic criterion that an individual must be assessed in his or her own terms, he devised his own test for eliciting a person's personal constructs, the **Role Construct Repertory Test** or "Rep Test." On this test, subjects or clients fill in a matrix or grid like the one shown in Figure 13-3.

Along the top of the grid is a list of people who are important to the individual. These might be supplied by the assessor or the subject, but they usually include "myself" and sometimes include "my ideal self." On each line of the grid, the assessor circles three of the cells. For example, in the first row of the figure, the assessor has circled the cells in the columns labeled "myself," "my mother," and "my best friend." The subject is asked to consider these three people and to place an "X" in the cells of the two people who are most similar to each other but different from the third. As shown in the first row, this (male) subject considers himself and his mother to be the most similar pair. He is then asked, "In what way are you and your mother alike but different from your best friend?" In this case, the subject has indicated that he and his mother are both *witty*. This description is called his *construct*. Next, he is asked "In what way is your friend different from you and your mother?" He has responded that his friend is *humorless*. This description is called his *contrast*. For this subject, then, the dimension *witty–humorless* is one of the personal constructs he uses to interpret or construe his interpersonal world.

Note that a construct–contrast pair need not constitute logical opposites. For example, this subject might have labeled himself and his mother as *witty*, but then labeled his best friend as *serious* or *introverted* or *prefers-to-listen-to-humor-rather-than-to-initiate-it*. If that is how he construes the two poles of the

FIGURE 13-3

Role Construct Repertory Test   *In each row, the subject compares three of the persons listed at the top of the grid, placing an "X" under the two who are most alike. He or she then describes how they are alike by writing in the* construct. *Finally, the subject describes how the third person is different from the other two by writing in the* contrast. *This subject indicates that he sees himself and his mother as both being* witty *and different from his best friend, who is seen as* humorless. *The procedure is repeated for each row in the matrix.*

dimension, then that is what Kelly wanted to know. The Rep Test is designed to assess the individual's constructs, not the psychologist's.

This procedure is repeated with several other triads in the set. By looking at the entire set, the investigator or therapist can explore a number of themes that seem to characterize the individual's construal of the world. For example, some clients will reveal through this procedure that they see the entire world in authoritarian terms; dimensions like *strong–weak, powerful–powerless,* and so forth might appear repeatedly. Or an individual might reveal that she always pairs herself with males on the construct end of dimensions while placing other women on the contrast end.

The Rep Test is a very general procedure and is not restricted to construing persons. For example, an individual may be asked to consider triads of situations or events. (Which two are alike but different from the third? Taking an examination; going out on a blind date; encountering a spider.) The technique has proved valuable both for research on people's constructs and for counseling. There are even specialized mathematical techniques for analyzing the grid and abstracting structural features of the individual's construct system, such as the degree of cognitive complexity it reveals.

PHENOMENOLOGICAL PORTRAIT OF HUMAN NATURE

As a matter of principle, phenomenological psychologists—especially humanistic psychologists—have been quite explicit about the values and philosophical presuppositions that underlie their approach to human personality. The four principles set forth by the Association of Humanistic Psychology, which we summarized earlier, draw sharp contrasts between the humanistic portrait of human personality and the portraits drawn by the psychoanalytic and behavioristic approaches.

Most humanistic psychologists do not dispute that biological and environmental variables can influence behavior, but they emphasize the individual's own role in defining and creating his or her destiny and thereby downplay the kind of determinism characteristic of the other approaches. Individuals are basically good, striving for growth and self-actualization. They are also modifiable and active. Humanistic psychologists set a particularly high criterion for psychological health.

Humanistic psychology prompts a more radical politics than the other orientations. For example, it provided support for the challenge to women's traditional sex-typed roles.

Mere ego control or adaptation to the environment is not sufficient. Only an individual who is growing toward self-actualization can be said to be psychologically healthy. In other words, psychological health is a process, not an end state.

Philosophical positions also have political implications. We pointed out earlier that the philosophical assumptions of behaviorism are quite compatible with American ideology. Its assumption that all humans are created equal and are infinitely modifiable by the environment provides a psychological rationale for politically liberal programs that seek to improve the environments of those who are disadvantaged.

In contrast, humanistic psychology provides support for a much more radical politics. Anything that retards the fulfillment of one's potential—that prevents any human being from becoming all he or she can be—should be challenged. If women in the 1950s were happy and well adjusted to traditional sex roles, the criterion of psychological health defined by behaviorism was satisfied. But from the humanistic perspective, consigning all women to the same role is undesirable—no matter how appropriate that role might be for some women—because it prevents many women from reaching their maximum potential. It is not accidental that the rhetoric of liberation movements—such as women's liberation and gay liberation—echoes the language of humanistic psychology. Betty Friedan's 1963 book, *The Feminine Mystique,* is often credited with initiating the contemporary feminist movement. Friedan criticizes the sexism of Freud and has little good to say about the bland liberalism of behaviorism, but she does have one major hero from the world of psychology: Abraham Maslow.

EVALUATION OF PHENOMENOLOGICAL APPROACH

By focusing on the individual's unique perception and interpretation of events, the phenomenological approach brings the role of private experience back to the study of personality. More than other theories we have discussed, the theories of Rogers and Maslow also concentrate on the whole, healthy person and emphasize a positive, optimistic view of human personality. Moreover, phenomenological psychologists emphasize that they study important problems even if they do not always have rigorous methods for investigating them. They have a point; investigating trivial problems just because one has a convenient method for doing so does little to advance the science of psychology. Moreover, phenomenological psychologists have been increasingly ingenious over the years at devising new methods for assessing self-concepts and conducting studies that treat the individual as an equal partner in the research enterprise. Nevertheless, critics can and do question the quality of the evidence in support of the humanistic claims. For example, to what extent are the characteristics of self-actualizers a consequence of a psychological process called self-actualization and to what extent are they merely reflections of the particular value systems held by Rogers and Maslow? Where, they ask, is the evidence for Maslow's hierarchy of needs?

Phenomenological psychologists are also vulnerable to a criticism that is the mirror image of a criticism they have leveled at Freud. They have criticized Freud for attempting to build a complete theory of personality on observations of neurotic individuals. But critics point out that Rogers, Maslow, and Kelly built their theories on observations of relatively healthy people (mainly college students in the case of Rogers and Kelly). Accordingly, their theories are best suited to well-functioning people who have the luxury of worrying about needs at the top of Maslow's hierarchy. The application of these theories to seriously malfunctioning individuals or to socially, culturally, or economically disadvantaged individuals is less apparent.

And finally, some have even criticized the values espoused by the humanistic theorists. Many observers believe that America already has too obsessive a concern with the individual and too little concern for the welfare of the larger society. A psychology that raises individual self-fulfillment and actualization to the top of the value hierarchy is *too* compatible with American ideology; some critics believe that it even provides a psychological "sanction for selfishness" (Wallach & Wallach, 1983). Although Maslow lists a concern for the welfare of humanity among his characteristics of self-actualizers (see Table 13-1) and some of the self-actualizers identified by Maslow—such as Eleanor Roosevelt—clearly possessed this characteristic, it is conspicuously absent from the hierarchy of needs that is so central to Maslow's formal theory.

BIOLOGICAL-PSYCHOLOGICAL PERSPECTIVES

Freud, who began his career as a neurologist, always believed that someday biological knowledge would ultimately explain the psychological phenomena of personality. In speaking of psychopathology, for example, he asserted that where there is a twisted thought, there is a twisted molecule. Although that day has not yet arrived—and many personality psychologists do not believe that it ever will—biology is playing an increasingly important role in the understanding of personality. For example, many studies have now related brain functioning to the traits of extraversion and neuroticism (Eysenck, 1990). In Chapter 12, we noted how the discipline of behavioral genetics is contributing to our knowledge of the origins of individual differences in personality. In Chapters 15 and 16, on abnormal behavior and methods of therapy, we will see that biological knowledge contributes substantially to the understanding and treatment of psychopathology—just as Freud envisioned. And finally, in Chapter 17, on social cognition and affect, we discuss how the relatively new discipline of sociobiology is generating theory and research on individual and group differences in social and sexual behaviors that are considered to be part of personality psychology.

 CHAPTER SUMMARY

1. *Personality* refers to the distinctive and characteristic patterns of thought, emotion, and behavior that define an individual's personal style of interacting with the physical and social environments. Personality psychology seeks (a) to describe and to explain individual differences, and (b) to synthesize the processes that can influence an individual's interactions with the environment into an integrated account of the total person.

2. Freud's *psychoanalytic theory* holds that many behaviors, including dreams and slips of the tongue, are caused by unconscious motivations. Personality is primarily determined by the biological drives of sex and aggression and by experiences that occur during the first 5 years of life. Freud's theory of *personality structure* views personality as composed of the *id,* the *ego,* and the *superego,* which are often in conflict. The id operates on the *plea-*sure principle, seeking immediate gratification of biological impulses. The ego obeys the *reality principle,* postponing gratification until it can be achieved in socially acceptable ways. The superego (conscience) imposes *moral standards* on the individual. In a well-integrated personality, the ego remains in firm but flexible control over the id and superego; the reality principle governs.

3. Freud's theory of *personality dynamics* proposes that there is a constant amount of psychic energy (*libido*) for each individual. If a forbidden act or impulse is suppressed, its energy will seek an outlet in some other form, such as dreams or neurotic symptoms. The theory assumes that unacceptable id impulses cause anxiety, which can be reduced by *defense mechanisms.*

4. Freud's theory of *personality development* proposes that individuals pass through *psy-*

chosexual stages (such as oral, anal, phallic) and must resolve the *Oedipal conflict,* in which the young child sees the same-sex parent as a rival for the affection of the opposite-sex parent. Freud's theory of anxiety and defense mechanisms has fared better over the years than his structural and developmental theories have. Psychoanalytic theory has been modified by others like Jung, Adler, Horney, Sullivan, Fromm, and Erikson—all of whom place more emphasis on functions of the ego and on motives other than sex and aggression.

5. *Social-learning theory* is the contemporary version of the *behavioristic approach* to personality. It assumes that personality differences result from variations in learning experiences—which includes learning by observation in addition to direct operant or classical conditioning. Social-learning theory, which has become increasingly cognitive over the past few decades, now emphasizes the reciprocal interaction between external determinants of behavior (such as rewards and punishments) and internal determinants (such as beliefs, thoughts, and expectations).

6. Social-learning theorists have challenged the underlying assumption of most personality theories—including the layperson's "intuitive" theory—that an individual's behavior is consistent across various situations. The low correlations between measures of the same trait in two different situations or between personality test scores and situational mea-

sures of the trait found in most empirical studies support the contention made by social-learning theorists that behavior is more dependent on the situation than it is on enduring traits.

7. In reply to the charge that behavior is not cross-situationally consistent, some theorists have pointed out that the correlations are higher when individual observations of behavior are aggregated in the same way that responses to items on a personality test are added together. Allport and others have argued that the low correlations demonstrate only that individuals are not consistent in the same way, not that they are inconsistent with themselves. A third reply suggests that because persons in everyday life select and shape the situations into which they enter, they will be more consistent than they would be in an experimental study, which randomly assigns persons to conditions.

8. The *phenomenological approach* is concerned with the individual's subjective experience. *Humanistic psychology,* a branch of the phenomenological approach, was founded as the "third force," an explicit alternative to psychoanalytic and behavioristic approaches. Humanistic psychologists like Carl Rogers and Abraham Maslow emphasize a person's self-concept and striving for growth, or self-actualization. George Kelly's *personal construct theory* focuses on the concepts or constructs individuals use to interpret or *construe* their world.

FURTHER READING

There are a number of good general books on personality. These include Hall, Lindzey, Loehlin, and Manosevitz, *Introduction to Theories of Personality* (1985); Mischel, *Introduction to Personality* (5th ed., 1993); McAdams, *The Person* (2nd ed., 1994; and Burger, *Personality* (3rd ed. 1993).

For an in-depth discussion of the social-learning approach to personality, see Bandura, *Social Learning Theory* (1989). Freud's theories are presented in their most readable form in his *New Introductory Lectures on Psychoanalysis* (1933; reprint ed., 1965). His *Psychopathology of Everyday Life* (1901/

1960)—in which he discusses what have come to be known as "Freudian slips," as well as dreams and humor—is both entertaining and well worth reading. Other comprehensive references for psychoanalytic theories of personality include Holzman, *Psychoanalysis and Psychopathology* (1970); and Eagle, *Recent Developments in Psychoanalysis: A Critical Evaluation* (1984).

The humanistic viewpoint is represented at length in Maddi and Costa, *Humanism in Personology: Allport, Maslow, and Murray* (1972). For Carl Rogers' influential views, see Rogers and Stevens, *Person to Person: The*

Problem of Being Human (1967); and Rogers, *Carl Rogers on Personal Power* (1977). *Personality and Personal Growth* (2nd ed., 1984) by Frager and Fadiman focuses on the personality theories that are most concerned with understanding human nature and includes a section on such Eastern theories of personality as yoga, Zen Buddhism, and Sufism.

STRESS, PSYCHOPATHOLOGY, AND PSYCHOTHERAPY

We all experience stress occasionally. Students may be stressed when their relationship with their roommates is not going well, when they must declare a course of study, or when final exams come. Today's rapidly paced society creates stress for many of us. We are constantly pressured to accomplish more and more in less and less time. Air and noise pollution, traffic congestion, crime, and excessive workload are increasingly present in our everyday lives. Finally, we sometimes face major stressful events, such as the death of a parent or a natural disaster. Exposure to stress can lead to painful emotions—for instance, anxiety or depression. It can also lead to physical illnesses, both minor and severe. But people's reactions to stressful events differ widely: Some people faced with a stressful event develop serious psychological or physical problems, whereas other people faced with the same stressful event develop no problems and may even find the event challenging and interesting. In this chapter we discuss the concept of stress and the effects of stress on the mind and the body. We also look at the differences between people's ways of thinking about and coping with stressful events, and how these differences contribute to adjustment.

Stress has become a popular topic. The media often attribute unusual behavior or illness in people to burn-out from stress or a nervous breakdown resulting from stress. For example, when a celebrity attempts suicide, it is often said that he or she was burnt out from the pressures of public life. In their daily lives at school, students often talk about each other's levels of stress. "I'm so stressed out!" is a common claim. But what is stress? In general terms, **stress** occurs when people are faced with events they perceive as endangering their physical or psychological well-being. These events are usually referred to as **stressors,** and people's reactions to them as **stress responses.**

There are some types of events that most people experience as stressful. We will describe the characteristics of such events below. Then we will describe the body's natural reaction to stress. This reaction is adaptive when it is possible to flee from, or attack, a stressor, but can become maladaptive when a stressor is chronic or uncontrollable. Stress can have both direct and indirect effects on health.

The study of how stress, and other social, psychological, and biological factors come together to contribute to illness is known as **behavioral medicine** or **health psychology.** In this chapter, we will review findings from this field on how psychosocial factors interact with biological vulnerabilities to affect cardiovascular health and the functioning of the immune system. Finally, we will describe ways that people can learn to manage stress better to improve their health.

CHARACTERISTICS OF STRESSFUL EVENTS

Countless events create stress. Some are major changes affecting large numbers of

The causes of stress vary from one person to the next. What is overwhelming to one person may be exciting and challenging to another.

people—events such as war, nuclear accidents, and earthquakes. Others are major changes in the life of individuals—for instance, moving to a new area, changing jobs, getting married, losing a friend, suffering a serious illness. Everyday hassles can also be experienced as stressors—losing your wallet, getting stuck in traffic, arguing with your professor, and so on. Finally, the source of stress can be within the individual in the form of conflicting motives or desires. Events that are perceived as stressful usually fall into one or more of the following categories: traumatic events outside the usual range of human experience, uncontrollable events, unpredictable events, events that challenge the limits of our capabilities and self-concept, or internal conflicts.

TRAUMATIC EVENTS

The most obvious sources of stress are traumatic events—situations of extreme danger that are outside the range of usual human experience. These include natural disasters, such as earthquakes and floods; man-made disasters, such as wars and nuclear accidents; catastrophic accidents, such as car or plane crashes; and physical assaults, such as rape or attempted murder.

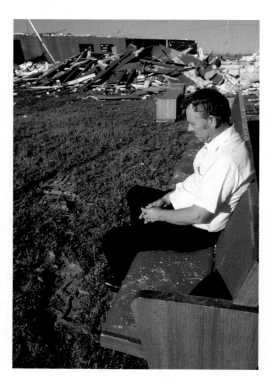

Victims of disasters are often stunned and disoriented shortly after the disaster. Later they become more responsive but may still have trouble initiating even simple activities. They may remain anxious and distracted long after the disaster.

There is a series of psychological reactions that many people experience following a traumatic event (Horowitz, 1986). At first, survivors are stunned, dazed, and appear to be unaware of their injuries or of the danger. They may wander around in a disoriented state, perhaps putting themselves at risk for further injury. For example, an earthquake survivor may wander through buildings that are on the verge of collapse, unaware of the obvious danger. In the next stage, survivors are still passive and unable to initiate even simple tasks, but they may follow orders readily. For example, a rape survivor days after her assault may not even think to fix herself food to eat, but if her close friend calls and insists they go out for food, she will comply. In the third stage survivors become anxious and apprehensive, have difficulty concentrating, and may repeat the story of the catastrophe over and over again. The survivor of a car crash may become extremely nervous when near a car, may be unable to go back to work because he or she cannot concentrate, and may tell friends about the details of the crash repeatedly.

Fortunately, most of us never experience traumatic events. More common events can lead to stress responses, however. Three characteristics of events lead to their being perceived as stressful: their controllability, predictability, and the extent to which they challenge the limits of our capabilities and our self-concept. Of course, the degree to which an event is stressful differs for each individual. That is, people differ in the extent to which they *appraise* the same event as controllable, predictable and a challenge to their capabilities and self-concept, and it is largely these appraisals that influence the perceived stressfulness of the event (Lazarus & Folkman, 1984).

CONTROLLABILITY

The more uncontrollable an event seems, the more likely it is perceived as stressful (see Chapter 7). Major uncontrollable events include the death of a loved one, being laid off from work, or serious illness. Minor uncontrollable events are such things as having a friend refuse to accept your apology for some misdeed or being bumped off a flight because the airline oversold tickets. One obvious reason uncontrollable events are stressful is that if we cannot control them, we cannot stop them from happening.

As we noted, however, it appears that our *perceptions* of the controllability of events are as important to our assessment of their stressfulness as is the actual controllability of those events. Consider this study. Subjects were shown color photographs of victims of violent deaths. The experimental group could terminate the viewing by pressing a button. The control subjects saw the same photographs for the time duration determined by the experimental group, but they could not terminate the exposure. The level of arousal or anxiety in both groups was measured by the galvanic skin response (GSR), a drop in the electrical resistance of the skin that is widely used as an index of autonomic arousal. The experimental group showed much less anxiety in response to the photographs than did the control group, even though the two groups were exposed to the photographs for the same amount of time (Geer & Maisel, 1972).

The belief that we can control events appears to reduce the impact of the events, even if we never exercise that control. This was demonstrated in a study in which two groups of subjects were exposed to a loud, extremely unpleasant noise. Subjects in one group were told that they could terminate the noise by pressing a button, but they were urged not to do so unless it was absolutely necessary. Subjects in the other group had no control over the noise. None of the subjects who had a control button actually pressed it, so the noise exposure was the same for both groups. Nevertheless, performance on subsequent problem-solving tasks was significantly worse for the group that had no control, indicating that they were more disturbed by the noise than was the group that had the potential for control (Glass & Singer, 1972).

PREDICTABILITY

Being able to predict the occurrence of a stressful event—even if the individual cannot control it—usually reduces the severity of the stress. As discussed in Chapter 7, laboratory experiments show that both humans and animals prefer predictable aversive events to unpredictable ones. In one study, rats were given a choice between a signaled shock and an unsignaled shock. If the rat pressed a bar at the start of a series of shock trials, each shock was preceded by a warning tone. If the rat failed to press the bar, no warning tones sounded during that series of trials. All of the rats quickly learned to press the bar, showing a marked preference for predictable shock (Abbott, Schoen, & Badia, 1984). Humans generally choose predictable over unpredictable shocks, too. They also show less emotional arousal and report less distress while waiting for predictable shocks to occur, and they perceive predictable shocks as less aversive than unpredictable ones of the same intensity (Katz & Wykes, 1985).

How do we explain these results? One possibility is that a warning signal before an aversive event allows the person or animal to initiate some sort of preparatory process that acts to lessen the effects of a noxious stimulus. An animal receiving the signal that a shock is about to happen may shift its feet in such a way as to reduce the experience of the shock. A man who knows he is about to receive a shot in the doctor's office can try to distract himself to lessen the pain. A woman who hears warnings of an impending hurricane can board up her windows in an attempt to prevent damage to her house. Another possibility is that with unpredictable shock, there is no safe period; with predictable shock, the subject (human or animal) can relax to some extent until the signal warns that shock is about to occur. Recall from Chapter 7 that this has been called the *safety signal hypothesis* (Seligman & Binik, 1977). A real-life example of the presence of a safety signal is when an employee's boss, who tends to criticize the employee in front of others, is out of town on a business trip. The boss's absence is a signal to the employee that he is safe to relax. An employee whose boss never goes out of town, and who criticizes him unpredictably throughout the day, has no safety signals, however, and may chronically feel stressed. An earthquake is one type of natural event for which there is no safety signal.

Some jobs are filled with unpredictability and are considered very stressful, such as fire fighting and emergency-room medicine. Serious illnesses often are very unpredictable. One of the major problems faced by cancer patients who receive treatment is that they cannot be sure whether or not they have been

TABLE 14-1

Life Events Scale   *This scale, also known as the Holmes and Rahe Social Readjustment Rating Scale, measures stress in terms of life changes.* (After Holmes & Rahe, 1967)

LIFE EVENT	VALUE
Death of spouse	100
Divorce	73
Marital separation	65
Jail term	63
Death of close family member	63
Personal injury or illness	53
Marriage	50
Fired from job	47
Marital reconciliation	45
Retirement	45
Change in health of family member	44
Pregnancy	40
Sex difficulties	39
Gain of new family member	39
Business readjustment	39
Change in financial state	38
Death of close friend	37
Change to different line of work	36
Foreclosure of mortgage	30
Change in responsibilities at work	29
Son or daughter leaving home	29
Trouble with in-laws	29
Outstanding personal achievement	28
Wife begins or stops work	26
Begin or end school	26
Change in living conditions	25
Revision of personal habits	24
Trouble with boss	23
Change in residence	20
Change in school	20
Change in recreation	19
Change in church activities	19
Change in social activities	18
Change in sleeping habits	16
Change in eating habits	15
Vacation	13
Christmas	12
Minor legal violations	11

cured until many years have passed. Every day they must confront the uncertainty of a potentially disastrous future.

Another example of chronic unpredictability is women whose husbands were reported missing in action in Vietnam. Not knowing whether their husbands were alive or dead made it difficult for them to resolve their grief and proceed with their lives. Compared with wives of men who were killed in action and with wives of men who were prisoners, women married to MIAs showed the poorest physical and emotional health (Hunter, 1979).

CHALLENGING OUR LIMITS

Some situations are largely controllable and predictable, but are still experienced as stressful because they push us to the limits of our capabilities and challenge our views of ourselves. Final exam week is a good example. Most students work much longer hours during final exam week than they do during the rest of the year. This physical and intellectual exertion is experienced as stressful by some people. Some students also find the limits of their knowledge and intellectual capabilities tested by exams. Even among students who are capable of doing well on exams, the possibility that they may fail important exams may challenge their view of themselves as competent and their decision to pursue a particular profession. A study of U.S. Military Academy cadets found that those who were high on motivation to pursue a military career but who were performing poorly in examinations were at increased risk to develop an illness, specifically mononucleosis (Kasl, Evans, & Niederman, 1979).

Although we enter some pressure situations enthusiastically and joyfully, they still may be stressful. Marriage is a good example; it entails many, many new adjustments. Individuals are often challenged to the limits of their patience and tolerance as they become accustomed to the idiosyncrasies of their new spouses (for example, his or her habit of leaving clothes lying around everywhere). When minor irritations or major disagreements over important matters (for instance, financial decisions) lead to arguments between newlyweds, they may find their beliefs that they married the right persons challenged.

Researchers Holmes and Rahe (1967) argued that any change in life that requires numerous readjustments can be perceived as stressful. In an attempt to measure the impact of life changes, they developed the *Life Events Scale,* shown in Table 14-1. The life events are ranked in order of the most stressful (death of a spouse) to the least stressful (minor violations of the law). To arrive at this scale, the investigators examined thousands of interviews and medical histories to identify the kinds of events that people found stressful. Because marriage appeared to be a critical event for most people, it was placed in the middle of the scale and was assigned an arbitrary value of 50. The investigators then

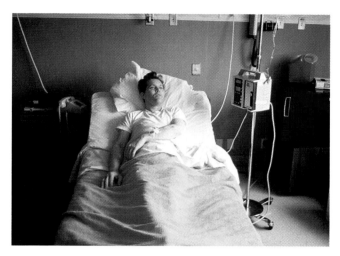

asked approximately 400 men and women of varying ages, backgrounds, and marital status to compare marriage with a number of life events. They were asked such questions as, "Does the event call for more or less readjustment than marriage?" Those interviewed were then asked to assign a point value to each event on the basis of their evaluation of its severity and the time required for adjustment. These ratings were used to construct the scale in Table 14-1.

Although positive events often require adjustment and are therefore sometimes stressful, most research indicates that negative events have a much greater impact on our psychological and physical health than positive events. In addition, there are large differences in how people are affected by events. Some of these differences are linked to age and cultural background (Masuda & Holmes, 1978; Ruch & Holmes, 1971). Also, some people do not find major changes or pressure situations such as exam week stressful. They experience such situations as challenging and are invigorated by them. Later we will discuss characteristics of individuals that affect whether situations are viewed as stressors or challenges.

INTERNAL CONFLICTS

So far, we have discussed only external events in which something or someone in the environment challenges our well-being. Stress can also be brought about by internal processes—unresolved conflicts that may be conscious or unconscious. Conflict occurs when a person must choose between in-compatible, or mutually exclusive, goals or courses of action. Many of the things people desire prove to be incompatible. You want to play on your college volleyball team but cannot devote the time required and still earn the grades necessary to apply to graduate school. You want to join your friends for a pizza party but are afraid you will fail tomorrow's exam if you don't stay home and study. You don't want to go to your uncle's for dinner but you don't want to listen to your parents' complaints if you reject the invitation. The goals in these instances are incompatible because the action needed to achieve one automatically prevents you from reaching the other.

Even if two goals are equally attractive— for example, you receive two good job offers— you may agonize over the decision and experience regrets after making a choice. This stress would not have occurred if you had been offered only one job.

Conflict may also arise when two inner needs or motives are in opposition. In our society, the conflicts that are the most pervasive and difficult to resolve generally occur between the following motives:

- *Independence versus dependence* Particularly when faced with a difficult situation, we may want someone to take care of us and solve our problems. But we are taught that we must stand on our own and assume responsibilities. At other times, we may wish for independence, but circumstances or other people force us to remain dependent.
- *Intimacy versus isolation* The desire to be close to another person and to share our

We often engage voluntarily in activities that others would find stressful but that we perceive as challenging and exciting. When an event is negative, uncontrollable, and unpredictable, however, most people perceive it as stressful.

CRITICAL DISCUSSION	*SEXUAL ABUSE AS A MAJOR STRESSOR*

One type of stress that is tragically common in our society is sexual abuse. Estimates of the incidence of sexual abuse vary, depending on the methods of individual studies (see Cutler & Nolen-Hoeksema, 1991). In one of the largest studies of sexual abuse, 3,132 randomly selected adults living in Los Angeles were interviewed in person (Burnam et al., 1988; Stein et al., 1988). Seventeen percent of the women and 9 percent of the men reported having had some type of experience of sexual assault at some time in their lives. Over 80 percent of the assaults occurred before the victims were 25 years old; 6.8 percent of the women and 3.8 percent of the men reported experiencing some type of sexual abuse involving physical contact before the age of 16. Kilpatrick and colleagues (1985) conducted telephone interviews with 2,004 randomly selected women in South Carolina and found that 14.5 percent reported one or more experiences of attempted or completed sexual assault, 5 percent reported they had been raped, and 4 percent reported they had been victims of attempted rape. Russell and Howell (1983) found a higher rate of rape experiences in a study using in-person interviews to gather information from a random sample of 930 adult women in San Francisco. Rather than simply asking women if they had ever been raped, the interviewers asked these women if they had ever had an experience of forced intercourse, intercourse obtained by threat of force, intercourse completed when they were drugged,

unconscious, asleep, or otherwise totally helpless and thus unable to consent (this is the legal definition of rape in California). Twenty-four percent of the women interviewed reported having had at least one such experience.

The impact of rape and other types of sexual violence on the victim's emotional health appears to be great (Kendall, Tuckett, Williams, & Finkelhart, 1993). Several studies have found that in the first six months after a rape or other assault, women and men show high levels of depression, anxiety, dismay, and many other indicators of emotional distress (Rothbaum et al., 1992; Wirtz & Harrell, 1987; Kilpatrick, Veronen & Resick, 1979). For some people, this emotional distress declines over time. For others, however, emotional distress is long-lasting. The following letter describes one rape survivor's lingering distress fear:

No one except someone who has experienced rape can know the late night, quiet playback and the thousands of stirring memories ready to rear up their ugly heads at the slightest incitement. Even almost a year later, as the "anniversary" draws near, I can feel all of my original reactions once again full force, and they are something which will not recede in time. Only women who have spent lonely nights such as this one trying to exorcise the ghosts can truly comprehend the insolence and hideousness of rape. And our number is growing, faster all the time. (J. Pilgrim, letter quoted by Thom, 1987, p. 222).

In their study, Burnam and colleagues (1988) found that assault victims were twice as likely as people

who had not been assaulted to have a diagnosable depressive disorder, anxiety disorder, or substance abuse disorder at some time after the assault. They were most likely to develop these disorders if they had been assaulted as a child. In fact, people who had been assaulted as children remained at higher risk than the non-assaulted people for developing a psychological disorder throughout their lives.

The stressfulness of sexual abuse comes not only from the abuse itself, but also from the blame society often lays upon survivors for having been abused. Particularly with regard to women and rape, cultural myths and stereotypes can lead survivors to conceal their experiences, in guilt and fear of being ridiculed for having "let themselves" be abused. Examples of these myths include "only bad girls get raped," "any woman can resist rape if she really wants to," "women ask for it," "when a woman says 'no' she really means 'yes,'" and "women cry rape to hurt men" (Burt, 1980).

As society's awareness of the high incidence of rape and sexual abuse increases, we can hope that more measures will be taken to stop abuse and that attitudes toward survivors will change for the better. In the meantime, abuse survivors can be helped through psychotherapy and through participation in support groups of other people who have shared their experiences.

---

innermost thoughts and emotions may conflict with the fear of being hurt or rejected if we expose too much of ourselves.

- *Cooperation versus competition* Our society places much emphasis on competi-

tion and success. Competition begins in early childhood among siblings, continues through school, and culminates in business and professional rivalry. At the same time, we are urged to cooperate and to help others.

- *Impulse expression versus moral standards* Impulses must be regulated to some degree in all societies. We noted in Chapter 3 that much of childhood learning involves internalizing cultural restrictions placed on impulses. Sex and aggression are two areas in which our impulses frequently conflict with moral standards, and violation of these standards can generate feelings of guilt.

These four areas present the greatest potential for serious conflict. Trying to find a workable compromise between opposing motives can create considerable stress.

PSYCHOLOGICAL REACTIONS TO STRESS

Stressful situations produce emotional reactions ranging from exhilaration (when the event is demanding but manageable) to the common emotions of anxiety, anger, discouragement, and depression. If the stressful situation continues, our emotions may switch back and forth among any of these, depending on the success of our coping efforts.

ANXIETY

The most common response to a stressor is **anxiety.** By anxiety, we mean the unpleasant emotion characterized by such terms as "worry," "apprehension," "tension," and "fear" that we all experience at times in varying degrees.

People who live through events that are beyond the normal range of human suffering (for example, natural disasters, rape, kidnapping) sometimes develop a severe set of anxiety-related symptoms known as **post-traumatic stress disorder.** The major symptoms include (a) feeling *numb* to the world, with a lack of interest in former activities and a sense of estrangement from others; (b) reliving the trauma repeatedly in memories and dreams; and (c) sleep disturbances, difficulty concentrating, and over-alertness. Some individuals also feel guilty about surviving when others did not.

Most young adults experience conflict and frustration when they wish for independence but must wait to achieve it.

Post-traumatic stress disorder may develop immediately after the disaster, or it may be brought on by some minor stress weeks, months, or even years later. And it may last a long time. A study of survivors of Nazi concentration camps found that 97 percent were still troubled with anxiety 20 years after they were freed from the camps. Many still relived the traumas of persecution in their dreams and were fearful that something terrible would happen to their spouses or their children whenever they were out of sight (Krystal, 1968).

Post-traumatic stress disorder affects about one-sixth of the Vietnam War veterans, and almost half of the vets still have memories about the war that they are trying to forget.

Post-traumatic stress disorder became widely accepted as a diagnostic category because of difficulties experienced by Vietnam veterans. Although stress reactions to the horrors of battle had been noted in earlier wars (in World War I it was called "shell shock" and in World War II "combat fatigue"), veterans of Vietnam seemed especially prone to develop the long-term symptoms we have described. A survey estimated that 15 percent of Vietnam veterans have suffered from post-traumatic stress disorder since their discharge (Centers for Disease Control, 1988). Substance abuse, violence and interpersonal problems are common correlates of post-traumatic stress disorder. In a study of 713 men who served in Vietnam, 16 percent reported having problems resulting from drinking heavily, such as trouble at school or work, problems with friends, and passing out. Sixteen percent had been arrested at least once; and 44 percent said that they had war memories that they were still trying to forget (Yager, Laufer, & Gallops, 1984).

The soldiers who fought in Vietnam were young (average age 19), and the conditions of warfare were unusual: absence of clear front lines, unpredictable attacks in dense jungle, difficulty in distinguishing between Vietnamese allies and enemies, and the lack of support for the war on the home front. To this day, some Vietnam veterans still re-experience in memories or in dreams the traumatic events that happened to them. As one veteran wrote: "The war is over in history. But it never ended for me" (Marbly, 1987, p. 193).

ANGER AND AGGRESSION

Another common reaction to a stressful situation is anger, which may lead to aggression. Laboratory studies have shown that some animals behave aggressively in response to a variety of stressors, including overcrowding, electric shock, and the failure to receive an expected food reward. If a pair of animals is shocked in a cage from which they cannot escape, they begin fighting when the shock starts and stop fighting when it ends.

Children often become angry and exhibit aggressive behavior when they experience **frustration**. As we noted in Chapter 11, the **frustration-aggression hypothesis** assumes that whenever a person's effort to reach a goal is blocked, an aggressive drive is induced that motivates behavior to injure the object—or the person—causing the frustration. While research has shown that aggression is not an inevitable response to frustration, it certainly is one of them. When one child takes a toy from another, the second is likely to attack the first in an attempt to regain the toy. In the late 1980s, some adults frustrated by interminable traffic jams on hot Los Angeles freeways began shooting at one another. Fortunately, adults usually express their aggression verbally rather than physically; they are more likely to exchange insults than blows.

Direct aggression toward the source of frustration is not always possible or wise. Sometimes the source is vague and intangible. The person does not know what to attack but feels angry and seeks an object on which to vent these feelings. Sometimes the individual responsible for the frustration is so powerful that an attack would be dangerous. When circumstances block direct attack on the cause of frustration, aggression may be *displaced:* The aggressive action may be directed toward an innocent person or object rather than toward the actual cause of the frustration. A man who is reprimanded at work may take out unexpressed resentment on his family. A student, angry at her professor for an unfair grade, may blow up at her roommate. A child frustrated by experiences at school may resort to vandalism of school property.

APATHY AND DEPRESSION

Although a common response to frustration is active aggression, the opposite response of withdrawal and apathy is also common. If the stressful conditions continue and the individual is not successful in coping with them, apathy may deepen into depression.

The theory of **learned helplessness** (Seligman, 1975) explains how experience with aversive, uncontrollable events can lead to apathy and depression (see also Chapter 7). A series of experiments showed that dogs placed in a shuttle box (an apparatus with two compartments separated by a barrier) quickly learn to jump to the opposite compartment to escape a mild electric shock delivered to their feet through a grid on the floor. If a light is turned on a few seconds before the grid is electrified, the dogs can learn to avoid the shock entirely by jumping to the safe compartment when signaled by the light. However, if the dog has had a previous history of being in another enclosure in which shocks were unavoidable and inescapable—in which nothing the animal did terminated the shock—then it is very difficult for the dog to learn the avoidance response in a new situation when it is appropriate. The animal simply sits and endures the shock in the shuttle box, even though an easy jump to the opposite compartment would eliminate discomfort. Some dogs never learn, even if the experimenter demonstrates the proper procedure by carrying them over the barrier. The experimenters concluded that the animals had learned through prior experience that they were helpless to avoid the shock and so gave up trying to do so, even in a new situation. This learned helplessness was difficult for the animals to overcome (Overmeier & Seligman, 1967).

Some humans also appear to develop learned helplessness, characterized by apathy, withdrawal, and inaction, in response to uncontrollable events. Not all do, however. The original learned helplessness theory has had to be modified to take into account the fact that some people become helpless following uncontrollable events, but other people are invigorated by the challenge that such events pose (Wortman & Brehm, 1975). This modified theory will be discussed in the section on personality style.

The original learned helplessness theory is useful, however, in helping us to understand why some people seem to give up and take it when exposed to difficult events. For example, the theory has been used to explain why prisoners in Nazi concentration camps did not revolt against their captors more often: They had come to believe that they were helpless to do anything about their captivity and thus did not try to escape. Women caught in marriages with a battering husband frequently do not try to escape. These women often say that they feel helpless to do anything about their situations because they fear what their husbands would do if they tried to leave, or because they do not have the economic resources to support themselves and their children.

Learned helplessness theory may explain why some battered women remain in battering relationships, even when they may have opportunities to leave.

COGNITIVE IMPAIRMENT

In addition to the emotional reactions to stress we have just discussed, people often show substantial cognitive impairment when faced with serious stressors. They find it hard to concentrate and to organize their thoughts logically. They may be easily distracted. As a result, their performance on tasks, particularly complex tasks, tends to deteriorate.

This cognitive impairment may come from two sources. High levels of emotional arousal can interfere with a mind's processing of information (recall Figure 11-5, page 395). So the more anxious, angry, or depressed we are following a stressor, the more likely we are to experience cognitive impairment. Cognitive impairment may also result from the distracting thoughts that go through our heads when faced with a stressor. We contemplate possible sources of action, we worry about the consequences of our actions, and we may berate ourselves for not being able to handle the situation better. For instance, students who have a condition called *test anxiety* tend to worry about possible failures and about their inadequacies while trying to work on a test. They can become so distracted by these negative thoughts that they fail to follow instructions and neglect or misinterpret obvious information provided by questions. As anxiety mounts, they have difficulty retrieving facts they had learned well. (See the discussion of emotion and memory in Chapter 8.)

Cognitive impairment during stressful periods often leads people to adhere rigidly to behavior patterns because they cannot consider alternative patterns. People have been trapped in flaming buildings because they persisted in pushing against exit doors that opened inward; in their panic, they failed to consider the possibility of an alternate action. Some people resort to old, childlike behavior patterns that are not appropriate to the situation. The cautious person may become even more cautious and withdraw entirely, whereas the aggressive person may lose control and strike out heedlessly in all directions.

PHYSIOLOGICAL REACTIONS TO STRESS

The body reacts to stressors by initiating a complex sequence of innate responses to a perceived threat. If the threat is resolved quickly, these emergency responses subside, and our physiological state returns to normal. If the stressful situation continues, a different set of internal responses occurs as we attempt to adapt to a chronic stressor.

PHYSIOLOGICAL STRESS RESPONSE

Whether you fall into an icy river, encounter a knife-wielding assailant, or are terrified by your first parachute jump, your body responds in similar ways. Regardless of the stressor, your body automatically prepares to handle the emergency. Recall from Chapter 11 that this has been called the **fight-or-flight response**. Quick energy is needed, so the liver releases extra sugar (glucose) to fuel the muscles, and hormones are released that stimulate the conversion of fats and proteins to sugar. The body's metabolism increases in preparation for expending energy on physical action. Heart rate, blood pressure, and breathing rate increase, and the muscles tense. At the same time, certain unessential activities, such as digestion, are curtailed. Saliva and mucus dry up, thereby increasing the size of air passages to the lungs. Thus, an early sign of stress is a dry mouth. The body's natural painkillers, *endorphins*, are secreted and the surface blood vessels constrict to reduce bleeding in case of

injury. The spleen releases more red blood cells to help carry oxygen, and the bone marrow produces more white corpuscles to fight infection.

Most of these physiological changes result from activation of two neuroendocrine systems controlled by the hypothalamus: the **sympathetic system** and the **adrenal-cortical system**. The hypothalamus has been called the brain's stress center because of its dual function in emergencies. Its first function is to activate the sympathetic division of the autonomic nervous system (see Chapter 2). The hypothalamus transmits nerve impulses to nuclei in the brain stem that control the functioning of the autonomic nervous system. The sympathetic division of the autonomic system acts directly on the smooth muscles and internal organs to produce some of the bodily changes described above—for example, increased heart rate, elevated blood pressure, dilated pupils. The sympathetic system also stimulates the inner core of the adrenal glands (the adrenal medulla) to release the hormones **epinephrine** (adrenaline) and **norepinephrine** into the blood stream. Epinephrine has the same effect on the muscles and organs as the sympathetic nervous system does (for example, it increases heart rate and blood pressure) and thus serves to perpetuate a state of arousal. Norepinephrine, through its action on the pituitary gland, is indirectly responsible for the release of extra sugar from the liver (see Figure 14-1).

The above events describe only the first function of the hypothalamus: activation of the sympathetic system. The hypothalamus carries out its second function (activation of the adrenal-cortical system) by signaling the **pituitary gland**, which lies just below it (recall Figure 2-9, page 46), to secrete **adrenocorticotrophic hormone (ACTH)**, the body's "major stress hormone" (see Chapter 2). ACTH stimulates the outer layer of the adrenal glands (the adrenal cortex) resulting in the release of a group of hormones (the major one is cortisol) that regulate the blood levels of glucose and of certain minerals. The amount of cortisol in blood or urine samples is often used as a measure of stress. ACTH also signals other endocrine glands to release about 30 hormones, each of which plays a role in the body's adjustment to emergency situations.

A wide variety of physical and psychological stressors triggers this response pattern. While the physiological components of the

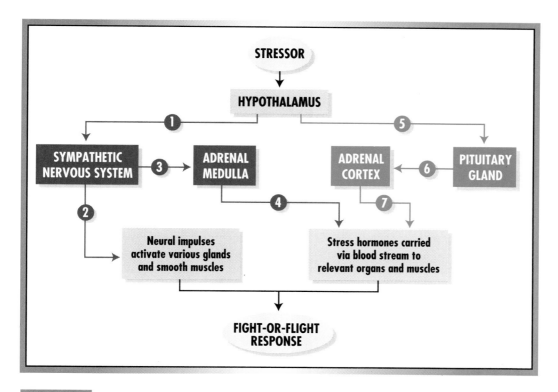

FIGURE 14-1

Fight-or-Flight Response   *A stressful situation activates the hypothalamus, which, in turn, controls two neuroendocrine systems: the sympathetic system (shown in red) and the adrenal-cortical system (shown in green). The sympathetic nervous system, responding to neural impulses from the hypothalamus (1), activates various organs and smooth muscles under its control (2). For example, it increases heart rate and dilates the pupils. The sympathetic nervous system also signals the adrenal medulla (3) to release epinephrine and norepinephrine into the bloodstream (4). The adrenal-cortical system is activated when the hypothalamus secretes CRF, a chemical that acts on the pituitary gland lying just below the hypothalamus (5). The pituitary gland, in turn, secretes the hormone ACTH, which is carried via the bloodstream to the adrenal cortex (6), where it stimulates the release of a group of hormones, including cortisol, that regulate blood glucose levels (7). ACTH also signals the other endocrine glands to release some 30 hormones. The combined effect of the various stress hormones carried via the bloodstream plus the neural activity of the sympathetic division of the autonomic nervous system constitute the fight-or-flight response.*

fight-or-flight response are valuable in helping an individual deal with physical threat requiring immediate action, they are not very adaptive for dealing with many modern-day sources of stress. In situations in which action is impossible or in which the threat continues and must be dealt with over an extended period of time, such intense physiological arousal can be harmful.

Laboratory studies with animals have shown that prolonged exposure to a stressor produces a number of bodily changes: enlarged adrenal glands, shrunken lymph nodes, and stomach ulcers (Selye, 1979). These changes decrease the organism's ability to resist other stressors, including infectious and disease-producing agents. As we will see later,

chronic arousal can make both animals and people susceptible to illness.

We have focused on the negative aspects of the physiological arousal elicited by stressors. Studies have shown, however, that exposure to intermittent stressors can have later benefits in the form of physiological toughness. In essence, intermittent stress (occasional exposure but with recovery periods) leads to stress tolerance later on (Dienstbier, 1989). For example, young rats that are removed from their cages and handled daily (a stressor for them) are less fearful when exposed to other stressors as adults and show a quicker return to their normal levels of the stress hormones (Meaney et al., 1987; Levine, 1960). Similarly, rats that were toughened by having to swim in cold water for a period of 14 consecutive days performed better on a later swim test and showed less depletion of epinephrine and norepinephrine than rats that had received no prior exposure to cold water (Weiss et al., 1975).

The physiological responses that appear to be beneficial involve arousal of the sympathetic system and occur when a person makes active efforts to cope with the stressful situation (Frankenhauser, 1983). Increases in epinephrine and norepinephrine correlate positively with performance on a variety of tasks (from students taking tests to paratroopers engaged in training jumps): High levels of these hormones in blood and urine were related to better performance (Ursin, 1978; Johansson & Frankenhaeuser, 1973). The physiological responses that appear to be harmful involve arousal of the adrenal-cortical system and occur when a person experiences distress but does not actively attempt to cope with the stressful situation.

Research on the positive aspects of stress arousal is still in an exploratory stage. The interaction between the sympathetic system and the adrenal-cortical system is exceedingly complex, and it is difficult to determine their separate effects using current research methods (primarily measures of chemistry of the blood and/or urine). However, the idea that stressors can have beneficial effects under certain circumstances has generated increased interest among researchers.

HOW STRESS AFFECTS HEALTH

Attempts to adapt to the continued presence of a stressor may deplete the body's resources and make it vulnerable to illness. Chronic stress can lead to such physical disorders as ulcers, high blood pressure, and heart disease. It may also impair the immune system, decreasing the body's ability to fight invading bacteria and viruses. Indeed, doctors estimate that emotional stress plays an important role in more than half of all medical problems.

Psychophysiological disorders are physical disorders in which emotions are believed to play a central role. A common misconception

is that people with psychophysiological disorders are not really sick and do not need medical attention. On the contrary, the symptoms of psychophysiological illness reflect physiological disturbances associated with tissue damage and pain; a peptic ulcer caused by stress is indistinguishable from an ulcer caused by a factor unrelated to stress, such as long-term heavy usage of aspirin.

Traditionally, research in psychophysiology focused on such illnesses as asthma, hypertension (high blood pressure), ulcers, colitis, and rheumatoid arthritis (see Taylor, 1991, for a review). Researchers looked for relationships between specific illnesses and characteristic attitudes toward, or ways of coping with, stressful life events. For example, individuals with hypertension were said to feel that life was threatening and, consequently, they must be on guard at all times. Those suffering from colitis were believed to be angry but unable to express their anger. However, most studies that reported characteristic attitudes to be related to specific illnesses have not been replicated. Thus, the hypothesis that people who share the same ways of reacting to stress will be vulnerable to the same illnesses has generally not been confirmed. An important exception is the research on coronary heart disease and Type A behavior patterns, as we will see shortly.

In this section, we consider how stress may directly affect the body's ability to fight disease, and how it can indirectly affect disease by leading us to engage in unhealthy behaviors.

DIRECT EFFECTS OF STRESS ON HEALTH

The physiological response the body undergoes in the face of a stressor may have a direct, negative effect on physical health if this response is chronically maintained. Long-term overarousal of the sympathetic system or the adrenal-cortical system can cause damage to arteries and organ systems. Stress may also have a direct effect on the immune system's ability to fight off disease.

CHRONIC OVERAROUSAL The chronic overarousal caused by chronic stressors may contribute to coronary heart disease. Coronary heart disease (CHD) occurs when the blood vessels that supply the heart muscles are narrowed or closed (by the gradual build-up of a hard, fatty substance called plaque), blocking the flow of oxygen and nutrients to the heart. This can lead to pain, called angina pectoris, that radiates across the chest and arm. When oxygen to the heart is completely blocked, it can cause a myocardial infarction—a heart attack.

Coronary heart disease is a leading cause of death and chronic illness in the United States. Nearly half of the deaths in the United States every year are caused by coronary heart disease, many before the age of 65 years. There seems to be a genetic contribution to coronary heart disease: People with family histories of CHD are at increased risk for CHD. CHD is also linked to high blood pressure, high serum cholesterol, diabetes, smoking, and obesity.

People in high-stress jobs are at increased risk for CHD, particularly jobs that are highly demanding (in terms of workload, responsibilities, and role conflicts) but that provide little control (the worker has little control over the speed, nature, and conditions of work). An example of such a high stress job is an assembly line in which rapid, high-quality production is expected and the work is machine-paced rather than self-paced.

In one study, 900 middle-aged men and women were followed over a 10-year period and examined for the development of heart disease. Two independent methods—occupational titles and the subjects' self-reports of their own feelings about their jobs—were used to classify workers along the dimensions of job demand and job control. The results showed that both men and women in occupations classified as "high strain" (high demand combined with low control) had a risk of coronary heart disease 1½ times greater than those in other occupations (Karasek et al., 1982; Karasek et al., 1981).

High family demands in addition to a stressful job can adversely affect a woman's cardiovascular health. Employed women in general are not at a higher risk of coronary heart disease than homemakers. However, employed mothers are more likely to develop heart disease. The likelihood of disease increases with the number of children for working women but not for homemakers (Haynes & Feinleib, 1980). The researchers did not examine the effects of children in the home on men's health.

One group that lives in chronically stressful settings and has particularly high rates of high blood pressure is low-income African-Americans. They often do not have adequate financial resources for daily living, may be poorly educated and therefore have trouble finding good employment, live in violent neighborhoods, and are frequently exposed to racism. All these conditions have been linked to higher blood pressure (Armstead et al., 1989).

Experimental studies with animals have shown that disruption of the social environment can induce pathology that resembles coronary artery disease (Sapolsky, 1990; Manuck, Kaplan, & Matthews, 1986). Some of the key experiments have been conducted with a

People who work in highly demanding jobs over which they have little control may be at increased risk for illness.

type of macaque monkey whose social organization involves the establishment of stable hierarchies of social dominance: dominant and submissive animals can be identified within a given group based on the animals' social behavior. The introduction of unfamiliar monkeys into an established social group is a stressor that leads to increased aggressive behavior as group members attempt to re-establish a social dominance hierarchy (Manuck, Kaplan, & Matthews, 1986).

In these studies, some monkey groups remained stable with fixed memberships; other groups were stressed by the repeated introduction of new members. After about two years under these conditions, the high ranking or dominant males in the unstable social condition showed more extensive atherosclerosis (the build-up of plaque on the artery walls) than the subordinate males (Sapolsky, 1990).

THE IMMUNE SYSTEM   One relatively new area of research in behavioral medicine is **psychoneuroimmunology**, the study of how the body's immune system is affected by stress and other psychological variables. The immune system, by means of specialized cells called lymphocytes, protects the body from disease-causing microorganisms. It affects our susceptibility to infectious diseases, allergies, cancers, and autoimmune disorders (that is, diseases such as rheumatoid arthritis, in which the immune cells attack the normal tissue of the body).

There is no single index of the quality of an individual's immune functioning, or *immunocompetence*. It is a complex system with many interacting components, and different investigators have chosen to focus on the different components of the system. Evidence from a number of areas suggests that stress affects the ability of the immune system to defend the body. Let us look at a few examples. One study indicates that the common belief that we are more likely to catch a cold when we are under stress is probably correct (Cohen, Tyrel, & Smith, 1991). Researchers exposed 400 healthy volunteers to a nasal wash containing one of five cold viruses or an innocuous salt solution. Each participant answered questions about the number of stressful events experienced in the past year, the degree to which they felt able to cope with daily demands, and the frequency of negative emotions such as anger and depression. Based on these data, each subject was assigned a stress index ranging from 3 (lowest stress) to 12 (highest stress). The volunteers were examined daily for cold symptoms and for the presence of cold viruses or virus-specific antibodies in their upper respiratory secretions.

The majority of the virus-exposed volunteers showed signs of infection, but only about a third actually developed colds. The rates of viral infection and of actual cold symptoms increased in accordance with the reported stress levels. Compared with the lowest stress group, volunteers who reported the highest stress were significantly more likely to become infected with the cold virus and almost twice as likely to develop a cold (see Figure 14-2). These results held even after controlling statistically for a number of variables that might influence immune functioning, such as age, allergies, cigarette and alcohol use, exercise, and diet. The two indicators of immunocompetence that were measured in this study did not show any specific change as a result of stress, so exactly how stress lowered the body's resistance to the cold virus remains to be determined.

This study is unusual in that the subjects were exposed to a virus, lived in special quar-

FIGURE 14-2

Stress and Colds
The graph shows the percentage of virus-exposed subjects who developed colds as a function of the degree of stress reported. (After Cohen, Tyrel, & Smith, 1991)

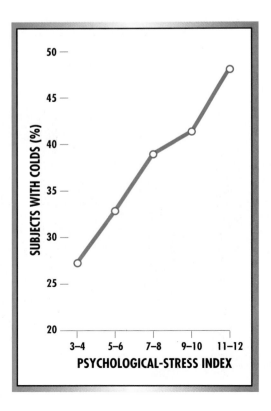

ters near the laboratory for a number of days both before and after exposure, and were carefully monitored. Such controlled conditions for studying the effects of stress on health are seldom feasible. Most studies look at individuals undergoing a particularly stressful event—such as academic pressures, bereavement, or marital disruption—and evaluate their immunocompetence, using various indices. For example, one study found that during examination periods college students have lower levels of an antibody in their blood that defends against respiratory infections (Jemmott et al., 1985), and another found that medical students show lowered immune functioning on a number of blood-sample measures (Glaser et al., 1986; Glaser et al., 1985). A study of men whose wives had died from breast cancer demonstrated that the responsiveness of the men's immune system functioning declined significantly within the month following their wives' deaths, and in some cases remained low for a year thereafter (Schleifer et al., 1979). Similarly, a series of studies revealed that individuals of both sexes who have recently been separated or divorced show poorer immune functioning than matched control subjects who are still married, even though no significant differences were found between the two groups in health-related behaviors such as smoking and diet (Kiecolt-Glaser et al., 1988, 1987).

Psychological factors that reduce stress can attenuate these adverse immunological changes. For example, Kiecolt-Glaser and colleagues (1985) trained older adults to use relaxation techniques to reduce stress. These adults showed improvement on a number of indices of immunological functioning, whereas a control group of older adults who received no relaxation training showed no improvement in immunocompetence over the same period of time.

One factor that appears to be important is the extent to which an individual can control the stress. Recall that controllability is one of the variables that determines the severity of stress. A series of animal studies demonstrates that uncontrollable shock has a much greater effect on the immune system than controllable shock (Laudenslager et al., 1983; Visintainer, Volpicelli, & Seligman, 1982). In these experiments, rats are subjected to electric shock. One group can press a lever to turn off the shock. The other animals, the

To programmer

FIGURE 14-3

Yoked Controls in a Stress Experiment   *A series of electrical shocks are preprogrammed to be delivered simultaneously to the tails of the two male rats. The rat on the left can terminate a shock when it occurs by pressing the lever in front of him. The rat on the right has no control in the situation (his lever is inoperative) but he is yoked to the first rat. That is, when the first rat receives a shock, the yoked rat simultaneously receives the same shock and it remains on until the first rat presses his lever. The lever presses of the yoked rat have no effect on the shock sequence for either animal.*

yoked controls, receive an identical sequence of shocks but their levers are ineffective (see Figure 14-3).

In one study using this procedure, the investigators looked at how readily the rats' T-cells multiplied when challenged by an invader. T-cells are lymphocytes that secrete chemicals that kill harmful cells, such as cancer cells. They found that the T-cells from rats that could control the shock multiplied as readily as did those from rats that were not stressed at all. T-cells from rats exposed to uncontrollable shock, on the other hand, multiplied only weakly. Thus, shock (stress) interfered with the immune response only in rats that could not control it (Laudenslager et al., 1983).

In another study, the investigators implanted tumor cells into rats, gave them shocks, and recorded whether the rats' natural defenses rejected the cells or whether they developed into tumors. Only 27 percent of the rats given uncontrollable shocks rejected the tumors, but 63 percent of the rats that could turn the shocks off rejected the tumors—even though the rats received identical amounts of shock (Visintainer, Volpicelli, & Seligman, 1982).

Perceptions of control also appear to mediate the influence of stress on the immune system in humans. In one study on the effects of marital separation or divorce on immune functioning, the partner who had initiated the separation (the one more in control of the situation) was less distressed, reported better health, and showed better immune system functioning than the non-initiator (Kiecolt-Glaser et al., 1988). Similarly, a study of women with breast cancer found that those with a pessimistic perspective—that is, who felt they had little control over events on the world—were the most likely to develop new tumors over a five-year period, even after the physical severity of their diseases was taken into account (Levy & Heiden, 1991).

The immune system is incredibly complicated, employing a number of different weapons that interact to defend the body. Much remains to be discovered about the immune system and even more about its relationship to the nervous system. Scientists once believed that the immune system operated quite independently, isolated from other physiological systems. But current studies are making it increasingly evident that the immune system and the nervous system have numerous anatomical and physiological connections. For example, researchers are discovering that lymphocytes have receptors for a number of different neurotransmitters. Thus, these immune system cells are equipped to receive messages from the nervous system that may alter the way they behave. One of the reasons a link between neurotransmitters and the immune system is important is that negative emotional states (for example, anxiety or depression) can affect neurotransmitter levels. Thus, stressful situations may affect immune system functioning only if these situations arouse negative emotional states.

As research on psychoneuroimmunology yields additional information about the links between the nervous and immune systems, we will gain a clearer understanding of how mental attitudes affect health.

HEALTH BEHAVIORS

Stress can also affect our health by leading us to engage in behaviors that undermine the body's ability to fight off disease. When we are feeling stressed, we often do not take proper care of ourselves. Students taking exams stay up all night, often for several nights in a row. They may skip meals, snacking only on junk food. Many men whose wives have died do not know how to cook for themselves, and thus may eat poorly or hardly at all. In their grief, some bereaved men increase alcohol consumption and smoking. People under stress cease normal exercise routines and become sedentary. Each of these *health behaviors* influences the body's ability to fight disease and its general functioning, and may contribute to the development of illness. Thus, stress may indirectly affect health by reducing positive health behaviors and increasing negative behaviors.

Health behaviors—that is, how we eat, how much we exercise, and how much sleep we get—influence our bodies abilities to fight disease.

APPRAISALS AND PERSONALITY AS MEDIATORS OF STRESS RESPONSES

As we have noted, events that are uncontrollable or unpredictable, or that challenge our views of ourselves, tend to be experienced as stressful. Some people appear more likely than others to appraise events in these ways, and thus to experience stress responses to the events. There are three basic theories about why some people are prone to appraise events as stressful: psychoanalytic theory, behavioral theory, and personality theory.

PSYCHOANALYTIC THEORY

Psychoanalysts make a distinction between **objective anxiety**, which is a reasonable response to a harmful situation, and **neurotic anxiety**, which is anxiety out of proportion to the actual danger. Freud believed that neurotic anxiety stems from unconscious conflicts within an individual between unacceptable **id** impulses (mainly sexual and aggressive) and the constraints imposed by the **ego** and **superego** (see Chapter 13). Many id impulses pose a threat to the individual because they are contradictory to personal or social values. A woman may not consciously acknowledge that she has strong hostile feelings toward her mother because these feelings conflict with her belief that a child should love her parents. If she acknowledged her true feelings, she would destroy her self-concept as a loving daughter and would risk the loss of her mother's love and support. When she begins to feel angry toward her mother, the aroused anxiety serves as a signal of potential danger. Thus, this woman may experience even a minor conflict with her mother, such as a disagreement about where the family should go for vacation or what to have for dinner, as a major stressor. A woman who is not so conflicted in her feelings about her mother would experience this as a less severe stressor.

According to psychoanalytic theory, we all have some unconscious conflicts. For some people, however, these conflicts are more severe and greater in number, and these people see more events in life as stressful.

BEHAVIORAL THEORY

While Freud saw unconscious conflicts as the internal source of stress responses, behaviorists have focused on ways in which individuals learn to associate stress responses with certain situations. People may also react to specific situations with fear and anxiety because those situations caused them harm or were stressful in the past. Some phobias develop through such **classical conditioning** (see Chapter 7). For example, a person whose car nearly slid off the road on the side of a steep mountain may experience anxiety now every time she is in a high place. Or a student who failed a final exam in a particular classroom may feel anxious the next year when he re-enters the room to take another class.

Sometimes fears are difficult to extinguish. If your first reaction is to avoid or escape the anxiety-producing situation, you may not be able to determine when the situation is no longer dangerous. The little girl who has been punished for assertive behavior in the past may never learn that it is acceptable for her to express her wishes in new situations because she never tries to. Thus, people can continue to have fears about particular situations because they chronically avoid the situation and therefore never challenge their fears.

COGNITIVE THEORY

A modification of the learned helplessness theory proposed by Abramson and her colleagues (1978) focuses on one type of personality style that relates to the attributions or causal explanations people give for important events. These researchers argued that when people attribute negative events to causes that are internal to them ("it's my fault"), that are stable in time ("it's going to last forever"), and that affect many areas of their lives ("it will impact everything I do"), they are most likely to show a helpless, depressed response to negative events. For example, if a person whose spouse left him attributed the break-up of his marriage to his "bad" personality (an internal, stable, and global attribution), he would tend to lose self-esteem and expect future relationships to fail as well. In turn, he would show lowered motivation, passivity, and sadness. In contrast, if he made a less pessimistic attribution, such as attributing the failure of his marriage to simple incompatibility between himself and his wife, he would tend to maintain his self-esteem and motivation for the future (for similar arguments, see Weiner, 1972).

Abramson and colleagues propose that people have consistent styles of making attributions for the events in their lives, which they called **attributional styles,** and that these styles influence the degree to which people view events as stressful and have helpless, depressive reactions to difficult events. A number of studies support this theory (Peterson & Seligman, 1984). In one study, researchers assessed the attributional styles of students a few weeks before they were to take a midterm exam. Just before the exam, they also asked the students what grade they would consider a failure and what grade they would be happy with. Then, after the students received their grades from the exam, they measured the students' levels of sadness and depression. Among students who received a grade below their standards, those who had a pessimistic style of attributing events were significantly more depressed than those who had a more optimistic attributional style (Metalsky, Halberstadt, & Abramson, 1987).

A pessimistic attributional style is also linked to physical illness (Peterson, Seligman, & Vaillant, 1988; Peterson & Seligman, 1987). Students with more pessimistic attributional styles report more illness and make more visits to the health center than students with a more optimistic attributional style. In a 35-year-long study of men in the Harvard classes of 1939–1940, researchers found that men who had a pessimistic attributional style at age 25 were more likely to develop physical illness over the subsequent years than men with a more optimistic attributional style. How does attributional style affect health? We do not know for sure yet. People with a pessimistic attributional style tend to feel they have little control over their lives and, as noted earlier, perceptions of uncontrollability have been linked to lowered immune system functioning. A study by Taylor and colleagues (1992) suggests that a pessimistic outlook may impair health by leading people to engage in unhealthy behaviors. The focus of this study was gay men, some of whom had the virus that causes AIDS (that is, were HIV-positive) and some of whom did not (they were HIV-negative). The researchers found that among both HIV-positive and HIV-negative men, those who were more pessimistic and fatalistic were less likely to engage in healthy behaviors, such as maintaining a proper diet, getting enough sleep, and exercising. This is particularly important for the HIV-positive men, because engaging in these healthy behaviors can reduce the risk of developing AIDS. Thus, a pessimistic outlook may affect health directly, by reducing immune system functioning, or indirectly, by reducing a person's tendency to engage in health-promoting behavior.

HARDINESS Another line of research has focused on people who are *most* resistant to stress—who do not become physically or emotionally impaired even in the face of major stressful events (Kobasa, Maddi, & Kahn, 1982; Kobasa, 1979). In one study, more than 600 men who were executives or managers in the same company were given checklists and were asked to describe all of the stressful events and illnesses they had experienced over the previous three years. Two groups were selected for comparison: The first group scored above average on both stressful events and illness; the second group scored equally high on stress but *below average* on illness. Members of both groups then filled out detailed personality questionnaires. Analysis of the results indicated that the high-stress/low-illness men differed from the men who became ill under stress on three major dimensions: They were more actively involved in their work and social lives, they were more oriented toward challenge and change, and they felt more in control of events in their lives (Kobasa, 1979).

Arguably, these personality differences could be the *result* rather than the *cause* of illness. For example, it is hard for people to be involved in work or in social activity when they are ill. The investigators therefore conducted a longitudinal study that considered the personality characteristics of business executives before they became ill, and then monitored their life stress and the extent of their illnesses for a period of two years. The results showed that the executives whose attitudes toward life could be rated high on involvement, feeling of control, and positive responses to change remained healthier over time than men who scored low on these dimensions (Kobasa, Maddi, & Kahn, 1982). The most important factors appear to be a sense of personal control and a commitment to personal goals (Cohen & Edwards, 1989). Although this study was conducted with men only, similar results have been found in a study of women (Wiebe & McCallum, 1986).

The personality characteristics of stress-resistant or hardy individuals are summarized by the terms "commitment," "control," and "challenge." These characteristics are interrelated with the factors we have discussed as influencing the perceived severity of stressors. For example, the sense of being in control of life events reflects feelings of competency and also influences the appraisal of stressful events. Challenge also involves cognitive evaluation, the belief that change is normal in life and should be viewed as an opportunity for growth rather than as a threat to security.

TYPE A PATTERN

One behavior pattern or personality style that has received a great deal of attention is the **Type A pattern**. Physicians noted over the years that heart attack victims tend to be hostile, aggressive, impatient persons who were overinvolved in their work. In the 1950s two cardiologists defined a constellation of behaviors (the Type A pattern) that seemed to characterize patients with coronary heart disease (Friedman & Rosenman, 1974). People who exhibit this Type A behavior pattern are extremely competitive and achievement oriented; they have a sense of time urgency, find it difficult to relax, and become impatient and angry when confronted with delays or with people they view as incompetent. Although outwardly self-confident, they are prey to constant feelings of self-doubt; they push themselves to accomplish more and more in less and less time. Some common Type A behaviors are listed in Table 14-2. Type B people are those who do not exhibit the characteristics listed for Type A. Type B people are able to relax without feeling guilty and to work without becoming agitated; they lack a sense of urgency, with its accompanying impatience, and are not easily roused to anger.

To examine the relationship between Type A behavior and coronary heart disease, more than 3,000 healthy, middle-aged men were

Hardy individuals—that is, those who do not become ill when stressed—are more actively involved in their work, are more oriented to challenge and change, and feel more in control of their lives than those who are vulnerable to the effects of stress.

Thinking of or doing two things at once

Scheduling more and more activities into less and less time

Failing to notice or be interested in the environment or things of beauty

Hurrying the speech of others

Becoming unduly irritated when forced to wait in line or when driving behind a car you think is moving too slowly

Believing that if you want something done well, you have to do it yourself

Gesticulating when you talk

Frequent knee jiggling or rapid tapping of your fingers

Explosive speech patterns or frequent use of obscenities

Making a fetish of always being on time

Having difficulty sitting and doing nothing

Playing nearly every game to win, even when playing with children

Measuring your own and others' success in terms of numbers (number of patients seen, articles written, and so on)

Lip clicking, head nodding, fist clenching, table pounding, or sucking in of air when speaking

Becoming impatient while watching others do things you think you can do better or faster

Rapid blinking or ticlike eyebrow lifting

TABLE 14-2

Type A Behaviors   *Some behaviors that characterize people prone to coronary heart disease.* (After Friedman & Rosenman, 1974)

evaluated by means of a structured interview. The interview was designed to be irritating. The interviewer kept the subject waiting without explanation and then asked a series of questions about being competitive, hostile, and pressed for time. Examples are: Do you ever feel rushed or under pressure? Do you eat quickly? Would you describe yourself as ambitious and hard driving or relaxed and easygoing? Do you resent it if someone is late? The interviewer interrupted, asked questions in a challenging manner, and threw in non sequiturs. The interview was scored more on the way the person behaved in answering the questions than on the answers themselves. For example, extreme Type A men spoke loudly in an explosive manner, talked over the interviewer so as not to be interrupted, appeared tense and tight-lipped, and described hostile incidents with great emotional intensity. Classic Type B men sat in a relaxed manner, spoke slowly and softly, were easily interrupted, and smiled often.

After the subjects were classified as Type A or Type B, they were studied for 8½ years. During that period, Type A men had twice as many heart attacks or other forms of coronary heart disease as Type B men. These results held up even after diet, age, smoking, and other variables were taken into account (Rosenman et al., 1975). Other studies confirmed this twofold risk and linked Type A behavior to heart disease in both men and women (Kornitzer et al., 1982; Haynes, Feinleib, & Kannel, 1980). In addition, Type A behavior correlates with severity of coronary

artery blockage as determined at autopsy or in X-ray studies of the inside of coronary blood vessels (Williams et al., 1988; Friedman et al., 1968).

After reviewing the evidence, in 1981 the American Heart Association decided that Type A behavior should be classified as a risk factor for coronary heart disease. However, two more recent studies failed to find a link between Type A behavior and heart disease (Case, Heller, Case & Moss, 1985; Shekelle et al., 1983). While some researchers attribute this failure to the way Type A individuals were assessed in these studies, others believe that the definition of Type A behavior, as originally formulated, is too diffuse. They argue that time urgency and competitiveness are *not* the most important components; the crucial variable may be hostility.

Several studies have found that a person's level of hostility is a better predictor of heart disease than is his or her overall level of Type A behavior (Booth-Kewley & Friedman, 1987; Dembroski et al., 1985; Thoresen, Telch, & Eagleston, 1981). To examine further the anger component of Type A behavior, several studies have used personality tests rather than interviews to measure hostility. For example, a 25-year study of 118 male lawyers found that those who scored high on hostility traits on a personality inventory taken in law school were five times as likely to die before age 50 as classmates who were not hostile (Barefoot et al., 1989). In a similar follow-up study of physicians, hostility scores obtained in medical school predicted the incidence of coronary heart disease as well as mortality from all causes (Barefoot, Williams, & Dahlstrom, 1983). In both studies, this relationship is independent of the effects of smoking, age, and high blood pressure. There is some evidence that when anger is repressed, or held in, it may be even more destructive to the heart than anger that is overtly expressed (Wright, 1988; Spielberger et al., 1985).

How does Type A behavior or its component trait of hostility lead to coronary heart disease? One plausible biological mechanism is the way the individual's sympathetic nervous system responds to stress. When exposed to stressful experimental situations (for example, when faced with threat of failure, harassment, or competitive task demands), most subjects report feeling angry, irritated, and tense. However, subjects who score high on

Type A individuals are hostile, pressured, and competitive, and are twice as likely to suffer coronary heart disease as Type B individuals.

hostility as a trait show much larger increases in blood pressure, heart rate, and the secretion of stress-related hormones than subjects with low hostility scores (Suarez & Williams, 1989). The same results are found when Type A subjects are compared with Type B subjects (Manuck & Kranz, 1986). The sympathetic nervous systems of hostile and/or Type A individuals appear to be hyper-responsive to stressful situations. All of these physiological changes can damage the heart and blood vessels.

Hostile and nonhostile people may have fundamentally different nervous systems. When nonhostile individuals are aroused and upset, their parasympathetic nervous systems act like a stop switch to calm them down. In contrast, hostile individuals may have a weak parasympathetic nervous system. When they are angered, their adrenalin fires off and they stay unpleasantly aroused. As a consequence, they interact differently with the world (Williams, 1989).

The good news about the Type A behavior pattern is that it can be modified through well-established therapy programs, and people who are able to reduce their Type A behavior show lowered risk of coronary heart disease. We will discuss this therapy later in the chapter.

COPING SKILLS

The emotions and physiological arousal created by stressful situations are highly uncomfortable, and this discomfort motivates the individual to do something to alleviate it. The process by which a person attempts to manage stressful demands is called *coping,* and it takes two major forms. A person can focus on the specific problem or situation that has arisen, trying to find some way of changing it or avoiding it in the future. This is called **problem-focused coping.** A person can also focus on alleviating the emotions associated with the stressful situation, even if the situation itself cannot be changed. This second process is called **emotion-focused coping** (Lazarus & Folkman, 1984). When dealing with a stressful situation, most people use both problem-focused coping and emotion-focused coping.

PROBLEM-FOCUSED COPING

Strategies for solving problems include defining the problem, generating alternative solutions, weighing the alternatives in terms of costs and benefits, choosing among them, and implementing the selected alternative. Problem-focused strategies can also be directed inward: The person can change something about himself or herself instead of changing the environment. Changing levels of aspiration, finding alternative sources of gratification, and learning new skills are examples. How skillfully the individual employs these strategies depends on his or her range of experiences and capacity for self-control.

Suppose you receive a warning that you are about to fail a course required for graduation. You might confer with the professor, devise a work schedule to fulfill the requirements, and then follow it; or you might decide that you cannot fulfill the requirements in the time remaining and so sign up to retake the course in summer school. Both of these actions are problem-focused methods of coping.

People who tend to use problem-focused coping in stressful situations show lower levels of depression both during and after the stressful situation (Billings & Moos, 1984). Of course, people who are less depressed may find it easier to use problem-focused coping. But longitudinal studies show that problem-focused coping leads to shorter periods of depression, even taking into account people's initial levels of depression. In addition, therapies that teach depressed people to use problem-focused coping can be effective in helping them to overcome their depressions and react more adaptively to stressors (Nezu, Nezu, & Perri, 1989).

EMOTION-FOCUSED COPING

People engage in emotion-focused coping to prevent their negative emotions from overwhelming them and preventing them from engaging in actions to solve their problems. They also use emotion-focused coping when a problem is uncontrollable.

There are many ways we try to cope with our negative emotions. Some researchers have divided these into behavioral strategies and cognitive strategies (Moos, 1988). *Behavioral strategies* include engaging in physical

Talking with supportive friends about your problems can be an adaptive coping strategy.

exercise to get our minds off a problem, using alcohol or other drugs, venting anger, seeking emotional support from friends. *Cognitive strategies* include temporarily setting aside thoughts about the problem (for example, "I decided it wasn't worth worrying about") and reducing the threat by changing the meaning of the situation (for instance, "I decided that her friendship wasn't that important to me"). Cognitive strategies often involve reappraising the situations. Obviously, some behavioral and cognitive strategies we would expect to be adaptive, but other strategies we would expect to only cause the person more stress (such as drinking heavily). One strategy for coping with negative emotions that appears to help people adjust emotionally and physically to a stressor is seeking emotional support from others. For example, in a study of women who had just received surgery for breast cancer, Levy and colleagues (1990) found that those who actively sought social support from others had higher natural killer cell activity, indicating that their immune system was more aggressively attacking their cancer (see also the Critical Discussion, Can Psychological Interventions Affect the Course of Cancer?). In a large series of studies, Pennebaker (1990) has found that people who reveal personal traumas, such as being raped or having a spouse commit suicide, to supportive others tend to show more positive physical health both shortly after the trauma and in the long run.

The quality of the social support a person receives from others following a trauma strongly influences the impact of social support on health, however (Rook, 1984). Some friends or relatives can be burdens instead of blessings in times of stress. Persons who have a high degree of conflict in their social networks tend to show poorer physical and emotional health following a major stressor, such as bereavement (Windholz et al., 1985). Conflictual social relationships may affect physical health through the immune system. Kiecolt-Glaser and colleagues (1993) found that newlywed couples who became hostile and negative toward each other while discussing a marital problem showed more decrements in four indicators of immune system functioning than couples who remained calm and nonhostile in discussing marital problems. Couples who became hostile during these discussions also showed elevated blood pressure for a longer period of time than those who did not become hostile.

Positive social support may help people to adjust better emotionally to stress by leading them to avoid rumination about the stressor (Nolen-Hoeksema, Parker, & Larson, 1994; Pennebaker & O'Heeron, 1984). Rumination involves isolating ourselves to think about how badly we feel, worrying about the consequences of the stressful event or our emotional state, or repetitively talking about how bad things are without taking any action to change them. One longitudinal study of recently bereaved people found that those who ruminated in response to their grief showed longer depressions (Nolen-Hoeksema, Parker & Larson, 1994). In addition, those who were more socially isolated or had a lot of conflict in their social network were most likely to ruminate.

Another longitudinal study was conducted quite by accident. A group of researchers at Stanford University just happened to have taken measures of emotion-focused coping tendencies and levels of depression and anxiety in a large group of students two weeks before the major earthquake that hit the San Francisco Bay Area in 1989. They remeasured students' levels of depression and anxiety again both 10 days and 7 weeks following the earthquake. They also estimated how much environmental stress the students experienced as a result of the earthquake (that is, injury to themselves, to their friends or family, and to their homes). The results showed that students who evidenced a ruminative style of coping with emotions before the earthquake were more likely to be depressed and anxious 10 days and still 7 weeks following the earthquake. This was true even after the students' levels of depression and anxiety before the earthquake were taken into account (Nolen-Hoeksema & Morrow, 1991a). Students who used dangerous activities to avoid their moods, such as drinking alcohol, also tended to remain depressed and anxious. In contrast, students who used pleasant activities to lift their moods and regain a sense of control had short and mild periods of depression and anxiety.

You might ask whether people who engage in ruminative coping are more sensitive to their own feelings and thus more likely to solve their problems. The evidence to date suggests that the answer is no. People who engage in ruminative coping are *less* likely also to engage in active problem-solving following stressors. In contrast, people who use pleasant activities to take a breather from their moods for a while are *more* likely to turn to active problem-solving to deal with their stressors (Nolen-Hoeksema, Parker, & Larson, 1992; Nolen-Hoeksema & Morrow, 1991a). In addition, people who use ruminative coping may actually do a *poorer* job of problem-solving when they do try. Two laboratory studies have shown that depressed people who have spent ten minutes ruminating and then go on to do a problem-solving task show poorer performance at problem-solving than depressed people who have spent ten minutes engaging in distraction before attempting the problem-solving task (Lynbomirsky & Nolen-Hoeksema, in press; Nolen-Hoeksema & Morrow, 1991b). Ruminating may get in the way of good problem-solving.

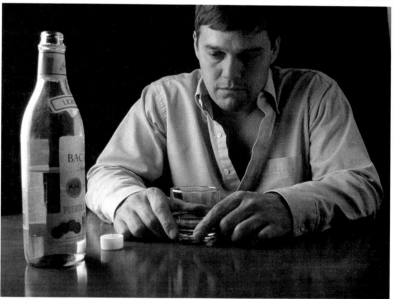

When confronted with negative emotions, some people isolate themselves and ruminate over the problem; some people distract themselves by, say, exercising or going to the movies; some people avoid the problem by engaging in harmful behaviors such as heavy drinking. How effective is each of these types of behaviors in coping with negative emotions?

DEFENSE MECHANISMS AS EMOTION-FOCUSED COPING

The coping strategies we have discussed thus far have been the focus of relatively recent research. There is a long history of thought on emotion-focused coping in the psychoanalytic literature, however (A. Freud, 1946/1967). Freud used the term **defense mechanisms** to refer to unconscious strategies that people use to deal with negative emotions. These emotion-focused strategies do not alter the stressful situation; they simply change the way the person perceives or thinks about

it. Thus, all defense mechanisms involve an element of *self-deception.*

We all use defense mechanisms at times. They help us over the rough spots until we can deal more directly with the stressful situation. Defense mechanisms indicate personality maladjustment only when they become the dominant mode of responding to problems. One difference between the defense mechanisms and the coping strategies we discussed earlier is that the defense mechanisms are unconscious processes, whereas the coping strategies are often engaged in consciously. As we describe below, however, some of the unconscious defense mechanisms, when taken to the extreme, may lead an individual to show some of the maladaptive conscious coping strategies described earlier.

REPRESSION   Freud considered **repression** to be the basic, and most important, defense mechanism. In repression, impulses or memories that are too frightening or painful are excluded from conscious awareness. Memories that evoke shame, guilt, or self-deprecation are often repressed. Freud believed that repression of certain childhood impulses is universal. He maintained that all young boys have feelings of sexual attraction toward the mother and feelings of rivalry and hostility toward the father (the **Oedipal conflict**); these impulses are repressed to avoid the painful consequences of acting on them. In later life, individuals may repress feelings and memories that could cause anxiety because they are inconsistent with their self-concepts. Feelings of hostility toward a loved one and experiences of failure may be banished from conscious memory.

Repression is different from **suppression**. Suppression is the process of deliberate self-control, keeping impulses and desires in check (perhaps holding them in privately while denying them publicly) or temporarily pushing aside painful memories. Individuals are aware of suppressed thoughts but are largely unaware of repressed impulses or memories.

Freud believed that repression is seldom completely successful. The repressed impulses threaten to break through into consciousness; the individual becomes anxious (although unaware of the reason) and employs several other defense mechanisms to keep the partially repressed impulses from awareness, as we will see below.

Interest in people who habitually repress or suppress painful thoughts and emotions has resurged in recent years. People with a repressive style appear to have a heightened vulnerability to illness in general, including more coronary heart disease and a more rapid course of cancer (Bonnano & Singer, 1990). Another line of research has shown that people who confide in others about traumatic events and the emotions they feel in reaction to those events tend to show better health than people who do not confide in others

(Pennebaker & Beall, 1986). For example, wives of men who died by suicide were more likely to be physically ill over the years following their husbands' deaths if they never confided to others that their husbands committed suicide (Pennebaker & O'Heeron, 1984).

How may repression or suppression contribute to poor physical health? First, as Freud suggested, suppression and repression seldom are completely satisfactory. People who try to suppress thoughts may actually ruminate more about the unwanted thoughts and emotions than people who express them to other people. Several studies have shown that trying to suppress thoughts actually leads us to think those thoughts more frequently than when we stop trying to suppress them (Wegner, Schneider, Carter, & White, 1987). In other words, there is a *rebound effect* whereby suppressed unwanted thoughts come back with greater force once the person's guard is down. In the study of widows of suicide victims, the researchers found that women who had not told anyone about their husbands' suicides actually ruminated more about it than women who had confided in others about the suicide (Pennebaker & O'Heeron, 1984). Thus, people who habitually try to push unwanted thoughts out of their minds might find these thoughts coming back with great force, causing them much distress. In turn, this heightened level of distress and the physiological arousal accompanying it could have negative effects on the body.

Second, the act of suppressing or repressing thoughts in itself may be physically taxing and thus have negative effects on the body. That is, constantly pushing thoughts out of our minds, and monitoring whether or not the thoughts are returning, may require physical energy and may lead to chronic arousal, which damages the body.

Pennebaker (1990) has shown that having people recount traumas and the emotions associated with them, whether in conversations with other people or simply by writing about them in diaries, reduces the people's tendencies to ruminate about the traumas, and may lead to improvements in their health. Expressing traumas and emotions about traumas may reduce ruminations and help a person's health in a number of ways. Verbally expressing fears and emotions may help to make them more concrete and thus somehow easier to deal with. When we tell others about our traumas and emotions, the listeners provide social support and validation for our feelings. Finally, talking about a trauma may help us to *habituate* to the trauma—to get used to the trauma so it does not create the same level of negative emotion every time we think about it.

RATIONALIZATION   When the fox in Aesop's fable rejected the grapes he could not reach because they were sour, he illustrated a defense mechanism known as **rationalization**. Rationalization does not mean "to act rationally," as we might assume; it is the assignment of logical or socially desirable motives to what we do so that we seem to have acted rationally. Rationalization serves two purposes: It eases our disappointment when we fail to reach a goal ("I didn't want it anyway"), and it provides us with acceptable motives for our behavior. If we act impulsively or on the basis of motives we do not wish to acknowledge even to ourselves, we rationalize what we have done to place our behavior in a more favorable light.

In the search for the good reason rather than the true reason, individuals make a number of excuses. These excuses are usually plausible; they simply do not tell the whole story. For example, "My roommate failed to wake me" or "I had too many other things to do" may be true, but they are perhaps not the real reasons for the individual's failure to perform the behavior in question. Individuals who are really concerned set an alarm clock or find the time.

An experiment involving posthypnotic suggestion (see Chapter 6) demonstrates the process of rationalization. A hypnotist instructs a subject under hypnosis that when he wakes from the trance he will watch the hypnotist, and when the hypnotist takes off her glasses, the subject will raise the window, but he will not remember that the hypnotist told him to do this. Aroused from the trance, the subject feels a little drowsy but soon circulates among the people in the room and carries on a normal conversation, furtively watching the hypnotist. When the hypnotist casually removes her glasses, the subject feels an impulse to open the window. He takes a step in that direction but hesitates. Unconsciously, he mobilizes his wishes to be a reasonable person; seeking a reason for his impulse to open the window, he says "Isn't it

a little stuffy in here?" Having found the needed excuse, he opens the window and feels more comfortable (Hilgard, 1965).

REACTION FORMATION   Sometimes individuals can conceal a motive from themselves by giving strong expression to the opposite motive. Such a tendency is called **reaction formation**. A mother who feels guilty about not wanting her child may become overindulgent and overprotective to assure the child of her love and to assure herself that she is a good mother. In one case, a mother who wished to do everything for her daughter could not understand why the child was so unappreciative. At great sacrifice, she had the daughter take expensive piano lessons and assisted her in the daily practice sessions. Although the mother thought she was being extremely kind, she was actually being very demanding—in fact, hostile. She was unaware of her own hostility, but when confronted with it, the mother admitted that she had hated piano lessons as a child. Under the conscious guise of being kind, she was unconsciously being cruel to her daughter. The daughter vaguely sensed what was going on and developed symptoms that required psychological treatment.

Some people who crusade with fanatical zeal against loose morals, alcohol, and gambling may be manifesting reaction formation. Some of these individuals may have a background of earlier difficulties with these problems, and their zealous crusading may be a means of defending themselves against the possibility of backsliding.

PROJECTION   All of us have undesirable traits that we do not acknowledge, even to ourselves. One unconscious mechanism, **projection**, protects us from recognizing our own undesirable qualities by assigning them in exaggerated amounts to other people. Suppose you have a tendency to be critical of or unkind to other people, but you would dislike yourself if you admitted this tendency. If you are convinced that the people around you are cruel or unkind, your harsh treatment of them is not based on *your* bad qualities—you are simply "giving them what they deserve." If you can assure yourself that everybody else cheats on college examinations, your unacknowledged tendency to take some academic shortcuts seems not so bad. Projection is really a form of rationalization, but it is so pervasive in our culture that it merits discussion in its own right.

INTELLECTUALIZATION   Intellectualization is an attempt to gain detachment from a stressful situation by dealing with it in abstract, intellectual terms. This kind of defense is frequently a necessity for people who must deal with life-and-death matters in their daily jobs. The doctor who is continually confronted with human suffering cannot afford to become emotionally involved with each patient. In fact, a certain amount of detachment may be essential for the doctor to function competently. This kind of intellectualization is a problem only when it becomes such a pervasive life-style that individuals cut themselves off from all emotional experiences.

DENIAL   When an external reality is too unpleasant to face, an individual may deny that it exists. The parents of a fatally ill child may refuse to admit that anything is seriously wrong, even though they are fully informed of the diagnosis and the expected outcome. Because they cannot tolerate the pain that acknowledging reality would produce, they resort to the defense mechanism of **denial**. Less extreme forms of denial may be seen in individuals who consistently ignore criticism, fail to perceive that others are angry with them, or disregard all kinds of clues suggesting that a marriage partner is having an affair.

Sometimes, denying facts may be better than facing them. In a severe crisis, denial may give the person time to face the grim facts at a more gradual pace. For example, victims of a stroke or a spinal cord injury might give up altogether if they were fully aware of the seriousness of their conditions. Hope gives them the incentive to keep trying. Servicemen who have faced combat or imprisonment report that denying the possibility of death helped them to function. In these situations, denial clearly has an adaptive value. On the other hand, the negative aspects of denial are evident when people postpone seeking medical help: For example, a woman may deny that a lump in her breast may be cancerous and so may delay going to a physician.

DISPLACEMENT   The last defense mechanism we consider fulfills its function (reduces anxiety) while partially gratifying the unacceptable motive. Through the mechanism of **displacement,** a motive that cannot be gratified in one form is directed into a new channel. An example of displacement was provided in our discussion of anger that could not be expressed toward the source of frustration and was redirected toward a less threatening object.

Freud felt that displacement was the most satisfactory way of handling aggressive and sexual impulses. The basic drives cannot be changed, but we can change the object toward which a drive is directed. For example, sexual impulses toward the parents cannot be safely gratified, but such impulses can be displaced toward a more suitable love object. Erotic impulses that cannot be expressed directly may be expressed indirectly in creative activities such as art, poetry, and music. Hostile impulses may find socially acceptable expression through participation in contact sports.

It seems unlikely that displacement actually eliminates the frustrated impulses, but substitute activities do help to reduce tension when a basic drive is thwarted. For example, the activities of taking care of others or seeking companionship may help reduce the tension associated with unsatisfied sexual needs.

MANAGING STRESS

Thus far we have primarily focused on factors within individuals that influence their perceptions and the impact of stressful events on them. The emotional support and concern of other people also can make stress more bearable. Divorce, the death of a loved one, or a serious illness is usually more devastating if an individual must face it alone. A study of Israeli parents who had lost a son (either through accidents or in the Yom Kippur War) found that bereavement exacted a heavier toll for those who were already widowed or divorced. Their mortality rate in the 10-year period following their loss was higher than the mortality rate for parents who could share their grief with each other (Levav, Friedlander, Kark & Peritz, 1988).

Numerous studies indicate that people who have many social ties (spouse, friends, relatives, and group memberships) live longer and are less apt to succumb to stress-related illnesses than are people who have few supportive social contacts (Cohen & Wills, 1985). Friends and family can provide support in many ways. They can bolster self-esteem by loving us despite our problems. They can provide information and advice, companionship to distract us from our worries, and financial or material aid. All of these tend to reduce feelings of helplessness and to increase our confidence in our ability to cope.

Stress is easier to tolerate when the cause of the stress is shared by others. Community disasters (floods, earthquakes, tornadoes, wars) often seem to bring out the best in people (Nilson et al., 1981). Individual anxieties and conflicts tend to be forgotten when people are working together against a common enemy or toward a common goal. For example, during the intensive bombing of London in World War II there was a marked decline in the number of people seeking help for emotional problems.

Sometimes, however, family and friends can increase the stress. Minimizing the seriousness of the problem or giving blind assurance that everything will be all right may produce more anxiety than failing to offer support at all. A study of graduate students facing crucial examination suggests that spouses who are realistically supportive ("I'm worried, but I know you'll do the best you can") are more helpful than spouses who deny any possibility of failure ("I'm not worried; I'm sure you'll pass). In the latter case, the student has to worry not only about failing the exam but also about losing respect in the eyes of the spouse (Mechanic, 1962). Other people can also make demands and create burdens on an individual at the very time he or she is dealing with other stressors (Rook, 1984). For example, a person who is caring for a terminally ill parent is more likely to suffer from depression if she is also being criticized and harassed by siblings for how she is caring for the parent (Nolen-Hoeksema, Parker, & Larson, 1994).

In addition to seeking positive social support in times of stress, people can learn other techniques to reduce the negative effects of stress on the body and the mind. Below we discuss some behavioral and cognitive techniques shown to help people reduce the effects of stress, then discuss in detail how these techniques are applied to reduce Type A behavior and coronary heart disease.

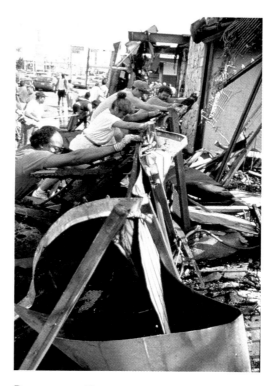

Disasters tend to rally individuals to work toward a common goal.

BEHAVIORAL TECHNIQUES

Among the behavioral techniques that have been used to help people control their physiological responses to stressful situations are *biofeedback, relaxation training,* and *aerobic exercise.*

In **biofeedback training**, individuals receive information (feedback) about an aspect of their physiological state and then attempt to alter that state. For example, in a procedure for learning to control tension headaches, electrodes are attached to the participant's forehead so that any movement in the forehead muscle can be electronically detected, amplified, and fed back to the person as an auditory signal. The signal, or tone, increases in pitch when the muscle contracts and decreases when it relaxes. By learning to control the pitch of the tone, the individual learns to keep the muscle relaxed. (Relaxation of the forehead muscle usually ensures relaxation of scalp and neck muscles also.) After 4 to 8 weeks of biofeedback training, the participant learns to recognize the onset of tension and to reduce it without feedback from the machine (Tarler-Benlolo, 1978).

Physiological processes that are controlled by the autonomic nervous system, such as heart rate and blood pressure, have traditionally been assumed to be automatic and not

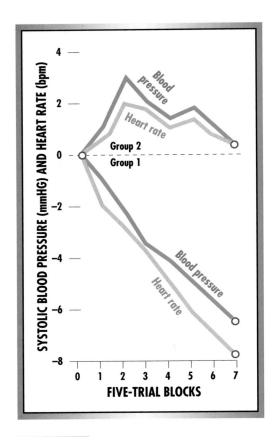

FIGURE 14-4

Operant Conditioning of Blood Pressure and Heart Rate   *One group of subjects received biofeedback (a light and a tone) whenever their blood pressure and heart rate decreased simultaneously (Group 1); the other group received the same feedback whenever their blood pressure and heart rate increased simultaneously (Group 2). The subjects achieved significant simultaneous control of blood pressure and heart rate during a single conditioning session. The group reinforced for lowering both functions achieved increasingly more control over trials; the group reinforced for raising both functions was less consistent. (After Schwartz, 1975)*

under voluntary control. However, laboratory studies have demonstrated that people can learn to modify heart rate and blood pressure (see Figure 14-4). The results of these studies have led to new procedures for treating patients with high blood pressure (hypertension). One procedure is to show patients a graph of their blood pressure while it is being monitored and to teach them techniques for relaxing different muscle groups. The patients are instructed to tense their muscles (for example, to clench a fist or to tighten the abdomen), release the tension, and notice

the difference in sensation. By starting with the feet and ankle muscles and progressing through the body to the muscles that control the neck and face, the patients learn to modify muscular tension. This combination of biofeedback with **relaxation training** has proved effective in lowering blood pressure for some individuals (Tarler-Benlolo, 1978).

Reviews of numerous studies using biofeedback and relaxation training to control headaches and hypertension conclude that the most important variable is *learning how to relax* (Runck, 1980). Some people may learn to relax faster when they receive biofeedback. Others may learn to relax equally well when they receive training in muscle relaxation without any specific biofeedback. The usefulness of relaxation training seems to depend on the individual. Some people who are not conscientious about taking drugs to relieve high blood pressure are more responsive to relaxation training, whereas others who have learned to control their blood pressure through relaxation may eventually drop the procedure because they find it too time-consuming.

Another factor important in controlling stress is physical fitness. Individuals who regularly engage in **aerobic exercise** (any sustained activity that increases heart rate and oxygen consumption, such as jogging, swimming, or cycling) show significantly lower heart rates and blood pressure in response to stressful situations than individuals who do not exercise regularly (Blumenthal et al., 1990; Holmes & McGilley, 1987; Holmes & Roth, 1985). In turn, Brown (1991) found that physically fit people were much less likely to become physically ill following stressful events than people who were not fit. Because of these findings, many stress management programs also emphasize physical fitness.

COGNITIVE TECHNIQUES

People who are able to control their physiological or emotional responses through biofeedback and relaxation training in the laboratory will have more difficulty doing so in actual stressful situations, particularly if they continue to interact in ways that make them tense. Consequently, an additional approach to stress management focuses on changing the individual's cognitive responses to stressful situations. **Cognitive behavior** therapy attempts to help people identify the kinds of stressful situations that produce their physiological or emotional symptoms and to alter the way they cope with these situations. For example, a man who suffers from tension headaches would be asked to begin by keeping a record of their occurrence and rating the severity of each headache and the circumstances in which it occurred. Next he is taught how to monitor his responses to these stressful events and is asked to record his feelings, thoughts, and behavior prior to, during, and following the event. After a period of self-monitoring, certain relationships often become evident among situational variables (for example, criticism by a supervisor or co-worker); thoughts ("I can't do anything right"); and emotional, behavioral, and physiological responses (depression, withdrawal, and headache).

The next step is trying to identify the expectations or beliefs that might explain the headache reactions (for example, "I expect to do everything perfectly, so the slightest criticism upsets me" or "I judge myself harshly, become depressed, and end up with a headache"). The final and most difficult step is trying to change something about the stressful situation, the individual's way of thinking about it, or the individual's behavior. The options might include finding a less stressful job, recognizing that the need to perform perfectly leads to unnecessary anguish over errors, or learning to behave more assertively in interactions instead of withdrawing.

This summary of cognitive therapy for coping with stressful situations does not do justice to the procedures involved. Chapter 16 provides a more detailed description. Biofeedback, relaxation training, and cognitive therapy have all proved useful in helping people control their physiological and emotional responses to stress. Some research suggests that the improvements gained is more likely to be maintained over time with a combination of cognitive and behavior therapy. (Holroyd, Appel, & Andrasik, 1983). This is not surprising, since the complex demands of everyday life often require flexible coping skills; being able to relax may not be an effective method of coping with some of life's stresses. Programs for stress management frequently employ a combination of biofeedback, relaxation training, and cognitive modification techniques.

In this biofeedback procedure for treating headaches, the sensors measure forehead muscle contractions and finger temperature. Cold fingers are often a sign of tension.

MODIFYING TYPE A BEHAVIOR

A combination of cognitive and behavioral techniques effectively reduces Type A behavior (Friedman et al., 1985). The subjects were more than 1,000 individuals who had experienced at least one heart attack. Subjects in the treatment group were helped to reduce their sense of time urgency by practicing standing in line (a situation Type A individuals find extremely irritating) and using the opportunity to reflect on things that they do not normally have time to think about, or to watch people, or to strike up a conversation with a stranger. Treatment also included learning to express themselves without exploding at people and to alter certain specific behaviors (such as interrupting the speech of others or talking or eating hurriedly). Therapists helped the subjects re-evaluate basic beliefs (such as the notion that success depends on the quantity of work produced) that might drive much of a Type A person's urgent and hostile behavior. Finally, subjects found ways to make the home and work environment less stressful (such as reducing the number of unnecessary social engagements).

The critical dependent variable in this study was the occurrence of another heart attack. By the end of the study, 4½ years later, the experimental group had a cardiac recurrence rate almost half that of control subjects who were not taught how to alter their lifestyles. Clearly, learning to modify Type A behavior was beneficial to these subjects' health (Friedman et al., 1985).

CAN PSYCHOLOGICAL INTERVENTIONS AFFECT THE COURSE OF CANCER?

CRITICAL DISCUSSION

Many scientists are skeptical that psychological interventions can significantly affect the course of major disease processes, such as cancer. They argue that suggestions that cancer patients can control their disease through the power of their will have done more harm than good, because cancer patients are made to feel they are to blame if they cannot cure themselves. However, evidence increasingly suggests that at least some types of supportive psychological interventions can slow the progress of cancer. David Spiegel and his colleagues (Spiegel, Bloom, Kraemer, & Gottheil, 1989) produced some of the best evidence, unintentionally. Several years ago, these researchers began a study in which they randomly assigned women with metastatic breast cancer either to a series of weekly support groups or to no support groups (all women were receiving standard medical care for their cancers). The focus of the groups was on facing death and learning to live one's remaining days to the fullest. Spiegel and colleagues had no intention of affecting the course of the cancers—they did not believe this was possible. They only wanted to improve the quality of life for these women.

The researchers were quite surprised when, 48 months after the study began, all of the women who had not been in the support groups had died of their cancers, whereas a third of the women in the support groups were still alive. The average survival (from the time the study began) for the women in the support groups was about 40 months, compared to about 19 months for the women who were not in the support groups.

There were no differences between the groups, other than their participation in the weekly support meetings, that could explain the differences in average survival time. That is, the two groups did not differ in the initial seriousness of their cancers, the type of therapy received, or other variables that might have affected their survival time. Spiegel and colleagues were forced to believe that their intervention actually increased the number of months that the women in the support group lived (for similar results, see Richardson, Shelton, Krailo, & Levine, 1990).

How did the intervention affect the progress of these women's cancers? It is not clear, but the women in the support groups gained a great deal of psychological strength from each other:

> The support groups were intensely emotional and supportive. Members discussed their deepest fears of dying and death, visited other members in the hospital, grieved when they died, attended their funerals, and mourned the loss of abilities and friendships. In addition to sharing grief, the women in these groups derived tremendous strength from one another. They came to feel like experts in living, a wisdom that grew from their confrontation with death. They chose new life projects, ranging from imparting life values to their children to writing books of poetry (Spiegel, 1991, p. 62)

In addition, support group members showed lower levels of emotional distress and learned how to control their physical pain better than women who did not participate in the support groups.

Further studies are under way to determine exactly how psychological interventions can affect the course of disease. It may be that reducing distress leads to improved immune system functioning, which slows the course of disease. Studies such as this one are intriguing, however, and hold promise for new ways of helping people facing serious illness.

BIOLOGICAL-PSYCHOLOGICAL PERSPECTIVES

The research described in this chapter is based on the premise that the mind and body influence each other. Simple models of how stress affects health are being replaced by complex models that explain how biological, psychological, and social factors intertwine to create disease or health. As we have seen, the body has characteristic physiological reactions to stress. For people with pre-existing biological vulnerabilities, such as a genetic predisposition to heart disease, these physiological reactions to stress can cause deteriorations in health. Yet, an individual's perception of stress is determined by characteristics of events in the environment, and by his or her personal history, appraisals of the event, and coping styles. Thus, the extent to which the individual experiences psychological distress or ill health following potentially stressful situations is determined by the biological and psychological vulnerabilities and strengths he or she brings to these situations.

The field of behavioral medicine is exciting because it explicitly pursues integrative biopsychosocial models of disease and health. This fast-emerging field is also exciting because its findings hold much promise for improving people's lives.

 CHAPTER SUMMARY

1. Events are often considered stressful when they are *traumas* outside the range of normal human experience, are perceived as *uncontrollable* or *unpredictable,* when they *challenge* the limits of our capabilities, and when they cause *internal conflicts* between competing goals.

2. Common psychological reactions to stress include anxiety, anger and aggression, apathy and depression, and cognitive impairment (for example, problems in concentration and performance).

3. The body reacts to stress with the *fight-or-flight response.* The *sympathetic nervous system* causes increased heart rate, elevated blood pressure, dilated pupils, and the release of extra sugar from the liver. The *adrenal-cortical system* causes the release of adrenocorticotropic hormone (ACTH), which stimulates the release of cortisol in the blood. These reactions prepare the body to fight the stressor or to flee from it. When chronically aroused, however, these physiological responses can cause wear and tear on the body.

4. Stress may affect health directly by creating chronic overarousal of the sympathetic system or the adrenal cortical system or by impairing the immune system. People under stress also may not engage in positive health behaviors, and this may lead to illness.

5. The ways humans *appraise* events may influence their vulnerability to illness following events. For example, people who tend to explain bad events by internal, stable, and global causes are more likely to develop *learned helplessness* following bad events and to become ill.

6. People with the *Type A behavior pattern* tend to be hostile, aggressive, impatient persons who are overinvolved in their work. Studies of men and women show that people with this style are at increased risk for coronary heart disease.

7. Coping strategies are divided into *problem-focused strategies* and *emotion-focused strategies.* People who take active steps to solve problems are less likely to show depression and illness following negative life events. People who use rumination or avoidance strategies to cope with negative emotions show longer and more severe distress following events. Psychoanalytic theory describes a number of unconscious strategies (*defense mechanisms*) people use to cope with negative emotions; repression, reaction formation, denial, and projection are examples.

8. Behavioral techniques, such as relaxation training, and cognitive techniques, such as challenging negative thoughts, can help people react more adaptively to stress. Type A behavior can be changed through behavioral and cognitive techniques, resulting in a reduction of people's risk for coronary heart disease.

FURTHER READING

Stress and Stress Management: Research and Applications (1984) by Hamberger and Lohr discusses the different models of stress, some relevant research findings, and various methods for controlling stress. *Stress, Appraisal, and Coping* (1984) by Lazarus and

Folkman emphasizes the role of cognitive appraisal in determining stress. For a cognitive behavior approach to stress prevention and management, see Meichenbaum and Jaremko (eds.), *Stress Reduction and Prevention* (1983); and a paperback, *Stress Inoculation Training* (1985), by Meichenbaum.

The developing field of health psychology is described in *Why Zebras Don't Get Ulcers* (1994) by Sapolsky and in *The Psychology of Health, Illness, and Medical Care* (1991) by DiMatteo. See also *Behavioral Medicine: The Biopsychological Approach* (1985), edited by Schneiderman and Tapp, and *Mechanisms of Psychological Influence on Physical Health* (1989), edited by Carstensen and Neale. Pennebaker (1990) summarizes his research on the effect of confiding in others on physical health in *Opening Up: The Healing Powers of Confiding in Others*. For a review of research on stress and heart disease, see *Handbook of Stress, Reactivity, and Cardiovascular Disease* (1986), edited by Matthews. For a comprehensive review of the literature on psychology and health, see Taylor's *Health Psychology* (1991).

A classic account of defense mechanisms is given by Anna Freud in *The Ego and the Mechanisms of Defense* (rev. ed., 1967).

15
CHAPTER

Abnormal Psychology

Most of us have periods when we feel anxious, depressed, unreasonably angry, or inadequate in dealing with life's complexities. Trying to lead a satisfying and meaningful life is not easy in an era of rapid social and technological change. Many of our traditional assumptions about work, religion, sex, marriage, and family are being questioned, and the social values that gave our grandparents a sense of security no longer provide clear guidelines for behavior. It is an unusual person who manages to get through life without periods of loneliness, self-doubt, and despair. In fact, nearly half of Americans will experience a severe enough mental or emotional problem at least once during their lifetime that, if diagnosed, would be classified as a mental disorder (Kessler et al., 1994).

A word of warning may be appropriate before proceeding further. It is common for students studying abnormal psychology for the first time to see signs of mental disorders in themselves, just as medical students diagnose themselves as suffering from every new disease they read about. Most of us at one time or another have had some of the symptoms we will be describing, and that is no cause for alarm. However, if you have been bothered by distressing feelings for quite a while, it never hurts to talk to someone about them—perhaps someone in your school's counseling service or student health service.

ABNORMAL BEHAVIOR

In this chapter, we look at some individuals who have serious mental disorders and some who have developed self-destructive lifestyles. The behaviors we discuss are classified as "abnormal," but as we will see, the dividing line between "normal" and "abnormal" behavior is far from clear.

DEFINING ABNORMALITY

What do we mean by "abnormal" behavior? By what criteria do we distinguish it from "normal" behavior? There is no general agreement, but most attempts to describe abnormality are based on one or more of the following definitions.

DEVIATION FROM STATISTICAL NORMS The word *abnormal* means "away from the norm." Many characteristics, such as height, weight, and intelligence, cover a range of values when measured over a population. Most people fall within the middle range of height, while a few individuals are abnormally tall or abnormally short. One definition of abnormality is based on *statistical frequency:* Abnormal behavior is statistically infrequent or deviant from the norm. But according to this definition, the person who is extremely intelligent or extremely happy would be classified as abnormal. Thus, in defining abnormal behavior, we must consider more than statistical frequency.

DEVIATION FROM SOCIAL NORMS Every society has certain standards, or norms, for acceptable behavior; behavior that deviates markedly from these norms is considered abnormal. Usually, but not always, such behavior is also statistically infrequent in that society. However, several problems arise when deviation from social norms is used as a criterion for defining abnormality.

Behavior that is considered normal by one society may be considered abnormal by another. For example, members of some African cultures do not consider it unusual to hear voices when no one is actually talking or to see visions when nothing is actually there, but such behaviors are considered abnormal in most societies. Another problem is that the concept of abnormality changes over time within the same society. Most Americans would have considered smoking marijuana or appearing nearly nude at the beach abnormal behaviors 40 years ago. Today, such behaviors tend to be viewed as differences in life-style rather than as signs of abnormality.

Thus, ideas of normality and abnormality differ from one society to another and over time within the same society. Any definition of abnormality must reflect more than social compliance.

MALADAPTIVENESS OF BEHAVIOR Rather than defining abnormal behavior in terms of deviance from either statistical or societal norms, many social scientists believe that the most important criterion is how the behavior affects the well-being of the individual or of the social group. According to this criterion, behavior is abnormal if it is *maladaptive,* if it has adverse effects on the individual or on society. Some kinds of deviant behavior interfere with the welfare of the individual (a man who is so fearful of crowds that he cannot ride the bus to work; an alcoholic who drinks so heavily that he or she cannot keep a job; a woman who attempts suicide). Other forms of deviant behavior are harmful to society (an adolescent who has violent aggressive outbursts; a paranoid individual who plots to assassinate national leaders). If we use the criterion of maladaptiveness, all of these behaviors would be considered abnormal.

PERSONAL DISTRESS   A fourth criterion considers abnormality in terms of the individual's subjective feelings of distress rather than the individual's behavior. Most people diagnosed as mentally ill feel acutely miserable. They are anxious, depressed, or agitated and many suffer from insomnia, loss of appetite, or numerous aches and pains. Sometimes personal distress may be the only symptom of abnormality; the individual's behavior may appear normal to the casual observer.

None of these definitions provides a completely satisfactory description of abnormal behavior. In most instances, all four criteria—statistical frequency, social deviation, maladaptive behavior, and personal distress—are considered in diagnosing abnormality.

WHAT IS NORMALITY?

Normality is even more difficult to define than abnormality, but most psychologists would agree that the following qualities indicate emotional well-being. These characteristics do not make sharp distinctions between the mentally healthy and the mentally ill; rather, they represent traits that the normal person possesses to a *greater degree* than the individual who is diagnosed as abnormal.

1. *Efficient perception of reality* Normal individuals are fairly realistic in appraising their reactions and capabilities and in interpreting what is going on in the world around them. They do not consistently misperceive what others say and do, and they do not consistently overevaluate their abilities and tackle more than they can accomplish, nor do they underestimate their abilities and shy away from difficult tasks.

Behaviors are often labeled abnormal if they violate social norms for appropriateness.

2. *An ability to exercise voluntary control over behavior* Normal individuals feel fairly confident about their ability to control their behavior. Occasionally, they may act impulsively, but they are able to restrain sexual and aggressive urges when necessary. They may fail to conform to social norms, but their decision to act as such is voluntary rather than the result of uncontrollable impulses.

3. *Self-esteem and acceptance* Well-adjusted people have some appreciation of their own self-worth and feel accepted by those around them. They are comfortable with other people and are able to react spontaneously in social situations. At the same time, they do not feel obligated to subjugate their opinions to those of the group. Feelings of worthlessness, alienation, and lack of acceptance are prevalent among individuals who are diagnosed as abnormal.

4. *An ability to form affectionate relationships* Normal individuals are able to form close and satisfying relationships with other people. They are sensitive to the feelings of others and do not make excessive demands on others to gratify their own needs. Often, mentally disturbed people are so concerned with protecting their own security that they become extremely self-centered. Preoccupied with their own feelings and strivings, they seek affection but are unable to reciprocate. Sometimes they fear intimacy because their past relationships have been destructive.

5. *Productivity* Well-adjusted people are able to channel their abilities into productive activity. They are enthusiastic

about life and do not need to drive themselves to meet the demands of the day. A chronic lack of energy and excessive susceptibility to fatigue are often symptoms of psychological tension resulting from unsolved problems.

CLASSIFYING ABNORMAL BEHAVIOR

A broad range of behaviors has been classified as abnormal. Some abnormal behaviors are acute and transitory, resulting from particularly stressful events, whereas others are chronic and lifelong. Each person's behavior and emotional problems are unique; no two individuals behave in exactly the same manner or share the same life experiences. However, enough similarities exist for mental health professionals to classify cases into categories.

A classification system has advantages and disadvantages. If the various types of abnormal behavior have different causes, we can hope to uncover them by grouping individuals according to similarities in behavior and then looking for other ways in which the persons may be similar. A diagnostic label also enables those who work with disturbed individuals to communicate information more quickly and concisely. The diagnosis of **schizophrenia** indicates quite a bit about a person's behavior. Knowing that an individual's symptoms are similar to those of other patients (whose progress followed a particular course or who benefited from a certain kind of treatment) is also helpful in deciding how to treat the patient.

Disadvantages arise, however, if we allow a diagnostic label to carry too much weight. Labeling induces us to overlook the unique features of each case and to expect the person to conform to the classification. We may also forget that a label for maladaptive behavior is not an explanation of that behavior; the classification does not tell us how the behavior originated or what maintains the behavior.

The classification of mental disorders used by most mental health professionals in this country is the *Diagnostic and Statistical Manual of Mental Disorders,* 4th edition, (DSM-IV for short), which corresponds generally to the international system formulated by the World Health Organization. The major categories of mental disorders classified by

DSM-IV are listed in Table 15-1. Some of these disorders will be discussed in more detail later in the chapter.

DSM-IV provides an extensive list of subcategories under each of these headings, as well as a description of the symptoms that must be present for the diagnosis to be applicable. The complete diagnosis for an individual is fairly comprehensive. Each person is evaluated on five separate dimensions or axes. Axis I includes the categories listed in Table 15-1, except for personality disorders and mental retardation that make up Axis II. Axes I and II were separated to ensure that the presence of long-term disturbances would be considered when attending to the present disturbance. For example, a person who is now a heroin addict would be diagnosed on Axis I as having a psychoactive substance use disorder; he might also have a long-standing antisocial personality disorder, which would be listed on Axis II.

The remaining three axes are not needed to make the actual diagnosis but are included to ensure that factors other than a person's symptoms are considered in the overall assessment. The five axes are listed below.

I: The diagnostic category listed in Table 15-1 with the appropriate subclassification. For example, "schizophrenia, paranoid type."

II: Personality disorders and mental retardation are listed here, if present.

III: A list of any current physical disorders that may be relevant to understanding and treating the person.

IV: Documentation of stressful events that may have precipitated the disorder (such as divorce, death of a loved one).

V: An evaluation of how well the individual has functioned socially and occupationally during the previous year.

All of these variables are helpful in determining treatment and prognosis.

You have probably heard the terms "neurosis" and "psychosis" and may be wondering where they fit into the categories of mental disorders listed in Table 15-1. Traditionally, these terms denoted major diagnostic categories. **Neuroses** (plural of *neurosis*) included a group of disorders characterized by anxiety,

1. **Disorders usually first evident in infancy, childhood, or adolescence**

   Includes mental retardation, autism, attention deficit disorder with hyperactivity, separation anxiety, speech disorders, and other deviations from normal development.

2. **Delirium, dementia, amnestic, and other cognitive disorders**

   Disorders in which the functioning of the brain is known to be impaired, either permanently or transiently; may be the result of aging, degenerative diseases of the nervous system (for example, syphilis or Alzheimer's disease), or the ingestion of toxic substances (for example, lead poisoning or drugs).

3. **Psychoactive substance use disorders**

   Includes excessive use of alcohol, barbiturates, amphetamines, cocaine, and other drugs that alter behavior. Marijuana and tobacco are also included in this category, which is controversial.

4. **Schizophrenia**

   A group of disorders characterized by loss of contact with reality, marked disturbances of thought and perception, and bizarre behavior. At some phase delusions or hallucinations almost always occur.

5. **Mood disorders**

   Disturbances of normal mood; the person may be extremely depressed, abnormally elated, or may alternate between periods of elation and depression.

6. **Anxiety disorders**

   Includes disorders in which anxiety is the main symptom (generalized anxiety or panic disorders) or anxiety is experienced unless the individual avoids feared situations (phobic disorders) or tries to resist performing certain rituals or thinking persistent thoughts (obsessive-compulsive disorders). Also includes post-traumatic stress disorder.

7. **Somatoform disorders**

   The symptoms are physical, but no organic basis can be found and psychological factors appear to play the major role. Included are conversion disorders (for example, a woman who resents having to care for her invalid mother suddenly develops a paralyzed arm) and hypochondriasis (excessive preoccupation with health and fear of disease when there is no basis for concern.) Does *not* include psychosomatic disorders that have an organic basis. (See Chapter 14.)

8. **Dissociative disorders**

   Temporary alterations in the functions of consciousness, memory, or identity due to emotional problems. Included are amnesia (the individual cannot recall anything about his or her history following a traumatic experience) and dissociative identity disorder (better known as multiple personality disorder, involving two or more independent personality systems existing within the same individual).

9. **Sexual disorders**

   Includes problems of sexual identity (for example, transsexualism), sexual performance (for example, impotence, premature ejaculation, and frigidity), and sexual aim (for example, sexual interest in children, sadism, and masochism).

10. **Eating disorders**

    Self-induced starvation (anorexia) or patterns of binge eating followed by self-induced purging (bulimia).

11. **Sleep disorders**

    Includes chronic insomnia, excessive sleepiness, sleep apnea, sleep-walking, and narcolepsy.

12. **Factitious disorders**

    Physical or psychological symptoms that are intentionally produced or feigned. Differs from malingering in that there is no obvious goal, such as disability payments or the avoidance of military service. The best-studied form of this disorder is called Münchausen syndrome: The individual's plausible presentation of factitious physical symptoms results in frequent hospitalizations.

13. **Impulse control disorder**

    Includes kleptomania (compulsive stealing of objects not needed for personal use or their monetary value), pathological gambling and pyromania (setting fires for the pleasure or relief of tension derived thereby).

14. **Personality disorders**

    Long-standing patterns of maladaptive behavior that constitute immature and inappropriate ways of coping with stress or solving problems. Antisocial personality disorder and narcissistic personality disorder are two examples.

15. **Other conditions that may be the focus of clinical attention**

    This category includes many of the problems for which people seek help, such as marital problems, parent-child difficulties, and academic or occupational problems.

TABLE 15-1

Categories of Mental Disorders *Listed are the main diagnostic categories of DSM-IV. Each category includes numerous subclassifications. Personality disorders and developmental disorders (such as mental retardation and delayed language) are coded on Axis II.* (After American Psychiatric Association, 1994) personal unhappiness, and maladaptive behavior that were seldom serious enough to require hospitalization. The individual could usually function in society, although not at full capacity. **Psychoses** (plural of *psychosis*) included more serious mental disorders. The individual's behavior and thought processes were so disturbed that he or she was out of touch with reality, could not cope with the demands of daily life, and usually had to be hospitalized.

Neither neuroses nor psychoses appear as major categories in DSM-IV. There are several reasons for this departure from earlier classification systems, but the main one concerns precision of diagnosis. Both categories were fairly broad and included a number of mental disorders with quite dissimilar symptoms. Consequently, mental health professionals did not always agree on the diagnosis for a particular case. DSM-IV attempts to achieve greater consensus by grouping disorders according to very specific behavioral symptoms, without implying anything about their origins or treatment. The intention is to describe what clinical workers *observe* about individuals who have psychological problems in a way that ensures accurate communication among mental health professionals. Consequently, DSM-IV includes many more categories than previous editions of the manual.

Although psychosis is no longer a major category, DSM-IV recognizes that people diagnosed as having schizophrenia, delusional dis-

orders, and some mood disorders exhibit **psychotic behavior** at some point during their illness. Their thinking and perception of reality are severely disturbed and they may have **hallucinations** (false sensory experiences, such as hearing voices or seeing strange visions) and/or **delusions** (false beliefs, such as the conviction that all thoughts are controlled by a powerful being from another planet).

These issues will become clearer as we look more closely at some of the mental disorders listed in Table 15-1. In the remainder of this chapter, we will examine anxiety disorders, mood disorders, schizophrenia, and two types of personality disorder. Alcoholism and drug dependence (both classified as psychoactive substance use disorders) are covered in Chapter 6. Multiple personality, a dissociative disorder, is also discussed in Chapter 6.

Table 15-2 gives the likelihood of the major mental disorders during one's lifetime. The study on which this table is based found that mental disorders are more common among people under age 45. Although the overall rates of disorders are not different in men and women, men are twice as likely as women to abuse alcohol or other drugs. Antisocial personality disorders affected four times as many men as women, but more women suffered from mood and anxiety disorders.

Many cultures recognize mental disorders that do not correspond to any disorders listed in the DSM-IV (see Table 15-3). Some of these disorders may have the same underlying causes as certain disorders recognized by the DSM-IV, but are manifested by different symptoms in other cultures. Other disorders may be truly unique to the cultures in which they are found.

DISORDER	RATE
Anxiety disorders	24.9
Mood disorders	19.3
Schizophrenia and related disorders	0.7
Antisocial personality	3.5
Substance use disorder	26.6

TABLE 15-2

Lifetime Prevalence Rates of Selected Disorders
Listed are the percentage of individuals in the United States population who have experienced one of these mental disorders during their lifetime. These percentages are based on interviews with a sample of 8,098 individuals, age 18 to 54, all around United States cities. (After Kessler et al., 1994)

PERSPECTIVE ON MENTAL DISORDERS

Attempts to understand the causes of mental disorders and proposals for treating them generally fall under one of the approaches to psychology described in Chapter 1. The **biological perspective**, also called the medical or disease model, emphasizes the idea that bodily disturbances cause disordered behavior. Researchers using this approach look for genetic irregularities that may predispose a person to develop a particular mental disorder. They also look for abnormalities in specific parts of the brain, defects in neurotransmission, and problems in the functioning of the autonomic nervous system. Drugs are pri-

SYNDROME	Cultures Where Found	Symptoms
amok	Malaysia, Laos, Phillipines, Papau New Guinea, Puerto Rico, Navajos	Brooding, followed by violent behavior, persecutory ideas, amnesia, exhaustion. More often seen in men than women.
ataque de nervios	Latin America	Uncontrollable shouting, crying, trembling, heat in the chest rising to the head, verbal or physical aggression, seizures, fainting.
ghost sickness	American Indians	Nightmares, weakness, feelings of danger, loss of appetite, fainting, dizziness, hallucinations, loss of consciousness, sense of suffocation.
koro	Malaysia, China, Thailand	Sudden and intense anxiety that the penis (in males) or the vulva and nipples (in females) will recede into body and cause death.
latah	East Asia	Hypersensitivity to sudden fright, trancelike behavior most often seen in middle-aged women.
susto	Mexico, Central America	Appetite disturbances, sleep disturbances, sadness, loss of motivation, low self-worth, following a frightening event. Sufferers believe their soul has left their body.
taijin kyofusho	Japan	Intense fear that one's body displeases, embarrasses, or is offensive to others.

TABLE 15-3

Culture-bound syndromes *Some cultures have syndromes or mental disorders that are only found in that culture, and that do not correspond to any DSM-IV categories.* Based on Robert C. Carson and James N. Butcher, Abnormal Psychology, 9th ed. (Glenview, Illinois: Scott, Foresman) 1992, p. 89.

marily used by proponents of this perspective to treat disorders.

The **psychoanalytic perspective** on mental disorders emphasizes the importance of unconscious conflicts, usually originating in early childhood, and the use of defense mechanisms to handle the anxiety generated by the repressed impulses and emotions. Bringing the unconscious conflicts and emotions into awareness presumably eliminates the need for the defense mechanisms and alleviates the disorder.

The **behavioral perspective** looks at mental disorders from the standpoint of learning theory and assumes that maladaptive behaviors are learned. This approach investigates how fears become conditioned to specific situations and the role that reinforcement plays in the origin and maintenance of inappropriate behaviors.

The **cognitive perspective**, like the psychoanalytic perspective, is concerned with internal processes. Rather than stressing hidden motivations, emotions, and conflicts, however, it emphasizes conscious mental processes. The way we think about ourselves (our **self-schema**), the way we appraise stressful situations, and our strategies for coping with them are all interrelated. From the cognitive viewpoint, some mental disorders stem from disordered cognitive processes and can be alleviated by changing these faulty cognitions.

The ideas embodied in these summaries will become clearer as we discuss them in relation to specific mental disorders. Each of these approaches has something important to say about mental disorders, but none has the complete answer. Some disorders, such as schizophrenia, have a stronger biological component than others. But psychological and environmental factors also play a role. One way of integrating these factors is the **vulnerability-stress model** which considers the interaction between a *predisposition* that makes a person vulnerable for developing an illness and stressful environmental conditions the individual encounters. On a biological level, vulnerability might be genetic. For some of the disorders we will discuss, having a close relative with the disorder increases the person's risk of developing it. On a psychological level, a chronic feeling of hopelessness and inadequacy might make an individual vulnerable for the development of depression.

Being vulnerable for a disorder does not, by any means, guarantee that the person will develop the disorder. Whether or not the predisposition leads to an actual disorder often depends on the kinds of stressors the individual encounters. These would include poverty, malnutrition, frustration, conflicts, and traumatic life events.

The key point of the vulnerability-stress model is that both vulnerability and stress are necessary. It helps explain why some people become mentally ill when confronted with a minimum of stress, while others remain healthy regardless of how difficult their lives may be.

ANXIETY DISORDERS

Most of us feel anxious and tense in the face of threatening or stressful situations. Such feelings are normal reactions to stress. Anxiety is considered abnormal only when it occurs in situations that most people can handle with little difficulty. *Anxiety disorders* include a group of disorders in which anxiety either is the main symptom (*generalized anxiety* and *panic disorders*) or is experienced when the individual attempts to control certain maladaptive behaviors (*phobic* and *obsessive-compulsive disorders*). (Posttraumatic stress disorder, which involves anxiety following a traumatic event, was discussed in Chapter 14.)

I am often bothered by the thumping of my heart.

Little annoyances get on my nerves and irritate me.

I often become suddenly scared for no good reason.

I worry continuously and that gets me down.

I frequently get spells of complete exhaustion and fatigue.

It is always hard for me to make up my mind.

I always seem to be dreading something.

I feel nervous and high-strung all the time.

I often feel I cannot overcome my difficulties.

I feel constantly under strain.

TABLE 15-4

Generalized Anxiety   *The statements listed in the table are self-descriptions by individuals who have chronically high levels of anxiety.* (After Sarason & Sarason, 1993)

GENERALIZED ANXIETY AND PANIC DISORDERS

A person who suffers from a **generalized anxiety disorder** lives each day in a state of high tension. She or he feels vaguely uneasy or apprehensive much of the time and tends to overreact even to mild stresses. An inability to relax, disturbed sleep, fatigue, headaches, dizziness, and rapid heart rate are the most common physical complaints. In addition, the individual continually worries about potential problems and has difficulty concentrating or making decisions. When the individual finally makes a decision, it becomes the source of further worry ("Did I foresee all possible consequences?" or "Will disaster result?"). Some self-descriptions provided by people with chronically high levels of anxiety appear in Table 15-4.

People who suffer generalized anxiety may also experience panic attacks—episodes of acute and overwhelming apprehension or terror. During panic attacks, the individual feels certain that something dreadful is about to happen. This feeling is usually accompanied by such symptoms as heart palpitations, shortness of breath, perspiration, muscle tremors, faintness, and nausea. The symptoms result from excitation of the sympathetic division of the autonomic nervous system (see Chapter 2) and are the same reactions an individual experiences when extremely frightened. During severe panic attacks, the person fears that he or she will die. The following personal account describes how terrifying such experiences can be:

> I remember walking up the street, the moon was shining and suddenly everything around me seemed unfamiliar, as it would be in a dream. I felt panic rising inside me, but managed to push it away and carry on. I walked a quarter of a mile or so, with the panic getting worse every minute. . . . By now, I was sweating, yet trembling; my heart was pounding and my legs felt like jelly. . . . Terrified, I stood, not knowing what to do. The only bit of sanity left in me told me to get home. Somehow this I did very slowly, holding onto the fence in the road. I cannot remember the actual journey back, until I was going into the house, then I broke down and cried helplessly. . . . I did not go out again for a few days. When I did, it was with my mother and baby to my grandmother's a few miles away. I felt panicky there and couldn't cope with the baby. My cousin suggested we go to my Aunt's house, but I had another attack there. I was sure I was going to

die. Following this, I was totally unable to go out alone, and even with someone else I had great difficulty. Not only did I get the panicky fainting spells, but I lived in constant fear of getting them. (Melville, 1977, pp. 1, 14)

People who experience generalized anxiety and **panic disorders** may have no clear idea of why they are frightened. This kind of anxiety is sometimes called "free-floating" because it is not triggered by a particular event; rather, it occurs in a variety of situations.

PHOBIAS

In contrast to the vague apprehension of generalized anxiety disorders, the fears in phobic disorders are more specific. Someone who responds with intense fear to a stimulus or situation that most people do not consider particularly dangerous is said to have a **phobia**. The individual usually realizes that his or her fear is irrational but still feels anxiety (ranging from strong uneasiness to panic) that can be alleviated only by avoiding the feared object or situation.

Many of us have an irrational fear or two—snakes, insects, and heights are common ones. However, a fear is usually not diagnosed as a phobic disorder unless it interferes considerably with the person's daily life. Examples of phobic disorders would be a woman whose fear of enclosed places prevents her from entering elevators or a man whose fear of crowds prevents him from attending the theater or walking along congested sidewalks.

DSM-IV divides phobic disorders into three broad categories: simple phobias, social phobias, and agoraphobia. A **simple phobia** is a fear of a specific object, animal, or situation. Irrational fears of snakes, germs, enclosed places, and darkness are examples. Some people may develop a simple phobia but be normal in other respects. In more serious cases, the individual has a number of phobias that interfere with many aspects of life and may be intertwined with obsessive or compulsive behavior.

People with **social phobias** feel extremely insecure in social situations and have an exaggerated fear of embarrassing themselves. Often they are fearful that they will betray their anxiety by such signs as hand tremors, blushing, or a quavering voice. These fears are usually unrealistic: Individuals who fear they might shake do not do so; those who fear they will stutter or quaver actually speak quite normally. Fear of public speaking or of eating in public are the most common complaints of socially phobic individuals.

Agoraphobia is the most common phobia among people seeking professional help. It is also the most disabling. The word is Greek for "fear of the marketplace." Individuals suffering from agoraphobia are afraid of entering unfamiliar settings. They avoid open spaces, crowds, and traveling. In extreme cases, the individual may be afraid to leave the familiar setting of home. The following incident in the life of a woman suffering from agoraphobia shows how distressing such fears can be.

The woman who lives next door is a very nice person and I like her. One day she asked me if I would drive over to a big shopping center that had recently opened about five miles from where we live. I didn't know how to tell her that there isn't a chance in the world that I'd go to that shopping center or any other place outside our neighborhood. She must have seen how upset I got, but I was shaking like a leaf even more inside. I imagined myself in the crowd, getting lost, or passing out. I was terrified by the openness of the shopping center and the crowds. I made an excuse this time, but I don't know what I'll say next time. Maybe I'll just have to let her in on my little bit of craziness. (Sarason & Sarason, 1989, p. 155)

Agoraphobics usually have a history of panic attacks. They become fearful of being

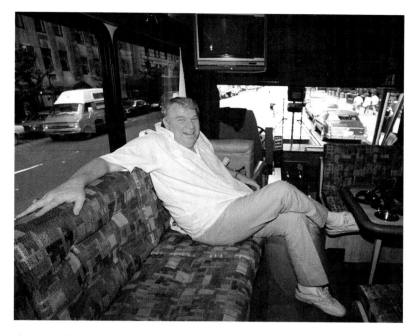

Sports commentator John Madden rides to sports events in a custom-built bus because he has a phobia of flying.

incapacitated by an attack away from the security of home and where no one may be available to help them. Crowded enclosed places where escape to safety would be difficult (such as a bus or a theater) are especially terrifying. But agoraphobics also fear open spaces (large bodies of water, bare landscapes, an empty street) and feel more comfortable when the space is circumscribed by trees, or when an enclosed space (perhaps symbolic of home) is easily reached. Agoraphobics are usually very dependent. A large percentage of them exhibited separation anxiety (fear of being away from mother) in childhood, long before developing agoraphobia (Gittelman & Klein, 1985). While simple phobias and social phobias are fairly easy to treat, agoraphobia is much more difficult.

OBSESSIVE-COMPULSIVE DISORDERS

A man gets out of bed several times each night and checks all the doors to make sure they are locked. On returning to bed he is tormented by the thought that he may have missed one. Another man takes three or four showers in succession, scrubbing his body thoroughly with a special disinfectant each time, fearful that he may be contaminated by germs. A woman has recurrent thoughts about stabbing her infant and feels panic-stricken whenever she has to handle scissors or knives. A teenage girl is always late to school because she feels compelled to repeat many of her ac-

An obsessive-compulsive person who fears contamination may spend hours every day performing cleaning rituals.

tions (replacing her brush on the dresser, arranging the school supplies in her bookbag, crossing the threshold to her bedroom) a set number of times, usually some multiple of the number four.

All of these people have symptoms of an **obsessive-compulsive disorder,** their lives are dominated by repetitive acts or thoughts. **Obsessions** are persistent intrusions of unwelcome thoughts, images, or impulses that elicit anxiety. **Compulsions** are irresistible urges to carry out certain acts or rituals that reduce anxiety. Obsessive thoughts are often linked with compulsive acts (for example, thoughts of lurking germs which lead to the compulsion to wash eating utensils many times before using them). Regardless of whether the repetitive element is a thought (obsession) or an act (compulsion), the central feature of the disorder is the subjective experience of loss of voluntary control. The victims struggle mightily to rid themselves of the troublesome thoughts or to resist performing the repetitive acts but are unable to do so.

At times, all of us have persistently recurring thoughts ("Did I leave the gas on?") and urges to perform ritualistic behavior (arranging the materials on a desk in a precise order before starting an assignment). But for people with obsessive-compulsive disorders, such thoughts and acts occupy so much time that they seriously interfere with daily life. The individuals recognize their thoughts as irrational and repugnant but are unable to ignore or suppress them. They realize the senselessness of their compulsive behavior but become anxious when they try to resist their compulsions, and feel a release of tension once the acts are carried out.

Obsessive thoughts cover a variety of topics, but most often they are concerned with causing harm to oneself or others, fear of contamination, and doubt that a completed task has been accomplished satisfactorily (Rachman & Hodgson, 1980; Stern & Cobb, 1978). Interestingly enough, the content of obsessions changes with the times. In earlier days obsessive thoughts about religion and sex were common—for example, blasphemous thoughts or impulses to shout obscenities in church or expose one's genitals in public. They are less frequent today. While obsessions about contamination used to focus on syphilis, AIDS has now become the object of many contamination fears (Rapaport, 1989).

BOX 1   ## *Obsessive-Compulsive Disorder*

Mike, a 32-year-old patient, engaged in checking rituals that were triggered by a fear of harming others. When driving he felt compelled to stop the car often to check whether he had run over people, particularly babies. Before flushing the toilet, Mike inspected the commode to be sure that a live insect had not fallen into the toilet—he did not want to be responsible for killing any living creature. In addition, he repeatedly checked the doors, stoves, lights, and windows, making sure that all were shut or turned off so that no harm, such as fire or burglary, would befall his family as a result of his "irresponsible" behavior. In particular he worried about the safety of his 15-month-old daughter, repeatedly checking the gate to the basement to be sure that it was locked. He did not carry his daughter while walking on concrete floors in order to avoid killing her by accidentally dropping her. Mike performed these and many other checking rituals for an average of four hours a day. Checking behavior started several months after his marriage, 6 years before treatment. It increased 2 years later, when Mike's wife was pregnant with their first child, and continued to worsen over the years.

Treatment for Mike included a form of systematic desensitization (see Chapter 16) in which he imagined scenes of his fears. For example, he was asked to imagine that he forgot to check the windows and doors; a burglar entered and stole his wife's jewelry; she blamed him for the theft. Or to imagine that he dropped his baby daughter on the concrete floor because he wasn't holding her properly and she suffered serious injuries. His homework involved actual exposure to the feared situation—for example, walking his daughter on a concrete floor until his anxiety subsides or closing doors and windows and checking only once.

At a 3-year follow-up, Mike reported 10 minutes of checking per day in contrast to 4 hours before treatment (Foa & Steketee, 1989, pp. 185, 200).

Some people with an obsessive-compulsive disorder have intrusive thoughts without overt repetitious actions. However, the majority of patients with obsessive thoughts also exhibit compulsive behavior (Akhtar et al., 1975). Compulsions take a variety of forms, of which the two most common are *washing* and *checking* (Foa & Steketee, 1989). "Washers" are individuals who feel contaminated when exposed to certain objects or thoughts and spend hours performing washing and cleaning rituals. "Checkers" are people who check doors, lights, ovens, the accuracy of a completed task—10, 20, or 100 times—or who repeat ritualistic acts over and over again. They believe that their actions will prevent future "disaster" or punishments. Sometimes these rituals are related to the anxiety-evoking obsessions in a direct way (for example, repeatedly checking to see if the stove is off to avoid possible fire); other rituals are not rationally related to the obsessions (for example, dressing and undressing to prevent one's husband from having an accident). The common theme behind all of these repetition behaviors is doubt. Obsessive-compulsive individuals cannot trust their senses or their judgment; they can't trust their eyes that see no dirt or really believe that the door is locked. The case described in Box 1 shows how time consuming and extensive checking rituals can be.

Obsessive-compulsive disorders are related to phobic disorders in that both involve severe anxiety and both may appear in the same patient. However, there are important differences. Phobic patients seldom ruminate constantly about their fears nor do they show ritualistic compulsive behavior. And the two disorders have different evoking stimuli. Dirt, germs, and harm to others—which are common obsessive-compulsive preoccupations—seldom cause major problems for phobic individuals.

UNDERSTANDING ANXIETY DISORDERS

We do not know why some people become chronically anxious, but their reactions seem to reflect feelings of inadequacy in situations that they perceive as threatening. Following the approaches to understanding mental disorders described earlier, theories of anxiety disorders have focused on internal conflicts, learned responses to external events, maladaptive cognitions, and biological factors.

PSYCHOANALYTIC PERSPECTIVE Psychoanalytic theory assumes that the major determinants of anxiety disorders are internal conflicts and unconscious motives. As we noted in Chapter 14, Freud distinguished between **objective anxiety,**

which is a reasonable response to a harmful situation, and **neurotic anxiety**, which is out of proportion to the actual danger. He believed that neurotic anxiety stems from unconscious conflicts within the individual between unacceptable **id** impulses (mainly sexual and aggressive) and the constraints imposed by the **ego** and **superego**. When these impulses come close to consciousness, anxiety is aroused and serves as a signal of potential danger. Because the source of anxiety is unconscious, the person does not know why he or she feels apprehensive.

Later psychoanalysts expanded the causes of neurotic anxiety to include the perception of oneself as helpless and unable to cope, fear of separation or being abandoned, and anticipation of disapproval and withdrawal of love. These feelings are assumed to be largely unconscious.

From a psychoanalytic viewpoint, phobias are ways of coping with anxiety by displacing it onto an object or situation that can be avoided. The classic example is the case of Little Hans, a 5-year-old who developed an intense fear of horses. Freud interpreted the boy's phobia in terms of Oedipal fears (see Chapter 13) by the following analysis. Hans was in love with his mother, jealously hated his father, and wanted to replace him (the **Oedipal Conflict**); he feared that his father would retaliate by castrating him; the anxiety produced by this conflict was enormous because the wishes were unacceptable to the child's conscious mind; the anxiety was displaced onto an innocent object (a large horse

To what extent is chronic anxiety a result of internal conflict, learned response, unrealistic appraisal, or genetic predisposition?

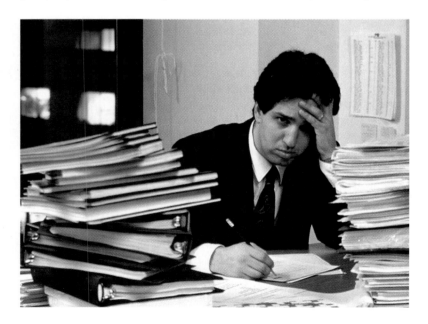

that Hans had seen fall down and thrash about violently in the street).

According to psychoanalytic theory, bringing the unconscious conflict to light and gaining insight into the fears that are being displaced onto the phobic object should cure the phobia. However, as we will see in Chapter 16, psychoanalysis has not proved very successful in treating phobias.

Obsessions and compulsions also serve to protect the individual from recognizing the true source of his or her anxiety. Obsessive thoughts are unacceptable impulses (hostility, destructiveness, inappropriate sexual urges) that have been repressed and somehow reappear in a disguised form. The individual feels that they are not a part of herself or himself and may commit compulsive acts to undo or atone for forbidden impulses. A mother who is obsessed with thoughts of murdering her infant may feel compelled to check many times during the night to assure herself that the child is well. Compulsive rituals also serve to keep threatening impulses out of the individual's conscious awareness: A person who is continually busy has little opportunity to think improper thoughts or commit improper actions.

BEHAVIORAL PERSPECTIVE   Psychologists who work within the framework of learning theory view anxiety as triggered more by specific external events than by internal conflicts. Generalized anxiety occurs when a person feels unable to cope with many everyday situations and consequently feels apprehensive much of the time. Phobias are viewed as avoidance responses that may be learned either directly from frightening experiences (developing a fear of dogs after being attacked by one) or vicariously by observing fearful responses in others.

The classical conditioning paradigm (see Chapter 7) provides an explanation of how innocuous objects or situations can become the focus of a phobia: A neutral object (the conditioned stimulus) paired with a traumatic event (the unconditioned stimulus) produces fear of the neutral object (the conditioned response). Learning theorists would explain the case of Little Hans according to this paradigm. The horse (the CS, previously a neutral object) paired with a traumatic event (the US, sight of the horse falling down and thrashing violently) produced a fear of horses (the CR, or phobia).

The precipitating trauma, when it can be identified in phobic cases, is well described by classical conditioning. And considerable evidence from laboratory experiments with animals and humans shows that pairing a neutral object with a frightening situation produces fear of the neutral object. However, there are problems with this explanation of phobias. Simple phobias almost always are restricted to a certain set of objects, rather than to any object that happens to be present at the same time as the traumatic event. Why, for example, are phobias of the dark common, but phobias of pajamas nonexistent, although both are paired with nighttime trauma? Why do we have phobias of snakes and insects but not phobias of kittens or lambs? And why are phobias of knives and guns rare, even though both objects are often paired with injury?

The notion of **prepared conditioning** has been proposed as an explanation. Humans are biologically predisposed, or prepared, to react with fear only to certain classes of dangerous objects or situations. When these objects or situations are paired with trauma, fear conditioning occurs rapidly and is very resistant to extinction (Seligman, 1971). The majority of common phobias were once actually dangerous to our early ancestors. Natural selection may have favored those ancestors who learned quickly (with only minimal exposure to trauma) that strangers, heights, snakes, large animals, and the dark were dangerous. Thus, there may be a select group of objects, all dangerous in an earlier time, that are readily conditionable to trauma. We are less likely to become conditioned to fear other objects (such as lambs, guns, and electric outlets) either because they were never dangerous or because their origin is too recent to have been subject to natural selection. Thus, phobias are instances not of ordinary classical conditioning but of prepared classical conditioning.

A series of laboratory experiments lends support to the idea that people are more prepared to learn to be afraid of certain objects than they are of others. Fear was conditioned in student volunteers using a variety of prepared conditioned stimuli (pictures of snakes or spiders) and unprepared stimuli (pictures of houses, faces, or flowers). The pictures were followed by a brief, painful electric shock. Fear conditioning, as measured by galvanic skin response (see Chapter 7), occurred much more rapidly to prepared stimuli than to unprepared ones. In fact, conditioning oc-

We may be biologically predisposed to phobias of things that have threatened our species for centuries.

curred in one pairing of electric shock with pictures of snakes and spiders, but it took four or five pairings for subjects' fear to be conditioned to faces, houses, or flowers. A subsequent experiment found the conditioning properties of guns to be similar to those for flowers, not snakes and spiders (Ohman, Fredrikson, Hugdahl, & Rimmo, 1976). Presumably, guns have not been around long enough for us to have become biologically prepared to develop phobias of them.

Viewing phobias as a form of prepared learning helps explain their irrationality and their resistance to extinction. With normal fear conditioning, once the unconditioned stimulus (for instance, the electric shock) is no longer paired with the conditioned stimulus, fear extinguishes rapidly. This does not appear to be the case for prepared fear conditioning. In one study, students were conditioned to fear either snakes and spiders or houses and faces by pairing each with shock. At the end of the conditioning (when the electrodes were removed), fear extinguished immediately to houses and faces but remained intense to snakes and spiders (Hugdahl & Ohman, 1977).

While some phobias appear to result from actual frightening experiences, others may be learned vicariously, through observation. Fearful parents tend to produce children who share their fears. A child who observes his or her parents react with fear to a variety of situations may accept such reactions as normal. Indeed, studies find a high correlation between the fears of a mother and those of her child.

As we will see in the next chapter, the treatment of phobias within the framework of learning theory uses various techniques to extinguish fear responses to the phobic object or situation.

COGNITIVE PERSPECTIVE   A cognitive analysis of anxiety disorders focuses on the way that anxious people think about situations and potential dangers. Individuals who suffer from generalized anxiety tend to make unrealistic appraisals of certain situations, primarily those in which the possibility of danger is remote. They consistently overestimate both the *degree* of harm and the *likelihood* of harm. This kind of mental set makes a person hypervigilant, always on the lookout for signs of danger. For example, a sudden noise in the house is interpreted as burglars; the screech of brakes in the street means one's child is in danger. This hypervigilance and expectation of harm result in continual bodily mobilization for danger. Thus, the physiological responses characteristic of the **fight-or-flight reaction** (tremors, rapid heart rate, clammy hands, muscle tension) are present much of the time.

The cognitive theory of obsessions assumes that we all have unwanted and repetitive thoughts on occasion. For example, song lyrics or advertising jingles often intrude unbidden into consciousness. But we are able to dismiss them, as well as the more abhorrent thoughts that occasionally run through our heads. The more anxiety-provoking the content of the obsession, the more difficult it is for anyone—obsessive or nonobsessive—to dismiss the thought. And the more stressed we are, the more frequent and intense are these thoughts. If a person is anxious to begin with, obsessive thoughts will be more disturbing and more difficult to dismiss.

If an event triggers a disturbing thought in a nonobsessive person, he or she may find the thought unacceptable but will not become anxious and will easily dismiss it. In contrast, the obsessive person will be made anxious by the thought, and the anxiety will reduce his or her ability to dismiss it. The thought will persist, and the obsessive's inability to disregard it will lead to further anxiety, which will increase his or her susceptibility to the intrusive thought.

Studies of obsessive-compulsive individuals have revealed that those persons hold unreasonable beliefs and assumptions. They believe that they (1) should be perfectly competent, (2) must avoid criticism or disapproval, and (3) will be severely punished for their mistakes and imperfections. At some level they also seem to believe that thinking certain thoughts or performing certain rituals will help them avoid the disastrous consequences that they imagine are just around the corner (Sarason & Sarason, 1993). Repetitive checking behaviors may be attempts to ensure that the task was done properly so that disaster is forestalled. Compulsive washing rituals may assure safety for the person obsessed with thoughts of disease and germs. These behaviors are reinforced by the relief from anxiety. But the relief is temporary. The obsessive thoughts return with increased frequency and intensity, and the individual must perform the ritual each time the thought recurs.

As we will see in the next chapter, the cognitive approach to treating obsessive disorders uses the technique of thought stopping to help the individual terminate obsessive thoughts. The treatment for generalized anxiety and phobias focuses on helping individuals develop more realistic and rational appraisals of themselves and the situations they encounter.

BIOLOGICAL PERSPECTIVE   Anxiety disorders tend to run in families. About 15 percent of parents and siblings of people who have anxiety disorders are similarly affected (Carey & Gottesman, 1981). This finding does not, of course, prove a hereditary basis for such disorders, since these individuals usually live together and thus experience similar environments. However, the results of twin studies provide firmer evidence for an inherited predisposition for panic attacks. Identical twins, as you recall, develop from the same egg and share the same heredity; fraternal twins develop from different eggs and are no more alike genetically than ordinary siblings. An identical twin is three times more likely to suffer from panic attacks if the other twin does than are fraternal twins (Torgersen, 1983).

Evidence for a biochemical basis for panic disorders comes from laboratory studies showing that a number of substances (including caffeine, sodium lactate, and the inhalation of a mixture of carbon dioxide and oxygen) can trigger panic attacks in individuals who suffer from spontaneous panic attacks. These same substances usually have no effect on normal individuals or on phobics who experience anxiety in response to an external stimulus (see McNally, 1990, for a review). In addition, scientists have identified a brain chemical (cholecystokinin) that will produce an attack in patients with panic disorders. Drugs that are capable of preventing panic attacks appear to block the effect of this chemical on neurons (Bradwejn, Koszycki, & Meterissian, 1989).

These and other data have convinced biological theorists that panic disorder is a disease of the body rather than a mental disorder. However, cognitive theorists are not so sure. They claim that panic disorder results from "catastrophic misinterpretation" of bodily sensations (Clark, 1988; Clark & Beck, 1988). For example, panic may arise when a person misinterprets rapid heartbeat and breathlessness as a sign of an impending heart attack or dizziness as a sign of a stroke. Catastrophic misinterpretation may also underlie panic attacks produced in the laboratory by the administration of sodium lactate or inhalation of an oxygen/carbon-dioxide mixture. These agents produce similar physiological effects in both panic patients and control subjects, yet only panic patients consistently respond with a panic attack (Yerazani, Balon, & Pohl, 1989).

What determines whether someone will panic in response to unusual bodily sensations? One possibility is that pre-existing beliefs about the harmfulness of such sensations may predispose individuals to interpret them catastrophically and thereby panic. If catastrophic misinterpretation is the cause of panic disorder, then teaching patients to correctly interpret their bodily sensations should cure the disorder. And apparently it does. In these treatment studies, patients brought to the clinic overbreathe (hyperventilate) into a bag. At first this will usually induce an immediate panic attack by producing shortness of breath. The patients are then taught to recognize that shortness of breath is simply the result of hyperventilating when they are under stress and not a sign of an impending heart attack or other catastrophe. Investigators using these treatment methods have reported complete reduction in panic at-

tacks in almost all patients, with no relapse (Beck, 1988; Clark, 1988).

The debate about a specific biochemical cause for panic disorders remains to be resolved by further research. It is clear, however, that both biological and psychological factors play a role. Genetic research suggests that individuals may inherit a general anxiety proneness that manifests itself in various anxiety disorders, including panic disorders.

The chemical systems in the brain that regulate feelings of anxiety undoubtedly involve the complex interaction of a number of neurotransmitters acting on different brain areas. In 1960, a group of drugs called **benzodiazepines** were developed and marketed under such trade names as Valium and Librium. These drugs proved effective in reducing anxiety (see Chapter 16 for a discussion of their merits and disadvantages). Researchers subsequently discovered that the drugs were effective because they bind to specific receptor molecules in certain neurons of the brain, thereby influencing neural transmission (see Chapter 2). The discovery of receptor sites for antianxiety drugs set off a search for a natural body substance that might act in the same way to keep anxiety in proper balance. So far, a natural Valium has not been found, but investigators have learned a great deal about the benzodiazepine receptors and how certain chemicals operate to increase or decrease anxiety (Costa, 1985).

There appear to be three specific docking areas on the benzodiazepine receptor site: one for the benzodiazepine molecule with its

This PET scan shows the metabolic differences between areas of the brain of a person with obsessive compulsive disorder and a normal control subject.

antianxiety effects, another for compounds that cause anxiety (the effects of which are blocked by administration of the benzodiazepines), and the third for a group of substances that block the effects of both the benzodiazepines and the anxiety-provoking compounds. The identification of these three receptor sites suggests that some substances secreted in the brain produce the subjective experience of fear and anxiety and other substances block this effect. The ratio of these substances may lead either to an emotionally stable or to an anxious individual (Agras, 1985).

The fact that head injuries, tumors, and encephalitis have all been associated with the development of obsessive-compulsive disorders has prompted the search for brain abnormalities that may make an individual vulnerable to repetitive thoughts and behaviors. PET scan studies (see Chapter 2) of obsessive-compulsive individuals have shown that the metabolic activity in a specific region of their brains (a circuit that runs between the frontal lobes and the basal ganglia) differs from that of normal individuals (Baxter et al., 1988). This region is believed to be involved in the brain's strategy for coping with repeated stimuli and in the control of repetitive movements. In essence, this part of the brain may play a role in telling the rest of the brain to stop worrying about contamination once the hands have been washed or about fire once the stove has been turned off. The exact nature of the brain chemistry abnormality is unknown, and such abnormalities may not be found in all cases of obsessive-compulsive disorders. Nevertheless, treatment with drugs that block the uptake of a neurotransmitter for which the basal ganglia have particularly dense receptors relieves obsessive-compulsive symptoms in about 60 percent of cases (Rapaport, 1989).

MOOD DISORDERS

In **mood disorders** the person may be severely depressed or manic (wildly elated), or may experience periods of depression as well as periods of mania. Mood disorders are divided into *depressive disorders,* in which the individual has one or more periods of depression without a history of manic episodes, and *bipolar disorders,* in which the individual alternates between periods of depression and periods of elation, usually with a return to normal mood in between the two extremes. Manic episodes without some history of depression are very uncommon.

DEPRESSION

Almost everyone gets depressed at times. Most of us have periods when we feel sad, lethargic, and not interested in any activities—even pleasurable ones. **Depression** is a normal response to many of life's stresses. Among the situations that most often precipitate depression are failure at school or at work, the loss of a loved one, and the realization that illness or aging is depleting one's resources. Depression is considered abnormal only when it is out of proportion to the event and continues past the point at which most people begin to recover.

Although depression is characterized as a disorder of mood, there are actually four sets of symptoms. In addition to emotional (mood) symptoms, there are cognitive, motivational, and physical symptoms. An individual need not have all of these to be diagnosed as depressed, but the more symptoms he or she has, and the more intense they are, the more certain we can be that the individual is suffering from depression.

Sadness and dejection are the most salient emotional symptoms in depression. The individual feels hopeless and unhappy, often has crying spells, and may contemplate suicide. Equally pervasive in depression is the loss of gratification or pleasure in life. Activities that used to bring satisfaction seem dull and joyless. The depressed person gradually loses interest in hobbies, recreation, and family activities. Most depressed patients report that they no longer derive gratification from what had been major interests in life, and many report losing interest in and affection for other people.

The cognitive symptoms consist primarily of negative thoughts. Depressed individuals tend to have low self-esteem, feel inadequate, and blame themselves for their failures. They feel hopeless about the future and are pessimistic that they can do anything to improve their life.

Motivation is at a low ebb in depression. The depressed person tends to be passive and has difficulty initiating activities. The following conversation between a patient and his therapist illustrates this passivity. The man, who had been hospitalized after a suicide attempt, spent his days sitting motionless in the lounge. His therapist decided to try to engage him in some activities:

THERAPIST: I understand that you spend most of your day in the lounge. Is that true?

PATIENT: Yes, being quiet gives me the peace of mind I need.

THERAPIST: When you sit here, how's your mood?

PATIENT: I feel awful all the time. I just wish I could fall in a hole somewhere and die.

THERAPIST: Do you feel better after sitting for 2 or 3 hours?

PATIENT: No, the same.

THERAPIST: So you're sitting in the hope that you'll find peace of mind, but it doesn't sound like your depression improves.

PATIENT: I get so bored.

THERAPIST: Would you consider being more active? There are a number of reasons why I think increasing your activity level might help.

PATIENT: There's nothing to do around here.

THERAPIST: Would you consider trying some activities if I could come up with a list?

PATIENT: If you think it will help, but I think you're wasting your time. I don't have any interests.

(Beck, Rush, Shaw, & Emery, 1979, p. 200)

The physical symptoms of depression include changes in appetite, sleep disturbances, fatigue, and loss of energy. Since a depressed person's thoughts are focused inward, rather than toward external events, he or she may magnify aches and pains and worry about health.

As we see from this description of its symptoms, depression can be a debilitating disor-

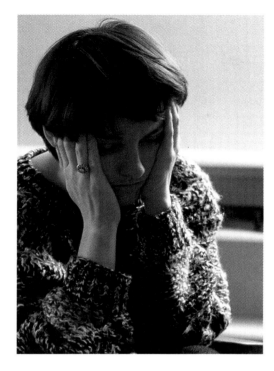

In addition to the emotional despair, physical aspects of depression include loss of appetite, sleep disturbances, fatigue, and loss of energy.

der. Unfortunately, severe depressions can also be long-lasting. One study of people with particularly severe depressions found that only 50 percent had recovered after one year (Keller et al., 1982). In addition, once they recovered, 50 percent of these people had another bout of depression within two years. Most of the people in this study were not receiving treatment for their depression. The good news is that most depressions can be successfully treated with either drugs or psychotherapy, as we will describe shortly.

BIPOLAR DISORDERS

The majority of depressions occur without episodes of mania. But between 5 and 10 percent of mood disorders involve both poles of the mood continuum and are classified as **bipolar disorders,** also known as **manic-depression.** The individual alternates between depression and extreme elation. In some cases the cycle between depressive episodes and manic episodes is swift with only a brief return to normality in between.

People experiencing manic episodes behave in a way that appears, on the surface, to be the opposite of depression. During mild manic episodes, the individual is energetic, enthusiastic, and full of self-confidence. He

DEPRESSION AND SUICIDE

The most disastrous consequence of depression is suicide. Of the reported 30,000 people who end their lives by suicide in the United States every year, the majority are suffering from depression. However, since suicide deaths are underreported (due to the stigma attached and the fact that many accidental deaths are probably suicides), the number of actual suicides per year may well be closer to 50,000. The number of people who attempt suicide but fail has been estimated at anywhere from two to eight times the number of suicides (Shneidman, 1985).

Women attempt to commit suicide about three times more often than men do, but men succeed more often than women in killing themselves. The greater number of suicide attempts by women is probably related to the greater incidence of depression among women. The fact that men are more successful in their attempts is related to the choice of method. Until recently, women have tended to use less lethal means, such as cutting their wrists or overdosing on sleeping pills; men are more likely to use firearms or carbon monoxide fumes or to hang themselves. However, with the marked increase in the number of women owning guns, suicide by firearms has now become the

woman's method of first choice (Wintemute, Teret, Kraus, & Wright, 1988). Consequently, the fatality rate for women is changing. (Attempted suicides are successful 80 percent of the time when firearms are involved, while only 10 percent of drug or poison ingestions are fatal—a powerful argument for not keeping firearms in the home.)

Among the reasons most frequently cited by those who have attempted suicide are depression, loneliness, ill health, marital problems, and financial or job difficulties (Petronis et al., 1990; Shneidman, 1985).

While elderly people have traditionally had the highest rate of suicide, and still do, their rate has been decreasing. In contrast, the suicide rate among adolescents and young adults (traditionally low) has been increasing. In fact, the incidence of suicide among 15- to 24-year-olds in the United States has quadrupled over the last four decades. In a recent national survey of high school seniors, 27 percent reported they had "thought seriously" about killing themselves, and one in 12 said they had actually tried (Centers for Disease Control, 1991).

College students are twice as likely to kill themselves as are nonstudents of the same age (Murphy & Wetzel, 1980). The increased suicide rate

among college students is found not only in the United States but in European countries, India, and Japan, as well. There are a number of possible reasons for the greater despair among college students: living away from home for the first time and having to cope with new problems; trying to stay at the top academically when the competition is much fiercer than it had been in high school; indecision about a career choice; loneliness caused by the absence of long-time friends and anxiety about new ones.

A study of the lives and academic records of college students who committed suicide found that they were moodier, drove themselves harder, and were depressed more frequently than their nonsuicidal classmates. They had also given recurrent warnings of their suicidal intent to others. The major precipitating events appear to have been worry about academic work and physical health and difficulties in their relationships with others (Seiden, 1966). However, we cannot be sure whether these factors caused the suicides or whether academic difficulties and interpersonal problems were secondary to a severe depression.

It may be that college students who contemplate suicide never learned how to deal with personal problems

---

or she talks continually, rushes from one activity to another with little need of sleep, and makes grandiose plans, paying little attention to their practicality. Unlike the kind if joyful exuberance that characterizes normal elation, manic behavior has a driven quality and often expresses hostility more than it does elation.

People experiencing severe manic episodes behave somewhat like the popular concept of a "raving maniac." They are extremely excited and constantly active. They may pace about, sing, shout, or pound the walls for hours. They are angered by attempts to interfere with their activities and may become abusive.

Impulses (including sexual ones) are immediately expressed in actions or words. These individuals are confused and disoriented and may experience delusions of great wealth, accomplishment, or power.

Tony was a middle-aged man, quite ragged in appearance, who was brought to the hospital by his family because he was "out of control" and "going crazy." Tony had been a sensible, rather subdued man until about a month ago, when his behavior changed dramatically. A bus driver in Philadelphia, Tony had taken to stopping his bus in busy traffic, turning to and emotions before going to college. One study, for example, found that students with suicidal thoughts were not faced with more stressful situations than other students but had fewer resources for dealing with problems and intense emotions (Carson & Johnson, 1985).

Suicidal college students, on the average, have higher records of academic achievement than their non-suicidal classmates, whereas most adolescents who commit suicide have exceptionally poor high-school records. Suicidal teenagers tend to be dropouts or to have behavior problems in school, although a few are academically gifted students who feel pressure to be perfect and to stay at the top of the class (Leroux, 1986).

The outstanding characteristic of adolescents who attempt suicide is social isolation: They describe themselves as loners, most have parents who were divorced or separated, a large number have alcoholic parents, and they report little parental affection (Berman & Jobes, 1991; Rohn et al., 1977).

A major factor contributing to suicide, in addition to depression, is drug abuse. For example, one study of 283 suicides found that nearly 60 percent were drug abusers and 84 percent abused both alcohol and other drugs (Rich, Fowler, Fogarty, & Young, 1988). It is not clear if the drug abuse caused these people to become depressed and kill themselves or if they turned to drugs as a way of coping with depression and killed themselves when the drugs did not help. But in many of the cases drug abuse appears to have preceded the psychological problems.

Young drug abusers (under age 30) who committed suicide had a greater than expected frequency of intense interpersonal conflict or the loss of a spouse or romantic partner in the weeks prior to killing themselves. They may have felt that they had lost their only source of support. And they might have been able to handle the stress without resorting to suicide had their personal resources not been depleted by drug use.

Some individuals commit suicide because they find their emotional distress intolerable and see no solution to their problems other than death. Their sole motivation is to end their life. In other cases, the person does not really wish to die but seeks to impress others with the seriousness of his or her dilemma. The suicide attempt is motivated by a desire to communicate feelings of despair and to change the behavior of other people. Examples would be a woman who takes an overdose of sleeping pills when her lover threatens to leave or a student who does the same when pressured by his parents to achieve beyond his abilities. The suicide attempt is a cry for help.

Some experts use the term *parasuicide* for nonfatal acts in which a person deliberately causes self-injury or ingests a substance in excess of any prescribed or generally recognized therapeutic dosage (Kreitman, 1977). The term "parasuicide" is preferred to "suicide attempt" because it does not necessarily imply a wish to die. As noted earlier, there are many more parasuicides than suicides. However, most people who commit suicidal acts are experiencing such turmoil and stress that their thinking is far from clear. They are not sure whether they want to live or die; they want to do both at the same time, usually one more than the other. Since the best predictor of a future suicide is a prior attempt, all parasuicides should be taken seriously. A person who talks about suicide may actually attempt it. Many communities have established suicide-prevention centers where troubled individuals can seek help, either through telephone contact or in person.

his passengers, and breaking into song. When asked about these incidents, Tony said that he had decided he wanted to be a nightclub singer and he was glad he had been fired from his bus-driving job because it gave him more time to devote to his singing career. By all accounts, Tony actually had a terrible singing voice. Two weeks ago, he had travelled to Las Vegas, where he tried to meet with managers of several casinos to convince them he should have a headline show at their casino. He was arrested for for making threatening remarks to these managers when they threw him out of their offices.

Tony then decided he should open his own casino in Philadelphia (although gambling was illegal there) so that he could sing every night. He cashed out the family savings accounts and put the house up for sale to finance his plan.

Manic episodes can occur without depression, but this is very rare. Usually a depressive episode will occur eventually, once a person has experienced a manic episode. The depression is similar to what we have already described.

Bipolar disorders are relatively uncommon. Whereas about 21 percent of adult females and 13 percent of adult males in the United States experienced a major depression at some time in their life, less than 2 percent of the adult population has had a bipolar disorder, which appears to be equally common in men and women (Kessler et al., 1994). Manic-depression differs from other mood disorders in that it tends to occur at an earlier age, is more likely to run in families, responds to different therapeutic medications, and almost always recurs unless treated. These facts suggest that biological variables play a more important role than psychological variables in bipolar disorders.

UNDERSTANDING MOOD DISORDERS

Depression is one of the most prevalent emotional disorders. Because depression is so common and can be so debilitating, much effort has been devoted to determining its causes. We will look briefly at several approaches to understanding mood disorders.

PSYCHOANALYTIC PERSPECTIVE   Psychoanalytic theories interpret depression as a *reaction to loss*. Whatever the nature of the loss (rejection by a loved one, loss of status, loss of moral support provided by a group of friends), the depressed person reacts to it intensely because the current situation brings back all the fears of an earlier loss that occurred in childhood—that being the loss of parental affection. For some reason, the individual's needs for affection and care were not satisfied in childhood. A loss in later life causes the individual to regress to his or her helpless, dependent state when the original loss occurred. Part of the depressed person's behavior, therefore, represents a cry for love—a display of helplessness and an appeal for affection and security (Blatt, 1974; Bibring, 1951).

Reaction to loss is complicated by angry feelings toward the deserting person. An underlying assumption of psychoanalytic theories is that people who are prone to depression have learned to repress their hostile feelings because they are afraid of alienating those on whom they depend for support. When things go wrong, they turn their anger inward and blame themselves. For example, a woman may feel extremely hostile toward the employer who fired her. But because her anger arouses anxiety, she internalizes her feelings: She is not angry; rather, others are angry at her. She assumes the employer had a reason for rejecting her: She is incompetent and worthless.

Psychoanalytic theories suggest that the depressed person's low self-esteem and feelings of worthlessness stem from a childlike need for parental approval. A small child's self-esteem depends on the approval and affection of the parents. But as a person matures, feelings of worth also should be derived from the individual's sense of his or her own accomplishments and effectiveness. The self-esteem of a person prone to depression depends primarily on external sources: the approval and support of others. When these supports fail, the individual may be thrown into a state of depression.

Psychoanalytic theories of depression, therefore, focus on loss, overdependence on external approval, and internalization of anger. They seem to provide a reasonable explanation for some of the behaviors exhibited by depressed individuals, but they are difficult to prove or to refute. Some studies indicate that people who are prone to depression are more likely than the average person to have lost a parent in early life (Barnes & Prosen, 1985; Roy, 1981). But parental loss (through death or separation) is also found in the case histories of people who suffer from other types of mental disorders, and most people who suffer such a loss do not develop emotional problems in adulthood (Tennant, Smith, Bebbington, & Hurry, 1981).

BEHAVIORAL PERSPECTIVE   Learning theorists assume that lack of reinforcement plays a major role in depression. The inactivity of the depressed person and the feelings of sadness are due to a low rate of positive reinforcement and/or a high rate of unpleasant experiences (Lewinsohn, Mischel, Chaplin, & Barton, 1980; Lewinsohn, Hoberman, Teri, & Hautziner, 1985). Many of the events that precipitate depression (such as the death of a loved one, loss of a job, or impaired health) reduce accustomed reinforcement. In addition, people prone to depression may lack the social skills either to attract positive reinforcement or to cope effectively with aversive events.

Once people become depressed and inactive, their main source of reinforcement is the sympathy and attention they receive from relatives and friends. This attention may initially reinforce the very behaviors that are maladaptive (weeping, complaining, criticizing themselves, talking about suicide). But because it is tiresome to be around someone who refuses to cheer up, the depressed person's behavior eventually alienates even close associates, producing a further reduction in reinforcement and increasing the individual's social isolation and unhappiness. A low rate of positive reinforcement further reduces the individual's activities and the expression of behaviors that might be rewarded. Both activities and rewards decrease in a vicious cycle.

COGNITIVE PERSPECTIVE Cognitive theories of depression focus not on what people *do* but on how they view themselves and the world. One of the most influential cognitive theories, developed by Aaron Beck, is derived from extensive therapeutic experience with depressed patients (Beck, 1976; Beck 1991; Beck, Rush, Shaw, & Emery, 1979). Beck was struck by how consistently these patients appraise events from a negative and self-critical viewpoint. They expect to fail rather than to succeed, and they tend to magnify failures and minimize successes in evaluating their performance. When things go wrong, they tend to blame themselves rather than the circumstances.

As we noted in Chapter 11, people's appraisals of a situation can determine their emotions. We all constantly appraise and evaluate what happens to us and what we do. Sometimes we are aware of our appraisals, but other times we are not. It seemed to Beck that the negative thoughts of depressed individuals tended to arise quickly and automatically, as though by reflex. Such thoughts were usually followed by unpleasant emotions (sadness, despair) of which the patients were very much aware, even though they were unaware of, or barely aware of, the preceding automatic thoughts. Later, in working with more severely depressed patients, Beck noted that the negative thoughts were no longer peripheral but occupied a dominant place in consciousness and were repetitive (Beck, 1991).

Beck grouped the negative thoughts of depressed individuals into three categories, which he called the **cognitive triad**: negative thoughts about the self, about present experiences, and about the future. Negative thoughts about the self (a negative self-schema) consist of the depressed person's belief that he is worthless and inadequate. Any present misfortune is blamed on these personal inadequacies or defects. Even in ambiguous situations, where there are more plausible explanation for why things went wrong, the depressed person will blame himself. The depressed person's negative view of the future is one of hopelessness. He believes that his inadequacies and defects will prevent him from ever improving his situation.

Beck proposes that the depressed person's negative self-schema ("I am worthless," "I can't do anything right," "I am unlovable") is formed during childhood or adolescence through such experiences as loss of a parent, social rejection by peers, criticism by parents or teachers, or a series of tragedies. These negative beliefs are activated whenever a new situation resembles in some way, perhaps only remotely, the conditions in which the beliefs were learned, and depression may result. Moreover, according to Beck, depressed individuals make some systematic errors in thinking (cognitive distortions) that lead them to misperceive reality in a way that contributes to their negative self-schema. These cognitive distortions are listed in Table 15-5. Note that the same distortions could be used by a person who has a positive self-schema to *enhance* his view of himself. But for the depressed person, these errors in thinking confirm his view that he is unworthy and responsible for calamities. As we will see in Chapter 16, cognitive therapy for depression attempts to identify and correct the individual's distorted thinking.

Another cognitive approach to depression, which focuses on the kinds of attributions, or causal explanations, that people make when bad things happen, was discussed in Chapter 14. This theory proposes that people who characteristically attribute negative events to causes that are internal ("it's my fault") are stable over time ("it's going to last forever"), and affect many areas of their lives ("it will impact everything I do") are more prone to depression than individuals who have a less pessimistic attributional style (Peterson & Seligman, 1984; Abramson et al., 1978). The theory does not claim that attributional style alone is enough to cause depression. A

OVERGENERALIZATION

Drawing a sweeping conclusion on the basis of a single event. For example, a student concludes from his poor performance in one class on a particular day that he is inept and stupid.

SELECTIVE ABSTRACTION

Focusing on an insignificant detail while ignoring the more important features of a situation. For example, from a conversation in which her boss praises her overall job performance, a secretary remembers the only comment that could be construed as mildly critical.

MAGNIFICATION AND MINIMIZATION

Magnifying small bad events and minimizing major good events in evaluating performance. For example, a woman gets a small dent in her car fender and views it as a catastrophe (magnification) while the fact that she gave an excellent presentation in class does nothing to raise her self-esteem (minimization).

PERSONALIZATION

Incorrectly assuming responsibility for bad events in the world. For example, when rain dampens spirits at an outdoor buffet, the host blames himself rather than the weather.

ARBITRARY INFERENCE

Drawing a conclusion when there is little evidence to support it. For example, a man concludes from his wife's sad expression that she is disappointed in him; if he had checked out the situation, he would have discovered she was distressed by her friend's illness.

TABLE 15-5

Cognitive Distortions in Depression *According to Beck's theory, these are the principal errors in thinking that characterize depressed individuals.*

pessimistic attributional style is important only when a person encounters intense or frequent negative events in his or her life (Abramson, Metalsky, and Alloy, 1989).

Cognitive theories of depression have stimulated a great deal of research. The results of some studies have been supportive, while others raise questions (see Haaga, Dyck, & Ernst, 1991 for a review). Depressed individuals score consistently higher on scales designed to measure negative thinking than do nondepressed people (both normal subjects and those suffering from mental disorders other than depression). And their negative thinking does encompass the three aspects of Beck's cognitive triad—the self, the present, and the future. However, evidence that de-

pressive thinking is especially inaccurate or illogical is weak. It is not clear that only those who are depressed distort information and evaluate themselves in illogical ways. Although depressed individuals are consistently pessimistic, in some instances they seem to perceive reality more accurately than normals (see the Critical Discussion on Illusion and Well-Being). In addition, the extent to which self-critical attitudes and/or a pessimistic attributional style *precede* rather than *accompany* a depressed episode is also unclear. A number of studies using mildly depressed individuals as subjects (mostly college students) have found a relationship between a pessimistic explanatory style and the degree of depression experienced when faced with bad events (Peterson & Seligman, 1984). However, studies of severely depressed, hospitalized patients found that depressive cognitions accompany depression but are *not* apparent after a depressive episode. Once the patient's depression had lifted, they did not differ from control subjects (who had near been depressed) in the way they interpreted bad events (Fennell & Campbell, 1984; Hamilton & Abramson, 1983). Thus a pessimistic attributional style may be a *symptom* rather than a *cause* of depression. It is an important symptom, however, because the intensity of a patient's negative beliefs does predict the speed of recovery from a period of depression (Brewin, 1985).

The way a person interprets bad events may be less important for the development of depression than is the belief that one has control over one's life. We noted in Chapter 14 that stressful situations are less disturbing if the individual believes that he or she can exert some control over them. Confidence in one's ability to cope with bad events may increase resistance to depression (Abramson, Metalsky, & Alloy, 1989).

BIOLOGICAL PERSPECTIVE A tendency to develop mood disorders, particularly bipolar disorders, appears to be inherited. Evidence from twin studies shows that if one identical twin is diagnosed as having bipolar disorder, there is a 69 percent chance that the other twin will suffer from the same disorder. The corresponding figure for fraternal twins is only 19 percent (Bertelsen et al., 1977). These figures, called *concordance rates,* represent the likelihood that both twins will have a specific characteristic, given that one of the twins has the characteristic. The concordance rate for identical twins suffering from depression (53 percent) also exceeds the rate for fraternal twins (28 percent), but the difference between these two rates is less than is the difference between the rates for bipolar twins (McGuffin et al., 1991). This comparison indicates that bipolar disorders are more closely related to genetic factors than are depressive disorders.

The specific role that genetic factors play in mood disorders is far from clear. However, it seems likely that a biochemical abnormality is involved. Mounting evidence indicates that our moods are influenced by the **neurotransmitters** that transmit nerve impulses from one neuron to another (see Chapter 2). A number of chemicals serve as neurotransmitters in different parts of the nervous system, and normal behavior requires a careful balance among them. Two neurotransmitters believed to play an important role in mood disorders are **norepinephrine** and **serotonin**. Both of these neurotransmitters, which belong to a class of compounds called *biogenic amines,* are localized in areas of the brain that regulate emotional behavior (the limbic system and the hypothalamus). The biological hypothesis is that depression is associated with a deficiency of one or both of these neurotransmitters and that mania is associated with an excess of one or both of them. However, the evidence is indirect, based largely on the effects that certain drugs have on behavior and on neurotransmitter activity. For example, the drug reserpine, which is used to treat high blood pressure, sometimes produces severe depression as a side effect. Animal research has shown that the drug causes a decrease in the brain levels of serotonin and norepinephrine.

Drugs that are effective in relieving depression may increase the availability of norepinephrine and serotonin in the nervous system. Three major classes of antidepressant drugs act in different ways to increase neurotransmitter levels. The **monoamine oxidase (MAO) inhibitors** block the activity of an enzyme that can destroy both norepinephrine and serotonin, thereby increasing the concentration of these two neurotransmitters in the brain. The **tricyclic antidepressants** prevent *reuptake* (the process by which neurotransmitters are taken back by the nerve terminals from which they were released) of norepi-

nephrine, thereby prolonging the duration of its activity. The **serotonin reuptake inhibitors** also block the reuptake of serotonin.

Research using new techniques is studying the long-term effects of antidepressants on the neuron's postsynaptic receptors. Antidepressant drugs require time to be effective: tricyclics, MAO inhibitors and serotonin reuptake inhibitors take from 1 to 3 weeks before they begin to relieve the symptoms of depression. These observations do not fit with the discovery that the drugs, when they are first taken, increase norepinephrine and serotonin levels only temporarily; after several days, the neurotransmitters return to their previous levels. Thus, an increase in norepinephrine or serotonin per se cannot be the mechanism that relieves depression. Preliminary evidence indicates that these antidepressants increase the sensitivity of both norepinephrine and serotonin postsynaptic receptors. The time frame within which this occurs corresponds well with the course of drug action on symptoms (Charney, Heninger, & Sternberg, 1984; Charney & Heninger, 1983). Thus, even though the patient's levels of norepinephrine or serotonin are low once again, they may be able to use these neurotransmitters more effectively because the receptors receiving them have become more sensitive.

The neurotransmitter systems that influence mood and emotion are incredibly complex, and we are only beginning to understand them. Several neurotransmitter systems, acting alone or in combination, may be responsible for depressive symptoms (McNeal & Cimbolic, 1986). And bipolar disorders may involve the malfunctioning of yet a different neurotransmitter system (Depue & Iacono, 1989).

There is no doubt that mood disorders involve biochemical changes in the nervous system. The unresolved question is whether the physiological changes are the cause or the result of the psychological changes. For example, people who deliberately behave as if they were experiencing a manic episode exhibit changes in neurotransmitter levels similar to those found among actual manic patients (Post, Kotin, Goodwin, & Gordon, 1973). The depletion of norepinephrine may cause certain kinds of depression, but an earlier link in the causal chain leading to depression may be feelings of helplessness or loss of emotional support.

ILLUSION AND WELL-BEING

In discussing cognitive theories of depression, we noted that depressed individuals appraise themselves and the world from a negative viewpoint. They are self-critical, expect to fail rather than succeed, magnify failures and minimize successes in evaluating their performance, and are pessimistic about the future. On the other hand, those of us who are not depressed may also suffer from illusions: We may look at ourselves and the world through rose-colored glasses.

Numerous studies indicate that most people have (a) unrealistically positive views of themselves, (b) exaggerated perceptions of how much control they have over events, and (c) unrealistic optimism about the future (Taylor & Brown, 1988). For example, when asked to indicate how accurately positive and negative personality adjectives describe themselves, normal subjects judged positive traits to be overwhelmingly more characteristic of themselves than negative attributes (Brown, 1986). In addition, most people recall positive information about themselves more readily than negative information (Kuiper, Olinger, MacDonald & Shaw, 1985); recall successes more often than failures (Silverman, 1964); tend to recall their performance on a task as better than it actually was (Crary, 1966); and attribute positive outcomes to their own ability and negative outcomes to chance factors (Zuckerman, 1979b). When college students, who were interacting on a group task, rated themselves along a number of personality dimensions (for example, friendly, assertive), their ratings were significantly more positive than the ratings of observers who had watched the group interac-

tion (Lewinsohn, Mischel, Chaplin, & Barton, 1980).

Moreover, there seems to be a pervasive tendency to see oneself as better than others. Individuals judge positive personality traits to be *more* descriptive of themselves than of the average person, but see negative personality attributes as *less* descriptive of themselves than of the average person (Brown, 1986). This effect has been documented for a wide range of traits; individuals even believe that their driving ability is superior to others (Svenson, 1981). Because it is logically impossible for most people to be better than the average, these positive views of the self are unrealistic and illusory.

Similarly, studies have shown that most people believe they have more control over situations than they actually do. For example, people believe that they have greater control if they personally throw the dice than if someone else does it for them (Fleming & Darley, 1986). People overestimate their degree of control over events that are largely determined by chance: When an expected outcome occurs, they often overestimate the degree to which they were instrumental in bringing it about (Miller & Ross, 1975).

Most people are more optimistic about the future than reality warrants. When college students were asked what was possible for them in the future, they reported four times as many positive as negative possibilities (Markus & Nurius, 1986). People estimated the likelihood that they would experience a variety of pleasant events (such as getting a high-salaried job or having a gifted child) as higher than those of their peers (Weinstein, 1980). Conversely, when asked about their

chances of experiencing negative events (a car accident, becoming ill), most people believed they are *less* likely than their peers to do so (Kuiper, MacDonald, & Deery, 1983).

To summarize, most of us have unrealistically positive views of ourselves, an exaggerated belief in our ability to control our environment, and a belief that our future will be better than that of the average person. These positive illusions enable us to cope with an uncertain, and sometimes frightening, world. They provide the motivation to persist in the face of obstacles, and they help us avoid depression.

Traditional views of mental health assert that well-adjusted individuals possess accurate perceptions of themselves and of their ability to control events in their lives. Indeed, the description of normality presented earlier in this chapter includes *efficient perception of reality* as one of the criteria that distinguishes between a normal person and one who is diagnosed as abnormal. The evidence presented here indicates that this criterion should be modified.

Clearly, we need to perceive what is going on in the world and what other people say and do with some degree of accuracy. Nevertheless, positive illusions about our personal qualities and about our ability to control events appear to make us happier, more optimistic, and more willing to undertake challenges. Such illusions may be especially adaptive under circumstances that tend to produce depression. The belief in ourselves as competent and effective, facing a future that is generally positive helps in overcoming setbacks and blows to our self-esteem (Taylor & Brown, 1988).

VULNERABILITY AND STRESS All of the theories we have discussed make important points about the nature of depression. Inherited physiological characteristics may predispose an in-

dividual to extreme mood changes. Early experiences (the loss of parental affection or the inability to gain gratification through one's own efforts) may also make a person vulnerable to depression in later life. The kinds of stressful events that depressed patients report precipitated their disorder are usually within the range of normal life experiences; they are experiences most people can handle without becoming abnormally depressed. Thus, the concept of vulnerability is helpful in understanding why some people develop depression but others do not when confronted with a particular stressful experience.

Some additional factors that have been found to increase vulnerability to depression include having few social skills, being poor, being very dependent on others, having children under the age of 7, and not having a close and intimate confidant. The last of these appears to be the most important, at least for women, since it has been the most consistently identified over various studies (Bebbington, Sturt, Tennant, & Hurry, 1984; Campbell, Cope, & Teasdale, 1983; Brown & Harris, 1978). Having an intimate, confiding relationship with a husband or friend decreased the risk of a woman's becoming depressed when confronted with a stressful life situation. This is consistent with the research (discussed in Chapter 14) indicating that social supports help to buffer the severity of stressful events.

Depression has many causes, which may range from being determined almost entirely by an inherited biochemical abnormality to being exclusively the result of psychological or environmental factors. Most cases fall in between the two extremes and involve a mixture of genetic, early developmental, and environmental factors.

SCHIZOPHRENIA

Schizophrenia is the label applied to a group of disorders characterized by severe personality disorganization, distortion of reality, and an inability to function in daily life. It occurs in all cultures, even those that are remote from the stresses of industrialized civilization, and appears to have plagued humanity for at least 200 years. The disorder affects about 1 percent of the population, occurs equally in men and women, and usually appears in late adolescence or early adulthood (most cases have their onset between the ages of 15 and 35).

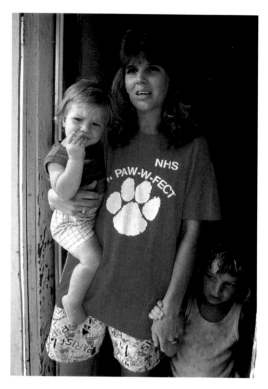

Being poor or having young children increases one's vulnerability to depression.

Although there do not appear to be ethnic or racial differences in the actual incidence of schizophrenia, African-Americans may often be misdiagnosed as having schizophrenia when they really have bipolar disorder (manic depression) (Snowden & Cheung, 1990). This is particularly likely when the person doing the assessment is white (Mukherjee et al., 1983). It is not clear just what leads to the misdiagnosis of African-Americans, but most investigators believe there are cultural differences in the presentation of the symptoms of schizophrenia. For example, African-Americans may present more intense symptoms than whites, which are misunderstood as representing more severe psychopathology by white assessors. Those labeled schizophrenic usually require hospitalization, sometimes for months or years. At any given time, this diagnostic group occupies about half of the beds in mental hospitals and constitutes a large proportion of outpatients. Sometimes schizophrenia develops slowly as a gradual process of increasing seclusiveness and inappropriate behavior. Sometimes the onset of schizophrenia is sudden, marked by intense confusion and emotional turmoil; such acute cases are usually precipitated by a period of stress in individuals whose lives have tended toward isolation, self-preoccupation, and feelings of insecurity.

CHARACTERISTICS OF SCHIZOPHRENIA

Whether schizophrenia develops slowly or suddenly, the symptoms are many and varied. The primary characteristics of schizophrenia can be summarized under the following headings, although not every person diagnosed as suffering from the disorder will exhibit all of these symptoms.

DISTURBANCES OF THOUGHT AND ATTENTION Whereas affective disorders are characterized by disturbances of mood, schizophrenia is characterized by disturbances of *thought*. Both the *process* of thinking and the *content* of thought may be disordered. The following excerpt from a patient's writings illustrates how difficult it is to understand schizophrenic thinking.

> If things turn by rotation of agriculture or levels in regards and timed to everything; I am referring to a previous document when I made some remarks that were facts also tested and there is another that concerns my daughter she has a lobed bottom right ear, her name being Mary Lou. Much of abstraction has been left unsaid and undone in these productmilk syrup, and others, due to economics, differentials, subsidies, bankruptcy, tools, buildings, bonds, national stocks, foundation craps, weather, trades, government in levels of breakages and fuses in electronics too all formerly states not necessarily factuated. (Maher, 1966, p. 395)

By themselves, the words and phrases make sense, but they are meaningless in relation to each other. The juxtaposition of unrelated words and phrases and the idiosyncratic word associations (sometimes called a "word salad") are characteristic of schizophrenic writing and speech. They reflect a *loosening of associations* in which the individual's ideas shift from one topic to another in ways that appear unrelated. Moreover, a schizophrenic's train of thought often seems influenced by the *sound* of words rather than by their meaning. The following account by a schizophrenic patient of her thoughts in response to her doctor's questions illustrates this tendency to form associations by rhyming words, referred to as clang associations.

DOCTOR:	How about the medication? Are you still taking the Haldol? (an antipsychotic drug)
PATIENT THINKS:	*Foul Wall.* She nods but does not reply.
DOCTOR:	What about the vitamins?
PATIENT THINKS:	*Seven sins. Has-beens.* She nods.
DOCTOR:	I don't think you're taking all your meds.
PATIENT THINKS:	*Pencil leads.*
	(North, 1987, p. 261)

The confused thought processes that are the hallmark of schizophrenia seem to stem from a general difficulty in focusing attention and filtering out irrelevant stimuli. Most of us are able to focus our attention selectively. From a mass of incoming sensory information, we are able to select the stimuli that are relevant to the task at hand and to ignore the rest. A person who suffers from schizophrenia is perceptually receptive to many stimuli at the same time and has trouble making sense of the profusion of inputs, as the following statement by a schizophrenic patient illustrates.

> I can't concentrate. It's diversions of attention that trouble me. I am picking up different conversations. It's like being a transmitter. The sounds are coming through to me, but I feel my mind cannot cope with everything. It's difficult to concentrate on any one sound. (McGhie & Chapman, 1961, p. 104)

A sense of being unable to control one's attention and to focus one's thoughts is central to the experience of schizophrenia.

In addition to the disorganized thought processes that make it difficult to understand what a schizophrenic is trying to say are disturbances in the *content* of thought. Most individuals suffering from schizophrenia show a *lack of insight*. When asked what is wrong or why they are hospitalized, they seem to have no appreciation of their condition and little realization that their behavior is unusual. They are also subject to **delusions**, holding beliefs that most people would view as misinterpretations of reality. The most common delusions are beliefs that external forces are trying to control the individual's thoughts and actions. These *delusions of influence* include the belief that one's thoughts are being broadcast to the world so that others can hear them, that strange thoughts (not one's own) are being inserted into the individual's mind, or that feelings and actions are being imposed on the person by some external force. Also frequent are beliefs that certain people or certain groups are threatening or plotting against the individual (*delusions of persecution*). Less common are beliefs that the person is powerful and important (*delusions of grandeur*).

A person who has persecutory delusions is called **paranoid**. He or she may become suspicious of friends and relatives, may fear being poisoned, or may complain of being watched, followed, and talked about. So-called motiveless crimes, when an individual attacks or kills someone for no apparent cause, are sometimes committed by people who are later diagnosed as suffering from paranoid schizophrenia. These incidents are quite rare, however. Most people with schizophrenia are not a danger to others, although their confusion may make them a danger to themselves.

DISTURBANCES OF PERCEPTION During acute schizophrenic episodes, people often report that the world appears *different* to them (noises seem louder; colors, more intense). Their own bodies may no longer appear the same (their hands may seem to be too large or too small; their legs, overly extended; their eyes, dislocated in the face). Some patients fail to rec-ognize themselves in a mirror or see their reflection as a triple image. The most dramatic disturbances of perception are called **hallucinations**, sensory experiences in the absence of relevant or adequate external stimulation. Auditory hallucinations (usually voices telling the person what to do or commenting on his or her actions) are the most common. Visual hallucinations (such as seeing strange creatures or heavenly beings) are somewhat less frequent. Other sensory hallucinations (a bad odor emanating from the individual's body, the taste of poison in food, the feeling of being pricked by needles) occur infrequently. Hallucinations may occur independently or as part of a delusional belief. An example would be a patient who hears voices threatening to kill him and believes they are part of a plot to eliminate him because of his powers.

In one sense, hallucinations are not that far removed from ordinary experiences. We all know what visual hallucinations are like because we have them in dreams. But for most people dreams only occur during sleep (see Chapter 6), not while awake. It is possible that some sort of neurotransmitter-mediated process inhibits dreams during the waking state and that this process has failed in schizophrenics who hallucinate (Assad and Shapiro, 1986).

German psychiatrist Hans Privizhorn is responsible for the most extensive collection of artwork by mental patients available. The painting from the collection, by August Neter, illustrates the hallucinations and paranoid fantasies from which many schizophrenic patients suffer.

Auditory hallucinations may have their origin in ordinary thought. We often carry on internal dialogues, for example, commenting on our actions or having an imaginary conversation with another person. We may even on occasion talk to ourselves aloud. The voices that schizophrenic patients hear, calling them bad names or telling them what to do, are similar to internal dialogues. But the patient experiencing an auditory hallucination does not believe that the voices originate within the self or that they can be controlled. The inability to distinguish between external and internal, real and imagined, is central to the schizophrenic experience.

DISTURBANCES OF AFFECT   Schizophrenic individuals usually fail to exhibit normal emotional responses. They often are withdrawn and unresponsive in situations that should make them sad or happy. For example, a man may show no emotional response when informed that his daughter has cancer. However, this blunting of emotional expression can conceal inner turmoil, and the person may erupt with angry outbursts.

Sometimes the schizophrenic individual expresses emotions that are inappropriately linked to the situation or to the thought being expressed. For instance, a patient may smile while speaking of tragic events. Since our emotions are influenced by cognitive processes, it is not surprising that disorganized thoughts and perceptions are accompanied by changes in emotional responses. This point is illustrated by the following comment of a schizophrenic patient.

> Half the time I am talking about one thing and thinking about half a dozen other things at the same time. It must look queer to people when I laugh about something that has got nothing to do with what I am talking about, but they don't know what's going on inside and how much of it is running around in my head. You see I might be talking about something quite serious to you and other things come into my head at the same time that are funny and this makes me laugh. If I could only concentrate on one thing at the one time I wouldn't look half so silly. (McGhie & Chapman, 1961, p. 104)

MOTOR SYMPTOMS AND WITHDRAWAL FROM REALITY
Schizophrenic patients often show bizarre motor activity. They may grimace or adopt strange facial expressions. They may gesture repeatedly using peculiar sequences of finger, hand, and arm movements. Some may become very agitated and move about in continual activity, as in a manic state. Some, at the other extreme, may become totally unresponsive and immobile, adopting an unusual posture and maintaining it for long periods of time. For example, a patient may stand like a statue with one foot extended and one arm raised toward the ceiling and maintain this state of *catatonic immobility* for hours. Such an individual, who appears completely withdrawn from reality, may be responding to inner thoughts and fantasies. The episode described in Box 2 gives a feeling for the kind of inner turmoil and distress that may underlie a schizophrenic patient's outward unresponsiveness and bizarre behavior.

DECREASED ABILITY TO FUNCTION   Besides the specific symptoms we have described, schizophrenics have many impairments in their ability to carry out the daily routines of living. If the disorder occurs in adolescence, the individual shows a decreasing ability to cope with school, has limited social skills, and few friends. The adult schizophrenic is often unsuccessful in obtaining or holding a job. Personal hygiene and grooming deteriorate. The individual becomes more and more seclusive and avoids the company of other people. The signs of schizophrenia are many and varied. Trying to make sense of the variety of symptoms is complicated by the fact that some may result directly from the disorder, while others may be a reaction to life in a mental hospital or to the effects of medication.

UNDERSTANDING SCHIZOPHRENIA

Although more research has been devoted to trying to understand the nature of schizophrenia than to any other mental disorder, the causes are still not understood. New evidence indicates that both the structure and activity of schizophrenic brains are abnormal. However, environmental factors also play a role in the development of the disorder. We will examine the biological evidence first and then consider social and psychological variables.

BIOLOGICAL PERSPECTIVE   Family studies show that there is a hereditary predisposition toward de-

BOX 2	*PSYCHOTIC EPISODE*

This account is by a schizophrenic patient who recovered and later became a psychiatrist. Her descriptions of her thoughts and emotions, drawn from memory and a diary, are interspersed with excerpts from her medical records (North, 1987, pp. 282–284).

The helicopters. Oh no, not the helicopters. Have come to tear the feathers out of my frontal lobes. Help me, nurse, help me, can't you hear them? Gotta get back into my body to save it. Am so far away. Out of reach of the neural connections. The doctor is thinking I would make good glue. He is a witch doctor. He is sending radio messages to the helicopters to help them find me.

Dr. Kopetti observed:

. . . still catatonic at this time. Totally unresponsive. . . . I would wonder if she'll be able to cope with the pressures of school again. . . . she apparently does not respond to antipsychotic agents and has a low threshold for extrapyramidal symptoms [muscular side effects].

Big pieces are cracking off the edge of my consciousness. I will never be back. The universe disappears with one slight wave of my hand.

A nurse observed in my chart:
Data: patient acting out in response to voices, i.e., posturing, crying out. States she's frightened, refused to undress for sleep for fear of needing to get out of room quickly. . . . was found standing in one place for long periods of time, eyes wide open, staring. . . . patient standing in room facing wall, arms outstretched to wall. . . . was not responsive to verbalization, responded with blank stare. . . . frequently pacing around room suspiciously, jumps when others approach her. Several times said, "Am I dead?" Seemed out of touch with her body at times, holding her hands in angular positions.

The pendulum has swung to the far side where everything dissipates into everything. It can't swing back. I am scared of the change. I am scared to move.
"Would you like to be made into hotdog meat?" Ah, the voices. Where have they been?

I must be on track again.
"Hotdogs for lunch!"
My head splits down the middle, brains falling out all over the floor, and I put out an awkward hand to catch them. They slip right through my metal fingers. Do they put brain meat in hotdogs?
"You can put down your hand, Carol. You don't have to hold it there." Had the nurse said that or had I said it? Or had the voices said it? Or was it a slice from another Dimension?
Hand back to my side. Try to think straight. There is a logical way out of this maze. Just don't forget your thoughts. Don't forget.

. . . Patient talked about having difficulty telling "where the voices ended and her thoughts begin." Thought that her skull was split in half and asked me to examine it—was reassured that I didn't see or feel a split. Also said she feels like she's going to "fall out of her body," but didn't know where she'd fall to. At one time, patient put her hands over her ears and said, "I don't want hotdogs for lunch" when it had nothing to do with the conversation.

veloping schizophrenia; relatives of schizophrenics are more likely to develop the disorder than are people from families free of schizophrenia. Figure 15-1 gives the lifetime risk of developing schizophrenia as a function of how closely an individual is genetically related to a person diagnosed as schizophrenic. Note that an identical twin of a schizophrenic is 3 times as likely as a fraternal twin to develop schizophrenia and 46 times as likely as an unrelated person to develop the disorder. However, fewer than half of the identical twins of schizophrenics develop schizophrenia themselves, even though they share the same genes. This fact demonstrates the importance of nongenetic variables.

Studies of the children of schizophrenic mothers and/or fathers who were adopted in early infancy and reared in foster homes provide further evidence for the heritability of

schizophrenia. Compared with matched control groups of normal adopted children, the children with a biological parent diagnosed as schizophrenic were much more likely to develop schizophrenia and to have siblings who developed the disorder (Kender & Gruenberg, 1984; Kety et al., 1988, 1978).

Although the tendency for schizophrenia to run in families has been recognized for many years, a search for the specific genes involved has become possible only recently with the development of new molecular biology techniques for genetic mapping. To locate the relevant genes, researchers find a family with a high incidence of schizophrenia over several generations. They examine the DNA of family members and search for a short sequence of DNA that is different in schizophrenic and in normal family members. If family members with a particular DNA sequence at a particular

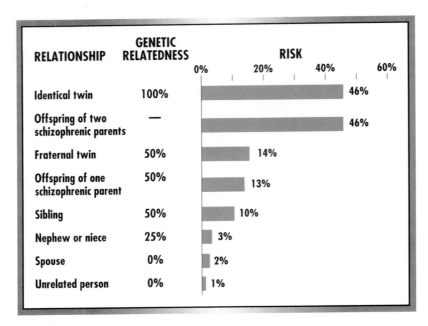

FIGURE 15-1

Genetic Relationships and Schizophrenia   *The lifetime risk of developing schizophrenia is largely a function of how closely an individual is genetically related to a schizophrenic and not a function of how much their environment is shared. In the case of an individual with two schizophrenic parents, genetic relatedness cannot be expressed in terms of percentage, but the regression of the individual's "genetic value" on that of the parents is 1, the same as it is for identical twins.* (After Gottesman, 1991; Gottesman & Shields, 1982)

location on a chromosome frequently have schizophrenia, but family members with a different sequence on that location never have the disease, then that DNA sequence may be either part of the disease-causing gene or very close to it on the chromosome (Byerly et al.,

The odds of all four identical quadruplets being diagnosed as schizophrenic are 1 in 2 billion—yet these quadruplets, the Genains, were. They have been in and out of hospitals since high school.

1989). Several studies of DNA samples from families with an unusually high incidence of schizophrenia found evidence of a defective gene, or cluster of genes, located on chromosome 5 (Bassett, 1989; Sherrington et al., 1988). However, other researchers studying a different group of high-incidence families found no evidence linking chromosome 5 with the disorder (Kennedy et al., 1988; McGuffin et al., 1990).

It may be that different genes are involved for different variants of the disorder. This idea is compatible with the view that schizophrenia is a group of disorders that produce similar symptoms but have different biological causes. Or, it may be that schizophrenia is a polygenic disorder, involving the accumulation of several defective genes. Whatever the means of genetic transmission, the familial data (in Figure 15-1) make it clear that we are not dealing with a genetic disorder that has a clear inheritance pattern such as Huntington's disease or phenylketonuria (PKU). As you may recall from Chapter 2, Huntington's disease is caused by a single dominant gene passed from parent to child; on the average, half of the offspring will develop the disease. PKU is associated with a recessive gene; on the average, a quarter of the offspring will be affected. The genetic component in the transmission of schizophrenia is probably similar to that associated with diabetes or coronary heart disease: A number of genes acting together may make an individual susceptible to the disorder, and environmental factors will determine whether the disorder develops and the degree of its severity.

How do the genetic abnormalities that predispose an individual to schizophrenia affect the brain? Current research focuses on two main areas: irregularities in neurochemistry and differences in brain structure between schizophrenics and normals. While neurochemical theories of mood disorders center on norepinephrine and serotonin, the culprit in schizophrenia is believed to be **dopamine**, a neurotransmitter active in an area of the brain that is involved in the regulation of emotion (the limbic system). The **dopamine hypothesis** proposes that schizophrenia is caused by too much dopamine at certain synapses in the brain. This excess may be due to overproduction of the neurotransmitter or to faulty regulation of the reuptake mechanism by which dopamine returns to and is stored by vesicles in the presynaptic neurons. It might also be due to oversensitive dopamine receptors or to too many dopamine receptors.

Evidence for the importance of dopamine comes from two sources. First, drugs that are effective in relieving the symptoms of schizophrenia, called **antipsychotic drugs**, reduce the amount of usable dopamine in the brain. Researchers believe that they do so by blocking the dopamine receptors. These drugs do not cure schizophrenia, but they do reduce hallucinations and delusions, improve concentration, and make many schizophrenic symptoms less bizarre. Moreover, the therapeutic effectiveness of a particular drug has been found to parallel its potency in blocking dopamine receptors (Creese, Burt, & Snyder, 1978).

Further evidence that an abnormality in dopamine metabolism may be the underlying cause of schizophrenia comes from observations of the effects of amphetamines, which increase the release of dopamine. Drug users who overdose on amphetamines exhibit psychotic behavior that closely resembles schizophrenia, and their symptoms can be relieved by the same antipsychotic drugs used to treat schizophrenia. When low doses of amphetamines are given to schizophrenic patients, their symptoms become much worse. In these cases, the drug does not produce a psychosis of its own; rather, it exacerbates whatever symptoms the patient may be experiencing (Snyder, 1980). For example, one patient entered the hospital claiming that spirits rose out of people's heads and spoke to him. After treatment with antipsychotics, he admitted that his talk about spirits had been "crazy talk," but within one minute of an amphetamine injection he again claimed that spirits were rising out of the interviewer's head (Janowsky, El-Yousef, Davis, & Sererke, 1973).

Thus, enhancing the action of dopamine aggravates schizophrenic symptoms, and blocking dopamine receptors alleviates them. Studies using positron emission tomography (PET), one of the techniques for obtaining detailed pictures of the living brain described in Chapter 2, have found the density of a certain class of dopamine receptors (called D2 receptors) to be significantly greater in a group of schizophrenics who had never been treated

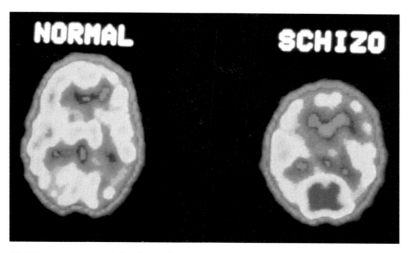

This PET scan shows the metabolic differences between areas of the brain of a schizophrenic subject and that of a normal subject.

with drugs than in either a group of drug-treated schizophrenics or normals (Wong et al., 1989; 1986). This, along with other findings, indicates that an excess of cells that are sensitive to dopamine may be the important neurochemical defect in schizophrenia.

As for structural abnormalities in the brain, studies using computer axial tomography (CAT) and magnetic resonance imagery (MRI) have found that some schizophrenics have significantly larger cerebral ventricles (the cavities that contain the cerebrospinal fluid) than nonschizophrenics. In several studies, patients with schizophrenia had larger ventricles than their brothers and sisters, including identical twins of the patients (Andreasen, 1988). By inference, if the ventricles are larger than normal, the brain tissue must be smaller than normal; ventricular enlargement suggests a process of deterioration or atrophy of brain tissue. The frontal lobes, the temporal lobes, and the hippocampus are brain areas that studies thus far have indicated may be smaller than normal in schizophrenics (Suddath et al., 1990). These areas of the brain are involved in thinking, concentration, memory, and perception.

The evidence from studies of brain structure and brain biochemistry has led some investigators to postulate that there may be two forms of schizophrenia. Type I schizophrenia is characterized by *positive symptoms* or behavioral excesses that include hallucinations, delusions, bizarre behavior, and confused thinking. Patients with positive symptoms usually functioned well before their schizophrenic symptoms first appeared; their disturbed behaviors tend to come and go so that at times their social behavior is reasonably effective; they usually respond well to antipsychotic drugs that block the transmission of the neurotransmitter dopamine; and their brain scans generally do not show structural abnormalities. Type II schizophrenia is characterized by *negative symptoms* or behavioral deficits such as poverty of speech, emotional unresponsiveness, seclusiveness, and impaired attention. Patients with negative symptoms usually have a history of poor social and educational functioning prior to their initial psychotic episode and continue to function poorly afterward (Fenton & McGlashan, 1992). They show little, if any, improvement with antipsychotic drugs, and their brain scans are likely to show structural abnormalities (Fenton & McGlashan, 1992).

Type I schizophrenia is assumed to result from difficulties in neurotransmission, and Type II from abnormalities in brain structure. One possible cause of the structural abnormality is damage to the brain by viral infection. Some data suggest that such an infection could occur during fetal development. In 1957 a major influenza epidemic occurred in Helsinki, Finland. Rates of schizophrenia were examined in adults who had been exposed during their mothers' pregnancies. Those exposed during the second trimester of pregnancy (which is a critical period of growth for cortical development) had much higher rates than those exposed during either of the other trimesters or in nonexposed controls (Mednick et al., 1988).

However, not all of the data support the distinctions between Type I and Type II schizophrenia. Some schizophrenic patients have both positive and negative symptoms, and the symptoms may change over the course of the illness. Nevertheless, investigators may be on the verge of isolating a subgroup of schizophrenic patients who have signs of brain pathology and suffer negative symptoms.

SOCIAL AND PSYCHOLOGICAL PERSPECTIVE   Numerous studies in the United States and other countries have revealed that the incidence of schizophrenia is significantly higher among the lower classes than among the middle and upper classes (Strauss, 1982; Dohrenwend, 1973). The highest rates of schizophrenia are found in central city areas inhabited by the lowest socioeconomic class. The relationship does not show a continuous progression of higher rates of schizophrenia as the social class becomes lower. Instead, there is a marked difference between the number of schizophrenics in the lowest social class and those in the others. No one knows why social class is related to schizophrenia. Two quite different types of explanation have been proposed: social selection and social causation.

1. *Social selection—downward mobility.* Because their coping skills are poor, individuals who suffer from schizophrenia have difficulty completing their education and getting a decent job. They gradually drift downward in society and become part of the lower classes.

2. *Social causation—adversity and stress.* Living under conditions of poverty in areas with high crime rates, run-down housing, and inadequate schools creates enough additional stress to precipitate schizophrenic disorders, particularly in individuals who are genetically predisposed to schizophrenia.

Evidence indicates that both explanations are true (Brenner, 1982; Fried, 1982; Kosa & Zola, 1975), with social selection probably playing the greater role (Dohrenwend et al., 1992).

Research on the role of psychological factors in the development of schizophrenia has focused on relationships within the family. During the 1950s and 1960s numerous investigators recorded detailed observations of families in which one member was diagnosed as schizophrenic in an attempt to determine the kinds of parental attitudes and behaviors that contributed to the disorder. They came to various conclusions, most of which proved difficult to replicate. A major problem was that the families were studied *after* a mental disorder in one family member had affected the entire family. While some of the atypical family interactions may have preceded the onset of the disorder, others may represent reactions to the stresses of living with a mentally ill person. For example, unclear or conflicting communications between parent and offspring has been identified as a factor that distinguishes between schizophrenic and normal families. The parents are described as communicating in ways that create confusion and uncertainty (Wynne, Singer, Bartko, & Toohey, 1977). However, the results of a related study suggest that the parents' communication problems may be a response to unclear communication from their schizophrenic children. In this study the experimenter asked parents and sons, independently, to describe specific objects so that someone listening to their descriptions could identify the objects without seeing them. The descriptions were tape-recorded and played for others in the experiment, including normal and schizophrenic sons and their parents. The investigator found that the parents of schizophrenic sons did not differ from parents of normals sons in their ability to communicate ideas. The poorest communicators were the schizophrenic sons. To quote the investigator, "The communication disorder of the schizophrenic sons had an immediate negative effect not only on the parents of schizophrenic sons but on all parents who heard and attempted to respond to them" (Liem, 1974, p. 445).

A longitudinal study attempted to eliminate the problem inherent in earlier studies by observing family relationships *before* a family member was diagnosed as schizophrenic. The study began with 64 families that contained at least one teenager referred to a psychology clinic for help with mild to moderately severe emotional problems. The adolescents and their families were studied intensively and then followed up for the next 15 years with periodic assessments. The highest incidence of schizophrenia occurred among families in which the parents (a) dealt with the adolescent in a critical and hostile manner, and (b) were confusing in their communications. The combination of negative parental attitudes and confused communication was more predictive of future schizophrenia than either variable alone (Goldstein, 1987). However, the causal relationship is still not clear. It is possible that communication problems and critical parental attitudes were a consequence of the parents' attempts to cope with a child whose behavior was disturbed or unusual even before he or she was diagnosed as schizophrenic. In other words, is the parents' deviance a cause of the child's maladaptive behavior, or are the child's atypical characteristics a cause of the parents' behavior? This question remains unanswered.

But whatever their role in causing the initial schizophrenic behavior, family disorganization and parental rejection are important in determining the severity of the illness and the prognosis for recovery (Anderson, Reiss, & Hogarty, 1986; Roff & Knight, 1981).

In addition to disturbed family relationships, other traumatic events (such as the early death of one or both parents) are found with greater than average frequency in the backgrounds of people who develop schizophrenia. Stressful childhoods of various kinds may contribute to the disorder. In general, the more stressful the childhood, the more severe the schizophrenic disorder.

VULNERABILITY AND STRESS Most individuals who live in poverty or who experience a disturbing and stressful childhood do *not* develop schizophrenia. While earlier theories of schizophrenia emphasized environmental factors, the explanation that currently has the greatest support views schizophrenia as an inherited brain disorder that makes the individual vulnerable to stresses of life. It remains to be seen whether the same brain abnormality is characteristic of all persons diagnosed as schizophrenic, whether there are different brain defects for different types of schizophrenia, or whether some cases of schizophrenia are due solely to environmental causes.

Currently, some 50 longitudinal studies are being conducted with children who have been identified as having a high risk of developing schizophrenia. The studies follow the children from their early years to adulthood in an attempt to pinpoint some of the factors that determine whether or not the disorder will develop. In most of these studies, the children are considered to have a high risk because they have at least one schizophrenic parent (Moldin et al., 1990; John, Mednick, & Schulsinger, 1982; Steffy et al., 1984; Marcus et al., 1987; Tienari et al., 1987; Mednick, Cannon, Parnas, & Schulsinger, 1989). Other investigators have selected their high-risk group of the basis of psychophysiological measures or behavioral characteristics that they believe to be precursors of schizophrenia (Garmezy & Devine, 1984; Garmezy, 1974).

The high-risk subjects are usually matched with a control group of children who have no family background of mental illness and who show no early signs of psychopathology. The development of both groups is carefully monitored through periodic testing and interviews with parents, teachers, and peers. Once a high-risk subject has a schizophrenic breakdown, he or she is matched both with a subject from the high-risk group who has remained well and with a well member of the control group. Thus, the background of the individual who develops schizophrenia can be compared with that of a nonschizophrenic high-risk subject and a normal, low-risk subject.

Most of these studies, started in the 1960s and 1970s, are still in progress, and the subjects are now young adults. Some have already become schizophrenic, and many more are expected to do so within the next decade. Consequently, the data available at present consist mainly of comparisons between high-risk and low-risk groups. These data indicate that the high-risk child is similar to an adult schizophrenic in many ways. For example, high-risk children are rated low in social competence and tend to perform poorly on tasks that require sustained attention or abstract thinking.

Preliminary data on high-risk subjects who later developed schizophrenia indicate that they differ from the high-risk subjects who have remained well in the following ways. The subjects who developed the disorder

1. Were more likely to have experienced birth complications that may have affected the functioning of their nervous system.

2. Were more likely to have been separated from their mothers at an early age.

3. Had fathers who were more likely to have been hospitalized, with diagnoses ranging from alcoholism to schizophrenia.

4. Were more likely to show inappropriate behavior in school. The boys were described by their teachers as anxious, lonely, and causing disciplinary problems; the girls, as withdrawn, isolated, and poorly controlled.

When more data from these ongoing high-risk studies become available, we should have a better understanding of how innate and environmental factors interact to produce schizophrenia. Recently, investigators have identified an atypical pattern of infant development (involving certain lags and spurts in the maturation of motor and visual abilities) that may prove useful as a screening test to identify children with a high risk of schizophrenia (Fish et al., 1992).

PERSONALITY DISORDERS

Personality disorders are long-standing patterns of maladaptive behavior. In Chapter 13, we described *personality traits* as enduring ways of perceiving or relating to the environment and thinking about oneself. When personality traits become so inflexible and maladaptive that they significantly impair the individual's ability to function, they are called personality disorders. Personality disorders constitute immature and inappropriate ways of coping with stress or solving problems. They are usually evident by early adolescence and may continue throughout adult life.

Unlike people with mood or anxiety disorders, which also involve maladaptive behavior, people who have personality disorders often do not feel upset or anxious and may not be motivated to change their behavior. They do not lose contact with reality or display marked disorganization of behavior, unlike individuals suffering from schizophrenia.

DSM-IV lists 11 personality disorders. For example, someone who has a *narcissistic personality disorder* is described as having an inflated sense of self-importance, being preoccupied with fantasies of success, constantly seeking admiration and attention, and being insensitive to the needs of others and often exploiting them. *Dependent personality disorders* are characterized by a passive orientation to life, an inability to make decisions or accept responsibility, a tendency to be self-deprecating, and a need for continual support from others.

Most of the personality disorders listed in DSM-IV have not been the subject of much research. The characteristics of the various personality disorders overlap, so that agreement in classifying individuals is poor. Moreover, it is even more difficult with the personality disorders to say when a person's behavior is simply different from other people's behaviors and when the behavior is so severe that it warrants a diagnosis. The personality disorder that has been studied the most and is the most reliably diagnosed is the antisocial personality (formerly called psychopathic personality, also sometimes called sociopathy).

ANTISOCIAL PERSONALITY

People who have **antisocial personalities** seem to have little sense of responsibility, morality, or concern for others. Their behavior is determined almost entirely by their own needs. In other words, they lack a *conscience*. Whereas the average person realizes at an early age that some restrictions are placed on behavior and that pleasures must sometimes be postponed in consideration of the needs of others, individuals who have antisocial personalities seldom consider any desires except their own. They behave impulsively, seek immediate gratification of their needs, and cannot tolerate frustration.

The term "antisocial personality" is somewhat misleading, because these characteristics do not describe most people who commit antisocial acts. Antisocial *behavior* results from a number of causes, including membership in a delinquent gang or a criminal subculture, the need for attention and status, loss of contact with reality, and an inability to control impulses. Most juvenile delinquents and adult criminals do have some concern for others (for family or gang members) and some code of moral conduct (you don't betray a friend). In contrast, antisocial *personalities* have little feeling for anyone except themselves and seem to experience little guilt or remorse, regardless of how much suffering their behavior may cause others. Other characteristics of the antisocial personality (sociopath, for short) include a great facility for lying, a need for thrills and excitement with little concern for possible injury, and an inability to alter behavior as a consequence of punishment. Such individuals are often attractive, intelligent, charming people who are quite facile in manipulating others—in other words, good con artists. Their façade of competence and sincerity wins them promising jobs, but they have little staying power. Their restlessness and impulsiveness soon lead them into an escapade that reveals their true nature; they accumulate debts, desert their families, squander company money, or commit crimes. When caught, their declarations of repentance are so convincing that

they often escape punishment and are given another chance. But antisocial personalities seldom live up to these declarations; what they say has little relation to what they feel or do (see Box 3).

The two characteristics considered most indicative of an antisocial personality disorder are: (a) lack of empathy and concern for others, and (b) lack of shame or guilt—the inability to feel remorse for one's actions, regardless of how reprehensible they may be (Hare, 1980).

UNDERSTANDING ANTISOCIAL PERSONALITIES

What factors contribute to the development of the antisocial personality? Current research focuses on biological determinants, on the quality of the parent-child relationship, and on thinking styles that promote antisocial behaviors.

BIOLOGICAL FACTORS There is substantial support for a genetic influence on antisocial behaviors, particularly criminal behaviors. Twin studies find that the concordance rate for criminal behaviors is twice as high in identical twins as in fraternal twins, suggesting that these behaviors are in part heritable (Rutter et al., 1990). Adoption studies find that the criminal records of adopted sons are more similar to the records of their biological fathers than their adoptive fathers (Cloninger & Gottesman, 1987; Mednick et al., 1987; Crow, 1983).

Many studies have investigated the hypothesis that persons with antisocial personality disorder show low levels of arousability, which then may lead them to seek stimulation and sensation through impulsive and dangerous acts (see Morey, 1993). For example, one study compared two groups of adolescent male delinquents selected from the detention unit of a juvenile court. One group had been diagnosed as having antisocial personality disorders; the other, adjustment reactions to negative life events. The experimenters measured galvinic skin response, or GSR, under stress (see Chapter 11). Dummy electrodes were attached to each subject's leg, and he was told that in 10 minutes he would be given a very strong but not harmful shock. A large clock was visible so that the subject knew precisely when the shock was supposed to occur. No shock was actually administered. The two

BOX 3 ANTISOCIAL PERSONALITY

A 40-year-old man was convicted of check forgery and embezzlement. He was arrested with a young woman, age 18, whom he had married bigamously some months before. She was unaware of the existence of any previous marriage. The subject in this case had already been convicted for two previous bigamous marriages and for 40 other cases of passing fraudulent checks.

The circumstances of his arrest illustrate the impulsivity and lack of insight characteristic of many antisocial personalities. He had gotten a job managing a small restaurant; the absentee owner, who lived in a neighboring town, had arranged to stop by at the end of each week to check on progress and to collect the income. The subject was provided with living quarters over the restaurant, a small salary, and a percentage of the cash register receipts. At the end of the first week, the subject took all the money (he had failed to bank it nightly as he had been instructed) and departed shortly before the employer arrived; he left a series of vulgar messages scribbled on the walls saying he had taken the money because the salary was "too low." He found lodgings with his wife a few blocks from the restaurant and made no effort to escape detection. He was arrested a few days later.

During the inquiry, it emerged that the subject had spent the past few months cashing checks in department stores in various cities. He would make out the check and send his wife in to cash it; he commented that her genuine innocence of the fact that he had no bank account made her very effective in not arousing suspicion. He had not bothered to use a false name when he signed the checks or the bigamous marriage contract, but he seemed surprised that the police discovered him so quickly.

Inquiry into the subject's history revealed that he had been educated mostly in private schools and that his parents were financially well-to-do. They had planned for him to go to college, but his academic record was not good enough (although on examination he proved to have superior intelligence). Failing to get into college, he started work as an insurance salesman trainee and did very well. He was a distinguished-looking young man and an exceptionally fluent speaker.

Just as it appeared that he could anticipate a successful career in the insurance business, he ran into trouble because he failed to turn in the checks that customers had given him to pay their initial premiums. He admitted to having cashed these checks and to spending the money (mostly on clothes and liquor). It apparently did not occur to him that the company's accounting system would quickly discern this type of embezzlement. In fact, he expressed amused indignation at the company's failure to realize that he intended to pay back the money from his salary. No legal action was taken, but he was requested to resign. His parents reimbursed the company for the missing money.

At this point, the subject enlisted in the army and was sent to Officer Candidate School, from which he graduated as a second lieutenant. He was assigned to an infantry unit, where he soon got into trouble that progressed from minor infractions (drunk on duty, smuggling women into his quarters) to cashing fraudulent checks. He was court-martialed and given a dishonorable discharge. From then on, his life followed a pattern of finding a woman to support him (with or without marriage) and then running off with her money to the next woman when life became too tedious.

At his trial, where he was sentenced to five years in prison, he gave a long and articulate speech, pleading clemency for the young woman who was being tried with him, expressing repentance for having ruined her life, and stating that he was glad to have the opportunity to repay society for his crimes (Maher, 1966, pp. 214–215).

groups showed no difference in GSR measures during periods of rest or in response to auditory or visual stimulation. However, during the 10 minutes of shock anticipation, the group with adjustment reactions showed significantly more tension than the antisocial group. At the moment when the clock indicated the shock was due, most of the group with adjustment reactions showed GSR responses indicating a sharp increase in anxiety. *None* of the antisocial subjects showed this reaction (Lippert & Senter, 1966). Low arousability to anxiety-provoking stimuli may also make it more difficult for people with antisocial personality disorder to learn from the punishments they do receive because they will not experience punishment to be as aversive as most people, and they will not be anxious in anticipation of the punishment.

More recent research has focused on the problems that people with antisocial personality disorder have in inhibiting impulsive behavior. Research with children who show antisocial tendencies indicates that a significant percentage, perhaps the majority, have an attention deficit disorder, which involves significant problems in maintaining attention and in inhibiting impulsive behaviors

(Moffitt & Silva, 1988). The disruptive behavior of these children leads to frequent punishment and rejection by peers, teachers, and other adults. In turn, these children then become even more disruptive and some become overtly aggressive and antisocial in their behaviors and attitudes.

Although children who develop antisocial personalities may have some biological predisposition to this disorder, studies suggest that they are unlikely to develop them unless they are also exposed to environments that promote antisocial behavior (Rutter, Quinton, & Hill, 1990; Cadoret & Cain, 1980; Cloninger & Gottesman, 1987). The characteristics of such environments are described in the next section.

PARENTAL FACTORS The quality of parenting a child receives, particularly a child with a vulnerability to hyperactivity and conduct disturbances, is strongly related to whether or not he develops a full-blown antisocial personality disorder (Loeber, 1990). One of the best predictors of children's conduct disturbances is parental supervision: Children who are frequently unsupervised or poorly supervised for long periods of time are much more likely to develop a pattern of delinquent behaviors than children who are seldom unsupervised. A related variable is parental uninvolvement: Children whose parents are not involved in their everyday life, for example, the parents do not know who their child's friends are, are more likely to develop antisocial personalities. When parents of children with conduct disturbances do interact with their children, these interactions are often characterized by hostility, physical violence, and ridicule (Patterson, DeBaryshe, & Ramsey, 1989). The picture one gets of these families is one in which parents frequently ignore a child or are absent from the home, but then when the child does transgress or annoy a parent in some way, the parent lashes out at the child violently. Evidence that these parenting deficits are a cause, and not just a correlate, of conduct disturbances in children comes from the fact that interventions designed to overcome these deficits can be effective in reducing the children's conduct disturbances (Lochman et al., 1991).

The biological factors and family factors that contribute to conduct disorders may often coincide. Children with conduct distur-

bances often suffer neuropsychological problems that are the result of maternal drug use, poor prenatal nutrition, pre- and post-natal exposure to toxic agents, child abuse, birth complications, and low birth weight (Moffitt, 1993). Children with these neuropsychological problems are more irritable, impulsive, awkward, overreactive, and innattentive, and slower learners than their peers. This makes them difficult for parents to care for, and they are at increased risk for maltreatment and neglect. In turn, the parents of these children are more likely to be teenagers or to have psychological problems of their own that contribute to ineffective or harsh or inconsistent parenting. Thus, these children may carry both a biological predisposition to disruptive, antisocial behaviors and experience parenting that contributes to these behaviors. In a study of 536 boys, Moffitt (1990) found that those who both had neuropsychological deficits and adverse home environments scored four times higher on an aggression scale than those boys with neither neuropsychological deficits or adverse home environments.

PERSONALITY FACTORS Children with conduct disturbances tend to process information about social interactions in ways that promote aggressive reactions to these interactions (Crick & Dodge, 1994). They assume that other children will be aggressive toward them, and interpret the actions of their peers in line with these assumptions rather than using cues from the specific situations they actually face. In addition, conduct-disordered children tend

Antisocial behaviors begin early in life and are often quite stable into adulthood.

INSANITY AS A LEGAL DEFENSE

How should the law treat a mentally disturbed person who commits a criminal offense? Should individuals whose mental faculties are impaired be held responsible for their actions? These questions are of concern to behavioral and social scientists, to members of the legal profession, and to individuals who work with criminal offenders.

Over the centuries, an important part of Western law has been the concept that a civilized society should not punish a person who is mentally incapable of controlling his or her conduct. In 1724, an English court maintained that a man was not responsible for an act if "he doth not know what he is doing, no more than . . . a wild beast." Modern standards of legal responsibility, however, have been based on the M'Naghten decision of 1843.

M'Naghten, a Scotsman, suffered the paranoid delusion that he was being persecuted by the English prime minister, Sir Robert Peel. In an attempt to kill Peel, he mistakenly shot Peel's secretary. Everyone involved in the trial was convinced by M'Naghten's senseless ramblings that he was insane. He was judged not responsible by reason of insanity and sent to a mental hospital, where he remained until his death. But Queen Victoria was not pleased with the verdict—apparently she felt that politi-

cal assassinations should not be taken lightly—and called on the House of Lords to review the decision. The decision was upheld, and rules for the legal definition of insanity were put into writing. The M'Naghten Rule states that a defendant may be found not guilty by reason of insanity only if he were so severely disturbed at the time of his act that he did not know what he was doing, or if he did know what he was doing, did not know that it was wrong.

The M'Naghten Rule was adopted in the United States, and the distinction of knowing right from wrong remained the basis of most decisions of legal insanity for over a century. Some states added to their statutes the doctrine of "irresistible impulse," which recognizes that some mentally ill individuals may respond correctly when asked if a particular act is morally right or wrong but may be unable to control their behavior.

During the 1970s, a number of state and federal courts adopted a broader legal definition of insanity proposed by the American Law Institute, which states: "A person is not responsible for criminal conduct if at the time of such conduct, as a result of mental disease or defect, he lacks substantial capacity either to appreciate the wrongfulness of his conduct or to conform his conduct to the requirements of the law." The word *substantial* suggests that any inca-

pacity is not enough to avoid criminal responsibility but that total incapacity is not required either. The use of the word *appreciate* rather than *know* implies that intellectual awareness of right or wrong is not enough; individuals must have some understanding of the moral or legal consequences of their behavior before they can be held criminally responsible.

The problem of legal responsibility in the case of mentally disordered individuals became a topic of increased debate in the wake of John Hinckley, Jr.'s, acquittal, by reason of insanity, for the attempted assassination of President Reagan in 1981. Many Americans were outraged by the verdict and felt that the insanity defense was a legal loophole that allowed too many guilty people to go free. In response, Congress enacted the Insanity Defense Reform Act (1984), which contains a number of provisions designed to make it more difficult to absolve a defendant of legal responsibility. For example, the act changes the American Law Institute's "lacks substantial capacity . . . to appreciate" to "unable to appreciate"; it stipulates that the mental disease or defect be "severe" (the intent being to exclude nonpsychotic disorders such as antisocial personality); and it shifts the burden of proof from the prosecution to the defense (instead of the prosecution having to prove that the person was sane beyond a reasonable

to believe that any negative actions a peer might take against them—for example, taking their favorite pencil—are intentional rather than accidental. When deciding upon what action to take in response to a perceived provocation by a peer, children with conduct disturbances tend to think of a narrow range of responses, usually including aggression. When pressed to consider responses other than aggression these children generate ineffective or vague responses, and often consider responses other than aggression to be useless or unattractive.

Children who think about their social interactions in this way are likely to engage in aggressive behaviors toward others. They then may be retaliated against: Other children will hit them, parents and teachers will punish them, and they will be more negatively perceived by others. In turn, these actions may feed the child's assumptions that the world is against him, causing him to misinterpret future actions by others. A cycle of interactions can be built that maintains and encourages aggressive, antisocial behaviors in a child.

doubt at the time of the crime, the defense must prove he or she was not sane, and must do so with "clear and convincing evidence"). This law applies to all cases tried in federal courts and about half the state courts. It is still too early to evaluate its impact.

Another attempt to clarify the legal defense of insanity is the verdict "guilty but mentally ill." Initially proposed by Michigan, it has been adopted by eleven states. (In some of these states this verdict replaces the not guilty by reason of insanity verdict; in other states it is an additional option.) Generally, the laws permit a finding of guilty but mentally ill when a defendant is found to have a substantial disorder of thought or mood that afflicted him at the time of the crime and that significantly impaired his judgment, behavior, capacity to recognize reality, or ability to cope with the ordinary demands of life. The effect of this mental illness, however, falls short of legal insanity. The guilty but mentally ill verdict allows jurors to convict a person they perceive as dangerous while attempting also to ensure that he or she receives psychotherapeutic treatment. The individual could be given treatment in prison or be treated in a mental hospital and returned to prison when deemed fit to complete the sentence. The problem remains as to whether treatment in either place would be sufficient to rehabilitate the person.

Public concern that the insanity defense may be a major loophole in the criminal law is largely groundless. The defense is rarely used, and actual cases of acquittal by reason of insanity are even rarer. Jurors seem reluctant to believe that people are not morally responsible for their acts, and lawyers, knowing that an insanity plea is apt to fail, tend to use it only as a last resort. Fewer than 1 percent of defendants charged with serious crimes are found not guilty by reason of insanity.

The question of mental disorder exerts its greatest impact earlier in the legal process. Many accused people who are mentally ill never come to trial. In the United States, the law requires that the defendant be *competent to stand trial*. An individual is judged competent to stand trial if he or she is able (a) to understand the charges, and (b) to cooperate with a lawyer in preparing a defense. The competency issue is basic to the American ideal of a fair trial and is quite separate from the question of whether the person was "insane" at the time the crime was committed. In a preliminary hearing, the judge receives evidence about the accused's mental competency. The judge may drop the charges and commit the individual to a psychiatric facility (if the crime is not serious) or commit the accused and file the charges until he or she is deemed competent to stand trial. Because court calendars are congested and trials are expensive, judges often prefer to deal with mentally disturbed defendants in this way, particularly if they believe that the mental hospital will provide adequate treatment and secure confinement.

Many more persons are confined to mental institutions because they are found incompetent to stand trial than because they are found not guilty by reason of insanity. These people, many of whom are not dangerous, often are confined longer than they would have been if they had been convicted of the crime in question. Indeed, before the widespread use of antipsychotic drugs, individuals deemed incompetent to stand trial were often committed to mental institutions for life. However, in 1972, the Supreme Court ruled that defendants found incompetent to stand trial due to mental illness could not be held indefinitely. Judges now attempt to bring such individuals to trial or to release them within 18 months. In deciding on release, the seriousness of the crime and the potential for future dangerous behavior are important considerations. Unfortunately, at present our data for predicting whether an individual is likely to commit a dangerous act are not very reliable.

BORDERLINE PERSONALITY DISORDER

Borderline personality disorder has been the focus of considerable attention in the popular press and in clinical and research writings in psychology in the last couple of decades. The diagnosis of borderline personality disorder was only added to the DSM in its third edition in 1980. Clinicians have long used the label "borderline," however, to refer to people who seem to teeter between severe neurotic traits (such as emotional instability) and bouts of psychosis (see Millon, 1981).

Instability is a key feature of borderline personality disorder. The mood of persons with borderline personality disorder is unstable, with bouts of severe depression, anxiety, or anger seeming to arise frequently and often without good reason. The self-concept of these people is unstable, with periods of extreme self-doubt and periods of grandiose self-importance. The interpersonal relationships of these people are extremely unstable, and they can switch from idealizing other people to despising them without provocation. Persons with borderline personality disorder often feel desperately empty and will initially cling to a new acquaintance or therapist in hopes that this person will fill the tremendous void they feel in themselves. They are nearly paranoid about abandonment, however, and misinterpret other people's innocent actions as abandonment or rejection. For example, if a therapist has to cancel an appointment because she is ill, a person with borderline personality disorder might interpret this as a rejection by the therapist and become extremely depressed or angry. Along with instability of mood, self-concept, and interpersonal relationships comes a tendency toward impulsive self-damaging behaviors, including self-mutilating behaviors and suicidal behavior. The self-mutilating behaviors often take the form of burning or cutting oneself. Finally, persons with borderline personality disorder are prone to transient episodes in which they feel unreal, lose track of time, and may even forget who they are. The following case describes a person with borderline personality disorder (McGlashan, 1984, pp. 87–88).

> *Ms. Q was a 28-year-old, white single woman when admitted voluntarily (to a psychiatric hospital). . . . In late adolescence, Ms. Q became romantically and sexually involved with a young artist. When he informed her that she was "just another woman" in his life, she became morose and moody. She began hallucinating his face on movie screens and newspapers. Shortly after the accidental drowning of a young boy from her neighborhood, Ms. Q started feeling guilty for his death and feared imminent apprehension by the police. In an act later described as a "manipulative gesture," she took an overdose of sleeping medication and was hospitalized briefly.*
>
> *Over the next five years, Ms. Q attended college sporadically. She moved often between a variety of living situations: alone in hotels or dormitories or with one or the other of her divorced parents. Changes of domicile were often precipitated by quarrels. Although seldom alone, she developed relatively superficial social relationships. The few women whom she befriended tended to be older. She would frequently become attached to their parents and call them "mama and papa." Sexually she had three or four intense affairs, each lasting*

> *less than six months and each terminating painfully with one or the other partner refusing to marry. In all of her relationships, Ms. Q was described as manipulative, dependent, masochistic, hostile, and derogatory.*
>
> *Mood swings between anger and despondency occurred weekly and sometimes daily. She frequently abused alcohol and barbituates and made numerous manipulative suicidal threats. For the latter she was hospitalized briefly on two more occasions (one month or less in duration). . . .*
>
> *In her mid-20s, Ms. Q joined the armed services. After an initial honeymoon period, she performed miserably. She cried "for hours over her typewriter and stayed in her room not eating." After 10 months, she received a "neuropsychiatric" medical discharge. She began moving around again, trying various jobs, which she was unable to hold for more than a few days. She became more seclusive, even with fellow employees.*
>
> *At age 26 Ms. Q began two years of intensive psychotherapy (up to four times per week). Her therapist recorded that Ms. Q tried "very hard to be sick" and was intent on causing "trouble with everyone she did not like" by "upsetting everyone during her bad spells."*
>
> *Her hospitalization at (the psychiatric hospital) arose out of a visit home to her mother. She felt slighted in several ways. First, her mother's welcome was less than "gushing." Second, she felt insulted when her mother's boyfriend showed her a brochure describing a psychiatric residential treatment facility. Third, she discovered that a certain choice piece of family real estate was being willed to her least favorite sibling. Feeling rejected, she took an overdose of aspirin and was hospitalized at (the psychiatric hospital) shortly thereafter.*

Persons with borderline personality disorder also tend to receive diagnoses of one of the acute disorders, including substance abuse, depression, and generalized anxiety disorder, simple phobias, and agoraphobia, post-traumatic stress disorder, panic disorder, somatization disorder (Weissman, 1993; Fabrega et al., 1991). Longitudinal studies of people with this disorder indicate that about 6 percent die by suicide (see Perry, 1993). The greatest risk of suicide appears to be in the first year or two after a person is diagnosed with borderline personality disorder. This may be because a person is often not diagnosed with this disorder until a crisis brings him or her into therapy.

Epidemiological studies suggest that the lifetime prevalence of borderline personality disorder is between 1 and 2 percent (Weissman, 1993). Borderline personality disorder is much more often diagnosed in women than men (Fabrega et al., 1991; Swartz et al., 1990). People with this disorder are high users of outpatient mental health services; one community study found that 50 percent had used some form of mental health service in the past six months (Swartz et al., 1990). They tend to have stormy marital relationships, more job difficulties, and a higher rate of physical disability than average.

UNDERSTANDING BORDERLINE PERSONALITIES

BIOLOGICAL PERSPECTIVES Several family history studies of borderline personality disorder have been conducted, and the evidence that this specific disorder is transmitted genetically is weak (Dahl, 1993). There are high rates of mood disorders in the families of persons diagnosed with borderline personality disorder, however (Kendler et al., 1993). Most researchers do not suggest that borderline personality disorder is simply a type of affective disorder, but there clearly are links between the two disorders. Drug treatments for persons with borderline personality disorder have focused on reducing their symptoms of anxiety and depression through anti-anxiety drugs and antidepressants and controlling their impulsive behaviors with serotonin reuptake inhibitors (see Chapter 16). The effectiveness of these drugs, even in the short term, is not yet clear.

PSYCHOANALYTIC PERSPECTIVES Psychoanalytic theorists suggest that persons with this disorder have just enough reality-testing to retain a foothold in the real world, but rely on primitive defenses such as denial rather than more advanced defenses against their conflicts (Kernberg, 1979). In addition, the borderline person has very poorly developed views of the

self and others, stemming from poor early relationships with caregivers. The caregivers of people with borderline personality disorder are characterized as deriving much gratification from the child's dependence on them early in life. Thus, they do not encourage the child to develop a separate sense of self and may punish the child's attempt at individuation and separation. As a result, the child never learns to fully differentiate her views of herself and her views of others. This makes her extremely reactive to others' opinions of her and to the possibility of being abandoned by others. When others are perceived as rejecting her, she rejects herself and may engage in self-punishment or self-mutilation. She also has never been able to integrate the positive and negative qualities of either her self-concept or her concept of others, because her early caregivers were comforting and rewarding when she remained dependent and compliant toward them, but hostile and rejecting when she tried to individuate from them. She tends to see herself and other people as either "all good" or "all bad" and vacillates between these two views. This process is referred to as "splitting." The lability in borderline persons' emotions and interpersonal relationships is caused by splitting—their emotions and their perspectives on their interpersonal relationships reflect their vacillation between the "all good" and the "all bad" self or other.

Psychodynamic treatment for people with borderline personality disorder involves helping the client clarify feelings, confronting the client with his tendency to split images of the self and other, and interpreting the client's transference relationship with the therapist (Kernberg, et al., 1989). The client may also be taught more adaptive means of solving everyday problems so that the world does not appear so overwhelming. Self-destructive tendencies are addressed, with the therapist helping the client identify the feelings leading to these acts and develop healthy ways of coping with these feelings.

COGNITIVE PERSPECTIVES Cognitive theorists (Beck et al., 1990) suggest that at the heart of borderline personality disorder is a set of maladaptive assumptions, specifically "The world is dangerous and malevolent," "I am powerless and vulnerable," and "I am inherently unacceptable." In addition, borderline persons are extremely susceptible to the cognitive distortion known as dichotomous thinking, seeing everything in terms of mutually exclusive categories, such as good or bad, success or failure, and trustworthy or deceitful. This results in extreme shifts of emotions and interpretations of situations.

Cognitive behavior therapies focus on helping the client gain a more realistic and positive sense of the self, learning adaptive skills at solving problems and regulating emotions, and correcting dichotomous thinking (Beck et al., 1990; Linehan, 1987; Millon, 1981). The therapist will teach the client to monitor self-disparaging thoughts and her black-or-white evaluations of people and situations and to challenge these thoughts and evaluations. The therapist will also help the client learn appropriate assertiveness skills for close relationships so that she can express her needs and feelings in a mature manner. Linehan et al. (1991) found that cognitive-behavioral therapy significantly reduced suicidal behaviors and the need for hospitalization in 44 women with severe borderline personality disorder.

STRESSFUL LIFE EVENTS Recent research suggests that many persons with borderline personality disorder have a history of physical and sexual abuse during childhood (Perry & Herman, 1993). This abuse could lead to the problems in self-concept that most theorists suggest is at the core of this disorder. In addition, a child whose parent alternates between being abusive and being loving could develop a fundamental mistrust of others and a tendency to see others as all good or all bad.

BIOLOGICAL-PSYCHOLOGICAL PERSPECTIVES

Although some researchers and clinicians who specialize in abnormal psychology still take the perspective that mental disorders are entirely caused by biological factors or entirely caused by psychological factors, many researchers and clinicians believe that most people who develop serious mental disorders probably have both biological and psychological vulnerabilities to these disorders, and that stressful events can trigger new epispdoes of the disorder. This is especially true of serious anxiety disorders and mood disorders. There is increasing evidence, as we discussed in this chapter, that people who develop serious anxiety or mood disorders in the face of stress differ from people who do not develop these disorders both in their biochemistry and in their ways of thinking about themselves and the world. It is often difficult to tell whether disordered biochemistry or disorder thinking processes are the cause or the consequence of an anxiety or mood disorder. But it is clear that disorders are phenomena of the whole person—they affect people at the biological, psychological, and social levels.

In the case of schizophrenia, where the evidence for genetic and biochemical theories of the disorder is strong, it is still clear that environmental stress and family support play a role in triggering new episodes or facilitating recovery. Although we know little about the causes of the personality disorders, the evidence suggests that both biological and psychological factors will be shown to play roles in the development and maintenance of the disorders.

Thus, it seems that advances in our understanding of mental disorders will necessarily involve models that integrate biological and psychological variables. These models may illuminate both how mental disorders are caused and how the mind and body work together in people considered mentally healthy.

📖 CHAPTER SUMMARY

1. The diagnosis of abnormal behavior is based on *statistical frequency, social norms, adaptiveness of behavior,* and *personal distress.* Characteristics indicative of good mental health include an *efficient perception of reality, control of behavior, self-esteem,* an *ability to form affectionate relationships,* and *productivity.*

2. DSM-IV classifies mental disorders according to specific behavioral symptoms.

Such a classification system helps to communicate information and provides a basis for research. However, each case is unique, and diagnostic labels should not be used to pigeonhole individuals.

3. Theories about the causes of mental disorders and proposals for treating them can be grouped under one of the following perspectives: *biological, psychoanalytic, behavioral,* and *cognitive.* The *vulnerability-stress model* emphasizes the interaction between a predisposition (biological and/or psychological) that makes a person vulnerable for developing a disorder and stressful environmental conditions the individual encounters.

4. Anxiety disorders include *generalized anxiety* (constant worry and tension), *panic disorders* (sudden attacks of overwhelming apprehension), *phobias* (irrational fears of specific objects or situations), and *obsessive-compulsive disorders* (persistent unwanted thoughts, or *obsessions,* combined with urges, or *compulsions,* to perform certain acts).

5. Psychoanalytic theories attribute anxiety disorders to unresolved *unconscious conflicts.* Behavioral theories focus on anxiety as a *learned response* to external events and invoke the concept of *prepared conditioning* to explain some phobias. Cognitive theories emphasize the way anxious people think about potential dangers: Their overestimation of the likelihood and degree of harm makes them tense and physiologically prepared for danger; they are unable to dismiss obsessive thoughts and believe that compulsive rituals will prevent disaster. Biological theories focus on the interaction of a number of *neurotransmitters* that regulate feelings of anxiety. Biochemical abnormalities have been identified for panic attacks and obsessive-compulsive disorders.

6. Mood disorders are divided into *depressive disorders* (the individual has one or more periods of depression) and *bipolar disorders* (the individual alternates between periods of depression and periods of elation, or mania). Sadness, loss of gratification in life, negative thoughts, and lack of motivation are the main symptoms of depression. Psychoanalytic theories view depression as a *reactivation of the loss of parental affection* in a person who is *dependent on external approval* and tends *to turn anger inward.* Learning theories focus on *reduced positive reinforcement.*

7. Beck's theory views depression as a *cognitive triad* of negative thoughts about the self, present experiences, and the future. The depressed person's *negative self-schema* is fueled by systematic errors in thinking that distort reality. The *attributional theory* of Seligman and Abramson proposes that a pessimistic explanatory style that invokes *internal, stable,* and *global causes for bad events* leads to depression. Negative cognitions and pessimistic attributions accompany depression but may not be a primary cause.

8. Some mood disorders may be influenced by inherited abnormalities in the metabolism of certain *neurotransmitters* (such as *norepinephrine* and *serotonin*). Inherited predispositions and early experiences may make people *vulnerable* to depression when under stress.

9. *Schizophrenia* is characterized by disturbances in the *form of thought* (disorganized thought processes that stem from difficulty in filtering out irrelevant stimuli) and in the *content of thought* (delusions and lack of insight). Other symptoms include perceptual disturbances (such as *hallucinations*), inappropriate affect, bizarre motor activity, withdrawal, and impaired functioning. Research on the causes of schizophrenia has focused on evidence for a hereditary disposition to the disorder, defects in the metabolism of neurotransmitters (the *dopamine hypothesis*), social factors, and deviant family relationships. Studies of high-risk children point to some predictors of schizophrenia.

10. *Personality disorders* are long-standing patterns of maladaptive behavior that constitute immature and inappropriate ways of coping with stress or solving problems. Individuals classified as having *antisocial personalities* are impulsive, show little guilt, are concerned only with their own needs, and are frequently in trouble with the law. People with *borderline personality disorder* show instability in mood, self-concept, and interpersonal relationships.

FURTHER READING

Mending Minds (1992), a paperback by Heston, provides a brief description of the major mental disorders, with case histories and descriptions of treatment options.

The hereditary aspects of mental illness are reviewed in Plomin De-Fries, and McClearn, *Behavioral Genetics: A Primer* (2nd ed., 1989). *Schizophrenia Genesis: The Origins of Madness* (1991), a paperback by Gottesman, presents the latest research findings on the genetics of this disorder, a discussion of social and psychological factors, and personal accounts by schizophrenic patients and their families.

Panic: Facing Fears, Phobias, and Anxiety (1985) by Agras provides an interesting discussion of the way fears develop into phobias. *The Boy Who Couldn't Stop Washing: The Experience and Treatment of Obsessive-Compulsive Disorder* (1989) by Rapaport provides a fascinating account of this disorder, including descriptions of clinical cases and research findings on treatment.

The world of psychosis from the patient's viewpoint is graphically described in Green, *I Never Promised You a Rose Garden* (1971); and in North, *Welcome Silence* (1987). In *Holiday of Darkness* (1982) by Endler, a well-known psychologist provides an account of his personal battle with depression and discusses the effects of various treatments. *The Three Faces of Eve* gives one of the first and most comprehensive accounts of a person with multiple personality disorder. Donna Williams writes of her childhood experiences with autism in two gripping books, *Nobody Nowhere* (1992) and *Somebody Somewhere* (1994).

Methods of Therapy

I n this chapter, we look at methods for treating abnormal behavior. Some of these methods focus on helping individuals gain an understanding of developmental experiences that may have contributed to their problems, some attempt to modify more current thoughts and behavior, some involve biological interventions, and some specify ways in which the community can help. The treatment of mental disorders is linked to theories about the causes of such disorders. A brief history of the treatment of the mentally ill will illustrate how methods change as theories about human nature and the causes of its disorders change.

HISTORICAL BACKGROUND

According to one of the earliest beliefs (espoused by the ancient Chinese, Egyptians, and Hebrews), a person with unusual behavior was possessed by evil spirits. These demons were exorcised by such techniques as prayer, incantation, magic, and the use of purgatives concocted from herbs. If these interventions were unsuccessful, more extreme measures were taken to ensure that the body would be an unpleasant dwelling place for the evil spirit. Flogging, starving, burning, and causing the person to bleed profusely were frequent forms of intervention.

In the Western world, the first progress in understanding mental disorders was made

by Hippocrates (circa 460–377 B.C.), who rejected demonology and maintained that unusual behaviors were the result of a disturbance in the balance of bodily fluids.

Hippocrates, and the Greek and Roman physicians who followed him, argued for a more humane treatment of the mentally ill. They stressed the importance of pleasant surroundings, exercise, proper diet, massage, and soothing baths, as well as some less desirable treatments, such as purging, and mechanical restraints. Although there were no institutions for the mentally ill during this period, many individuals were cared for with great kindness by physicians in temples dedicated to the Greek and Roman gods.

This progressive view of mental illness did not continue, however. Primitive superstitions and a belief in demonology were revived during the Middle Ages. The mentally ill were considered to be in league with Satan and to possess supernatural powers with which they could cause floods, pestilence, and injuries to others. Seriously disturbed individuals were treated cruelly: People believed that by beating, starving, and torturing the mentally ill, they were punishing the devil. This type of cruelty culminated in the witchcraft trials that sentenced to death thousands of people (many of them mentally ill) during the fifteenth, sixteenth, and seventeenth centuries.

EARLY ASYLUMS

In the latter part of the Middle Ages, cities created asylums to cope with the mentally ill. These asylums were simply prisons; the inmates were chained in dark, filthy cells and were treated more as animals than as human beings. It was not until 1792, when Philippe Pinel was placed in charge of an asylum in Paris, that some improvements were made. As an experiment, Pinel removed the chains that restrained the inmates. Much to the amazement of skeptics who thought Pinel was mad to unchain such "animals," the experiment was a success. When released from their restraints, placed in clean, sunny rooms, and treated kindly, many people who for years had been considered hopelessly insane improved enough to leave the asylum.

By the beginning of the twentieth century, the fields of medicine and psychology were making great advances. In 1905, a mental dis-

Phillipe Pinel in the courtyard of the hospital of Salpetriere.

order known as *general paresis* was shown to have a physical cause: a syphilis infection acquired many years before the symptoms of the disorder appeared. General paresis is characterized by a gradual decline in mental and physical functions, marked personality changes, and delusions and hallucinations. Without treatment, death occurs within a few years. The syphilis spirochete remains in the body after the initial genital infection disappears, and it gradually destroys the nervous system. At one time, general paresis accounted for more than 10 percent of all admissions to mental hospitals, but today few cases are reported, due to the effectiveness of penicillin in treating syphilis (Dale, 1975).

The discovery that general paresis was the result of a disease encouraged those who believed that mental illness was biological in origin. At about the same time, Sigmund Freud and his followers laid the groundwork for understanding mental illness in terms of psychological factors; likewise Pavlov's laboratory experiments demonstrated that animals could become emotionally disturbed if forced to make decisions beyond their capacities.

Despite these scientific advances, in the early 1900s the public still did not understand mental illness and viewed mental hospitals and their inmates with fear and horror. Clifford Beers undertook the task of educating the public about mental health. As a young man, Beers developed a bipolar disorder and was confined for 3 years in several private and state hospitals. Although chains and other methods of torture had been abandoned long before, the straitjacket was still widely used to restrain excited patients. Lack of funds made the average state mental hospital—with its overcrowded wards, poor food, and unsympathetic attendants—a far from pleasant place

Early forms of "treatment" for mental illness often included floggings.

to live. After his recovery, Beers wrote about his experiences in the now-famous book *A Mind That Found Itself* (1908), which aroused considerable public interest. Beers worked ceaselessly to educate the public about mental illness and helped to organize the National Committee for Mental Hygiene. In 1950, this organization joined with two related groups to form the National Association for Mental Health. The mental hygiene movement played an invaluable role in stimulating the organization of child-guidance clinics and community mental health centers to aid in the prevention and treatment of mental disorders.

MODERN TREATMENT FACILITIES

Mental hospitals have been upgraded markedly since the time of Beers, but there is still much room for improvement. The best of these hospitals are comfortable and well-kept

THE CRIB

The "crib"—a restraining device used in a New York mental institution in 1882.

places that provide a number of therapeutic activities: individual and group psychotherapy, recreation, occupational therapy (designed to teach skills, as well as to provide relaxation), and educational courses to help patients prepare for a job upon release from the hospital. The worst are primarily custodial institutions where patients lead a boring existence in run-down, overcrowded wards and receive little treatment except for medication. Most mental hospitals fall somewhere in between these two extremes.

Beginning in the early 1960s emphasis shifted from treating mentally disturbed individuals in hospitals to treating them in their own communities. This movement toward *deinstitutionalization* was motivated partly by the recognition that hospitalization has some inherent disadvantages, regardless of how good the facilities may be. Hospitals remove people from the social support of family and friends and from their patterns of daily life; they tend to make people feel "sick" and unable to cope with the world; and they encourage dependency. They are also very expensive.

During the 1950s psychotherapeutic drugs (discussed later in this chapter) were discovered that could relieve depression and anxiety and reduce psychotic behavior. When these drugs became widely available in the 1960s, it was possible for many hospitalized patients to be discharged and returned home to be treated as outpatients. The Community Mental Health Centers Act of 1963 made federal funds available for the establishment of community treatment centers. These community mental health centers were designed to provide outpatient treatment and a number of other services, including short-term hospitalization and partial hospitalization. Partial hospitalization is more flexible than traditional hospitalization: Individuals may receive treatment at the center during the day and return home in the evening or may work during the day and spend nights at the center.

As Figure 16-1 shows, the number of patients treated in state and county mental hospitals has decreased dramatically over the past 35 years. For some patients deinstitutionalization has worked. The services of the mental health centers and private care clinicians, along with help from their families and the use of psychotherapeutic drugs, have enabled them to resume a satisfactory life. For others, however, deinstitutionalization has had unfortunate consequences, largely because the facilities in most communities are far from adequate.

Many individuals who improve with hospitalization and could manage on their own with assistance do not receive adequate follow-up care in terms of outpatient therapy or help in finding friends, housing, and jobs. As a consequence, they lead a revolving-door existence, going in and out of institutions between unsuccessful attempts to cope on their own. About half of all patients discharged from state hospitals are readmitted within a year.

Some discharged patients are too incapacitated to even attempt to support themselves or to function without custodial care; they may live in dirty, overcrowded housing or roam the streets. The disheveled man standing on the corner talking to himself and shouting gibberish may be one victim of deinstitutionalization. The woman with all of her worldly possessions in a shopping bag who spends one night in the doorway of an office building and the next in a subway station may be another. At least one third of street people suffer from some sort of mental disorder (Rossi, 1990).

The increasing visibility of homeless mentally ill individuals, particularly in large cities, has aroused public concern and prompted a

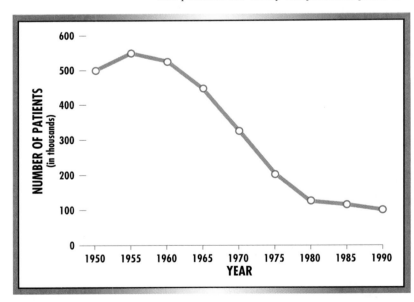

FIGURE 16-1

Patients in Mental Hospitals   *The number of patients cared for in United States state and county mental hospitals has decreased dramatically over the past 35 years.*

move toward reinstitutionalization. However, an important ethical issue is involved. If such people are not readjusting to society, should they be involuntarily committed to a mental hospital? One of the most cherished civil rights in a democratic society is the right to liberty. It is essential that any commitment proceedings safeguard this right.

Some experts believe that legal action is warranted only if a person is potentially dangerous to others. The rare, but highly publicized, occasions when a mentally ill person experiencing a psychotic episode attacks an innocent bystander have generated fears for public safety. But dangerousness is difficult to predict. Studies have shown that mental health professionals are poor at predicting whether a person will commit a dangerous act (Monahan, 1976). Moreover, our legal system is designed to protect people from preventative detention. A person is assumed innocent until proven guilty by the courts, and prisoners are released from penitentiaries even though statistics show that most will commit additional crimes. Should mentally ill individuals not have the same rights? And what about the person who appears self-destructive, more dangerous to himself than to others? Should he or she be committed? These complex issues have yet to be resolved.

Aside from the legal issues, the problem of providing care for the mentally ill remains. Society has to be willing to pay for appropriate care of persons with mental disorders. Many of them might voluntarily seek treatment, but cannot because they do not have the means to pay for good treatment.

PROFESSIONS INVOLVED IN PSYCHOTHERAPY

Whether a person receives therapy in a hospital, a community mental health center, or a private office, several different types of professionals may be involved.

A **psychiatrist** has an M.D. degree and has completed a three-year residency (after medical school) in a mental health facility, during which he or she received supervision in the diagnosis of abnormal behavior, drug therapy, and psychotherapy. As a physician, the psychiatrist can prescribe medication and, in most states, hospitalization.

The term **psychoanalyst** is reserved for individuals who have received specialized train-

A child psychiatrist works with a young patient.

ing at a psychoanalytic institute learning the methods and theories derived from Freud. The program usually takes several years, during which the trainees must undergo their own psychoanalysis as well as treat several clients psychoanalytically while under supervision. Until recently, most psychoanalytic institutes required their graduates to have an M.D. degree. Thus, most psychoanalysts are psychiatrists. However, the vast majority of psychiatrists are not psychoanalysts.

Psychologists who work as therapists have obtained graduate training in clinical, counseling, or school psychology. Usually, they hold a Ph.D. (Doctor of Philosophy) or Psy.D. (Doctor of Psychology) degree. The Ph.D. emphasizes training in research as well as diagnosis and therapy. The Psy.D. is a more applied degree, focusing mainly on diagnosis and therapy. Both degrees require four or five years of postgraduate study plus a year or more of internship. In addition, most states require psychologists to pass a licensing or certification examination.

Clinical psychologists work with people suffering from a broad range of mental disorders. **Counseling psychologists** focus more on problems of adjustment and often concentrate on specific areas such as student, marriage, or family counseling. **School psychologists** are concerned with young people who have academic difficulties.

Psychiatric social workers have completed a two-year master's degree program (M.S.W.), which includes training in interviewing,

A clinical psychologist talking with a client.

therapy, and in extending treatment procedures to the home and community. The psychiatric social worker is often called on to collect information about a patient's home situation and to assist the patient in getting help from community resources (such as hospitals, clinics, and social agencies).

Sometimes these professionals work as a team. The psychiatrist prescribes psychotherapeutic medications and monitors their effectiveness; the psychologist sees the same client in individual or group psychotherapy; the social worker monitors the home environment and acts as a liaison with community agencies for the client. In mental hospitals a fourth professional is available: the **psychiatric nurse**. Psychiatric nursing is a field within the nursing profession that requires special training in the understanding and treatment of mental disorders. In our discussion of psychotherapeutic techniques, we will not specify the profession of the psychotherapists; we will assume that they are trained and competent members of any one of these professions.

TECHNIQUES OF PSYCHOTHERAPY

Psychotherapy refers to the treatment of mental disorders by psychological (rather than physical or biological) means. The term embraces a variety of techniques, all of which are intended to help emotionally disturbed individuals modify their behavior, thoughts, and emotions so that they can develop more useful ways of dealing with stress and with other people. Some psychotherapists believe that modification of behavior is dependent on the individual's understanding of his or her unconscious motives and conflicts (psychoanalysts, for example). Others focus on changing habitual patterns of thinking and behavior rather than on unconscious conflicts (behavior therapists and cognitive behavior therapists, for example). Despite differences in techniques, most methods of psychotherapy have certain basic features in common. They involve a helping relationship between two people: the client (patient) and the therapist. The client is encouraged to discuss intimate concerns, emotions, and experiences freely without fear of being judged by the therapist or having confidences betrayed. The therapist, in turn, offers sympathy and understanding, engenders trust, and tries to help the client develop more effective ways of handling his or her problems.

PSYCHOANALYSIS

Psychoanalytic theories of personality (see Chapter 13) assume that within each individual are opposing forces (the **id**, the **ego**, and the **superego**) that make internal conflicts inevitable. These conflicts, of which the person may or may not be aware, have a powerful influence on personality development and on the ability to handle life stresses. Freud believed that psychological disorders are the result of conflicts, usually originating in early childhood, of which the individual is *not* aware; the impulses and emotions involved have been repressed to the unconscious.

Unconscious conflicts between the aggressive and sexual impulses of the id and the constraints imposed by the ego and superego were considered by Freud to be the most crucial for later maladjustment. For example, a young boy may naturally feel hostile toward the new baby brother who usurps some of the parental love that was once exclusively his. If the parents refuse to acknowledge the boy's feelings and severely punish any expression of anger toward the baby, the boy must deny these impulses in order to retain his parents' love. The unwanted impulse to hurt the baby (and any emotions or memories associated with this impulse) may be pushed out of consciousness. These unconscious feelings of sibling rivalry may influence relationships in later life, perhaps taking the form of intense jealousy of and competition with friends and co-workers. Because the original conflict was repressed, the individual will have no awareness of the source of these emotions.

A key assumption of psychoanalysis is that a person's current problems cannot be successfully resolved without a thorough understanding of their unconscious basis in the early relationships with parents and siblings. The goal of psychoanalysis is to bring conflicts (repressed emotions and motives) into awareness so that they can be dealt with in a more rational and realistic way.

FREE ASSOCIATION AND DREAM ANALYSIS   One of the main techniques psychoanalysts use to facilitate the recovery of unconscious conflicts is **free association**. The client is encouraged to give free rein to thoughts and feelings and to say whatever comes to mind without editing or censoring. This is not easy to do, however. In conversation, we usually try to keep a connecting thread running through our remarks and to exclude irrelevant ideas. In addition,

most of us have spent a lifetime learning to be cautious and to think before speaking; thoughts that strike us as inappropriate, stupid, or shameful usually remain unspoken.

With practice, however, and with encouragement from the analyst, free association becomes easier. But even individuals who conscientiously try to give free rein to their thoughts will occasionally find themselves blocked. When a patient remains silent, abruptly changes the subject, or is unable to recall the details of an event, the analyst assumes that the person is resisting the recall of certain thoughts or feelings. Freud believed that blocking, or *resistance,* results from the individual's unconscious control over sensitive areas and that these are precisely the areas that should be explored.

Another technique often used with free association is *dream analysis.* Freud believed that dreams were "the royal road to the unconscious"; they represented an unconscious wish or fear in disguised form. He distinguished between the *manifest* (obvious, conscious) *content* and the *latent* (hidden, unconscious) *content* of dreams (see Chapter 6). By talking about the manifest content of a dream and then free associating to that content, the analyst and client attempt to discern the unconscious meaning.

Freud's office of Vienna offered the comfort of his famous couch, as well as a collection of Egyptian, Greek, and Roman antiquities.

TRANSFERENCE In psychoanalysis, the patient's attitudes toward the analyst are considered to be an important part of treatment. Sooner or later, the client develops strong emotional responses to the psychoanalyst. Sometimes the responses are positive and friendly; sometimes, negative and hostile. Often these reactions are inappropriate to what is taking place in the therapy sessions. The tendency for the client to make the therapist the object of emotional responses is known as **transference**: The client expresses attitudes toward the analyst that the client actually feels toward other people who are, or were, important in his or her life. Freud assumed that transference represents relics of childhood reactions to parents, and he utilized this transference of attitudes as a means of explaining to patients the childhood origin of many of their concerns and fears. By pointing out how their clients are reacting to them, analysts help their patients achieve a better understanding of how they react to others. The following excerpt shows an analyst's use of transference, followed by the use of free association.

> PATIENT: I don't understand why you're holding back on telling me if this step is the right one for me at this time in my life.
>
> ANALYST: This has come up before. You want my approval before taking some action. What seems to be happening here is that one of the conflicts you have with your wife is trying to get her approval of what you have decided you want to do, and that conflict is occurring now between us.
>
> PATIENT: I suppose so. Other people's approval has always been very important to me.
>
> ANALYST: Let's stay with that for a few minutes. Would you free associate to that idea of getting approval from others. Just let the associations come spontaneously—don't force them.
>
> (Woody & Robertson, 1988, p. 129)

INTERPRETATION The analyst helps the client gain **insight** into the nature of the uncon-

scious conflicts that are the source of his or her difficulties through **interpretation**. An interpretation is a hypothesis that summarizes a segment of the client's behavior and offers an explanation of its motivation. In the previous excerpt, the analyst offers an interpretation by comparing the patient's behavior in the therapy situation (seeking approval for a proposed action) to the kind of approval-seeking behavior that causes conflict with his wife. The client appears to tentatively accept the interpretation.

Interpretation may also take the form of calling attention to the patient's resistances—a sudden blocking of free association, changing the subject, or forgetting an appointment. All of these behaviors may indicate that the client is trying to avoid uncomfortable topics. Interpretations must be skillfully timed; that is, made at a point when unconscious material is close to awareness and the patient is ready to accept painful insights. An interpretation offered before a client is ready to accept it may only arouse anxiety and defensiveness.

WORKING THROUGH As an analysis progresses, the patient goes through a lengthy process of reeducation known as **working through**. By examining the same conflicts over and over as they have appeared in a variety of situations, the client comes to understand them and to see how pervasive certain of his attitudes and behaviors are. By working through painful childhood emotions during therapy, the person becomes strong enough to face these emotions with less anxiety and to deal with them in a more realistic manner.

Psychoanalysis is a lengthy, intensive, and expensive process. Client and analyst usually meet for 50-minute sessions several times a week for at least a year, and often several years. Psychoanalysis is thought to be most successful with individuals who are highly motivated to solve their problems, who can verbalize their feelings with some ease, and who can afford it.

PSYCHOANALYTIC THERAPIES

Since Freud's time, numerous forms of psychotherapy based on Freudian concepts have developed. They share in common the premise that mental disorders stem from unconscious conflicts and fears, but they differ from classical psychoanalysis in a number of ways and are usually called **psychoanalytic therapies.** (The term *psychodynamic therapies* is also used.) As noted in Chapter 13, the ego analysts (such as Karen Horney and Heinz Hartman) placed greater emphasis on the role of the rational, problem-solving ego in directing behavior and correspondingly less emphasis on the role of unconscious sexual and aggressive drives. They sought to strengthen the functions of the ego, in particular self-esteem and feelings of competency, so that the individual could deal more constructively with current anxieties and interpersonal relationships. Their general strategy was (a) to give the client insight into how the past continues to influence the present and (b) to develop the client's awareness of what can be done in the present to correct the harmful effects of the past.

The techniques of psychoanalysis have been modified too. Contemporary psychoanalytic therapy is usually briefer, more flexible, and less intense. Sessions are scheduled less frequently, usually once a week. There is less emphasis on a complete reconstruction of childhood experiences and more attention to problems arising from the way the individual is currently interacting with others. Free association is often replaced with a direct discussion of critical issues, and the psychoanalytic therapist may be more direct, raising pertinent topics when it seems appropriate rather than waiting for the client to bring them up. While transference is still considered an important part of the therapeutic process, the therapist may try to limit the intensity of the transference feelings.

Still central, however, is the psychoanalytic therapist's conviction that unconscious motives and fears are at the core of most emotional problems and that insight and the working-through process are essential to a cure (Auld and Hyman, 1991). As we will see in the next section, behavior therapists do not agree with these views.

Behavior Therapies

The term **behavior therapy** includes a number of different therapeutic methods based on the principles of learning and conditioning discussed in Chapter 7. Behavior therapists assume that maladaptive behaviors are learned ways of coping with stress and that some of the techniques developed in experimental work on learning can be used to substitute more appropriate responses for maladaptive ones. Whereas psychoanalysis is concerned with understanding how the individual's past conflicts influence behavior, behavior therapy focuses more directly on the behavior itself.

Behavior therapists point out that, although the achievement of insight is a worthwhile goal, it does not ensure behavior change. Often we understand why we behave the way we do in a certain situation but are not able to change our behavior. If you are unusually timid about speaking in class, you may be able to trace this fear to past events (your father criticized your opinions whenever you expressed them, your mother made a point of correcting your grammar, you had little experience in public speaking during high school because you were afraid to compete with your older brother who was captain of the debate team). Understanding the reasons behind your fear does not necessarily make it easier for you to contribute to class discussions.

In contrast to psychodynamic therapy, which attempts to change certain aspects of the individual's personality, behavior therapies tend to focus on the modification of maladaptive behaviors in specific situations. Behavior therapists are also more concerned than psychoanalysts with obtaining experimental evaluations of their techniques.

In the initial therapy session a behavior therapist listens carefully to the client's statement of the problem. What exactly does the client want to change? Is it a fear of flying or of speaking in public? A problem with uncontrolled eating or drinking? Feelings of inadequacy and helplessness? An inability to concentrate and get work done? The first step is to define the problem clearly and to break it down into a set of specific therapeutic goals. If, for example, the client complains of general feelings of inadequacy, the therapist will try to get the client to describe these feelings more specifically: to pinpoint the kinds of situations in which they occur and the kinds of behaviors associated with them. Inadequate to do what? To speak up in class or in social situations? To get assignments completed on time? To control eating? Once the behaviors that need changing are specified, the therapist and client work out a treatment program employing some of the procedures we will describe. The therapist chooses the treatment method that is appropriate for the particular problem.

SYSTEMATIC DESENSITIZATION AND IN VIVO EXPOSURE Systematic desensitization and in vivo exposure can be viewed as a *deconditioning* or counterconditioning processes (Wolpe, 1958). These procedures are highly effective in eliminating fears or phobias. The principle of the treatment is to substitute a response that is incompatible with anxiety—namely, relaxation. It is difficult to be both relaxed and anxious at the same time. The client is first trained to relax deeply. One way is to progressively relax various muscles, starting, for example, with the feet and ankles and proceeding up the body to neck and facial muscles. The person learns what muscles feel like when they are truly relaxed and how to discriminate various degrees of tension. Sometimes drugs and hypnosis are used to help people who cannot relax otherwise.

The next step is to make up a hierarchy of the anxiety-producing situations. The situations are ranked in order from the one that produces the least anxiety to the one that is most fearful. In systematic desensitization, the client is then asked to relax and imagine each situation in the hierarchy, starting with the one that is least anxiety-producing. In vivo exposure requires the client to actually experience the anxiety-producing situations. In vivo exposure is a more effective procedure than simply imagining anxiety-producing situations, but some clients need to begin with imagination and eventually move to experiencing feared situations.

An example will make these procedures clearer. Suppose the client is a woman who suffers from a phobia of snakes. This phobia is so strong that the woman is afraid to walk in her own back yard for fear of encountering a snake, let alone going for a walk in the countryside or on a vacation to a resort in the woods. Her anxiety hierarchy might begin with a picture of a snake in a book. Somewhere around the middle of her hierarchy list might be viewing a snake in a glass cage at the zoo. At the top of her list would be actually handling a large snake. After this woman has learned to relax and has constructed the hierarchy, the therapist would begin to take her through her list. In systematic desensitiza-

tion, she would sit with her eyes closed in a comfortable chair while the therapist describes the least anxiety-provoking situation to her. If she can imagine herself in the situation without any increase in muscle tension, the therapist proceeds to the next item on the list. If the woman reports any anxiety while visualizing a scene, she concentrates on relaxing; the same scene is visualized until all anxiety is neutralized. This process continues through a series of sessions until the situation that originally provoked the most anxiety now elicits only relaxation. At this point, the woman has been systematically desensitized to anxiety-provoking situations through the strengthening of an incompatible response—relaxation.

During in vivo exposure, the woman would actually experience each of the situations on her list, beginning with the least feared and with the coaching of the therapist. Before the woman actually handled a snake herself the therapist might *model* handling the snake without being fearful—the therapist would hold the snake in the client's presence, displaying confidence and no anxiety. Eventually, the woman would handle the snake herself, allowing the snake to crawl on her, while using relaxation to control her anxiety. In vivo exposure therapy of this sort has proven extremely effective in the treatment of phobias (Bandura, Blanchard, & Rifter, 1969).

The specific learning process and in vivo exposure may be **extinction**, rather than counterconditioning. Exposing oneself to a fear-arousing stimulus and discovering that nothing bad happens extinguishes the conditioned fear response. Relaxation may be merely a useful way to encourage a person to confront what he or she fears. Indeed, if phobic individuals can force themselves to stay in the feared situation for a long period (for example, a claustrophobic sits in a closet for hours or someone who fears contamination goes for days without washing), the initial terror gradually subsides. This procedure, exposing a phobic individual to the most feared situation or object for an extended length of time without the opportunity to escape, is called **flooding**. It has proved particularly effective in treating agoraphobia (which involves a fear of leaving secure places such as one's home) and obsessive-compulsive disorders (Steketee & White, 1990; Emmelkamp & Kuipus, 1979).

Selective Reinforcement Whether the underlying learning process is counterconditioning or extinction, systematic desensitization and exposure are based on principles of classical conditioning. Selective reinforcement, based on the principles of operant conditioning (see Chapter 7), has also proved to be an effective method of modifying behavior, especially with children.

The procedure can be illustrated by the case of a third-grade student who was inattentive in school, refused to complete assignments or to participate in class, and spent most of her time daydreaming. In addition, her social skills were poor and she had few friends. The behavior to be reinforced was defined as "on task" behavior, which included paying attention to schoolwork or instructions from the teacher, completing reading assignments, and taking part in class discussions. The reinforcement consisted of beans that were used as tokens to be exchanged for special privileges that the girl valued, such as standing first in line (three beans) or being allowed to stay after school to help the teacher with special projects (nine beans). Anytime the teacher observed the student performing on-task behaviors, she placed one bean in a jar.

During the first 3 months of treatment, the girl completed 12 units of work, compared to 0 units during the 3 months before the reinforcement regime started. In the final 3 months, she completed 36 units and was performing at the same level as the rest of the class. A follow-up the next year showed that the girl was maintaining her academic performance. She also showed a marked improvement in social skills and was accepted more by the other children (Walker, Hedberg, Clement, & Wright, 1981). This is a common finding: Improving behavior in one area of life often produces added benefits (Kazdin, 1982).

Reinforcement of desirable responses can be accompanied by extinction of undesirable ones. For example, a young boy who habitually shouts to get his mother's attention could be ignored whenever he does so and reinforced by her attention only when he comes to where she is and speaks in a conversational tone.

Operant conditioning procedures involving rewards for desirable responses and no rewards for undesirable ones have been used successfully in dealing with a broad range of childhood problems, including bed-wetting, aggression, tantrums, disruptive classroom behavior, poor school performance, and social withdrawal. Similar procedures have been used with autistic children, retarded adults and severely disordered mental patients.

A number of mental hospitals have instituted "token economies" on wards with very impaired, chronic patients to induce socially appropriate behavior. Tokens (which can later be exchanged for food and privileges such as watching television) are given for dressing properly, interacting with other patients, eliminating "psychotic talk," helping on the wards, and so on. Such programs have proved successful in improving both the patients' behavior and the general functioning of the ward (Paul and Lentz, 1977).

Modeling Another effective means of changing behavior that we mentioned briefly earlier is modeling. Modeling makes use of observational learning. Since observing other models is a principal way in which humans learn, watching people who are displaying adaptive behavior should teach people with maladaptive responses better coping strategies. Observing the behavior of a model (either live or videotaped) has proved effective in reducing fears and teaching new skills.

Selective reinforcement can be used to help children learn to control tantrums.

FIGURE 16-2

Treatment of Snake Phobia *The mean number of snake-approach responses by subjects before and after they received different behavior therapy treatments.* (After Bandura, Blanchard, & Ritter, 1969)

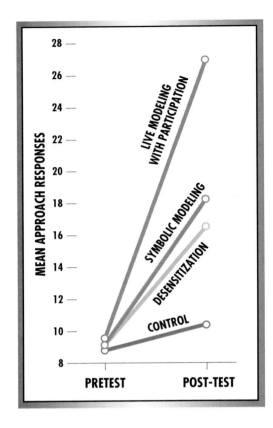

Figure 16-2 shows the results of a study in which modeling was combined with gradual practice in the treatment of snake phobia.

Modeling is effective in overcoming fears and anxieties because it gives the person a chance to observe someone else go through the anxiety-provoking situation without getting hurt. Watching videotapes of models enjoying a visit to the dentist or going through various hospital procedures has proved successful in helping both children and adults overcome their fears of such experiences (Melamed & Siegel, 1975; Shaw & Thoresen, 1974).

BEHAVIORAL REHEARSAL In a therapy session modeling is often combined with role-playing, or **behavioral rehearsal**. The therapist helps the individual rehearse or practice more adaptive behaviors. In the following excerpt, a therapist helps a young man overcome his anxieties about asking women for dates. The young man has been pretending to talk to a woman over the phone and finishes by asking for a date.

CLIENT: Um, I was wondering, you wouldn't want to go out on a date Saturday night, or anything, would you?

THERAPIST: Okay, that's a start. Can you think of another way of asking her out that sounds a bit more positive and confident? For example, "There's a concert I'd like to see on Saturday night and I'd like very much to take you, if you are free."

CLIENT: That's great!

THERAPIST: Okay, you try it.

CLIENT: Um, I've got two tickets to the concert Saturday night. If you don't have anything to do, you might want to come along.

THERAPIST: That's better. Try it one more time, but this time try to convey to her that you'd really like her to go.

CLIENT: I've got two tickets for Saturday's concert. It would be great if you'd go with me, if you're not busy.

THERAPIST: Great! Just practice it a couple of more times, and you're ready to pick up the phone.

This example illustrates the use of behavioral rehearsal in one type of *assertiveness training*. Like the young man in the example, many people have trouble asking for what they want or refusing to allow others to take advantage of them. By practicing *assertive responses* (first in role-playing with the therapist and then in real-life situations), the individual not only reduces anxiety but also develops more effective coping techniques. The therapist determines the kinds of situations in which the person is passive and then helps him or her to think of and to practice some assertive responses that might be effective. The following situations might be worked through during a sequence of therapy sessions:

- Someone steps in front of you in line.
- A friend asks you to do something you do not want to do.

- Your boss criticizes you unjustly.
- You return defective merchandise to a store.
- You are annoyed by the conversation of people behind you in the movies.
- The mechanic did an unsatisfactory job of repairing your car.

Most people do not enjoy dealing with such situations, but some individuals are so fearful of asserting themselves that they say nothing and instead build up feelings of resentment and inadequacy. In assertiveness training, the client rehearses with the therapist effective responses that could be made in such situations and gradually tries them in real life. The therapist tries to teach the client to express his needs in a way that is straightforward and forceful, but not seen by others as hostile or threatening (see Table 16-1).

SELF-REGULATION   Because client and therapist seldom meet more than once per week, the client must learn to control or regulate his or her own behavior so that progress can be made outside the therapy hour. Moreover, if people feel they are responsible for their own improvement, they are more likely to maintain such gains. **Self-regulation** involves monitoring, or observing, one's own behavior and using various techniques—*self-reinforcement, self-punishment, control of stimulus conditions, development of incompatible responses*—to change the maladaptive behavior. An individual monitors his or her behavior by keeping a careful record of the kinds of situations that elicit the maladaptive behavior and the kinds of responses that are incompatible with it. A person concerned with alcohol abuse would note the kinds of situations in which he or she is most tempted to drink and would try to control such situations or to devise a response that is incompatible with drinking. A man who finds it hard not to join his co-workers in a noontime cocktail might plan to eat lunch at his desk, thereby controlling his drinking behavior by controlling his environment. If he is tempted to relax with a drink on arriving home from work, he might substitute a game of tennis or a jog around the block as a means of relieving tension. Both of these activities would be incompatible with drinking.

Self-reinforcement is rewarding yourself immediately for achieving a specific goal; the

*Decide what you want to say and stick with it rather than giving into others the minute they disagree with you. For example, when a clerk says you cannot return a defective product, say "This is defective and I want to return it" repeatedly until the clerk allows you to return it or at least calls the manager, whom you tell "This is defective and I want to return it" until you get your money back.
 	
*Ask for small, specific changes in a situation or another person's behavior rather than requesting global changes. For example, rather than saying, "I want you to be more loving," say, "I want you to listen to me when I talk."
 	
*Use "I" phrases instead of accusatory phrases when discussing a difficult situation with another person. Four pieces to an "I" statement are:
 	
   I feel . . .
   when you . . .
   because . . .
   what I want . . .
 	
For example, "*I feel* angry *when you* don't show up for an appointment *because* it wastes my time. *What I want* is for you to call me and cancel our appointment when you think you won't be able to make it."

TABLE 16-1

Some Elements of an Assertive Response

reward could be praising yourself, watching a favorite television program, telephoning a friend, eating a favorite food. Self-punishment is arranging some aversive consequence for failing to achieve a goal, such as depriving yourself of something you enjoy (*not* watching a favorite television program, for instance) or making yourself do an unpleasant task (such as cleaning your room). Depending on the kind of behavior the individual wants to change, various combinations of self-reinforcement, self-punishment, or control of stimuli and responses may be used. Table 16-2 outlines a program for self-regulation of eating.

COGNITIVE BEHAVIOR THERAPIES

The behavior therapy procedures we have discussed thus far have focused on modifying behavior directly with little attention paid to the individual's thinking and reasoning processes. Initially, behavior therapists discounted the importance of cognition, preferring a strict stimulus-response approach. They regarded any consideration of beliefs and attitudes as a return to the kind of unscientific introspection that Watson objected to at the beginning of this century (see Chapter 1). However, in

TABLE 16-2

Self-Regulation of Eating
The program illustrates the use of learning principles to help control food intake. (After Stuart & Davis, 1972; O'Leary & Wilson, 1975)

SELF-MONITORING

DAILY LOG

Keep a detailed record of everything you eat. Note amount eaten, type of food and caloric value, time of day, and the circumstances of eating. This record will establish the caloric intake that is maintaining your present weight. It will also help to identify the stimuli that elicit and reinforce your eating behavior.

WEIGHT CHART

Decide how much you want to lose and set a weekly goal for weight loss. Your weekly goal should be realistic (between 1 and 2 pounds). Record your weight each day on graph paper. In addition to showing how your weight varies with food intake, this visual record will reinforce your dieting efforts as you observe progress toward your goal.

CONTROLLING STIMULUS CONDITIONS

Use these procedures to narrow the range of stimuli associated with eating:

1. Eat only at predetermined times, at a specific table, using a special place mat, napkin, dishes, and so forth. Do *not* eat at other times or in other places (for example, while standing in the kitchen).

2. Do *not* combine eating with other activities, such as reading or watching television.

3. Keep in the house only those foods that are permitted on your diet.

4. Shop for food only after having had a full meal; buy only those items that are on a previously prepared list.

MODIFYING ACTUAL EATING BEHAVIOR

Use these procedures to break the chain of responses that makes eating automatic:

1. Eat very slowly, paying close attention to the food.

2. Finish chewing and swallowing before putting more food on the fork.

3. Put your utensils down for periodic short breaks before continuing to eat.

DEVELOPING INCOMPATIBLE RESPONSES

When tempted to eat at times other than those specified, find a substitute activity that is incompatible with eating. For example, exercise to music, go for a walk, talk with a friend (preferably one who knows you are dieting), study your diet plan and weight graph, noting how much weight you have lost.

SELF-REINFORCEMENT

Arrange to reward yourself with an activity you enjoy (watching television, reading, planning a new wardrobe, visiting a friend) when you have maintained appropriate eating behavior for a day. Plan larger rewards (for example, buying something you want) for a specified amount of weight loss. Self-punishment (other than forgoing a reward) is probably less effective because dieting is a fairly depressing business anyway. But you might decrease the frequency of binge eating by immediately reciting to yourself the aversive consequences or by looking at an unattractive picture of yourself in a bathing suit.

response to evidence that cognitive factors—the individual's thoughts, expectations, and interpretation of events—are important determinants of people's behaviors, many behavior therapists have incorporated a focus on cognitions into therapy (Bandura, 1986).

Cognitive behavior therapy is a general term for treatment methods that use behavior modification techniques but also incorporate procedures designed to change maladaptive beliefs. The therapist attempts to help people control disturbing emotional reactions, such as anxiety and depression, by

teaching them more effective ways of interpreting and thinking about their experiences. For example, as we noted in discussing Beck's cognitive theory of depression (see Chapter 15), depressed individuals tend to appraise events from a negative and self-critical viewpoint. They expect to fail rather than to succeed, and they tend to magnify failures and to minimize successes in evaluating their performance. In treating depression, cognitive behavior therapists try to help their clients recognize the distortions in their thinking and make changes that are more in line with reality. The following dialogue illustrates how a therapist, by carefully directed questioning, makes a client aware of the unrealistic nature of her beliefs.

THERAPIST: Why do you want to end your life?

CLIENT: Without Raymond, I am nothing. . . . I can't be happy without Raymond. . . . But I can't save our marriage.

THERAPIST: What has your marriage been like?

CLIENT: It has been miserable from the very beginning. . . . Raymond has always been unfaithful. . . . I have hardly seen him in the past five years.

THERAPIST: You say that you can't be happy without Raymond. . . . Have you found yourself happy when you are with Raymond?

CLIENT: No, we fight all the time and I feel worse.

THERAPIST: You say you are nothing without Raymond. Before you met Raymond, did you feel you were nothing?

CLIENT: No, I felt I was somebody.

THERAPIST: If you were somebody before you knew Raymond, why do you need him [in order] to be somebody now?

CLIENT: (puzzled) Hmmm. . . .

THERAPIST: If you were free of the marriage, do you think that men might be interested in you—knowing that you were available?

CLIENT: I guess that maybe they would be.

THERAPIST: Is it possible that you might find a man who would be more constant than Raymond?

CLIENT: I don't know. . . . I guess it's possible. . . .

THERAPIST: Then what have you actually lost if you break up the marriage?

CLIENT: I don't know.

THERAPIST: Is it possible that you'll get along better if you end the marriage?

CLIENT: There is no guarantee of that.

THERAPIST: Do you have a *real* marriage?

CLIENT: I guess not.

THERAPIST: If you don't have a real marriage, what do you actually lose if you decide to end the marriage?

CLIENT: (long pause) Nothing, I guess.

(Beck, 1976, pp. 280–291)

The behavioral component of the treatment comes into play when the therapist encourages the client to formulate alternative ways of viewing her situation and then test the implications. For example, the woman in this dialogue might be asked to record her moods at regular intervals and then to note how her depression and feelings of self-esteem fluctuate as a function of what she is doing. If she finds she feels worse after interacting with her husband than when she is alone or is interacting with someone else, this information could serve to challenge her belief that she "can't be happy without Raymond."

A cognitive-behavioral program to help someone overcome agoraphobia might include training in positive thinking, along with in vivo exposure (accompanied excursions that take the individual progressively further from home). The therapist teaches the client to replace self-defeating internal dialogues ("I'm so nervous, I know I'll faint as soon as I leave the house") with positive self-instructions ("Be calm; I'm not alone; even if I have a panic attack, I can cope"). Table 16-3 describes a program for the treatment of depression that includes techniques for modifying behavior and for changing attitudes.

Cognitive behavior therapists agree that it is important to alter a person's beliefs in order to bring about an enduring change in behavior. Most maintain that behavioral procedures are more powerful than strictly verbal ones in affecting cognitive processes. For example, to overcome anxiety about giving a speech in class, it is helpful to think positively: "I know the material well, and I'm sure I can present my ideas effectively"; "The topic is interesting,

INSTRUCTION IN SELF-CHANGE SKILLS

Pinpointing the target behavior and recording its baseline rate of occurrence; discovering the events or situations that precede the target behavior and the consequences (either positive or negative) that follow it; setting goals for change and choosing reinforcers

RELAXATION TRAINING

Learning progressive muscle relaxation to handle the anxiety that often accompanies depression; monitoring tension in daily situations and applying relaxation techniques

INCREASING PLEASANT EVENTS

Monitoring the frequency of enjoyable activities and planning weekly schedules so that each day contains a balance between negative/neutral activities and pleasant ones

COGNITIVE STRATEGIES

Learning methods for increasing positive thoughts and decreasing negative thoughts; for identifying irrational thoughts and challenging them; and for using self-instructions to help handle problem situations

ASSERTIVENESS TRAINING

Identifying situations in which being nonassertive adds to feelings of depression; learning to handle social interactions more assertively via modeling and role-playing

INCREASING SOCIAL INTERACTION

Identifying the factors that are contributing to low social interaction (such as getting in the habit of doing things alone, feeling uncomfortable due to few social skills); deciding on activities that need to be increased (such as calling friends to suggest getting together) or decreased (such as watching television) in order to improve the level of pleasant social interaction

and the other students will enjoy what I have to say." But successfully presenting the speech to a roommate and again before a group of friends will probably do more to reduce anxiety. Successful performance increases our feeling of mastery. In fact, it has been suggested that all therapeutic procedures that are effective give the person a sense of mastery or *self-efficacy*. Observing others cope and succeed, being verbally persuaded that we can handle a difficult situation, and judging from internal cues that we are relaxed and in control contribute to our feelings of self-efficacy. But the greatest sense of efficacy comes from actual performance, from personal mastery experiences. In essence, nothing succeeds like success (Bandura, 1995).

HUMANISTIC THERAPIES

Humanistic therapies are based on the phenomenological approach to personality discussed in Chapter 13. While there are different varieties of humanistic therapies, they all emphasize the individual's natural tendency toward growth and self-actualization. Psychological disorders are assumed to arise when the process of reaching one's potential is blocked by circumstances or by other people (parents, teachers, spouses) who try to channel the person's development along lines they find acceptable. When this occurs, the person begins to deny his true desires. The person's awareness of his uniqueness becomes narrowed and the potential for growth is reduced. Humanistic therapies seek to help people get in touch with their real selves and to make deliberate choices regarding their lives and behavior, rather than letting external events determine their behavior. The goal of humanistic therapy is to help the client to become more the person he or she is capable of becoming.

Like the psychoanalyst, the humanistic therapist attempts to increase the person's awareness of underlying emotions and motives. But the emphasis is on what the individual is experiencing in the here and now, rather than in the past. The humanistic therapist does not interpret the person's behavior (as a psychoanalyst might) or try to modify it (as a behavior therapist would) because such actions would impose the therapist's own views on the patient. The goal of the humanistic therapist is to facilitate exploration of the individual's own thoughts and feelings and to assist the individual in arriving at his or her own solutions. This approach will become clearer as we look at **client-centered therapy** (also called **nondirective therapy**), one of the first humanistic therapies.

Client-centered therapy, developed in the 1940s by the late Carl Rogers, is based on the assumption that the individual is the best expert on himself or herself and that people are capable of working out solutions to their own problems. The task of the therapist is to facilitate this progress—not to ask probing questions, to make interpretations, or to suggest courses of action. In fact, Rogers preferred the term "facilitator" to "therapist," and he called the people he worked with "clients" rather than "patients" because he did not view emotional difficulties as an indication of an illness to be cured.

The therapist facilitates the client's progress toward self-insight by restating to the client what the therapist hears the client saying about his needs and emotions, in order to help the client *clarify* his feelings.

Rogers believed that the most important qualities for a therapist are empathy, warmth, and genuineness. *Empathy* refers to the ability to understand the feelings the client is trying to express *and* the ability to communicate this understanding to the client. The therapist must adopt the client's frame of reference and must strive to see the problems as the client sees them. By *warmth*, Rogers meant a deep acceptance of the individual as he or she is, including the conviction that this person has the capacity to deal constructively with his or her problems. A therapist who is *genuine* is open and honest and does not play a role or operate behind a professional façade. People are reluctant to reveal themselves to those they perceive as phony. Rogers believed that a therapist who possesses these attributes will facilitate the client's growth and self-exploration (Truax & Mitchell, 1971; Rogers, 1970).

Rogers was the first to make tape recordings of therapy sessions and to permit them to be studied and analyzed. He and his colleagues have contributed much to the field of psychotherapy research. Client-centered therapy has some limitations, however. Like psychoanalysis, it appears to be successful only with individuals who are fairly verbal and who are motivated to discuss their problems. For people who do not voluntarily seek help or who are seriously disturbed and are unable to discuss their feelings, more directive methods are usually necessary. In addition, by using the client's self-reports as the only measure of psychotherapeutic effectiveness, the client-centered therapist ignores behavior outside of the therapy session. Individuals who feel insecure and ineffective in their interpersonal relationships often need more structured help in modifying their behavior.

AN ECLECTIC APPROACH

There are many variations of psychotherapy in addition to the ones we have discussed here. Several are listed in Table 16-4. Most psychotherapists do not adhere strictly to any *single* method. Instead, they take an *eclectic approach,* selecting from the different techniques the ones they feel are most appropriate given the client's personality and specific symptoms. Although their theoretical orientation may be toward a particular method or school (for example, more psychoanalytic than behaviorist), eclectic psychotherapists feel free to discard the concepts they view as not especially helpful and to select techniques from other schools. In addition, many psychotherapists use both psychotherapeutic techniques and drug therapies in treating clients with more severe problems. (Psychotherapists who are not physicians will work with a psychiatrist who will prescribe drugs for their patients.)

In dealing with a highly anxious individual, for instance, an eclectic psychotherapist might first prescribe tranquilizers or relaxation training to help reduce the person's level of anxiety. (Most psychoanalysts would not take this approach, however, because they believe that anxiety is necessary to motivate the client to explore his or her conflicts.) To help the client understand the origins of his or her problems, the eclectic therapist might discuss certain aspects of the patient's history but might feel it unnecessary to explore childhood experiences to the extent that a psychoanalyst would. The therapist might use educational techniques, such as providing information about sex and reproduction to help relieve the anxieties of an adolescent boy who feels guilty about his sexual impulses or explaining the functioning of the autonomic nervous system to reassure an

TABLE 16-4

Other Approaches to Psychotherapy
Listed are several psychotherapies not discussed in the text.

NAME	FOCUS OF THERAPY	PRINCIPLE METHODS
Gestalt therapy	To become aware of the whole personality by working through unresolved conflicts and discovering those aspects of the individual's being that are blocked from awareness. Emphasis is on becoming intensely aware of how one is feeling and behaving at the moment.	Therapy in a group setting, but therapist works with one individual at a time. Acting out fantasies, dreams or the two sides to a conflict are methods used to increase awareness. Combines psychoanalytic emphasis on resolving internal conflicts with behaviorist emphasis on awareness of one's behavior and humanistic concern for self-actualization.
Reality therapy	To clarify the individual's values and to evaluate current behavior and future plans in relation to these values. To force the individual to accept responsibility.	Therapist helps the individual perceive the consequences of possible courses of action and decide on a realistic solution or goal. Once a plan of action is chosen, a contract may be signed in which the client agrees to follow through.
Rational-emotive therapy	To replace certain irrational ideas (It is essential to be loved and admired by everyone all the time; I should be competent in all respects; People have little control over their sorrow and unhappiness) with more realistic ones. Assumes that cognitive change will produce emotional changes.	Therapist attacks and contradicts the individual's ideas (sometimes subtly, sometimes directly) in an attempt to persuade her or him to take a more rational view of the situation. Similar to Beck's cognitive therapy but therapist is more direct and confrontive.
Transactional analysis	To become aware of the intent behind the individual's communications; to eliminate subterfuge and deceit so that the individual can interpret his or her behavior accurately.	Therapy in a group setting. Communications between married couples or group members are analyzed in terms of the part of the personality that is speaking—"parent," or "child," or "adult" (similar to Freud's supergo, id, and ego)—and the intent of the message. Destructive social interactions or games are exposed for what they are.
Hypnotherapy	To relieve the symptoms and strengthen ego processes by helping the individual set reality aside and make constructive use of imagery.	Therapist uses various hypnotic procedures in an attempt to reduce conflict and doubt by focusing the individual's attention, to modify symptoms through direct suggestion or displacement, and to strengthen the individual's ability to cope.

anxious woman that some of her symptoms, such as heart palpitations and hand tremors, are not indications of a disease.

Recognizing that often no single therapeutic approach deals successfully with all aspects of a problem, more and more therapists are specializing in specific problems. For example, some clinicians specialize in problems of sexual dysfunction. They learn all they can about the physiological processes that lead to orgasm; the effect of drugs (such as alcohol, tranquilizers, and other medications) on sexual performance; and the way in which such factors as anxiety, sexual traumas, and poor communication between partners contribute to sexual dysfunction. Once sex therapists have learned all there is to know about the variables involved in normal and abnormal sexual functioning, they examine the various therapeutic systems to see what techniques can be applied to specific problems. Although

sex therapists may draw on all of the approaches we have discussed, biological and cognitive behavioral methods are most often used in treating sexual dysfunctions.

Other therapists specialize in anxiety, depression, alcoholism, and marital problems. Some concentrate on certain age groups, seeking to learn all they can about the problems of children, adolescents, or the aged. Within their special areas, therapists generally use an eclectic, or integrative, approach.

GROUP AND FAMILY THERAPY

Many emotional problems involve an individual's difficulties in relating to others, including feelings of isolation, rejection, and loneliness and the inability to form meaningful relationships. Although the therapist can help the individual to work out some of these problems, the final test lies in how well the person can apply the attitudes and responses learned in therapy to relationships in everyday life. **Group therapy** permits clients to work out their problems in the presence of others, to observe how other people react to their behavior, and to try out new methods of responding when old ones prove unsatisfactory. It is often used as a supplement to individual psychotherapy.

Therapists of various orientations (psychoanalytic, humanistic, and cognitive behaviorist) have modified their techniques to be applicable to therapy groups. Group therapy has been used in a variety of settings: in hospital wards and outpatient psychiatric clinics, with parents of disturbed children, and with teenagers in correctional institutions, to name a few. Typically, the groups consist of a small number of individuals (6 to 8 is considered optimal) who have similar problems. The therapist usually remains in the background, allowing the members to exchange experiences, to comment on one another's behavior, and to discuss their own problems as well as those of the other members. However, in some groups the therapist is quite active. For example, in a group desensitization session, people who share the same phobias (such as fear of flying or anxieties about tests) may be led together through a systematic desensitization hierarchy. Or in a session for training social skills, a group of shy and unassertive individuals may be coached by the therapist in a series of role-playing scenes. Group therapy has several advantages over individual therapy. It uses the therapist's resources more efficiently because one therapist can help several people at once. An individual can derive comfort and support from observing that others have similar, perhaps more severe problems. A person can learn vicariously by watching how others behave and can explore attitudes and reactions by interacting with a variety of people, not just with the therapist. Groups are particularly effective when they provide the participants with opportunities to acquire new social skills through modeling and to practice these skills in the group.

Most groups are led by a trained therapist. However, the number and variety of self-help groups—groups that are conducted without a professional therapist—are increasing. Self-help groups are voluntary organizations of people who meet regularly to exchange information and to support each other's efforts to overcome a common problem. *Alcoholics Anonymous* is the best known of the self-help groups. Another is *Recovery, Inc.,* an organization open to former mental patients. Other groups help people cope with specific stressful situations such as bereavement, divorce, and single parenthood. Table 16-5 lists a variety of self-help groups.

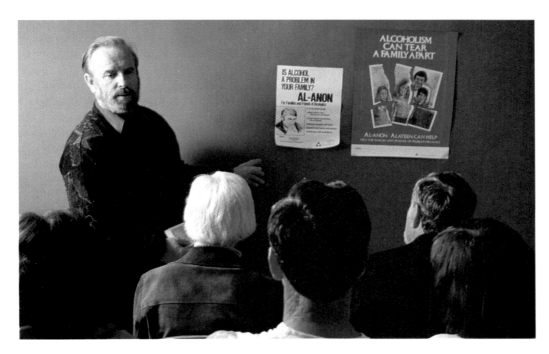

Alcoholics Anonymous is an example of a self-help group.

TABLE 16-5

Examples of Self-Help
Groups   *Listed are some
of the self-help groups
available in one large
community.* (After San
Diego Mental Health
Association, 1989)

AIDS Counseling Program	Lesbian Support Group
AIRS (teenage chemical dependency)	Loss Support (grief recovery)
Adult Children of Alcoholics	Make Today Count (breast cancer support)
Adults Molested as Children	PMS Association (Pre-menstrual syndrome)
Affective Disorders Group (mood disorders)	Parent Aid (parents at risk for child abuse)
Al-Anon (families of alcoholics)	Parents United (sexual abuse)
Ala-Teen (teenage alcohol abuse)	Parkinson's Disease Support Group
Alcoholics Anonymous	Pre Ala-Teen (child alcohol dependency)
Alzheimer's Disease Family Support Group	Project Return (recovering mental patients)
Arthritis Support Group	Recovery, Inc.
Battered Women's Support Group	Phobia Foundation
Bi-Polar Support Group (manic-depression)	Single Parent Support Group
CREATE (college students recovering from mental illness)	Survivors of Suicide
Emotional Health Anonymous	Teen Mothers Support Group
Epilepsy Support Group	Victims of Homicide (family and loved ones)
Gay Men's Coming Out-Group	Voices (schizophrenic support group)
Grandmothers' Support Group (mothers of teenage mothers)	

MARITAL AND FAMILY THERAPY   Problems in communicating feelings, satisfying one's needs, and responding appropriately to the needs and demands of others become intensified in the intimate context of marriage and family life. To the extent that they involve more than one client and focus on interpersonal relationships, **marital therapy** and **family therapy** can be considered specialized forms of group therapy.

The high divorce rate and the number of couples seeking help for difficulties centering around their relationship have made marital, or couple, therapy a growing field. Studies show that joint therapy for both partners is more effective in solving marital problems than is individual therapy for only one partner (Gurman & Kniskern, 1981).

There are many approaches to marital therapy, but most focus on helping the partners communicate their feelings, develop greater understanding and sensitivity to each other's needs, and work on more effective ways of handling their conflicts. Some couples enter marriage with very different, and often unrealistic, expectations about the roles of husband and wife, which can wreak havoc

with their relationship. The therapist can help them clarify their expectations and work out a mutually agreeable compromise. Sometimes the couple negotiates *behavioral contracts,* agreeing on the behavior changes each person is willing to make in order to create a more satisfying relationship and specifying the rewards and penalties they can use with each other to ensure the changes.

Family therapy overlaps with marital therapy but has a somewhat different origin. It developed in response to the discovery that many people who improved in individual therapy while away from their family—often in institutional settings—relapsed when they returned home. It became apparent that many of these people came from a disturbed family setting that required modification itself if the individual's gains were to be maintained. When the person with a psychological problem is a child, it is particularly important that the family be treated, because children are entirely dependent on their families. The basic premise of family therapy is that the problem shown by the identified patient is a sign that something is wrong with the entire family; the *family system* is not operating properly. The difficulty may lie in poor communication among family members or in an alliance between some family members that excludes others. For example, a mother whose relationship with her husband is unsatisfactory may focus all her attention on her son. As a result, the husband and daughter feel neglected and the son, upset by his mother's smothering and the resentment directed toward him by his father and sister, develops problems in school. While the boy's school difficulties may be the reason for seeking treatment, it is clear that they are only a symptom of a more basic family problem.

In family therapy, the family meets regularly with one or two therapists (usually a male and a female). The therapist, while observing the interactions among family members, tries to help each member become aware of the way he or she relates to the others and how his or her actions may be contributing to the family's problems. Sometimes videotape recordings are played back to make the family members aware of how they interact with each other. Other times, the therapist may visit the family in the home to observe conflicts and verbal exchanges as they occur in their natural setting. It often becomes apparent that problem behaviors are being reinforced by the responses of family members. For example, a young child's temper tantrums or a teenager's eating problems may be inadvertently reinforced by the attention they elicit from the parents. The therapist can teach the parents to monitor their own and their children's behavior, to determine how their reactions may be reinforcing the problem behavior, and then to alter the reinforcement contingencies.

One important application of family therapy involves teaching families of people with schizophrenia to communicate more positively and clearly with one another (Goldstein, 1987). Schizophrenics in families in which conflict and hostility are expressed in hurtful ways and in which family members are overinvolved in each other's lives tend to have more frequent relapses than schizophrenics in families in which conflict and hostility are expressed more calmly and family members respect each other's independence. Training programs that enhance families' skills at expression of negative emotion and positive interactions can reduce relapse rates for people with schizophrenia.

Family therapy.

EFFECTIVENESS OF PSYCHOTHERAPY

How effective is psychotherapy? Which methods work best? These questions are not easy to answer. Research into the effectiveness of psychotherapy is hampered by several major difficulties. How do we decide whether an individual has improved? What measures of improvement are valid? How do we know what caused the change?

EVALUATING PSYCHOTHERAPY

Evaluating the effectiveness of psychotherapy is a difficult task because so many variables must be considered. For instance, some people with psychological problems get better

Marriage counseling.

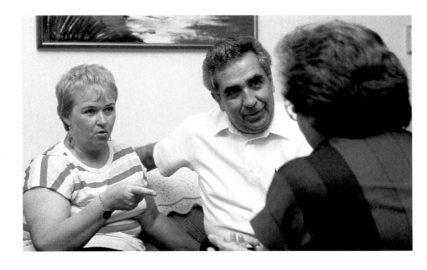

without any professional treatment. This phenomenon is called **spontaneous remission.** Some mental disorders do improve by themselves, simply with the passage of time—much like the common cold. But more often, improvement that occurs in the absence of treatment is not spontaneous; rather, it is the result of external events—usually changes in the individual's life situation or with the help of another person.

Many emotionally disturbed people who do not seek professional assistance are able to improve with the help of a nonprofessional, such as a friend, teacher, or religious adviser. We cannot consider these recoveries to be spontaneous; but since they are not due to psychotherapy, they are included in the rate of spontaneous remission, which ranges from about 30 to 60 percent, depending on the particular disorder being studied (Bergin & Lambert, 1978). To allow for those who would have improved without treatment, any evaluation of psychotherapy must compare a treated group with an untreated control group. Psychotherapy is judged to be effective if the client's improvement after therapy is greater than any improvement that occurs without therapy over the same period. The ethical problem of allowing someone to go without treatment is usually resolved by composing the control group of individuals on a waiting list. Members of the waiting-list

control group are interviewed at the start of the study to gather baseline information but receive no treatment until after the study. Unfortunately, the longer the study (and time is needed to measure improvement, especially with insight therapies), the harder it is to keep people on a waiting list.

A second major problem in evaluating psychotherapy is measuring the outcome. How do we decide whether a person has been helped by therapy? We cannot always rely on the individual's own assessment. Some people report that they are feeling better simply to please the therapist or to convince themselves that their money was well spent. The therapist's evaluation of the treatment as successful cannot always be considered an objective criterion, either. The therapist has a vested interest in proclaiming that the client is better. And sometimes the changes that the therapist observes during the therapy session do not carry over into real-life situations. Assessment of improvement, therefore, should include at least three independent measures: the client's evaluation of progress; the therapist's evaluation; and the judgment of a third party, such as family members and friends or a clinician not involved in the treatment.

Despite these problems, researchers have been able to conduct many psychotherapy evaluation studies. Rather than discuss individual studies, we will look at a major evaluation that attempted to answer the question of whether psychotherapy works. The investigators located 475 published studies that compared at least one therapy group with an untreated control group. Using a complicated statistical procedure called meta-analysis (see Chapter 6), they determined the magnitude of effect for each study by comparing the average change produced in treatment (on measures such as self-esteem, anxiety, and achievement in work and school) with that of the control group. They concluded that individuals receiving therapy were better off than those who had received no treatment. The average psychotherapy patient showed greater improvement than 80 percent of the untreated control-group patients (Smith, Glass, & Miller, 1980).

A subsequent review that analyzed a new sample of studies yielded comparable results (Shapiro & Shapiro, 1982). When we look at improvement rates as a function of the number of therapy sessions (see Figure 16-3), it

FIGURE 16-3

Improvement with Psychotherapy   *The figure shows the relationship between the number of sessions of individual psychotherapy and the percentage of patients improved. Improvement was rated by indpendent researchers following the termination of treatment.* (After Howard, Kopta, Krause, & Orlinsky, 1986)

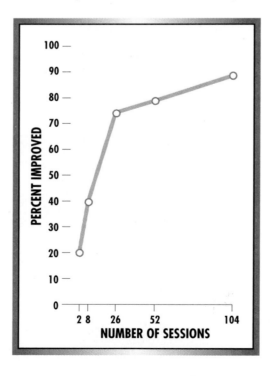

is clear that treated groups show a rate of change that is above and beyond spontaneous remission estimates. By the eight therapy session approximately 50 percent of patients are measurably improved, and 75 percent have shown improvement by the end of 6 months of weekly psychotherapy.

COMPARING PSYCHOTHERAPIES

Psychotherapy produces greater improvement than no treatment, but are the different therapeutic approaches equally effective? A number of reviews have analyzed studies in which the results of different psychotherapies were compared (for example, Smith, Glass, & Miller, 1980; Rachman & Wilson, 1980; Bergin & Lambert, 1978). The conclusion of most of these reviews is that there is little difference in effectiveness between therapies. How can therapies that espouse such different methods produce such similar results? Numerous possible explanations have been suggested (see Stiles, Shapiro, & Elliott, 1986). We will mention only two.

Perhaps certain therapies are effective for certain problems or disorders but are relatively ineffective for others. When specific therapies are used to treat a wide range of disorders, they may help some cases but not others. Thus, averaging results over cases may conceal the special strengths of a particular therapy. We need to know which treatment is effective for which problem.

Another reason why different psychotherapies may be equally effective in helping clients is because they all share certain factors. It may be these common factors, rather than the specific therapeutic techniques employed, that promote positive change.

COMMON FACTORS IN PSYCHOTHERAPIES

One school of therapy emphasizes insight; another, modeling and reinforcement; and yet another, rational cognitions. But perhaps these variables are not the crucial ones. Other factors that are common to most psychotherapies, but which receive little emphasis when therapists write about what they do, may be more important (Garfield, 1980; Orlinsky & Howard, 1987).

AN INTERPERSONAL RELATIONSHIP OF WARMTH AND TRUST
Regardless of the type of therapy provided, in a good therapeutic relationship, client and therapist have mutual respect and regard for each other. The client must believe that the therapist understands and is concerned with his or her problems. Although behavior therapy may sound like a rather impersonal procedure when it is described in a textbook, studies indicate that experienced behavior therapists show as much empathy and depth of interpersonal involvement as experienced psychoanalytically oriented therapists (Sloane et al., 1975). A therapist who understands our problems and believes we can solve them earns our trust, which increases our sense of competence and our confidence that we can succeed.

REASSURANCE AND SUPPORT Our problems often seem insurmountable and unique to us. Discussing them with an expert who accepts our difficulties as not unusual and indicates that they can be resolved is reassuring. Having someone help us with problems we have not been able to solve alone also provides a sense of support and a feeling of hope. In fact, the most successful therapists, regardless of their method of psychotherapy, are those who form a helpful, supportive relationship with their clients (Luborsky et al., 1985).

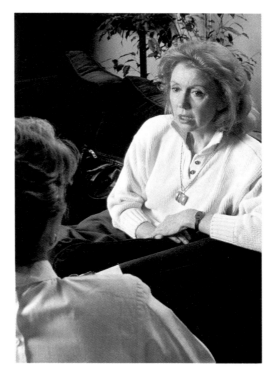

A relationship of mutual respect and trust is important to successful psychotherapy.

DESENSITIZATION   We have already talked about systematic desensitization, the specific techniques of behavior therapy aimed at helping individuals to lose their fear of certain objects or situations. But many types of psychotherapy can encourage a broader kind of desensitization. When we discuss events and emotions that have been troubling us in the accepting atmosphere of a therapy session, they gradually lose their threatening quality. Problems that we brood about alone can become magnified beyond proportion; sharing problems with someone else often makes them seem less serious. Several other hypotheses can also explain how desensitization occurs in psychotherapy. For example, putting events that are disturbing into words may help us reappraise the situation in a more realistic manner. From the viewpoint of learning theory, repeatedly discussing distressing experiences in the security of a therapeutic setting (where punishment is not forthcoming) may gradually extinguish the anxiety associated with them. Whatever the process, desensitization does appear to be a factor common to many kinds of psychotherapy.

REINFORCEMENT OF ADAPTIVE RESPONSES   Behavior therapists use reinforcement as a technique to increase positive attitudes and actions. But any therapist in whom a client places trust and confidence functions as a reinforcing agent; that is, the therapist tends to express approval of the behaviors or attitudes deemed conducive to better adjustment and to ignore or express disapproval of maladaptive attitudes or responses. Which responses are reinforced depends on the therapist's orientation and therapeutic goals. The use of reinforcement may be intentional or unintentional; in some instances, the therapist may be unaware that he or she is reinforcing or failing to reinforce a particular client behavior. For example, client-centered therapists believe in letting the client determine what is discussed during the therapy sessions and do not wish to influence the trend of the client's conversation. However, reinforcement can be subtle; a smile, a nod of the head, or a simple "um hmm" following certain client statements may increase the likelihood of their recurrence.

Since the goal of all psychotherapies is to bring about a change in the client's attitudes and behaviors, some type of learning must take place in therapy. The therapist needs to be aware of his or her role in influencing the client by means of reinforcement and should use this knowledge consciously to facilitate desired changes.

UNDERSTANDING OR INSIGHT   All of the psychotherapies we have been discussing provide the client with an *explanation* of his or her difficulties—how they arose, why they persist, and how they can be changed. For the individual in psychoanalysis, this explanation may take the form of a gradual understanding of repressed childhood fears and the ways in which these unconscious feelings have contributed to current problems. A behavior therapist might inform the client that current fears are the result of previous conditioning and can be conquered by learning responses that are incompatible with the current ones. A client seeing a cognitive behavior therapist might be told that his or her difficulties stem from the irrational belief that one must be perfect or must be loved by everyone.

How can such different explanations all produce positive results? Perhaps the precise nature of the insights and understanding provided by the therapist is relatively unimportant. It may be more important to provide the client with an explanation for the behavior or feelings that he or she finds so distressing and to present a set of activities (such as free association or relaxation training) that both therapist and client believe will alleviate the distress. When a person is experiencing disturbing symptoms and is unsure of their cause or how serious they might be, he or she will feel reassured contacting a professional who seems to know what the problem is and offers ways of relieving it. The knowledge that change is possible gives the individual hope, and hope is an important variable in facilitating change. (See the Critical Discussion, The Placebo Response.)

Our discussion of common factors among psychotherapies is not intended to deny the value of some specific treatment methods. Perhaps the most effective therapist is one who recognizes the importance of the common factors and utilizes them in a planned manner for all patients, but who also selects the specific procedures most appropriate for each individual case.

BIOLOGICAL THERAPIES

The biological approach to abnormal behavior assumes that mental disorders, like physical illnesses, are caused by biochemical or physiological dysfunctions of the brain. Several biological theories were mentioned in discussing the etiology of schizophrenia and the mood disorders in Chapter 15. Biological therapies include the use of drugs and electroconvulsive shock.

Psychotherapeutic Drugs

By far the most successful biological therapy is the use of drugs to modify mood and behavior. The discovery in the early 1950s of drugs that relieved some of the symptoms of schizophrenia represented a major breakthrough in the treatment of severely disturbed individuals. Intensely agitated patients no longer had to be physically restrained by straitjackets, and patients who had been spending most of their time hallucinating and exhibiting bizarre behavior became more responsive and functional. As a result, psychiatric wards became more manageable, and patients could be discharged more quickly. A few years later, the discovery of drugs that could relieve severe depression had a similar beneficial effect on hospital management and population. We saw in Figure 16-1 the reduction in the number of mental-hospital residents that occurred following the introduction of antipsychotic and antidepressant drugs. About the same time, drugs were being developed to relieve anxiety.

ANTIANXIETY DRUGS   Most drugs that reduce anxiety belong to the family called benzodiazepines. They are commonly known as **tranquilizers** and are marketed under such trade names as Valium (diazepam), Librium (chlordiazepoxide), and Xanax (alprazolam). Antianxiety drugs reduce tension and cause drowsiness. Like alcohol and the barbiturates, they depress the action of the central nervous system. Family physicians often prescribe tranquilizers to help people cope during difficult periods in their lives. The drugs are also used to treat anxiety disorders, withdrawal from alcohol, and physical disorders related to stress. For example, antianxiety drugs may be combined with systematic desensitization in the treatment of a phobia to help the individual relax when confronting the feared situation.

Although tranquilizers may be useful on a short-term basis, the overall benefits are debatable, and such drugs clearly are overprescribed and misused. Until quite recently (before some of the dangers became apparent), Valium and Librium were the two most widely prescribed drugs in this country (Julien, 1992). The dangers of tranquilizer overuse are several. Depending on a pill to relieve anxiety may prevent a person from exploring the *cause* of the anxiety and from learning more effective ways of coping with tension. More importantly, long-term use of tranquilizers can lead to physical dependency, or addiction (see Chapter 6). Although tranquilizers are not as addictive as barbiturates, tolerance does develop with repeated use and the individual experiences severe withdrawal symptoms if the drug is discontinued. In addition, tranquilizers impair concentration, including driving performance, and can cause death if combined with alcohol.

In recent years, researchers have discovered that certain drugs thought previously to be antidepressant drugs also reduce symptoms of anxiety. This is particularly true of the serotonin reuptake inhibitors (see below). These drugs may relieve anxiety as well as depression because they affect biochemical disturbances that are common to anxiety and depression.

ANTIPSYCHOTIC DRUGS   Most of the **antipsychotic drugs** that relieve the symptoms of schizophrenia belong to the family called **phenothiazines**. Examples are Thorazine (chlorpromazine) and Prolixin (fluphenazine). These drugs have been called "major tranquilizers," but the term is not really appropriate, because they do not act on the nervous system in the same way as barbiturates or antianxiety drugs. They may cause some drowsiness and lethargy, but they do not induce deep sleep even in massive doses (the person can be easily aroused). They also seldom create the pleasant, slightly euphoric feeling associated with low doses of antianxiety drugs. In fact, the psychological effects of the antipsychotic drugs when administered to normal individuals are usually unpleasant. Hence, these drugs are seldom abused.

In Chapter 15, we discussed the theory that schizophrenia is caused by excessive activity

THE PLACEBO RESPONSE

Placebos are commonly used in research on the effectiveness of drugs. A placebo is an inert substance (known to have no pharmacological effect) that is made to look like an active drug—in essence, a sugar pill. Placebos are used in drug research as controls (a) for the patients' expectations that the medicine will make them feel better, (b) for the researcher's belief that the medicine is effective, and (c) for the beneficial effects of extra attention from nurses and other personnel that stem from being a research subject. A **double-blind** procedure is usually employed: One group of patients is given the drug and a comparable group is given the placebo, but neither the patients nor the researchers (or whoever judges the results) knows until the end of the study which pills contain the active medication and which are the placebos. Since both the patients and the researchers are blind to the nature of the pills, the method is termed double-blind. If the rate of improvement is greater in those who received the drug, then the drug is considered to be therapeutically effective. If both groups of patients show similar improvement, then whatever positive response occurs with the drug is

considered to be a placebo effect and the drug is judged to be ineffective.

All responses that cannot be explained on the basis of actual drug effects are considered to be placebo responses—that is, due to unknown and nonpharmacological causes. Such unknown causes are generally assumed to be psychological in nature.

Placebo responses can be very powerful. For example, 40 percent of patients who were suffering from a painful heart disease (angina pectoris) reported marked relief from their symptoms after undergoing a diagnostic procedure that they believed was an operation to cure the problem (Beecher, 1961). In treating psychological disorders, placebos are often as effective as medication. For example, a large study of drug therapies and psychotherapies for depression found that patients responded nearly as well to a pill placebo as they did to antidepressant drugs or to psychotherapy (Elkin et al., 1984).

Until the beginning of modern scientific medicine, almost all medications were placebos. Patients were given every conceivable substance—crocodile dung, lozenges of dried vipers, spermatic fluid of frogs, spiders, worms, and human excrement—

prepared in every possible manner to treat their symptoms. Throughout medical history, patients have been purged, poisoned, leached, bled, heated, frozen, sweated, and shocked (Shapiro & Morris, 1978). Since physicians and healers traditionally have held positions of honor and respect, their "treatments" must have helped at least some of their patients. We assume their effectiveness was due to the placebo response. Scientists also attribute documented cases of faith healing and various forms of miraculous cures to placebo effects.

Some clinicians have suggested that the placebo response may be one of the reasons why psychotherapy works (Wilkins, 1984; Lieberman & Dunlap, 1979). According to this view, almost any method of psychotherapy should show positive results if the client believes it will be effective. If this is true, it becomes important for the therapist to convey to the client his or her conviction that the method of treatment will be successful.

The idea that placebo response play a central role in psychotherapy is disturbing to some clinicians. They feel that it links psychotherapy with quackery or charlatanism and implies that the process is one of self-

---

of the neurotransmitter dopamine. Antipsychotic drugs block dopamine receptors. Because the drugs' molecules are structurally similar to dopamine molecules, they bind to the postsynaptic receptors of dopamine neurons, thereby blocking the access of dopamine to its receptors. (The drug itself does not activate the receptors.) A single synapse has many receptor molecules. If all of them are blocked, transmission across the synapse will fail. If only some of them are blocked, transmission will be weakened. The clinical potency of an antipsychotic drug is directly related to its ability to compete for dopamine receptors.

Neurons that have receptors for dopamine are concentrated in the reticular system, the limbic system, and the hypothalamus. The reticular system selectively filters the flow of

messages from the sense organs to the cerebral cortex and controls the individual's state of arousal. The limbic system and the hypothalamus are important in the regulation of emotion. Alteration of neural activity in these areas may account for the calming effects of antipsychotic drugs, although we have no idea as yet of the processes involved.

Whatever their method of action, antipsychotic drugs are effective in alleviating the hallucinations and confusion of an acute schizophrenia episode and in restoring rational thought processes. These drugs do not cure schizophrenia; most patients must continue to receive a maintenance dosage in order to function outside of a hospital. Many of the characteristic symptoms of schizophrenia—emotional blunting, seclusiveness, deception. This is not the case. Physicians and psychotherapists have known for a long time that a patient's attitudes and beliefs are very important in determining the effectiveness of treatment. Any treatment will be more effective if the patient believes in it and is motivated to use it in the proper manner. Rather than deny the importance of the placebo effect, it would be better to continue investigating the variables that contribute to it.

In addition, researchers who wish to demonstrate the effectiveness of a specific therapeutic technique should control for the placebo response. Sophisticated studies do this by including a placebo control group, as well as an untreated control group. For example, an experiment designed to test the efficacy of systematic desensitization in reducing anxiety about public speaking included the following groups: systematic desensitization, insight therapy, attention-placebo, and untreated control. The subjects in the attention-placebo group met with a sympathetic therapist who led them to believe that a pill would reduce their overall sensitivity to stress. To convince them, the therapist had them listen to a "stress tape" (pre-

sumably one used in training astronauts to function under stress) for several sessions after ingesting the "tranquilizer." In reality, the pill was a placebo and the tape contained nonverbal sounds that had been found in other research to be boring rather than stressful. In this way, the researcher raised the subjects' expectations that their speech anxiety would be lessened by taking a pill. The results of this study revealed that the systematic desensitization group improved (they reduced their speech anxiety) much more than the no-treatment group and more than the attention-placebo and insight therapy groups, who reacted about the same to their forms of therapy. The latter two groups, however, did show significant improvement (Paul, 1967). By including the attention-placebo group, the experimenter was able to conclude that the success of the systematic desensitization procedure was not due solely to the placebo effect.

The mechanism that causes placebo responses is unknown. Numerous hypotheses have been proposed, but so far there is little empirical verification for any of them. One group of explanations focuses on social influence (see Chapter 18). Because patients

tend to view physicians and therapists as socially powerful individuals, they may be very suggestible to the influence of such authorities and may be easily persuaded that beneficial results will occur. In addition, the role of patient entails certain prescribed behaviors. A good patient is one who gets better; getting better justifies the therapists' initial concern and subsequent interest.

Other explanations focus on the individual's expectations. The person who administers the treatment may communicate, by intended or unintended means, expectations about the effects of the treatment. The patients also arrive with certain expectations, based on their previous experiences. Expectations that one will get better and a strong desire that it happen are the essential ingredients of hope. And hope can have a powerful influence on our emotions and bodily processes. Some researchers speculate that this influence may be mediated by the endorphin group of neurotransmitters. We noted in Chapter 2 how endorphins, the "brain's natural opiates," affect mood and the subjective experience of pain. Endorphins may turn out to play an important role in the placebo response.

difficulties in sustaining attention—remain. Nevertheless, antipsychotic drugs shorten the length of time patients must be hospitalized, and they prevent relapse. Studies of schizophrenics living in the community find that the relapse rate for those taking one of the phenothiazines is typically half the relapse rate of those receiving a placebo (Hogarty et al., 1979).

Unfortunately, antipsychotic drugs do not help all schizophrenic patients. In addition, the drugs have unpleasant side effects—dryness of the mouth, blurred vision, difficulty concentrating, and sometimes neurological symptoms—that prompt many patients to discontinue their medication. With long-term usage, more serious side effects may also occur (for example, low blood pressure and a

muscular disorder in which there are involuntary movements of the mouth and chin). Researchers continue to search for drugs that will relieve the symptoms of schizophrenia with fewer side effects.

ANTIDEPRESSANT DRUGS   Antidepressant drugs help to elevate the mood of depressed individuals. These drugs energize rather than tranquilize, apparently by increasing the availability of two neurotransmitters (norepinephrine and serotonin) that are deficient in some cases of depression (see Chapter 15). Antidepressant drugs act in different ways to increase neurotransmitter levels. The **monoamine oxidase** (MAO) **inhibitors** (examples are Nardil and Parnate) block the activity of an enzyme that can destroy both norepinephrine and serotonin, thereby increasing the concentration of these two neurotransmitters in the brain. The **tricyclic antidepressants** (examples are Tofranil and Elavil) prevent the **reuptake** of serotonin and norepinephrine, thereby prolonging the duration of the neurotransmitters' actions. (Recall that *reuptake* is the process by which neurotransmitters are drawn back into the nerve terminals that released them.) Both classes of drugs have proved effective in relieving certain types of depression, presumably those caused more by biological factors than environmental ones. However, like the antipsychotic drugs, the antidepressants can produce some undesirable side effects. The most common of these are dry mouth, blurred vision, constipation, and urinary retention. They can also cause a severe drop in blood pressure upon standing up and changes in heart rate and rhythm. The tricyclic antidepressants can be fatal if taken in an overdose, a severe concern when a depressed patient may be suicidal. The MAO inhibitors can interact with certain foods, including cheese, chocolate, and red wine, to create severe cardiac problems.

Antidepressants are not stimulants, as amphetamines are (see Chapter 6); they do not produce feelings of euphoria and increased energy. In fact, a patient may undergo several weeks of medication before a change in mood is observed. This is one reason why electroconvulsive therapy, which acts more quickly, is sometimes the preferred treatment for severely depressed, suicidal individuals. We will discuss electroconvulsive therapy in the next section.

The search for drugs that are more effective, have fewer side effects, and act more quickly than the tricyclic antidepressants and MAO inhibitors has intensified in the past few years. As a result, new drugs appear on the market almost daily. Among these newer drugs (called **serotonin reuptake inhibitors**) are several that selectively increase serotonin levels, by blocking its reuptake, without affecting norepinephrine. Examples are fluoxetine (Prozac), clomipramine (Anafranil) and setraline (Zoloft). In addition to relieving depression, these drugs have also proved helpful in treating both obsessive-compulsive disorders and panic disorders (see Lickey & Gordon, 1991). They tend to produce fewer side effects than the other antidepressants, although they do have some side effects, in-

cluding inhibited orgasm, nausea and diarrhea, dizziness, and nervousness.

Another drug, lithium, has proved very successful in treating bipolar disorder. Lithium reduces extreme mood swings and returns the individual to a more normal state of emotional equilibrium. Although the effectiveness of this drug has been known for more than 40 years, researchers have only recently discovered how its complex action on certain neurotransmitters achieves this normalizing effect (Worley, Heller, Snyder, & Baraban, 1988).

Drug therapy has reduced the severity of some types of mental disorders. Many individuals who would require hospitalization otherwise can function within the community with the help of these drugs. On the other hand, there are limitations to the application of drug therapy. All therapeutic drugs can produce undesirable side effects. Many people with medical problems, and women who are pregnant or nursing, often cannot take psychoactive drugs. In addition, many psychologists feel that these drugs alleviate symptoms without requiring the individual to face the personal problems that may be contributing to the disorder or that may have been caused by the disorder (such as marital problems caused by the behaviors of a manic person). When therapeutic drugs are prescribed, psychotherapeutic help is usually also required.

ELECTROCONVULSIVE THERAPY

In electroconvulsive therapy (ECT), also known as **electroshock therapy**, a mild electric current is applied to the brain to produce a seizure similar to an epileptic convulsion. ECT was a popular treatment from about 1940 to 1960, before antipsychotic and antidepressant drugs became readily available. Today, ECT is used primarily in cases of severe depression when patients fail to respond to drug therapy.

ECT has been the subject of much controversy and public apprehension for several reasons. At one time, it was used indiscriminately in mental hospitals to treat such disorders as alcoholism and schizophrenia, for which it produced no beneficial results. Before more refined procedures were developed, ECT was a frightening experience for the patient, who was often awake until the electric current triggered the seizure and produced momentary unconsciousness. The patient frequently suffered confusion and memory loss afterward. Occasionally, the intensity of the muscle spasms accompanying the brain seizure resulted in physical injuries.

Today, ECT involves little discomfort. The patient is given a short-acting anesthesia and then is injected with a muscle relaxant. A brief, very weak electric current is delivered to the brain, typically to the temple on the side of the nondominant cerebral hemisphere. The minimum current required to produce a brain seizure is administered, since the seizure itself—*not* the electricity—is therapeutic. The muscle relaxant prevents the convulsive spasm of body muscles and possible injury. The individual awakens within a few minutes and remembers nothing about the treatment. Four to six treatments are usually administered over a period of several weeks.

The most troublesome side effect of ECT is memory loss. Some patients report a gap in memory for events that occurred up to 6 months before ECT, as well as an impaired ability to retain new information for a month or two following treatment. However, if very low dosages of electricity are used (the amount is carefully calibrated for each patient to be just sufficient to produce a seizure), and the electricity is administered to the nondominant side of the brain only, memory problems are minimal (Sackeim & Malitz, 1985).

No one knows how the electrically induced seizures relieve depression. Brain seizures do cause the massive release of a number of neurotransmitters, including norepinephrine and serotonin; deficiencies of these two neurotransmitters may be an important factor in some cases of depression (see Chapter 15). Currently researchers are trying to determine the similarities and dissimilarities between ECT and antidepressant drugs in terms of the way each affects neurotransmitters. However it works, ECT is effective in bringing people out of severe, immobilizing depression and does so faster than drug therapy (Janicak et al., 1985).

THE EFFECTS OF CULTURE AND GENDER ON THERAPY

Each year, over 2 million people in the United States are hospitalized for a mental disorder (Kiesler & Sibulkin, 1987). African-Americans and Native Americans are considerably more likely than white Americans to be hospitalized in an inpatient mental health facility (Snowden & Cheung, 1990). Asian-Americans are much less likely than whites or any of the other groups to be hospitalized. These ethnic differences in hospitalization do not appear to be due to ethnic differences in socioeconomic

A patient being prepared for electroconvulsive therapy.

status, which can affect the availability of alternatives to hospitalization, such as seeking private care outside a hospital.

Do African-Americans suffer from severe mental disorders that require hospitalization more frequently than other groups? The answer from national epidemiological studies seems to be "no." The rates of the major types of psychopathology that most frequently result in hospitalization, namely severe mood disorders and schizophrenia, are very similar among African-Americans, whites and Hispanics (Robins et al., 1984). (Rates of these disorders from large scale-studies of Native Americans and Asian-Americans are not available.) Recall from the previous chapter, however, that African-Americans may be more frequently *mis*diagnosed as suffering from schizophrenia than whites (Mukherjee et al., 1983). Since this diagnosis often leads to hospitalization, it may explain the overrepresentation of African-Americans among hospitalized mental paitents.

In the United States, men and women are hospitalized at about the same rate for mental disorders (National Institute of Mental Health, 1987), but the types of disorders for which they are hospitalized differ considerably. Men are more often hospitalized for substance abuse than women, but women are more often hospitalized for a mood disorder than men. There do not tend to be gender differences in the rate of hospitalization for schizophrenia (NIMH, 1987).

Most people who seek treatment for a psychological disorder are not hospitalized. They are more likely to receive treatment from private-practice psychologists, psychiatrists, or general practice physicians. In fact, one large study found that people in the United States are twice as likely to seek help for emotional or mental problems from their general practice physicians than from a mental health professional (Leaf & Bruce, 1987). This study also found that women are much more likely than men to talk to their general practice physicians about mental and emotional problems, and somewhat more likely to seek a mental health professional for these problems (see also Kessler, Brown, & Broman, 1981; Russo & Sobel, 1981).

Hispanics and Asian-Americans appear more likely to care for a member of the family who is suffering from a major mental disorder in the home than non-Hispanic whites in the United States (Gaw, 1993; Snowden, 1988). These trends may be due both to an emphasis on the family as the center of problem solving and stigma associated with seeking mental health care. In contrast, African-Americans tend to seek mental health treatment more quickly after the onset of symptoms than other groups (Broman, 1987).

Several cross-cultural theorists have made recommendations about the type of psychotherapy that might prove most acceptable to specific ethnic groups (see Sue & Zane, 1987). For example, more structured and action-oriented therapies such as behavior or cognitive-behavior therapies have been recommended for Hispanics, African-Americans and Asian-Americans, on the premise that these groups may be less inclined to the intrapsychic explorations of psychodynamic therapies. Asian-Americans are said to prefer therapists who provide structure, guidance, and direction, rather than nondirective therapies such as psychoanalysis or client-centered therapy (Atkinson, Maruyama, & Matsui, 1978). Most of these assertions have not been put to rigorous empirical tests, however (Sue & Zane, 1987). Similarly, although some clinicians have suggested that women will find therapies that focus on interpersonal relationships and expression of feelings more appealing and helpful than other types of therapies, there is little evidence for or against this assertion (McGrath et al., 1990).

The specific form of therapy may not matter so much as the cultural and gender sensitivity the therapist shows the client, whatever therapy is being used. People from ethnic minority groups in the United States are much more likely than whites to drop out of psychosocial therapy (Sue & Zane, 1987). One study of 13,450 therapy clients found that the dropout rate for Hispanics was 42 percent, Native Americans 55 percent, and African-Americans 52 percent, compared to only 30 percent in whites (Sue, Allen, & Conaway, 1978). In most of these cases, the therapist was white. Ethnic minority clients may often find the suggestions of therapists strange and unhelpful.

The fact that a therapist is from the same ethnic or racial group as the client, however, does not ensure that they share the same value system. For example, a fourth-generation Japanese-American who has fully adopted American competitive and individualistic values may clash badly with a recent immigrant from Japan who ascribes to the self-sacrificing, community-oriented values of Japanese culture. Similarly, a woman therapist who has strong feminist values may clash with a woman client who holds traditional sex-role expectations. These value differences among people of the same ethnic/racial group or the same gender may explain why studies show that matching the ethnicity or race or gender of the therapist and client does not necessarily lead to a better outcome for the client (Atkinson, 1986, 1983; Jones, 1978; Lerner, 1972).

Some clients care deeply about having a therapist of the same ethnic group or gender, but other clients may only trust a therapist who corresponds to their stereotype of a "doctor," and other clients have no preferences regarding the ethnicity or gender of their therapist. For clients who wish to be matched with a therapist of the same ethnic or gender group, this matching may be necessary for the client to trust the therapist and have faith in the therapy. And, as we noted earlier, the relationship between a client and therapist and a client's beliefs about the likely effectiveness of a therapy contribute strongly to the client's full engagement in the therapy and the effectiveness of the therapy.

ENHANCING MENTAL HEALTH

The prevention and treatment of mental disorders is a problem of tremendous concern for both the community and the nation. Early in this chapter, we noted that the Community Mental Health Centers Act, passed by Congress in 1963, provided funds for the establishment of community mental health centers so that people could be treated close to family and friends rather than in large state psychiatric hospitals. These community centers provide short-term hospitalization, outpatient treatment, and a 24-hour emergency service. They are also concerned with preventing emotional problems and so consult with schools, juvenile courts, and other community agencies.

Federal funding for community mental health centers has been cut drastically in recent years, greatly diminishing services for the poor. Increased efforts by states, commu-

nities, and volunteer organizations are essential to help fill the void.

COMMUNITY RESOURCES AND PARAPROFESSIONALS

A variety of community resources has been developed in response to the psychological needs of different groups. One such resource is the *halfway house,* where patients who have been hospitalized can live while making the transition back to an independent life in the community. Residential centers are also available to people recovering from alcohol and drug problems, to delinquent or runaway youths, and to battered wives. *Rap centers,* where troubled teenagers can discuss their problems with each other and with sympathetic counselors, play an important role in many communities; *youth centers* provide job counseling, remedial education, and help with family and personal problems.

CRISIS INTERVENTION *Crisis intervention* provides immediate help for individuals and families undergoing intense stress. During periods of acute emotional turmoil, people often feel overwhelmed and incapable of dealing with the situation. They may not be able to wait for a therapy appointment, or they may not know where to turn. One form of crisis intervention is provided by 24-hour, walk-in services, often in a community mental health center, where the individual receives immediate attention. There, a therapist helps to clarify the problem, provides reassurance, suggests a plan of action, and mobilizes the support of

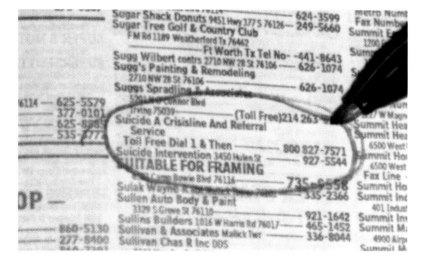

A telephone hotline for suicide prevention.

A telephone hotline for suicide prevention.

other agencies or family members. This kind of therapy is usually short-term (five or six sessions) and provides the support the person requires to handle the crisis at hand. Such short-term intervention often prevents the need for hospitalization.

Another form of crisis intervention is the *telephone hot line*. Telephone crisis centers are usually staffed by volunteers under the direction of mental health professionals. Some focus specifically on suicide prevention; others are more general and help distressed callers find the particular kind of assistance they need. The volunteers usually receive training that emphasizes listening with care, evaluating the potential for suicide, conveying empathy and understanding, providing information about community resources, giving hope and reassurance, and recording the caller's name and phone number before he or she hangs up so that a professional can follow up on the problem. Most major cities in the United States have developed some form of telephone hot line to help people who are undergoing periods of severe stress, as well as specialized hot lines to deal with child

abuse, rape victims, battered wives, and runaways. The phone numbers are widely publicized in the hope of reaching those who need help.

PARAPROFESSIONALS AS THERAPISTS   Most of the community programs we have discussed could not function without the help of paraprofessionals. Because the need for psychological services outstrips the supply of available therapists, concerned citizens can play a valuable role. People of all ages and backgrounds have been trained to work in the area of community mental health. College students have served as companions for hospitalized patients. Older individuals who have successfully raised families have been trained as mental health counselors to work with adolescents in community clinics, to counsel parents of youngsters who have behavior problems, and to work with schizophrenic children. Former mental patients, recovered drug addicts, and ex-convicts have been trained to help those faced with problems similar to the ones they have experienced.

Many residential mental health programs are run by nonprofessionals in consultation with trained therapists. An outstanding example is Achievement Place, which is a home-style facility in Kansas where couples act as surrogate parents for a group of youngsters referred by the courts because of their delinquent behavior. Behavior therapy methods are used to extinguish aggressive behavior and to reward social skills. Follow-up data show that youths who graduate from Achievement Place have fewer contacts with courts and police and achieve slightly higher grades than do individuals who are placed on probation or in a traditional institution for delinquents (Fixsen, Phillips, Phillips, & Wolf, 1976). At present, there are 80 Achievement Places throughout the United States modeled after the original Kansas facility.

PROMOTING YOUR OWN EMOTIONAL WELL-BEING

Aside from seeking professional help, there are many ways that each of us can positively influence our own psychological well-being. By monitoring our feelings and behavior we can determine the kinds of actions and situations that cause us pain or get us into difficulty, and, conversely, the kinds that benefit us the most. By trying to analyze our motives and abilities, we can enhance our capacity to make active choices in our lives, instead of passively accepting what comes.

The problems that people face vary greatly, and there are no universal guidelines for staying psychologically healthy. However, a few general suggestions have emerged from the experiences of therapists.

ACCEPT YOUR FEELINGS Anger, sorrow, fear, and a feeling of having fallen short of ideals or goals are all unpleasant emotions, and we may try to escape anxiety by denying these feelings. Sometimes we try to avoid anxiety by facing situations unemotionally, which leads to a false kind of detachment or cool that may be destructive. We may try to suppress all emotions, thereby losing the ability to accept as normal the joys and sorrows that are a part of our involvement with other people.

Unpleasant emotions are a normal reaction to many situations. There is no reason to be ashamed of feeling homesick, of being afraid when learning to ski, or of becoming angry at someone who has disappointed us. These emotions are natural, and it is better to recognize them than to deny them. When emotions cannot be expressed directly (for example, it may not be wise to tell off your boss), it helps to find another outlet for releasing tension.

Taking a long walk, pounding a tennis ball, or discussing the situation with a friend can help to dissipate anger. As long as you accept your right to feel emotion, you can express it in indirect or substitute ways when direct channels of expression are blocked.

KNOW YOUR VULNERABILITIES Discovering the kinds of situations that upset you or cause you to overreact may help to guard against stress. Perhaps certain people annoy you. You could avoid them, or you could try to understand just what it is about them that disturbs you. Maybe they seem so poised and confident that they make you feel insecure. Trying to pinpoint the cause of your discomfort may help you to see the situation in a new light. Perhaps you become very anxious when you have to speak in class or present a paper. Again, you could try to avoid such situations, or you could gain confidence by taking a course in public speaking. (Many colleges offer courses specifically aimed at learning to control speech anxiety.) You could also reinterpret the situation. Instead of thinking "Everyone is waiting to criticize me as soon as I open my mouth," you could tell yourself "The class will be interested in what I have to say, and I'm not going to let it worry me if I make a few mistakes."

Many people feel especially anxious when they are under pressure. Careful planning and spacing of work can help you avoid

Troubled adolescents work with caring adults in group homes.

feeling overwhelmed at the last minute. The strategy of purposely allowing more time than you think you need to get to classes or to appointments can eliminate one source of stress.

DEVELOP YOUR TALENTS AND INTERESTS   People who are bored and unhappy seldom have many interests. Today's college and community programs offer almost unlimited opportunities for people of all ages to explore their talents in many areas, including sports, academic interests, music, art, drama, and crafts. Often, the more you know about a subject, the more interesting it (and life) becomes. In addition, the feeling of competency gained from developing skills can do a great deal to bolster self-esteem.

BECOME INVOLVED WITH OTHER PEOPLE   Feelings of isolation and loneliness form the core of most emotional disorders. We are social beings, and we need the support, comfort, and reassurance provided by other people. Focusing all of your attention on your own problems can lead to an unhealthy preoccupation with yourself. Sharing your concerns with others often helps you to view your troubles in a clearer perspective. Also, being concerned for the welfare of other people can reinforce your feelings of self-worth.

KNOW WHEN TO SEEK HELP   Although these suggestions can help to promote emotional well-being, there are limits to self-understanding and self-help. Some problems are difficult to solve alone. Our tendency toward self-deception makes it hard to view problems objectively, and we may not know all of the possible solutions. When you feel that you are making little headway in gaining control over a problem, it is time to seek professional help from a counseling or clinical psychologist, a psychiatrist, or some other trained therapist. The willingness to seek help is a sign of emotional maturity, not a sign of weakness; do not wait until you feel overwhelmed. Obtaining psychological help when it is needed should be as accepted a practice as going to a physician for medical problems.

BIOLOGICAL-PSYCHOLOGICAL PERSPECTIVES

Although in this chapter we divided therapies into psychological therapies and biological therapies, the movement these days in the treatment of people with mental disorders is toward combined biological and psychological treatments. In depression and the anxiety disorders, often the person's biochemistry and his or her functioning in social and occupational settings are affected by the disorder, and it can be helpful to treat people at both the biological and psychosocial levels. Even in disorders like schizophrenia, where the primary cause of the disorder is biological, the person often experiences severe losses in his or her social skills and network and in his or her ability to function on a job. Supplementing antipsychotic drugs with psychotherapy designed to help the person cope with the consequences of schizophrenia can be very useful.

The fact that a wide range of both psychotherapies and drugs are effective in the treatment of some disorders (especially depression) suggests that intervening at one level of a person's bio-psycho-social system can affect all levels of the system. For example, intervening at the psychological level may cause changes in the person's biochemistry and in his or her social behaviors. When this occurs, it is because our biochemistry, our personalities and thought processes and our social behaviors are so intertwined that each can affect the other in both positive and negative ways.

📖 CHAPTER SUMMARY

1. Treatment of the mentally ill has progressed from the ancient notion that abnormal behavior resulted from the possession of evil spirits that needed to be punished, to custodial care in ill-kept and isolated asylums, to modern mental hospitals and community mental health centers. The policy of *deinstitutionalization* (despite its good intentions) has created the problem of homeless mentally ill, causing concern about civil rights and adequate care.

2. *Psychotherapy* is the treatment of mental disorders by psychological means. One type of psychotherapy is *psychoanalysis,* which was developed by Freud. He believed that unconscious conflicts between the aggressive and sexual impulses of the id and the constraints imposed by the ego and superego were the cause of most mental disorders. Through the methods of *free association* and *dream analysis,* repressed thoughts and feelings are brought to the patient's awareness. By *interpreting* these dreams and associations, the analyst helps the individual gain *insight* into his or her problems. *Transference,* the tendency to express feelings toward the analyst that the client has for important people in his or her life, provides another source of interpretation. Through the processes of *working through,* the individual becomes able to cope with problems more realistically.

3. *Psychoanalytic therapies,* based on Freudian concepts, are briefer than psychoanalysis and place more emphasis on the problem-solving functions of the ego (as opposed to the id's sexual and aggressive impulses) and the individual's current interpersonal problems (as opposed to a complete reconstruction of childhood experiences).

4. *Behavior therapies* apply methods based on learning principles to *modify* the individual's behavior. These methods include *systematic desensitization* (the individual learns to relax in situations that previously produced anxiety), *reinforcement* of adaptive behaviors, *modeling* and *rehearsal* of appropriate behavior, and techniques for *self-regulation* of behavior.

5. *Cognitive behavior therapies* use behavior modification techniques but also incorporate procedures for changing maladaptive beliefs. The therapist helps the individual to replace irrational interpretations of events with more realistic ones.

6. *Humanistic therapies* help individuals to become aware of their real selves and to solve their problems with a minimum of therapist intervention. Carl Rogers, who developed *client-centered psychotherapy,* believed that the therapist's characteristics necessary for the client's growth and self-exploration are *empathy, warmth,* and *genuineness.*

7. Rather than adhering strictly to any single method, many therapists take an *eclectic* approach, selecting from the different techniques the ones most appropriate for a given client. Some therapists specialize in treating specific problems, such as alcoholism, sexual dysfunction, or depression.

8. *Group therapy* provides an opportunity for the individual to explore his or her attitudes and behavior in interaction with others who have similar problems. *Marital therapy* and *family therapy* are specialized forms of group therapy that help couples, or parents and children, to learn more effective ways of relating to one another and of handling their problems.

9. The effectiveness of psychotherapy is hard to evaluate because of the difficulty of defining a *successful outcome* and of controlling for *spontaneous remission.* Research indicates that psychotherapy does help but that different approaches do not differ greatly in effectiveness. Factors common to the various psychotherapies—a *warm and trustful interpersonal relationship, reassurance and support, desensitization, insight,* and *reinforcement of adaptive responses*—may be more important in producing positive change than are specific therapeutic methods.

10. *Biological therapies* include *electroconvulsive therapy* (ECT) and the use of *psychotherapeutic drugs.* Of the two, drug therapy is by far the most widely used. *Antianxiety drugs* are used to reduce severe anxiety and to help individuals cope with life crises. *Antipsychotic drugs* have proved effective in the treatment of schizophrenia, *antidepressants* help to elevate the mood of depressed patients, and *lithium* has been successful in treating bipolar disorders.

11. African-Americans and Native Americans are more likely than other ethnic groups in

the United States to be hospitalized for a psychological disorder or to seek outpatient mental health services for a psychological problem. Hispanics and whites are similar in their hospitalization rates, but Asian-Americans are much less likely than other ethnic groups to be hospitalized for psychological problems. These ethnic differences may be caused by differences in attitudes toward hospitalization and in the availability of nonprofessional sources of care (for example, caring for the person in the family). In addition, African-Americans may be overdiagnosed with schizophrenia, which leads to their more frequent hospitalization, compared to other groups.

Men and women are equally likely to be hospitalized or to seek a mental health professional for psychological problems, but men more frequently seek care for substance abuse than women, and women more frequently seek care for a mood disorder than men. Women are also more likely than men to talk with their general practice physician about mental health problems.

Some clients may wish to work with therapists of the same culture or gender, but it is unclear whether matching therapist and client is necessary for therapy to be effective. It is important for therapists to be sensitive to the influences of culture and gender on a client's attitudes toward therapy and on the acceptability of different types of solutions to their problems.

12. The prevention and treatment of mental disorders is of great concern in our society. Community resources that offer help include *halfway houses, residential centers* for people who have special problems, and various forms of *crisis intervention*. We can promote our own emotional health by accepting our feelings as natural, discovering our vulnerabilities, developing talents and interests, becoming involved with others, and recognizing when to seek professional help.

FURTHER READING

Interesting material on the historical treatment of the mentally ill can be found in Veith, *Hysteria: The History of a Disease* (1970); and Bell, *Treating the Mentally Ill: From Colonial Times to the Present* (1980).

A review of the various methods of psychotherapy is provided by Woody and Robertson, *Becoming a Clinical Psychologist* (1988); and Corsini, *Current Psychotherapies* (1984). *Psychotherapy: An Eclectic Approach* (1980) by Garfield describes the process of psychotherapy, the features common to most psychotherapies, and psychotherapy research. Seligman reviews the effectiveness of therapies for a wide range of psychological disorders in *What You Can Change and What You Can't* (1993).

For an introduction to psychoanalytic methods, see Luborsky, *Principles of Psychoanalytic Psychotherapy* (1984) and Auld and Hyman, *Resolution of Inner Conflict: An Introduction to Psychoanalytic Therapy* (1991). For client-centered therapy, see *On Becoming a Person: A Therapist's View of Psychotherapy* (1970) and *Carl Rogers on Personal Power* (1977), both by Rogers. The principles of behavior therapy are presented in Bellack, Hersen, and Kazdin (eds.), *International Handbook of Behavior Modification and Therapy,* (2nd ed., 1990); and Suinn, *Anxiety Management Training: A Behavior Therapy* (1990). The application of cognitive-behavior therapy to a variety of mental disorders is described in *Cognitive Psychotherapy: Theory and Practice* (1988), edited by Perris, Blackburn, and Perris. *Panic: Facing Fears, Phobias, and Anxiety* (1985) by Agras describes behavior therapy methods for overcoming fears.

An overview of group therapy is presented in Yalom, *The Theory and Practice of Group Psychotherapy* (3rd ed., 1985). For a cognitive-behavioral approach to marital and couple therapy, see Beck, *Love Is Never Enough* (1988).

Medicine and Mental Illness (1991), a paperback by Lickey and Gordon, presents a very readable summary of biological research on the major mental disorders. It describes symptoms and DSM-III-R diagnostic criteria, evidence of drug effectiveness, and how psychotherapeutic drugs affect the brain.

For ways to modify your own behavior, see Watson and Tharp, *Self-Directed Behavior: Self-Modification for Personal Adjustment* (5th ed., 1989). *Feeling Good* (1981), a paperback by Burns, provides a step-by-step program for using cognitive therapy techniques to understand and to change feelings of depression, anxiety, and anger. *Necessary Losses* (1986) by Viorst, written from a psychoanalytic viewpoint, is a sensitive and wise analysis of how we grow and change through the losses that are an inevitable part of life.

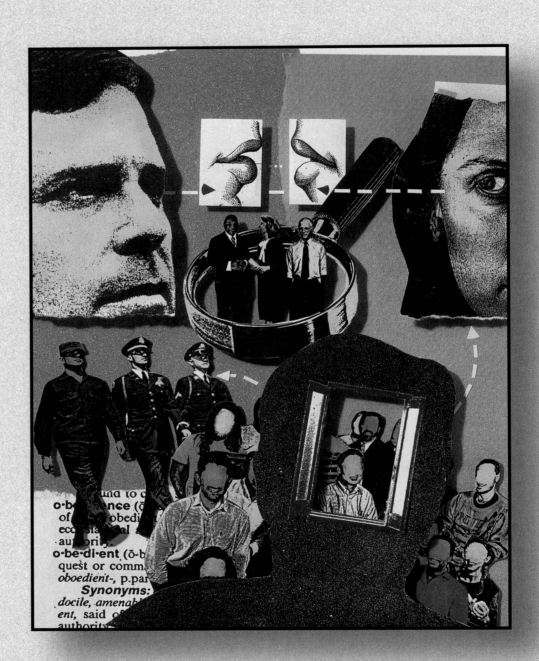

SOCIAL BEHAVIOR

8
PART

17
CHAPTER

SOCIAL COGNITION AND AFFECT

Social psychology is the study of how people think and feel about their social world and how they interact and influence one another. How do we form our impressions of people and come to interpret their actions? How are our social beliefs and attitudes—including our stereotypes and prejudices—formed and changed? What determines whom we like, love, or choose as a romantic partner? How do we influence one another?

In seeking answers to such questions, social psychologists begin with the basic observation that human behavior is a function of both the person and the situation. Each individual brings a unique set of personal attributes to a situation, leading different persons to act in different ways in the same situation. But each situation also brings a unique set of forces to bear on an individual, leading him or her to act in different ways in different situations. Research in social psychology has repeatedly shown situations be to more powerful determinants of behavior than our intuitions lead us to believe.

Individuals, however, do not react simply to the objective features of situations but to their subjective interpretations of them. The person who interprets an offensive act as the product of hostility reacts differently from the person who interprets that same act as the product of ignorance. Accordingly, this chapter begins our two-chapter discussion of social behavior by examining the ways in which we think and feel about our social environments. Chapter 18 deals with social interaction and influence.

INTUITIVE THEORIES OF SOCIAL BEHAVIOR

We are all psychologists. In attempting to understand people, we are like informal scientists who construct our own intuitive theories of human behavior. In doing so, we face the same basic tasks as the formal scientist (Nisbett & Ross, 1980). First, we collect data ("My friend Chris asserts that women should have the right to obtain abortions"; "Lee Yamuri achieved the highest score on the math test"). Second, we attempt to detect covariation or correlation, to discern what goes with what ("Do most people who support the right to abortion also oppose the death penalty?" "On the average, do Asians seem to do better in math and science than non-Asians?"). And third, we try to infer cause and effect, to evaluate what causes what ("Does Chris support the right to abortion out of genuine conviction or because of peer pressure to express liberal attitudes?" "Do Asian students excel in math and science because they are inherently smarter or because their families stress the value of education?").

We go through the same processes in trying to understand ourselves: We observe our own thoughts, feelings, or actions ("My heart seems to be pounding"), attempt to detect covariation ("My heart always seems to pound when I'm with Robin"), and try to infer cause and effect ("Am I in love with Robin or is it just sexual passion?").

Our intuitive attempts to apply scientific reasoning to everyday life work surprisingly well. Social interaction would be chaos if our informal theories of human behavior did not possess substantial validity. But we also make a number of systematic errors in arriving at social judgments, and, ironically, our intuitive theories themselves often interfere with making accurate judgments. As we shall see, our theories can actually shape our perceptions of the data, distort our estimates of covariation, and bias our evaluations of cause and effect.

STORING AND RETRIEVING DATA: SCHEMAS

The first difficulty we face as informal scientists is collecting data in a systematic and unbiased way. When a survey researcher wants to estimate how many Americans support a woman's right to abortion, he or she takes great care to ensure that a random or representative sample of people are contacted so that the numbers of Catholics, Protestants, men, women, and so forth are interviewed in proportion to their percentage of the total population. But when we, as informal survey researchers, try to make this estimate intuitively, our major source of data is likely to be the people we know personally. Obviously this is not a representative sample of the population.

Another major source of data for us is the mass media, which also provide a nonrandom and nonrepresentative sample of data. For example, the media necessarily give more attention to a small number of antiabortion protesters publicly demonstrating at a medical clinic than they do to a larger number of people who silently support the clinic's abortion service. The media are not being biased here in the usual sense; they are simply reporting the news. But the data they give us are still not a reliable sample from which to estimate public opinion.

A survey researcher also keeps accurate records of the data. But in everyday life, we constantly accumulate information in our heads and then attempt to recall it from memory when we are later called upon to make some judgment. Thus, not only are the data we collect a biased sample in the first place, but the data we actually bring to bear on our social judgments are further biased by problems of selective recall.

VIVIDNESS One of the factors that influences the information we notice and remember is its *vividness*. Research has shown that when both vivid and nonvivid information compete for our attention, our estimates and judgments are more influenced by the vivid information—even when the nonvivid information is more reliable and potentially more informative (Taylor & Thompson, 1982; Nisbett & Ross, 1980).

In one study, introductory psychology students who planned to major in psychology were given information about upper-level psychology courses and then asked to indicate which courses they planned to take. The subjects either heard two or three students make some informal remarks about each course in a face-to-face session or they saw a statistical summary of course evaluations made by past students in the courses. The subjects were more influenced in their choices by the face-to-face remarks than by the statistical summary—even when the summary was accompanied by written quotations of those same remarks. The vivid face-to-face information was more influential than the nonvivid written information even though it was based on less complete and representative data (Borgida & Nisbett, 1977).

The vividness effect is a particular problem with information from the mass media. Even if reporters scrupulously gave equal coverage to both the vivid and nonvivid sides of an issue, our own information-processing tendencies would supply the bias. Thus, even if a television newscast reports the results of a survey showing that a national majority supports abortion rights, we are still more likely to store and later recall the vivid pictures of the antiabortion protest when we intuitively try to estimate public opinion.

SCHEMAS Even if we could collect data in a systematic and unbiased way, our perceptions of the data can still be biased by our existing expectations and preconceptions—our theories—of what the data *should* look like. Whenever we perceive any object or event, we compare the incoming information with our memories of previous encounters with similar

Vivid events influence our judgments more than nonvivid events.

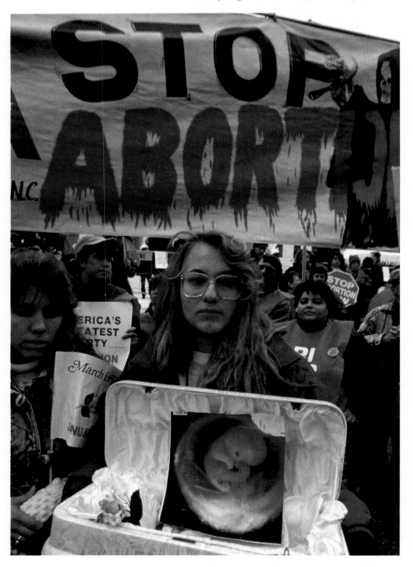

objects and events. In earlier chapters, we saw that our memories of objects and events are not usually photographlike reproductions of the original stimuli, but simplified reconstructions of our original perceptions. As noted in Chapter 8, such representations or memory structures are called *schemas* (singular, **schema**), organized beliefs and knowledge we hold about people, objects, events, and situations. The process of searching for the schema in memory that is most consistent with the incoming data is called **schematic processing**. Schemas and schematic processing permit us to organize and process an enormous amount of information with great efficiency. Instead of having to perceive and remember all the details of each new object or event, we can simply note that it is like one of our preexisting schemas and encode or remember only its most prominent features. Schematic processing typically occurs rapidly and automatically; usually we are not even aware that any processing of information is taking place at all (Fiske, 1993; Fiske & Taylor, 1991).

For example, we have schemas for different kinds of people. When someone tells you that you are about to meet an extravert, you retrieve your extravert schema in anticipation of the coming encounter. The extravert schema consists of a set of interrelated traits such as sociability, warmth, and possibly loudness and impulsiveness. As we shall discuss later, general person-schemas such as these are sometimes called **stereotypes**. We also have schemas of particular persons, such as the president of the United States or our parents. We even have a schema about ourselves—a set of organized self-concepts stored in memory (Markus, 1977). When you see a job advertisement for a peer counselor, you can evaluate the match between your counselor schema and your **self-schema** to decide whether you should apply.

Research confirms that schemas help us to process information. For example, if people are explicitly instructed to remember as much information as they can about a person, they actually remember less than if they are simply told to try to form an impression of him or her (Hamilton, 1979). The instruction to form an impression induces the subjects to search for various person-relevant schemas that help them organize and recall material better. The self-schema also permits

us to organize and process information efficiently. For example, people can recall a list of words better if they are told to decide whether each word describes themselves as they go through the list (Ganellen & Carver, 1985; Rogers, Kuiper, & Kirker, 1977). This has become known as the *self-reference effect* and occurs both because relating each word to the self leads the person to think more deeply and elaborately about it as he or she ponders whether or not it is self-relevant and because the self-schema serves to link in memory what would otherwise be unrelated information (Klein, Loftus, & Burton, 1989; Klein & Loftus, 1989).

SCHEMAS AND PERCEPTION   Without schemas and schematic processing, we would simply be overwhelmed by the information that inundates us. We would be very poor information processors. But the price we pay for such efficiency is a bias in both our perception and our memories of the data. Consider, for example, the impression you form of Jim from the following observations of his behavior.

> Jim left the house to get some stationery. He walked out into the sun-filled street with two of his friends, basking in the sun as he walked. Jim entered the stationery store, which was full of people. Jim talked with an acquaintance while he waited to catch the clerk's eye. On his way out, he stopped to chat with a school friend who was just coming into the store. Leaving the store, he walked toward the school. On his way he met the girl to whom he had been introduced the night before. They talked for a short while, and then Jim left for school. After school Jim left the classroom alone. Leaving the school, he started on his long walk home. The street was brilliantly filled with sunshine. Jim walked down the street on the shady side. Coming down the street toward him, he saw the pretty girl whom he had met on the previous evening. Jim crossed the street and entered a candy store. The store was crowded with students, and he noticed a few familiar faces. Jim waited quietly until he caught the counterman's eye and then gave his order. Taking his drink, he sat down at a side table. When he had finished his drink he went home. (Luchins, 1957, pp. 34–35)

What impression do you have of Jim? Do you think of him as friendly and outgoing or shy and introverted? If you think of him as friendly, you agree with 78 percent of people who read this description. But examine the description closely; it is actually composed of two very different portraits. Up to the sentence that begins "After school, Jim left . . . ," Jim is portrayed in several situations as fairly friendly. After that point, however, a nearly identical set of situations shows him to be much more of a loner. Whereas 95 percent of the people who are shown only the first half of the description rate Jim as friendly, only 3 percent of the people who are shown only the second half do so. Thus, in the combined description that you read, Jim's friendliness dominates the overall impression. But when individuals read the same description with the unfriendly half of the paragraph appearing first, only 18 percent rate Jim as friendly; his nonfriendliness leaves the major impression (see Table 17-1). in general, the first information we receive has the greater impact on our overall impressions. This is known as the **primacy effect.**

The primacy effect has been found repeatedly in several different kinds of impression formation studies, including studies using real rather than hypothetical persons (Jones, 1990). For example, subjects who watched a male student attempt to solve a series of difficult multiple-choice problems were asked to assess his general ability (Jones et al., 1968). Although the student always solved exactly 15 of the 30 problems correctly, he was judged more capable if the successes came mostly at the beginning of the series than if they came near the end. Moreover, when asked to recall how many problems the student had solved, subjects who had seen the 15 successes bunched at the beginning estimated an average of 21, but subjects who had seen the

successes at the end estimated an average of 13.

Although several factors contribute to the primacy effect, it appears to be primarily a consequence of schematic processing. When we are first attempting to form our impressions of a person, we actively search in memory for the person schema or schemas that best match the incoming data. At some point we make a preliminary decision: This person is friendly (or some such judgment). We then assimilate any further information to that judgment and dismiss any discrepant information as not representative of the real person we have come to know. For example, when explicitly asked to reconcile the apparent contradictions in Jim's behavior, subjects sometimes say that Jim is really friendly but was probably tired by the end of the day (Luchins, 1957). Our theory of Jim, which has already been established, shapes our perception of all subsequent data about him. More generally, our subsequent perceptions become schema-driven and therefore relatively impervious to new data. There is truth to the conventional warning that first impressions are important.

SCHEMAS AND MEMORY   The way in which schematic processing affects our memories was demonstrated in a study in which subjects viewed a videotape of a woman celebrating her birthday by having dinner with her husband. Some subjects were told that she was a librarian; others were told that she was a waitress. Some of her behaviors were designed to be consistent with the common stereotype of a librarian; for example, she wore glasses, liked classical music, had spent the day reading, and had traveled in Europe. An equal number of behaviors were consistent with a waitress stereotype; for example, she drank beer, liked popular music, and owned a bowling ball.

After viewing the videotape, subjects were given a questionnaire that tested their memories. For example, subjects were asked whether the woman had drunk beer or wine with her dinner. Subjects correctly remembered schema-consistent behaviors 88 percent of the time but schema-inconsistent behaviors only 78 percent of the time. Thus, subjects who had been told that the woman was a librarian were more likely to remember that she had traveled in Europe than to

CONDITIONS	PERCENTAGE RATING JIM AS FRIENDLY
Friendly description only	95
Friendly first—unfriendly last	78
Unfriendly first—friendly last	18
Unfriendly description only	3

TABLE 17-1

Schematic Processing and the Primacy Effect
Once a schema of Jim has been established, later information is assimilated to it. (After Luchins, 1957)

remember that she owned a bowling ball (Cohen, 1981).

As with the primacy effect, there is more than one possible explanation for memory effects like those just described (Stangor & McMillan, 1992). For example, if subjects are unsure about the relevant fact, they may simply use their knowledge that she was a librarian or a waitress to make an educated—that is, a stereotyped—guess. Another explanation is that our schemas are like file folders in a file cabinet. They help us retrieve information by providing a path to the relevant items. Our "waitress" schema (file folder) is more likely to contain the "bowling ball" item than the "classical music" item.

Although this suggests that we are more likely to remember information that is consistent rather than inconsistent with our schemas, this is not always the case (Stangor & McMillan, 1992) For example, if someone does something startlingly at odds with our expectations (the librarian burns a book), we are likely to remember that even better than something that is consistent (she spent the day reading) or only mildly inconsistent (she drank a beer).

PERSISTENCE OF SCHEMAS Because they affect our perceptions and memories in schema-consis-

tent ways, schemas tend to persist in the face of disconfirming data. If we remember that the librarian spent the day reading but fail to remember that she drank beer at dinner, then we will not retain any uncomfortable facts that might otherwise prompt us to modify our librarian stereotype.

More elaborate belief-schemas are similarly resistant to data. In an elegant demonstration of this, students who held strongly divergent beliefs about whether or not capital punishment (the death penalty) acts as a deterrent against homicide read a summary of two purportedly authentic studies. One of the studies appeared to show that capital punishment was a deterrent, and the other appeared to show that it was not. The students also read a critique of each study that criticized its methodology. You will not be surprised to learn that students on each side of the issue found the study supporting their own position to be significantly more convincing and better conducted than the other study. But the more surprising and unsettling result was that after reading all the evidence on both sides, students were actually more convinced about the correctness of their initial position than they were at the beginning of the study (Lord, Ross, & Lepper, 1979). This implies that evidence introduced into public

We are more likely to remember facts about people that are consistent with our schemas of them. For example, we are more likely to remember that the woman on the left drank wine at her birthday party than that she owns a bowling ball. We are more likely to remember that the woman on the right drank beer at her birthday party than that she likes classical music.

debate in the hope of resolving an issue—or at least moderating extreme views—will tend instead to polarize public opinion even further. Proponents of each side will pick and choose from the evidence so as to bolster their initial opinions (Nisbett & Ross, 1980).

PERSISTENCE OF A SELF-SCHEMA   A similar effect has been shown with the self-schema. In an experiment, subjects were asked to distinguish between genuine and fake suicide notes. Some of the subjects were led to believe that they had done very well at the task; others were led to believe they had done badly. They were then "debriefed," that is, they were told that the feedback had actually been manipulated and that the experimenter actually had no idea how well they had done. Despite this, the "successful" subjects persisted in the belief that they had, in fact, probably done quite well and were good at the task; similarly, the "unsuccessful" subjects continued to believe that they had done badly and were not good at the task (Ross, Lepper, & Hubbard, 1975). This has been called the *perseverance effect*. Why does it occur?

One compelling explanation is that, upon learning that they had done well, subjects tried to come up with an explanation for their performance ("Well, I have been a peer counselor, and so I am probably pretty sensitive to other people's moods; it's not surprising I did well"). Similarly, those who were told they had done badly might have reviewed their past and discovered reasons for their poor performance ("This person in my dorm who I thought was the picture of mental health had to take medical leave for psychiatric reasons; I guess I'm not very good at spotting someone else's emotional troubles"). When they then learned that, in fact, the experimenter did not know how they had done, they were left with their causal explanations, which still seemed valid. And so they continued to predict that they had done well or badly on the basis of their new self-schema for the task (Nisbett & Ross, 1980).

Subsequent research supports this explanation of the perseverance effect. Subjects were asked to place themselves in the position of a clinical psychologist and try to explain an event in a person's life on the basis of his or her previous history. All subjects read an authentic clinical case history of either an unhappy and somewhat neurotic young

woman or a chronically unemployed and depressed middle-aged man. Each subject was then told about a later event in the person's life (for example, committing suicide, being involved in a hit-and-run accident, joining the Peace Corps, running for public office) and asked to explain why it might have occurred. Subjects were then "debriefed" and told that the later event was purely hypothetical and that, in fact, there was no available information about the later life of the patient whose history they had read. Each subject was then asked to assess the likelihood of a number of possible events in the patient's later life, including the critical event that had been explained.

It was found that subjects predicted that the event they had explained was much more likely to occur than did subjects who had explained some other event. For example, those who had explained why, on the basis of her earlier case history, the young woman might have joined the Peace Corps now thought it much more likely that she had actually done so than those who had explained why she might have been involved in a hit-and-run accident (Ross, Lepper, Strack, & Steinmetz, 1977).

We will see additional reasons for the persistence of schemas in the following section when we again discuss stereotypes.

PERCEIVING COVARIATION: STEREOTYPES

Detecting covariation or correlation—discovering what goes with what—is a fundamental task in every science. Discovering that symptoms of an illness covary with the amount of environmental pollution or correlate with the presence of a virus is the first step toward a cure. And as intuitive scientists of human behavior, we perceive—or think we perceive—such correlations all the time ("People who are against capital punishment seem more likely to hold a pro-choice position on abortion"; "Asians seem to do better in math and science than non-Asians"). Our schemas of classes of persons—stereotypes—are actually minitheories of covariation: The stereotype of an extravert, a gay person, or a college professor is a theory of what particular traits or behaviors go with certain other traits or behaviors.

Research shows that we are not very accurate at detecting covariations. Once again, our theories mislead us. When our schemas or theories lead us to expect two things to covary, we overestimate the correlation between them, even seeing illusory correlations that do not exist. But when we do not have a theory that leads us to expect them to covary, we underestimate the correlation, even failing to detect a correlation that is strongly present in the data.

This was demonstrated by two researchers who were intrigued by the fact that clinical psychologists routinely report correlations between their clients' responses to projective tests (see Chapter 12) and their personality characteristics, even though research studies fail to find such correlations. For example, experienced clinicians have often reported that gay men are more likely than heterosexual men to see anal images, feminine clothing, and three other, similar kinds of images in Rorschach inkblots. Controlled studies, however, have not found any of these images to be correlated with a homosexual orientation (Chapman & Chapman, 1969). The researchers hypothesized that psychologists see these correlations because the reported images fit a popular stereotype, or schema, of male homosexuality. Several experiments have now confirmed this hypothesis.

In one, college students were asked to study a set of Rorschach cards. Each card contained the inkblot, a description of the image a client had reported seeing in it, and a statement of two personal characteristics that the client possessed. The images described included the five stereotyped images reported by clinical psychologists to be correlated with male homosexuality plus a number of other unrelated images (for example, images of food). The characteristics reported were either homosexuality ("has sexual feelings toward other men") or unrelated characteristics (for example, "feels sad and depressed much of the time"). The cards were carefully constructed so that no image was systematically associated with homosexuality.

After studying all the cards, subjects were asked to report if they had noticed "any general kind of thing that was seen most often by men" with the different characteristics. The results revealed that the students in this study—like experienced clinical psychologists—erroneously reported a correlation between the stereotyped images and homosexuality. They did not report any correlations between the nonstereotyped images and homosexuality.

The researchers then repeated the study, modifying the cards so that two of the nonstereotyped images (a monster image in one inkblot and an animal-human image in another) *always* appeared with the characteristic of homosexuality—a perfect correlation. Despite this, subjects still reported seeing the nonexistent correlation with the stereotyped images more than twice as often as the perfect, correlation with the nonstereotyped images.

As intuitive scientists, we are schema- or theory-driven. We see covariations our theories have prepared us to see and fail to see covariations our theories have not prepared us to see.

PERSISTENCE OF STEREOTYPES Perhaps it is not surprising that the inexperienced students in the study just described are misled by their stereotypes to see nonexistent correlations in the data. But why should this be true of experienced clinical psychologists? Why doesn't their daily contact with real data correct their mistaken perceptions of covariation? More generally, why do our stereotypes persist in the face of nonconfirming data?

We can illustrate some of the factors involved by representing the covariation task in a 2 × 2 table, as shown in Figure 17-1. It displays some hypothetical data relevant to a popular stereotype similar to that explored in the Rorschach inkblot study: the stereotype that gay men display effeminate gestures. The table classifies a hypothetical sample of 1,100 men into the 4 cells of the table according to

FIGURE 17-1

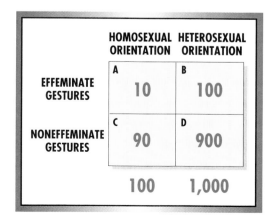

Stereotypes as Covariations *To determine whether there is a correlation between sexual orientation and effeminate gestures, we need to know whether the proportion of men with effeminate gestures differs as a function of sexual orientation. This requires taking all four cells into account so that the column totals can be computed. Invalid stereotypes often persist because we attend only to cell A and neglect the other cells. There is, in fact, no correlation between the two factors in these hypothetical data.*

whether they have a homosexual or a heterosexual orientation and whether they do or do not display effeminate gestures.

The correct way to assess whether the two factors are correlated is to examine whether the *proportion* of gay men who display effeminate gestures (the left-hand column) is different from the *proportion* of heterosexual men who display effeminate gestures (the right-hand column). To do this, we must first add up the two cells in each column to find how many men with each kind of orientation there are in the sample. When we do this, we see that 10 out of 100, or 10 percent, of the gay men display effeminate gestures and 100 out of 1,000, or 10 percent, of the heterosexual men do so. In other words, there is *no* correlation in these data between sexual orientation and effeminate gestures. It is important to note that to assess the correlation, we had to take into account all four cells of the table. Now consider what our intuitions would tell us if we encountered these data in daily life—where we do not have the data neatly laid out in front of us.

In our society, men with a homosexual orientation are in a minority, as are men who display effeminate gestures. When the two occur together (as in cell A, gay men with effeminate gestures), it is a particularly distinctive occurrence. This has two consequences. First, research has shown that people *overestimate* the frequency with which they have actually encountered such distinctive combinations (Hamilton & Sherman, 1989; Hamilton & Gifford, 1976). Second, even if we did not overestimate their frequency, we are still most likely to notice and to remember instances that fall into cell A and to remain oblivious to the instances that fall into the other cells of the table.

Part of the reason for this is that the relevant information is almost never available to us. In particular, we rarely have the opportunity to assess the frequency of cell C, the number of gay men who do *not* display effeminate gestures. Cell B also provides an inferential trap for some people. When they observe a man with effeminate gestures, they may simply *assume* he is gay even though they have no knowledge of his actual sexual orientation. He might belong to either cell A or cell B. But through circular reasoning, they illegitimately convert cell B disconfirmations of their stereotype into cell A confir-

mations. Note that it is the stereotype itself that leads them to make this inferential error—another instance of how our information processing is schema- or theory-driven.

But even if the data from cells other than cell A were available to us, it would not typically occur to us that we need to know this other information. We find it particularly difficult to take into account—or to understand why we *need* to take into account—cell D, the frequency of *non*gay men who do *not* display effeminate gestures. Why is this difficult?

We noted earlier in this chapter that we are more likely to notice and to remember vivid rather than nonvivid information. This is why cell A is noticed, remembered, and overestimated: Gay men with effeminate gestures are distinctive and, hence, vivid. In contrast, there are not many events that are less vivid—and hence, less noticeable and less memorable—than events that do *not* occur. But this is precisely what cell D events are: nonevents. The *non*gay man who does *not* display effeminate gestures does not constitute a psychological event for us. It is difficult to notice or to appreciate the relevance of nonevents in daily life.

This difficulty was cleverly employed by Arthur Conan Doyle in his Sherlock Holmes story, "The Adventure of Silver Blaze," in which the famous detective is asked to discover who had stolen a prize race horse from its private stable during the night. Holmes draws the police inspector's attention to "the curious incident of the dog in the night-time." Puzzled, the inspector says, "The dog did nothing in the night-time." To which Holmes replies: "That was the curious incident." Holmes then deduces correctly that the horse was stolen by its own trainer—because the dog had *not* barked and, hence, must have known the intruder (Doyle, 1892/1981, p. 197).

The nonvividness of nonevents also leads the news media to promote and sustain stereotypes. When a gay man commits a murder—especially one with sexual overtones—both the sexual orientation and the murder are featured in the news story; when a heterosexual man commits a murder—even one with sexual overtones—sexual orientation is not mentioned. Thus cell A events are widely publicized—thereby fueling the stereotype—whereas cell B events are not seen as relevant to sexual orientation. And, of course, cell C and D events—men of any sexual orientation who do *not* commit murder—are not news. They are nonevents.

Self-fulfilling Stereotypes Our schemas influence not only our perceptions and inferential processes, but also our behavior and social interactions. And this, too, can sustain our stereotypes. In particular, our stereotypes can lead us to interact with those we stereotype in ways that cause them to fulfill our expectations. Thus, our stereotypes can become both self-perpetuating and self-fulfilling. Two studies illustrate this process.

In one, the investigators first noted that white job interviewers displayed a less friendly manner when interviewing African-American applicants than when interviewing white applicants. They hypothesized that this could cause African-American applicants to come off less well in the interviews. To test this hypothesis, they trained interviewers to reproduce both the less friendly and the more friendly interviewing styles. Applicants (all white) were then videotaped while being interviewed by an interviewer using one of these two styles. Judges who later viewed the tapes rated applicants who had been interviewed in a less friendly manner significantly lower on their interview performance than those who had been interviewed in the more friendly manner (Word, Zanna, & Cooper, 1974). The study thus confirmed the hypothesis that prejudiced individuals can interact in ways that actually evoke the stereotyped behaviors that sustain their prejudice.

A commonly held stereotype is that physically attractive people are more sociable, poised, and outgoing (Dion, Berscheid, & Walster, 1972). To find out if this stereotype could be self-fulfilling, researchers had unacquainted male and female college students talk to each other over the telephone for about 10 minutes. Before each conversation, the man was shown a photograph of either an attractive or an unattractive woman and told (falsely) that it was a photograph of his phone partner.

The conversations were recorded on two-track tapes, and analyses of the men's side of the conversations showed that those who believed they were talking to an attractive woman were friendlier, more outgoing, and more sociable than were men who believed they were talking to a less attractive woman.

More interestingly, judges who listened to the woman's half of each conversation without hearing the male partner or knowing his belief about the woman's attractiveness rated women whose partners believed they were attractive as more sociable, poised, and humorous than women whose partners believed they were unattractive. The men's stereotype of physically attractive women became self-fulfilling in a 10-minute telephone conversation (Snyder, Tanke, & Berscheid, 1977).

Inferring Causality: Attributions

The heart of most sciences is the discovery of causes and effects. Similarly, as intuitive scientists, we feel we truly understand some instance of human behavior when we know why it occurred or what caused it. Suppose, for example, a famous athlete endorses a breakfast cereal on television. Why does she do it? Does she really like the cereal or is she doing it for the money? You give a $5 donation to Planned Parenthood. Why? Are you altruistic? Were you being pressured? Do you need a tax writeoff? Do you believe in the work of the organization?

Each of these cases creates an attribution problem. We see some behavior—perhaps our own—and must decide to which of many possible causes the action should be attributed. Our intuitive attempts to infer the causes of behavior has been a central topic in social psychology for a long time now (Kelley, 1967; Heider, 1958).

Fundamental Attribution Error As the two examples above illustrate, one of the major attribution tasks we face daily is deciding whether an observed behavior reflects something unique about the person (his or her attitudes, personality characteristics, and so forth) or something about the situation in which we observe the person. If we infer that something about the person is primarily responsible for the behavior (for instance, the athlete really loves the cereal), then our inference is called an *internal* or **dispositional attribution** ("disposition" here refers to a person's beliefs, attitudes, and personality characteristics). If, however, we conclude that some external cause is primarily responsible for the behavior (for instance, money, social norms, threats), it is called an *external* or **situational attribution**.

Fritz Heider, the founder of attribution theory, noted that an individual's behavior is so compelling to us that we take it at face value and give insufficient weight to the circumstances surrounding it (1958). Research has confirmed Heider's observation. We underestimate the situational causes of behavior, jumping too easily to conclusions about the disposition of the person. If we observe someone behaving aggressively, we too readily assume that the person has an aggressive personality rather than that the situation might have provoked the aggression in anyone. Another way of stating it is that we have a schema of cause and effect for human behavior that gives too much weight to the person and too little to the situation. One psychologist has termed this bias toward dispositional attributions rather than situational attributions the **fundamental attribution error** (Ross, 1977).

In one of the first studies to reveal this bias, subjects read a debater's speech that either supported or attacked Cuban leader Fidel Castro. The subjects were explicitly told that the debater had been assigned which side of the issue to argue by the debate coach; the debater had no choice. Despite this knowledge, when asked to estimate the debater's actual attitude toward Castro, subjects inferred that he or she held a position close to the one

argued in the debate. In other words, the subjects made a dispositional attribution even though situational forces were fully sufficient to account for the behavior (Jones & Harris, 1967). This effect is quite powerful. Even when the subjects themselves get to designate which side of the issue that a speaker is to argue, they still tend to see him or her as actually holding that opinion (Gilbert & Jones, 1986). The effect occurs even if the presentations are deliberately designed to be drab and unenthusiastic and the speaker simply reads a transcribed version of the speech in a monotone and uses no gestures (Schneider & Miller, 1975).

SELF-ATTRIBUTIONS As informal scientists of human behavior, one of our major tasks is understanding ourselves. As we shall see, the judgments we make about our own thoughts, emotions, behaviors, motives, and personalities are governed by many of the same processes that govern our judgments of others.

We saw in Chapter 11 that we often judge our emotions through a process of cognitive appraisal. Although the physiological arousal of our autonomic nervous system provides the information that we are experiencing an emotion, the more subtle judgment of *which* emotion it is often depends on our perceptions—our cognitive appraisals—of the surrounding circumstances. This suggests the more general possibility that we may rely on external cues in order to make judgments about many of our inner states.

This possibility is the basis for **self-perception theory** by Daryl Bem (1972), who proposes that we make judgments about ourselves using the same inferential processes—and making the same kinds of errors—that we use for making judgments about others. Specifically, the theory proposes that individuals come to know their own attitudes, emotions, and other internal states partially by inferring them from observations of their own behavior and the circumstances in which the behavior occurs. Thus to the extent that internal cues are weak, ambiguous, or uninterpretable, the individual is like any outside observer who must rely on external cues to infer the individual's inner states.

These propositions are illustrated by the common remark, "This is my second sandwich; I guess I was hungrier than I thought." Here the speaker has decided on the basis of a self-observation that he or she had originally

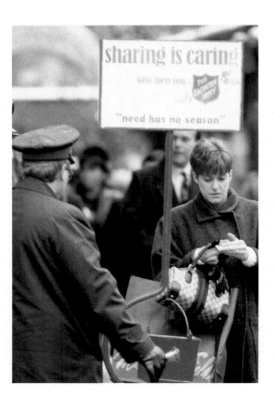

We often observe a behavior—perhaps our own—and must decide to what causes it should be attributed. Is this woman giving money to the Salvation Army because she supports its work, because she feels pressured, or because she is generally altruistic?

CROSS-CULTURAL DIFFERENCES IN ATTRIBUTION PROCESSES

Most Western industrialized nations, especially the United States, have an individualist orientation, which values independence and self-assertiveness. In contrast, many non-Western cultures have a more collectivist orientation, which stresses the interdependence of persons with others in the community. This suggests the possibility that some of the attributional effects that we have been discussing may not be universal but simply reflect the individualist orientation of the societies in which most of the research has been conducted. For example, it may be our individualist orientation rather than a universal feature of human information processing that prompts us to describe people in terms of personality traits or to attribute actions to an individual's personality rather than to the situation.

To test this possibility, individuals from Japan (a society with a collectivist orientation) and the United States were asked to respond repeatedly to the question "Who am I?" The Japanese subjects listed only a fourth as many psychological traits (for example, "I am optimistic") as the American subjects but three times as many social roles and contexts (for example, "I am a member of the drama club"). Interestingly, when a social context was specified, the Japanese were actually more likely than the Americans to use psychological traits to describe themselves (for example, "at home I am sometimes lazy" or "in school I am hard-working"), thereby indicating that they view their behavior as dependent on the situation (Cousins, 1989). Other, similar studies confirm that individuals in Europe and North America are significantly more likely than Asians to describe themselves in dispositional terms (Trafimow, Triandis, & Goto, 1991; Triandis, 1989).

Individuals in collectivist cultures are more likely than individuals in individualistic cultures to describe and explain behaviors in terms of social roles and situations than in personality or dispositional terms.

Another cross-cultural study sought to determine whether individuals in the United States would be more likely than Hindu individuals in India to favor dispositional explanations of behavior over situational explanations. Each subject was asked to "describe something a person you know well did recently that you considered a wrong thing to have done" and also to "describe something a person you know well did recently that you considered good for someone else." Subjects were then asked to explain why each behavior occurred.

As predicted, subjects in the United States offered dispositional explanations (for example, "he is rather careless and inconsiderate") more frequently and situational explanations (for example, "it was hard to see, and the other bicycle was going very fast") less frequently than did Hindu subjects. To determine whether these differences were simply due to the kinds of behaviors selected by members of each culture, the United States subjects were also asked to explain the behaviors mentioned by the Hindu subjects. This made no difference; they continued to favor dispositional explanations over situational ones to the same extent (Miller, 1984).

At first glance, these results would seem to imply that individuals in collectivist Asian cultures are less likely to commit the fundamental attribution error than are individuals from the United States or other individualist cultures. But it may also be that situational factors actually do play more of a role in determining behavior in collectivist cultures. This is, in fact, the basic assumption of scholars who contrast individualist and collectivist cultures. These explanations are not mutually exclusive, however. Situational influences in collectivist cultures may be both more powerful determinants of behavior and, therefore, also more cognitively available as explanations for behavior (Ross & Nisbett, 1991).

misjudged an internal state. Similarly, the self-observation "I've been biting my nails all day; something must be bugging me" is based on the same external evidence that might lead a friend to remark, "You've been biting your nails all day; something must be bugging you."

A more formal and surprising illustration of self-perception theory is provided by an *induced-compliance* experiment originally conducted in order to test Festinger's theory of *cognitive dissonance* (1957)—which we will discuss later in the section on attitudes. Male college students participated one at a time in an experiment in which they worked on dull, repetitive tasks. After completing the tasks, some subjects were offered $1 to tell the next subject that the tasks had been fun and interesting. Others were offered $20 to do this. All subjects complied with the request. Later they were asked how much they had enjoyed the tasks. As shown in Figure 17-2, subjects who had been paid only $1 stated that they had, in fact, enjoyed the tasks. But subjects who had been paid $20 did not find them significantly more enjoyable than control subjects who never spoke to another subject (Festinger & Carlsmith, 1959). The small incentive for complying with the experimenter's request—but not the large incentive—led individuals to *believe* what they had heard themselves say. Why should this be so?

Just as we try to decide whether an athlete on television really loves the cereal she endorses or whether she is just saying so for the money, so too self-perception theory proposes that subjects in this experiment looked at their own behavior (telling another subject that the tasks were interesting) and implicitly asked themselves, "Why did I do this?" It further proposes that they sought an answer the same way an outside observer would, by trying to decide whether to make a dispositional attribution (he did it because he really did enjoy the tasks) or a situational attribution (he did it for the money). When the individual is paid only $1, the observer is more likely to make a dispositional attribution: "He wouldn't be willing to say it for only $1, so he must have actually enjoyed the tasks." But if the individual is paid $20, the observer is more likely to make a situational attribution: "Anyone would have done it for $20, so I can't judge his attitude toward the tasks on the basis of his statement." If the individual follows the same inferential process as this hypothetical outside observer, then subjects paid $1 make a dispositional attribution about their own behavior: "I must think the tasks were enjoyable; otherwise, I would not have said so." But subjects paid $20 attribute their behavior to the money and thus express the same attitudes toward the tasks as the control subjects who made no statements to another subject.

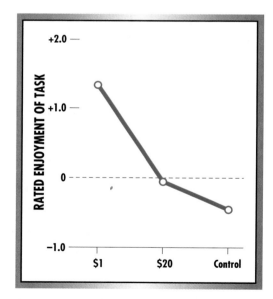

FIGURE 17-2

Induced-Compliance Experiment   *The smaller incentive for agreeing to say the tasks were interesting led subjects to infer that they had actually enjoyed the tasks. The larger incentive did not.* (After Festinger & Carlsmith, 1959)

FUNDAMENTAL ATTRIBUTION ERROR IN SELF-PERCEPTION
There is a subtle point about the findings in this experiment. We know that all the subjects were willing to tell the next subject that the tasks were enjoyable—even subjects who were offered only $1 to do so. But the subjects themselves do not know this. Thus, when subjects paid $1 infer that they must think the tasks are enjoyable because otherwise they would not have said so, they are wrong. They should be inferring that they talked to the next subject because they were paid $1 to do so. In other words, the subjects are making a dispositional attribution about their own behavior when they should be making a situational attribution. They are committing the fundamental attribution error.

An experiment designed as a quiz game illustrates how both participants and observers make the same fundamental attribution error in the same setting. Pairs of male or female subjects were recruited to participate in a question-and-answer game of general knowledge. One member of the pair was randomly assigned to be the questioner and to make up 10 difficult questions to which he or she knew the answers (for example, "What is the world's largest glacier?"). The other subject served as the contestant and attempted to answer the questions. When the contestant failed a question, the questioner would give the answer. In a reenactment of the study, observers also watched the contest. After the game was completed, both participants and observers were asked to rate the level of general knowledge possessed by the questioner and the contestant, relative to the "average student." It is important to note that participants and observers all knew that the roles of questioner and contestant had been assigned randomly.

As Figure 17-3 shows, questioners judged both themselves and the contestant to be about average in level of general knowledge. But contestants rated the questioner as superior and themselves as inferior to the average student. They attributed the outcome of the game to their (and the questioner's) level of knowledge rather than taking into account the overwhelming situational advantage enjoyed by the questioner, who gets to decide which questions to ask and gets to omit any questions to which he or she does not know the answer. Observers, aware that the questioner could ask questions which neither they nor the contestant could answer, rated the questioner's level of knowledge even higher. In other words, both contestants and observers gave too much weight to dispositional causes and too little to situational causes—the fundamental attribution error (Ross, Amabile, & Steinmetz, 1977).

One implication of this study is that people who select the topics discussed in a conversation will be seen as more knowledgeable than those who passively let others set the agenda, even if everyone is aware of the differential roles being played. This, in turn, has implications for contemporary sex roles. Research has shown that men talk more than women in mixed-sex interactions (Henley, Hamilton, & Thorne, 1985); they interrupt more (West & Zimmerman, 1983); and they are more likely to raise the topics discussed (Fishman, 1983). The questioner-contestant

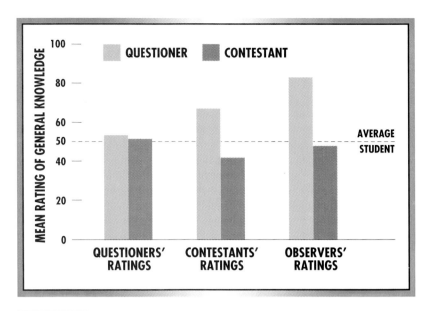

FIGURE 17-3

Fundamental Attribution Error *Ratings of questioners and contestants after they had participated in a quiz game. The questioner is rated as superior by both the contestant and observers even though the questioner had an overwhelming situational advantage. Both contestants and observers gave too much weight to dispositional causes and too little to situational causes.* (After Ross, Amabile, & Steinmetz, 1977)

study implies that one consequence of these sex-role patterns is that women leave most mixed-sex interactions thinking themselves less knowledgeable than the men, with bystanders of both sexes sharing this illusion. The moral is clear: The fundamental attribution error can work for or against you. If you want to appear knowledgeable both to yourself and to others, learn how to structure the situation so that you control the choice of topics discussed. Be the questioner, not the contestant.

THEORIZING ABOUT ONESELF Self-perception theory draws a portrait of two selves in one, a subject-self and a psychologist-self. The subject-self behaves and the psychologist-self attempts to interpret or explain the behavior, displaying the same biases and making the same kinds of errors as any intuitive scientist. We saw a similar idea in Chapter 6, where we discussed Hilgard's *neodissociation theory* of hypnosis. According to this theory, there is a "hidden observer," a mental structure that monitors everything that happens during hypnosis, including events that the subject is not consciously aware of perceiving.

Research in neuropsychology suggests that the concept of an observing self and an observed self may be more than a simple metaphor. In Chapter 2, we reported research on patients who had the two hemispheres of their brains surgically separated for medical reasons. Because the language area of the brain is located in the left hemisphere, such patients cannot verbally describe visual stimuli presented to the right cerebral hemisphere. Subsequent experiments have suggested to one neuropsychologist that there is a "left-brain interpreter" that attempts to understand feelings and behaviors originating in other parts of the brain (Gazzaniga, 1985).

In one of Gazzaniga's experiments, a picture of a chicken claw was presented to the left hemisphere of a split-brain patient while a picture of a snow scene was presented to the right hemisphere. Under these conditions, the left hemisphere does not register the snow scene. The patient was then shown an array of pictures and asked to choose those associated with the pictures presented. The obviously correct associations were a picture of a chicken for the chicken claw and a shovel for the snow scene. The patient chose both of the correct pictures, pointing to the shovel with the left hand (which is controlled by the right hemisphere) and the chicken with the right hand. When asked why he chose these items, he replied, "Oh, that's simple. The chicken claw goes with the chicken, and you need a shovel to clean out the chicken shed." The left-brain interpreter—ignorant of the snow scene but seeing his hand choose the picture of the shovel—made up a plausible theory to explain the behavior.

In another experiment, the written command "laugh" was presented to a patient's right hemisphere. The patient laughed, and when asked why, said, "You guys come up and test us every month. What a way to make a living!" When the command "walk" was flashed to the right hemisphere of another patient, he stood up and began to leave, explaining that he had decided to get a Coke.

Understanding our emotions also appears to require the left-brain interpreter. In one experiment, a film depicting one person throwing another into a fire was shown to the right hemisphere of a split-brain patient. As expected, she could not describe what she saw, but she described herself as feeling kind of scared and jumpy. As an aside to a colleague, she then said, "I know I like Dr. Gazzaniga, but right now I'm scared of him for some rea-son." Denied a knowledge of the source of the emotion, the left-brain interpreter came up with a plausible theory to explain the felt emotional state.

In general, when people are asked to account for their preferences, behaviors, and emotional states, they tend to identify causes that seem plausible—even when those causes are not operative—and to overlook actual causes that seem less plausible (Nisbett & Wilson, 1977). For example, several studies have asked individuals to keep daily records of their moods and the factors that might affect them (the day of the week, the weather, the amount they slept, and so forth). At the end of each study, the individuals were asked to judge how much each of the factors had affected their moods. There was little relationship between their perceptions of how important a factor was and how well it actually correlated with their moods. In fact, individuals were no better at estimating how well the day of the week or the weather had predicted their moods than strangers who were simply asked to make plausible intuitive estimates (Wilson, Laser, & Stone, 1982).

ATTITUDES

So far our discussion has focused exclusively on cognitive functioning, the processes of perceiving and thinking. With the concept of **attitude**, one of social psychology's most central concepts, we can begin to incorporate affective functioning—emotions and feelings—into our discussion of social behavior.

Attitudes are likes and dislikes—favorable or unfavorable evaluations of and reactions to objects, people, situations, or any other aspects of the world, including abstract ideas and social policies. We often express our attitudes in opinion statements: "I love oranges" or "I can't abide Republicans." But even though attitudes express feelings, they are often linked to cognitions, specifically to beliefs about the attitude objects ("Oranges contain lots of vitamins"; "Republicans have no compassion for the poor"). Moreover, attitudes are sometimes linked to actions we take with respect to the attitude objects ("I eat an orange every morning"; "I never vote for Republicans").

Accordingly, social psychologists usually conceive of attitudes as comprising a *cognitive* component, an *affective* component, and a *behavioral* component. For example, in studying negative attitudes toward groups, social psychologists distinguish between negative **stereotypes** (negative beliefs and perceptions about a group—the cognitive component), **prejudice** (negative feelings toward the group—the affective component), and **discrimination** (negative actions against members of the group—the behavioral component). Some theorists prefer to define an attitude as comprising only the cognitive and affective components; others include only the affective component. But despite differing definitions, all share a concern with the interrelationships among the pertinent beliefs, feelings, and behaviors.

CONSISTENCY OF ATTITUDES

Certain attitudes seem to go together. For example, people who support affirmative action seem likely to advocate stronger gun control, to oppose capital punishment, and to hold a pro-choice position on abortion. On the surface these diverse attitudes do not seem to follow one another logically. Yet knowing that a person holds one of the attitudes often permits us to guess the others with fair accuracy, and there does seem to be a kind of logic involved. The attitudes all appear to follow more or less from a common set of underlying values that we might label as "liberal."

The same kind of logic can be discerned among "conservative" attitudes. Many people who oppose affirmative action and gun control laws cite their belief in the value of individual freedom as the basis for their opinions. Even those who disagree with such opinions can appreciate the logic involved. But many such freedom-loving individuals also feel that women belong in the home, that marijuana use should be more heavily penalized, and that homosexual behavior should be illegal. Here the logic is less than clear, yet these attitudes, too, seem strangely predictable.

In short, people's attitudes often appear to have a kind of internal logic to them, but it is not usually a strict kind of formal logic. Instead, it is a kind of psycho-logic, and it is this psycho-logic that social psychologists have studied under the label of *cognitive consis-*

tency. The basic premise of cognitive consistency theories is that we all strive to be consistent in our beliefs, attitudes, and behaviors, and that inconsistency acts as an irritant or a stimulus that motivates us to modify or change them until they form a coherent, if not logical, package. Throughout the years, the consistency theorists have amassed a great deal of evidence for this basic premise (Abelson et al., 1968).

But most of the research on consistency has been conducted with college students in laboratory studies. Psychologists and political scientists who have analyzed the public mind outside the social psychology laboratory are divided in their views about the ideological coherence of public opinion on social and political issues (Kinder & Sears, 1985). One of those who believes the public to be ideologically innocent has said:

> As intellectuals and students of politics we are disposed by training and sensibility to take political ideas seriously. . . . We are therefore prone to forget that most people take them less seriously than we do, that they pay little attention to issues, rarely worry about the consistency of their opinions, and spend little or no time thinking about the values, presuppositions and implications that distinguish one political orientation from another. (McClosky, quoted by Abelson, 1968)

Examples of such nonconsistency have been around for decades. For example, in a national survey taken by the *New York Times* and CBS News in the late 1970s, a majority of Americans said they disapprove of "most government-sponsored welfare programs." Yet over 80 percent said they supported: the government's "program providing financial assistance for children raised in low-income homes where one parent is missing" (Aid to Families with Dependent Children, a major welfare program); the government's program for "helping poor people buy food for their families at cheaper prices" (the essence of the federal food-stamp program); and the government's program for paying for health care for poor people (the Medicaid program). The strong support for these major welfare programs was similar among all types of people—rich and poor, liberal and conservative, Democrat and Republican. And despite the recent push to reform the welfare system, people are still more likely to oppose the general concept of welfare than they are to

Another person's beliefs may seem inconsistent to us because they may not fit our own ideologies. For example, a Catholic priest's or nun's opposition to both capital punishment and legalized abortion reflects a consistent pro-life ideology. Yet their views may appear inconsistent to those who hold the more common political position of opposing either capital punishment or legalized abortion, but not both.

oppose specific programs. (Moreover, government subsidies that benefit the middle class—Medicare, subsidized college loans, tax deductions for mortgage interest payments— are rarely defined by the public as welfare.)

An early national survey designed specifically to probe this kind of inconsistency found a similar contradiction between an *ideological* conservatism and an *operational* liberalism in attitudes toward welfare. One out of four Americans was conservative on questions concerning the general concept of welfare but simultaneously liberal on questions concerning specific welfare programs (Free & Cantril, 1967).

Despite these findings, we need to be cautious about accusing someone of being inconsistent, because his or her attitudes may simply be inconsistent with our own ideological framework; inconsistency may be in the eye of the beholder. For example, opposition to capital punishment is usually characterized as a liberal position, whereas opposition to legalized abortion is usually thought of as a conservative position. Yet there is a quite logical coherence to the views of a person who, being against all taking of life, opposes both capital punishment and legalized abortion. (Catholic clergy often hold this set of views, for example.) Another example is provided by libertarians, who are opposed to any government interference in our lives. They are conservative on economic issues— the free market, not the government, should

control the economic system—and in their opposition to government-enforced civil rights laws and affirmative action programs. But they are liberal on personal social issues, believing, for example, that the government should not criminalize the use of marijuana or concern itself with our private sexual behavior. To libertarians, both conservatives and liberals are inconsistent.

Nevertheless, the evidence suggests that most citizens do not organize their beliefs and attitudes according to any kind of overall ideology; nonconsistency, if not inconsistency, seems more prevalent than consistency. This has led one psychologist to propose that many of our attitudes come packaged as **opinion molecules**. Each molecule is made up of (a) a belief, (b) an attitude, and (c) a perception of social support for the opinion. In other words, each opinion molecule contains a fact, a feeling, and a following (Abelson, 1968): "It's a fact that when my Uncle Charlie had back trouble, he was cured by a chiropractor [*fact*]"; "You know, I feel that chiropractors have been sneered at too much [*feeling*], and I'm not ashamed to say so because I know a lot of people who feel the same way [*following*]." Or, "Americans don't really want universal health insurance [*following*], and neither do I [*feeling*]. It would lead to socialized medicine [*fact*]."

Opinion molecules serve important social functions. First, they act as conversational units, giving us something coherent to say when a particular topic comes up in conversation. They also give a rational appearance to our unexamined agreement with friends and neighbors on social issues. But most important, they serve as badges of identification with our important social groups, reinforcing our sense of belonging to a social community. Thus, the fact and the feeling are less important ingredients of an opinion molecule than the following.

FUNCTIONS OF ATTITUDES

Attitudes serve a number of different psychological functions for us. Different people might hold the same attitude for different reasons, and a person might hold a particular attitude for more than one reason. The functions that an attitude serves for the person also influence how consistent it is with his or her other attitudes and how easily it can be changed. Over the years attitude theorists have identified and discussed a number of the functions that attitudes might serve (for example, Herek, 1986; Katz, 1960; Smith, Bruner, & White, 1956). We discuss five of them here.

INSTRUMENTAL FUNCTION Attitudes that we hold for practical or utilitarian reasons are said to serve an *instrumental* function. They simply express specific instances of our general desire to obtain benefits or rewards and avoid punishment. For example, most Americans favor more government services but oppose higher taxes. As this example indicates, such attitudes are not necessarily consistent with one another. To change such attitudes, the person needs only to be convinced that some alternative would bring more benefits.

KNOWLEDGE FUNCTION Attitudes that help us to make sense of the world, that bring order to the diverse information we must assimilate in our daily lives, are said to serve a *knowledge* function. Such attitudes are essentially schemas that permit us to organize and process diverse information efficiently without having to attend to its details. For example, until its recent demise, negative attitudes toward the Soviet Union helped many Americans to organize and interpret world events in terms of the cold war. The belief that Democrats just want to "tax and spend" or that Republicans care only for the wealthy provides a quick schematic way of interpreting and evaluating the proposals and candidates offered by the two parties. Like other schemas, such attitudes often oversimplify reality and bias our perception of events.

VALUE-EXPRESSIVE FUNCTION Attitudes that express our values or reflect our self-concepts are said to serve a *value-expressive* function. For example, a person might have positive attitudes toward gay people because of deeply held values about diversity, personal freedom, and tolerance; another person might have negative attitudes because of deeply held religious convictions that condemn homosexuality. Because value-expressive attitudes derive from a person's underlying values or self-concept, they tend to be consistent with one another. As we noted earlier, broad political values, such as liberalism or conservatism, can serve as a basis for value-expressive attitudes. Such attitudes do not change easily; the individual has to be convinced that an alternative attitude would be more consistent with his or her underlying values or self-concept.

EGO-DEFENSIVE FUNCTION Attitudes that protect us from anxiety or from threats to our self-esteem are said to serve an *ego-defensive* function. The concept of ego defensiveness comes from Sigmund Freud's psychoanalytic theory (see Chapter 13). One of the mechanisms of ego defense Freud describes is **projection**: The individual represses his or her own unacceptable impulses and then expresses hostile attitudes toward others who are perceived to possess those same impulses. For example, a person who is fearful of his or her own possible homosexual feelings is likely to deny and repress such feelings and then to display hostility toward gay people. (The term "homophobia" accurately describes anti-gay prejudice that serves such an ego-defensive function; it is less accurate when used more broadly to refer to all anti-gay attitudes.) In one study, students at a liberal California university were asked to write essays describing their attitudes toward lesbians and gay men. A content analysis of the essays revealed negative attitudes serving an ego-defensive function in about 35 percent of the essays (Herek, 1987).

The notion that negative attitudes toward minority groups can serve an ego-defensive function is called the **scapegoat theory of prejudice**, because the person's hostility often takes the form of blaming the groups for both personal and societal problems. The theory was tested in the late 1940s by a group of psychologists at the University of California at Berkeley. The researchers sought to discover whether psychoanalytic theory could explain the kind of anti-Semitism and fascist ideology that had emerged in Nazi Germany and whether one could identify individuals who would be particularly susceptible to such an ideology. The research, described in the book *The Authoritarian Personality,* has become a classic in social psychology (Adorno, Frenkel-Brunswick, Levinson, & Sanford, 1950).

Using attitude questionnaires, the investigators first confirmed their hypothesis that individuals who were anti-Semitic were also likely to be prejudiced against many groups other than their own—called "outgroups." In interviews, such individuals recalled rigidly moralistic parental discipline, a hierarchical family structure, and an anxious concern about the family's socioeconomic status.

According to the investigators, such home environments produce individuals with "authoritarian personalities"—individuals who are submissive and obedient to those they consider their superiors (including authority figures), but contemptuous of and aggressive toward those they consider inferior. As the psychoanalytic theory of prejudice predicts, authoritarian individuals repress knowledge of their own undesirable characteristics, projecting them instead onto members of "inferior" outgroups.

Although the authoritarian personality study has been criticized for a number of shortcomings (Christie & Jahoda, 1954), many of its original conclusions have withstood the test of continued research. In particular, there does appear to be an authoritarian personality type that seems particularly susceptible to a fascist ideology that has hostility toward outgroups at its core. More recent research does suggest, however, that prejudice and authoritarian attitudes may be acquired more directly in the home environment through the usual learning processes rather than through the more involved psychoanalytic processes described in the original research (Altemeyer, 1988). Also, the specific political content of an authoritarian outlook can differ from one society to another. In a survey conducted in 1991, it was found that highly authoritarian Russians tended to oppose individualism but supported equality (such as free and equal medical care for everybody), a pattern opposite that displayed by authoritarian individuals in the United States (McFarland, Ageyev, & Abalakina-Paap, 1992).

SOCIAL ADJUSTMENT FUNCTION Attitudes that help us feel that we are a part of a social community are said to serve a *social adjustment* function. The opinion molecules we discussed earlier provide one example. Another example is provided by people who hold the prescribed beliefs and attitudes of a particular church or political party because their

Hostile attitudes toward "outgroups" may be serving an ego-defensive function in which the person blames them for personal and societal problems. This is called the scapegoat theory of prejudice.

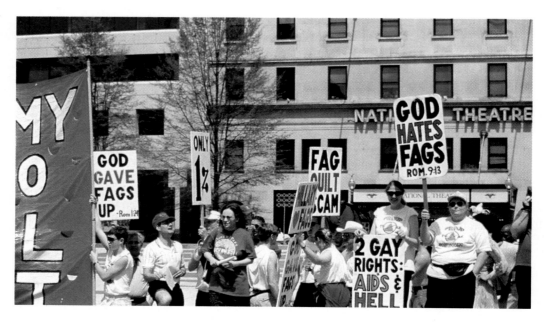

friends, families, and neighbors do; the actual content of the beliefs and attitudes is less important than the social bonds they provide. To the extent that attitudes serve primarily a social adjustment function, they are likely to change if the social norms change.

This was strikingly shown in the American South during the 1950s, when legalized racial segregation was being dismantled. Surveys showed that Americans in the South were generally opposed to desegregation and were more likely than Americans in the North to express negative attitudes toward African-Americans. Some psychologists suggested that Southern Americans might be more authoritarian than Northern Americans—that racial attitudes in the South were serving an ego-defensive function. But Thomas Pettigrew, a social psychologist who specializes in race relations, argued that racial attitudes in the South were being sustained primarily by simple conformity to the prevailing social norms of the region—a social adjustment function (Pettigrew, 1959).

Using the questionnaire developed for measuring authoritarianism, Pettigrew found that Southerners were no more authoritarian than Northerners (although authoritarian individuals in both regions were more prejudiced against African-Americans than nonauthoritarian individuals). Moreover, Southerners who were prejudiced against African-Americans were not necessarily prejudiced against other outgroups—which is contrary to what the theory of authoritarianism predicts. In fact, the South has historically been one of the least anti-Semitic regions in the United States, and one survey at the time showed Southern whites to be unfavorable toward African-Americans but quite favorable toward Jews (Prothro, 1952). Also, veterans from the South—whose military experience had exposed them to different social norms—were considerably less prejudiced than nonveterans, even though veterans from both South and North were more authoritarian than nonveterans.

The subsequent history of desegregation confirmed Pettigrew's analysis. As desegregation progressed, surveys showed that attitudes toward a particular desegregation step tended to be unfavorable just before the change had been implemented but then became favorable soon afterward (Pettigrew, 1959). Thus some communities had accepted the desegregation of public accommodations but were still op-

posed to school desegregation; other communities showed just the reverse pattern. In one study, it was estimated that about 40 percent of the sample had firm opinions favoring or opposing desegregation, but that the remaining 60 percent favored whatever the social norms happened to be at the time (Minard, 1952).

It is often said that one cannot legislate attitudes. In the literal sense this is obviously true. But legislation and judicial decrees change public policies and practices, and these, in turn, frequently lead to changes in the social norms. To the extent that a citizen's attitudes are serving a social adjustment function, they, too, will change. Under these conditions, the quickest path to changing "hearts and minds" is to change behavior first by changing the social norms.

ATTITUDES AND BEHAVIOR

A major reason for studying attitudes is the expectation that they will enable us to predict a person's future behavior. A political candidate is interested in a survey of voters' opinions only if the attitudes expressed relate to voting behavior. The assumption that a person's attitudes determine his or her behavior is deeply ingrained in Western thinking, and in many instances the assumption holds.

But research has shown that the relationship between attitudes and behavior is complex. A classic study conducted during the 1930s was the first to question the link. A white professor traveled across the United States with a young Chinese couple. At that time, there was quite strong prejudice against Asians and there were no laws against racial discrimination in public accommodations. The three travelers stopped at over 200 hotels, motels, and restaurants and were served at all the restaurants and all but one of the hotels and motels without problem. Later, a letter was sent to all of the establishments visited asking them whether or not they would accept a Chinese couple as guests. Of the 128 replies received, 92 percent said they would not. In other words, these proprietors expressed attitudes that were much more prejudiced than their behavior (LaPiere, 1934).

This study illustrates that behavior is determined by many factors other than attitudes, and these other factors affect attitude-behavior consistency. One obvious factor is the degree of constraint in the situation: We must often act in ways that are not consistent with what we feel or believe. As children, we ate asparagus that we detested, and as adults we attend lectures and dinner parties that we would compare unfavorably to our experience with asparagus. In the racial discrimination study, the prejudiced proprietors may have found it difficult to act on their prejudices when actually faced with an Asian couple seeking service. Public accommodation laws against discrimination now make it even more difficult than it was in 1934 to display such prejudices. Peer pressure can exert similar influences on behavior. For example, a teenager's attitude toward marijuana is moderately correlated with his or her actual use of marijuana, but the number of marijuana-using friends the teenager has is an even better predictor of his or her marijuana use (Andrews & Kandel, 1979).

In general, attitudes tend to predict behavior best when (a) they are strong and consistent; (b) they are specifically related to the behavior being predicted; (c) they are based on the person's direct experience; and (d) the individual is self-aware of his or her attitudes. We shall look briefly at each of these.

Strong and consistent attitudes predict behavior better than weak or ambivalent attitudes. Surveys of presidential elections show that individuals whose attitudes fail to predict how they vote are likely to hold weak or ambivalent attitudes (Kelley & Mirer, 1974). Many such voters experience ambivalence because they are cross-pressured by friends and associates who do not agree with one another. For example, a Jewish businessperson belongs to an ethnic group that generally holds liberal political positions, but she also belongs to a business community that frequently holds conservative political positions, particularly on economic issues. When it comes time to vote, such a person is subjected to conflicting pressures. Ambivalence and conflict can arise from within the person as well. When the affective and cognitive components of an attitude are not consistent with each other—for example, when we like something we know is bad for us—then it is often difficult to predict the behavior (Norman, 1975). In general, when the components are inconsistent, it is the one that is most closely related to the behavior that will best predict it (Millar & Tesser, 1989).

Relevant to this last point is the frequent finding that attitudes specifically related to the behavior being assessed predict better than attitudes only generally related. For example, general environmental attitudes in one study were not related to a willingness to take action on behalf of the Sierra Club, but attitudes specifically toward the Sierra Club were strongly related (Weigel, Vernon, & Tognacci, 1974). Attitudes toward birth control correlated only .08 with a woman's use of oral contraceptives over a 2-year span, but attitudes toward the pill in particular correlated .7 with that behavior (Davidson & Jaccard, 1979). In a more recent study, students in the United States, Britain, and Sweden were asked both general attitudes toward nuclear war and specific attitudes toward nuclear war, nuclear weapons, and nuclear power plants. Again, specific attitudes were much better predictors of activist behaviors (such as writing a letter to a newspaper or signing a petition) than more general attitudes (Newcomb, Rabow, & Hernandez, 1992).

Attitudes based on direct experience predict behavior better than do attitudes formed from just reading or hearing about an issue (Fazio, 1990). For example, during a housing shortage at a university, many freshmen had to spend the first few weeks of the term in crowded temporary housing. Researchers measured attitudes of students toward the housing crisis and their willingness to sign and distribute petitions or to join committees to study it. For students who actually had to live in the temporary housing, there was a high correlation between their attitude toward the crisis and their willingness to take action to solve it. But for students who had not directly experienced the temporary housing, no such correlation existed (Regan & Fazio, 1977). There are many more examples of a strong relationship between behaviors and attitudes based on direct experiences, and these have been interpreted as evidence for the self-perception process, described earlier, in which individuals infer their attitudes from observations of their own behaviors (Fazio & Zanna, 1981).

One reason that attitudes formed through direct experience may relate more closely to behavior is that they tend to be highly *accessible* to the individual, that is, they come quickly and readily to mind (Fazio, 1989). This was illustrated in a study of voters in the 1984 presidential election between Republican Ronald Reagan and his Democratic opponent, Walter Mondale. The researchers asked people in a shopping mall to respond to a number of attitude statements about Reagan by pressing one of five buttons labeled "Strongly agree" to "Strongly disagree." The faster they pushed a button, the more accessible the attitude was considered to be. When contacted after the election, it was found that voters with highly accessible attitudes showed a correlation of .89 between their attitudes and their presidential vote, compared with a correlation of .66 for voters with less accessible attitudes (Fazio & Williams, 1986).

And finally, there is evidence that people who are more aware of their attitudes are more likely to show attitude-behavior consistency. This is true for people who are generally more focused on their thoughts and feelings as part of their personalities (Scheier, Buss, & Buss, 1978) and for people who are placed in situations designed to make them more aware (for example, in front of a mirror or video camera) (Hutton & Baumeister, 1992; Carver & Scheier, 1981; Pryor, 1977).

Interestingly, however, when people are first asked to ponder the *reasons* for their attitudes, their attitudes become less predictive of their behavior. Apparently, when we first analyze how we feel, we cognitively "derive" our attitudes on the basis of our intuitive theories of what attitudes *should* plausibly follow from such reasons. This logically derived attitude is frequently different from our actual affective feelings (Wilson, Dunn, Kraft, & Lisle, 1989). This is similar to an effect we discussed earlier: When people are asked to account for their preferences, behaviors, and emotional states, they tend to identify causes that seem plausible—even when those causes are not operative—and to overlook actual causes that seem less plausible (Nisbett & Wilson, 1977).

COGNITIVE DISSONANCE THEORY   Our discussion of attitude-behavior consistency has covered only half the topic so far. We have examined how attitudes might lead to behavior, but it is also possible for behavior to lead to attitudes. The most influential theory of this sequence of events has been Leon Festinger's theory of cognitive dissonance. Like cognitive consistency theories in general, cognitive dissonance theory assumes that there is a drive toward cognitive consistency; two cognitions that are inconsistent with one another will

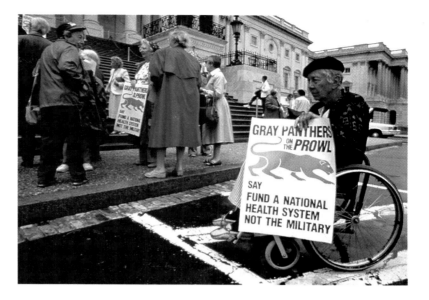

produce discomfort that motivates the person to remove the inconsistency and bring the cognitions into harmony. This inconsistency-produced discomfort is called **cognitive dissonance** (Festinger, 1957).

Although cognitive dissonance theory addresses several kinds of inconsistency, it has been the most provocative in predicting that engaging in behavior that is counter to one's attitudes creates dissonance pressure to change the attitudes so they are consistent with the behavior. The theory further states that engaging in counterattitudinal behavior produces the most dissonance, and hence the most attitude change, when there are no compensating consonant (that is, consistent) reasons for engaging in the behavior. This was illustrated in an experiment that we have already discussed in the context of self-perception theory, the $1–$20 induced-compliance experiment by Festinger and Carlsmith (1959).

Recall that subjects in this study were induced to tell a waiting subject that a series of dull tasks had been fun and interesting. Subjects who had been paid $20 to do this did not change their attitudes, but subjects who had been paid only $1 came to believe that the tasks had, in fact, been enjoyable. According to cognitive dissonance theory, being paid $20 provides a very consonant reason for complying with the experimenter's request to talk to the waiting subject, and hence the person experiences little or no dissonance. The inconsistency between the person's behavior and his or her attitude toward the tasks is outweighed by the far greater consistency between the

Attitudes based on direct experience predict behavior better than do attitudes formed from just reading or hearing about an issue.

compliance and the incentive for complying. Accordingly, the subjects who were paid $20 did not change their attitudes; the subjects who were paid $1, however, had no consonant reason for complying. Accordingly, they experienced dissonance, which they reduced by coming to believe that they really did enjoy the tasks. The general conclusion is that dissonance-causing behavior will lead to attitude change in induced-compliance situations when the behavior can be induced with a *minimum* amount of pressure, whether in the form of reward or punishment.

Experiments with children have confirmed the prediction about minimal punishment. If children obey a very mild request not to play with an attractive toy, they come to believe that the toy is not as attractive as they first thought—a belief that is consistent with their observation that they are not playing with it. But if the children refrain from playing with the toy under a strong threat of punishment, they do not change their liking for the toy (Freedman, 1965; Aronson & Carlsmith, 1963).

Cognitive dissonance theory successfully predicts a number of other attitude change phenomena as well and is one of the best-known theories in social psychology. Over the years, alternative explanations have been offered for some of its findings. For example, we have seen that both cognitive dissonance theory and self-perception theory claim to explain the results of induced-compliance studies.

In general, each of the alternative theories has generated data that the other theories cannot explain and several investigators have now concluded that all the theories may be correct—each under slightly different circumstances—and that the focus of research should be on specifying when and where each theory applies (Baumeister & Tice, 1984; Paulhus, 1982; Fazio, Zanna, & Cooper, 1977).

INTERPERSONAL ATTRACTION

In our discussion of attitudes, we distinguished between the cognitive and affective components—thinking and feeling. There is, however, no area of human behavior in which

cognitions and affects are more complexly intertwined than in interpersonal attraction—liking, loving, and sexual desire. Research in these areas has often confirmed common knowledge, but it has also produced a number of surprises and contradictions. We begin with liking—namely, friendship and the early stages of more intimate relationships.

LIKING

When Great Britain's Prince Charles married Lady Diana Spencer, social psychologists were not surprised that he married "the girl next door," an attractive woman whom he had known for years and who shared many of his social background characteristics and attitudes. As we shall see, these are precisely the determinants of interpersonal attraction: physical attractiveness, proximity, familiarity, and similarity. As this ill-fated couple also illustrates, however, these factors are not always sufficient to sustain a long-term relationship.

PHYSICAL ATTRACTIVENESS   To most of us there is something mildly undemocratic about the possibility that a person's physical appearance is a determinant of how well others like him or her. Unlike character and personality, physical appearance is a factor over which we have little control, and hence it seems unfair to use it as a criterion for liking someone. In fact, surveys taken over a span of several decades have shown that people do not rank physical attractiveness as very important in their liking of other people (Buss & Barnes, 1986; Hudson & Hoyt, 1981; Tesser & Brodie, 1971; Perrin, 1921).

But research on actual behavior shows otherwise (see Brehm, 1992, for a review). One group of psychologists set up a "computer dance" in which college men and women were randomly paired with one another. At intermission everyone filled out an anonymous questionnaire evaluating his or her date. In addition, the experimenters obtained several personality test scores for each person, as well as an independent estimate of his or her physical attractiveness. The results showed that only physical attractiveness played a role in how much the person was liked by his or her partner. None of the measures of intelligence, social skills, or personality was related to the partners' liking for one another (Walster,

Aronson, Abrahams, & Rottmann, 1966). This experiment has now been replicated many times, including one that focused on gay men (Sergios & Cody, 1985), and all have shown similar results. Moreover, the importance of physical attractiveness continues to operate not only on first dates but on subsequent ones as well (Mathes, 1975).

The importance of physical attractiveness is not confined just to dating and mating patterns. For example, physically attractive boys and girls (5 and 6 years of age) are more popular with their peers than are less attractive children (Dion & Berscheid, 1972). Even adults are affected by a child's physical attractiveness. One investigator had women read a description of an aggressive act committed by a 7-year-old child. The description was accompanied by a photograph of either an attractive or an unattractive child. The women believed that the attractive child was less likely than the unattractive child to commit a similar aggressive act in the future (Dion, 1972).

Why is physical attractiveness so important? Part of the reason is that our own social standing and self-esteem are enhanced when we are seen with physically attractive companions. Both men and women are rated more favorably when they are with an attractive romantic partner or friend than when they are with an unattractive companion (Sheposh, Deming, & Young, 1977; Sigall & Landy, 1973). But there is an interesting twist to this: Both men and women are rated less favorably when they are seen with a *stranger* who is physically more attractive than they (Kernis & Wheeler, 1981). Apparently they suffer by comparison when compared with the other person. This effect has been found in other studies. For example, male college students who had just watched a television show starring beautiful young women gave lower attractiveness ratings to a photograph of a more typical-looking woman—as did both men and women who were first shown a photograph of a highly attractive woman (Kenrick & Gutierres, 1980).

Fortunately, there is hope for the unbeautiful among us. First of all, physical attractiveness appears to decline in importance when a permanent partner is being chosen (Stroebe, Insko, Thompson, & Layton, 1971). And, as we shall see, several other factors can work in our favor.

PROXIMITY An examination of 5,000 marriage license applications in Philadelphia in the 1930s found that one-third of the couples lived within five blocks of each other (Rubin, 1973). Research shows that the best single predictor of whether two people are friends is how far apart they live. In a study of friendship patterns in apartment houses, residents were asked to name the three people they saw socially most often. Residents mentioned 41 percent of neighbors who lived in the apartment next door, 22 percent of those who lived two doors away (about 30 feet) and only 10 percent of those who lived at the other end of the hall (Festinger, Schachter, & Back, 1950).

Studies of college dormitories show the same effect. After a full academic year, roommates were twice as likely as floormates to be friends, and floormates were more than twice as likely as dormitory residents in general to be friends (Priest & Sawyer, 1967). A study of male trainees at the training academy of the Maryland State Police is even more striking. The academy assigns trainees to dormitory rooms and classroom seats by name in alphabetical order. Thus the closer two trainees' last names are alphabetically, the more likely they are to spend time in close proximity to one another. The researchers asked trainees who had been at the academy for 6 months to name their three closest friends there. Despite an intensive training course in which all trainees get to know one another quite well, there was a strong alphabetical proximity effect. On the average, each person chosen as a best friend was only 4.5 letters away from the person who chose him—an alphabetical proximity significantly closer than the 15.3 letters expected by chance (Segal, 1974).

There are cases, of course, in which neighbors and roommates hate one another, and

Certainly, unbeknownst to William Evans, the perfect woman for him is a waitress in Caracas named Ramona. Good luck, Bill.

the major exception to the friendship-promoting effect of proximity seems to occur when there are initial antagonisms. In a test of this, a subject waited in a laboratory with a female confederate who treated the subject pleasantly or unpleasantly. When she was pleasant, the closer she sat to the subject the better she was liked; when she was unpleasant, the closer she sat to the subject, the less she was liked. Proximity simply increased the intensity of the initial reaction (Schiffenbauer & Schiavo, 1976). But because most initial encounters probably range from neutral to pleasant, the most frequent result of sustained proximity is friendship.

Those who believe in miracles when it comes to matters of the heart may believe that there is a perfect mate chosen for each of us waiting to be discovered somewhere in the world. But if this is true, the far greater miracle is the frequency with which fate conspires to place this person within walking distance.

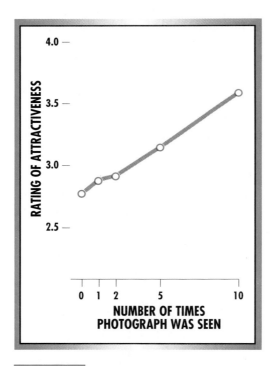

FIGURE 17-4

Familiarity Breeds Liking *Subjects were asked to rate photographs of unknown faces according to how much they thought they would like the person. The lowest ratings of liking were made by subjects who had never seen the photograph before; the highest ratings of liking were made by subjects who had seen the photograph most often.* (After Zajonc, 1968)

FAMILIARITY One of the major reasons that proximity creates liking is that it increases *familiarity,* and there is now abundant evidence that familiarity all by itself—sheer exposure—increases liking (Zajonc, 1968). This *familiarity-breeds-liking* effect is a very general phenomenon. For example, rats repeatedly exposed to either the music of Mozart or Schoenberg enhance their liking for the composer they have heard, and humans repeatedly exposed to selected nonsense syllables or Chinese characters come to prefer those they have seen most often. The effect even occurs when individuals are unaware that they have been previously exposed to the stimuli (Bornstein, 1992; Bornstein & D'Agostino, 1992; Moreland & Zajonc, 1979; Wilson, 1979). More germane to the present discussion is a study in which subjects were exposed to pictures of faces and then asked how much they thought they would like the person shown. The more frequently they had seen a particular face, the more they said they liked it and thought they would like the person (Zajonc, 1968)—see Figure 17-4. Similar results are obtained when individuals are exposed to one another in real life (Moreland & Beach, 1992).

In one clever demonstration of the familiarity-breeds-liking effect, the investigators took photographs of college women and then prepared prints of both the original face and its mirror image. These prints were then shown to the women themselves, their female friends, and their lovers. The women themselves preferred the mirror-image prints by a margin of 68 percent to 32 percent, but the friends and lovers preferred the nonreversed prints by a margin of 61 percent to 39 percent (Mita, Dermer, & Knight, 1977). Can you guess why?

The moral is clear. If you are not beautiful or you find your admiration of someone unreciprocated, be persistent and hang around. Proximity and familiarity are your most powerful weapons.

SIMILARITY An old saying declares that opposites attract, and lovers are fond of recounting how different they are from each other: "I love boating, but she prefers mountain climbing." "I'm in engineering, but he's a history major." What such lovers overlook is that they both like outdoor activities; they are both preprofessionals; they are both Democrats; they are both the same nationality; the same religion; the same social class; the same educational level; and they are probably within 3 years of each other in age and within 5 IQ points of each other in intelligence. In short, the old saying is mostly false.

Research all the way back to 1870 supports this conclusion. Over 99 percent of the married couples in the United States are of the same race, and most are of the same religion. Moreover, statistical surveys show that husbands and wives are significantly similar to each other not only in sociological characteristics—such as age, race, religion, education, and socioeconomic class—but also with respect to psychological characteristics like intelligence and physical characteristics such as height and eye color (Rubin, 1973). A study of dating couples finds the same patterns, in addition to finding that couples were also similar in their attitudes about sexual behavior and sex roles. Moreover, couples who were most similar in background at the beginning of the study were most likely to be together a year later (Hill, Rubin, & Peplau, 1976). Of particular pertinence to our earlier discussion is the finding that couples are closely matched on physical attractiveness as well (Feingold, 1988).

For example, in one study, judges rated photographs of each partner of 99 couples for physical attractiveness without knowing who was paired with whom. The physical attrac-tiveness ratings of the couples matched each other significantly more closely than did the ratings of photographs that were randomly paired into couples (Murstein, 1972). Similar results were obtained in a real-life field study in which separate observers rated the physical attractiveness of members of couples in bars and theater lobbies and at social events (Silverman, 1971).

This matching of couples on physical attractiveness appears to come about because we weigh a potential partner's attractiveness against the probability that the person would be willing to pair up with us. Put bluntly, less attractive people seek less attractive partners because they expect to be rejected by someone more attractive than themselves. A study of a video dating service found that both men and women were most likely to pursue a relationship with someone who matched them in physical attractiveness. Only the most attractive people sought dates with the most attractive partners (Folkes, 1982). The overall result of this chilling marketplace process is attractiveness similarity: Most of us end up with partners who are about as attractive as we are.

But similarities on dimensions other than physical attractiveness are probably even more important over the long-term course of a relationship. A longitudinal study of 135 married couples, discussed in Chapter 12, found that spouses who were more similar to

Partners in successful long-term relationships tend to be similar to one another on sociological characteristics (such as age, race, education), interests, personality traits, and even physical attractiveness.

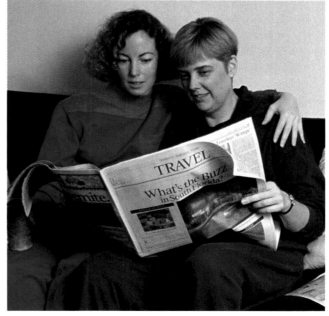

each other in personality also resembled each other more in terms of how much they enjoyed similar daily activities like visiting friends, going out for dinner, and participating in community activities and professional meetings. These couples also reported less marital conflict and greater closeness, friendliness, and marital satisfaction than less similar spouses (Caspi & Herbener, 1990).

In an ambitious study of similarity and friendship, male students received free room for the year in a large house at the University of Michigan in exchange for their participation. On the basis of information from tests and questionnaires, some men were assigned roommates who were quite similar to them and others were assigned roommates who were quite dissimilar. The investigator observed the friendship patterns that developed over the course of the year, obtaining more questionnaire and attitude data from the participants at regular intervals. In all other respects the men lived as they would in any dormitory.

Roommates who were initially similar generally liked each other and ended up as better friends than those who were dissimilar. When the study was repeated with a new group of men the next year, however, the familiarity-breeds-liking effect turned out to be even more powerful than similarity. Regardless of whether low or high similarity had been the basis for room assignments, roommates came to like each other (Newcomb, 1961).

One reason that similarity produces liking is probably that people value their own opinions and preferences and enjoy being with others who validate their choices, possibly boosting their self-esteem in the process. But perhaps the major reason that similarity produces liking is just a repeat of factors we have seen before—proximity and familiarity. Both social norms and situational circumstances throw us together with people who are like us. Most religious groups prefer (or insist) that their members date and mate within the religion, and cultural norms regulate what is considered acceptable in terms of race and age matches—a couple comprising an older woman and a younger man is still viewed as inappropriate. Situational circumstances also play an important role. Many couples meet in college or graduate school, thus ensuring that they will be similar in educational level,

general intelligence, professional aspirations, and probably in age and socioeconomic status. Moreover, tennis players will have met on the tennis courts, political liberals at a pro-choice rally, and gay people at a gay pride parade or a meeting of the Lesbian, Gay, and Bisexual Task Force.

Despite all this, it is often suggested that the saying that opposites attract may still apply to certain complementary personality traits (Winch, Ktsanes, & Ktsanes, 1954). To take the most obvious example, one partner may be quite dominant and thus require someone who is relatively more submissive. A person with strong preferences may do best with someone who is very flexible or even wishy-washy. But despite the plausibility of this complementarity hypothesis, there is not much evidence for it (Levinger, Senn, & Jorgensen, 1970). In one study, marital adjustment among couples married for up to 5 years was found to depend more on similarity than on complementarity (Meyer & Pepper, 1977). Attempts to identify the pairs of personality traits that bring about complementarity have not been very successful (Strong et al., 1988). But there is one notable exception: sex. Most people choose members of the opposite sex to be their romantic and sexual partners. We will return to this apparent paradox later.

ROMANTIC/SEXUAL ATTRACTION AND LOVE

Love is more than just strong liking. Most of us know people we like very much but do not love, and some of us have felt even passionate attraction for someone we did not particularly like. Research confirms these everyday observations. One of the first researchers to study romantic love compiled a number of statements that people thought reflected liking and loving and constructed separate scales to measure each (Rubin, 1973). Items on the liking scale tap the degree to which the other person is regarded as likable, respected, admired, and having maturity and good judgment. Items on the love scale tap three main themes: a sense of attachment ("It would be hard for me to get along without _____"), a sense of caring for the other person ("I would do almost anything for _____"), and a sense of trust ("I feel that I can confide in _____ about virtually everything"). The two scales are only moderately correlated with each other: .56 for men and .36 for women.

LOVE AND MARRIAGE The concept of romantic love is an old one, but the belief that it has much to do with marriage is more recent and far from universal. In some non-Western cultures, marriage is still considered to be a contractual or financial arrangement that has nothing whatever to do with love. In our own society, the link between love and marriage has actually become stronger over the past 30 years. In 1976, college students were asked "if a man (woman) had all the other qualities you desired, would you marry this person if you were not in love with him (her)?" About 65 percent of the men said no, but only 24 percent of the women said no (only 4 percent actually said yes; the majority of women were undecided) (Kephart, 1967). The recent feminist movement had just begun at that time, and it may be that women were then more likely than now to consider marriage a necessary condition for their own financial security. When the survey was repeated in 1984, 85 percent of both men and women said that they would refuse to marry without being in love (Simpson, Campbell, & Berscheid, 1986).

PASSIONATE AND COMPANIONATE LOVE Several social scientists have attempted to distinguish different kinds of love. One of the most widely accepted distinctions is between *passionate*

love and *companionate* love (Hatfield, 1988; Peele, 1988).

Passionate love is defined as an intensely emotional state in which "tender and sexual feelings, elation and pain, anxiety and relief, altruism and jealousy coexist in a confusion of feelings" (Berscheid & Walster, 1978, p. 177). It has been proposed that the experience of passionate love combines physiological arousal with the perception that the arousal is evoked by the beloved (Berscheid & Walster, 1974). (See the Critical Discussion, Producing Passion with Extrinsic Arousal.)

In contrast, **companionate love** is defined as "the affection we feel for those with whom our lives are deeply intertwined" (Hatfield, 1988, p. 205; Berscheid & Walster, 1978, p. 177). The characteristics of companionate love are trust, caring, tolerance of the partner's flaws and idiosyncrasies, and an emotional tone of warmth and affection rather than high-pitched emotional passion. As a relationship continues over time, interdependence grows and the potential for strong emotion actually increases. This can be seen when long-time partners experience intense feelings of loneliness and desire when temporarily separated from each other or in the emotional devastation typically experienced by someone who loses a long-time partner. But, paradoxically, because companionate couples become so compatible and coordinated in their daily routines, the actual frequency of strong emotions is usually fairly low (Berscheid, 1983).

The passionate component of romantic love becomes less important than the companionate component in later life.

In his first-century Roman handbook *The Art of Love,* Ovid offered advice on romantic conquest to both men and women. Among his more intriguing suggestions to a man was that he take a woman in whom he is interested to the gladiator contests, where she could be easily aroused to passion. He did not say why this should be so, however. It was not until 1887 that a psychological explanation for this bit of wisdom was offered:

Love can only be excited by strong and vivid emotion, and it is almost immaterial whether these emotions are agreeable or disagreeable. The Cid wooed the proud heart of Donna Ximene, whose father he had slain, by shooting one after another of her pet pigeons. (Adolf Horwicz, quoted in Finck, 1887, p. 240)

These romantic tactics should strike a familiar chord. As discussed both in Chapter 11 and earlier in this chapter in the discussion of self-perception, we often judge what emotion we are experiencing through a process of cognitive appraisal. Although the physiological arousal of our autonomic nervous system provides the cues that we are experiencing an emotion, the more subtle judgment of *which* emotion we are experiencing often depends on our cognitive appraisals of the surrounding circumstances.

Ovid and Horwicz were thus suggesting that a person who is physiologically aroused (by whatever means) might attribute that arousal to love or sexual passion—to the advantage of any would-be lover who happens to be at hand.

There is now solid experimental evidence for this phenomenon but disagreement about the process underlying it. In one set of studies, male subjects were physiologically aroused

by running in place, by hearing an audiotape, of a comedy routine, or by hearing an audiotape of a grisly killing. They then viewed a taped interview with a woman who was either attractive or unattractive. Finally, they rated the woman on several dimensions, including her attractiveness, her sexiness, and the degree to which they would be interested in dating her and kissing her. The results showed that no matter how the arousal had been elicited, subjects were more sexually responsive to the attractive woman and less sexually responsive to the unattractive women than were control subjects who had not been aroused. In other words, the arousal intensified both positive or negative reactions to the woman, depending on which was cognitively appropriate (White, Fishbein, & Rutstein, 1981).

This effect of extrinsic arousal is not limited to the individual's cognitive appraisal of his or her emotional state. In two studies, men or women watched a sequence of two videotapes. The first portrayed either an anxiety-inducing or non-anxiety-inducing scene; the second videotape portrayed a nude heterosexual couple engaging in sexual foreplay. Preexposure to the anxiety-inducing scene produced greater penile tumescence in men and greater vaginal blood volume increases in women in response to the erotic scene than did preexposure to non-anxiety-inducing tapes (Wolchik et al., 1980; Hoon, Wincze, & Hoon, 1977).

Several explanations for this effect have been offered. The attribution (or misattribution) explanation is that the individual mistakenly attributes his or her arousal to the target person, thereby interpreting it as roman-

tic or sexual feelings (or possibly as revulsion in the presence of a particularly unattractive person). A second explanation is that the effect reflects *excitation transfer*—discussed briefly in Chapter 11—in which arousal from one source can carry over to intensify the arousal experienced from a different source. For example, a man will show more aggression when provoked if he has first been exposed to sexually stimulating materials, including nonviolent materials (Zillmann, 1984, 1978; Zillmann & Bryant, 1974). By extension, arousal produced by exercise might carry over to intensify sexual arousal.

A third explanation is *response facilitation,* a well known phenomenon in psychology. When an organism is aroused, whatever response it is most likely to make in the situation—called the dominant response—will be facilitated or intensified. If the subject's dominant response in these studies is attraction to the woman, then this will be intensified by the additional arousal. If the subject's dominant response in the situation is *not* to be attracted to the woman, then the arousal would intensify this negative response, exactly what was found in the study described above (Allen, Kenrick, Linder, & McCall, 1989).

Experimental attempts to determine which explanation is the most valid have produced mixed results and the dispute is not yet settled (McClanahan et al., 1990; Allen, Kenrick, Linder, & McCall, 1989; White & Kight, 1984). But whatever the specific mechanism, the phenomenon itself appears to be genuine and solidly established. Would-be lovers of both sexes should feel encouraged to buy a pair of tickets to the hockey game.

Many of the young men and women in the survey cited above stated that if love disappears from a marriage, that is sufficient reason to end it. Those young people who equate

love with only its passionate variant, however, are likely to be disappointed. Most successful long-term couples emphasize the companionate elements of their relationship, and both theory and research suggest that the intense feelings that characterize passionate love are unlikely to persist over time (Berscheid, 1983; Solomon & Corbit, 1974). As the sixteenth century writer Giraldi put it: "The history of a love affair is in some sense the drama of its fight against time."

This is illustrated in a study that compared long-term marriages in the United States—where couples claim to marry for love—with marriages in Japan that had been arranged by the couples' parents. As expected, the American marriages started out with a higher level of expressed love and sexual interest than did the Japanese arranged marriages. But the amount of love expressed decreased in both groups until there were no differences between the two groups after 10 years. Nevertheless, many couples in this study reported quite gratifying marriages, marriages that had evolved into a deep companionate love characterized by communication between the partners, an equitable division of labor, and equality of decision-making power (Blood, 1967).

The moral is that passionate love might be terrific for starters, but the sustaining forces of a good long-term relationship are less exciting, undoubtedly require more work, and have more to do with equality than with passion. In fact, there may even be a built-in incompatibility between passionate and companionate love—as we shall now see.

FAMILIARITY, SIMILARITY, AND SEXUAL ATTRACTION We saw earlier that two of the best predictors of whether or not two people will like each other are familiarity and similarity. Paradoxically, however, most people do not choose members of their own sex to be their romantic and sexual partners. Similarly, boys and girls who are raised collectively on communes in Israel rarely marry one another; they feel *too* familiar with one another, more like brothers and sisters than potential lovers (Shepher, 1971). Thus it may be that, although familiarity and similarity promote friendship and compatibility, it is necessary to have some degree of *unfamiliarity* or *dissimilarity* to spark passionate love or sexual attraction (D. Bem, 1995; Tripp, 1987; Bell, 1982).

This hypothesis has now been elaborated into a developmental theory of sexual attraction by Daryl Bem (1995), which we introduced in Chapter 10 when we discussed sexual orientation. The theory begins with the observation that the sex-based division of labor and sex-role norms in most cultures prompt most boys and girls to see each other as very different from one another. To the extent that they engage in sex-typical and sex-segregated activities and play groups, children will be more familiar with same-sex peers than with opposite-sex peers. Thus most children will feel more comfortable with children of their own sex and more uncomfortable with children of the opposite sex.

The theory next proposes that this discomfort produces generalized (nonsexual) arousal. For the typical girl this arousal may be felt as mild fear or apprehension in the presence of boys; for the typical boy, it may be felt as awkwardness or contempt in the presence of girls ("girls are yucky"). Finally, the theory generalizes the findings of the studies discussed in the Critical Discussion (Producing Passion With Extrinsic Arousal) by proposing that this generalized arousal of childhood is transformed in later years into erotic arousal or sexual attraction—long after the original reason for the arousal has been forgotten. Thus sex-typical children will come to feel sexual attraction for persons of the opposite sex while feeling comfortable but nonerotic friendship with persons of the same sex. Thus does "exotic become erotic."

As we discuss in detail in Chapter 10, research on gay men and lesbians provides additional support for the theory. They are much more likely than heterosexual men and women to report that, as children, they had enjoyed activities typical of the opposite sex, had been "pals" with opposite-sex peers, and had "felt different" from same-sex peers as early as grade school (Bell, Weinberg, & Hammersmith, 1981a, 1981b). Thus, like heterosexual men and women, gay men and lesbians choose their romantic and sexual partners from the less familiar, more "exotic" set of potential lovers.

TRIANGULAR THEORY OF LOVE Since the distinction between passionate and companionate love was introduced, similar but more differentiated classifications have been proposed. One of these divides love into three components: *intimacy, passion,* and *commitment* (Sternberg, 1986). Intimacy is the emotional component and involves closeness and sharing of feelings. Passion is the motivational component that captures sexual attraction and the

TABLE 17-2

Triangular Theory of Love   *The three dimensions of love combine to produce eight types of love relationships.* (After Sternberg, 1986)

	INTIMACY	**PASSION**	**COMMITMENT**
Nonlove	Low	Low	Low
Liking	High	Low	Low
Infatuated love	Low	High	Low
Romantic love	High	High	Low
Empty love	Low	Low	High
Companionate love	High	Low	High
Fatuous love	Low	High	High
Consummate love	High	High	High

romantic feeling of being "in love." Commitment is the cognitive component that reflects the person's intention to remain in the relationship. Combining these components in different ways yields the eight kinds of relationships shown in Table 17-2. As can be seen, passionate love is split in this scheme into two types: *infatuated* love and *romantic* love. Both are characterized by high passion and low commitment, but infatuated love is low on intimacy, whereas romantic love is high on intimacy. Companionate love is characterized by high intimacy and commitment but low passion.

ATTACHMENT STYLES   One recent classification of love proposes that adult love styles recapitulate the three kinds of attachment that infants show toward their primary caregivers (see Chapter 3): securely attached, insecurely attached/avoidant, and insecurely attached/anxious-ambivalent. After being separated from the primary caregiver—usually the mother—securely attached children seek to interact with her upon her return; insecurely attached/avoidant children show conspicuous avoidance of interaction upon her return; and insecurely attached/anxious-ambivalent children show resistance to her upon her return (for example, they may cry to be picked up but then squirm angrily to get down).

Two researchers developed a method of assessing whether adult romantic relationships show these same patterns (Shaver, Hazan, & Bradshaw, 1988; Hazan & Shaver, 1987). They created brief descriptions of each style and asked subjects to check which one best fit them:

(Secure) I find it relatively easy to get close to others and am comfortable depending on them and having them depend on me. I don't often worry about being abandoned or about someone getting too close to me.

(Avoidance) I am somewhat uncomfortable being close to others; I find it difficult to trust them completely, difficult to allow myself to depend on them. I am nervous when anyone gets too close, and often, love partners want me to be more intimate than I feel comfortable with.

(Ambivalent) I find that others are reluctant to get as close as I would like. I often worry that my partner doesn't really love me or won't want to stay with me. I want to merge completely with another person, and this desire sometimes scares people away.

When a large sample of adults were asked to identify their love styles, about 56 percent were in the secure category, 25 percent were avoidant, and 19 percent were anxious/ambivalent. These percentages are quite similar to those obtained in studies of children. They also found that secure adults reported warmer and more loving relationships with their parents than adults in the other two categories. Avoidant adults tended to report that their mothers had been cold and rejecting. Again, these tend to parallel findings from studies of children.

More recent research suggests that there may be two kinds of avoidant people: those who strive for independence and self-sufficiency and play down the importance of close relationships and dependency on others, and those who want to have close relationships but fear being hurt (Bartholomew & Horowitz, 1991).

Still other classifications of love have been proposed. For example, one draws an analogy with colors, proposing three primary and three secondary "colors" of love (Lee, 1988, 1977, 1973; Hendrick & Hendrick, 1986). Recent attempts to integrate these several classification systems, however, have produced inconsistent results (Hendrick & Hendrick, 1989; Levy & Davis, 1988). At the moment, the distinction between passionate and companionate love has the widest consensus behind it (Brehm, 1992).

PAIR BONDING AND MATING STRATEGIES

One of the newest approaches to romantic and sexual attraction is also one of the oldest: Darwin's theory of evolution. As we noted in Chapter 1, evolutionary psychology is concerned with the origins of psychological mechanisms. The key idea is that, just like biological mechanisms, psychological mechanisms must have evolved over millions of years by a process of natural selection, which means that they have a genetic basis and have proved useful to the human species in the past for solving some problems of survival or in increasing the chances of reproducing.

The application of evolutionary principles to social behavior is part of a relatively new discipline known as sociobiology, and the renewed interest in evolution among social psychologists has led to a (sometimes controversial) reexamination of several behavioral phenomena. Among these are pair bonding in humans and differences between men and women in sexual behavior and mating strategies.

From the perspective of evolution, men and women mate in order to produce offspring who will pass down their genes to future generations. To do this, individuals must solve several problems, including: (a) winning out over competitors in gaining access to fertile members of the opposite sex; (b) selecting mates who have the greatest reproductive potential; (c) engaging in the necessary social and sexual behavior to achieve conception; (d) preventing the mate from defecting or deserting; (e) ensuring the survival and reproductive success of one's offspring (Buss, 1991).

According to sociobiologists, humans have evolved to form intense, long-term bonds with a partner to ensure that human offspring survive to reproductive age. As we noted in Chapter 3, the more complex an organism's nervous system is, the longer the time required to reach maturity. A chimpanzee will be a functioning adult member of its species years before a human of the same age is ready

One theory of love suggests that adult love relationships recapitulate the styles of attachment that the individuals showed as infants toward their primary care givers. For example, adults who form secure romantic relationships report that they had warm, loving, relationships with their parents.

to fend for itself. Accordingly, it has been important in the history of our species to have the male stick around to defend, provide for, and help rear the young. In contrast to humans, both male and female chimpanzees are quite promiscuous, and males have little or no involvement in rearing the young.

Sociobiologists further argue that because men and women play different roles in reproduction, the mating tactics and strategies used by the two sexes might also have evolved to be different as well. Because it is theoretically possible for a man to father hundreds of children, it is to his evolutionary advantage to impregnate as many women as possible to pass down the greatest number of his own genes. The woman, however, must invest a great deal of time and energy in each birth and can have only a limited number of offspring. Thus, it is to her advantage to be careful to select a mate who is most willing and best able to assist in protecting and raising her children, thereby maximizing the likelihood of passing down her own genes to future generations. This reasoning suggests that evolution would have made men more promiscuous and less discriminating in their choice of sexual partners than women. In fact, it has been documented repeatedly that men are more promiscuous than women in most societies, and societies that permit one man to mate with more than one woman far outnumber those in which one woman may mate with many different men (Wilson, 1978).

Sociobiological theory also predicts that a man should prefer to mate with the most fertile young women available because they are most likely to bear his children. A woman should prefer to mate with a man of high social status and solid material resources, one who can best ensure the survival of the children to adulthood and reproductive success of their own. As a result, sociobiologists predict that men will prefer younger women (with many more years of fertile years ahead of them), whereas woman will prefer older men (who have more resources). This sex difference in mate preference was strongly confirmed in a study of 37 cultures (Buss, 1989).

Sociobiological theorizing has not gone unchallenged. Some critics argue that even if a behavioral pattern appears across many or all cultures, it does not necessarily follow that it is programmed into the human genes.

For example, some universal cross-cultural sex differences may have arisen historically simply because women had less upper body strength and—until very recently in technological societies—were pregnant or nursing during most of their adult lives. This created sex-based divisions of labor in virtually all societies, which placed political power and decision making in the hands of men and confined women to the domestic sphere (S. Bem, 1993). Greater sexual freedom for men could easily emerge from such power differences.

Some critics have also accused sociobiologists of circular reasoning: Sociobiologists, they argue, sometimes observe a behavior and make it a *premise* that the behavior has a genetic basis; they then construct a speculative story to explain how that behavior could have served to maximize the reproductive success of the individual and could thereby have been selected during the course of evolution *if* it were genetically based; this *conjecture* then becomes evidence for the *premise* that the behavior is genetically based (Bleier, 1984).

Accordingly, it is often instructive to ask whether sociobiological reasoning could also have predicted a different or opposite outcome. For example, we have seen the argument that a male's ability to produce many hundreds of offspring would create an evolutionary push toward male promiscuity. But the need to ensure that one's offspring survive to reproductive age—the same need that presumably gave rise to human pair bonding in the first place—would provide an opposing evolutionary push toward monogamy. In other words, sociobiological theorizing could be invoked to explain either male promiscuity or male sexual fidelity.

Despite these criticisms, however, there is no doubt that evolutionary thinking has re-invigorated both personality and social psychology. In addition to its provocative analysis of sex differences in mating strategies, it has prompted new thinking and research about shyness (Baumeister & Tice, 1990), parent-offspring conflict (Daly & Wilson, 1990), and individual differences in sociosexual behavior *within* sex (Simpson & Gangestad, 1992). There is probably no other single principle in the behavioral sciences with as much potential explanatory power as the principle of evolution.

BIOLOGICAL-PSYCHOLOGICAL PERSPECTIVES

With its strong emphasis on the situational control of behavior, social psychology would appear to be the subfield of psychology for which a biological perspective would be the least relevant. And, except for some early speculation about social "instincts" at the turn of the century, this has generally been true. But as we have just seen, the emergence of sociobiological theorizing seems likely to change that. Even social psychologists who study the processes of social cognition now theorize about how and why our strategies for processing social information might have evolved (Nisbett & Ross, 1980). Social psychologists are now more likely than in the past to ask, for example, why schematic processing might have evolved as one of our cognitive strategies—especially when it appears to produce so many perceptual and inferential biases and errors. And this questioning, in turn, leads to experiments that demonstrate how schematic processing enables us to process otherwise overwhelming amounts of information efficiently with only a small sacrifice in accuracy.

Similarly, many social psychological topics, such as sexual attraction and orientation, raise nature-nurture questions—discussed more extensively in Chapter 10—that require both a biological and psychological perspective if they are to be fully answered. In short, there is now virtually no major subfield of psychology that is not aided in its quest for understanding by both biological and psychological perspectives.

CHAPTER SUMMARY

1. *Social psychology* is the study of how people perceive, think, and feel about their social world and how they interact and influence one another. Beginning with the premise that human behavior is a function of both the person and the situation, social psychologists emphasize the *power of a situation* and the importance of the person's *interpretation of a situation* in determining social behavior.

2. In attempting to understand others and ourselves, we construct intuitive theories of human behavior by performing the same tasks as a formal scientist: *collecting data, detecting covariation,* and *inferring causality.* Our theories themselves, however, can shape our perceptions of the data, distort our estimates of covariation, and bias our evaluations of cause and effect. For example, we tend to notice and recall vivid information more than nonvivid information, and this biases our social judgments.

3. *Schematic processing* is the perceiving and interpreting of incoming information in terms of simplified memory structures called *schemas.* Schemas constitute minitheories of everyday objects and events. They allow us to process social information efficiently by permitting us to encode and to remember only the unique or most prominent features of a new object or event.

4. Because schemas constitute simplifications of reality, schematic processing produces biases and errors in our processing of social information. In forming impressions of other people, for example, we are prone to the *primacy effect;* the first information we receive evokes an initial schema and, hence, becomes more powerful in determining our impression than does later information. In general, schematic processing produces perceptions that are resistant to change and relatively impervious to new data.

5. We are not very accurate at detecting covariations or correlations between events in everyday life. When our schemas or theories lead us to expect two things to covary, we overestimate their actual correlation; but when we do not have a theory, we underestimate their correlation.

6. *Stereotypes* can be thought of as theories or schemas of covariation. Like other schemas, they are resistant to change. In particular, they lead us overlook the very data that would disconfirm them. Moreover, they can be self-perpetuating and self-fulfilling, because they influence those who hold them to

behave in ways that actually evoke the stereo-typed behavior.

7. *Attribution* is the process by which we attempt to interpret and to explain the behavior of other people—that is, to discern the causes of their actions. One major attribution task is to decide whether someone's action should be attributed to *dispositional* causes (the person's personality or attitudes) or to *situational* causes (social forces or other external circumstances). We tend to give too much weight to dispositional factors and too little to situational factors. This bias has been called the *fundamental attribution error.*

8. *Self-perception theory* proposes that we make judgments about ourselves using the same inferential processes—and making the same kinds of errors—that we use for making judgments about others. For example, we often commit the fundamental attribution error when interpreting our own behavior.

9. *Attitudes* are likes and dislikes—favorable or unfavorable evaluations of and reactions to objects, people, events, or ideas. Attitudes comprise a *cognitive* component, an *affective* component, and a *behavioral* component. A major issue in attitude research is the degree of consistency among a person's attitudes. Despite evidence for attitude consistency in laboratory studies, social scientists are divided in their views about the degree to which citizens hold coherent opinions about social and political issues.

10. Attitudes serve many functions: Attitudes that we hold for practical reasons serve an *instrumental* function; those that help us make sense of the world serve a *knowledge* function; those that express our values or reflect our self-concepts serve a *value-expressive* function; those that protect us from anxiety or threats to our self-esteem serve an *ego-defensive* function; those that help us feel that we are a part of a social community serve a *social adjustment* function.

11. The *scapegoat theory of prejudice* holds that negative attitudes toward groups sometimes serve an ego-defensive function, leading individuals to *repress* their own undesirable characteristics and to *project* those same characteristics onto other groups. *The Authoritarian Personality* is a classic study in social psychology that tested this theory and described the kind of person who would be particularly likely to hold this kind of prejudice. Negative attitudes toward desegregation

and African-Americans in the American South in the 1950s served primarily a social adjustment function and, hence, changed relatively easily as the social norms changed.

12. Attitudes tend to predict behavior best when they are (a) strong and consistent; (b) specifically related to the behavior being predicted; (c) based on the person's direct experience; and (d) when the individual is self-aware of his or her attitudes. *Cognitive dissonance theory* proposes that when a person's behaviors are inconsistent with his or her attitudes, the discomfort produced by this dissonance leads the person to change the attitudes to be consistent with the behavior.

13. Many factors influence whether we will be attracted to someone. The most important are *physical attractiveness, proximity, familiarity,* and *similarity.* The old saying that "opposites attract" has not been upheld by research—except that most people choose members of the opposite sex to be their romantic and sexual partners. One theory suggests that although similarity increases liking and compatibility, a certain amount of *dissimilarity* is required to spark romantic and sexual attraction; studies of gay men and lesbians provide additional support for the theory.

14. The link between love and marriage is historically recent and far from universal. In our own society the link has become closer over the past 30 years, with more women and men today refusing to marry someone they do not love. There have been several attempts to classify types of love. *Passionate* love is characterized by intense and often conflicting emotions, whereas *companionate* love is characterized by trust, caring, tolerance of the partner's flaws, and an emotional tone of warmth and affection. Even though passionate love decreases over time in long-term relationships, the potential for strong emotion actually increases. But because companionate couples become so compatible in their daily routines, the actual frequency of strong emotions is fairly low.

15. One classification of love divides it into the components of intimacy, passion, and commitment. Another suggests that adult love styles recapitulate the kinds of attachments that individuals had to their primary caregivers as children.

16. Sociobiological theorizing—based on Darwin's theory of evolution—suggests that

humans have evolved to form long-term bonds with a partner because historically such pair bonds have operated to ensure the survival of offspring to reproductive age. A more controversial sociobiological hypothesis is that men and women have evolved to pursue different mating strategies, with men evolving to be more promiscuous and to seek out younger women.

FURTHER READING

Three comprehensive textbooks in social psychology are Aronson, Wilson, and Akert, *Social Psychology* (1994); Baron and Byrne, *Social Psychology* (7th ed., 1994); and Lippa, *Introduction to Social Psychology* (2nd ed., 1994). More advanced treatments are available in Lindzey and Aronson (eds.), *The Handbook of Social Psychology* (3rd ed., 1985).

A major theme of this chapter—that persons act as informal scientists in arriving at social judgments—is treated in detail in Nisbett and Ross, *Human Inference: Strategies and Shortcomings of Social Judgment* (1980). A delightful extension of this basic theme is presented by Gilovich, *How We Know What Isn't So: The Fallibility of Human Reason in Everyday Life* (1991).

A number of books deal in more depth with the other topics discussed. Recommended are Aronson, *The Social Animal* (7th ed., 1995); Brehm, *Intimate Relationships* (2nd ed., 1992); and Ross and Nisbett, *The Person and the Situation: Perspectives of Social Psychology* (1991).

SOCIAL INTERACTION AND INFLUENCE

In Chapter 17, we discussed the part of social psychology that deals with how people think and feel about their social world—their social cognitions and affects. In this chapter we examine how people interact and influence one another. To most people, the term *social influence* connotes direct and deliberate attempts to change our beliefs, attitudes, or behaviors. Parents attempt to get their children to eat spinach; television commercials attempt to induce us to buy a product or vote for a candidate; a religious cult attempts to persuade a person to abandon school, job, or family and serve a "higher" mission.

We react to such social influences in many ways. In some cases, we publicly comply with the wishes of the influencer but do not necessarily change our private beliefs or attitudes— the child eats the spinach but may continue to dislike it. Social psychologists often call this **compliance**. In other cases, we are convinced that the influencer is correct and change our private beliefs and attitudes as well. This has been called **internalization**. And in some cases, we resist the influence, possibly even showing overt rebellion. In this chapter, we shall see instances of compliance, internalization, and resistance.

But many forms of social influence are indirect or unintentional; for example, just being with other people can affect us in diverse ways. And even when we are alone, we continue to be influenced by **social norms**— implicit rules and expectations that dictate what we ought to think and how we ought to behave; these range from the trivial to the profound. Social norms tell us to face forward when riding in an elevator, and they govern how long we can gaze at a stranger before being considered rude. More profoundly, social norms can create and maintain racism, sexism, or homophobia in a society. As we shall see, compliance with orders or requests often depends on our unwitting allegiance to social norms.

Social interaction and influence are central to communal life. Cooperation, altruism, and love all involve social interaction and influence. But practical social problems have historically prompted social psychologists to focus much of their attention on the negative effects of social influence. Accordingly, just as the chapter on psychopathology dwells on the dark side of individual behavior, this chapter focuses disproportionately on the dark side of social behavior. Some of the findings are disturbing, even depressing. But just as the study of psychopathology has led to effective therapies, so too the study of problematic social interactions has led us to more effective ways of dealing with them. By understanding the principles underlying many of our social problems, we simultaneously understand the principles underlying their solutions.

PRESENCE OF OTHERS

SOCIAL FACILITATION

In 1898, the psychologist Norman Triplett was examining the speed records of bicycle racers and he noticed that many cyclists achieved better times when they raced against each other than when they raced against the clock. This led him to perform one of social psychology's earliest laboratory experiments. He instructed children to turn a fishing reel as fast

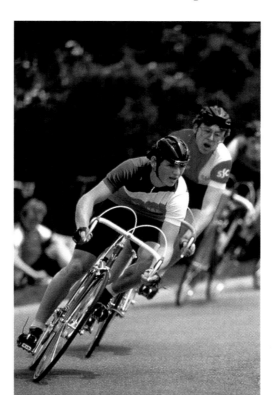

In 1898, psychologist Norman Triplett noticed that cyclists achieved better times when they raced against other cyclists than when they raced against the clock. This led him to study the phenomenon of social facilitation in one of social psychology's earliest laboratory experiments.

as possible for a fixed period of time. Sometimes two children worked at the same time in the same room, each with his or her own reel. Other times they worked alone. Although his published data are difficult to evaluate, Triplett reported that many children worked faster in *coaction*—that is, when another child doing the same task was present—than when they worked alone.

Since this experiment, many studies have demonstrated the facilitating effects of coaction with both human and animal subjects. For example, worker ants in groups will dig more than three times as much sand per ant than when alone (Chen, 1937), many animals will eat more food if other members of their species are present (Platt, Yaksh, & Darby, 1967), and college students will complete more multiplication problems in coaction than when alone (F. H. Allport, 1920, 1924). Soon after Triplett's experiment on coaction, psychologists discovered that the presence of a passive spectator—an audience rather than a coactor—also facilitates performance. For example, the presence of an audience had the same facilitating effect on students' multiplication performance as did that of the coactors in the earlier study (Dashiell, 1930). These coaction and audience effects have been called **social facilitation.**

But even this simple case of social influence turned out to be more complicated than social psychologists first thought. For example, researchers found that subjects made more errors on the multiplication problems when in coaction or in the presence of an audience than when they performed alone (Dashiell, 1930). In other words, the quality of performance declined even though quantity increased. In other studies, however, the quality of performance improved when coactors or audiences were present (for example, Cottrell, 1972; Dashiell, 1935). How can these contradictions be reconciled?

In examining the findings, psychologist Robert Zajonc (1980, 1965) noted that simple responses, highly practiced responses, or instinctive responses (such as eating) were typically facilitated in the presence of coactors or audiences, whereas complex or newly learned responses were typically impaired. He proposed that a long-known principle of motivation could account for the findings: A high level of drive or arousal tends to energize the dominant responses of an organism. If the

mere presence of another member of the species raises the general arousal or drive level of an organism, then the dominant response will be facilitated. For simple or well-learned behaviors, the dominant response is most likely to be the correct response, and performance should be facilitated. For complex behaviors or behaviors just being learned, the dominant or most probable response is likely to be incorrect. On a multiplication problem, for example, there are many wrong responses but only one correct one. Performance should therefore be impaired.

A number of experiments have confirmed these predictions. For example, human subjects learn simple mazes or easy word lists more quickly but complex mazes or difficult word lists more slowly when an audience is present than when it is not (Hunt & Hillery, 1973; Cottrell, Rittle, & Wack, 1967). There is even a study with cockroaches that finds that they run an easy route to escape light more quickly but a difficult route more slowly when other roaches watch from the sidelines (or run with them) than when they run without other roaches present (Zajonc, Heingartner, & Herman, 1969).

Because social facilitation occurs in nonhuman species, it would not seem to require complex cognitive processes. But one theory suggests that social facilitation in humans is due not to the mere presence of others but to feelings of competition or to concerns about being evaluated, and it is these cognitive concerns that raise the drive level. Even the early studies of coaction found that, if all elements of rivalry and competition were removed, social facilitation effects were reduced or eliminated (Dashiell, 1930). Other studies show that audience effects vary depending on how much the person feels that he or she is being evaluated. For example, social facilitation effects are enhanced if an expert watches but diminished if the audience consists only of "undergraduates who want to watch a psychology experiment" (Paulus & Murdock, 1971; Henchy & Glass, 1968). In one study, when the audience wore blindfolds and hence could not watch or evaluate the individual's performance, no social facilitation effects were found (Cottrell, Wack, Sekerak, & Rittle, 1968).

But subjects in these experiments still knew that their performances were being recorded by the experimenter and, accordingly, may still have felt concern about being evaluated even when in the alone or mere presence conditions. Thus, these studies still leave open the question of whether or not social facilitation effects in humans ever arise purely from the mere presence of others. This problem was overcome in a study in which subjects were asked to sit at a computer and provide some "background information before the experiment begins." In the evaluation condition, the experimenter stood behind them and watched; in the mere presence condition, there was a blindfolded person in the room who also wore headphones, faced away from the subject, and was said to be waiting to be in a sensory deprivation experiment.

The computer automatically recorded both how long it took the subject to type his or her name (an easy task) and to type a complex code name (a difficult task). Compared with subjects in the alone condition, subjects in both the evaluation and mere presence conditions performed the easy task more quickly but the difficult task more slowly, thereby demonstrating that social facilitation in humans can, in fact, be produced by the mere presence of others (Schmitt, Gilovich, Goore, & Joseph, 1986).

Two other theories have been proposed to account for social facilitation effects. *Distraction-conflict theory* suggests that the presence of others distracts the person, causing a conflict over how to allocate attention between the others and the task to be performed. It is this attentional conflict—rather than the mere presence of another person or a concern over being evaluated—that raises the drive level and causes social facilitation effects (Baron, 1986; Sanders & Baron, 1975). *Self-presentation theory* proposes that the presence of others enhances the individual's desire to present a favorable image. On easy tasks this leads to more effort and concentration and thus to improved performance. On difficult tasks, however, this desire magnifies the frustrations imposed by the tasks and leads to embarrassment, withdrawal, or excessive anxiety, all of which lead to poorer performance (Bond, 1982). There are research results that support each of these theories, and it seems likely that all of the proposed processes—mere presence, concern over evaluation, distraction-conflict, and desire to present a favorable image—contribute to social facilitation effects (Sanders, 1984).

DEINDIVIDUATION

At about the same time that Triplett was performing his laboratory experiment on social facilitation, another observer of human behavior, Gustave LeBon, was taking a less dispassionate view of group coaction. In his book, *The Crowd* (1895), he complained that "the crowd is always intellectually inferior to the isolated individual. . . . The mob man is fickle, credulous, and intolerant, showing the violence and ferocity of primitive beings . . . women, children, savages, and lower classes . . . operating under the influence of the spinal cord." LeBon believed that the aggressive and immoral behaviors shown by lynch mobs (and, in his view, French revolutionaries) spread by contagion through a mob or crowd like a disease, breaking down a man's moral sense and self-control. This caused crowds to commit destructive acts that no lone individuals—except, of course, women, children, savages, and lower classes—would commit.

Despite his obvious prejudices, LeBon's observations have some validity. The modern counterpart to his theory is built on the concept of **deindividuation,** a concept first proposed by Festinger, Pepitone, and Newcomb (1952) and extended by Zimbardo (1970) and Diener (1980, 1979). Their theories propose that certain conditions that are sometimes present in groups can lead individuals to experience a psychological state of deindividuation, a feeling that they have lost their personal identities and merged anonymously into the group. This produces diminished restraints against impulsive behavior and the other cognitive and emotional conditions associated with unruly mob behavior. The several antecedents and consequences of deindividuation proposed by Diener are illustrated in Figure 18-1. Note that antecedent conditions lead to deindividuation by producing a state of reduced self-awareness in the individual.

In one study of deindividuation, college women, participating in groups of four, were required to deliver electric shocks to another woman who was supposedly in a learning experiment. Half of the women were deindividuated by making them feel anonymous. They were dressed in bulky laboratory coats and hoods that hid their faces, and the experimenter spoke to them only as a group, never referring to any of them by name (see Figure

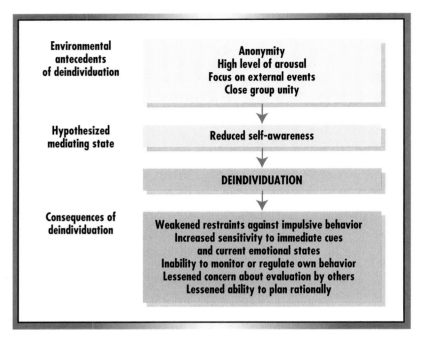

FIGURE 18-1

Antecedents and Consequences of Deindividuation   *One explanation of crowd behavior traces it to a loss of personal identity in certain group situations.* (After Diener, 1979)

18-2). The remaining women were individuated by having them remain in their own clothes and wear large identification tags. In addition, the women in the second group were introduced to one another by name. During the experiment, each woman had a

shock button in front of her that she was to push when the learner made an error. Pushing the button appeared to deliver a shock to the learner. The results showed that the deindividuated women delivered twice as much shock to the learner as did the individuated groups (Zimbardo, 1970).

One clever study was conducted simultaneously at several homes in a community on Halloween. Children out trick-or-treating were greeted at the door by a woman who asked that each child take only one piece of candy. The woman then disappeared into the house briefly, giving the children the opportunity to take more candy. Some of the children had been asked their names while others remained anonymous. Children who came in groups or who remained anonymous stole more candy than did children who came alone or who had given their names to the adult (Diener, Fraser, Beaman, & Kelem, 1976).

These experiments are not definitive, however. For example, you can see from Figure 18-2 that the laboratory coats and hoods in the first study resembled Ku Klux Klan outfits. Similarly, Halloween costumes often represent witches, monsters, or ghosts. These all carry aggressive or negative connotations. It may be that the roles suggested by the costumes rather than the anonymity they provided produced the behavior. To test this possibility, the shock experiment was repeated, but this time each subject wore one of

FIGURE 18-2

Anonymity Produces Deindividuation   *When women were disguised so they felt anonymous, they delivered more shock to another subject than did nondisguised subjects.*

three outfits: a Ku Klux Klan-type costume, a nurse's uniform, or the subject's own clothes. The results of the revised experiment did not replicate those of the original study: Wearing a Ku Klux Klan-type costume had only a small effect on the level of shock the subjects administered. More significantly, those wearing nurses' uniforms actually gave fewer shocks than did the control group who wore their own clothes, suggesting that a uniform encourages the person to play the kind of role it connotes. This study shows that anonymity does not inevitably lead to enhanced aggression (Johnson & Downing, 1979). A more recent study showed that deindividuation led subjects to be both more aggressive and more generous in the same study (Spivey & Prentice-Dunn, 1990).

A second qualification also has emerged from the research: Being in a group is not itself a critical variable in producing deindividuation. Being in a group produces deindividuation only when it provides the other antecedent conditions listed in Figure 18-2, especially anonymity and a reduction of self-awareness (Diener, 1980). Most of the initial studies of deindividuation included both a group context and anonymity, so that it was not possible to identify which was the critical variable.

BYSTANDER INTERVENTION

In earlier chapters, we noted that people do not react simply to the objective features of a situation but to their own subjective interpretations of it. In this chapter we have seen that even social facilitation, a primitive kind of social influence, depends in part on the individual's interpretation of what others are doing or thinking. But as we shall now see, defining or interpreting the situation is often the very mechanism through which individuals influence one another.

In 1964, Kitty Genovese was murdered outside her home in New York City late at night. She fought back, and the murder took over half an hour. At least 38 neighbors heard her screams for help, but nobody came to her aid. No one even called the police.

The American public was horrified by this incident, and social psychologists began to investigate the causes of what at first was termed "bystander apathy." Their work showed that "apathy" was not a very accurate term, however. It is not simple indifference that prevents bystanders from intervening in emergencies. First, there are realistic deterrents such as physical danger. Second, getting involved may mean lengthy court appearances or other entanglements. Third, emergencies are unpredictable and require quick, unplanned action; few of us are prepared for such situations. Finally, one risks making a fool of oneself by misinterpreting a situation as an emergency when it is not. Researchers concluded that "the bystander to an emergency situation is in an unenviable position. It is perhaps surprising that anyone should intervene at all" (Latané & Darley, 1970, p. 247).

Although we might suppose that the presence of other bystanders would embolden an individual to act despite the risks, research demonstrates the reverse: Often it is the very presence of other people that prevents us from intervening. In fact, by 1980, there were more than 50 studies of bystander intervention, most of them showing that people are *less* likely to help when others are present (Latané Nida, & Wilson, 1981). Latané and Darley (1970) suggest that the presence of others deters an individual from intervening by (a) defining the situation as a nonemergency, and (b) diffusing the responsibility for acting.

DEFINING THE SITUATION Many emergencies begin ambiguously. Is the man who is staggering about ill or simply drunk? Is the woman being threatened by a stranger or is she arguing with her husband? Is that smoke from a fire or just steam pouring out the window? One common way to deal with such dilemmas is to postpone action, to act as if nothing is wrong, and to look around to see how others are reacting. What you are likely to see, of course, are other people who, for the same reasons, are also acting as if nothing is wrong. A state of **pluralistic ignorance** develops—that is, everybody in the group misleads everybody else by defining the situation as a nonemergency. We have all heard about crowds panicking because each person leads everybody else to overreact. The reverse situation—in which a crowd lulls its members into inaction—may be even more common. Several experiments demonstrate this effect.

In one experiment, male college students were invited to an interview. As they sat in a

Although many passers-by have noticed the man lying on the sidewalk, no one has stopped to help—to see if he is asleep, sick, drunk, or dead. Research shows that someone is more likely to help if other bystanders are not present.

The results confirmed the findings of the smoke study. Of the subjects who were alone, 70 percent came to the woman's aid, but only 40 percent of those in two-person groups offered help. Again, those who had not intervened claimed later that they were unsure of what had happened but had decided that it was not serious (Latané & Rodin, 1969). The presence of others in these experiments produced pluralistic ignorance; each person, observing the calmness of the others, resolved the ambiguity of the situation by deciding no emergency existed.

DIFFUSION OF RESPONSIBILITY Pluralistic ignorance can lead individuals to define a situation as a nonemergency, but this process does not explain such incidents as the Genovese murder, in which the emergency is abundantly clear. Moreover, Kitty Genovese's neighbors could not observe one another behind their curtained windows and hence could not tell whether others were calm or panicked. The crucial process here was **diffusion of responsibility**. When each individual knows that many others are present, the burden of responsibility does not fall solely on him or her. Each can think, "Someone else must have done something by now; someone else will intervene."

To test this hypothesis, experimenters placed subjects in individual booths and told them that they would participate in a group discussion about personal problems faced by college students. To avoid embarrassment, the discussion would be held through an intercom. Each person would speak for 2 minutes. The microphone would be turned on only in the booth of the person speaking, and the experimenter would not be listening. Actually, the voices of all participants except the subject's were tape recordings. On the first round, one of the taped participants mentioned that he had problems with seizures. On the second round, this individual sounded as if he were actually starting to have a seizure and begged for help. The experimenters waited to see if the subject would leave the booth to report the emergency and how long it would take. Note that (a) the emergency is not at all ambiguous, (b) the subject could not tell how the bystanders in the other booths were reacting, and (c) the subject knew the experimenter could not hear the emergency. Some subjects were led to believe that the discussion group consisted only of themselves and the seizure

small waiting room, a stream of smoke began to pour through a wall vent. Some subjects were alone in the waiting room when this occurred; others were in groups of three. The experimenters observed them through a one-way window and waited 6 minutes to see if anyone would take action or report the situation. Of the subjects tested alone, 75 percent reported the smoke within about 2 minutes. In contrast, fewer than 13 percent of the people tested in groups reported the smoke within the entire 6-minute period, even though the room was filled with smoke. Those who did not report the smoke subsequently reported that they decided that it must have been steam, air conditioning vapors, or smog—practically anything but a real fire or an emergency. This experiment thus showed that bystanders can define situations as nonemergencies for one another (Latané & Darley, 1968).

But perhaps these subjects were simply afraid to appear cowardly. To check this out, a similar study was designed in which the "emergency" did not involve personal danger. Subjects in the testing room heard a female experimenter in the next office climb up on a chair to reach a bookcase, fall to the floor, and yell, "Oh my God—my foot. . . . I can't move it. Oh . . . my ankle. . . . I can't get this thing off me." She continued to moan for about a minute longer. The entire incident lasted about 2 minutes. Only a curtain separated the woman's office from the testing room in which subjects waited, either alone or in pairs.

victim. Others were told that they were part of a three-person group; and still others, that they were part of a six-person group.

Of the subjects who thought that they alone knew of the victim's seizure, 85 percent reported it; of those who thought they were in a three-person group, 62 percent reported the seizure; and, of those who thought they were part of a six-person group only 31 percent reported it (see Figure 18-3). Interviews showed that all the subjects perceived the situation to be a real emergency. Most were very upset by the conflict between letting the victim suffer and rushing for help. In fact, subjects who did not report the seizure appeared more upset than those who did. Clearly we cannot interpret their nonintervention as apathy or indifference. Instead, the presence of others diffused the responsibility for acting (Darley & Latané, 1968; Latané & Darley, 1968).

If pluralistic ignorance and diffusion of responsibility are minimized, will people help one another? To find out, three psychologists used the New York City subway system as their laboratory (Piliavin, Rodin, & Piliavin, 1969). Two male and two female experimenters boarded a subway train separately. The female experimenters took seats and recorded the results, while the two men remained standing. As the train moved along, one of the men staggered forward and collapsed, remaining prone and staring at the ceiling until he received help. If no help came, the other man finally helped him to his feet. Several variations of the study were tried: The victim either carried a cane (so he would appear ill) or smelled of alcohol (so he would appear drunk). Sometimes the victim was white; other times, black. There was no ambiguity; clearly the victim needed help. Diffusion of responsibility was minimized because each bystander could not continue to assume that someone else was intervening. Therefore, people should help.

The results supported this optimistic expectation. The victim with the cane received spontaneous help on over 95 percent of the trials, within an average of 5 seconds. The drunk victim received help in half of the trials, on the average within 2 minutes. Both black and white cane victims were aided by black and white bystanders. There was no relationship between the number of bystanders and the speed of help, suggesting that diffu-

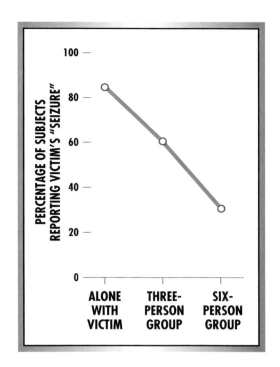

FIGURE 18-3

Diffusion of Responsibility *The percentage of subjects who reported a victim's apparent seizure declined as the number of other people the subject believed were in his or her discussion group increased.* (After Darley & Latané, 1968)

sion of responsibility had indeed been minimized. And all of this occurred on the New York City subway system. This not only tends to support the proposed explanations of bystander nonintervention but also may disconfirm some of our stereotypes about New York City subway riders.

ROLE OF HELPING MODELS In the subway study, as soon as one person moved to help, many others followed. This suggests that just as individuals use other people as models to define a situation as a nonemergency (pluralistic ignorance), they also use other people as models to indicate when to be helpful. This possibility was tested by counting the number of drivers who would stop to help a woman parked on the side of a road with a flat tire. It was found that significantly more drivers would stop to help if they had seen a another woman with car trouble receiving help about a quarter mile earlier. Similarly, people are more likely to donate to a person soliciting for charity if they observe others doing so (Macauley, 1970; Bryan & Test, 1967). These experiments indicate that others not only help us decide when *not* to act in an emergency but also serve as models to show us how and when to be good Samaritans.

Even role models on television can promote helping. In one study, 6-year-old children were shown an episode of *Lassie* in which a child rescues one of Lassie's pups from a mine shaft. Children in two control groups saw either a scene from *Lassie* that did not show a rescue scene or a scene from *The Brady Bunch*. Later, when the children were playing a game in which the winner would be given a prize, they were exposed to some unhappy whining puppies. Even though helping the puppies would diminish their chances of winning the prize, children who had watched the rescue episode spent more time comforting the puppies than did the children who had seen the control episodes (Sprafkin, Liebert, & Poulous, 1975). Another study found that children exposed to programs such as *Mister Rogers' Neighborhood* or *Sesame Street* were more likely to behave in giving ways than children who were not exposed to the shows (Forge & Phemister, 1987).

ROLE OF INFORMATION   Now that you have read about the factors that deter bystanders from intervening in an emergency, would you be more likely to act in such a situation? An experiment at the University of Montana suggests that you would. Undergraduates were either given a lecture or shown a film based on the material discussed in this section. Two weeks later, each undergraduate was confronted with a simulated emergency while walking with one other person (a confederate of the experimenters). A male victim was sprawled on the floor of a hallway. The confederate did not react as if the situation were an emergency. Those who had heard the lecture or seen the film were significantly more likely than others to offer help (Beaman, Barnes, Klentz, & McQuirk, 1978). For society's sake, perhaps you should reread this section!

COMPLIANCE AND RESISTANCE

CONFORMITY TO A MAJORITY

When we are in a group, we may find ourselves in the minority on some issue. This is a fact of life to which most of us have become accustomed. If we decide that the majority is a more valid source of information than our own experience, we may change our minds and conform to the majority opinion. But imagine yourself in a situation in which you are sure that your own opinion is correct and that the group is wrong. Would you yield to social pressure and conform under those circumstances? This is the kind of conformity that social psychologist Solomon Asch decided to investigate in a series of classic studies (1952, 1955, 1958).

In Asch's standard procedure, a single subject was seated at a table with a group of seven to nine others (all confederates of the experimenter). The group was shown a display of three vertical lines of different lengths, and members of the group were asked to judge which line was the same length as a standard drawn in another display (see Figure 18-4). Each individual announced his or her decision in turn, and the subject sat in the next to the last seat. The correct judgments were obvious, and on most trials everyone gave the same response. But on several predetermined

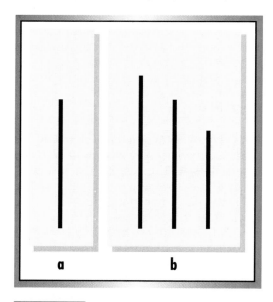

FIGURE 18-4

Representative Stimulus in Asch's Study   *After viewing display A, the subjects were told to pick the matching line from display B. The displays shown here are typical in that the correct decision is obvious.* (After Asch, 1958)

critical trials, the confederates had been instructed to give the wrong answer. Asch then observed the amount of conformity this procedure would elicit from his subjects.

The results were striking. Even though the correct answer was always obvious, the average subject conformed to the incorrect group consensus about one-third of the time; about 75 percent of the subjects conformed at least once. Moreover, the group did not have to be large to obtain such conformity. When Asch varied the size of the group from 2 to 16, he found that a group of 3 or 4 confederates was just as effective at producing conformity as were larger groups (Asch, 1958).

Why didn't the obviousness of the correct answer provide support for the individual's independence from the majority? Why isn't a person's confidence in his or her ability to make simple sensory judgments a strong force against conformity?

According to one line of argument, it is precisely the obviousness of the correct answer in the Asch experiment that produces the strong forces toward conformity (Ross, Bierbrauer, & Hoffman, 1976). Disagreements in real life typically involve difficult or subjective judgments such as which economic policy will best reduce inflation or which of two paintings is more aesthetically pleasing. In these cases, we expect to disagree with others occasionally; we even know that being a minority of one in an otherwise unanimous group is a plausible, if uncomfortable, possibility.

The Asch situation is much more extreme. Here the individual is confronted with unanimous disagreement about a simple physical fact, a bizarre and unprecedented occurrence that appears to have no rational explanation. Subjects are clearly puzzled and tense. They rub their eyes in disbelief and jump up to look more closely at the lines. They squirm, mumble, giggle in embarrassment, and look searchingly at others in the group for some clue to the mystery. After the experiment, they offer halfhearted hypotheses about optical illusions or suggest—quite aptly—that perhaps the first person occasionally made a mistake, and each successive person followed suit because of conformity pressures (Asch, 1952).

Consider what it means to dissent from the majority under these circumstances. Just as the judgments of the group seem incomprehensible to the subject, so the subject believes that his or her dissent will be incomprehensible to the group. Group members will surely judge him or her to be incompetent, even out of touch with reality. Similarly,

In a study of conformity to majority opinion, (top) all of the group members except the man sixth from the left are confederates previously instructed to give uniformly wrong answers on 12 of the 18 trials. Number 6, who has been told he is participating in an experiment in visual judgment, therefore finds himself a lone dissenter when he gives the correct answers. (bottom left) The subject, showing the strain of repeated disagreement with the majority, leans forward anxiously to look at the exhibit in question. (bottom right) This particular subject persists in his opinion, saying that "he has to call them as he sees them." (After Asch, 1958)

if the subject dissents repeatedly, this will seem to constitute a direct challenge to the group's competence, a challenge that requires enormous courage when one's own perceptual abilities are suddenly and inexplicably called into question. Such a challenge violates a strong social norm against insulting others. This fear of "What will they think of me?" and "What will they think I think of them?" inhibits dissent and generates the strong pressures to conform in the Asch situation.

Conformity pressures are far less strong when the group is not unanimous. If even one confederate breaks with the majority, the amount of conformity drops from 32 percent of the trials to about 6 percent. In fact, a group of eight containing only one dissenter produces less conformity than a unanimous majority of three (Allen & Levine, 1969; Asch, 1958). Surprisingly, the dissenter does not even have to give the correct answer. Even when the dissenter's answers are more inaccurate than the majority's, their influence is broken and subjects are more inclined to give their own, correct judgments (Asch, 1955). Nor does it matter who the dissenter is. An African-American dissenter reduces the conformity rate among racially prejudiced white subjects just as effectively as a white dissenter (Malof & Lott, 1962). In a variation that approaches the absurd, conformity was significantly reduced even though the subjects thought the dissenter was so visually handicapped that he could not see the stimuli (Allen & Levine, 1971). It seems clear that the presence of but one other deviant to share the potential disapproval or ridicule of the group permits the subject to dissent without feeling totally isolated.

If Asch's conformity situation is unlike most situations in real life, why did Asch use a task in which the correct answer was obvious? The reason is that he wanted to study pure public conformity, uncontaminated by the possibility that subjects were actually changing their minds about the correct answers. (However, Asch reports that a few subjects actually did decide that the group was correct on some of the critical trials.) Several variations of Asch's study have used more difficult or subjective judgments, and although they may reflect life more faithfully, they do not permit us to assess the effects of pure pressure to conform to a majority when we are certain that our own minority judgment

is correct (Ross, Bierbrauer, & Hoffman, 1976).

MINORITY INFLUENCE

A number of European scholars have been critical of social psychological research in North America because of its preoccupation with conformity and the influence of the majority on the minority. As they correctly point out, intellectual innovation, social change, and political revolution often occur because an informed and articulate minority—sometimes a minority of one—begins to convert others to its point of view (Moscovici, 1976). Why not study innovation and the influence that minorities can have on the majority?

To make their point, these European investigators deliberately began their experimental work by setting up a laboratory situation virtually identical to Asch's conformity situation. Subjects were asked to make a series of simple perceptual judgments in the face of confederates who consistently gave the incorrect answer. But instead of placing a single subject in the midst of several confederates, these investigators planted two confederates, who consistently gave incorrect responses, in the midst of four real subjects. The experimenters found that the minority was able to influence about 32 percent of the subjects to make at least one incorrect judgment. For this to occur, however, the minority had to remain consistent throughout the experiment. If they wavered or showed any inconsistency in their judgments, they were unable to influence the majority (Moscovici, Lage, & Naffrechoux, 1969).

Since this initial demonstration of minority influence, more than 90 related studies have been conducted in both Europe and North America, including several that required groups to debate social and political issues rather than to make simple perceptual judgments (for a recent review, see Wood et al., 1994). The general finding is that minorities can move majorities toward their point of view if they present a consistent position without appearing rigid, dogmatic, or arrogant. Such minorities are perceived to be more confident and, occasionally, more competent than the majority (Maass & Clark, 1984). Minorities are also more effective if they argue a position that is consistent with the developing social norms of the larger society. For example, in two experiments in which feminist issues were discussed, subjects were moved significantly more by a minority position that was in line with recent social norms (feminist) than by one opposed to these new norms (antifeminist) (Paicheler, 1977, 1976).

But the most interesting finding from this research is that the majority members in these studies show a change of private attitude—internalization—not just the public conformity that was found in the Asch conformity experiments. In fact, minorities sometimes obtain private attitude change from majority members even when they fail to obtain public conformity. In one study, groups of subjects read a purported summary of a group discussion of gay rights held by five undergraduates like themselves. In all cases four discussants had favored one position and a minority of one had consistently favored the opposite position. In some discussions, the majority had been for gay rights and the minority against; in other discussions, the majority and minority positions were reversed. After reading the summary, subjects voiced considerable public agreement with the majority view—regardless of whether it had been for or against gay rights—but written ratings revealed that opinions had shifted toward the minority position (Maass & Clark, 1983).

One investigator has suggested that minorities are able to produce attitude change because they lead majority individuals to rethink the issues. Even when they fail to convince the majority, they broaden the range of acceptable opinions. In contrast, unanimous majorities are rarely prompted to think carefully about their position (Nemeth, 1986).

These findings serve to remind us that the majorities of the world typically have the social power to approve and disapprove, to accept or reject, and it is this power that can obtain public compliance or conformity. In contrast, minorities rarely have such social power. But if they have credibility, then they have the power to produce genuine attitude change and, hence, innovation, social change, and revolution.

OBEDIENCE TO AUTHORITY

In Nazi Germany from 1933 to 1945, millions of innocent people were systematically put to death in concentration camps. The master-

mind of this horror, Adolf Hitler, may well have been a psychopathic monster. But he could not have done it alone. What about all those who ran the day-to-day operations, who built the ovens and gas chambers, filled them with human beings, counted bodies, and did the necessary paperwork? Were they all monsters, too?

Not according to social philosopher Hannah Arendt (1963), who covered the trial of Adolf Eichmann, a Nazi war criminal who was found guilty and was executed for causing the murder of millions of Jews. She described him as a dull, ordinary bureaucrat who saw himself as a little cog in a big machine. The publication of a partial transcript of Eichmann's pretrial interrogation supports Arendt's view. Several psychiatrists found Eichmann to be quite sane, and his personal relationships were quite normal. In fact, he believed that the Jews should have been allowed to emigrate to a separate territory and had argued that position within Hitler's security service. Moreover, he had a Jewish mistress in secret—a crime for an SS officer—and a Jewish half-cousin whom he arranged to have protected during the war (Von Lang & Sibyll, 1983).

Arendt subtitled her book about Eichmann *A Report on the Banality of Evil* and concluded that most of the "evil men" of the Third Reich were just ordinary people following orders from superiors. This suggests that all of us might be capable of such evil and

Social change is sometimes brought about, in part, because a few persons manage to persuade the majority to change its attitudes.

that Nazi Germany was an event less wildly alien from the normal human condition than we might like to think. As Arendt put it, "in certain circumstances the most ordinary decent person can become a criminal." This is not an easy conclusion to accept because it is more comforting to believe that monstrous evil is done only by monstrous persons. In fact, our emotional attachment to this explanation of evil was vividly shown by the intensity of the attacks on Arendt and her conclusions.

The problem of obedience to authority arose again in Vietnam in 1969, when a group of American soldiers, claiming that they were simply following orders, killed a number of civilians in the community of My Lai. Again the public was forced to ponder the possibility that ordinary citizens are willing to obey authority in violation of their own moral consciences.

This issue was explored empirically in a series of important and controversial studies conducted by Stanley Milgram (1963, 1974) at Yale University. Ordinary men and women were recruited through a newspaper ad that offered $4 for one hour's participation in a "study of memory." On arriving at the laboratory, the subject was told that he or she would be playing the role of teacher in the study. The subject was to read a series of word pairs to another subject and then test that learner's memory by reading the first word of each pair and asking him to select the correct second word from four alternatives. Each time the learner made an error, the subject was to press a lever that delivered an electric shock to him.

The subject watched while the learner was strapped into a chair and an electrode was attached to his wrist. The subject was then seated in an adjoining room in front of a shock generator whose front panel contained 30 lever switches set in a horizontal line. Each switch was labeled with a voltage rating, ranging in sequence from 15 to 450 volts, and groups of adjacent switches were labeled descriptively, ranging from "Slight Shock" up to "Danger: Severe Shock." When a switch was depressed, an electric buzzer sounded, lights flashed, and the needle on a voltage meter deflected to the right. To illustrate how it worked, the subject was given a sample shock of 45 volts from the generator. As the procedure began, the experimenter instructed the subject to move one level higher on the shock generator after each successive error (see Figure 18-5).

(top left) The "shock generator" used in Milgram's experiment on obedience. (top right) The victim is strapped into the "electric chair." (bottom left) A subject receives the sample shock before starting the "teaching session." (bottom right) A subject refuses to go on with the experiment. Most subjects became deeply disturbed by the role they were asked to play, whether they continued in the experiment to the end or refused at some point to go on. (From the film Obedience, *distributed by New York University Film Library; copyright © 1965 by Stanley Milgram)*

The learner did not actually receive any shocks. He was a 47-year-old, mild-mannered man who had been specially trained for his role. As he began to make errors and the shock levels escalated, he could be heard protesting through the adjoining wall. As the shocks became stronger, he began to shout and curse. At 300 volts he began to kick the wall, and at the next shock level (marked "Extreme Intensity Shock"), he no longer answered the questions or made any noise. As you might expect, many subjects began to object to this excruciating procedure, pleading with the experimenter to call a halt. But the experimenter responded with a sequence of prods, using as many as necessary to get the subject to go on: "Please continue"; "The experiment requires that you continue"; "It is absolutely essential that you continue"; and "You have no other choice—you must go on." Obedience to authority was measured by the maximum amount of shock the subject would administer before refusing to continue.

Milgram found that 65 percent of the subjects continued to obey throughout, going all the way to the end of the shock series (450 volts). Not one subject stopped prior to administering 300 volts, the point at which the learner began to kick the wall (see Figure 18-6). What produces such obedience?

Milgram suggests that the potential for obedience to authority is such a necessary requirement for communal life that it has probably been built into our species by evolution. The division of labor in a society requires that individuals be willing at times to subordinate and coordinate their own independent actions to serve the goals and purposes of the larger social organization. Parents, school systems, and businesses all nurture this willingness further by reminding the individual about the importance of following the directives of others who "know the larger picture." To understand obedience in a particular situation, then, we need to understand the factors that persuade individuals to relinquish their autonomy and become voluntary agents of the system. Milgram's experiments nicely illustrate four such factors: social norms, surveillance, buffers, and ideological justification.

SOCIAL NORMS By replying to the advertisement and agreeing to be in the study, subjects in Milgram's experiments had voluntarily assented to an implicit contract to

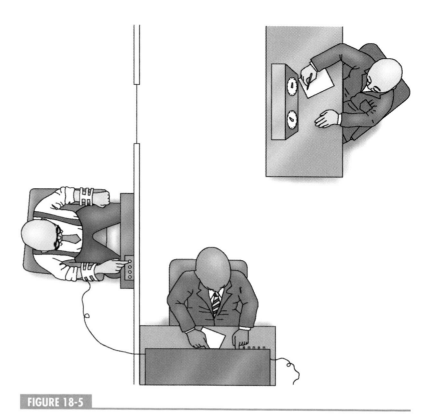

FIGURE 18-5

Milgram Obedience Experiment *The subject was told to give the learner a more intense shock after each error. If the subject objected, the experimenter insisted it was necessary to go on.* (After Milgram, 1974)

FIGURE 18-6

Obedience to Authority *The percentage of subjects willing to administer a punishing shock did not begin to decline until the intensity level of the shock reached 300 volts (the danger level).* (After Milgram, 1963)

cooperate with the experimenter, to follow the directions of the person in charge, and to see the job through to completion. This is a very strong social norm, and we tend to underestimate how difficult it is to break such an agreement and to go back on our implied word to cooperate.

The experiment was also designed to reinforce this norm by making it particularly difficult to stop once it had begun. The procedure starts rather innocently as an experiment in memory and then gradually escalates. Once subjects begin to give shocks and to raise the shock levels, there is no longer a natural stopping point. By the time they want to quit, they are trapped. The experimenter makes no new demands, only that they continue to do what they are already doing. In order to break off, they must suffer the guilt and embarrassment of acknowledging that they were wrong to begin at all. And the longer they put off quitting, the harder it is to admit their misjudgment in going as far as they have. It is easier to continue. Imagine how much less obedience there would be if subjects had to begin by giving the strongest shock first.

Finally, the potential quitter faces a dilemma over violating a social norm of etiquette (not being rude) similar to the one confronting a subject in the Asch situation. Dissenting in that case implied that the subject thought the group was incompetent. Dissenting in the Milgram situation is equivalent to accusing the experimenter of being immoral—an even more compelling force that pushes the subject to stay in line and go along with the experiment.

Modern warfare now permits us to destroy fellow humans at a distance, thereby providing a buffer between us and the final act of violence. Buffers make it psychologically easier to kill thousands of people by pushing a button than it would be to kill one individual in direct contact.

If social norms like these can produce so much obedience in Milgram's studies, then it is easy to imagine how much more powerful the penalties for quitting would be in Nazi Germany or in military service once one has already "signed on."

SURVEILLANCE An obvious factor in the Milgram experiment is the constant presence or surveillance of the experimenter. When the experimenter left the room and issued his orders by telephone, obedience dropped from 65 percent to 21 percent (Milgram, 1974). Moreover, several of the subjects who continued under these conditions cheated by administering shocks of lower intensity than they were supposed to.

BUFFERS Milgram's subjects believed that they were committing acts of violence, but there were several buffers that obscured this fact or diluted the immediacy of the experience. For example, the learner was in the next room, out of sight and unable to communicate. Milgram reports that obedience drops from 65 percent to 40 percent if the learner is in the same room as the subject. If the subject must personally ensure that the learner holds his hand on a shock plate, obedience declines to 30 percent. The more direct the person's experience with the victim—the fewer buffers between the person and the consequences of his or her act—the less the person will obey.

The most common buffer found in warlike situations is the remoteness of the person from the final act of violence. Thus, Adolf Eichmann argued that he was not directly responsible for killing Jews; he merely arranged for their deaths indirectly. Milgram conducted an analog to this "link-in-the-chain" role by requiring a subject only to pull a switch that enabled another teacher (a confederate) to deliver the shocks to the learner. Under these conditions, obedience soared: A full 93 percent of the subjects continued to the end of the shock series. In this situation, the subject can shift responsibility to the person who actually delivers the shock.

The shock generator itself served as a buffer—an impersonal mechanical agent that actually delivered the shock. Imagine how obedience would have declined if subjects were required to hit the learner with their fists. In real life, we have analogous technologies that permit us to destroy distant fellow humans by remote control, thereby removing us from the sight of their suffering. Although we probably all agree that it is worse to kill thousands of people by pushing a button that releases a guided missile than it is to beat one individual to death with a rock, it is still psychologically easier to push the button. Such are the effects of buffers.

IDEOLOGICAL JUSTIFICATION The fourth and most important factor producing voluntary obedience is the individual's acceptance of an *ideology*—a set of beliefs and attitudes—that legitimates the authority of the person in charge and justifies following his or her directives. Nazi officers such as Eichmann believed in the primacy of the German state and hence in the legitimacy of orders issued in its name. Similarly, the American soldiers who followed orders to shoot enemy civilians in Vietnam had already committed themselves to the premise that national security requires strict obedience to military commands.

In the Milgram experiments, the "importance of science" is the ideology that legitimates even quite extraordinary demands. Some critics have argued that the Milgram experiments were artificial, that the prestige of a scientific experiment led people to obey without questioning the dubious procedures in which they participated, and that people in real life would never do such a thing (for example, see Baumrind, 1964). Indeed, when Milgram repeated his experiment in a rundown set of offices and removed any association with Yale University from the setting, obedience dropped from 65 percent to 48 percent (Milgram, 1974).

But this criticism misses the major point. The prestige of science is not an irrelevant artificiality but an integral part of Milgram's demonstration. Science serves the same legitimating role in the experiment that the German state served in Nazi Germany and that national security serves in wartime killing. It is precisely their belief in the importance of scientific research that prompts individuals to subordinate their personal moral autonomy and independence to those who claim to act on science's behalf.

OBEDIENCE IN EVERYDAY LIFE Because the Milgram experiments have been criticized for being artificial (for example, Orne & Holland, 1968), it is instructive to look at an example of obedience to authority under more ordinary conditions. Researchers investigated whether nurses in public and private hospitals would obey an order that violated hospital rules and professional practice (Hofling et al., 1966). While on regular duty, the subject (a nurse) received a phone call from a doctor she knew to be on the staff but had not met: "This is Dr. Smith from Psychiatry calling. I was asked to see Mr. Jones this morning, and I'm going to have to see him again tonight. I'd like him to have had some medication by the time I get to the ward. Will you please check your medicine cabinet and see if you have some Astroten? That's ASTROTEN." When the nurse checked the medicine cabinet, she saw a pillbox labeled:

ASTROTEN

5 mg. capsules

Usual dose: 5 mg.

Maximum daily dose: 10 mg.

After she reported that she had found it, the doctor continued, "Now will you please give Mr. Jones a dose of 20 milligrams of Astroten. I'll be up within 10 minutes; I'll sign the order then, but I'd like the drug to have started taking effect." A staff psychiatrist, posted unobtrusively nearby, terminated each trial by disclosing its true nature when the nurse either poured the medication (actually a harmless placebo), refused to accept the order, or tried to contact another professional.

This order violated several rules: The dose was clearly excessive. Medication orders are not permitted to be given by telephone. The medication was unauthorized—that is, it was not on the ward stock list clearing it for use.

Over the years, Milgram's obedience experiments have become as well known for the ethical questions they raise about the conduct of psychological research as they have for their results. The first published criticism appeared soon after Milgram published his early findings (Baumrind, 1964), and an entire book has now been written about the controversy itself (Miller, 1986). The criticisms primarily concern the welfare of those who served as subjects.

First, critics argue that Milgram's procedures created an unacceptable level of stress in the subjects during the experiment itself. In support of this claim, they quote Milgram's own description:

> In a large number of cases, the degree of tension reached extremes that are rarely seen in sociopsychological laboratory studies. Subjects were observed to sweat, tremble, stutter, bite their lips, groan, and dig their fingernails into their flesh. These were characteristic rather than exceptional responses to the experiment.
> One sight of tension was the regular occurrence of nervous laughing fits. Fourteen of the 40 subjects showed definite signs of nervous laughing and smiling. The laughter seemed entirely out of place, even bizarre. Full-blown, uncontrollable seizures were observed for 3 subjects. On one occasion we observed a seizure so violently convulsive that it was necessary to call a halt to the experiment. . . . Milgram, 1963, p. 375)

Second, critics express concern about the long-term psychological effects on subjects and their self-esteem of having learned that they would be willing to give potentially lethal shocks to a fellow human being. And finally, critics argue that subjects are likely to feel foolish and "used" when told the true nature of the experiment, thereby making them less

trusting of psychologists in particular and of authority in general.

Milgram has replied to these and other criticisms of his experiments. His major defense is that, in general, the subjects themselves do not agree with the critics. After each session, Milgram conducted a careful "debriefing," explaining the reasons for the procedures and reestablishing positive rapport with the subject. This included a reassuring chat with the "victim" who the subject had thought was receiving the shocks. After the completion of an experimental series, subjects were sent a detailed report of the results and purposes of the experimental project. Milgram then conducted a survey of the subjects, asking them how they felt about their participation "now that [you] have read the report, and all things considered."

Milgram found that 84 percent of the subjects indicated that they were glad to have taken part in the study; 15 percent reported neutral feelings; and 1 percent stated that they were sorry to have participated. These percentages were about the same for those who had obeyed and those who had defied the experimenter during the experiment itself. In addition, 80 percent felt that more experiments of this sort should be carried out, and 74 percent indicated that they had learned something of personal importance as a result of being in the study. Milgram also hired a psychiatrist to interview 40 of the subjects in person to determine whether the study had any injurious effects. This follow-up revealed no indications of long-term distress or traumatic reactions among subjects; typically they felt that their participation was instructive and enriching (Milgram, 1964).

With respect to the concern that subjects might be less trusting of authority in the future, Milgram noted that "the experimenter is not just any authority: he is an authority who tells the subject to act harshly and inhumanely against another man. I would consider it of the highest value if participation in the experiment could inculcate a skepticism of this kind of authority" (1964, p. 852).

In Chapter 1, we noted that research guidelines set forth by the United States government and the American Psychological Association emphasize two major principles. The principle of *minimal risk* specifies that the risks anticipated in a research study should be no greater than those ordinarily encountered in daily life. The principle of *informed consent* specifies that subjects must enter a study voluntarily and be permitted to withdraw from it at any time without penalty if they so desire. They must also be told ahead of time about any aspects of the study that could be expected to influence their willingness to cooperate. When this requirement cannot be strictly met, a thorough "debriefing" must adequately eliminate any negative feelings the subject might have experienced.

Milgram's studies were conducted in the early 1960s, before these guidelines were in effect. Despite the importance of the research and the precautions that Milgram took, it seems likely that most of the review boards that must now approve federally funded research projects would not permit these experiments to be conducted today. Although many replications of Milgram's experiments were conducted in earlier years, the last one conducted in the United States was published in 1976 (for a review, see Blass, 1991).

Finally, the order was given by an unfamiliar person. Despite all this, 95 percent of the nurses started to give the medication. Moreover, the telephone calls were all brief, and the nurses put up little or no resistance. None of them insisted on a written order, although several sought reassurance that the doctor would arrive promptly. In interviews after the experiment, all the nurses stated that such orders had been received in the past and that doctors became annoyed if the nurses balked.

POWER OF SITUATIONS

In Chapter 17, we saw that people typically overestimate the role of personal dispositional factors and underestimate the role of situational factors in controlling behavior—the **fundamental attribution error**. Studies on conformity and obedience illustrate this point—not through their results, but through our surprise at their results. We simply do not expect the situational forces to be as effective as they are. When college students are told about Milgram's procedures (but not given the results) and are asked whether they would continue to administer the shocks in the Milgram situation after the learner begins to pound on the wall, about 99 percent of the students say they would not (Aronson, 1995). Milgram himself surveyed psychiatrists at a leading medical school. They predicted that most subjects would refuse to go on after reaching 150 volts, that only about 4 percent would go beyond 300 volts, and that fewer than 1 percent would go all the way to 450 volts. In one study, subjects were asked to estimate obedience rates after they had reenacted the entire Milgram procedure, complete with shock apparatus and a tape recording of the protesting learner. Whether they played the role of the actual subject or the role of an observer, all subjects continued to vastly underestimate the compliance rates actually obtained by Milgram, as shown in Figure 18-7 (Bierbrauer, 1973).

The nursing study on administering medication yields comparable results. When nurses who had not been subjects were given a complete description of the situation and asked how they themselves would respond, 83 percent reported that they would not have given the medication, and most of them thought a majority of nurses would also

refuse. Of 21 nursing students asked the same question, all of them reported that they would not have given the medication as ordered.

There is an amusing footnote to the nursing study. The study was conducted and reported by psychiatrists, and they offer a psychoanalytic explanation for the nurses' compliance, complete with references to Oedipal feelings that female nurses are likely to have for male doctors. Most contemporary social psychologists are likely to regard such a dispositional explanation as superfluous—even silly—and to believe that the situational forces in this study were quite sufficient to account for the 95 percent compliance rate observed. In short, they are likely to believe that the authors of the nursing study are themselves committing the fundamental attribution error.

In sum, our reactions to conformity and obedience experiments dramatically illustrate a major lesson of social psychology: We seriously underestimate the extent and power of social and situational forces on human behavior.

REBELLION

One reason the experiments on conformity and obedience obtain such high compliance

Predicted and Actual Compliance *The upper curve presents the Milgram data and shows the percentage of subjects who remained obedient in the situation, continuing to administer shocks as the voltage increased. The lower curve is from a study in which role-playing subjects reenacted the Milgram experiment and attempted to predict what percentage of the actual subjects would continue to be obedient as shock increased. The role-playing subjects vastly underestimated the magnitude of the situational forces and the likelihood of obedience in the Milgram situation.* (After Bierbrauer, 1973)

is that the social pressures in these studies are directed toward a lone individual. If the subject were not alone would he or she be less obedient? We have already seen some data to support this possibility: A subject in the Asch conformity situation is less likely to go along with the group's incorrect judgments if there is at least one other dissenter.

A similar phenomenon occurs in the Milgram obedience situation. In one variation of the procedure, two additional confederates were employed. They were introduced as subjects who would also play teacher roles. Teacher 1 would read the list of word pairs; Teacher 2 would tell the learner if he was right or wrong; and Teacher 3 (the subject) would deliver the shocks. The confederates complied with the instructions through the 150-volt shock, at which point Teacher 1 informed the experimenter that he was quitting. Despite the experimenter's insistence that he continue, Teacher 1 got up from his chair and sat in another part of the room. After the 210-volt shock, Teacher 2 also quit. The experimenter then turned to the subject and ordered him to continue alone. Only 10 percent of the subjects were willing to complete the series in this situation. In a second variation, there were two experimenters rather than two additional teachers. After a few shocks, they began to argue—one of them saying that they should stop the experiment; the other saying they should continue. Under these circumstances, not a single subject would continue despite the orders to do so by the second experimenter (Milgram, 1974).

A more recent experiment examined more directly the possibility that *groups* of subjects might actually be moved to rebel against unjust authority. Citizens from a nonuniversity community were recruited by phone for $10 to spend 2 hours at a local motel assisting in research on "group standards" sponsored by a fictitious company, the Manufacturer's Human Relations Consultants, or MHRC (Gamson, Fireman, & Rytina, 1982). Nine subjects, both male and female, were recruited for each group session. When they arrived, they were given a letter explaining that legal cases sometimes hinge on the notion of community standards and that MHRC collects evidence on such standards by bringing together concerned citizens for group discussion. The subjects were then seated in front of video cameras and microphones at a U-shaped table, where they filled out a background questionnaire and signed a "participation agreement" giving MHRC permission to videotape them as they engaged in group discussion. The man in charge, who introduced himself as the coordinator, then read the background of a pending court case. The basic facts were as follows:

> A service station manager was suing an oil company because it had canceled the franchise on his service station. The oil company had conducted an investigation of the man and discovered that he was living with a woman to whom he was not married. The company claimed that his lifestyle violated the moral standards of the local community and that he would therefore not be able to maintain good relations with customers; accordingly, they decided to revoke his franchise license. The man sued for breach of contract and invasion of privacy, arguing that the company was out to get him because he had publicly criticized the company's gas pricing policies in a local television interview.

After presenting the case, the coordinator asked the group to discuss it while being videotaped. After a general discussion, the cameras were turned off and the group was given a short break. Before resuming the videotaping, the coordinator requested three of the group members to argue as if they were personally offended by the station manager's lifestyle. This second discussion was taped, there was another break, and three additional individuals were designated to argue in the same way in the next discussion. Finally, the coordinator asked each individual to go on camera alone and voice objections to the station manager's affair, stating an intention to boycott the station and arguing that the manager should lose his franchise. Group members were also told that they would be asked to sign notarized affidavits giving MHRC the right to introduce the tapes as evidence in court after editing them as it saw fit.

As MHRC's motives began to dawn on them, all but one of the 33 groups in this experiment began to dissent: "Can you assure us that the court is going to know these aren't our real opinions?"; "Would you mind leaving the tape on while you give us these instructions, so that it doesn't appear. . ."; "Do these professional people know what you're doing in fact is suborning perjury?" (Gamson, Fireman, & Rytina, 1982, pp. 62, 65). One group even decided to take direct action by gathering up materials from the table and taking them to the local newspaper.

Overall, 16 of the 33 groups rebelled completely—all members refused to sign the final affidavit—and a majority refused to do so in 9 additional groups. Only a minority refused in the remaining 8 groups, although a number of dissenting comments were voiced. Compared with the Milgram situation, then, obedience to authority had clearly been undermined in this study. But why?

The two studies differ in several respects, so we cannot be certain that the important difference was having a group rather than a lone individual as the target. Nevertheless, this seems to be the most likely factor. In fact, the circumstances producing rebellion in the MHRC study appear to be the same ones we have seen operating in other group contexts: defining the situation and conformity.

In the bystander intervention studies, we noted that individuals in a group define an ambiguous situation for one another. Subjects in the MHRC study were given ample opportunity during the breaks to define and clarify the situation for one another by sharing their suspicions of MHRC's motives. Some of the comments were "How are people going to know that these aren't our opinions?"; "We don't want to be faced with the situation where you read in the *New York Times* one day that thanks to a new method of litigation [group laughter] that this poor schnook [group laughter] lost his license" (Gamson, Fireman, & Rytina, 1982, pp. 101–102).

The preliminary questionnaires also indicated that 80 to 90 percent of the subjects initially disagreed with the position they were asked to take: They saw nothing wrong with an unmarried man and woman living together; they were critical of large oil companies; and they believed that an employee's private life was none of a company's business. The group members could also share these opinions with one another. The researchers compared the 23 groups in which a majority of subjects initially held dissenting opinions with the 10 groups that initially held fewer dissenting opinions. They found that 65 percent of the former groups produced complete rebellion—nobody signed the affidavits—but only 10 percent of the latter groups rebelled completely. A majority of the groups also contained some individuals who had been active in past protests and strikes, and these groups were also more likely to rebel than groups without such role models. Lone subjects in the Milgram obedience studies obviously had none of these opportunities for sharing information, receiving social support for dissent, or seeing role models for disobedience.

But before we congratulate the human species for bold independence and autonomy in the face of social pressure, we should consider the implication of these findings more closely. They suggest that many of the individuals in the groups were not choosing between obedience and autonomy but between obedience and conformity: Obey the coordinator or conform to the group's norm to disobey. As the researchers observed, "Many were uncertain at this point, waiting to see what others would do, delaying decision as long as possible. Ultimately, they were faced with an unavoidable choice—to sign or not to sign—and loyalty to the group became one major factor in their decision." Some who had already signed the affidavit crossed out their names or tore up the form. As one subject told the coordinator, "I didn't personally say anything I didn't believe, but I'm not going to sign this either, if the rest of the group isn't signing" (Gamson, Fireman, & Rytina, 1982, p. 99).

Morally or politically motivated disobedience to authority is usually a collective act that is justified by the shared values of a group.

Obeying or conforming may not strike you as a very heroic choice. But these are among the processes that provide the social glue for the human species. Several years before this study was conducted, a social historian noted that "disobedience when it is not criminally but morally, religiously or politically motivated is always a collective act and it is justified by the values of the collectivity and the mutual engagements of its members" (Walzer, 1970, p. 4).

IDENTIFICATION AND INTERNALIZATION

Most studies of conformity and obedience focus on whether or not individuals overtly comply with the influence. In everyday life, however, those who attempt to influence us usually want to change our private attitudes, not just our public behaviors, to obtain changes that will be sustained even after they are no longer on the scene. As we noted in the introduction to this chapter, such change is called *internalization*. Certainly the major goal of parents, educators, clergy, politicians, and advertisers is internalization, not just compliance. In general, internalization is obtained by an influence source who either (a) presents a persuasive message that is itself compelling or (b) is perceived as credible, possessing both expertise and trustworthiness. In this section, we examine influence that persuades rather than coerces.

PERSUASIVE COMMUNICATION

Just as the practices of Nazi Germany under Hitler prompted social psychologists to be interested in obedience to authority, so propaganda efforts on both sides in World War II prompted them to study persuasion. Intensive research began in the late 1940s at Yale University, where investigators sought to determine the characteristics of successful persuasive communicators, successful communications, and the kinds of persons who are most easily persuaded (Hovland, Janis, & Kelley, 1953). As research on these topics continued over the years, a number of interesting phenomena were discovered but few general principles emerged. The results became increasingly complex and difficult to summarize, and every conclusion seemed to require several "it depends" qualifications. Beginning in the 1970s, however, social psychology's interest in information processing (see Chapter 17) gave rise to theories of persuasion that began to provide a more unified framework for understanding its many complexities.

Among the new approaches to persuasion were several variations of **cognitive response theory**. This theory proposes that persuasion induced by a communication is actually self-persuasion produced by the thoughts that the person generates while reading, listening to, or even just anticipating the communication. These thoughts can be about the content of the communication itself or about other aspects of the situation, such as the credibility of the communicator. If the communication evokes thoughts supportive of the position being advocated, the individual will move toward that position; if the communication evokes unsupportive thoughts (such as counterarguments or disparaging thoughts about the communicator), the individual will remain unconvinced or even *boomerang*—shift away from the position being advocated (Petty, Ostrom, & Brock, 1981; Greenwald, 1968).

A number of studies support this theory. In one, each subject read a communication containing arguments on a controversial issue and wrote a one-sentence reaction (cognitive response) to each argument. One week later the subjects were unexpectedly given a memory test asking them to recall both the arguments in the communication and their written reactions to those arguments. Subjects' opinions on the issue were assessed both before receiving the communication and then, again, at the time of the memory test one week later. The results showed that the amount of opinion change produced by the communication was significantly correlated with both the supportiveness of subjects' reactions to the communication and with subjects' later recall of those reactions, but it was *not* significantly correlated with subjects' recall of the arguments themselves (Love & Greenwald, 1978). This experiment not only supports the theory, but it also explains what had previously been a puzzling observation—that the persistence of opinion change is often unrelated to an individual's memory for the arguments that produced that change.

Cognitive response theory also proposes that a persuasive communication will be unsuccessful to the extent that the target individual is both motivated to generate counterarguments against the position being advocated and has the ability and opportunity to do so. As we shall now see, the theory provides a unified explanation for several long-standing phenomena of persuasion.

ONE-SIDED VERSUS TWO-SIDED COMMUNICATION A tactical decision facing any persuasive communicator is whether to present only the side of the issue favorable to his or her conclusions or to present both sides of the issue and to argue explicitly against the opposing side. This was explored empirically as early as 1945 by psychologists in the United States Army's Information and Education Division. After the Allies defeated Germany in World War II, the Army did not want soldiers to be overconfident about the ease of defeating the Japanese, with whom the United States was still at war. The psychologists designed two radio broadcasts that argued that the war would last at least 2 more years. One broadcast presented only arguments in favor of that conclusion. The other broadcast presented arguments on both sides; for example, it raised and responded to the counterargument that the United States now had the advantage of fighting the war on only one front.

The researchers found that for soldiers who already agreed that the war would last a long time, the one-sided broadcast was more effective than the two-sided broadcast. The two-sided broadcast apparently alerted them to counterarguments they would not have thought of otherwise and thus weakened the effect of the broadcast. But for soldiers who initially disagreed with the communication's conclusion, the one-sided broadcast was less effective (Hovland, Lumsdaine, & Sheffield, 1949). These soldiers already possessed a set of counterarguments that they could generate while hearing the broadcast. Moreover, they were more likely to perceive the one-sided broadcast as biased and hence to generate unfavorable thoughts about its credibility. Later research has shown that just being aware that opposing arguments exist renders a one-sided communication less persuasive than a two-sided one (Jones & Brehm, 1970).

There is an additional advantage to two-sided communications. Regardless of whether they agree or disagree with the position advocated, individuals exposed to two-sided communications are more resistant to later counterarguments than are individuals exposed to one-sided communications (Lumsdaine & Janis, 1953). Two-sided communications expose individuals not only to counterarguments but to the refutations of those counterarguments as well, giving those individuals a new set of contrary cognitive responses to generate when later exposed to communications from the opposing side.

INOCULATION AGAINST PERSUASION As we have just seen, two-sided communications can serve to immunize an individual's newly acquired opinions against counterattack. Psychologist William McGuire decided to pursue this biological analogy by asking whether it was possible to inoculate people against persuasion as we inoculate them against a virus. Would a weak attack on an individual's beliefs stimulate him or her to marshal counterarguments against a full-blown attack the same way a vaccination containing a weakened form of a virus stimulates the body to produce antibodies against it?

To perform this feat, McGuire needed "germ-free" beliefs—beliefs that had not previously been exposed to attack. For this purpose, he selected *cultural truisms,* beliefs that are so widely believed that nobody thinks of questioning them (for example, "It's a good idea to brush your teeth after every meal if at all possible"). First, he confirmed that attacking such beliefs with strong arguments could markedly diminish an individual's belief in them. ("Did you know that the American Dental Association has warned that too much tooth brushing can damage your gums?") He then showed that subjects who first received a mild attack on their belief in a truism and then read or wrote an essay refuting this attack were better able to resist a subsequent strong attack. Moreover, this inoculation defense was more effective than a supportive defense in which subjects simply read paragraphs presenting arguments in favor of the truism—analogous to giving a person vitamins to bolster the body's general resistance (McGuire, 1964; Papageorgis & McGuire, 1961; McGuire & Papageorgis, 1961).

FOREWARNING Mildly attacking individuals' beliefs is not the only way to stimulate them to marshal counterarguments against persuasion. A simple *forewarning* that they are about to receive a communication with which they will disagree is also sufficient. Even a warning issued only 2 minutes before receiving the communication is sufficient to produce resistance to it (Hass & Grady, 1975; Freedman & Sears, 1965), and research shows that forewarned subjects do, in fact, use this time to construct counterarguments (Petty & Cacioppo, 1977). Unwarned subjects will also show resistance to a communication if they are simply instructed to list their thoughts on the topic beforehand. This demonstrates that it is not forewarning per se that induces resistance to a communication but the anticipatory thinking about the topic.

PRACTICAL APPLICATIONS As we noted earlier, social psychologists initiated research on persuasion in response to practical problems involved in the prosecution of World War II. Although much of the subsequent research has been conducted in laboratories, exposing college students to communications on relatively unimportant issues, there has always been an interest in the practical applications of the findings. Cognitive response theory is no exception.

For example, one education program has been designed to inoculate junior high school

Learning how to generate counterarguments can inoculate young people against peer pressure to use drugs.

students against peer pressure to smoke. High school students conducted sessions in which they taught seventh-graders how to generate counterarguments. For example, in role-playing sessions they were taught to respond to being called "chicken" for not taking a cigarette by saying things like "I'd be a real chicken if I smoked just to impress you." They were also taught to respond to advertisements implying that liberated women smoke by saying, "She's not really liberated if she is hooked on tobacco." Several inoculation sessions were held during seventh and eighth grades, and records were kept of how many of the students smoked from the beginning of the study through the ninth grade. The results show that inoculated students were half as likely to smoke as students at a matched junior high school that used a more typical smoking education program (McAlister et al., 1980). Similar programs have been designed to inoculate elementary school children against being taken in by deceptive television commercials (Cohen, 1980; Feshbach, 1980).

CENTRAL VERSUS PERIPHERAL ROUTES OF PERSUASION Although research on cognitive response theory has focused primarily on the individual's thoughts about the substantive arguments in a communication, the individual can also respond to other features of the situation—such as cues about the communicator's credibility. Richard Petty and John Cacioppo, two major contributors to cognitive response theory, have clarified the persuasion domain even further by demonstrating the importance of distinguishing between two routes that persuasion can take in producing belief and attitude change (Petty & Cacioppo, 1986, 1981).

Persuasion is said to follow the *central route* when the individual responds to substantive information about the issue under consideration. This can be information contained in the persuasive communication itself or information that is part of the individual's preexisting knowledge. Most of the research on cognitive response theory explores this route. Persuasion is said to follow the *peripheral route* when the individual responds instead to noncontent cues in a communication (such as the sheer number of arguments it contains) or to the context of the communication (such as the credibility of the communicator or the pleasantness of the surroundings).

The central route to persuasion is taken only when the individual is both motivated to generate thoughts in response to the substantive contents of a communication and has the ability and opportunity to do so. The peripheral route is taken when the individual is unable or unwilling to put in the cognitive work required to carefully evaluate the content of the communication. Several factors can influence which route will be taken. One such factor is personal involvement. If a communication addresses an issue in which the individual has a personal stake, he or she is more likely to attend carefully to the arguments. In such a case, the individual is also likely to have a rich store of prior information and opinion on the issue—which can provide many cognitive responses to the communication. On the other hand, if an issue has no personal relevance for the individual, he or she is not likely to make much of an effort either to support or to refute arguments about it. What happens then?

According to one recent theory, when we are unwilling or unable to process the content of a communication, we may use simple rules of thumb—called *heuristics*—to infer the validity of its arguments. Examples of such rules might include "Messages with many arguments are more likely to be valid than messages with few arguments"; "Politicians always lie"; or "College professors know what they are talking about." This special case of cognitive response theory is called the **heuristic theory of persuasion** (Chaiken, 1987, 1980; Eagly & Chaiken, 1984).

This line of reasoning about the two routes of persuasion has been tested in several studies. In one rather complex study, college undergraduates read an essay allegedly written by the chairperson of a university committee charged with advising the chancellor on changes in academic policy. The essay advocated that the university institute a comprehensive examination that every undergraduate would have to pass in his or her major field before being permitted to graduate. In order to manipulate the personal involvement of the students in the issue, half of them were told that any policy changes adopted by the chancellor would be instituted the following year (high involvement), and the other half were told that any changes would take effect in 10 years (low involvement). Different forms of the essay were also

used. Some contained strong arguments; others contained weak arguments. Some contained only three arguments; others contained nine.

The postcommunication attitudes of students in the high-involvement conditions are shown in Figure 18-8. It can be seen that strong arguments produced more favorable attitudes overall than did weak arguments. But more importantly, nine strong arguments produced greater agreement with the essay than did three strong arguments, whereas nine weak arguments produced less agreement with the essay than did three weak arguments. How do the theories account for these patterns?

The theory about routes of persuasion predicts that students in the high-involvement conditions will be motivated to process the essay's substantive arguments and thus generate topic-relevant cognitive responses. This is the central route of persuasion, and cognitive response theory predicts that strong arguments will evoke more supportive cognitive

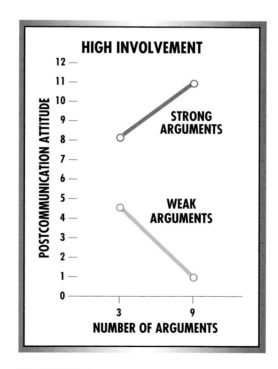

FIGURE 18-8

Postcommunication Attitudes *When subjects have high involvement in the issue, nine strong arguments produce more agreement with the essay than three strong arguments, but nine weak arguments produce less agreement than three weak arguments.* (After Petty & Cacioppo, 1984)

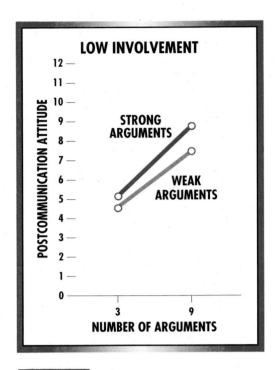

LOW INVOLVEMENT

POSTCOMMUNICATION ATTITUDE

STRONG ARGUMENTS

WEAK ARGUMENTS

NUMBER OF ARGUMENTS

FIGURE 18-9

Postcommunication Attitudes   *When subjects have low involvement in the issue, nine arguments produce more agreement than three arguments, regardless of whether the arguments are strong or weak.*

responses and fewer counterarguments than will weak arguments and will thus produce more agreement with the essay—as, indeed, they did. Moreover, nine strong arguments should be more persuasive than three strong arguments because the more strong arguments the individual encounters, the more supportive cognitive responses he or she will generate. In contrast, nine weak arguments should be less persuasive than three weak arguments because the more weak arguments the individual encounters, the more counterarguments he or she will generate. These predictions accord with the findings displayed in Figure 18-8.

As shown in Figure 18-9, a different pattern emerges for students in the low-involvement conditions. Here the theory about routes of persuasion predicts that students in the low-involvement conditions will not be motivated to scrutinize the essay's arguments closely and will instead rely on simple heuristics to evaluate its merits and form their attitudes. This is the peripheral route, and the heuristic theory of persuasion predicts that an individ-

ual in this setting will not even bother to determine whether the arguments are strong or weak but will simply invoke the heuristic rule: "Messages with many arguments are more likely to be valid than messages with few arguments." Thus, strong arguments will be no more effective than weak arguments, and nine arguments will be more persuasive than three arguments—regardless of whether they are strong or weak. This is precisely the pattern shown in Figure 18-9: Overall, there were no significant differences between strong and weak arguments, but nine arguments were more effective than three arguments in both conditions (Petty & Cacioppo, 1984).

An experiment that varied the expertise of the communicator rather than the number of arguments found similar results: Subjects in the high-involvement conditions were more influenced by the strength of the arguments, but subjects in the low-involvement conditions relied more on the heuristic "Arguments made by an expert are more valid than arguments made by a nonexpert" (Petty, Cacioppo, & Goldman, 1981).

The complexity of the results in these studies should give you some idea of how chaotic the findings from persuasion research must have appeared before the recent theories imposed some order on them. The findings remain complex, but at least they now fall into sensible patterns.

REFERENCE GROUPS

Nearly every group to which we belong, from our family to the society as a whole, has an implicit or explicit set of beliefs, attitudes, and behaviors that it considers correct. Any member of the group who strays from these social norms risks isolation and social disapproval. Thus, through social rewards and punishments, the groups to which we belong obtain compliance from us. In addition, if we respect or admire other individuals or groups, we may obey their norms and adopt their beliefs, attitudes, and behaviors in order to be like them, to identify with them. This process is called **identification.**

Groups with whom we identify are called our **reference groups,** because we refer to them in order to evaluate and to regulate our opinions and actions. Reference groups can also serve as a frame of reference by providing us not only with specific beliefs and attitudes but also with a general perspective from which we view the world—an ideology or set of ready-made interpretations of social issues and events. If we eventually adopt these views and integrate the group's ideology into our own value system, then the reference group will have produced internalization. The process of identification, then, can provide a bridge between compliance and internalization.

An individual does not necessarily have to be a member of a reference group in order to be influenced by its values. For example, lower-middle-class individuals often use the middle class as a reference group. A young, aspiring athlete may use professional athletes as a reference group, adopting their views and otherwise trying to model himself or herself after them.

Life would be simple if each of us identified with only one reference group. But most of us identify with several reference groups, which often leads to conflicting pressures on us. We noted in Chapter 17, for example, that a Jewish businessperson might experience cross-pressures because his or her ethnic reference group usually holds more liberal political positions than does his or her business reference group. But perhaps the most enduring example of competing reference groups is the conflict that many young people experience between their family reference group and their college or peer reference group. The most extensive study of this conflict is Theodore Newcomb's classic Bennington Study—an examination of the political attitudes of the entire population of Bennington College, a small, politically liberal college in Vermont. The dates of the study (1935–1939) are a useful reminder that this is not a new phenomenon.

Today, Bennington College tends to attract liberal students, but in 1935 most students came from wealthy, conservative families. (It is also coed today, but in 1935, it was a women's college.) Over two-thirds of the parents of Bennington students were affiliated with the Republican party. The Bennington College community was liberal during the 1930s, but this was not why most of the women selected the college.

Newcomb's main finding was that with each year at Bennington, students moved further away from their parents' attitudes and closer to the attitudes of the college community. For example, in the 1936 presidential

campaign about 66 percent of parents favored the Republican candidate, Alf Landon, over the Democratic candidate, Franklin Roosevelt. Landon was supported by 62 percent of the Bennington freshmen and 43 percent of the sophomores, but only 15 percent of the juniors and seniors.

For most of the women, increasing liberalism reflected a deliberate choice between the two competing reference groups for most women. Two women discuss how they made this choice:

> All my life I've resented the protection of governesses and parents. At college I got away from that, or rather, I guess I should say, I changed it to wanting the intellectual approval of teachers and more advanced students. Then I found that you can't be reactionary and be intellectually respectable.

> Becoming radical meant thinking for myself and, figuratively, thumbing my nose at my family. It also meant intellectual identification with the faculty and students that I most wanted to be like. (Newcomb, 1943, pp. 134, 131)

Note that the second woman uses the term "identification" in the sense that we have been using it. Note, too, how the women describe a mixture of change produced by social rewards and punishments (compliance) and change produced by an attraction to an admired group whom they strive to emulate (identification).

FROM IDENTIFICATION TO INTERNALIZATION As mentioned earlier, reference groups also serve as frames of reference by providing their members with new perspectives on the world. The Bennington community, particularly the faculty, gave students a perspective on the depression of the 1930s and the threat of World War II that their wealthy and conservative home environments had not, and this began to move them from identification to internalization:

> It didn't take me long to see that liberal attitudes had prestige value. . . . I became liberal at first because of its prestige value; I remain so because the problems around which my liberalism centers are important. What I want now is to be effective in solving problems.

> Prestige and recognition have always meant everything to me. . . . But I've sweat[ed] blood in trying to be honest with myself, and the result is that I really know what I want my attitudes to be, and I see what their consequences will be in my own life. (Newcomb, 1943, pp. 136–37)

Many of our most important beliefs and attitudes are probably based initially on identification. Whenever we start to identify with a new reference group, we engage in a process of "trying on" the new set of beliefs and attitudes they prescribe. What we "really believe" is in flux, capable of changing from day to day. The first year of college often has this effect on students; many of the views students bring from the family reference group are challenged by students and faculty from very different backgrounds, with different beliefs. Students often "try on" the new beliefs with great intensity and strong conviction, only to discard them for still newer beliefs when the first set does not quite fit. This is a natural process of growth. Although the process never really ends for people who remain open to new experiences, it is greatly accelerated during the college years, before the person has formed a nucleus of permanent beliefs on which to build more slowly and less radically. The real work of college is to evolve an ideological identity from the several beliefs and attitudes that are tested in order to move from identification to internalization.

As noted earlier, one advantage of internalization over compliance is that the changes are self-sustaining. The original source of influence does not have to monitor the individual to maintain the induced changes. The test of internalization, then, is the long-term stability of the induced beliefs, attitudes, and behaviors. Was the identification-induced liberalism of Bennington women maintained when the students returned to the "real world"? The answer is yes. Two follow-up studies of the Bennington women 25 and 50 years later found they had remained liberal. For example, in the 1984 presidential election, 73 percent of Bennington alumnae preferred the Democratic candidate, Walter Mondale, over the Republican candidate, Ronald Reagan, compared with fewer than 26 percent of women of the same age and educational level. Moreover, about 60 percent of Bennington alumnae were politically active, most (66 percent) within the Democratic party (Alwin, Cohen, & Newcomb, 1991; Newcomb, Koening, Flacks, & Warwick, 1967).

But we never outgrow our need for identification with supporting reference groups. The political attitudes of Bennington women remained stable, in part, because they selected new reference groups—friends and husbands—after college who supported the attitudes they developed in college. Those who married more conservative men were more likely to be politically conservative in later life. As Newcomb noted, we often select our reference groups because they share our attitudes, and then our reference groups, in turn, help to develop and to sustain our attitudes. The relationship is circular. The distinction between identification and internalization is a useful one for understanding social influence, but in practice it is not always possible to disentangle them.

COLLECTIVE DECISION MAKING

Many decisions in everyday life are made not by individuals but by groups. Members of a family jointly decide where to spend their vacation; a jury judges a defendant to be guilty; a city council votes to raise property taxes; or the president and the Joint Chiefs of Staff decide to commit troops to an area of international conflict. How do such decisions compare with those that might have been made by individual decision makers? Are group decisions better or worse, more risky or cautious, more prudent or reckless? These are the questions that concern us in this section.

GROUP POLARIZATION

In the 1950s, the conventional wisdom was that decisions made by groups were typically cautious and conservative. For example, it was argued that because business decisions were increasingly being made by committees, the bold, innovative risk-taking of entrepreneurs such as Andrew Carnegie was a thing of the past (for example, Whyte, 1956). James Stoner, then a graduate business student at MIT, decided to test this assumption (1961).

In his study, subjects were asked to consider a number of hypothetical dilemmas. In one, an electrical engineer must decide whether to stick with his present job at a modest but adequate salary or to take a job with a new firm offering more money and a possible partnership in the new venture if it succeeds, but no long-term security. In another, a man with a severe heart ailment must seriously curtail his customary way of life or he can choose to undergo a medical operation that would either cure him completely or prove fatal. Subjects were asked to decide how good the odds of success would have to be before they would advise the person to try the riskier course of action. For example, they could recommend that the engineer go for the riskier job if the chances that the new venture would succeed were 5 in 10, or 3 in 10, or only 1 in 10. By using numerical odds like these, Stoner was able to compare the riskiness of different decisions quantitatively.

In the study, subjects first made their decisions alone, as individuals. They then met in groups and arrived at a group decision for each dilemma. After the group discussion, they again considered the dilemmas privately as individuals. When Stoner compared the group's decisions with the average of the individuals' pregroup decisions, he found that the group's decisions were *riskier* than the individual's initial decisions. Moreover, this shift reflected genuine opinion change on the part of group members, not just public conformity to the group decision: The private individual decisions after the group discussion were significantly riskier than the initial decisions. These findings were subsequently replicated by other researchers, even in situations that presented subjects with real rather than hypothetical risks (Bem, Wallach, & Kogan, 1965; Wallach, Kogan, & Bem, 1964, 1962). The phenomenon was initially called the "risky shift" effect.

This turned out not to be an accurate characterization. Even in the early studies, group decisions tended to shift slightly but consistently in the cautious direction on one or two of the hypothetical dilemmas (Wallach, Kogan, & Bem, 1962). After many more studies, it became clear that group discussion leads to decisions that are not necessarily more risky but are *more extreme* than the individual decisions: If group members are initially inclined to be risky on a particular dilemma, then the group will become more risky; if group members are initially inclined to be cautious, the group will be even more cautious. Accordingly, the phenomenon is now called the **group polarization** effect (Myers & Lamm, 1976).

There are now more than 300 studies of the group polarization effect, with a dazzling array of variations. For example, in one recent study, active burglars actually cased houses and then provided individual and group estimates of how easy each would be to burglarize. Compared with the individual estimates, the group estimates were more conservative; that is, they rated the homes to be more difficult to break into successfully (Cromwell, Marks, Olson, & Avary, 1991).

Group polarization extends beyond issues of risk and caution. For example, group discussion caused French students' initially positive attitudes toward the country's premier to become even more positive and their initially negative attitudes toward Americans to become even more negative (Moscovici & Zavalloni, 1969). Jury decisions can be similarly affected, leading to more extreme verdicts (Isozaki, 1984). Polarization in juries is more likely to occur on judgments concerning values and opinions (for example, in deciding what would be an appropriate punishment for a guilty defendant) than on judgments concerning matters of fact (for example, the defendant's guilt), and they are most likely to show polarization when they are required to reach unanimous decisions—as juries often are (Kaplan & Miller, 1987).

Many explanations for the group polarization effect have been offered over the years, but the two that have best survived intensive testing are *informational influence* and *normative influence* (Isenberg, 1986). *Informational influence* occurs when people learn new information and hear novel arguments relevant to the decision under discussion. For

Juries often arrive at decisions that are more extreme than the average of jury members' individual decisions—the group polarization effect.

example, in discussing whether the electrical engineer should go with the new venture—a decision that almost always shifts in the risky direction—it is quite common for someone in the group to argue that riskiness is warranted because electrical engineers can always find good jobs. A shift in the conservative direction occurred in the burglar study after one of the group noted that it was nearly 3:00 P.M. and that children would soon be returning from school and playing nearby.

The more arguments raised in the discussion in favor of a position, the more likely it is that the group will move toward that position. And this is where the bias enters: Members of a group are most likely to present points in favor of the position they initially favor and to discuss repeatedly information they already share (Stasser, Taylor, & Hanna, 1989; Stasser & Titus, 1985). Accordingly, the discussion will be biased in favor of the group's initial position, and the group will move toward that position as more of the group members become convinced. Interestingly, the polarization effect still occurs even when everybody is given an extensive list of arguments before the experiment begins—a finding that some believe casts doubt on the informational explanation of the effect (Zuber, Crott, & Werner, 1992).

Normative influence occurs when people compare their own views with the norms of the group. During discussion, they may learn that others have similar attitudes or even more extreme views than they themselves do. If they are motivated to be seen positively by the group, they may conform to the group's position or even express a position that is more extreme than the group's. As one researcher noted, "To be virtuous . . . is to be different from the mean—in the right direction and to the right degree" (Brown, 1974, p. 469).

But normative influence is not simply pressure to conform. Often the group provides a frame of reference for its members, a context within which they can reevaluate their initial positions. This is illustrated by a common and amusing event that frequently occurs in group polarization experiments. For example, in one group, a subject began the discussion of the dilemma facing the electrical engineer by confidently announcing, "I feel this guy should really be willing to take a risk here. He should go with the new job even if it has only a

5 in 10 chance of succeeding." Other group members were incredulous: "You think that 5 in 10 is being risky? If he has any guts, he should give it a shot even if there is only 1 chance in 100 of success. I mean, what has he really got to lose?" Eager to reestablish his reputation as a risk-taker, the original individual quickly shifted his position further in the risky direction. By redefining the meaning of "risky," the group thus moved both its own decision and its members' postdiscussion attitudes further toward the risky extreme of the scale (Wallach, Kogan, & Bem, 1962; from the authors' private notes).

As this example illustrates, both informational and normative influence occur simultaneously in group discussions, and several studies have attempted to untangle them. Some studies have shown that the polarization effect occurs if subjects simply hear the arguments of the group, without knowing the actual positions of others members of the group (Burnstein & Vinokur, 1977, 1973). This demonstrates that informational influence by itself is sufficient to produce polarization. Other studies have shown that the polarization effect also occurs when people learn others' positions but do not hear any supporting arguments, demonstrating that normative influence by itself is sufficient (Goethals & Zanna, 1979; Sanders & Baron, 1977). Typically, the information effect is greater than the normative effect (Isenberg, 1986).

GROUPTHINK

"How could we have been so stupid?" This was President John Kennedy's reaction to the disastrous failure of his administration's attempt to invade Cuba at the Bay of Pigs in 1961 and overthrow the government of Fidel Castro. The plan was badly conceived at many levels. For example, if the initial landing were unsuccessful, the invaders were supposed to retreat into the mountains. But no one in the planning group had studied the map closely enough to realize that no army could have gotten through the 80 miles of swamp that separated the mountains from the landing area. As it turned out, this didn't matter, because other miscalculations caused the invading force to be wiped out long before the retreat would have taken place.

The invasion had been conceived and planned by the president and a small group of his advisers. Writing four years later, one of these advisers, the historian Arthur Schlesinger, Jr., blamed himself

> for having kept so silent during those crucial discussions in the Cabinet Room, though my feelings of guilt were tempered by the knowledge that a course of objection would have accomplished little save to gain me a name as a nuisance. I can only explain my failure to do more than raise a few timid questions by reporting that one's impulse to blow the whistle on this nonsense was simply undone by the circumstances of the discussion. (1965, p. 255)

What were these "circumstances of the discussion" that led the group to pursue such a disastrous course of action? After reading Schlesinger's account, social psychologist Irving Janis proposed a theory of groupthink, a phenomenon in which members of a group are led to suppress their own dissent in the interests of group consensus (Janis, 1982). After analyzing several other foreign-policy decisions, Janis set forth the antecedent conditions and symptoms of groupthink as well as the symptoms of defective decision making that result from it. These are outlined in Figure 18-10.

As shown in the figure, the stage for groupthink is set when a cohesive group of decision makers assembles in isolation from outside influences and without systematic procedures for considering both the pros and cons of different courses of action. It is further fostered by a directive leader who explicitly favors a particular course of action and by high stress—often due to an external threat, recent failures, moral dilemmas, and an apparent lack of viable alternatives. Recent research has confirmed that groupthink is particularly likely to develop in situations that involve external threats to the group (McCauley, 1989). All these conditions foster a strong desire to achieve and maintain group consensus and to avoid "rocking the boat" with dissent.

The symptoms of groupthink include group-shared illusions of invulnerability, morality, and unanimity. These are achieved by direct pressure on dissenters or—as Schlesinger's account notes—self-censorship. As a result, the group members spend more time rationalizing their decision rather

FIGURE 18-10

The Causes and Consequences of Groupthink (After Janis, 1982)

ANTECEDENT CONDITIONS
1. A cohesive group
2. Isolation of the group from outside influences
3. No systematic procedures for considering both the pros and cons of different courses of action
4. A directive leader who explicitly favors a particular course of action
5. High stress

GROUPTHINK
The desire to achieve consensus and avoid dissent

SYMPTOMS OF GROUPTHINK
1. Illusion of invulnerability, morality, and unanimity
2. Pressure on dissenters
3. Self-censorship of dissent
4. Collective rationalization
5. Self-appointed mindguards

FLAWS OF DECISION MAKING PROCESS UNDER GROUPTHINK
1. Incomplete survey of the group's objectives and alternative courses of action
2. Failure to examine the risks of the preferred choice
3. Poor and incomplete search for relevant information
4. Selective bias in processing the information at hand
5. Failure to reappraise rejected alternatives
6. Failure to develop contingency plans in case of failure

than realistically examining its strengths and weaknesses. Moreover, there are often self-appointed *mindguards,* group members who actively attempt to prevent the group from considering information that would challenge the effectiveness or morality of its decisions. For example, the attorney general

Unless precautions are taken, group decision making can be distorted by Groupthink, in which members are led to suppress reservations about a course of action in order to avoid "rocking the boat" by disrupting consensus.

(President Kennedy's brother Robert) privately warned Schlesinger, "The President has made his mind up. Don't push it any further." The secretary of state withheld information from the group that had been provided by intelligence experts who warned against an invasion of Cuba (Janis, 1982). Finally, figure 18-10 lists the flaws of decision making that follow from groupthink and lead ultimately to poor decisions.

Janis has also analyzed two successful group decisions: the Truman administration's decision to implement the Marshall Plan (which helped Europe recover from World War II) and the Kennedy administration's handling of the Soviet Union's attempts to install missiles in Cuba. In later publications, Janis spelled out some of the safeguards groups could use to avoid the hazards of groupthink.

First, of course, he thinks that group members should be told about groupthink, its causes, and its consequences. Among his more specific suggestions are that the group leader foster an atmosphere of open debate and not openly endorse any position before the discussion begins; that one or more members be assigned explicitly to play the role of "devil's advocate," actively questioning the group's decisions throughout; that outside experts be brought in to challenge the group and give it fresh perspectives; and finally, once the group has arrived at a consensus, that there be a "second chance" meeting in which members can rediscuss any lingering doubts or reservations (Janis, 1985, 1982).

There has also been criticism of Janis's theory. First, it is based on historical analysis more than on laboratory experimentation. Experiments that have been done have yielded mixed results (for example, Turner, Pratkanis, & Leve, 1992; McCauley, 1989; Calloway, Marriott, & Esser, 1985; Longley & Pruitt, 1980; Courtright, 1978; Flowers, 1977). The processes that Janis calls groupthink are clearly quite complex, and recent work has been directed toward trying to integrate it into a more general theory of group decision making (Aldag & Fuller, 1993).

BIOLOGICAL-PSYCHOLOGICAL PERSPECTIVES

We noted at the end of Chapter 17 that social psychology's strong emphasis on the situational control of behavior has tended to discourage it from taking a biological perspective on social psychological phenomena. Nevertheless, the increasing popularity of sociobiological or evolutionary theorizing has been changing that. For example, we pointed out that social psychologists are now more likely than in the past to ask how our ways of processing social information might have evolved and to debate the evolutionary and biological foundations of such social psychological phenomena as sexual attraction and orientation.

In this chapter, we have seen that the phenomenon of social facilitation is shared by human and nonhuman creatures, suggesting a common underlying biology—such as the arousal-producing effects of being in the presence of other members of the species. In trying to account for the high obedience rates in his experiments, Milgram speculated that obedience to authority is so important for communal life that the tendency to give over one's autonomy to an authority figure has probably been built in to our species by evolution.

In sum, social psychologists, too, are coming to appreciate that a broader understanding of social influence and interaction can be facilitated by adopting both a biological and psychological perspective.

CHAPTER SUMMARY

1. To most people, the term *social influence* connotes direct and deliberate attempts to change our beliefs, attitudes, or behaviors. If we respond to such influence by complying with the wishes of an influencer—without necessarily changing our private beliefs or attitudes—our reaction is called *compliance.* If we change our private beliefs and attitudes as well, our reaction is called *internalization.* Many forms of social influence are indirect or unintentional. Even the mere physical presence of other persons can affect us. We are also influenced by *social norms,* implicit rules and expectations of how we ought to think and behave. The success of direct and deliberate social influence often depends on our allegiance to social norms.

2. Both humans and animals respond more quickly when in the presence of other members of their species. This *social facilitation* occurs whether the others are performing the same task (coactors) or are simply watching (an audience). The presence of others appears to raise the organism's drive level. This facilitates the correct performance of simple response but hinders the performance of complex responses. For humans, cognitive factors, such as a concern with evaluation, also play a role.

3. The uninhibited aggressive behavior sometimes shown by mobs and crowds may be the result of a state of *deindividuation,* in which individuals feel that they have lost their personal identities and have merged into the group. Anonymity reduces self-awareness and contributes to deindividuation. Some of the consequences of deindividuation are weakened restraints against impulsive behavior, increased sensitivity to immediate cues and current emotional states, and a lessened concern about the evaluation by others. Being in a group and feeling anonymous do not inevitably lead to increased aggressiveness, however.

4. A bystander to an emergency is less likely to intervene or help if in a group than if alone. Two major factors that deter intervention are *defining the situation* and *diffusion of responsibility.* By attempting to appear calm, bystanders may define the situation for each other as a nonemergency, thereby producing a state of *pluralistic ignorance.* The presence of other people also diffuses responsibility so that no one person feels the necessity to act. Bystanders are more likely to intervene when these factors are minimized, particularly if at least one person begins to help.

5. In a series of classic studies on *conformity,* Solomon Asch found that a unanimous group exerts strong pressure on an individual to conform to the group's judgments—even when those judgments are clearly wrong. Much less conformity is observed if even one person dissents from the group.

6. In a series of classic studies on *obedience,* Stanley Milgram demonstrated that ordinary people would obey an experimenter's order to deliver strong electric shocks to an innocent victim. Factors conspiring to produce the high obedience rates include *social norms* (for example, the implied contract to continue the experiment until completed); the *surveillance* of the experimenter; *buffers* that distance the person from the consequences of his or her acts; and the *legitimating role of science,* which leads people to abandon their autonomy to the experimenter. There has also been controversy about the ethics of the experiments themselves.

7. Obedience to authority can be undermined—and rebellion provoked—if the individual is with a group whose members have the opportunity to share their opinions, can give each other social support for dissenting, and can provide role models for disobedience. But the individual may then have to choose between obedience to the authority and conformity to the group that has decided to rebel.

8. Studies of conformity and obedience reveal that situational factors exert more influence over behavior than most of us realize. We tend to underestimate situational forces on behavior.

9. A minority of persons within a larger group can move the majority toward its point of view if it maintains a consistent dissenting position without appearing to be rigid, dogmatic, or arrogant. Minorities sometimes obtain private attitude change from majority members even when they fail to obtain public conformity.

10. *Cognitive response theory* proposes that persuasion induced by a communication is actually self-persuasion produced by the thoughts that the person generates while reading or hearing the communication. If the communication evokes thoughts supportive of the position being advocated, the individual will move toward that position; if the communication evokes unsupportive thoughts—such as counterarguments or disparaging thoughts about the communicator—the individual will remain unpersuaded. The theory provides a unified explanation for several previously discovered phenomena of persuasion.

11. Persuasion can take two routes in producing belief and attitude change: the *central route,* in which the individual responds to the substantive arguments of a communication, and the *peripheral route,* in which the individual responds to noncontent cues in a communication (such as the number of arguments) or to context cues (such as the credibility of the communicator or the pleasantness of the surroundings). A communication about an issue of personal relevance is more likely to generate thoughts in response to the communication's substantive arguments. When an issue is of little personal relevance or when people are unwilling or unable to respond to the substantive content of a communication, they tend to use simple *heuristics*—rules of thumb—to judge the merits of the communication.

12. In the process of *identification,* we obey the norms and adopt the beliefs, attitudes, and behaviors of groups that we respect and admire. We use such *reference groups* to evaluate and regulate our opinions and actions. A reference group can regulate our attitudes and behavior by administering social rewards and punishments or by providing us with a frame of reference, a ready-made interpretation of events and social issues.

13. Most of us identify with more than one reference group, and this can lead to conflicting pressures on our beliefs, attitudes, and behaviors. College students frequently move away from the views of their family reference group toward the college reference group. These new views are usually sustained in later life because (a) they become internalized and (b) we tend to select new reference groups after college—spouses and friends—who share our views.

14. When groups make decisions, they often display *group polarization:* The group decision is in the same direction but is more extreme than the average of the group members' initial positions. This is not just public conformity; group members' private attitudes typically shift in response to the group discussion as well. The effect is due, in part, to *informational influence,* in which group members learn new information and hear novel arguments relevant to the decision under discussion. Group members tend to raise more arguments in favor of their initial position than against it, thus biasing the discussion and pushing the final decision further in the direction of the initial positions. Group polarization is also produced by *normative influence,* in which people compare their own initial views with the norms of the group. They may then adjust their position to conform to the group's majority position. In addition, the group can provide a frame of reference that causes its members to perceive their initial position as too weak or too moderate as an expression of their actual attitude.

15. An analysis of disastrous foreign-policy decisions reveals that a cohesive group of decision makers with a directive leader can fall into the trap of *groupthink,* in which members of the group suppress their own dissenting opinions in the interest of group consensus. This gives rise to a group-shared illusion of invulnerability, morality, and unanimity. This, in turn, produces a flawed decision-making process and bad decisions. It has been suggested that groupthink can be avoided if: The leader fosters an atmosphere of open debate and does not endorse any position before discussion begins; some group members are assigned to be "devil's advocates"; outside experts are brought in; and there is a "second chance" meeting at which members can reconsider any lingering doubts or reservations about their decision.

FURTHER READING

The three comprehensive textbooks in social psychology listed at the end of Chapter 17 also cover the topics discussed in this chapter. They are Aronson, Wilson, and Akert, *Social Psychology* (1994); Baron and Byrne, *Social Psychology* (7th ed., 1994); and Lippa, *Introduction to Social Psychology* (2nd ed., 1994). Aronson, *The Social Animal* (7th ed., 1995), covers several topics in social influence. More advanced treatments are available in Lindzey and Aronson (eds.), *The Handbook of Social Psychology* (3rd ed., 1985).

Many of the topics in this chapter are covered in paperback books written for general audiences, often by the original investigators. Milgram, *Obedience to Authority* (1974) is well worth reading, especially before forming an opinion about this controversial series of studies. Latané and Darley, *The Unresponsive Bystander: Why Doesn't He Help?* (1970) is a report by two of the original researchers in that area. Petty and Cacioppo, *Attitudes and Persuasion: Classic and Contemporary Approaches* (1981) is a good summary of both earlier and current work on persuasion written by two major contributors to this field. Janis, *Groupthink: Psychological Studies of Policy Decisions and Fiascoes* (2nd ed., 1982) is the major source for the groupthink phenomenon. And finally, LeBon's classic book, *The Crowd* (1895), is available in several editions.

BRIEF HISTORY
OF PSYCHOLOGY

Psychology has rich roots dating back to the views of early Greek philosophers, such as Socrates, Plato, and Aristotle, on the nature of the mind, the soul, the body, and of human experience. One of the earliest debates about human psychology is still raging today—the question of whether human capabilities are inborn or acquired through experience. The *nativist* view is that human beings enter the world with an inborn store of knowledge and understanding of reality. Early philosphers believed that this knowledge and understanding could be accessed through careful reasoning and introspection. Descartes, in the seventeenth century, supported the nativist view by arguing that some ideas (such as God, the self, geometric axioms, perfection, and infinity) are innate at birth. Descartes is also notable for his conception of the body as a machine that can be studied much as other machines are studied. This is the root of modern-day information-processing perspectives on the mind, which we will describe shortly.

The *empiricist* view is that knowledge is acquired through experiences and interactions with the world. Although this view was held by some of the early Greek philosophers, it is most strongly associated with the seventeenth-century English philosopher John Locke. According to Locke, humans are born *tabula rasa,* or with a blank slate, onto which experience in the world writes all knowledge and understanding. This perspective gave birth to *associationist psychology.* The associationists denied inborn ideas or capabilities of the mind. Instead, they argued that the mind was filled with ideas that entered by way of the senses and then became associated through such principles as similarity, contrast, and contiguities. Current research on memory and learning is related to earlier association theory.

These days, the debate between nativism and empiricism is referred to as the *nature versus nurture* debate. Although some psychologists would still argue that human thought and behavior is the result primarily of biology or primarily of experience, most psychologists take a more integrated approach, acknowledging that biological processes (such as heredity or processes in the brain) affect thoughts and behavior, but expe-

Wilhelm Wundt

rience also leaves its mark on thoughts and behavior.

WUNDT'S LABORATORY

Wilhelm Wundt is given credit for founding psychology as an academic discipline. The founding date is usually cited as 1879, the year that Wundt established the first formal psychological laboratory at the University of Leipzig in Germany. Wundt's research was primarily concerned with the senses, especially vision, but he and his co-workers also studied attention, emotion, and memory.

Wundt's psychology relied on *introspection* as a method of studying mental processes. The introspective method was inherited from philosophy, but Wundt added a new dimension to the concept. Pure self-observation was not sufficient; it had to be supplemented by experiments. His experiments systematically varied some physical dimension of a stimulus, and the introspective method was used to determine how these physical changes modified consciousness.

Wundt's approach to research can be illustrated by one of his experiments on *reaction time.* In this experiment, the subject was required to press a key as quickly as possible after the onset of a light, and the subject's reaction time was carefully measured. Wundt found that the response time was longer when a subject paid careful attention to detecting the onset of light than it was when the subject's attention was directed to making a quick finger movement to press the key. The subject reacted very quickly in both cases, but there was a difference in reaction time of about .1 second. To explain this strange finding, Wundt distinguished between *perception* and *apperception*. When attention was focused on the finger movement, simple perception occurred and the light triggered the response promptly. But when attention was focused on the stimulus, an additional activity of apperception occurred, which involved a "richer" perception of the light. Wundt decided that this apperception required about .1 second. His interpretation is no longer accepted, for we now know that the processes intervening between stimulus and response are organized in more complex ways; but such studies helped to launch psychology as an experimental science.

Until his death in 1920, Wundt's personal influence on psychology was singularly important. Many pioneers in American psychology were trained in Wundt's laboratory. The first formal psychology laboratory in the United States was established in 1883 at Johns Hopkins University by G. Stanley Hall (who had studied with Wundt), although William James had set up a small demonstration laboratory at Harvard by 1875. The first person to be called "professor of psychology" in the United States was J. McKeen Cattell, another Wundt student, who acquired that title at the University of Pennsylvania in 1888. Before the end of the 1890s, Wundt's students were to be found in many American universities.

Sir Francis Galton

OTHER ROOTS OF CONTEMPORARY PSYCHOLOGY

Although the impetus for establishing psychological laboratories came largely from Germany, there were other influences. In England, Sir Francis Galton was a pioneer in the study of individual differences and exerted an important influence on the development of intelligence tests. Galton invented the statistical technique of correlation and developed the index that later became known as the *coefficient of correlation*.

The influence of the theory of evolution through natural selection, propounded by Charles Darwin, also came from England. Darwin's theory established the continuity between animals and human beings and thus led to comparative studies in psychology.

Another area of influence on psychology came from medicine, especially from the treatment of the mentally ill. Hypnotism, for example, has a long history as a form of therapy, dating from the work of Anton Mesmer in the late 1700s. Another Viennese physician, Sigmund Freud, founded psychoanalysis early in the present century.

SCHOOLS OF PSYCHOLOGY

STRUCTURALISM AND FUNCTIONALISM

When scientific psychology emerged in the latter part of the nineteenth century, researchers were making great advances in chemistry and physics by analyzing complex compounds (molecules) into their elements (atoms). These successes encouraged psychologists to look for the mental elements of which more complex experiences were composed. If the chemist made headway by analyzing water into hydrogen and oxygen, perhaps the psychologist could make progress by considering the taste of lemonade (perception) as a molecule of conscious experience to be analyzed into elements (sensations)—such as sweet, bitter, cold, and whatever—that could be identified by introspection. This was the approach taken by Wundt and his students; its major proponent in the United

States was E. B. Titchener, a Wundt-trained psychologist at Cornell University. Since the goal was to specify mental structures, Titchener introduced the term *structuralism* to describe this brand of psychology.

But there was vigorous opposition to the purely analytical character of structuralism. William James—a distinguished psychologist at Harvard University—was impatient with the restrictions on psychology as it was developing under the structuralists. James felt that less emphasis should be placed on analyzing the elements of consciousness and more emphasis should be placed on understanding its fluid, streaming, personal character. His principal interest was in studying how the mind worked so that an organism could adapt to its environment. Because James asked how consciousness functions (particularly in the adaptive process), his approach to psychology was named *functionalism*. James' writing on *habits* as a mode of adaptation helped set the stage for a psychology that included the learning process as a central topic of study.

Interest in adaptation was influenced by Darwin's theory of natural selection. Consciousness evolved, so the argument ran, only because it served some purpose in guiding the activities of the individual. With this emphasis on the functional role of consciousness came a recognition that the introspetive method of structuralism was too restrictive. To find out how the organism adapts to its environment, the functionalists argued that data derived from introspection had to be supplemented by observations of actual behavior, including the study of animal behavior and the development of behavior (developmental psychology). Thus, functionalism broadened the scope of psychology to include behavior as a dependent variable. But along with the structuralists, functionalists still regarded psychology as the science of conscious experience and the principal investigative method as introspection.

Structuralism and functionalism played important roles in the early development of psychology. Because each viewpoint provided a systematic approach to the field, the two were considered competing *schools of psychology*. As psychology developed, other schools evolved and vied for leadership. By 1920, structuralism and functionalism were being displaced by three newer schools: be-

William James

haviorism, Gestalt psychology, and psychoanalysis.

BEHAVIORISM

Of the three new schools, behaviorism had the greatest influence on scientific psychology. Its founder, John B. Watson, reacted against the tradition of his time—that conscious experience was the province of psychology—and boldly proclaimed a psychology *without* introspection. Watson made no assertions about consciousness when he studied the behavior of animals and infants. He decided not only that the results of animal psychology and child psychology could stand on their own as a science, but also that they set a pattern that adult psychology might well follow.

John B. Watson

In order to make psychology a science, Watson said, psychological data must be open to public inspection like the data of any other science. Behavior is public; consciousness is private. Science should deal with public facts. Because psychologists were growing impatient with introspection, the new behaviorism caught on rapidly, particularly in the 1920s; for a time, most of the younger psychologists in the United States called themselves "behaviorists." In Russia, the work of Ivan Pavlov on the conditioned response was regarded as an important area of research by the behaviorists. The conditioned response was being investigated in the United States in a limited way before the advent of behaviorism, but Watson was responsible for its subsequent widespread influence on psychology.

Watson argued that nearly all behavior is the result of conditioning, and that the environment shapes our behavior by reinforcing specific habits. The conditioned response was viewed as the smallest indivisible unit of behavior, an "atom of behavior" from which more complicated behaviors could be built. All types of complex behavioral repertoires arising from special training or education were regarded as nothing more than an interlinked fabric of conditioned responses.

Behaviorists found it congenial to discuss psychological phenomena as beginning with a stimulus and ending with a response—giving rise to the term *stimulus-response (S-R) psychology*. S-R psychologists went beyond the earlier behaviorists in their willingness to infer hypothetical processes between the stimulus input and the response output,

processes that were called *intervening variables*.

If broad definitions are used, so that "stimulus" refers to a whole class of antecedent conditions and "response" refers to a whole class of outcomes (actual behavior and products of behavior), S-R psychology becomes merely a psychology of independent and dependent variables. Viewed in this way, S-R psychology is not a particular theory but a *language* that can be used to make psychological information explicit and communicable. As such, the S-R outlook is widely prevalent in psychology today.

GESTALT PSYCHOLOGY

At about the same time that Watson announced behaviorism in America, Gestalt psychology was appearing in Germany. The word *Gestalt* translates from the German as "form" or "configuration," and the psychology announced by Max Wertheimer in 1912 was a psychology concerned with the organization of mental processes. The position came to be identified most closely with Wertheimer and his colleagues Kurt Koffka and Wolfgang Köhler, all of whom migrated to the United States.

The earliest Gestalt experiments dealt with perceived motion, particularly the *phi phenomenon*. When two separated lights are flashed in succession (provided the timing and spatial locations are proper), the subject sees a single light moving from the position of the first light to that of the second. The phenomenon of apparent motion was familiar, but the Gestalt psychologists sensed the theoretical importance of the patterning of stimuli in producing the effect. Our experiences depend on the *patterns* formed by stimuli and on the *organization* of experience, they decided. What we see is relative to background, to other aspects of the whole. The whole is different from the sum of its parts; the whole consists of parts in relationship.

Although the Gestalt psychologists did not subscribe to the introspective psychology of their day any more than Watson did, they were vigorous opponents of behaviorism. They did not want to give up a kind of free introspection that goes by the name of *phenomenology*. They wanted to be able to ask a person what something looked like, what

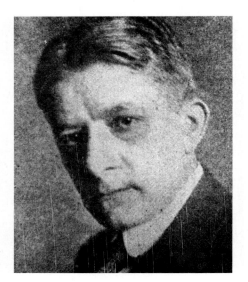

Wolfgang Köhler

it meant. They were interested in the perception of motion, in how people judged sizes, and in the appearance of colors under changes in illumination.

The importance of perception in all psychological events has led those influenced by Gestalt psychology to a number of perception-centered interpretations of learning, memory, and problem solving. These interpretations, spoken of as forms of cognitive theory, were instrumental in laying the groundwork for current developments in cognitive psychology.

PSYCHOANALYSIS

Sigmund Freud introduced psychoanalytic psychology to the United States in a series of lectures given at Clark University in 1909 on the invitation of psychologist G. Stanley Hall. Thus, the first scholarly recognition of Freud's work in the United States came from psychologists. Freud's influence became so pervasive that those who know nothing else about psychology have at least a nodding acquaintance with psychoanalysis.

If one of Freud's theories is to be singled out for consideration along with behaviorism and Gestalt psychology, it is his interpretation of the *unconscious*. Basic to Freud's theory of the unconscious is the conception that the unacceptable (forbidden, punished) wishes of childhood are driven out of awareness and become part of the unconscious, where they remain influential. The unconscious presses to find expression, which it

does in numerous ways, including dreams, slips of speech, and unconscious mannerisms. The method of psychoanalysis—free association under the guidance of the analyst—is itself a way of helping unconscious wishes find verbal expression. In classical Freudian theory, these unconscious wishes were almost exclusively sexual. This emphasis on childhood sexuality was one of the barriers to the acceptance of Freud's theories when they were first announced.

RECENT DEVELOPMENTS

Despite the important contribution of Gestalt psychology and psychoanalysis, psychology was dominated by behaviorism until World War II, particularly in the United States. With the end of the war, interest in psychology increased and many people were attracted to careers in the field. Sophisticated instruments and electronic equipment became available, and a wider range of problems could be examined. This expanded program of research made it evident that earlier theoretical approaches were too restrictive.

This viewpoint was strengthened by the development of computers in the 1950s. Computers, properly programmed, were able to perform tasks—such as playing chess and proving mathematical theorems—that previously could be done only by human beings. It became apparent that the computer offered psychologists a powerful tool with which to

Sigmund Freud
Herbert Simon

theorize about psychological processes. A series of brilliant papers, published in the late 1950s by Herbert Simon (who was later awarded the Nobel prize) and his colleagues, indicated how psychological phenomena could be *simulated* using the computer. Many old psychological issues were recast in terms of *information-processing systems*. The human being could now be viewed as a processor of information. The senses provide an input channel for information; mental operations are applied to the input; the transformed input creates a mental structure that is stored in memory; that structure interacts with others in memory to generate a response. The power of the computer permitted psychologists to theorize about complex mental processes and investigate the implications of the theory by simulating it on a computer. If the response (output) stage of the computer simulation agreed with the observed behavior of actual people, the psychologist could have some confidence in the theory.

The information-processing approach provided a richer and more dynamic approach to psychology than S-R theory with its intervening variables. Similarly, the information-processing approach permitted some of the speculations of Gestalt psychology and psychoanalysis to be formulated in a precise fashion as programs in a computer; in this way, earlier ideas about the nature of the mind could be made concrete and checked against actual data.

Another factor that led to a changing viewpoint in psychology in the 1950s was the development of modern linguistics. Prior to that time, linguists were primarily concerned with a description of a language; now they began to theorize about the mental structures required to comprehend and to speak a language. Work in this area was pioneered by Noam Chomsky, whose book *Syntactic Structures,* published in 1957, provided the basis for an active collaboration between psychologists and linguists. A rapid development of the field of *psycholinguistics* followed, providing the first significant psychological analyses of language.

At the same time, important advances were occurring in neuropsychology. A number of discoveries about the brain and the nervous system established clear relationships between neurobiological events and mental processes. It became increasingly dif-

ficult to assert, as some of the early behaviorists had, that a science of psychology could be established without links to neurophysiology. In the last decade, advances in biomedical technology have contributed to an explosion of research on neurophysiological correlates of normal and abnormal thought and behavior. In 1981, Roger Sperry won the Nobel prize for his work demonstrating the interconnections of the brain and the links between certain regions of the brain and basic thought or behavioral processes.

The development of information-processing models, psycholinguistics, and neuropsychology has produced a psychology that is highly cognitive in orientation. There is no agreed-on definition of *cognitive psychology,* but its principal concern is the scientific analysis of mental processes and mental structures. Cognitive psychology is not exclusively concerned with thought and knowledge. Its early concerns with the representation of knowledge and human thought led to the label "cognitive psychology," but the approach has been expanded to all areas of psychology, including motivation, perception, psychopathology, and social psychology.

During this century, the focus of psychology has come full circle. After rejecting conscious experience as ill-suited to scientific investigation and turning to the study of behavior, psychologists are once again theorizing about the mind, but this time with new and more powerful tools. The gain from behaviorism has been an emphasis on the objectivity and reproducibility of findings—an emphasis that has found a place in cognitive psychology.

From a historical perspective, it is too early to judge the long-term significance of recent developments in psychology. What is evident, however, is that there is great excitement in the field today, and many psychologists believe that it is in a period of revolutionary change and progress. Understanding how the mind works is a challenge that deserves the best intellectual effort we can put forth.

FURTHER READING

For a general survey of the history of psychology, see Hilgard, *Psychology in America: A Historical Survey* (1987); Watson, *The*

Great Psychologists: From Aristotle to Freud (4th ed., 1978); Wertheimer, *A Brief History of Psychology* (rev. ed., 1979); and Schultz, *A History of Modern Psychology* (6th ed., 1990). See also Boring, *A History of Experimental Psychology* (2nd ed., 1950); and Herrnstein and Boring, *A Source Book in the History of Psychology* (1965).

For a discussion of prominent women in the history of psychology, see Stevens and Gardner (1982), *The Women of Psychology*, Vols. I and II.

Important Dates in the History of Psychology

400 B.C.	Hippocrates relates personality characteristics to body types and proposes a physiological (as opposed to demonological) theory of mental illness.
350 B.C.	Aristotle stresses the objective observation of man's behavior and proposes three principles to account for the association of ideas.
A.D. 400	Saint Augustine, influenced by Platonic ideas, makes careful introspections in his *Confessions*.
1650	René Descartes characterizes the mind-body relationship as one of interaction.
1651	Thomas Hobbes foreshadows associationism by declaring that all ideas come from sensory experience.
1690	John Locke carries Hobbes' notion a step further by declaring that at birth the mind is a blank slate (*tabula rasa*).
1749	David Hartley formalizes a doctrine of associationism and suggests a neurological basis for memory.
1781	Immanuel Kant's *Critique of Pure Reason* attacks associationism and the nativistic approach; it strongly influences later philosophers and psychologists.
1809	Franz Gall and Johann Spurzheim give prominence through phrenology to the study of mental faculties and brain function.
1821	Pierre Flourens performs the first significant experiments in localization of brain functions.
1838	Johannes Müller formulates the doctrine of specific nerve energies.
1846	Ernst Weber derives the first quantitative law in psychology.
1850	Hermann von Helmholtz measures the rates of conduction of nerve impulses.
1859	Charles Darwin publishes *The Origin of Species*, propounding the theory of evolution through natural selection.
1860	Gustav Fechner publishes *Elements of Psychophysics*, in which he presents various methods for measuring the relationship between physical stimuli and sensations.
1869	Sir Francis Galton studies individual differences and applies Darwin's concept of selective adaptation to the evolution of races.
1879	Wilhelm Wundt opens the first formal psychological laboratory at the University of Leipzig.
1883	G. Stanley Hall establishes the first psychological laboratory in America at Johns Hopkins University.
1885	Hermann Ebbinghaus publishes the first experimental studies of memory.
1890	William James' *Principles of Psychology* is published in the United States.
1892	Edward Titchener at Cornell University establishes "structuralism" as a major influence in American psychology.
1892	Mary Calkins publishes her work on memorization by rote, establishing important experimental procedures for the study of cognition.
1898	Edward Thorndike performs some of the first controlled experiments on animal learning.
1900	Sigmund Freud publishes *The Interpretation of Dreams*, which presents many of his ideas on psychoanalysis.
1905	Alfred Binet and Theodore Simon devise the first intelligence test.
1906	Ivan Pavlov publishes the results of his studies on classical conditioning.

(continued)

1908	William McDougall's publication of *An Introduction to Social Psychology* marks the formal inauguration of the field of social psychology.
1912	Max Wertheimer publishes the first formulation of Gestalt psychology.
1913	John B. Watson exerts a major force on the course of psychology with his behaviorist manifesto.
1917	Wolfgang Köhler publishes the results of his studies on problem solving in primates.
1922	Edward Tolman presents his initial ideas on purposive behaviorism.
1929	Karl Lashley publishes *Brain Mechanisms and Intelligence.*
1932	Karen Horney moves to the United States and continues writing feminist critiques and reformulations of psychoanalysis.
1938	B. F. Skinner publishes *The Behavior of Organisms,* which summarizes early research on operant conditioning.
1942	Carl Rogers publishes *Counseling and Psychotherapy,* setting forth his humanistic approach to therapy.
1949	Donald Hebb, in *Organization of Behavior,* presents a theory that bridges the gap between neurophysiology and psychology.
1950	William Estes lays the foundation for a mathematical approach to theories of learning.
1954	The Swiss psychologist Jean Piaget publishes *The Construction of Reality in the Child,* which focuses attention on cognitive development.
1957	Noam Chomsky publishes *Syntactic Structures,* a book that presents a cognitive approach to language behavior.
1958	Herbert Simon and colleagues publish *Elements of a Theory of Human Problem Solving,* which reformulates classical psychological problems in terms of information-processing models.
1962	David Hubel and Torsten Weisel discover the relationship between the activity of individual neurons in the visual cortex to specific features of a visual stimulus.
1981	Roger Sperry wins the Nobel prize for physiology for his research on split-brain patients, demonstrating the interconnections of the brain.
	More recent events are not listed because not enough time has elapsed to judge their long-term impact on the field.

Statistical Methods and Measurement

Much of the work of psychologists calls for making measurements—either in the laboratory or under field conditions. This work may involve measuring the eye movements of infants when first exposed to a novel stimulus, recording the galvanic skin response of people under stress, counting the number of trials required to condition a monkey that has a prefrontal lobotomy, determining achievement test scores for students using computer-assisted learning, or counting the number of patients who show improvement following a particular type of psychotherapy. In all these examples, the *measurement operation* yields numbers; the psychologist's problem is to interpret them and to arrive at some general conclusions. Basic to this task is *statistics*—the discipline that deals with collecting numerical data and with making inferences from such data. The purpose of this appendix is to review certain statistical methods that play an important role in psychology.

This appendix is written on the assumption that the problems students have with statistics are essentially problems of clear thinking about data. An introductory acquaintance with statistics is *not* beyond the scope of anyone who understands enough algebra to use plus and minus signs and to substitute numbers for letters in equations.

DESCRIPTIVE STATISTICS

Statistics serves, first of all, to provide a shorthand description of large amounts of data. Suppose that we want to study the college entrance examination scores of 5,000 students recorded on cards in the registrar's office. These scores are the raw data. Thumbing through the cards will give us some impressions of the students' scores, but it will be impossible for us to keep all of them in mind. So we make some kind of summary of the data, possibly averaging all the scores or finding the highest and lowest scores. These statistical summaries make it easier to remember and to think about the data. Such summarizing statements are called *descriptive statistics*.

FREQUENCY DISTRIBUTIONS

Items of raw data become comprehensible when they are grouped in a *frequency distribution*. To group data, we must first divide the scale along which they are measured into intervals and then count the number of items that fall into each interval. An interval in which scores are grouped is called a class interval. The decision of how many *class intervals* the data are to be grouped into is not fixed by any rules but is based on the judgment of the investigator.

Table 1 provides a sample of raw data representing college entrance examination scores for 15 students. The scores are listed in the order in which the students were tested (the first student tested had a score of 84; the second, 61; and so on). Table 2 shows these data arranged in a frequency distribu-

84	75	91
61	75	67
72	87	79
75	79	83
77	51	69

TABLE 1

Raw Scroes   *College entrance examination scores for 15 students, listed in the order in which they were tested.*

CLASS INTERVAL	NUMBER OF PERSONS IN CLASS
50–59	1
60–69	3
70–79	7
80–89	3
90–99	1

TABLE 2

Frequency Distribution
Scores from Table 1 accumulated by class intervals.

tion for which the class interval has been set at 10. One score falls in the interval from 50 to 59, three scores fall in the interval from 60 to 69, and so on. Note that most scores fall in the interval from 70 to 79 and that no scores fall below the 50 to 59 interval or above the 90 to 99 interval.

A frequency distribution is often easier to understand if it is presented graphically. The most widely used graph form is the *frequency histogram;* an example is shown in the top panel of Figure 1. Histograms are constructed by drawing bars, the bases of which are given by the class intervals and the heights of which are determined by the corresponding class frequencies. An alternative way of presenting frequency distributions in graph form is to use a *frequency polygon,* an example of which is shown in the bottom panel of Figure 1. Frequency polygons are constructed by plotting the class frequencies at the center of the class interval and connecting the points obtained by straight lines. To complete the picture, one extra class is added at each end of the distribution; since these classes have zero frequencies, both ends of the figure will touch the horizontal axis. The frequency polygon gives the same information as the frequency histogram but by means of a set of connected lines rather than bars.

In practice, we would obtain a much greater number of items than those plotted in Figure 1, but a minimum amount of data is shown in all of the illustrations in this appendix so that you can easily check the steps in tabulating and plotting.

Measures of Central Tendency

A *measure of central tendency* is simply a representative point on our scale—a central point that summarizes important information about the data. Three such measures are commonly used: the *mean,* the *median,* and the *mode.*

The mean is the familiar arithmetic average obtained by adding the scores and dividing by the number of scores. The sum of the raw scores in Table 1 is 1,125. If we divide this by 15 (the number of students' scores), the mean turns out to be 75.

The median is the score of the middle item, which is obtained by arranging the scores in order and then counting into the

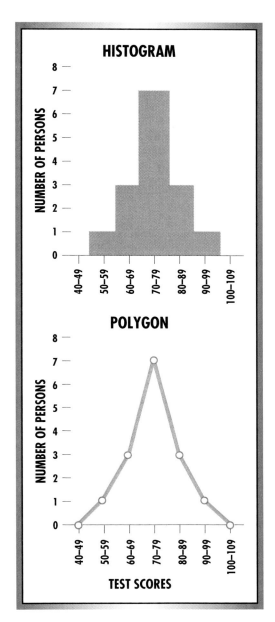

FIGURE 1

Frequency Diagrams   *The data from Table 2 are plotted here. A frequency histogram is on the top; a frequency polygon, on the bottom.*

middle from either end. When the 15 scores in Table 1 are placed in order from highest to lowest, the eighth score from either end turns out to be 75. If the number of cases is even, we simply average the two cases on each side of the middle.

The mode is the most frequent score in a given distribution. In Table 1, the most frequent score is 75; hence, the mode of the distribution is 75.

In a *normal distribution,* in which the scores are distributed evenly on either side of the middle (as in Figure 1), the mean, median, and mode all fall together. This is not true for distributions that are *skewed,* or unbalanced. Suppose we want to analyze the departure times of a morning train. The train usually leaves on time; occasionally it leaves late, but it never leaves early. For a train with a scheduled departure time of 8:00 A.M., one week's record might be as follows:

M	8:00	Mean	=	8:07
Tu	8:04	Median	=	8:02
W	8:02	Mode	=	8:00
Th	8:19			
F	8:22			
Sat	8:00			
Sun	8:00			

The distribution of departure times in this example is skewed because of the two late departures; they raise the mean departure time but do not have much effect on the median or the mode.

Skewness is important because, unless it is understood, the differences between the median and the mean may sometimes be misleading (see Figure 2). If, for example, company executives and the company's union are arguing about the prosperity of the company's work force, it is possible for the mean and median incomes to move in opposite directions. Suppose that a company raises the wages of most of its employees, but cuts the wages of its top executives, who were at the extremely high end of the pay scale. The median income of the company might have gone up while the mean went down. The party wanting to show that incomes were getting higher would choose the median, and the party wanting to show that incomes were getting lower would choose the mean.

The mean is the most widely used measure of central tendency, but there are times when the mode or the median is a more meaningful measure.

MEASURES OF VARIATION

Usually more information is needed about a distribution than can be obtained from a measure of central tendency. For example, we need a measure to tell us whether scores cluster closely around their average or whether they scatter widely. A measure of the spread of scores around the average is called a *measure of variation.*

Measures of variation are useful in at least two ways. First, they tell us how representative the average is. If the variation is small, we know that individual scores are close to it. If the variation is large, we cannot use the mean as a representative value with as much assurance. Suppose that clothing is being designed for a group of people without the benefit of precise measurements. Knowing their average size would be helpful, but it also would be important to know the spread of sizes. The second measure provides a yardstick that we can use to measure the amount of variability among the sizes.

To illustrate, consider the data in Figure 3, which show frequency distributions of entrance examination scores for two classes of 30 students. Both classes have the same mean of 75, but they exhibit clearly different degrees of variation. The scores of all the students in Class I are clustered close to the mean, whereas the scores of the students in Class II are spread over a wide range. Some measure is required to specify more exactly how these two distributions differ. Three measures of variation frequently used by psychologists are the *range,* the *variance,* and the *standard deviation.*

FIGURE 2

Skewed Distribution Curves *Note that skewed distributions are designated by the direction in which the tail falls. Also note that the mean, median, and mode are not identical for a skewed distribution; the median commonly falls between the mode and the mean.*

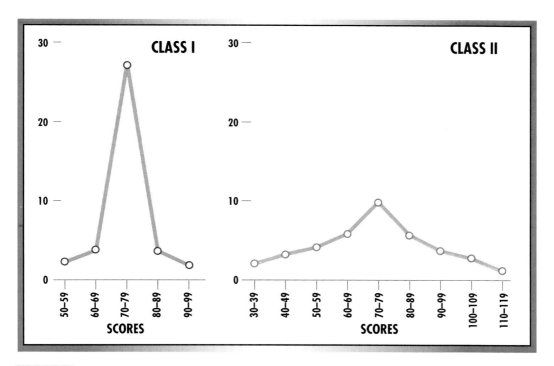

FIGURE 3

Distributions Differing in Variation *It is easy to see that the scores for Class 1 cluster closer to the mean than the scores for Class II, even though the means of the two classes are identical (75). For Class I, all the scores fall between 60 and 89, with most of the scores falling in the interval from 70 through 79. For Class II, the scores are distributed fairly uniformly over a wide range from 40 through 109. This difference in variability between the two distributions can be measured using the standard deviation, which is smaller for Class I than for Class II.*

To simplify arithmetic computation, we will suppose that five students from each class seek entrance to college and that their entrance examination scores are as follows:

Student scores from Class I:
73, 74, 75, 76, 77 (mean = 75)

Student scores from Class II:
60, 65, 75, 85, 90 (mean = 75)

We will now compute the measures of variation for these two samples.

The *range* is the spread between the highest score and the lowest score. The range of scores for the five students from Class I is 4 (from 73 to 77); the range of scores from Class II is 30 (from 60 to 90).

The range is easy to compute, but the variance and standard deviation are more frequently used. They are more sensitive measures of variation because they account for every score, not just extreme values as the range does. The variance measures how far the scores making up a distribution depart from that distribution's mean. To compute

the variance, first compute the deviation d of each score from the mean of the distribution by subtracting each score from the mean (see Table 3). Then, each of the deviations is squared to get rid of negative numbers. Finally, the deviations are added together and divided by the total number of deviations to obtain the average deviation. This average deviation is the variance. When this is done for the data in Figure 3, we find that the variance for Class I is 2.0 and the variance for Class II is 130. Obviously, Class II has much more variability in its scores than Class I.

One disadvantage of the variance is that it is expressed in squared units of measurement. Thus, to say that Class I has a variance of 2 does not indicate that, on average, scores varied an average of 2 points from the mean. Instead, it indicates that 2 is the average of the squared number of points that scores varied from the mean. In order to obtain a measure of variability that is expressed in the original units of measurement (in this case, points on an exam), simply take the square

TABLE 3

Computation of the
Variance and Standard
Deviation

CLASS I SCORES (MEAN = 75)

	d	d^2
77 − 75 =	2	4
76 − 75 =	1	1
75 − 75 =	0	0
74 − 75 =	−1	1
73 − 75 =	−2	4
		10

Sum of d^2 = 10

Variance = Mean of d^2 = $^{10}/_5$ = 2.0

Standard deviation (σ) = $\sqrt{2.0}$ = 1.4

CLASS II SCORES (MEAN = 75)

	d	d^2
90 − 75 =	15	225
85 − 75 =	10	100
75 − 75 =	0	0
65 − 75 =	−10	100
60 − 75 =	−15	225
		650

Sum of d^2 = 650

Variance = Mean of d^2 = $^{650}/_5$ = 130

Standard deviation (σ) = $\sqrt{130}$ = 11.4

root of the variance. This is known as the standard deviation. The standard deviation is denoted by the lowercase Greek letter *sigma* (σ), which also is used in several other statistical calculations, as we will discuss shortly. The formula for the standard deviation is

$$\sigma = \sqrt{\frac{\text{sum of } d^2}{N}}$$

Specimen Computation of the Standard Deviation The scores for the samples from the two classes are arranged in Table 3 for easy computation of the standard deviation. The first step involves subtracting the mean from each score (the mean is 75 for both classes). This operation yields positive d values for scores above the mean and negative d values for scores below the mean. The minus signs disappear when the d values are squared in

the next column. The squared deviations are added and then divided by N, the number of cases in the sample; in our example, N = 5. Taking the square root yields the standard deviation.*

STATISTICAL INFERENCE

Now that we have become familiar with statistics as a way of describing data, we are ready to turn to the processes of interpretation—to the making of inferences from data.

POPULATIONS AND SAMPLES

First, it is necessary to distinguish between a *population* and a *sample* drawn from that population. The United States Census Bureau attempts to describe the whole population by obtaining descriptive material on age, marital status, and so on from everyone in the country. The word *population* is appropriate to the census because it represents *all* the people living in the United States.

In statistics, the word "population" is not limited to people or animals or things. The population may be all of the temperatures registered on a thermometer during the last decade, all of the words in the English language, or all of any other specified supply of data. Often we do not have access to the total population, and so we try to represent it by a sample drawn in a *random* (unbiased) fashion. We may ask some questions of a random fraction of the people, as the Census Bureau has done as part of recent censuses; we may derive average temperatures by reading the thermometer at specified times, without taking a continuous record; we may estimate the number of words in the encyclopedia by counting the words on random pages. These illustrations all involve the selection of a *sample* from the population. If any of these

---

* For this introductory treatment, we will use *sigma* (σ) throughout. However, in the scientific literature, the lowercase letter *s* is used to denote the standard deviation of a *sample* and σ is used to denote the standard deviation of the *population*. Moreover, in computing the standard deviation of a sample *s*, the sum of d^2 is divided by $N-1$ rather than by N. For reason-

ably large samples, however, the actual value of the standard deviation is only slightly affected whether we divide by $N-1$ or N. To simplify this presentation, we will not distinguish between the standard deviation of a sample and that of a population; instead, we will use the same formula to compute both. For a discussion of this point, see Phillips (1992).

processes are repeated, we will obtain slightly different results due to the fact that a sample does not fully represent the whole population and therefore contains *errors of sampling.* This is where statistical inference enters.

A sample of data is collected from a population in order to make inferences about that population. A sample of census data may be examined to see whether the population is getting older, for example, or whether there is a trend of migration to the suburbs. Similarly, experimental results are studied to determine what effects experimental manipulations have had on behavior—whether the threshold for pitch is affected by loudness, whether child-rearing practices have detectable effects later in life. To make *statistical inferences,* we have to evaluate the relationships revealed by the sample data. These inferences are always made under some degree of uncertainty due to sampling errors. If the statistical tests indicate that the magnitude of the effect found in the sample is fairly large (relative to the estimate of the sampling error), then we can be confident that the effect observed in the sample holds for the population at large.

Thus, statistical inference deals with the problem of making an inference or judgment about a feature of a population based solely on information obtained from a sample of that population. As an introduction to statistical inference, we will consider the normal distribution and its use in interpreting standard deviations.

NORMAL DISTRIBUTION

When large amounts of data are collected, tabulated, and plotted as a histogram or polygon, they often fall into a roughly bell-shaped symmetrical distribution known as the *normal distribution.* Most items fall near the mean (the high point of the bell), and the bell tapers off sharply at very high and very low scores. This form of curve is of special interest because it also arises when the outcome of a process is based on a large number of *chance* events all occurring independently. The demonstration device displayed in Figure 4 illustrates how a sequence of chance events gives rise to a normal distribution. The chance factor of whether a steel ball will fall to the left or right each time it encounters a point where the channel branches results in a sym-

metrical distribution: More balls fall straight down the middle, but occasionally one reaches one of the end compartments. This is a useful way of visualizing what is meant by a chance distribution closely approximating the normal distribution.

The normal distribution (Figure 5) is the mathematical representation of the idealized distribution approximated by the device shown in Figure 4. The normal distribution represents the likelihood that items within a normally distributed population will depart from the mean by any stated amount. The percentages shown in Figure 5 represent the *percentage of the area* lying under the curve between the indicated scale values; the total area under the curve represents the whole population. Roughly two-thirds of the cases (68 percent) will fall between plus and minus one standard deviation from the mean ($\pm$ 1σ); 95 percent of the cases within $\pm 2\sigma$ and virtually all cases (99.7 percent) within $\pm 3\sigma$. A more detailed listing of areas under portions of the normal curve is given in Table 4.

FIGURE 4

Device to Demonstrate a Chance Distribution
The board is held upside down until all the steel balls fall into the reservoir. Then the board is turned over and held vertically until the balls fall into the nine columns. The precise number of balls falling into each column will vary from one demonstration to the next. On the average, however, the heights of the columns of balls will approximate a normal distribution, with the greatest height in the center column and gradually decreasing heights in the outer columns.

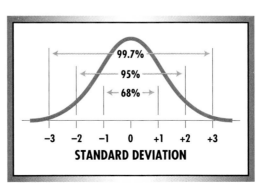

FIGURE 5

Normal Distribution
The normal distribution curve can be constructed using the mean and the standard deviation. The area under the curve below -3σ and above $+3\sigma$ is negligible.

TABLE 4

Area of the Normal Distribution as Proportion of Total Area

STANDARD DEVIATION	(1) AREA TO THE LEFT OF THIS VALUE	(2) AREA TO THE RIGHT OF THIS VALUE	(3) AREA BETWEEN THIS VALUE AND MEAN
-3.0σ	.001	.999	.499
-2.5σ	.006	.994	.494
-2.0σ	.023	.977	.477
-1.5σ	.067	.933	.433
-1.0σ	.159	.841	.341
-0.5σ	.309	.691	.191
0.0σ	.500	.500	.000
$+0.5\sigma$	.691	.309	.191
$+1.0\sigma$	.841	.159	.341
$+1.5\sigma$	.933	.067	.433
$+2.0\sigma$	.977	.023	.477
$+2.5\sigma$	.994	.006	.494
$+3.0\sigma$	.999	.001	.499

Using Table 4, let us trace how the 68 percent and 95 percent values in Figure 5 are derived. We find from Column 3 of Table 4 that between -1σ and the mean lies .341 of the total area and between $+1\sigma$ and the mean also lies .341 of the area. Adding these values gives us .682, which is expressed in Figure 5 as 68 percent. Similarly, the area between -2σ and $+2\sigma$ is $2 \times 477 = .954$, which is expressed as 95 percent.

These percentages have several uses. One is in connection with the interpretation of standard scores, to which we turn next. Another is in connection with tests of significance.

SCALING OF DATA

In order to interpret a score, we often need to know whether it is high or low in relation to other scores. If a person taking a driver's test requires .500 seconds to brake after a danger signal, how can we tell whether the performance is fast or slow? Does a student who scores 60 on a physics examination pass the course? To answer questions of this kind, we have to derive a *scale* against which the scores can be compared.

RANKED DATA By placing scores in rank order from high to low, we derive one kind of scale. An individual score is interpreted on the basis of where it ranks among the group of scores. For example, the graduates of West Point know where they stand in their class—perhaps 35th or 125th in a class of 400.

STANDARD SCORES The standard deviation is a convenient unit to use in scaling because we can interpret how far away 1σ or 2σ is from the mean (see Table 4). A score based on a multiple of the standard deviation is known as a *standard score*. Many scales used in psychological measurement are based on the principle of standard scores.

Specimen Computations of Standard Scores Table 1 presented college entrance scores for 15 students. Without more information, we do not know whether these scores are representative of the population of all college applicants. On this examination, however, we will assume that the population mean is 75 and the standard deviation is 10.

What, then, is the *standard score* for a student who had 90 on the examination? We must express how far this score lies above the mean in multiples of the standard deviation.

Standard score for grade of 90:

$$\frac{90 - 75}{10} = \frac{15}{10} = 1.5\sigma$$

As a second example, consider a student with a score of 53.

Standard score for grade of 53.

$$\frac{53 - 75}{10} = \frac{-22}{10} = -2.2\sigma$$

In this case, the minus sign tells us that the student's score is below the mean by 2.2 standard deviations. Thus, the sign of the standard score (+ or −) indicates whether the score is above or below the mean, and its value indicates how far from the mean the score lies in standard deviations.

HOW REPRESENTATIVE IS A MEAN?

How useful is the mean of a sample in estimating the population mean? If we measure the height of a random sample of 100 college students, how well does the sample mean predict the true population mean (that is, the mean height of *all* college students)? These questions raise the issue of making an *inference* about a population based on information from a sample.

The accuracy of such inferences depends on *errors of sampling*. Suppose we were to select two random samples from the same population and compute the mean for each sample. What differences between the first and the second mean could be expected to occur by chance?

Successive random samples drawn from the same population will have different means, forming a distribution of *sample means* around the *true mean* of the population. These sample means are themselves numbers for which the standard deviation can be computed. We call this standard deviation the *standard error of the mean,* or σ_M, and can estimate it on the basis of the following formula:

$$\sigma_M = \frac{\sigma}{\sqrt{N}}$$

where σ is the standard deviation of the sample and N is the number of cases from which each sample mean is computed.

According to the formula, the size of the standard error of the mean decreases as the sample size increases; thus, a mean based on a large sample is more trustworthy (more likely to be close to the actual population mean) than a mean based on a smaller sample. Common sense would lead us to expect this. Computations of the standard error of the mean permit us to make clear assertions about the degree of uncertainty in our computed mean. The more cases in the sample, the more uncertainty has been reduced.

SIGNIFICANCE OF A DIFFERENCE

In many psychological experiments, data are collected on two groups of subjects; one group is exposed to certain specified experimental conditions, and the other serves as a control group. The question is whether there is a difference in the mean performance of the two groups, and if such a difference is observed, whether it holds for the population from which these groups of subjects have been sampled. Basically, we are asking whether a difference between two sample means reflects a true difference or whether this difference is simply the result of sampling error.

As an example, we will compare the scores on a reading test for a sample of first-grade boys with the scores for a sample of first-grade girls. The boys score lower than the girls as far as mean performances are concerned, but there is a great deal of overlap; some boys do extremely well, and some girls do very poorly. Thus, we cannot accept the obtained difference in means without making a test of its *statistical significance*. Only then can we decide whether the observed differences in sample means reflect true differences in the population or are due to sampling error. If some of the brighter girls and some of the duller boys are sampled by sheer luck, the difference could be due to sampling error.

As another example, suppose that we have set up an experiment to compare the grip strength of right-handed and left-handed men. The top panel of Table 5 presents hypothetical data from such an experiment. A sample of five right-handed men averaged 8 kilograms stronger than a sample of five left-handed men. In general, what can we infer from these data about left-handed and right-handed men? Can we argue that right-handed men are stronger than left-handed men? Obviously not, because the averages derived from most of the right-handed men would not differ from those from the left-handed men; the one markedly deviant score of 100 tells us we are dealing with an uncertain situation.

Now suppose that the results of the experiment were those shown in the bottom panel of Table 5. Again, we find the same mean difference of 8 kilograms, but we are now inclined to have greater confidence in the results, because the left-handed men scored consistently lower than the right-handed men. Statistics provides a precise way of taking into account the reliability of the mean differences so that we do not have to depend

TABLE 5

Significance of a Difference *Two examples that compare the difference between means are shown. The difference between means is the same (8 kilograms) in both the top and the bottom panel. However, the data in the bottom panel indicate a more reliable difference between means than do the data in the top panel.*

STRENGTH OF GRIP IN KILOGRAMS, RIGHT-HANDED MEN	STRENGTH OF GRIP IN KILOGRAMS, LEFT-HANDED MEN
40	40
45	45
50	50
55	55
100	60
Sum 290	Sum 250
Mean 58	Mean 50

STRENGTH OF GRIP IN KILOGRAMS, RIGHT-HANDED MEN	STRENGTH OF GRIP IN KILOGRAMS, LEFT-HANDED MEN
56	48
57	49
58	50
59	51
60	52
Sum 290	Sum 250
Mean 58	Mean 50

solely on intuition to determine that one difference is more reliable than another.

These examples suggest that the significance of a difference will depend on both the size of the obtained difference and the variability of the means being compared. From the standard error of the means, we can compute the *standard error of the difference between two means* σD_M. We can then evaluate the obtained difference by using a *critical ratio*—the ratio of the obtained difference between the means D_M to the standard error of the difference between the means:

$$\text{Critical ratio} = \frac{D_M}{\sigma_{D_M}}$$

This ratio helps us to evaluate the significance of the difference between the two means. As a rule of thumb, a critical ratio should be 2.0 or larger for the difference between means to be accepted as significant. Throughout this book, statements that the difference between means is "statistically significant" indicate that the critical ratio is at least that large.

Why is a critical ratio of 2.0 selected as statistically significant? Simply because a value this large or larger can occur by chance only

5 out of 100 times. Where do we get the 5 out of 100? We can treat the critical ratio as a standard score because it is merely the difference between two means, expressed as a multiple of its standard error. Referring to Column 2 in Table 4, we note that the likelihood is .023 that a standard deviation as high as or higher than +2.0 will occur by chance. Because the chance of deviating in the opposite direction is also .023, the total probability is .046. This means that 46 times out of 1,000, or about 5 times out of 100, a critical ratio as large as 2.0 would be found by chance if the population means were identical.

The rule of thumb that says a critical ratio should be at least 2.0 is just that—an arbitrary but convenient rule that defines the "5 percent level of significance." Following this rule, we will make fewer than 5 errors in 100 decisions by concluding on the basis of sample data that a difference in means exists when in fact there is none. The 5 percent level need not always be used; a higher level of significance may be appropriate in certain experiments, depending on how willing we are to make an occasional error in inference.

Specimen Computation of the Critical Ratio The computation of the critical ratio calls for finding the *standard error of the difference between two means*, which is given by the following formula:

$$\sigma_{D_M} = \sqrt{(\sigma_{M_1})^2 + (\sigma_{M_2})^2}$$

In this formula, σ_{M_1}, and σ_{M_2} are the standard errors of the two means being compared.

As an illustration, suppose we wanted to compare reading achievement test scores for first-grade boys and girls in the United States. A random sample of boys and girls would be identified and given the test. We will assume that the mean score for the boys was 70 with a standard error of .40 and that the mean score for the girls was 72 with a standard error of .30. On the basis of these samples, we want to decide whether there is a real difference between the reading achievement of boys and girls in the population as a whole. The sample data suggest that girls do achieve better reading scores than boys, but can we infer that this would have been the case if we had tested all the girls and all the boys in the United States? The critical ratio helps us make this decision.

$$\begin{aligned} \sigma_{D_M} &= \sqrt{(\sigma_{M_1})^2 + (\sigma_{M_2})^2} \\ &= \sqrt{.16 + .09} = \sqrt{.25} \\ &= .5 \end{aligned}$$

Critical ratio $= \dfrac{D_M}{\sigma_{D_M}} = \dfrac{72 - 70}{.5} = \dfrac{2.0}{.5} = 4.0$

Because the critical ratio is well above 2.0, we may assert that the observed mean difference is statistically significant at the 5 percent level. Thus, we can conclude that there is a reliable difference in performance on the reading test between boys and girls. Note that the sign of the critical ratio could be positive or negative, depending on which mean is subtracted from which; when the critical ratio is interpreted, only its magnitude (not its sign) is considered.

COEFFICIENT OF CORRELATION

Correlation refers to the parallel variation of two measures. Suppose that a test is designed to predict success in college. If it is a good test, high scores on it will be related to high performance in college and low scores will be related to poor performance. The *coefficient of correlation* gives us a way of stating the degree of relationship more precisely.

PRODUCT-MOMENT CORRELATION

The most frequently used method of determining the coefficient of correlation is the *product-moment method*, which yields the index conventionally designated by the lowercase letter *r*. The product-moment coefficient *r* varies between perfect positive correlation

$(r = +1.00)$ and perfect negative correlation $(r = -1.00)$. Lack of any relationship yields $r = .00$.

The formula for computing the product-moment correlation is

$$r = \frac{\text{Sum } (dx)(dy)}{N\sigma_2 \sigma_y}$$

Here, one of the paired measures has been labeled the x-score; the other, the y-score. The dx and dy refer to the deviations of each score from its mean, N is the number of paired measures, and σ_x and σ_y are the standard deviations of the x-scores and the y-scores.

The computation of the coefficient of correlation requires the determination of the sum of the $(dx)(dy)$ products. This sum, in addition to the computed standard deviations for the x-scores and y-scores, can then be entered into the formula.

Specimen Computation of Product-Moment Correlation Suppose that we have collected the data shown in Table 6. For each subject, we have obtained two scores—the first being a score on a college entrance test (to be labeled arbitrarily the *x*-score) and the second being freshman grades (the *y*-score).

Figure 6 is a *scatter diagram* of these data. Each point represents the *x*-score and *y*-score for a given subject; for example, the uppermost right-hand point is for Adam (labeled A). Looking at these data, we can easily detect that there is some positive correlation between the *x*-scores and the *y*-scores. Adam attained the highest score on the entrance test and also earned the highest freshman grades; Edward received the lowest scores on both. The other students' test scores and grades are a little irregular, so we know that the correlation is not perfect; hence, *r* is less than 1.00.

TABLE 6

Computation of a Product-Moment Correlation

STUDENT	ENTRANCE TEST (x-score)	FRESHMAN GRADES (y-score)	(dx)	(dy)	(dx)(dy)
Adam	71	39	6	9	+54
Bill	67	27	2	−3	−6
Charles	65	33	0	3	0
David	63	30	−2	0	0
Edward	59	21	−6	−9	+54
Sum	325	150	0	0	+102
Mean	65	30			

$\sigma_x = 4$
$\sigma_y = 6$

$r = \dfrac{\text{Sum } (dx)(dy)}{N\sigma_x\sigma_y} = \dfrac{+102}{5 \times 4 \times 6} = +.85$

FIGURE 6

Scatter Design   *Each point represents the x- and y-scores for a particular student. The letters next to the points identify the students in the data table (A = Adam, B = Bill, and so on).*

We will compute the correlation to illustrate the method, although no researcher would consent, in practice, to determining a correlation for so few cases. The details are given in Table 6. Following the procedure outlined in Table 3, we compute the standard deviation of the *x*-scores and then the standard deviation of the *y*-scores. Next, we compute the $(dx)(dy)$ products for each subject and total the five cases. Entering these results in our equation yields an *r* of $+.85$.

INTERPRETING A CORRELATION COEFFICIENT

We can use correlations in making predictions. For example, if we know from experience that a certain entrance test correlates with freshman grades, we can predict the freshman grades for beginning college students who have taken the test. If the correlation were perfect, we could predict their grades without error. But *r* is usually less than 1.00, and some errors in prediction will be made; the closer *r* is to 0, the greater the sizes of the errors in prediction.

Although we cannot go into the technical problems of predicting freshman grades from entrance examinations or of making other similar predictions, we can consider the meanings of correlation coefficients of different sizes. It is evident that with a correlation of 0 between *x* and *y*, knowledge of *x* will not help to predict *y*. If weight is unrelated to intelligence, it does us no good to know a subject's weight when we are trying to predict his or her intelligence. At the other extreme, a perfect correlation would mean 100 percent predictive efficiency—knowing *x*, we can predict *y* perfectly. What about intermediate values of *r*? Some appreciation of the meaning of correlations of intermediate sizes can be gained by examining the scatter diagrams in Figure 7.

In the preceding discussion, we did not emphasize the sign of the correlation coefficient, since this has no bearing on the strength of a relationship. The only distinction between a correlation of $r = +.70$ and $r = -.70$ is that increases in *x* are accompanied by increases in *y* for the former, and increases in *x* are accompanied by decreases in *y* for the latter.

Although the correlation coefficient is one of the most widely used statistics in psychology, it is also one of the most widely misused procedures. Those who use it sometimes overlook the fact that *r* does not imply a cause-and-effect relationship between *x* and *y*. When two sets of scores are correlated, we may suspect that they have some causal factors in common, but we cannot conclude that one of them causes the other.

Correlations sometimes appear paradoxical. For example, the correlation between study time and college grades has been found to be slightly negative (about $-.10$). If a causal interpretation were assumed, we might conclude that the best way to raise grades would be to stop studying. The negative correlation arises because some students have advantages over others in grade making (possibly due to better college preparation), so that often those who study the hardest are those who have difficulty earning the best grades.

This example provides sufficient warning against assigning a causal interpretation to a coefficient of correlation. It is possible, however, that when two variables are correlated, one may be the cause of the other. The search for causes is a logical one, and correlations can help us by providing leads to experiments that can verify cause-and-effect relationships.

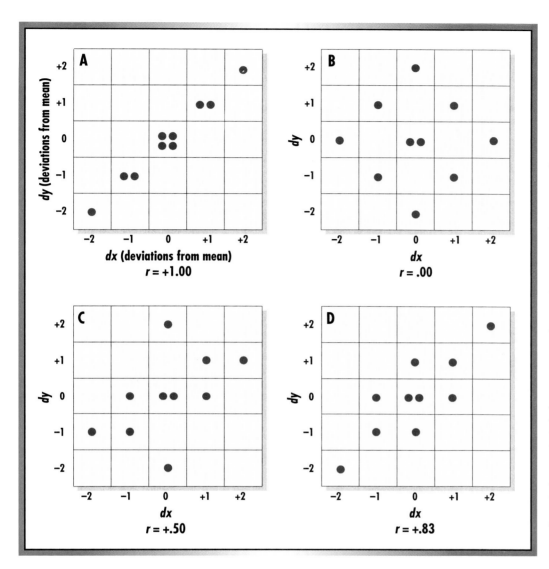

FIGURE 7

Scatter Diagrams Illustrating Correlations of Various Sizes *Each dot represents one individual's score on two tests, x and y. In A, all cases fall on the diagonal and the correlation is perfect (r = +1.00); if we know a subject's score on x, we know that it will be the same on y. In B, the correlation is 0; knowing a subject's score on x, we cannot predict whether it will be at, above, or below the mean on y. For example, of the four subjects who score at the mean of x (dx = 0), one makes a very high score on y (dy = +2), one a very low score (dy = −2), and two remain average. In both C and D, there is a diagonal trend to the scores, so that a high score on x is associated with a high score on y and a low score on x with a low score on y, but the relationship is imperfect. It is possible to check the value of the correlations by using the formulas given in the text for the coefficient of correlation. The computation has been greatly simplified by presenting the scores in the deviation form that permits entering them directly into the formulas. The fact that the axes do not have conventional scales does not change the interpretation. For example, if we assigned the values 1 through 5 to the x and y coordinates and then computed r for these new values, the correlation coefficients would be the same.*

FURTHER READING

There are a number of textbooks on statistics written from the viewpoint of psychological research. Examples are McCall, *Fundamental Statistics for Behavioral Sciences* (5th ed., 1990); Welkowitz, Ewen, and Cohen, *Introductory Statistics for the Behavioral Sciences* (3rd ed., 1982); Hinkle, Wiersma, and Jurs, *Applied Statistics for the Behavioral Sciences* (2nd ed., 1988); and Phillips, *How to Think About Statistics* (rev. ed., 1992).

The role of statistics in the design of psychological experiments is discussed in Keppel, Saufley, and Tokunaga, *Introduction to Design and Analysis* (2nd ed., 1992).

GLOSSARY

The glossary defines the technical words that appear in the text and some common words that have special meanings when used in psychology. No attempt is made to give the range of meanings beyond those used in the text. For fuller definitions and other shades of meaning, consult any standard dictionary of psychology.

A

ability. Demonstrable knowledge or skill. Ability includes aptitude and achievement. See also *achievement, aptitude.*

abreaction. In psychoanalysis, the process of reducing emotional tension by reliving (in speech or action or both) the experience that caused the tension.

absolute threshold. The intensity or frequency at which a stimulus becomes effective or ceases to become effective, as measured under experimental conditions. See also *difference threshold, threshold.*

accommodation. (1) The process by which the lens of the eye varies its focus. (2) In Piaget's theory of cognitive development, the process by which an infant modifies a pre-existing schema in order to include a novel object or event. See also *assimilation, schema.*

acetylcholine. The most common of the neurotransmitters. It is found in many synapses in the brain and spinal cord, and is particularly prevalent in an area of the brain called the hippocampus, which plays a key role in the formation of new memories. See also *neurotransmitter.*

achievement. Acquired ability, such as school attainment in spelling. See also *aptitude.*

achromatic colors. Black, white, and gray. See also *chromatic colors.*

acoustic buffer. In short-term memory, a hypothesized component of the encoding process which briefly stores information in an acoustic code (i.e., the sound of the digit, letter, or word). See also *central executive, encoding, short-term memory, visual buffer.*

acquisition. The stage during which a new response is learned and gradually strengthened. See also *classical conditioning.*

ACTH. See *adrenocorticotropic hormone.*

action potential. Synonymous with *nerve impulse.* The wave of electrical activity that is transmitted down the axon of the neuron when the cell membrane becomes depolarized. See also *depolarization, graded potentials, resting potential.*

activation model. In memory, the proposal that retrieval of an item depends on the activation of that item reaching a critical level.

acupuncture. A healing procedure developed in China in which needles are inserted in the skin at critical points and twirled, eliminating pain. See also *gate control theory of pain.*

addiction. See *drug dependence.*

additive mixture. The mixture of colored lights; two spotlights of different colors focused on the same spot yield an additive color mixture. See also *subtractive mixture.*

ADH. See *antidiuretic hormone.*

adipocytes. Special fat cells in the body. Obese individuals have many more of them and thus, perhaps, a higher body fat base line.

adolescence. The period of transition from childhood to adulthood during which the individual develops to sexual maturity. See also *puberty.*

adolescent growth spurt. A period of rapid physical growth that accompanies the onset of puberty.

adrenal gland. One of a pair of endocrine glands located above the kidneys. The medulla of the gland secretes the hormones epinephrine and norepinephrine. The cortex of the gland secretes a number of hormones, collectively called the *adrenocortical hormones*, which include cortisol. See also *endocrine system.*

adrenalin. See *epinephrine.*

adrenal-cortical-system. A neuro-endocrine system activated in response to stress. On a signal from the hypothalamus, the pituitary gland secretes a number of hormones. One stimulates the thyroid gland to make more energy available; the other (adrenocorticotropic hormone, ACTH) triggers the outer layer of the adrenal gland (the adrenal cortex) to release some 30 hormones (including cortisol) which play a role in the body's adjustment to emergencies. See also *adrenocorticotropic hormone, cortisol.*

adrenocorticotropic hormone (ACTH). A hormone released by the pituitary gland in response to stress; known as the body's major "stress" hormone. It is carried by the bloodstream to the adrenal glands and various other organs of the body, causing the release of some 30 hormones, each of which plays a role in the body's adjustment to emergency situations. See also *corticotropin-release factor.*

aerobic exercise. Any sustained activity that increases oxygen consumption, such as jogging, swimming, cycling, or fast walking.

affect. The experience of (hedonic) pleasure or of (aversive) displeasure or pain.

affective experience. An emotional experience, whether pleasant or unpleasant, mild or intense. See also *emotion.*

afferent neuron. See *sensory neuron.*

afterimage. The sensory experience that remains when a stimulus is withdrawn. Usually refers to visual experience—for example, the negative afterimage of a picture or the train of colored images that results after staring at the sun.

age regression. In hypnosis, the reliving through fantasy of experiences that are based on early memories or that are appropriate to a younger age. See also *hypnosis.*

aggregated score. A combination of several measures of the same behavior or characteristic.

aggression. Behavior intended to harm another person.

agnosia. A perceptual disturbance, resulting from damage to the cerebral cortex, in which the individual has difficulty identifying familiar objects even though visual acuity is normal. People suffering from agnosia appear to perceive but are not capable of understanding the information presented to them. See also *associative agnosia, prosopagnosia.*

agoraphobia. Fear of being alone or being in a public place where escape might be difficult or help unavailable should the individual be incapacitated by a panic attack. See also *panic disorder, phobia.*

AI. See *artificial intelligence.*

all-or-none principle. The rule that the nerve impulse in a single neuron is independent of the strength of stimulation; the neuron either responds completely (fires its action potential) or not at all.

alpha waves. See *electroencephalogram.*

alternate form reliability. The consistency between two or more versions of the same test when given to the same person. See also *reliability.*

ambivalence. Simultaneous liking and disliking of an object or person; the conflict caused by an incentive that is at once positive and negative. See also *conflict.*

Ames room. A perceptual illusion; specifically, a room that when viewed through a peephole leads to distortions in size judgments. See also *size constancy.*

amnesia. A partial or complete loss of memory. May be due to psychological factors (for example, emotional trauma) or physiological factors (some form of brain damage) and may involve loss of memory for events occurring prior to or subsequent to the amnesia-causing trauma. See also *anterograde amnesia, retrograde amnesia.*

amphetamines. Central nervous system stimulants that produce restlessness, irritability, anxiety, and rapid heart rate. Dexedrine sulfate ("speed") and methamphetamine ("meth") are two types of amphetamines. See also *depressants, stimulants.*

amygdala. A brain structure located below the cerebral cortex that is involved in consolidation of emotional memories. See also *diencephalon, hippocampus.*

anal stage. The second stage in Freud's psychoanalytic theory of psychosexual development, following the oral stage. The sources of gratification and conflict have to do with the expulsion and retention of feces. See also *psychosexual development.*

androgen. A male hormone.

androgens. The collective name for male sex hormones, of which testosterone, secreted by the testes, is best known. See also *gonads.*

angiotensin. A hormone that induces the feeling of thirst as well as an appetite for salt, which leads to behavioral adjustments.

Anorexia nervosa. A pathological desire *not* to gain weight; distinguished by an extreme, self-imposed weight loss. Dangerous side effects include emaciation, susceptibility to infection, and other symptoms of undernourishment.

anterior attentional system. Neural structures in the front of the brain that mediate our ability to selectively attend to some attribute of an object (other than its location).

anterograde amnesia. Loss of memory for events and experiences occurring subsequent to an amnesia-causing trauma; the patient is unable to acquire new information, although recall of information learned prior to the onset may be largely unaffected. See also *amnesia, retrograde amnesia.*

anthropology. The science that studies chiefly preliterate societies. Its main divisions are archaeology (the study of the physical monuments and remains from earlier civilizations), physical anthropology (concerned with the anatomical differences among people and their evolutionary origins), linguistic anthropology, and social anthropology (concerned with social institutions and behavior). See also *behavioral sciences.*

antianxiety drug. Central nervous system depressant (belonging to the family of drugs called benzodiazapines) that reduces anxiety and tension. Causes some drowsiness but less than barbituates. Diazepam (Valium) and alprozolam (Xanax) are examples (syn. *tranquilizer*).

antidepressant. Drug used to elevate the mood of depressed individuals, presumably by increasing the availability of the neurotransmitters norepinephrine and/or serotonin. Examples are imipramine (Tofranil), isocarboxazid (Marplan), and tranylcypromine (Parnate).

antidiuretic hormone (ADH). A hormone that regulates the kidneys so they release water back into the bloodstream and form only very concentrated urine.

antipsychotic drug. A drug that reduces psychotic symptoms, used more frequently in the treatment of schizophrenia. The phenothiazines, such as chlorpromazine (Thorazin) and fluphenazine (Prolixin), are examples (syn. *neuroleptic drug*). See also *phenothiazines, psychotic behavior.*

antisocial personality. A type of personality disorder marked by impulsivity, inability to abide by the customs and laws of society, and lack of anxiety or guilt regarding behavior (syn. *sociopathic personality, psychopathic personality*).

anxiety. A state of apprehension, tension, and worry. Synonymous with fear for some theorists, although others view the object of anxiety (such as a vague danger or foreboding) as less specific than the object of a fear (such as a vicious animal). See also *neurotic anxiety, objective anxiety.*

anxiety disorders. A group of mental disorders characterized by intense anxiety or by maladaptive behavior designed to relieve anxiety. Includes generalized anxiety and panic disorders, phobic and obsessive-compulsive disorders. Major category of DSM-IV covering most of the disorders formerly called neuroses. See also *generalized anxiety disorder, neurosis, obsessive-compulsive disorder, panic disorder, phobic disorder, posttraumatic stress disorder.*

anxiety hierarchy. A list of situations or stimuli to which a person responds with anxiety ranked in order from the least anxiety-producing to the most fearful. Used by behavior therapists in systematically desensitizing patients to feared stimuli by associating deep relaxation with the situations rather than anxiety. See also *behavior therapy, systematic desensitization.*

apathy. Listlessness, indifference; one of the consequences of frustration. See also *frustration.*

aphagia. Inability to eat. See also *hyperphagia.*

aphasia. Impairment or loss of ability to articulate words or comprehend speech.

apnea. A sleep disturbance characterized by inhibited breathing during sleep.

apparent motion. See *phi phenomenon, stroboscopic motion.*

appetitive behavior. Seeking behavior. See also *aversive behavior.*

appraisals. Evaluations of a situation, event, person, or the self.

appraisal theories of emotion. A group of theories of emotions stating that people's cognitive appraisals of situations determine the emotions they experience in response to the situations.

aptitude. The capacity to learn—for instance, a person's typing aptitude prior to practice on a typewriter. Aptitude tests are designed to predict the outcome of training, hence to predict future ability on the basis of present ability. See also *achievement.*

arousal level. The principle according to which people seek an optimal level of drive or arousal.

artificial intelligence (AI). A field of research combining computer science and cognitive psychology; it is concerned with (a) using computers to simulate human thought processes and (b) devising computer programs that act "intelligently" and can adapt to changing circumstances. In essence, it is the science of making machines (computers) do things that are normally done by the human mind. See also *cognitive psychology, cognitive science, computer simulation.*

assertiveness training. The use of behavioral rehearsal to help an individual learn to express his or her needs in an effective, nonhostile manner. See also *behavioral rehearsal.*

assimilation. In Piaget's theory of cognitive development, the process by which an infant comprehends a novel object or event in terms of a pre-existing schema. See also *accommodation, schema.*

association areas. Areas of the cerebral cortex that are not directly concerned with sensory or motor processes; they integrate inputs from various sensory channels and presumably function in learning, memory, and thinking.

associative agnosia. A perceptual disturbance, resulting from damage to specific areas of the cerebral cortex, in which the individual has difficulty recognizing familiar objects presented visually, although he or she can readily name the objects if allowed to touch or hear them. See also *agnosia, prosopagnosia.*

associative learning. Learning that certain contingencies (or relations) exist between events; learning that one event is associated with another.

astigmatism. In vision, an optical defect that prevents horizontal and vertical contours from being in focus simultaneously. See also *strabismus.*

attachment. The tendency of the young organism to seek closeness to particular individuals and to feel more secure in their presence.

attention. The focusing of perception leading to heightened awareness of a limited range of stimuli. It has both overt behavioral components and internal components. See also *orienting reflex.*

attitude. A like or dislike; a favorable or unfavorable evaluation of and reaction to an object, person, event, or idea: An attitude comprises a *cognitive* component, an *affective* component, and a *behavioral* component.

attribution. The process by which we attempt to explain the behavior of other people. Attribution theory deals with the rules people use to infer the causes of observed behavior. See also *dispositional attribution, situational attribution.*

attributional style. A person's characteristic way of giving causal explanations (attributions) for important events. People with a pessimistic attributional style, who attribute negative events to causes that are internal, stable over time, and global are presumably more prone to depression than people with a more optimistic style who attribute such events to external, temporary, and specific causes. See also *attribution*.

auditory area. A brain region located at the top of the temporal lobe of each cerebral hemisphere where auditory signals carried by the acoustic nerve are analyzed. Because nerve fibers from each side of the head cross over at the brain stem before reaching the auditory area, signals from each ear reach both temporal lobes. Thus, damage to one lobe does not produce deafness in one ear.

authoritarian personality. A personality type who is submissive and obedient to superiors but contemptuous of and aggressive toward those he or she considers inferior. Shows prejudice against minority groups. The *Authoritarian Personality* is a classic social psychological study, based in psychoanalytic theory, which examined this personality type. See also *scapegoat theory of prejudice*.

autism. A mental disorder, first evident during early childhood, in which the child shows significant deficits in communication, social interaction, and bonding and play activities, and engages in repetitive stereotyped behaviors and self-damaging acts.

automatic writing. Writing that the writer is unaware of (does not know that he or she is producing); familiar in hypnosis. See also *hypnosis*.

autonomic nervous system. The division of the peripheral nervous system that regulates smooth muscle (organ and glandular) activities. It is divided into the sympathetic and parasympathetic divisions. See also *parasympathetic system, peripheral nervous system, sympathetic system*.

average. See *measure of central tendency*.

aversive behavior. Avoidance behavior. See also *appetitive behavior*.

aversive conditioning. A form of conditioning in which an undesirable response is extinguished through association with punishment; has been used in behavior therapy to treat alcoholism, smoking, and sexual problems. See also *behavior therapy, counterconditioning*.

avoidance learning. Learning to make a response to a warning signal in order to avoid an aversive event. See also *escape learning*.

awareness. See *consciousness*.

axon. That portion of a neuron that transmits impulses to other neurons. See also *dendrite, neuron*.

B

BAC. See *blood alcohol concentration*.

basal mental age. In individual tests of the Binet type, the highest age level at which, and below which, all tests are passed. See also *mental age*.

base-rate rule. A rule in probability theory, which states that the probability of something (e.g., a person or object) being a member of a class is greater the more class members there are. People frequently violate this rule when reasoning about real-world situations.

basic level. In a hierarchy of concepts, the level at which one first categorizes an object.

basilar membrane. A membrane of the ear within the coils of the cochlea supporting the organ of Corti. Movements of the basilar membrane stimulate the hair cells of the organ of Corti, producing the neural effects of auditory stimulation. See also *cochlea*.

behavior. Those activities of an organism that can be observed by another organism or by an experimenter's instruments. Included within behavior are verbal reports made about subjective, conscious experiences. See also *conscious processes*.

behavior genetics. The study of the inheritance of behavioral characteristics.

behavior modification. See *behavior therapy*.

behavior therapy. A method of psychotherapy based on learning principles. It uses such techniques as counterconditioning, reinforcement, and shaping to modify behavior (syn. *behavior modification*). See also *cognitive behavior therapy*.

behavioral medicine. The study of how social, psychological, and biological factors interact to contribute to physical illness (syn. *health psychology*).

behavioral perspective. An approach to psychology that focuses only on observable behavior, and tries to explain it in terms of its relation to environmental events. See also *behaviorism*.

behavioral rehearsal. A technique used by behavior therapists in which the therapist helps the individual rehearse, or role-play, more adaptive behaviors. Practicing assertive response in situations where a person tends to be timid is an example. See also *assertiveness training*.

behavioral sciences. The sciences concerned in one way or another with the behavior of humans and lower organisms (especially social anthropology, psychology, and sociology but including some aspects of biology, economics, political science, history, philosophy, and other fields of study.)

behaviorism. A school or system of psychology associated with the name of John B. Watson; it defined psychology as the study of behavior and limited the data of psychology to observable activities. In its classical form it was more restrictive than the contemporary behavioral viewpoint in psychology.

belief-driven learning. A kind of associative learning in which people have prior beliefs about the relation that has to be learned; learning is driven by the beliefs as well as by the input. See also *data-driven learning*.

benzodiazepines. A class of drugs with similar chemical structures that are effective in reducing anxiety. Examples are diazepam (Valium) and alprazolam (Xanax). See *anti-anxiety drug*.

binocular cues. See *distance cues*.

binocular disparity. A cue to depth perception that arises because an object projects slightly different images on the two retinas (due to the different positions of the right and left eyes).

binocular parallax. A cue to depth perception that arises because any visible point will differ slightly in its direction to the two eyes. See also *binocular disparity*.

biofeedback. A procedure that permits individuals to monitor their own physiological processes (such as heart rate, blood pressure) which they are normally unaware of, to learn to control them.

biological perspective. An approach to psychology that tries to explain behavior in terms of electrical and chemical events taking place inside the body, particularly within the brain and nervous system.

biological psychologist. A psychologist concerned with the relationship between biological processes and behavior. Same as *physiological psychologist*.

biological therapy. Treatment of emotional problems or mental disorders by drugs, electric shock, or other methods directly affecting bodily processes. See also *psychotherapy*.

bipolar cells. Cells in the retina that transmit electrical impulses from photoreceptors to ganglion cells. See also *ganglia, photoreceptors, retina*.

bipolar disorder. A mood disorder in which people experience episodes of depression and mania (exaggerated excitement) or of mania alone. Typically the individual alternates between the two extremes, often with periods of normal mood in between (syn. *manic-depression*). See also *depression, mood disorder*.

blind spot. An insensitive area of the retina where the nerve fibers from the ganglion cells join to form the optic nerve.

blocking. A phenomenon in classical conditioning: if one conditioned stimulus reliably predicts an unconditioned stimulus, and another conditioned stimulus is added, the relation between the added conditioned stimulus and the unconditioned stimulus will not be learned.

blood alcohol concentration (BAC). The concentration, in milligrams, of alcohol per 100 milliliters of blood. The legal definition of intoxication in most states is a blood alcohol concentration of .10 percent (100 milligrams of alcohol per 100 milliliters of blood).

blood pressure. The pressure of the blood against the walls of the blood vessels. Changes in blood pressure following stimulation serve as one indicator of emotion.

borderline personality disorder. A mental disorder in which the individual has manifested unstable moods, relationships with others, and self-perceptions chronically since adolescence or childhood.

bottom-up processes. Processes in perception, learning, memory, and comprehension that are driven solely by the information input, and that do not involve the organism's prior knowledge and expectations. See also *top-down processes*.

brain stem. The structures lying near the core of the brain; essentially all of the brain with the exception of the cerebrum and the cerebellum and their dependent parts.

Broca's area. A portion of the left cerebral hemisphere involved in the control of speech. Individuals with damage in this area have difficulty enunciating words correctly and speak in a slow and labored way; their speech often makes sense, but it includes only key words.

bulimia. A pathological desire *not* to gain weight; characterized by recurrent episodes of *binge eating* (rapid consumption of a large amount of food in a discrete period of time), followed by attempts to purge the excess eating by means of vomiting and laxatives.

C

cannabis. The hemp plant from which marijuana is obtained. See also *marijuana*.

Cannon-Bard theory. A classical theory of emotion proposed by Cannon and Bard. The theory states that an emotion-producing stimulus activates the cortex and bodily responses at the same time; bodily changes and the experience of emotion occur simultaneously. See also *cognitive-appraisal theory, James-Lange theory*.

cardiac muscle. A special kind of muscle found only in the heart. See also *smooth muscle, striate muscle*.

case history. A biography obtained for scientific purposes; the material is sometimes supplied by interview, sometimes collected over the years. See also *longitudinal study*.

castration. Surgical removal of the gonads; in the male, removal of the testes; in the female, removal of the ovaries.

catatonic immobility. A fixity of posture maintained for long periods with accompanying muscular rigidity and a trance-like state of consciousness. A symptom in some cases of schizophrenia. See also *schizophrenia*.

categorization. Assigning an object to a concept. See also *concept*.

catharsis. Reduction of an impulse or emotion through direct or indirect expression, particularly verbal and fantasy expression.

central core. The most central and the evolutionally oldest portion of the brain. It includes structures that regulate basic life processes, including most of the brain stem. See also *brain stem, cerebellum, hypothalamus, reticular formation*.

central executive. In short-term memory, a hypothesized component of the encoding process that coordinates the acoustic and visual buffers. See also *acoustic buffer, encoding, short-term memory, visual buffer*.

central fissure. A fissure of each cerebral hemisphere that separates the frontal and parietal lobes (syn. *fissure of Rolando*).

central nervous system. In vertebrates, the brain and spinal cord, as distinct from the nerve trunks and their peripheral connections. See also *autonomic nervous system, peripheral nervous system*.

cerebellum. Lobed structure attached to the rear of the brain stem that regulates muscle tone and coordination of intricate movements.

cerebral cortex. The surface layer of the cerebral hemispheres in higher animals, including humans. It is commonly called gray matter because its many cell bodies give it a gray appearance in cross section, in contrast with the myelinated nerve fibers that make up the white matter in the center.

cerebral hemisphere. Two large masses of nerve cells and fibers constituting the bulk of the brain in humans and other higher animals. The hemispheres are separated by a deep fissure, but connected by a broad band of fibers, the corpus callosum (syn. *cerebrum*). See also *cerebral cortex, left hemisphere, right hemisphere, split-brain subject*.

cerebrum. See *cerebral hemispheres*.

childhood amnesia. The inability to recall events from the first years of one's life.

chlorpromazine. See *antipsychotic drug*.

chromatic colors. All colors other than black, white, and gray; for instance, red, yellow, blue. See also *achromatic colors*.

chromosome. Rodlike structures found in pairs in all the cells of the body, carrying the genetic determiners (genes) that are transmitted from parent to offspring. A human cell has 46 chromosomes, arranged in 23 pairs, one member of each pair deriving from the mother, one from the father. See also *gene*.

chronological age (CA). Age from birth; calendar age. See also *mental age*.

chunk. The largest meaningful unit of information that can be stored in short-term memory; short-term memory holds 7 ± 2 chunks. See also *short-term memory*.

cilia. Hairlike structures that are sometimes parts of receptors.

circadian rhythm. A cycle or rhythm that is roughly 24 hours long. Sleep-wakefulness, body temperature, and water excretion follow a circadian rhythm, as do a number of behavioral and psychological variables.

clairvoyance. Perception of objects or events that do not provide a stimulus to the known senses (for example, identifying a concealed playing card, the identity of which is unknown). See also *extrasensory perception, parapsychology, precognition, psi, psychokinesis, telepathy*.

classical concept. A concept where an instance must have every property mentioned in the concept. An example is the concept of *bachelor*; every instance must have the properties of being adult, male, and unmarried. See also *fuzzy concept*.

classical conditioning. Conditioned response conforming to the pattern of Pavlov's experi-

ment. The main feature is that the originally neutral conditioned stimulus, through repeated pairing with the unconditioned one, becomes associated with the unconditioned stimulus. See also *operant conditioning*.

claustrophobia. Fear of closed places. See also *phobia*.

client-centered therapy. A method of psychotherapy developed by Carl Rogers in which the therapist is nondirective and reflective and does not interpret or advise. The operating assumption is that the client is the best expert on his or her problems and can work them out in a nonjudgmental, accepting atmosphere. (syn. *nondirective counseling*). See also *humanistic therapies*.

clinical psychologist. A psychologist, usually with a Ph.D. or Psy.D. degree, trained in the diagnosis and treatment of emotional or behavioral problems and mental disorders. See also *counseling psychologist, psychiatrist*.

cocaine. A central nervous system stimulant derived from leaves of the coca plant. Increases energy, produces euphoria, and in large doses causes paranoia.

cochlea. The portion of the inner ear containing the receptors for hearing. See also *basilar membrane*.

coding. See *encoding*.

coding by pattern. Coding the quality of a sensation in terms of the pattern of neural firing. See also *coding by specificity*.

coding by specificity. Coding the quality of a sensation in terms of the specific neurons involved. See also *coding by pattern, specific nerve energies*.

coefficient of correlation. A numerical index used to indicate the degree of correspondence between two sets of paired measurements. The most common kind is the product-moment coefficient designated by *r*.

cognition. An individual's thoughts, knowledge, interpretations, understandings, or ideas. See also *cognitive processes*.

cognitive appraisal. The interpretation of an event or situation with respect to one's goals and well-being. The cognitive appraisal of an event influences both the quality and intensity of the emotion experienced and the degree of perceived threat.

cognitive-appraisal theory. A theory of emotion that proposes that the subjective emotional state is a function of the individual's appraisal, or analysis, of the emotion-arousing situation. A state of physiological arousal can produce different emotions (even antithetical ones) depending on how the person appraises the situation. See also *Cannon-Bard theory, James-Lange theory*.

cognitive behavior therapy. A psychotherapy approach that emphasizes the influence of a person's beliefs, thoughts, and self-statements on behavior. Combines behavior therapy methods with techniques designed to change the way the individual thinks about self and events. See also *behavior therapy*.

cognitive dissonance. The condition in which one has beliefs or attitudes that disagree with each other or with behavioral tendencies; when such cognitive dissonance arises, the subject is motivated to reduce the dissonance through changes in behavior or cognition.

cognitive distortions. In Beck's theory of depression, systematic errors in thinking that lead depressed individuals to misperceive reality in a way that contributes to their negative self-schema. Examples are overgeneralization (drawing a sweeping conclusion on the basis of a single negative event) and selective abstraction (focusing on an insignificant negative detail while ignoring the more important positive features of a situation). See also *depression, self-schema.*

cognitive map. A hypothetical structure in memory that preserves and organizes information about the various events that occur in a learning situation; a mental picture of the learning situation. See also *schema.*

cognitive neuroscience. An interdisciplinary approach that combines aspects of cognitive psychology and neuroscience to study how mental activities are executed in the brain.

cognitive perspective. An approach to psychology that focuses on mental processes such as perceiving, remembering, reasoning, deciding, and problem solving, and tries to explain behavior in terms of these mental processes. See also *cognitive psychology, cognitive science.*

cognitive processes. Mental processes of perception, memory, and information processing by which the individual acquires information, makes plans, and solves problems.

cognitive psychology. A general approach to psychology that stresses the role of mental processes in understanding behavior. The cognitive psychologist explains behavior at the level of mental representations and the mental processes that operate on these representations to produce products (including responses). The approach is not restricted to the study of thought and knowledge; its early concerns with these topics led to the label "cognitive psychology," but in recent years the approach has been generalized to all areas of psychology. See also *artificial intelligence, cognitive science, information-processing model, mental representation.*

cognitive response theory. A theory that proposes that persuasion induced by a communication is actually self-persuasion produced by the thoughts that the individual generates while receiving or even just anticipating the communication.

cognitive science. A term introduced in the 1970s to focus attention on how humans acquire and organize knowledge; a "new" science dedicated to understanding cognition. In addition to psychology, the disciplines relevant to cognitive science are neuroscience, linguistics, philosophy, mathematics, and computer science (particularly that branch of computer science known as artificial intelligence). See also *artificial intelligence, cognitive psychology.*

cognitive triad. In Beck's theory, the major concommitant, and possibly cause, of depression. Consists of negative thoughts about the self, the present situation, and the future. See also *depression.*

color blindness. Defective discrimination of chromatic colors. See also *dichromatism, monochromatism, red-green color blindness, trichromatism.*

color circle. An arrangement of chromatic colors on the circumference of a circle in the order in which they appear in the spectrum but with the addition of nonspectral reds and purples. The colors are so arranged that those opposite each other are complementaries in additive mixture. See also *color solid.*

color constancy. The tendency to see a familiar object as of the same color, regardless of changes in illumination on it that alter its stimulus properties. See also *perceptual constancy.*

color solid. A three-dimensional representation of the psychological dimensions of color, with hue around the circumference, saturation along each radius, and brightness from top to bottom. See also *color circle.*

color-opponent cells. In color vision, cells that respond only to their two opponent colors. See also *opponent-color theory.*

companionate love. An affection people feel for those with whom their lives are deeply intertwined. Characterized by trust, caring, tolerance of the partner's flaws and idiosyncrasies, and an emotional tone of warmth and affection. Contrasted with *passionate love.* See also *passionate love.*

complementary colors. Two colors that in additive mixture yield either a gray or an unsaturated color of the hue of the stronger component.

complex cell. A cell in the visual cortex that responds to a bar of light or straight edge of a particular orientation located anywhere in the visual field. See also *simple cell.*

complex learning. Learning that involves more than forming associations; for example, using a strategy to solve a problem or forming a mental map of one's surroundings. Contrasted with habituation and conditioning which are simpler types of learning. See also *classical conditioning, habituation, operant conditioning.*

compliance. Publicly conforming to the wishes of an influencing source but not necessarily changing one's private beliefs or attitudes. See also *identification, internalization.*

compulsion. A repetitive action that a person feels driven to make and is unable to resist; ritualistic behavior. See also *obsession, obsessive-compulsive disorder.*

computer program. See *program.*

computer simulation. The use of a computer to simulate a phenomenon or system in order to study its properties. In psychology, the simulation usually involves an attempt to program a computer to mimic how the mind processes information and solves problems. In this sense, the computer program is literally a theory of how the mind functions. See also *artificial intelligence, cognitive psychology, information-processing model.*

computerized axial tomography (CT). A computer-based procedure that analyzes data obtained by a scanning beam of X rays to provide a picture of a cross-sectional slice through the body or brain.

concept. The properties or relationships common to a class of objects or ideas. Concepts may be of concrete things (such as the concept *poodle* referring to a given variety of dog) or of abstract ideas (such as *equality, justice, number*). See also *classical concept, fuzzy concept.*

concrete operational stage. Piaget's third stage of cognitive development (ages 7 to 11 years) during which a child becomes capable of logical thought and achieves conservation concepts. See also *conservation.*

conditioned emotion. An emotional response acquired by conditioning: one aroused by a stimulus that did not originally evoke it. See also *conditioning.*

conditioned fear. A fear acquired by classical conditioning. The object that the organism comes to fear was originally neutral, but when it is repeatedly paired with an aversive stimulus it becomes an object of fear.

conditioned reinforcer. A stimulus that has become reinforcing through prior association with a reinforcing stimulus (syn. *secondary reinforcer*). See also *reinforcing stimulus.*

conditioned response (CR). In classical conditioning, the learned or acquired response to a conditioned stimulus; in other words, to a stimulus that did not evoke the response originally. See also *conditioned stimulus, unconditioned response, unconditioned stimulus.*

conditioned stimulus (CS). In classical conditioning, a stimulus previously neutral that comes to elicit a conditioned response through association with an unconditioned stimulus. See also *conditioned response, unconditioned response, unconditioned stimulus.*

conditioning. The process by which conditioned responses are learned. See also *classical conditioning, operant conditioning.*

conduction loss. A hearing deficit in which threshold elevation (loss of sensitivity) occurs equally at all frequencies as the result of poor conduction in the middle ear. See also *sensory-neural loss.*

cone. In the eye, a specialized cell of the retina found predominantly in the fovea and more sparsely throughout the retina. The cones mediate both chromatic and achromatic sensations. See also *fovea, retina, rod.*

conflict. The simultaneous presence of opposing or mutually exclusive impulses, desires, or tendencies. See also *ambivalence.*

conjunction rule. A rule in probability theory, which states that the probability of a proposition cannot be less than the probability of that proposition conjoined with another proposition. People frequently violate the rule when reasoning about real-world situations.

connectionist models. Models of cognitive processes (like perception) that incorporate a network of nodes, with excitatory and inhibitory connections between them.

connotative meaning. The suggestive and emotional meanings of a word or symbol, beyond its denotative meaning. Thus, *naked* and *nude* both refer to an unclothed body (denotative meaning), but they have somewhat different connotations. See also *denotative meaning.*

conscience. An internal recognition of standards of right and wrong by which the individual judges his or her conduct. See also *superego.*

conscious. In Freud's topographic model, the part of the mind containing thoughts and memories of which the individual is currently aware. See also *preconscious, topographic model, unconscious.*

conscious processes. Events such as perceptions, private thoughts, and dreams, of which only the person is aware. They are accessible to others through verbal report or by way of inference from other behavior (syn. *experience, awareness*).

consciousness. We are conscious when we are aware of external events, reflect on past experiences, engage in problem solving, are selective in attending to some stimuli rather than others, and deliberately choose an action in response to environmental conditions and personal goals. In short, consciousness has to do with a) *monitoring* ourselves and our environment so that percepts, memories, and thoughts are accurately represented in awareness; and b) *controlling* ourselves and our environment so that we are able to initiate and terminate behavioral and cognitive activities. In some contexts, the term is used as a synonym for *awareness.*

conservation. Piaget's term for the ability of the child to recognize that certain properties of objects (such as mass, volume, number) do not change despite transformations in the appearance of the objects. See also *preoperational stage.*

construct validity. The ability of a test or assessment instrument to confirm predictions of the theory underlying some theoretical concept or construct. Confirming results validate both the concept and the assessment instrument simultaneously. See also *criterion problem, validity.*

constructive memory. The memory that results when we use general knowledge construct and elaborate a more complete and detailed account of some event.

contrast sensitivity. In visual perception, the ability to discriminate between dark and light stripes under various conditions.

control group. In an experimental design contrasting two groups, that group not given the treatment whose effect is under study. See also *experimental group.*

control processes. Regulatory processes that serve to establish equilibrium or monitor goal-directed activities. See also *homeostasis.*

controlled stimulation. Conditions in which the perceptual experiences of an organism are systematically varied in order to determine the effect on subsequent performance. For example, rearing kittens in an environment where they see only vertical stripes for the first few months of life or having humans wear prism goggles that distort the directions of objects.

core. The part of a concept that contains the properties that are more essential for determining membership in the concept. See also *prototype.*

cornea. The transparent surface of the eye through which light enters and rays are bent inward to begin image formation. See also *lens, pupil, retina.*

corpus callosum. A large band of nerve fibers connecting the two cerebral hemispheres.

correlation. See *coefficient of correlation.*

correlational method. A research method used to determine whether some difference that is not under the researcher's control is associated, or correlated, with another difference of interest. See also *coefficient of correlation.*

corticotropin-release factor (CRF). A substance secreted by neurons in the hypothalamus in response to stress. It, in turn, is carried through a channel-like structure to the pituitary gland, causing ACTH (the body's major "stress" hormone) to be released. See also *adrenocorticotropic hormone.*

cortisol. One of the steroid hormones produced by the adrenal glands. It has many effects on the body, including the formation of glucose, the reduction of inflammation, and the retention of water. Its level in the blood is used as a measure of stress. See also *adrenal gland, adrenal-cortical system.*

counseling psychologist. A trained psychologist, usually with a Ph.D. or Psy.D. degree, who deals with personal problems not classified as illness, such as academic, social, or vocational problems of students. He or she has skills similar to those of the clinical psychologist but usually works in a nonmedical setting. See also *clinical psychologist, psychiatrist.*

counterconditioning. In behavior therapy, the replacement of a particular response to a stimulus by the establishment of another (usually incompatible) response.

CRF. See *corticotropin-release factor.*

criterion. (a) A set of scores or other records against which the success of a predictive test is verified. (b) A standard selected as the goal to be achieved in a learning task; for example, the number of runs through a maze to be made without error as an indication that the maze has been mastered.

criterion-keyed method of test construction. Selecting items for a test or assessment instrument by comparing the responses of some criterion group (for example, paranoid individuals) with a control group and retaining only those that discriminate between the two groups.

criterion problem. The difficulty that arises in validating a test or assessment instrument when there is no criterion behavior the investigator is willing to accept as the "true" measure of the concept being evaluated. See also *construct validity, validity.*

criterion validity. The ability of a test or assessment instrument to predict the behavior it is designed to predict (syn. *empirical validity*). See also *criterion, validity.*

critical period. Crucial time periods in a person's life during which specific events must occur for development to proceed normally.

cross-pressure. Conflicting social influences on an individual's beliefs, attitudes, or behaviors. Usually arises when a person identifies with more than one reference group.

cues to distance. See *distance cues.*

cultural psychology. An interdisciplinary approach involving psychologists, anthropologists, sociologists, and other social scientists that is concerned with how an individual's culture influences his or her mental representations and psychological processes.

cumulative curve. A graphic record of the responses emitted during an operant conditioning session. The slope of the cumulative curve indicates the rate of response.

D

dark adaptation. The increased sensitivity to light when the subject has been continuously in the dark or under conditions of reduced illumination. See also *light adaptation.*

data-driven learning. A kind of associative learning in which people have no prior beliefs about the relation that has to be learned; learning is driven only by the input or data. See also *belief-driven learning.*

db. See *decibel.*

decibel (db). A measure of sound intensity. A change of 10 decibels corresponds to a change in sound power of 10 times; 20 decibels, a change of 100 times; and so forth.

deductive reasoning. Reasoning about arguments in which the conclusion cannot be false if the premises are true. See also *inductive reasoning.*

defense mechanisms. In Freud's psychoanalytic theory, the strategies used by the ego to ward off or to reduce anxiety. These consist of adjustments made unconsciously, either through action or the avoidance of action, to keep from recognizing personal motives that might threaten self-esteem or heighten anxiety. Repression, denial, and projection are examples.

degradation. The process in which enzymes in the membrane of a receiving neuron react with a neurotransmitter to break it up chemically and make it inactive; one method (in addition to reuptake) of terminating a neurotransmitter's action. See also *neurotransmitter, reuptake.*

deindividuation. A psychological state in which persons feel that they have lost their personal identities and have merged anonymously into a group. Hypothesized to be the basis for the impulsive, aggressive behaviors sometimes shown by mobs and crowds.

delayed conditioning. A classical conditioning procedure in which the CS begins several seconds or more before the onset of the UCS and continues with it until the response occurs. See also *trace conditioning.*

delta waves. See *electroencephalogram.*

delusion. False beliefs characteristic of some forms of psychotic disorder. They often take the form of delusions of grandeur or delusions of persecution. See also *hallucination, illusion, paranoid schizophrenia.*

dendrite. The specialized portion of the neuron that (together with the cell body) receives impulses from other neurons. See also *axon, neuron.*

denial. A defense mechanism by which unacceptable impulses or ideas are not perceived or allowed into full awareness. See also *defense mechanisms.*

denotative meaning. The primary meaning of a symbol, something specific to which the symbol refers or points (for example, my street address is denotative; whether I live in a desirable neighborhood is a connotative meaning secondary to the address itself). See also *connotative meaning.*

deoxyribonucleic acid (DNA). The basic hereditary material of all organisms; a nucleic acid polymer incorporating the sugar deoxyribose. In higher organisms, the great bulk of DNA is located within the chromosomes.

dependent variable. The variable whose measured changes are attributed to (or correspond to) changes in the independent variable. In psychological experiments, the dependent variable is often a response to a stimulus. See also *independent variable.*

depolarization. Change in the resting potential of the nerve cell membrane in the direction of the action potential; the inside of the membrane becomes more positive. See also *action potential, resting potential.*

depressants. Psychoactive drugs that tend to reduce arousal. Alcohol, barbiturates, and opiates are examples.

depression. A mood disorder characterized by sadness and dejection, decreased motivation and interest in life, negative thoughts (for example, feelings of helplessness, inadequacy, and low self-esteem) and such physical symptoms as sleep disturbances, loss of appetite, and fatigue. See also *mood disorder.*

depth perception. The perception of the distance of an object from the observer. See also *distance cues.*

determinism. See *psychological determinism.*

developmental psychologist. A psychologist whose research interest lies in studying the changes that occur as a function of the growth and development of the organism, in particular the relationship between early and later behavior.

diathesis-stress model. See *vulnerability-stress model.*

dichromatism. Color blindness in which either the red-green or the blue-yellow system is lacking. The red-green form is relatively common; the blue-yellow form is the rarest of all forms of color blindness. See also *monochromatism, red-green color blindness, trichromatism.*

diencephalon. A cluster of nuclei, located below the cerebral cortex, that is involved in memory. See also *amygdala, hippocampus.*

difference reduction. A problem-solving strategy in which one sets up subgoals that, when obtained, put one in a state closer to the goal. See also *means-ends analysis, working backwards.*

difference threshold. The minimum difference between a pair of stimuli that can be perceived under experimental conditions. See also *absolute threshold, just noticeable difference, threshold, Weber's law.*

differential reinforcement. A procedure in conditioning in which reinforcement is given only in the presence of a certain stimulus. The outcome of this procedure is a conditioned discrimination.

diffusion of responsibility. The tendency for persons in a group situation to fail to take action (as in an emergency) because others are present, thus diffusing the responsibility for acting. A major factor in inhibiting bystanders from intervening in emergencies.

disaster syndrome. A three-stage behavior pattern that is a common reaction to a traumatic event. The person is at first dazed and disoriented, then passive but able to respond to instructions, and finally anxious, apprehensive, and unable to concentrate.

discrimination. (a) In perception, the detection of differences between two stimuli. (b) In conditioning, the differential response to the positive (reinforced) stimulus and to the negative (nonreinforced) stimulus. See also *generalization.* (c) In social psychology, prejudicial treatment, as in racial discrimination. See also *prejudice.*

discriminative stimulus. A stimulus that becomes an occasion for an operant response; for example, a knock that leads one to open the door. See also *operant behavior.*

dishabituation. A return in strength of a response following habituation to a repeated stimulus. Indicates renewed attention on the part of the organism to a change in the stimulus situation. See also *habituation.*

displaced aggression. Aggression against a person or object other than that which was

(or is) the source of frustration. See also *scapegoat.*

displacement. a) A defense mechanism whereby a motive that may not be directly expressed (such as sex or aggression) appears in a more acceptable form. See also *defense mechanism.* b) The principle of loss of items from short-term memory as too many new items are added. See also *chunk, short-term memory.*

display rules. A culture's rules for the types of emotions people should experience in certain situations, and the behaviors (including facial expressions) appropriate for each emotion.

dispositional attribution. Attributing a person's actions to internal dispositions (attitudes, traits, motives), as opposed to situational factors. See also *situational attribution.*

dissociation. The process whereby some ideas, feelings, or activities lose relationship to other aspects of consciousness and personality and operate automatically or independently.

dissociative identity disorder. The existence of two or more distinct identities or personalities within the same individual. Each identity has its own set of memories and characteristic behaviors. Typically, the attitudes and behaviors of the alternating personalities are markedly different. Formerly called multiple personality disorder.

dissonance. (a) In music, an inharmonious combination of sounds; contrasted with consonance. (b) In social psychology, Festinger's term for discomfort arising from a perceived inconsistency between one's attitudes and one's behavior. See also *cognitive dissonance.*

distance cues. (a) In vision, the monocular cues according to which the distance of objects is perceived—such as superposition of objects, perspective, light and shadow, and relative movement—and the binocular cues used in stereoscopic vision. See also *stereoscopic vision.* (b) In audition, the corresponding cues governing perception of distance and direction, such as intensity and time differences of sound reaching the two ears.

dizygotic (DZ) twins. Twins developed from separate eggs. They are no more alike genetically than ordinary brothers and sisters and can be of the same or different sexes (syn. *fraternal twin*). See also *monozygotic twins.*

DNA. See *deoxyribonucleic acid.*

dominance. The higher status position when social rank is organized according to a dominance–submission hierarchy; commonly found in human societies and in certain animal groups.

dominant gene. A member of a gene pair which, if present, determines that the individual will show the trait controlled by the gene, regardless of whether the other member of the pair is the same or different (that is, recessive). See also *recessive gene.*

dopamine. A neurotransmitter of the central nervous system believed to play a role in schizophrenia. It is synthesized from an amino acid by the action of certain body enzymes and, in turn, is converted into norepinephrine. See also *neurotransmitter, norepinephrine.*

dopamine hypothesis. The hypothesis that schizophrenia is related to an excess of the neurotransmitter dopamine; either schizophrenics produce too much dopamine or have an abnormally large number of dopamine receptors. See also *dopamine, schizophrenia.*

double blind. An experimental design, often used in drug research, in which neither the investigator nor the patients know which subjects are in the treatment and which in the nontreatment condition until the experiment has been completed.

Down's syndrome. A form of mental deficiency produced by a genetic abnormality (an extra chromosome on pair 21). Characteristics include a thick tongue, extra eyelid folds, and short, stubby fingers (syn. *mongolism*).

drive. An internal cause for motivation, which arises independent of events outside the individual. Drive theories of motivation stress the role of physiological states and of homeostasis.

drive-reduction theory. The theory that a motivated sequence of behavior can be best explained as moving from an aversive state of heightened tension (or drive) to a goal state in which the drive is reduced. The goal of the sequence, in other words, is drive reduction. See also *drive, incentive theory, motive, need.*

drug abuse. Continued use of a drug despite serious consequences in the absence of signs of dependency (i.e., no symptoms of tolerance, withdrawal, or compulsive craving). See also *drug dependence.*

drug dependence. A pattern of compulsive drug use usually characterized by tolerance (the need to consume more and more of the drug to achieve the same effect) and withdrawal (unpleasant reactions if use is discontinued). See also *drug abuse.*

DSM-IV. The fourth edition of the *Diagnostic and Statistical Manual of the American Psychiatric Association,* revised.

dual-memory theory. A theory that distinguishes between a short-term memory of limited capacity and a virtually unlimited long-term memory. Information is encoded into longterm memory via short-term memory. See also *long-term memory, short-term memory.*

DZ twins. See *dizygotic twins.*

E

eardrum. The membrane at the inner end of the auditory canal, leading to the middle ear. See also *middle ear.*

early selection. Selective attention that occurs in the early stages of recognition, when the organism is constructing a description of the input and before the meaning of the input has been determined. See also *late selection, selective attention.*

educational psychologist. A psychologist whose research interest lies in the application of psychological principles to the education of children and adults in schools. See also *school psychologist.*

EEG. See *electroencephalogram.*

efferent neuron. See *motor neuron.*

ego. In Freud's tripartite division of the personality, the rational part or controlling self. Operates on the *reality principle,* holding back the impulses of the id until they can be satisfied in socially approved ways. See also *id, reality principle, superego.*

ego analyst. A psychoanalyst, who focuses on the integrative, positive functions of the ego (for example, coping with the environment) rather than the functions of the id (for example, gratifying sexual impulses). Heinz Hartman and David Rapaport are considered ego analysts. See also *ego, id, psychoanalyst.*

eidetic imagery. The ability to retain visual images of pictures that are almost photographic in clarity. Such images can be described in far greater detail than would be possible from memory alone. See also *mental imagery.*

elaboration. A memory process wherein one expands verbal material so as to increase the number of ways to retrieve the material.

electroconvulsive therapy (ECT). A treatment for severe depression in which a mild electric current is applied to the brain, producing a seizure similar to an epileptic convulsion. Also known as *electroshock therapy.*

electroencephalogram (EEG). A record obtained by attaching electrodes to the scalp (or occasionally to the exposed brain). Among the brain waves observed are alpha waves (8-13 Hz), characteristic of relaxed wakefulness; delta waves (1-3 Hz), a slower wave of high amplitude that occurs during deep sleep; and theta waves (4-7 Hz), a pattern characteristic of the EEG of the hippocampus and indicative of behavioral arousal.

electroshock therapy. See *electroconvulsive therapy.*

emotion. The condition of the organism during affectively toned experience, whether mild or intense. See also *affective experience.*

emotion-focused coping. Ways of reducing anxiety or stress that do not deal directly with the anxiety-producing situation; defense mechanisms are a form of emotion-focused coping. See also *problem-focused coping.*

empirical validity. See *criterion validity.*

empiricism. The view that behavior is learned as a result of experience. See also *nativism.*

encoding. Transforming a sensory input into a form (code) that can be processed by the memory system.

endocrine system. A system of ductless glands that discharge their secretions (hormones) into the extracellular fluid around capillaries and hence into the bloodstream. The hormones secreted by the endocrine glands are important integrators of bodily functions. See also *hormone.*

endorphins. Chemicals produced by our own body that act like morphine to reduce pain.

engineering psychologist. A psychologist who specializes in the relationship between people and machines, seeking, for example, to design machines that minimize human error.

epinephrine. The principal hormone secreted by the adrenal medulla in response to stressful situations. Its effects are similar to those brought about by stimulation of the sympathetic division of the autonomic nervous system (for example, arousal, increased heart rate and blood pressure). It is also an excitatory neurotransmitter in the central nervous system (syn. *adrenalin*). See also *adrenal gland, norepinephrine.*

episodic memory. A type of memory that stores facts about personal episodes. The fact or episode is encoded with respect to the memorizer, and often with respect to the specific time and place as well. See also *semantic memory.*

equilibratory senses. The senses that give discrimination of the position of the body in space and of the movement of the body as a whole. See also *kinesthesis, semicircular canals, vestibular sacs.*

escape learning. Learning to make a response in order to escape from an aversive event. See also *avoidance learning.*

ESP. See *extrasensory perception.*

estrogen. A female hormone.

estrogens. A group of female sex hormones produced principally by the ovaries. They are responsible for the development of female body characteristics and hair distribution, and for preparing the reproductive system for pregnancy. See also *androgens.*

estrous cycle. Recurring episodes of sexual receptivity that precede ovulation in most female mammals. They are characterized by rising and falling levels of estrogens and progesterone in the bloodstream. See also *estrogens, progesterone.*

ethology. The study of animal behavior in the natural environment.

evocative interaction. The interaction between individuals and their environments that arises because the behavior of different individuals evokes different responses from others. See also *proactive interaction, reactive interaction.*

evoked potential. An electric discharge in some part of the nervous system produced by stimulation elsewhere. The measured potential is commonly based on response averaging by a computer.

evolutionary psychology. An area of research that studies how psychological processes have evolved by means of natural selection; those behaviors that aided survival or increased the chance of reproduction have tended to persist through the course of evolutionary history.

exemplar strategy. A categorization strategy in which (a) old instances of a concept are memorized and (b) a new item is declared a member of that concept if it is sufficiently similar to the memorized instances.

excitatory synapse. A synapse at which the neurotransmitter changes the membrane permeability of the receiving cell in the direction of depolarization. See also *depolarization, inhibitory synapse, synapse.*

expectation. An anticipation or prediction of future events based on past experience and present stimuli.

experimental design. A plan for collecting and treating the data of a proposed experiment. The design is evolved after preliminary exploration, with the aims of economy, precision, and control, so that appropriate inferences and decisions can be made from the data.

experimental group. In an experimental design contrasting two groups, that group of subjects given the treatment whose effect is under investigation. See also *control group.*

experimental method. The method of investigation of natural events that seeks to control the variables involved so as to more precisely define cause-and-effect relationships. Most frequently done in a laboratory, but need not be. See also *observational method, variable.*

experimental psychologist. A psychologist who uses experimental methods to study how people (and other animals) react to sensory stimuli, perceive the world, learn and remember, reason and respond emotionally.

explicit memory. The kind of memory that underlies a conscious recollection of something in the past. See also *implicit memory.*

extinction. (a) The experimental procedure, following classical or operant conditioning, of presenting the conditioned stimulus without the usual reinforcement. (b) The reduction in response that results from this procedure. See also *reinforcement.*

extracellular fluid. Fluid, including the blood, outside the cells; one of the critical variables monitored in the control of thirst.

extracellular reservoir. Water outside the body's cells, including blood.

extrasensory perception (ESP). Response to external stimuli without any known sensory contact. See also *clairvoyance, parapsychology, precognition, psi, psychokinesis, telepathy.*

F

facial feedback hypothesis. The hypothesis that people's subjective experience of an emotion is determined by feedback from the physiological arousal caused by engaging in specific facial expressions.

factor analysis. A statistical method used in test construction and in interpreting scores from batteries of tests. The method enables the investigator to compute the minimum number of determiners (factors) required to account for the intercorrelations among the scores on the tests making up the battery.

family therapy. Psychotherapy with the family members as a group rather than treatment of the patient alone. See also *group therapy.*

feature detector. A general term for any perceptual mechanism that detects distinctive features in a complex display. An example is a line (or edge) detector in vision. Since anything we see can be approximated by a series of line segments at angles to each other, feature detectors have been postulated to be the building blocks for recognizing more complex forms.

Fechner's law. The assertion that the perceived magnitude of a stimulus increases in proportion to the logarithm of its physical intensity.

fetal alcohol syndrome. Abnormal development of the fetus and infant caused by maternal alcohol consumption during pregnancy. Features of the syndrome include retarded growth, small head circumference, a flat nasal bridge, a small midface, shortened eyelids, and mental retardation.

fight-or-flight response. A pattern of bodily responses that prepares the organism for an emergency. Most of these physiological changes result from activation of the sympathetic system and the adrenalcortical system. Includes increases in pupil size, heart rate, blood pressure, respiration, muscle tension, and the secretion of epinephrine, norepinephrine, ACTH and other hormones; decreases in saliva, mucous, digestive activity, and the size of blood vessels. See also *ACTH, adrenal-cortical system, epinephrine, norepinephrine, sympathetic system.*

figure-ground organization. Perceiving a pattern as foreground against a background. Patterns are commonly perceived this way even when the stimuli are ambiguous and the foreground–background relationships are reversible.

file-drawer problem. A problem that arises because studies that fail to obtain positive results are less likely to be published than studies that do obtain positive results. (Failed studies are thus said to "go into the file drawer" rather than being published.) The file-drawer effect causes the database of known studies to be biased toward confirming studies.

filter. Any device that allows some things to pass through it and not others; for example, an electronic device that allows only particular sound frequencies to pass or an optical lens that transmits only certain wavelengths of light. Various types of filters are embedded in the sensory system (optical, mechanical, chemical, neural) that pass some signals and not others. A neuron in the sensory system that is preceded by a filter will respond only to signals that pass through the filter; such a neuron is said to be "tuned" to those signals.

fixation. In Freud's psychoanalytic theory, arrested development through failure to pass beyond one of the earlier stages of psychosexual development or to change the objects of attachment (such as fixation at the oral stage or fixation on the mother).

flashbulb memory. A vivid and relatively permanent record of the circumstances in which one learned of an emotionally charged, significant event.

flooding. A behavior therapy procedure in which a fearful person exposes himself or herself to what is frightening, in reality or in imagination, for extended periods of time without opportunity to escape. See also *behavior therapy.*

flow chart. A diagramatic representation of the sequence of choices and actions in an activity.

formal operational stage. Piaget's fourth stage of cognitive development (age 11 and up) in which the child becomes able to use abstract rules.

fovea. In the eye, a small area in the central part of the retina, packed with cones; the most sensitive part of the retina for detail vision and color vision in daylight. See also *cone, retina.*

fraternal twins. See *dizygotic twins.*

free association. (a) The form of word-association experiment in which the subject gives any word he or she thinks of in response to the stimulus word. (b) In psychoanalysis, the effort to report without modification everything that comes into awareness.

free recall. A memory task in which a subject is given a list of items (usually one at a time) and is later asked to recall them in any order.

frequency theory of pitch. Same as *temporal theory of pitch.*

Freudian slip. In psychoanalytic theory, a mistake or substitution of words in speaking or writing that is contrary to the speaker's conscious intention and presumably expresses wishes or thoughts repressed to the unconscious.

frontal lobe. A portion of each cerebral hemisphere, in front of the central fissure. See also *occipital lobe, parietal lobe, temporal lobe.*

frustration. (a) As an event, the thwarting circumstances that block or interfere with goal-directed activity. (b) As a state, the annoyance, confusion, or anger engendered by being thwarted, disappointed, defeated.

frustration-aggression hypothesis. The hypothesis that frustration (thwarting a person's goal-directed efforts) induces an aggressive drive, which, in turn, motivates aggressive behavior.

fundamental. The frequency being played in a musical note.

fundamental attribution error. The tendency to underestimate situational influences on behavior and assume that some personal characteristic of the individual is responsible; the bias toward dispositional rather than situational attributions. See also *attribution, dispositional attribution, situational attribution.*

fuzzy concept. A concept in which one primarily relies on prototype properties in determining membership, and hence cannot always be sure of one's decisions. See also *prototype.*

G

GABA. See *gamma-aminobutyric acid.*

galvanic skin response (GSR). Changes in electrical conductivity of, or activity in, the skin, detected by a sensitive galvanometer. The reactions are commonly used as an emotional indicator.

gamma-aminobutyric acid (GABA). An important inhibitory neurotransmitter.

ganglia (sing. *ganglion*). A collection of nerve cell bodies and synapses, constituting a center lying outside the brain and spinal cord, as in the sympathetic ganglia. See also *nuclei.*

gate control theory of pain. According to this theory, the sensation of pain requires not only that pain receptors be activated, but also that a neural gate in the spinal cord allow these signals to continue to the brain. Pressure stimulation tends to close the gate; this is why rubbing a hurt area can relieve pain. Attitudes, suggestions, and drugs may act to close the gate.

gender constancy. A child's realization that a person's sex does not change with age or appearance (e.g., wearing opposite-sex clothes). A direct analogue to Piaget's concept of *conservation* in the child's understanding of the physical world.

gender identity. The sense of one's self as either male or female.

gender schema. A mental structure that organizes the person's perceptual and conceptual world into gender categories (male-female, masculine-feminine). *Gender schema theory* holds that society produces gender identity and sex typing by teaching individuals to use the gender schema as a set of "lenses" through which to view reality. See also *gender identity, schema, sex typing.*

gene. The basic unit of hereditary transmission, localized within the chromosomes. Each chromosome contains many genes. Genes are typically in pairs, one member of the pair being found in the chromosome from the father, the other in the corresponding chromosome from the mother. See also *chromosome, dominant gene, recessive gene.*

General Problem Solver (GPS). A computer program to simulate human problem solving

by setting up subgoals and reducing the discrepancies to each subsequent subgoal. See also *simulation.*

generalization. (a) In concept formation, problem solving, and transfer of learning, the detection by the learner of a characteristic or principle common to a class of objects, events, or problems. (b) In conditioning, the principle that once a conditioned response has been established to a given stimulus, similar stimuli will also evoke that response. See also *discrimination.*

generalized anxiety disorder. An anxiety disorder characterized by persistent tension and apprehension. May be accompanied by such physical symptoms as rapid heart rate, fatigue, disturbed sleep, and dizziness. See also *anxiety disorders.*

genetics. That branch of biology concerned with heredity and the means by which hereditary characteristics are transmitted.

genital stage. In Freud's psychoanalytic theory, the final stage of psychosexual development, beginning at puberty and culminating in mature adult sexuality. See also *psychosexual development.*

genotype. In genetics, the characteristics that an individual has inherited and will transmit to his or her descendants, whether or not the individual manifests these characteristics. See also *phenotype.*

geon. In perception, geometric forms (such as cylinders, cones, blocks, and wedges) that comprise the features of objects. Recognition of an object is good to the extent that the geons of the object can be recovered.

Gestalt psychology. A system of psychological theory concerned primarily with perception that emphasizes pattern, organization, wholes, and field properties.

glia cells. Supporting cells (not neurons) composing a substantial portion of brain tissue; recent speculation suggests that they may play a role in neural conduction.

glutamate. An amino acid that serves as an important excitatory neurotransmitter. See also *neurotransmitter.*

gonads. Sexual organs that secrete sexual hormones and that manufacture reproductive cells. Female gonads, called ovaries, secrete estrogen and produce egg cells. Male gonads, called testes, secrete androgen (especially testosterone) and produce sperm cells.

graded potentials. Potential changes of varying size induced in a neuron's dendrites or cell body by stimulation from synapses from other neurons. When the graded potentials reach a threshold of depolarization, an action potential occurs. See also *action potential, depolarization.*

group polarization. The tendency of groups to arrive at decisions that are in the same direction but are more extreme than the mean of the pre-discussion decisions of the individuals in the group.

group therapy. A group discussion or other

group activity with a therapeutic purpose participated in by more than one client or patient at a time. See also *psychotherapy.*

groupthink. The tendency of members of some decision-making groups to suppress their own dissenting opinions in the interests of group consensus, thereby producing an inadequate decision-making process and poor decisions.

GSR. See *galvanic skin response.*

gustation. The sense of taste.

H

habit. A learned stimulus-response sequence. See also *conditioned response.*

habituation. The reduction in the strength of a response to a repeated stimulus. In general, almost any stimulus will produce habituation; for example, a pure tone sounded for a half-hour may decrease as much as 20 db in perceived loudness. See also *dishabituation.*

habituation method. A technique used to study perception in infants. It is based on the fact that while infants look directly at novel objects they soon tire of doing so (habituation). Hence one can determine the degree to which an infant perceives an object as novel by measuring the time spent looking at it.

hair cells. In audition, hairlike receptors in the cochlea that bend due to vibration of the basilar membrane and then send electrical impulses to the brain. See also *basilar membrane, cochlea.*

hallucination. A sense experience in the absence of appropriate external stimuli; a misinterpretation of imaginary experiences as actual perceptions. See also *delusion, illusion, schizophrenia.*

hallucinogens. Drugs whose main effect is to change perceptual experience and "expand consciousness." LSD and marijuana are examples (syn. *psychedelic drugs*).

halo effect. The tendency to bias our perception of another person in the direction of one particular characteristic that we like or dislike.

hashish. See *marijuana.*

health psychology. See *behavioral medicine.*

heritability. The proportion of the total variability of a trait in a given population that is attributable to genetic differences among individuals within the population.

hermaphrodite. An individual born with genitals that are ambiguous in appearance or that are in conflict with the internal sex glands. See also *transsexual.*

heroin. An extremely addictive central nervous system depressant derived from opium. See also *opiates.*

hertz (Hz). The unit used to measure the frequency of a sound wave, specifically the number of cycles per second.

heterosexual. When a person is sexually attracted primarily to members of the opposite sex.

heuristic. In problem solving, a strategy that

can be applied to a variety of problems and that usually, but not always, yields a correct solution.

heuristic theory of persuasion. A theory that proposes that when we are unwilling or unable to process the content of a persuasive communication, we evaluate its validity by utilizing simple rules of thumb (*heuristics*). One such rule might be "messages with many arguments are more likely to be valid than messages with few arguments."

hidden observer. A metaphor to describe the concealed consciousness in hypnosis, inferred to have experiences differing from, but parallel to, the hypnotic consciousness.

hierarchies of concepts. The relationships among individual concepts. See also *concept*.

hierarchy of needs. Maslow's way of classifying needs and motives, ascending from basic biological needs to a peak of self-actualization, supposedly the highest human motive.

hippocampus. A brain structure located below the cerebral cortex that is involved in the consolidation of new memories; its role seems to be that of a cross-referencing system, linking together aspects of a particular memory that are stored in separate parts of the brain.

home sign. A system of gestures used by deaf children that initially functions as a kind of simple pantomime but eventually takes on the properties of a language.

homeostasis. A motivational control system based on negative feedback, which maintains a constant physiological or psychological state. Homeostatic systems keep body temperature, water balance, energy balance, etc., close to critical goal values. When the state deviates from the goal value, the homeostatic system activates a response that will correct the deviation.

homosexual. When a person is sexually attracted primarily to members of the same sex; the term can be applied to a man or a woman.

hormone. A chemical messenger produced by an organ in one part of the body and transported through the bloodstream to other parts of the body where it has a specific effect on cells that recognize its message. See also *endocrine system*.

hue. The dimension of color from which the major color names are derived (red, yellow, green, and so on), corresponding to wavelength of light. See also *saturation*.

humanistic psychology. A psychological approach that emphasizes the uniqueness of human beings; it is concerned with subjective experience and human values. See also *phenomenology*.

humanistic therapies. A general term for approaches to psychotherapy that emphasize the individual's subjective experiences, free will, and ability to solve his or her own problems. Client-centered therapy and Gestalt therapy are examples. See also *client-centered therapy*.

hunger drive. A drive based on food deprivation. See also *drive, specific hunger*.

hypercomplex cell. A cell in the visual cortex that responds to a particular orientation and length. See also *complex cell, feature detector, simple cell*.

hyperphagia. Pathological overeating. See also *aphagia*.

hypnosis. The responsive state achieved following a hypnotic induction or its equivalent. In this state, one person (the subject) responds to suggestions offered by another person (the hypnotist) and experiences alterations in perception, memory, and voluntary action.

hypnotic induction. The procedure used in establishing hypnosis in a responsive person. It usually involves relaxation and stimulated imagination. See also *hypnosis*.

hypnotic trance. The dreamlike state of heightened suggestibility induced in a subject by a hypnotist. See also *posthypnotic suggestion*.

hypothalamus. A small but very important structure located just above the brain stem and just below the thalamus. Considered a part of the central core of the brain, it includes centers that govern motivated behavior such as eating, drinking, sex, and emotions; it also regulates endocrine activity and maintains body homeostatis. See also *lateral hypothalamus, ventromedial hypothalamus*.

hypothesis testing. Gathering information and testing alternative explanations of some phenomenon.

hypothetical construct. One form of inferred intermediate mechanism. The construct is conceived of as having properties of its own, other than those specifically required for the explanation; for example, drive that is inferred from the behavior of a deprived organism and is used in the explanation of later behavior.

Hz. See *hertz*.

I

id. In Freud's tripartite division of the personality, the most primitive part, consisting of the basic biological impulses (or drives). The source of psychic energy or *libido*. Operates on the *pleasure principle*, endeavoring to obtain pleasure and to avoid pain, regardless of external circumstances. See also *ego, libido, pleasure principle, superego*.

identical twins. See *monozygotic twins*.

identification. Changing one's beliefs, attitudes, or behaviors in order to be like an admired reference group. See also *compliance, internalization, reference group*.

identification figures. Adult models (especially parents) copied, partly unconsciously, by the child. See also *identification*.

identity crisis. In Erikson's theory of psychosocial development, a period of self-doubt and active questioning about one's definition of self ("Who am I?" "Where am I going?") which typically takes place during adolescence. See also *identity status, psychosocial stages*.

identity status. An individual's position on Erikson's identity-formation continuum, which includes *identity achievement, foreclosure, moratorium,* and *identity diffusion (or confusion)*. See also *identity crisis*.

illusion. In perception, a misinterpretation of the relationships among presented stimuli so that what is perceived does not correspond to physical reality; especially, but not exclusively, an optical or visual illusion. See also *delusion, hallucination*.

imitation. Behavior that is modeled on or copies that of another. See also *identification*.

implicit memory. The kind of memory that underlies perceptual and cognitive skills. It is often expressed as an improvement on some perceptual or cognitive task without any conscious recollection of the experiences that led to the improvement. See also *explicit memory*.

impossible figures. A figure in which recognition is normal when attending to each part, but the parts do not fuse into a single coherent picture.

imprinting. A type of early learning in which a newborn forms an attachment with some kind of model (normally, a parent).

incentive. An external event or stimulus that is the target of a motivation, and that can serve as a reward. Incentive theories of motivation stress the role of external targets in eliciting and satisfying motivational states.

incentive theory. A theory of motivation that emphasizes the importance of negative and positive incentives in determining behavior; internal drives are not the sole instigators of activity. See also *drive-reduction theory*.

independent variable. The variable under experimental control with which the changes studied in the experiment are correlated.

individual differences. Relatively persistent dissimilarities in structure of behavior among persons or members of the same species.

induced motion. The perception of motion caused when a larger object surrounding a smaller object moves; the smaller object may appear to be the one that is moving even if it is stationary. See also *stroboscopic motion*.

inductive reasoning. Reasoning about arguments in which it is improbable that the conclusion is false if the premises are true. See also *deductive reasoning*.

industrial psychologist. A psychologist who is concerned with such problems as selecting people most suitable for particular jobs, developing job training programs, and figuring out the determinants of consumer behavior.

infancy. The period of helplessness and dependency in humans and other organisms; in humans, roughly the first 2 years.

information-processing model. In general, a model based on assumptions regarding the flow of information through a system; usually best realized in the form of a computer program. In cognitive psychology, theories of how the mind functions are often represented in the form of an information-processing model. By simulating the model on a computer, one can study the properties and implications of the theory. See also *cognitive psychology, computer simulation, model.*

inhibitory synapse. A synapse at which the neurotransmitter changes the membrane permeability of the receiving cell in the direction of the resting potential; in other words, keeps it from firing. See also *excitatory synapse, synapse.*

inner ear. The internal portion of the ear containing, in addition to the cochlea, the vestibular sacs and the semicircular canals. See also *cochlea, semicircular canals, vestibular sacs.*

insight. (a) In problem-solving experiments the perception of relationships leading to solution. Such a solution can be repeated promptly when the problem is again confronted. (b) In psychotherapy, the discovery by the individuals of dynamic connections between earlier and later events so that they come to recognize the roots of their conflicts.

insomnia. Dissatisfaction with the amount or quality of one's sleep. The diagnosis is subjective because many people who complain of insomnia are found to have normal sleep when studied in the laboratory, whereas others who do not complain of insomnia are found to have detectable sleep disturbances. See also *apnea.*

instinct. An innately determined behavior that is specific to a certain species and appears in the same form in all members of the species.

insulin. The hormone secreted by the pancreas. See also *hormone.*

intellectualization. A defense mechanism whereby a person tries to gain detachment from an emotionally threatening situation by dealing with it in abstract, intellectual terms. See also *defense mechanisms.*

intelligence. (a) That which a properly standardized intelligence test measures. (b) The ability to learn from experience, think in abstract terms, and deal effectively with one's environment. See also *intelligence quotient, mental age.*

intelligence quotient (IQ). A scale unit used in reporting intelligence test scores, based on the ratio between mental age and chronological age. The decimal point is omitted so that the average IQ for children of any one chronological age is set at 100. See also *chronological age, deviation IQ, mental age.*

interactionism. (a) Within personality-development theory, a framework in which personality is seen as resulting from the interaction between the child's genotype (inherited characteristics) and the environment in which he or she is raised. (b) In personality theory, a framework in which behavior is seen as resulting from the interaction between consistent personality dispositions or traits and the situations in which people find themselves. See also *evocative interaction, proactive interaction, reactive interaction.*

interaural intensity difference. The difference in intensity of sounds reaching the two ears; it aids in the localization of sounds at high frequencies. See also *interaural time difference.*

interaural time difference. The difference in time between the arrival of sound waves at the two ears; it aids in the localization of sounds at low frequencies. See also *interaural intensity.*

interference. A factor that can impair retrieval from long-term memory. It arises when different items are associated with the same retrieval cue; attempted retrieval of one of these items can be blocked by the inadvertent retrieval of the other item. See also *long-term memory, retrieval cue.*

interjudge reliability. The consistency achieved by two or more observers when assessing or rating some behavior (for example, in rating the aggressiveness of nursery-school children). Also called inferater agreement. See also *reliability.*

intermittent reinforcement. See *partial reinforcement.*

internalization. Changing one's beliefs, attitudes, and behaviors because one genuinely believes in them. Incorporating them into one's own value system. See also *compliance, identification.*

internal consistency. A form of test reliability. Specifically, the homogeneity of a set of items on a test, the degree to which they are all measuring the same variable. See also *reliability.*

interneurons. Neurons in the central nervous system that receive messages from sensory neurons and send them to other interneurons or to motor neurons. See also *motor neuron, sensory neuron.*

interpretation. In psychoanalysis, the analyst's calling attention to the patient's resistances in order to facilitate the flow of associations; also the explanation of symbols, as in dream interpretation. See also *resistance.*

interrater agreement. See *interjudge reliability.*

interval schedules. In operant conditioning, reinforcement schedules in which reinforcement occurs only after a certain time interval has elapsed. On a fixed interval (FI) schedule, the organism is reinforced for its first response only after a certain amount of time has passed since its last response. On a variable interval (VI) schedule, reinforcement still depends on time since last response, but the interval's duration varies unpredictably. See also *ratio schedules.*

intervening variable. A process inferred to occur between stimulus and response, thus accounting for one response rather than another to the same stimulus. The intervening variable may be inferred without further specification, or it may be given concrete properties and become an object of investigation.

interview. A conversation between an investigator (the interviewer) and a subject (the respondent) used for gathering pertinent data for the subject's benefit (as in the psychotherapeutic interview) or for information-gathering (as in a sample survey).

intracellular fluid. Water contained within the body's cells; one of the critical variables monitored in the control of thirst.

intracellular reservoir. Water inside the body's cells.

introspection. (a) A form of trained self-observation, in which individuals describe the content of their consciousness without the intrusion of meanings or interpretations. (b) Any form of reporting on subjective (conscious) events or experiences. See also *phenomenology.*

introspective method. See *introspection.*

introversion–extraversion. The personality dimension first identified by Carl Jung that refers to the degree to which a person's basic orientation is turned inward toward the self or outward toward the external world. At the introversion end are shy individuals who tend to withdraw into themselves; at the extraversion end are sociable individuals who prefer to be with others.

ion channel. A specialized protein molecule that permits specific ions to enter or leave cells. Some ion channels open or close in response to appropriate neurotransmitter molecules; others open or close in response to voltage changes across the cell membrane. This process regulates depolarization and the firing of nerve impulses.

ion pump. A protein molecule that helps to maintain an uneven distribution of electrically charged ions across the cell membrane of a neuron by pumping them into or out of the cell. Ion pumps work with ion channels to regulate depolarization and firing of nerve impulses. See also *depolarization, ion channel.*

J

James–Lange theory. A classical theory of emotion, named for the two men who independently proposed it. The theory states that the stimulus first leads to bodily responses, and then the awareness of these responses constitutes the experience of emotion. See also *Cannon-Bard theory, cognitive-appraisal theory.*

jnd. See *just noticeable difference.*

just noticeable difference (jnd). A barely perceptible physical change in a stimulus; a measure of the difference threshold. The term is used also as a unit for scaling the steps of sensation corresponding to increases in the magnitude of stimulation. See also *difference threshold, Weber's law.*

K

key-word method. A technique for learning vocabulary of a foreign language via an intermediate key word related to the sound of the foreign word and the meaning of the English equivalent. See also *mnemonics.*

kinesthesis. The muscle, tendon, and joint senses, yielding discrimination of position and movement of parts of the body. See also *equilibratory senses.*

L

late selection Selective attention that occurs in the later stages of recognition, after the organism has determined the meaning of the input. See also *early selection.*

latency. A temporal measure of response, referring to the time delay between the occurrence of the stimulus and the onset of the response. See also *psychosexual development.*

latency period. In Freud's psychoanalytic theory, a period in middle childhood, roughly the years 6–12, when both sexual and aggressive impulses are said to be in a quiescent state.

latent content. The underlying significance of a dream (such as the motives of wishes being expressed by it) as interpreted from the manifest content. See also *manifest content.*

lateral fissure. A deep fissure at the side of each cerebral hemisphere, below which lies the temporal lobe (syn. *fissure of Sylvius*).

lateral hypothalamus (LH). An area of the hypothalamus important to the regulation of food intake. Electrical stimulation of this area will make an experimental animal start to eat; destruction of brain tissue here causes an animal to stop eating. See also *hypothalamus, ventromedial hypothalamus.*

law of effect. The phenomenon that any behavior that is followed by reinforcement is strengthened; from the infinite pool of possible responses, those that lead to reinforcement are repeated, whereas those that do not are extinguished. See also *reinforcement.*

learned helplessness. A condition of apathy or helplessness created experimentally by subjecting an organism to unavoidable trauma (such as shock, heat, or cold). Being unable to avoid or escape an aversive situation produces a feeling of helplessness that generalizes to subsequent situations.

learning. A relatively permanent change in behavior that occurs as the result of practice. Behavior changes due to maturation or temporary conditions of the organism (such as fatigue, the influence of drugs, adaptation) are not included.

learning curve. A graph plotting the course of learning, in which the vertical axis (ordinate) plots a measure of proficiency (amount per unit time, time per unit amount, errors made, and so on), while the horizontal axis

(abscissa) represents some measure of practice (trials, time, and so on.)

left hemisphere. The left cerebral hemisphere. Controls the right side of the body and, for most people, speech and other logical, sequential activities (syn. *major hemisphere*). See also *cerebral hemispheres, corpus callosum, right hemisphere, split-brain subject.*

lens. The part of the eye that helps focus light rays on a single point of the retina. See also *cornea, pupil, retina.*

lesbian. See *homosexual.*

LH. See *lateral hypothalamus.*

libido. (Latin for lust). In Freud's psychoanalytic theory, the psychic energy of the id. See also *id.*

lie detector. See *polygraph, voice stress analyzer.*

light adaptation. The decreased sensitivity of the eye to light when the subject has been continuously exposed to high levels of illumination. See also *dark adaptation.*

lightness. In sensory psychology, the degree to which a light appears white (which is different from brightness, in that a dimly lit object can still appear white).

lightness constancy. The tendency to see a familiar object as of the same lightness, regardless of light and shadow that change its stimulus properties. See also *perceptual constancy.*

limbic system. A set of structures in and around the midbrain, forming a functional unit regulating motivational and emotional types of behavior, such as waking and sleeping, excitement and quiescence, feeding, and mating.

linear perspective. In perspective, a monocular cue for depth. When parallel lines appear to converge, they are perceived as vanishing in the distance. See also *relative height, relative size, superposition.*

linguistic relativity hypothesis. The proposition that one's thought processes, the way one perceives the world, are determined by one's language.

lithium carbonate. A compound based on lithium, an element related to sodium. Has been successful in treating bipolar disorders. See also *bipolar disorder.*

localized functions. Behavior controlled by known areas of the brain; for example, vision is localized in the occipital lobes.

location constancy. The tendency to perceive the place at which a resting object is located as remaining the same even though the relationship to the observer has changed. See also *perceptual constancy.*

long-term memory (LTM). The relatively permanent component of the memory system, as opposed to short-term memory. See also *short-term memory.*

long-term potentiation. A phenomenon concerning the neural bases of learning. Once stimulated, neurons will show an increase in their rate of activity when subsequently stimulated (at least up to a period of months).

longitudinal study. A research method that studies an individual through time, taking measurements at periodic intervals. See also *case history.*

loudness. An intensity dimension of hearing correlated with the amplitude of the sound waves that constitute the stimulus. Greater amplitudes yield greater loudnesses. See also *pitch, timbre.*

LSD. See *lysergic acid diethylamide.*

LTP. See *long-term potentiation.*

lucid dream. A dream in which events seem so normal (lacking the bizarre and illogical character of most dreams) that the dreamer believes he or she is awake and conscious.

lunch-line effect. An example of peripheral attention. Even though you may be absorbed in conversation in a room full of people, the sound of your name in another conversation will usually attract your attention; this phenomenon suggests a nonconscious monitoring of that conversation.

lysergic acid diethylamide. A powerful psychoactive drug capable of producing extreme alterations in consciousness, hallucinations, distortions in perception, and unpredictable mood swings.

M

magnetic resonance imaging (MRI). A computer-based scanning procedure that uses strong magnetic fields and radio-frequency pulses to generate a picture of a cross section of the brain or body. Provides greater precision than the CT scanner.

major hemisphere. See *left hemisphere.*

manic-depression. See *bipolar disorder.*

manifest content. The remembered content of a dream, the characters, and their actions, as distinguished from the inferred latent content. See also *latent content.*

mantra. See *meditation.*

MAO. See *monamine oxidase.*

MAOI. See *monoamine oxidase inhibitor.*

marijuana. The dried leaves of the hemp plant (canabis); also known as hashish, "pot," or "grass." Hashish is actually an extract of the plant material and, hence, is usually stronger than marijuana. Intake may enhance sensory experiences and produce a state of euphoria.

marital therapy. Psychotherapy with both members of a couple aimed at resolving problems in their relationship (syn. *couples therapy*). See also *psychotherapy.*

masochism. A pathological desire to inflict pain on oneself or to suffer pain at the hands of others. See also *sadism.*

maternal drive. The drive, particularly in animals, induced in the female through bearing and nursing young, leading to nestbuilding, retrieving, and other forms of care. See also *drive.*

maturation. Growth processes in the individual that result in orderly changes in behavior, whose timing and patterning are relatively independent of exercise or experience though they may require a normal environment.

maze. A device use in the study of animal and human learning, consisting of a correct path and blind alleys.

mean. The arithmetical average; the sum of all scores divided by their number. See also *measure of central tendency.*

means-ends analysis. A problem-solving strategy in which one compares one's current state to the goal state in order to find the most important difference between them; eliminating this difference then becomes the main subgoal. See also *difference reduction, working backwards.*

measurement. Assigning numbers to different levels, amounts, or sizes of a variable.

measure of central tendency. A value representative of a frequency distribution, around which other values are dispersed; for example, the mean, the median, or mode of a distribution of scores. See also *mean, median, mode.*

measure of variation. A measure of the dispersion or spread of scores in a frequency distribution, such as the range or the standard deviation. See also *standard deviation.*

mechanisms of defense. See *defense mechanisms.*

medial-temporal-lobe amnesia. A form of amnesia or memory loss that results from damage to the middle of the temporal lobe of the brain.

median. The score of the middle case when cases are arranged in order of size of score. See also *measure of central tendency.*

meditation. An altered state of consciousness in which the individual is extremely relaxed and feels divorced from the outside world; the individual loses self-awareness and gains a sense of being involved in a wider consciousness. This meditative state is achieved by performing certain rituals, including regulating breathing, sharply restricting one's field of attention, and assuming yogic body positions. A commercialized form of meditation has been widely promoted under the name of *transcendental meditation or TM.*

medulla. The lowest section of the brainstem, a slight enlargement of the spinal cord as it enters the skull; the point at which the major nerve tracts cross over so that the right cerebral hemisphere controls the left side of the body, and the left cerebral hemisphere controls the right side.

memory decay. A major cause of forgetting in short-term memory in which information simply fades with time.

memory span. The number of items (digits, letters, words) that can be reproduced in order after a single presentation; usually 7 ± 2. See also *chunk, short-term memory.*

memory trace. The inferred change in the nervous system that persists between the time something is learned and the time it is recalled.

menarche. The first menstrual period, indicative of sexual maturation in a girl.

mental age (MA). A scale unit proposed by Binet for use in intelligence testing. If an intelligence test is properly standardized, a representative group of children of age 6 should earn an average mental age of 6, those of age 7, a mental age of 7, and so on. A child whose MA is above his or her chronological age (CA) is advanced; one whose MA lags behind is retarded. See also *chronological age, intelligence quotient.*

mental imagery. Mental representations that are picture-like. Not the same as eidetic imagery. See also *eidetic imagery.*

mental model. A concrete mental representation of a problem situation that may be useful in solving the problem. See also *mental representation.*

mental practice. The imagined rehearsal of a perceptual-motor skill in the absence of gross body movements. For example, picturing yourself serving a tennis ball and making mental corrections when the movement seems faulty, without actually moving your arm.

mental representation. A hypothesized "inner representation" of objects and events in human memory. Some theorists endow mental representations with the very properties they are alleged to represent (a "picture of the mind"); others argue that they involve an abstract characterization much like the propositional logic used by mathematicians (the way information is represented in a digital computer); and yet others believe that they are best thought of as a kind of private symbol system that may vary from person to person. The general concept is pervasive in cognitive psychology. See also *mental imagery.*

mental retardation. Subnormal intellectual functioning with impairment in social adjustment.

mental rotation. The notion that a mental image of an object can be rotated in the mind in fashion analogous to rotating the real object.

mesolimbic dopamine system. A set of neurons in the upper brainstem that is crucial to incentive motivation for food and other rewards. The neurons begin in the midbrain and project their axons upward to limbic structures in the forebrain, where they release dopamine as a neurotransmitter.

meta-analysis. A statistical technique that treats the accumulated studies of a particular phenomenon as a single grand experiment and each study as a single observation.

method of constant stimuli. A psychophysical method for determining sensory thresholds. Stimuli with magnitudes varying around the threshold are presented to a subject many times to see what percentage of the time the subject detects them. See also *psychophysical methods.*

method of loci. An aid to serial memory. Verbal

material is transformed into mental images, which are then located at successive positions along a visualized route, such as an imaged walk through the house or down a familiar street.

middle ear. The part of the ear that transmits sound waves from the eardrum to the oval window of the inner ear by means of three tiny connecting bones (malleus, incus, and stapes). See also *cochlea, eardrum, inner ear, oval window.*

minor hemisphere. See *right hemisphere.*

mnemonics. A system for improving memory often involving a set of symbols that can substitute for the material to be remembered; for example, in attempting to remember a number sequence, one may translate the sequence into letters of the alphabet that in turn approximate words that are easily remembered.

mode. The most frequent score in a distribution, or the class interval in which the greatest number or cases fall. See also *measure of central tendency.*

model. (a) Miniature systems are often constructed according to a logical, mathematical, or physical model. That is, the principles according to which data are organized and made understandable parallel those of the model; for instance, the piano keyboard is a model for understanding the basilar membrane; the thermostat is a model for the feedback principle of homeostasis. (b) In behavior therapy, one who *models* or performs behaviors that the therapist wishes the patient to imitate.

modeling. In social learning theory, the process by which a person learns social and cognitive behaviors by observing and imitating others.

mongolism. See *Down's syndrome.*

monoamine oxidase (MAO). One of the enzymes responsible for the breakdown of a group of neurotransmitters called biogenic amines (norepinephrine, dopamine, and serotonin are examples); believed to be important in the regulation of emotion. Drugs that inhibit the action of this enzyme (MAO inhibitors) are used in treating depression. See also *antidepressant, monamine oxidase inhibitor, neurotransmitter.*

monoamine oxidase inhibitor (MAOI). A class of drugs used to treat depression; the drug inhibits the action of an enzyme (monoamine oxidase) that breaks down certain neurotransmitters (such as dopamine, norepinephrine, and serotonin), thereby prolonging the action of these neurotransmitters. See also *antidepressant, monoamine oxidase, neurotransmitter.*

monochromatism. Total color blindness, the visual system being achromatic. A rare disorder. See also *dichromatism, trichromatism.*

monocular cues. See *distance cues.*

monozygotic (MZ) twins. Twins developed from a single egg. They are always of the same sex and commonly much alike in appearance, although some characteristics may be in mirror image; for example one right-handed, the other left-handed (syn. *identical twins*). See also *dizygotic twins*.

mood disorder. A mental disorder characterized by disturbances of mood. Depression, mania (exaggerated excitement), and bipolar disorders in which the individual experiences both extremes of mood are examples. See also *bipolar disorder, depression*.

moon illusion. A perceptual illusion that makes the moon appear as much as 50 percent larger when it is near the horizon than when it is at its zenith, even though at both locations the moon produces the same retinal image.

moral realism. In Piaget's theory of cognitive development, the preoperational child's treatment of social rules as absolute and unchangeable. Also see *preoperational stage*.

morpheme. The smallest meaningful unit in the structure of a language, whether a word, base, or affix; such as *man, strange, ing, pro*. See also *phoneme*.

motion aftereffect. The illusion of movement in a static object that occurs after viewing motion for an extended period of time; the aftereffect occurs in the opposite direction of the viewed motion.

motion parallax. A monocular cue to depth perception. When you are moving rapidly, nearby objects appear to move more quickly in the opposite direction than distant objects do. This difference in apparent speed provides a cue to the respective depths of the objects.

motivation. Factors that energize behavior and give it direction.

motive. Any condition of the organism that affects its readiness to start on or continue in a sequence of behavior.

motor neuron. A neuron, or nerve cell, that conveys messages from the brain or spinal cord to the muscles and glands (syn. *efferent neuron*). See also *sensory neuron*.

MRI. See *magnetic resonance imaging*.

multiple personality. See *dissociative identity disorder*.

multivariate experiment. A type of experiment that involves the simultaneous manipulation of several independent variables. See also *independent variable*.

myelin sheath. The fuzzy sheath surrounding certain nerve fibers known as myelinated fibers. Impulses travel faster and with less energy expenditure in myelinated fibers than in unmyelinated fibers.

MZ twins. See *monozygotic twins*.

N

nanometer (nm). A billionth of a meter. Wavelength of light is measured in nanometers.

narcissism. Self-love; in Freud's psychoanalytic theory, the normal expression of pregenital development.

narcolepsy. A sleep disturbance characterized by an uncontrollable tendency to fall asleep for brief periods at inopportune times.

narcotics. See *opiates*.

nativism. The view that behavior is innately determined. See also *empiricism*.

nature-nurture issue. The problem of determining the relative importance of heredity (nature) and the result of upbringing in a particular environment (nurture) on mature ability.

need. A physical state involving any lack or deficit within the organism. See also *drive, motive*.

negative incentive. An object or circumstance away from which behavior is directed when the object or circumstance is perceived or anticipated. See also *positive incentive*.

negative reinforcement. Reinforcing a response by the removal of an aversive stimulus. See also *negative reinforcer*.

negative reinforcer. Any stimulus that, when removed following a response, increases the probability of the response. Loud noises, electric shock, and extreme heat or cold classify as negative reinforcers. See also *punishment*.

negative symptoms. In schizophrenia, behavioral deficits such as flattened affect, apathy, and poverty of speech. Presumed to result from abnormalities in brain structure. See also *positive symptoms, schizophrenia*.

nerve. A bundle of elongated axons belonging to hundreds or thousands of neurons, possibly both afferent and efferent neurons. Connects portions of the nervous system to other portions and to receptors and effectors. See also *axon, neuron*.

nerve cell. See *neuron*.

neuroimaging. Newly developed techniques that can create visual images of a brain in action, with an indication of which regions of the brain show the most neural activity during a particular task. One of the most widely used neuroimaging techniques is positron emission tomography (PET).

neuron. The nerve cell; the basic unit of a synaptic nervous system.

neuroreceptor molecule. A protein molecule in a cell membrane that is sensitive to a particular chemical, such as a neurotransmitter. When the appropriate chemical activates a neuroreceptor molecule, changes occur in the cell membrane that either increase or decrease its permeability. Some neurotransmitters have an excitatory effect when locked to their neuroreceptors; others have an inhibitory effect. See also *neurotransmitter*.

neurosis (pl. *neuroses*). A mental disorder in which the individual is unable to cope with anxieties and conflicts and develops symptoms that he or she finds distressing, such as obsessions, compulsions, phobias, or anxiety attacks. In Freud's psychoanalytic theory, neurosis results from the use of defense mechanisms to ward off anxiety caused by

unconscious conflicts. No longer a diagnostic category of DSM-IV. See also *anxiety disorders, obsessive-compulsive disorder, phobia*.

neurotic anxiety. Fear that is out of proportion to the actual danger posed (such as stage fright). See also *anxiety, objective anxiety*.

neuroticism. The name of the emotional instability–stability dimension in Eysenck's factor-analytic theory of personality. Moody, anxious, and maladjusted individuals are at the neurotic or unstable end; calm, well-adjusted individuals are at the other. See also *introversion–extraversion*.

neurotransmitter. A chemical involved in the transmission of nerve impulses across the synapse from one neuron to another. Usually released from small vesicles in the synaptic terminals of the axon in response to the action potential; diffuses across synapse to influence electrical activity in another neuron. See also *dopamine, epinephrine, norepinephrine, serotonin*.

NMDA. See *N-methyl D-aspartate receptor*.

N-methyl D-aspartate receptor (NMDA receptor). A receptor molecule that requires two successive chemical signals to activate it; the first signal makes the receptor more responsive (a phenomenon known as long-term potentiation) so that when a second chemical signal occurs (the neurotransmitter glutanate), the receptor is activated. NMDA receptors are particularly dense in the hippocampus and may explain how memories are stored by linking neurons to form new neural circuits. See also *hippocampus, neurotransmitter, neuroreceptor molecule*.

nonconscious processes. A considerable body of research indicates that we register and evaluate stimuli that we are not consciously aware of. The stimuli are said to influence us unconsciously or to operate at an unconscious (or subconscious) level of awareness. See also *consciousness*.

noradrenalin. See *norepinephrine*.

norepinephrine. One of the hormones secreted by the adrenal medulla; its action in emotional excitement is similar in some, but not all, respects to that of epinephrine. It is also a neurotransmitter of the central nervous system. Norepinephrine synapses can be either excitatory or inhibitory. Believed to play a role in depression and bipolar disorders (syn. *noradrenaline*). See also *adrenal gland, epinephrine*.

normal curve. The plotted form of the normal distribution.

normal distribution. The standard symmetrical bell-shaped frequency distribution, whose properties are commonly used in making statistical inferences from measures derived from samples. See also *normal curve*.

nuclei (sing. *nucleus*). A collection of nerve cell bodies grouped in the brain or spinal cord. See also *ganglia*.

null hypothesis. A statistical hypothesis that any difference observed among treatment conditions occurs by chance and does not reflect a true difference. Rejection of the null hypothesis means that we believe the treatment conditions are actually having an effect.

O

obesity. A condition of being 30 percent or more in excess of one's appropriate body weight.

object constancy. See *perceptual constancy*.

object permanence. Piaget's term for the child's realization that an object continues to exist even though it is hidden from view. See also *sensorimotor stage*.

object relations theory. An outgrowth of psychoanalytic theory that deals with the person's attachments to others over the course of development. Emphasizes ego functioning more than did classical psychoanalytic theory.

object size. The size of an object as determined from measurement at its surface. When size constancy holds, the observer perceives a distant object as being near its object size. See also *retinal size*.

objective anxiety. Fear that is proportionate to the danger posed.

observational method. Studying events as they occur in nature, without experimental control of variables; for instance, studying the nest-building of birds, or observing children's behavior in a play situation. See also *experimental method*.

obsession. A persistent, unwelcome, intrusive thought, often suggesting an aggressive or sexual act. See also *compulsion, obsessive-compulsive disorder*.

obsessive-compulsive disorder. An anxiety disorder taking one of three forms: (a) recurrent thoughts, often disturbing and unwelcome (obsessions); (b) irresistible urges to repeat stereotyped or ritualistic acts (compulsions); (c) both of these in combination. See also *anxiety disorders*.

occipital lobe. A portion of the cerebral hemisphere, behind the parietal and temporal lobes. See also *frontal lobe, parietal lobe, temporal lobe*.

Oedipal conflict. In Freud's psychoanalytic theory, the conflict that arises during the phallic stage of psychosexual development in which the individual is sexually attracted to the parent of the opposite sex and perceives the same-sex parent as a rival. See also *phallic stage, psychosexual development*.

olfaction. The sense of smell.

olfactory bulb. A region of the brain involved in olfaction (smell); it is a way station between the receptors in the nasal passage and the olfactory cortex.

olfactory epithelium. The specialized skin within the nasal cavity that contains the receptors for the sense of smell.

operant behavior. Behavior defined by the stimulus to which it leads rather than by the stimulus that elicits it; such as behavior leading to reward (syn. *instrumental behavior*).

operant conditioning. The strengthening of an operant response by presenting a reinforcing stimulus if, and only if, the response occurs (syn. *instrumental conditioning, reward learning*). See also *classical conditioning*.

opiates. Opium or one of its chemical derivatives: codeine, morphine, or heroin. Central nervous system depressants that relieve pain and produce euphoria, all highly addictive (syn. *narcotics*). See also *heroin*.

opinion molecule. A cognitive unit comprising a belief, an attitude, and a perception of social support for the individual's view on the matter. For example, "I believe that Democrats are compassionate toward the poor" (*belief*); "I prefer having Democrats in office" (*attitude*); "And I think the American people agree with me" (*perception of social support*).

opioid receptors. Neuroreceptor molecules in specific areas of the brain and spinal cord to which a group of neurotransmitters, called endorphins, bind. These molecules also have an affinity for opiates. There are several distinct types of opioid receptors; each has a different affinity for binding with various opiates. See also *neurotransmitter, neuroreceptor molecule*.

opponent-color theory. A theory of color perception that postulates two types of color-sensitive units that respond in opposite ways to the two colors of an opponent pair. One type of unit responds to red or green, the other to blue or yellow. Since a unit cannot respond in two ways at once, reddish-greens and yellowish-blues cannot occur. See also *trichromatic theory, two-stage color theory*.

optic chiasma. A cross-over junction of the optic nerves, located near the base of the brain, where nerve fibers from the inner half of each retina (nearest the nose) cross to the opposite side of the brain. The resulting left optic tract carries data about objects seen in the right-hand side of the field of vision, and the right optic tract carries signals from objects seen on the left.

optic nerve. In vision, a nerve formed out of axons of the ganglion cells, which leads to the brain. See also *bipolar cells. ganglia, photoreceptors, retina*.

oral stage. In Freud's psychoanalytic theory, the first stage of psychosexual development; pleasure derives from the lips and mouth, as in sucking at the mother's breast. See also *psychosexual development*.

organizational psychologist. See *industrial psychologist*.

orienting reflex. (a) A nonspecific response to change in stimulation involving depression of cortical alpha rhythm, galvanic skin response, pupillary dilation, and complex vasomotor responses (a term introduced by Russian psychologists). (b) Head or body movements that orient the organism's receptors to those parts of the environment in which stimulus changes are occurring.

osmoreceptors. Hypothesized cells in the hypothalamus that respond to dehydration by stimulating the release of ADH by the pituitary gland, which, in turn, signals the kidneys to reabsorb water into the bloodstream. See also *antidiuretic hormone, volumetric receptors*.

otoliths. "Ear stones." See *vestibular sacs*.

outer ear. The external ear and auditory canal, whose purpose is to funnel sound waves towards the inner ear. See also *inner ear, middle ear*.

oval window. A membrane on the cochlea of the inner ear that receives vibrations from the ear drum via three connecting bones (malleus, incus, and stapes). Vibrations at the oval window set up similar vibrations in the internal fluid of the cochlea, ultimately activating the hair cells that serve as auditory receptors. See also *cochlea, hair cells*.

ovarian hormones. See *estrogen, progesterone*.

overextension. The tendency of a child, in learning a language, to apply a new word too widely; for example, to call all animals "doggie."

overtone. A higher frequency tone, a multiple of the fundamental frequency, that occurs when a tone is sounded by a musical instrument. See also *timbre*.

P

PAG. A region of the midbrain called the perioqueductal gray, or PAG for short, that is involved in sensing pain. When PAG neurons are active, a neural gate is closed and consequently the sensation of pain is diminished.

pancreas. A bodily organ situated near the stomach. As a duct gland, it secretes pancreatic juice into the intestines, but some specialized cells function as an endocrine gland, secreting the hormone insulin into the bloodstream. See also *endocrine gland*.

panic disorder. An anxiety disorder in which the individual has sudden and inexplicable episodes of terror and feelings of impending doom accompanied by physiological symptoms of fear (such as heart palpitations, shortness of breath, muscle tremors, faintness). See also *anxiety, anxiety disorders*.

parallel processing. A theoretical interpretation of information processing in which several sources of information are all processed simultaneously. See also *serial processing*.

paranoid schizophrenia. A schizophrenic reaction in which the patient has delusions of persecution. See also *schizophrenia*.

paraphilias. Same as sexual perversions. Sexual attraction to unusual objects as well as sexual activities that are unusual in nature. Examples are fetishism (sexual attractions to an inanimate object or some specific nongenital part of a person), exhibitionism (obtaining sexual gratification by exposing one's genitals to an unwilling observer), and pedophilia (a preference for obtaining sexual gratification through contact with youngsters who are legally underage).

parapsychology ("beside psychology"). A subfield of psychology that studies psi phenomena (extrasensory perception and psychokinesis). See also *clairvoyance, extrasensory perception, precognition, psi, psychokinesis, telepathy.*

parasympathetic system. A division of the automatic nervous system, the nerve fibers of which originate in the cranial and sacral portions of the spinal cord. Active in relaxed or quiescent states of the body and to some extent antagonistic to the sympathetic division, or system. See also *sympathetic system.*

parathyroid glands. Endocrine glands adjacent to the thyroid gland in the neck, whose hormones regulate calcium metabolism, thus maintaining the normal excitability of the nervous system. Parathyroid inadequacy leads to tetany. See also *endocrine system.*

parietal lobe. A portion of the cerebral hemisphere, behind the central fissure and between the frontal and occipital lobes. See also *frontal lobe, occipital lobe, temporal lobe.*

partial reinforcement. Reinforcing a given response only some proportion of the times it occurs (syn. *intermittent reinforcement*). See also *reinforcement, reinforcement schedule.*

passionate love. An intensely emotional state in which tender and sexual feelings, elation and pain, anxiety and relief, altruism and jealousy coexist in a confusion of feelings. Combines physiological arousal with perception that the arousal is evoked by the beloved. Contrasted with *companionate love.* See also *companionate love.*

path analysis. A correlational procedure that divides an overall correlation between two variables into separate components or paths. For example, path analysis can help to determine whether a link between childhood temper tantrums and later occupational problems is direct or is due to some intervening link like dropping out of school.

pattern recognition. The perceptual process of determining what an object is.

PCP. See *phenycyclidine.*

percept. The result of the perceptual process; that which the individual perceives.

perception. A general term to describe the whole process of how we come to know what is going on around us; the entire sequence of events from the presentation of a physical stimulus to the phenomenological experiencing of it. Perception is viewed as a set of subprocesses that occur in a multilevel, interactive system. The lower levels in this system, the parts closely associated with the sense organs, are called sensory processes. See also *sensory processes.*

perceptual constancy. The tendency to see objects as relatively unchanged under widely altered conditions of illumination, distance, and position. See also *color constancy, lightness constancy, location constancy, shape constancy, size constancy.*

perceptual defense. The supposed prevention of an individual's conscious perceptual system from recognizing an anxiety-producing situation perceived by the individual's unconscious perceptual system.

perceptual patterning. The tendency to perceive stimuli according to principles such as proximity, similarity, continuity, and closure. Emphasized by Gestalt psychologists. See also *figure-ground organization, gestalt psychology.*

performance. Overt behavior, as distinguished from knowledge or information not translated into action. The distinction is important in theories of learning.

peripheral nervous system. That part of the nervous system outside the brain and spinal cord; it includes the autonomic nervous system and the somatic nervous system. See also *autonomic nervous system, somatic nervous system.*

personal construct. In George Kelly's theory of personality, a dimension used by an individual to interpret or "construe" his or her environment. Considered by Kelly to be the basic unit of personality organization. See also *Role Construct Repertory Test.*

personality. The distinctive and characteristic patterns of thought, emotion, and behavior that define an individual's personal style of interacting with the physical and social environment.

personality assessment. The measurement or appraisal of personality.

personality disorders. Ingrained habitual, and rigid patterns of behavior or character that severely limit the individual's adaptive potential; often society sees the behavior as maladaptive whereas the individual does not.

personality inventory. An inventory for self-appraisal, consisting of many statements or questions about personal characteristics and behavior that the person judges to apply or not to apply to him or her. See also *projective test.*

personality psychologist. A psychologist whose area of interest focuses on classifying individuals and studying the differences between them. This specialty overlaps both developmental and social psychologists to some extent. See also *developmental psychologist, social psychologist.*

person-centered therapy. See *client-centered therapy.*

PET scan. See *positron emission tomography.*

phallic stage. In Freud's psychoanalytic theory, the third stage of psychosexual development in which gratification is associated with stimulation of the sex organs and sexual attach-

ment is to the parent of the opposite sex. See also *Oedipal conflict, psychosexual development.*

phasic pain. The kind of sharp pain experienced immediately upon suffering an injury; usually brief with a rapid increase in intensity followed by a decrease. See also *tonic pain.*

phencyclidine (PCP). Originally developed as an anesthetic but discontinued because of the bizarre reactions it produced, this drug causes an insensitivity to pain and makes the users feel dissociated from themselves and from their environments. Overdoses result in prolonged periods of stupor or coma.

phenomenological perspective. An approach to psychology that focuses on subjective experience and tries to describe it from each individual's unique perspective. See also *humanistic psychology.*

phenomenology. The study of an individual's subjective experience or unique perception of the world. Emphasis is on understanding events from the subject's point of view rather than focusing on behavior. See also *humanistic psychology, introspection.*

phenothiazines. A group of antipsychotic drugs that relieve the symptoms of schizophrenia by blocking the access of the neurotransmitter dopamine to its receptors. Chlorpromazine (Thorazine) and fluphenazine (Prolixin) are examples. See also *antipsychotic drug, dopamine, neurotransmitter.*

phenotype. In genetics, the characteristics that are displayed by the individual organism—such as eye color or intelligence—as distinct from those traits that one may carry genetically but not display. See also *genotype.*

pheromones. Special chemicals secreted by many animals that float through the air to attract other members of the same species. They represent a primitive form of communication.

phi phenomenon. Stroboscopic motion is its simpler form. Commonly produced by successively turning on and off two separated stationary light sources; as the first is turned off and the second turned on, the subject perceives a spot of light moving from the position of the first to that of the second. See also *stroboscopic motion.*

phobia. Excessive fear in the absence of real danger. See also *agoraphobia, claustrophobia.*

phobic disorder. An anxiety disorder in which phobias are severe or pervasive enough to interfere seriously with the individual's daily life. See also *anxiety disorders, phobia.*

phoneme. The smallest unit in the sound system of a language; it serves to distinguish utterances from one another. See also *morpheme.*

photopigments. Chemicals contained in the rods and cones (the receptor cells in the eye). These chemicals absorb light, which starts a process that results in a neural impulse.

physiological motive. A motive based on an evident bodily need, such as the need for food or water.

physiological psychologist. See *biological psychologist.*

pitch. A qualitative dimension of hearing correlated with the frequency of the sound waves that constitute the stimulus. Higher frequencies yield higher pitches. See also *loudness, timbre.*

pituitary gland. An endocrine gland joined to the brain just below the hypothalamus. It consists of two parts, the anterior pituitary and the posterior pituitary. The anterior pituitary is the more important part because of its regulation of growth and of other endocrine glands (syn. *hypophysis*). See also *endocrine system.*

place theory of pitch. A theory of hearing that associates pitch with the place on the basilar membrane where activation occurs. See also *temporal theory of pitch.*

placebo. An inert substance used in place of an active drug; given to the control group in an experimental test.

pleasure principle. In Freud's psychoanalytic theory, the strategy followed by the *id*, seeking to obtain pleasure and to avoid pain regardless of external circumstances. See also *id, reality principle.*

pluralistic ignorance. The tendency for persons in a group to mislead each other about a situation; for example, to define an emergency as a nonemergency because others are remaining calm and are not taking action.

polygenic traits. Characteristics—intelligence, height, emotional stability—determined by many sets of genes.

polygraph. A device that measures simultaneously several physiological responses that accompany emotion; for instance, heart and respiration rate, blood pressure, and GSR. Commonly known as a "lie detector" because of its use in determining the guilt of a subject through responses while he or she answers questions. See also *GSR, voice stress analyzer.*

pop-out effect. A phenomenon in perception, wherein when searching for a primitive feature in a large array, the target feature seems to "pop out."

population. The total universe of all possible cases from which a sample is selected. The usual statistical formulas for making inferences from samples apply when the population is appreciably larger than the sample—for instance, 5 to 10 times larger than the sample. See also *sample.*

positive incentive. An object or circumstance toward which behavior is directed when the object or circumstance is perceived or anticipated. See also *negative incentive.*

positive reinforcement. Reinforcing a response by the presentation of a positive stimulus. See also *positive reinforcer.*

positive reinforcer. Any stimulus that, when applied following a response, increases the probability of the response (syn. *reward*). See also *negative reinforcer.*

positive symptoms. In schizophrenia, behavioral excesses such as hallucinations and bizarre behavior. Contrasted with negative symptoms and presumed to be caused by irregularities in neural transmission. See also *negative symptoms, schizophrenia.*

positron emission tomography (PET). A computer-based scanning procedure that measures regional changes in blood flow to map the neural activities of the living brain.

posterior attentional system. Neural structures in the back of the brain that mediate our ability to selectively attend to a particular location.

posthypnotic amnesia. A particular form of posthypnotic suggestion in which the hypnotized person forgets what has happened during the hypnosis until signaled to remember. See also *posthypnotic suggestion.*

posthypnotic response. See *posthypnotic suggestion.*

posthypnotic suggestion. A suggestion made to a hypnotized person that he or she will perform in a prescribed way (commonly to a prearranged signal) when no longer hypnotized. The activity, the posthypnotic response, is usually carried out without the subject's awareness of its origin. See also *hypnosis.*

post-traumatic stress disorder. An anxiety disorder in which a stressful event that is outside the range of usual human experience, such as military combat or a natural disaster, brings in its aftermath such symptoms as a re-experiencing of the trauma and avoidance of stimuli associated with it, a feeling of estrangement, a tendency to be easily startled, nightmares, recurrent dreams, and disturbed sleep. See also *anxiety disorder.*

PQRST method. A technique for reading and studying information presented in textbook form. The method takes its name from the first letter of the five steps one follows in reading a textbook chapter: *Preview, Question, Read, Self-recitation, Test.*

pragmatic rules. Rules used in deductive reasoning that are less abstract than logical rules, but still applicable to many different domains of life. An example is the *permission* rule.

precognition. Perception of a future event that could not be anticipated through any known inferential process (for example, predicting that a particular number will come up on the next throw of dice). See also *clairvoyance, extrasensory perception, parapsychology, psi, psychokinesis, telepathy.*

preconscious. In Freud's topograhic model, the part of the mind containing thoughts and memories that are not part of conscious awareness at the moment, but which can be brought to awareness when needed. See also *conscious, topographic model, unconscious.*

preferential looking method. A method of examining infants' perceptual preferences by presenting them two stimuli simultaneously and noting the amount of time the infants gaze at each object.

prejudice. Negative feelings toward a group. Derived from "pre-judgment," usually implies negative feelings not based on adequate or valid data about the group. See also *attitude, discrimination, stereotype.*

preoperational stage. Piaget's second stage of cognitive development (ages 2–7 years). The child can think in terms of symbols but does not yet comprehend certain rules or operations, such as the principle of conservation. See also *conservation.*

prepared conditioning. The proposal that humans are biologically predisposed, or prepared, by evolutionary selection to associate fear with objects or situations that were dangerous in earlier times. Explains why people develop phobias (conditioned fears) of snakes and heights but not of lambs or guns. See also *classical conditioning.*

primacy effect. (a) In memory experiments, the tendency for initial words in a list to be recalled more readily than later words. (b) In studies of impression formation, the tendency for initial information to carry more weight than information received later.

primary abilities. The abilities, discovered by factor analysis, that underlie intelligence test performance. See also *factor analysis.*

primary auditory area. A brain region located at the top of the temporal lobe of each cerebral hemisphere where auditory signals carried by the acoustic nerve are analyzed. Because nerve fibers from each side of the head cross over at the brain stem before reaching the auditory area, signals from each ear reach both temporal lobes. Thus, damage to one lobe does not produce deafness in one ear.

primary motor area. A projection area in the brain lying in front of the central fissure. Electrical stimulation commonly results in movement, or motor, responses. See also *primary somatosensory area.*

primary sex characteristics. The structural or physiological characteristics that make possible sexual union and reproduction. See also *secondary sex characteristics.*

primary somatosensory area. Area in the parietal lobe of the brain that registers sensory experiences, such as heat, cold, touch, and pain (syn. *body-sense area*). See also *primary motor area.*

primary visual area. A projection area lying in the occipital lobe. In humans, damage to this area produces blindness in portions of the visual field corresponding to the amount and location of the damage.

priming. The increased accessibility or retrievability of information stored in memory produced by the prior presentation of relevant cues.

proactive interaction. The interaction between

individuals and their environments that arises because different individuals choose to enter different situations and to shape those situations differently after entering them. See also *evocative interaction, reactive interaction.*

proactive interference. The interference of earlier learning with the learning and recall of new material. See also *retroactive interference.*

probe. In studies of memory, an item from a list to be remembered that is presented as a cue to the subject; for example, the subject could be asked to give the next item in the list.

problem-focused coping. Reducing anxiety or stress by dealing in some way with the anxiety-producing situation. Escaping the situation or finding a way to alter it are examples. See also *emotion-focused coping.*

problem-solving strategies. The various strategies that can be employed in solving a problem. Of special interest are a class of strategies that involve breaking the solution to a problem into a series of subgoals. The subgoals are to be accomplished as intermediate steps toward ultimately reaching the final goal.

product-moment correlation. See *coefficient of correlation.*

progesterone. A female hormone secreted by the ruptured follicle.

program. (a) A plan for the solution of a problem; often used interchangeably with "routine" to specify the precise sequence of instructions enabling a computer to solve a problem. (b) In teaching, a set of materials arranged so as to maximize the learning process.

projection. A defense mechanism by which people protect themselves from awareness of their own undesirable traits by attributing those traits excessively to others. See also *defense mechanisms.*

projective test. A personality test in which subjects reveal ("project") themselves through imaginative productions. The projective test gives much freer possibilities of response than the fixed-alternative personality inventory. Examples of projective tests are the Rorschach Test (ink blots to be interpreted) and the Thematic Apperception Test (pictures that elicit stories). See also *personality inventory.*

prolactin. Pituitary hormone prompting the secretion of milk. See also *hormones.*

proposition. A sentence or component of a sentence that asserts something, the predicate, about somebody (or something), the subject. All sentences can be broken into propositions.

prosopagnosia. A loss in the ability to recognize faces that results from brain damage.

prototype. The part of a concept that contains the properties that describe the best examples of the concept. See also *core.*

psi. Processes of information and/or energy ex-

change not currently explicable in terms of known physical mechanisms. See also *clairvoyance, extrasensory perception, parapsychology, precognition, psychokinesis, telepathy.*

psychedelic drugs. See *hallucinogens.*

psychiatric nurse. A nurse specially trained to deal with patients suffering from mental disorders.

psychiatric social worker. A social worker trained to work with patients and their families on problems of mental health and illness, usually in close relationship with psychiatrists and clinical psychologists. See also *clinical psychologist, psychiatrist.*

psychiatrist. A medical doctor specializing in the treatment and prevention of mental disorders both mild and severe. See also *clinical psychologist, psychoanalyst.*

psychiatry. A branch of medicine concerned with mental health and mental illness. See also *psychiatrist, psychoanalyst.*

psychoactive drugs. Drugs that affect one's behavior and thought processes. See also *depressants, hallucinogens, stimulants.*

psychoanalysis. (a) The method developed by Freud and extended by his followers for treating mental disorders. (b) The theory of personality which grew out of experiences with the psychoanalytic method of treatment. The theory emphasizes the role of unconscious processes in personality development and in motivation.

psychoanalyst. A psychotherapist, usually trained as a psychiatrist, who uses methods related to those originally proposed by Freud for treating neuroses and other mental disorders. See also *clinical psychologist, psychiatrist.*

psychoanalytic perspective. An approach to psychology that tries to explain certain kinds of behaviors in terms of unconscious beliefs, fears, and desires. See also *psychoanalysis.*

psychoanalytic psychotherapy. A method of treating mental disorders based on the theories of Freud but briefer and less intense than psychoanalysis. Less emphasis on exploration of childhood experiences and more attention to the client's current interpersonal problems. See also *psychoanalysis.*

psychoanalytic theory. See *psychoanalysis.*

psychoimmunology. An area of research in behavioral medicine that studies how the body's immune system is affected by psychological variables. See also *behavioral medicine.*

psychokinesis (PK). Mental influence over physical events without the intervention of any known physical force (for example, willing that a particular number will come up on the throw of dice). See also *clairvoyance, extrasensory perception, parapsychology, precognition, psi, telepathy.*

psycholinguistics. The study of the psychological aspects of language and its acquisition.

psychological dependence. Habitual use of a

drug to relieve anxiety even though no physical dependence (addiction) has developed.

psychological determinism. The doctrine that all thoughts, emotions, and actions have causes.

psychological motive. A motive that is primarily learned rather than based on biological needs.

psychology. The science that studies behavior and mental processes.

psychometric function. A curve plotting the percentage of times the subject reports detecting a stimulus against a measure of the physical energy of the stimulus.

psychopathic personality. See *antisocial personality.*

psychopharmacology. The study of the effects of drugs on behavior.

psychophysical methods. Procedures used to determine thresholds of sensory modalities.

psychophysics. A name used by Fechner for the science of the relationship between mental processes and the physical world. Now usually restricted to the study of the sensory consequences of controlled physical stimulation.

psychosexual development. In Freud's psychoanalytic theory, the idea that development takes place through stages (oral, anal, phallic, latent, genital), each stage characterized by a zone of pleasurable stimulation and appropriate objects of sexual attachment, culminating in adult sexuality. See also *anal stage, genital stage, latency, oral stage, psychosocial stages.*

psychosexual stages. See *psychosexual development.*

psychosis. (pl. *psychoses*). A severe mental disorder in which thinking and emotion are so impaired that the individual is seriously out of contact with reality. No longer a major diagnostic category in DSM-IV. See also *psychotic behavior.*

psychosocial stages. A modification by Erikson of the psychoanalytic theory of psychosexual development, giving more attention to the social and environmental problems associated with the various stages of development and adding some adult stages beyond genital maturing. See also *psychosexual development.*

psychosomatic disorder. Physical illness that has psychological causes (syn. *psychophysiological disorder*).

psychotherapy. Treatment of personality maladjustment or mental disorders by psychological means, usually, but not exclusively, through personal consultation. See also *biological therapy.*

psychotic behavior. Behavior indicating gross impairment in reality contact as evidenced by delusions and/or hallucinations. May result from damage to the brain or from a mental disorder such as schizophrenia or a bipolar disorder. See also *psychosis.*

puberty. The period during which the reproductive organs become functionally mature. The development of the secondary sex characteristics (particularly the growth and pigmentation of underarm and pubic hair) marks the onset of puberty and the capacity for reproduction, the culmination. See also *adolescent growth spurt, secondary sex characteristics.*

punishment. A procedure used to decrease the strength of a response by presenting an aversive stimulus whenever the response occurs. Note that such a stimulus when applied would be a punisher; when removed, it would act as a negative reinforcer, reinforcing whatever led to its removal. See also *negative reinforcer.*

pupil. In the eye, a circular opening in the iris (the colored part of the eye) that expands and contracts, varying according to the intensity of light present. See also *cornea, lens, retina.*

pure alexia. A loss of the ability to recognize words that results from brain damage (in the left occipital lobe).

Q

Q sort. An assessment technique by which a rater provides a systematic description of an individual's personality by sorting a set of personality statements (for example, "Has a wide range of interests") into groups, ranging from those that are least descriptive to those that are most descriptive of the individual.

R

rapid eye movements (REMS). Eye movements that usually occur during dreaming and that can be measured by attaching small electrodes laterally to and above the subject's eye. These register changes in electrical activity associated with movements of the eyeball in its socket.

rapport. (a) A comfortable relationship between the subject and the tester, ensuring cooperation in replying to test questions. (b) A similar relationship between therapist and patient. (c) A special relationship of hypnotic subject to hypnotist.

rating scale. A device by which raters can record their judgments of others (or of themselves) on the traits defined by the scale.

ratio schedules. In operant conditioning, reinforcement schedules where reinforcement depends on the number of responses the organism makes. On a fixed ratio (FR) schedule, the number of responses required is fixed at a particular value (for example, five responses for a reinforcement). On a variable ratio (VR) schedule, reinforcement occurs only after a certain number of responses, but that number varies unpredictably (for example, sometimes one response, other times ten, but with an average of five). See also *interval schedules.*

rationalization. A defense mechanism in which self-esteem is maintained by assigning plausible and acceptable reasons for conduct entered on impulsively or for less acceptable reasons. See also *defense mechanisms.*

reaction formation. A defense mechanism in which a person denies a disapproved motive through giving strong expressions to its opposite. See also *defense mechanisms.*

reaction time. The time between the presentation of a stimulus and the occurrence of a response. See also *latency.*

reactive interaction. The interaction between individuals and their environments that arises because different individuals interpret, experience, and react to situations in different ways. See also *evocative interaction, proactive interaction.*

reality principle. In Freud's psychoanalytic theory, the strategy followed by the ego, holding back the impulses of the id until they can be satisfied in socially approved ways. See also *ego, pleasure principle.*

receiver-operating-characteristic curve (ROC curve). The function relating the probability of hits and false alarms for a fixed signal level in a detection task. Factors influencing response bias may cause hits and false alarms to vary, but their variation is constrained to the ROC curve. See also *signal detection task.*

recency effect. In memory experiments, the tendency for the last words in a list to be recalled more readily than other list words.

receptive field. In vision, a region of the retina that is associated with a specific cortical neuron; when a stimulus appears anywhere in the field, the associated neuron fires. See also *feature detector.*

receptor. A specialized cell sensitive to particular kinds of stimuli and connected to nerves composed of afferent neurons (such as the retina of the eye). Used more loosely, the organ containing these sensitive portions (such as the eye or the ear).

recessive gene. A member of a gene pair that determines the characteristic trait or appearance of the individual only in the other member of the pair is recessive. If the other member of the pair is dominant, the effect of the recessive gene is masked. See also *dominant gene.*

recoding. A process for improving short-term memory by grouping items into a familiar unit or chunk.

recognition. To recognize something is to associate it correctly with a category, such as "chair," or with a specific name, such as "John Jones." It is a high-level process that requires learning and remembering.

red-green color blindness. The commonest form of color blindness, a variety of dichromatism. See also *color blindness, dichromatism.*

reduced stimulation study. An experimental situation in which sensory stimulation is markedly reduced (syn. *sensory deprivation study*).

reductionism. In psychology, a kind of explanation that tries to explain (or reduce) psychological notions to biological ones.

reference group. Any group to which an individual refers for comparing, judging, and deciding on his or her opinions and behaviors. We are said to "identify" with such groups. See also *identification.*

refractory phase. The period of temporary inactivity in a neuron after it has fired once.

registration. A term to describe receptive processing in which information is processed but not perceived. See also *perception.*

regression. A return to more primitive or infantile modes of response.

rehearsal. The conscious repetition of information in short-term memory, usually involving speech. The process facilitates the short-term recall of information and its transfer to long-term memory. See also *dual-memory theory.*

reincarnation. The belief in rebirth; in other words, that a person has lived before.

reinforcement. (a) In classical conditioning, the experimental procedure of following the conditioned stimulus by the unconditioned stimulus. (b) In operant conditioning, the analogous procedure of following the occurrence of the operant response by the reinforcing stimulus. (c) The process that increases the strength of conditioning as a result of these arrangements. See also *negative reinforcement, partial reinforcement, positive reinforcement.*

reinforcement schedule. A well-defined procedure for reinforcing a given response only some proportion of the time it occurs. See also *interval schedules, partial reinforcement, ratio schedules.*

reinforcing stimulus. (a) In classical conditioning, the unconditioned stimulus. (b) In operant conditioning, the stimulus that reinforces the operant (typically, a reward) (syn. *reinforcer*). See also *negative reinforcer, positive reinforcer.*

relative height. In perception, a monocular cue for depth. Among identical objects, those that are higher in an image are perceived as being farther away. See also *distance cues, linear perspective, relative height, superposition.*

relative size. In perception, a monocular cue for depth. If an image contains an array of objects of similar shape, the smaller objects are perceived as being farther away. See also *distance cues, linear perspective, relative height, superposition.*

relaxation training. Training in various techniques for relaxing muscle tension. The procedure is based on Jacobson's progressive relaxation method, in which the person learns how to relax muscle groups one at a time, the assumption being that muscular relaxation is effective in bringing about emotional relaxation.

releaser. A term used by ethologists for a stimulus that sets off a cycle of instinctive behavior. See also *ethology, instinct.*

reliability. The self-consistency of a test as a measuring instrument. Reliability is measured by a coefficient of correlation between scores on two halves of a test, alternate forms of the test, or retests with the same test; a high correlation signifies high consistency of scores for the population tested. See also *validity*.

REMs. See *rapid eye movements*.

repression. (a) A defense mechanism in which an impulse or memory that is distressing or might provoke feelings of guilt is excluded from conscious awareness. See also *defense mechanisms, suppression*. (b) A theory of forgetting.

Rescorla–Wagner model. A model of classical conditioning. It assumes that the amount of conditioning between a conditioned stimulus and an unconditioned stimulus on any trial depends on the predictability of the unconditioned stimulus; the less predictable the unconsitioned stimulus, the greater the amount of conditioning.

resistance. In psychoanalysis, a blocking of free association; a psychological barrier against bringing unconscious impulses to the level of awareness. Resistance is part of the process of maintaining repression. See also *interpretation, repression*.

respondent behavior. A type of behavior corresponding to reflex action, in that it is largely under the control of and predictable from the stimulus (syn. *elicited behavior*). See also *operant behavior*.

response. (a) The behavioral result of stimulation in the form of a movement or glandular secretion. (b) Sometimes, any activity of the organism, including central responses (such as an image or fantasy) regardless of whether the stimulus is identified and whether identifiable movements occur. (c) Products of the organism's activity, such as words typed per minute.

resting potential. The electrical potential across the nerve cell membrane when it is in its resting state (in other words, not responding to other neurons); the inside of the cell membrane is slightly more negative than the outside. See also *action potential*.

reticular formation. A system of ill-defined nerve paths and connections within the brain stem, lying outside the well-defined nerve pathways, and important as an arousal mechanism.

retina. The portion of the eye sensitive to light, containing the rods and the cones. See also *cone, rod*.

retinal image. The image projected onto the retina by an object in the visual field.

retinal size. The size of the retinal image of an object; retinal size decreases in direct proportion to the object's distance. See also *object size*.

retrieval. Locating information in memory.

retrieval cue. Anything that can help you retrieve information from memory.

retroactive interference. The interference in recall of something earlier learned by something subsequently learned. See also *proactive interference*.

retrograde amnesia. Loss of memory for events and experiences occurring in a period of time prior to the amnesia-causing trauma. See also *amnesia, anterograde amnesia*.

reuptake. The process by which a neurotransmitter is "taken up" again (reabsorbed) by the synaptic terminals from which it had been released. See also *neurotransmitter, synaptic terminals*.

reward. A synonym for *positive reinforcement*. See also *positive reinforcement*.

right hemisphere. The right cerebral hemisphere. Controls the left side of the body and, for most people, spatial and patterned activities (syn. *minor hemisphere*). See also *cerebral hemispheres, corpus callosum, left hemisphere, split-brain subject*.

ROC curve. See *receiver-operating-characteristic curve*.

rod. In the eye, an element of the retina mediating achromatic sensation only; particularly important in peripheral vision and night vision. See also *cone, retina*.

Role Construct Repertory Test. A measuring instrument devised by George Kelly for eliciting a person's constructs. Also called the *Rep Test*. See also *personal construct*.

role-playing. A method for teaching attitudes and behaviors important to interpersonal relations by having the subject assume a part in a spontaneous play, whether in psychotherapy or in leadership training.

Rorschach Test. See *projective test*.

S _____

Saccade. The quick movement of the eyes between eye fixations.

sadism. A pathological motive that leads to inflicting pain on another person. See also *masochism*.

safety signal hypothesis. The suggestion that the reason organisms prefer predictable to unpredictable aversive events is because predictability provides a safe period.

sample. A selection of scores from a total set of scores known as the "population." If selection is random, an unbiased sample results; if selection is nonrandom, the sample is biased and unrepresentative. See also *population*.

satiety sensors. Detectors located in different parts of the digestive or thirst systems that signal that the needed nutrients or fluids are on their way and that feeding or drinking can stop.

saturation. The dimension of color that describes its purity; if highly saturated, it appears to be pure hue and free of gray, but if of low saturation, it appears to have a great deal of gray mixed with it. See also *hue*.

scaling. Converting raw data into types of

scores more readily interpreted, such as ranks, centiles, standard scores.

scapegoat. A form of displaced aggression in which an innocent but helpless victim is blamed or punished as the source of the scapegoater's frustration. See also *displaced aggression, scapegoat theory of prejudice*.

scapegoat theory of prejudice. The theory that some hostility toward minority groups arises because prejudiced individuals repress their own unacceptable impulses and then express hostile attitudes toward others who are perceived to possess those same impulses. The hostility often takes the form of blaming the group for both personal and societal problems.

Schacter-Singer theory. A theory of emotions stating that environmental stimuli lead to general physiological arousal; the individual's cognitive appraisal of the arousal then leads to the subjective experience of a specific emotion.

schedule of reinforcement. The frequency and/or timing with which reinforcement occurs. See also *ratio schedules, interval schedules*.

schema. (pl. *schemas*). The term refers to cognitive structures stored in memory that are abstract representations of events, objects, and relationships in the real world. It is a key ingredient of cognitive theories of psychological phenomena. See also *cognitive map, schematic processing*.

schematic processing. The cognitive process of searching for the schema in memory that is most consistent with the incoming information. See also *schema*.

schizoid. Having some characteristics that resemble schizophrenia but are less severe. Occurs with higher frequency in families of schizophrenics and thus tends to support a genetic basis for schizophrenia. See also *schizophrenia*.

schizophrenia. A group of mental disorders characterized by major disturbances in thought, perception, emotion, and behavior. Thinking is illogical and usually includes delusional beliefs; distorted perceptions may take the form of hallucinations; emotions are flat or inappropriate; bizarre behavior includes unusual postures, stereotyped movements, and "crazy talk." The individual withdraws from other people and from reality. Inherited brain or biochemical abnormalities are implicated.

school psychologist. A professional psychologist employed by a school or school system, with responsibility for testing, guidance, research, and so on. See also *educational psychologist*.

second order conditioning. Conditioning in which the UCS is *not* biologically significant (such as food, water, or shock) but gains power as a UCS by being consistently paired with a biologically significant UCS. See also *classical conditioning, unconditioned stimulus*.

secondary sex characteristics. The physical features distinguishing the mature male from the mature female, apart from the reproductive organs. In humans, the deeper voice of the male and the growth of the beard are illustrative. See also *primary sex characteristics.*

selective adaptation. In perception, a loss of sensitivity to motion that occurs when we view motion. The adaptation is selective because we lose sensitivity to the motion viewed, and to similar motions, but not to motion that differs significantly in direction or speed. Presumably the result of fatigued neurons in the cerebral cortex.

selective attention. The perceptual processes by which we select certain input, but not others, for recognition.

selective breeding. A method of studying genetic influences by mating animals that display certain traits and selecting for breeding from among their offspring those that express the trait. If the trait is primarily determined by heredity, continued selection for a number of generations will produce a strain that breeds true for that trait.

self-actualization. A person's fundamental tendency toward maximal realization of his or her potentials; a basic concept in humanistic theories of personality such as those developed by Maslow and Rogers.

self-concept. The composite of ideas, feelings, and attitudes people have about themselves. For some theorists, self-concept is synonymous with the *self.*

self-consciousness. A state of heightened self-awareness; the disposition to be self-attentive.

self-perception. The individual's awareness of himself or herself; differs from self-consciousness because it may take the form of objective self-appraisal. See also *self-consciousness.*

self-perception theory. The theory that attitudes and beliefs are influenced by observations of one's own behavior; sometimes we judge how we feel by observing how we act.

self-regulation. In behavior therapy, monitoring one's own behavior and using techniques such as self-reinforcement or controlling stimulus conditions to modify maladaptive behavior. See also *behavior therapy.*

self-schema. (pl. *self-schemas*). A generalization or theory about oneself derived from past experience. Self-schemata are assumed to influence the way we selectively attend to, process, and recall personally relevant information (syn. *self-concept*). See also *schema.*

semantic memory. A type of memory that stores general knowledge, such as the meanings of words. Knowledge is encoded in relation to other knowledge rather than in relation to the memorizer. See also *episodic memory.*

semicircular canals. Three curved tubular canals, in three planes, which form part of the labyrinth of the inner ear and are concerned with equilibrium and motion. See also *equilibratory senses.*

sensation. The conscious experience associated with a very simple stimulus like the onset of a tone or light. At one time, the distinction between sensation and perception had great theoretical importance with perception viewed as a combination of sensations. Today, the dividing line between sensation and perception is much less clear, and it seems best to view such experiences as lying along a continuum.

sensitive period. See *critical period.*

sensitization. A simple form of learning in which an organism learns to strengthen its reaction to a weak stimulus if a threatening or painful stimulus follows.

sensorimotor stage. Piaget's first stage of cognitive development (birth–2 years) during which the infant discovers relationships between sensations and motor behavior. See also *object permanance.*

sensory adaptation. The reduction in sensitivity that occurs with prolonged stimulation and the increase in sensitivity that occurs with lack of stimulation; most noted in vision, smell, taste, and temperature sensitivity. See also *dark adaptation, light adaptation.*

sensory modalities. The individual senses.

sensory-neural loss. A hearing deficit in which threshold elevation (loss of sensitivity) is greater at high rather than low frequencies. See also *conduction loss.*

sensory neuron. A neuron, or nerve cell, that conveys messages to the brain or spinal cord from the sense receptors informing the organism about events in the environment or within the body (syn. *afferent neuron*). See also *motor neuron, receptor.*

sensory processes. The subprocesses of the perceptual system that are closely associated with the sense organs. Sensory processes provide selectively filtered information about the stimuli that impinge on us; higher-level processes use this information to form a mental representation of the scene. See also *filter, perception.*

septal area. A portion of the brain deep in the central part, between the lateral ventricles, that appears to yield a state akin to pleasure when stimulated electrically (in a rat, at least).

serial memory search. Comparing a test stimulus in sequence to each item in short-term memory. See also *short-term memory.*

serial processing. A theoretical interpretation of information processing in which several sources of information are processed in a serial order; only one source being attended to at a time. See also *parallel processing.*

serotonin. A neurotransmitter in both the peripheral and central nervous systems. It is an inhibitory transmitter whose actions have been implicated in various processes including sleep, the perception of pain, and mood disorders (depression and manic-depression). See also *neurotransmitter.*

serotonin reuptake inhibitors. A class of antidepressant drugs that work by increasing levels of the neurotransmitter serotonin in the synapse.

set point. The weight at which an individual body functions best.

sex role. The full complement of attitudes and behaviors that a society considers appropriate for the individual because of his or her sex. See also *sex typing.*

sex typing. The acquisition of attitudes and behaviors that a society considers appropriate for the individual because of his or her sex. Distinguished from *gender identity,* which is the degree to which one regards oneself as male or female. See also *sex role.*

sex-linked trait. A trait determined by a gene transmitted on the same chromosomes that determine sex, such as red-green color blindness. See also *X, Y chromosome.*

shape constancy. The tendency to see a familiar object as of the same shape regardless of the viewing angle. See also *perceptual constancy.*

shaping of behavior. Modifying operant behavior by reinforcing only those variations in response that deviate in the direction desired by the experimenter.

shock therapy. See *electroconvulsive therapy.*

short-term memory (STM). The component of the memory system has limited capacity and maintains information for only a brief time. See also *long-term memory.*

sibling. A brother or sister.

signal detection theory. A theory of the sensory and decision processes involved in psychophysical judgments, with special reference to the problem of detecting weak signals in noise. See also *signal detection task.*

signal detection task. A procedure whereby the subject must judge on each trial whether a weak signal was embedded in a noise background. Saying "yes" when the signal was presented is called a *hit* and saying "yes" when the signal was not presented is called a *false alarm.* See also *receiver-operating-characteristic curve.*

simple cell. A cell in the visual cortex that responds to a bar of light or straight edge of a particular orientation and location in the visual field. See also *complex cell.*

simple phobia. Excessive fear of a specific object, animal, or situation in the absence of real danger. See also *phobia, phobic disorder.*

simulation. See *computer simulation.*

sine wave. A cyclical wave that when plotted corresponds to the plot of the trigonometric sine function. The sound waves of pure tones yield this function when plotted.

situational attribution. Attributing a person's actions to factors in the situation or environment, as opposed to internal attitudes and motives. See also *dispositional atttribution.*

size constancy. The tendency to see a familiar object as of its actual size regardless of its distance. See also *perceptual constancy.*

size-distance invariance principle. The proposal that the perceived size of an object is equal to the product of the retinal size of the object and the perceived distance of the object.

smooth muscle. The type of muscle found in the digestive organs, blood vessels, and other internal organs. Controlled via the autonomic nervous system. See also *cardiac muscle, striate muscle.*

social facilitation. The phenomenon in which an organism performs responses more rapidly when other members of its species are present.

social-learning theory. The application of learning theory to the problems of personal and social behavior (syn. *social behavior theory*).

social norms. A group or community's unwritten rules that govern its members' behavior, attitudes, and beliefs.

social phobia. Extreme insecurity in social situations accompanied by an exaggerated fear of embarrassing oneself. See also *phobia, phobic disorder.*

social psychologist. A psychologist who studies social interaction and the ways in which individuals influence one another.

socialization. The shaping of individual characteristics and behavior through the training that the social environment provides.

sociology. The science dealing with group life and social organization in literate societies. See also *behavioral sciences.*

sociopathic personality. See *antisocial personality.*

somatic nervous system. A division of the peripheral nervous system consisting of nerves that connect the brain and spinal cord with the sense receptors, muscles, and body surface. See also *autonomic nervous system, peripheral nervous system.*

spatial frequency. In perception, the distance between successive dark bars in a grating consisting of alternating dark and light bars. Spatial frequency is a determinant of visual resolution. See also *contrast sensitivity.*

spatial localization. The perceptual process of determining where in the visual field an object is. See also *pattern recognition.*

spatial resolution. The ability to see spatial patterns. Visual actuity and the contrast threshold are measures of spatial resolution.

speaker's intention. The speaker's goal in uttering a particular sentence, which is distinct from the actual content of the sentence.

species-specific behavior. See *instinct.*

specific hunger. Hunger for a specific food incentive, such as a craving for sweets. See also *hunger drive.*

specific nerve energies. Johannes Müller's proposal that the brain codes qualitative differences between sensory modalities by the specific neural pathways involved.

spindle. An EEG characteristic of Stage 2 sleep, consisting of short bursts of rhythmical responses of 13–16 Hz; slightly higher than alpha. See also *electroencephalogram.*

split-brain subject. A person who has had an operation that severed the corpus callosum, thus separating the functions of the two cerebral hemispheres. See also *cerebral hemispheres, corpus callosum.*

spontaneous recovery. A phenomenon in classical conditioning discovered by Pavlov. When an organism undergoes execution of a conditioned response and is then moved to a new context, the conditioned response may reappear.

spontaneous remission. Recovery from an illness or improvement without treatment.

sports psychology. The study of human behavior in sport. The goal of much of the work is to help athletes develop psychological skills that maximize performance and enhance the sport experience. For example, hypnosis and biofeedback have been used to control an athlete's anxiety level during competition and mental imagery has been employed to help perfect the synchrony and flow of certain body movements.

spreading activation. A proposed model of retrieval from long-term memory in which activation subdivides among paths emanating from an activated mental representation.

spurious association. A plausible but nonexistent relation between two stimuli. Human learners frequently report such relations when trying to learn less-than-perfect relations.

S-R psychology. See *stimulus-response psychology.*

stabilized retinal image. The image of an object on the retina when special techniques are used to counteract the minute movements of the eyeball that occur in normal vision. When an image is thus stabilized it quickly disappears, suggesting that the changes in stimulation of retinal cells provided by the eye movements are necessary for vision.

stages of development. Developmental periods, usually following a progressive sequence, that appear to represent qualitative changes in either the structure or the function of the organism (such as Freud's psychosexual stages, Piaget's cognitive stages).

standard deviation. The square root of the mean of the squares of the amount by which each case departs from the mean of all the cases (syn. *root mean square deviation*).

state-dependent learning. Learning that occurs during a particular biological state—such as when drugged—so that it can best be demonstrated or is most effective when the person is put in the same state again.

statistical significance. The trustworthiness of an obtained statistical measure as a statement about reality; for example, the probability that the population mean falls within the limits determined from a sample. The expression refers to the reliability of the statistical finding and not to its importance.

statistics. The discipline that deals with sampling data from a population of individuals, and then drawing inferences about the population from the sample. See also *statistical significance.*

stereoscopic vision. (a) The binocular perception of depth and distance of an object owing to the overlapping fields of the two eyes. (b) The equivalent effect when slightly unlike pictures are presented individually to each eye in a stereoscope. See also *distance cues.*

stereotype. A schema of the personality traits or physical attributes of a class or group of people. The schema is usually an overgeneralization, leading us to assume that every member of the group possesses the particular characteristic; for instance the false stereotype that all homosexual males are effeminate. See also *schema.*

steroids. Complex chemical substances, some of which are prominent in the secretions of the adrenal cortex and may be related to some forms of mental illness. See also *adrenal gland.*

stimulants. Psychoactive drugs that increase arousal. Amphetamines, cocaine, and caffeine are examples.

stimulation-produced analgesia. An analgesic effect produced by the stimulation of a region of the midbrain. See also *gate control theory of pain.*

stimulus (pl. *stimuli*). (a) Some specific physical energy impinging on a receptor sensitive to that kind of energy. (b) Any objectively describable situation or event (whether outside or inside the organism) that is the occasion for an organism's response. See also *response.*

stimulus-response (S-R) psychology. A psychological view that all behavior is in response to stimuli and that the appropriate tasks of psychological science are those identifying stimuli, the responses correlated with them, and the processes intervening between stimulus and response.

STM. See *short-term memory.*

strabismus. In vision, a lack of binocular depth perception caused by a person's eyes not pointing in the same direction early in life. See also *astigmatism.*

stress. A state that occurs when people encounter events that they perceive as endangering their physical or psychological well-being.

stress responses. Reactions to events an individual perceives as endangering his or her well-being. These may include bodily changes that prepare for emergency (the fight-or-flight response) as well as such psychological reactions as anxiety, anger and aggression, apathy and depression, and cognitive impairment. See also *fight-or-flight response.*

stressors. Events that an individual perceives as endangering his or her physical or psychological well-being.

striate muscle. Striped muscle; the characteristic muscles controlling the skeleton, as in the arms and legs. Activated by the somatic, as opposed to the autonomic, nervous system. See also *cardiac muscle, smooth muscle.*

stroboscopic motion. An illusion of motion resulting from the successive presentation of discrete stimulus patterns arranged in a progression corresponding to movement, such as motion pictures. See also *phi phenomenon.*

subtractive mixture. Color mixture in which the results differ from additive mixture obtained by mixing projected lights. Subtractive mixture occurs when transparent colored filters are placed one in front of the other and when pigments are mixed. See also *additive mixture.*

superego. In Freud's tripartite division of the personality, the part that represents the internalization of the values and morals of society; the conscience that controls the expression of the id's impulses through moral scruples. See also *conscience, ego, id.*

superposition. In perception, a monocular cue for depth. If an object has contours that cut through those of another, obstructing the other object's view, the overlapping object is perceived as being nearer. See also *distance cues, linear perceptive, relative height, relative size.*

suppression. A process of self-control in which impulses, tendencies to action, and wishes to perform disapproved acts are in awareness but not overtly revealed. See also *repression.*

survey method. A method of obtaining information by questioning a large sample of people.

symbol. Anything that stands for or refers to something other than itself.

sympathetic system. A division of the autonomic nervous system, characterized by a chain of ganglia on either side of the spinal cord, with nerve fibers originating in the thoracic and lumbar portions of the spinal cord. Active in emotional excitement and to some extent antagonistic to the parasympathetic division. See also *parasympathetic system.*

synapse. The close functional connection between the axon of one neuron and the dendrites or cell body of another neuron. See also *excitatory synapse, inhibitory synapse.*

synaptic gap. The space between the presynaptic cell membrane and the post-synaptic cell membrane; the space across a synapse. See also *synapse.*

synaptic terminals. Small swellings at the end of axon branches that enclose synaptic vesicles containing neurotransmitters. See also *neurotransmitter, synapse, synaptic vesicles.*

synaptic vesicles. Small spherical or irregularly shaped structures within a synaptic terminal that contain neurotransmitters; when stimulated, they discharge the neurotransmitters.

See also *neurotransmitter, synapse, synaptic terminals.*

syntactic analysis. In language, an analysis that divides a sentence into noun phrases and verb phrases, and then divides these phrases into smaller units like nouns, adjectives, and verbs.

systematic desensitization. A behavior therapy technique in which hierarchies of anxiety-producing situations are imagined (or sometimes confronted in reality) while the person is in a state of deep relaxation. Gradually the situations become dissociated from the anxiety response. See also *anxiety hierarchy, behavior therapy, counterconditioning.*

systematic reinforcement. A method for modifying behavior by reinforcing desirable responses (with praise or tangible rewards) and ignoring undesirable ones. Used in behavior therapy. See also *behavior therapy.*

T

tabula rasa. Latin, meaning *blank slate.* The term refers to the view that human beings are born without any innate knowledge or ideas; all knowledge is acquired through learning and experience. Proposed by the 17th- and 18th-century British empiricists (Locke, Hume, Berkeley, Hartley).

tachistoscope. An instrument for the brief exposure of words, symbols, pictures, or other visually presented material; sometimes called a T-scope.

taste buds. Receptors for taste located in clusters on the tongue and around the mouth.

T-cell (thymus-dependent cell). A type of lymphocyte that recognizes and destroys foreign antigens (enzymes, toxins, or other substances) and thus plays an important role in the body's immune response.

telegraphic speech. A stage in the development of speech in which the child preserves only the most meaningful and perceptually salient elements of adult speech. The child tends to omit prepositions, articles, prefixes, suffixes, and auxiliary words.

telepathy. Thought transference from one person to another without the mediation of any known channel of sensory communication (for example, identifying a playing card merely being thought of by another person). See also *clairvoyance, extrasensory perception, parapsychology, precognition, psi, psychokinesis.*

temperament. An individual's characteristic mood, sensitivity to stimulation, and energy level. Temperament is usually conceptualized as a genetic predisposition because striking differences in reactivity to stimulation, general mood, and activity level can be observed in newborns.

temperature regulation. The process by which an organism keeps its body temperature relatively constant.

temporal lobe. A portion of the cerebral hemi-

sphere, at the side below the lateral fissure and in front of the occipital lobe. See also *frontal lobe, occipital lobe, parietal lobe.*

temporal theory of pitch. A theory of pitch perception which assumes that the frequency of neural impulses traveling up the auditory nerve correspond to the frequency of a tone. See also *place theory of pitch.*

temporal stability. See *test-retest reliability.*

test battery. A collection of tests whose composite scores are used to appraise individual differences.

test profile. A chart plotting scores from a number of tests given to the same individual (or group of individuals) in parallel rows on a common scale, with the scores connected by lines, so that high and low scores can be readily perceived.

test-retest reliability. The consistency of a test when given over successive occasions to the same person (syn. *temporal stability*). See also *reliability.*

testosterone. A kind of androgen that is responsible during puberty for the sudden growth of facial, underarm, and pubic hair; it also causes a deepening of the voice, the development of muscles that lead to a more masculine form, and the growth of the external genitals.

texture gradient. A cue for perceiving depth directly. When viewing a surface in perspective, the elements that make up the surface appear to be packed closer and closer together, giving an impression of depth. See also *distance cues.*

thalamus. Two groups of nerve cell nuclei located just above the brain stem and inside the cerebral hemispheres. Considered a part of the central core of the brain. One area acts as a sensory relay station, the other plays a role in sleep and waking; this portion is considered part of the limbic system. See also *hypothalamus.*

Thematic Apperception Test (TAT). See *projective test.*

theory. A set of assumptions advanced to explain existing data and predict new events; usually applicable to a wide array of phenomena.

theta rhythm. See *electroencephalogram.*

thinking. The ability to imagine or represent objects or events in memory and to operate on these representations.

three primaries law. A basic law about color vision. Three wavelengths of light can be combined to match almost any color of light, as long as one light is drawn from the long-wave end of the spectrum, another light is drawn from the middle, and the third light is drawn from the short end.

threshold. The transitional point at which an increasing stimulus or an increasing difference not previously perceived becomes perceptible (or at which a decreasing stimulus or previously perceived difference becomes imperceptible). The value obtained depends in part on the methods used in determining it. See also *absolute threshold, difference threshold.*

thyroid gland. An endocrine gland located in the neck, whose hormone thyroxin is important in determining metabolic rate. See also *endocrine gland.*

timbre. The quality distinguishing a tone of a given pitch sounded by one instrument from that sounded by another. The differences are due to overtones and other impurities. See also *overtone.*

tip-of-the-tongue phenomenon. The experience of failing to recall a word or a name when we are quite certain we know it.

TM. See *meditation.*

tolerance. The need to take more and more of a drug to achieve the same effect. An important factor in drug dependence.

tonic pain. The kind of steady, long-lasting pain experienced after an injury has occurred; usually produced by swelling and tissue damage. In contrast to phasic pain. See also *phasic pain.*

top-down processes. Processes in perception, learning, memory, and comprehension that are driven by the organism's prior knowledge and expectations, rather than by the input. See also *bottom-up processes.*

topographic model. Freud's model of the human mind, containing the conscious, preconscious, and the unconscious. See also *conscious, preconscious, unconscious.*

trace conditioning. A classical conditioning procedure in which the CS terminates before the onset of the UCS. See also *delayed conditioning.*

tranquilizer. A drug that reduces anxiety and agitation. See *antianxiety drug.*

transcendental meditation (TM). See *meditation.*

transducer. A device such as an electrode or gauge that, in psychophysiology, converts physiological indicators into other forms of energy that can be recorded and measured.

transduction. The translation of a physical energy into electrical signals by specialized receptor cells. See also *receptor cells.*

transference. In psychoanalysis, the patient's unconsciously making the therapist the object of emotional response, transferring to the therapist responses appropriate to other persons important in the patient's life history.

transsexual. An individual who is physically one sex but psychologically the other. Transsexuals sometimes resort to surgery and hormonal treatment to change their physical appearance. They do not, however, consider themselves to be homosexual. See also *homosexual.*

trichromatic theory. A theory of color perception that postulates three basic color receptors (cones), a "red" receptor, a "green" receptor, and a "blue" receptor. The theory

explains color blindness by the absence of one or more receptor types (syn. *Young-Helmholtz theory*). See also *opponent-color theory, two-stage color theory.*

trichromatism. Normal color vision, based on the classification of color vision according to three color systems: black-white, blue-yellow, and red-green. The normal eye sees all three; the colorblind eye is defective in one or two of the three systems. See also *dichromatism, monochromatism.*

tricyclic antidepressant. A class of antidepressants that relieve the symptoms of depression by preventing the reuptake of the neurotransmitters serotonin and norepinephrine, thereby prolonging their action. Imipramine (brand names, Tofranil and Elavil) is one drug commonly prescribed. See also *antidepressant.*

two-point threshold. A kind of pressure threshold; it is the minimum distance by which two thin rods touching the skin must be separated before they are felt as two points rather than one.

two-stage color theory. A theory of color vision that postulates three types of cones (in agreement with trichromatic theory) followed by red-green and yellow-blue opponent processes (in agreement with opponent-color theory). This theory accounts for much of what is known about color vision, and serves as a prototype for the analysis of other sensory systems. See also *opponent-color theory, trichromatic theory.*

type A and type B. Two contrasting behavior patterns found in studies of coronary heart disease. Type A people are rushed, competitive, aggressive, and overcommitted to achieving; type Bs are more relaxed and feel less pressure. Type As are at risk for heart disease.

U

unconditioned response (UCR). In classical conditioning, the response given originally to the unconditioned stimulus used as the basis for establishing a conditioned response to a previously neutral stimulus. See also *conditioned response, conditioned stimulus, unconditioned stimulus.*

unconditioned stimulus (UCS). In classical conditioning, a stimulus that automatically elicits a response, typically via a reflex, without prior conditioning. See also *conditioned response, conditioned stimulus, unconditioned response.*

unconscious. In Freud's topographic model, that part of the mind containing repressed thoughts and memories of which the individual is unaware. See also *conscious, preconscious, repression, topographic model.*

unconscious inference. A term used by the German scientist Hermann von Helmholtz to describe the process by which the perceiver progresses from experiencing sensations

evoked by an object to recognizing the properties of the object. We make this inference automatically and unconsciously, and eventually we do not even notice the sensations on which it is based. Helmholtz argued that unconscious inference is the basis of many perceptual phenomena, including distance and object perception.

unconscious motive. A motive of which the subject is unaware or aware of in distorted form. Because there is no sharp dividing line between conscious and unconscious, many motives have both conscious and unconscious aspects.

unconscious processes. Memories, impulses, and desires that are not available to consciousness. According to the psychoanalytic theories of Sigmund Freud, painful memories and wishes are sometimes repressed—that is, diverted to the unconscious where they continue to influence our actions even though we are not aware of them. See also *conscious, unconscious.*

V

validity. The predictive significance of a test for its intended purposes. Validity can be measured by a coefficient of correlation between scores on the test and the scores that the test seeks to predict; in other words, scores on some criterion. See also *criterion, reliability.*

validity coefficient. The correlation between a test score and some criterion to which the test is supposed to predict. See also *criterion, validity.*

variable. One of the conditions measured or controlled in an experiment. See also *dependent variable, independent variable.*

variance. The square of a standard deviation.

ventromedial hypothalamus (VMH). Area of the hypothalamus important to the regulation of food intake. Electrical stimulation of this area will make an experimental animal stop eating; destruction of brain tissue here produces voracious eating, eventually leading to obesity. See also *hypothalamus, lateral hypothalamus.*

vestibular apparatus. An organ in the inner ear that contains receptors for body movement and kinesthesis.

vestibular sacs. Two sacs in the labyrinth of the inner ear, called the *saccule* and *utricle,* which contain the otoliths ("ear stones"). Pressure of the otoliths on the hair cells in the gelatinous material of the utricle and saccule gives us the sense of body tilt or linear acceleration. See also *equilibratory senses.*

vicarious learning. Learning by observing the behavior of others and noting the consequences of that behavior (syn. *observational learning*).

visual acuity. The ability to detect visual detail.

visual area. A projection area lying in the occipital lobe. In humans, damage to this area produces blindness in portions of the visual field corresponding to the amount and location of the damage.

visual buffer. In short-term memory, a hypothesized component of the encoding process that briefly stores information in a visual code (i.e., a visual representation of verbal and nonverbal items). See also *acoustic buffer, central executive, encoding, short-term memory.*

visual cliff. An experimental apparatus with glass over a patterned surface, one half of which is just below the glass and the other half, several feet below. Used to test the depth perception of animals and human infants.

visual field. The total visual array acting on the eye when it is directed toward a fixation point.

visual-evoked potentials. A method of studying perception using electrodes placed on the back of the head over the visual cortex. The electrodes record electrical responses related to how well the observer can discriminate a presented stimulus.

VMH. See *ventromedial hypothalamus.*

voice stress analyzer. A device that graphically represents changes in a person's voice associated with emotion. Used in lie detection. See also *polygraph.*

volumetric receptors. Hypothesized receptors that regulate water intake by responding to the volume of blood and body fluids. Renin, a substance secreted by the kidneys into the bloodstream, may be one volumetric receptor; it constricts the blood vessels and stimulates the release of the hormone, angiotensin, which acts on cells in the hypothalamus to produce thirst. See also *osmoreceptors.*

voluntary processes. Activities selected by choice and controlled or monitored according to intention or plan. See also *control processes.*

vulnerability-stress model. An interactive model of physical or mental disorders that proposes that an individual will develop a disorder only when he or she has both some constitutional vulnerability (predisposition) and experiences stressful circumstances. Same as *diathesis-stress model.*

W

weak methods. General problem-solving strategies that do not depend on specific knowledge of a problem. Examples are difference reduction, means-ends analysis, and working backwards. See also *difference reduction, means-ends analysis,* and *working backwards.*

Weber's constant. See *Weber's law.*

Weber's law. The observation that the difference threshold is a fixed proportion of the stimulus magnitude at which it is measured. The proportion is constant over a wide range of stimulus magnitudes, and is called Weber's constant. The value of Weber's constant depends on the sensory modality; the smaller the constant, the more sensitive the modality. See also *difference threshold.*

Wernicke's area. A portion of the left cerebral hemisphere involved in language understanding. Individuals with damage in this area are not able to comprehend words; they can hear words, but they do not know their meanings.

withdrawal symptoms. Unpleasant physiological and psychological reactions that occur when a person suddenly stops taking an addictive drug; these range from nausea, anxiety, mild tremors, and difficulty sleeping at low levels of dependence to vomiting, cramps, hallucinations, agitation, and severe tremors or seizures at higher levels. See also *drug dependence.*

working backwards. A problem-solving strategy in which one works backwards from the goal towards the current state. See also *difference reduction, means-ends analysis.*

working through. In psychoanalytic therapy, the process of reeducation by having patients face the same conflicts over and over in the consultation room, until they can independently face and master the conflicts in ordinary life.

X

X chromosome. A chromosome that, if paired with another X chromosome, determines that the individual will be a female. If it is combined with a Y chromosome, the individual will be a male. The X chromosome transmits sex-linked traits. See also *chromosome, sex-linked trait, Y chromosome.*

XYY syndrome. An abnormal condition in which a male has an extra Y sex chromosome; reputedly associated with unusual aggressiveness, although the evidence is not conclusive. See also *Y chromosome.*

Y

Y chromosome. The chromosome that, combined with an X chromosome, determines maleness. See also *chromosome, sex-linked trait, X chromosome.*

Young-Helmholtz theory. See *trichromatic theory.*

Z

zygote. A fertilized ovum or egg. See also *dizygotic twins, monozygotic twins.*

REFERENCES

Citations in the text are made by author and date of publication.

ABBOTT, B. B., SCHOEN, L. S., & BADIA, P. (1984). Predictable and unpredictable shock: Behavioral measures of aversion and physiological measures of stress. PSYCHOLOGICAL BULLETIN, 96, 45–71.

ABELSON, R. P. (1968). Computers, polls, and public opinion—Some puzzles and paradoxes. TRANSACTION, 5, 20–27.

ABELSON, R. P., ARONSON, E., MCGUIRE, W. J., NEWCOMB, T. M., ROSENBERG, M. J., & TANNENBAUM, P. H. (Eds.). (1968). THEORIES OF COGNITIVE CONSISTENCY: A SOURCEBOOK (pp. 112–39) Chicago: Rand McNally.

ABRAMSON, L. Y., GARBER, J., EDWARDS, N., & SELIGMAN, M. E. P. (1978). Expectancy change in depression and schizophrenia. JOURNAL OF ABNORMAL PSYCHOLOGY, 87, 165–179.

ABRAMSON, L. Y., METALSKY, G. I., & ALLOY, L. B. (1989). Hopelessness depression: A theory-based subtype of depression. PSYCHOLOGICAL REVIEW, 96, 358–372.

ABRAMSON, L. Y., SELIGMAN, M. E. P., & TEASDALE, J. (1978). Learned helplessness in humans: critique and reformulation. JOURNAL OF ABNORMAL PSYCHOLOGY, 87, 49–74.

ABRAVANEL, E., & SIGAFOOS, A. D. (1984). Exploring the presence of imitation during early infancy. CHILD DEVELOPMENT, 55, 381–392.

ADAMS, J. L. (1974). CONCEPTUAL BLOCKBUSTING. Stanford, CA: Stanford Alumni Association.

ADAMS, M., & COLLINS, A. (1979). A schema-theoretic view of reading. In R. O. Freedle (Ed.), NEW DIRECTIONS DISCOURSE PROCESSING, Vol. 12. Norwood, NJ: Ablex.

ADKINS-REGAN, E. (1988). Sex hormones and sexual orientation in animals. PSYCHOBIOLOGY, 16, 335–347.

ADORNO, T. W., FRENKEL-BRUNSWIK, E., LEVINSON, D. J., & SANFORD, R. N. (1950). THE AUTHORITARIAN PERSONALITY. New York: Harper.

AGRAS, W. S. (1985). PANIC: FACING FEARS, PHOBIAS, AND ANXIETY. New York: Freeman.

AINSWORTH, M. D. S. (1989). Attachments beyond infancy. AMERICAN PSYCHOLOGIST, 44, 709–716.

AINSWORTH, M. D. S., BLEHAR, M. C., WALTERS, E., & WALL, S. (1978). PATTERNS OF ATTACHMENT: A PSYCHOLOGICAL STUDY OF THE STRANGE SITUATION. Hillsdale, NJ: Erlbaum.

AKERS, C. (1984). Methodological criticisms of parapsychology. In S. Krippner (Ed.), ADVANCES IN PARAPSYCHOLOGICAL RESEARCH (Vol. 4). Jefferson, NC: McFarland.

AKHTAR, S., WIG, N. N., VARMA, V. K., PERSHARD, D., & VERMA, S. K. (1975). A phenomenological analysis of symptoms in the obsessive-compulsive neurosis. BRITISH JOURNAL OF PSYCHIATRY, 127, 342–348.

ALBERTS, B., BRAY, D., LEWIS, J., RAFF, M., ROBERTS, K., & WATSON, J. D. (1989). MOLECULAR BIOLOGY OF THE CELL. New York: Garland.

ALDAG, R. J., & FULLER, S. R. (1993). Beyond fiasco: A reappraisal of the groupthink phenomenon and a new model of group decision processes. PSYCHOLOGICAL BULLETIN, 113, 533–552.

ALEXANDER, C. N., RAINFORTH, M. V., & GELDERLOOS, P. (1991). Transcendental meditation, self-actualization, and psychological health: A conceptual overview and statistical meta-analysis. JOURNAL OF SOCIAL BEHAVIOR AND PERSONALITY, 6(5), 189–247.

ALLEN, J. B., KENRICK, D. T., LINDER, D. E., & MCCALL, A. M. (1989). Arousal and attraction: A response-facilitation alternative to misattribution and negative-reinforcement models. JOURNAL OF PERSONALITY AND SOCIAL PSYCHOLOGY, 57, 261–270.

ALLEN, M. G. (1976). Twin studies of affective illness. ARCHIVES OF GENERAL PSYCHIATRY, 35, 1476–1478.

ALLEN, V. L., & LEVINE, J. M. (1969). Consensus and conformity. JOURNAL OF EXPERIMENTAL SOCIAL PSYCHOLOGY, 5, (No. 4), 389–399.

ALLEN, V. L., & LEVINE, J. M. (1971). Social support and conformity: The role of independent assessment of reality. JOURNAL OF EXPERIMENTAL SOCIAL PSYCHOLOGY, 7, 48–58.

ALLOY, L. B., & TABACHNIK, N. (1984). Assessment of covariation by animals and humans: Influence of prior expectations and current situational information. PSYCHOLOGICAL REVIEW, 91, 112–149.

ALLPORT, F. H. (1920). The influence of the group upon association and thought. JOURNAL OF EXPERIMENTAL PSYCHOLOGY, 3, 159–182.

ALLPORT, F. H. (1924). SOCIAL PSYCHOLOGY. Boston: Houghton Mifflin.

ALLPORT, G. W., & ODBERT, H. S. (1936). Trait-names: A psycholexical study. PSYCHOLOGICAL MONOGRAPHS, 47, (1, Whole No. 211.).

ALLPORT G. W. (1937). PERSONALITY: A PSYCHOLOGICAL INTERPRETATION. New York: Henry Holt.

ALTEMEYER, B. (1988). ENEMIES OF FREEDOM: UNDERSTANDING RIGHT-WING AUTHORITARIANISM. San Francisco: Jossey-Bass.

ALWIN, D. F., COHEN, R. L., & NEWCOMB, T. M. (1991). PERSONALITY AND SOCIAL CHANGE: ATTITUDE PERSISTENCE AND CHANGES OVER THE LIFESPAN. Madison: University of Wisconsin Press.

AMERICAN PSYCHIATRIC ASSOCIATION. (1987). DIAGNOSTIC AND STATISTICAL MANUAL OF MENTAL DISORDERS (3rd ed., rev.). Washington, DC: American Psychiatric Association.

AMERICAN PSYCHIATRIC ASSOCIATION. (1994). DIAGNOSTIC AND STATISTICAL MANUAL OF MENTAL DISORDERS (4th ed.). Washington, DC: American Psychiatric Association.

AMERICAN PSYCHOLOGICAL ASSOCIATION. (1990). Ethical principles of psychologists. AMERICAN PSYCHOLOGIST, 45, 390–395.

ANASTASI, A. (1989). PSYCHOLOGICAL TESTING (6th ed.). New York: MacMillan.

ANCH, M. A., BROWMAN, C. P., MITLER, M. M., & WALSH, J. K. (1988). SLEEP: A SCIENTIFIC PERSPECTIVE. Englewood Cliffs, NJ: Prentice-Hall.

ANCOLI-ISRAEL, S., KRIPKE, D. F., & MASON, W. (1987). Characteristics of obstructive and central sleep apnea in the elderly: An interim report. BIOLOGICAL PSYCHIATRY, 22, 741–750.

ANDERSON, C. M., REISS, D. J., & HOGARTY, G. E. (1986). SCHIZOPHRENIA AND THE FAMILY. New York: Guilford Press.

ANDERSON, J. R. (1983). THE ARCHITECTURE OF COGNITION. Cambridge, MA: Harvard University Press.

ANDERSON, J. R. (1987). Skill acquisition: Compilation of weak-method problem solutions. PSYCHOLOGICAL REVIEW, 94, 192–210.

ANDERSON, J. R. (1990). COGNITIVE PSYCHOLOGY AND ITS IMPLICATIONS (3rd ed.). New York: Freeman.

ANDREASEN, N. C. (1988). Brain imaging: Applications in psychiatry. SCIENCE, 239, 1381–1388.

ANDREWS, K. H., & KANDEL, D. B. (1979). Attitude and behavior. AMERICAN SOCIOLOGICAL REVIEW, 44, 298–310.

ANGOFF, W. H. (1988). The nature-nurture debate, aptitudes, and group differences. AMERICAN PSYCHOLOGIST, 43, 713–720.

ARDREY, R. (1966). THE TERRITORIAL IMPERATIVE. New York: Dell.

ARENDT, H. (1963). EICHMANN IN JERUSALEM: A REPORT ON THE BANALITY OF EVIL. New York: Viking Press.

ARMSTEAD, C., LAWLER, K., GORDEN, G., & CROSS, J. (1989). Relationship of racial stressors to blood pressure responses and anger expression in Black college students. HEALTH PSYCHOLOGY, 8(5), 541–556.

ARMSTRONG, S. L., GLEITMAN, L. R., & GLEITMAN, H. (1983). What some concepts might not be. COGNITION, 13, 263–308.

ARNOLD, M. (1949). A demonstrational analysis of the TAT in a clinical setting. JOURNAL OF ABNORMAL AND SOCIAL PSYCHOLOGY, 44, 97–111.

ARONSON, E. (1995). THE SOCIAL ANIMAL (7th ed.). San Francisco: Freeman.

ARONSON, E., & CARLSMITH, J. M. (1963). The effect of the severity of threat on the devaluation of forbidden behavior. JOURNAL OF ABNORMAL AND SOCIAL PSYCHOLOGY, 66, 584–588.

ARONSON, E., WILSON, T. D., & AKERT, R. M. (1994). SOCIAL PSYCHOLOGY. New York: Harper-Collins.

ASCH, S. E. (1952). SOCIAL PSYCHOLOGY. Englewood Cliffs, NJ: Prentice-Hall.

ASCH, S. E. (1955). Opinions and social pressures. SCIENTIFIC AMERICAN, *193*, 31–35.

ASCH, S. E. (1958). Effects of group pressure upon modification and distortion of judgments. In E. E. Maccoby, T. M. Newcomb, & E. L. Hartley (Eds.), READINGS IN SOCIAL PSYCHOLOGY (3rd ed.). New York: Holt, Rinehart & Winston.

ASLIN, R. N. (1987). Visual and auditory development in infancy. In J. D. Osofsky (Ed.), HANDBOOK OF INFANT DEVELOPMENT (2nd ed.). New York: Wiley.

ASLIN, R. N. & BANKS, M. S. (1978). Early visual experience in humans: Evidence for a critical period in the development of binocular vision. In S. Schneider, H. Liebowitz, H. Pick, & H. Stevenson (Eds.), PSYCHOLOGY: FROM BASIC RESEARCH TO PRACTICE. New York: Plenum.

ASSAD, G., & SHAPIRO, B. (1986). Hallucinations: Theoretical and clinical overview. AMERICAN JOURNAL OF PSYCHIATRY, *143*, (9), 1088–1097.

ATKINSON, D. (1983). Ethnic similarity in counseling psychology: A review of the research. COUNSELING PSYCHOLOGIST, *11*(3), 79–92.

ATKINSON, D., MARUYAMA, M., & MATSUI, S. (1978). The effects of counselor race and counseling approach on Asian Americans' perceptions of counselor credibility and utility. JOURNAL OF COUNSELING PSYCHOLOGY, *25*, 76–83.

ATKINSON, R. C. (1975). Mnemotechnics in second-language learning. AMERICAN PSYCHOLOGIST, *30*, 821–828.

ATKINSON, R. C. (1974). Teaching children to read using a computer. AMERICAN PSYCHOLOGIST, *29*, 169–178.

ATKINSON, R. C., HERRNSTEIN, R. J., LINDZEY, G., & LUCE, R. D. (Eds.). (1988). STEVENS' HANDBOOK OF EXPERIMENTAL PSYCHOLOGY (Vols. 1 and 2). New York: Wiley.

ATKINSON, R. C., & SHIFFRIN, R. M. (1968). Human memory: A proposed system and its control processes. In K. W. Spence (Ed.), THE PSYCHOLOGY OF LEARNING AND MOTIVATION: ADVANCES IN RESEARCH AND THEORY, *2*, (89–195).

AULD, F., & HYMAN, M. (1991). RESOLUTION OF INNER CONFLICT: AN INTRODUCTION TO PSYCHOANALYTIC THERAPY. Washington, DC: American Psychological Association. 708–709.

AVERILL, J. R. (1982). ANGER AGGRESSION: AN ESSAY ON EMOTION. New York: Springer-Verlag.

AVERILL, J. R. (1983). Studies on anger and agression: Implications for theories of emotion. AMERICAN PSYCHOLOGIST, *38*, 1145–1160.

AWAYA, S. MIYAKE, Y., IMAYUMI, Y., SHIOSE, Y., KNADA, T., & KOMURO, K. (1973). Amblyopia. JAPANESE JOURNAL OF OPHTHALMOLOGY, *17*, 69–82.

AX, A. (1953). The physiological differentiation between fear and anger in humans. PSYCHOSOMATIC MEDICINE, *15*, 433–442.

BAARS, B. J. (1988). COGNITIVE THEORY OF CONSCIOUSNESS. New York: Cambridge University Press.

BADDELEY, A. D. (1990). HUMAN MEMORY: THEORY AND PRACTICE. Boston: Allyn and Bacon.

BADDELEY, A. D., & HITCH, G. J. (1974). Working memory. In G. H. Bower (Ed.), THE PSYCHOLOGY OF LEARNING AND MOTIVATION (Vol. 8). New York: Academic Press.

BADDELEY, A. D., THOMPSON, N., & BUCHANAN, M. (1975). Word length and the structure of short-term memory. JOURNAL OF VERBAL LEARNING AND VERBAL BEHAVIOR, *14*, 575–589.

BAER, P. E. & FUHRER, M. J. (1968). Cognitive processes during differential trace and delayed conditioning of the G. S. R. JOURNAL OF EXPERIMENTAL PSYCHOLOGY, *78*, 81–88.

BAHRICK, H. P., & PHELPHS, E. (1987). Retention of Spanish vocabulary over eight years. JOURNAL OF EXPERIMENTAL PSYCHOLOGY: LEARNING, MEMORY AND COGNITION, *13*, 344–349.

BAILLARGEON, R. (1987). Object permanence in 3-1/2- and 4-1/2-month-old infants. DEVELOPMENTAL PSYCHOLOGY, *23*, 655–664.

BAILLARGEON, R., SPELKE, E. S., & WASSERMAN, S. (1985). Object permanence in five-month-old infants. COGNITION, *20*, 191–208.

BAILEY, C. H., CHEN, M., KELLER, F., & KANDEL, E. R. (1992). Serotonin-mediated endocytosis of apCAM: an early step of learning-related synaptic growth in aplysia. SCIENCE, *256*, 645–649.

BAILEY, J. M., & PILLARD, R. C. (1991). A genetic study of male sexual orientation. ARCHIVES OF GENERAL PSYCHIATRY, *48*, 1089–1096.

BAILEY, J. M., PILLARD, R. C., NEALE, M. C., & AGYEI, Y. (1993). Heritable factors influence sexual orientation in women. ARCHIVES OF GENERAL PSYCHIATRY, *50*, 217–223.

BALTES, P. B., & BALTES, M. M. (EDS.). (1990). SUCCESSFUL AGING: PERSPECTIVES FROM THE BEHAVIORAL SCIENCES. Cambridge: Cambridge University Press.

BANDURA, A. (1973). AGGRESSION: A SOCIAL LEARNING ANALYSIS. Englewood Cliffs, NJ: Prentice-Hall.

BANDURA, A. (1984). Recycling misconceptions of perceived self-efficacy. COGNITIVE THERAPY AND RESEARCH, *8*, 231–255.

BANDURA, A. (1986). SOCIAL FOUNDATIONS OF THOUGHT AND ACTION: A SOCIAL COGNITIVE THEORY. Englewood Cliffs, NJ: Prentice-Hall.

BANDURA, A. (1989). SOCIAL LEARNING THEORY. Englewood Cliffs, NJ: Prentice-Hall.

BANDURA, A. (1992). Self-efficacy mechanism in psychobiologic functioning. In R. Schwarzer (Ed.), SELF EFFICACY: THOUGHT CONTROL OF ACTION (pp. 356–394). Washington, Philadelphia, London: Hemisphere Publishing Corporation.

BANDURA, A., BLANCHARD, E. B., & RITTER, B. (1969). The relative efficacy of desensitization and modeling approaches for inducing behavioral, affective, and attitudinal changes. JOURNAL OF PERSONALITY AND SOCIAL PSYCHOLOGY, *13*, 173–199.

BANDURA, A., TAYLOR, C. B., EWART, C. K., MILLER, N. M., & DEBUSK, R. F. (1985). Exercise testing to enhance wives' confidence in their husbands' cardiac capability soon after clinically uncomplicated acute myocardial infarction. AMERICAN JOURNAL OF CARDIOLOGY, *55*, 635–638.

BANKS, W. P., & PRINTZMETAL, W. (1976). Configurational effects in visual information processing. PERCEPTION AND PSYCHOPHYSICS, *19*, 361–367.

BANKS, W. P., & SALAPATEK, P. (1983). Infant visual perception. In P. H. Mussen (Ed.), HANDBOOK OF CHILD PSYCHOLOGY (Vol. 2). New York: Wiley.

BANYAI, E. I., & HILGARD, E. R. (1976). A comparison of active-alert hypnotic induction with traditional relaxation induction. JOURNAL OF ABNORMAL PSYCHOLOGY, *85*, 218–224.

BARBOUR, H. G. (1912). Die wirkung unmittelbarer erwarmung und abkuhlung der warmenzentrum auf die korpertemperatur. ACHIV FUR EXPERIMENTALLE, PATHOLOGIE UND PHARMAKOLOGIE, *70*, 1–26.

BAREFOOT, J. C., DODGE, K. A., PETERSON, B. L., DAHLSTROM, W. G., & WILLIAMS, R. B., Jr. (1989) The Cook-Medley hostility scale: Item content and ability to predict survival. PSYCHOSOMATIC MEDICINE, *51*, 46–57.

BAREFOOT, J. C., WILLIAMS, R. B., & DAHLSTROM, W. G. (1983). Hostility, CHD incidence and total mortality: A 25-year follow-up study of 255 physicians. PSYCHOSOMATIC MEDICINE, *45*, 59–63.

BARKOW, J., COSMIDES, L., & TOOBY, J. (1990). THE ADAPTED MIND: EVOLUTIONARY PSYCHOLOGY AND THE GENERATION OF CULTURE. Oxford University Press.

BARLOW, H. B., & MOLLON, J. D. (1982). THE SENSES. Cambridge: Cambridge University Press.

BARNES, G. E., & PROSEN, H. (1985). Parental death and depression. JOURNAL OF ABNORMAL PSYCHOLOGY, *94*, 64–69.

BARON, R. A., & BYRNE, D. (1994). SOCIAL PSYCHOLOGY (7th ed.). Boston: Allyn and Bacon.

BARON, R. S. (1986). Distraction-conflict theory: Progress and problems. In L. Berkowitz (Ed.), ADVANCES IN EXPERIMENTAL SOCIAL PSYCHOLOGY (Vol. 19). New York: Academic Press.

BARRERA, M. E., & MAURER, D. (1981). Recognition of mother's photographed face by the three-month-old infant. CHILD DEVELOPMENT, *52*, 714–716.

BARSALOU, L. W. (1985). Ideals, central tendency, and frequency of instantiation as determinants of graded structure in categories. JOURNAL OF EXPERIMENTAL PSYCHOLOGY: LEARNING, MEMORY, AND COGNITION, *11*, 629–654.

BARSALOU, L. W. (1992). COGNITIVE PSYCHOLOGY: AN OVERVIEW FOR COGNITIVE SCIENTISTS. Hillsdale, NJ: Erlbaum Press.

BARTHOLOMEW, K., & HOROWITZ, L. M. (1991). Attachment styles among young adults: A test of a four-category model. JOURNAL OF PERSONALITY AND SOCIAL PSYCHOLOGY, *61*, 226–244.

BARTLETT, F. C. (1932). REMEMBERING: A STUDY IN EXPERIMENTAL AND SOCIAL PSYCHOLOGY. Cambridge: Cambridge University Press.

BARTOSHUK, L. M. (1979). Bitter taste of saccharin: Related to the genetic ability to taste the bitter substance propylthiourial (PROP). SCIENCE, *205*, 934–935.

BASS, E., & DAVIS, L. (1988). THE COURAGE TO HEAL. New York: Harper & Row.

BASSETT, A. S. (1989). Chromosome 5 and schizophrenia: Implications for genetic linkage studies, current and future. SCHIZOPHRENIA BULLETIN, *15*, 393–402.

BATESON, P. (1978). Sexual imprinting and optimal outbreeding. NATURE, *273*(5664), 659–60.

BAUM, A., GATCHEL, R. J., FLEMING, R., & LAKE, C. R. (1981). CHRONIC AND ACUTE STRESS ASSOCIATED WITH THE THREE MILE ISLAND ACCIDENT AND DECONTAMINATION: PRELIMINARY FINDINGS OF A LONGITUDINAL STUDY. Technical report submitted to the U.S. Nuclear Regulatory Commission.

BAUMEISTER, R. F., & TICE, D. M. (1984). Role of self-presentation and choice in cognitive dissonance under forced compliance: Necessary or sufficient causes? JOURNAL OF PERSONALITY AND SOCIAL PSYCHOLOGY, *43*, 838–852.

BAUMEISTER, R. F., & TICE, D. M. (1990). Anxiety and social exclusion. JOURNAL OF SOCIAL AND CLINICAL PSYCHOLOGY, *9*, 165–195.

BAUMRIND, D. (1971). Current patterns of parental authority. DEVELOPMENTAL PSYCHOLOGY MONOGRAPHS, *1*, 1–103.

BAXTER, L. R., JR., SCHWARTZ, J. M., MAZZIOTTA, J. C., PHELPS, M. E., PAHL, J. J., GUZE, M. D., & FAIRBANKS, L. (1988). Cerebral glucose metabolic rates in nondepressed patients with obsessive-compulsive disorder. AMERICAN JOURNAL OF PSYCHIATRY, *145*, 1560–1563.

BEAMAN, A. L., BARNES, P. J., KLENTZ, B., & MCQUIRK, B. (1978). Increasing helping rates through information dissemination: Teaching pays. PERSONALITY AND SOCIAL PSYCHOLOGY BULLETIN, *4*, 406–411.

BEATON, A. (1986). LEFT SIDE/RIGHT SIDE: A REVIEW OF LATERALITY RESEARCH. New Haven: Yale University Press.

BEBBINGTON, P., STURT, E., TENNANT, C., & HURRY, J. (1984). Misfortune and resilience: A community study of women. PSYCHOLOGICAL MEDICINE, *14*, 347–363.

BECK, A. T. (1976). COGNITIVE THERAPY AND THE EMOTIONAL DISORDER. New York: International Universities Press.

BECK, A. T. (1988a). LOVE IS NEVER ENOUGH. New York: Harper & Row.

BECK, A. T. (1988b). Cognitive approaches to panic disorder: Theory and therapy. In S. Rachman & J. D. Maser (Eds.), PANIC: PSYCHOLOGICAL PERSPECTIVES. Hillsdale, NJ: Erlbaum.

BECK, A. T. (1991). Cognitive therapy. AMERICAN PSYCHOLOGIST, *46* (4), 368–375.

BECK, A. T., RUSH, A. J., SHAW, B. F., & EMERY, G. (1979). COGNITIVE THERAPY OF DEPRESSION. New York: Guilford Press.

BEECHER, H. K. (1961). Surgery as placebo. JOURNAL OF AMERICAN MEDICAL ASSOCIATION, *176*, 1102–1107.

BEERS, C. W. (1908). A MIND THAT FOUND ITSELF. New York: Doubleday.

BÉKÉSY, G. Von (1960). EXPERIMENTS IN HEARING, (E. G. Weaver, Trans). New York: McGraw-Hill.

BELL, A. P. (1982, November). Sexual preference: A postscript. SIECUS REPORT, *11*, 1–3.

BELL, A. P., & WEINBERG, M. S. (1978). HOMOSEXUALITIES: A STUDY OF DIVERSITY AMONG MEN AND WOMEN. New York: Simon & Schuster.

BELL, A. P., WEINBERG, M. S., & HAMMERSMITH, S. K. (1981a). SEXUAL PREFERENCE: ITS DEVELOPMENT IN MEN AND WOMEN. Bloomington: Indiana University Press.

BELL, A. P., WEINBERG, M. S., & HAMMERSMITH, S. K. (1981b). SEXUAL PREFERENCE, ITS DEVELOPMENT IN MEN AND WOMEN. STATISTICAL APPENDIX. Bloomington: Indiana University Press.

BELL, L. V. (1980). TREATING THE MENTALLY ILL: FROM COLONIAL TIMES TO THE PRESENT. New York: Praeger.

BELL, S. M., & AINSWORTH, M. D. (1972). Infant crying and maternal responsiveness. CHILD DEVELOPMENT, *43*, 1171–1190.

BELLACK, A. S., HERSEN, M., & KAZDIN, A. E. (Eds.) (1990). INTERNATIONAL HANDBOOK OF BEHAVIOR MODIFICATION AND THERAPY. New York: Plenum Press.

BELSKY, J., & ROVINE, M. J. (1987). Temperament and attachment security in the strange situation: An empirical rapprochement. CHILD DEVELOPMENT, *58*, 787–795.

BELSKY, J., ROVINE, M., & TAYLOR, D. G. (1984). The Pennsylvania infant and family development project III: The origins of individual differences in infant-mother attachment: Maternal and infant contributions. CHILD DEVELOPMENT, *55*, 718–728.

BEM, D. J. (1970). BELIEFS, ATTITUDES, AND HUMAN AFFAIRS. Belmont, CA: Brooks/Cole.

BEM, D. J. (1972). Self-perception theory. In L. Berkowitz (Ed.), ADVANCES IN EXPERIMENTAL SOCIAL PSYCHOLOGY (Vol. 6). New York: Academic Press.

BEM, D. J. (1983). Toward a response style theory of persons in situations. In R. A. Dienstbier & M. M. Page (Eds.), NEBRASKA SYMPOSIUM ON MOTIVATION 1982: PERSONALITY—CURRENT THEORY AND RESEARCH (Vol. 30, pp. 201–231). Lincoln: University of Nebraska Press.

BEM, D. J. (1995). EXOTIC BECOMES EROTIC: A DEVELOPMENTAL THEORY OF SEXUAL ORIENTATION. Unpublished manuscript, Cornell University at Ithaca, New York.

BEM, D. J., & ALLEN, A. (1974). On predicting some of the people some of the time: The search for cross-situational consistencies in behavior. PSYCHOLOGICAL REVIEW, *81*, 506–520.

BEM, D. J., & HONORTON, C. (1994). Does psi exist? Replicable evidence for an anomalous process if information transfer. PSYCHOLOGICAL BULLETIN, *115*, 4–18.

BEM, D. J., WALLACH, M. A., & KOGAN, N. (1965). Group decision-making under risk of aversive consequences. JOURNAL OF PERSONALITY AND SOCIAL PSYCHOLOGY, *1*, 453–460.

BEM, S. L. (1981). Gender schema theory: A cognitive account of sex typing. PSYCHOLOGICAL REVIEW, *88*, 354–364.

BEM, S. L. (1985). Androgyny and gender schema theory: A conceptual and empirical integration. In T. B. Sonderegger (Ed.), NEBRASKA SYMPOSIUM ON MOTIVATION 1984: PSYCHOLOGY AND GENDER (pp. 179–226). Lincoln, NE: University of Nebraska Press.

BEM, S. L. (1987). Gender schema theory and the romantic tradition. In P. Shaver, & C. Hendrick (Eds.), REVIEW OF PERSONALITY AND SOCIAL PSYCHOLOGY (Vol. 7, pp. 251–271). Newbury Park, CA: Sage.

BEM, S. L. (1989). Genital knowledge and gender constancy in preschool children. CHILD DEVELOPMENT, *60*, 649–662.

BEM, S. L. (1993). THE LENSES OF GENDER: TRANSFORMING THE DEBATE ON SEXUAL INEQUALITY. New Haven, CT: Yale University Press.

BEM, S. L., MARTYNA, W., & WATSON, C. (1976). Sex typing and androgyny: Further explorations of the expressive domain. JOURNAL OF PERSONALITY AND SOCIAL PSYCHOLOGY, *34*, 1016–1023.

BENSON, D. F. (1985). Aphasia. In K. M. Heilman & E. Valenstein (Eds.), CLINICAL NEUROPSYCHOLOGY (2nd Ed). In New York: Oxford University Press.

BENSON, H. (1976). THE RELAXATION RESPONSE. New York: Morrow.

BENSON, H., KOTCH, J. B., CRASSWELLER, K. D., & GREENWOOD, M. M. (1977). Historical and clinical considerations of the relaxation response. AMERICAN SCIENTIST, *65*, 441–443.

BERGER, T. W. (1984). Long-term potentiation of hippocampal synaptic transmission affects rate of behavioral learning. SCIENCE, *224*, 627–630.

BERGIN, A. E., & LAMBERT, M. J. (1978). The evaluation of therapeutic outcomes. In S. L. Garfield & A. E. Bergin (Eds.), HANDBOOK OF PSYCHOTHERAPY AND BEHAVIOR CHANGE (2nd ed.). New York: Wiley.

BERKOWITZ, L. (1965). The concept of aggressive drive. In L. Berkowitz (Ed.), ADVANCES IN EXPERIMENTAL SOCIAL PSYCHOLOGY (Vol. 2). New York: Academic Press.

BERKOWITZ, L. (1989). Frustration-aggression hypothesis: Examination and reformulation. PSYCHOLOGICAL BULLETIN, *106*, 59–73.

BERLIN, B., & KAY, P. (1969). BASIC COLOR TERMS: THEIR UNIVERSALITY AND EVOLUTION. Los Angeles: University of California Press.

BERMAN, A. L., & JOBES, D. A. (1991). ADOLESCENT SUICIDE ASSESSMENT AND INTERVENTION. Washington, DC: American Psychological Association.

BERRIDGE, K. C., & VALENSTEIN, E. S. (1991). What psychological process mediates feeding evoked by electrical stimulation of the lateral hypothalamus? BEHAV NEUROSCI *105*(1), 3–14.

BERSCHEID, E. (1983). Emotion. In H. H. Kelley, E. Berscheid, A. Christensen, J. H. Harvey, T. L. Hutson, G. Levinger, E. McClintock, L. A. Peplau, & D. R. Peterson (Eds.), CLOSE RELATIONSHIPS (pp. 110–168). New York: Freeman.

BERSCHEID, E., & WALSTER, E. H. (1974). A little bit about love. In T. Huston (Ed.), FOUNDATION OF INTERPERSONAL ATTRACTION. New York: Academic Press.

BERSCHEID, E., & WALSTER, E. H. (1978). INTERPERSONAL ATTRACTION (2nd ed.). Menlo Park, CA: Addison-Wesley.

BERTELSEN, A., HARVALD, B., & HAUGE, M. A. (1977). A Danish twin study of manic-depressive disorders. BRITISH JOURNAL OF PSYCHIATRY, *130*, 330–351.

BEST, J. B. (1992). COGNITIVE PSYCHOLOGY. New York: West Publishing.

BETTELHEIM, B. (1967). THE EMPTY FORTRESS. New York: Free Press.

BIBRING, E. (1953). The mechanism of depression. In P. Greenacre (Ed.), AFFECTIVE DISORDERS (pp. 13–48). New York: International Universities Press.

BIEDERMAN, I. (1987). Recognition by components: A theory of human image understanding. PSYCHOLOGICAL REVIEW, *94*, 115–1947.

BIEDERMAN, I. (1990). Higher-level vision. In D. N. Osherson, S. M. Kossyln, & J. M. Hollerbach (Eds.), AN INVITATION TO COGNITIVE SCIENCE: VISUAL COGNITION AND ACTION (Vol. 2). Cambridge, MA: MIT press.

BIEDERMAN, I., & JU, G. (1988). Surface versus edge-based determinants of visual recognition. COGNITIVE PSYCHOLOGY, *20*, 38–64.

BIERBRAUER, G. (1973). ATTRIBUTION AND PERSPECTIVE: EFFECTS OF TIME, SET, AND ROLE ON INTERPERSONAL INFERENCE. Unpublished Ph.D. dissertation, Stanford University.

BILLINGS, A. G., & MOOS, R. H. (1984). Coping, stress, and social resources among adults with unipolar depression. JOURNAL OF PERSONALITY AND SOCIAL PSYCHOLOGY, *46*, 887–891.

BINET, A., & SIMON, T. (1905). New methods for the diagnosis of the intellectual level of subnormals. ANNALS OF PSYCHOLOGY, *11*, 191.

BIRNHOLZ, J. C., & BENACERRAF, B. R. (1983). The development of human fetal hearing. SCIENCE, *222*, 516–518.

BISIACH, E., & LUZZATI, C. (1978). Unilateral neglect of representational space. CORTEX, *14*, 129–133.

BLAKEMORE, C., & COOPER, G. F. (1970). Development of the brain depends on the visual environment. NATURE, *228*, 477–478.

BLASS, E. M., & EPSTEIN, A. N. (1971). A lateral preoptic osmosensitive zone for thirst in the rat. JOURNAL OF COMPARATIVE AND PHYSIOLOGICAL PSYCHOLOGY, *76*, 378–394.

BLASS, T. (1991). Understanding behavior in the Milgram obedience experiment: The role of personality, situations, and their interactions. JOURNAL OF PERSONALITY AND SOCIAL PSYCHOLOGY, *60*, 398–413.

BLATT, S. J. (1974). Levels of object representation in anaclitic and introjective depression. PSYCHOANALYTIC STUDY OF THE CHILD, *29*, 107–159.

BLEIER, R. (1984). SCIENCE AND GENDER: A CRITIQUE OF BIOLOGY AND ITS THEORIES ON WOMEN. New York: Pergamon.

BLISS, E. L. (1980). Multiple personalities: Report of fourteen cases with implications for schizophrenia and hysteria. ARCHIVES OF GENERAL PSYCHIATRY, *37*, 1388–1397.

BLISS, T. V. P. & LMO, T. (1973). Long-lasting potentiation of synaptic transmission in the dentate area of the anesthetized rabbit following stimulation of the preforant path. JOURNAL OF PHYSIOLOGY, *232*, 331–356.

BLOCK, J. (1961/1978). THE Q-SORT METHOD IN PERSONALITY ASSESSMENT AND PSYCHIATRIC RESEARCH. Palo Alto: Consulting Psychologists Press.

BLOCK, J. (1971). LIVES THROUGH TIME. Berkeley: Bancroft.

BLOOD, R. O. (1967). LOVE MATCH AND ARRANGED MARRIAGE. New York: Free Press.

BLUM, G. S. (1953). PSYCHOANALYTIC THEORIES OF PERSONALITY. New York: McGraw-Hill.

BLUMENTHAL, J. A., FREDRIKSON, M., KUHN, C. M., ULMER, R. L., WALSH-RIDDLE, M., & APPELBAUM, M. (1990). Aerobic exercise reduces levels of cardiovascular and sympathoadrenal responses to mental stress in subjects without prior evidence of myocardial ischemia. AMERICAN JOURNAL OF CARDIOLOGY, *65*, 93–98.

BOFF, K. R., KAUFMAN, L., & THOMAS, J. P. (Eds.) (1986). HANDBOOK OF PERCEPTION AND HUMAN PERFORMANCE (Vol. 1). New York: Wiley.

BOLLES, R. C. (1970). Species-specific defense reactions and avoidance learning. PSYCHOLOGICAL REVIEW, *77*, 32–48.

BONANNO, G. A., & SINGER, J. L. (1990). Repressive personality style: Theoretical and methodological implications for health and pathology. In J. L. Singer (Ed.), REPRESSION AND DISSOCIATION (pp. 435–465). Chicago: University of Chicago Press.

BOND, C. F. (1982). Social facilitation: A self-presentational view. JOURNAL OF PERSONALITY AND SOCIAL PSYCHOLOGY, *42*, 1042–1050.

BOON, S., & DRAIJER, N. (1993). Multiple personality disorder in The Netherlands: a clinical investigation of 71 patients. AMERICAN JOURNAL OF PSYCHIATRY, *150*, 489–494.

BOOTH, D. (1990). Learned role of tastes in eating motivation. In E. D. Capaldi & P. T. L. (Eds.), TASTE, EXPERIENCE, AND FEEDING (pp. 179–194). Washington, DC: American Psychological Association.

BOOTH, D. A. (1991). Learned Ingestive Motivation and the Pleasures of the Palate. In R. C. Bolles (Eds.), THE HEDONICS OF TASTE (pp. 29–58). Hillsdale: Lawrence Erlbaum Associates.

BOOTH-KEWLEY, S., & FRIEDMAN, H. S. (1987). Psychological predictors of heart disease: A quantitative review. PSYCHOLOGICAL BULLETIN, *101*, 343–362.

BOOTZIN, R. R., KIHLSTROM, J. F., & SCHACTER, D. L. (Eds.) (1990). Sleep and Cognition. Washington, DC: American Psychological Assoc.

BORGIDA, E., & NISBETT, R. E. (1977). The differential impact of abstract vs. concrete information on decisions. JOURNAL OF APPLIED SOCIAL PSYCHOLOGY, *7*, 258–271.

BORING, E. G. (1930). A new ambiguous figure. AMERICAN JOURNAL OF PSYCHOLOGY, *42*, 444–445.

BORNSTEIN, R. F. (1992). Subliminal mere exposure effects. In R. F. Bornstein & T. S. Pittman (Eds.), PERCEPTION WITHOUT AWARENESS: COGNITIVE, CLINICAL AND SOCIAL PERSPECTIVES (pp. 191–210). New York: Guilford.

BORNSTEIN, R. F., & D'AGOSTINO, P. R. (1992). Stimulus recognition and the mere exposure effect. JOURNAL OF PERSONALITY AND SOCIAL PSYCHOLOGY, *63*, 545–552.

BOUCHARD, C. et al (1990). The response to long-term overeating in identical twins. NEW ENGLAND JOURNAL OF MEDICINE, *322*, 1477–1482.

BOUCHARD, T. J., JR. (1984). Twins reared apart and together: What they tell us about human diversity. In S. Fox (Ed.), THE CHEMICAL AND BIOLOGICAL BASES OF INDIVIDUALITY. New York: Plenum.

BOUCHARD, T. J., JR., LYKKEN, D. T., MCGUE, M., SEGAL, N. L., & TELLEGEN, A. (1990). Sources of human psychological differences: The Minnesota study of twins reared apart. SCIENCE, *250*, 223–228.

BOUCHARD, T. J., & MGGUE, M. (1981). Familial studies of intelligence: A review. SCIENCE, *212*, 1055–1059.

BOUTON, M. E. (1994). Context, ambiguity, and classical conditioning. CURRENT DIRECTIONS IN PSYCHOLOGICAL SCIENCE, *3*, 49–52.

BOWER, G. H. (1981). Mood and Memory. AMERICAN PSYCHOLOGIST, *6*, 129–148.

BOWER, G. H., BLACK, J. B., & TURNER, T. R. (1979). Scripts in memory for text. COGNITIVE PSYCHOLOGY, *11*, 177–220.

BOWER, G. H., & CLARK, M. C. (1969). Narrative stories as mediators for serial learning. PSYCHONOMIC SCIENCE, *14*, 181–182.

BOWER, G. H., CLARK, M. C., WINZENZ, D., & LESGOLD, A. (1969). Hierarchical retrieval schemes in recall of categorized word lists. JOURNAL OF VERBAL LEARNING AND VERBAL BEHAVIOR, *8*, 323–343.

BOWER, G. H. & SPRINGSTON, F. (1970). Pauses as recoding points in letter series. JOURNAL OF EXPERIMENTAL PSYCHOLOGY, *83*, 421–430.

BOWERS, K. S., & MEICHENBAUM, D. H. (Eds.) (1984). THE UNCONSCIOUS RECONSIDERED. New York: Wiley.

BOWLBY, J. (1973). ATTACHMENT AND LOSS: SEPARATION, ANXIETY AND ANGER (Vol. 2). London: Hogarth Press.

BOYNTON, R. M. (1979). HUMAN COLOR VISION. New York: Holt, Rinehart & Winston.

BOYNTON, R. M. (1988). Color vision. ANNUAL REVIEW OF PSYCHOLOGY, *39*, 69–100.

BRADSHAW, G. L., & ANDERSON, J. R. (1982). Elaborative encoding as an explanation of levels of processing. JOURNAL OF VERBAL LEARNING AND VERBAL BEHAVIOR., *21*, 165–174.

BRADWEJN, J., KOSZYCKI, D., & METERISSIAN, G. (1990). Cholescystokinin tetrapeptide induces panic attacks identical to spontaneous panic attacks in patients suffering from panic disorder. CANADIAN JOURNAL OF PSYCHIATRY, *35*, 83–85.

BRANSFORD, J. D., & JOHNSON, M. K. (1973). Considerations of some problems of comprehension. In W. G. Chase (Ed.), VISUAL INFORMATION PROCESSING. New York: Academic Press.

BRAUN, B. G. (1986). TREATMENT OF MULTIPLE PERSONALITY DISORDER. Washington, DC: American Psychiatric Press.

BRAZELTON, T. B. (1978). The remarkable talents of the newborn. BIRTH & FAMILY JOURNAL, *5*, 4–10.

BREEDLOVE, S. M. (1994). Sexual differentiation of the human nervous system. ANNU REV PSYCHOL, *45*, 389–418.

BREGMAN, A. S., & REIDNICKY, A. I. (1975). Auditory segregation: Stream of streams? JOURNAL OF EXPERIMENTAL PSYCHOLOGY: HUMAN PERCEPTION AND PERFORMANCE, *1*, 263–267.

BREHM, S. S. (1992). INTIMATE RELATIONSHIPS (2nd ed.). New York: McGraw-Hill.

BRELAND, K., & BRELAND, M. (1966). ANIMAL BEHAVIOR. New York: Macmillan.

BRENNER, C. (1980). A psychoanalytic theory of affects. In R. Plutchik & H. Kellerman (Eds.), EMOTION: THEORY, RESEARCH, AND EXPERIENCE (Vol. 1). New York: Academic Press.

BRENNER, M. H. (1982). Mental illness and the economy. In D. L. Parron, F. Solomon & C. D. Jenkins (Eds.), BEHAVIOR, HEALTH RISKS, AND SOCIAL DISADVANTAGE, Washington, DC: National Academy Press.

BREWER, W. F., & NAKAMURA, G. V. (1984). The nature and functions of schemas. In R. S. Wyer & T. K. Srull (Eds.), HANDBOOK OF SOCIAL COGNITION (Vol. 1). Hillsdale, NJ: Erlbaum.

BREWIN, C. R. (1985). Depression and causal attributions: What is their relationship? PSYCHOLOGICAL BULLETIN, *98*, 297–300.

BRIDGER, W. H. (1961). Sensory habituation and discrimination in the human neonate. AMERICAN JOURNAL OF PSYCHIATRY, *117*, 991–996.

BROADBENT, D. E. (1958). PERCEPTION AND COMMUNICATION. London: Pergamon Press.

BRODY, N. (1992). INTELLIGENCE (2nd ed.). San Diego: Academic Press.

BROMAN, C. L. (1987). Race differences in professional help seeking. AMERICAN JOURNAL OF COMMUNITY PSYCHOLOGY, *15*(4), 473–489.

BROOKS-GUNN, J., & RUBLE, D. N. (1983). The experience of menarche from a developmental perspective. In J. Brooks-Gunn & A. C. Petersen (Eds.), GIRLS AT PUBERTY: BIOLOGICAL AND PSYCHOLOGICAL PERSPECTIVES. New York: Plenum.

BROWN, A. E. (1936). Dreams in which the dreamer knows he is asleep. JOURNAL OF ABNORMAL PSYCHOLOGY, *31*, 59–66.

BROWN, D. P. (1977). A model for the levels of concentrative mediation. INTERNATIONAL JOURNAL OF CLINICAL AND EXPERIMENTAL HYPNOSIS, *25*, 236–273.

BROWN, E. L., & DEFFENBACHER, K. (1979). PERCEPTION AND THE SENSES. Oxford: Oxford University Press.

BROWN, G. W., & HARRIS, T. (1978). SOCIAL ORIGINS OF DEPRESSION: A STUDY OF PSYCHIATRIC DISORDER IN WOMEN. London: Tavistock.

BROWN, J. (1991). Staying fit and staying well: Physical fitness as a moderator of life stress. JOURNAL OF PERSONALITY AND SOCIAL PSYCHOLOGY, *60*, 555–561.

BROWN, J. D. (1986). Evaluations of self and others: Self-enhancement biases in social judgments. SOCIAL COGNITION, *4*, 353–376.

BROWN, R. (1973). A FIRST LANGUAGE: THE EARLY STAGES. Cambridge, MA: Harvard University Press.

BROWN, R. (1974). Further comment on the risky shift. AMERICAN PSYCHOLOGIST, *29*, 468–470.

BROWN, R. (1986). SOCIAL PSYCHOLOGY: THE SECOND EDITION. New York: Free Press.

BROWN, R., CAZDEN, C. B., & BELLUGI, U. (1969). The child's grammar from 1 to 3. In J. P. Hill (Ed.), MINNESOTA SYMPOSIUM ON CHILD PSYCHOLOGY (Vol. 2). Minneapolis: University of Minnesota Press.

BROWN, R., & KULIK, J. (1977). Flashbulb memories. COGNITION, *5*, 73–99.

BROWN, R. W., & McNEILL, D. (1966). The "tip-of-the-tongue" phenomenon. JOURNAL OF VERBAL LEARNING AND VERBAL BEHAVIOR, *5*, 325–337.

BROWNELL, K. (1988). Yo-yo dieting. PSYCHOLOGY TODAY, *22*(Jan), 20–23.

BROWNELL, K. D., & RODIN, J. (1994). The dieting maelstrom: is it possible and advisable to lose weight? AMERICAN PSYCHOLOGIST, *49*, 781–791.

BRUCH, H. (1973). EATING DISORDERS: OBESITY, ANOREXIA NERVOSA, AND THE PERSON WITHIN. New York: Basic Books.

BRUNER, J. S. (1957). Going beyond the information given. In CONTEMPORARY APPROACHES TO COGNITION: A SYMPOSIUM HELD AT THE UNIVERSITY OF COLORADO. Cambridge, MA: Harvard University Press.

BRUNER, J. S., GOODNOW, J. J., & AUSTIN, G. A. (1956). A STUDY OF THINKING, New York: Wiley.

BRUNER, J. S., OLVER, R. R., GREENFIELD, P. M., & collaborators (1966). STUDIES IN COGNITIVE GROWTH. New York: Wiley.

BRUYER, R., LATERRE, C., SERON, X., & collaborators (1983). A case of prosopagnosia with some preserved covert remembrance of familiar faces. BRAIN AND COGNITION, *2*, 257–284.

BRYAN, J. H., & TEST, M. A. (1967). Models and helping: Naturalistic studies in aiding behavior. JOURNAL OF PERSONALITY AND SOCIAL PSYCHOLOGY, *6*, 400–407.

BUB, D., BLACKS, S., & HOWELL, J. (1989). Word recognition and orthographic context effects in a letter-by-letter reader. BRAIN AND LANGUAGE, *36*, 357–376.

BUCHANAN, ECCLES, & BECKER (1992). Are adolescents the victims of raging hormones? Evidence for activational effects of hormones on moods and behavior at adolescence. PSYCHOLOGICAL BULLETIN, *111*, 62–107.

BUCK, L., & AXEL, R. (1991). A novel multigene family may encode odorant receptors: A molecular basis for odor recognition. CELL, *65*, 175–187.

BURGESS, A. W., & HOLMSTROM, L. (1974). Rape trauma syndrome. AMERICAN JOURNAL OF PSYCHIATRY, *131*, 981–986.

BURNAM, M. A., STEIN, J. A., GOLDING, J. M., SIEGEL, J. M., SORENSON, S. B., FORSYTHE, A. B., & TELLES, C. A. (1988). Sexual assault and mental disorders in a community population. JOURNAL OF CONSULTING AND CLINICAL PSYCHOLOGY, *56*, 843–850.

BURNS, D. D. (1981). FEELING GOOD: THE NEW MOOD THERAPY. New York: Penguin Books.

BURNSTEIN, E., & VINOKUR, A. (1973). Testing two classes of theories about group-induced shifts in individual choice. JOURNAL OF EXPERIMENTAL SOCIAL PSYCHOLOGY, *9*, 123–137.

BURNSTEIN, E., & VINOKUR, A. (1977). Persuasive arguments and social comparison as determinants of attitude polarization. JOURNAL OF EXPERIMENTAL SOCIAL PSYCHOLOGY, *13*, 315–332.

BURT, M. R. (1980). Cultural myths and supports for rape. JOURNAL OF PERSONALITY AND SOCIAL PSYCHOLOGY, *38*, 217–230.

BUSS, A. H., & PLOMIN, R. (1975). A TEMPERAMENT THEORY OF PERSONALITY DEVELOPMENT. New York: Wiley.

BUSS, D. M. (1989). Sex differences in human mate preference: Evolutionary hypotheses tested in 37 cultures. BRAIN AND BEHAVIOR SCIENCES, *12*, 1–49.

BUSS, D. M. (1994). THE EVOLUTION OF DESIRE: STRATEGIES OF HUMAN MATING. New York: Basic Books.

BUSS, D. M., & BARNES, M. (1986). Preferences in human mate selection. JOURNAL OF PERSONALITY AND SOCIAL PSYCHOLOGY, *50*, 559–570.

BUSS, D. M., LARSEN, R. J., WESTERN, D., & SEMMELROTH, J. (1992). Sex differences in jealousy: evolution physiology, and psychology. PSYCHOLOGICAL SCIENCE, *3*, 251–255.

BUTLER, J. M., & HAIGH, G. V. (1954). Changes in the relation between self-concepts and ideal concepts consequent upon client centered counseling. In C. R. Rogers & R. F. Dymond (Eds.), PSYCHOTHERAPY AND PERSONALITY CHANGE: COORDINATED STUDIES IN THE CLIENT-CENTERED APPROACH, 55–76. Chicago: University of Chicago Press.

BUTT, D. S. (1988). THE PSYCHOLOGY OF SPORT: THE BEHAVIOR, MOTIVATION, PERSONALITY AND PERFORMANCE OF ATHLETES (2nd ed.). New York: Van Nostrand Reinhold.

BUTTERFIELD, E. L., & SIPERSTEIN, G. N. (1972). Influence of contingent auditory stimulation on nonnutritional sucking. In J. Bosma (Ed.), ORAL SENSATION AND PERCEPTION: THE MOUTH OF THE INFANT. Springfield, IL: Charles B. Thomas.

BYERLY, W. B. et al. (1989). Mapping genes for manic-depression and schizophrenia with DNA markers. TRENDS IN NEUROSCIENCES, *12*, 46–48.

CABANAC, M. (1979). Sensory pleasure. Q REV BIOL, *54*(1), 1–29.

CABANAC, M. (1992). Pleasure: the common currency. JOURNAL OF THEORETICAL BIOLOGY, *155*, 173–200.

CAGGIULA, A. R., & HOEBEL, B. G. (1966). A "copulation-reward site" in the posterior hypothalamus. SCIENCE, *153*, 1284–1285.

CAHILL, L., PRINS, B., WEBER, M., & McGAUGH, J. L. (1994). Adrenergic activation and memory for emotional events. NATURE, *371*.

CAIN, W. S. (1988). Olfaction. In R. C. Atkinson, R. J. Hernstein, G. Lindzey, & R. D. Luce (Eds.), STEVENS' HANDBOOK OF EXPERIMENTAL PSYCHOLOGY (Vol. 1). New York: Wiley, 409–459.

CALLAWAY, M. R., MARRIOTT, R. G., & ESSER, J. K. (1985). Effects of dominance on group decision making: Toward a stress-reduction explanation of group-think. JOURNAL OF PERSONALITY AND SOCIAL PSYCHOLOGY, *49*, 949–952.

CAMPBELL, E. A., COPE, S. J., & TEASDALE, J. D. (1983). Social factors and affective disorder: An investigation of Brown and Harris's model. BRITISH JOURNAL OF PSYCHIATRY, *143*, 548–553.

CAMPOS, J. J., BARRETT, K. C., LAMB, M. E., GOLDSMITH, H. H., & STENBERG, C. (1983). Socioemotional development. In P. Mussen (Ed.), HANDBOOK OF CHILD PSYCHOLOGY (Vol. 1, 1–101). New York: Wiley.

CANNON, W. B. (1927). The James-Lange theory of emotions: A critical examination and an alternative theory. AMERICAN JOURNAL OF PSYCHOLOGY, *39*, 106–124.

CANTOR, N., MARKUS, H., NIEDENTHAL, P., & NURIUS, P. (1986). On motivation and the self-concept. In R. M. Sorrentino & E. T. Higgins (Eds.), HANDBOOK OF MOTIVATION AND COGNITION: FOUNDATIONS OF SOCIAL BEHAVIOR (pp. 96–121). New York: Guilford.

CARAMAZZA, A., & ZURIF, E. B. (1976). Dissociation of algorithmic and heuristic processes in language comprehension: Evidence from aphasia. BRAIN AND LANGUAGE, *3*, 572–582.

CAREY, G., & GOTTESMAN, I. I. (1981). Twin and family studies of anxiety, phobic, and obsessive disorders. In D. F. Klein & J. Rabkin (Eds.). ANXIETY: NEW RESEARCH AND CHANGING CONCEPTS. New York: Haven Press.

CARLSON, N. R. (1988). FOUNDATIONS OF PHYSIOLOGICAL PSYCHOLOGY. Boston: Allyn & Bacon.

CARLSON, N. R. (1986). PHYSIOLOGY OF BEHAVIOR, (3rd ed.). Boston, MA: Allyn & Bacon.

CARLSON, R. (1971). Where is the person in personality research? PSYCHOLOGICAL BULLETIN, *75*, 203–219.

CARLSON, W. R. (1986). PHYSIOLOGY OF BEHAVIOR (3rd ed.). Boston: Allyn & Bacon.

CARPENTER, P. A., JUST, M. A., & SHELL, P. (1990). What one intelligence test measures: A theoretical account of the processing in the Raven Progressive Matrices Test. PSYCHOLOGICAL REVIEW, *97*, 404–431.

CARROL, E. N., ZUCKERMAN, M., & VOGEL, W. H. (1982). A test of the optimal level of arousal theory of sensation seeking. JOURNAL OF PERSONALITY AND SOCIAL PSYCHOLOGY, *42*, 572–575.

CARROLL, D. W. (1985). PSYCHOLOGY OF LANGUAGE. Monterey, CA: Brooks/Cole.

CARROLL, J. B. (1988). Individual differences in cognitive functioning. In R. C. Atkinson, R. J. Herrnstein, G. Lindzey, & R. D. Luce (Eds.), STEVENS' HANDBOOK OF EXPERIMENTAL PSYCHOLOGY (Vol. 2). New York: Wiley.

CARSKADON, M. A., MITLER, M. M., & DEMENT, W. C. (1974). A comparison of insomniacs and normals: Total sleep time and sleep latency. SLEEP RESEARCH, *3*, 130.

CARSON, N. D., & JOHNSON, R. E. (1985). Suicidal thoughts and problem-solving preparations among college students. JUNIOR COLLEGE STUDENT PERSONNEL, *26*(6), 484–487.

CARSON, R. C. & BUTCHER, J. N. (1992). ABNORMAL PSYCHOLOGY AND MODERN LIFE. Glenview, IL: Scott, Foresman & Co.

CARSTENSEN, L. L., & NEALE, J. M. (1989). MECHANISMS OF PSYCHOLOGICAL INFLUENCE ON PHYSICAL HEALTH. New York: Plenum.

CARTER, J. E., & HEALTH, B. (1971). Somatotype methodology and kinesiology research. KINESIOLOGY REVIEW, *2*, 10.

CARTERETTE, E. C., & FRIEDMAN, M. P. (Eds.) (1974–1978) HANDBOOK OF PERCEPTION, Vols. 1–11. New York: Academic Press.

CARTWRIGHT, R. D. (1974). The influence of a conscious wish on dreams. A methodological study of dream meaning and function. JOURNAL OF ABNORMAL PSYCHOLOGY, *83*, 387–393.

CARVER, C. S., & SCHEIER, M. F. (1981). ATTENTION AND SELF-REGULATION: A CONTROL-THEORY APPROACH TO HUMAN BEHAVIOR. New York: Springer-Verlag.

CASE, R. (1985). INTELLECTUAL DEVELOPMENT: A SYSTEMATIC REINTERPRETATION. New York: Academic Press.

CASE, R. B., HELLER, S. S., CASE, N. B., & MOSS, A. J. (1985). Type A behavior and survival after acute myocardial infarction. NEW ENGLAND JOURNAL OF MEDICINE, *312*, 737.

CASPI, A., BEM, D. J., & ELDER, G. H., JR. (1989). Continuities and consequences of interactional styles across the life course. JOURNAL OF PERSONALITY, *56*, 375–406.

CASPI, A., ELDER, G. H., JR., & BEM, D. J. (1987). Moving against the world: Life-course patterns of explosive children. DEVELOPMENTAL PSYCHOLOGY, *22*, 303–308.

CASPI, A., ELDER, G. H., JR., & BEM, D. J. (1989). Moving toward the world: Life-course patterns of dependent children. Unpublished manuscript, Harvard University.

CASPI, A., & HERBENER, E. S. (1990). Continuity and change: Assortative marriage and the consistency of personality in adulthood. JOURNAL OF PERSONALITY AND SOCIAL PSYCHOLOGY, *58*, 250–258.

CASPI, A., & MOFFIT, T. E. (1991). Individual differences are accentuated during periods of social change: The sample case of girls at puberty. JOURNAL OF PERSONALITY AND SOCIAL PSYCHOLOGY, *61*, 157–168.

CASTELLUCI, V., & KANDEL, E. R. (1976). Presynaptic facilitation as a mechanism for behavioral sensitization in Aplysia. SCIENCE, *194*, 1176–1178.

CATTELL, R. B. (1957). PERSONALITY AND MOTIVATION STRUCTURE AND MEASUREMENT. Yonkers-on-Hudson, NY: World Publishers.

CATTELL, R. B. (1966). THE SCIENTIFIC ANALYSIS OF PERSONALITY. Chicago: Aldine.

CAVE, K. R., & WOLFE, J. M. (1989). Modeling the role of parallel processing in visual search. COGNITIVE PSYCHOLOGY, *22*, 225–271.

CECI, S. J., CAVES, R. D., & HOWE, M. J. (1981). Children's long-term memory for information that is incongruous with their prior knowledge. BRITISH JOURNAL OF PSYCHOLOGY. *72*(4), 443–450.

CENTERS FOR DISEASE CONTROL (1988) Health status of Vietnam veterans: Psychosocial characteristics. JOURNAL OF THE AMERICAN MEDICAL ASSOCIATION, *259*, 2701–2707.

CHAIKEN, S. (1980). Heuristic versus systematic information processing and the use of source versus message cues in persuasion. JOURNAL OF PERSONALITY AND SOCIAL PSYCHOLOGY, *39*, 752–766.

CHAIKEN, S. (1987). The heuristic model of persuasion. In M. P. Zanna, J. N. Olson, & C. P. Herman (Eds.), SOCIAL INFLUENCE: THE ONTARIO SYMPOSIUM (Vol. 5, pp. 3–39). Hillsdale, NJ: Erlbaum.

CHAPMAN, L. J., & CHAPMAN, J. P. (1969). Illusory correlation as an obstacle to the use of valid psychodiagnostic signs. JOURNAL OF ABNORMAL PSYCHOLOGY, *74*, 271–280.

CHARNEY, D. S., & HENINGER, G. R. (1983). Monoamine receptor sensitivity and depression: Clinical studies of antidepressant effects on serotonin and noradrenergic function. PSYCHOPHARMACOLOGY BULLETIN, *20*, 213–223.

CHARNEY, D. S., HENINGER, G. R., & STERNBERG, D. E. (1984). Serotonin function and mechanism of action of antidepressant treatment: Effects of amitriptyline and desipramine. ARCHIVES OF GENERAL PSYCHIATRY, *41*, 359–365.

CHASE, W. G., & SIMON, H. A. (1973a). The mind's eye in chess. In W. G. Chase (Ed.), VI-

SUAL INFORMATION PROCESSING. New York: Academic Press.

CHASE, W. G., SIMON, H. A. (1973b.) Perception in Chess. COGNITIVE PSYCHOLOGY, *4*, 55–81.

CHAUDURI, H. (1965). PHILOSOPHY OF MEDITATION. New York: Philosophical Library.

CHEN, S. C. (1937). Social modification of the activity of ants in nest-building. PHYSIOLOGICAL ZOOLOGY, *10*, 420–436.

CHENG, P. W., HOLYOAK, K. J., NISBETT, R. E., & OLIVER, L. (1986). Pragmatic versus syntactic approaches to training deductive reasoning. COGNITIVE PSYCHOLOGY, *18*, 293–328.

CHESS, S., & THOMAS, A. (1984). ORIGINS AND EVOLUTION OF BEHAVIOR DISORDERS: INFANCY TO EARLY ADULT LIFE. New York: Brunner/Mazel.

CHI, M. (1978). Knowledge structures and memory development. In R. S. Siegler (Ed.), CHILDREN'S THINKING: WHAT DEVELOPS? Hillsdale, NJ: Erlbaum.

CHI, M., GLASER, R., & REES, E. (1982). Expertise in problem solving. In R. Sternberg (Ed.), ADVANCES IN THE PSYCHOLOGY OF HUMAN INTELLIGENCE (Vol. 1). Hillsdale, NJ: Erlbaum.

CHOMSKY, N. (1965). ASPECTS OF THE THEORY OF SYNTAX. Cambridge, MA: MIT Press.

CHOMSKY, N. (1972). LANGUAGE AND MIND (2nd ed.). New York: Harcourt Brace Jovanovich.

CHOMSKY, N. (1980). RULES AND REPRESENTATIONS. New York: Columbia University Press.

CHOMSKY, N. (1991, March). Quoted in DISCOVER.

CHRISTIE, R., & JOHODA, M. (Eds.). (1954). STUDIES IN THE SCOPE AND METHOD OF "THE AUTHORITARIAN PERSONALITY." New York: Free Press.

CHURCHLAND, P. M. (1988). MATTER AND CONSCIOUSNESS. Cambridge: MIT Press.

CHURCHLAND, P. M. (1995) THE ENGINE OF REASON, THE SEAT OF THE SOUL. (Cambridge: MIT Press).

CHURCHLAND, P. S., & SEJNOWSKI, T. J. (1988). Perspectives on cognitive neuroscience, SCIENCE, *242*, 741–745.

CLARK, D. M. (1988). A cognitive model of panic attacks. In S. Rachman & J. D. Maser (Eds.), PANIC: PSYCHOLOGICAL PERSPECTIVES. Hillsdale, NJ: Erlbaum

CLARK, D. M., & BECK, A. T. (1988). Cognitive approaches. In C. G. Last & M. Hersen (Eds.), HANDBOOK OF ANXIETY DISORDERS. Elmsford, NY: Pergamon Press.

CLARK, E. V. (1983). Meanings and concepts. In P. H. Mussen (Ed.), HANDBOOK OF CHILD PSYCHOLOGY (Vol. 3). New York: Wiley.

CLARK, H. H. (1984). Language use and language users. In G. Lindzey & E. Aronson (Eds.), THE HANDBOOK OF SOCIAL PSYCHOLOGY (Vol. 2, 3rd. ed.). New York: Harper & Row.

CLARK, H. H., & CLARK, E. V. (1977). PSYCHOLOGY AND LANGUAGE: AN INTRODUCTION TO PSYCHOLINGUISTICS. New York: Harcourt Brace Jovanovich.

CLARKE-STEWART, K. A. (1973). Interactions between mothers and their young children:

Characteristics and consequences. MONOGRAPHS OF THE SOCIETY FOR RESEARCH IN CHILD DEVELOPMENT, *38* (6 & 7, Serial No. 153).

COHEN, C. E. (1981). Person categories and social perception: Testing some boundaries of the processing effects of prior knowledge. JOURNAL OF PERSONALITY AND SOCIAL PSYCHOLOGY, *40*, 441–452.

COHEN, N. J., & SQUIRE, L. R. (1980). Preserved learning and retention of pattern analyzing skill in amnesia: Dissociation of knowing how and knowing that. SCIENCE, *210*, 207–209.

COHEN, S. (1980, September). Training to understand TV advertising: Effects and some policy implications. Paper presented at the American Psychological Association convention, Montreal.

COHEN, S., & EDWARDS, J. R. (1989). Personality characteristics as moderators of the relationship between stress and disorder. In R. J. Neufeld (Ed.), ADVANCES IN THE INVESTIGATION OF PSYCHOLOGICAL STRESS (pp. 235–283). New York: Wiley.

COHEN, S., TYRRELL, D. A. J., & SMITH, A. P. (1991). Psychological stress and susceptibility to the common cold. THE NEW ENGLAND JOURNAL OF MEDICINE, *325*, 606–612.

COHEN, S., & WILLIAMSON, G. M. (1991). Stress and infectious disease in humans. PSYCHOLOGICAL BULLETIN, *109*, 5–24.

COHEN, S., & WILLS, T. A. (1985). Stress, social support, and the buffering hypothesis. PSYCHOLOGICAL BULLETIN, *98*, 310–357.

COLBY, A., KOHLBERG, L., GIBBS, J., & LIEBERMAN, M. A. (1983). A longitudinal study of moral judgment. MONOGRAPHS OF THE SOCIETY FOR RESEARCH IN CHILD DEVELOPMENT, *48* (No. 200), 1–2.

COLE, M., & COLE, S. R. (1993). THE DEVELOPMENT OF CHILDREN. (2nd ed.) New York: Scientific American Books.

COLEGROVE, F. W. (1899). Individual Memories. AMERICAN JOURNAL OF PSYCHOLOGY, *10*, 228–255.

COLLINS, A. M., & LOFTUS, E. G. (1975). A spreading-activation theory of semantic processing. PSYCHOLOGICAL REVIEW, *82*, 407–428.

COLLINS, H. M. (1974). The TEA set: Tacit knowledge and scientific networks. SCIENCE STUDIES, *4*, 165–186.

COMREY, A. L., & LEE, H. B. (1992). A FIRST COURSE IN FACTOR ANALYSIS (2nd ed.). Hillsdale, NJ: Erlbaum.

CONDRY, J., & CONDRY, S. (1976). Sex differences: A study in the eye of the beholder. CHILD DEVELOPMENT, *47*, 812–819.

CONRAD, R. (1964). Acoustic confusions in immediate memory. BRITISH JOURNAL OF PSYCHOLOGY, *55*, 75–84.

COOPER, L. A., & SHEPARD, R. N. (1973). Chronometric studies of the rotation of mental images. In W. G. Chase (Ed.), VISUAL INFORMATION PROCESSING. New York: Academic Press.

COOPER, L. M. (1979). Hypnotic amnesia. In E.

Fromm & R. E. Shor (Eds.), HYPNOSIS: DEVELOPMENTS IN RESEARCH AND NEW PERSPECTIVES (rev. ed.). New York: Aldine.

CORBETTA, M., MIEZIN, F. M., SHULMAN, G. L., & PETERSEN, S. E. (1993). A PET study of visuospatial attention. THE JOURNAL OF NEUROSCIENCE, *13*, 1202–1226.

CORDUA, G. D., MCGRAW, K. O., & DRABMAN, R. S. (1979). Doctor or nurse: Children's perception of sextyped occupations. CHILD DEVELOPMENT, *50*, 590–593.

COREN, S., & WARD, L. M. (1989). SENSATION & PERCEPTION (3rd ed.). San Diego: Harcourt Brace Javanovich.

CORSINI, R. J. (1984). CURRENT PSYCHOTHERAPIES (3rd ed.). Itasca, IL: Peacock.

COSCINA, D. V., & DIXON, L. M. (1983). Body weight regulation in anorexia nervosa: Insights from an animal model. In F. L. Darby, P. E. Garfinkel, D. M. Garner, & D. V. Coscina, (Eds.), ANOREXIA NERVOSA: RECENT DEVELOPMENTS. New York: Allan R. Liss.

COSTA, E. (1985). Benzodiazepine/GABA interactions: A model to investigate the neurobiology of anxiety. In A. H. Tuma & J. D. Maser (Eds.), ANXIETY AND THE ANXIETY DISORDERS. Hillsdale, NJ: Erlbaum.

COSTA, P. T., & MCCRAE, R. R. (1980). Still stable after all thee years: Personality as a key to some issues in aging. In P. B. Bolles & O. G. Brim (Eds.), LIFESPAN DEVELOPMENT AND BEHAVIOR (Vol. 3). New York: Academic Press.

COTTRELL, N. B. (1972). Social facilitation. In C. G. McClintock (Ed.), EXPERIMENTAL SOCIAL PSYCHOLOGY. New York: Holt, Rinehart & Winston.

COTTRELL, N. B., & RITTLE, R. H., & WACK, D. L. (1967). Presence of an audience and list type (competitional or noncompetitional) as joint determinants of performance in paired-associates learning. JOURNAL OF PERSONALITY, *25*, 425–434.

COTTRELL, N. B., WACK, D. L., SEKERAK, G. J., & RITTLE, R. H. (1968). Social facilitation of dominant responses by the presence of an audience and the mere presence of others. JOURNAL OF PERSONALITY AND SOCIAL PSYCHOLOGY, *9*, 245–250.

COURTRIGHT, J. A. (1978). A laboratory investigation of groupthink. COMMUNICATIONS MONOGRAPHS, *43*, 229–246.

COUSINS, S. D. (1989). Culture and self-perception in Japan and the U.S. JOURNAL OF PERSONALITY AND SOCIAL PSYCHOLOGY, *56*, 124–131.

COX, R. H., QIU, Y., & LIU, Z. (1993). Overview of sport psychology. In R. N. Singer, M. Murphey, & L. K. Tennant (eds.), HANDBOOK OF RESEARCH ON SPORT PSYCHOLOGY. New York: MacMillan.

CRAIGHEAD, L. W., STUNKARD, A. J., & O'BRIEN, R. M. (1981). Behavior therapy and pharmacotherapy for obesity. ARCHIVES OF GENERAL PSYCHIATRY, *38*, 763–768.

CRAIK, F. I. M., & TULVING, E. (1975). Depth of processing and the retention of words in episodic memory. JOURNAL OF EXPERIMENTAL PSYCHOLOGY: GENERAL, *104*, 268–294.

CRARY, W. G. (1966). Reactions to incongruent self-experiences. JOURNAL OF CONSULTING PSYCHOLOGY, *30*, 246–252.

CRASILNECK, H. B., & HALL, J. A. (1985). CLINICAL HYPNOSIS: PRINCIPLES AND APPLICATIONS (2nd ed.). Orlando, FL: Grune & Stratton.

CRAWFORD, H. J. (1989). Cognitive and physiological flexibility: Multiple pathways to hypnotic responsiveness. In V. A. Gheorghiu, P. Netter, H. J. Eysenck, & R. Rosenthal (Eds.), SUGGESTION AND SUGGESTIBILITY: THEORY AND RESEARCH. New York: Springer-Verlag.

CREESE, I., BURT, D. R., & SYNDER, S. H. (1978). Biomechanical actions of neuroleptic drugs. In L. L. Iversen, S. D. Iversen, & S. H. Snyder (Eds.), HANDBOOK OF PSYCHOPHARMACOLOGY (Vol. 10). New York: Plenum.

CRICK, F. (1994). THE ASTONISHING HYPOTHESIS: THE SCIENTIFIC SEARCH FOR THE SOUL. New York: Macmillan Publishing Company.

CRICK, F., & MITCHISON, G. (1983). The function of dream sleep. NATURE, *304*, 111–114.

CRICK, F., & MITCHISON, G. (1986) REM sleep neural nets. JOURNAL OF MIND AND BEHAVIOR, *7*, 229–250.

CROMWELL, P. F., MARKS, A., OLSON, J. N., & AVARY, D. W. (1991). Group effects on decision-making by burglars. PSYCHOLOGICAL REPORTS, *69*, 579–588.

CRONBACH, L. J. (1984). ESSENTIALS OF PSYCHOLOGICAL TESTING (4th ed.). New York: Harper & Row.

CUTLER, S. E., & NOLEN-HOEKSEMA, S. (1991). Accounting for sex differences in depression through female victimization: Childhood sexual abuse. SEX ROLES, *24*, 425–438.

DABBS, J. M., & MORRIS, R., JR. (1990). Testosterone, social class, and antisocial behavior in a sample of 4,462 men. PSYCHOLOGICAL SCIENCE, *1*, 209–211.

DALE, A. J. D. (1975). Organic brain syndromes associated with infections. In A. M., Freeman, H. I. Kaplan, & B. J. Sadock (Eds.), COMPREHENSIVE TEXTBOOK OF PSYCHIATRY (Vol. 2). *1*, 1121–1130. Baltimore, MD: Williams Wilkins.

DALY, M., & WILSON, W. (1990). Is parent-offspring conflict sex-linked? Freudian and Darwinian models. JOURNAL OF PERSONALITY, *58*, 165–189.

DAMASIO, A.R. (1985). Disorders of complex visual processing: Agnosia, achromatopsia, Balint's syndrome, and related difficulties of orientation and construction. In M. M. Mesulam (Ed.). PRINCIPLES OF BEHAVIORAL NEUROLOGY, 259–288. Philadelphia, PA: F. A. Davis Company.

DAMASIO, A. R. (1990). Category-related recognition defects as a clue to the neural substrates of knowledge. TRENDS IN NEUROSCIENCES, *13*, 95–98.

DAMON, W. (1977). THE SOCIAL WORLD OF THE CHILD. San Francisco: Jossey-Bass.

DAMON, W. (1983). SOCIAL AND PERSONALITY DEVELOPMENT. New York: Norton & Company.

DANEMAN, M., & CARPENTER, P. A. (1980). Individual differences in working memory and reading. JOURNAL OF VERBAL LEARNING AND VERBAL BEHAVIOR, *19*, 450–466.

DARIAN-SMITH, I. (Ed.) (1984). HANDBOOK OF PHYSIOLOGY: THE NERVOUS SYSTEM: SECTION 1, VOL. 3. SENSORY PROCESSES. Bethesda, MD: American Physiological Society.

DARLEY, C. F., TINKLENBERG, J. R., ROTH, W. T., HOLLISTER, L. E., & ATKINSON, R. C. (1973a). Influence of marijuana on storage and retrieval processes in memory. MEMORY AND COGNITION, *1*, 196–200.

DARLEY, C. F., TINKLENBERG, J. R., HOLLISTER, L. E., & ATKINSON, R. C. (1973b). Marijuana and retrieval from short-term memory. PSYCHOPHARMACOLOGIA, *29*, 231–238.

DARLEY, C. F., TINKLENBERG, J. R., ROTH, W. T., VERNON, S., & KOPELL, B. S. (1977). Marijuana effects on long-term memory assessment and retrieval. PSYCHOPHARMACOLOGY, *52*, 239–241.

DARLEY, J. M., & LATANÉ, B. (1968). Bystander intervention in emergencies: Diffusion of responsibility. JOURNAL OF PERSONALITY AND SOCIAL PSYCHOLOGY, *8*, 377–383.

DARO, D. (1988). CONFRONTING CHILD ABUSE. New York: The Free Press.

DARWIN, C. (1859). ON THE ORIGIN OF THE SPECIES. London: Murray.

DARWIN, C. (1872). THE EXPRESSION OF EMOTION IN MAN AND ANIMALS. New York: Philosophical Library.

DASHIELL. J. F. (1930). An experimental analysis of some group effects. JOURNAL OF ABNORMAL AND SOCIAL PSYCHOLOGY, *25*, 190–199.

DASHIELL, J. F. (1935). Experimental studies of the influence of social situations on the behavior of individual human adults. In C. Murchison (Ed.), HANDBOOK OF SOCIAL PSYCHOLOGY. Worcester, MA: Clark University.

DAUBER, R. B. (1984). Subliminal psychodynamic activation in depression: On the role of autonomy issues in depressed college women. JOURNAL OF ABNORMAL PSYCHOLOGY, *93*, 9–18.

DAVIDSON, A. R., & JACCARD, J. J. (1979). Variables that moderate the attitude-behavior relations: Results of a longitudinal survey. JOURNAL OF PERSONALITY AND SOCIAL PSYCHOLOGY, *37*, 1364–1376.

DAVIDSON, E. S., YASUNA, A., & TOWER, A. (1979). The effects of television cartoons on sex-role stereotyping in young girls. CHILD DEVELOPMENT, *50*, 597–600.

DAVIDSON, G. C. & NEALE, J. M. (1990). ABNORMAL PSYCHOLOGY (5th ed.). New York: John Wiley & Sons.

DECASPER, A. J., & FIFER, W. P. (1980). Of human bonding: Newborns prefer their mothers' voices. SCIENCE, *208*, 1174–1176.

DECASPER, A. J., & PRESCOTT, P. A. (1984). Human newborns' perception of male voices: Preference, discrimination and reinforcing

value. DEVELOPMENTAL PSYCHOBIOLOGY, *17*, 481–491.

DECASPER, A. J., & SIGAFOOS, A. D. (1983). The intrauterine heartbeat: A potent reinforcer for newborns. INFANT BEHAVIOR AND DEVELOPMENT, *6*, 19–25.

DECASPER, A. J., & SPENCE, M. J. (1986). Prenatal maternal speech influences newborns' perception of speech sounds. INFANT BEHAVIOR AND DEVELOPMENT, *9*, 133–150.

DEIKMAN, A. J. (1963). Experimental meditation. JOURNAL OF NERVOUS AND MENTAL DISEASE, *136*, 329–373.

DEMBROSKI, T. M., MACDOUGALL, J. M., WILLIAMS, B., & HANEY, T. L. (1985). Components of Type A hostility and anger: Relationship to angiographic findings. PSYCHOSOMATIC MEDICINE, *47*, 219–233.

DEMENT, W. C. & KLEITMAN, N. (1957). The relation of eye movements during sleep to dream activity: An objective method for the study of dreaming. JOURNAL OF EXPERIMENTAL PSYCHOLOGY, *53*, 339–346.

DEMENT, W. C., & WOLPERT, E. (1958). The relation of eye movements, bodily motility, and external stimuli to dream content. JOURNAL OF EXPERIMENTAL PSYCHOLOGY, *55*, 543–553.

DENNIS, W., & DENNIS, M. (1940). The effects of cradling practices upon the onset of walking in Hopi children. JOURNAL OF GENETIC PSYCHOLOGY, *56*, 77–86.

DEPUE, R. A., & IACONO, W. G. (1989). Neurobehavioral aspects of affective disorders. In M. R. Rosenzweig & L. W. Porter (Eds.), ANNUAL REVIEW OF PSYCHOLOGY (Vol. 40). Palo Alto, CA: Annual Reviews, Inc.

DEVALOIS, R. L., & DEVALOIS, K. K. (1980). Spatial vision. ANNUAL REVIEW OF PSYCHOLOGY, *31*, 309–341.

DEVALOIS, R. L., & JACOBS, G. H. (1984). Neural mechanisms of color vision. In I. Darian-Smith (Ed.), HANDBOOK OF PHYSIOLOGY (Vol. 3). Bethesda, MD: American Physiological Society.

DEVANE, W. A., LUMIR, H., BREUER, A., PERTWEE, R. G., STEVENSON, L. A., GRIFFIN, G. BIGSON, D., MANDELBAUM, A., ETINGER, A., & MECHOULAN, R. (1992). Isolation and structure of a brain constituent that binds to the cannabinoid receptor. SCIENCE, 258, 1946–1949.

DIAMOND, M. (1982). Sexual identity, monozygotic twins reared in discordant sex roles and a BBC follow-up. ARCH SEX BEHAV, *11*(2), 181–6.

DIENER, E. (1979). Deindividuation, self-awareness, and disinhibition. JOURNAL OF PERSONALITY AND SOCIAL PSYCHOLOGY, *37*, 1160–1171.

DIENER, E. (1980). Deindividuation: The absence of self-awareness and self-regulation in group members. In P. B. Paulus (Ed.), THE PSYCHOLOGY OF GROUP INFLUENCE. Hillsdale, NJ: Erlbaum.

DIENER, E., FRASER, S. C., BEAMAN, A. L., & KELEM, R. T. (1976). Effects of deindividuation variables on stealing among Halloween trick-or-treaters. JOURNAL OF PERSONALITY AND SOCIAL PSYCHOLOGY, *33*, 178–183.

DIENSTBIER, R. A. (1989). Arousal and physiological toughness: Implications for mental and physical health. PSYCHOLOGICAL REVIEW, *96*, 84–100.

DIGMAN, J. M., & INOUYE, J. (1986). Further specification of the five robust factors of personality. JOURNAL OF PERSONALITY AND SOCIAL PSYCHOLOGY, *50*, 116–123.

DILLBECK, M. C., & ORME-JOHNSON, D. W. (1987). Physiological differences between transcendental meditation and rest. AMERICAN PSYCHOLOGIST, *42*(9), 879–881.

DIMATTEO, M. R. (1991). THE PSYCHOLOGY OF HEALTH, ILLNESS, AND MEDICAL CARE—AN INDIVIDUAL PERSPECTIVE. Pacific Grove, CA: Brooks/Cole.

DION, K. K. (1972). Physical attractiveness and evaluations of children's transgressions. JOURNAL OF PERSONALITY AND SOCIAL PSYCHOLOGY, *24*, 207–213.

DION, K. K. & BERSCHEID, E. (1972). Physical attractiveness and social perception of peers in preschool children. Unpublished manuscript, University of Minnesota, Minneapolis.

DION, K. K., BERSCHEID, E., & WALSTER, E. (1972). What is beautiful is good. JOURNAL OF PERSONALITY AND SOCIAL PSYCHOLOGY, *24*, 285–290.

DOBELLE, W. H., MEADEJOVSKY, M. G., & GIRVIN, J. P. (1974). Artificial vision for the blind: Electrical stimulation of visual cortex offers hope for a functional prosthesis. SCIENCE, *183*, 440–444.

DOHRENWEND, B. P., LEVAV, I., SHROUT, P. E., SCHWARTZ, S., NAVEH, G., LINK, B. G., SKODOL, A. E., & STUEVE, A. (1992). Socioeconomic status and psychiatric disorders: the causation-selection issue. SCIENCE, *255*, 946–952.

DOHRENWEND, B. S. (1973). Social status and stressful life events. JOURNAL OF PERSONALITY AND SOCIAL PSYCHOLOGY, *28*, 225–235.

DOLLARD, J., DOOB, L. W., MILLER, N. E., MOWRER, O. H., & SEARS, R. R. (1939). FRUSTRATION AND AGGRESSION. New Haven: Yale University Press.

DOMJAN, M., & BURKHARD, B. (1986). THE PRINCIPLES OF LEARNING AND BEHAVIOR. Monterey, CA: Brooks/Cole.

DOWLING, J. E., & BOYCOTT, B. B. (1966). Organization of the primate retina. PROCEEDINGS OF THE ROYAL SOCIETY OF LONDON, SERIES B, *166*, 80–111.

DOYLE, A. C. (1892/1981). THE ORIGINAL ILLUSTRATED SHERLOCK HOLMES. Secaucus, NJ: Castle Books. (Originally published in America by Harper & Bros. in *McClure's Magazine*, 1893).

DUCLAUX, R., & KENSHALO, D. R. (1980). Response characteristics of cutaneous warm fibers in the monkey. JOURNAL OF NEUROPHYSIOLOGY, *43*, 1–15.

DUJARDIN, K., GUERRIEN, A., & LECONTE, P. (1990). Sleep, brain activation and cognition.

In PHYSIOLOGY & BEHAVIOR, *47*, 1271–1278.

DUNN, J., & PLOMIN, R. (1990). SEPARATE LIVES: WHY SIBLINGS ARE SO DIFFERENT. New York: Basic Books.

DUTTON, D. G., & ARON, A. P. (1974). Some evidence for heightened sexual attraction under conditions of high anxiety. JOURNAL OF PERSONALITY AND SOCIAL PSYCHOLOGY, *30*, 510–517.

EAGLE, M. N. (1984). RECENT DEVELOPMENTS IN PSYCHOANALYSIS: A CRITICAL EVALUATION. New York: McGraw-Hill.

EAGLY, A. H., & CHAIKEN, S. (1984). Cognitive theories of persuasion. In L. Berkowitz (Ed.), ADVANCES IN EXPERIMENTAL SOCIAL PSYCHOLOGY (Vol. 17, pp. 267–359). New York: Academic Press.

EBBESEN, E., DUNCAN, B., & KONECNI, V. (1975). Effects of content of verbal aggression on future verbal aggression: A field experiment. JOURNAL OF EXPERIMENTAL PSYCHOLOGY, *11*, 192–204.

EBBINGHANS, H. (1885). Uber das Gedachthis, Leipzig: Dunckes and Humblot.

EGAN, J. P. (1975). SIGNAL DETECTION THEORY AND ROC ANALYSIS. New York: Academic Press.

EHRHARDT, A. A., MEYER-BAHLBURG, H. F., ROSEN, L. R., FELDMAN, J. F., VERIDIANO, N. P., ELKIN, E. J., & McEWEN, B. S. (1989). The development of gender-related behavior in females following prenatal exposure to diethylstilbestrol (DES). HORM BEHAV, *23*(4), 526–41.

EIBL-EIBESFELDT, I. (1970). ETHOLOGY: THE BIOLOGY OF BEHAVIOR, (E. Klinghammer, Trans.). New York: Holt, Rinehart & Winston.

EICH, J. E. (1980). The cue-dependent nature of state-dependent retrieval. MEMORY AND COGNITION, *8*, 157–173.

EICHORN, D. H., CLAUSSEN, J. A., HAAN, N., HONZIK, M. P., & MUSSEN, P. H. (Eds.) (1981). PRESENT AND PAST IN MIDDLE LIFE. New York: Academic Press.

EIMAS, P. D. (1975). Speech perception in early infancy. In L. B. Cohen & P. Salapatek (Eds.), INFANT PERCEPTION: FROM SENSATION TO COGNITION (Vol. 2). New York: Academic Press.

EIMAS, P. D. (1985). The perception of speech in early infancy. SCIENTIFIC AMERICAN, *252*, 46–52.

EKMAN, P. (1982). EMOTION IN THE HUMAN FACE (2nd ed.). New York: Cambridge University Press.

EKMAN, P. (1985). TELLING LIES; CLUES TO DECEIT IN THE MARKETPLACE, POLITICS, AND MARRIAGE. New York: Norton.

EKMAN, P., LEVENSON, R. W., & FRIESON, W. V. (1983). Autonomic nervous system activity distinguishes among emotions. SCIENCE, *221*, 1208–1210.

EKSTROM, R. B., FRENCH, J. W., HARMAN, H. H., & DERMAN, D. (1976). MANUAL FOR KIT OF FACTOR-REFERENCED COGNITIVE TESTS, 1976. Princeton, NJ: Educational Testing Service.

EKSTROM, R. B., FRENCH, J. W., & HARMAN, H. H. (1979). Cognitive factors: Their identification and replication. MULTIVARIATE BE-

HAVIORAL RESEARCH MONOGRAPHS. Ft. Worth, TX: Society for Multivariate Experimental Psychology.

ELKIN, I., SHEA, T., WATKINS, J., IMBER, S., SOTSKY, S., COLLINS, J., GLASS, D., PILKONIS, P., LEBER, W., DOCHERTY, J., FIESTER, S., & PARLOFF, M. (1989, November). National Institutes of Mental Health treatment of depression collaborative research program. ARCHIVES OF GENERAL PSYCHIATRY, *46*, 971–982.

ELLIS, H. C., & HUNT, R. R. (1989). FUNDAMENTALS OF HUMAN MEMORY AND COGNITION (4th ed.). Dubuque, Iowa: Wm. C. Brown.

ELLIS, L., & AMES, M. A. (1987). Neurohormonal functioning and sexual orientation: A theory of homosexuality-heterosexuality. PSYCHOLOGICAL BULLETIN, *2*, 233–258.

ELLSWORTH, P. (1991). Some implications of cognitive appraisals on theories of emotion. In K. T. Strongman (Ed.), INTERNATIONAL REVIEW OF STUDIES ON EMOTION (Vol. 1). New York: Wiley.

ELMES, D. G., KANTOWITZ, B. H., & ROEDIGER, H. L. (1989). RESEARCH METHODS IN PSYCHOLOGY (3rd ed.). St. Paul, MN: West.

EMMELKAMP, P., & KUIPERS, A. (1979). Agoraphobia: a follow-up study four years after treatment. BRITISH JOURNAL OF PSYCHIATRY, *134*, 352–355.

ENDLER, N. S. (1982). HOLIDAY OF DARKNESS. New York: Wiley.

ENGEN, T. (1982). THE PERCEPTION OF ODORS. New York: Academic Press.

EPPLEY, K. R., ABRAMS, A. I., & SHEAR, J. (1987). Differential effects of relaxation techniques on trait anxiety: a meta-analysis. JOURNAL OF CLINICAL PSYCHOLOGY, *45*, 957–974.

EPSTEIN, A. (1982). The physiology of thirst. In D. W. Pfaff (Eds.), PHYSIOLOGICAL MECHANISMS OF MOTIVATION. (pp. 25–55). New York: Springer-Verlag.

EPSTEIN, S. (1977). Traits are alive and well. In D. Magnusson & N. S. Endler (Eds.), PERSONALITY AT THE CROSSROADS: CURRENT ISSUES IN INTERACTIONAL PSYCHOLOGY. Hillsdale, NJ: Erlbaum.

ERDELYI, M. H. (1985). PSYCHOANALYSIS: FREUD'S COGNITIVE PSYCHOLOGY. New York: Freeman.

ERICSSON, K. A., CHASE, W. G., & FALOON, S. (1980). Acquisition of a memory skill. SCIENCE, *208*, 1181–1182.

ERICSSON, K. A., & SIMON, H. A. (1993). PROTOCOL ANALYSIS: VERBAL REPORTS AS DATA (rev. ed.). Cambridge, MA: MIT Press.

ERIKSON, E. H. (1963). CHILDHOOD AND SOCIETY (2nd ed.). New York: Norton.

ERIKSON, E. H. (1968). IDENTITY: YOUTH AND CRISIS. New York: Norton.

ERON, L. D. (1987). The development of aggressive behavior from the perspective of a developing behaviorism. AMERICAN PSYCHOLOGIST, *42*, 435–442.

ERON, L. D., HUESMANN, L. R., LEFKOWITZ, M. M., & WALDER, L. O. (1972). Does television violence cause aggression? AMERICAN PSYCHOLOGIST, *27*, 253–263.

ERVIN-TRIPP, S. (1964). Imitation and structural change in children's language. In E. H. Lenneberg (Ed.), NEW DIRECTIONS IN THE STUDY OF LANGUAGE. Cambridge, MA: MIT Press.

ESTERSON, A. (1993). SEDUCTIVE MIRAGE: AN EXPLORATION OF THE WORK OF SIGMUND FREUD. Chicago: Open Court Publishing Company.

ESTES, W. K. (1972). An associative basis for coding and organization in memory. In A. W. Melton & E. Martin (Eds.), CODING PROCESSES IN HUMAN MEMORY. Washington, DC: Winston.

ESTES, W. K. (Ed.). (1975–1979) HANDBOOK OF LEARNING AND COGNITIVE PROCESSES (Vols. 1–6). Hillsdale, NJ: Erlbaum.

ETCOFF, N. L. (1985). The neuropsychology of emotional expression. In G. Goldstein & R. E. Tarter, (Eds.), ADVANCES IN CLINICAL NEUROPSYCHOLOGY (Vol. 3). New York: Plenum.

EVANS, C. (1984). LANDSCAPES OF THE NIGHT: HOW AND WHY WE DREAM. New York: Viking.

EVANS, C. J., KEITH, D. E., MORRISON, H., MAGENDZO, D., & EDWARDS, R. H. (1992). Cloning of a delta opioid receptor by functional expression. SCIENCE, *258*, 1952–1955.

EXNER, J. (1986). THE RORSCHACH: A COMPREHENSIVE SYSTEM (2nd ed., Vol. 1). New York: Wiley.

EYSENCK, H. J. (1953). THE STRUCTURE OF HUMAN PERSONALITY. New York: Wiley.

EYSENCK, H. J. (1990). Biological dimensions of personality. In L. A. Pervin (Ed.), HANDBOOK OF PERSONALITY: THEORY AND RESEARCH (pp. 244–276). New York: Guilford Press.

EYSENCK, H. J., & EYSENCK, S. B. G. (1976). PSYCHOTICISM AS A DIMENSION OF PERSONALITY. London: Hoder & Stroughton.

EYSENCK, H. J., & KAMIN, L. (1981). THE INTELLIGENCE CONTROVERSY. New York: Wiley.

EYSENCK, H. J., & RACHMAN, S. (1965). THE CAUSES AND CURES OF NEUROSIS: AN INTRODUCTION TO MODERN BEHAVIOR THERAPY BASED ON LEARNING THEORY AND THE PRINCIPLES OF CONDITIONING. San Diego: Knapp.

FAGOT, B. I. (1978). The influence of sex of child on parenteral reactions to toddler children. CHILD DEVELOPMENT, *49*, 459–465.

FAGOT, B. I., & LEINBACH, M. D. (1989). The young child's gender schema: Environmental input, internal organization. CHILD DEVELOPMENT, *60*, 663–672.

FALLON, A. E., & ROZIN, P. (1985). Sex differences in perceptions of desirable body shape. JOURNAL OF ABNORMAL PSYCHOLOGY, *94*, 102–105.

FANCHER, R. E. (1985). THE INTELLIGENCE MEN: MAKERS OF THE IQ CONTROVERSY. New York: Norton.

FANTZ, R. L. (1961). The origin of form perception. SCIENCE, *204*, 66–72.

FANTZ, R. L. (1970). Visual perception and experience in infancy: Issues and approaches. In NATIONAL ACADEMY OF SCIENCE, EARLY EXPERIENCE AND VISUAL INFORMATION PROCESSING IN PERCEPTUAL AND READING DISORDERS, 351–381. New York: National Academy of Science.

FARAH, M. J., & MCCLELLAND, J. L. (1991). A computational model of semantic memory impairment. JOURNAL OF EXPERIMENTAL PSYCHOLOGY: GENERAL, *120*, 339–357.

FARAH, M. J. (1990). VISUAL AGNOSIA: DISORDERS OF OBJECT RECOGNITION AND WHAT THEY TELL US ABOUT NORMAL VISION. Cambridge, MA: MIT Press.

FARBEROW, N. L., & SCHNEIDMAN, E. S. (1965). THE CRY FOR HELP. New York: McGraw-Hill.

FARTHING, G. W. (1992). THE PSYCHOLOGY OF CONSCIOUSNESS. Englewood Cliffs, NJ: Prentice-Hall.

FAUST, I. M. (1984). Role of the fat cell in energy balance physiology. in A. T. Stunkard & E. Stellar (Eds.), EATING AND ITS DISORDERS. New York: Raven Press.

FAZIO, R. H. (1989). On the power and functionality of attitudes: The role of attitude accessibility. In A. R. Pratkanis & A. G. Greenwald (Eds.), ATTITUDE STRUCTURE AND FUNCTION. Hillsdale, NJ: Erlbaum.

FAZIO, R. H. (1990). Multiple processes by which attitudes guide behavior: The MODE model as an integrative framework. In M. P. Zanna (Ed.), ADVANCES IN EXPERIMENTAL SOCIAL PSYCHOLOGY (Vol. 23,). San Diego: Academic Press.

FAZIO, R. H., & WILLIAMS, C. J. (1986). Attitude accessibility as a moderator of the attitude-perception and attitude-behavior relations: An investigation of the 1984 presidential election. JOURNAL OF PERSONALITY AND SOCIAL PSYCHOLOGY, *51*, 505–514.

FAZIO, R., & ZANNA, M. P. (1981). Direct experience and attitude-behavior consistency. In L. Berkowitz (Ed.), ADVANCES IN AN EXPERIMENTAL SOCIAL PSYCHOLOGY (Vol. 14). New York: Academic Press.

FAZIO, R., ZANNA, M. P., & COOPER, J. (1977). Dissonance and self-perception: An integrative view of each theory's proper domain of application. JOURNAL OF EXPERIMENTAL SOCIAL PSYCHOLOGY, *13*, 464–479.

FECHNER, G. T. (1860/1966). ELEMENTS OF PSYCHOPHYSICS (H. E. Adler, Trans.). New York: Holt, Rinehart & Winston.

FEINGOLD, A. (1988). Cognitive gender differences are disappearing. AMERICAN PSYCHOLOGIST, *43*, 95–103.

FEINGOLD, A. (1990). Matching for attractiveness in romantic partners and same-sex friends: A meta-analysis and theoretical critique. PSYCHOLOGICAL BULLETIN, *104*, 226–235.

FELDMAN, H., GOLDIN-MEADOW, S., & GLEITMAN, L. R. (1978). Beyond Herodotus: The creation of language by linguistically deprived children. In A. Lock (Ed.), ACTION, GESTURE, AND SYMBOL: THE EMERGENCE OF LANGUAGE. London: Academic Press.

FENNELL, M. J. V., & CAMPBELL, E. H. (1984). The cognitions questionnarie: Specific thinking errors in depression. BRITISH JOURNAL OF CLINICAL PSYCHOLOGY, *23*, 81–92.

FENTON, W. S., & MCGLASHAN, T. H. (1992). TESTING SYSTEMS FOR ASSESSMENT OF NEGATIVE SYMPTOMS IN SCHIZOPHRENIA, ARCHIVES OF GENERAL PSYCHIATRY, *49*, 179–184.

FENWICK, P. (1987). Mediation and the EEG. In M. A. West (Ed.), THE PSYCHOLOGY OF MEDITATION. Oxford, England: Oxford University Press.

FESHBACH, N. D. (1980, September). The child as psychologist and economist: Two curricula. Paper presented at the American Psychological Association convention. Montreal.

FESHBACH, S., & WEINER, B. (1991). PERSONALITY (3rd ed.). Lexington, MA: Heath.

FESTINGER, L. (1957). A THEORY OF COGNITIVE DISSONANCE. Stanford: Stanford University Press.

FESTINGER, L., & CARLSMITH, J. M. (1959). Cognitive consequences of forced compliance. JOURNAL OF ABNORMAL AND SOCIAL PSYCHOLOGY, *58*, 203–210.

FESTINGER, L., PEPITONE, A., & NEWCOMB, T. M. (1952). Some consequences of deindividuation in a group. JOURNAL OF ABNORMAL AND SOCIAL PSYCHOLOGY, *47*, 383–389.

FESTINGER, L., SCHACHTER, S., & BACK, K. (1950). SOCIAL PRESSURES IN INFORMAL GROUPS: A STUDY OF HUMAN FACTORS IN HOUSING. New York: Harper & Row.

FIELD, J. (1987). The development of auditory-visual localization in infancy. In B. E. McKenzie & R. H. Day (Eds.), PERCEPTUAL DEVELOPMENT IN EARLY INFANCY. Hillsdale, NJ: Erlbaum.

FIELD, T. M., WOODSON, R., GREENBERG, R., & COHEN, D. (1982). Discrimination and imitation of facial expressions by neonates. SCIENCE, *218*, 179–181.

FINCK, H. T. (1887). ROMANTIC LOVE AND PERSONAL BEAUTY: THEIR DEVELOPMENT, CAUSAL RELATIONS, HISTORIC AND NATIONAL PECULARITIES. London: Macmillan.

FINKE, R. A. (1985). Theories relating mental imagery to perception. PSYCHOLOGICAL BULLETIN, *98*, 236–259.

FISH, B., MARCUS, J., HANS, S. L., AUERBACH, J. G., & PERDUE, S. (1992). Infants at risk for schizophrenia: sequelae of a genetic neurointegrative defect. ARCHIVES OF GENERAL PSYCHIATRY, *49*, 221–235.

FISHER, G. H. (1967). Preparation of ambiguous stimulus materials. PERCEPTION AND PSYCHOPHYSICS, *2*, 421–422.

FISHMAN, P. (1983). Interaction: The work women do. In B. Thorne, C. Kramarae & N. Henley (Eds.), LANGUAGE, GENDER, AND SOCIETY. Rowley, MA: Newbury House.

FISKE, S. T. (1993). Social cognition and social perception. In L. Porter & M. R. Rosenzweig (Eds.), ANNUAL REVIEW OF PSYCHOLOGY (Vol. 44, pp. 155–194).

FISKE, S. T., & TAYLOR, S. E. (1991). SOCIAL COGNITION (2nd ed.). New York: McGraw-Hill.

FITZSIMONS, J. T. (1969). The role of a renal thirst factor in drinking induced by extra cellular stimuli. JOURNAL OF PHYSIOLOGY, London, *201*, 349–368.

FITZSIMONS, J. T. (1990). Thirst and sodium appetite. In E. M. Stricker (Eds.), NEUROBIOLOGY OF FOOD AND FLUID INTAKE (pp. 23–44). New York: Plenum.

FIVUSH, R., & HAMOND, N. R. (1991). Autobiographical memory across the preschool years: Toward reconceptualizing childhood memory. In R. Fivush & N. R. Hamond (Eds.). KNOWING AND REMEMBERING IN YOUNG CHILDREN. New York: Cambridge University Press.

FIXSEN, D. L., PHILLIPS, E. L., PHILLIPS, E. A., & WOLF, M. M. (1976). The teaching-family model of group home treatment. In W. E. Craighead, A. E. Kazdin, & M. J. Mahoney (Eds.), BEHAVIOR MODIFICATION: PRINCIPLES, ISSUES, AND APPLICATIONS. Boston: Houghton Mifflin.

FLAVELL, J. H. (1992). COGNITIVE DEVELOPMENT (3rd ed.). Englewood Cliffs, NJ: Prentice-Hall.

FLEMING, J., & DARLEY, J. M. (1986). Perceiving Intention in Constrained Behavior: The Role of Purposeful and Constrained Action Cues in Correspondence Bias Effects. Unpublished manuscript, Princeton University, Princeton, NJ.

FLODERUS-MYRED, B., PETERSEN, N., & RASMUSON, I. (1980). Assessment of heritability for personality based on a short form of the Eysenck Personality Inventory. BEHAVIOR GENETICS, 10, 153–161.

FLOWERS, M. L. (1977). A laboratory test of some implications of Janis's groupthink hypothesis. JOURNAL OF PERSONALITY AND SOCIAL PSYCHOLOGY, 35, 888–896.

FLYNN, J. R. (1984). The mean IQ of Americans: Massive gains 1932 to 1978. PSYCHOLOGICAL BULLETIN, 95, 29–51.

FLYNN, J. R. (1987). Massive IQ gains in 14 nations: What IQ tests really measure. PSYCHOLOGICAL BULLETIN, 101, 171–191.

FOA, E., & STEKETEE, G. (1989). Obsessive-compulsive disorder. In C. Lindemann (Ed.) HANDBOOK OF PHOBIA THERAPY. Northvale, NJ: Jason Aronson Inc.

FODOR, J. A. (1981). REPRESENTATIONS: PHILOSOPHICAL ESSAYS ON THE FOUNDATIONS OF COGNITIVE SCIENCE. Cambridge, MA: MIT Press.

FODOR, J. A., BEVER, T. G., & GARRETT, M. F. (1974). THE PSYCHOLOGY OF LANGUAGE: AN INTRODUCTION TO PSYCHOLINGUISTICS AND GENERATIVE GRAMMAR. New York: McGraw-Hill.

FOLKES, V. S. (1982). Forming relationships and the matching hypothesis. PERSONALITY AND SOCIAL PSYCHOLOGY BULLETIN, 8, 631–636.

FOLSTEIN, S., & RUTTER, M. (1977). Infantile autism: A genetic study of 21 twin pairs. JOURNAL OF CHILD PSYCHOLOGY AND PSYCHIATRY, 18, 297–322.

FOREM, J. (1973). TRANSCENDENTAL MEDITATION: MAHARISHI MAHESH YOGI AND THE SCIENCE OF CREATIVE INTELLIGENCE. New York: Dutton.

FORGE, K. L., & PHEMISTER, S. (1987). The effect off prosocial cartoons on preschool children. CHILD DEVELOPMENT JOURNAL, 17, 83–88.

FOSS, D. J., & HAKES, D. T. (1978). PSYCHOLOLINGUISTICS: AN INTRODUCTION TO THE PSYCHOLOGY OF LANGUAGE. Englewood Cliffs, NJ: Prentice-Hall.

FRAGER, R., & FADIMAN, J. (1984). PERSONALITY AND PERSONAL GROWTH (2nd ed.). New York: Harper & Row.

FRANKENHAEUSER, M. (1983). The sympathetic-adrenal and pituitary-adrenal response to challenge: Comparison between the sexes. In T. M. Dembroski, T. H. Schmidt, & G. Blumchen (Eds.), BIOBEHAVIROAL BASES OF CORONARY HEART DISEASE. Basel: Karger.

FRANKLIN, J. (1987). MOLECULES OF THE MIND. New York: Atheneum.

FRANTZ, R. L. (1966). Pattern discrimination and selective attention as determinants of perceptual development from birth. In A. H. Kikk & J. F. Rivoire (Eds.), DEVELOPMENT OF PERCEPTION: VOL. 2. THE VISUAL SYSTEM (pp. 143–173). New York: International University Press.

FRAUMAN, D. C., LYNN, S. J., HARDAWAY, R., & MOLTENI, A. (1984). Effect of subliminal symbiotic activation on hypnotic rapport and susceptibility. JOURNAL OF ABNORMAL PSYCHOLOGY, 93, 481–483.

FRAZIER, K. (Ed.). (1985). SCIENCE CONFRONTS THE PARANORMAL. Buffalo: Prometheus Books.

FRAZIER, K. (1987). Psychic's imagined year fizzles (again). SKEPTICAL INQUIRER, 11, 335–336.

FREDERIKSEN, N., MISLEVY, R. J., & BEJAR, I. (Eds.) (1992). TEST THEORY FOR A NEW GENERATION OF TESTS. Hillsdale, NJ: Erlbaum

FREE, L. A., & CANTRIL, H. (1967). THE POLITICAL BELIEFS OF AMERICANS. New Brunswick, NJ: Rutgers University Press.

FREEDMAN, J. L. (1965). Long-term behavioral effects of cognitive dissonance. JOURNAL OF EXPERIMENTAL SOCIAL PSYCHOLOGY, 1, 145–155.

FREEDMAN, J. L., & SEARS, D. O. (1965). Warning, distraction, and resistance to influence. JOURNAL OF PERSONALITY AND SOCIAL PSYCHOLOGY, 1, 262–266.

FRENCH, G. M., & HARLOW, H. F. (1962). Variability of delayed-reaction performance in normal and brain-damaged rhesus monkeys. JOURNAL OF NEUROPHYSIOLOGY, 25, 585–599.

FREUD, A. (1958). Adolescence. THE PSYCHOANALYTIC STUDY OF THE CHILD, 13, 255–278.

FREUD, A. (1946/1967). THE EGO AND THE MECHANISMS OF DEFENSE (rev. ed.). New York: International Universities Press.

FREUD, S. (1885). UEBER COCA. Vienna: Mortiz Perles. (Translated in Freud, 1974).

FREUD, S. (1885/1974). COCAINE PAPERS (edited and introduction by R. Byck; notes by A. Freud). New York: Stonehill.

FREUD, S. (1900/1953). THE INTERPRETATION OF DREAMS (Reprint ed., Vol. 4, 5). London: Hogarth Press.

FREUD, S. (1901/1960). PSYCHOPATHOLOGY OF EVERYDAY LIFE (Standard ed., Vol. 6). London: Hogarth Press.

FREUD, S. (1905/1948). THREE CONTRIBUTIONS TO THEORY OF SEX (4th ed.; A. A. Brill, Trans.) New York: Nervous and Mental Disease Monograph.

FREUD, S. (1915/1976). Repression. In J. Strachey (Ed. and Trans.), THE COMPLETE PSYCHOLOGICAL WORKS: STANDARD EDITION (Vol. 14). London: Hogarth Press.

FREUD, S. (1920/1975). BEYOND THE PLEASURE PRINCIPLE. New York: Norton.

FREUD, S. (1925/1961). Some psychical consequences of the anatomical distinctions between the sexes. In J. Strachey (Ed. and Trans.) THE COMPLETE PSYCHOLOGICAL WORKS: STANDARD EDITION (Vol. 18) London: Hogarth Press.

FREUD, S. (1933/1964). NEW INTRODUCTORY LECTURES ON PSYCHOANALYSIS (J. Strachey, Ed. and Trans.). New York: Norton.

FREUD, S. (1933/1965). Revision of the theory of dreams. In J. Strachey (Ed. and Trans.), NEW INTRODUCTORY LECTURES ON PSYCHOANALYSIS, (Vol. 22, Lect. 29). New York: Norton.

FREUD, S. (1940). An outline of psychoanalysis. INTERNATIONAL JOURNAL OF PSYCHOANALYSIS, 21, 27–84.

FRIED, I., MATEER, C., OJEMANN, G., WHONS, R., & FEDIO, P. (1982). Organization of visuospatial functions in human cortex. BRAIN, 105, 349–371.

FRIED, M. (1982). Disadvantage, vulnerability, and mental illness. In D. L. Parron, F. Solomon, & C. D. Jenkins (Eds.), BEHAVIOR, HEALTH RISKS, AND SOCIAL DISADVANTAGE. Washington, DC: National Academy Press.

FRIEDAN, B. (1963). THE FEMININE MYSTIQUE. New York: Dell Publishing.

FRIEDMAN, M., & ROSENMAN, R. H. (1974). Type A Behavior. New York: Knopf.

FRIEDMAN, M., ROSENMAN, R. H., STRAUS, R., WURM, M., & KOSITCHECK, R. (1968). The relationship of behavior pattern A to the state of coronary vasculature. AMERICAN JOURNAL OF MEDICINE, 44, 525–537.

FRIEDMAN, M., THORESEN, C. E., GILL, J. J., & collaborators (1985, March), Alteration of Type A behavior and its effect upon cardiac recurrences in post-myocardial infarction subjects: Summary results of the recurrent coronary prevention project. Paper presented at meetings of the Society of Behavioral Medicine, New Orleans.

FRIEDMAN, M. I. (1990). Making sense out of calories. In E. M. Stricker (Eds.), NEUROBIOLOGY OF FOOD AND FLUID INTAKE (pp. 513–528). New York: Plenum.

FRIEDMAN, M. I., & STRICKER, E. M. (1976). The physiological psychology of hunger: A physiological perspective. PSYCHOLOGICAL REVIEW, 83, 401–431.

FRIDJA, N. (1986). THE EMOTIONS. Cambridge, England: Cambridge University Press.

FRISCHHOLZ, E. J. (1985). The relationship among dissociation, hyponosis, and child abuse in the development of multiple personality disorder. In R. P. Kluft (Ed.), CHILDHOOD ANTECEDENTS OF MULTIPLE PERSONALITY. Washington, DC: American Psychiatric Press.

FRODI, A., & THOMPSON, R. (1985). Infants' affective responses in the strange situation: Effects of prematurity and of quality of attachment. CHILD DEVELOPMENT, *56*, 1280–1290.

FROMM, E. (1970). Age regression with unexpected reappearance of a repressed childhood language. INTERNATIONAL JOURNAL OF CLINICAL AND EXPERIMENTAL HYPNOSIS, *18*, 79–88.

FROMM, E., & SHOR, R. E. (Eds.) (1979). HYPNOSIS: DEVELOPMENTS IN RESEARCH AND NEW PERSPECTIVES (2nd. ed.). Chicago: Aldine.

FUNKENSTEIN, D. (1955). The physiology of fear and anger. SCIENTIFIC AMERICAN, *192*, 74–80.

GADOW, K. D. (1992). Pediatric psychopharmacotherapy: A review of recent research. JOURNAL OF CHILD PSYCHOLOGY AND PSYCHIATRY, 153–195.

GALANTER, E. (1962). Contemporary psychophysics. In R. Brown & collaborators (Eds.), NEW DIRECTIONS IN PSYCHOLOGY (Vol. 1). New York: Holt, Rinehart & Winston.

GALOTTI, K. M. (1989). Approaches to studying formal and everyday reasoning. PSYCHOLOGICAL BULLETIN, *105*, 331–351.

GAMSON, W. B., FIREMAN, B., & RYTINA, S. (1982). ENCOUNTERS WITH UNJUST AUTHORITY, Homewood, IL: Dorsey Press.

GANAWAY, G. K. (1989). Historical versus narrative truth: Clarifying the role of exogenous trauma in the etiology of MPD and its variants. DISSOCIATION, *2*, 205–220.

GANELLEN, R. J., & CARVER, C. S. (1985). Why does self-reference promote incidental encoding? JOURNAL OF PERSONALITY AND SOCIAL PSYCHOLOGY, *21*, 284–300.

GARCIA, J. (1990). Learning without memory. JOURNAL OF COGNITIVE NEUROSCIENCE, *2*, 287–305.

GARCIA, J., & KOELLING, R. A. (1966). The relation of cue to consequence in avoiding learning. PSYCHONOMIC SCIENCE, *4*, 123–124.

GARDNER, B. T., & GARDNER, R. A. (1972). Two-way communication with an infant chimpanzee. In A. M. Schrier & F. Stollnitz (Eds.), BEHAVIOR OF NONHUMAN PRIMATES (Vol. 4). New York: Academic Press.

GARDNER, E. L. (1992). Brain reward mechanisms. In J. H. Lowinson, P. Ruiz, & R. B. Millman (Eds.), SUBSTANCE ABUSE: A COMPREHENSIVE TEXTBOOK (2nd ed.). Baltimore, MD: Williams & Wilkins.

GARDNER, H. (1975). THE SHATTERED MIND. New York: Knopf.

GARDNER, H. (1983). FRAMES OF MIND: THE THEORY OF MULTIPLE INTELLIGENCE. New York: Basic Books.

GARDNER, H. (1985). THE MIND'S NEW SCIENCE: A HISTORY OF THE COGNITIVE REVOLUTION. New York: Basic Books.

GARDNER, M. (1981). SCIENCE: GOOD, BAD, AND BOGUS. New York: Prometheus.

GARFIELD, S. L. (1980). PSYCHOTHERAPY: AN ECLECTIC APPROACH. New York: Wiley-Interscience.

GARFINKEL, P. E., & GARDNER, D. M. (1982). ANOREXIA NERVOSA: A MULTIDISCIPLINARY PERSPECTIVE. New York: Brunner/Mazel.

GARMEZY, N. (1974). Children at risk: The search for the antecedents of schizophrenia: Pt. 2. Ongoing research programs, issues and intervention. SCHIZOPHRENIA BULLETIN, *1*, 55–125.

GARMEZY, N., & DEVINE, E. (1984). Project competence: The Minnesota studies of children vulnerable to psychopathology. In N. F. Watt, E. J. Anthony, N. F. Wynne, & J. E. Rolf (Eds.), CHILDREN AT RISK FOR SCHIZOPHRENIA: A LONGITUDINAL PERSPECTIVE. Cambridge: Cambridge University Press.

GARRETT, M. F. (1990). Sentence processing. In D. N. Osherson & H. Lasnik, AN INVITATION TO COGNITIVE SCIENCE: LANGUAGE (Vol. 1). Cambridge, MA: MIT Press.

GATES, A. I. (1917). Recitation as a factor in memorizing. ARCHIVES OF PSYCHOLOGY, No. 40.

GAW, A. (1993). CULTURE, ETHNICITY, AND MENTAL ILLNESS. Washington, DC: American Psychiatric Press.

GAZZANIGA, M. S. (1985). THE SOCIAL BRAIN: DISCOVERING THE NETWORKS OF MIND. New York: Basic Books.

GEEN, R. G., & QUANTY, M. B. (1977). The catharsis of aggression. In L. Berkowitz (Ed.), ADVANCES IN EXPERIMENTAL SOCIAL PSYCHOLOGY, (Vol. 10). New York: Academic Press.

GEEN, R. G., BEATTY, W. W., & ARKIN, R. M. (1984). HUMAN MOTIVATION: PHYSIOLOGICAL, BEHAVIORAL, AND SOCIAL APPROACHES. Boston: Allyn & Bacon.

GEER, J., & MAISEL, E. (1973). Evaluating the effects of the prediction-control confound. JOURNAL OF PERSONALITY AND SOCIAL PSYCHOLOGY, *23*, 314–319.

GEISLER, C. (1986). The use of subliminal psychodynamic activation in the study of repression. JOURNAL OF PERSONALITY AND SOCIAL PSYCHOLOGY, *51*, 844–451.

GEISLER, W. S. (1978). Adaptation, afterimages and cone saturation. VISION RESEARCH, *18*, 279–289.

GELMAN, R., & GALLISTEL, C. R. (1978). THE YOUNG CHILD'S UNDERSTANDING OF NUMBER: A WINDOW ON EARLY COGNITIVE DEVELOPMENT. Cambridge, MA: Harvard University Press.

GENTER, D., & STEVENS, A. L. (1983). MENTAL MODELS. Hillsdale, NJ: Erlbaum Press.

GESCHWIND, N. (1972). Language and the brain. SCIENTIFIC AMERICAN, *226*, 76–83.

GESCHWIND, N. (1979). Specializations of the human brain. SCIENTIFIC AMERICAN, *241*, 180–199.

GESCHWIND, N., & GALABURDA, A. M. (1987). CEREBRAL LATERALIZATION.. Cambridge: MIT Press.

GESELL, A., & THOMPSON, H. (1929). Learning and growth in identical twins: An experimental study by the method of co-twin control. GENETIC PSYCHOLOGY MONOGRAPHS, *6*, 1–123.

GHEORGHIU, V. A., NETTER, P. EYSENCK, H. J., & ROSENTHAL, R. (Eds.) (1989). SUGGESTION AND SUGGESTIBILITY: THEORY AND RESEARCH. New York: Springer-Verlag.

GIBBS, J., YOUNG, R. C., & SMITH, G. P. (1973). Cholecystokinin decreases food intake in rats. JOURNAL OF COMPARATIVE AND PHYSIOLOGICAL PSYCHOLOGY, *84*, 484–495.

GIBSON, E. J., & WALK, R. D. (1960). The "visual cliff." SCIENTIFIC AMERICAN, *202*, 64–71.

GIBSON, J. J. (1950). THE PERCEPTION OF THE VISUAL WORLD. Boston: Houghton Mifflin.

GIBSON, J. J. (1966). THE SENSES CONSIDERED AS PERCEPTUAL SYSTEMS. Boston: Houghton Mifflin.

GIBSON, J. J. (1979). THE ECOLOGICAL APPROACH TO VISUAL PERCEPTION. Boston: Houghton Mifflin.

GILBERT, D. T., & JONES, E. E. (1986). Perceiver-induced constraint: Interpretations of self-generated reality. JOURNAL OF PERSONALITY AND SOCIAL PSYCHOLOGY, *50*, 269–280.

GILLBERG, C. (1991). Outcome in autism and autistic-like conditions. JOURNAL OF THE AMERICAN ACADEMY OF CHILD AND ADOLESCENT PSYCHIATRY, *30*(3), 375–382.

GILLBERG, C., & STEFFENBURG, S. (1987). Outcome and prognostic factors in infantile autism and similar conditions: A population-based study of 46 cases followed through poverty. JOURNAL OF AUTISM AND DEVELOPMENTAL DISORDERS, *17*(2), 173–287.

GILLBERG, C., & SVENNERHOLM, L. (1987). CSF monoamines in autistic syndromes and other pervasive developmental disorders of early childhood. BRITISH JOURNAL OF PSYCHIATRY, *151*, 89–94.

GILLIGAN, C. (1982). IN A DIFFERENT VOICE. Cambridge, MA: Harvard University Press.

GILLIN, J. C. (1985). Sleep and Dreams. In G. L. Klerman, M. M. Weissman, P. S. Applebaum, & L. H. Roth (Eds.), PSYCHIATRY (Vol. 3). Philadelphia: Lippincott.

GILOVICH, T. (1991). HOW WE KNOW WHAT ISN'T SO: THE FALLIBILITY OF HUMAN REASON IN EVERYDAY LIFE. New York: Free Press.

GINSBERG, A. (1983). Contrast perception in the human infant. Unpublished manuscript.

GITTELMAN, R., & KLEIN, D. F. (1985). Childhood separation anxiety and adult agoraphobia. In A. H. Tuma & J. D. Maser (Eds.), ANXIETY AND THE ANXIETY DISORDERS. Hillsdale, NJ: Erlbaum.

GLADUE, B. A. (1994). The biopsychology of sexual orientation. CURRENT DIRECTIONS IN PSYCHOLOGICAL SCIENCE, *3*, 150–154.

GLANZER, M. (1972). Storage mechanisms in recall. In G. H. Bower & J. T. Spence (Eds.), THE PSYCHOLOGY OF LEARNING AND MOTIVATION (Vol. 5). New York: Academic Press.

GLASER, R., RICE, J., SPEICHER, C. E., STOUT, J. C., & KIECOLT-GLASER, J. K. (1986). Stress depresses interferon production by leukocytes concomitant with a decrease in natural killer cell activity. BEHAVIORAL NEUROSCIENCE, *100*, 675–678.

GLASS, D. C., & SINGER, J. E. (1972). URBAN STRESS: EXPERIMENTS ON NOISE AND SOCIAL STRESSORS. New York: Academic Press.

GLASS, G. V., MCGAW, B., & SMITH, M. L. (1981). Meta-analysis in Social Research. Beverly Hills, CA: Sage

GLEITMAN, H. (1986). PSYCHOLOGY (2nd ed.). New York: Norton.

GLEITMAN, L. R. (1986). Biological predispositions to learn language. In P. Marler & H. S. Terrace (Eds.), THE BIOLOGY OF LEARNING. New York: Springer-Verlag.

GODDEN, D., & BADDELEY, A. D. (1975). Context-dependent memory in two natural environments: On land and under water. BRITISH JOURNAL OF PSYCHOLOGY, 66, 325–331.

GOETHALS, G. P., & ZANNA, M. P. (1979). The role of social comparison in choice shifts. JOURNAL OF PERSONALITY AND SOCIAL PSYCHOLOGY, 37, 1469–1476.

GOLDHABER, D. (1986). LIFE-SPAN HUMAN DEVELOPMENT. San Diego: Harcourt Brace Jovanovich.

GOLDIN-MEADOW, S. (1982). The resilience of recursion: A structure within a conventional model. In E. Wanner & L. R. Gleitman (Eds.), LANGUAGE ACQUISITION: THE STATE OF THE ART. Cambridge: Cambridge University Press.

GOLDMAN-RAKIC, P. S. (1987). Circuitry of primate prefrontal corex and regulation of behavior by representational memory. In F. Plum (Ed.), HANDBOOK OF PHYSIOLOGY: THE NERVOUS SYSTEM. Bethesda, MD: American Physiology Society.

GOLDSTEIN, AVRAM (1994). ADDICTION: FROM BIOLOGY TO DRUG POLICY. New York: Freeman.

GOLDSTEIN, E. B. (1989). SENSATION AND PERCEPTION (3rd ed.). Belmont, CA: Wadsworth.

GOLDSTEIN, M. (1987). Family interaction patterns that antedate the onset of schizophrenia and related disorders: A further analysis of data from a longitudinal prospective study. In K. Hahlweg, & M. Goldstein (Eds.), UNDERSTANDING MAJOR MENTAL DISORDERS: THE CONTRIBUTION OF FAMILY INTERACTION RESEARCH (pp. 11–32). New York: Family Process Press.

GOLDSTEIN, M. J. (1987). The UCLA high risk project. SCHIZOPHRENIA BULLETIN, 13, 505–514.

GOLEMAN, D. J. (1977). THE VARIETIES OF MEDITATIVE EXPERIENCE. New York: Dutton.

GOLEMAN, D. J. (1988, October 18). Chemistry of sexual desire yields its elusive secret. NEW YORK TIMES.

GOODALL, J. (1978). Chimp killings: Is it the man in them? SCIENCE NEWS, 113, 276.

GOODGLASS, H., & BUTTERS, N. (1988). Psychobiology of cognitive processes. In R. C. Atkinson, R. J. Hernstein, G. Lindzey, & R. D. Luce (Eds.), STEVENS' HANDBOOK OF EXPERIMENTAL PSYCHOLOGY (Vol. 2). New York: Wiley.

GORDON, W. (1989). LEARNING & MEMORY. Pacific Grove, CA: Brooks/Cole.

GORENSTEIN, E. E. (1982). Frontal lobe functions in psychopaths. JOURNAL OF ABNORMAL PSYCHOLOGY, 91, 368–379.

GORTMAKER, S. L., ECKENRODE, J., & GORE, S. (1982). Stress and the utilization of health services: A time series and cross-sectional analysis. JOURNAL OF HEALTH AND SOCIAL BEHAVIOR, 23, 25–38.

GOTTESMAN, I. I., (1991). SCHIZOPHRENIA GENESIS: THE ORIGINS OF MADNESS. New York: W. H. Freeman.

GOTTESMAN, I. I., & BERTELSEN, A. (1989). Confirming unexpressed genotypes for schizophrenia. ARCHIVES OF GENERAL PSYCHIATRY, 46, 867–872.

GOTTESMAN, I. I., & SHIELDS, J. (1982). SCHIZOPHRENIA: THE EPIGENETIC PUZZLE. New York: Cambridge University Press.

GOY, R. W. (1968). Organizing effect of androgen on the behavior of rhesus monkeys. In R. F. Michael (Ed.), ENDOCRINOLOGY OF HUMAN BEHAVIOUR. London: Oxford University Press.

GRADY, C. L., HAXBY, J. V., HORWITZ, B., SCHAPIRO, M. B., RAPOPORT, S. I., UNGERLEIDER, L. G., MISHKIN, M., CARSON, R. E., & HERSCOVITCH, P. (1992). Dissociation of object and spatial vision in human extrastriate cortex: Age-related changes in activation of regional cerebral blood flow measured with [^{15}O] Water and Positron Emission Tomography. JOURNAL OF COGNITIVE NEUROSCIENCE, 4, 23–34.

GRAF, P., & MANDLER, G. (1984). Activation makes words more accessible, but not necessarily more retrievable. JOURNAL OF VERBAL LEARNING AND VERBAL BEHAVIOR, 23, 553–568.

GRAHAM, J. R. (1990). THE MIMPI-2: ASSESSING PERSONALITY AND PSYCHOPATHOLOGY. New York: Oxford University Press.

GRANRUD, C. E. (1986). Binocular vision and spatial perception in 4- and 5-month old infants. JOURNAL OF EXPERIMENTAL PSYCHOLOGY: HUMAN PERCEPTION AND PERFORMANCE, 12, 36–49.

GREEN, D. M., & SWETS, J. A. (1966). SIGNAL DETECTION THEORY AND PSYCHOPHYSICS. New York: Wiley.

GREEN, D. M., & WIER, C. C. (1984). Auditory perception. In I. Darian-Smith (Ed.), HANDBOOK OF PHYSIOLOGY (Vol. 3). Bethesda, MD: American Physiological Society.

GREEN, H. (1971). I NEVER PROMISED YOU A ROSE GARDEN. New York: New American Library.

GREEN, R. (1987). THE "SISSY BOY SYNDROME" AND THE DEVELOPMENT OF HOMOSEXUALITY. New Haven: Yale University Press.

GREENFIELD, P. M., & SAVAGE-RUMBAUGH, S. (1990). Grammatical combination in Pan Paniscus: Processes of learning and invention in the evolution and development of language. In S. Parker & K. Gibson (Eds.), "LANGUAGE" AND INTELLIGENCE IN MONKEYS AND APES: COMPARATIVE DEVELOPMENTAL PERSPECTIVES. New York: Cambridge University Press.

GREENWALD, A. G. (1968). Cognitive learning, cognitive response to persuasion, and attitude change. In A. G. Greenwald, T. C. Brock, & T. M. Ostrom (Eds.), PSYCHOLOGICAL FOUNDATIONS OF ATTITUDES. New York: Academic Press.

GREENWALD, A. G. (1992). Unconscious cognition reclaimed. AMERICAN PSYCHOLOGIST, 47, 766–779.

GRICE, H. P. (1975). Logic and conversation. In G. Harman, & D. Davidson (Eds.), THE LOGIC OF GRAMMAR. Encino, CA: Dickinson.

GRIGGS, R. A., & COX, J. R. (1982). The elusive thermatic-materials effect in Watson's selection task. BRITISH JOURNAL OF PSYCHOLOGY, 73, 407–420.

GRILL, H. J., & KAPLAN, J. M. (1990). Caudal brainstem participates in the distributed neural control of feeding. In E. M. Stricker (Eds.), NEUROBIOLOGY OF FOOD AND FLUID INTAKE (pp. 125–149). New York: Plenum Press.

GRODZINSKY, Y. (1984). The syntactic characterization of agrammatism. COGNITION, 16, 99–120.

GROVES, P. M., & REBEC, G. V. (1992). INTRODUCTION TO BIOLOGICAL PSYCHOLOGY (4th ed.). Dubuque, IA: Brown.

GRÜNBAUM, A. (1984). THE FOUNDATIONS OF PSYCHOANALYSIS. Berkeley, CA: University of California Press.

GUILFORD, J. P. (1982). Cognitive psychology's ambiguities: Some suggested remedies. PSYCHOLOGICAL REVIEW, 89, 48–49.

GURMAN, A. S., & KNISKERN, D. P. (1981). HANDBOOK OF FAMILY THERAPY. New York: Brunner/Mazel.

GURNEY, R. (1936). The hereditary factor in obesity. ARCHIVES OF INTERNAL MEDICINE, 57, 557–561.

HAAGA, D. A. F., DYCK, M. J., & ERNST, D. (1991). Empirical status of cognitive theory of depression. PSYCHOLOGICAL BULLETIN, 110, 215–236.

HABER, R. N. (1969). Eidetic images. SCIENTIFIC AMERICAN, 220, 36–55.

HABER, R. N. (1979). Twenty years of haunting edetic imagery: Where's the ghost? BEHAVIORAL AND BRAIN SCIENCES, 24, 583–629.

HABERLANDT, K. (1993). COGNITIVE PSYCHOLOGY. Boston, MA: Allyn and Bacon.

HAITH, M. M., BERGMAN, T., & MOORE, M. J. (1977). Eye contact and face scanning in early infancy. SCIENCE, 198, 853–855.

HALIKAS, J. A., GOODWIN, D. W., & GUZE, S. B. (1971). Marijuana effects: A survey of regular users. JOURNAL OF AMERICAN MEDICAL ASSOCIATION, 217, 692–694.

HALL, C. S., LINDZEY, G., LOEHLIN, J. C., & MANOSEVITZ, M. (1985). INTRODUCTION TO THEORIES OF PERSONALITY. New York: Wiley.

HAMBERGER, L. K., & LOHR, J. M. (1984). STRESS AND STRESS MANAGEMENT: RESEARCH AND APPLICATIONS. New York: Springer.

HAMBURG, D., & TRUDEAU, M. B. (Eds.). (1981). BIOBEHAVIORAL ASPECTS OF AGGRESSION. New York: Alan Liss.

HAMER, D. H., HU, S., MAGNUSON, V. L., HU, N., & PATTATUCCI, A. M. L. (1993). A linkage between DNA markers on the X chromosome and male sexual orientation. SCIENCE, 261, 321–327.

HAMER, D., & COPELAND, P. (1994). THE SCIENCE OF DESIRE: THE SEARCH FOR THE GAY GENE AND THE BIOLOGY OF BEHAVIOR. New York: Simon & Schuster.

HAMILTON, D. L. (1979). A cognitive-attributional analysis of stereotyping. In L. Berkowitz (Ed.), ADVANCES IN EXPERIMENTAL SOCIAL PSYCHOLOGY (Vol. 12). New York: Academic Press.

HAMILTON, D. L., & GIFFORD, R. K. (1976). Illusory correlation in interpersonal perception: A cognitive basis of stereotypic judgments. JOURNAL OF EXPERIMENTAL SOCIAL PSYCHOLOGY, *12*, 392–407.

HAMILTON, D. L., & SHERMAN, S. J. (1989). Illusory correlations: Implications for stereotype theory and research. In D. Bar-Tal, C. F. Gravmann, A. W. Kruglanski, & W. Stroebe (Eds.), STEREOTYPES AND PREDJUDICE: CHANGING CONCEPTIONS. New York: Springer-Verlag.

HAMILTON, E. W., ABRAMSON, L. Y. (1983). Cognitive patterns and major depressive disorder: A longitudinal study in a hospital setting. JOURNAL OF ABNORMAL PSYCHOLOGY, *92*, 173–184.

HARE, R. D. (1970). PSYCHOPATHY: THEORY AND RESEARCH. New York: Wiley.

HARE, R. D. (1980). A research scale for the assessment of psychopathy in criminal populations. PERSONALITY AND INDIVIDUAL DIFFERENCES, *1*, 111–119.

HARE, R. D. (1988). Male psychopaths and their criminal careers. JOURNAL OF CONSULTING AND CLINICAL PSYCHOLOGY, *56*, 710–714.

HARLOW, H. F. (1971). LEARNING TO LOVE. San Francisco: Albion.

HARLOW, H. F., & HARLOW, M. K. (1969). Effects of various mother-infant relationships on rhesus monkey behaviors. In B. M. Foss (Ed.), DETERMINANTS OF INFANT BEHAVIOR (Vol. 4). London: Methuen.

HARLOW, H. F., HARLOW, M. K., & MEYER, D. R. (1950). Learning motivated by a manipulation drive. JOURNAL OF EXPERIMENTAL PSYCHOLOGY, *40*, 228–234.

HARRÉ, R., & LAMB, R. (Eds.) (1983). THE ENCYCLOPEDIC DICTIONARY OF PSYCHOLOGY. Cambridge, MA: MIT Press.

HARRIS, M. J., & ROSENTHAL, R. (1988). INTERPERSONAL EXPECTANCY EFFECTS AND HUMAN PERFORMANCE RESEARCH. Washington, DC: National Academy Press.

HARTSHORNE, H., & MAY, M. A. (1929). STUDIES IN THE NATURE OF CHARACTER II: STUDIES IN SERVICE AND SELF-CONTROL. New York: Macmillan.

HARTUP, W. W., & MOORE, S. G. (1963). Avoidance of inappropriate sex-typing by young children. JOURNAL OF CONSULTING PSYCHOLOGY, *27*, 467–473.

HASPEL, K. C., & HARRIS, R. S. (1982). Effect of tachistoscopic stimulation of subconscious Oedipal wishes on competitive performance: A failure to replicate. JOURNAL OF ABNORMAL PSYCHOLOGY, *91*, 437–443.

HASS, R. G., & GRADY, K. (1975). Temporal delay, type of forewarning and resistance to influence. JOURNAL OF EXPERIMENTAL SOCIAL PSYCHOLOGY, *11*, 459–469.

HATFIELD, E. (1988). Passionate and companionate love. In R. J. Sternberg, & M. L. Barnes (Eds.), THE PSYCHOLOGY OF LOVE (pp. 191–217). New Haven, CT: Yale University Press.

HATHAWAY, S. R., & MCKINLEY, J. C. (1943).

MANUAL FOR THE MINNESOTA MULTIPHASIC PERSONALITY INVENTORY. New York: Psychological Corporation.

HAWKINS, R. D., & KANDEL, E. R. (1984). Is there a cell-biological alphabet for simple forms of learning? PSYCHOLOGICAL REVIEW, *91*, 375–391.

HAXBY, J. V., GRADY, C. L., HORWIZ, B., UNGERLEIDER, L. G., MISHKIN, M., CARSON, R. E., HERSCOVITCH, P., SCHAPIRO, M. B., & RAPOPORT, S. I. (1991). Dissociation of object and spatial visual processing pathways in human extrastriate cortex. NEUROBIOLOGY, *88*, 1621–1625.

HAYES, J. R. (1989). THE COMPLETE PROBLEM SOLVER (2nd edition). Hillsdale, NJ: Erlbaum.

HAYES, L. A., & WATSON, J. S. (1981). Neonatal imitation: Fact or artifact. DEVELOPMENTAL PSYCHOLOGY, *17*, 655–660.

HAYNES, S. G., & FEINLEIB, M. (1980). Women, work, and coronary heart disease: Prospective findings from the Framingham heart study. AMERICAN JOURNAL OF PUBLIC HEALTH, *70*, 133–141.

HAYNES, S. G., FEINLEIB, M., & KANNEL, W. B. (1980). The relationship of psychosocial factors to coronary heart disease in the Framingham Study: Pt. 3. Eight-year incidence of coronary heart disease. AMERICAN JOURNAL OF EPIDEMIOLOGY, *111*(No. 1), 37–58.

HAZAN, C., & SHAVER, P. (1987). Romantic love conceptualized as an attachment process. JOURNAL OF PERSONALITY AND SOCIAL PSYCHOLOGY, *52*, 511–524.

HEATH, R. G. (1972). Pleasure and brain activity in man. Deep and surface electroencephalograms during orgasm. J NERV MENT DIS, *154*(1), 3–18.

HEBB, D. O. (1972). TEXTBOOK OF PSYCHOLOGY (3rd ed.). Philadelphia: Saunders.

HEBB, D. O. (1982). Understanding psychological man: A state-of-the science report. PSYCHOLOGY TODAY, *16*, 52–53.

HECHT, S., SHALER, S., & PIREENE, M. H. (1942). Energy, quanta, and vision. JOURNAL OF GENERAL PHYSIOLOGY, *25*, 819–840.

HEIDER, F. (1958). THE PSYCHOLOGY OF INTERPERSONAL RELATIONS. New York: Wiley.

HEILBRUN, K. S. (1982). Silverman's subliminal psychodynamic activation: A failure to replicate. JOURNAL OF ABNORMAL PSYCHOLOGY, *89*, 560–566.

HELD, R. (1965). Plasticity in sensory motor systems. SCIENTIFIC AMERICAN, *21*(No. 5), 84–94.

HELD, R., & HEIN, A. (1963). Movement produced stimulation in the development of visually guided behavior. JOURNAL OF COMPARATIVE AND PHYSIOLOGICAL PSYCHOLOGY, *56*, 872–876.

HEMMI, T. (1969). How we have handled the problem of drug abuse in Japan. In F. Sjoqvist & M. Tottie (Eds.), ABUSE OF CENTRAL STIMULANTS. New York: Raven Press.

HENCHY, T., & GLASS, D. C. (1968). Evaluation apprehension and social facilitation of

dominant and subordinate responses. JOURNAL OF PERSONALITY AND SOCIAL PSYCHOLOGY, *10*, 445–454.

HENDRICK, C., & HENDRICK, S. S. (1986). A theory and method of love. JOURNAL OF PERSONALITY AND SOCIAL PSYCHOLOGY, *50*, 392–402.

HENDRICK, C., & HENDRICK, S. S. (1989). Research on love: Does it measure up? JOURNAL OF PERSONALITY AND SOCIAL PSYCHOLOGY, *56*, 784–794.

HENLEY, N., HAMILTON, M., & THORNE, B. (1985). Womanspeak and manspeak: Sex differences and sexism in communication, verbal and nonverbal. In A. G. Sargent (Ed.), BEYOND SEX ROLES. St. Paul, MN: West.

HENSEL, H. (1973). Cutaneous thermoreceptors. In A. Iggo (Ed.), HANDBOOK OF SENSORY PHYSIOLOGY (Vol. 2). Berlin: Springer-Verlag.

HERBERT, N. (1987). QUANTUM REALITY: BEYOND THE NEW PHYSICS. Garden City, NY: Anchor.

HERDT, G. H. (Ed.) (1984). RITUALIZED HOMOSEXUALITY IN MELANESIA. Berkeley: University of California Press.

HEREK, G. M. (1986). The instrumentality of attitudes: Toward a neofunctional theory. JOURNAL OF SOCIAL ISSUES, *42*, 99–114.

HEREK, G. M. (1987). Can functions be measured? A new perspective on the functional approach to attitudes. SOCIAL PSYCHOLOGY QUARTERLY, *50*, 285–303.

HERING, E. (1878). OUTLINES OF A THEORY OF THE LIGHT SENSE (L. M. Hurvich & D. Jameson, Trans.). Cambridge, MA: Harvard University Press.

HERING, E. (1920). Memory as a universal function of organized matter. In S. Butler (Ed.) UNCONSCIOUS MEMORY. London: Jonathon Cape.

HERMAN, C. P., & POLIVY, J. (1980). Retrained eating. In A. J. Stunkard (Ed.), OBESITY. Philadelphia: Saunders.

HERRNSTEIN, R. J., & MURRAY, C. (1994). THE BELL CURVE: INTELLIGENCE AND CLASS STRUCTURE IN AMERICAN LIFE. New York: The Free Press.

HERZOG, D. B., NORMAN, D. K., GORDON, C., & PEPOSE, M. (1984). Sexual conflict and eating disorders in 27 males. AM J PSYCHIATRY, *141*(8), 989–90.

HESS, E. H. (1958). "Imprinting" in animals. SCIENTIFIC AMERICAN, *198*, 81–90.

HESS, E. H. (1972). "Imprinting" in a natural laboratory. SCIENTIFIC AMERICAN, *227*, 24–31.

HESTON, L. L. (1966). Psychiatric disorders in foster home reared children of schizophrenic mothers. BRITISH JOURNAL OF PSYCHIATRY, *112*, 819–825.

HESTON, L. L. (1992). Mending Minds, A Guide to the New Psychiatry of Depression, Anxiety, and Other Serious Mental Disorders. New York: W. H. Freeman.

HILGARD, E. R. (1965). HYPNOTIC SUSCEPTIBILITY. New York: Harcourt Brace Jovanovich.

HILGARD, E. R. (1968). THE EXPERIENCE OF HYPNOSIS. New York: Harcourt Brace Jovanovich.

HILGARD, E. R. (1986). DIVIDED CONSCIOUSNESS: MULTIPLE CONTROLS IN HUMAN THOUGHT AND ACTION. New York: Wiley-Intercience.

HILGARD, E. R. (1987). PSYCHOLOGY IN AMERICAN: A HISTORICAL SURVEY. San Diego: Harcourt Brace Javanovich.

HILGARD, E. R., & HILGARD, J. R. (1975). HYPNOSIS IN THE RELIEF OF PAIN. Los Altos, CA: Kaufmann.

HILGARD, E. R., HILGARD, J. R., MACDONALD, H., MORGAN, A. H., & JOHNSON, L. S. (1978). Covert pain in hypnotic analgesia: Its reality as tested by the real-simulator design. JOURNAL OF ABNORMAL PSYCHOLOGY, 87, 655–663.

HILGARD, J. R. (1979). PERSONALITY AND HYPNOSIS: A STUDY OF IMAGINATIVE INVOLVEMENT (2nd ed.). Chicago: University of Chicago Press.

HILL, C., RUBIN, Z., & PEPLAU, L. A. (1976). Breakups before marriage: The end of 103 affairs. JOURNAL OF SOCIAL ISSUES, 32, 147–168.

HILLYARD, S. A. (1985). Electrophysiology of human selective attention. TRENDS IN NEUROSCIENCE, 8, 400–406.

HIRSCH, J., & BATCHELOR, B. R. (1976). Adipose tissue cellularity and human obesity. CLINICAL ENDOCRINOLOGY AND METABOLISM, 5, 299–311.

HIRSCH, H. V., B., & SPINELLI, D. N. (1970). Visual experience modifies distribution of horizontally and vertically oriented receptive fields in cats. SCIENCE, 168, 869–871.

HOBSON, J. A. (1988). THE DREAMING BRAIN. New York: Basic Books.

HOBSON, J. A. (1989). SLEEP. New York: Freeman.

HOBSON, J. A. (1994). THE CHEMISTRY OF CONSCIOUS STATES, HOW THE BRAIN CHANGES ITS MIND. New York: Little, Brown & Company.

HOEBEL, B. G., & TEITELBAUM, P. (1966). Effects of force-feeding and starvation on food intake and body weight on a rat with ventromedial hypothalamic lesions. JOURNAL OF COMPARATIVE AND PHYSIOLOGICAL PSYCHOLOGY, 61, 189–193.

HOFLING, C. K. (1975). TEXTBOOK OF PSYCHIATRY FOR MEDICAL PRACTICE (3rd ed.). Philadelphia: Lippincott.

HOFLING, C. K., BROTZMAN, E., DALRYMPLE, S., GRAVES, N., & PIERCE, C. M. (1966). An experimental study in nurse-physician relationships. JOURNAL OF NERVOUS AND MENTAL DISEASE, 143, 171–180.

HOGARTY, G. E., SCHOOLER, N. R., ULRICH, R., MUSSARE, F., FERRO, P., & HERRON, E. (1979). Fluphenazine and social therapy in the after care of schizophrenic patients. ARCHIVES OF GENERAL PSYCHIATRY, 36, 1283–1294.

HOHMANN, G. W. (1962). Some effects of spinal cord lesions on experienced emotional feelings. PSYCHOPHYSIOLOGY, 3, 143–156.

HOLDEN, C. (1975). Lie detectors: PSE gains audience despite critic's doubt. SCIENCE, 190, 359–362.

HOLLAND, J. H., HOLYOAK, K. J., NISBETT, R. E., & THAGARD, P. R. (1986). INDUCTION: PROCESSES OF INFERENCE, LEARNING, AND DISCOVERY. Cambridge, MA: MIT Press.

HOLMES, D. S. (1974). Investigations of repression: Differential recall of material experimentally or naturally associated with ego threat. PSYCHOLOGICAL BULLETIN, 81, 632–653.

HOLMES, D. S., & MCGILLEY, B. M. (1987). Influence of a brief aerobic training program on heart rate and subjective response to stress. PSYCHOSOMATIC MEDICINE, 49, 366–374.

HOLMES, D. S., & ROTH, D. L. (1985). Association of aerobic fitness with pulse rate and subjective responses to psychological stress. PSYCHOPHYSIOLOGY, 22, 525–529.

HOLMES, T. H. (1979). Development and application of a quantitative measure of life change magnitude. In J. E. Barrett (Ed.), STRESSFUL LIFE EVENTS: THEIR NATURE AND EFFECTS. New York: Wiley.

HOLMES, T. H., & RAHE, R. H. (1967). The social readjustment rating scale. JOURNAL OF PSYCHOSOMATIC RESEARCH, 11, 213–218.

HOLROYD, K. A., APPEL, M. A., & ANDRASIK, F. (1983). A cognitive behavioral approach to psychophysiological disorders. In D. Meichenbaum & M. E. Jaremko (Eds.), STRESS REDUCTION AND PREVENTION. New York: Plenum.

HOLYOAK, K., KOH, K., & NISBETT, R. E. (1989). A theory of conditioning: Inductive learning within rule-based default hierarchies. PSYCHOLOGICAL REVIEW, 96, 315–340.

HOLZMAN, P. S. (1970). PSYCHOANALYSIS AND PSYCHOPATHOLOGY. New York: McGraw-Hill.

HONIG, W. K., & STADDON, J. E. R. (Eds.) (1977). HANDBOOK OF OPERANT BEHAVIOR. Englewood Cliffs, NJ: Prentice-Hall.

HONORTON, C. (1985). Meta-analysis of psi ganzfeld research: A response to Hyman. JOURNAL OF PARAPSYCHOLOGY, 49, 51–91.

HONORTON, C., BERGER, R. E., VARVOGLIS, M. P., QUANT, M., DERR, P., SCHECHTER, E., & FERRARI, D. C. (1990). Psi communication in the ganzfeld: Experiments with an automated testing system and a comparison with a meta-analysis of earlier studies. JOURNAL OF PARAPSYCHOLOGY, 54, 99–139.

HOON, P. W., WINCZE, J. P., & HOON, E. F. (1977). A test of reciprocal inhibition: Are anxiety and sexual arousal in women mutually inhibitory? JOURNAL OF ABNORMAL PSYCHOLOGY, 86, 65–74.

HOPKINS, J. R. (1977). Sexual behavior in adolescence. JOURNAL OF SOCIAL ISSUES, 33, 67–85.

HORM, J., & ANDERSON, K. (1993). Who in America is trying to lose weight? ANN INTERN MED, 119(7 Pt 2), 672–6.

HORNE, J. A., & MCGRATH, M. J. (1984). The consolidation hypothesis for REM sleep function: Stress and other confounding factors—A review. BIOLOGICAL PSYCHOLOGY, 18, 165–84.

HOROWITZ, F. D. (1974). Visual attention, auditory stimulation, and language stimulation in young infants. MONOGRAPHS OF THE SOCIETY FOR RESEARCH IN CHILD DEVELOPMENT, 31, Serial Number 158.

HOROWITZ, M. (1986). Stress-response syndromes: A review of postraumatic and adjustment disorders. HOSPITAL & COMMUNITY PSYCHIATRY, 37(3), 241–249.

HOVLAND, C., JANIS, I., & KELLEY, H. H. (1953). COMMUNICATION AND PERSUASION. New Haven: Yale University Press.

HOVLAND, C. I., LUMSDAINE, A. A., & SHEFFIELD, F. D. (1949). Experiments on mass communication. STUDIES IN SOCIAL PSYCHOLOGY IN WORLD WARD II (Vol. III). Princeton, NJ: Princeton University Press.

HOWARD, K. I., KOPTA, S. M., KRAUSE, M. S., & ORLINSKY, D. E. (1986). The dose-effect relationship in psychotherapy. AMERICAN PSYCHOLOGIST, 41, 159–164.

HSER, Y. I., ANGLIN, D., & POWERS, K. (1993). A 24-year follow-up of California narcotics addicts. ARCHIVES OF GENERAL PSYCHIATRY, 50, (Issue 7), 577–584.

HUBEL, D. H., & WIESEL, T. N. (1963). Receptive fields of cells in striate cortex of very young visually inexperienced kittens. JOURNAL OF NEUROPHYSIOLOGY, 26, 994–1002.

HUDSON, J. W., & HOYT, L. L. (1981). Personal characteristics important in mate preference among college students. SOCIAL BEHAVIOR AND PERSONALITY, 9, 93–96.

HUGDAHL, K., & OHMAN, A. (1977). Effects of instruction on acquisition and extinction of electrodermal response to fear-relevant stimuli. JOURNAL OF EXPERIMENTAL PSYCHOLOGY: HUMAN LEARNING AND MEMORY, 3, 608–618.

HUMMEL, J. E., & BIEDERMAN, I. (1992). Dynamic binding in a neutral network for shape recognition. PSYCHOLOGICAL REVIEW, 99, 480–517.

HUNT, D. D., & HAMPSON, J. L. (1980). Follow up of 17 biologic male transsexuals after sex reassignment surgery. AMERICAN JOURNAL OF PSYCHIATRY, 137, 432–438.

HUNT, E. (1990). A modern arsenal for mental assessment. EDUCATIONAL PSYCHOLOGIST, 25, 223–241.

HUNT, M. (1974). SECUAL BEHAVIOR IN THE 1970'S. Chicago: Playboy Press.

HUNT, P. J., & HILLERY, J. M. (1973). Social facilitation at different stages in learning. Paper presented at the Midwestern Psychological Association Meetings, Cleveland.

HUNTER, E. J. (1979, May). Combat casualities who remain at home. Paper presented at Western Regional Conference of the Interuniversity Seminar, "Technology in Combat." Navy Postgraduate School, Monterey, CA.

HUNTER, I. M. L. (1974). MEMORY. Baltimore: Penguin.

HURVICH, L. M., & JAMESON, D. (1957). An opponent process theory of color vision. PSYCHOLOGICAL REVIEW, 64 384–404.

HUTTON, D. C., & BAUMEISTER, R. F. (1992). Self-awareness and attitude change: Seeing oneself on the central route to persuasion. PERSONALITY AND SOCIAL PSYCHOLOGY BULLETIN, 18, 68–75.

HYMAN, R. (1985). The ganzfield psi experiment: A critical appraisal. JOURNAL OF PARAPSYCHOLOGY, 49, 3–49.

HYMAN, R. (1994). Anomaly or Artifact? Comments on Bem and Honorton. PSYCHOLOGICAL BULLETIN, *115*, 19–24.

HYMAN, R., & HONORTON, C. (1986). A joint communique: The psi ganzfeld controversy. JOURNAL OF PARAPSYCHOLOGY, *50*, 351–364.

IMPERATO-MCGINLEY, J., PETERSON, R. E., GAUTIER, T., & STURLA, E. (1979). Androgens and the evolution of male gender identity among male pseudohermaphrodites with 5 alpha reductase deficiency. NEW ENGLAND JOURNAL OF MEDICINE, *300*, 1233–1237.

INSTITUTE OF MEDICINE (1982). MARIJUANA AND HEALTH. Washington, DC: National Academy Press.

INSTITUTE OF MEDICINE (1990). TREATING DRUG PROBLEMS. Washington, DC: National Academy Press.

ISEN, P. M. (1985). The assymmetry of happiness and sadness in effects on memory in normal college students. JOURNAL OF EXPERIMENTAL PSYCHOLOGY: GENERAL, *114*, 388–391.

ISEN, P. M., SHALKER, T. E., CLARK, M., & KARP, L. (1978). Affect, accessibility of material in memory, and behavior: A cognitive loop? JOURNAL OF PERSONALITY AND SOCIAL PSYCHOLOGY, *36*, 1–12.

ISENBERG, D. J. (1986). Group polarization: A critical review and meta-analysis. JOURNAL OF PERSONALITY AND SOCIAL PSYCHOLOGY, *50*, 1141–1151.

ISOZAKI, M. (1984). The effect of discussion on polarization of judgments. JAPANESE PSYCHOLOGICAL RESEARCH, *26*, 187–193.

JACKENDOFF, R. (1990). CONSCIOUSNESS AND THE COMPUTATIONAL MIND. Cambridge: MIT Press.

JACKLIN, C. N., & MACCOBY, E. E. (1978). Social behavior at 33 months in same-sex and mixed-sex dyads. CHILD DEVELOPMENT, *49*, 557–569.

JACOBS, W. J., & NADEL, W. (1985). Stress-induced recovery of fears and phobias. PSYCHOLOGICAL REVIEW, *92* 512–531.

JACOBSON, A. L., FRIED, C., & HOROWITZ, S. D. (1967). Classical conditioning, pseudoconditioning, or sensitization in the planarian. JOURNAL OF COMPARATIVE AND PHYSIOLOGICAL PSYCHOLOGY, *64*, 73–79.

JACOBSON, S. W. (1979). Matching behavior in the young infant. CHILD DEVELOPMENT, *50*, 425–430.

JACOBY, L. L., & DALLAS, M. (1981). On the relationship between biographical memory and perceptual learning. JOURNAL OF EXPERIMENTAL PSYCHOLOGY: GENERAL, *110*, 306–340.

JAHN, R. G., & DUNNE, B. J. (1987). MARGINS OF REALITY. San Diego: Harcourt Brace & Jovanovich.

JAMES, W. (1884). What is an emotion? MIND, *9*, 188–205.

JANET, P. (1889). L'AUTOMISMEPSYCHOLOGIGUE. Paris: Felix Alcan.

JANICAK, P. C., DAVIS, J. M., GIBBONS, R. D., ERICKSEN, S., CHANG, S., & GALLAGHER, P. (1985). Efficacy of ECT: A meta-analysis.

AMERICAN JOURNAL OF PSYCHIATRY, *142*, 297–302.

JANIS, I. L. (1982). GROUPTHINK: PSYCHOLOGICAL STUDIES OF POLICY DECISIONS AND FIASCOES (2nd ed.). Boston, Houghton Mifflin.

JANIS, I. L. (1985). Sources of error in strategic decision making. In J. M. Pennings (Ed.), ORGANIZATIONAL STRATEGY AND CHANGE. San Francisco: Jossey-Bass.

JANOWITZ, H. D., & GROSSMAN, M. I. (1949). Some factors affecting the food intake of normal dogs and dogs esophagostomy and gastric fistula. AMERICAN JOURNAL OF PHYSIOLOGY, *159*, 143–148.

JANOWSKY, D. S., EL-YOUSEF, M. F., DAVIS, J. M., & SERERKE, H. S. (1973). Provocation of schizophrenic symptoms by intravenous injection of methylphenidate. ARCHIVES OF GENERAL PSYCHIATRY, *28*, 185–191.

JASMOS, T. M., & HAKMILLER, K. L. (1975). Some effects of lesion level, and emotional cues on affective expression in spinal cord patients. PSYCHOLOGICAL REPORTS, *37*, 859–870.

JEMMOTT, J. B., III, BORYSENKO, M., MCCLELLAND, D. C., CHAPMAN, R., MEYER, D., & BENSON, H. (1985). Academic stress, power motivation, and decrease in salivary secretory immunoglubulin: A secretion rate. LANCET, *1*, 1400–1402.

JENNINGS, D., AMABILE, T. M., & ROSS, L. (1982). Informal covariation assessment: Data-based vs. theory-based judgments. In A. Tversky, D. Kahneman, & P. Slovic (Eds.), JUDGMENT UNDER UNCERTAINTY: HEURISTICS AND BIASES. New York: Cambridge University Press.

JESELL & KELLY, (1991).

JOHANSSON, G., & FRANKENHAEUSER, J. (1973). Temporal factors in sympatho-adrenomedullary activity following acute behavioral activation. BIOLOGICAL PSYCHOLOGY, *1*, 63–73.

JOHN, O. P. (1990). The "Big Five" factor taxonomy: Dimension of personality in the natural language and in questionnaires. In L. A. Pervin (Ed.), HANDBOOK OF PERSONALITY: THEORY AND RESEARCH (pp. 66–100). New York: Guilford Press.

JOHN, R. S., MEDNICK, S. A., & SCHULSINGER, F. (1982). Teacher reports as a predictor of schizophrenia and borderline schizophrenia: A Bayesian decision analysis. JOURNAL OF ABNORMAL PSYCHOLOGY, *91*, 399–413.

JOHNSON, C., & LARSON, R. (1982). Bulimia: An analysis of moods and behavior. PSYCHOSEMATIC MEDICINE, *44*, 341–351.

JOHNSON, E. J., & TVERSKY, A. (1983). Affect, generalization, and the perception of risk. JOURNAL OF PERSONALITY AND SOCIAL PSYCHOLOGY, *45*, 20–31.

JOHNSON, L. D., O'MALLEY, P. M., & BACHMAN, J. G. (1995). NATIONAL SURVEY RESULTS ON DRUG USE. Rockville, MD: National Institute on Drug Abuse.

JOHNSON, M. K., & RAYE, C. L. (1981). Reality monitoring. PSYCHOLOGICAL REVIEW, *88*, 67–85.

JOHNSON, R. D., & DOWNING, L. L. (1979). Deindividuation and valence of cues: Effect on prosocial and antisocial behavior. JOURNAL OF PERSONALITY AND SOCIAL PSYCHOLOGY, *37*, 1532–1538.

JOHNSON-LAIRD, P. N. (1985). The deductive reasoning ability. In R. J. Sternberg (Ed.), HUMAN ABILITIES: AN INFORMATION PROCESSING APPROACH. New York: Freeman.

JOHNSON-LAIRD, P. N. (1988). THE COMPUTER AND THE MIND: AN INTRODUCTION TO COGNITIVE SCIENCE. Cambridge: Harvard University Press.

JOHNSON-LAIRD, P. (1988). A computational analysis of consciousness. In A. J. Marcel & E. Bisiach (Eds.), CONSCIOUSNESS IN CONTEMPORARY SCIENCE. New York: Oxford University Press.

JOHNSON-LAIRD, P. N. (1989). Mental models. In M. I. Posner (Ed.), FOUNDATIONS OF COGNITIVE SCIENCE. Cambridge, MA: MIT Press.

JOHNSON-LAIRD, P. N., & BYRNE, R. M. J. (1991). DEDUCTION. Hillsdale, NJ: Erlbaum.

JOHNSTON, L. E., O'MALLEY, P. M., & BACHMAN, J. G. (1992). ILLICIT DRUG USE, SMOKING, AND DRINKING BY AMERICA'S HIGH SCHOOL STUDENTS, COLLEGE STUDENTS, AND YOUNG ADULTS, 1975–1991. Rockville, MD: National Institute on Drug Abuse DHHS publication nos. (ADM) 92-1920 & (ADM) 92-1940, in press.

JONES, E. E. (1978). Effects of race on psychotherapy process and outcome: An exploratory investigation. PSYCHOTHERAPY: THEORY, RESEARCH, AND PRACTICE, *15*, 226–236.

JONES, E. E. (1990). INTERPERSONAL PERCEPTION. New York: Freeman.

JONES, E. E., & HARRIS, V. A. (1967). The attribution of attitudes. JOURNAL OF EXPERIMENTAL SOCIAL PSYCHOLOGY, *3*, 1–24.

JONES, E. E., ROCK, L., SHAVER, K. G., GOETHALS, G. R., & WARD, L. M. (1968). Pattern of performance and ability attribution: An unexpected primacy effect. JOURNAL OF PERSONALITY AND SOCIAL PSYCHOLOGY, *9*, 317–340.

JONES, H. C., & LOVINGER, P. W. (1985). THE MARIJUANA QUESTION AND SCIENCE'S SEARCH FOR AN ANSWER. New York: Dodd, Mead.

JONES, R. A., & BREHM, J. W. (1970). Persuasiveness of one- and two-sided communications as a function of awareness there are two sides. JOURNAL OF EXPERIMENTAL SOCIAL PSYCHOLOGY, *6*, 47–56.

JULIEN, R. M. (1988). DRUGS AND THE BODY. New York: Freeman.

JULIEN, R. M. (1992). A PRIMER OF DRUG ACTION: A CONCISE, NONTECHNICAL GUIDE TO THE ACTIONS, USES, AND SIDE EFFECTS OF PSYCHOACTIVE DRUGS (6th ed.). New York: Freeman.

JUST, M. A., & CARPENTER, P. A. (1980). A theory of reading: From eye fixations to comprehension. PSYCHOLOGICAL REVIEW, *87*, 329–354.

JUTAI, J. W., & HARE, R. D. (1983). Psychopathy and selective attention during performance of a complex perceptual-motor task. PSYCHOPHYSIOLOGY, *20*, 140–151.

KAGAN, J. (1979). Overview: Perspectives on human infancy. In J. D. Osofsky (Ed.), HANDBOOK OF INFANT DEVELOPMENT. New York: Wiley-Interscience.

KAGAN, J., KEARSLEY, R. B., & ZELAZO, P. (1978). INFANCY: ITS PLACE IN HUMAN DEVELOPMENT. Cambridge, MA: Harvard University Press.

KAGAN, N. (1984). THE NATURE OF THE CHILD. New York: Basic Books.

KAGAN, N., & MOSS, H. A. (1962). BIRTH TO MATURITY. New York: Wiley.

KAHNEMAN, D., SLOVIC, P., & TVERSKY, A. (Eds.) (1982). JUDGMENT UNDER UNCERTAINTY: HEURISTICS AND BIASES. New York: Cambridge University Press.

KAIL, R. (1989). THE DEVELOPMENT OF MEMORY IN CHILDREN (3rd ed.). New York: Freeman.

KAIL, R., & PELLEGRINO, J. W. (1985). HUMAN INTELLIGENCE: PERSPECTIVES AND PROSPECTS. New York: Freeman.

KAMERMAN, S. B. (1980). PARENTING IN AN UNRESPONSIVE SOCIETY. New York: Free Press.

KAMIN, L. J. (1969). Predictability, surprise, attention, and conditioning. In B. A. Campbell & R. M. Church (Eds.), PUNISHMENT AND AVERSIVE BEHAVIOR. New York: Appleton-Century-Crofts.

KAMIN, L. J. (1974). THE SCIENCE AND POLITICS OF IQ. Hillsdale, NJ: Erlbaum.

KANDEL, D. B. (1975). Stages in adolescent involvement in drug use. SCIENCE, 190, 912–914.

KANDEL, D. B., DAVIES, M., KARUS, D. K., & YAMAGUCHI, K. (1986). The consequences in young adulthood of adolescent drug involvement. ARCHIVES GENERAL PSYCHIATRY, 43, 746–754.

KANDEL, E. R. (1979). Small systems of neurons. In R. Thompson (Ed.), THE BRAIN. San Francisco: Freeman.

KANDEL, E. R. & SCHWARTZ, J. H. (1985) PRINCIPLES OF NEURAL SCIENCE (2nd Edition). New York: Elsevier/North Holland.

KANNER, L. (1943). Autistic disturbances of affective contact. NERVOUS CHILD, 2, 217–250.

KAPLAN, J. (1985). THE HARDEST DRUG: HEROIN AND PUBLIC POLICY. Chicago: University of Chicago Press.

KAPLAN, M. R., & MILLER, C. E. (1987). Group decision making and normative versus informational influence: Effects of type of issue and assigned decision rule. JOURNAL OF PERSONALITY AND SOCIAL PSYCHOLOGY, 53, 306–313.

KAPLAN, R. M., & SACCUZZO, D. (1993). PSYCHOLOGICAL TESTING: PRINCIPLES AND ISSUES (3rd ed.). Pacific Grove, CA: Brooks/Cole.

KARASEK, R., BAKER, D., MARXER, F., AHLBOM, A., & THEORELL, T. (1981). Job decision latitude, job demands, and cardiovascular disease: A prospective study of Swedish men. AMERICAN JOURNAL OF PUBLIC HEALTH, 71, 694–705.

KARASEK, R. A., THEORELL, T. G., SCHWARTZ, J., PIEPER, C., & ALFREDSSON, L. (1982). Job, psychological factors and coronary heart disease: Swedish prospective findings and U.S. prevalence findings using a new occupation inference method. ADVANCES IN CARDIOLOGY, 29, 62–67.

KARNI, A., TANNE, D., RUBENSTEIN, B. S., ASKENASY, J. J. M., & SAGI, D. (1994). Dependence on REM sleep of overnight improvement of a perceptual skill. SCIENCE, 265, 679–682.

KASL, S. V., EVANS, A. S., & NIEDERMAN, J. C. (1979). Psychosocial risk factors in the development of infectious mononucleosis. PSYCHOSOMATIC MEDICINE, 41, 445–466.

KATZ, D. (1960). The functional approach to the study of attitudes. PUBLIC OPINION QUARTERLY, 24, 163–204.

KATZ, R., & WYKES, T. (1985). The psychological difference between temporally predictable and unpredictable stressful events: Evidence for information control theories. JOURNAL OF PERSONALITY AND SOCIAL PSYCHOLOGY, 48, 781–790.

KAZDIN, A. E. (1982). Symptom substitution, generalization, and response covariation: Implications for psychotherapy outcome. PSYCHOLOGICAL BULLETIN, 91, 349–365.

KEESEY, R. E., & POWLEY, T. L. (1975). Hypothalamic regulation of body weight. AMERICAN SCIENTIST, 63, 558–565.

KEIL, F. C. (1989). CONCEPTS, KINDS, AND COGNITIVE DEVELOPMENT. Cambridge, MA: MIT Press.

KEIL, F. C., & BATTERMAN, N. A. (1984). Characteristic-to-defining shift in the development of word meaning. JOURNAL OF VERBAL LEARNING AND VERBAL BEHAVIOR, 23, 221–236.

KELLER, M., SHAPIRO, R., LAVORI, P., & WOLFE, N. (1982, August). Recovery in major depressive disorder. ARCHIVES OF GENERAL PSYCHIATRY, 39, 905–910.

KELLEY, H. H. (1967). Attribution theory in social psychology. In D. Levine (Ed.), NEBRASKA SYMPOSIUM ON MOTIVATION (Vol. 15). Lincoln: University of Nebraska Press.

KELLMAN, P. J. (1984). Perception of three-dimensional form by human infants. PERCEPTION AND PSYCHOPHYSICS, 36, 353–358.

KELLY, G. A. (1955). THE PSYCHOLOGY OF PERSONAL CONSTRUCTS. New York: Norton.

KELTNER, D., ELLSWORTH, P., & EDWARDS, K. (1992). BEYOND SIMPLE PESSIMISM: EFFECTS OF SADNESS AND ANGER ON SOCIAL PERCEPTION. Manuscript submitted for publication.

KENDALL-TACKETT, K., WILLIAMS, L., & FINKELHOR, D. (1993). Impact of sexual abuse on children: A review and synthesis of recent empirical studies. PSYCHOLOGICAL BULLETIN, 113(1), 164–180.

KENDLER, K. S., & GRUENBERG, A. M. (1984). An independent analysis of the Copenhagen sample of the Danish adoption study of schizophrenia: IV. The pattern of psychiatric illness, as defined by DSM-III in adoptees and relatives. ARCHIVES OF GENERAL PSYCHIATRY, 41, 555–564.

KENNEDY, J. L., GIUFFRA, L. A., & collaborators (1988). Evidence against linkage of schizophrenia to markers on chromosome 5 in northern Swedish pedigree. NATURE, 336, 167–170.

KENDRICK, D. T., & CIALDINI, R. B. (1977). Romantic attraction: Misattribution versus reinforcement explanations. JOURNAL OF PERSONALITY AND SOCIAL PSYCHOLOGY, 35, 381–391.

KENDRICK, D. T., & GUTIERRES, S. E. (1980). Contrast effects and judgments of physical attractiveness: When beauty becomes a social problem. JOURNAL OF PERSONALITY AND SOCIAL PSYCHOLOGY, 38, 131–140.

KENSHALO, D. R., NAFE, J. P., & BROOKS, B. (1961). Variations in thermal sensitivity. SCIENCE, 134, 104–105.

KEPHART, W. M. (1967). Some correlates of romantic love. JOURNAL OF MARRIAGE AND THE FAMILY, 29, 470–474.

KERNIS, M. H., & WHEELER, L. (1981). Beautiful friends and ugly strangers: Radiation and contrast effects in perception of same-sex pairs. JOURNAL OF PERSONALITY AND SOCIAL PSYCHOLOGY, 7, 617–620.

KESSLER, R. C., BROWN, R. L., & BROMAN, C. L. (1981). Sex differences in psychiatric help-seeking: Evidence from four large-scale surveys. JOURNAL OF HEALTH AND SOCIAL BEHAVIOR, 22, 49–64.

KESSLER, R. C., MCGONAGLE, K. A., ZHAO, S., NELSON, C., HUGHES, M., ESHLEMAN, S., WITTCHEN, H., & KENDLER, K. (1994). Lifetime and 12-month prevalence of DSM-III-R psychiatric disorders in the United States. ARCHIVES OF GENERAL PSYCHIATRY, 51, 8–19.

KETY, S. S. (1988). Schizophrenic illness in the families of schizophrenic adoptees: findings from the Danish national sample. SCHIZOPHRENIA BULLETIN, 14, 217–222.

KETY, S. S., ROSENTHAL, D., WENDER, P. H., SCHULSINGER, F., & JACOBSEN, B. (1978). The biological and adoptive families of adopted individuals who become schizophrenic. In L. C. Wynne, R. L. Cromwell, & S. Matthysse (Eds.), THE NATURE OF SCHIZOPHRENIA. New York: Wiley.

KIECOLT-GLASER, J. K., FISHER, B. S., OGROCKI, P., STOUT, J. C., SPEICHER, C. E., & GLASER, R. (1987). Marital quality, marital disruption, and immune function. PSYCHOSOMATIC MEDICINE, 49, 13–33.

KIECOLT-GLASER, J. K., KENNEDY, S., MALKOFF, S., FISHER, L., SPEICHER, C. E., & GLASER, R. (1988). Marital discord and immunity in males. PSYCHOSOMATIC MEDICINE, 50, 213–229.

KIECOLT-GLASER, J., MALARKEY, W., CHEE, M., NEWTON, T., CACIOPPO, J., MAO, H., & GLASER, R. (1993). Negative behavior during marital conflict is associated with immunological down-regulation. PSYCHOSOMATIC MEDICINE, 55, 395–409.

KIESLER, C. A. (1982). Mental hospitals and alternative care: Noninstitutionalization as potential policy for mental patients. AMERICAN PSYCHOLOGIST, 34, 349–360.

KIESLER, C. A., & SIBULKIN, A. E. (1987). MENTAL HOSPITALIZATION: MYTHS AND FACTS ABOUT A NATIONAL CRISIS. Newbery Park, CA: Sage.

KIHLSTROM, J. F. (1984). Conscious, subconscious, unconscious: A cognitive view. In K. S. Bowers & D. Meichenbaum, (Eds.). THE UNCONSCIOUS: RECONSIDERED. New York: Wiley.

KIHLSTROM, J. F. (1985). Hypnosis. ANNUAL REVIEW OF PSYCHOLOGY, *36*, 385–235.

KIHLSTROM, J. F. (1987). The Cognitive Unconscious. SCIENCE, *237*, 1445–1452.

KILPATRICK, D., VERONEN, L., & RESICK, P. (1979). The aftermath of rape: recent empirical findings. AMERICAN JOURNAL OF ORTHOPSYCHIATRY, *49*, 658–669.

KILPATRICK, D., RESICK, P., & VERONEN, L. (1981). Effects of a rape experience: A longitudinal study. JOURNAL OF SOCIAL ISSUES, *37*, 105–122.

KIMMEL, D. C., & WEINER, I. B. (1985). ADOLESCENCE: A DEVELOPMENTAL TRANSITION. Hillsdale, NJ: Erlbaum.

KINDER, D. R., & SEARS, D. O. (1985). Public opinion and political action. In G. Lindzey & E. Aronson, (Eds.), THE HANDBOOK OF SOCIAL PSYCHOLOGY (3rd ed., Vol. 2). New York: Random House.

KLAHR, D. (1982). Nonmonotone assessment of monotone development: An information processing analysis. In S. Strauss (Ed.), U-SHAPED BEHAVIORAL GROWTH. New York: Academic Press.

KLATZKY, R. L., LEDERMAN, S. J., & METZGER, V. A. (1985). Identifying objects by touch: An expert system. PERCEPTION AND PSYCHOPHYSICS, *37*, 299–302.

KLEIN, S. B., & LOFTUS, J. (1988). The nature of self-referent encoding: The contributions of elaborative and organizational processes. JOURNAL OF PERSONALITY AND SOCIAL PSYCHOLOGY, *55*, 5–11.

KLEIN, S. B., LOFTUS, J., & BURTON, H. A. (1989). Two self-reference effects: The importance of distinguishing between self-descriptiveness judgments and autobiographical retrieval in self-referent encoding. JOURNAL OF PERSONALITY AND SOCIAL PSYCHOLOGY, *56*, 853–865.

KLEINMUNTZ, B. (1985). PERSONALITY AND PSYCHOLOGICAL ASSESSMENT. Malabar, FL: Robert E. Krieger.

KLINE, P. (1972). FACT AND FANCY IN FREUDIAN THEORY. London: Methuen.

KLINEBERG, O. (1938). Emotional expression in Chinese literature. JOURNAL OF ABNORMAL AND SOCIAL PSYCHOLOGY, *33*, 517–520.

KLUFT, R. P. (Ed.) (1985). CHILDHOOD ANTECEDENTS OF MULTIPLE PERSONALITY. Washington, DC: American Psychiatric Press.

KNITTLE, J. L., & HIRSCH, J. (1968). Effect of early nutrition on the development of rat epididymal fat pads: Cellularity and metabolism. JOURNAL OF CLINICAL INVESTIGATION, *47*, 2091.

KNOX, V. J., CRUTCHHELD, L., & HILGARD, E. R. (1975). The nature of task interference in hypnotic dissociation: An investigation of hypnotic behavior. INTERNATIONAL JOURNAL OF CLINICAL AND EXPERIMENTAL HYPNOSIS, *23*, 305–323.

KOBASA, S. C. (1979). Stressful life events, personality, and health: An inquiry into hardiness. JOURNAL OF PERSONALITY AND SOCIAL PSYCHOLOGY, *37*, 1–11.

KOBASA, S. C., MADDI, S. R., & KAHN, S. (1982). Hardiness and health: A prospective study. JOURNAL OF PERSONALITY AND SOCIAL PSYCHOLOGY, *42*, 168–177.

KOBASIGAWA, A., ARAKAKI, K., & AWIGUNI, A. (1966). Avoidance of feminine toys by kindergarten boys: The effects of adult presence or absence, and an adult's attitudes toward sextyping. JAPANESE JOURNAL OF PSYCHOLOGY, *37*, 96–103.

KOHLBERG, L. (1966). A cognitive-developmental analysis of children's sexrole concepts and attitudes. In E. E. Maccoby (Ed.), THE DEVELOPMENT OF SEX DIFFERENCES (pp. 82–173). Stanford, CA: Stanford University Press.

KOHLBERG, L. (1969). Stage and sequence: The cognitive-developmental approach to socialization. In D. A. Goslin (Ed.), HANDBOOK OF SOCIALIZATION THEORY AND RESEARCH. Chicago: Rand McNally.

KOHLBERG, L. (1976). Moral stages and moralization: The cognitive-developmental approach. In T. Lickong (Ed.), MORAL DEVELOPMENT AND BEHAVIOR. New York: Holt, Rinehart & Winston.

KOHLER, W. (1925). THE MENTALITY OF APES. New York: Harcourt Brace. (Reprint ed., 1976. New York: Liveright.)

KOHNSTAMM, G. A., BATES, J. E., & ROTHBART, M. K. (Eds.). (1989). Temperament in childhood . Chichester: John Wiley & Sons.

KOHOUT, J. (1991). CHANGES IN SUPPLY: WOMEN IN PSYCHOLOGY. Paper presented at the meeting of the American Psychological Association, San Francisco, California. Data compiled by Office of Demographic, Employment and Educational Research, Education Directorate American Psychological Association 8/91.

KOLB, B., & WHISHAW, I. Q. (1985). FUNDAMENTALS OF HUMAN NEUROPSYCHOLOGY (2nd ed.). San Francisco: Freeman.

KOLODNY, J. A., (1994). Memory processes in classification learning. PSYCHOLOGICAL SCIENCE, *5*, 164–169.

KOOB, G. F., & BLOOM, F. E. (1988). Cellular and molecular mechanisms of drug dependence. SCIENCE, *242*, 715–723.

KORNER, A. F. (1973). Individual differences at birth: Implications for early experience and later development. In J. C. Westman (Ed.), INDIVIDUAL DIFFERENCES IN CHILDREN. New York: Wiley.

KORNHABER, M., KRECHEVSKY, M., & GARDNER, H. (1990). Engaging intelligence. EDUCATIONAL PSYCHOLOGIST, *25* (3 & 4), 177–199.

KORNITZER, M., MAGOTTEAU, V., & collaborators. (1982). Angiographic findings and the Type A pattern assessed by means of the Bortner scale. JOURNAL OF BEHAVIORAL MEDICINE, *5*, 313–320.

KOSA, J., & ZOLA, I. K. (Eds.) (1975). POVERTY AND HEALTH: A SOCIOLOGICAL ANALYSIS. Cambridge, MA: Harvard University Press.

KOSAMBI, D. D. (1967). Living prehistory in India. SCIENTIFIC AMERICAN, *215*, 105.

KOSSLYN, S. M. (1980). IMAGE AND MIND. Cambridge, MA: Harvard University Press.

KOSSLYN, S. M. (1983). GHOSTS IN THE MIND'S MACHINE. New York: Norton.

KOSSLYN, S. M. (1988). Aspects of a cognitive neuroscience of mental imagery: SCIENCE, *240*, 1621–1626.

KOSSLYN, S. M. (1994). THE RESOLUTION OF THE IMAGERY DEBATE. Cambridge, MA: MIT Press.

KOSSLYN, S. M., ALPERT, N. M., THOMPSON, W. L., MALJKOVIC, V., WEISE, S. B., CHABRIS, C. F., HAMILTON, S. E., RAUCH, S. L., & BUONANNO, F. S. (1993). Visual mental imagery activates topographically organized visual cortex. JOURNAL OF COGNITIVE NEUROSCIENCE, *5*, 263–287.

KOSSLYN, S. M., BALL, T. M., & REISER, B. J. (1978). Visual images preserve metric spatial information: Evidence from studies of image scanning. JOURNAL OF EXPERIMENTAL PSYCHOLOGY: HUMAN PERCEPTION AND PERFORMANCE, *4*, 47–60.

KOSSLYN, S. M. & KOENIG, O. (1992). WET MIND: THE NEW COGNITIVE NEUROSCIENCE. The Free Press, New York.

KOULACK, D., & GOODENOUGH, D. R. (1976). Dream recall and dream recall failure: An arousal-retrieval model. PSHCHOLOGICAL BULLETIN, *83*, 975–984.

KRAUT, (1982). Social presence, facial feedback, and emotion. JOURNAL OF PERSONALITY AND SOCIAL PSYCHOLOGY, *42*, 853–863.

KREITMAN, N. (1977). PARASUICIDE. London: Wiley.

KRIPKE, D. F. (1985). Biological Rythms. In G. L. Klerman, M. M. Weissman, P. S. Applebaum, & L. H. Roth, (Eds.), PSYCHIATRY (Vol. 3). Philadelphia: Lippincott.

KRIPKE, D. F., & GILLIN, J. C. (1985). Sleep disorders. In G. L. Klerman, M. M. Weissman, P. S. Applebaum, & L. N. Roth (Eds.), PSYCHIATRY (Vol. 3). Philadelphia: Lippincott.

KRYSTAL, H. (1968). MASSIVE PSYCHIC TRAUMA. New York: International University Press.

KUBIS, J. F. (1962). Cited in B. M. Smith (1967), The polygraph. SCIENTIFIC AMERICAN, *216*, 21, 25–31, 146.

KUIPER, N. A., MACDONALD, M. R., & DERRY, P. A. (1983). Parameters of a depressive self-schema. In J. Suls, & A. G. Greenwald (Eds.), PSYCHOLOGICAL PERSPECTIVES ON THE SELF (Vol. 2). Hillsdale, NJ: Erlbaum.

KUIPER, N. A., OLINGER, L. J., MACDONALD, M. R., & SHAW, B. F. (1985). Self-schema processing of depressed and nondepressed content: The effects of vulnerability on depression. SOCIAL COGNITION, *3*, 77–93.

KUMAN, I. G., FEDROV, C. N., & NOVIKOVA, L.

A. (1983). Investigation of the sensitive period in the development of the human visual system. ZH. VYSSH. NERV. DEYAT (JOURNAL OF HIGHER NERVOUS ACTIVITY), *33*, 434–441.

KURTINES, W., & GREIF, E. B. (1974). The development of moral thought: Review and evaluation of Kohlberg's approach. PSYCHOLOGICAL BULLETIN, *81*, 453–470.

KURTZ, P. (Ed.). (1985). A SKEPTIC'S HANDBOOK OF PARAPSYCHOLOGY. Buffalo: Prometheus Books.

LACKNER, J., & GARRETT, M. (1973). Resolving ambiguity: Effects of biasing context in the unattended ear. COGNITION, *1*, 359–372.

LAGERSPETZ, K., VIEMERO, V., & AKADEMI, A. (1986). Television and aggressive behavior among Finnish children. In L. R. Huesmann & L. D. Eron (Eds.), TELEVISION AND THE AGGRESSIVE CHILD. New York: Erlbaum.

LAMB, M. E., & BORNSTEIN, M. H. (1987). DEVELOPMENT IN INFANCY: AN INTRODUCTION (2nd ed.). New York: Random House.

LAND, E. H. (1977). The retinex theory of color vision. SCIENTIFIC AMERICAN, *237*, 108–128.

LANGLOIS, J. H., & DOWNS, A. C. (1980). Mothers, fathers, and peers as socialization agents of sex-typed play behaviors in young children. CHILD DEVELOPMENT, *51*, 1237–1247.

LAPIERE, R. (1934). Attitudes versus actions. SOCIAL FORCES, *13*, 230–237.

LARKIN, J. H., MCDERMOTT, J., SIMON, D. P., & SIMON, H. A. (1980). Expert and novice performance in solving physics problems. SCIENCE, *208*, 1335–1342.

LATANÉ, B., & DARLEY, J. M. (1968). Group inhibition of bystander intervention in emergencies. JOURNAL OF PERSONALITY AND SOCIAL PSYCHOLOGY, *10*, 215–221.

LATANÉ, B., & DARLEY, J. M. (1970). THE UNRESPONSIVE BYSTANDER: WHY DOESN'T HE HELP? New York: Appleton-Century-Crofts.

LATANÉ, B., NIDA, S. A., & WILSON, D. W. (1981). The effects of group size on helping behavior. In J. P. Rushton & R. M. Sorrentino (Eds.), ALTRUISM AND HELPING BEHAVIOR: SOCIAL PERSONALITY, AND DEVELOPMENTAL PERSPECTIVES. Hillsdale, NJ: Erlbaum.

LATANÉ, B., & RODIN, J. (1969). A lady in distress: Inhibiting effects of friends and strangers on bystander intervention. JOURNAL OF EXPERIMENTAL AND SOCIAL PSYCHOLOGY, *5*, 189–202.

LATANÉ, B., WILLIAMS, K. D., & HARKINS, S. G. (1979). Many hands make light work: The causes and consequences of social loafing. JOURNAL OF PERSONALITY AND SOCIAL PSYCHOLOGY, *37*, 822–832.

LAUDENSLAGER, M. L., RYAN, S. M., DRUGAN, R. C., HYSON, R. L., & MAIER, S. F. (1983). Coping and immunosuppression: Inescapable but not escapable shock suppresses lymphocyte proliferation. SCIENCE, *221*, 568–570.

LAUMANN, E. O., GAGNON, J. H. MICHAEL, R. T., & MICHAELS, S. (1994). THE SOCIAL ORGANIZATION OF SEXUALITY: SEXUAL PRACTICES IN THE UNITED STATES. Chicago: University of Chicago Press.

LAURENCE, J. R. (1980). DUALITY AND DISSOCIATION IN HYPNOSIS. Unpublished M. A. thesis, Concordia University, Montreal.

LAWLER, R. W., & YAZDANI, M. (Eds.) (1987). ARTIFICIAL INTELLIGENCE AND EDUCATION (Vol. 1). Norwood, NJ: Ablex.

LAZARUS, R. S. (1961). Group therapy of phobic disorders by systematic densensitization. JOURNAL OF ABNORMAL AND SOCIAL PSYCHOLOGY, *63*, 504–510.

LAZARUS, R. S. (1991 a). Cognition and motivation in emotion. AMERICAN PSYCHOLOGIST, *46*, 352–367.

LAZARUS, R. S. (1991 b). EMOTION AND ADAPTATION. New York: Oxford University Press.

LAZARUS, R. S., & FOLKMAN, S. (1984). STRESS, APPRAISAL, AND COPING. New York: Springer.

LAZARUS, R. S., KANNER, A. D., & FOLKMAN, S. (1980). Emotions: A cognitive-phenomenological analysis. In R. Plutchik & H. Kellerman (Eds.), EMOTION: THEORY, RESEARCH, AND EXPERIENCE (Vol. 1). New York: Academic Press.

LEAF, P. J., & BRUCE, M. L. (1987). Gender differences in the use of mental health-related services: A re-examination. JOURNAL OF HEALTH AND SOCIAL BEHAVIOR, *28*, 171–183.

LE BON, G. (1985). THE CROWD. London: Ernest Benn.

LE DEOX, J. E. (1989). Cognitive-emotional interactions in the brain. COGNITION AND EMOTION, *3*, 267–289.

LEE, J. A. (1973). THE COLORS OF LOVE: AN EXPLORATION OF THE WAYS OF LOVING. Don Mills, Ontario: New Press.

LEE, J. A. (1977). A typology of styles of loving. PERSONALITY AND SOCIAL PSYCHOLOGY BULLETIN, *3*, 173–182.

LEE, J. A. (1988). Love-styles. In R. J. Sternberg & M. L. Barnes (Eds.), THE PSYCHOLOGY OF LOVE (pp. 38–67). New Haven, CT: Yale University Press.

LEFF, J., & VAUGHN, C. (1985). EXPRESSED EMOTION IN FAMILIES. New York: Guilford Press.

LENNEBERG, E. H. (1967). BIOLOGICAL FOUNDATIONS OF LANGUAGE. New York: Wiley.

LERNER, R., KARSON, M., MEISELS, M., & KNAPP, J. R. (1975). Actual and perceived attitudes of late adolescents: The phenomenon of the generation gaps. JOURNAL OF GENETIC PSYCHOLOGY, *126*, 197–207.

LEROUX, J. A. (1986). Suicidal behavior and gifted adolescents. Roeper Rev., *9*(2), 77–79.

LESLIE, A. M. (1987). Do infants perceive causality? COGNITION, *22*, 127–139.

LEVAV, I., FRIEDLANDER, Y., KARK, J. D., & PERITZ, E. (1988). An epidemiologic study of mortality among bereaved parents. THE NEW ENGLAND JOURNAL OF MEDICINE, *319*, 457–461.

LEVAY, S. (1991). A difference in hypothalmic structure between heterosexual and homosexual men. SCIENCE, *253*, 1034–1037.

LEVENSON, R., EKMAN, P., FRIESEN, W., FRIJDA, N., KUIPERS, P., & SCHURE, E. (1989, August). Relations among emotion, appraisal, and emotional action readiness. JOURNAL OF PERSONALITY AND SOCIAL PSYCHOLOGY, *57*(2), 212–228.

LEVENSON, R. W., EKMAN, P., HEIDER, K., & FRIESIN, W. V. (1992). Emotion and autonomic nervous system activity in an Indonesian culture. JOURNAL OF PERSONALITY AND SOCIAL PSYCHOLOGY, *62*, 927–988.

LEVINE, D. N., WARACH, J., & FARAH, M. J. (1988). Two visual systems in mental imagery: Dissociation of "what" and "where" in imagery disorders due to bilateral posterior cerebral lesions. NEUROLOGY, *35*, 1010–1018.

LEVINE, S. (1960). Stimulation in infancy. SCIENTIFIC AMERICAN, *202*, 80–86.

LEVINGER, G., SENN, D. J., & JORGENSEN, B. W. (1970). Progress toward permanence in courtship: A test of the Kerckhoff-Davis hypotheses. SOCIOMETRY, *33*, 427–443.

LEVINSON, D. J., DARROW, C., KLEIN, E. B., LEVINSON, M. H., & McKEE, B. (1978). THE SEASONS OF A MAN'S LIFE. New York: Knopf.

LEVY, J. (1985). Right brain, left brain: Facts and fiction. PSYCHOLOGY TODAY, *19*, 38–44.

LEVY, M. B., & DAVIS, K. E. (1988). Love styles and attachment styles compared: Their relation to each other and to various relationship characteristics. JOURNAL OF SOCIAL AND PERSONAL RELATIONSHIPS, *I*, 439–471.

LEVY, S. M., & HEIDEN, I., (1991). Depression, distress and immunity: Risk factors for infectious disease. STRESS MEDICINE, *7*, 45–51.

LEVY, S., HERBERMAN, R., WHITESIDE, T., SANZO, K., LEE, J., & KIRKWOOD, J. (1990). Perceived social support and tumor estrogen/progesterone receptor status as predictors of natural killer cell activity in breast cancer patients. PSYCHOSOMATIC MEDICINE, *52*, 73–85.

LEWINSOHN, P. M., ANTONUCCIO, D. O, STEINMETZ, J. L., & TERI, L. (1984). THE COPING WITH DEPRESSION COURSE: PSYCHOEDUCATIONAL INTERVENTION FOR UNIPOLAR DEPRESSION. Eugene, OR: Castalia.

LEWINSOHN, P. M., FENN, D., & FRANKLIN, J. (1982). The relationship of age of onset to duration of episode in unipolar depression. Unpublished manuscript, University of Oregon.

LEWINSOHN, P. M., HOBERMAN, H., TERI, L., HAUTZINER, M. (1985). An integrative theory of depression. In S. Reiss & R. Bootsin, (Eds.), THEORETICAL ISSUES IN BEHAVIOR THERAPY. New York: Academic Press.

LEWINSOHN, P. M., MISCHEL, W., CHAPLIN, W., & BARTON, R. (1980). Social competence and depression: The role of illusory self-perceptions. JOURNAL OF ABNORMAL PSYCHOLOGY, *89*, 203–212.

LEY, R. G., & BRYDEN, M. P. (1982). A dissociation of right and left hemispheric effects for recognizing emotional tone and verbal content. BRAIN AND COGNITION, *I*, 3–9.

LIBERMAN, A. M., COOPER, F., SHANK-

WEILER, D., & STUDERT-KENNEDY, M. (1967). Perception of the speech code. PSYCHOLOGICAL REVIEW, *74*, 431–459.

LICKEY, M. E. & GORDON, B. (1991). MEDICINE AND MENTAL ILLNESS. New York: Freeman.

LIEBERMAN, L. R., & DUNLAP, J. T. (1979). O'Leary and Borkovec's conceptualization of placebo: The placebo paradox. AMERICAN PSYCHOLOGIST, *34*, 553–554.

LIEM, J. H. (1974). Effects of verbal communications of parents and children: A comparison of normal and schizophrenic families. JOURNAL OF CONSULTING AND CLINICAL PSYCHOLOGY, *42*, 438–450.

LINDZEY, G., & ARONSON, E. (Eds.) (1985). THE HANDBOOK OF SOCIAL PSYCHOLOGY (3rd ed.). Hillsdale, NJ: Erlbaum.

LINN, R. L. (1982). Ability Testing: Individual differences, prediction, and differential prediction. In A. Wigdor & W. Gardner, (Eds.), ABILITY TESTING: USES, CONSEQUENCES, AND CONTROVERSIES. Washington, DC: National Academy Press.

LIPPA, R. A. (1994). INTRODUCTION TO SOCIAL PSYCHOLOGY (2nd ed.). Belmont, CA: Wadsworth.

LIPPERT, W. W., & SENTER, R. J. (1966). Electrodermal responses in the sociopath. PSYCHONOMIC SCIENCE, *4*, 25–26.

LIVINGSTONE, M., & HUBEL, D. (1988). Segregation of form, color, movement, and depth: Anatomy, physiology, and perception. SCIENCE, *240*, 740–750.

LOEB, G. (1985). The functional replacement of the ear. SCIENTIFIC AMERICAN, *252*, 104–111.

LOFTUS, E. F. (1993). The reality of repressed memories, AMERICAN PSYCHOLOGIST, *48*, 518–537.

LOFTUS, E. F. & COAN, D. (1994). The construction of childhood memories. In D. Peters (Ed.), THE CHILD WITNESS IN CONTEXT: COGNITIVE, SOCIAL, AND LEGAL PERSPECTIVES. New York: Kluwer.

LOFTUS, E. F., & LOFTUS, G. R. (1980). On the permanence of stored informaiton in the human brain. AMERICAN PSYCHOLOGIST, *35*, 409–420.

LOFTUS, E. F., SCHOOLER, J. W., & WAGENAAR, W. A. (1985). The fate of memory: Comment on McCloskey and Zaragoza. JOURNAL OF EXPERIMENTAL PSYCHOLOGY: GENERAL, *114* 375–380.

LOFTUS, G. R., & LOFTUS, E. F. (1975). HUMAN MEMORY: THE PROCESSING OF INFORMATION. New York: Halstead Press.

LOGUE, A. W. (1991). THE PSYCHOLOGY OF EATING AND DRINKING: AN INTRODUCTION (2nd edition). New York: Freeman.

LONGLEY, J., & PRUITT, D. G. (1980). Groupthink: A critique of Janis's theory. In L. Wheeler (Ed.), REVIEW OF PERSONALITY AND SOCIAL PSYCHOLOGY (Vol. 1). Beverly Hills, CA: Sage.

LOOMIS, A. L., HARVEY, E. N., & HOBART, G. A. (1937). Cerebral states during sleep as studied by human potentials. JOURNAL OF EXPERIMENTAL PSYCHOLOGY, *21*, 127–144.

LOPEZ, A., ATRAN, S., MEDIN, D. L., SMITH, E. E., & COLEY, J. (1994). The tree of life: Universals of folkbiological taxonomies and inductions. Unpublished manuscript, University of Michigan.

LORD, C. G., ROSS, L., & LEPPER, M. R. (1979). Biased assimilation and attitude polarization: The effects of prior theories on subsequently considered evidence. JOURNAL OF PERSONALITY AND SOCIAL PSYCHOLOGY, *37*, 2098–2109.

LORENZ, K. (1966). ON AGGRESSION. New York: Harcourt Brace Jovanovich.

LORENZ, K. (1981). THE FOUNDATIONS OF ETHOLOGY. New York: Springer-Verlag.

LOVAAS, O. I. (1987). Behavioral treatment and abnormal education and intellectual functioning in young autistic children. JOURNAL OF CONSULTING AND CLINICAL PSYCHOLOGY, *55*, 3–9.

LOVAAS, O. I., FREITAG, G., GOLD, V. J., & KASSORLA, I. C. (1965). Recording apparatus for observation of behaviors of children in free play settings. JOURNAL OF EXPERIMENTAL CHILD PSYCHOLOGY, *2*, 108–120.

LOVE, R. E., & GREENWALD, A. C. (1978). Cognitive responses to persuasion as mediators of opinion change. JOURNAL OF SOCIAL PSYCHOLOGY, *104*, 231–241.

LOWINGER, P., & DOBIE, S. (1969). What makes the placebo work? A study of placebo response rate. ARCHIVES OF GENERAL PSYCHIATRY, *20*, 84–88.

LUBORSKY, L. (1984). PRINCIPLES OF PSYCHOANALYTIC PSYCHOTHERAPY: A MANUAL FOR SUPPORTIVE-EXPRESSIVE TREATMENT. New York: Basic Books.

LUBORSKY, L. L., MCLELLAN, A. T., WOODY, G. E., O'BRIEN, E. P., & AUERBACH, A. (1985). Therapist success and its determinants. ARCHIVES OF GENERAL PSYCHIATRY, *42*, 602–611.

LUCHINS, A. (1957). Primacy-recency in impression formation. In C. L. Hovland, (Ed.), THE ORDER OF PRESENTATION IN PERSUASION. New Haven: Yale University Press.

LUDWIG, A. M., BRANDSMA, J. M., WILBUR, C. B., BENDFELDT, F., & JAMESON, D. H. (1972). The objective study of a multiple personality. ARCHIVES OF GENERAL PSYCHIATRY, *26*, 298–310.

LUMSDAINE, A. A., & JANIS, I. L. (1953). Resistance to "counter-propaganda" produced by one-sided and "two-sided propaganda" presentations. PUBLIC OPINION QUARTERLY, *17*, 311–318.

LUNDIN, R. W. (1985). THEORIES AND SYSTEMS OF PSYCHOLOGY, (3rd ed.). Lexington, MA: Heath.

LURIA, Z., & RUBIN, J. Z. (1974). The eye of the beholder: Parents' views on sex of newborns. AMERICAN JOURNAL OF ORTHOPSYCHIATRY, *44*, 512–519.

LYCAN, W. G. (1987). CONSCIOUSNESS. Cambridge: MIT Press.

LYKKEN, D. T. (1957). A study of anxiety in the sociopathic personality. JOURNAL OF ABNORMAL AND SOCIAL PSYCHOLOGY, *55*, 6–10.

LYKKEN, D. T. (1980). TREMOR IN THE BLOOD: USES AND ABUSES OF THE LIE DETECTOR. New York: McGraw-Hill.

LYKKEN, D. T. (1982). Research with twins: The concept of emergenesis. THE SOCIETY FOR PSYCHOPHYSIOLOGICAL RESEARCH, *19*, 361–373.

LYKKEN, D. T. (1984). Polygraphic interrogation. NATURE, *307*, 681–684.

LYKKEN, D. T., MCGUE, M., TELLEGEN, A., & BOUCHARD, T. J., JR. (1992). Emergenesis: Genetic traits that may not run in families. AMERICAN PSYCHOLOGIST, *47*, 1565–1577.

LYONS-RUTH, K., CONNELL, D. B., ZOLL, D., & STAHL, J. (1987). Infants at social risk: Relations among infant maltreatment, maternal behavior, and infant attachment behavior. DEVELOPMENTAL PSYCHOLOGY, *23*, 223–232.

MAASS, A., & CLARK, R. D., III (1983). Internalization versus compliance: Differential processes underlying minority influence and conformity. EUROPEAN JOURNAL OF SOCIAL PSYCHOLOGY, *13*, 45–55.

MAASS, A., & CLARK, R. D., III (1984). Hidden impact of minorities: Fifteen years of minority influence research. PSYCHOLOGICAL BULLETIN, *95*, 428–450.

MACAULAY, J. (1970). A shill for charity. In J. Macaulay & L. Berkowitz (Eds.), ALTRUISM AND HELPING BEHAVIOR (pp. 43–59). New York: Academic Press.

MACCOBY, E. E. (1980). SOCIAL DEVELOPMENT: PSYCHOLOGICAL GROWTH AND THE PARENT-CHILD RELATIONSHIP. New York: Harcourt Brace Jovanovich.

MACCOBY, E. E., & JACKLIN, C. N. (1974). THE PSYCHOLOGY OF SEX DIFFERENCES. Stanford: Stanford University Press.

MACK, J. E. (1980). Psychoanalysis and biography: Aspects of a developing affinity. JOURNAL OF AMERICAN PSYCHOANALYTIC ASSOCIATION, *28*, 543–562.

MADDI, S., & COSTA, P. (1972). HUMANISM IN PERSONOLOGY: ALLPORT, MASLOW, AND MURRAY. Chicago: Aldine.

MAHER, B. A. (1966). PRINCIPLES OF PSYCHOTHERAPY: AN EXPERIMENTAL APPROACH. New York: McGraw-Hill.

MAIER, S. F., & SELIGMAN, M. E. P. (1976). Learned helplessness: Theory and evidence. JOURNAL OF EXPERIMENTAL PSYCHOLOGY: GENERAL, *105*, 3–46.

MAIN, M., & CASSIDY, J. (1988). Categories of response to reunion with parents at age 6: Predictable from infant attachment classifications and stable over a 1-month period. DEVELOPMENTAL PSYCHOLOGY, *24*, 415–426.

MAIN, M., & SOLOMON, J. (1986). Discovery of an insecure-disorganized/disoriented attachment pattern: Procedures, findings and implications for the classification of behavior. In T. B. Brazelton, & M. Yogman (Eds.), AFFECTIVE DEVELOPMENT IN INFANCY (pp. 95–124). Norwood, NJ: Ablex.

MALINOWSKI B. (1927). SEX AND REPRESSION IN SAVAGE SOCIETY. London: Humanities Press.

MALOF, M., & LOTT, A. J. (1962). Ethnocentrism and the acceptance of Negro support in a group pressure situation. JOURNAL OF ABNORMAL AND SOCIAL PSYCHOLOGY, *65*, 254–258.

MALONEY, L. T., & WANDELL, B. A. (1986). Color constancy: A method for recovering surface spectral reflectance. JOURNAL OF THE OPTICAL SOCIETY OF AMERICA, *3*, 29–33.

MALT, B. C. (1985). The role of discourse structure in understanding anaphora. JOURNAL OF MEMORY AND LANGUAGE, *24*, 271–289.

MANDLER, G. (1982). MIND AND EMOTION. New York: Norton.

MANDLER, J. (1983). Representation. In P. H. Mussen (Ed.) HANDBOOK OF CHILD PSYCHOLOGY (Vol. 3). New York: Wiley.

MANUCK, S. B., KAPLAN, J. R., & MATTHEWS, K. A. (1986). Behavioral antecedents of coronary heart disease and atherosclerosis. ARTERIOSCLEROSIS, *6*, 1–14.

MANUCK, S. B., & KRANTZ, D. S. (1986). Psychophysiologic reactivity in coronary heart disease and essential hypertension. In K. A. Matthews, S. M. Weiss, T. Detre, T. M. Dembroski, B. Falkner, S. B. Manuck, & R. B. Williams J. (Eds.), HANDBOOK OF STRESS, REACTIVITY, AND CARDIOVASCULAR DISEASE. New York: Wiley.

MARBLY, N. (1987). But you weren't there. In T. Williams (Ed.) POSTTRAMUATIC STRESS DISORDERS: A HANDBOOK FOR CLINICIANS. Cincinati, OH: Disabled American Veterans.

MARCEL, A. M., & BISIACH, E. (Eds.) (1988). CONSCIOUSNESS IN CONTEMPORARY SCIENCE. New York: Oxford Unversity Press.

MARCIA, J. E. (1966). Development and validation of ego identify status. JOURNAL OF PERSONALITY AND SOCIAL PSYCHOLOGY, *3*, 551–558.

MARCIA, J. E. (1980). Identity in adolescence. In J. Adelson (Ed.) HANDBOOK OF ADOLESCENT PSYCHOLOGY New York: Wiley.

MARCUS, J., HANS, S. L. NAGLER, S., AUERBACK, J. G., MIRSKY, A. F., & AUBREY, A. (1987). A review of the NIMH Israeli Kibbutz-city study. SCHIZOPHRENIA BULLETIN, *13*, 425–438.

MARDSEN, G. (1971). Content analysis studies of psychotherapy: 1954 through 1968. In A. E. Bergin & S. L. Garfield (Ed.), HANDBOOK OF PSYCHOTHERAPY AND BEHAVIOR CHANGE. New York: Wiley.

MARKMAN, E. M. (1979). Classes and collections: Conceptual organization and numerical abilities. COGNITIVE PSYCHOLOGY, *11*, 395–411.

MARKMAN, E. M. (1987). How children constrain the possible meanings of words. In U. Neisser (Ed.), CONCEPTS AND CONCEPTUAL DEVELOPMENT: ECOLOGICAL AND INTELLECTUAL FACTORS IN CATEGORIZATIONS. New York: Cambridge University Press.

MARKUS, H. (1977). Self-schemata and processing information about the self. JOURNAL OF PERSONALITY AND SOCIAL PSYCHOLOGY, *35*, 63–78.

MARKUS, H., & NURIUS, P. (1986). Possible selves. AMERICAN PSYCHOLOGIST, *41*, 954–969.

MARLATT, G. A., BAER, J. S., DONOVAN, D. M., & KIVLAHAN, D. R. (1988). Addictive behaviors: Etiology and treatment. In M. R. Rosenzweig & L. W. Porter, (Eds.), ANNUAL REVIEW OF PSYCHOLOGY (Vol. 39). Palo Alto, CA: Annual Reviews.

MARR, D. (1982). VISION. San Francisco: Freeman.

MARSHALL, G., & ZIMBARDO, P. G. (1979). Affective consequences of inadequately explained physiological arousal. JOURNAL OF PERSONALITY AND SOCIAL PSYCHOLOGY, *37*, 970–988.

MARTIN, C. L., & HALVERSON, C. F. (1983). A schematic processing model of sex typing and stereotyping in children. CHILD DEVELOPMENT, *52*, 1119–1134.

MASLACH, C. (1979). The emotional consequences of arousal without reason. In Izard, C. E. (Ed.), EMOTION IN PERSONALITY AND PSYCHOPATHOLOGY. New York: Plenum.

MASLOW, A. H. (1967). Self-actualization and beyond. In J. F. T. Bugenthal (Ed.), CHALLENGES OF HUMANISTIC PSYCHOLOGY. New York: McGraw-Hill.

MASLOW, A. H. (1970). MOTIVATION AND PERSONALITY (2nd ed.). New York: Harper and Row.

MASSON, J. M. (1984). THE ASSAULT ON TRUTH. New York: Farrar, Straus & Giroux, Inc.

MASTERS, W. H., & JOHNSON, V. E. (1966). HUMAN SEXUAL RESPONSE. Boston: Little, Brown.

MASUDA, M. & HOLMES, T. H. (1978). Life events: perceptions and frequencies. PSYCHOSOMATIC MEDICINE, *40*, 236–261.

MATAS, L., AREND, R. A., & SROUFE, L. A. (1978). Continuity of adaption in the second year: The relationship between quality of attachment and later competence. CHILD DEVELOPMENT, *49*, 547–556.

MATHES, E. W. (1975). The effects of physical attractiveness and anxiety on heterosexual attraction over a series of five encounters. JOURNAL OF MARRIAGE AND THE FAMILY, *37*, 769–773.

MATTHEWS, D. F. (1972). Response patterns of single neurons in the tortoise olfactory epithelium and olfactory bulb. JOURNAL OF GENERAL PHYSIOLOGY, *60*, 166–180.

MATTHEWS, K. A., WEISS, S. M., DETRE, T., DEMBROSKI, T. M., FALKNER, B., MANUCK, S., & WILLIAMS, R. B., JR. (Eds.) (1986). HANDBOOK OF STRESS REACTIVITY AND CARDIOVASCULAR DISEASE. New York: Wiley.

MAYER, R. E. (1983). THINKING, PROBLEM SOLVING AND COGNITION. New York: Freeman.

MCALISTER, A., PERRY, C., KILLEN, J., SLINKARD, L. A., & MACCOBY, N. (1980). Pilot study of smoking, alcohol and drug abuse prevention. AMERICAN JOURNAL OF PUBLIC HEALTH, *70*, 719–721.

MCBURNEY, D. H. (1978). Psychological dimensions and the perceptual analysis of taste. In E. C. Carterette, & M. P. Friedman (Eds.), HANDBOOK OF PERCEPTION (Vol. 6). New York: Academic Press.

MCCARTHY, R. A., & WARRINGTON, E. K. (1987a). The double dissociation of short-term memory for lists and sentences. BRAIN, *10*, 1545–1563.

MCCARTHY, R. A., & WARRINGTON, E. K. (1987b). Understanding: A function of short-term memory? BRAIN, *110*, 1565–1578.

MCCAULEY, C. (1989). The nature of social influence in groupthink: Compliance and internalization. JOURNAL OF PERSONALITY AND SOCIAL PSYCHOLOGY, *57*, 250–260.

MCCLANAHAN, K. K., GOLD, J. A., LENNEY, E., RYCKMAN, R. M., & KULBERG, G. E. (1990). Infatuation and attraction to a dissimilar other: Why is love blind? JOURNAL OF SOCIAL PSYCHOLOGY, *130*, 433–445.

MCCLELLAND, J. L., & RUMELHART, D. E. (1981). An interactive model of context effects in letter perception: Pt. 1. An account of basic findings. PSYCHOLOGICAL REVIEW, *88*, 375–407.

MCCLELLAND, J. L., RUMELHART, D. E., & THE PDP RESEARCH GROUP (1986). PARALLEL DISTRIBUTED PROCESSING: EXPLORATIONS IN THE MICROSTRUCTURE OF COGNITION (Vol. 2). Cambridge, MA: Bradford Brooks/MIT Press.

MCCLINTOCK, M. K. (1971). Menstrual synchrony and suppression. NATURE, *229*, 244–245.

MCCLOSKEY, M., WIBLE, C. G., & COHEN, N. J. (1988). Is there a flashbulb-memory system? JOURNAL OF EXPERIMENTAL PSYCHOLOGY, *117*, 171–181.

MCCLOSKEY, M., & COHEN, N. J. (1989). Castastrophic interference in connectionist networks: The sequential learning problem. In G. H. Bower (Ed.). THE PSYCHOLOGY OF LEARNING AND MOTIVATION (Vol. 24, pp. 109–164). New York: Academic Press.

MCCONAGHY, M. J. (1979). Gender permanence and the genital basis of gender. Stages in the development of constancy of gender identity. CHILD DEVELOPMENT, *50*, 1223–1226.

MCCRAE, R. R., & COSTA, P. T., JR. (1987). Validation of the five-factor model of personality across instruments and observers. JOURNAL OF PERSONALITY AND SOCIAL PSYCHOLOGY, *52*, 81–90.

MCDOUGALL, W. (1908). SOCIAL PSYCHOLOGY. New York: G. P. Putnam's Sons.

MCELREE, B. DOSHER, B. A. (1989). Serial position and set size in short-term memory. The time course of recognition. JOURNAL OF EXPERIMENTAL PSYCHOLOGY: GENERAL, *118*, 346–373.

MCFARLAND, D. (1985). ANIMAL BEHAVIOUR: PSYCHOBIOLOGY, ETHOLOGY AND EVOLUTION. Menlo Park, CA: Benjamin-Cummings.

MCFARLAND, S. G., AGEYEV, V. S., & ABALAKINA-PAAP, M. A. (1992). Authoritarianism in the former Soviet Union. JOURNAL OF PERSONALITY AND SOCIAL PSYCHOLOGY, *63*, 1004–1010.

MCGHIE, A., & CHAPMAN, J. (1961). Disorders of attention and perception in early schizophrenia. BRITISH JOURNAL OF MEDICAL PSYCHOLOGY, *34*, 103–116.

MCGRATH, E., KEITA, G. P., STRICKLAND, B. R., & RUSSO, N. F. (1990). WOMEN AND DEPRESSION: RISK FACTORS AND TREATMENT ISSUES. Washington, DC: American Psychological Association.

MCGRAW, M. B. (1975). GROWTH: A STUDY OF JOHNNY AND JIMMY. New York: Acno Press (Originally published 1935).

MCGUFFIN, P., KATZ, R., & RUTHERFORD, J. (1991). Nature, nurture and depression: A twin study. PSYCHOLOGICAL MEDICINE, *21*, 329–335.

MCGUFFIN, P., SARGEANT, M., HETT, G., TIDMARSH, S., WHATLEY, S., & MARCHBANKS, R. M. (1990). Exclusion of a schizophrenia susceptibility gene from the chromosome 5q11-q13 region. New data and a reanalysis of previous reports. AMERICAN JOURNAL OF HUMAN GENETICS. *47*, 524–535.

MCGUIRE, W. J. (1964). Inducing resistance to persuasion: some contemporary approaches. In L. Berkowitz (Ed.), ADVANCES IN EXPERIMENTAL SOCIAL PSYCHOLOGY (Vol. 1). Academic Press.

MCGUIRE, W. J., & PAPAGEORGIS, D. (1961). The relative efficacy of various types of prior belief-defense in producing immunity against persuasion. JOURNAL OF ABNORMAL AND SOCIAL PSYCHOLOGY, *62*, 327–337.

MCHUGH, P. R. (1990). Clinical issues in food ingestion and body weight maintenance. In E. M. Stricker (Ed.), NEUROBIOLOGY OF FOOD AND FLUID INTAKE (pp. 531–547). New York: Plenum.

MCKENNA, R. J. (1972). Some effects of anxiety level and food cues on the eating behavior of obese and normal subjects. JOURNAL OF PERSONALITY AND SOCIAL PSYCHOLOGY, *22*, 311–319.

MCKENZIE, B., & OVER, R. (1983). Young infants fail to imitate facial and manual gestures. INFANT BEHAVIOR AND DEVELOPMENT, *6*, 85–95.

MCNALLY, R. J. (1990). Psychological approaches to panic disorder: A review. PSYCHOLOGY BULLETIN, *108*, 403–419.

MCNEAL, E. T., & CIMBOLIC, P. (1986). Antidepressants and biochemical theories of depression. PSYCHOLOGICAL BULLETIN, *99*, 361–374.

MCNEILL, D. (1966). Developmental psycholinguistics. In F. Smith & G. A. Miller (Eds.), THE GENESIS OF LANGUAGE: A PSYCHOLINGUISTIC APPROACH. Cambridge, MA: MIT Press.

MEANEY, M. J., AITKENS, D. H., BERKEL, C., BHATNAGAR, S., SARRIEAU, A., & SAPOLSKY, R. M. (1987). POST-NATAL HANDLING ATTENUATES AGE-RELATED CHANGES IN THE ADRENOCORTICAL STRESS RESPONSE AND SPATIAL MEMORY DEFICITS IN THE RAT. Paper presented at the 17th Annual Meeting of the Society of Neuroscience, New Orleans.

MECHANIC, D. (1962). STUDENTS UNDER STRESS. New York: Free Press.

MEDCOF, J., & ROTH, J. (Eds.) (1988). APPROACHES TO PSYCHOLOGY. Philadelphia: Open University Press, Milton Keynes.

MEDIN, D. L., & ROSS, B. H. (1992). COGNITIVE PSYCHOLOGY Fort Worth, TX: Harcourt Brace College Publishers.

MEDNICK, S. A., CANNON, T. PARNAS, J., & SCHULSINGER, F. (1989). 27 year follow-up of the Copenhagen high-risk for schizophrenia project: Why did some of the high-risk offspring become schizophrenic? (Abstract) SCHIZOPHRENIA RESEARCH, *2*, 14.

MEDNICK, S. A., MACHON, R., HUTTUNEN, M. O., & BONETT, D. (1988). Fetal viral infection and adult schizophrenia. ARCHIVES OF GENERAL PSYCHIATRY, *45*, 189–192.

MEEHL, P. E., & DAHLSTROM, W. G. (1960). Objective configural rules for discriminating psychotic from neurotic MMPI profiles. JOURNAL OF CONSULTING PSYCHOLOGY, *24*, 375–387.

MEGARGEE, E. I. (1972). THE CALIFORNIA PSYCHOLOGICAL INVENTORY HANDBOOK. San Francisco: Jossey-Bass.

MEICHENBAUM, D. H. (1985). STRESS INOCULATION TRAINING. New York: Pergamon.

MEICHENBAUM, D. H., & JAREMKO, M. E. (Eds.) (1983). STRESS REDUCTION AND PREVENTION. New York: Plenum.

MEIER, R. P. (1991). Language acquisition by deaf children. AMERICAN SCIENTIST, *79*, 60–76.

MELAMED, B. G., & SIEGEL, L. J. (1975). Reduction of anxiety in children facing hospitalization and surgery by use of filmed modeling. JOURNAL OF CONSULTING AND CLINICAL PSYCHIATRY, *43*, 511–521.

MELTON, A. W. (1963). Implications of short-term memory for a general theory of memory. JOURNAL OF VERBAL LEARNING AND VERBAL BEHAVIOR, *1*, 1–21.

MELTZOFF, A. N., & MOORE, M. K. (1977). Imitation of facial and manual gestures by human neonates. SCIENCE, *198*, 75–78.

MELTZOFF, A. N., & MOORE, M. K. (1983). Newborn infants imitate adult facial gestures. CHILD DEVELOPMENT, *54*, 702–709.

MELVILLE, J. (1977). PHOBIAS AND OBSESSIONS. New York: Coward, McCannn, & Geoghegan.

MELZAK, R. (1973). THE PUZZLE OF PAIN. New York: Basic Books.

MERVIS, C. B., & PANI, J. R. (1981). Acquisition of basic object categories. COGNITIVE PSYCHOLOGY, *12*, 496–522.

MERVIS, C. B., & ROSCH, E. (1981). Categorization of natural objects. In M. R. Rosenz & L. W. Porter (Eds.), ANNUAL REVIEW OF PSYCHOLOGY (Vol. 21). Palo Alto, CA: Annual Reviews.

METALSKY, G. I., HALBERSTADT, L. J., & ABRAMSON, L. Y. (1987). Vulnerability to depressive mood reactions: Toward a more powerful test of the diathesis-stress and causal meditation components of the reformulated theory of depression. JOURNAL OF PERSONALITY AND SOCIAL PSYCHOLOGY, *52*, 386–393.

MEYER, J. P., & PEPPER, S. (1977). Need compatability and marital adjustment in young married couples. JOURNAL OF PERSONALITY AND SOCIAL PSYCHOLOGY, *8*, 331–342.

MICHAELS, S., GAGNON, J. H., LAUMANN, E. O., & KOLATA, G. (1994). SEX IN AMERICA. Boston: Little, Brown.

MICHOTTE, A. (1963). THE PERCEPTION OF CAUSALITY. New York: Basic Books.

MIDDLETON, F. A., & STRICK, P. L. (1994). Anatomic evidence for cerebellar and basal ganglia involvement in higher cognitive function. SCIENCE, *266*, 458–463.

MILES, L. E., RAYNAL, D. M., & WILSON, M. A. (1977). Blind man living in normal society has circadian rhythm of 24.9 hours. SCIENCE, *198*, 421–423.

MILGRAM, S. (1963). Behavioral study of obedience. JOURNAL OF ABNORMAL AND SOCIAL PSYCHOLOGY, *67*, 371–378.

MILGRAM, S. (1974). OBEDIENCE TO AUTHORITY: AN EXPERIMENTAL VIEW. New York: Harper & Row.

MILLAR, M. G., & TESSER, A. (1989). The effects of affective-cognitive consistency and thought on the attitude-behavior relation. JOURNAL OF EXPERIMENTAL SOCIAL PSYCHOLOGY, *25*, 189–202.

MILLER, A. (1984). A transitional phase in gender constancy and its relationship to cognitive level and sex identification. CHILD STUDY JOURNAL, *13*, 259–275.

MILLER, D. T., & ROSS, M. (1975). Self-serving biases in attribution of causality: Fact or fiction? PSYCHOLOGICAL BULLETIN, *82*, 213–225.

MILLER, G. A. (1956). The magical number seven plus or minus two: Some limits on our capacity for processing information. PSYCHOLOGICAL REVIEW, *63*, 81–97.

MILLER, G. A., & GILDEA, P. M. (1987). How children learn words. SCIENTIFIC AMERICAN, *257*, 94–99.

MILLER, J. G. (1984). Culture and the development of everyday social explanation. JOURNAL OF PERSONALITY AND SOCIAL PSYCHOLOGY, *46*, 961–978.

MILLER, N. E., & KESSEN, M. L. (1952). Reward effects of food via stomach fistula compared with those of food via mouth. JOURNAL OF COMPARATIVE AND PHYSIOLOGICAL PSYCHOLOGY, *45*, 555–564.

MILLER, P. H. (1989). THEORIES OF DEVELOPMENTAL PSYCHOLOGY (2nd ed.). New York: Freeman.

MILNER, B. (1964). Some effects of frontal lobectomy in man. In J. M. Warren & K. Akert (Eds.), THE FRONTAL GRANULAR CORTEX AND BEHAVIOR. New York: McGraw-Hill.

MILNER, B., CORKIN, S., & TUEBER, H. L. (1968). Further analysis of the hippocampal amnesic syndrome: 14-year follow-up study of H. M. NEUROPSYCHOLOGIA, *6*, 215–234.

MINARD, R. D. (1952). Race relations in the Pocahontas coal field. JOURNAL OF SOCIAL ISSUES, *8*, 29–44.

MISCHEL, W. (1966). A social learning view of sex differences in behavior. In E. E. Maccoby (Ed.), THE DEVELOPMENT OF SEX DIFFERENCES. Stanford: Stanford University Press.

MISCHEL, W. (1968). PERSONALITY AND ASSESSMENT. New York: Wiley.

MISCHEL, W. (1973). Toward a cognitive social learning reconceptualization of personality. PSYCHOLOGICAL REVIEW, *80*, 272–283.

MISCHEL, W. (1993). INTRODUCTION TO PERSONALITY (5th ed.). Forth Worth: Harcourt Brace Jovanovich.

MISHKIN, M., & APPENZELLER, T. (1987). The anatomy of memory. SCIENTIFIC AMERICAN, *256*, 80–89.

MITA, T. H., DERMER, M., & KNIGHT, J. (1977). Reversed facial images and the mere-exposure hypthoses. JOURNAL OF PERSONALITY AND SOCIAL PSYCHOLOGY, *35*, 597–601.

MITCHEL, J. S., & KEESEY, R. E. (1974). The effects of lateral hypothalamic lesions and castration upon the body weight of male rats. BEHAVIORAL BIOLOGY, *11*, 69–82.

MOERMAN, D. E. (1981). Edible symbols: The effectiveness of placebos. In T. A. Sebok & R. Rosenthal (Eds.), THE CLEVER HANS PHENOMENON Annals of the New York Academy of Sciences (Vol. 364). New York: New York Academy of Science.

MOLDIN, S., GOTTESMAN, I. I., ERLENMEYER-KIMLING, L., & CORNBLATT, B. A. (1990). Psychometric deviance in offspring at risk for schizophrenia. PSYCHIATRY RESEARCH, *32*, 297–322.

MONAHAN, J. (1976). The prevention of violence. In J. Monahan (Ed.), COMMUNITY MENTAL HEALTH AND THE CRIMINAL JUSTICE SYSTEM. Elmsford, NY: Pergamon Press.

MONEY, J. (1980). Endocrine influences and psychosexual status spanning the life cycle. In H. M. Van Praag (Ed.), HANDBOOK OF BIOLOGICAL PSYCHIATRY (Part 3). New York: Marcel Dekker.

MONEY, J. (1987). Sin, sickness, or status? Homosexual gender identity and psychoneuroendocrinology. AMERICAN PSYCHOLOGIST, *42*, 384–400.

MONEY, J., & EHRHARDT, A. A. (1972). MAN AND WOMAN, BOY AND GIRL: THE DIFFERENTIATION AND DIMORPHISM OF GENDER IDENTITY FROM CONCEPTION TO MATURITY. Baltimore: Johns Hopkins Press.

MONEY, J. & LAMACZ, M. (1989). VANDALIZED LOVEMAPS: PARAPHILLIC OUTCOME OF SEVEN CASES IN PEDIATRIC SEXOLOGY. Buffalo, NY: Prometheus.

MONEY, J., SCHWARTZ, M., & LEWIS, V. G. (1984). Adult heterosexual status and fetal hormonal masculinization and demasculinization: 46, XX congenital virilizing adrenal hyperplasia and 46, XY androgen-insensitivity syndrome compared. PSYCHONEUROENDOCRINOLOGY, *9*, 405–414.

MONEY, J., WEIDEKING, C., WALKER, P. A., & GAIN, D. (1976). Combined antiandrogenic and counseling programs for treatment for 46 XY and 47 XXY sex offenders. In E. Sacher (Ed.), HORMONES, BEHAVIOR AND PSYCHOPATHOLOGY. New York: Raven Press.

MONSELL, S. (1979). Recency, immediate recognition memory, and reaction time. COGNITIVE PSYCHOLOGY, *10*, 465–501.

MONTAIGNE, M. de (1580/1943). Of the inconsistency of our actions. In D. M. Frame (Trans. Ed.), SELECTED ESSAYS. Roslyn, NY: Walter J. Black.

MOOK, D. C. (1987). MOTIVATION: THE ORGANIZATION OF ACTION. New York: Norton.

MOORE, B. C. J. (1982). AN INTRODUCTION TO THE PSYCHOLOGY OF HEARING (2nd ed.). New York: Academic Press.

MOOS, R. H. (1988). COPING RESPONSES INVENTORY MANUAL. Social Ecology Laboratory, Department of Psychiatry, Stanford University and Veterans Administration Medical Centers, Palo Alto, CA.

MORAN, J., & DESIMONE, R. (1985). Selective attention gates visual processing in the extrastriate cortex. SCIENCE, *229*, 782–784.

MORAY, N. (1969). ATTENTION: SELECTIVE PROCESSES IN VISION AND HEARING. London: Hutchinson.

MORELAND, R. L., & BEACH, S. R. (1992). Exposure effects in the classroom: The development of affinity among students. JOURNAL OF EXPERIMENTAL SOCIAL PSYCHOLOGY, *28*, 255–276.

MORELAND, R. L., & ZAJONC, R. B. (1979). Exposure effects may not depend on stimulus recognition. JOURNAL OF PERSONALITY AND SOCIAL PSYCHOLOGY, *37*, 1085–1089.

MORRIS, M., & PENG, K. (1995). Culture and cause: American and Chinese attributions for social and physical events. JOURNAL OF PERSONALITY AND SOCIAL PSYCHOLOGY.

MORROW, J., & NOLEN-HOEKSEMA, S. (1990). Effects of responses to depression on the remediation of depressive affect. JOURNAL OF PERSONALITY AND SOCIAL PSYCHOLOGY, *58*, 519–527.

MOSCOVICI, S. (1976). SOCIAL INFLUENCE AND SOCIAL CHANGE. London: Academic Press.

MOSCOVICI, S., LAGE, E., & NAFFRECHOUX, M. (1969). Influence of a consistent minority on the responses of a majority in a color perception task. SOCIOMETRY, *32*, 365–379.

MOSCOVICI, S., & ZAVALLONI, M. (1969). The group as a polarizer of attitudes. JOURNAL OF PERSONALITY AND SOCIAL PSYCHOLOGY, *12*, 125–135.

MOSKOWITZ, H. R., KUMRAICH, V., SHARMA, H., JACOBS, L., & SHARMA, S. D. (1975). Cross-cultural difference in simple taste preference. SCIENCE, *190*, 1217–1218.

MOWRER, O. H. (1947). On the dual nature of learning—A reinterpretation of "conditioning" and "problem-solving". HARVARD EDUCATIONAL REVIEW, *17*, 102–148.

MUKHERJEE, S., SHUKLA, S., WOODLE, J., ROSEN, A. M., & OLARTE, S. (1983). Misdiagnosis of schizophrenia in bipolar patients: A multiethnic comparison. AMERICAN JOURNAL OF PSYCHIATRY, *140*(2), 1571–1574.

MURDOCK, B. B., JR. (1962). The serial position effect in free recall. JOURNAL OF EXPERIMENTAL PSYCHOLOGY, *64*, 482–488.

MURPHY, G. E., & WETZEL, R. D. (1980). Suicide risk by birth cohort in the United States, 1949 to 1974. ARCHIVES OF GENERAL PSYCHIATRY, *37*, 519–523.

MURPHY, G. L., & BROWNELL, H. H. (1985). Category differentiation in object recognition: Typicality constraints on the basic category advantage. JOURNAL OF EXPERIMENTAL PSYCHOLOGY, *11*, 70.

MURPHY, K. R., & DAVIDSHOFER, C. O. (1991). PSYCHOLOGICAL TESING: PRINCIPLES AND APPLICATIONS (2nd ed.). Englewood Cliffs, NJ: Prentice Hall.

MURSTEIN, B. I. (1972). Physical attractiveness and marital choice. JOURNAL OF PERSONALITY AND SOCIAL PSYCHOLOGY, *22*, 8–12.

MUSSEN, P. H. (Ed.) (1983). HANDBOOK OF CHILD PSYCHOLOGY (4th ed.). New York: Wiley.

MUSSEN, P. H., CONGER, J. J., KAGAN, J., & HUSTON, A. C. (1990). CHILD DEVELOPMENT AND PERSONALITY (7th ed.). New York: Harper & Row.

MYERS, D. G., & LAMM, H. (1976). The group polarization phenomenom. PSYCHOLOGICAL BULLETIN, *83*, 602–627.

NARANJO, C., & ORNSTEIN, R. E. (1977). ON THE PSYCHOLOGY OF MEDITATION. New York: Penguin.

NATHANS, J., THOMAS, D., & HOGNESS, D. S. (1986). Molecular genetics of human color vision: The genes encoding blue, green, and red pigments. SCIENCE, *232*, 193–202.

NATIONAL INSTITUTES OF MENTAL HEALTH. (1987). Pyschiatric hospitalizations in 1980. Unpublished data, Survey and Reports Branch, Division of Biometry and Applied Sciences.

NEBES, R. D., & SPERRY, R. W. (1971). Cerebral dominance in perception. NEUROPSYCHOLOGIA, *9*, 247.

NEGRETE, J. C., & KWAN, M. W. (1972). Relative value of various etiological factors in short-lasting, adverse psychological reactions to cannabis smoking. INTERNAL PHARMACOPSYCHIATRY, *7*, 249–259.

NEMETH, C. (1986). Differential contributions of majority and minority influence. PSYCHOLOGICAL REVIEW, *93*, 23–32.

NEUGARTEN, B. (1968). Adult personality: Toward a psychology of the life cycle. In B. Neugarten, (Ed.), MIDDLE AGE AND AGING. Chicago: University of Chicago Press.

NEWCOMB, M. D., & BENTLER, P. M. (1988). CONSEQUENCES OF ADOLESCENT DRUG USE. Newbury Park, CA: Sage.

NEWCOMB, M. D., RABOW, J., & HERNANDEZ, A. C. R. (1992). A cross-national study of nuclear attitudes, normative support, and activist behavior: Additive and interactive effects. JOURNAL OF APPLIED SOCIAL PSYCHOLOGY, *22*, 780–200.

NEWCOMB, T. M. (1943). PERSONALITY AND SOCIAL CHANGE. New York: Dryden Press.

NEWCOMB, T. M. (1961). THE ACQUAINTANCE PROCESS. New York: Holt, Rinehart & Winston.

NEWCOMB, T. M., KOENING, K. E., FLACKS, R., & WARWICK, D. P. (1967). PERSISTENCE

AND CHANGE: BENNINGTON COLLEGE AND ITS STUDENTS AFTER TWENTY-FIVE YEARS. New York: Wiley.

NEWELL, A., & SIMON, H. A. (1972). HUMAN PROBLEM SOLVING. Englewood Cliffs, NJ: Prentice-Hall.

NEWPORT, E. L. (1990). Maturational constraints on language learning. COGNITIVE SCIENCE, *14*, 11–28.

NEZU, A. M., NEZU, C. M., & PERRI, M. G. (1989). PROBLEM-SOLVING THERAPY FOR DEPRESSION: THEORY, RESEARCH, AND CLINICAL GUIDELINES. New York: Wiley.

NICKLAUS, J. (1974). GOLF MY WAY. New York: Simon & Schuster.

NILSON, D. C., NILSON, L B., OLSON, R. S., & MCALLISTER, B. H. (1981). THE PLANNING ENVIRONMENT REPORT FOR THE SOUTHERN CALIFORNIA EARTHQUAKE SAFETY ADVISORY BOARD. Redlands, CA: Social Research Advisory & Policy Research Center.

NININGER, H. H. (1933). OUR STONEPELTED PLANET. Boston: Houghton Mifflin.

NISAN, M., & KOHLBERG, L. (1982). Universality and variation in moral judgment: A longitudinal and cross-sectional study in Turkey. CHILD DEVELOPMENT, *53*, 865–876.

NISBETT, R. E. (1968). Taste, deprivation, and weight determinants of eating behavior. JOURNAL OF PERSONALITY AND SOCIAL PSYCHOLOGY, *10*, 107–116.

NISBETT, R. E. (1972). Hunger, obesity, and the ventromedial hypothalamus. PSYCHOLOGICAL REVIEW, *79*, 433–453.

NISBETT, R. E., KRANZ, D. H., JEPSON, D., & KUNDA, Z. (1983). The use of statistical heuristics in everyday inductive reasoning. PSYCHOLOGICAL REVIEW, *90*, 339–363.

NISBETT, R. E., & ROSS, L. (1980). HUMAN INFERENCE: STRATEGIES AND SHORTCOMINGS OF SOCIAL JUDGMENT. Englewood Cliffs, NJ: Prentice-Hall.

NISBETT, R. E., & WILSON, T. D. (1977). Telling more than we can know: Verbal reports on mental processes. PSYCHOLOGICAL REVIEW, *84*, 231–259.

NOLEN-HOEKSEMA, S. (1991). Responses to depression and their effects on the duration of depressive episodes. JOURNAL OF ABNORMAL PSYCHOLOGY, *100*, 569–582.

NOLEN-HOEKSEMA, S., & LYUBOMIRSKY, S. (1992). Effects of ruminative and distracting responses on problem-solving and attributions. Manuscript submitted for publication.

NOLEN-HOEKSEMA, S., & MORROW, J. (1991). A prospective study of depression and distress following a natural disaster: The 1989 Loma Prieta earthquake. JOURNAL OF PERSONALITY AND SOCIAL PSYCHOLOGY, *61*, 105–121.

NOLEN-HOEKSEMA, S., PARKER, L., & LARSON, J. (1992). Pyschosocial predictors of depression in family members of the terminally ill. Manuscript submitted for publication.

NOLEN-HOEKSEMA, S., PARKER, L., & LARSON, J. (1994, July). Ruminative coping with depressed mood following loss. JOURNAL OF PERSONALITY AND SOCIAL PSYCHOLOGY, *67*(1), 92–104.

NORMAN, R. (1975). Affective-cognitive consistency, attitudes, conformity, and behavior. JOURNAL OF PERSONALITY AND SOCIAL PSYCHOLOGY, *32*, 83–91.

NORMAN, W. T. (1963). Toward an adequate taxonomy of personality attributes: Replicated factor structure in peer nomination personality ratings. JOURNAL OF ABNORMAL AND SOCIAL PSYCHOLOGY, *66*, 574–583.

NORTH, C. (1987). WELCOME SILENCE. New York: Simon and Schuster.

NUCCLI, L. (1981). The development of personal concepts: A domain distinct from moral or societal concepts. CHILD DEVELOPMENT, *52*, 114–121.

O'DONNELL, J. A., & CLAYTON, R. R. (1982). The stepping stone hypothesis: Marijuana, heroin, and causality. CHEMICAL DEPENDENCIES, *4*(No. 3).

OFFIR, C. (1982). HUMAN SEXUALITY. San Diego: Harcourt Brace Jovanovich.

OGBU, J. U. (1986). The consequences of the American caste system. In Neisser, U. (ed.), THE SCHOOL ACHIEVEMENT OF MINORITY CHILDREN. Hillsdale, NJ: Erlbaum.

O'HARA, M. W., NEUNABER, D. J., & ZEKOWSKI, E. M. (1984). Prospective study of postpartum depression: prevalence, course and predictive factors. JOURNAL OF ABNORMAL PSYCHOLOGY, *93*, 158–171.

OHMAN, A., FREDRIKSON, M., HUGDAHL, K., & RIMMO, P. (1976). The premise of equipotentiality in human classical conditioning: Conditioned electrodermal responses to potentially phobic stimuli. JOURNAL OF EXPERIMENTAL PSYCHOLOGY: GENERAL, *105*, 313–337.

O'LEARY, K. D., & WILSON, G. T. (1975). BEHAVIOR THERAPY: APPLICATION AND OUTCOME. Englewood Cliffs, NJ: Prentice-Hall.

OLIO, K. A. (1989). Memory retrieval in the treatment of adult survivors of sexual abuse. TRANSACTIONAL ANALYSIS JOURNAL, *19*, 93–94.

OLTON, D. S. (1978). Characteristics of spatial memory. In S. H. Hulse, H. F. Fowler, & W. K. Honig (Eds.), COGNITIVE PROCESSES IN ANIMAL BEHAVIOR. Hillsdale, NJ: Erlbaum.

OLTON, D. S. (1979). Mazes, maps, and memory. AMERICAN PSYCHOLOGIST, *34*, 583–596.

OLWEUS, D. (1969). PREDICTION OF AGGRESSION. Scandanavian Test Corporation.

ORLINSKY, D. E., & HOWARD, K. I. (1987). A generic model of psychotherapy. JOURNAL OF INTEGRATIVE AND ECLECTIC PSYCHOTHERAPY, *6*, 6–27.

ORNE, M. T., & HOLLAND, C. C. (1968). On the ecological validity of laboratory deceptions. INTERNATIONAL JOURNAL OF PSYCHIATRY, *6*, 282–293.

ORTONY, A., CLORE, G. L., & COLLINS, A. (1988). THE COGNITIVE STRUCTURE OF EMOTIONS. Cambridge: Cambridge University Press.

OSHERSON, D. N., KOSLYN, S. M. & HOLLERBACH, J. M. (1990). AN INVITATION TO COGNITIVE SCIENCE (Vol. 2). Cambridge, MA: MIT Press.

OSHERSON, D. N., & LASNIK, H. (1990). AN INVITATION TO COGNITIVE SCIENCE (Vol. 1). Cambridge, MA: MIT Press.

OSHERSON, D. N. & SMITH, E. E. (1990). AN INVITATION TO COGNITIVE SCIENCE (Vol. 3). Cambridge, MA: MIT Press.

OSHERSON, D. N., SMITH, E. E., WILKIE, O., LOPEZ, A., & SHAFIR, E. B. (1990). Category based induction. PSYCHOLOGICAL REVIEW, *97*, 185–200.

OSOFSKY, J. D. (Ed.) (1987). HANDBOOK OF INFANT DEVELOPMENT (2nd ed.). New York: Wiley.

OVERMEIER, J. B., & SELIGMAN, M. E. P. (1967). Effects of inescapable shock upon subsequent escape and avoidance responding. JOURNAL OF COMPARATIVE AND PHYSIOLOGICAL PSYCHOLOGY, *63*, 28.

PAICHELER, G. (1976). Norms and attitude change: Pt. 2. The Phenomenon of Bipolarization. EUROPEAN JOURNAL OF SOCIAL PSYCHOLOGY, *6*, 405–427.

PAICHELER, G. (1977). Norms and attitude change: Pt. 1 Polarization and styles of behavior. EUROPEAN JOURNAL OF SOCIAL PSYCHOLOGY, *7*, 5–14.

PALLIS, C. A. (1955). Impaired identification of faces and places with agnosia for colors. JOURNAL OF NEUROLOGY, NEUROSURGERY, AND PSYCHIATRY, *18*, 218–224.

PALMER, J. A., HONORTON, C., & UTTS, J. (1989). REPLY TO THE NATIONAL RESEARCH COUNCIL STUDY ON PARAPSYCHOLOGY. Journal of the American Society for Psychical Research, *83*, 31–49.

PALMER, S. E. (1975). The effect of contextual scenes on the identification of objects. MEMORY AND COGNITION, *3*, 519–526.

PAPAGEORGIS, D., & MCGUIRE, W. J. (1961). The generality of immunity to persuasion produced by pre-exposure to weakened counterarguments. JOURNAL OF ABNORMAL AND SOCIAL PSYCHOLOGY, *62*, 475–481.

PATEL, V. L., & GROEN, G. J. (1986). Knowledge based solution strategies in medical reasoning. COGNITIVE SCIENCE, *10*, 91.

PATTERSON, F. G. (1978). The gestures of a gorilla: Language acquisition in another pongid. BRAIN AND LANGUAGE, *5*, 72–97.

PATTERSON, F. G., & LINDEN, E. (1981). THE EDUCATION OF KOKO. New York: Holt, Rinehart & Winston.

PATTERSON, G. R. (1976). The aggressive child: Victim and architect of a coercive system. In L. A. Hamerlynck, L. C. Handy, & E. J. Mash, (Eds.), BEHAVIOR MODIFICATION AND FAMILIES: 1. THEORY AND RESEARCH. New York: Brunner/Mazel.

PATTERSON, G. R., & LITTMAN, R. A., & BRICKER, W. A. (1967). Assertive behavior in children: A step toward a theory of aggression. MONOGRAPHS OF THE SOCIETY FOR RESEARCH IN CHILD DEVELOPMENT, (Serial No. 113), 5.

PAUL, G. L. (1967). Insight versus desensitization in psychotherapy two years after termination. JOURNAL OF CONSULTING PSYCHOLOGY, *31*, 333–348.

PAUL, G. L., & LENTZ, R. J. (1977). PSYCHO-SOCIAL TREATMENT OF CHRONIC MENTAL PATIENTS: MILIEU VERSUS SOCIAL LEARNING PROGRAMS. Cambridge, MA: Harvard University Press.

PAULHUS, D. (1982). Individual differences, self-presentation, and cognitive dissonance: Their concurrent operation in forced compliance. JOURNAL OF PERSONALITY AND SOCIAL PSYCHOLOGY, *43*, 838–852.

PAULUS, P. B., & MURDOCK, P. (1971). Anticipated evaluation and audience presence in the enhancement of dominant responses. JOURNAL OF EXPERIMENTAL SOCIAL PSYCHOLOGY, *7*, 280–291.

PAVLOV, I. P. (1927). CONDITIONED REFLEXES. New York: Oxford University Press.

PECHURA, C. M., & MARTIN, J. B. (Eds.) (1991). MAPPING THE BRAIN AND ITS FUNCTIONS. Washington, D.C.: National Academy Press.

PECK, J. W., & NOVIN, D. (1971). Evidence that osmoreceptors mediating drinking in rabbits are in the lateral preoptic area. JOURNAL OF COMPARATIVE AND PHYSIOLOGICAL PSYCHOLOGY, *74*, 134–147.

PEDERSEN, N. L., PLOMIN, R., MCCLEARN, G. E., & FRIBERG, L. (1988). Neuroticism, extraversion and related traits in adult twins reared apart and reared together. JOURNAL OF PERSONALITY AND SOCIAL PSYCHOLOGY, *55*, 905–957.

PEDERSEN, N. L., PLOMIN, R., NESSELROADE, J. R., & MCCLEARN, G. E. (1992). A quantitative genetic analysis of cognitive abilities during the second half of the life span. PSYCHOLOGICAL SCIENCE, *3*, 346–353.

PEELE, S. (1988). Fools for love: The romantic ideal, psychological theory, and addictive love. In R. J. Sternberg, & M. L. Barnes (Eds.), THE PSYCHOLOGY OF LOVE (pp. 159–188). New Haven, CT: Yale University Press.

PELLEGRINO, J. W. (1985). Inductive reasoning ability. In R. J. Sternberg (Ed.), HUMAN ABILITIES: AN INFORMATION-PROCESSING APPROACH. New York: Freeman.

PENNEBAKER, J. W. (1990). OPENING UP: THE HEALING POWER OF CONFIDING IN OTHERS. New York: William Morrow and Company.

PENNEBAKER, J. W., & BEALL, S. K. (1986). Confronting a traumatic event: toward an understanding of inhibition and disease. JOURNAL OF ABNORMAL PSYCHOLOGY, *95*, 274–281.

PENNEBAKER, J. W., & O'HEERON, R. C. (1984). Confiding in others and illness rates among spouses of suicide and accidental-death victims. JOURNAL OF ABNORMAL PSYCHOLOGY, *93*, 473–476.

PEPLAU, L. A., RUBIN, Z., & HILL, C. T. (1977). Sexual intimacy in dating relationships. JOURNAL OF SOCIAL ISSUES, *33*, 86–109.

PERLMUTTER, M., & HALL, E. (1992). ADULT DEVELOPMENT AND AGING (2nd ed.). New York: Wiley.

PERRIN, F. A. C. (1921). Physical attractiveness and repulsiveness. JOURNAL OF EXPERIMENTAL PSYCHOLOGY, *4*, 203–217.

PERRY, D. G., & BUSSEY, K. (1984). SOCIAL DEVELOPMENT. Englewood Cliffs, NJ: Prentice-Hall.

PERRIS, C., BLACKBURN, I. M., & PERRIS, H. (Eds.) (1988). COGNITIVE PSYCHOTHERAPY: THEORY & PRACTICE. New York: Springer-Verlag.

PETERSEN, A. C. (1988). Adolescent development. In M. R. Rosenzweig, & L. W. Porter (Eds.), ANNUAL REVIEW OF PSYCHOLOGY (Vol. 39). Palo Alto, CA: Annual Reviews.

PETERSEN, A. C. (1989). Adolescent development. In M. R. Rosenzweig & L. W. Porter (Eds.), ANNUAL REVIEW OF PSYCHOLOGY (Vol. 39). Palo Alto, CA: Annual Reviews.

PETERSON, C., & SELIGMAN, M. E. P. (1984). Causal explanations as a risk factor for depression: Theory and evidence. PSYCHOLOGICAL REVIEW, *91*, 347–374.

PETERSON, C., & SELIGMAN, M. E. P. (1987). Explanatory style and illness. Special illness: personality and physical health. JOURNAL OF PERSONALITY, *55*, 237–265.

PETERSON, C., SELIGMAN, M., & VAILLANT, G. (1988). Pessimistic explanatory style as a risk factor for physical illness: a thirty-five-year longitudinal study. JOURNAL OF PERSONALITY AND SOCIAL PSYCHOLOGY, *55*, 23–27.

PETRONIS, K. R., SAMUELS, J. F., MOSCICKI, E. K., & ANTHONY, J. C. (1990). An epidemiologic investigation of potential risk factors for suicide attempts. SOCIAL PSYCHIATRY AND PSYCHIATRIC EPIDEMIOLOGY, *25*, 193–199.

PETTIGREW, T. F. (1959). Regional differences in anti-Negro prejudice. JOURNAL OF ABNORMAL AND SOCIAL PSYCHOLOGY, *59*, 28–36.

PETTY, R. E., & CACIOPPO, J. T. (1977). Forewarning, cognitive responding, and resistance to persuasion. JOURNAL OF PERSONALITY AND SOCIAL PSYCHOLOGY, *35*, 645–655.

PETTY, R. E., & CACIOPPO, J. T. (1981). ATTITUDES AND PERSUASION: CLASSIC AND CONTEMPORARY APPROACHES. Dubuque, IA: Wm. C. Brown.

PETTY, R. E., & CACIOPPO, J. T. (1984). The effects of involvement on responses to argument quantity and quality: Central and peripheral routes to persuasion. JOURNAL OF PERSONALITY AND SOCIAL PSYCHOLOGY, *46*, 69–81.

PETTY, R. E., & CACIOPPO, J. T. (1986). Elaboration likelihood model of persuasion. In L. Berkowitz, (Ed.), ADVANCES IN EXPERIMENTAL SOCIAL PSYCHOLOGY (Vol. *19*, pp. 123–205). New York: Academic Press.

PETTY, R. E., CACIOPPO, J. T., & GOLDMAN, R. (1981). Personal involvement as a determinant of argument-based persuasion. JOURNAL OF PERSONALITY AND SOCIAL PSYCHOLOGY, *41*, 847–855.

PETTY, R. E., OSTROM, T. M., & BROCK, T. C. (1981). Historical foundations of the cognitive response approach to attitudes and persuasion. In R. E. Petty, T. M. Ostrom, & T. C. Brock (Eds.) COGNITIVE RESPONSES IN PERSUASION. Hillsdale, NJ: Erlbaum.

PHILLIPS, J. L., JR (1981). PIAGET'S THEORY: A PRIMER. San Francisco: Freeman.

PHILLIPS, J. L., JR. (1992). HOW TO THINK ABOUT STATISTICS (revised ed.). New York: Freeman.

PHOENIX, C. H., GOY, R. H., & RESKO, J. A. (1968). Psychosexual differentiation as a function of androgenic stimulation. In M. Diamond (Ed.), REPRODUCTION AND SEXUAL BEHAVIOR. Bloomington: Indiana University Press.

PIAGET, J. (1932/1965). THE MORAL JUDGMENT OF THE CHILD. New York: Free Press.

PIAGET, J. (1952). THE ORIGINS OF INTELLIGENCE IN CHILDREN. New York: International Universities Press.

PIAGET, J. (1962). PLAY, DREAMS, AND IMITATION. New York: Norton.

PIAGET, J., & INHELDER, B. (1969). THE PSYCHOLOGY OF THE CHILD. New York: Basic Books.

PICCIONE, C., HILGARD, E. R., & ZIMBARDO, P. G. (1989). On the degree of stability of measured hyponotizability over a 25-year period. JOURNAL OF PERSONALITY AND SOCIAL PSYCHOLOGY, *56*, 289–95.

PILIAVIN, I. M., RODIN, J., & PILIAVIN, J. A. (1969). Good Samaritanism: An underground phenomenon: JOURNAL OF PERSONALITY AND SOCIAL PSYCHOLOGY, *13*, 289–299.

PILLARD, R. C., & WEINRICH, J. D. (1986). Evidence of familial nature of male homosexuality. ARCHIVES OF GENERAL PSYCHIATRY, *43*, 808–812.

PINKER, S. (1984). LANGUAGE LEARNABILITY AND LANGUAGE DEVELOPMENT. Cambridge, MA: Harvard University Press.

PINKER, S., & PRINCE, A. (1988). On language and connectionism: Analysis of a parallel distributed processing model of language acquisition. COGNITION, *28*, 71–193.

PION, G. M. (1991). Psychologists wanted: employment trends over the past decade. In R. R. Kilburg, Ed., HOW TO MANAGE YOUR CAREER IN PSYCHOLOGY. Washington, D.C.: American Psychological Association.

PIRKE, K. M., KELLNER, M. B., FRIESS, E., KRIEG, J. C., & FICHTER, M. M. (1994). Satiety and cholecystokinin. INT J EAT DISORD, *15*(1), 63–9.

PLATT, J. J., YAKSH, T., & DARBY, C. L. (1967). Social facilitation of eating behavior in armadillos. PSYCHOLOGICAL REPORTS, *20*, 1136.

PLOMIN, R. (1990). NATURE AND NUTURE. Pacific Grove, CA: Brooks/Cole.

PLOMIN, R. (1991). Behavioral genetics. In P. R. McHugh & V. A. McKusick (Eds.), GENES, BRAIN, AND BEHAVIOR. New York: Raven Press.

PLOMIN, R., & BERGEMAN, C. S. (1991). The nature of nurture: Genetic influence on "environmental" measures. BEHAVIORAL & BRAIN SCIENCES, *14*(3), 373–427.

PLOMIN, R., & DANLIES, D. (1987). Why are children in the same family so different from one another? BEHAVIORAL AND BRAIN SCIENCES, *10*, 1–60.

PLOMIN, R., DEFRIES, J. C., & LOEHLIN, J. C. (1977). Genotype-environment interaction and correlation in the analysis of human behavior. PSYCHOLOGICAL BULLETIN, *84*, 309–322.

PLUTCHIK, R., & KELLERMAN, H. (Eds.)

(1980). EMOTION: THEORY, RESEARCH, AND EXPERIENCE (Vol. 1). New York: Academic Press.

POLIVY, J., & HERMAN, C. P. (1985). Dieting and binging: A causal analysis. AMERICAN PSYCHOLOGIST, 40, 193–201.

POMEROY, J. C. (1990). Infantile autism and childhood psychosis. In B. D. Garfinkel, G. A. Carlson, & E. B. Weller (Eds.), PSYCHIATRIC DISORDERS IN CHILDREN AND ADOLESCENTS (pp. 271–290). Philadelphia: W. B. Saunders.

POPE, K. S., & SINGER, J. L. (Eds.) (1978). THE STREAM OF CONSCIOUSNESS. New York: Plenum.

POSNER, M. I. (1980). Orienting of attention. QUARTERLY JOURNAL OF EXPERIMENTAL PSYCHOLOGY, 32, 3–25.

POSNER, M. I. (1988). Structures and functions of selective attention. In T. Boll & B. K. Bryant (Eds.), CLINICAL NEUROPSYCHOLOGY AND BRAIN FUNCTION: RESEARCH, MEASUREMENT, AND PRACTICE. Washington, DC: American Psychological Association.

POSNER, M. I., & DEHAENE, S. (1994). Attentional networks. TRENDS IN NEUROSCIENCE, 17, 75–79.

POSNER, M. I., & KEELE, S. W. (1967). Decay of visual information from a single letter. SCIENCE, 158, 137–139.

POSNER, M. I., & MARIN, O. S. M. (Eds.) (1985). MECHANISMS OF ATTENTION: Vol. 11. ATTENTION AND PERFORMANCE. Hillsdale, NJ: Erlbaum.

POSNER, M. I., PETERSEN, S. E., FOX, P. T., & RAICHLE, M. E. (1988). Localization of cognitive operations in the human brain. SCIENCE, 240, 1627–1631.

POST, R. M., & KOTIN, J., GOODWIN, F. K., & GORDON, E. (1973). Psychomotor activity and cerebrospinal fluid amine metabolites in effective illness. AMERICAN JOURNAL OF PSYCHIATRY, 130, 67–72.

POWELL, R. A., & BOER, D. P. (1994). Did Freud mislead patients to confabulate memories of abuse? PSYCHOLOGICAL REPORTS, 74, 1283–1298.

POWLEY, T. L., & KEESEY, R. E. (1970). Relationship of body weight to the lateral hypothalamic feeding syndrome. JOURNAL OF COMPARATIVE AND PSYCHOLOGICAL PSYCHOLOGY, 70, 25–36.

PREMACK, D. (1971). Language in chimpanzees? SCIENCE, 172, 808–822.

PREMACK, D. (1985) "Gavagi!" Or the future history of the animal language controversy. COGNITION, 19, 207–296.

PREMACK, D., & PREMACK, A. J. (1983). THE MIND OF AN APE. New York: Norton.

PRESSLEY, M., LEVIN, J. R., & DELANEY, H. D. (1982). The mnemonic keyword method. REVIEW OF EDUCATIONAL RESEARCH, 52, 61–91.

PRIEST, R. F., & SAWYER, J. (1967). Proximity and peership: Bases of balance in interpersonal attraction. AMERICAN JOURNAL OF SOCIOLOGY, 72, 633–649.

PRINTZMETAL, W., & BANKS, W. P. (1977). Good continuation affects visual detection. PERCEPTION & PSYCHOPHYSICS, 21, 389–395.

PRIOR, M. R. (1987). Biological and neuropsychological approaches to childhood autism. BRITISH JOURNAL OF PSYCHIATRY, 150, 8–17.

PROTHRO, E. T., (1952). Ethnocentrism and anti-Negro attitudes in the deep South. JOURNAL OF ABNORMAL AND SOCIAL PATHOLOGY, 47, 105–108.

PRYOR, J. B., BIGGONS, F. X., WICKLUND, R. A., FAZIO, R. H. , & HOOD, R. (1977). Self-focused attention and self-report validity. JOURNAL OF PERSONALITY, 45, 514–527.

PUTNAM, F. W., JR. (1984). Cited in R. M. Restak THE BRAIN. New York: Bantam.

RAAIJMAKERS, J. G., & SHIFFRIN, R. M. (1981). Search of associative memory. PSYCHOLOGICAL REVIEW, 88, 93–134.

RACHMAN, S. J., & HODGSON, R. J. (1980). OBSESSIONS AND COMPULSIONS. Englewood Cliffs, NJ: Prentice-Hall.

RACHMAN, S. J., & WILSON, G. T. (1980). THE EFFECTS OF PSYCHOLOGICAL THERAPY (2nd ed.). Elmsford, NY: Pergamon Press.

RAMACHANDRAN, V. S., & GREGORY, R. L. (1991). Perceptual filling in of artificially induced scotomas in human vision. NATURE, 350, 699–702.

RANDI, J. (1982). FLIM-FLAM! PSYCHICS, ESP, UNICORNS AND OTHER DELUSIONS. Buffalo: Prometheus Books.

RAPAPORT, D. (1942). EMOTIONS AND MEMORY. Baltimore: Williams & Wilkins.

RAPOPORT, J. L. (1989). THE BOY WHO WOULDN'T STOP WASHING. New York: Dutton.

RAVENS, J. C. (1965). ADVANCED PROGRESSIVE MATRICES, SETS I AND II. London: H. K. Lewis. (Distributed in the U.S. by The Psychological Corporation, San Antonio, TX).

RAVUSSIN, E., & collaborators (1988). Reduced rate of energy expenditure as a risk factor for body-weight gain. THE NEW ENGLAND JOURNAL OF MEDICINE, 318, 467–472.

RAY, W. J., & RAVIZZA, R. (1988). METHODS TOWARD A SCIENCE OF BEHAVIOR AND EXPERIENCE (3rd ed.). Belmont, CA: Wadsworth.

RAYNER, K. (1978). Eye movements, reading and information processing. PSYCHOLOGICAL BULLETIN, 6, 618–660.

REGAN, D., BEVERLEY, K. I., & CY NADER, (1979). The visual perception of motion depth. SCIENTIFIC AMERICAN, 241(No. 1), 136–151.

REGAN, D. T., & FAZIO, R. (1977). On the consistency between attitudes and behavior: Look to the method of attitude information. JOURNAL OF EXPERIMENTAL SOCIAL PSYCHOLOGY, 13, 28–45.

REGIER, D. A., BOYD, J. H., & collaborators. (1988). One-month prevalence of mental disorders in the United States. ARCHIVES OF GENERAL PSYCHIATRY. 45, 977–986.

REICHER, G. M. (1969). Perceptual recognition as a function of the meaningfulness of the material. JOURNAL OF EXPERIMENTAL PSYCHOLOGY, 81, 275–280.

REISENZEIN, R. (1983). The Schachter theory emotion: Two decades later. PSYCHOLOGICAL BULLETIN, 94, 239–264.

REISER, B. J., KIMBERG, D. Y., LOVETT, M. C., & RANNEY, M. (1989). KNOWLEDGE REPRESENTATION AND EXPLANATION IN GIL, AN INTELLIGENCE TUTOR FOR PROGRAMMING. Technical Report 37, Cognitive Science Laboratory, Princeton University.

RESCORLA, R. A. (1967). Pavlovian conditioning and its proper control procedures. PSYCHOLOGICAL REVIEW, 74, 71–80.

RESCORLA, R. A. (1972). Informational variables in Pavlovian conditioning. In Bower, G. H. (Ed.), PSYCHOLOGY OF LEARNING AND MOTIVATION (Vol. 6). New York: Academic Press.

RESCORLA, R. A. (1980). Overextension in early language development. JOURNAL OF CHILD LANGUAGE, 7, 321–335.

RESCORLA, R. A. (1987). A Pavlovian analysis of goal-directed behavior. AMERICAN PSYCHOLOGIST, 42, 119–129.

RESCORLA, R. A. & SOLOMON, R. L. (1967). Two-process learning theory: Relations between Pavlovian conditioning and instrumental learning. PSYCHOLOGICAL REVIEW, 74, 151–182.

RESCORLA, R. A., & WAGNER, A. R. (1972). A theory of Pavlovian conditioning. Variations in the effectivness of reinforcement and non-reinforcement. In P. H. Black & W. F. Prokasy (Eds.). CLASSICAL CONDITIONING II. New York: Appleton-Century-Crofts

REUBENS, A. B., & BENSON, D. F. (1971). Associative visual agnosia. ARCHIVES OF NEUROLOGY, 24, 305–316.

REYNOLDS, D. V. (1969). Surgery in the rat during electrical analgesia induced by focal brain stimulation. SCIENCE, 164, 444–445.

RHEINGOLD, H. F., & COOK, K. V. (1975). The content of boys' and girls' rooms as an index of parent behavior. CHILD DEVELOPMENT, 46, 459–463.

RICE, B. (1978). The new truth machine. PSYCHOLOGY TODAY, 12, 61–78.

RICH, C. L., FLOWLER, R. C., FOGARTY, L. A., & YOUNG, D. (1988). San Diego suicide study. ARCHIVES OF GENERAL PSYCHIATRY, 45, 589–592.

RICHARDSON, J. L., SHELTON, D. R., KRAILO, M., & LEVINE, A. M. (1990). The effect of compliance with treatment in survival among patients with hematologic malignancies. JOURNAL OF CLINICIAL ONCOLOGY, 8, 356.

RIESEN, A. H. (1947). The development of visual perception in man and chimpanzee. SCIENCE, 106, 107–108.

RIMM, D. C., & MASTERS, J. C. (1979). BEHAVIOR THERAPY: TECHNIQUES AND EMPIRICAL FINDINGS (2nd ed.). New York: Academic Press.

RIORDAN, C. A., & TEDESCHI, J. T. (1983). Attraction in aversive environments: Some evidence for classical conditioning and negative reinforcement. JOURNAL OF PERSONALITY AND SOCIAL PSYCHOLOGY, 44, 683–692.

RIPS, L. J. (1983). Cognitive processes in propositional reasoning. PSYCHOLOGICAL REVIEW, 90, 38–71.

RITVO, E. R., & FREEMAN, B. J. (1978). National Society for Autistic Children definition of the syndrome of autism. JOURNAL OF AUTISM AND CHILD SCHIZOPHRENIA, *8*, 162–167.

RITVO, E. R., FREEMAN, B. J., PINGREE, C., MASON-BROTHERS, A., JORDE, L., JENSON, W. R., MCMAHON, W. M., PETERSEN, P. B., MO, A., & RITVO, A. (1989). The UCLA-University of Utah epidemiology survey of autism: Prevalence. AMERICAN JOURNAL OF PSYCHIATRY, *146*(2), 194–199.

ROBINS, L. N. (1966). DEVIANT CHILDREN GROWN UP. Baltimore, MD: Williams & Wilkins.

ROBINS, L. N., HELZER, J. E., WEISSMAN, M. M., ORVASCHEL, H., GRUENBERG, E., BURKE, J. D., & REGIER, D. A. (1984). Lifetime prevalence of specific psychiatric disorders in three sites. ARCHIVES OF GENERAL PSYCHIATRY, *41*, 949–958.

ROBINSON, T. E., & BERRIDGE, K. C. (1993). The neural basis of drug craving: an incentive-sensitization theory of addiction. BRAIN RES BRAIN RES REV, *18*(3), 247–91.

ROCK, I. (1983). THE LOGIC OF PERCEPTION. Cambridge, MA: MIT Press.

RODIN, J. (1981). Current status of the internal-external hypothesis of obesity: What went wrong? AMERICAN PSYCHOLOGIST, *36*, 361–372.

ROEDIGER, H. L. (1990). Implicit memory: Retention without remembering. AMERICAN PSYCHOLOGIST, *45*, 1043–1056.

ROFF, J. D., & KNIGHT, R. (1981). Family characteristics, childhood symptoms, and adult outcome in schizophrenia. JOURNAL OF ABNORMAL PSYCHOLOGY, *90*, 510–520.

ROFFWARG, H. P., HERMAN, J. H., BOWER-ANDERS, C., & TAUBER, E. S. (1978). The effects of sustained alterations of waking visual input on dream content. In A. M. Arkin, J. S. Antrobus, & S. J. Ellman (Eds.), THE MIND IN SLEEP. Hillsdale, NJ: Erlbaum.

ROGERS, C. R. (1959). A theory of therapy, personality, and interpersonal relationships as developed in the client-centered framework. In S. Koch (Ed.), PSYCHOLOGY: A STUDY OF A SCIENCE: VOL. 3. FORMULATIONS OF THE PERSON AND THE SOCIAL CONTEXT. New York: McGraw-Hill.

ROGERS, C. R. (1951). CLIENT-CENTERED THERAPY. Boston: Houghton Mifflin.

ROGERS, C. R. (1963). The actualizing tendency in relation to motives and to consciousness. In M. Jones (Ed.), NEBRASKA SYMPOSIUM ON MOTIVATION (pp. 1–24). Lincoln: University of Nebraska Press.

ROGERS, C. R. (1970). ON BECOMING A PERSON: A THERAPIST'S VIEW OF PSYCHOTHERAPY. Boston: Houghton Mifflin.

ROGERS, C. R. (1977). CARL ROGERS ON PERSONAL POWER. New York: Delacorte Press.

ROGERS, C. R., & STEVENS, B. (1967). PERSON TO PERSON: THE PROBLEM OF BEING HUMAN. New York: Pocket Books.

ROGERS, T. B., KUIPER, N. A., & KIRKER, W. S. (1977). Self-reference and the encoding of personal information. JOURNAL OF PERSONALITY AND SOCIAL PSYCHOLOGY, *35*, 677–688.

ROHN, R. D., SARTES, R. M., KENNY, T. J., REYNOLDS, B. J., & HEALD, F. P. (1977). Adolescents who attempt suicide. JOURNAL OF PEDIATRICS, *90*, 636–638.

ROITBLAT, H. L. (1986). INTRODUCTION TO COMPARATIVE COGNITION. New York: Freeman.

ROLAND, P. E., & FRIBERG, L. (1985). Localization of cortical areas activated by thinking. JOURNAL OF NEUROPHYSIOLOGY, *53*, 1219–1243.

ROOK, K. (1984). The negative side of social interaction: impact on psychological well-being JOURNAL OF PERSONALITY AND SOCIAL PSYCHOLOGY, *46*, 1097–1108.

ROSCH, E. (1974). Linguistic relativity. In A. Sliverstein (Ed.), HUMAN COMMUNICATION: THEORETICAL PERSPECTIVES. New York: Halsted Press.

ROSCH, E. (1978). Principles of categorization. In E. Rosch & B. L. Lloyd, (Eds.), COGNITION AND CATEGORIZATION. Hillsdale, NJ: Erlbaum.

ROSE, J. E., BRUGGE, J. F., ANDERSON, D. J., & HIND, J. E. (1967). Phase-locked response to lower frequency tones in single auditory nerve fibers of the squirrel monkey. JOURNAL OF NEUROPHYSIOLOGY, *390*, 769–793.

ROSEMAN, I. J. (1984). Cognitive determinants of emotions: A structural theory. In P. Shaver (Ed.), REVIEW OF PERSONALITY AND SOCIAL PSYCHOLOGY: VOL. 5, EMOTIONS, RELATIONSHIPS, AND HEALTH. Beverly Hills, CA: Sage.

ROSENBLITH, J. F. (1992). IN THE BEGINNING: DEVELOPMENT FROM CONCEPTION TO AGE TWO YEARS (2nd ed.). Newbury Park, CA: Sage.

ROSENBLOOM, P. S., LAIRD, J. E., NEWELL, A., & McCARL, R. (1991). A preliminary analysis of the foundations of Soar. ARTIFICIAL INTELLIGENCE, *47*, 289–325.

ROSENHAN, D. L., & SELIGMAN, M. E. P. (1989). Abnormal Psychology (2nd ed.). New York: W. W. Norton.

ROSENMAN, R. H., BRAND, R. J., JENKINS, C. D., FRIEDMAN, M., STRAUS, R., & WRUM, M. (1976). Coronary heart disease in the Western Collaborative Group Study: Final follow-up experience of 8-1/2 years. JOURNAL OF THE AMERICAN MEDICAL ASSOCIATION, *233*, 878–877.

ROSENTHAL, R. (1966). EXPERIMENTER EFFECTS IN BEHAVIORAL RESEARCH. New York: Appleton-Century-Crofts.

ROSENTHAL, R. (1984). META-ANALYTIC PROCEDURES FOR SOCIAL RESEARCH. Beverly Hills, CA: Sage.

ROSENZWEIG, M. R., & LEIMAN, A. L. (1989). PHYSIOLOGICAL PSYCHOLOGY (2nd ed.). Lexington, MA: Health.

ROSS, L. (1977). The intuitive psychologist and his shortcomings: Distortions in the attribution process. In L. Berkowitz, (Ed.), ADVANCES IN EXPERIMENTAL SOCIAL PSYCHOLOGY (Vol. 10). New York: Academic Press.

ROSS, L., AMABILE, T. M., & STEINMETZ, J. L. (1977). Social roles, social control, and biases in social-perception processes. JOURNAL OF PERSONALITY AND SOCIAL PSYCHOLOGY, *35*, 485–494.

ROSS, L., BIERBRAUER, G., & HOFFMAN, S. (1976). The role of attribution processes in conformity and dissent. Revisiting the Asch Situation. AMERICAN PSYCHOLOGIST, *31*, 148–157.

ROSS, L., LEPPER, M. R., & HUBBARD, M. (1975). Perseverance in self perception and social perception: Biased attributional processes in the debriefing paradigm. JOURNAL OF PERSONALITY AND SOCIAL PSYCHOLOGY, *32*, 880–892.

ROSS, L., LEPPER, M. R., STRACK, F., & STEINMETZ, J. L. (1977). Social explanation and social expectation: The effects of real and hypothetical explanations upon subjective likelihood. JOURNAL OF PERSONALITY AND SOCIAL PSYCHOLOGY, *35*, 817–829.

ROSS, L., & NISBETT, R. E. (1991). THE PERSON AND THE SITUATION: PERSPECTIVES OF SOCIAL PSYCHOLOGY. New York: McGraw-Hill.

ROSSI, P. (1990). The old homelessness and the new homelessness in historical perspective. AMERICAN PSYCHOLOGIST, *45*(8), 954–959.

ROTHBAUM, B., & FOA, E. (1992). Exposure therapy for rape victims with post-traumatic stress disorder. THE BEHAVIOR THERAPIST, OCTOBER, 219–222.

ROTTER, J. B. (1954). SOCIAL LEARNING AND CLINICAL PSYCHOLOGY. Englewood Cliffs, NJ: Prentice-Hall.

ROTTER, J. B. (1982). THE DEVELOPMENT AND APPLICATIONS OF SOCIAL LEARNING THEORY: SELECTED PAPERS. New York: Praeger.

ROVEE-COLLIER, C., & HAYNE, H. (1987). Reactivation of infant memory: Implications for cognitive development. In H. W. Reese (Ed.), ADVANCES IN CHILD DEVELOPMENT AND BEHAVIOR (Vol. 20). New York: Academic Press.

ROWLAND, N. E., & ANTELMAN, S. M. (1976). Stress-induced hyperphagia and obesity in rats: a possible model for understanding human obesity. SCIENCE, *191*(4224), 310–12.

ROY, A. (1981). Role of past loss in depression. ARCHIVES OF GENERAL PSYCHIATRY, *38*, 301–302.

ROYCE, J. R., & MOS, L. P. (Eds.) (1981). HUMANISTIC PSYCHOLOGY: CONCEPTS AND CRITICISMS. New York: Plenum.

ROZIN, P. N., & SCHULKIN, J. (1990). Food selection. In E. M. Stricker (Eds.), NEUROBIOLOGY OF FOOD AND FLUID INTAKE (pp. 297–328). New York: Plenum.

RUBIN, D. C. (Ed.). (1986). AUTOBIOGRAPHICAL MEMORY. New York: Cambridge University Press.

RUBIN, Z. (1973). LIKING AND LOVING. New York: Holt, Rinehart & Winston.

RUCH, J. C. (1975). Self-hypnosis: The result of heterohypnosis or vice versa? INTERNATIONAL JOURNAL OF CLINICAL AND EXPERIMENTAL HYPNOSIS, *23*, 282–304.

RUCH, J. C., MORGAN, A. H., & HILGARD, E. R. (1973). Behavioral predictions from hypnotic responsiveness scores when obtained with and without prior induction procedures. JOURNAL OF ABNORMAL PSYCHOLOGY, *82*, 543–546.

RUCK, B. (1980). Biofeedback: Issues in Treatment Assessment. National Institute of Mental Health Science Reports.

RUDERMAN. A. J. (1986). Dietary restraint: A theoretical and empirical review. PSYCHOLOGICAL BULLETIN, *99*, 247–262.

RUMELHART, D. E., & MCCLELLAND, J. L. (1987). Learning the past tenses of English verbs: Implicit rules or parallel distributed processing? In B. MacWhinney (Ed.), MECHANISMS OF LANGUAGE ACQUISITION. Hillsdale, NJ: Erlbaum.

RUMELHART, D. E., MCCLELLAND, J. L., & THE PDP RESEARCH GROUP (1986). PARALLEL DISTRIBUTED PROCESSING: EXPLORATIONS IN THE MICROSTRUCTURE OF COGNITION. VOLUME 1: FOUNDATIONS. Cambridge, MA: Bradford Books/MIT Press.

RUSHTON, J. P., JACKSON, D. N., & PAUNONEN, S. V. (1981). Personality: Nomothetic or idiographic? A response to Kenrick and Stringfield. PSYCHOLOGICAL REVIEW, *88*, 582–589.

RUSSEK, M. (1971). Hepatic receptors and the neurophysiological mechanisms controlling feedback behavior. In S. Ehreupreis (Ed.), NEUROSCIENCES RESEARCH (Vol. 4). New York: Academic Press.

RUSSELL, D. E. H., & HOWELL, N. (1983). The prevalence of rape in the United States revisted. JOURNAL OF WOMEN IN CULTURE AND SOCIETY, *8*, 688–695.

RUSSELL, M. J. (1976). Human olfactory communication. NATURE, *260*, 520–522.

RUSSELL, M. J., SWITZ, G. M., & THOMPSON, K. (1980). Olfactory influence on the human menstrual cycle. PHARMACOLOGY, BIOCHEMISTRY AND BEHAVIOR, *13*, 737–738.

RUSSO, N. F., & SOBEL, S. B. (1981). Sex differences in the utilization of mental health facilities. PROFESSIONAL PSYCHOLOGY, *12*, 7–19.

RUTTER, M., MACDONALD, H., CONTEUR, A. LE, HARRINGTON, R., BOLTON, P., & BAILEY, A. (1990). Genetic factors in child psychiatric disorders: II. Empirical findings. JOURNAL OF CHILD PSYCHOLOGY AND PSYCHIATRY, *31*(1), 39–83.

SACHS, J. D. S. (1967). Recognition memory for syntactic and semantic aspects of connected discourse. PERCEPTION AND PSYCHOPHYSICS, *2*, 437–442.

SACKEIM, H. A., PORTNOY, S., NEELEY, P., STEIF, B. L., DECINA, P., & MALITZ, S. (1985). Cognitive consequences of low dosage ECT. In S. Malitz & H. A. Sackeim (Eds.) ELECTROCONVULSIVE THERAPY: CLINICAL AND BASIC RESEARCH ISSUES. Annals of the New York Academy of Science.

SACKS, O. (1985). THE MAN WHO MISTOOK HIS WIFE FOR A HAT AND OTHER CLINICAL TALES. New York: Harper Perennial.

SALAMY, J. (1970). Instrumental responding to internal cues associated with REM sleep. PSYCHONOMIC SCIENCE, *18*, 342–343.

SALAPATEK, P. (1975). Pattern perception in early infancy. In L. B. Cohen & P. Salapatek (Eds.), INFANT PERCEPTION: FROM SENSATION TO COGNITION (Vol. 1). New York: Academic Press.

SALK, L. (1973). The role of the heartbeat in the relationship between mother and infant. SCIENTIFIC AMERICAN, *228*, 24–29.

SANDERS, G. S. (1984). Self-presentation and drive in social facilitation. JOURNAL OF EXPERIMENTAL SOCIAL PSYCHOLOGY, *20*, 312–322.

SANDERS, G. S., & BARON, R. S. (1975). The motivating effects of distraction on task performance. JOURNAL OF PERSONALITY AND SOCIAL PSYCHOLOGY, *32*, 956–963.

SANDERS, G. S., & BARON, R. S. (1977). Is social comparison irrelevant for producing choice shifts? JOURNAL OF EXPERIMENTAL SOCIAL PSYCHOLOGY, *13*, 303–314.

SAPOLSKY, R. M. (1990). Stress in the wild. SCIENTIFIC AMERICAN, *262*, 116–123.

SARASON, I., & SARASON, B. (1993). ABNORMAL PSYCHOLOGY: THE PROBLEM OF MALADAPTIVE BEHAVIOR (7th ed.). Englewood Cliffs, NJ: Prentice-Hall.

SATINOFF, E. (1964). Behavioral thermoregulation in reponse to local cooling of the rat brain. AMERICAN JOURNAL OF PHYSIOLOGY, *206*, 1389–1394.

SATINOFF, E. (1983). A reevaluation of the concept of the homeostatic organization of temperature regulation. In E. Satinoff & P. Teitelbaum (Eds.), MOTIVATION (pp. 443–474). New York: Plenum Press.

SATINOFF, E., & RUTSTEIN, J. (1970). Behavioral thermoregulations in rats with anterior hypothalamic lesions. JOURNAL OF COMPARATIVE AND PHYSIOLOGICAL PSYCHOLOGY, *71*, 72–82.

SATINOFF, E., & SHAN, S. Y. (1971). Loss of behavioral thermoregulation after lateral hypothalamic lesions in rats. JOURNAL OF COMPARATIVE PHYSIOLOGICAL PSYCHOLOGY, *72*, 302–312.

SATTLER, J. M. (1988). ASSESSMENT OF CHILDREN. San Diego: Jerome M. Sattler.

SAUNDERS, D. R. (1985). On Hyman's factor analyses. JOURNAL OF PARAPSYCHOLOGY, *49*, 86–88.

SAVIN-WILLIAMS, R. C., & JAQUISH, G. A. (1981). The assessment of adolescent self-esteem: A comparison of methods. JOURNAL OF PERSONALITY, *49*, 324–336.

SAXE, L., DOUGHERTY, D., & CROSS, T. (1985). The validity of polygraph testing. AMERICAN PSYCHOLOGIST, *40*, 355–366.

SCARR, S. (1988). How genotypes and environments combine: Development and invidual differences. In N. Bolger, A. Caspi, G. Downey, & M. Moorehouse (Eds.), PERSONS IN CONTEXT: DEVELOPMENTAL PROCESSES (pp. 217–244). New York: Cambridge University Press.

SCARR, S., & MCCARTNEY, K. (1983). How people make their own environments: A theory of genotype-environment effects. CHILD DEVELOPMENT, *54*, 424–435.

SCARR, S., WEINBERG, R. A., & LEVINE, A. (1986). UNDERSTANDING DEVELOPMENT. San Diego: Harcourt Brace Javanovich.

SCHACHTEL, E. G. (1982). On memory and childhood amnesia. In U. Neisser (Ed.), MEMORY OBSERVED: REMEMBERING IN NATURAL CONTEXTS. San Francisco: Freeman.

SCHACHTER, S. (1971). EMOTION, OBESITY, AND CRIME. New York: Academic Press.

SCHACHTER, S., & SINGER, J. E. (1962). Cognitive, social and physiological determinants of emotional state. PSYCHOLOGICAL REVIEW, *69*, 379–399.

SCHACTER, D. L. (1989). Memory. In M. Posner (Ed.), FOUNDATIONS OF COGNITIVE SCIENCE. Cambridge, MA: MIT Press.

SCHAFER, R. (1976). A NEW LANGUAGE FOR PSYCHOANALYSIS. New Haven: Yale University Press.

SCHAIE, K. W., & WILLIS, S. L. (1991). ADULT DEVELOPMENT AND AGING (3rd ed.). New York: Harper Collins.

SCHARNBERG, M. (1993). THE NONAUTHENTIC NATURE OF FREUD'S OBSERVATIONS: VOL. 1. THE SEDUCTION THEORY. Philadelphia: Coronet Books.

SCHEIER, M. F., BUSS, A. H., & BUSS, D. M. (1978). Self-consciousness, self-reports of aggressiveness, and aggressions. JOURNAL OF RESEARCH IN PERSONALITY, *12*, 133–140.

SCHERER, K., & WALLBOTT, H. (1994, February). Evidence for universality and cultural variation of differential emotion response patterning. JOURNAL OF PERSONALITY AND SOCIAL PSYCHOLOGY, *66*(2), 310–328.

SCHIFF, W., & FOULKE, E. (Eds.) (1982). TACTUAL PERCEPTION: A SOURCEBOOK. Cambridge: Cambridge University Press.

SCHIFFENBAUER, A., & SCHIAVO, R. S. (1976). Physical distance and attraction: An intensification effect. JOURNAL OF EXPERIMENTAL SOCIAL PSYCHOLOGY, *12*, 274–282.

SCHIFFMAN, H. R. (1990). SENSATION AND PERCEPTION: AN INTEGRATED APPROACH (3rd ed.). New York: Wiley.

SCHLEIFER, S. J., KELLER, S. E., MCKEGNEY, F. P., & STEIN, M. (1979 March). The influence of stress and other psychosocial factors on human immunity. Paper presented at the 36th Annual Meeting of the Psychosomatic Society, Dallas.

SCHLESINGER, A. M., JR. (1965). A THOUSAND DAYS. Boston: Houghton Mifflin.

SCHMITT, B. H., GILOVICH, T., GOORE, N., & JOSEPH, L. (1986). Mere presence and social facilitation: One more time. JOURNAL OF EXPERIMENTAL SOCIAL PSYCHOLOGY, *22*, 242–248.

SCHNEIDER, A. M., & TARSHIS, B. (1986). AN INTRODUCTION TO PHYSIOLOGICAL PSYCHOLOGY (3rd ed.). New York: Random House.

SCHNEIDER, D. J., & MILLER, R. S. (1975). The effects of enthusiasm and quality of arguments on attitude attribution. JOURNAL OF PERSONALITY, *43*, 693–708.

SCHNEIDERMAN, N. S., & TAPP, J. T. (Eds.) (1985). BEHAVIORAL MEDICINE: THE BIOPSYCHOSOCIAL APPROACH. New York: Erlbaum.

SCHNEIDMAN, E. A. (1985). DEFINITION OF SUICIDE. New York: Wiley.

SCHUCKIT, M. A. (1989). DRUG AND ALCOHOL

ABUSE: A CLINICAL GUIDE TO DIAGNOSIS AND TREAT-MENT (3rd ed.) New York: Plenum.

SCHULTZ, D. (1987). A HISTORY OF MODERN PSYCHOLOGY (4th ed.). New York: Academic Press.

SCHWARTZ, B. & REISBERG, D. (1991). LEARNING AND MEMORY. New York: Norton.

SCHWARTZ, G. E. (1975). Biofeedback, self-regulation, and the patterning of physiological processes. AMERICAN SCIENTIST, 63, 314–324.

SCHWARZ, C. S. (1983, April). Infant day care: effects at 2, 4, and 8 years. Paper presented at the meeting of the Society for Research on Child Development, Detroit. (Abstract published by ERIC Clearinghouse on Elementary and Early Education, #PS013805).

SCOTT, T. R., & MARK, G. P. (1986). Feeding and taste. PROG NEUROBIOL, 27(4), 293–317.

SEARS, D. O., PEPLAU, L. A., & TAYLOR, S. E. (1991). SOCIAL PSYCHOLOGY (7th ed.). Englewood Cliffs, NJ: Prentice-Hall.

SEARS, R. R. (1943). Survey of objective studies of psychoanalytic concepts. SOCIAL SCIENCE RESEARCH COUNCIL BULLETIN, No. 51.

SEARS, R. R. (1944). Experimental analyses of psychoanalytic phenomena. In J. Hunt (Ed.), PERSONALITY AND THE BEHAVIOR DISORDERS (Vol. 1, pp. 306–332). New York: Ronald.

SEEMAN, J. (1949). A study of the process of nondirective therapy. JOURNAL OF CONSULTING PSYCHOLOGY, 13, 157–168.

SEGAL, M. W. (1974). Alphabet and attraction: An unobstrusive measure of the effect of propinquity in a field setting. JOURNAL OF PERSONALITY AND SOCIAL PSYCHOLOGY, 30, 654–657.

SEIDEN, R. H. (1966). Campus tragedy: A study of student suicide. JOURNAL OF ABNORMAL PSYCHOLOGY, 71, 388–399.

SEIFERT, C. M., ROBERTSON, S. P., & BLACK, J. B. (1985). Types of inferences generated during reading. JOURNAL OF MEMORY AND LANGUAGE, 24, 405–422.

SEKULER, R., & BLAKE, R. (1985). PERCEPTION. New York: Knopf.

SEKULER, R., & GANZ, L. (1963). A new after-effect of seen movement with a stabilized retinal image. SCIENCE, 139, 1146–1148.

SELFRIDGE, O., & NEISSER, U. (1960). Pattern recognition by machine. SCIENTIFIC AMERICAN, 203, 60–80.

SELIGMAN, M. E. P. (1975). HELPLESSNESS. San Francisco: Freeman.

SELIGMAN, M. E. P. & BINIK, Y. M. (1977). The safety signal hypothesis. In H. Davis & H. Hurwitz (Eds.), PAVLOVIAN OPERANT INTERACTIONS. Hillsdale, NJ: Erlbaum.

SELIGMAN, M. E. P. & JOHNSTON, J. C. (1973). A cognitive theory of avoidance learning. In F. J. McGuigan & D. B. Lumsden (Eds.), CONTEMPORARY APPROACHES TO CONDITIONING AND LEARNING. Washington, D.C.: Winston-Wiley.

SELYE, H. (1979). THE STRESS OF LIFE (rev. ed.). New York: Van Nostrand Reinhold.

SERGIOS, P. A., & CODY, J. (1985). Physical attractiveness and socia: Assertiveness skills in male homosexual dating behavior and partner selection. JOURNAL OF SOCIAL PSYCHOLOGY, 125, 505–514.

SHAFER, L. F. (1947). Fear and courage in aerial combat. JOURNAL OF CONSULTING PSYCHOLOGY, 11, 137–143.

SHALLICE, T. (1988). FROM NEUROPSYCHOLOGY TO MENTAL STRUCTURE. Cambridge: Cambridge University Press.

SHALLICE, T., FLETCHER, P., FRITH, C. D., GRASBY, P., FRACKOWIAK, R. S. J., & DOLAN, R. J. (1994). Brain regions associated with acquisition and retrieval of verbal episodic memory. NATURE, 368, 633–635.

SHANKS, D. R., & DICKINSON, A., (1987). Associative accounts of causality judgment. THE PSYCHOLOGY OF LEARNING AND MOTIVATION, 21, 229–261.

SHAPIRO, A. K., & MORRIS, L. A. (1978). The placebo effect in medical and psychological therapies. In S. L. Garfield & A. E. Bergin (Eds.), HANDBOOK OF PSYCHOTHERAPY AND BEHAVIOR CHANGE, (2nd ed.) New York: Wiley.

SHAPIRO, D. A., & SHAPIRO, D. (1982). Meta-analysis of comparative therapy outcome studies: A replication and refinement. PSYCHOLOGICAL BULLETIN, 92, 581–604.

SHAPLEY, R., & LENNIE, P. (1985). Spatial frequency analysis in the visual system. ANNUAL REVIEW OF NEUROSCIENCES, 8, 547–583.

SHAVER, P., HAZAN, C., & BRADSHAW, D. (1988). Love as attachment: The integration of three behavioral systems. In R. J. Sternberg, & M. L. Barnes (Eds.), THE PSYCHOLOGY OF LOVE (pp. 68–99). New Haven, CT: Yale University Press.

SHAW, D. W., & THORESEN, C. E. (1974). Effects of modeling and desensitization in reducing dentist phobia. JOURNAL OF COUNSELING PSYCHOLOGY, 21, 415–420.

SHEEHY, G. (1976). PASSAGES. New York: Dutton.

SHEINGOLD, K., & TENNEY, Y. J. (1982). Memory for a salient childhood event. In U. Neisser (Ed.), MEMORY OBSERVED: REMEMBERING IN NATURAL CONTEXTS. San Francisco: Freeman.

SHEKELLE, R., NEATON, J. D., JACOBS, D., HULLEY, S., & BLACKBURN, H. (1983). Type A behavior pattern in MRFIT. A paper presented to the American Heart Association Council on Epidemiology Meetings, San Diego.

SHEPARD, R. N., & COOPER, L. A. (1982). MENTAL IMAGES AND THEIR TRANSFORMATIONS. Cambridge, MA: MIT Press, Bradford Books.

SHEPHER, J. (1971). Mate selection among second generation kibbutz adolescents and adults: Incest avoidance and negative imprinting. ARCHIVES OF SEXUAL BEHAVIOR, 1, 293–307.

SHEPOSH, J. P., DEMING, M., & YOUNG, L. E. (1977, April). The radiating effects of status and attractiveness of a male upon evaluating his female partner. Paper presented at the annual meeting of the Western psychological Association, Seattle.

SHERMAN, A. R. (1972). Real-life exposure as a primary therapeutic factor in the desensitization treatment of fear. JOURNAL OF ABNORMAL PSYCHOLOGY. 79, 19–28.

SHERRINGTON, R., BRYNJOLFSSON, J., & collaborators (1988). Localization of a susceptibility locus for schizophrenia on chromsome 5. NATURE, 336, 164–167.

SHERWIN, B. (1988a). A comparative analysis of the role of androgen in human male and female sexual behavior: Behavioral specificity, critical thresholds, and sensitivity. PSYCHOBIOLOGY, 16, 416–425, 1988.

SHERWIN, B. (1988b). Critical analysis of the role of androgens in human male and female sexual behavior: Behavioral specificity, critical thresholds, and sensitivity. PSYCHOBIOLOGY, 16, 416–423.

SHWEDER, R. A. (1984). Anthropology's romantic rebellion against the enlightenment, or there's more to thinking than reason and evidence. In R. A. Shweder, & R. A. LeVine (Eds.), CULTURE THEORY: ESSAYS ON MIND, SELF, AND EMOTION (pp. 27–66). Cambridge: Cambridge University Press.

SIEGEL, S. (1979). The Role of Conditioning, Drug Tolerance and Addiction. In J. D. Keehn (Ed.), PSYCHOPATHOLOGY IN ANIMALS: RESEARCH AND CLINICAL IMPLICATIONS. New York: Academic Press.

SIEGEL, S. (1983). Classical conditioning, drug tolerance, and drug dependence. In Y. Israel, F. B. Glaser, H. Kalant, R. E. Popham, W. Schmidt, & R. G. Smart (Eds.). RESEARCH ADVANCES IN ALCOHOL AND DRUG PROBLEMS (Vol. 7). New York: Plenum.

SIEGLER, R. S. (1986). CHILDREN'S THINKING. Englewood Cliffs: NJ: Prentice-Hall.

SIGALL, H., & LANDY, D. (1973). Radiating beauty: The effects of having a physically attractive partner on person perception. JOURNAL OF PERSONALITY AND SOCIAL PSYCHOLOGY, 31, 410–414.

SILVERMAN, I. (1964). Self-esteem and differential responsiveness to success and failure. JOURNAL OF ABNORMAL AND SOCIAL PSYCHOLOGY, 69, 115–119.

SILVERMAN, I. (1971). Physical attractiveness and courtship. SEXUAL BEHAVIOR, 1, 22–25.

SILVERMAN, L. H., & FISHEL, A. K. (1981). The Oedipus Complex: Studies in adult male behavior. In L. Wheeler (Ed.), REVIEW OF PERSONALITY AND SOCIAL PSYCHOLOGY (Vol. 2, pp. 43–67). Beverly Hills, CA: Sage.

SILVERMAN, L. H., ROSS, D. L., ADLER, J. M., & LUSTIG, D. A. (1978). Simple research paradigm for demonstrating subliminal psychodynamic activation: Effects of Oedipal stimuli on dart-throwing accuracy in college males. JOURNAL OF ABNORMAL PSYCHOLOGY, 87, 341–357.

SILVERMAN, L. B. (1991). Transforming the debate about child care and maternal employment. AMERICAN PSYCHOLOGIST, 46, 1025–1032.

SIMMONS, J. V. (1981). PROJECT SEA HUNT: A RE-

PORT ON PROTOTYPE DEVELOPMENT AND TESTS. Technical Report 746, Naval Ocean Systems Center, San Diego.

SIMMONS, R. G., & BLYTH, D. A. (1988). MOVING INTO ADOLESCENCE: THE IMPACT OF PUBERTAL CHANGE AND SCHOOL CONTEXT. New York: Aldine.

SIMON, H. A. (1985, June). Using Cognitive Science to Solve Human Problems. Paper presented at Science and Public Policy Seminar, Federation of Behavioral, Psychological, and Cognitive Sciences.

SIMON, H. A. (1989). The scientist as problem solver. In D. Klar & K. Kotovsky (Eds.), COMPLEX INFORMATION PROCESSING: THE IMPACT OF HERBERT A. SIMON. Hillsdale, NJ: Erlbaum Press.

SIMON, H. A., & GILMARTIN, K. (1973). A simulation of memory for chess positions. COGNITIVE PSYCHOLOGY, 5, 29–46.

SIMPSON, J. A., & GANGESTAD, S. W. (1992). Sociosexuality and romantic partner choice. JOURNAL OF PERSONALITY, 60, 31–51.

SIMPSON, J. A., CAMPBELL, B., & BERSCHEID, E. (1986). The association between romantic love and marriage: Kephart (1967) twice revisited. PERSONALITY AND SOCIAL PSYCHOLOGY BULLETIN, 12, 363–372.

SINGER, J. L., & SINGER, D. G. (1981). TELEVISION, IMAGINATION AND AGGRESSION. Hillsdale, NJ: Erlbaum.

SINGER, R. N., MURPHEY, M., & TENNANT, L. K. (Eds.) (1993). HANDBOOK OF RESEARCH ON SPORT PSYCHOLOGY. New York: Macmillan.

SIQUELAND, E. R., & LIPSITT, J. P. (1966). Conditioned head-turning in human newborns. JOURNAL OF EXPERIMENTAL CHILD PSYCHOLOGY, 3, 356–376.

SIZEMORE, C. C., & PITTILLO, E. S. (1977). I'M EVE. Garden City, NY: Doubleday.

SKINNER, B. F. (1938). THE BEHAVIOR OF ORGANISMS. New York: Appleton-Century-Crofts.

SKINNER, B. F. (1948). "Superstition" in the pigeon. JOURNAL OF EXPERIMENTAL PSYCHOLOGY, 38, 168–172.

SKINNER, B. F. (1971). BEYOND FREEDOM AND DIGNITY. New York: Knopf.

SKINNER, B. F. (1981). Selection by consequences. SCIENCE, 213, 501–504.

SKYRMS, B. (1986). CHOICE AND CHANCE: AN INTRODUCTION TO INDUCTIVE LOGIC. Belmont, CA: Dickenson.

SLOANE, R. B., STAPLES, F. R., CRISTOL, A. H., YORKSTON, N. J., & WHIPPLE, K. (1975). PSYCHOTHERAPY VS. BEHAVIOR THERAPY. Cambrige, MA: Harvard University Press.

SLOBIN, D. I. (1971). Cognitive prerequisites for the acquisition of grammar. In C. A. Ferguson, & D. I. Slobin (Eds.), STUDIES OF CHILD LANGUAGE DEVELOPMENTS. New York: Holt, Rinehart & Winston.

SLOBIN, D. I. (1979). PSYCHOLINGUISTICS (2nd. ed.). Glenville, IL: Scott, Foresman.

SLOBIN, D. I. (Ed.) (1985). THE CROSS-LINGUISTIC STUDY OF LANGUAGE ACQUISITION. Hillsdale, NJ: Erlbaum.

SLOMAN, S. & RUMELHART, D. E. (1992). Reducing interference in distributed memories through episodic gating. In A. Healy, S. Kosslyn, & R. Shiffrin (Eds.) FROM LEARNING THEORY TO CONNECTIONIST THEORY: ESSAYS IN HONOR OF W. K. ESTES. Hillsdale, NJ: Erlbaum.

SMITH, C. A., & ELLSWORTH, P. C. (1985). Patterns of cognitive appraisal in emotion. JOURNAL OF PERSONALITY AND SOCIAL PSYCHOLOGY, 48, 813–848.

SMITH, C. A., & ELLSWORTH, P. C. (1987). Patterns of appraisal and emotion related to taking an exam. JOURNAL OF PERSONALITY AND SOCIAL PSYCHOLOGY, 52, 475–488.

SMITH, D., KING, M., & HOEBEL, B. G. (1970). Lateral hypothalamic control of killing: Evidence for a cholinoceptive mechanism. SCIENCE, 167, 900–901.

SMITH, E. E. (1989). Concepts and induction. In M. I. Posner (Ed.), FOUNDATIONS OF COGNITIVE SCIENCE. Cambridge, MA: MIT Press.

SMITH, E. E., & JONIDES, J. (1994). Neuropsychological studies of working memory. In M. Gazzaniga (Ed.), THE COGNITIVE NEUROSCIENCES. Cambridge, MA: MIT Press.

SMITH, E. E., JONIDES, J., & KOEPPE, R. A. (1996). Dissociating verbal and spatial working memory using PET.

SMITH, E. E., & MEDIN, D. L. (1981). CATEGORIES AND CONCEPTS. Cambridge, MA: Harvard University Press.

SMITH, G. M. (1986). Adolescent personality traits that predict adult drug use. COMPREHENSIVE THERAPY, 22, 44–50.

SMITH, G. P., & GIBBS, J. (1994). Satiating effect of cholecystokinin. ANN NY ACAD SCI, 713, 236–41.

SMITH, M. B., BRUNER, J. S., & WHITE, R. W. (1956). OPINIONS AND PERSONALITY. New York: Wiley.

SMITH, M. L., GLASS, G. V., & MILLER, T. I. (1980). THE BENEFITS OF PSYCHOTHERAPY. Baltimore: Johns Hopkins University Press.

SMUTS, B. B. (1986). Gender, aggression, and influence. In B. Smuts, D. Cheney, R. Seyfarth, R. Wrangham, T. Struhsaker (Eds.), PRIMATE SOCIETIES. Chicago: University of Chicago Press.

SNODGRASS, J. G., LEVY-BERGER, G., & HAYDON, M. (1985). HUMAN EXPERIMENTAL PSYCHOLOGY. New York: Oxford University Press.

SNOW, C. (1987). Relevance of the notion of a critical period to language acquisition. In M. H. Bornstein (Ed.), SENSITIVE PERIODS IN DEVELOPMENT: INTERDISCIPLINARY PERSPECTIVES. Hillsdale, NJ: Erlbaum.

SNOWDEN, L. R. (1988). Ethnicity and utilization of mental health services: An overview of current findings. In OKLAHOMA MENTAL HEALTH RESEARCH INSTITUTE, 1988 PROFESSIONAL SYMPOSIUM (pp. 227–238). Oklahoma City: Oklahoma Mental Health Research Institute.

SNOWDEN, L., & CHEUNG, F. (March 1990). Use of inpatient mental health services by members of ethnic minority groups. AMERICAN PSYCHOLOGIST, 45(3), 347–355.

SNYDER, M. L., TANKE, E. D., & BERSCHEID, E. (1977). Social perception and interpersonal behavior: On the self-fulfilling nature of social stereotypes. JOURNAL OF PERSONALITY AND SOCIAL PSYCHOLOGY, 35, 656–666.

SNYDER, S. H. (1980). BIOLOGICAL ASPECTS OF MENTAL DISORDERS. New York: Oxford University Press.

SOLOMON, R. L., & CORBIT, J. D. (1974). An opponent-process theory of motivation: I. Temporal dynamics of affect. PSYCHOLOGICAL REVIEW, 81, 119–145.

SPANOS, N. P. (1986). Hypnotic behavior: A social-psychological interpretation of amnesia, analgesia, and "trance logic". THE BEHAVIORAL AND BRAIN SCIENCES, 9, 449–502.

SPANOS, N. P., & HEWITT, E. C. (1980). The hidden observer in hypnotic analgesia: Discovery or experimental creation? JOURNAL OF PERSONALITY AND SOCIAL PSYCHOLOGY, 39, 1201–1214.

SPEARMAN, C. (1904). "General intelligence" objectively determined and measured. AMERICAN JOURNAL OF PSYCHOLOGY, 15, 201–293.

SPENCE, K. W. (1964). Anxiety (Drive) level and performance in eyelid conditioning. PSYCHOLOGICAL BULLETIN, 61, 129–139.

SPERRY, R. W. (1968). Perception in the absence of neocortical commissures. In PERCEPTION AND ITS DISORDERS (Res. Publ. A.R.N.M.D., Vol. 48). New York: The Association for Research in Nervous & Mental Disease.

SPIEGEL, D. (1991). Mind matters: Effects of group support on cancer patients. JOURNAL OF NIH RESEARCH, 3, 61–63.

SPIEGEL, D., BLOOM, J. R., KRAEMER, H. C., & GOTTHEIL, E. (1989). Psychological support for cancer patients. LANCET, II, 1447.

SPIELBERGER, C. D., JOHNSON, E. H., RUSSELL, S. F., CRANE, R. S., JACOBS, G. A., & WORDEN, T. J. (1985). The Experience and Expression of Anger: Construction and validation of an anger expression scale. In M. A. Chesney & R. H. Rosenman (Eds.), ANGER AND HOSTILITY IN CARDIOVASCULAR AND BEHAVIORAL DISORDERS. New York: Hemisphere/McGraw-Hill.

SPOEHR, K. T., & LEHMKUHLE, S. W. (1982). VISUAL INFORMATION PROCESSING. San Francisco: Freeman.

SPRAFKIN, J. N., LIEBERT, R. M., & POULOUS, R. W. (1975). Effects of a prosocial televised example on children's helping. JOURNAL OF PERSONALITY AND SOCIAL PSYCHOLOGY, 48, 35–46.

SPRINGER, S. P., & DEUTSCH, G. (1989). LEFT BRAIN, RIGHT BRAIN (3rd ed.). San Francisco: Freeman.

SQUIRE, L. R. (1987). MEMORY AND BRAIN. New York: Oxford University Press.

SQUIRE, L. R. (1992). Memory and the hippocampus: A synthesis from findings with rats, monkeys, and humans. PSYCHOLOGICAL REVIEW, 99, 195–231.

SQUIRE, L. R., & BUTTERS, N. (Eds.) (1984). THE NEUROPSYCHOLOGY OF MEMORY. New York: Guilford Press.

SQUIRE, L. R., & FOX, M. M. (1980). Assessment of remote memory: Validation of the television test by repeated testing during a seven-day period. BEHAVIORAL RESEARCH METHODS AND INSTRUMENTATION, *12*, 583–586.

SQUIRE, L. R., OJEMANN, J. G., MIEZIN, F. M., PETERSEN, S. E., VIDEEN, T. O., & RAICHLE, M. E. (1992). Activation of the hippocampus in normal humans: A functional anatomical study of memory, PROCEEDINGS OF THE NATIONAL ACADEMY OF SCIENCE, *89*, 1837–1841.

SQUIRE, L. R., ZOLA-MORGAN, S., CAVE, C. B. HAIST, F., MUSEN, G., & SUZUKI, W. A. (1990). MEMORY: ORGANIZATION OF BRAIN SYSTEMS AND COGNITION. In Symposium on quantiative biology, the brain. Vol. 55, Cold Spring Harbor Laboratory, Cold Spring Harbor, NY.

STAATS, A. W. (1968). LANGUAGE, LEARNING, AND COGNITION. New York: Holt, Rinehart & Winston.

STALLER, S. J., DOWELL, R. C., BEITER, A. L., & BRIMACOMBE, J. A. (1991). Perceptual abilities of children with the Nucleus 22-channel cochlear implant. EAR HEAR, *12*, (supplement) 34–47.

STANLEY, B. G., ANDERSON, K. C., GRAYSON, M. H., & LIEBOWITZ, S. F. (1989). Repeated hypothalamic stimulation with neuropeptide Y increases daily carbohydrate and fat intake and body weight gain in female rats. PHYSIOLOGY AND BEHAVIOR, *46*, 173–177.

STASSER, G., TAYLOR, L. A., & HANNA, C. (1989). Information sampling in structured and unstructured discussion of three- and six-person groups. JOURNAL OF PERSONALITY AND SOCIAL PSYCHOLOGY, *57*, 67–78.

STASSER, G., & TITUS, W. (1985). Pooling of unshared information in group decision making: Biased information sampling during discussion. JOURNAL OF PERSONALITY AND SOCIAL PSYCHOLOGY, *48*, 1467–1478.

STATTIN, H., & MAGNUSSON, D. (1990). PUBERTAL MATURATION IN FEMALE DEVELOPMENT. Hillsdale, NJ: Erlbaum.

STAYTON, D. J. (1973, March). Infant responses to brief everyday separations: Distress, following, and greeting. Paper presented at the meeting of the Socity for Research in Child Development.

STEERING COMMITTEE OF THE PHYSICIANS' HEALTH STUDY RESEARCH GROUP (1988). Preliminary report: findings from the aspirin component of the ongoing Physicians' Health Study. NEW ENGLAND JOURNAL OF MEDICINE, *318*, 262–264.

STEFFY, R. A., ASARNOW, R. F., ASARNOW, J. R., MACcRIMMON, D. J., & CLEGHORN, J. M. (1984). The McMaster-Waterloo High-Risk Project: Multifaced strategy for high-risk research. In H. F. Watt, E. J. Anthony, L. C. Wynne, & J. E. Rolf (Eds.), CHILDREN AT RISK FOR SCHIZOPHRENIA. New York: Cambridge University Press.

STEIN, J. A., GOLDING, J. M., SIEGEL, J. M., BURNAM, M. A., & SORENSEN, S. B. (1988). Long-term psychological sequelae of child sexual abuse: the Los Angeles epidemiologic catchment area study. In G. E. Wyatt & G. J. Powell (Eds.), LASTING EFFECTS OF CHILD SEXUAL ABUSE. Newbury Park: Sage Publications.

STEINBERG, L. (1989). ADOLESCENCE (2nd ed.). New York: Knopf.

STEINBERG, L. (1987). Impact of puberty on family relations: Effects of pubertal status and pubertal timing. DEVELOPMENTAL PSYCHOLOGY, *23*, 451–460.

STEINER, J. E. (1979). Human facial expressions in response to taste and smell stimulation. ADV CHILD DEV BEHAV, *13*, 257–95.

STEKETEE, G., & WHITE, K. (1990). WHEN ONCE IN NOT ENOUGH. Oakland, CA: New Harbinger Publications.

STELLAR, E. (1954). The physiology of motivation. PSYCHOLOGICAL REVIEW, *61*, 5–22.

STELLAR, J. R., & STELLAR, E. (1985). THE NEUROBIOLOGY OF MOTIVATION AND REWARD. New York: Springer-Verlag.

STERN, D. B. (1978). Phenomenology of obsessive-compulsive neurosis. BRITISH JOURNAL OF PSYCHIATRY, *132*, 233–234.

STERNBACH, R. A. (Ed.) (1986). THE PSYCHOLOGY OF PAIN (2nd ed.). New York: Raven.

STERNBERG, R. J. (Ed.) (1984). HUMAN ABILITIES: AN INFORMATION-PROCESSING APPROACH. New York: Freeman.

STERNBERG, R. (1986). A triangular theory of love. PSYCHOLOGICAL REVIEW, *93*, 119–135.

STERNBERG, R. J. (1985). BEYOND IQ: A TRIARCHIC THEORY OF HUMAN INTELLIGENCE. New York: Cambridge University Press.

STERNBERG, R. J. (1986). INTELLIGENCE APPLIED: UNDERSTANDING AND INCREASING YOUR INTELLECTUAL SKILLS. San Diego: Harcourt Brace Jovanovich.

STERNBERG, S. (1966). Highspeed scanning in human memory. SCIENCE, *153*, 652–654.

STERNBERG, S. (1969). Memory-scanning: Mental processes revealed by reaction-time experiments. AMERICAN SCIENTIST, *57*, 421–457.

STERNBERG, S. (1975). Memory scanning: New findings and current controversies. QUARTERLY JOURNAL OF EXPERIMENTAL PSYCHOLOGY, *27*, 1–32.

STERNGLANZ, S. H., & SERBIN, L. A. (1974). Sex-role stereotyping in children's television programs. DEVELOPMENTAL PSYCHOLOGY, *10*, 710–715.

STEUER, F. B., APPLEFIELD, J. M., & SMITH, R. (1971). Televised aggression and the interpersonal aggression of preschool children. JOURNAL OF EXPERIMENTAL CHILD PSYCHOLOGY, *11*, 422–447.

STEVENS, S. S. (1957). On the psychophysical law. PSYCHOLOGICAL REVIEW, *64*, 153–181.

STEVENSON, H. W., LEE, S., & GRAHAM, T. (1993). Chinese and Japanese kindergartens: Case study in comparative research. In B. Spodek (Ed.), HANDBOOK OF RESEARCH ON THE EDUCATION OF YOUNG CHILDREN. New York: Macmillan.

STILES, W. B., SHAPIRO, D. A., & ELLIOTT, R. (1986). Are all psychotherapies equivalent? AMERICAN PSYCHOLOGIST, *41*, 165–180.

STOKES, D. M. (1987). Theoretical parapsychology. In S. Krippner (Ed.), ADVANCES IN PARAPSYCHOLOGICAL RESEARCH (Vol. 5). Jefferson, NC: McFarland.

STONER, J. A. F. (1961). A COMPARISON OF INDIVIDUAL AND GROUP DECISIONS INVOLVING RISK. Unpublished masters' thesis, Massachusetts Institute of Technology.

STRACK, F., MARTIN, L. L., & STEPPER, S. (1988). Inhibiting and facilitating conditions of the human smile: A non-obtrusive test of the facial feedback hypothesis. JOURNAL OF PERSONALITY AND SOCIAL PSYCHOLOGY, *54*, 768–777.

STRAUSS, J. S. (1982). Behavioral aspects of being disadvantaged and risk for schizophrenia. In D. L. Parron, F. Solomon, & C. D. Jenkins (Eds.), BEHAVIOR, HEALTH RISKS, AND SOCIAL DISADVANTAGE. Washington, DC: National Academy Press.

STREISSGUTH, A. P., CLARREN, S. K., & JONES, K. L. (1985). Natural history of the fetal alcohol syndrome: A 10-year follow-up of eleven patients. THE LANCET, *2*, 85–91.

STRICKER, E. M. (1983). Thirst and sodium appetite after colloid treatment in rats: Role of the renin-angiotensin-aldosterone system. BEHAVIORAL NEUROSCIENCE, *97*, 725–737.

STRICKER, E. M., & ROWLAND, N., SALLER, C. F., & FRIEDMAN, M. I. (1977). Homeostasis during hypglycemia: Central control of adrenal secretion and peripheral control of feeding. SCIENCE, *196*, 79–81.

STRICKER, E. M., & VERGALIS, J. G. (1988). Hormones and behavior: The biology of thirst and sodium appetite. AMERICAN SCIENTIST, *76*, 261–268.

STROEBE, W., INSKO, C. A. THOMPSON, V. D., & LAYTON, B. D. (1971). Effects of physical attractiveness, attitude similarity and sex on various aspects of interpersonal attraction. JOURNAL OF PERSONALITY AND SOCIAL PSYCHOLOGY, *18*, 79–91.

STRONG, S. R., HILLS, H. J., KILMARTIN, C. T., DEVRIES, H., LANIER, K., NELSON, B. N., STRICKLAND, D., & MEYER, C. W., III (1988). The dynamic relations among interpersonal behaviors: A test of complementarity and anti-complementarity. JOURNAL OF PERSONALITY AND SOCIAL PSYCHOLOGY, *54*, 798–810.

STUART, R. B., & DAVIS, B. (1972). SLIM CHANCE IN A FAT WORLD. Champaign, IL: Research Press.

STUNKARD, A. J. (1982). Obesity. In M. Hersen, A. Bellack, A. Kazdin (Eds.), INTERNATIONAL HANDBOOK OF BEHAVIOR MODIFICATION AND THERAPY. New York: Plenum.

SUAREZ, E. C., & WILLIAMS, R. B. (1989). Situational determinants of cardiovascular and emotional reactivity in high and low hostile men. PSYCHOSOMATIC MEDICINE. *51*, 404–418.

SUDDATHG, R. L. CHRISTISON, G. W., TORREY, E. F., CASANOVA, M. F., & WEIN-

BERGER, D. R. (1990). Anatomical abnormalities in the brains of monozygotic twins discordant for schizophrenia. NEW ENGLAND JOURNAL OF MEDICINE, *322*, 789–794.

SUE, S., ALLEN, D., & CONAWAY, L. (1978). The responsiveness and equality of mental health care to Chicanos and native Americans. AMERICAN JOURNAL OF COMMUNITY PSYCHOLOGY, *6*, 137–146.

SUE, S., & ZANE, N. (1987). The role of culture and cultural techniques in psychotherapy: A critique and reformulation. AMERICAN PSYCHOLOGIST, *42*(1), 37–51.

SUEDFELD, P. (1975). The benefits of boredom: Sensory deprivation considered. AMERICAN SCIENTIST, *63*, 60–69.

SULLIVAN, H. S. (1953). THE INTERPERSONAL THEORY OF PSYCHIATRY. New York: Norton.

SUINN, R. M. (1990). ANXIETY MANAGEMENT TRAINING: A BEHAVIOR THERAPY. New York: Plenum Press.

SUOMI, S. J., HARLOW, H. F., & MCKINNEY, W. T. (1972). Monkey psychiatrist. AMERICAN JOURNAL OF PSYCHIATRY, *28*, 41–46.

SWETS, J. A., & BJORK, R. A. (1990). Enhancing human performance: An evaluation of "new age" techniques considered by the U.S. Army. PSYCHOLOGICAL SCIENCE. *1*, 85–96.

SWINNEY, D. A. (1979). Lexical access during sentence comprehension: Consideration of context effects. JOURNAL OF VERBAL LEARNING AND VERBAL BEHAVIOR, *18*, 645–659.

SWINNEY, D. A. ZURIF, E. B., & NICOL, J. (1989). The effects of focal brain damage on sentence processing: An examination of the neurological organization of a mental module. JOURNAL OF COGNITIVE NEUROSCIENCE, *1*, 25–37.

SYER, J., & CONNOLLY, C. (1988). SPORTING BODY SPORTING MIND: AN ATHLETE'S GUIDE TO MENTAL TRAINING. Englewood Cliffs, NJ: Prentice Hall.

SZATMARI, P., BARTOLUCCI, G., BRENNER, R., BOND, S., & RICH, S. (1989). A follow-up study of high-functioning autistic children. JOURNAL OF AUTISM AND DEVELOPMENTAL DISORDERS, *19*, 213–225.

TALLENT, N. (1992). THE PRACTICE OF PSYCHOLOGICAL ASSESSMENT. Englewood Cliffs, NJ: Prentice-Hall.

TANENHAUS, M. G., LEIMAN, J., & SEIDENBERG, M. (1979). Evidence for multiple stages in the processing of ambiguous words in syntactic contexts. JOURNAL OF VERBAL LEARNING AND VERBAL BEHAVIOR, *18*, 427–441.

TARLER-BENLOLO, L. (1978). The role of relaxation in biofeedback training. PSYCHOLOGICAL BULLETIN, *85*, 727–755.

TART, C. T., & DICK, L. (1970). Conscious control of dreaming. Pt. 1. The post-hypnotic dream. JOURNAL OF ABNORMAL PSYCHOLOGY, *76*, 304–315.

TARTTER, V. C. (1986). LANGUAGE PROCESSES. New York: Holt, Rinehart & Winston.

TAVRIS, C. (1984). ANGER: THE MISUNDERSTOOD EMOTION. New York: Simon & Schuster.

TAVRIS, C., & SADD, S. (1977). THE REDBOOK REPORT ON FEMALE SEXUALITY. New York: Dell.

TAYLOR, S. (1986). Stress and development of illness. In S. E. Taylor, HEALTH PSYCHOLOGY. New York: Random House.

TAYLOR, S. E., & BROWN, J. D. (1988). Illusion and well-being: A social psychological perspective on mental health. PSYCHOLOGICAL BULLETIN, *103*, 193–210.

TAYLOR, S., KEMENY, M., ASPINWALL, L., SCHNEIDER, S., RODRIGUEZ, R., & HERBERT, M. (1992). Optimism, coping, psychological distress, and high-risk sexual behavior among men at risk for acquired immunodeficiency syndrome (AIDS). JOURNAL OF PERSONALITY AND SOCIAL PSYCHOLOGY, *63*(3), 460–473.

TAYLOR, S. E., & THOMPSON, S. C. (1982). Stalking the elusive "vividness" effect. PSYCHOLOGICAL REVIEW, *89*, 155–181.

TEDESCHI, J. T., & ROSENFELD, P. (1981). Impression management and the forced compliance situation. In J. T. Tedeschi (Ed.) IMPRESSION MANAGEMENT THEORY AND SOCIAL PSYCHOLOGICAL RESEARCH. New York: Academic Press.

TEITELBAUM, P., & EPSTEIN, A. N. (1962). The lateral hypothalamic syndrome: Recovery of feeding and drinking after lateral hypothalamic lesions. PSYCHOLOGICAL REVIEW, *69*, 74–90.

TELLEGEN, A., LYKKEN, D. T., BOUCHARD, T. J., JR., WILCOX, K. J., SEGAL, N. L., & RICH, S. (1988). Personality similarity in twins reared apart and together. JOURNAL OF PERSONALITY AND SOCIAL PSYCHOLOGY, *54*, 1031–1039.

TEMPLIN, M. C. (1957). CERTAIN LANGUAGE SKILLS IN CHILDREN: THEIR DEVELOPMENT AND INTERRELATIONSHIPS. Minneapolis: University of Minnesota Press.

TENNANT, C., SMITH, A., BEBBINGTON, P., & HURRY, J. (1981). Parental loss in childhood: Relationship to adult psychiatric impairment and contact with psychiatric services. ARCHIVES OF GENERAL PSYCHIATRY, *38*, 309–314.

TERKEL, J., & ROSENBLATT, J. S. (1972). Humoral factors underlying maternal behavior at parturition: Cross transfusion between freely moving rats. JOURNAL OF COMPARATIVE AND PHYSIOLOGICAL PSYCHOLOGY, *80*, 365–371.

TERRACE, H. S., PETITTO, L. A. SANDERS, D. J., & BEVER, T. G. (1979). Can an ape create a sentence? SCIENCE, *206*, 891–902.

TESSER, A., & BRODIE, M. (1971). A note on the evaluation of a "computer date." PSYCHONOMIC SCIENCE. *23*, 300.

THIGPEN, C. H., & CLECKLEY, H. (1957). THE THREE FACES OF EVE. New York: McGraw-Hill.

THOM, M. (Ed.) (1987). LETTERS TO *MS*. 1972–1987. New York: Holt.

THOMAS, A., & CHESS, S. (1977). TEMPERAMENT AND DEVELOPMENT, New York: Brunner/Mazel.

THOMAS, A., & CHESS, S. (1986). The New York longitudinal study: From infancy to early adult life. In R. Plomin, & J. Dunn (Eds.), THE STUDY OF TEMPERAMENT: CHANGES, CONTINUITIES AND CHALLENGES (pp. 39–52). Hillsdale, NJ: Erlbaum.

THOMAS, A., CHESS, S., BIRCH, H., HERTZIG, M., & KORN, S. (1963). BEHAVIORAL INDIVIDUALITY IN EARLY CHILDHOOD. New York: New York University Press.

THOMAS, E. L., & ROBINSON, H. A. (1982). IMPROVING READING IN EVERY CLASS. Boston: Allyn & Bacon.

THOMPSON, R. A., LAMB, M., & ESTES, D. (1982). Stability of infant-mother attachment and its relationship to changing life circumstances in an unselected middle-class sample. CHILD DEVELOPMENT, *53*, 144–148.

THOMPSON, S. K. (1975). Gender labels and early sex role development. CHILD DEVELOPMENT, *46*, 339–347.

THOMPSON, W. R. (1954). The inheritance and development of intelligence. PROCEEDINGS OF THE ASSOCIATION FOR RESEARCH ON NERVOUS AND MENTAL DISEASE, *33*, 209–231.

THORESEN, C. E., TELCH, M. J., & EAGLESTON, J. R. (1981). Altering Type A behavior. PSYCHOSOMATICS, *8*, 472–482.

THORNDIKE, R. L., HAGEN, E. P., & SATTLER, J. M. (1986). STANFORD-BINET INTELLIGENCE SCALE: GUIDE FOR ADMINISTERING AND SCORING THE FOURTH EDITION. Chicago: Riverside.

THORNDYKE, E. L. (1898). Animal intelligence: An experimental study of the associative processes in animals. PSYCHOLOGICAL MONOGRAPHS, *2* (No. 8).

THURSTONE, L. L. (1938). Primary mental abilities. PSYCHOMETRIC MONOGRAPHS, No. 1, Chicago: University of Chicago Press.

TIENARI, P., SORRI, A., LAHTI, I., NAARALA, M., WAHLBERG, K., et al. (1987). Interaction of genetic and psychosocial factors in schizophrenia. The Finnish adoptive family study: A longitudinal combination of the adoptive family strategy and the risk research strategy. SCHIZOPHRENIA BULLETIN, *13*, 477–484.

TIME (1983, August 15). Babies: What do they know? When do they know it? (p. 5).

TOATES, F. (1986). MOTIVATIONAL SYSTEMS. Cambridge: Cambridge University Press.

TOLMAN, E. C. (1932). Purpose Behavior in Animals and Men. New York: Appleton-Century-Crofts. (Reprinted, 1967. New York: Irvington.)

TOMKINS, S. S. (1962). AFFECT, IMAGERY, CONSCIOUSNESS: VOL. 1 THE POSITIVE AFFECTS. New York: Springer.

TOMPKINS, S. S. (1980). Affect as amplification: Some modifications in theory. In R. Plutchik & H. Kellerman (Eds.), EMOTION: THEORY, RESEARCH AND EXPERIENCE (Vol. 1). New York: Academic Press.

TORGERSEN, S. (1983). Genetic factors in axiety disorders. ARCHIVES OF GENERAL PSYCHIATRY, *40*, 1085–1089.

TRAFIMOW, D., TRIANDIS, H. C., & GOTO, S. G. (1991). Some tests of the distinction between the private self and the collective self.

JOURNAL OF PERSONALITY AND SOCIAL PSYCHOLOGY, *60*, 649–655.

TREISMAN, A. (1969). Strategies and models of selective attention. PSYCHOLOGICAL REVIEW, *76*, 282–299.

TREISMAN, A., & GORMICAN, S. (1988). Feature analysis in early vision: Evidence from search asymmetries. PSYCHOLOGICAL REVIEW, *95*, 15–48.

TRIANDIS, H. C. (1989). The self and social behavior in different cultures. PSYCHOLOGICAL REVIEW, *96*, 506–520.

TRINDER, J. (1988). Subjective insomnia without objective findings: A pseudodiagnostic classification. PSYCHOLOGICAL BULLETIN, *103*, 87–94.

TRIPP, C. A. (1987). THE HOMOSEXUAL MATRIX (2nd ed.). New York: New American Library.

TRIPLETT, N. (1898). The dynamogentic factors in pacemaking and competition. AMERICAN JOURNAL OF PSYCHOLOGY, *9*, 507–533.

TULVING, E. (1974). Cue-dependent forgetting. AMERICAN SCIENTIST, *62*, 74–82.

TULVING, E. (1983). THE ELEMENTS OF EPISODIC MEMORY. New York: Oxford University Press.

TULVING, E. (1985). How many memory systems are there? AMERICAN PSYCHOLOGIST, *40*, 385–398.

TULVING, E., KAPUR, S., CRAIK, F. I. M., MOSCOVITCH, M., & HOULE, S. (1994). Hemispheric encoding/retrieval asymmetry in episodic memory: Positron emission tomography findings. PROCEEDINGS OF THE NATIONAL ACADEMY OF SCIENCE USA, *91*, 2016–2020.

TULVING, E., KAPUR, S., MARKOWITSCH, H. J., CRAIK, F. I. M., HABIB, R., & HOULE, S. (1994). Neuroanatomical correlates of retrieval in episodic memory: Auditory sentence recognion. PROCEEDINGS OF THE NATIONAL ACADEMY OF SCIENCE USA, *91*, 2012–2015.

TULVING, E., & PEARLSTONE, Z. (1966). Availability versus accessibility of information in memory for words. JOURNAL OF VERBAL LEARNING AND VERBAL BEHAVIOR, *5*, 381–391.

TULVING, E., SCHACTER, D. L., & STARK, H. A. (1982). Priming effects in word-fragment completion are independent of recognition memory. JOURNAL OF EXPERIMENTAL PSYCHOLOGY: LEARNING, MEMORY, AND COGNITION, *8*, 336–342.

TURIEL, E. (1983). THE DEVELOPMENT OF SOCIAL KNOWLEDGE: MORALITY AND CONVENTION. Cambridge: Cambridge University Press.

TURNER, M. E., PRATKANIS, A. R., PROBASCO, P., & LEVER, C. (1992). Threat, cohesion, and group effectiveness: Testing a social identity maintenance perspective in groupthink. JOURNAL OF PERSONALITY AND SOCIAL PSYCHOLOGY, *63*, 781–796.

TVERSKY, A., & KAHNEMAN, D. (1973). On the psychology of prediction. PSYCHOLOGICAL REVIEW, *80*, 237–251.

TVERSKY, A., & KAHNEMAN, D. (1983). Extensional versus intuitive reasoning: The conjunction fallacy in probability judgment. PSYCHOLOGICAL REVIEW, *90*, 293–315.

TYHURST, J. S. (1951). Individual reactions to community disaster. AMERICAN JOURNAL OF PSYCHIATRY, *10*, 746–769.

TYLER, H. (1977). The unsinkable Jeane Dixon. THE HUMANIST, *37*, 6–9.

ULRICH, R. E., STACHNIK, T. J., & STAINTON, N. R. (1963). Student acceptance of generalized personality interpretations. PSYCHOLOGICAL REPORTS, *13*, 831–834.

URSIN, H. (1978). Activation, coping, and psychosomatics. In H. Ursin, E. Baade, & S. Levine (Eds.), PSYCHOBIOLOGY OF STRESS: A STUDY OF COPING MEN. New York: Academic Press.

UTTS, J. (1986). The gansfeld debate: A statistician's perspective. JOURNAL OF PARAPSYCHOLOGY, *50*, 393–402.

VALLIANT, G. (1977). ADAPTATION TO LIFE. Boston: Little, Brown.

VAN EEDEN, F. (1913). A study of dreams. PROCEEDINGS OF THE SOCIETY FOR PHYSICAL RESEARCH, *26*, 431–461.

VAN VORT, W., & SMITH, G. P. (1987). Sham feeding experience produces a conditioned increase of meal size. APPETITE, *9*(1), 21–9.

VAUGHN, B. E., LEFEVER, G. B., SEIFER, R., & BARGLOW, P. (1989). Attachment behavior, attachment security, and temperament during infancy. CHILD DEVELOPMENT, *60*, 728–737.

VIETH, I. (1970). HYSTERIA: THE HISTORY OF A DISEASE. Chicago: University of Chicago Press.

VELMANS, M. (1991). Is human information processing conscious? BEHAVIORAL AND BRAIN SCIENCES, *14*, 651–726.

VENTER, A., LORD, C., & SCHOPLER, E. (1992). A follow-up study of high-functioning autistic children. JOURNAL OF CHILD PSYCHOLOGY AND PSYCHIATRY, *33*(3), 489–507.

VIORST, J. (1986). NECESSARY LOSSES. New York: Faucett Gold Medal.

VISINTAINER, M. A., VOLPICELLI, J. R., & SELIGMAN, M. E. P. (1982). Tumor rejection in rats after inescapable or escapable shock. SCIENCE, *216*, 437–439.

VOGT, T., & BELLUSCIO, D. (1987). Controversies in plastic surgery: suction-assisted lipectomy (SAL) and the hCG (human chorionic gonadotropin) protocol for obesity treatment. AESTHETIC PLAST SURG, *11*(3), 131–56.

VON LANG, J., & SIBYLL, C. (Eds.) (1983). EICHMANN INTERROGATED (R. Manheim, Trans.). New York: Farrar, Straus & Giroux.

WAGNER, A. R. (1981). SOP: A model of automatic memory processing in animal behavior. In N. E. Spear & R. R. Miller (Eds.), INFORMATION PROCESSING IN ANIMALS: MEMORY MECHANISMS. Hillsdale, NJ: Erlbaum.

WAGNER, W. M., & MONNET, M. (1979). Attitudes of college professors toward extrasensory perception. ZETETIC SCHOLAR, *5*, 7–17.

WALD, G., & BROWN, P. K. (1965). Human color vision and color blindness. COLD SPRING HARBOR SYMPOSIA ON QUANTITATIVE BIOLOGY, *30*, 345–359.

WALDROP, M. M. (1987). The workings of working memory. SCIENCE, *237*, 1564–1567.

WALKER, C. E., HEDBERG, A., CLEMENT, P. W., & WRIGHT, L. (1981). CLINICAL PROCEDURES FOR BEHAVIOR THERAPY. Englewood Cliffs, NJ: Prentice-Hall.

WALKER, E. (1978). EXPLORATIONS IN THE BIOLOGY OF LANGUAGE. Montgomery, VT: Bradford Books.

WALLACH, M. A., KOGAN, N., & BEM, D. J. (1962). Group influence on individual risk taking. JOURNAL OF ABNORMAL AND SOCIAL PSYCHOLOGY, *65*, 75–86.

WALLACH, M. A., KOGAN, N., & BEM, D. J. (1964). Diffusion of responsibility and level of risk taking in groups. JOURNAL OF ABNORMAL AND SOCIAL PSYCHOLOGY, *68*, 263–274.

WALLACH, M. A., & WALLACH, L. (1983). PSYCHOLOGY'S SANCTION FOR SELFISHNESS. San Francisco: Freeman.

WALSTER, E., ARONSON, E., ABRAHAMS, D., & ROTTMAN, L. (1966). Importance of physical attractiveness in dating behavior. JOURNAL OF PERSONALITY AND SOCIAL PSYCHOLOGY, *4*, 508–516.

WALZER, M. (1970). OBLIGATIONS. Cambridge, MA: Harvard University Press.

WARD, I. L. (1992). Sexual behavior: the products of perinatal hormonal and prepubertal social factors. In A. A. Gerall, H. Motz, & I. L. Ward (Eds.), SEXUAL DIFFERENTIATION (pp. 157–179). New York: Plenum.

WARRINGTON, E. K., & WEISKRANTZ, L. (1978). Further analysis of the prior learning effect in amnesic patients. NEUROPSYCHOLOGICA, *16*, 169–177.

WASON, P. C., & JOHNSON-LAIRD, P. N. (1972). PSYCHOLOGY OF REASONING: STRUCTURE AND CONTENT. London: Batsford.

WASSERMAN, E. A. (1990). Detecting response-outcome relations: Toward an understanding of the causal texture of the environment. THE PSYCHOLOGY OF LEARNING AND MOTIVATION, *26*, 27–82.

WATERMAN, A. S. (1985). Identity in the context of adolescent psychology. In A. S. Waterman (Ed.), IDENTITY IN ADOLESCENCE: PROGRESS AND CONTENTS: (NEW DIRECTIONS FOR CHILD DEVELOPMENT, NO. 30). San Francisco: Jossey-Bass.

WATERS, E., WIPPMAN, J., & SROUFE, L. A. (1979). Attachment, positive affect, and competence in the peer group: Two studies in construct validation. CHILD DEVELOPMENT, *50*, 821–829.

WATSON, D., & PENNEBAKER, J. W. (1989). Health complaints, stress, and distress: exploring the central role of negative affectivity. PSYCHOLOGICAL REVIEW, *96*, 234–254.

WATSON, D. L., & THARP, R. G. (1989). SELF-DIRECTED BEHAVIOR: SELF-MODIFICATION FOR PERSONAL ADJUSTMENT (5th ed.). Belmont, CA: Wadsworth.

WATSON, J. B. (1930). BEHAVIORISM (Rev. ed.). New York: Norton.

WEAVER, E. G. (1949). THEORY OF HEARING. New York: Wiley.

WEBB, W. B. (1975). SLEEP THE GENTLE TYRANT. Englewood Cliffs, NJ: Prentice-Hall.

WECHSLER, D. (1939). THE MEASUREMENT OF ADULT INTELLIGENCE. Baltimore: Williams and Wilkins.

WECHSLER, D. (1955). MANUAL FOR THE WECHSLER ADULT INTELLIGENCE SCALE. San Antonio: The Psychological Corporation.

WECHSLER, D. (1958). THE MEASUREMENT AND APPRAISAL OF ADULT INTELLIGENCE. Baltimore: Williams.

WECHSLER, D. (1974). WECHSLER INTELLIGENCE SCALE FOR CHILDREN, REVISED. New York: Psychological Corporation.

WECHSLER, D. (1981). MANUAL FOR THE WECHSLER ADULT INTELLIGENCE SCALE—REVISED. San Antonio: The Psychological Corporation.

WECHSLER, C. (1991). WECHSLER INTELLIGENCE SCALE FOR CHILDREN, REVISED. San Antonio: The Psychological Corporation.

WECHSLER, H., DAVENPORT, A., DOWDALL, G., MOEYKENS, B., & CASTILLO, S. (1994). Health and behavioral consequences of binge drinking in college, a national survey of students at 140 campuses. JOURNAL OF THE AMERICAN MEDICAL ASSOCIATION, *272*(21), 1672–1677.

WEGNER, D. M., SCHNEIDER, D. J., CARTER III, S., & WHITE, L. (1987). Paradoxical consequences of thought suppression. JOURNAL OF PERSONALITY AND SOCIAL PSYCHOLOGY, *53*, 1–9.

WEIGEL, R. H., VERNON, D. T. A., & TOGNACCI, L. N. (1974). Specificity of the attitude as a determinant of attitude-behavior congruence. JOURNAL OF PERSONALITY AND SOCIAL PSYCHOLOGY, *30*, 724–728.

WEIGLE, D. S. (1994). Appetite and the regulation of body composition. FASEB J, *8*(3), 302–10.

WEINBERGER, J. L., & SILVERMAN, L. H. (1987). Subliminal psychodynamic activation: A method for studying psychoanalytic dynamic propositions. In R. Hogan & W. H. Jones (Eds.), PERSPECTIVES ON PERSONALITY (Vol. 2, pp. 251–287). Greenwich, CT: JAI Press.

WEINER, E. (1972). THEORIES OF MOTIVATION: FROM MECHANISM TO COGNITION. Chicago: Rand McNally.

WEINSTEIN, N. D. (1980). Unrealistic optimism about future events. JOURNAL OF PERSONALITY AND SOCIAL PSYCHOLOGY, *39*, 806–820.

WEISS, J. M., GLAZER, H. I., POHORECKY, L. A., BRICK, J., & MILLER, N. E. (1975). Effects of chronic exposure to stressors on avoidance-escape behavior and on brain norepinephrine. PSYCHOSOMATIC MEDICINE, *37*, 522–534.

WEISS, R. D., MIRIN, S. M., & BARTEL, R. L. (1994). COCAINE (2nd ed.). Washington, DC: American Psychiatric Press, Inc.

WERTHEIMER, M. (1912/1932). Experimentelle Studien uber das Sehen von Beuegung. ZEITSCHRIFT FUER PSYCHOLOGIE, *61*, 161–265.

WERTHEIMER, M. (1987). A BRIEF HISTORY OF PSYCHOLOGY. (3rd ed.). San Diego: Harcourt Brace.

WEST, C., & ZIMMERMAN, D. H. (1983). Small insults: A study of interruptions in cross-sex conversations between unacquainted persons. In B. Thorne, C. Kramarae, N. Henley (Eds.), LANGUAGE, GENDER, AND SOCIETY. Rowley, MA: Newbury House.

WEST, M. A. (Ed.) (1987). THE PSYCHOLOGY OF MEDITATION. New York: Oxford University Press.

WESTON, D., & TURIEL, E. (1980). Act-rule relations: Children's concepts of social rules. DEVELOPMENTAL PSYCHOLOGY, *16*, 417–424.

WHITAM, F. L., DIAMOND, M., & MARTIN, J. (1993). Homosexual orientation in twins: A report on 61 pairs and 3 triplet sets. ARCHIVES OF SEXUAL BEHAVIOR, *22*, 187–206.

WHITE, C. (1977). Unpublished Ph.D. dissertation, Catholic University, Washington, DC.

WHITE, G. L., FISHBEIN, S., & RUTSTEIN, J. (1981). Passionate love and the misattribution of arousal. JOURNAL OF PERSONALITY AND SOCIAL PSYCHOLOGY, *41*, 56–62.

WHITE, G. L., KIGHT, T. D. (1984). Misattribution of arousal and attraction: Effects of salience of explanations for arousal. JOURNAL OF EXPERIMENTAL SOCIAL PSYCHOLOGY, *20*, 55–64.

WHITE, R. W., & WATT, N. F. (1981). THE ABNORMAL PERSONALITY (5th ed.). New York: Wiley.

WHYTE, W. H. (1956). THE ORGANIZATION MAN. New York: Simon & Schuster.

WHORF, B. L. (1956). Science and linguistics. In J. B. Carroll (Ed.), LANGUAGE, THOUGHT AND REALITY: SELECTED WRITINGS OF BENJAMIN LEE WHORF. Cambridge, MA: MIT Press.

WIEBE, D. J., & MCCALLUM, D. M. (1986). Health practices and hardiness as mediators in the stress-illness relationship. HEALTH PSYCHOLOGY, *5*, 425–438.

WILCOXIN, H. C., DRAGOIN, W. B., & KRAL, P. A. (1971). Illness-induced aversions in rat and quail: Relative salience of visual and gustatory cues. SCIENCE, *171*, 823–828.

WILKES, A. L., & KENNEDY, R. A. (1969). Relationship between pausing and retrieval latency in sentences of varying grammatical form. JOURNAL OF EXPERIMENTAL PSYCHOLOG, *79*, 241–245.

WILKINS, W. (1984). Psychotherapy: The powerful placebo. JOURNAL OF CONSULTING AND CLINICAL PSYCHOLOGY, *52*, 570–573.

WILLIAMS, D. C. (1959). The elimination of tantrum behavior by extinction procedures. JOURNAL OF ABNORMAL AND SOCIAL PSYCHOLOGY, *59*, 269.

WILLIAMS, M. D., & HOLLAN, J. D. (1981). The process of retrieval from very long-term memory. COGNITIVE SCIENCE, *5*, 87–119.

WILLIAMS, R. (1989). THE TRUSTING HEART: GREAT NEWS ABOUT TYPE A BEHAVIOR. New York: Random House.

WILLIAMS, R. B., JR., BAREFOOT, J. C., HANEY, T. L., HARRELL, F. E., BLUMENTHAL, J. A., PRYOR, D. B., & PETERSON, B. (1988). Type A behavior and angiographically documented coronary atherosclerosis in a sample of 2,289 patients. PSYCHOSOMATIC MEDICINE, *50*, 139–152.

WILLIS, S. L. (1985). Towards an educational psychology of the older adult learner: Intellectual and cognitive bases. In J. E. Birren & K. W. Schaie (Eds.), HANDBOOK OF THE PSYCHOLOGY OF AGING (2nd ed.). New York: Van Nostrand Reinhold.

WILLSHAW, D. J. (1981). Holography, associative memory, and inductive generalization. In G. E. Hinton & J. A. Anderson (Eds.), PARALLEL MODELS OF ASSOCIATIVE MEMORY. Hillsdale, NJ: Erlbaum.

WILSON, E. O. (1978). ON HUMAN NATURE. Cambridge, MA: Harvard University Press.

WILSON, E. O. (1963). Pheromones. SCIENTIFIC AMERICAN, *208*(5), 100–114.

WILSON, M. A., & MCNAUGHTON, B. L. (1994). Reactivation of hippocampal ensemble memories during sleep. SCIENCE, *265*, 676–679.

WILSON, T. D., DUNN, D. S., KRAFT, D., & LISLE, D. J. (1989). Introspection, attitude change, and attitude-behavior consistency: The disruptive effects of explaining why we feel the way we do. In L. Berkowitz (Ed.), ADVANCES IN EXPERIMENTAL SOCIAL PSYCHOLOGY (Vol. 22,). San Diego: Academic Press.

WILSON, T. D., LASER, P. S., & STONE, J. I. (1982). Judging the predictors of one's mood: Accuracy and the use of shared theories. JOURNAL OF EXPERIMENTAL SOCIAL PSYCHOLOGY, *18*, 537–556.

WILLIAMS, D. (1992). NOBODY NOWHERE. New York: Avon Books.

WILLIAMS, D. (1994). SOMEBODY SOMEWHERE. New York: Times Books.

WILSON, W. R. (1979). Feeling more than we can know: Exposure effects without learning. JOURNAL OF PERSONALITY AND SOCIAL PSYCHOLOGY, *37*, 811–821.

WINCH, R. F., KTSANES, T., & KTSANES, V. (1954). The theory of complementary needs in mate selection: An analytic and descriptive study. AMERICAN SOCIOLOGICAL REVIEW, *29*, 241–249.

WINDHOLZ, M. J., MARMAR, C. R., & HOROWITZ, M. J. (1985). A review of the research on conjugal bereavement: Impact on health and efficacy of intervention. COMPREHENSIVE PSYCHIATRY, *26*, 433–447.

WINGER, G., HOFFMAN, F. G., & WOODS, J. H. (1992). A HANDBOOK ON DRUG AND ALCOHOL ABUSE (3rd ed.). New York: Oxford University Press.

WINSBERG, B. G., SVERD, J., CASTELLS, S., HURWIC, M., & PEREL, J. M. (1980). Estimation of monoamine and cyclic-AMP turnover and aminoacid concentrations of spinal fluid in autistic children. NEUROPEDIATRICS, *11*, 250–255.

WINSON, J. (1990). The meaning of dreams. SCIENTIFIC AMERICAN, *262*, 86–96.

WINTEMUTE, G. J., TERET, S. P., KRAUS, J. F., & WRIGHT, M. W. (1988). The choice of weapons in firearm suicides. AMERICAN JOURNAL OF PUBLIC HEALTH, *18*, 824–826.

WIRTZ, P. W., & HARRELL, A. V. (1987). Effects of postassault exposure to attack-similar stimuli on long-term recovery of victims. JOURNAL OF CONSULTING AND CLINICAL PSYCHOLOGY, *55*, 10–16.

WISE, R. A. (1982). Neuroleptics and operant behavior: the anhedonia hypothesis. BEHAVIORAL AND BRAIN SCIENCES, 539–87.

WISNIEWSKI, E. J., & MEDIN, D. L. (1991). Harpoons and longsticks: The interaction of theory and similarity in rule induction. In D. Fisher, M. Pazzani, & P. Langley (Eds.), CONCEPT FORMATION: KNOWLEDGE AND EXPERIENCE IN UNSUPERVISED LEARNING. San Mateo, CA: Morgan-Kaufman.

WOLCHIK, S. A., BEGGS, V. E., WINCZE, P. P., SAKHEIM, D. K., BARLOW, D. H., & MAVIS-SAKALIAN, M. (1980). The effect of emotional arousal on subsequent sexual arousal in men. JOURNAL OF ABNORMAL PSYCHOLOGY, *89*, 595–598.

WOLFE, D. A. (1985). Child-abusive parents: An empirical review and analysis. PSYCHOLOGICAL BULLETIN, *97*, 462–482.

WOLMAN, B. B., DALE, L. A., SCHMEIDLER, G. R., & ULLMAN, M. (Eds.) (1986). HANDBOOK OF PARAPSYCHOLOGY. New York: Van Nostrand & Reinhold.

WOLPE, J. (1958). PSYCHOTHERAPY BY RECIPROCAL INHIBITION. Stanford: Stanford University Press.

WONG, D. F., PEARLSON, G. D., TUNE, L. E., YOUNG, C., ROSS, C., VILLEMAGNE, V., DANNALS, R. F., YOUNG, D., PARKER, R., WILSON, A. A., RAVERT, H. T., LINKS, J., MIDHA, K., WAGNER, H. N., & GJEDDE, A. (1989). Update on PET methods for D2 dopamine receptors in schizophrenia and bipolar disorder (Abstract). SCHIZOPHRENIA RESEARCH, *2*, 115.

WONG, D. F., PEARLSON, G. D., TUNE, L. E., YOUNG, C., ROSS, C., VILLEMAGNE, V., DANNALS, R. F., YOUNG, D., PARKER, R., WILSON, A. A., RAVERT, H. T., LINKS, J. MIDHA, K., WAGNER, H. N., & GJEDDE, A. (1986). Positron Emission Tomography reveals elevated D2 dopamine reception in drug-naive schizophrenics. SCIENCE, *234*, 1558–1563.

WOOD, G. (1986). FUNDAMENTALS OF PSYCHOLOGICAL RESEARCH (3rd ed.). Boston: Little, Brown.

WOOD, W., LUNDGREN, S., OUELLETTE, J. A., BUSCEME, S., & BLACKSTONE, T. (1994). Minority influence: A meta-analytic review of social influence processes. PSYCHOLOGICAL BULLETIN, *115*, 323–345.

WOOD, W., WANG, F. Y. & CHACHERIE, J. G. (1991). Effects of media violence on viewers' aggression in unconstrained social situations. PSYCHOLOGICAL BULLETIN, *109*, 371–383.

WOODRUFF, D. S., & BIRREN, J. E. (1983). AGING: SCIENTIFIC PERSPECTIVES AND SOCIAL ISSUES (2nd ed.). Belmont, CA: Wadsworth.

WOODY, R. H., & ROBERTSON, M. (1988). BECOMING A CLINICAL PSYCHOLOGIST. Madison, CT: International Universities Press.

WORD, C. O., ZANNA, M. P., & COOPER, J. (1974). The nonverbal mediation of self-fulfilling prophecies in interracial interaction. JOURNAL OF EXPERIMENTAL SOCIAL PSYCHOLOGY, *10*, 109–120.

WORLEY, P. F., HELLER, W. A., SNYDER, S. H., & BARABAN, J. M. (1988). Lithium blocks a phosphoinositide-mediated cholinergic response in hippocampal slices. SCIENCE, *239*, 1428–1429.

WORTMAN, C. B., BREHM, J. W. (1975). Responses to uncontrollable outcomes: An integration of reactance theory and the learned helplessness model. ADVANCES IN EXPERIMENTAL AND SOCIAL PSYCHOLOGY, *8*, 277–236.

WRIGHT, L. (1988). The Type A behavior pattern and coronary artery disease, quest for the active ingredients and the elusive mechanism. AMERICAN PSYCHOLOGIST, *43*, 2–14.

WRIGHT, W. D. (1946). RESEARCHES ON NORMAL AND COLOR DEFECTIVE VISION. London: Henry Kimpton.

WUNDT, W. (1904). PRINCIPLES OF PHYSIOLOGICAL PSYCHOLOGY (Titchener, E. B., Trans.). (5 ed.). New York: MacMillan.

WYNNE, L. C., SINGER, M. T., BARTKO, J., & TOOHEY, M. L. (1977). Schizophrenics and their families: Research on parenteral communication. In J. Tanner (Ed.), DEVELOPMENTS IN PSYCHIATRIC RESEARCH. London: Hodder & Stoughton.

YAGER, T., LAUFER, R., & GALLOPS, M. (1984). Some problems associated with war experience in men of the Vietnam generation. ARCHIVES OF GENERAL PSYCHIATRY, *41*, 327–333.

YALOM, I. D. (1985). THE THEORY AND PRACTICE OF GROUP PSYCHOTHERAPY (3rd ed.). New York: Basic Books.

YARBUS, D. L. (1967). EYE MOVEMENTS AND VISION. New York: Plenum.

YERAGANI, V., BALON, R., & POHL, R. (1989). Lactate infusions in panic disorder patients and normal controls: Autonomic measures and subjective anxiety. ACTA PSYCHIATRICA SCANDINAVICA, *79*, 32–40.

YESAVAGE, J. A., LEIER, V. O., DENARI, M., & HOLLISTER, L. E. (1985). Carry-over effect of marijuana intoxication on aircraft pilot performance: A preliminary report. AMERICAN JOURNAL OF PSYCHIATRY, *142*, 1325–1330.

YOST, W. A., & NIELSON, D. W. (1985). FUNDAMENTALS OF HEARING (2nd ed.). New York: Holt, Rinehart & Winston.

YU, B., ZHANG, W., JING, Q., PENG, R., ZHANG, G., & SIMON, H. A. (1985). STM capacity for Chinese and English language materials. MEMORY AND COGNITION, *13*, 202–207.

ZAJONC, R. B. (1965). Social facilitation. SCIENCE, *149*, 269–274.

ZAJONC, R. B. (1968). Attitudinal effects of mere exposure. JOURNAL OF PERSONALITY AND SOCIAL PSYCHOLOGY, Monograph Supplement *9* (No. 2), 1–29.

ZAJONC, R. B. (1980). Compresence. In P. B. Paulus (Ed.), PSYCHOLOGY OF GROUP INFLUENCE. Hillsdale, NJ: Erlbaum.

ZAJONC, R. B. (1984). On the primacy of affect. AMERICAN PSYCHOLOGIST, *39*, 117–123.

ZAJONC, R. B., HEINGARTNER, A., & HERMAN, E. M. (1969). Social enhancement and impairment of performance in the cockroach. JOURNAL OF PERSONALITY AND SOCIAL PSYCHOLOGY, *13*, 83–92.

ZAJONC, R. B., MURPHY, S. T., & INGLEHART, M. (1989). Feeling and facial efference: Implications of the vascular theory of emotion. PSYCHOLOGICAL REVIEW, (in press).

ZALUTSKY, R. A., & NICOLL, R. A. (1990). Comparison of two forms of longterm potentiation in single hippocampal neurons. SCIENCE, *248*, 1619–1624.

ZAMANSKY, H. S., & BARTIS, S. P. (1985). The dissociation of an experience: The hidden observer observed. JOURNAL OF ABNORMAL PSYCHOLOGY, *94*, 243–248.

ZEKI, S. (1992). The visual image in mind and brain. SCIENTIFIC AMERICAN, *267*, 68–77.

ZELAZO, P. R., ZELAZO, N. A., & KOLB, S. (1972). Walking in the newborn. SCIENCE, *176*, 314–315.

ZHANG, Y. PROENCA, R., MAFFEI, M., BARONE, M., LEOPOLD, L., & FRIEDMAN, J. M. Positional cloning of the mouse *obese* gene and its human homologue. NATURE, *372*, 425–431, 1994.

ZILLMANN, D. (1984). CONNECTIONS BETWEEN SEX AND AGGRESSION. Hillsdale, NJ: Erlbaum.

ZILLMANN, D., & BRYANT, J. (1974). Effect of residual excitation on the emotional response to provocation and delayed aggressive behavior. JOURNAL OF PERSONALITY AND SOCIAL PSYCHOLOGY, *30*, 782–791.

ZIMBARDO, P. G. (1970). The human choice: Individuation, reason and order versus deindividuation, impulse and chaos. In W. J. Arnold & D. Levine (Eds.), NEBRASKA SYMPOSIUM ON MOTIVATION (Vol. 16). Lincoln: University of Nebraska Press.

ZOLA-MORGAN, S., & SQUIRE, L. R. (1985). Medial-temporal lesions in monkeys impair memory on a variety of tasks sensitive to human amnesia. BEHAVIORAL NEUROSCIENCE, *99*, 22–34.

ZOLA-MORGAN, S. M., SQUIRE, L. R., & AMARAL, D. G. (1989). Lesions of the hippocampal formation but not lesions of the fornix or the mamalary nuclei produce long-lasting memory impairments in monkeys. JOURNAL OF NEUROSCIENCE, *9*, 898–913.

ZOLA-MORGAN, S. M., & SQUIRE, L. R. (1990). The primate hippocampal formation: Evidence for a time-limited role in memory storage. SCIENCE, *250*, 228–290.

ZUBEK, J. P. (1969). SENSORY DEPRIVATION: FIFTEEN YEARS OF RESEARCH. New York: Appleton-Century Crofts.

ZUBER, J. A., CROTT, H. W., & WERNER, J. (1992). Choice shift and group polarization: An analysis of the status of arguments and social decision schemes. JOURNAL OF PERSONALITY AND SOCIAL PSYCHOLOGY, *62*, 50–61.

ZUCKER, K. J. (1990). Gender identity disorders in children: Clinical descriptions and natural history. In R. Blanchard & B. W. Steiner (Eds.), CLINICAL MANAGEMENT OF GENDER IDENTITY DISORDERS IN CHILDREN AND ADULTS (pp. 1–23). WASHINGTON, DC: AMERICAN PSYCHIATRIC PRESS.

ZUCKERMAN, M. (1979A). SENSATION SEEKING: BEYOND THE OPTIMAL LEVEL OF AROUSAL. HILLSDALE, NJ: ERLBAUM.

ZUCKERMAN, M. (1979B). ATTRIBUTION OF SUCCESS AND FAILURE REVISITED, OR: THE MOTIVATIONAL BIAS IS ALIVE AND WELL IN ATTRIBUTION THEORY. JOURNAL OF PERSONALITY, *47*, 245–287.

ZUKERMAN, M., & NEEB, M. (1980). DEMOGRAPHIC INFLUENCES IN SENSATION-SEEKING AND EXPRESSIONS OF SENSATION-SEEKING IN RELIGION, SMOKING AND DRIVING HABITS. PERSONALITY AND INDIVIDUAL DIFFERENCES, *19*, 197–206.

ZURIF, E. B., (1990). LANGUAGE AND THE BRAIN. In D. N. OSHERSON & H. LASNIK (EDS.) AN INVITATION TO COGNITIVE SCIENCE: LANGUAGE (VOL. 1). CAMBRIDGE, MA: MIT PRESS.

ZURIF, E. B., CARAMAZZA, A., MYERSON, R., & GALVIN. J. (1974). SEMANTIC FEATURE REPRESENTATIONS FOR NORMAL AND APHASIC LANGUAGE. BRAIN AND LANGUAGE, *1*, 167–187.

COPYRIGHTS AND ACKNOWLEDGMENTS AND ILLUSTRATION CREDITS

Figures, Boxes, and Tables

Figure 1-2, Sheingold, K. and Tenney, Y. J. (1982) "Memory for a salient childhood event." In U. Neisser (ed), *Memory Observed: Remembering In Natural Contexts.*Copyright © by W. F. Freeman and Company. Adapted by permission of the publisher.

Figure 1-3, Eron, L., et al. (1972) "Does television cause aggression? *American Psychologist,* 2:253-63. Copyright © 1972 by The American Psychological Association. Adapted by permission.

Figure 1-5, Darley, C. F. et al. (1973) "Influence of marijuana on storage and retrieval processes in memory," *Memory and Cognition,*1:196-200. Reprinted by permission of the Psychonomic Society.

Box 1-1, (Item #1) G. M. Pion (1991) "Psychologist Wanted: Employment Trends over the Past Decade." In R. R. Kilburg (ed), *How To Manage Your Career in Psychology.* Copyright © 1991 by the American Psychological Association. Adapted by permission.

Box1-1, (Item # 2), Compiled by Research Office, American Psychological Association, based upon data from The National Science Foundation (1988), *Science and Engineering Doctorates: 1960-1986* (NSF 88-309), Washington D. C., and the National Research Council, *Survey of Earned Doctorates, 1994*

Figure1-8, Courtesy of Alfred P. Sloan Foundation.

Figures 2-1, 2-2, & 2-3, Adapted from *Human Anatomy* by Anthony J. Gaudin and Kenneth C. Jones. Copyright © 1988 by Anthony J. Gaudin and Kenneth C. Jones. Reprinted by permission of the authors.

Figure2-5, Adapted from In *Search for the Human Mind* by Robert Sternberg.

copyright © 1994 by Harcourt Brace & Company, reproduced by permission of the publisher.

Figures 2-6, 2-9, 2-10,& 2-12 Adapted from *Human Anatomy* by Anthony . Gaudin and Kenneth C. Jones. Copyright © 1988 by Anthony J. Gaudin and Kenneth C. Jones. Reprinted by permission of the authors.

Figures 2-13 & 2-14, Reprinted from *Neuropsychologia, Volume* 9, by R. D. Nebes and W. Sperry, page 247, Copyright © 1971, with kind permission from Elsevier Science, Ltd., The Boulevard, Langford Lane, Kidlington OX5 1GB UK.

Figures 2-15 & 2-16, Adapted from *Human Anatomy* by Anthony J. Gaudin and Kenneth C. Jones. Copyright © 1988 by Anthony J. Gaudin and Kenneth C. Jones. Reprinted by permission of the authors.

Figure 2-20, Reprinted from *Proceedings of the Association for Research in Nervous an*d *Mental Diseases,* Volume 33, by R. W. Thompson, pages 209-231, Copyright © 1954, with kind permission from Elsevier Science, Ltd, The Boulevard, Langford Lane, Kidlington OX5 1GB UK.

Figure 3-1, Adapted from "The origin of form perception," from *Scientific American,* Volume 204, by R. L .Fantz, pages 66-72. Copyright © 1961 by Scientific American, Inc. All rights reserved.

Table 3-1, From *Review of Child Development Research,* Volume 1, edited by M. L. Hoffman and L. W. Hoffman. Copyright © 1964 by the Russell Sage Foundation. Reprinted by permission of the Russell Sage Foundation.

Table 3-2, Kohlberg, L. (1969), "Stage and sequence: The cognitive-developmental approach to socialization." In D. A. Goslin (ed), *Handbook of Socialization Theory and Research.* Reprinted by permission of Rand McNally.

Figure 3-7, Adapted from Balliargeon, R. (1987), "Object permanence in 31/2 and 41/2 month old infants," *Developmental Psychology,* 23:655-664. Reprinted by permission of the Academic Press.

Figure 3-9, Reprinted by permission of the publishers from *Infancy: Its Place in Human Development* by Jerome Kagan, Richard B. Kearsley and Philip R. Zelazo, Cambridge, Mass: Harvard University Press, Copyright © 1978 by the President and Fellows of Harvard Collge.

Table 3-3, Adapted from *Childhood and Society* by Erik H. Erikson, with the permission of W. W. Norton & Company, Inc. Copyright 1950, © 1963 by W. W. Norton & Company, Inc.

Table 4-1, Galanter, E. (1962), "Contemporary Psychophysics." In R. Brown & collaborators (eds.), *New Directions in Psychology,* Volume I. Reprinted by permission of Roger Brown.

Figure 4-2, Reprinted from *Vision Research,* Volume 18, by W. S. Geisler, "Adaptation, afterimages, and cone saturation," pages 279-289, Copyright © 1978, with kind permission from Elsevier Science, Ltd, The Boulevard, Langford Lane, Kidlington OX5 1GB UK.

Figure 4-5, From *Sensation and Perception* by E. Bruce Goldstein. Copyright © 1989, 1984, 1980 by Wadsworth Publishing Company. Reprinted by permission of Brooks/Cole Publishing Company, a division of International Thomson Publishing Inc., Pacific Grove, CA 93950.

Figures 4-6 & 4-7, Adapted from *Human Color Vision* by Robert M. Boynton, copyright © 1979 by Holt, Rinehart and

Winston, Inc., reprinted by permission of Harcourt Brace & Company, Inc.

Figure 4-8, Dowling, J. E. and Boycott, B. B. (1969), "Organization of the primate retina," *Proceedings of the Royal Society of London,* Series B, 166:80-111. Adapted by permission of the Royal Society.

Figure 4-14, Wright, W. D. (1946) *Researches on Normal and Color Defective Vision,* London: Harry Kimpton Medical Publications.

Figure 4-18,Wald, G. and Brown, P. K. (1965), "Human Color Vision and Color Blindness," *Cold Spring Harbor Symposia On Quantitative Biology,* 30:345-359.

Figure 4-20, Hurvich, L. M. and Jameson, D. (1957) "An opponent process theory of color vision," *Psychological Review,* 64:384-404. Copyright © 1957 by the American Psychological Association. Adapted by permission.

Figure 4-22, Adapted from *Human Anatomy* by Anthony J. Gaudin and Kenneth C. Jones. Copyright © 1988 by Anthony J. Gaudin and Kenneth C. Jones. Reprinted by permission of the authors.

Figure 4-23, Figure from *Sensation and Perception,* Third Edition by Stanley Coren and Lawrence M. Ward, copyright © 1989 by Harcourt Brace & Company, reproduced by permission of the publisher.

Figure 4-25, Adapted from *Human Anatomy* by Anthony J. Gaudin and Kenneth C. Jones. Copyright © 1988 by Anthony J. Gaudin and Kenneth C. Jones. Reprinted by permission of the authors.

Figure 4-26, Erickson, E. H. (1963) "Sensory neural patterns and gustation." In Zotterman (ed), *Olfaction and Taste,* Volume I, pp. 205-213.

Figure 4-27, Kosambi, D. D. (1967) "Living prehistory in India," *Scientific American,* 215: 105. Copyright © by D. D. Kosambi. Reprinted by permission of Dr. Meera Kosambi and Mr. Bijoy B. Surkar.

Figure 5-1, Mishkin, Mortimer Ungerleider, Leslie, G., and Macko, Kathleen A. (1983), "Object Vision and Spatial Vision: Two cortical pathways," *Trends in Neurosciences,* 6(10):414-417.

Figure 5-6, Banks, W. P. and Prinzmetal, W. (1976) "Configurational effects in visual information processing," *Perception and Psychophysics,* 19:361-367. Reprinted by permission of Psychonomic Society.

Figure 5-12, Triesman, A. and Gormican, S. (1988) "Feature analysis in early vision: Evidence from search asymmetries," *Psychological Review,* 95:15-48. Copyright © 1988 by the American Psychological Association. Adapted by permission.

Figure 5-16, Riecher, G. M. (1969), "Perceptual recognition as a function of the meaningfulness of the material," *Journal of Experimental Psychology,* 81:275-280. Copyright © 1969 by American Psychological Association. Adapted by permission.

Figures 5-18 & 5-19, Biederman, I. (1987), "Recognition of components: A theory of human image understanding," *Computer Vision, Graphics and Image Processing,* 32:29-73. Reprinted by permission of the Academic Press.

Figure 5-20, Boring, E. G. (1930) "A new ambiguous figure," *American Journal of Psychology,* 42:444-445.Copyright © 1930 by the Board of trustees of the University of Illinois. Used with permission of the University of Illinois Press.

Figure 5-21, Fisher, G. H. . (1967). "Perception of ambiguous stimulus materials," Perception and Psychophysics, 2: 421-422. Reprinted by permission of the Psychonomic Society.

Figure 5-28 From *Sensation and Perception* by E. Bruce Goldstein. Copyright © 1989, 1984, 1980 by Wadsworth Publishing Company. Reprinted by permission of Brooks/Cole Publishing Company, a division of International Thomson Publishing Inc. Pacific Grove, CA 93950

Figure 5-33, Held, R. and Hein, A. (1963), "Movement-Produced Stimulation in the development of visually guided behavior," *Journal of Comparative and Physiological Psychology*, 56:872-876. Copyright © 1963 by the American Psychological Association. Adapted with permission.

Figure 6-1, Ludwig, A. M., Brandsma, J. M. , Wilbur, C. B., Bendfeldt, F., and Jameson, D. H. (1972), "The objective study of multiple personality," *Archives of General Psychiatry*, 26:298-310. Copyright © 1972 by the American Medical Association.

Table 6-1, Pion, G. M. (1991), "Psychologists wanted: employment trends over the post decade." In R. R. Kilburg (ed), Copyright © 1991 by the American Psychological Association. Reprinted by permission.

Figure6-5, From *Illicit Drug Use, Smoking, and Drinking by America's High School Students, College Students, and Young Adults 1975-1995*, by Jerome Johnson, P. M. O'Malley and Jerald G. Bachman. Rockville, MD: National Institute on Drug Abuse.

Figure 6-6, Data from the National Highway and Traffic Safety Administration.

Critical Discussion, "Steps in trancendental mediation." From Benson, H. Kotch, J. B. , Crassweller, K. D., and Greenwood, M. M. (1977), Historical and clincial considerations of the relaxation response," *American Scientist*, 65:441-443. Reprinted by permission of the Scientific Research Society.

Figure 6-9, From *Hypnotic Susceptibilty* by Ernest Hilgard, copyright © 1965 by Harcourt Brace & Company, reprinted by permission of the publisher.

Figure 6-10, Cooper, L. M. (1979) "Hypnotic Amnesia." In Fromm, Erika, and Shor, Ronald E. (ed.), *Hypnosis: Developments in Research and New Perspectives* (New and revised 2nd edition). Copyright © 1979 by Erika Fromm and Ronald E. Shor. Reprinted by permission of Erika Fromm and Ronald E. Shor.

Figure 7-2, Adapted from *Conditioned Reflexes* by E. P. Pavlov. Copyright © 1927 by Oxford University Press. Reprinted by permission of Oxford University Press

Figure 7-3, "The sensory generalization of conditioned responses with varying frequencies of tone," *Journal of General Psychology*, Volume 17,pages 125-148, 1937. Reprinted with permissions of the Helen Dwight Reid Educational Foundation. Published by Heldref Publications, 1219 Eighteenth St., N.W., Washington, D. C.,20036-1802. Copyright © 1939.

Figure 7-4. Adapted from article, "Differential Classical Conditioning: Verbalization of Stimulus Contingencies," Reprinted with permission from *Science*, Volume 10, December 10, 1975, pages 1479-1481, by M. J. Fuhrer and P. E. Baer. Copyright © 1965 American Association for the Advancement of Science.

Figure 7-5, Rescorla, R. a. (1967), "Pavlovian conditioning and its proper control procedures," *Psychological Review*, 74:71-80. Copyright © 1967 by the American

Psychological Association. Adapted by permission.

Table 7-1, Leon J. Kamin, "Predictability, Surprise, Attention, & Conditioning," in *Punishment And Aversive Behavior*, Campbell/Church eds., © 1969, pp. 279-296. Adapted by permission of Prentice-Hall, Englewood Cliffs, New Jersey.

Table 7.2, Garcia, J. and Koelling, R. A. (1966), "The relation of cue to consequence in avoidance learning," *Psychonomic Science*, 4:123-124. Reprinted by permission of the Psychonomic Society.

Box 7-1, Item #1, Kandel, E. R. (1979) "Small systems of neurons." In R. Thompson, *The Brain*. Copyright © 1979 by W. H. Freeman and Company. Adapted with permission of the publisher.

Box 7-1, Item #2, Hawkins, R. D. and Kandel, E. R. (1984), "Is there a cell-biological alphabet for simple forms of learning?," *Psychological Review*, 91:375-391. Copyright © 1984 by the American Psychological Association. Adapted with permission.

Figure 7-8, Adapted from *Psychology of Learning and Behavior*, Third Edition by Barry Schwartz, with the permission of W. W. Norton & Company, Inc. Copyright © 1989, 1984, 1978 by W. W Norton & Company, Inc.

Figure 7-9, From *Brain, Mind and Behavior* by Bloom and Lazerson. Copyright © 1988 by Educational Broadcasting Corporation. Used with permission of W. H. Freeman and Company.

Figure 8-1, Melton, A. W. (1963), "Implication of short-term memory for a general theory of memory," *Journal of Verbal Learning and Verbal Behavior*, 2:1-21. Adapted by permission of the Academic Press.

Figure 8-3, Jonides, John, Smith, Edward, E., Koeppe, Robert A. , and Awh, Edward (1994), "Spatial working memory in humans as revealed by PET," *Nature*, 363:623-625. Reprinted with permission from *Nature*. Copyright © 1994 by Macmillan Magazines Limited.

Figure 8-4, Adapted from article, "High speed scanning in human memory." Reprinted with permission from *Science*, Volume 153, August 5, 1966, pages 652-654, by S. Sternberg. Copyright © 1966 American Association for the Advancement of Science.

Figure 8-6, Murdock, B. B. (1962) "The serial position effect in free recall," *Journal of Experimental Psychology*, 64: 482-488. Copyright © 1962 by the American Psychological Association. Adapted by permission.

Table 8-1, Tulving, E. and Pearlstone, Z. (1976), "Availability and Accessibility," *Journal of Memory and Language*, 5:381-391. Reprinted by permission of the Academic Press.

Figure8-9, Godden, D. and Baddeley, A. D. (1975), "Context-dependent memory in two natural environments: On land and under water. *British Journal of Psychology*, 66:325-331.

Critical Discussion, Table of "Recall of an early memory," Adapted from Sheingold, K. and Tenney, Y. J. (1982), "Memory for a salient childhood event." In U Neisser, *Memory Observed: Remembering in Natural Contexts*, Copyright © 1982 by W. H. Freeman & Company, Inc. Adapted by permission of the publisher.

Table 8-2, Reprinted from *Neuropsychologia*, Volume 16, by W. K. Warrinton and L. Weiskrantz, "Further

Analysis of the Prior learning effect in amnesic patients," pages 169-197, Copyright © 1978, with kind permission from Elsevier Science, Ltd, The Boulevard, Langford Lane, Kidlington OX5 1GB UK.

Figure 8-11, Adapted from article, "Acquisition of a memory skill." Reprinted with permission from *Science*, Volume 208, pages 1181-1182, by I. A. Ericson et al. Copyright © 1980 by American Association for the Advancement of Science.

Figure 8-14, Bower, G. H. and Clark, M. C. (1969), "Narrative stories as mediators for serial learning," *Psychonomic Science*, 14:181-182. Reprinted by permission of the Psychonomic Society.

Figure 9-2, Wisniewski, E. J. and Medin, D. L. (1991), "Harpoons and longsticks: The interaction of theory and similarity in rule reduction." In P. Langley (eds) *Concept Formation: Knowledge and Experience in Unsupervised Learning*. Copyright © 1991 by Morgan and Kaufman Publishers, Inc. Reprinted by permission of the publisher."

Figure 9-3, Griggs, R. A. and Cox, J. R. (1982), "The elusive thematic-materials effect in Watson's selection task," *British Journal of Psychology*, 73:407-420. Adapted by permission of the British Psychological Society.

Table 9-1, Slobin, D. I. (1971), "Developmental Psycholinguistics." In W. O. Dingwall (ed), *A Survey of Linguistic Science*, pages 298-400.

Figures 9-8& 9-9, Cooper, L. A. and Shepard, R. N. (1973), "Chronometric studies of the rotation of mental images." In W. G. Chase (ed) *Visual Information Processing*. Adapted by permission of the Academic Press.

Figure 9-10, Kosslyn, S. M, et al. (1978), "Visual images preserve metric spatial information: Evidence from studies of image scanning," *Journal of Experimental Psychology: Human Perception and Performance*,4:46-60. Copyright © 1978 by the American Psychological Association. Adapted by permission.

Table 9-2, From *Beyond IQ: A Triarchic Theory of Human Intelligence* by Robert J. Sternberg. Copyright © 1985 by Robert J. Sternberg. Reprinted by permission of Cambridge University Press.

Figure 10-1, Adapted from *Motivational Systems*, by F. Toates. Copyright © 1986 by F. Toates. Reprinted by permission of Cambridge University Press.

Figure 10-5, Powley, T. L. and Keesey, R. E. (1970), "Body weight and the lateral hypothalmic feeding syndrome," *Journal of Comparative and Physiological Psychology*, 70:25-26. Copyright © 1970 by the American Psychological Association. Adapted by permission.

Figure 10-6, Hoebel, B. G. and Teitebaum, P. (1970), "Effects of force feeding and starvation, food intake and body weight of a rat with ventromedial hypothalamic lesions," *Journal of Comparative and Physiological Psychology*, 61"189-193. Copyright © 1966 by the American Psychological Association. Adapted by permission.

Figure 10-7, From "Taste, deprivation and weight determinants of eating behavior," by R. C. Nisbett in *Nerophysiology and Emotion*, edited by D. C. Glass. Copyright © 1967 by the Russell Sage Foundation. Reprinted by permission of the Russell Sage Foundation.

Table 10-1, Craighead, L. W., Stunkard, A. J. and O'Brien, R. M. (1981) "Behavior therapy and pharmacotherapy for obesity," *Archives*

of General Psychiatry, 38:763-768. Copyright © 1981 by the American Medical Association.

Figure 10-9, Fallon, A. E. and P. Rozin (1985), "Sex differences in perceptions of desirable body shape," *Journal of Abnormal Psychology*, 94:102-105. Copyright © 1985 by the American Psychological Association. Adapted by permission.

Figure 10-12, Hopkins, J. R. (1977), "Sexual Behavior in Adolescence," *Journal of Social Issues*, 33(2):67-85. Adapted with permission of the Society for the Psychological Study of Social Issues.

Table 10-2, From *Sexual Preference: Its Development in Men and Women*, by A. P. Bell, M. A. Weinberg, and S.K. Hammersmith. Copyright © 1981 by Indiana University Press. Reprinted by permission of the publisher.

Table 11-1, Shafer, L. F. (1947), "Fear and Courage in aerial combat," *Journal of Consulting Psychology*, 11:137-143.

Box 11-1, Item #1, Kubis, J. F. (1962),cited in B. M. Smith (1967), "The Polygraph." In R.C. Atkinson (ed), *Contemporary Psychology*. Adapted by permission of the publisher.

Box 11-2, Item #2, Adapted from article, "Lie detectors: PSE gains audience despite critics' doubt," Reprinted with permission from *Science*, Volume 190, pages 1208-1210, by C. Holden. Copyright © 1975 bt the American Association for the Advancement of Science.

Figure 11-1, Schachter, S. (1964) "The interaction of Cognitive and Physiological determinates of emotional state." In P. H. Leiderman and D. Shapiro (eds), *Psychobiological Approaches to Human Behavior*. Stanford: Stanford University Press. Adapted from G. W. Hohmann, "The effect of dysfunctions of the autonomic nervous system on experienced feelings and emotions," paper read at Conference on Emotions and feelings at New School for Social Research, New York, October 1962.

Figure 11-2, Adapted from article, "Autonomic Nervous System Activity Distinguishes Among Emotions." Reprinted with permission from *Science*, Volume 221, September 16 , 1983, pages 1208-1210, by P. Ekman, et al. Copyright © 1983 by American Association for the Advancement of Science.

Table 11-2, From Emotion: Theory, Research, and Experience. edited by R. Plutchnik and H. Kellerman. Copyright © 1980 by R. Plutchnik and H. Kellerman. Reprinted by permission of the Academic Press.

Table 11-3, Roseman, I. J. (1984), "Cognitive determinants of emotions: A Structural Theory." In P. Shaver (ed), *Review of Personality and Social Psychology: Volume 5 Emotions, Relationships, and Health*. Copyright © 1984 by P. Shaver. Reprinted by permission of Sage Publications, Inc.

Figure 11-4, Adapted from *Textbook of Psychology*, by Donald O. Hebb, copyright © 1973 by Donald O. Hebb. Reprinted by permission of W. B. Saunders Company.

Figure 11-8, Bandura, A. et al. (1963), "Imitation of film mediated aggressive models," *Journal of Abnormal Psychology*, 66:8. Copyright © 1963 by the American Psychological Assocition. Adapted by permission.

Figure 11-9, Eron, L. et al (1972), "Does television violence cause aggression?," *American Psychologist*, 27:253-263. Copyright © 1972 by the American Psychological Association. Adapted by permission.

NAME INDEX

Subject Index